P9-CLI-685

FINANCIAL MODELING

FINANCIAL MODELING

Simon Benninga

with a section on Visual Basic for Applications
by Benjamin Czaczkes

THIRD EDITION

The MIT Press
Cambridge, Massachusetts
London, England

This book was set in Times Roman by SNP Best-set Typesetter Ltd., Hong Kong, and was printed and bound in the United States of America.

Library of Congress Cataloging-in-Publication Data

Benninga, Simon.
Financial modeling / Simon Benninga.—3rd ed.
p. cm.
Includes bibliographical references and index.
ISBN 978-0-262-02628-4
1. Finance—Mathematical models. I. Title.
HG173.B46 2008
332.01′5118—dc22

2007038629

10 9 8 7 6 5 4

To our parents: Helen and Noach Benninga; Esther and Alfred Czaczkes

Contents

Preface

The two previous editions of *Financial Modeling* have received a gratifyingly positive response from readers. The "cookbook combination" that mixes explanation and implementation using Excel fulfills a need in both the academic and practitioner markets for readers who realize that the implementation of the finance basics typically studied in an introductory finance course requires another, more heavily computational and implementational, approach. Excel, the most widely used computational tool in finance, is a natural vehicle for deepening our understanding of the materials.

Financial Modeling is organized along six different subject areas. Each of the first four sections of the book relates to a specific area of finance. These sections are independent of each other, though the reader should realize that they all assume some familiarity with the finance area—*Financial Modeling* is not an introductory text. Section I (Chapters 1–7) deals with corporate finance topics; Section II (Chapters 8–15) with portfolio models; Section III (Chapters 16–24) with option models; and Section IV (Chapters 25–28) with bond-related topics.

The last two sections of *Financial Modeling* are technical in nature. Section V (Chapters 29–35) relates to various Excel topics that are used throughout the book. Chapters in this section can be read and accessed as necessary. Section VI (Chapters 36–41) deals with Excel's programming language, Visual Basic for Applications (VBA). VBA is used throughout *Financial Modeling* to create functions and routines that make life easier, but it is never intrusive—in principle the reader can understand the materials in all of the other chapters of *Financial Modeling* without needing the VBA chapters.

New Chapters

Finance is a very dynamic area. The new edition of *Financial Modeling* contains many updates and changes that track new developments in the area of computational finance. In addition, almost all the chapters have been revised to make explanations more up-to-date. The third edition of *Financial Modeling* contains eight completely new chapters:

• Chapter 5 discusses bank valuation. The basic valuation framework of Chapter 3 is applied to the valuation of financial institutions.

- Chapter 13 adds an exposition of the Black-Litterman model of portfolio choice to the section on portfolio models. This model, widely used in asset allocation, is not discussed in any major textbook.
- Chapter 14 discusses event studies, the most prominent tool for judging the effect of market events on the returns of individual stocks.
- Chapter 20, on Greeks, has been added to Section III, on options.
- Chapters 22 and 23 discuss the implementation of Monte Carlo methods to option valuation.
- Chapter 34 discusses array functions, both those included with Excel and the construction of homemade array functions.
- Chapter 41 shows how to use VBA to extract Web information to Excel.

In addition to the new chapters, many of the *Financial Modeling* chapters have been substantially rewritten. Following are a few examples:

Chapter 2 includes a number of new cases used to illustrate the estimation of the cost of capital.

Chapter 4 has a new example (PPG Corporation) for the implementation of pro forma models and valuation.

Chapter 10 now includes a discussion of shrinkage methods and their use in the estimation of the variance-covariance methods.

Chapter 17 shows how to use the binomial option pricing model to price employee stock options.

Chapter 19 adds discussions of structured securities and the Merton model within the framework of Black-Scholes.

Chapter 27, on polynomial term structure models, is based on new materials and a new data set of zero-coupon bonds from the Federal Reserve.

Getformula

The Excel files with this edition include a function called **Getformula** that enables the user to track cell contents. The disk that comes with *Financial Modeling* has a document on how users can add **Getformula** to their files. In order to allow **Getformula** to work, you must set your

Excel security settings (**Tools|Macro|Security**) to **Medium**. If you have done this, then when opening an Excel notebook, you will be confronted by the following screen:

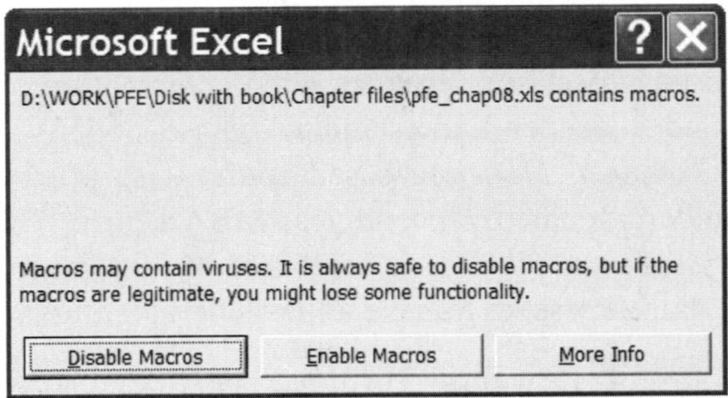

You can safely click **Enable Macros**, which enables the formulas on the notebook. A separate file on the CD-ROM tells you how to implant this useful program on your own Excel notebooks.

Excel 2007

As this book went to press in late 2007, Excel 2007 was starting to be used on many computer systems. The differences between Excel 2007 and previous versions of Excel are largely esthetic and not substantive. Since most readers of this book are likely to have older versions of Excel on their computers, I have chosen to continue using Excel 2003 in this edition. A document relating to Excel 2007 is on the disk with *Financial Modeling*.

The Disk

The CD-ROM included with *Financial Modeling* provides files that give all the Excel contents of each chapter as well as files that give the answers to each of the end-of-chapter questions. All the book's files have been checked and work with Excel 2007. The disk also includes documents on the differences between Excel 2003 and Excel 2007, on adding **Getfor-**

mula to spreadsheets, and on some problems encountered with Excel's **XNPV** and **XIRR** functions.

Using *Financial Modeling* in a University Course

Financial Modeling has become the book of choice in many intermediate and advanced finance classes that stress the combination of modeling/Excel skills and a deeper understanding of the underlying financial models. The *Financial Modeling*–based courses are often a third- or fourth-year undergraduate or second-year MBA course. These courses are often very different from each other and include much instructor-specific input, but they seem to have a few general features:

- A typical course starts with two or three classes that stress the Excel skills needed for financial modeling. Often these classes are held in a computer lab. Though almost all business school students know Excel, they may not know how to finesse data tables (Chapter 30) or some of the basic financial functions (Chapters 1 and 33) and array functions (Chapter 34). The initial classes give the instructor a chance to level the playing field.
- Most one-semester courses then cover, at most, one of the *Financial Modeling* sections. If we assume that in a typical university course, covering one chapter per week is an upper limit (and many chapters will require two weeks), then a typical course might concentrate on either corporate finance (Chapters 1–7), portfolio models (Chapters 8–15), or options (Chapters 16–24). At a stretch, the instructor could perhaps throw in the shorter bond section (Chapters 25–28).
- I suggest that after the initial classes in a computer lab, the instructor move to a regular classroom. This enables the classroom emphasis to be on discussions of theory and implementation, with student homework concentrating on actual spreadsheets.

An alternative to the preceding structure is to build an even more advanced course around VBA. I teach a financial engineering course that starts with binomial option pricing, proceeds to cover some of the VBA chapters (36–38), and then covers Black-Scholes and Monte Carlo methods (Chapters 18–23).

A major problem with a computer-based course is how to structure the final examination. Two solutions seem to work well. One alternative is to have students (whether alone or in teams) submit a final project. Examples might be a corporate valuation if the course is based on Section I of the book, an event study for Section II, an option-based project for Section III, or the computation of a bond expected return if the emphasis is on Section IV. A second alternative is to have students submit, by e-mail, a spreadsheet-based examination with severe time limits. One instructor using this book sends his class the final exam (a compendium of spreadsheet problems) at nine o'clock in the morning and requires an e-mail with a spreadsheet answer by noon.

Acknowledgments

I want to start by thanking a group of wonderful editors: John Covell, Nancy Lombardi, Elizabeth Murry, Ellen Pope, and Peter Reinhart. My next thanks go to a dedicated group of colleagues who read the typescripts for *Financial Modeling*: Arindam Bandopadhyaya, Michael Chau, Jaksa Cvitanic, Richard Harris, Aurele Houngbedji, Iordanis Karagiannidis, Yvan Lengwiler, Nejat Seyhun, Gökçe Soydemir, and David Y. Suk.

Many of the changes in this edition of Financial Modeling are due to the comments of readers, who have been assiduous in offering suggestions and improvements for the book. I follow a tradition started with the first two editions of Financial Modeling by acknowledging those readers whose comments have been incorporated into this edition: Meni Abudy, Zvika Afik, Gordon Alexander, Apostol Bakalov, Naomi Belfer, David Biere, Vitaliy Bilyk, Oded Braverman, Roeland Brinkers, Craig Brody, Salvio Cardozo, Sharad Chaudhary, Israel Dac, Jeremy Darhansoff, Toon de Bakker, Govindvyas Dharwada, Davey Disatnik, Kevin Dowd, Brice Dupoyet, Cederik Engel, Orit Eshel, Yaara Geyra, Rana P. Ghosh, Bjarne Jensen, Marek Jochec, Milton Joseph, Erez Kamer, Saggi Katz, Emir Kiamilev, Brennan Lansing, Paul Ledin, Paul Legerer, Quinn Lewis, David Martin, Tom McCurdy, Tsahi Melamed, Tal Mofkadi, Geoffrey Morrisett, Sandip Mukherji, Max Nokhrin, Michael Oczkowski, David Pedersen, Mikael Petitjean, Georgio Questo, Alex Riahi, Arad Rostampour, Joseph Rubin, Andres Rubio, Ofir Shatz, Natalia Simakina, Ashutosh Singh, Permjit Singh, Gerald Strever, Shavkat Sultanbekov,

Ilya Talman, Mel Tukman, Daniel Vander, Guy Vishnia, Torben Voetmann, Chao Wang, James Ward, Roberto Wessels, Geva Yaniv, Richard Yeh, and Werner Zitzman.

Finally, I want to thank my very patient wife Terry, who has maintained her own and my equilibrium through two books and a business school deanship in the past five years.

As always, I welcome comments and corrections!

Simon Benninga
benninga@wharton.upenn.edu

Preface to the Second Edition

The purpose of this book remains to provide a "cookbook" for implementing common financial models in Excel. This edition has been expanded by six additional chapters, covering financial calculations, cost of capital, value at risk (VaR), real options, early exercise boundaries, and term-structure modeling. There is also an additional technical chapter containing a potpourri of Excel hints.

I am indebted to a number of people (in addition to those mentioned in the previous preface) for help and suggestions: Andrew A. Adamovich, Alejandro Sanchez Arevalo, Yoni Aziz, Thierry Berger-Helmchen, Roman Weissman Bermann, Michael Giacomo Bertolino, John Bollinger, Enrico Camerini, Manuel Carrera, John Carson, Roy Carson, Lydia Cassorla, Philippe Charlier, Michael J. Clarke, Alvaro Cobo, Beni Daniel, Ismail Dawood, Ian Dickson, Moacyr Dutra, Hector Tassinari Eldridge, Shlomy Elias, Peng Eng, Jon Fantell, Erik Ferning, Raz Gilad, Nir Gluzman, Michael Gofman, Doron Greenberg, Phil Hamilton, Morten Helbak, Hitoshi Hibino, Foo Siat Hong, Marek Jochec, Russell W. Judson, Tiffani Kaliko, Boris Karasik, Rick Labs, Allen Lee, Paul Legerer, Guoli Li, Richard Liu, Moti Marcus, Gershon Mensher, Tal Mofkadi, Glenn Morley, Stephen O'Neil, Steven Ong, Oren Ossad, Jackie Rosner, Steve Rubin, Dvir Sabah, Ori Salinger, Meir Shahar, Roger Shelor, David Siu, Maja Sliwinski, Bob Taggart, Maurry Tamarkin, Mun Hon Tham, Efrat Tolkowsky, Mel Tukman, Sandra van Balen, Michael Verhofen, Lia Wang, Roberto Wessels, Ethan Weyand, Ubbo Wiersema, Weiqin Xie, Ke Yang, Ken Yook, George Yuan, Khurshid Zaynutdinov, Ehud Ziegelman, and Eric Zivot. I also want to thank my editors, who again have been a great help: Nancy Lombardi, Peter Reinhart, Victoria Richardson, and Terry Vaughn.

As always I welcome suggestions and comments.

Simon Benninga
http://finance.wharton.upenn.edu/~benninga
benninga@post.tau.ac.il

Preface to the First Edition

Like its predecessor *Numerical Techniques in Finance*, this book presents some important financial models and shows how they can be solved numerically and/or simulated using Excel. In this sense this is a finance "cookbook"; like any cookbook, it gives recipes with a list of ingredients and instructions for making and baking. As any cook knows, a recipe is just a starting point; having followed the recipe a number of times, you can think of your own variations and make the results suit your tastes and needs.

Financial Modeling covers standard financial models in the areas of corporate finance, financial statement simulation, portfolio problems, options, portfolio insurance, duration, and immunization. Clear and concise explanations are provided in each case for the implementation of the models using Excel. Very little theory is offered except where necessary to understand the numerical implementations.

While Excel is often inappropriate for high-level, industrial-strength calculations (portfolios are an example), it is an excellent tool for understanding the computational intricacies involved in financial modeling. It is often the case that the fullest understanding of the models comes by calculating them, and Excel is one of the most accessible and powerful tools available for this purpose.

Along the way a lot of students, colleagues, and friends (these are nonexclusive categories) have helped me with advice and comments. In particular I would like to thank Olivier Blechner, Miryam Brand, Elizabeth Caulk, John Caulk, Benjamin Czaczkes, John Ferrari, John P. Flagler, Kunihiko Higashi, Julia Hynes, Don Keim, Anthony Kim, Ken Kunimoto, Philippe Nore, Nir Sharabi, Mark Thaler, Terry Vaughn, and Xiaoge Zhou.

Finally, my thanks go to a wonderful set of editors: Nancy Lombardi, Peter Reinhart, Victoria Richardson, and Terry Vaughn.

I Corporate Finance Models

The seven chapters that open the third edition of *Financial Modeling* cover basic problems and techniques in corporate finance. Chapters 1 and 2 are both review chapters. Chapter 1 is an introduction to basic financial calculations using Excel. Almost all of the applications discussed center on variations of the discounted cash flow method. The cost of capital, discussed in Chapter 2, is the rate at which corporate cash flows are discounted to arrive at enterprise value. Calculating this rate is not trivial and involves a combination of theoretical models and numerical computation, both discussed in the chapter.

Chapter 3 shows how to build pro forma models, which simulate the corporate income statement and balance sheets. Pro forma models are at the heart of many corporate finance applications, including business plans, credit analyses, and valuations. The models require a mixture of finance, accounting, and Excel. Chapter 4 develops a pro forma model to value PPG Corporation. The example we develop is typical of an exercise that accompanies many merger and acquisition valuations. Chapter 5 shows how to apply the valuation technology to banks; it also includes a short discussion of applying price-earnings techniques to bank valuation.

Chapters 6 and 7 discuss the financial analysis of leasing. In Chapter 6 we concentrate on the basic lease/purchase decision using the equivalent loan method. An appendix to Chapter 6 discusses some tax and accounting considerations relating to leases. Chapter 7 discusses the financial analysis of leveraged lease arrangements, including a discussion of the multiple-phases method of FASB 13. The multiple-phases method rate of return is a hybrid IRR, and Excel can easily be used to calculate this return.

1 Basic Financial Calculations

1.1 Overview

This chapter aims to give you some finance basics and their Excel implementation. If you have had a good introductory course in finance, this chapter is likely to be at best a refresher.[1]

This chapter covers

- Net present value (NPV)
- Internal rate of return (IRR)
- Payment schedules and loan tables
- Future value
- Pension and accumulation problems
- Continuously compounded interest

Almost all financial problems center on finding the *value today* of a series of *cash receipts over time.* The cash receipts (or cash flows, as we will call them) may be certain or uncertain. The *present value* of a cash flow CF_t anticipated to be received at time t is $\frac{CF_t}{(1+r)^t}$. The numerator of this expression is usually understood to be the *expected time-t cash flow*, and the discount rate r in the denominator is adjusted for the riskiness of this expected cash flow—the higher the risk, the higher the discount rate.

The basic concept in present-value calculations is the concept of *opportunity cost.* Opportunity cost is the return that would be required of an investment to make it a viable alternative to other, similar, investments. In the financial literature there are many synonyms for opportunity cost, among them discount rate, cost of capital, and interest rate. When the opportunity cost is applied to risky cash flows, we will sometimes call it the risk-adjusted discount rate (RADR) or the weighted average cost of capital (WACC). It goes without saying that this discount rate should be risk adjusted, and much of the standard finance literature discusses how to make this adjustment. As illustrated in this chapter, when we calculate the net present value, we use the investment's opportunity cost as a discount rate. When we calculate the internal rate of

1. In my book *Principles of Finance with Excel* (Oxford University Press, 2006), I have discussed many basic Excel/finance topics at greater length.

return, we compare the calculated return to the investment's opportunity cost to judge its value.

1.2 Present Value and Net Present Value

Both concepts, present value and net present value, are related to the value *today* of a set of future anticipated cash flows. As an example, suppose we are valuing an investment that promises $100 per year at the end of this and the next four years. We suppose that there is no doubt that this series of five payments of $100 each will actually be paid. If a bank pays an annual interest rate of 10 percent on a five-year deposit, then this 10 percent is the investment's opportunity cost, the alternative benchmark return to which we want to compare the investment. We may calculate the value of the investment by discounting its cash flows using this opportunity cost as a discount rate:

	A	B	C	D
1	**COMPUTING THE PRESENT VALUE**			
2	Discount rate	10%		
3				
4	**Year**	**Cash flow**	**Present value**	
5	1	100	90.9091	<-- =B5/(1+$B$2)^A5
6	2	100	82.6446	<-- =B6/(1+$B$2)^A6
7	3	100	75.1315	<-- =B7/(1+$B$2)^A7
8	4	100	68.3013	<-- =B8/(1+$B$2)^A8
9	5	100	62.0921	<-- =B9/(1+$B$2)^A9
10				
11	Net present value			
12	Summing cells C5:C9	379.08	<-- =SUM(C5:C9)	
13	Using Excel's NPV function	379.08	<-- =NPV(B2,B5:B9)	
14	Using Excel's PV function	379.08	<-- =PV(B2,5,-100)	

The *present value*, 379.08, is the *value today* of the investment. In a competitive market, the present value should correspond to the market price of the cash flows. The spreadsheet illustrates three ways of obtaining this value:

- Summing the individual present values in cells C5:C9. To simplify the copying, note the use of "^" to represent the power and the use of both the relative and absolute references; for example: = B5/(1 + $B$2)^A5 in cell C5.

• Using the Excel **NPV** function. As we will soon show, Excel's **NPV** function is unfortunately misnamed—it actually computes the present value and not the net present value (discussed in section 1.2.2).

• Using the Excel **PV** function. This function computes the present value of a series of constant payments. **PV(B2,5,–100)** is the present value of five payments of 100 each at the discount rate in cell B2. The **PV** function returns a negative value for positive cash flows; to prevent this unfortunate occurrence, we have made the cash flows negative.[2]

1.2.1 The Difference Between Excel's PV and NPV Functions

The preceding spreadsheet may leave the impression that **PV** and **NPV** perform exactly the same computation. But this is not true—whereas **NPV** can handle any series of cash flows, **PV** can handle only constant cash flows:

	A	B	C	D
1	**COMPUTING THE PRESENT VALUE** **In this example the cash flows are not equal** **Either discount each cash flow separately or use Excel's NPV function** **Excel's PV doesn't work for this case**			
2	Discount rate	10%		
3				
4	**Year**	**Cash flow**	**Present value**	**Present value of each cash flow**
5	1	100	90.9091	<-- =B5/(1+$B$2)^A5
6	2	200	165.2893	<-- =B6/(1+$B$2)^A6
7	3	300	225.3944	<-- =B7/(1+$B$2)^A7
8	4	400	273.2054	<-- =B8/(1+$B$2)^A8
9	5	500	310.4607	<-- =B9/(1+$B$2)^A9
10				
11	Net present value			
12	Summing cells C5:C9	1065.26	<-- =SUM(C5:C9)	
13	Using Excel's NPV function	1065.26	<-- =NPV(B2,B5:B9)	

2. This strange property—returning negative values for positive cash flows—is shared by a number of otherwise impeccable Excel functions such as PMT and PV. The somewhat convoluted logic which led Microsoft to write these functions this way is not worth explaining.

1.2.2 Excel's NPV Function Is Misnamed!

In standard finance terminology, the *present value* of a series of cash flows is the value today of the cash flows starting in year 1:

$$\text{Present value} = \sum_{t=1}^{N} \frac{CF_t}{(1+r)^t}$$

The *net present value* is the present value and the cost of acquiring the asset (the cash flow at time zero):

$$\text{Net present value} = \sum_{t=0}^{N} \frac{CF_t}{(1+r)^t} = \underbrace{CF_0}_{\substack{\uparrow \\ \text{In many cases} \\ CF_0 < 0\text{, meaning} \\ \text{that it represents the} \\ \text{price paid for the asset.}}} + \underbrace{\sum_{t=1}^{N} \frac{CF_t}{(1+r)^t}}_{\substack{\uparrow \\ \text{This is the present} \\ \text{value, given by Excel's} \\ \text{NPV function}}}$$

Excel's language about discounted cash flows differs somewhat from the standard finance nomenclature. To calculate the finance net present value of a series of cash flows using Excel, we have to calculate the present value of the future cash flows (using the Excel **NPV** function), taking into account the time-zero cash flow (this is often the cost of the asset in question).

1.2.3 Net Present Value

Suppose that the investment of section 1.2 is sold for $400. Clearly it would not be worth its purchase price, since—given the alternative return (discount rate) of 10 percent—the investment is worth only $379.08. The net present value (NPV) is the applicable concept here. Denoting by r the discount rate applicable to the investment, the NPV is calculated as follows:

$$NPV = CF_0 + \sum_{t=1}^{N} \frac{CF_t}{(1+r)^t}$$

where CF_t is the investment's cash flow at time t and CF_0 is today's cash flow.

Suppose, for example, that the series of five cash flows of $100 is sold for $250. Then, as shown in the following spreadsheet, the NPV = 129.08.

	A	B	C	D
1	**COMPUTING THE NET PRESENT VALUE**			
2	Discount rate	10%		
3				
4	**Year**	**Cash flow**	**Present value**	
5	0	-250	-250.00	<-- =B5/(1+$B$2)^A5
6	1	100	90.91	<-- =B6/(1+$B$2)^A6
7	2	100	82.64	<-- =B7/(1+$B$2)^A7
8	3	100	75.13	<-- =B8/(1+$B$2)^A8
9	4	100	68.30	<-- =B9/(1+$B$2)^A9
10	5	100	62.09	<-- =B10/(1+$B$2)^A10
11				
12	Net present value			
13	Summing cells C5:C10	129.08	<-- =SUM(C5:C10)	
14	Using Excel's NPV function	129.08	<-- =B5+NPV(B2,B6:B10)	

The NPV represents the *wealth increment* that accrues to the purchaser of the cash flows. If you buy the series of five cash flows of 100 for 250, then you have gained 129.08 in wealth today. In a competitive market the NPV of a series of cash flows ought to be zero: Since the present value should correspond to the market price of the cash flows, the NPV should be zero. In other words, the market price of our five cash flows of 100—in a competitive market, assuming that 10 percent is the correct risk-adjusted discount rate—ought to be 379.08.

1.2.4 Present Value of an Annuity—Some Useful Formulas

An *annuity* is a security that pays a constant sum in each period in the future.[3] Annuities may have a finite or infinite series of payments. If the annuity is finite and the appropriate discount rate is r, then the value today of the annuity is its present value:

$$\text{PV of finite annuity} = \frac{C}{1+r} + \frac{C}{(1+r)^2} + \ldots + \frac{C}{(1+r)^n}$$

$$= C\left(\frac{1-\dfrac{1}{(1+r)^n}}{r}\right)$$

This formula can also be computed using Excel's **PV** function. The following illustration also shows the use of Excel's **NPV** function in valuing a finite annuity:

3. All the formulas in this subsection depend on some well-known but oft-forgotten high school algebra. See box on the Euler formula in Chapter 2 (pp. 41–42).

	A	B	C
1	**COMPUTING THE VALUE OF A FINITE ANNUITY**		
2	Periodic payment, C	1,000	
3	Number of future periods paid, n	5	
4	Discount rate, r	12%	
5	Present value of annuity		
6	Using formula	3,604.78	<-- =B2*(1-1/(1+B4)^B3)/B4
7	Using Excel's **PV** function	3,604.78	<-- =PV(B4,B3,-B2)
8			
9	**Period**	**Annuity payment**	
10	1	1,000.00	<-- =B2
11	2	1,000.00	
12	3	1,000.00	
13	4	1,000.00	
14	5	1,000.00	
15			
16	Present value using Excel's **NPV** function	3,604.78	<-- =NPV(B4,B10:B14)

If the annuity promises an infinite series of constant future payments, then this formula reduces to

$$\text{PV of infinite annuity} = \frac{C}{1+r} + \frac{C}{(1+r)^2} + \ldots = \frac{C}{r}$$

	A	B	C
1	**COMPUTING THE VALUE OF AN INFINITE ANNUITY**		
2	Periodic payment, C	1,000	
3	Discount rate, r	12%	
4	Present value of annuity	8,333.33	<-- =B2/B3

A *growing annuity* pays out a sum C that grows at a periodic growth rate g. If the annuity is finite, its value today is given by

$$\begin{aligned}\text{PV of finite growing annuity} &= \frac{C}{1+r} + \frac{C(1+g)}{(1+r)^2} + \frac{C(1+g)^2}{(1+r)^3} + \ldots \\ &+ \frac{C(1+g)^{n-1}}{(1+r)^n} \\ &= \frac{C\left[1-\left(\frac{1+g}{1+r}\right)^n\right]}{r-g}\end{aligned}$$

This formula can easily be implemented in Excel, and—as shown here—can also be computed using the Excel **NPV** function:

	A	B	C
1	**COMPUTING THE VALUE OF A GROWING FINITE ANNUITY**		
2	First payment, C	1,000	
3	Growth rate of payments, g	6%	
4	Number of future periods paid, n	5	
5	Discount rate, r	12%	
6	Present value of annuity		
7	Using formula	4,010.91	<-- =B2*(1-((1+B3)/(1+B5))^B4)/(B5-B3)
8			
9	**Period**	**Annuity payment**	
10	1	1,000.00	<-- =B2
11	2	1,060.00	<-- =$B$2*(1+$B$3)^(A11-1)
12	3	1,123.60	<-- =$B$2*(1+$B$3)^(A12-1)
13	4	1,191.02	<-- =$B$2*(1+$B$3)^(A13-1)
14	5	1,262.48	<-- =$B$2*(1+$B$3)^(A14-1)
15			
16	Present value using Excel's **NPV** function	4,010.91	<-- =NPV(B5,B10:B14)

Taking the previous formula and letting $n \to \infty$, we can compute the value of an *infinite growing annuity*:

$$\text{PV of infinite growing annuity} = \frac{C}{1+r} + \frac{C(1+g)}{(1+r)^2} + \frac{C(1+g)^2}{(1+r)^3} + \ldots$$

$$= \frac{C}{r-g}, \text{ provided } \left|\frac{1+g}{1+r}\right| < 1$$

Here is an illustration in Excel:

	A	B	C
1	**COMPUTING THE VALUE OF A GROWING INFINITE ANNUITY**		
2	Periodic payment, C	1,000	<-- Starting at date 1
3	Growth rate of payments, g	6%	
4	Discount rate, r	12%	
5	Present value of annuity	16,666.67	<-- =B2/(B4-B3)

1.3 Internal Rate of Return and Loan Tables

The *internal rate of return* (IRR) is defined as the compound rate of return r that makes the NPV equal to zero:

$$CF_0 + \sum_{t=1}^{N} \frac{CF_t}{(1+r)^t} = 0$$

To illustrate, consider the following example given in rows 2–10. A project costing 800 in year zero returns a variable series of cash flows at the end of years 1–5. The IRR of the project (cell B10) is 22.16 percent.

	A	B	C
1	**INTERNAL RATE OF RETURN**		
2	**Year**	**Cash flow**	
3	0	-800	
4	1	200	
5	2	250	
6	3	300	
7	4	350	
8	5	400	
9			
10	Internal rate of return	22.16%	<-- =IRR(B3:B8)

Note that the Excel **IRR** function includes as arguments *all* the cash flows of the investment, including the first—in this case negative—cash flow of –800.

1.3.1 Determining the IRR by Trial and Error

There is no simple formula to compute the IRR. Excel's **IRR** function uses trial and error, which can be simulated as shown in the following spreadsheet:

	A	B	C
1	**INTERNAL RATE OF RETURN**		
2	Discount rate	12%	
3			
4	**Year**	**Cash flow**	
5	0	-800	
6	1	200	
7	2	250	
8	3	300	
9	4	350	
10	5	400	
11			
12	Net present value (NPV)	240.81	<-- =B5+NPV(B2,B6:B10)

By playing with the discount rate or by using Excel's **Goal Seek**, we can determine that at 22.16 percent the NPV in cell B12 is zero.

	A	B	C
1	**INTERNAL RATE OF RETURN**		
2	Discount rate	22.16%	
3			
4	**Year**	**Cash flow**	
5	0	-800	
6	1	200	
7	2	250	
8	3	300	
9	4	350	
10	5	400	
11			
12	Net present value (NPV)	0.00	<-- =B5+NPV(B2,B6:B10)

Here's the way the **Goal Seek** screen looked before we got the correct answer:

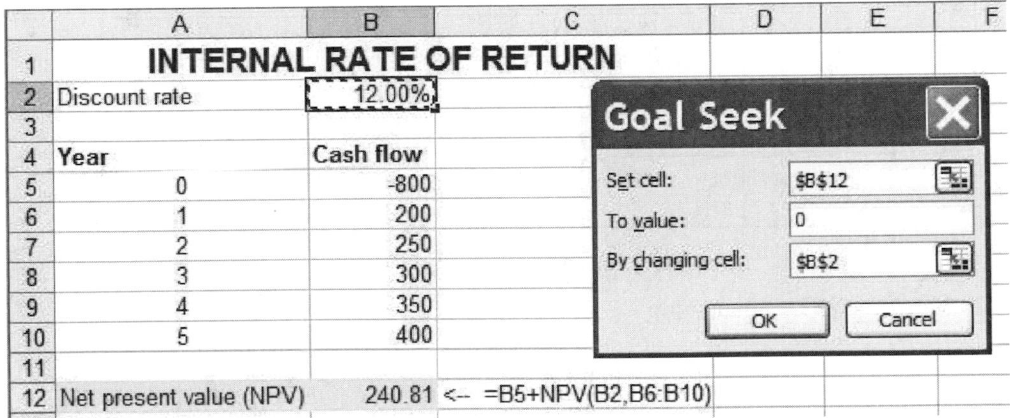

	A	B	C
1	**INTERNAL RATE OF RETURN**		
2	Discount rate	12.00%	
3			
4	**Year**	**Cash flow**	
5	0	-800	
6	1	200	
7	2	250	
8	3	300	
9	4	350	
10	5	400	
11			
12	Net present value (NPV)	240.81	<-- =B5+NPV(B2,B6:B10)

1.3.2 Loan Tables and the Internal Rate of Return

The IRR is the compound *rate of return paid by the investment*. To understand this point fully, it helps to make a *loan table*, which shows the division of the investment's cash flows between investment income and the return of the investment principal:

	A	B	C	D	E	F
1	**INTERNAL RATE OF RETURN**					
2	**Year**	**Cash flow**				
3	0	-800				
4	1	200				
5	2	250				
6	3	300				
7	4	350				
8	5	400				
9						
10	Internal rate of return	22.16%	<-- =IRR(B3:B8)			
11						
12	**USING THE IRR IN A LOAN TABLE**					
13	=-B3		=$B$10*B15	**Division of cash flow between investment income and return of principal**		
14	**Year**	**Investment at beginning of year**	**Cash flow at end of year**	**Income**	**Return of principal**	
15	1	800.00	200.00	177.28	22.72	<-- =C15-D15
16	2	777.28	250.00	172.25	77.75	
17	3	699.53	300.00	155.02	144.98	
18	4	554.55	350.00	122.89	227.11	
19	5	327.44	400.00	72.56	327.44	
20	6	0.00				
21	=B15-E15					
22			The remaining investment principal in the year after the last cash flow is zero, indicating that all the principal has been repaid.			
23						
24						
25						
26						

The loan table divides each of the cash flows of the asset into an income component and a return-of-principal component. The income component at the end of each year is IRR times the principal balance at the beginning of that year. Notice that the principal at the beginning of the last year ($327.44 in the example) exactly equals the return of principal at the end of that year.

We can actually use the loan table to find the internal rate of return. Consider an investment costing $1,000 today that pays off the cash flows indicated at the end of years 1, 2, 5. At a rate of 15 percent (cell B2), the principal at the beginning of year 6 is negative, indicating that too little has been paid out in income. Thus the IRR must be larger than 15 percent.

	A	B	C	D	E	F
1	**USING A LOAN TABLE TO FIND THE IRR**					
2	IRR?	15.00%				
3						
4				**Division of cash flow between investment income and return of principal**		
5	**Year**	**Principal at beginning of year**	**Cash flow at end of year**	**Income**	**Principal**	
6	1	1,000.00	300	150.00	150.00	<-- =C6-D6
7	2	850.00	200	127.50	72.50	
8	3	777.50	150	116.63	33.38	
9	4	744.13	600	111.62	488.38	
10	5	255.74	900	38.36	861.64	
11	6	-605.89				
12			=$B$2*B6			
13	=B6-E6					

If the interest rate in cell B2 is indeed the IRR, then cell B11 should be 0. We can use Excel's **Goal Seek** (found on the **Tools** menu) to calculate the IRR:

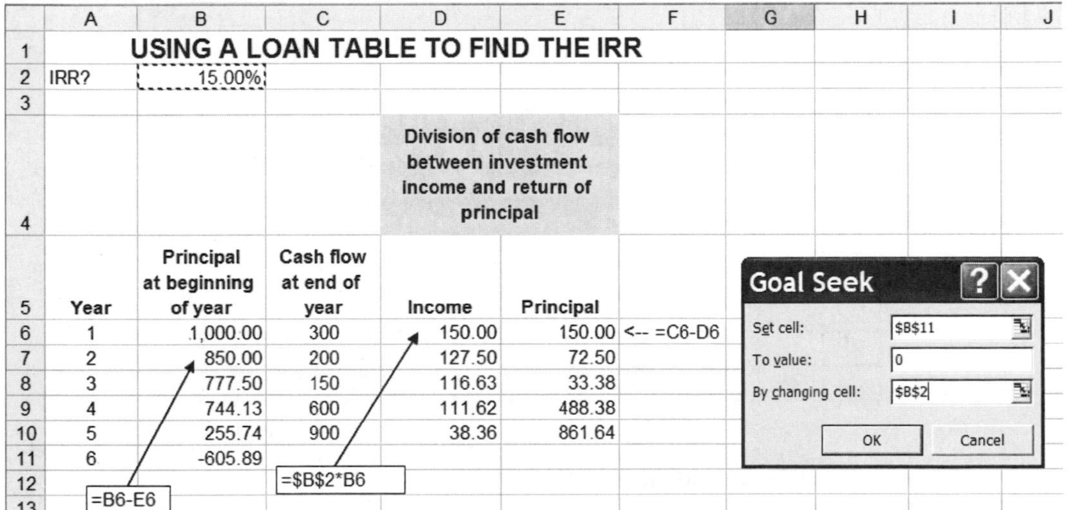

	A	B	C	D	E	F
1	**USING A LOAN TABLE TO FIND THE IRR**					
2	IRR?	15.00%				
3						
4				**Division of cash flow between investment income and return of principal**		
5	**Year**	**Principal at beginning of year**	**Cash flow at end of year**	**Income**	**Principal**	
6	1	1,000.00	300	150.00	150.00	<-- =C6-D6
7	2	850.00	200	127.50	72.50	
8	3	777.50	150	116.63	33.38	
9	4	744.13	600	111.62	488.38	
10	5	255.74	900	38.36	861.64	
11	6	-605.89				
12			=$B$2*B6			
13	=B6-E6					

As shown here, the IRR is 24.44 percent:

	A	B	C	D	E	F
1	USING A LOAN TABLE TO FIND THE IRR					
2	IRR?	24.44%				
3						
4				Division of cash flow between investment income and return of principal		
5	Year	Principal at beginning of year	Cash flow at end of year	Income	Principal	
6	1	1,000.00	300	244.36	55.64	<-- =C6-D6
7	2	944.36	200	230.76	-30.76	
8	3	975.13	150	238.28	-88.28	
9	4	1,063.41	600	259.86	340.14	
10	5	723.26	900	176.74	723.26	
11	6	0.00				
12			=$B$2*B6			
13	=B6-E6					

Of course, we could have simplified life by just using the **IRR** function:

	A	B	C	D
15	Direct calculation of IRR			
16	Year	Cash flow		
17	0	-1,000		
18	1	300		
19	2	200		
20	3	150		
21	4	600		
22	5	900		
23				
24	IRR	24.44%	<-- =IRR(B17:B22)	

1.3.3 Excel's Rate Function

Excel's **Rate** function computes the IRR of a series of constant future payments. In the following example, we pay $1,000 today for an annual payment of $100 for the next 30 years. **Rate** shows that the IRR is 9.307 percent:

	A	B	C
1	**USING EXCEL'S RATE FUNCTION TO COMPUTE THE IRR**		
2	Initial investment	1,000	
3	Periodic cash flow	100	
4	Number of payments	30	
5	IRR	9.307%	<-- =RATE(B4,B3,-B2)

Note: **Rate** works much like **PMT** and **PV**, discussed elsewhere in this chapter; it requires a sign change between the initial investment and the periodic cash flow (note that we have used –B2 in cell B5). It also has switches to allow for payments that start today and payments that start one period from now (not shown in the example).

1.4 Multiple Internal Rates of Return

Sometimes a series of cash flows has more than one IRR. In the next example we can tell that the cash flows in cells B6:B11 have two IRRs, since the NPV graph crosses the x-axis twice:

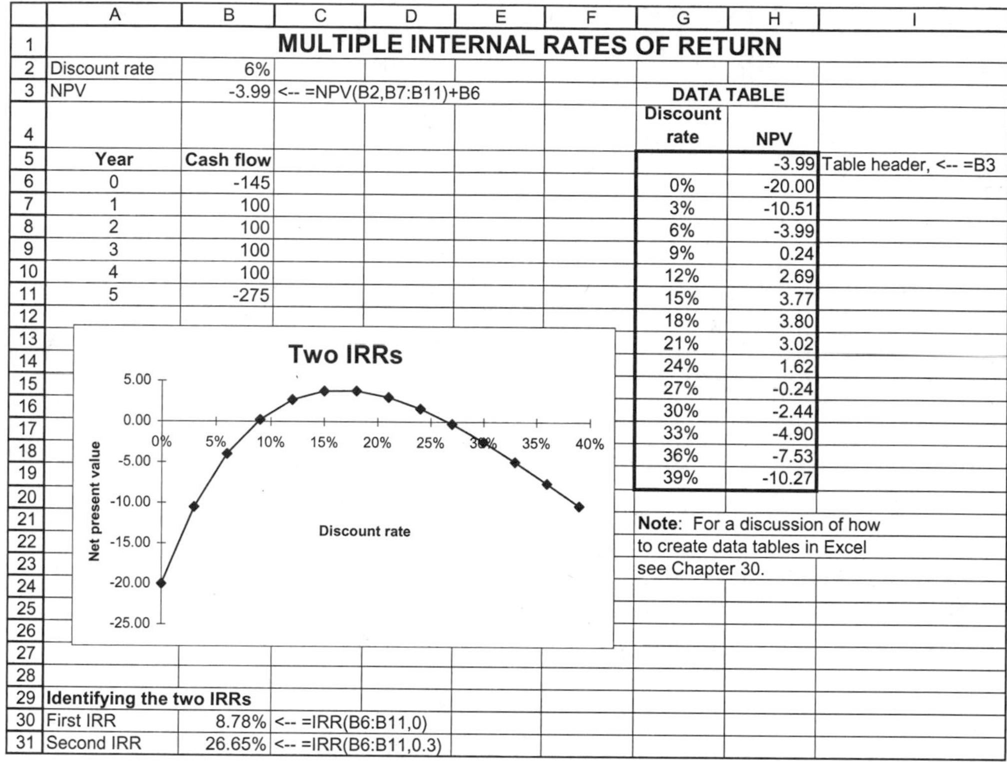

	A	B	C	D	E	F	G	H	I
1			MULTIPLE INTERNAL RATES OF RETURN						
2	Discount rate	6%							
3	NPV	-3.99	<-- =NPV(B2,B7:B11)+B6				DATA TABLE		
4							Discount rate	NPV	
5	Year	Cash flow						-3.99	Table header, <-- =B3
6	0	-145					0%	-20.00	
7	1	100					3%	-10.51	
8	2	100					6%	-3.99	
9	3	100					9%	0.24	
10	4	100					12%	2.69	
11	5	-275					15%	3.77	
12							18%	3.80	
13							21%	3.02	
14							24%	1.62	
15							27%	-0.24	
16							30%	-2.44	
17							33%	-4.90	
18							36%	-7.53	
19							39%	-10.27	
20									
21							**Note**: For a discussion of how		
22							to create data tables in Excel		
23							see Chapter 30.		
24									
25									
26									
27									
28									
29	**Identifying the two IRRs**								
30	First IRR	8.78%	<-- =IRR(B6:B11,0)						
31	Second IRR	26.65%	<-- =IRR(B6:B11,0.3)						

Excel's **IRR** function allows us to add an extra argument that will help us find both IRRs. Instead of writing **=IRR(B6:B11)**, we write =**IRR(B6:B11,guess)**. The argument **guess** is a starting point for the algorithm that Excel uses to find the IRR; by adjusting the **guess**, we can identify both the IRRs. Cells B30 and B31 give an illustration.

There are two things to note about this procedure:

- The argument **guess** merely has to be close to the IRR; it is not unique. For example by setting the guesses equal to 0.1 and 0.5, we will still get the same IRRs:

	A	B	C	D
29	**Identifying the two IRRs**			
30	First IRR	8.78%	<-- =IRR(B6:B11,0.1)	
31	Second IRR	26.65%	<-- =IRR(B6:B11,0.5)	

• In order to identify the number and the approximate value of the IRRs, it helps greatly to graph (as we did above) the NPV of the investment as a function of various discount rates. The internal rates of return are then the points where the graph crosses the x-axis, and the approximate location of these points should be used as the guesses in the IRR function.[4]

From a purely technical point of view, a set of cash flows can have multiple IRRs only if it has at least two changes of sign. Many "typical" cash flows have only one change of sign. Consider, for example, the cash flows from purchasing a bond having a 10 percent coupon, a face value of $1,000, and eight more years to maturity. If the current market price of the bond is $800, then the stream of cash flows changes signs only once (from negative in year 0 to positive in years 1–8). Thus there is only one IRR:

	A	B	C	D	E	F	G	H	I	J	K
1	BOND CASH FLOWS: NPV CROSSES x-AXIS ONLY ONCE, SO THERE IS ONLY ONE IRR										
2	Year	Cash flow			Data table: Effect of						
3	0	-800			discount rate on NPV						
4	1	100				1,000.00	<-- =NPV(E4,B4:B11)+B3, table header				
5	2	100			0%	1,000.00					
6	3	100			2%	786.04					
7	4	100			4%	603.96					
8	5	100			6%	448.39					
9	6	100			8%	314.93					
10	7	100			10%	200.00					
11	8	1100			12%	100.65					
12					14%	14.45					
13	IRR	14.36%	<-- =IRR(B3:B11)		16%	-60.62					
14					18%	-126.21					
15					20%	-183.72					
16											
17											

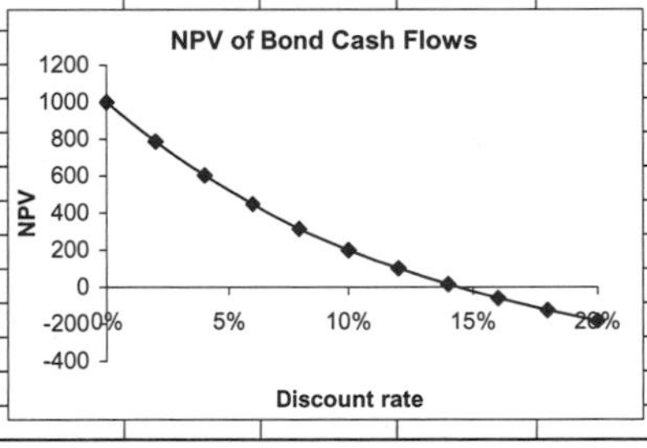

NPV of Bond Cash Flows

NPV: 1200, 1000, 800, 600, 400, 200, 0, -200, -400

0%, 5%, 10%, 15%, 20%

Discount rate

1.5 Flat Payment Schedules

Another common problem is to compute a "flat" repayment for a loan. For example, you take a loan for $10,000 at an interest rate of 7 percent per year. The bank wants you to make a series of payments that will pay off the loan and the interest over six years. We can use Excel's **PMT** function to determine how much each annual payment should be:

4. If you don't put in a guess (as we did in the example), Excel defaults to a guess of 0. Thus, in this case, IRR(B6:B11) will return 8.78 percent.

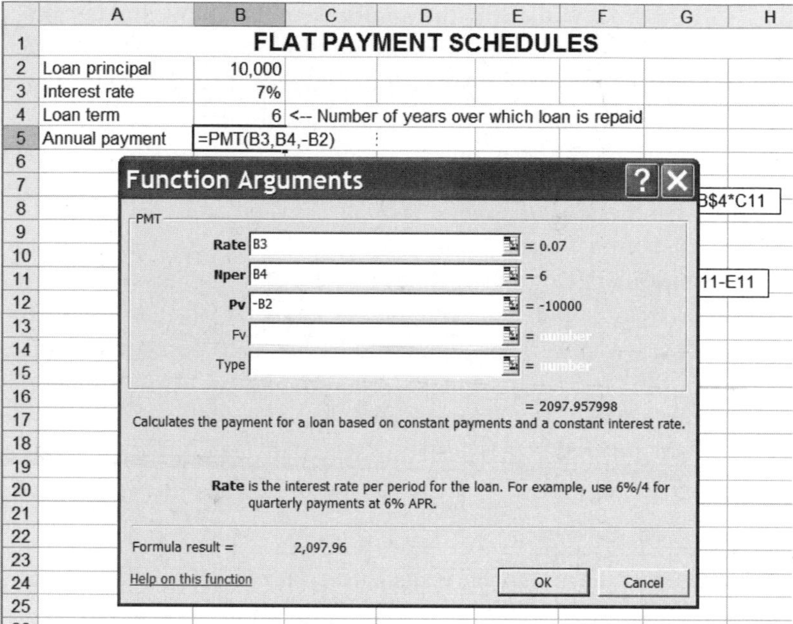

Notice that we have put a minus sign in the space labeled **Pv**—Excel's nomenclature for the initial loan principal. As discussed in footnote 3, if we do not do so, Excel returns a negative payment (a minor irritant). You can confirm that the answer of $2,097.96 is correct by creating a loan table:

	A	B	C	D	E	F	G
1	FLAT PAYMENT SCHEDULES						
2	Loan principal	10,000					
3	Interest rate	7%					
4	Loan term	6	<-- Number of years over which loan is repaid				
5	Annual payment	2,097.96	<-- =PMT(B3,B4,-B2)				
6							
7					Split payment into:		=$B$3*C9
8		Year	Principal at beginning of year	Payment at end of year	Interest	Return of principal	
9		1	10,000.00	2,097.96	700.00	1,397.96	
10		2	8,602.04	2,097.96	602.14	1,495.82	=D9-E9
11		3	7,106.23	2,097.96	497.44	1,600.52	
12	=C9-F9	4	5,505.70	2,097.96	385.40	1,712.56	
13		5	3,793.15	2,097.96	265.52	1,832.44	
14		6	1,960.71	2,097.96	137.25	1,960.71	
15		7	0.00				

The zero in cell C15 indicates that the loan is fully repaid over its term of six years. You can easily confirm that the present value of the payments over the six years is the initial principal of $10,000.

1.6 Future Values and Applications

We start with a triviality. Suppose you deposit $1,000 in an account today, leaving it there for 10 years. Suppose the account draws annual interest of 10 percent. How much will you have at the end of 10 years? The answer, as shown in the following spreadsheet, is $2,593.74:

	A	B	C	D	E
1	SIMPLE FUTURE VALUE				
2	Interest	10%			
3					
4	Year	Account balance, beginning of year	Interest earned during year	Total in account, end year	
5	1	1,000.00	100.00	1,100.00	<-- =C5+B5
6	2	1,100.00	110.00	1,210.00	<-- =C6+B6
7	3	1,210.00	121.00	1,331.00	
8	4	1,331.00	133.10	1,464.10	=$B$2*B5
9	5	1,464.10	146.41	1,610.51	
10	6	1,610.51	161.05	1,771.56	
11	7	1,771.56	177.16	1,948.72	
12	8	1,948.72	194.87	2,143.59	
13	9	2,143.59	214.36	2,357.95	
14	10	2,357.95	235.79	2,593.74	
15	11	2,593.74		=D5	
16					
17	A simpler way		2,593.74	<-- =B5*(1+B2)^10	

As cell C17 shows, you don't need all these complicated calculations: The *future value* of $1,000 in 10 years at 10 percent per year is given by

$$FV = 1{,}000 * (1+10\%)^{10} = 2{,}593.74$$

Now consider the following, slightly more complicated, problem: Again, you intend to open a savings account. Your initial deposit of \$1,000 today will be followed by a similar deposit at the beginning of years 1 to 9. If the account earns 10 percent per year, how much will you have in the account at the start of year 10?

This problem is easily modeled in Excel:

	A	B	C	D	E	F
1	FUTURE VALUE WITH ANNUAL DEPOSITS					
2	Interest	10%				
3	Annual deposit	1,000	<-- Made today and at beginning of each of next 9 years			
4	Number of deposits	10				
5						
6	Year	Account balance, beginning of year	Deposit at beginning of year	Interest earned during year	Total in account, end year	
7	1	0.00	1,000	100.00	1,100.00	<-- =D7+C7+B7
8	2	1,100.00	1,000	210.00	2,310.00	<-- =D8+C8+B8
9	3	2,310.00	1,000	331.00	3,641.00	
10	4	3,641.00	1,000	464.10	5,105.10	=\$B\$2*(B7+C7)
11	5	5,105.10	1,000	610.51	6,715.61	
12	6	6,715.61	1,000	771.56	8,487.17	
13	7	8,487.17	1,000	948.72	10,435.89	
14	8	10,435.89	1,000	1,143.59	12,579.48	
15	9	12,579.48	1,000	1,357.95	14,937.42	
16	10	14,937.42	1,000	1,593.74	17,531.17	
17						
18	Future value	17,531.17	<-- =FV(B2,B4,-B3,,1)		=E7	

Thus the answer is that we will have \$17,531.17 in the account at the end of year 10. This same answer can be represented as a formula that sums the future values of each deposit:

$$\text{Total at beginning of year } 10 = 1{,}000*(1+10\%)^{10} + 1{,}000*(1+10\%)^{9} + \ldots + 1{,}000*(1+10\%)^{1} = \sum_{t=1}^{10} 1{,}000*(1+10\%)^{t}$$

An Excel Function Note from cell B18 that Excel has a function **FV** that gives this sum. The dialog box brought up by **FV** is the following:

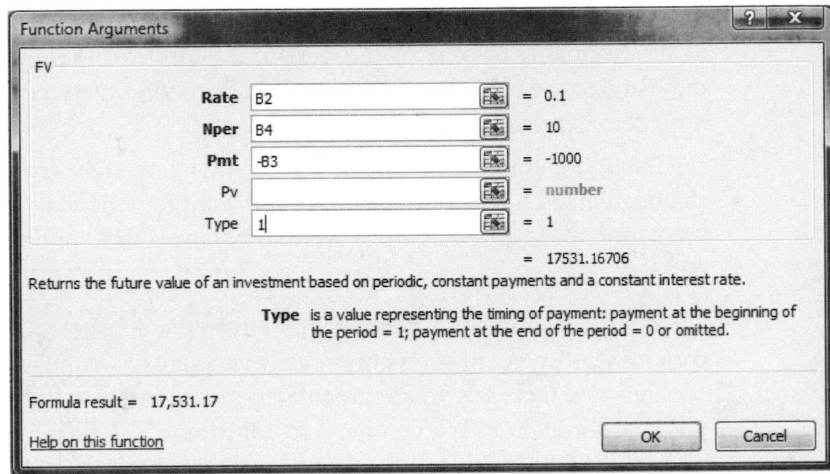

We note three things about this function:

1. For positive deposits **FV** returns a negative number (look back at footnote 2). This is an irritating property of this function that it shares with **PV** and **PMT**. To avoid negative numbers, we have put the **Pmt** in as –1,000.

2. The line **Pv** in the dialog box refers to a situation where the account has some initial value other than 0 when the series of deposits is made. In this example, this space has been left blank, indicating that the initial account value is zero.

3. As noted in the picture, "Type" (either 1 or 0) refers to whether the deposit is made at the beginning or the end of each period (in our example the former is the case).

1.7 A Pension Problem—Complicating the Future-Value Problem

A typical exercise is the following: You are currently 55 years old and intend to retire at age 60. To make your retirement easier, you intend to start a retirement account.

• At the beginning of each of years 1, 2, 3, 4 (that is, starting today and at the beginning of each of the next four years), you intend to make a deposit into the retirement account. You think that the account will earn 8 percent per year.

• After retirement at age 60, you anticipate living eight more years.[5] At the beginning of each of these years you want to withdraw $30,000 from your retirement account. Your account balances will continue to earn 8 percent.

How much should you deposit annually in the account? The following spreadsheet fragment shows how easily you can go wrong in this kind of problem—in this case, you've calculated that in order to provide $30,000 per year for eight years, you need to contribute $240,000/5 = $48,000 in each of the first five years. As the spreadsheet shows, you'll end up with a lot of money at the end of eight years! (The reason—you've ignored the powerful effects of compound interest. If you set the interest rate in the spreadsheet equal to 0 percent, you'll see that you're right.)

	A	B	C	D	E	F
1	**A RETIREMENT PROBLEM**					
2	Interest	8%				
3	Annual deposit	48,000.00				
4	Annual retirement withdrawal	30,000.00				
5						=$B$2*(C7+B7)
6	**Year**	**Account balance, beginning of year**	**Deposit at beginning of year**	**Interest earned during year**	**Total in account, end year**	
7	1	0.00	48,000.00	3,840.00	51,840.00	<-- =D7+C7+B7
8	2	51,840.00	48,000.00	7,987.20	107,827.20	
9	3	107,827.20	48,000.00	12,466.18	168,293.38	
10	4	168,293.38	48,000.00	17,303.47	233,596.85	
11	5	233,596.85	48,000.00	22,527.75	304,124.59	
12	6	304,124.59	-30,000.00	21,929.97	296,054.56	
13	7	296,054.56	-30,000.00	21,284.36	287,338.93	
14	8	287,338.93	-30,000.00	20,587.11	277,926.04	
15	9	277,926.04	-30,000.00	19,834.08	267,760.12	
16	10	267,760.12	-30,000.00	19,020.81	256,780.93	
17	11	256,780.93	-30,000.00	18,142.47	244,923.41	
18	12	244,923.41	-30,000.00	17,193.87	232,117.28	
19	13	232,117.28	-30,000.00	16,169.38	218,286.66	
20						
21	**Note**: This problem has five deposits and eight annual withdrawals, all made at the beginning of the year. The beginning of year 13 is the last year of the retirement plan; if the annual deposit is correctly computed, the balance at the beginning of year 13 after the withdrawal should be zero.					

5. Of course you're going to live much longer! And I wish you good health! The dimensions of this problem have been chosen to make it fit nicely on a page.

There are several ways to solve this problem. The first involves Excel's **Solver**. This can be found on the **Tools** menu.[6]

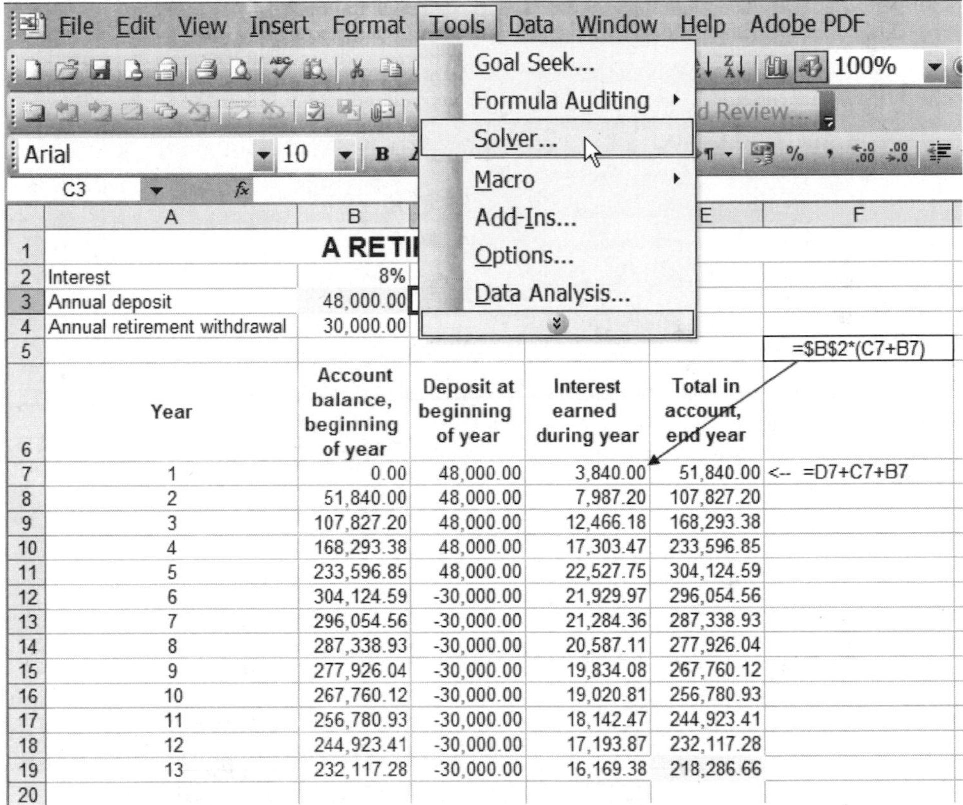

	A	B	C	D	E	F
1		A RETI				
2	Interest	8%				
3	Annual deposit	48,000.00				
4	Annual retirement withdrawal	30,000.00				
5						=$B$2*(C7+B7)
6	Year	Account balance, beginning of year	Deposit at beginning of year	Interest earned during year	Total in account, end year	
7	1	0.00	48,000.00	3,840.00	51,840.00	<-- =D7+C7+B7
8	2	51,840.00	48,000.00	7,987.20	107,827.20	
9	3	107,827.20	48,000.00	12,466.18	168,293.38	
10	4	168,293.38	48,000.00	17,303.47	233,596.85	
11	5	233,596.85	48,000.00	22,527.75	304,124.59	
12	6	304,124.59	-30,000.00	21,929.97	296,054.56	
13	7	296,054.56	-30,000.00	21,284.36	287,338.93	
14	8	287,338.93	-30,000.00	20,587.11	277,926.04	
15	9	277,926.04	-30,000.00	19,834.08	267,760.12	
16	10	267,760.12	-30,000.00	19,020.81	256,780.93	
17	11	256,780.93	-30,000.00	18,142.47	244,923.41	
18	12	244,923.41	-30,000.00	17,193.87	232,117.28	
19	13	232,117.28	-30,000.00	16,169.38	218,286.66	
20						

Clicking on the **Solver** makes a dialog box appear. In the following illustration we've filled it in.

6. If the **Solver** does not appear on the Tools menu, then you have to load it. Go **Tools|Add-Ins** and click **Solver Add-In** on the list of programs. Note that you could also use the **Goal Seek** tool to solve this problem. For simple problems such as this one, there is not much difference between the **Solver** and **Goal Seek**; the one (not inconsiderable) advantage of the **Solver** is that it remembers its previous arguments, so that if you bring it up again on the same spreadsheet, you can see what you did in the previous iteration. In later chapters we will illustrate problems that cannot be solved by **Goal Seek** and where the use of the **Solver** is a necessity. **Solver** and **Goal Seek** are compared in Chapter 6, page 210.

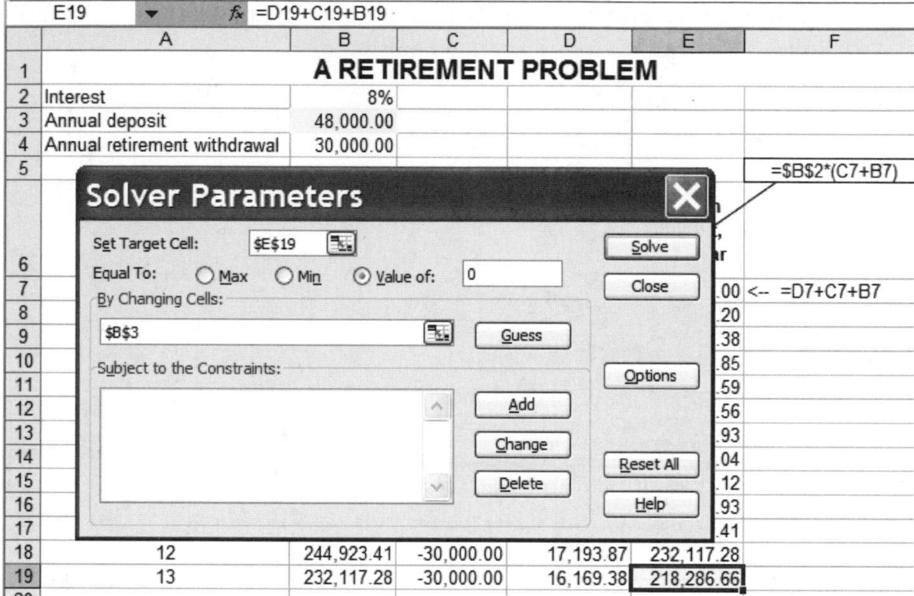

If we now click on the **Solve** box, we get the answer:

	A	B	C	D	E	F
1	**A RETIREMENT PROBLEM**					
2	Interest	8%				
3	Annual deposit	29,386.55				
4	Annual retirement withdrawal	30,000.00				
5						=$B$2*(C7+B7)
6	**Year**	**Account balance, beginning of year**	**Deposit at beginning of year**	**Interest earned during year**	**Total in account, end year**	
7	1	0.00	29,386.55	2,350.92	31,737.48	<-- =D7+C7+B7
8	2	31,737.48	29,386.55	4,889.92	66,013.95	
9	3	66,013.95	29,386.55	7,632.04	103,032.54	
10	4	103,032.54	29,386.55	10,593.53	143,012.62	
11	5	143,012.62	29,386.55	13,791.93	186,191.10	
12	6	186,191.10	-30,000.00	12,495.29	168,686.39	
13	7	168,686.39	-30,000.00	11,094.91	149,781.30	
14	8	149,781.30	-30,000.00	9,582.50	129,363.81	
15	9	129,363.81	-30,000.00	7,949.10	107,312.91	
16	10	107,312.91	-30,000.00	6,185.03	83,497.94	
17	11	83,497.94	-30,000.00	4,279.84	57,777.78	
18	12	57,777.78	-30,000.00	2,222.22	30,000.00	
19	13	30,000.00	-30,000.00	0.00	0.00	

1.7.1 Solving the Retirement Problem Using Financial Formulas

We can solve this problem in a more intelligent fashion if we understand the discounting process. The present value of the whole series of payments, discounted at 8 percent, must be zero:

$$\sum_{t=0}^{4} \frac{\text{Initial deposit}}{(1.08)^t} - \sum_{t=5}^{12} \frac{30{,}000}{(1.08)^t} = 0$$

$$\Rightarrow \text{Initial deposit} = \left[\sum_{t=5}^{12} \frac{30{,}000}{(1.08)^t} \right] \Big/ \left[\sum_{t=0}^{4} \frac{1}{(1.08)^t} \right]$$

Both the numerator on the right-hand side as $\sum_{t=5}^{12} \frac{30{,}000}{(1.08)^t} = \frac{1}{(1.08)^4} \sum_{t=1}^{8} \frac{30{,}000}{(1.08)^t}$ and the denominator $\sum_{t=0}^{4} \frac{1}{(1.08)^t}$ can be calculated using Excel's **PV** function:

	A	B	C
1	**A RETIREMENT PROBLEM** **Solution using formulas**		
2	Interest	8%	
3	Annual deposit	48,000.00	
4	Annual retirement withdrawal	30,000.00	
5			
6	Numerator	126,718.54	<-- =1/(1+B2)^4*PV(B2,8,-B4)
7	Denominator	4.31	<-- =PV(B2,5,-1,,1)
8	Annual deposit	29,386.55	<-- =B6/B7

1.8 Continuous Compounding

Suppose you deposit $1,000 in a bank account that pays 5 percent per year. At the end of the year you will have $1,000 ∗ (1.05) = $1.050. Now suppose that the bank interprets "5 percent per year" to mean that it pays you 2.5 percent interest twice a year. Thus after six months you'll have $1,025, and after one year you will have $\$1{,}000 * \left(1 + \frac{0.05}{2}\right)^2 = \$1{,}050.625$. By this logic, if you get paid interest n times per year, your accretion at the end of the year will be $\$1{,}000 * \left(1 + \frac{0.05}{n}\right)^n$. As n increases, this amount gets larger, converging (rather quickly, as you will soon see) to $e^{0.05}$, which in Excel is written as the function **Exp**. When n is infinite, we refer to this practice as *continuous compounding*. (By typing **Exp(1)** in a spreadsheet cell, you can see that $e = 2.7182818285. \ldots$)

As you can see in the next display, \$1,000 continuously compounded for one year at 5 percent grows to \$1,000 $* e^{0.05}$ = \$1,051.271 at the end of the year. Continuously compounded for t years, it will grow to \$1,000 $* e^{005*t}$, where t need not be a whole number (for example, when $t = 4.25$, then the accumulation factor $e^{0.05*4.25}$ measures the growth of the initial investment at 5 percent annually, continuously compounded for four years and three months).

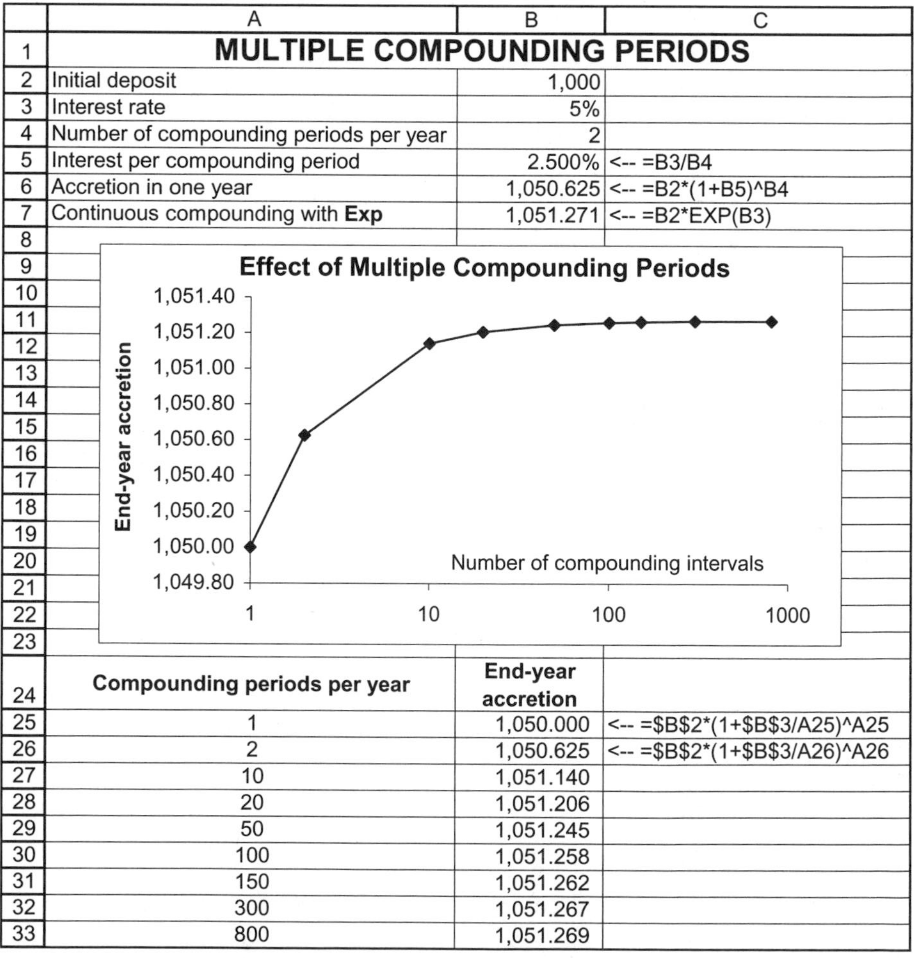

	A	B	C
1	**MULTIPLE COMPOUNDING PERIODS**		
2	Initial deposit	1,000	
3	Interest rate	5%	
4	Number of compounding periods per year	2	
5	Interest per compounding period	2.500%	<-- =B3/B4
6	Accretion in one year	1,050.625	<-- =B2*(1+B5)^B4
7	Continuous compounding with **Exp**	1,051.271	<-- =B2*EXP(B3)
8			

24	**Compounding periods per year**	**End-year accretion**	
25	1	1,050.000	<-- =\$B\$2*(1+\$B\$3/A25)^A25
26	2	1,050.625	<-- =\$B\$2*(1+\$B\$3/A26)^A26
27	10	1,051.140	
28	20	1,051.206	
29	50	1,051.245	
30	100	1,051.258	
31	150	1,051.262	
32	300	1,051.267	
33	800	1,051.269	

1.8.1 A Technical Note on the Graph

The graph is an Excel XY (Scatter) chart; the x-axis in the chart has been set to be in logarithmic scale. This emphasizes the compounding process. The following picture shows the graph's x-axis marked and the relevant dialog box (right-click after marking the axis and go to **Format Axis**).

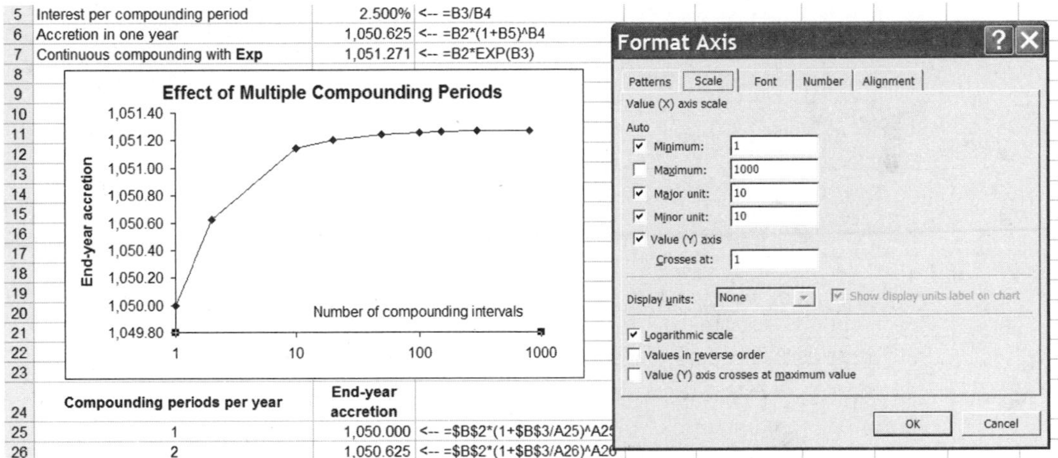

1.8.2 Back to Finance—Continuous Discounting

If the accretion factor for continuous compounding at interest r over t years is e^{rt}, then the discount factor for the same period is e^{-rt}. Thus a cash flow C_t occurring in year t and discounted at continuously compounded rate r will be worth $C_t e^{-rt}$ today, as follows:

	A	B	C	D
1	**CONTINUOUS DISCOUNTING**			
2	Interest	8%		
3				
4	**Year**	**Cash flow**	**Continously discounted PV**	
5	1	100	92.312	<-- =B5*EXP(-$B$2*A5)
6	2	200	170.429	<-- =B6*EXP(-$B$2*A6)
7	3	300	235.988	
8	4	400	290.460	
9	5	500	335.160	
10				
11	Present value		1,124.348	<-- =SUM(C5:C9)

1.8.3 Calculating the Continuously Compounded Return from Price Data

Suppose at time 0 you had $1,000 in the bank and suppose that one year later you had $1,200. What was your percentage return? Although the answer may appear obvious, it actually depends on the compounding method. If the bank paid interest only once a year, then the return would be 20 percent:

$$\frac{1{,}200}{1{,}000}-1=20\%$$

However, if the bank paid interest twice a year, you would need to solve the following equation to calculate the return:

$$1{,}000*\left(1+\frac{r}{2}\right)^2=1{,}200 \Rightarrow \frac{r}{2}=\left(\frac{1{,}200}{1{,}000}\right)^{1/2}-1=9.5445\%$$

The annual percentage return when interest is paid twice a year is therefore $2*9.5445\%=19.089\%$.

In general, if there are n compounding periods per year, you have to solve $\frac{r}{n}=\left(\frac{1{,}200}{1{,}000}\right)^{1/n}-1$ and then multiply the result appropriately. If n is very large, this converges to $r=\ln\left(\frac{1{,}200}{1{,}000}\right)=18.2322\%$:

	A	B	C
1	**CALCULATING RETURNS FROM PRICES**		
2	Initial deposit	1,000	
3	End-of-year value	1,200	
4	Number of compounding periods	2	
5	Implied annual interest rate	19.09%	<-- =((B3/B2)^(1/B4)-1)*B4
6			
7	Continuous return	18.23%	<-- =LN(B3/B2)
8			
9	**Implied annual interest rate with n compounding periods**		
10	Number of compounding periods	Rate	
11		19.09%	<-- =B5, data table header
12	1	20.00%	
13	2	19.09%	
14	4	18.65%	
15	8	18.44%	
16	20	18.32%	
17	1,000	18.23%	

1.8.4 Why Use Continuous Compounding?

All this may seem somewhat esoteric. However, continuous compounding/discounting is often used in financial calculations. In this book, it is used to calculate portfolio returns (Chapters 8–15) and in practically all of the options calculations (Chapters 16–24).

There's another reason to use continuous compounding—its ease of calculation. Suppose, for example, that your $1,000 grew to $1,500 in one year and nine months. What's the annualized rate of return? The easiest—and most consistent—way to find this answer is to calculate the continuously compounded annual return. Since 1 year and 9 months equals 1.75 years, this return is

$$1{,}000 * \exp[r * 1.75] = 1{,}500 \Rightarrow r = \frac{1}{1.75} \ln\left[\frac{1{,}500}{1{,}000}\right] = 23.1694\%$$

1.9 Discounting Using Dated Cash Flows

Most of the computations in this chapter consider cash flows that occur at fixed periodic intervals. Typically we look at cash flows that occur on dates 0, 1, . . . , n, where the period indicates an annual, semiannual, or other fixed interval. Two Excel functions, **XIRR** and **XNPV**, allow us to do computations on cash flows which occur on specific dates that need not be at even intervals.[7]

In the following example we compute the IRR of an investment of $1,000 made on 1 January 2006 with payments on specific dates:

	A	B	C
1	**USING XIRR TO COMPUTE THE ANNUALIZED INTERNAL RATE OF RETURN**		
2	**Date**	**Cash flow**	
3	1-Jan-06	-1,000	
4	3-Mar-06	150	
5	4-Jul-06	100	
6	12-Oct-06	50	
7	25-Dec-06	1,000	
8			
9	IRR	37.19%	<-- =XIRR(B3:B7,A3:A7)

The function **XIRR** outputs an annualized return. It works by computing the daily IRR and annualizing it, $XIRR = (1 + DailyIRR)^{365} - 1$.

XNPV computes the net present value of a series of cash flows occurring on specific dates.

7. If you do not see these functions, add them in by going to **Tools|Add-ins** on the tool bar and checking **Analysis ToolPak**.

	A	B	C
1	**USING XNPV TO COMPUTE THE NET PRESENT VALUE**		
2	Annual discount rate	12%	
3			
4	**Date**	**Cash flow**	
5	1-Jan-06	-1,000	
6	3-Mar-07	100	
7	4-Jul-07	195	
8	12-Oct-08	350	
9	25-Dec-09	800	
10			
11	Net present value	16.80	<-- =XNPV(B2,B5:B9,A5:A9)
12			
13	Note that **XNPV** has a different syntax from **NPV**! **XNPV** requires all the cash flows, including the initial cash flow, whereas **NPV** assumes that the first cash flow occurs one period hence.		

Exercises

1. You are offered an asset costing \$600 that has cash flows of \$100 at the end of each of the next 10 years.

   a. If the appropriate discount rate for the asset is 8 percent, should you purchase it?

   b. What is the IRR of the asset?

2. You just took a \$10,000, five-year loan. Payments at the end of each year are flat (equal in every year) at an interest rate of 15 percent. Calculate the appropriate loan table, showing the breakdown in each year between principal and interest.

3. You are offered an investment with the following conditions:

   - The cost of the investment is \$1,000.
   - The investment pays out a sum X at the end of the first year; this payout grows at the rate of 10 percent per year for 11 years.

   If your discount rate is 15 percent, calculate the smallest X that would entice you to purchase the asset. For example, as you can see in the following display, $X = \$100$ is too small—the NPV is negative.

	A	B	C
1	Discount rate	15%	
2	Initial payment	129.2852	
3	NPV	-226.52	<-- =B6+NPV(B1,B7:B17)
4			
5	**Year**	**Cash flow**	
6	0	-1,000.00	
7	1	100.00	<-- 100
8	2	110.00	<-- =B7*1.1
9	3	121.00	<-- =B8*1.1
10	4	133.10	
11	5	146.41	
12	6	161.05	
13	7	177.16	
14	8	194.87	
15	9	214.36	
16	10	235.79	
17	11	259.37	

4. The following cash-flow pattern has two IRRs. Use Excel to draw a graph of the NPV of these cash flows as a function of the discount rate. Then use the IRR function to identify the two IRRs. Would you invest in this project if the opportunity cost were 20 percent?

	A	B
4	**Year**	**Cash flow**
5	0	-500
6	1	600
7	2	300
8	3	300
9	4	200
10	5	-1,000

5. In this exercise we solve iteratively for the internal rate of return. Consider an investment that costs 800 and has cash flows of 300, 200, 150, 122, 133 in years 1–5 (see cells A8:B13 in the following spreadsheet). Setting up the loan table shows that 10 percent is greater than the IRR (since the return of principal at the end of year 5 is less than the principal at the beginning of the year).

	A	B	C	D	E	F	G	H
1	**IRR?**	10.00%						
2				**LOAN TABLE**			Division of payment between:	
3	**Year**	**Cash flow**		**Year**	**Principal at beginning of year**	**Payment at end of year**	**Interest**	**Principal**
4	0	-800		1	800.00	300.00	80.00	220.00
5	1	300		2	580.00	200.00	58.00	142.00
6	2	200		3	438.00	150.00	43.80	106.20
7	3	150		4	331.80	122.00	33.18	88.82
8	4	122		5	242.98	133.00	24.30	108.70
9	5	133		6	134.28	<-- Should be zero for IRR		

Setting the **IRR**? cell equal to 3 percent shows that 3 percent is less than the IRR, since the return of principal at the end of year 5 is greater than the principal at the beginning of year 5:

	A	B	C	D	E	F	G	H
1	**IRR?**	3.00%						
2				**LOAN TABLE**			Division of payment between:	
3	**Year**	**Cash flow**		**Year**	**Principal at beginning of year**	**Payment at end of year**	**Interest**	**Principal**
4	0	-800		1	800.00	300.00	24.00	276.00
5	1	300		2	524.00	200.00	15.72	184.28
6	2	200		3	339.72	150.00	10.19	139.81
7	3	150		4	199.91	122.00	6.00	116.00
8	4	122		5	83.91	133.00	2.52	130.48
9	5	133		6	-46.57	<-- Should be zero for IRR		

By changing the **IRR**? cell, find the internal rate of return of the investment.

6. An alternative definition of the IRR is the rate that makes the principal at the beginning of year 6 equal to zero.[9] In the preceding printout cell E9 gives the principal at the beginning of year 6. Using the **Goal Seek** function of Excel, find the rate that changes this figure to zero (the following picture shows how the screen should look).

---

9. In general, of course, the IRR is the rate of return that makes the principal in the year *following* the last payment equal to zero.

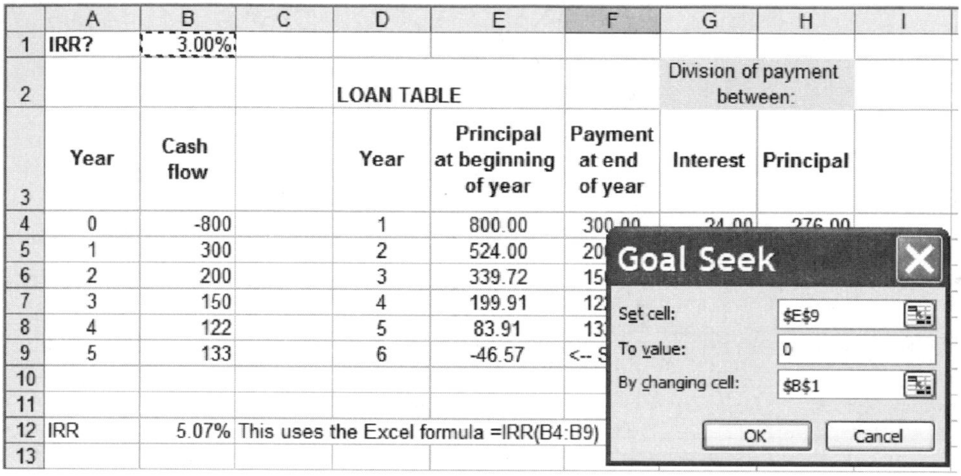

	A	B	C	D	E	F	G	H	I
1	IRR?	3.00%							
2				LOAN TABLE			Division of payment between:		
3	Year	Cash flow		Year	Principal at beginning of year	Payment at end of year	Interest	Principal	
4	0	-800		1	800.00	300.00	24.00	276.00	
5	1	300		2	524.00	20			
6	2	200		3	339.72	15			
7	3	150		4	199.91	12			
8	4	122		5	83.91	13			
9	5	133		6	-46.57	<-- S			
10									
11									
12	IRR	5.07%	This uses the Excel formula =IRR(B4:B9)						
13									

Goal Seek
Set cell: $E$9
To value: 0
By changing cell: $B$1
OK Cancel

(Of course you should check your calculations by using the Excel **IRR** function.)

7. Calculate the flat annual payment required to pay off a five-year loan of $100,000 bearing an interest rate of 13 percent.

8. You have just taken a car loan of $15,000. The loan is for 48 months at an annual interest rate of 15 percent (which the bank translates to a monthly rate of 15%/12 = 1.25%). The 48 payments (to be made at the end of each of the next 48 months) are all equal.

   a. Calculate the monthly payment on the loan.
   b. In a loan table calculate, for each month, the principal remaining on the loan at the beginning of the month and the split of that month's payment between interest and repayment of principal.
   c. Show that the principal at the beginning of each month is the present value of the remaining loan payments at the loan interest rate (use the **PV** function).

9. You are considering buying a car from a local auto dealer. The dealer offers you one of two payment options:

   • You can pay $30,000 cash.
   • The "deferred payment plan": You can pay the dealer $5,000 cash today and a payment of $1,050 at the end of each of the next 30 months.

   As an alternative to the dealer financing, you have approached a local bank, which is willing to give you a car loan of $25,000 at the rate of 1.25 percent per month.

   a. Assuming that 1.25 percent is the opportunity cost, calculate the present value of all the payments on the dealer's deferred payment plan.
   b. What is the effective interest rate being charged by the dealer? Do this calculation by preparing a spreadsheet like the one that follows (only part of the spreadsheet is shown—you have to do this calculation for all 30 months).

	D	E	F	G	H
2	**Month**	**Cash payment**	**Payment under deferred payment plan**	**Difference**	
3	0	30,000	5,000	25,000	<-- =E3-F3
4	1	0	1,050	-1,050	<-- =E4-F4
5	2	0	1,050	-1,050	
6	3	0	1,050	-1,050	
7	4	0	1,050	-1,050	
8	5	0	1,050	-1,050	
9	6	0	1,050	-1,050	
10	7	0	1,050	-1,050	
11	8	0	1,050	-1,050	

Now calculate the IRR of the numbers in column F; this is the monthly *effective interest rate* on the deferred payment plan.

10. You are considering a savings plan that calls for a deposit of $15,000 at the end of each of the next five years. If the plan offers an interest rate of 10 percent, how much will you accumulate at the end of year 5?

    Do this calculation by completing the following spreadsheet. This spreadsheet does the calculation twice—once using the **FV** function and once using a simple table that shows the accumulation at the beginning of each year.

	A	B	C	D
1	Annual payment	15,000		
2	Interest rate	10%		
3	Number of years	5		
4	Total value	$91,576.50	<-- =FV(B2,B3,-B1,,0)	
5				
6	**Year**	**Accumulation at begining of year**	**Payment at end of year**	**Annual interest**
7	1	0	15,000	0.00
8	2	15,000	15,000	1,500.00
9	3	31,500		
10	4			
11	5			
12	6			

11. Redo the previous calculation, this time assuming that you make five deposits at the *beginning* of this year and the following four years. How much will you accumulate by the end of year 5?

12. A mutual fund has been advertising that, had you deposited $250 per month in the fund for the last 10 years, you would now have accumulated $85,000. Assuming that these deposits were made at the beginning of each month for a period of 120 months, calculate the effective annual return fund investors got.

Hint: Set up the following spreadsheet and then use **Goal Seek**.

	A	B	C
1	Monthly payment	250	
2	Number of months	120	
3			
4	Effective monthly return?		
5	Accumulation		<-- =FV(B4,B2,-B1,,1)

The effective annual return can then be calculated in one of two ways:

- $(1 + \text{Monthly return})^{12} - 1$: This is the compound annual return, which is preferable, since it makes allowance for the reinvestment of each month's earnings.
- 12*Monthly return: This method is often used by banks.

13. You have just turned 35, and you intend to start saving for your retirement. Once you retire in 30 years (when you turn 65), you would like to have an income of $100,000 per year for the next 20 years. Calculate how much you would have to save between now and age 65 in order to finance your retirement income. Make the following assumptions:

- All savings draw compound interest of 10 percent per year.
- You make the first payment today and the last payment on the day you turn 64 (30 payments).
- You make the first withdrawal when you turn 65 and the last withdrawal when you turn 84 (20 payments).

14. You currently have $25,000 in the bank, in a savings account that draws 5 percent interest. Your business needs $25,000, and you are considering two options: (a) Use the money in your savings account or (b) borrow the money from the bank at 6 percent, leaving the money in the savings account.

Your financial analyst suggests that solution (b) is better. His logic: The sum of the interest paid on the 6 percent loan is lower than the interest earned at the same time on the $25,000 deposit. His calculations are illustrated in the following spreadsheet. Show that this logic is wrong. (If you think about it, it couldn't be preferable to take a 6 percent loan when you are getting 5 percent interest from the bank. However, the explanation may not be trivial.)

	A	B	C	D	E	F
1	EXERCISE 14, financial analyst's calculations					
2	Interest earned	5%				
3	Interest paid	6%				
4	Initial deposit	25,000				
5					=PMT($B$3,2,-$B$4)	
6	THE 6% LOAN					
7	Year	Principal at beginning of year	Payment at end of year	Interest paid	Repayment of principal	
8	1	25,000.00	13,635.92	1,500.00	12,135.92	<-- =C8-D8
9	2	12,864.08	13,635.92	771.84	12,864.08	
10		Total interest paid		2,271.84		
11						
12	Savings Account					
13	Year	In savings account at beginning of year	End-year interest earned	In account at end of year		
14	1	25,000.00	1,250.00	26,250.00		
15	2	26,250.00	1,312.50	27,562.50		
16		Interest earned	2,562.50			

15. Use **XIRR** to compute the internal rate of return for the following investment:

	A	B
1	Date	Cash flow
2	30-Jun-07	-899
3	14-Feb-08	70
4	14-Feb-09	70
5	14-Feb-10	70
6	14-Feb-11	70
7	14-Feb-12	70
8	14-Feb-13	1,070

16. Use **XNPV** to value the following investment. Assume that the annual discount rate is 15 percent.

	A	B
4	Date	Cash flow
5	30-Jun-07	-500
6	14-Feb-08	100
7	14-Feb-09	300
8	14-Feb-10	400
9	14-Feb-11	600
10	14-Feb-12	800
11	14-Feb-13	-1,800

17. Identify the two internal rates of return of the investment in exercise 16.

2 Calculating the Cost of Capital

2.1 Overview

In this chapter we discuss the calculation of the firm's weighted average cost of capital (WACC). The WACC has two important uses in finance:

- When used as the discount rate for a firm's anticipated free cash flows (FCF), the WACC gives the enterprise value of the firm. FCF is discussed at length in Chapters 3 and 4. At this point it suffices to say that the FCF is the cash flow generated by the firm's core business activities. These chapters also show how to apply the WACC to the valuation of firms.
- The WACC is also the appropriate risk-adjusted discount rate for firm projects whose riskiness is similar to the average riskiness of the firm's cash flows. When used in this context, the WACC is often referred to as the firm's *hurdle rate*.

The WACC is a weighted average of the firm's cost of equity r_E and its cost of debt r_D, with the weights created by the market values of the firm's equity (E) and debt (D):

$$WACC = \frac{E}{E+D} r_E + \frac{D}{E+D} r_D (1 - T_C)$$

where r_E is the firm's cost of equity, r_D is the firm's cost of debt, E is the market value of the firm's equity, D is the market value of the firm's debt, and T_C is the firm's corporate tax rate.

This chapter discusses the computation of r_E and r_D and shows detailed examples of how to compute the firm's WACC. The reader should be warned that the application of the models discussed requires a good deal of judgment—computing the WACC is equal parts science and art!

We consider two models for calculating the cost of equity r_E, the discount rate applied to equity cash flows. Each model has variations that are explored throughout the chapter:

- The Gordon model calculates the cost of equity based on the anticipated cash flows paid to the shareholders of the firm. Variations on this model include multiple growth rates and the definition of the equity cash flows.
- The capital asset pricing model (CAPM) calculates the cost of equity based on the correlation between the firm's equity returns and the

returns of a large, diversified, market portfolio. As we will see, the CAPM can also be used to calculate the cost of the firm's debt. Variations on this model include the tax framework in which the model is defined.

The other component of the cost of capital is the cost of debt r_D, the anticipated future cost of the firm's borrowing. This book contains three models to calculate the cost of debt; two of these models are discussed in this chapter and a third method is discussed separately in Chapter 28:

- The cost of debt r_D is most commonly computed by using the firm's current interest payments divided by its average debt.
- An alternative method is to compute r_D by imputing the firm's cost of debt from a rating-adjusted yield curve.
- Finally, we can compute the expected return on the firm's bonds as a proxy for its cost of debt; we discuss this method separately in Chapter 28.

A Terminological Note As noted in Chapter 1, "cost of capital" is a synonym for the "appropriate discount rate" to be applied to a series of cash flows. In finance "appropriate" is most often a synonym for "risk-adjusted." Hence another name for the cost of capital is the "risk-adjusted discount rate" (RADR).

2.2 The Gordon Dividend Model

The Gordon dividend model[1] derives the cost of equity from the following deceptively simple statement:

The value of a share is the present value of the future anticipated dividend stream from the share, where the future anticipated dividends are discounted at the appropriate risk-adjusted cost of equity r_E.

The simplest application of the Gordon model is the case where the anticipated future growth rate of dividends is constant. Suppose that the

1. This model is named after M. J. Gordon, who first published this formula in a paper entitled "Dividends, Earnings, and Stock Prices," *Review of Economics and Statistics* 41.

current stock price is P_0, the current dividend is Div_0, and the anticipated growth rate of future dividends is g. The Gordon model states that the stock price equals the discounted (at the appropriate cost of equity r_E) future dividends:

$$P_0 = \frac{\text{Div}_0 (1+g)}{1+r_E} + \frac{\text{Div}_0 * (1+g)^2}{(1+r_E)^2} + \frac{\text{Div}_0 * (1+g)^3}{(1+r_E)^3} + \frac{\text{Div}_0 * (1+g)^4}{(1+r_E)^4} + \dots$$
$$= \sum_{t=1}^{\infty} \frac{\text{Div}_0 * (1+g)^t}{(1+r_E)^t}$$

Provided that $|g| < r_E$, the expression $\sum_{t=1}^{\infty} \frac{\text{Div}_0 * (1+g)^t}{(1+r_E)^t}$ can be reduced to $\frac{\text{Div}_0 (1+g)}{r_E - g}$ (see the following box for derivation). Thus, given a constant anticipated dividend growth rate, we derive the Gordon model cost of equity:

$$P_0 = \frac{\text{Div}_0 (1+g)}{r_E - g}, \quad \text{provided} \quad |g| < r_E$$

Note the proviso at the end of this formula: In order for the infinite sum on the first line of the formula to have a finite solution, the growth rates of the dividends must be less than the discount rate. In our discussion of the Gordon model with supernormal growth rates (section 2.4), we return to the case where this condition is not satisfied.

Euler's Formula for the Sum of a Geometric Series: Recalling High School Algebra

The Gordon formula in this chapter, both in its standard form and for supernormal growth (section 2.4), derives from a formula for the sum of a geometric series due to the Swiss mathematician Leonhard Euler (1707–83). This formula is a staple of high school algebra. Euler showed that the sum of a geometric series:

$$S = a + aq + aq^2 + \dots + aq^{n-1}$$
$$= \frac{a(1-q^n)}{1-q}, \text{ provided } |q| < 1$$

The term a is the *first term* of the series, q is commonly called the *ratio* of the terms, and n is the number of terms. We leave the derivation to you; the application to the Gordon formula is

$$\sum_{t=1}^{\infty}\frac{\text{Div}_0 * (1+g)^t}{(1+r_E)^t} = \lim_{n\to\infty}\frac{\text{Div}_0\left(\frac{1+g}{1+r_E}\right)\left[1-\left(\frac{1+g}{1+r_E}\right)^n\right]}{1-\left(\frac{1+g}{1+r_E}\right)}$$

$$= \frac{\text{Div}_0\,(1+g)}{r_E - g}, \text{ provided}\left|\frac{1+g}{1+r_E}\right| < 1$$

Note that in this formulation $a = \text{Div}_0\left(\frac{1+g}{1+r_E}\right)$, $q = \left(\frac{1+g}{1+r_E}\right)$, and $n = \infty$.

Solving the previous expression for r_E gives a simple expression for the Gordon-model cost of capital:

$$r_E = \frac{\text{Div}_0\,(1+g)}{P_0} + g$$

To apply this formula, consider a firm whose current dividend is Div_0 = \$3 per share and whose share price is P_0 = \$60. Suppose the dividend is anticipated to grow by 12 percent per year. Then the firm's cost of equity r_E is 17.6 percent:

	A	B	C
1	**THE GORDON MODEL COST OF EQUITY**		
2	Current share price, P_0	60	
3	Current dividend, D_0	3	
4	Anticipated dividend growth rate	12%	
5	Gordon model cost of equity, r_E	17.60%	<-- =B3*(1+B4)/B2+B4

2.2.1 Using the Gordon Model to Compute the Cost of Equity for Kellogg

We apply the Gordon model to Kellogg, whose 10-year dividend history is given in the following spreadsheet (note that some of the data have been hidden):

	A	B	C
1	**KELLOGG DIVIDENDS, MAY1996 - MAY2006**		
2	Dividend growth rate, quarterly		
3	last 5 years	0.47%	<-- =(B51/B31)^(1/20)-1
4	last 10 years	0.89%	<-- =(B51/B11)^(1/40)-1
5			
6	Dividend growth rate, annualized		
7	Last 5 years	1.90%	<-- =(1+B3)^4-1
8	Last 10 years	3.61%	<-- =(1+B4)^4-1
9			
10	**Date**	**Dividends**	
11	29-May-96	0.195	
12	28-Aug-96	0.210	
13	26-Nov-96	0.210	
43	27-May-04	0.253	
44	27-Aug-04	0.253	
45	23-Nov-04	0.253	
46	25-Feb-05	0.253	
47	27-May-05	0.253	
48	30-Aug-05	0.278	
49	29-Nov-05	0.278	
50	27-Feb-06	0.278	
51	30-May-06	0.278	

The annualized growth rate of Kellogg's historical dividends may be either 1.90 percent or 3.61 percent, depending on the period taken. For purposes of computing the cost of equity r_E, the question is which of these rates better predicts future anticipated dividend growth rates.[2] In the following spreadsheet we allow for both possibilities. The calculations use Kellogg's stock price at the end of May 2006, $P_0 = \$48.28$.

2. Or perhaps neither does! Perhaps we are better off using another story altogether to predict *future anticipated* dividend growth. We could use a pro forma model (discussed in Chapter 3) to predict the firm's anticipated dividend payout.

	A	B	C
1	**COMPUTING KELLOGG'S r_E WITH THE GORDON MODEL**		
2	Kellogg stock price, P_0, 30 May 2006	48.28	
3	Current dividend		
4	Quarterly	0.278	
5	Annualized dividend, Div_0	1.112	<-- =B4*4
6	Dividend growth rate, g		
7	Last 5 years	1.90%	
8	Last 10 years	3.61%	
9			
10	Gordon model cost of equity r_E		
11	Using last 5 years' growth	4.25%	<-- =B5*(1+B7)/B2+B7
12	Using last 10 years' growth	6.00%	<-- =B5*(1+B8)/B2+B8

2.3 Adjusting the Gordon Model to Account for All Cash Flows to Equity

As illustrated in the preceding section, the Gordon model is computed on a per-share basis and for dividends only. However, for purposes of valuing the firm's equity, the Gordon model should be extended to include all cash flows to equity. In addition to dividends, cash flows to equity include at least two additional components:

• Share repurchases now account for around 50 percent of the total cash disbursed by American corporations to their shareholders.[3]

• The issuance of stock by the firm is an important *negative cash flow to equity*. In many firms the most important instance of stock issuance is the exercise by employees of their stock options. On occasion companies both issue stock and repurchase it; Johnson & Johnson (discussed in this section) and Wachovia Bank (discussed in section 2.4.1) are both cases in point.

In order to account for these additional cash flows to equity, we have to rewrite the Gordon model in terms of total equity value. The basic valuation model of Gordon now becomes

3. Dittmar, A. K., and R. F. Dittmar, 2004. "Stock Repurchase Waves: An Explanation of the Trends in Aggregate Corporate Payout Policy." Working paper, University of Michigan.

$$\text{Market value of equity} = \sum_{t=1}^{\infty} \frac{\text{Cash flow to equity}_0 * (1+g)^t}{(1+r_E)^t}$$

where g is anticipated growth rate of cash flow to equity.

This gives the formula for the cost of equity r_E as

$$r_E = \frac{\text{Cash flow to equity}_0\,(1+g)}{\text{Market value of equity}} + g,\ if\ |g| < r_E$$

As an example, we consider the following data for Johnson & Johnson:

	A	B	C	D	E	F	G
1	**JOHNSON & JOHNSON, CASH FLOW TO EQUITY, 1995–2005**						
2	**Year ending**	**Dividends**	**Repurchase of common stock**	**Stock issues**	**Cash flow to equity**	**Year on year growth**	
3	31-Dec-95	827,000,000	322,000,000	-112,000,000	1,037,000,000	<-- =SUM(B3:D3)	
4	31-Dec-96	974,000,000	412,000,000	-149,000,000	1,237,000,000	19.29%	<-- =E4/E3-1
5	31-Dec-97	1,137,000,000	628,000,000	-225,000,000	1,540,000,000	24.49%	<-- =E5/E4-1
6	31-Dec-98	1,305,000,000	930,000,000	-269,000,000	1,966,000,000	27.66%	<-- =E6/E5-1
7	31-Dec-99	1,479,000,000	840,000,000	-221,000,000	2,098,000,000	6.71%	
8	31-Dec-00	1,724,000,000	973,000,000	-387,000,000	2,310,000,000	10.10%	
9	31-Dec-01	2,047,000,000	2,570,000,000	-514,000,000	4,103,000,000	77.62%	
10	31-Dec-02	2,381,000,000	6,538,000,000	-390,000,000	8,529,000,000	107.87%	
11	31-Dec-03	2,746,000,000	1,183,000,000	-311,000,000	3,618,000,000	-57.58%	
12	31-Dec-04	3,251,000,000	1,384,000,000	-642,000,000	3,993,000,000	10.36%	
13	31-Dec-05	3,793,000,000	1,717,000,000	-696,000,000	4,814,000,000	20.56%	
14							
15	**End 2005 equity data**						
16	Stock price	61.07					
17	Number of shares	3,119,842,000					
18	Equity value	190,528,750,940	<-- =B16*B17				
19							
20	Equity cash flow, end 2005	4,814,000,000	<-- =E13				
21	Future growth rate						
22	Based on 10-year growth rate	16.59%	<-- =(E13/E3)^(1/10)-1				
23	Based on 5-year growth rate	15.82%					
24							
25	Gordon cost of equity, r_E						
26	Based on 10-year growth rate	19.54%	<-- =B20*(1+B22)/B18+B22				
27	Based on 5-year growth rate	18.75%	<-- =B20*(1+B23)/B18+B23				

If we assume that J&J's historic growth rate of cash flow to equity, 16.59 percent, will persist in the indefinite future, then its cost of equity is $r_E = 19.54$ percent (cell B26).[4]

4. A major problem of computing the total equity cash flows is that stock repurchases and employee stock exercises are only reported in the annual financial statements. Thus the only data available for these numbers are annual data, whereas dividends are reported quarterly, and stock price data—used to compute the CAPM beta discussed in section 2.5—are available on a daily basis.

The following graph displays the components of the equity cash flows for JNJ. You can see that the dividends paid out by JNJ are very smooth, whereas the variabilities of the stock repurchases and stock issuance are much larger. This is often the case—companies attach great importance to maintaining a steady, seemingly predictable, dividend, whereas the true variability of their equity payouts is hidden in other items such as stock issues and repurchases:

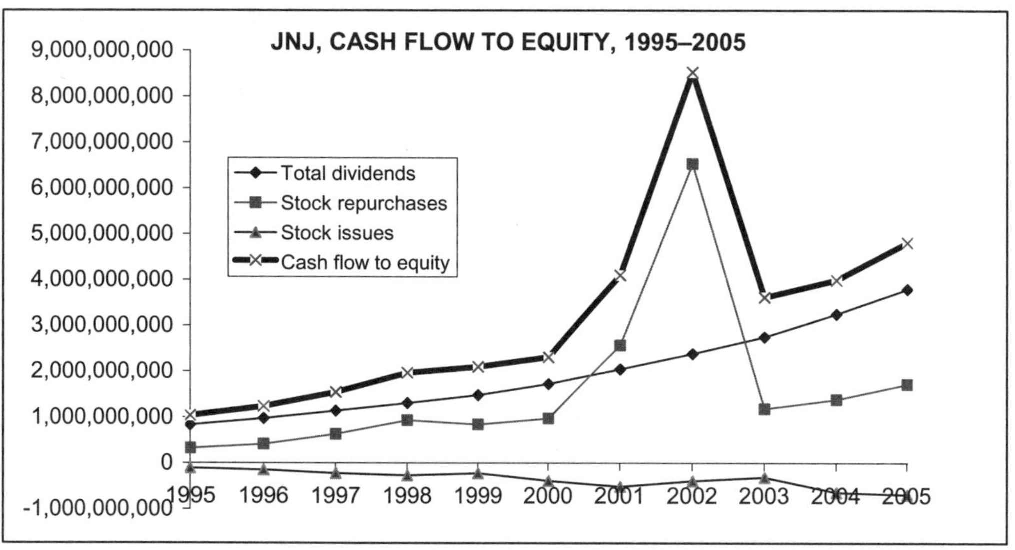

2.3.1 Is JNJ's r_E Different When Computed on a Dividend-per-Share Basis Versus Total Equity Cash Flows?

In this particular case, this cost of equity does not deviate much from the cost of equity computed on a dividend-per-share basis (though the opposite is often the case):

	A	B	C	D
1	**COMPUTING JNJ's r_E BASED ON DIVIDENDS PER SHARE**			
2	JNJ's stock price, P_0, 31 Dec 2005	61.07		
3	Current dividend			
4	Quarterly	0.33	<-- =B36	
5	Annualized dividend, Div_0	1.32	<-- =B4*4	
6				
7	Dividend growth rate, g	**Quarterly**	**Annualized**	
8	Growth since 17-Nov-00	3.69%	15.58%	<-- =(1+B8)^4-1
9	Growth since 14-Nov-03	4.06%	17.26%	<-- =(1+B9)^4-1
10				
11	Gordon model cost of equity r_E			
12	Growth since 17-Nov-00	18.08%	<-- =B5*(1+C8)/B2+C8	
13	Growth since 14-Nov-03	19.79%	<-- =B5*(1+C9)/B2+C9	
14				
15	**Date**	**Dividend per share**		
16	17-Nov-00	0.160		
17	15-Feb-01	0.160		
18	18-May-01	0.180		
19	17-Aug-01	0.180		
20	16-Nov-01	0.180		
21	14-Feb-02	0.180		
22	17-May-02	0.205		
23	16-Aug-02	0.205		
24	15-Nov-02	0.205		
25	13-Feb-03	0.205		
26	16-May-03	0.240		
27	15-Aug-03	0.240		
28	14-Nov-03	0.240		
29	12-Feb-04	0.240		
30	14-May-04	0.285		
31	13-Aug-04	0.285		
32	12-Nov-04	0.285		
33	11-Feb-05	0.285		
34	13-May-05	0.330		
35	19-Aug-05	0.330		
36	18-Nov-05	0.330		

2.4 "Supernormal Growth" and the Gordon Model

A basic condition of the Gordon formula $r_E = \frac{\text{Div}_0(1+g)}{P_0} + g$ is the condition $|g| < r_E$.[5] In finance examples, violations of $|g| < r_E$ usually occur for very fast-growing firms, in which—at least for short periods of time—we anticipate very high growth rates, so that $g > r_E$. If such "supernormal" growth were the case in the long run, the original dividend discount formula shows that P_0 would have an infinite value, since, when $g > r_E$, the expression $\sum_{t=1}^{\infty} \frac{\text{Div}_0 * (1+g)^t}{(1+r_E)^t} = \infty$. Thus a period of very high dividend growth rates (where $g > r_E$) must be followed by a period in which the long-term growth rate of dividends is less than the cost of equity, $g < r_E$.

Suppose that the firm is anticipated to pay high-growth dividends during periods 1, . . . , m, and that for subsequent periods the growth rate of dividends will be lower. A little algebra yields the following formula:

Share value today

= Present value of dividends

$$= \underbrace{\sum_{t=1}^{m} \frac{\text{Div}_0 * (1+g_1)^t}{(1+r_E)^t}}_{\substack{\text{PV of m years} \\ \text{of high-growth } g_1 \\ \text{dividends}}} + \underbrace{\sum_{t=m+1}^{\infty} \frac{\text{Div}_5 * (1+g_2)^{t-m}}{(1+r_E)^t}}_{\substack{\text{PV of remaining} \\ \text{normal-growth } g_2 \\ \text{dividends}}}$$

$$= \sum_{t=1}^{m} \frac{\text{Div}_0 * (1+g_1)^t}{(1+r_E)} + \frac{1}{(1+r_E)^m} \sum_{t=1}^{\infty} \frac{\text{Div}_m * (1+g_2)^t}{(1+r_E)^t}$$

$$= \frac{\text{Div}_0 * \left(\frac{1+g_1}{1+r_E}\right) * \left[1 - \left(\frac{1+g_1}{1+r_E}\right)^m\right]}{1 - \frac{1+g_1}{1+r_E}} + \frac{1}{(1+r_E)^m} \sum_{t=1}^{\infty} \frac{\text{Div}_m * (1+g_2)^t}{(1+r_E)^t}$$

$$= \frac{\text{Div}_0 * \left(\frac{1+g_1}{1+r_E}\right) * \left[1 - \left(\frac{1+g_1}{1+r_E}\right)^m\right]}{1 - \frac{1+g_1}{1+r_E}} + \frac{1}{(1+r_E)^m} \frac{\text{Div}_0 (1+g_1)^m (1+g_2)}{r_E - g_2}$$

5. In this section we interpret Div_0 in the Gordon formula to denote either dividends per share or total equity payouts.

The following spreadsheet uses this formula. It gives a numerical illustration of initially high growth rates of dividends followed by lower, more normal, rates. We consider a firm whose current dividend is $8 per share. The firm's dividend is expected to grow at 35 percent for the next five years, after which the growth rate will slow down to 8 percent per year. The cost of equity, the discount rate for all the dividends, is 18 percent:

	A	B	C
1	**THE GORDON MODEL WITH TWO GROWTH RATES**		
2	Current dividend, Div_0	8.00	
3	Growth rate g_1, years 1-m ("supernormal")	35%	
4	Growth rate g_2, years 6 - ∞	8%	
5	Number of supernormal growth years, m	5	
6	Cost of equity	18%	
7			
8	**Dividend valuation**		
9	PV of supernormal growth years		
10	Using Excel NPV	60.99	<-- =NPV(B6,B16:B20)
11	Check: Using book formula	60.99	<-- =B2*(1+B3)/(1+B6)*(1-((1+B3)/(1+B6))^B5)/(1-(1+B3)/(1+B6))
12	PV of normal growth years, after year 5	169.35	<-- =B20*(1+B4)/(B6-B4)/(1+B6)^B5
13	Share value	230.33	<-- =SUM(B11:B12)
14			
15	**Year**	**Anticipated dividend**	
16	1	10.80	<-- =B2*(1+$B$3)
17	2	14.58	<-- =B16*(1+$B$3)
18	3	19.68	<-- =B17*(1+$B$3)
19	4	26.57	<-- =B18*(1+$B$3)
20	5	35.87	<-- =B19*(1+$B$3)
21	6	38.74	<-- =B20*(1+$B$4)
22	7	41.84	<-- =B21*(1+$B$4)
23	8	45.19	
24	9	48.80	
25	10	52.71	
26	11	56.92	
27	12	61.48	
28	etc.	etc.	

The value of the firm's share is $230.33, which is the sum of

• Five years of supernormal growth, computed either by Excel's **NPV** function (cell B10) or by the formula $\left\{ \text{Div}_0 * \left(\frac{1+g_1}{1+r_E} \right) * \left[1 - \left(\frac{1+g_1}{1+r_E} \right)^5 \right] \right\} \Big/ \left(1 - \frac{1+g_1}{1+r_E} \right)$ derived previously (cell B11).

• The remaining dividends at a normal growth rate (cell B12), computed by the formula derived previously $\frac{1}{(1+r_E)^5} \frac{\text{Div}_0 (1+g_1)^5 (1+g_2)}{r_E - g_2}$.

2.4.1 Computing the Cost of Equity for a Firm with Supernormal Growth Rates

The supernormal growth model can be used to compute the cost of equity r_E for companies whose historical equity payout data overstate any anticipation of future growth rates. Consider, for example, the annual data for Wachovia Bank:

	A	B	C	D	E	F
1	**WACHOVIA BANK--DIVIDENDS, STOCK ISSUED, AND STOCK REPURCHASED** **Does historical growth overstate the cost of equity?**					
2		**Common stock issued**	**Total dividend payments**	**Common stock repurchased**	**Total equity cash flow**	
3	1991	16,462,000	150,730,000	1,215,000	135,483,000	<-- =D3+C3-B3
4	1992	29,717,000	170,756,000	31,197,000	172,236,000	<-- =D4+C4-B4
5	1993	24,961,000	191,488,000	98,804,000	265,331,000	
6	1994	25,339,000	210,503,000	52,908,000	238,072,000	
7	1995	24,115,000	235,495,000	65,032,000	276,412,000	
8	1996	25,826,000	254,458,000	376,716,000	605,348,000	
9	1997	59,281,000	327,303,000	532,682,000	800,704,000	
10	1998	80,375,000	381,798,000	531,122,000	832,545,000	
11	1999	59,478,000	418,447,000	634,623,000	993,592,000	
12						
13	Compound growth rate	17.42%	13.61%	118.65%	28.28%	<-- =(E11/E3)^(1/8)-1
14						
15	**Cost of capital using the Gordon model** **Using total equity payout and total equity value**					
16	End 1999 stock price	68.00				
17	Number of shares outstanding, end 1999	202,795,000				
18	Future dividend growth, g?	28.28%	<-- =E13			
19	End 1999 equity value, P_0	13,790,060,000	<-- =B16*B17			
20	Projected next total equity cash flow, D_1	1,274,598,774	<-- =E11*(1+B18)			
21	Gordon model cost of equity, r_E	37.52%	<-- =B20/B19+B18			

Based on the historical growth rate of the equity payout of 28.28 percent (cell E13), the Gordon model cost of equity is $r_E = 37.52$ percent. This astoundingly large number is based on the assumption that the historical equity payout growth rate will continue forever.

The two-stage Gordon model may be the answer to this conundrum: Perhaps the large historical equity payout growth rate is unsustainable in the long run and will slow down to "normal" growth rates after a number of years. If this is the case, we have to solve the following equation for r_E:

$$P_0 = \text{Current equity value}$$
$$= \sum_{t=1}^{m} \frac{\text{Div}_0 (1+g_{\text{High}})^t}{(1+r_E)^t} + \sum_{t=m+1}^{\infty} \frac{\text{Div}_0 (1+g_{\text{High}})^m (1+g_{\text{Normal}})^{t-m}}{(1+r_E)^t}$$

(Note that we now use P_0 to stand for total equity value at time 0 and Div_0 for total equity payouts at time 0.) As shown previously, we can simplify this expression as follows:

$$P_0 = \text{Div}_0 \left(\frac{1+g_{\text{High}}}{1+r_E}\right) * \frac{1-\left(\frac{1+g_{\text{High}}}{1+r_E}\right)^m}{1-\frac{1+g_{\text{High}}}{1+r_E}} + \text{Div}_0 \left(\frac{1+g_{\text{High}}}{1+r_E}\right)^m (1+g_{\text{Normal}}) * \frac{1}{r_E - g_{\text{Normal}}}$$

Given the dividend growth rates g_{High} and g_{Normal}, the current dividend D_0, and the number of years m of supernormal growth, the cost of equity r_E is the internal rate of return of the preceding expression.

Here's an implementation for Wachovia that assumes three years of $g_{\text{High}} = 28.28$ percent, after which the growth rate will be $g_{\text{Normal}} = 4$ percent. This gives the cost of equity for Wachovia of $r_E = 17.251$ percent:

	A	B	C
1	**WACHOVIA, TWO-STAGE GORDON MODEL**		
2	End-1999 equity value, P_0	13,790,060,000	
3	End 1999 total equity payout	993,592,000	
4			
5	High growth rate, g_{High}	28.28%	
6	Number of high-growth years, m	3	
7	Normal growth rate, g_{Normal}	4%	
8			
9	Cost of equity, r_E using the function **TwoStageGordon**	17.251%	<-- =TwoStageGordon(B2,B3,B5,B6,B7)

The function **TwoStageGordon** (on the file with this chapter, **fm3_chapter02.xls**) computes the cost of equity r_E for a two-stage Gordon model. The function computes the discount rate r_E that equates the current share price to the present value of future equity cash flows:

```
Function TwoStageGordon(P0, Div0, Highgrowth,
Highgrowthyrs, Normalgrowth)
    High = 4
    Low = 0

    Do While (High - Low) > 0.0000001
    Estimate = (High + Low) / 2
    factor = (1 + Highgrowth) / _
      (1 + Estimate)
    Term1 = Div0 * factor * _
      (1 - factor ^ Highgrowthyrs) / _
      (1 - factor)
    Term2 = Div0 * factor ^ Highgrowthyrs * _
      (1 + Normalgrowth) / _
      (Estimate - Normalgrowth)
    If (Term1 + Term2) > P0 Then
        Low = (High + Low) / 2
        Else:  High = (High + Low) / 2
    End If
    Loop
    TwoStageGordon = Estimate
End Function
```

2.5 Using the Capital Asset Pricing Model to Determine the Cost of Equity r_E

Sections 2.2 and 2.3 explored the Gordon dividend model as a means of computing the firm's cost of equity r_E. The capital asset pricing model (CAPM) is a viable alternative to the Gordon model for calculating the cost of capital.[6] It is also the most widely used cost-of-equity model,

6. This chapter does not discuss the derivation of the CAPM. For many more details, see Chapters 8–12.

because of both its theoretical elegance and its implementational simplicity. The CAPM derives the firm's cost of capital from its covariance with the market return.[7] The classic CAPM formula for the firm's cost of equity is

$$r_E = r_f + \beta\left[E(r_M) - r_f\right]$$

where r_f is the market risk-free rate of interest, $E(r_M)$ is the expected return on the market portfolio, and β is a firm-specific risk measure $\dfrac{\text{Cov}(r_{stock}, r_M)}{\text{Var}(r_M)}$.

In the remainder of this section we focus on measuring the firm's β; the next section shows how to apply the CAPM to find the firm's cost of equity r_E.

2.5.1 Beta Is the Regression Coefficient of the Firm's Stock Returns on the Market Returns

In the following spreadsheet, we show the five-year monthly prices and returns for Intel Corporation and the S&P 500 returns, which we take as proxy for the stock market as a whole. In cells B2:B6 we have regressed the Intel returns on those of the S&P 500:

$$\begin{aligned} r_{\text{Intel},t} &= \alpha_{\text{Intel}} + \beta_{\text{Intel}} r_{SP,t} \\ &= -0.0029 + 2.2516 r_{SP,t} R^2 = 0.5304 \end{aligned}$$

7. The CAPM is discussed in detail in Chapters 7–11. At this point we outline the application of the model to finding the cost of capital without entering into the theory.

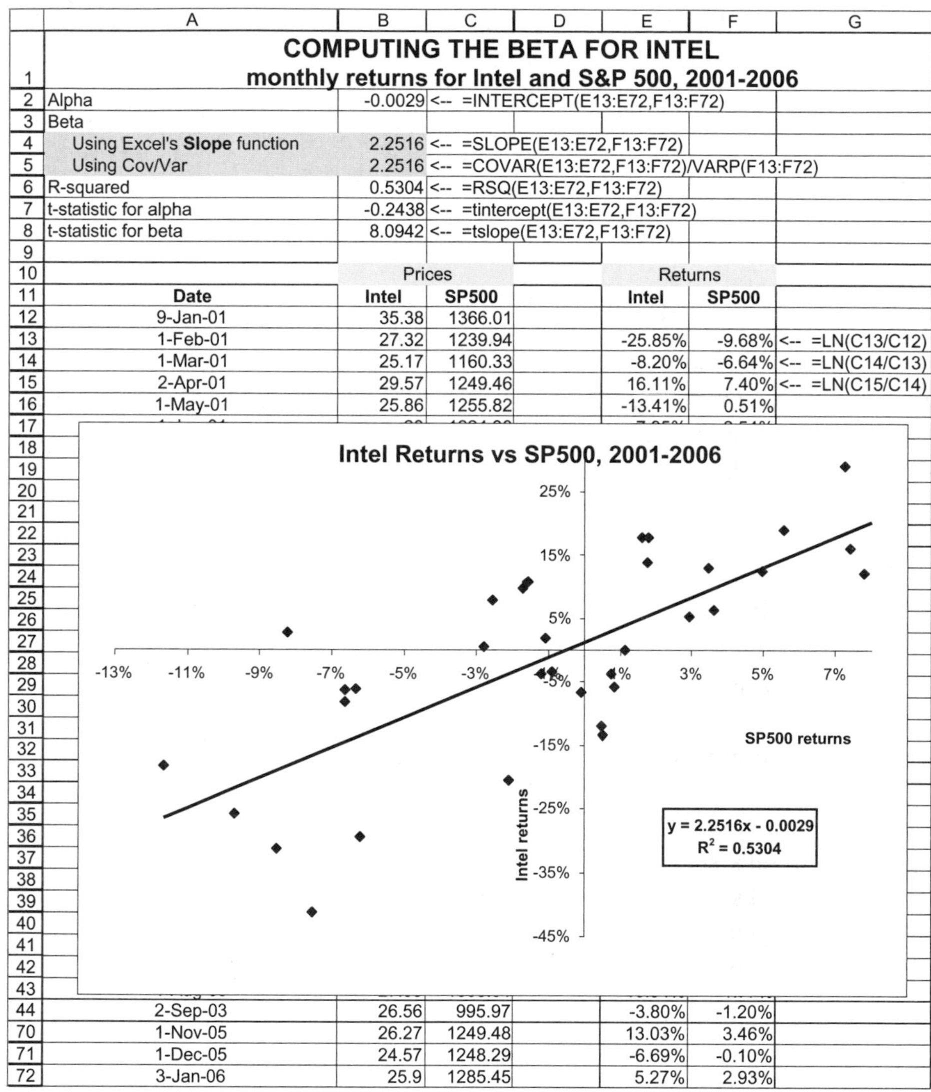

	A	B	C	D	E	F	G
1	**COMPUTING THE BETA FOR INTEL** monthly returns for Intel and S&P 500, 2001-2006						
2	Alpha	-0.0029	<-- =INTERCEPT(E13:E72,F13:F72)				
3	Beta						
4	Using Excel's **Slope** function	2.2516	<-- =SLOPE(E13:E72,F13:F72)				
5	Using Cov/Var	2.2516	<-- =COVAR(E13:E72,F13:F72)/VARP(F13:F72)				
6	R-squared	0.5304	<-- =RSQ(E13:E72,F13:F72)				
7	t-statistic for alpha	-0.2438	<-- =tintercept(E13:E72,F13:F72)				
8	t-statistic for beta	8.0942	<-- =tslope(E13:E72,F13:F72)				
9							
10		Prices			Returns		
11	**Date**	**Intel**	**SP500**		**Intel**	**SP500**	
12	9-Jan-01	35.38	1366.01				
13	1-Feb-01	27.32	1239.94		-25.85%	-9.68%	<-- =LN(C13/C12)
14	1-Mar-01	25.17	1160.33		-8.20%	-6.64%	<-- =LN(C14/C13)
15	2-Apr-01	29.57	1249.46		16.11%	7.40%	<-- =LN(C15/C14)
16	1-May-01	25.86	1255.82		-13.41%	0.51%	
44	2-Sep-03	26.56	995.97		-3.80%	-1.20%	
70	1-Nov-05	26.27	1249.48		13.03%	3.46%	
71	1-Dec-05	24.57	1248.29		-6.69%	-0.10%	
72	3-Jan-06	25.9	1285.45		5.27%	2.93%	

Here's what we can learn from this regression:

- Intel's *beta*, β_{Intel}, shows the sensitivity of its stock return to the market return. It is calculated by the following formula.

$$\beta_{\text{Intel}} = \frac{\text{Covariance(SP500 returns, Intel returns)}}{\text{Variance(SP500 returns)}}$$

We can compute β either by using this formula directly (cell B5) or by using the Excel **Slope** function (cell B4). Over the period covered, a 1 percent increase or decrease in the monthly returns of the S&P 500 was accompanied by a 2.25 percent increase or decrease in Intel's returns. The statistic **TSlope** (cell B8) shows that the β_{Intel} is highly significant (see section 2.5.2 for how this function was constructed).[8]

• Intel's alpha, α_{Intel}, shows that irrespective of changes in the S&P 500, the monthly return on Intel over the period was $\alpha_{\text{Intel}} = -0.29$ percent. On an annual basis, this is $12 * -0.29 = -3.5$ percent; this seems to indicate that, in the jargon of financial markets, Intel had negative performance over the period. Note, however, the **TIntercept** (cell B7): This function (its construction in Excel is discussed in section 2.5.2) shows that the negative intercept is not significantly different from zero.

• The R^2 of the regression shows that 53 percent of the variation in Intel's returns is accounted for by variability in the S&P 500. An R^2 of 53 percent may seem low, but in the CAPM literature this is actually quite a respectable number. It says that roughly 53 percent of the variation in Intel's returns is explicable by the variation in the S&P 500 return. The rest of the variability in the Intel returns can be diversified away by including Intel's shares in a diversified portfolio of shares. The average R^2 for stocks is approximately 30–40 percent, meaning that market factors account for approximately this percentage of a stock's variability, with factors idiosyncratic to the stock accounting for the rest.

The spreadsheet shows three ways of doing the regression: One way is to use the functions **Intercept**, **Slope**, **Rsq**. A second method involves

8. For the precise meaning of a *t*-statistic, you should refer to a good statistics text. For our purposes, a *t*-statistic over 1.96 indicates that with 95 percent probability the variable under discussion (the intercept when using **TIntercept** or the slope when using **TSlope**) is significantly different from zero. Thus the *t*-statistic for the intercept of –0.2438 indicates that the intercept is not significantly different from zero, whereas the *t*-statistic for the slope of 8.0942 indicates that the slope is significantly different from zero.

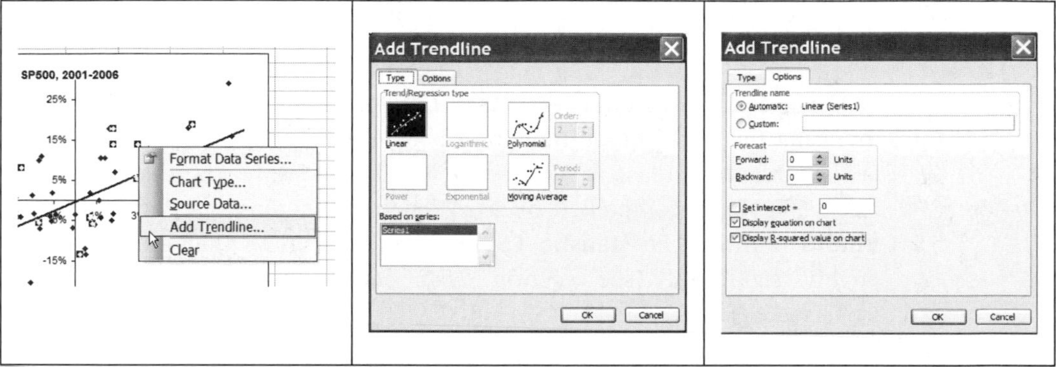

Figure 2.1
The sequence of commands for producing regression results from the **XY Scatter Plot** in Excel. Having marked the points, we right-click to select **Add Trendline** (left panel). We choose the linear regression (middle panel) and then click on the **Options** tab to indicate that the regression equation and the R^2 should be indicated on the graph.

using the Excel functions **Covar** and **VarP**. A third way involves Excel's **Trendline** function. Having graphed the returns of Intel and the S&P 500 on an **XY Scatter** plot, we then follow the procedure described in Figure 2.1.

2.5.2 The Homemade Functions TIntercept and TSlope

The preceding spreadsheet uses two functions to compute the *t*-statistics for the intercept and slope. These functions are built on the **Linest** function discussed in Chapter 33. Applying **Linest** to the return data, we get the following:

	I	J	K	L
10		Cells J14:K18created with the		
11		formula		
12		=LINEST(E12:E71,F12:F71,,1)}		
13		Slope	Intercept	
14	Slope -->	2.2516	-0.0029	<-- Intercept
15	Standard error of slope -->	0.2782	0.0120	<-- Standard error of intercept
16	R-squared -->	0.5304	0.0927	<-- Standard error of y values
17	F statistic -->	65.5155	58.0000	<-- Degrees of freedom
18	SS_{xy} -->	0.5627	0.4982	<-- SSE = Residual sum of squares

By using the Excel function **Index** we define a function **TIntercept** that divides the value of the intercept term produced by **Linest** (first row, second column of **Linest** output) by the standard error of the intercept (second row, second column):

```
Function tintercept(yarray, xarray)
     tintercept = Application.
Index(Application.
       LinEst(yarray, xarray, , 1), 1, 2) / _
     Application.Index(Application.
LinEst(yarray,
       xarray, , 1), 2, 2)
End Function
```

Similarly we can define a function **TSlope** that gives the *t*-statistic for the slope:

```
Function tslope(yarray, xarray)
     tslope = Application.Index(Application.
       LinEst(yarray, xarray, , 1), 1, 1) / _
     Application.Index(Application.
LinEst(yarray,
       xarray, , 1), 2, 1)
End Function
```

2.5.3 Using Excel's Data Analysis Add-in

There's a fourth way to produce the regression output: By clicking on **Tools|Data Analysis|Regression**, we can use a sophisticated Excel routine that computes more statistics, including the *t*-statistics. The output for this routine is illustrated as follows:

	A	B	C	D	E	F	G	H	I
1	**COMPUTING BETA FOR INTEL** **Monthly returns for Intel and SP500, 2001-2006**								
2	Alpha	-0.0029	<-- =INTERCEPT(E11:E70,F11:F70)						
3	Beta	2.2516	<-- =SLOPE(E11:E70,F11:F70)						
4	R-squared	0.5304	<-- =RSQ(E11:E70,F11:F70)						
5	t for alpha	-0.243762	<-- =tintercept(E11:E70,F11:F70)						
6	t for beta	8.094164	<-- =tslope(E11:E70,F11:F70)						
7									
8		**Prices**			**Returns**				
9	**Date**	**Intel**	**SP500**		**Intel**	**SP500**			
10	9-Jan-01	35.38	1366.01						
11	1-Feb-01	27.32	1239.94		-0.2585	-0.0968	<-- =LN(C11/C10)		
12	1-Mar-01	25.17	1160.33		-0.0820	-0.0664	<-- =LN(C12/C11)		
13	2-Apr-01	29.57	1249.46		0.1611	0.0740	<-- =LN(C13/C12)		
14	1-May-01	25.86	1255.82		-0.1341	0.0051			
15	1-Jun-01	28	1224.38		0.0795	-0.0254			
16	2-Jul-01	28.54	1211.23		0.0191	-0.0108			
65	1-Aug-05	25.24	1220.33		-0.0506	-0.0113			
66	1-Sep-05	24.19	1228.81		-0.0425	0.0069			
67	3-Oct-05	23.06	1207.01		-0.0478	-0.0179			
68	1-Nov-05	26.27	1249.48		0.1303	0.0346			
69	1-Dec-05	24.57	1248.29		-0.0669	-0.0010			
70	3-Jan-06	25.9	1285.45		0.0527	0.0293			
71									
72									
73	SUMMARY OUTPUT								
74									
75	*Regression Statistics*								
76	Multiple R	0.728302							
77	R Square	0.530423							
78	Adjusted R Square	0.522327							
79	Standard Error	0.092677							
80	Observations	60							
81									
82	ANOVA								
83		*df*	*SS*	*MS*	*F*	*Significance F*			
84	Regression	1	0.5627	0.5627	65.5155	0.0000			
85	Residual	58	0.4982	0.0086					
86	Total	59	1.0609						
87									
88		*Coefficients*	*Standard Erro*	*t Stat*	*P-value*	*Lower 95%*	*Upper 95%*	*Lower 95.0%*	*Upper 95.0%*
89	Intercept	-0.0029	0.0120	-0.2438	0.8083	-0.0269	0.0210	-0.0269	0.0210
90	X Variable 1	2.2516	0.2782	8.0942	0.0000	1.6948	2.8084	1.6948	2.8084

Rows 73–90 were produced from **Tools|Data Analysis|Regression** using the following values:

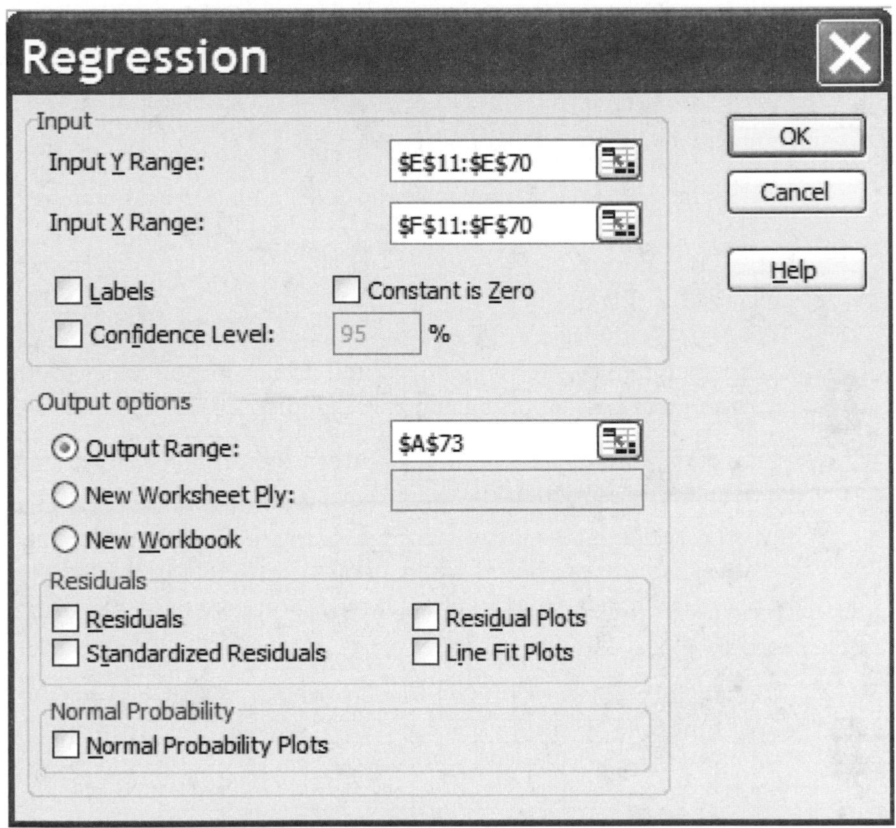

While **Tools|Data Analysis|Regression** produces a lot of data, it has one major drawback: The output is not automatically updated when the underlying data changes. For this reason we prefer to use the other methods illustrated.

2.6 Using the Security Market Line to Calculate Intel's Cost of Equity

In the capital asset pricing model, the security market line (SML) is used to calculate the risk-adjusted cost of capital. In this section we consider two SML formulations. The difference between these two methods has to do with the way taxes are incorporated into the cost-of-capital equation.

2.6.1 Method 1: The Classic Security Market Line

The classic CAPM formula uses an SML equation that ignores taxes:

Cost of equity, $r_E = r_f + \beta[E(r_M) - r_f]$

Here r_f is the risk-free rate of return in the economy, and $E(R_M)$ is the expected rate of return on the market. The choice of values for the SML parameters is often problematic. A common approach is to choose

- r_f equal to the risk-free interest rate in the economy (for example, the yield on Treasury bills).
- $E(r_M)$ equal to the historic average of the market return, defined as the average return of a broad-based market portfolio. There is an alternative approach based on market multiples; both of these are discussed in section 2.7.

The following spreadsheet fragment illustrates the classic CAPM cost of equity:

	A	B	C
1	**COMPUTING THE COST OF EQUITY FOR INTEL** **Classic CAPM: $r_E = r_f + \beta$*[$E(r_M)$-r_f]**		
2	Intel beta	2.2516	
3	Risk free rate, r_f	4.93%	
4	Expected market return, $E(r_M)$	9.88%	
5	Intel cost of equity, $r_{E,Intel}$	16.31%	<-- =B3+B2*(B4-B3)

The computation of $E(r_M)$ is discussed in section 2.7. The risk-free rate r_f is computed from Yahoo data—we take the yield on the short-term Treasury bills as a proxy for the market risk-free rate:

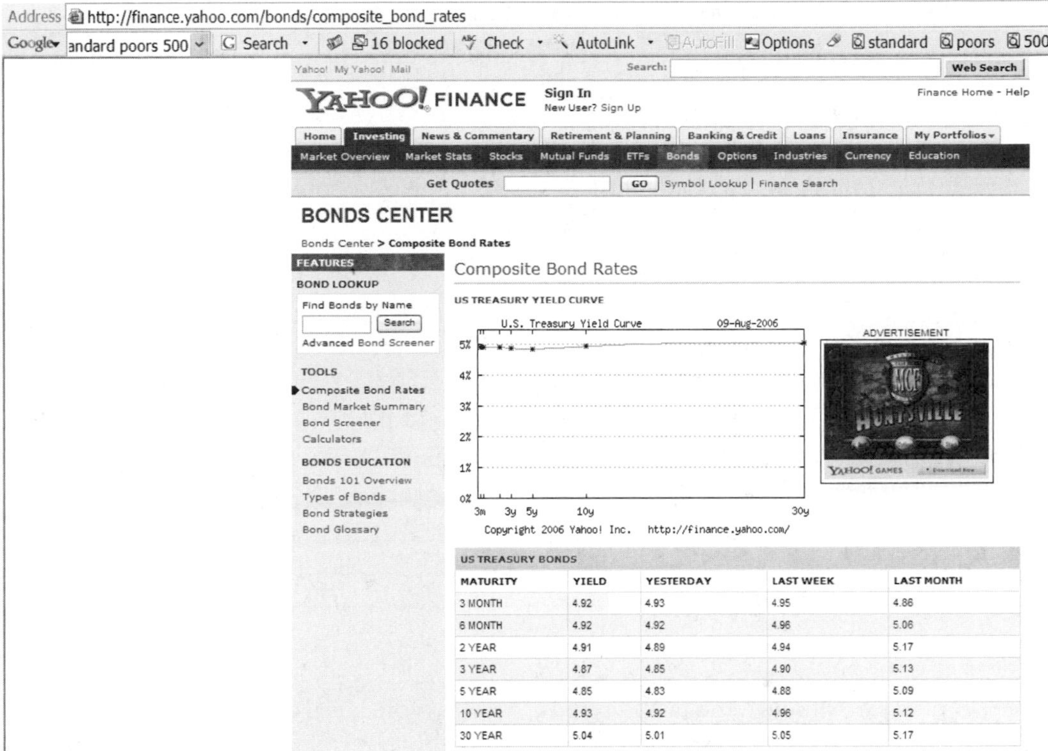

MATURITY	YIELD	YESTERDAY	LAST WEEK	LAST MONTH
3 MONTH	4.92	4.93	4.95	4.86
6 MONTH	4.92	4.92	4.96	5.06
2 YEAR	4.91	4.89	4.94	5.17
3 YEAR	4.87	4.85	4.90	5.13
5 YEAR	4.85	4.83	4.88	5.09
10 YEAR	4.93	4.92	4.96	5.12
30 YEAR	5.04	5.01	5.05	5.17

2.6.2 Method 2: The Tax-Adjusted Security Market Line

The classic CAPM approach makes no allowance for taxation. Benninga and Sarig (1997) show that the SML has to be adjusted for the marginal corporate tax rate in the economy.[9] Denoting the corporate tax rate by T_C, the tax-adjusted SML is

$$\text{Cost of equity} = r_f(1-T_C)+\beta[E(r_M)-r_f(1-T_C)]$$

This formula can be applied by substituting $r_f(1-T_C)$ for r_f in the classic CAPM. Note that the tax-adjusted cost of equity has a lower intercept and a higher slope than the classic CAPM.

9. The logic of the Benninga-Sarig approach is outlined in our book *Corporate Finance: A Valuation Approach* (McGraw-Hill, 1997). A more formal derivation of the model is given in "Risk, Returns and Values in the Presence of Differential Taxation," co-authored with Oded Sarig. *Journal of Banking and Finance* 27.

- The intercept is $r_f(1 - T_C)$ instead of r_f.
- The slope is $E(r_M) - r_f(1 - T_C)$ instead of $E(r_M) - r_f$. Note that the slope can be written as the classic CAPM slope plus $T_C r_f$:

$E(r_M) - r_f(1 - T_C) = [E(r_M) - r_f] + T_C r_f$

For Intel, the tax-adjusted approach gives a somewhat higher cost of equity:

	A	B	C
1	**COMPUTING THE COST OF EQUITY FOR INTEL** **Tax-adjusted CAPM: $r_E = r_f(1-T_C) + \beta$*$[E(r_M)-r_f(1-T_C)]$**		
2	Intel beta	2.2516	
3	Intel tax rate, T_C	31.29%	<-- Computed from Intel financials
4	Risk free rate, r_f	4.93%	
5	Expected market return, $E(r_M)$	9.88%	
6	Intel cost of equity, $r_{E,Intel}$	18.00%	<-- =B4*(1-B3)+B2*(B5-B4*(1-B3))

Although the tax-adjusted CAPM is more consistent with an economy with taxation, we confess that—given the uncertainties surrounding cost-of-capital computations—the difference between the classic CAPM and the tax-adjusted CAPM may not be worth the trouble.

2.7 Three Approaches to Computing the Expected Return on the Market $E(r_M)$

A critical computation for the CAPM cost of equity is the expected return on the market $E(r_M)$. There are three major approaches to computing this number:

1. The historical return on a major market index
2. The historical market risk premium
3. The Gordon model

All three approaches are illustrated in this section, and their effect on computing the Intel cost of equity is illustrated at the end of this section.

2.7.1 $E(r_M)$ as the Historical Average Return on a Market Portfolio

A simple approach to computing $E(r_M)$ is to take it as the average of the historical returns of a major market index. In the following computation we illustrate this approach by using Vanguard's 500 Index Fund as a proxy for the market.[10] The annualized return on this fund since 1987 is 9.98 percent:

	A	B	C	D
1	**MEASURING E(r$_M$) USING HISTORICAL DATA** **Derived from prices for the Vanguard 500 Index Fund (symbol: VFINX)** **These prices include dividends; April 1987–August 2006**			
2	Average monthly return	0.83%	<-- =AVERAGE(C10:C241)	
3	Monthly standard deviation	4.34%	<-- =STDEVP(C10:C241)	
4				
5	Annualized return	9.98%	<-- =12*B2	
6	Annualized standard deviation	15.05%	<-- =SQRT(12)*B3	
7				
8	**Date**	**Price**	**Return**	
9	1-Apr-87	17.32		
10	1-May-87	17.49	0.98%	<-- =LN(B10/B9)
11	1-Jun-87	18.37	4.91%	<-- =LN(B11/B10)
12	1-Jul-87	19.28	4.83%	<-- =LN(B12/B11)
13	3-Aug-87	20.02	3.77%	<-- =LN(B13/B12)
14	1-Sep-87	19.56	-2.32%	
15	1-Oct-87	15.31	-24.50%	
16	2-Nov-87	14.06	-8.52%	
17	1-Dec-87	15.12	7.27%	
18	4-Jan-88	15.75	4.08%	
19	1-Feb-88	16.48	4.53%	
20	1-Mar-88	15.98	-3.08%	
21	4-Apr-88	16.14	1.00%	

2.7.2 Computing the Market Risk Premium $E(r_M) - r_f$ Directly

We can also compute the market risk premium directly. This procedure requires a bit more work: In the following spreadsheet we add to the preceding Vanguard data, data from the St. Louis Federal Reserve Bank on three-month Treasury bill rates.

10. The Vanguard fund's prices incorporate dividends on the S&P 500.

	A	B	C	D	E	F
1	**MEASURING THE MARKET RISK PREMIUM $E(r_M)$ - r_f USING HISTORICAL DATA** **Vanguard 500 Index Fund (symbol: VFINX) minus Treasury Bills** **April 1987 - August 2006** **All measurements relate to monthly returns on SP500, r_{Mt}, and the Treasury bill rate r_{ft}**					
2	Average monthly risk premium	0.46%	<-- =AVERAGE(E10:E241)			Methodological note: I have used the St. Louis FRED data for 3-month Treasury bills; this data is annualized, and I have divided it by 12 to get the monthly returns. Since the data can be taken as an ex ante return, the April 1987 rate is attributed to May 1987. I've use 3-month instead of 1-month because there are lots of data problems with the latter.
3	Monthly standard deviation	4.34%	<-- =STDEVP(E10:E241)			
4						
5	Annualized risk premium	5.50%	<-- =12*B2			
6	Annualized standard deviation	15.04%	<-- =SQRT(12)*B3			
7						
8	**Date**	**Price**	**Return**	**Treasury bill rate**	**Market risk premium**	
9	1-Apr-87	17.32				
10	1-May-87	17.49	0.98%	0.47%	0.51%	<-- =C10-D10
11	1-Jun-87	18.37	4.91%	0.47%	4.44%	<-- =C11-D11
12	1-Jul-87	19.28	4.83%	0.47%	4.36%	
13	3-Aug-87	20.02	3.77%	0.47%	3.29%	
14	1-Sep-87	19.56	-2.32%	0.50%	-2.83%	
15	1-Oct-87	15.31	-24.50%	0.53%	-25.03%	
16	2-Nov-87	14.06	-8.52%	0.51%	-9.03%	

Applying the risk premium directly to the computation of Intel's cost of equity gives the following:

	A	B	C
1	**COMPUTING THE COST OF EQUITY FOR INTEL USING THE MARKET RISK PREMIUM $E(r_M)$ - r_f**		
2	Intel beta	2.2516	
3	Historical market risk premium	5.50%	
4	Intel tax rate, T_C	31.29%	<-- Computed from Intel financials
5	Risk free rate, r_f	4.93%	
6	Intel cost of equity, $r_{E,Intel}$		
7	Classic CAPM	17.31%	<-- =B5+B2*B3
8	Tax-adjusted CAPM	19.24%	<-- =B5*(1-B4)+B2*(B3+B4*B5)
9			
10	**Note**: The tax-adjusted model in cell B8 uses the equivalence $E(r_M) - r_f (1-T_C) = E(r_M) - r_f + T_C{*}r_f$		

2.7.3 Calculating the Expected Return on the Market $E(r_M)$ Using the Gordon Model

The 9.98 percent return for $E(r_M)$ approximates the historic market return in the United States for 1987–2006. Historic averages are appropriate if we think that the future anticipated rates of return will correspond to the historic average. However, we may want to take current market data to calculate directly the future anticipated market yield.

As Benninga and Sarig show, the Gordon model gives us an approach for doing so.[11] Recall that the model says that the cost of equity r_E is given by

$$r_E = \frac{\text{Div}_0(1+g)}{P_0} + g$$

This formula also applies to the market portfolio, so that we can write

$$r_M = \frac{\text{Div}_0(1+g)}{P_0} + g$$

interpreting Div_0, P_0, and g to be the current dividend, price, and growth rate of the market portfolio. Rewriting this formula, assuming that the firm pays out a constant proportion a of its earnings as dividends, indicating by EPS_0 the current earnings per share, and interpreting g to be the earnings growth of the firm, gives us

$$E(r_M) = \frac{a * EPS_0(1+g)}{P_0} + g = \frac{a*(1+g)}{P_0/EPS_0} + g$$

The term on the right-hand side of this equation, P_0/EPS_0, is the price-earnings ratio of the market. We can use this formula to compute $E(r_M)$ and thus tie the cost of equity to currently observable market parameters. Here is an implementation:

	A	B	C
1	**COMPUTING THE COST OF EQUITY FOR INTEL USING THE MARKET PRICE/EARNINGS MULTIPLE TO COMPUTE E(r_M)**		
2	Market price/earnings multiple, August 2006	17	
3	Equity cash flow payout ratio	50.00%	
4	Anticipated growth of market equity cash flow	6.00%	
5	Expected market return, E(r_M)	9.12%	<-- =B3*(1+B4)/B2+B4
6			
7	**Intel cost of equity calculations**		
8	Intel beta	2.2516	
9	Intel tax rate, T_C	31.29%	<-- Computed from Intel financials
10	Risk free rate, r_f	4.93%	
11	Intel cost of equity, $r_{E,Intel}$		
12	Classic CAPM	14.36%	<-- =B10+B8*(B5-B10)
13	Tax-adjusted CAPM	16.29%	<-- =B10*(1-B9)+B8*(B5-B10*(1-B9))
14			
15	**Note**: Price/Earnings ratio for S&P 500 from http://www.bullandbearwise.com		

11. A fuller exposition of this model can be found in Chapter 9 of Benninga and Sarig (1997).

2.8 Calculating the Cost of Debt

Thus far in this chapter we have shown several methods for computing the cost of equity r_E. We now turn to calculating the cost of debt r_D. In principle, r_D is the marginal cost to the firm (before corporate taxes) of borrowing an additional dollar. In practice the cost of debt often turns out to be more difficult to calculate than the cost of equity. There are at least three ways of calculating the firm's cost of debt. We will state them briefly and then go on to illustrate the application of two of the methods that, although they may not be theoretically perfect, are often used in practice:

- As a practical matter, the cost of debt can often be approximated by taking the *average cost* of the firm's existing debt. The problem with this method is that it runs the danger of confusing the *past costs* with the *future anticipated* cost of debt that we actually want to measure.
- We can use the yield of similar-risk, newly issued corporate securities. If a company is rated A and has mostly medium-term debt, then we can use the average yield on medium-term, A-rated debt as the firm's cost of debt. Note that this method is somewhat problematic because the yield on a bond is its *promised return*, whereas the cost of debt is the *expected return* on a firm's debt. Since there is usually a risk of default, the promised return is generally higher than the expected return.
- We can use a model that estimates the cost of debt from data about the firm's bond prices, the estimated probabilities of default, and the estimated payoffs to bondholders in case of default. This method requires a lot of work and is mathematically nontrivial; we postpone its discussion until Chapter 28. For cost of capital calculations it would be used in practice only if the firm we are analyzing has significant amounts of risky debt.

The first two methods are relatively easy to apply, and in many cases the problems or errors that are encountered in these methods are not critical.[12] As a matter of theory, however, both these methods fail to make

12. It bears repeating that calculating the cost of capital requires a large number of assumptions and does not necessarily give a precise answer. Thus cost of capital estimation is part science and part art. Users of cost of capital estimates should always do a sensitivity analysis around the numbers calculated. Given the data on the company you are analyzing, some sloppiness in the cost of capital calculations (with its accompanying savings in time) may be expedient.

proper risk adjustments for the cost of the firm's debt. The third method, which involves computing the expected return on a firm's debt, is more in line with standard financial theory, but it is also more difficult to apply. It may not, therefore, be worth the effort. In the remainder of this section, we apply the first two of these methods to calculate the cost of debt for Kraft.

2.8.1 Method 1: Kraft's Average Cost of Debt

The average cost of Kraft's debt in 1998 can be calculated from the financial statements as somewhere between 5.50 and 5.73 percent:

	A	B	C	D
1	COMPUTING THE COST OF DEBT FOR KRAFT			
2		2005/12/31	2004/12/31	
3	Cash and cash equivalents	316,000,000	282,000,000	
4				
5	Short-term borrowings	805,000,000	1,818,000,000	
6	Current portion of long-term debt	1,268,000,000	750,000,000	
7	Due to Altria Group, Inc., and affiliates	652,000,000	227,000,000	
8	Long-term debt	8,475,000,000	9,723,000,000	
9				
10	Interest and other debt expense, net	636,000,000	666,000,000	
11				
12	Net debt	10,884,000,000	12,236,000,000	<-- =SUM(C5:C8)-C3
13	Net interest cost	5.50%		<-- =B10/AVERAGE(B12:C12)
14				
15	Total debt	11,200,000,000	12,518,000,000	
16	Cash paid:			
17	Interest	679,000,000	633,000,000	
18				
19	Interest cost	5.73%		<-- =B17/AVERAGE(B15:C15)

Several aspects of our calculations are worth noting:

- When calculating the cost of debt r_D from the financial statements, it is important to include all financial debt, without distinguishing between short-term and long-term items. In Kraft's case we have identified four such items (rows 5–8). When—in the next chapter—we treat the case of corporate valuation, we will see that the nonfinancial items of the firm's short-term assets and short-term liabilities are included in the free cash flows that are discounted to arrive at the corporate value.
- In principle, liquid assets such as cash and cash equivalents are *negative debt* and should be subtracted from the firm's debt. The idea here is that

Kraft could use its cash to pay off part of its debt, so that the effective debt financing of the firm is its financial debt minus cash. However, the implementation of this particular piece of theory is largely a judgment call—we may not want to attribute all cash to the possibility of paying off debt, and we may want to compute the firm's cost of borrowing as opposed to the interest it earns on cash. In the preceding spreadsheet we illustrated both methods (cells B13 and B19).

2.8.2 Method 2: The Rating-Adjusted Yield on Kraft's Debt

From Kraft's financial statements, we learn that in August 2006, Kraft was rated BBB+ (see box).

Kraft's Financial Rating

The following is taken from Kraft's financial statements and shows that Kraft is rated approximately BBB+:

Credit Ratings. Following a $10.1 billion judgment on March 21, 2003, against Altria Group, Inc.'s domestic tobacco subsidiary, Philip Morris USA Inc., the three major credit rating agencies took a series of ratings actions resulting in the lowering of the Company's short-term and long-term debt ratings, despite the fact the Company is neither a party to, nor has exposure to, this litigation. The Company's credit ratings by Moody's at December 31, 2005, were "P-2" for short-term debt and "A3" for long-term debt, with stable outlook. The Company's credit ratings by Standard & Poor's at December 31, 2005 were "A-2" for short-term debt and "BBB+" for long-term debt, with stable outlook. The Company's credit ratings by Fitch Rating Services at December 31, 2005 were "F-2" for short-term debt and "BBB+" for long-term debt, with stable outlook. As a result of the rating agencies' actions, borrowing costs have increased. None of the Company's debt agreements requires accelerated repayment in the event of a decrease in credit ratings. The credit rating downgrades by Moody's, Standard & Poor's and Fitch Rating Services had no impact on any of the Company's other existing third-party contracts.

We can impute the marginal cost of Kraft's debt from a yield curve for the appropriate debt. Following is such a yield curve, compiled from data available on Yahoo:

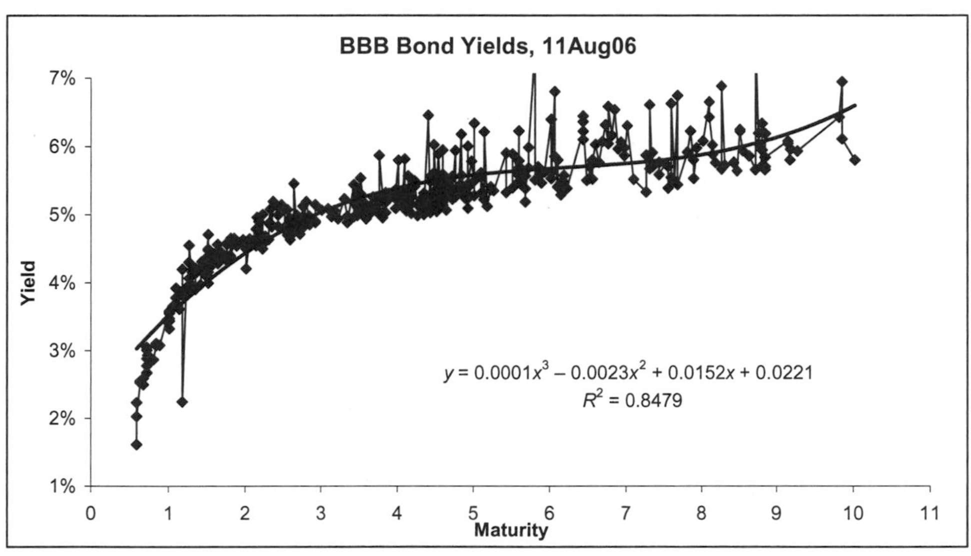

The polynomial regression line describes about 85 percent of the variability of the yields as a function of the time to maturity.[13] Assuming a five-year average maturity for Kraft's debt, the cost of borrowing for Kraft is 5.31 percent.

	A	B	C
1	**COMPUTING KRAFT'S r_D FROM A YIELD CURVE** **YTM=0.0001*time^3-0.0023*time^2+0.0152*time+0.0221**		
2	Average time to maturity (years)	5	
3	Yield	5.31%	<-- =0.0001*B2^3-0.0023*B2^2+0.0152*B2+0.0221

13. For more details, see Chapter 27.

2.9 Computing the WACC: Three Cases

In each the next three sections we compute the weighted average cost of capital for a different company. Each case illustrates some pitfalls of WACC computations. We make no claims for scientific accuracy—instead we are trying to show you, the financial analyst, that the computation of a firm's cost of capital requires a considerable number of judgment calls.

Here are the three cases:

1. Kraft Corporation (section 2.10) illustrates a large divergence between the Gordon r_E and the CAPM r_E. The question ultimately is what shareholders expect—do they think that the market variability of their stock investment is indicative of the riskiness of the stock, or did they invest in Kraft because of its history of payouts to shareholders?

2. Tyson Foods (section 2.11) has not changed its dividend payout per share for four years. Its equity payouts, however, exhibit considerable growth but also large variations over time. On a before-tax basis, the company's cost of equity r_E appears to be lower than its cost of debt r_D.

3. Cascade Corporation (section 2.12) illustrates a case of negative leverage: The company has more cash than it does debt.

2.10 Computing the WACC for Kraft Corporation

In section 2.8 we discussed Kraft's cost of debt r_D . In this section we restrict ourselves to the discussion of the firm's cost of equity r_E and its WACC.

2.10.1 Computing the Kraft r_E Using the Gordon Model

The computation of Kraft's cost of equity using the Gordon model for only its per-share dividends gives a very high r_E, as shown in the following spreadsheet:

	A	B	C
1	**KRAFT: COST OF EQUITY r_E BASED ON DIVIDENDS**		
2	Stock price, end 2005	27.75	
3	Current dividend, D_0	0.92	<-- =B25*4
4	Gordon cost of equity, r_E		
5	Using growth rate Dec01-Dec05	19.15%	<-- =B3*(1+B29)/B2+B29
6	Using growth rate Dec03-Dec05	16.79%	<-- =B3*(1+B32)/B2+B32
7			
8	**Date**	**Dividends per share**	
9	20-Dec-01	0.130	
10	13-Mar-02	0.130	
11	26-Jun-02	0.130	
12	12-Sep-02	0.150	
13	19-Dec-02	0.150	
14	12-Mar-03	0.150	
15	25-Jun-03	0.150	
16	11-Sep-03	0.180	
17	18-Dec-03	0.180	
18	11-Mar-04	0.180	
19	23-Jun-04	0.180	
20	10-Sep-04	0.205	
21	20-Dec-04	0.205	
22	11-Mar-05	0.205	
23	24-Jun-05	0.205	
24	2-Sep-05	0.230	
25	22-Dec-05	0.230	
26			
27	**Computing the growth rate of dividends**		
28	Quarterly growth, Dec01-Dec05	3.63%	<-- =(B25/B9)^(1/16)-1
29	Annualized	15.33%	<-- =(1+B28)^4-1
30			
31	Quarterly growth, Dec03-Dec05	3.11%	<-- =(B25/B17)^(1/8)-1
32	Annualized	13.04%	<-- =(1+B31)^4-1

When we examine the cash flows to equity holders, the picture becomes even more complicated. Kraft has paid out hefty amounts to shareholders over the past four years, but it has financed these payouts at least partially by a huge stock offering in 2002:

	A	B	C	D	E	F
1	**KRAFT: COST OF EQUITY r_E BASED ON CASH FLOW TO EQUITY**					
2	Shares outstanding	1,669,880,755				
3	Share price, end 2005	27.75				
4	Equity value, E	46,339,190,951	<-- =B2*B3			
5	End 2005 total equity payout	2,612,000,000	<-- =E18			
6						
7	High growth rate, g_{high}	10.00%	<-- Guess			
8	Number of high-growth years	3	<-- Guess			
9	Normal growth rate, g_{normal}	6%	<-- Guess			
10						
11	Cost of equity, r_E, using the function **twostagegordon**	14.46%	<-- =twostagegordon(B4,B5,B7,B8,B9)			
12						
13	**Date**	**Stock repurchases**	**Dividends paid**	**Stock issuance**	**Cash flow to equity holders**	
14	31-Dec-01	170,000,000	225,000,000		395,000,000	<-- =B14+C14-D14
15	31-Dec-02	372,000,000	936,000,000	8,425,000,000	-7,117,000,000	<-- =B15+C15-D15
16	31-Dec-03	372,000,000	1,089,000,000		1,461,000,000	
17	31-Dec-04	688,000,000	1,280,000,000		1,968,000,000	
18	31-Dec-05	1,175,000,000	1,437,000,000		2,612,000,000	
19	Growth rates					
20	Four year	62.14%	58.97%		60.36%	<-- =(E18/E14)^(1/4)-1
21	Two year	77.72%	14.87%		33.71%	<-- =(E18/E16)^(1/2)-1

Using our formula for a two-stage Gordon model (see Section 2.2) we arrive at a cost of equity r_E of 12.64 percent. This formula incorporates a guesstimate of 10 percent for a high growth rate of equity payouts over the next three years, followed by a normal growth rate of 6 percent. Were we to use 20 percent and 6 percent we would get $r_E = 14.46$ percent (not shown).

2.10.2 Kraft's r_E Using the CAPM

Kraft has a β equal to 0.47. Using a market price-earnings multiple to compute $E(r_M)$ as illustrated on page 65, we compute $r_E = 6.82$ percent using the classic CAPM and 6.05 percent using the tax-adjusted CAPM:

	A	B	C
1	**COMPUTING THE COST OF EQUITY r_E FOR KRAFT USING THE MARKET PRICE/EARNINGS MULTIPLE TO COMPUTE $E(r_M)$**		
2	Market price/earnings multiple, December 2005	18	
3	Equity cash flow payout ratio	50.00%	
4	Anticipated growth of equity cash flow	6.00%	
5	Expected market return, $E(r_M)$	8.94%	<-- =B3*(1+B4)/B2+B4
6			
7	**Kraft cost of equity calculations**		
8	Kraft beta	0.4700	<-- From Yahoo
9	Kraft tax rate, T_C	29.37%	<-- Computed from Kraft financials
10	Risk free rate, r_f	4.93%	
11	Kraft cost of equity, $r_{E,Kraft}$		
12	Classic CAPM	6.82%	<-- =B10+B8*(B5-B10)
13	Tax-adjusted CAPM	6.05%	<-- =B10*(1-B9)+B8*(B5-B10*(1-B9))

2.10.3 So What Is Kraft's WACC?

The preceding analysis produces four estimates for the WACC of Kraft—the Gordon estimates are high and the CAPM estimates are low:

	A	B	C
1	**COMPUTING THE WACC FOR KRAFT**		
2	Shares outstanding	1,669,880,755	
3	Share price, end 2005	27.75	
4	Equity value, E	46,339,190,951	
5	Net debt, D	10,884,000,000	
6			
7	**WACC based on Gordon per-share dividends and interest from financial statements**		
8	Cost of equity, r_E	16.79%	<-- ='Page 71'!B6
9	Cost of debt, r_D	5.50%	<-- ='Page 67'!B13
10	Tax rate, T_C	29.37%	<-- ='Kraft 10K, 2005'!B160
11	WACC	14.33%	<-- =$B$4/($B$4+$B$5)*B8+$B$5/($B$4+$B$5)*B9*(1-$B$10)
12			
13	**WACC based on Gordon equity payouts and interest from financial statements**		
14	Cost of equity, r_E	14.46%	<-- ='Page 72, top'!B11
15	Cost of debt, r_D	5.50%	<-- ='Page 67'!B13
16	Tax rate, T_C	29.37%	<-- ='Kraft 10K, 2005'!B160
17	WACC	12.45%	<-- =$B$4/($B$4+$B$5)*B14+$B$5/($B$4+$B$5)*B15*(1-$B$10)
18			
19	**WACC based on classic CAPM and interest from financial statements**		
20	Cost of equity, r_E	6.82%	<-- ='Page 72, bottom'!B12
21	Cost of debt, r_D	5.50%	<-- ='Page 67'!B13
22	Tax rate, T_C	29.37%	<-- ='Kraft 10K, 2005'!B160
23	WACC	6.26%	<-- =$B$4/($B$4+$B$5)*B20+$B$5/($B$4+$B$5)*B21*(1-$B$10)
24			
25	**WACC based on tax-adjusted CAPM and interest from financial statements**		
26	Cost of equity, r_E	6.05%	<-- ='Page 72, bottom'!B13
27	Cost of debt, r_D	5.50%	<-- ='Page 67'!B13
28	Tax rate, T_C	29.37%	<-- ='Kraft 10K, 2005'!B160
29	WACC	5.64%	<-- =$B$4/($B$4+$B$5)*B26+$B$5/($B$4+$B$5)*B27*(1-$B$10)

So what is Kraft's WACC? Is it in the range of 5–6 percent or in the range of 12–14 percent? One way to get a feel for the answer to this question is to look at other companies in the same sector. In section 2.11 we examine the WACC for Tyson's, another company in the food sector. All of the estimates for Tyson's WACC are in the lower range of Kraft's estimates. If this is indicative (and we think it is), then we conclude that Kraft's WACC is somewhere between 5.64 and 6.26 percent.

2.11 Computing the WACC for Tyson Foods

Tyson Foods (stock symbol TSN) is primarily a producer of meats, but the company also has a large processed foods segment. Tyson's dividends per share have stood still for the past four years, though its cash flows to equity show some growth over this same period. As we will see, the correspondence between the Gordon estimate for the company's cost of equity r_E and the CAPM estimates are much closer for Tyson than for Kraft.

2.11.1 Computing Tyson's r_E Using the Gordon Model

Tyson hasn't changed its per-share dividend in five years. This fact makes the computation of the cost of equity r_E using the dividend model very simple:

	A	B	C
1	**TYSON: COST OF EQUITY r_E BASED ON DIVIDENDS**		
2	Stock price, 11Aug06	13.45	
3	Current dividend, D_0	0.16	<-- =B25*4
4	Dividend growth rate	0%	
5	Gordon cost of equity, r_E	1.19%	<-- =B3*(1+B4)/B2+B4
6			
7	**Date**	**Dividends per share**	
8	29-Aug-01	0.04	
9	28-Nov-01	0.04	
10	27-Feb-02	0.04	
11	29-May-02	0.04	
12	28-Aug-02	0.04	
13	26-Nov-02	0.04	
14	26-Feb-03	0.04	
15	28-May-03	0.04	
16	27-Aug-03	0.04	
17	26-Nov-03	0.04	
18	26-Feb-04	0.04	
19	27-May-04	0.04	
20	30-Aug-04	0.04	
21	29-Nov-04	0.04	
22	25-Feb-05	0.04	
23	30-Aug-05	0.04	
24	27-Feb-06	0.04	
25	30-May-06	0.04	

When we examine the cash flows to equity holders, the picture becomes somewhat more interesting. Tyson's annual cash flows to equity are shown in the following spreadsheet; these show a more variable payout pattern than the per-share dividends:

	A	B	C	D	E	F
1	**TYSON: COST OF EQUITY r_E BASED ON CASH FLOW TO EQUITY**					
2	Shares outstanding	354,820,000				
3	Share price, 11Aug06	13.45				
4	Equity value, E	4,772,329,000	<-- =B2*B3			
5	Current (Aug06) total equity payout	81,631,562	<-- =E18*(1+B7)^0.75			
6						
7	High growth rate, g_{high}	10.00%	<-- Guess			
8	Number of high-growth years	3	<-- Guess			
9	Normal growth rate, g_{normal}	2%	<-- Guess			
10						
11	Cost of equity, r_E, using the function **twostagegordon**	4.18%	<-- =twostagegordon(B4,B5,B7,B8,B9)			
12						
13	**Date**	**Stock repurchases**	**Dividends paid**	**Stock issuance**	**Cash flow to equity holders**	
14	2001	48,000,000	35,000,000	34,000,000	49,000,000	<-- =B14+C14-D14
15	2002	19,000,000	58,000,000	0	77,000,000	<-- =B15+C15-D15
16	2003	41,000,000	54,000,000	0	95,000,000	
17	2004	72,000,000	55,000,000	43,000,000	84,000,000	
18	2005	45,000,000	55,000,000	24,000,000	76,000,000	
19	Growth rates					
20	Four year	-1.60%	11.96%		11.60%	<-- =(E18/E14)^(1/4)-1
21	Two year	4.76%	0.92%		-10.56%	<-- =(E18/E16)^(1/2)-1

In cell B5 we assume that the August 2006 equity payout is the payout for the financial year ending October 2005 multiplied by the high growth rate to the power 0.75. Using the two-stage Gordon model, we arrive at a cost of equity $r_E = 4.18$ percent. This formula incorporates a guesstimate of 10 percent for a high growth rate of equity payouts over the next three years, followed by a normal growth rate of 2 percent. Were we to use 10 percent and 5 percent, we would get $r_E = 7.06$ percent.

2.11.2 Tyson's r_E Using the CAPM

Tyson has a $\beta = 0.20$. Using a market price-earnings multiple to compute $E(r_M)$ as illustrated on page 65, we compute $r_E = 5.77$ percent using the classic CAPM and 4.60 percent using the tax-adjusted CAPM:

	A	B	C
1	**COMPUTING THE COST OF EQUITY r_E FOR TYSON USING THE MARKET PRICE/EARNINGS MULTIPLE TO COMPUTE $E(r_M)$**		
2	Market price/earnings multiple, August 2006	17	
3	Equity cash flow payout ratio	50.00%	
4	Anticipated growth of equity cash flow	6.00%	
5	Expected market return, $E(r_M)$	9.12%	<-- =B3*(1+B4)/B2+B4
6			
7	**Tyson cost of equity calculations**		
8	Tyson beta	0.20	<-- From Yahoo
9	Tyson tax rate, T_C	29.55%	<-- Computed from Tyson financials
10	Risk free rate, r_f	4.93%	
11	Tyson cost of equity, $r_{E,Kraft}$		
12	Classic CAPM	5.77%	<-- =B10+B8*(B5-B10)
13	Tax-adjusted CAPM	4.60%	<-- =B10*(1-B9)+B8*(B5-B10*(1-B9))

2.11.3 Method 1: Tyson's Cost of Debt r_D

The average cost of Tyson's debt in 2005 can be calculated from the financial statements as 7.22 percent:

	A	B	C	D
1	**COMPUTING THE COST OF DEBT FOR TYSON**			
2		**2005**	**2004**	
3	Cash and cash equivalents	40,000,000	33,000,000	
4	Current debt	126,000,000	338,000,000	
5	Long term debt	2,869,000,000	3,024,000,000	
6	Net debt	2,955,000,000	3,329,000,000	<-- =C5+C4-C3
7				
8	Interest paid	227,000,000		
9				
10	Interest cost	7.22%	<-- =B8/AVERAGE(B6:C6)	

2.11.4 Method 2: The Rating-Adjusted Yield on Tyson's Debt

In August 2006, Tyson was rated BBB. As we did for Kraft, we can impute a cost of debt for Tyson based on the yield curve of $r_D = 5.31$ percent.

2.11.5 Tyson's WACC

The preceding analysis produces four estimates for the WACC of Tyson. We have used the company's historical cost of debt ($r_D = 7.22\%$) instead of its rating-adjusted yield, our excuse being that we think the BBB rating understates the company's risk.

	A	B	C
1	COMPUTING THE WACC FOR TYSON		
2	Shares outstanding	354,820,000	
3	Share price, end 2005	13.45	
4	Equity value, E	4,772,329,000	
5	Net debt, D	2,955,000,000	
6			
7	**WACC based on Gordon per-share dividends and interest from financial statements**		
8	Cost of equity, r_E	1.19%	<-- ='Page 74'!B5
9	Cost of debt, r_D	7.22%	<-- ='Page 76, bottom'!B10
10	Tax rate, T_C	29.55%	<-- ='Tyson income statement'!B31
11	WACC	2.68%	<-- =$B$4/($B$4+$B$5)*B8+$B$5/($B$4+$B$5)*B9*(1-$B$10)
12			
13	**WACC based on Gordon equity payouts and interest from financial statements**		
14	Cost of equity, r_E	4.18%	<-- ='Page 75'!B11
15	Cost of debt, r_D	7.22%	<-- ='Page 76, bottom'!B10
16	Tax rate, T_C	29.55%	<-- ='Tyson income statement'!B31
17	WACC	4.53%	<-- =$B$4/($B$4+$B$5)*B14+$B$5/($B$4+$B$5)*B15*(1-$B$10)
18			
19	**WACC based on classic CAPM and interest from financial statements**		
20	Cost of equity, r_E	5.77%	<-- ='Page 76, top'!B12
21	Cost of debt, r_D	7.22%	<-- ='Page 76, bottom'!B10
22	Tax rate, T_C	29.55%	<-- ='Tyson income statement'!B31
23	WACC	5.51%	<-- =$B$4/($B$4+$B$5)*B20+$B$5/($B$4+$B$5)*B21*(1-$B$10)
24			
25	**WACC based on tax-adjusted CAPM and interest from financial statements**		
26	Cost of equity, r_E	4.60%	<-- ='Page 76, top'!B13
27	Cost of debt, r_D	7.22%	<-- ='Page 76, bottom'!B10
28	Tax rate, T_C	29.55%	<-- ='Tyson income statement'!B31
29	WACC	4.79%	<-- =$B$4/($B$4+$B$5)*B26+$B$5/($B$4+$B$5)*B27*(1-$B$10)
30			
31	**Estimated WACC?**	4.94%	<-- =AVERAGE(B29,B23,B17)

With the exception of the very low WACC produced by the dividend r_E, all the estimates are within the same range. We would feel comfortable declaring that Tyson's WACC is somewhere between 5 and 6 percent. If pressed to come up with a point estimate of the WACC, we would use the average of the three estimates, 4.94 percent (cell B31).

2.12 Computing the WACC for Cascade Corporation

Cascade Corporation (stock symbol CAE) makes materials-handling equipment—forks for forklifts, side shifters, paper-roll clamps, rotators, multiple-load handlers, carton clamps, and other technical equipment. The company has annual sales of around $500 million and is listed on the New York Stock Exchange.

2.12.1 Computing Cascade's r_E Using the Gordon Model

Cascade's dividends are approximately quarterly but somewhat irregular. In 2001, for example, the company paid no dividends. In the following spreadsheet we have calculated three dividend growth rates, using the daily growth as a basis for the annual growth rate. Not only is the dividend irregular, but also annual growth rates (and, of course, the corresponding Gordon model r_E) differ widely depending on the base date used:

	A	B	C	D
1	**CASCADE: COST OF EQUITY r_E BASED ON DIVIDENDS** **Dividend growth rate computed on daily basis**			
2	Share price, 31-Jan-06	50.69		
3	Current dividend, D_0	0.60	<-- =B29*4	
4	Gordon cost of equity, r_E			
5	Using growth since 16-Feb-99	7.32%	<-- =B3*(1+B33)/B2+B33	
6	Using growth since 02-Jan-04	18.11%	<-- =B3*(1+B36)/B2+B36	
7	Using growth since 29-Dec-04	26.10%	<-- =B3*(1+B39)/B2+B39	
8				
9	**Date**	**Dividends per share**	**Days between dividend payments**	
10	16-Feb-99	0.10		
11	18-May-99	0.10	91	<-- =A11-A10
12	17-Aug-99	0.10	91	<-- =A12-A11
13	1-Dec-99	0.10	106	
14	22-Feb-00	0.10	83	
15	16-May-00	0.10	84	
16	24-Aug-00	0.10	100	
17	29-Nov-02	0.10	827	
18	26-Mar-03	0.10	117	
19	25-Jun-03	0.10	91	
20	18-Sep-03	0.10	85	
21	2-Jan-04	0.11	106	
22	29-Mar-04	0.11	87	
23	23-Jun-04	0.11	86	
24	20-Sep-04	0.11	89	
25	29-Dec-04	0.12	100	
26	28-Mar-05	0.12	89	
27	1-Jul-05	0.12	95	
28	4-Oct-05	0.15	95	
29	3-Jan-06	0.15	91	
30				
31	**Computing the growth rate of dividends**			
32	Daily growth, 16-Feb-99 - 03-Jan-06	0.0161%	<-- =(B29/B10)^(1/(A29-A10))-1	
33	Annualized	6.07%	<-- =(1+B32)^365-1	
34				
35	Daily growth, 02-Jan-04 - 03-Jan-06	0.0424%	<-- =(B29/B21)^(1/(A29-A21))-1	
36	Annualized	16.73%	<-- =(1+B35)^365-1	
37				
38	Daily growth, 29-Dec-04 - 03-Jan-06	0.060%	<-- =(B29/B25)^(1/(A29-A25))-1	
39	Annualized	24.62%	<-- =(1+B38)^365-1	

Annual cash flows to equity are smoother than the dividend payouts. The cost of equity r_E based on the annual cash flow to equity is 10.46 percent:

	A	B	C	D	E	F
1	**CASCADE: COST OF EQUITY r_E BASED ON CASH FLOW TO EQUITY**					
2	Shares outstanding	12,536,000				
3	Share price, 31-Jan-06	50.69				
4	Equity value, E	635,449,840	<-- =B2*B3			
5	2005 total equity payout	3,904,000	<-- =E16			
6	Growth rate of payouts	9.78%	<-- =E17			
7	Cost of equity, r_E	10.46%	<-- =B5*(1+B6)/B4+B6			
8						
9						
10	**Date**	**Stock repurchases**	**Dividends paid**	**Stock issuance**	**Cash flow to equity holders**	
11	1/31/2001	0	2,448,000		2,448,000	
12	1/31/2002	1,354,000	0		1,354,000	
13	1/31/2003	1,396,000	1,200,000	73,000	2,523,000	
14	1/31/2004	0	4,936,000	1,299,000	3,637,000	
15	1/31/2005		5,478,000	1,616,000	3,862,000	
16	1/31/2006		6,691,000	2,787,000	3,904,000	
17				Growth rate	9.78%	<-- =(E16/E11)^(1/5)-1

2.12.2 Cascade's r_E Using the CAPM

Cascade has a β equal to 1.65. Using a market price-earnings multiple to compute $E(r_M)$ as illustrated on page 65, we compute $r_E = 11.55$ percent using the classic CAPM and 12.59 percent using the tax-adjusted CAPM:

	A	B	C
1	**COMPUTING THE COST OF EQUITY r_E FOR CASCADE USING THE MARKET PRICE/EARNINGS MULTIPLE TO COMPUTE $E(r_M)$**		
2	Market price/earnings multiple, December 2005	18	
3	Equity cash flow payout ratio	50.00%	
4	Anticipated growth of equity cash flow	6.00%	
5	Expected market return, $E(r_M)$	8.94%	<-- =B3*(1+B4)/B2+B4
6			
7	**Cascade cost of equity calculations**		
8	Cascade beta	1.65	<-- From Yahoo
9	Cascade tax rate, T_C	32.42%	<-- Computed from Cascade financials
10	Risk free rate, r_f	4.93%	
11	Cascade cost of equity, $r_{E,Cascade}$		
12	Classic CAPM	11.55%	<-- =B10+B8*(B5-B10)
13	Tax-adjusted CAPM	12.59%	<-- =B10*(1-B9)+B8*(B5-B10*(1-B9))

2.12.3 Cascade's Cost of Debt r_D

Looking at the following spreadsheet, it is obvious that there are conceptual problems computing Cascade's cost of debt:

	A	B	C	D
1	**COMPUTING THE COST OF DEBT r_D FOR CASCADE**			
2		2006/01/31	2005/01/31	
3	Cash and cash equivalents	35,493,000	30,482,000	
4	Marketable securities	23,004,000	1,503,000	
5				
6				
7	Notes payable to banks	4,741,000	2,461,000	
8	Current portion of long-term debt	12,681,000	12,916,000	
9	Long-term debt, net of current portion	12,500,000	25,187,000	
10	Total debt	29,922,000	40,564,000	
11				
12	Interest expense	2,741,000	3,570,000	
13	Interest income	979,000	562,000	
14				
15	Interest cost	7.78%	<-- =B12/AVERAGE(B10:C10)	
16	Interest income	2.97%	<-- =B13/AVERAGE(B3:C3)	
17				
18	Debt net of cash	-5,571,000	10,082,000	<-- =C10-C3
19	Debt net of cash and marketable securities	-28,575,000	8,579,000	

The problems are these:

- Cascade has large amounts of cash. Taking this cash into account, the company—as of 31 January 2006—has negative leverage (cell B18).
- Cascade also has large amounts of marketable securities, which—if we think of them as essentially liquid assets that could be used to pay off debt—make the leverage even more negative (cell B19). We could be less aggressive about the company's negative leverage by excluding the company's marketable securities from its net debt, but we consider that this item also reflects a "cashlike" asset and hence should be subtracted from Cascade's debt (another judgment call!).

These considerations force us to make a decision about Cascade's cost of debt r_D and its leverage for purpose of computing its WACC.[14]

14. The company's financial statements do not report its debt rating, so we do not use this method for computing r_D.

2.12.4 Cascade's WACC

Here are our estimates of the WACC for Cascade. In line with our analysis of the company's financial structure, we conclude that it has negative leverage. We reject the Gordon r_E based solely on dividends as unreasonably high and conclude that Cascade's WACC is 11.83 percent.

	A	B	C
1	**COMPUTING THE WACC FOR CASCADE** **The company has negative leverage**		
2	Shares outstanding	12,536,000	<-- ='Page 79, top'!B2
3	Share price, end 2005	50.69	<-- ='Page 78'!B2
4	Equity value, E	635,449,840	<-- =B2*B3
5	Net debt, D	-28,575,000	<-- ='Page 80'!B19
6			
7	**WACC based on Gordon per-share dividends and interest from financial statements**		
8	Cost of equity, r_E	18.11%	<-- ='Page 78'!B6
9	Cost of debt, r_D	7.78%	<-- ='Page 80'!B15
10	Tax rate, T_C	32.42%	<-- ='Page 79, bottom'!B9
11	WACC	18.71%	<-- =$B$4/($B$4+$B$5)*B8+$B$5/($B$4+$B$5)*B9*(1-B10)
12			
13	**WACC based on Gordon equity payouts and interest from financial statements**		
14	Cost of equity, r_E	10.46%	<-- ='Page 79, top'!B7
15	Cost of debt, r_D	7.78%	<-- ='Page 80'!B15
16	Tax rate, T_C	32.42%	<-- ='Page 79, bottom'!B9
17	WACC	10.70%	<-- =$B$4/($B$4+$B$5)*B14+$B$5/($B$4+$B$5)*B15*(1-B16)
18			
19	**WACC based on classic CAPM and interest from financial statements**		
20	Cost of equity, r_E	11.55%	
21	Cost of debt, r_D	7.78%	
22	Tax rate, T_C	32.42%	
23	WACC	11.85%	<-- =$B$4/($B$4+$B$5)*B20+$B$5/($B$4+$B$5)*B21*(1-B22)
24			
25	**WACC based on tax-adjusted CAPM and interest from financial statements**		
26	Cost of equity, r_E	12.59%	
27	Cost of debt, r_D	7.78%	
28	Tax rate, T_C	32.42%	
29	WACC	12.94%	<-- =$B$4/($B$4+$B$5)*B26+$B$5/($B$4+$B$5)*B27*(1-B28)
30			
31	**Estimated WACC?**	11.83%	<-- =AVERAGE(B29,B23,B17)

2.13 When the Models Don't Work

All models have problems, and nothing is perfect.[15] In this section we discuss some of the potential problems with the Gordon model and with the capital asset pricing model.

15. "Happiness is the maximum agreement of reality and desire."—Stalin.

2.13.1 Problems with the Gordon Model

Obviously the Gordon model doesn't work if a firm doesn't pay dividends and appears to have no intention—in the immediate future—of paying dividends.[16] But even for dividend-paying firms, it may be difficult to apply the model. Particularly problematic, in many cases, is the extraction of the future dividend payout rate from past dividends.

Consider, for example, the dividend history of Ford Motor Company in the years 1989–98:

	A	B	C
1	FORD MOTOR CO. DIVIDEND HISTORY 1989-1998		
2	Year	Dividend	
3	1989	3.00	
4	1990	3.00	
5	1991	1.95	
6	1992	1.60	
7	1993	1.60	
8	1994	1.33	
9	1995	1.23	
10	1996	1.46	
11	1997	1.64	
12	1998	22.81	
13	Growth rate, 1989-1997	-7.27%	<-- =(B11/B3)^(1/8)-1
14	Growth rate, 1989-1998	25.28%	<-- =(B12/B3)^(1/9)-1

The problem here is easily identifiable: Ford, whose dividends were in steady decline until 1997, paid a cash dividend on $21.09 in 1998, in addition to its regular quarterly dividends (which summed to $1.72 in 1998). If we use past history to predict the future, any inclusion of the extraordinary cash dividend will cause us to overestimate the future dividend growth. Excluding the $21.09 dividend, however, also does not reflect the actual situation.

It appears that the 10-year history of Ford's dividends is not, perhaps, the best guide to its future dividend payout. Several solutions are available to those wishing to use the Gordon model:

16. Firms cannot intend *never* to pay dividends, because such an intention would rationally mean that the value of the shares is zero.

• If we exclude the extraordinary dividend of $21.09 in 1998, then the dividend growth over the four years ending in 1998 is a respectable 6.64 percent. If Ford's anticipated future dividend growth is estimated to be this rate, then—given its end-1998 stock price of $58.69—the Gordon model cost of equity is 9.77 percent:

	A	B	C
17	FORD'S DIVIDENDS EXCLUDING THE 1998 $21.09 DIVIDEND		
18	Year	Dividend	
19	1989	3.00	
20	1990	3.00	
21	1991	1.95	
22	1992	1.60	
23	1993	1.60	
24	1994	1.33	
25	1995	1.23	
26	1996	1.46	
27	1997	1.64	
28	1998	1.72	
29	Growth rate, 1994-1998	6.64%	<-- =(B28/B24)^(1/4)-1
30	Ford's stock price, end-1998	58.69	
31	Gordon cost of equity	9.77%	<-- =B28*(1+B29)/B30+B29

• A better alternative might be to use Ford's total payouts to equity, as illustrated in this chapter. This method does not mean, however, that we can get away from judgment calls (witness our extensive use of the two-stage Gordon model).

• A last alternative to finding Ford's cost of capital is to predict its future dividends by doing a full-blown financial model for the company. Such models—illustrated in Chapters 3 and 4—are often used by analysts. Though they are complicated and time-consuming to build, they take into account all of the firm's productive and financial activities. Potentially they are, therefore, a more accurate predictor of the dividend.

2.13.2 Problems with the CAPM

In the following spreadsheet you will find the return of the S&P 500 and Big City Bagels. Superimposed on the spreadsheet is a calculation of Big City's β, which is computed to be –0.0542.

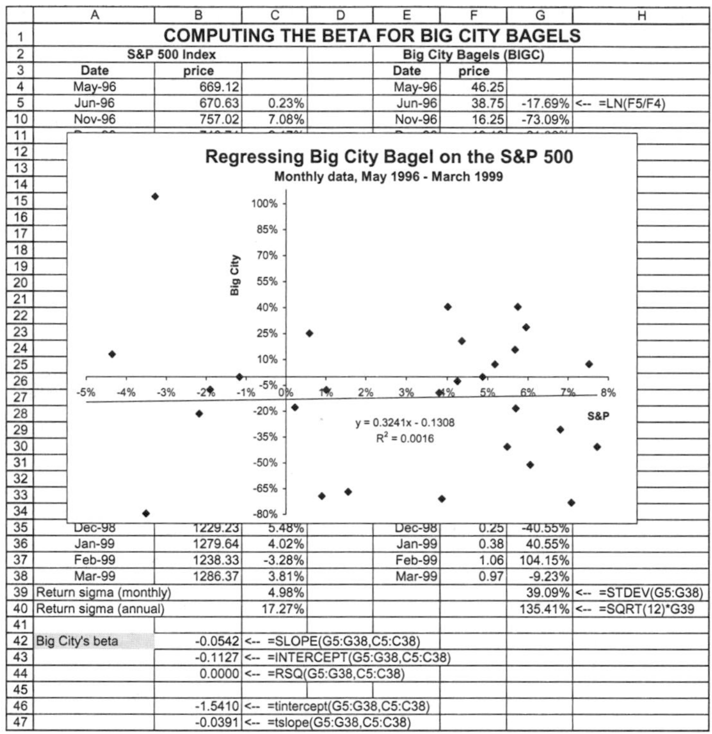

	A	B	C	D	E	F	G	H
1	**COMPUTING THE BETA FOR BIG CITY BAGELS**							
2	S&P 500 Index				Big City Bagels (BIGC)			
3	Date	price			Date	price		
4	May-96	669.12			May-96	46.25		
5	Jun-96	670.63	0.23%		Jun-96	38.75	-17.69%	<-- =LN(F5/F4)
10	Nov-96	757.02	7.08%		Nov-96	16.25	-73.09%	
35	Dec-98	1229.23	5.48%		Dec-98	0.25	-40.55%	
36	Jan-99	1279.64	4.02%		Jan-99	0.38	40.55%	
37	Feb-99	1238.33	-3.28%		Feb-99	1.06	104.15%	
38	Mar-99	1286.37	3.81%		Mar-99	0.97	-9.23%	
39	Return sigma (monthly)		4.98%				39.09%	<-- =STDEV(G5:G38)
40	Return sigma (annual)		17.27%				135.41%	<-- =SQRT(12)*G39
41								
42	Big City's beta	-0.0542	<-- =SLOPE(G5:G38,C5:C38)					
43		-0.1127	<-- =INTERCEPT(G5:G38,C5:C38)					
44		0.0000	<-- =RSQ(G5:G38,C5:C38)					
45								
46		-1.5410	<-- =tintercept(G5:G38,C5:C38)					
47		-0.0391	<-- =tslope(G5:G38,C5:C38)					

Big City Bagel's stock is clearly risky—the annualized standard deviation of its returns is 135 percent as compared to about 17 percent for the S&P 500 over the same period. However, the β of Big City Bagels is –0.0542, which indicates that Big City has—in a portfolio context—*negative risk*. Were this true, it would mean that adding Big City to a portfolio would lower the portfolio variance enough to justify a below-risk-free return for Big City. While this might be true for some stocks, it is hard to believe that—in the long run—the β of Big City is indeed negative.[17]

The R^2 of the regression between Big City's returns and the S&P 500 is essentially zero, meaning that the S&P 500 simply doesn't explain any of the variation in Big City returns. For statistics mavens, the t-statistics

17. A more plausible explanation is that—for the period covered—Big City's return has *nothing whatsoever* to do with the market return.

of the intercept and the slope indicate that neither differs significantly from zero. In short, the regression of Big City Bagel's historic returns on the S&P 500 indicates no connection between the two whatsoever.

What are we to make of this situation? How should we calculate the cost of capital for Big City? There are several alternatives:

• We could assume that the Big City β is –0.0542. The company's tax rate in March 1999 was essentially zero, so that the classical CAPM and the tax-adjusted version coincide:

	A	B	C
1	**COMPUTING THE COST OF EQUITY r_E FOR BIG CITY BAGELS March 1999**		
2	Big City's beta	-0.0542	
3			
4	Risk-free rate, r_f	4.29%	
5	Expected market return, $E(r_M)$	9.08%	
6	Cost of equity, r_E	4.03%	<-- =B4+B2*(B5-B4)

• We could assume that the β of Big City is in fact 0; given the standard deviation of the β estimate for Big City, the β is not statistically different from zero, so that this assumption makes sense. This means that all of Big City's risk is diversifiable and that the correct cost of equity for Big City is the riskless rate of interest.

• We could assume that the covariance (or lack thereof) between Big City and the S&P 500 is not indicative of their future correlation. This assumption would eventually lead us to conclude that Big City's risk is comparable to that of similar companies. A small study of the βs of snack food companies during the same period shows their βs to be well over 1: New World Coffee has a β of 1.15; Pepsico has a β of 1.42; Starbucks has a β of 1.84. Thus we might conclude that the β of Big City (in the sense of its *future* correlation with the market) would be somewhere between 1.15 and 1.84. This approach, of course, would give a radically different cost of equity for Big City:

	A	B	C
1	**COMPUTING THE COST OF EQUITY r_E FOR BIG CITY BAGELS** **Assumes that forward-looking beta = 1.3**		
2	Big City's beta	1.3000	
3			
4	Risk-free rate, r_f	4.29%	
5	Expected market return, $E(r_M)$	9.08%	
6	Cost of equity, r_E	10.52%	<-- =B4+B2*(B5-B4)

(For what it's worth, this author would follow the latter case.)

2.14 Conclusion

In this chapter we have illustrated in detail the application of two models for calculating the cost of equity: the Gordon dividend model and the CAPM. We have also considered three of the four practicable models for calculating the cost of debt. Because the application of these models includes many judgment calls, our advice is to

- Always use several models to calculate the cost of capital.
- If you have time, try to calculate the cost of capital not only for the firm you are analyzing, but also for other firms in the same industry.
- From your analysis try to pick out a *consensus* estimate of the cost of capital. Don't hesitate to exclude numbers (such as Big City's negative cost of equity) that strike you as unreasonable.

In sum, the calculation of the cost of capital is not just a mechanistic exercise!

Exercises

1. ABC Corporation has a stock price $P_0 = 50$. The firm has just paid a dividend of \$3 per share, and intelligent shareholders think that this dividend will grow by a rate of 5 percent per year. Use the Gordon dividend model to calculate the cost of equity of ABC.

2. Unheardof, Inc., has just paid a dividend of \$5 per share. This dividend is anticipated to increase at a rate of 15 percent per year. If the cost of equity for Unheardof is 25 percent, what should be the market value of a share of the company?

3. Dismal.Com is a producer of depressing Internet products. The company is currently not paying dividends, but its chief financial officer thinks that starting in three years it can pay a dividend of \$15 per share, and that this dividend will grow by 20 percent per year. Assuming that the cost of equity of Dismal.Com is 35 percent, value a share based on the discounted dividends.

4. Consider the following dividend and price data for Chrysler:

	A	B	C	D	E
1	**CHRYSLER CORPORATION (C)**				
2	**Year**	**Year-end stock price**	**Dividend per share**	**Growth rate**	
3	1986		0.40		
4	1987		0.50	25.00%	<-- =C4/C3-1
5	1988		0.50	0.00%	<-- =C5/C4-1
6	1989		0.60	20.00%	<-- =C6/C5-1
7	1990		0.60	0.00%	<-- =C7/C6-1
8	1991		0.30	-50.00%	<-- =C8/C7-1
9	1992		0.30	0.00%	
10	1993		0.33	10.00%	
11	1994		0.45	36.36%	
12	1995		1.00	122.22%	
13	1996	35.00	1.40	40.00%	

Use the Gordon model to calculate Chrysler's cost of equity at the end of 1996.

5. The current stock price of TransContinental Airways is $65 per share. TCA currently pays an annual per-share dividend of $3. Over the past five years this dividend has grown annually at a rate of 23 percent. A respected analyst assumes that the current growth rate of dividends will hold up for the next five years, after which dividend growth will slow to 5 percent annually. Use the **twostagegordon** function to compute the cost of equity.[18]

6. ABC Corporation has just paid a dividend of $3 per share. You—an experienced analyst—feel quite sure that the growth rate of the company's dividends over the next ten years will be 15 percent per year. After ten years you think that the company's dividend growth rate will slow to the industry average, which is about 5 percent per year. If the cost of equity for ABC is 12 percent, what is the value today of one share of the company?

7. The cash flow to equity holders for Merck, Inc. during the years 1991–2000 is given in the following chart. Compute Merck's cost of equity r_E at year-end 2000 on the assumption that the equity cash flow growth will be 20.15 percent for the following four years, followed by a long-term growth rate of 6 percent.

   Notes:

   - The numbers are taken from Merck's financial statements for 1991–2000. When employee stock options are exercised, the company gets a tax shield on the benefit accruing to the option holders. This benefit, measured as $T_c\left(\begin{matrix}\text{Stock price}\\ \text{at option exercise}\end{matrix} - \begin{matrix}\text{Option}\\ \text{exercise price}\end{matrix}\right)$, is computed in column E.
   - At the end of 2000, Merck had 2,307,599,179 shares and the stock price was 93.625 per share.

18. To do this problem you will have to copy the formula from the spreadsheet **fm3_chapter02.xls** to your answer spreadsheet. See the file "Adding Getformula to your spreadsheet" on the disk that comes with *Financial Modeling* for details.

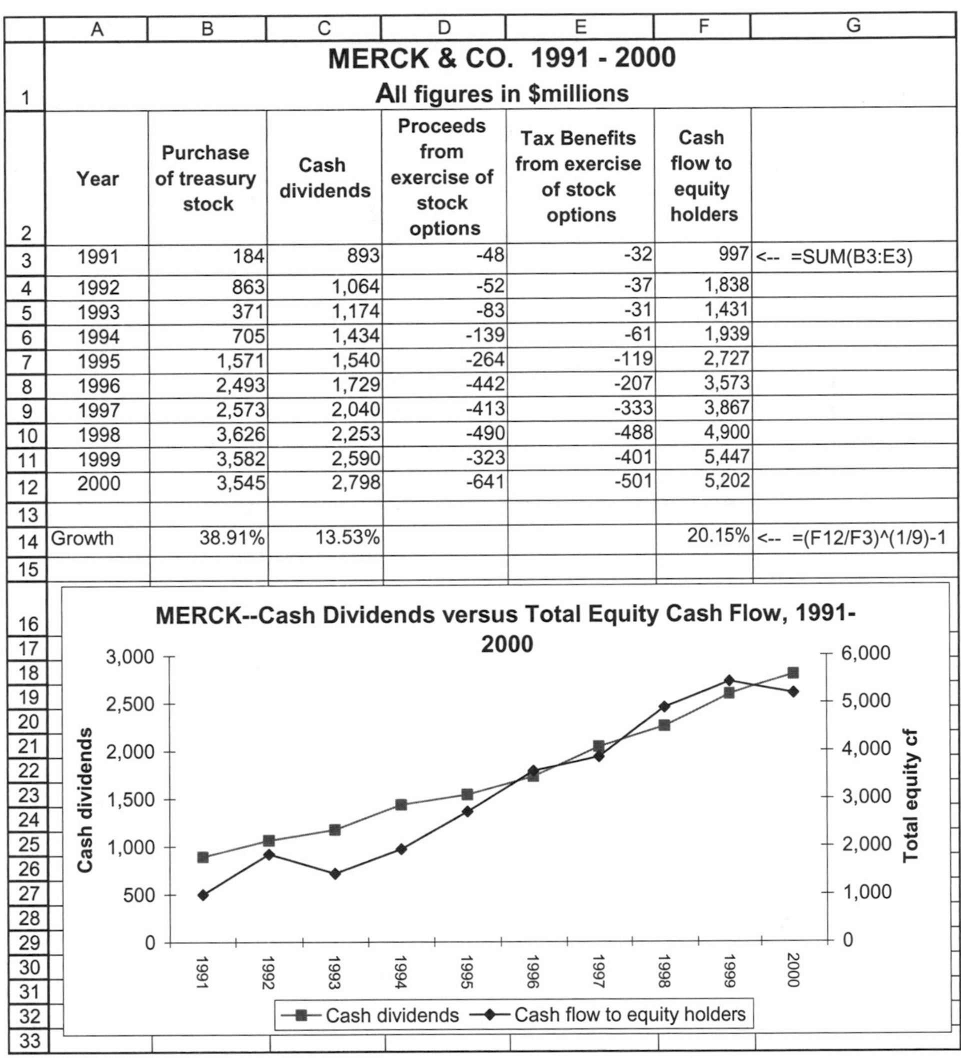

	A	B	C	D	E	F	G
1	**MERCK & CO. 1991 - 2000** All figures in $millions						
2	**Year**	**Purchase of treasury stock**	**Cash dividends**	**Proceeds from exercise of stock options**	**Tax Benefits from exercise of stock options**	**Cash flow to equity holders**	
3	1991	184	893	-48	-32	997	<-- =SUM(B3:E3)
4	1992	863	1,064	-52	-37	1,838	
5	1993	371	1,174	-83	-31	1,431	
6	1994	705	1,434	-139	-61	1,939	
7	1995	1,571	1,540	-264	-119	2,727	
8	1996	2,493	1,729	-442	-207	3,573	
9	1997	2,573	2,040	-413	-333	3,867	
10	1998	3,626	2,253	-490	-488	4,900	
11	1999	3,582	2,590	-323	-401	5,447	
12	2000	3,545	2,798	-641	-501	5,202	
13							
14	Growth	38.91%	13.53%			20.15%	<-- =(F12/F3)^(1/9)-1
15							

8. Consider a company that has $\beta_{equity} = 1.5$ and $\beta_{debt} = 0.4$. Suppose that the risk-free rate of interest is 6 percent, the expected return on the market $E(r_M) = 15$ percent, and the corporate tax rate is 40 percent. If the company has 40 percent equity and 60 percent debt in its capital structure, calculate its weighted average cost of capital using both the classic CAPM and the tax-adjusted CAPM.

9. On the spreadsheet **fm3_problems02.xls** you will find the following monthly data for Cisco's stock price and the S&P 500 index. Compute the equation $r_{CSCO,t} = \alpha_{CSCO} + \beta_{CSCO} r_{SP,t}$ and include the R^2 and t-statistics for the equation and its coefficients.[19]

	A	B	C
1	**CISCO (CSCO) AND S&P 500 PRICES July 2002 - June 2007**		
2	**Date**	**S&P 500**	**CSCO**
3	3-Jul-02	911.62	13.19
4	1-Aug-02	916.07	13.82
5	3-Sep-02	815.28	10.48
6	1-Oct-02	885.76	11.18
7	1-Nov-02	936.31	14.92
8	2-Dec-02	879.82	13.10
9	2-Jan-03	855.70	13.37
10	3-Feb-03	841.15	13.98
11	3-Mar-03	848.18	12.98
12	1-Apr-03	916.92	15.00
13	1-May-03	963.59	16.41
14	2-Jun-03	974.50	16.79
15	1-Jul-03	990.31	19.49
16	1-Aug-03	1008.01	19.14
17	2-Sep-03	995.97	19.59
18	1-Oct-03	1050.71	20.93
19	3-Nov-03	1058.20	22.70
20	1-Dec-03	1111.92	24.23
21	2-Jan-04	1131.13	25.71
22	2-Feb-04	1144.94	23.16

10. You are considering buying the bonds of a very risky company. A bond with a $100 face value, a one-year maturity, and a coupon rate of 22 percent is selling for $95. You consider the probability that the company will actually survive to pay off the bond 80 percent. With 20 percent probability, you think that the company will default, in which case you think that you will be able to recover $40. What is the expected return on the bond?

19. To do this problem you will have to copy the functions **tintercept** and **tslope** from the spreadsheet **fm3_chapter02.xls** to your answer spreadsheet. See previous footnote.

11. It is January 1, 1997. Normal America, Inc. (NA) has paid a year-end dividend in each of the last ten years, as shown by the following table:

	A	B	C	D	E	F
1	**NORMAL AMERICA, INC.**					
2	**Year**	**Dec. 31 stock price**	**Dec. 15 dividend per share**			**S&P 500 return**
3	1986	33.00				
4	1987	30.69	2.50		1987	4.7%
5	1988	35.38	2.50		1988	16.2%
6	1989	42.25	3.00		1989	31.4%
7	1990	34.38	3.00		1990	-3.3%
8	1991	36.25	1.60		1991	30.2%
9	1992	32.25	1.40		1992	7.4%
10	1993	43.00	0.80		1993	9.9%
11	1994	42.13	0.80		1994	1.2%
12	1995	52.88	1.10		1995	37.4%
13	1996	55.75	1.60		1996	22.9%

a. Calculate NA's β with respect to the S&P 500.

b. Suppose that the Treasury bill rate is 5.5 percent and that the expected return on the market is $E(r_M) = 13$ percent. If the corporate tax rate $T_C = 35$ percent, calculate NA's cost of equity using both the classic CAPM and the tax-adjusted model.

c. Assume that NA's cost of debt is 8 percent. If the company is financed by 1/3 equity and 2/3 debt, what is its weighted average cost of capital using each of the two CAPM models?

12. The file **fm3_problems03.xls** with *Financial Modeling* gives data (see following) for monthly returns on the Vanguard Index 500 fund for December 2000–June 2007. Assuming that this fund proxies for the market as a whole compute the following:

a. $E(r_M)$ based on the whole sample of returns

b. $E(r_M)$ based on the last two years of monthly returns

	A	B	C	D
1	**RETURN DATA FOR VANGUARD INDEX 500 FUND December 2000 - June 2007**			
2	**Date**	**Vanguard Index 500**	**Return**	
3	1-Dec-00	110.75		
4	2-Jan-01	114.68	3.49%	<-- =LN(B4/B3)
5	1-Feb-01	104.2	-9.58%	<-- =LN(B5/B4)
6	1-Mar-01	97.32	-6.83%	<-- =LN(B6/B5)
7	2-Apr-01	104.88	7.48%	<-- =LN(B7/B6)
8	1-May-01	105.57	0.66%	
9	1-Jun-01	102.98	-2.48%	
10	2-Jul-01	101.96	-1.00%	

13. At the end of June 2007, the price-earnings ratio of the S&P 500 was 17.5. Assume that the index proxies for the market, that it has a 50 percent dividend payout ratio, and that dividends are expected to grow at 7 percent. Compute $E(r_M)$.

Appendix 1: Why Is β a Good Measure of Risk? Portfolio β versus Individual Stock β

Although β may not be a very good measure of the riskiness of an individual stock, the average β is a very good measure of the riskiness of a diversified portfolio. This point is illustrated in this appendix. However, before we fire into the illustration, we want to stress the meaning of the previous sentence:

If portfolio β is a good measure of portfolio risk, then—for the holder of a diversified portfolio (and this includes most investors)—the individual share β is a good measure of the risk of a share, *when this share is ultimately held in a diversified portfolio.*

To illustrate, consider the following data—prices for the components of the Dow-Jones 30 Industrials (DJ30) over the 60 months between April 2002 and April 2007 (some are not shown):

PRICE DATA FOR DOW-JONES INDUSTRIAL 30 COMPONENTS, APRIL 2002 - APRIL 2007													
Date	Alcoa AA	American International AIG	American Express AXP	Boeing BA	Citigroup C	Caterpillar CAT	DuPont DD	Disney DIS	General Electric GE	General Motors GM	Home Depot HD	Honeywell HON
4/2/2002	30.54	67.13	34.27	40.92	34.28	24.70	37.72	22.04	27.56	50.54	43.85	32.59
5/1/2002	31.54	65.04	35.52	39.27	34.33	23.64	39.29	21.79	27.20	49.33	39.42	35.00
6/3/2002	29.89	66.31	30.35	41.44	30.81	22.14	37.92	17.97	25.53	42.43	34.77	31.46
7/1/2002	24.53	62.12	29.53	38.23	26.66	20.38	35.80	16.86	28.30	36.95	29.24	28.89
8/1/2002	22.75	61.03	30.20	34.29	28.07	19.90	34.72	14.91	26.50	38.43	31.18	26.90
9/3/2002	17.50	53.20	26.11	31.57	25.41	16.97	31.07	14.40	21.82	31.24	24.75	19.45
10/1/2002	20.00	60.84	30.53	27.52	31.83	18.79	35.53	15.88	22.35	26.70	27.38	21.50
11/1/2002	23.32	63.37	32.68	31.67	33.49	22.96	38.75	18.85	24.00	32.35	25.03	23.55
12/2/2002	20.79	56.31	29.74	30.68	30.31	21.03	36.82	15.70	21.72	30.03	22.83	21.73
1/2/2003	18.04	52.68	29.89	29.38	29.75	20.39	32.89	16.85	20.64	29.60	19.86	22.13
2/3/2003	18.86	47.98	28.25	25.77	28.88	21.79	32.16	16.42	21.62	27.90	22.29	20.89
3/3/2003	17.82	48.18	27.96	23.43	29.84	22.81	34.08	16.39	22.92	27.78	23.21	19.50
4/1/2003	21.23	56.46	31.93	25.51	34.00	24.54	37.30	17.97	26.47	29.78	26.81	21.54
5/1/2003	22.79	56.39	35.14	28.85	35.71	24.33	37.25	18.92	25.80	29.60	30.96	24.10
2/1/2007	33.41	67.11	56.72	87.26	50.37	64.43	50.73	34.25	34.91	31.90	39.36	46.40
3/1/2007	33.90	67.22	56.25	88.91	51.34	67.03	49.43	34.43	35.36	30.64	36.74	46.06
4/2/2007	34.59	67.23	55.96	90.50	51.57	67.63	49.32	34.91	35.02	31.90	38.02	47.26

In the next spreadsheet, we compute, for each of the components of the DJ30, the equations $r_{it} = \alpha_{it} + \beta_{it} r_{SP,t}$. We indicate the *r*-squared and the *t*-statistics of the intercept α and the slope β for each equation:

	A	B	C	D	E	F	G	H	I	J	K	L	M
1	RETURN DATA, ALPHA, BETA, R-SQUARED For Dow-Jones 30 Industrials, April 2002 - April 2007												
2													
3			=INTERCEPT(B16:B75,$AH$16:$AH$75)										
4				=SLOPE(B16:B75,$AH$16:$AH$75)									
5				=RSQ(B16:B75,$AH$16:$AH$75)									
6		Alcoa AA	American International AIG	American Express AXP	Boeing BA	Citigroup C	Caterpillar CAT	DuPont DD	Disney DIS	General Electric GE	General Motors GM	Home Depot HD	Noneywell HON
7	Alpha	-0.0074	-0.0058	0.0020	0.0097	0.0009	0.0100	-0.0007	0.0017	0.0003	-0.0140	-0.0098	-0.0018
8	Beta	1.9446	1.1873	1.2615	0.7304	1.2086	1.3915	1.0488	1.2131	0.7474	1.2860	1.5274	1.6276
9	R-squared	0.5646	0.3906	0.6987	0.1442	0.5050	0.4328	0.4114	0.3699	0.2533	0.1869	0.4791	0.6100
10	T-Alpha	-0.9545	-0.8548	0.5325	1.1917	0.1653	1.3765	-0.1147	0.2410	0.0583	-1.1417	-1.3563	-0.2964
11	T-Beta	8.6724	6.0965	11.5982	3.1260	7.6922	6.6532	6.3675	5.8350	4.4352	3.6511	7.3042	9.5241
12													
13			=tintercept(B16:B75,$AH$16:$AH$75)										
14				=tslope(B16:B75,$AH$16:$AH$75)									
15	Date												
16	5/1/2002	3.22%	-3.16%	3.58%	-4.12%	0.15%	-4.39%	4.08%	-1.14%	-1.31%	-2.42%	-10.65%	7.13%
17	6/3/2002	-5.37%	1.93%	-15.73%	5.38%	-10.82%	-6.56%	-3.55%	-19.27%	-6.34%	-15.07%	-12.55%	-10.66%
18	7/1/2002	-19.76%	-6.53%	-2.74%	-8.06%	-14.47%	-8.28%	-5.75%	-6.38%	10.30%	-13.83%	-17.32%	-8.52%

Here are the averages of the *r*-squared and the *t*-statistics when done on an individual basis:

	A	B	C
1	**REGRESSING THE DJ30 COMPONENTS ON THE S&P500** **Averages**		
2	Average alpha	-0.0005	<-- =AVERAGE('Page 87, bottom'!B7:AE7)
3	Average beta	1.1421	<-- =AVERAGE('Page 87, bottom'!B8:AE8)
4	Average r-squared	0.3508	<-- =AVERAGE('Page 87, bottom'!B9:AE9)
5	Average t-statistic, intercept	0.0052	<-- =AVERAGE('Page 87, bottom'!B10:AE10)
6	Average t-statistic, slope	5.7859	<-- =AVERAGE('Page 87, bottom'!B11:AE11)

If, however, we regress the returns of a portfolio of the Dow-Jones components on the S&P 500, we find a dramatic increase in the R^2:

	A	B	C
1	**REGRESSING PORTFOLIOS OF THE DJ30 COMPONENTS ON THE S&P500**		
2	Alpha	-0.0020	<-- {=INTERCEPT(MMULT('Page 87, bottom'!B16:AE75,'Page 88, bottom'!B9:B38),'Page 87, bottom'!AH16:AH75)}
3	Beta	1.1747	<-- {=SLOPE(MMULT('Page 87, bottom'!B16:AE75,'Page 88, bottom'!B9:B38),'Page 87, bottom'!AH16:AH75)}
4	R-squared	0.8191	<-- {=RSQ(MMULT('Page 87, bottom'!B16:AE75,'Page 88, bottom'!B9:B38),'Page 87, bottom'!AH16:AH75)}
5	T-Alpha	-0.7772	<-- {=tintercept(MMULT('Page 87, bottom'!B16:AE75,'Page 88, bottom'!B9:B38),'Page 87, bottom'!AH16:AH75)}
6	T-Beta	16.2082	<-- {=tslope(MMULT('Page 87, bottom'!B16:AE75,'Page 88, bottom'!B9:B38),'Page 87, bottom'!AH16:AH75)}
7			
8	**Portfolio weights**		
9	AA	0.1000	
10	AIG	0.0000	
11	AXP	0.0000	
12	BA	0.0000	
13	C	0.1000	
14	CAT	0.0000	
15	DD	0.1000	
16	DIS	0.1000	
17	GE	0.0000	
18	GM	0.0000	
19	HD	0.0000	
20	HON	0.0000	
21	HPQ	0.0000	
22	IBM	0.0000	
23	INTC	0.1000	
24	JNJ	0.0000	
25	JPM	0.0000	
26	KO	0.1000	
27	MCD	0.0000	
28	MMM	0.1000	
29	MO	0.0000	
30	MRK	0.1000	
31	MSFT	0.0000	
32	PFE	0.0000	
33	PG	0.0000	
34	T	0.0000	
35	UTX	0.0000	
36	VZ	0.1000	
37	WMT	0.0000	
38	XOM	0.1000	
39	**Sum of portfolio weights**	**1.00**	<-- =SUM(B9:B38)

By changing the portfolio weights, you can see that this increase is characteristic of almost all well-diversified portfolios (even those not including all of the DJ30 components):

	A	B	C
1	REGRESSING PORTFOLIOS OF THE DJ30 COMPONENTS ON THE S&P500		
2	Alpha	-0.0005	<-- {=INTERCEPT(MMULT('Page 87, bottom'!B16:AE75,'Page 89'!B9:B38),'Page 87, bottom'!AH16:AH75)}
3	Beta	1.1421	<-- {=SLOPE(MMULT('Page 87, bottom'!B16:AE75,'Page 89'!B9:B38),'Page 87, bottom'!AH16:AH75)}
4	R-squared	0.9460	<-- {=RSQ(MMULT('Page 87, bottom'!B16:AE75,'Page 89'!B9:B38),'Page 87, bottom'!AH16:AH75)}
5	T-Alpha	-0.3669	<-- {=tintercept(MMULT('Page 87, bottom'!B16:AE75,'Page 89'!B9:B38),'Page 87, bottom'!AH16:AH75)}
6	T-Beta	31.8910	<-- {=tslope(MMULT('Page 87, bottom'!B16:AE75,'Page 89'!B9:B38),'Page 87, bottom'!AH16:AH75)}
7			
8	Portfolio weights		
9	AA	0.0333	
10	AIG	0.0333	
11	AXP	0.0333	
12	BA	0.0333	
13	C	0.0333	
14	CAT	0.0333	
15	DD	0.0333	
16	DIS	0.0333	
17	GE	0.0333	
18	GM	0.0333	
19	HD	0.0333	
20	HON	0.0333	
21	HPQ	0.0333	
22	IBM	0.0333	
23	INTC	0.0333	
24	JNJ	0.0333	
25	JPM	0.0333	
26	KO	0.0333	
27	MCD	0.0333	
28	MMM	0.0333	
29	MO	0.0333	
30	MRK	0.0333	
31	MSFT	0.0333	
32	PFE	0.0333	
33	PG	0.0333	
34	T	0.0333	
35	UTX	0.0333	
36	VZ	0.0333	
37	WMT	0.0333	
38	XOM	0.0333	
39	**Sum of portfolio weights**	**1.00**	<-- =SUM(B9:B38)

The meaning of this result is that, when we invest in large diversified portfolios, almost all of the risk is due to the individual assets' βs.

Appendix 2: Getting Data from the Internet

All the data used in this chapter were retrieved from Yahoo. This appendix provides a brief description of how they were gotten. Keep in mind that since the Internet is a very lively place, it may be that by the time you read this book, some of the technical details and addresses will have changed.

1. Yahoo's financial information is most conveniently accessed by clicking on the **Finance** link on the Yahoo home page.

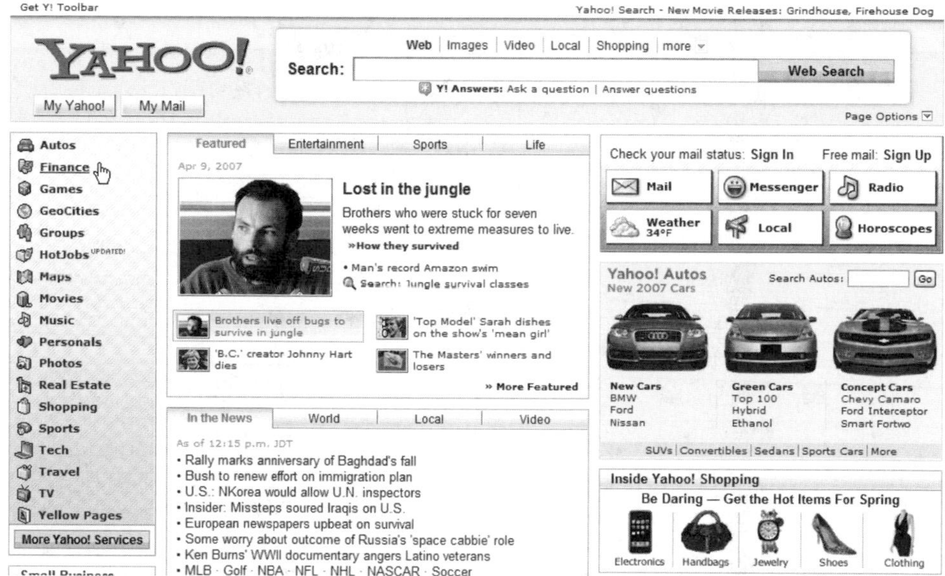

2. Putting the stock symbol in the **Get Quotes** box takes you to information about a particular company. Here we have asked for information on General Motors (stock symbol, GM):

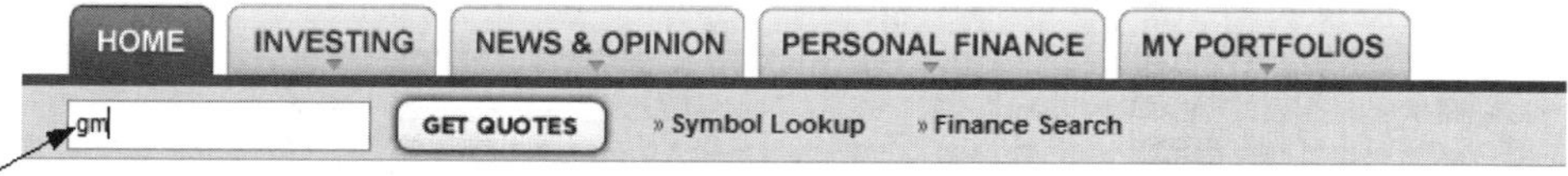

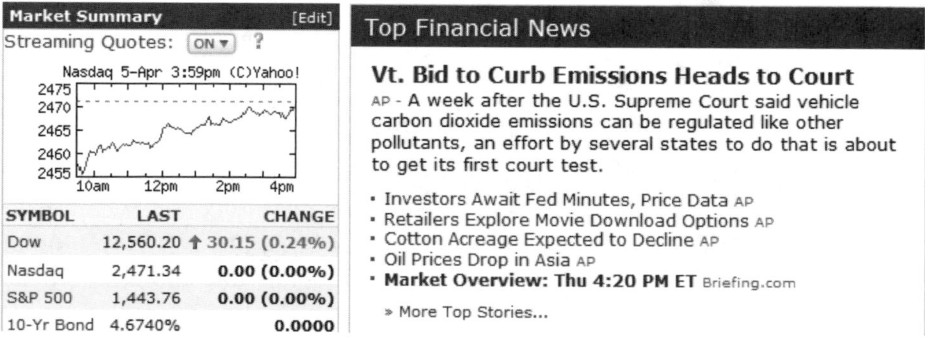

3. In this book we most commonly use **Historical Prices** to download price and dividend information about the stock and **Key Statistics** to access a wealth of information about the company.

4. **Key Statistics** gives much information about General Motors. Of particular interest to readers of this chapter is the computation of beta, based on 60 months of monthly return data versus the S&P 500 index:

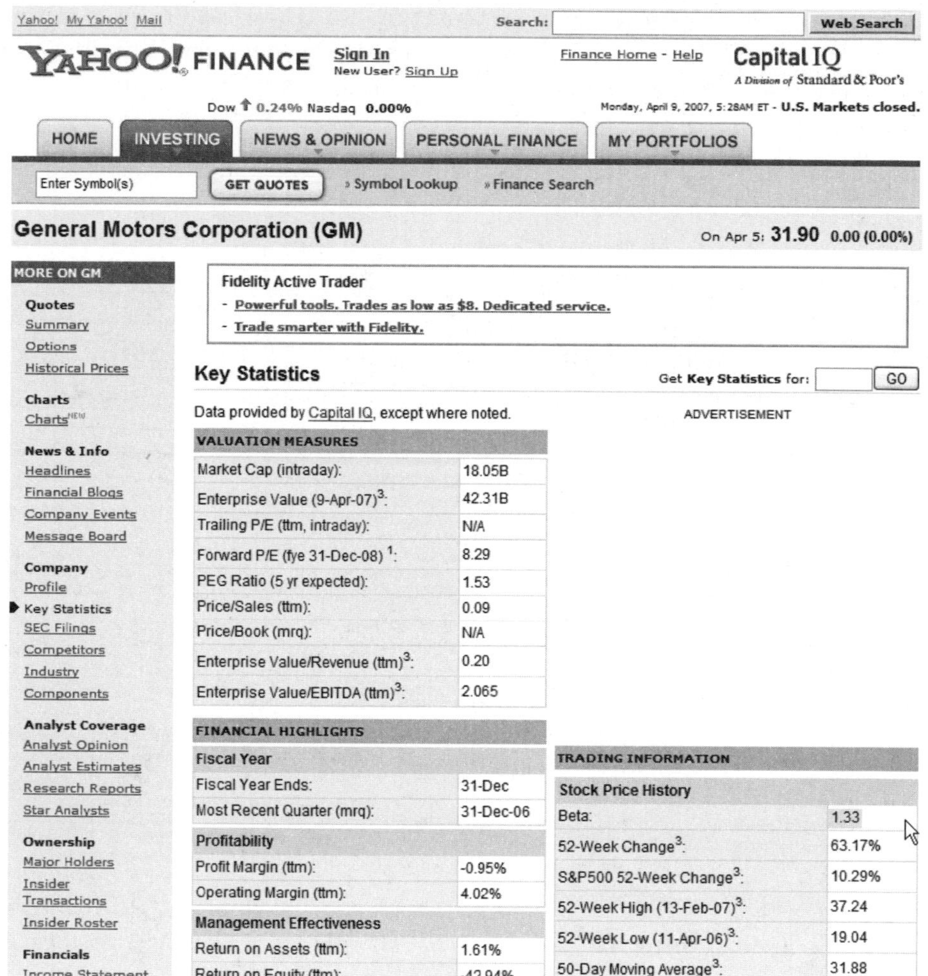

5. Clicking on **Historical Prices** accesses a page from which prices and dividend data may be downloaded. In this case we have asked to see 10 years of monthly price information for GM.

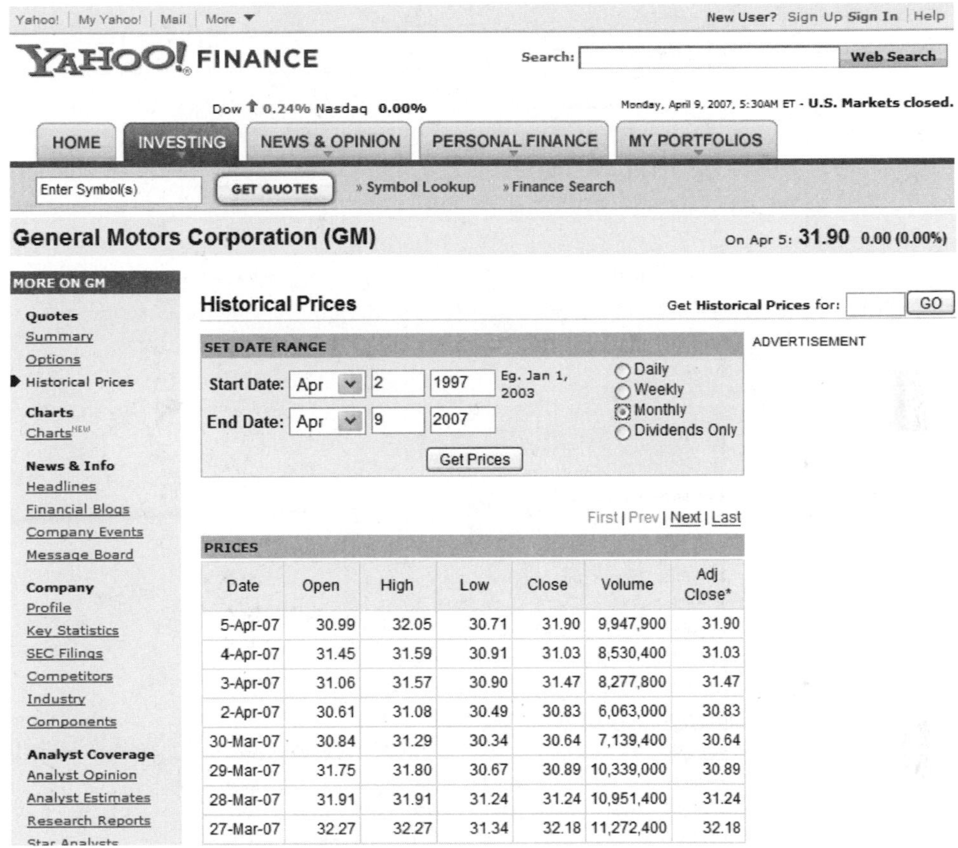

Date	Open	High	Low	Close	Volume	Adj Close*
5-Apr-07	30.99	32.05	30.71	31.90	9,947,900	31.90
4-Apr-07	31.45	31.59	30.91	31.03	8,530,400	31.03
3-Apr-07	31.06	31.57	30.90	31.47	8,277,800	31.47
2-Apr-07	30.61	31.08	30.49	30.83	6,063,000	30.83
30-Mar-07	30.84	31.29	30.34	30.64	7,139,400	30.64
29-Mar-07	31.75	31.80	30.67	30.89	10,339,000	30.89
28-Mar-07	31.91	31.91	31.24	31.24	10,951,400	31.24
27-Mar-07	32.27	32.27	31.34	32.18	11,272,400	32.18

When we click on **GetPrices**, Yahoo shows us price and dividend information for the period requested. The **Adjusted Close** is the stock price adjusted for stock splits and dividends:

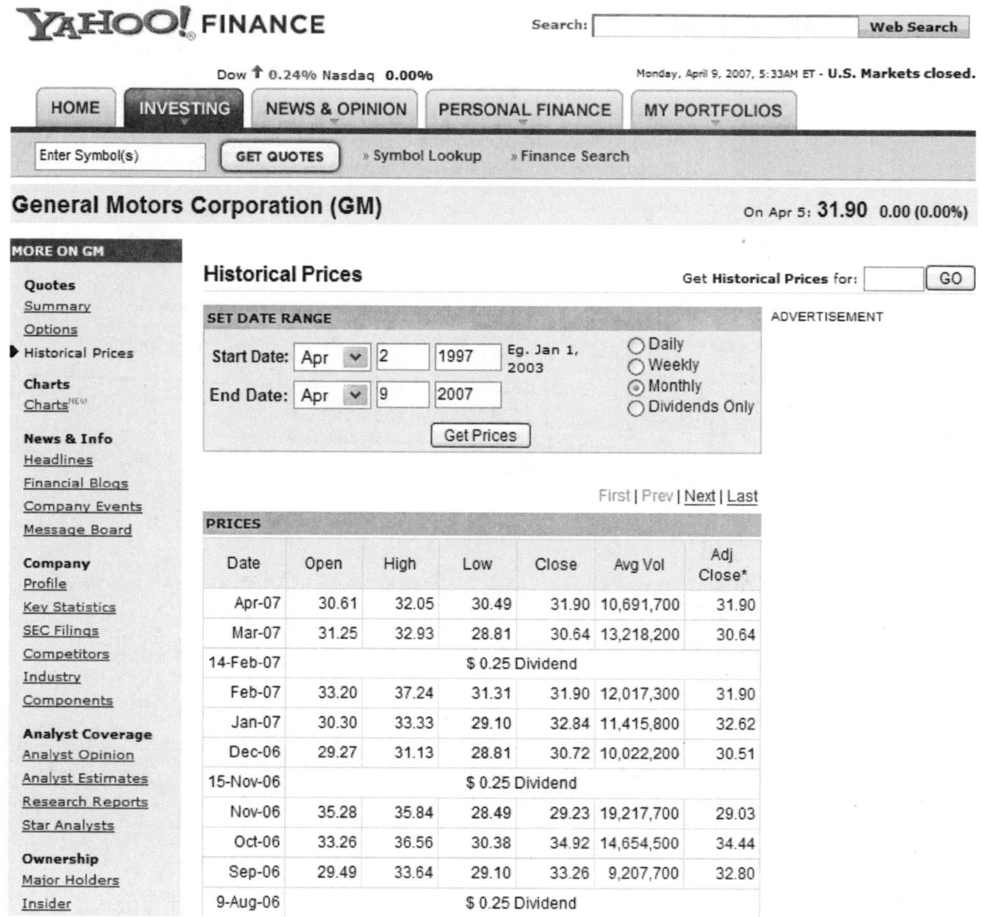

General Motors Corporation (GM) On Apr 5: 31.90 0.00 (0.00%)

Historical Prices

PRICES

Date	Open	High	Low	Close	Avg Vol	Adj Close*
Apr-07	30.61	32.05	30.49	31.90	10,691,700	31.90
Mar-07	31.25	32.93	28.81	30.64	13,218,200	30.64
14-Feb-07	$ 0.25 Dividend					
Feb-07	33.20	37.24	31.31	31.90	12,017,300	31.90
Jan-07	30.30	33.33	29.10	32.84	11,415,800	32.62
Dec-06	29.27	31.13	28.81	30.72	10,022,200	30.51
15-Nov-06	$ 0.25 Dividend					
Nov-06	35.28	35.84	28.49	29.23	19,217,700	29.03
Oct-06	33.26	36.56	30.38	34.92	14,654,500	34.44
Sep-06	29.49	33.64	29.10	33.26	9,207,700	32.80
9-Aug-06	$ 0.25 Dividend					

6. Clicking on **Download to Spreadsheet** gives the data (already adjusted for dividends and splits) in a file that can be opened with Excel.

13-Feb-02			$ 0.50 Dividend			
Feb-02	51.24	55.80	48.07	52.98	5,321,500	41.74
Jan-02	48.75	51.16	47.92	51.14	3,244,300	39.89
Dec-01	48.50	53.22	46.82	48.60	3,085,200	37.91
13-Nov-01			$ 0.50 Dividend			
Nov-01	41.32	50.17	40.69	49.70	2,588,000	38.76
Oct-01	41.82	42.01	41.30	41.32	5,737,000	31.85

* Close price adjusted for dividends and splits.

First | Prev | Next | Last

Download To Spreadsheet

Here's the way this file looks:

	A	B	C	D	E	F	G	H
1	Date	Open	High	Low	Close	Volume	Adj Close	
2	4/2/2007	30.61	32.05	30.49	31.9	10691700	31.9	
3	3/1/2007	31.25	32.93	28.81	30.64	13218200	30.64	
4	2/1/2007	33.2	37.24	31.31	31.9	12017300	31.9	
5	1/3/2007	30.3	33.33	29.1	32.84	11415800	32.62	
6	12/1/2006	29.27	31.13	28.81	30.72	10022200	30.51	
7	11/1/2006	35.28	35.84	28.49	29.23	19217700	29.03	
8	10/2/2006	33.26	36.56	30.38	34.92	14654500	34.44	
9	9/1/2006	29.49	33.64	29.1	33.26	9207700	32.8	
10	8/1/2006	32.1	32.23	29.05	29.18	7523400	28.78	
11	7/3/2006	30.3	33.06	27.12	32.23	10428900	31.53	
12	6/1/2006	27.09	30.56	24.52	29.79	16064000	29.14	
13	5/1/2006	23.2	29.1	22.29	26.93	14313500	26.34	
14	4/3/2006	21.75	23.4	19	22.88	13235900	22.17	
15	3/1/2006	20.51	23.25	19.02	21.27	12575300	20.61	
16	2/1/2006	24.05	24.6	19.99	20.31	10339200	19.68	
17	1/3/2006	19.12	24.55	18.47	24.06	20530100	23.04	
18	12/1/2005	22.16	23.41	18.33	19.42	19591900	18.6	
19	11/1/2005	27.52	27.61	20.6	21.9	16852800	20.97	
20	10/3/2005	30.36	31.5	25.48	27.4	14787700	25.76	
21	9/1/2005	34.19	34.44	30.21	30.61	7234800	28.78	

7. Final note: The ticker symbols for two commonly used indexes are ^GSPC (S&P 500) and ^DJI (Dow-Jones 30 Industrials).

3 Financial Statement Modeling

3.1 Overview

The usefulness of financial-statement projections for corporate financial management is undisputed. Such projections, termed *pro forma financial statements*, are the bread and butter of much corporate financial analysis. In this and the next chapter we will focus of the use of pro formas for valuing the firm and its component securities, but pro formas also form the basis for many credit analyses; by examining pro forma financial statements we can predict how much financing a firm will need in future years. We can play the usual "what if" games of simulation models, and we can use pro formas to ask what strains on the firm may be caused by changes in financial and sales parameters.

In this chapter we present a variety of financial models. All the models are sales driven, in that they assume that many of the balance-sheet and income-statement items are directly or indirectly related to sales. The mathematical structure of solving the models involves finding the solution to a set of simultaneous linear equations predicting both the balance sheets and the income statements for the coming years. However, the user of a spreadsheet need never worry about the solution of the model; the fact that spreadsheets can solve—by iteration—the financial relations of the model means that we only have to worry about correctly stating the relevant accounting relations in our Excel model.[1]

3.2 How Financial Models Work: Theory and an Initial Example

Almost all financial-statement models are *sales driven*; this term means that as many as possible of the most important financial statement variables are assumed to be functions of the sales level of the firm. For example, accounts receivable are often taken as a direct percentage of the sales of the firm. A slightly more complicated example might postulate that the fixed assets (or some other account) are a step function of the level of sales:

1. The mathematics of balance-sheet spreadsheets involve an iterative method for solving simultaneous equations known as the Gauss-Seidel method. Although you do not need to know this method to understand the contents of this chapter, it may be interesting to know that Gauss-Seidel can be implemented directly in Excel. For details, see Chapter 32.

$$\text{Fixed assets} = \begin{cases} a \rightarrow \text{if Sales} < A \\ b \rightarrow \text{if } A \leq \text{Sales} < B \\ \text{etc.} \end{cases}$$

In order to solve a financial-planning model, we must distinguish between those financial-statement items that are functional relationships of sales and perhaps of other financial-statement items and those items that involve policy decisions. The asset side of the balance sheet is usually assumed to be dependent only on functional relationships. The current liabilities may also be taken to involve functional relationships only, leaving the mix between long-term debt and equity as a policy decision.

A simple example is the following. We wish to predict the financial statements for a firm whose current balance sheet and income statement are as follows:

	A	B
13	**Year**	**0**
14	**Income statement**	
15	Sales	1,000
16	Costs of goods sold	(500)
17	Interest payments on debt	(32)
18	Interest earned on cash and marketable securities	6
19	Depreciation	(100)
20	Profit before tax	374
21	Taxes	(150)
22	Profit after tax	225
23	Dividends	(90)
24	Retained earnings	135
25		
26	**Balance sheet**	
27	Cash and marketable securities	80
28	Current assets	150
29	Fixed assets	
30	At cost	1,070
31	Depreciation	(300)
32	Net fixed assets	770
33	**Total assets**	1,000
34		
35	Current liabilities	80
36	Debt	320
37	Stock	450
38	Accumulated retained earnings	150
39	**Total liabilities and equity**	1,000

The current (year 0) level of sales is 1,000. The firm expects its sales to grow at a rate of 10 percent per year, and it anticipates the following financial-statement relations:

Current assets	Assumed to be 15 percent of end-of-year sales
Current liabilities	Assumed to be 8 percent of end-of-year sales
Net fixed assets	77 percent of end-of-year sales
Depreciation	10 percent of the average value of assets on the books during the year
Fixed assets at cost	Sum of net fixed assets plus accumulated depreciation
Debt	The firm neither repays any existing debt nor borrows any more money over the five-year horizon of the pro formas
Cash and marketable securities	This is the balance-sheet *plug* (see the explanation that follows). Average balances of cash and marketable securities are assumed to earn 8 percent interest.

3.2.1 The "Plug"

Perhaps the most important financial policy variable in the financial statement modeling is the "plug"—that is, the balance-sheet item that will "close" the model:

- How do we guarantee that assets and liabilities are equal (this is "closure" in the accounting sense)?
- How does the firm finance its incremental investments (this is "financial closure").

In general the plug in a pro forma model will be one of three financial balance-sheet items: (1) cash and marketable securities, (2) debt, or (3) stock.[2] As an example, consider the balance sheet of our first pro forma model:

2. We will see in section 3.5.2 that cash and debt are in many senses the *same financial item*. Cash can often be considered negative debt and vice versa.

Assets	Liabilities and Equity
Cash and marketable securities	Current liabilities
Current assets	Debt
Fixed assets	Equity
Fixed assets at cost	Stock (net funds directly provided by shareholders)
—Accumulated depreciation	Accumulated retained earnings (profits not paid out)
Net fixed assets	
Total assets	**Total liabilities and equity**

In the current example we assume that cash and marketable securities will be the plug. This assumption has two meanings:

1. The *mechanical* meaning of the plug: Formally, we define

$$\text{Cash and marketable securities} = \text{Total liabilities and equity} - \text{Current assets} - \text{Net fixed assets}$$

By using this definition, we guarantee that assets and liabilities will always be equal.

2. The *financial* meaning of the plug: By defining the plug to be cash and marketable securities, we are also making a statement about how the firm finances itself. In our following model, for example, the firm sells no additional stock, does not pay back any of its existing debt, and does not raise any more debt. This definition means that all incremental financing (if needed) for the firm will come from the cash and marketable securities account; it also means that if the firm has additional cash, it will go into this account.[3]

3.2.2 Projecting Next Year's Balance Sheet and Income Statement

We have given the financial statement for year 0. We now project the financial statement for year 1:

3. The cash and marketable securities account can be viewed as a kind of "negative debt." We will return to this point later when we use the pro forma model to value the firm.

	A	B	C	D
1	**SETTING UP THE FINANCIAL STATEMENT MODEL**			
2	Sales growth	10%		
3	Current assets/Sales	15%		
4	Current liabilities/Sales	8%		
5	Net fixed assets/Sales	77%		
6	Costs of goods sold/Sales	50%		
7	Depreciation rate	10%		
8	Interest rate on debt	10.00%		
9	Interest paid on cash and marketable securities	8.00%		
10	Tax rate	40%		
11	Dividend payout ratio	40%		
12				
13	**Year**	**0**	**1**	
14	**Income statement**			
15	Sales	1,000	1,100	<-- =B15*(1+$B$2)
16	Costs of goods sold	(500)	(550)	<-- =-C15*$B$6
17	Interest payments on debt	(32)	(32)	<-- =-$B$8*(B36+C36)/2
18	Interest earned on cash and marketable securities	6	9	<-- =$B$9*(B27+C27)/2
19	Depreciation	(100)	(117)	<-- =-$B$7*(C30+B30)/2
20	Profit before tax	374	410	<-- =SUM(C15:C19)
21	Taxes	(150)	(164)	<-- =-C20*$B$10
22	Profit after tax	225	246	<-- =C21+C20
23	Dividends	(90)	(98)	<-- =-$B$11*C22
24	Retained earnings	135	148	<-- =C23+C22
25				
26	**Balance sheet**			
27	Cash and marketable securities	80	144	<-- =C39-C28-C32
28	Current assets	150	165	<-- =C15*$B$3
29	Fixed assets			
30	At cost	1,070	1,264	<-- =C32-C31
31	Depreciation	(300)	(417)	<-- =B31+C19
32	Net fixed assets	770	847	<-- =C15*$B$5
33	**Total assets**	1,000	1,156	<-- =C32+C28+C27
34				
35	Current liabilities	80	88	<-- =C15*$B$4
36	Debt	320	320	<-- =B36
37	Stock	450	450	<-- =B37
38	Accumulated retained earnings	150	298	<-- =B38+C24
39	**Total liabilities and equity**	1,000	1,156	<-- =SUM(C35:C38)

The formulas are mostly obvious. (The dollar signs—indicating that when the formulas are copied, the cell references to the model parameters should not change—are very important! If you fail to put them in, the model will not copy correctly when you project years 2 and beyond.) Model parameters are in boldface in the following list:

Income Statement Equations

- Sales = Initial sales * (1+ **Sales growth**)^{year}
- Costs of goods sold = sales * **Costs of goods sold/Sales**

The assumption is that the only expenses related to sales are costs of goods sold. Most companies also book an expense item called *selling, general, and administrative expenses* (SG&A). The change you would have to make to accommodate this item is obvious (see an exercise at the end of this chapter).

- Interest payments on debt = **Interest rate on debt** * Average debt over the year

This formula allows us to accommodate changes in the model for repayment of debt, as well as rollover of debt at different interest rates. Note that in the current version of the model debt stays constant, but in other versions of the model to be discussed later debt will vary over time.

- Interest earned on cash and marketable securities = **Interest rate on cash** * Average cash and marketable securities over the year
- Depreciation = **Depreciation rate** * Average fixed assets at cost over the year

This calculation assumes that all new fixed assets are purchased during the year. We also assume that there is no disposal of fixed assets.

- Profit before taxes = Sales – Costs of goods sold – Interest payments on debt + Interest earned on cash and marketable securities – Depreciation
- Taxes = **Tax rate** * Profit before taxes
- Profit after taxes = Profit before taxes – Taxes
- Dividends = **Dividend Payout ratio** * Profit after taxes

The firm is assumed to pay out a fixed percentage of its profits as dividends. An alternative would be to assume that the firm has a target for its dividends per share.

- Retained earnings = Profit after taxes – Dividends

Balance Sheet Equations

- Cash and marketable securities = Total liabilities and equity – Current assets – Net fixed assets

As explained earlier, this formula means that cash and marketable securities are the balance-sheet plug.

- Current assets = **Current assets/Sales** * Sales
- Net fixed assets = **Net fixed assets/Sales** * Sales[4]
- Accumulated depreciation = Previous year's accumulated depreciation + **Depreciation rate** * Average fixed assets at cost over the year
- Fixed assets at cost = Net fixed assets + Accumulated depreciation

Note that this model does not distinguish between plant property and equipment (PP&E) and other fixed assets such as land.

- Current liabilities = **Current liabilities/Sales** * Sales
- Debt is assumed to be unchanged. An alternative model, which we will explore later, assumes that debt is the balance-sheet plug.
- Stock doesn't change. (Shareholders provide no additional direct financing: the company is assumed to issue no new stock or repurchase any stock.)
- Accumulated retained earnings = Previous year's accumulated retained earnings + Current year's additions to retained earnings

Circular References in Excel

Financial statement models in Excel always involve cells that are mutually dependent. As a result the solution of the model depends on the ability of Excel to solve circular references. To make sure your spreadsheet recalculates, you have to go to the **Tools|Options|Calculation** box and click **Iteration**. If you open a spreadsheet that involves iteration and if this box is not clicked, you will see the following Excel error message:

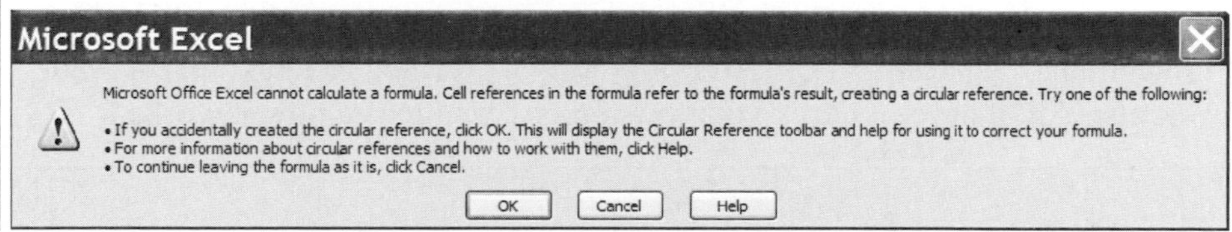

4. This is not the only way to model fixed assets. An alternative method assumes that *net* fixed assets is constant; see section 3.9 for an implementation.

Depending on where you are in Excel when you open the file with the circular references, you may get a slightly different version of this message. Whatever message you see, get out of it by clicking on **Cancel** and go to **Tools|Options|Calculation|Iteration**. In this dialog box click the box labeled **Iteration**:

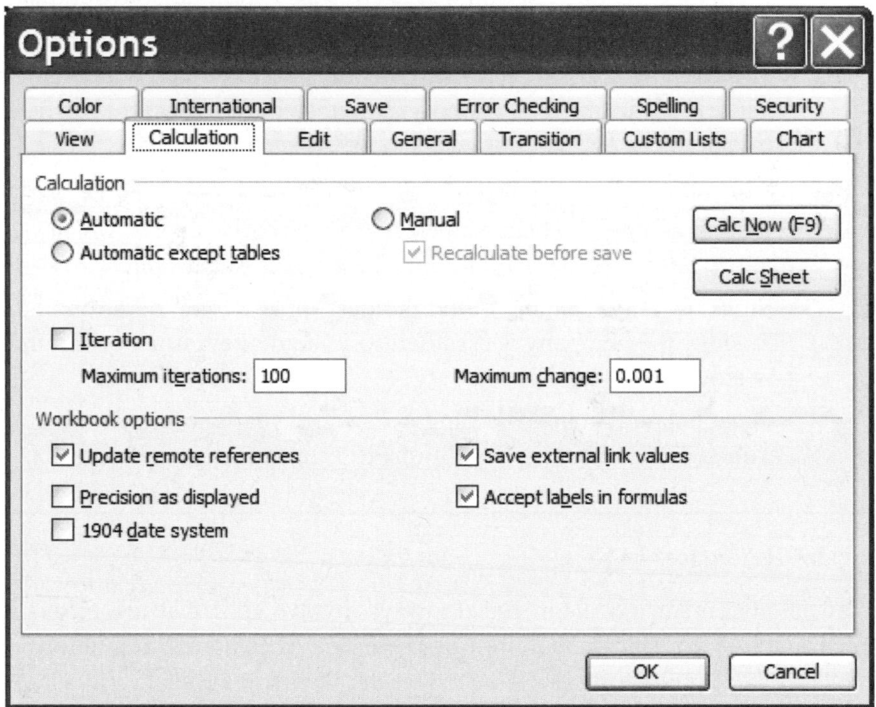

A somewhat irritating feature of Excel is the inability of some versions of the program to attach the **Iteration** feature to individual spreadsheets: In some versions of Excel the **Tools|Options|Calculation|Iteration** feature is universal to all the spreadsheets—it is turned either off or on; in other versions (including the latest version), **Iteration** can be attached to individual spreadsheets. You'll have to check your version of Excel to see how it works.

3.2.3 Extending the Model to Years 2 and Beyond

Now that you have the model set up, you can extend it by copying the columns.

	A	B	C	D	E	F	G
1	FIRST FINANCIAL MODEL						
2	Sales growth	10%					
3	Current assets/Sales	15%					
4	Current liabilities/Sales	8%					
5	Net fixed assets/Sales	77%					
6	Costs of goods sold/Sales	50%					
7	Depreciation rate	10%					
8	Interest rate on debt	10.00%					
9	Interest paid on cash and marketable securities	8.00%					
10	Tax rate	40%					
11	Dividend payout ratio	40%					
12							
13	**Year**	**0**	**1**	**2**	**3**	**4**	**5**
14	**Income statement**						
15	Sales	1,000	1,100	1,210	1,331	1,464	1,611
16	Costs of goods sold	(500)	(550)	(605)	(666)	(732)	(805)
17	Interest payments on debt	(32)	(32)	(32)	(32)	(32)	(32)
18	Interest earned on cash and marketable securities	6	9	14	20	26	33
19	Depreciation	(100)	(117)	(137)	(161)	(189)	(220)
20	Profit before tax	374	410	450	492	538	587
21	Taxes	(150)	(164)	(180)	(197)	(215)	(235)
22	Profit after tax	225	246	270	295	323	352
23	Dividends	(90)	(98)	(108)	(118)	(129)	(141)
24	Retained earnings	135	148	162	177	194	211
25							
26	**Balance sheet**						
27	Cash and marketable securities	80	144	213	289	371	459
28	Current assets	150	165	182	200	220	242
29	Fixed assets						
30	At cost	1,070	1,264	1,486	1,740	2,031	2,364
31	Depreciation	(300)	(417)	(554)	(715)	(904)	(1,124)
32	Net fixed assets	770	847	932	1,025	1,127	1,240
33	**Total assets**	1,000	1,156	1,326	1,513	1,718	1,941
34							
35	Current liabilities	80	88	97	106	117	129
36	Debt	320	320	320	320	320	320
37	Stock	450	450	450	450	450	450
38	Accumulated retained earnings	150	298	460	637	830	1,042
39	**Total liabilities and equity**	1,000	1,156	1,326	1,513	1,718	1,941

Note that the most common mistake to make in the transition between the two-columned financial model and this one is the failure to mark the model parameters with dollar signs. If you commit this error, you will get zeros in places where there should be numbers.

3.3 Free Cash Flow: Measuring the Cash Produced by the Business

Now that we have the model, we can use it to make financial predictions. The most important calculation for valuation purposes is the *free cash flow* (FCF). FCF—the cash produced by a business without taking into account the way the business is financed—is the best measure of the cash produced by a business.[5] The easiest way to define the free cash flow is as follows:

Defining the Free Cash Flow

Profit after taxes	This is the basic measure of the profitability of the business, but it is an accounting measure that includes financing flows (such as interest), as well as noncash expenses such as depreciation. Profit after taxes does not account for either changes in the firm's working capital or purchases of new fixed assets, both of which can be important cash drains on the firm.
+Depreciation	This noncash expense is added back to the profit after tax.
+After tax interest payments (net)	FCF is an attempt to measure the cash produced by the business activity of the firm. To neutralize the effect of interest payments on the firm's profits, we • Add back the after-tax cost of interest on debt (*after-tax* since interest payments are tax deductible). • Subtract out the after-tax interest payments on cash and marketable securities.
–Increase in current assets	When the firm's sales increase, more investment is needed in inventories, accounts receivable, etc. This increase in current assets is not an expense for tax purposes (and is therefore ignored in the profit after taxes), but it is a cash drain on the company.
+Increase in current liabilities	An increase in the sales often causes an increase in financing related to sales (such as accounts payable or taxes payable). This increase in current liabilities—when related to sales—provides cash to the firm. Since it is directly related to sales, we include this cash in the free cash flow calculations.
–Increase in fixed assets at cost	An increase in fixed assets (the long-term productive assets of the company) is a use of cash, which reduces the firm's free cash flow.

Here is the calculation for our firm:

	A	B	C	D	E	F	G
40							
41	**Year**	**0**	**1**	**2**	**3**	**4**	**5**
42	**Free cash flow calculation**						
43	Profit after tax		246	270	295	323	352
44	Add back depreciation		117	137	161	189	220
45	Subtract increase in current assets		(15)	(17)	(18)	(20)	(22)
46	Add back increase in current liabilities		8	9	10	11	12
47	Subtract increase in fixed assets at cost		(194)	(222)	(254)	(291)	(333)
48	Add back after-tax interest on debt		19	19	19	19	19
49	Subtract after-tax interest on cash and mkt. securities		(5)	(9)	(12)	(16)	(20)
50	**Free cash flow**		176	188	201	214	228

5. Extensive discussions of free cash flow and its uses in a valuation context can be found in books by Benninga and Sarig (1997) and by McKinsey & Company, Inc., et al. (2005).

3.3.1 Reconciling the Cash Balances

The free cash flow calculation is different from the "consolidated statement of cash flows" that is a part of every accounting statement. The purpose of the consolidated statement of cash flows is to explain the increase in the cash accounts in the balance sheet as a function of the cash flows from the firm's operating, investing, and financing activities. In the pro forma example of this section we treat the cash and marketable securities as the balance-sheet plug; however, it can also be derived from a standard accounting statement of cash flows.

	A	B	C	D	E	F	G	H
53	**CONSOLIDATED STATEMENT OF CASH FLOWS: RECONCILING THE CASH BALANCES**							
54	**Cash flow from operating activities**							
55	Profit after tax		246	270	295	323	352	<-- =G22
56	Add back depreciation		117	137	161	189	220	<-- =-G19
57	Adjust for changes in net working capital:							
58	Subtract increase in current assets		(15)	(17)	(18)	(20)	(22)	<-- =-(G28-F28)
59	Add back increase in current liabilities		8	9	10	11	12	<-- =G35-F35
60	Net cash from operating activities		356	400	448	502	562	<-- =SUM(G55:G59)
61								
62	**Cash flow from investing activities**							
63	Aquisitions of fixed assets--capital expenditures		(194)	(222)	(254)	(291)	(333)	<-- =-(G30-F30)
64	Purchases of investment securities		0	0	0	0	0	<-- Not in our model
65	Proceeds from sales of investment securities		0	0	0	0	0	<-- Not in our model
66	Net cash used in investing activities		(194)	(222)	(254)	(291)	(333)	<-- =SUM(G63:G65)
67								
68	**Cash flow from financing activities**							
69	Net proceeds from borrowing activities		0	0	0	0	0	<-- =G36-F36
70	Net proceeds from stock issues, repurchases		0	0	0	0	0	<-- =G37-F37
71	Dividends paid		(98)	(108)	(118)	(129)	(141)	<-- =G23
72	Net cash from financing activities		(98)	(108)	(118)	(129)	(141)	<-- =SUM(G69:G71)
73								
74	Net increase in cash and cash equivalents		64	70	76	82	88	<-- =G72+G66+G60
75	Check: changes in cash and mkt. securities		64	70	76	82	88	<-- =G27-F27

Line 75 checks that the changes in the cash accounts derived through the consolidated statement of cash flows match those derived in the financial model (which uses cash as a plug). As you can see, the model works, in the sense that changes in cash balances from the consolidated statement of cash flows in fact match those in the projected balance sheets of the pro forma model.

3.4 Using the Free Cash Flow to Value the Firm and Its Equity

The *enterprise value* of the firm is the present value of the firm's future anticipated free cash flows. We can use the pro forma FCF projections and a cost of capital to determine the enterprise value of the firm. Suppose we have determined that the firm's weighted average cost of capital (WACC) is 20 percent (recall that the calculation of the WACC was discussed in Chapter 2). Then the *enterprise value* of the firm is the discounted value of the firm's projected FCFs plus its terminal value:

$$\text{Enterprise value} = \sum_{t=1}^{\infty} \frac{FCF_1}{(1+WACC)^t}$$

Most financial analysts consider it presumptuous to project an infinite number of free cash flows; therefore, the projected cash-flow stream is often cut off at some arbitrary date, and a *terminal value* is substituted for the cash flows beyond this date:

$$\text{Enterprise value} = \frac{FCF_1}{(1+WACC)^1} + \frac{FCF_2}{(1+WACC)^2} + \ldots + \frac{FCF_5}{(1+WACC)^5} + \frac{\text{Year-5 terminal value}}{(1+WACC)^5}$$

In this formula, the year-5 terminal value is a proxy for the present value of all FCFs from year 6 onward. Instead of projecting the FCFs from year 6 onward, we use the most common terminal-value model:

$$\begin{aligned}\text{Terminal value at end of year 5} &= \sum_{t=1}^{\infty} \frac{FCF_{t+5}}{(1+WACC)^t} \\ &= \sum_{t=1}^{\infty} \frac{FCF_5 * (1+\text{Long-term FCF growth})^t}{(1+WACC)^t} \\ &= \frac{FCF_5 * (1+\text{Long-term FCF growth})}{WACC - \text{Long-term FCF growth}}\end{aligned}$$

This model (based on the formula for the present value of a growing annuity, see Chapter 1, p. 9) assumes that the year-5 cash flow will continue to grow at a constant long-term growth rate.[6]

Here's an example that uses our projections:

	A	B	C	D	E	F	G	H	I	J
53	**Valuing the firm**									
54	Weighted average cost of capital	20%								
55	Long-term free cash flow growth rate	5%	<-- real growth 2% + inflation 3%?							
56										
57	**Year**	**0**	**1**	**2**	**3**	**4**	**5**			
58	FCF		176	188	201	214	228			
59	Terminal value						1,598	<-- =G58*(1+B55)/(B54-B55)		
60	Total		176	188	201	214	1,826			
61										
62	Enterprise value, present value of row 60	1,231	<-- =NPV(B54,C60:G60)							
63	Add in initial (year 0) cash and mkt. securities	80	<-- =B27							
64	Asset value in year 0	1,311	<-- =B63+B62							
65	Subtract out value of firm's debt today	(320)	<-- =-B36							
66	Equity value	991	<-- =B64+B65							

6. The same method underlies the Gordon model in Chapter 2.

Note that the long-term FCF growth rate in cell B55 is different from the sales growth in cell B2. The sales growth is the anticipated growth over the years 1–5; the long-term growth rate is probably better estimated by making a more realistic estimate of the growth of the firm's market sector. For firms operating in a mature market, we often estimate the long-term FCF growth as the sum of real growth plus anticipated inflation.

3.5 Some Notes on the Valuation Procedure

In this section we cover some issues related to the valuation procedure outlined in section 3.4.

3.5.1 Terminal Value

In determining the terminal value we used a version of the growing annuity model described in Chapter 1. We have assumed that—after the year-5 projection horizon—the cash flows will grow at a long-term rate of growth of 5 percent. This assumption gives the terminal value as

$$\text{Terminal value at end of year 5} = \frac{FCF_5 * (1 + \text{Long-term FCF growth})}{WACC - \text{Long-term FCF growth}}$$

There are other ways of calculating the terminal value. All of the following are common variations that can be implemented in the framework of our model (see end-of-chapter exercises):

- Terminal value = Year-5 book value of debt + Equity

  This calculation assumes that the book value correctly predicts the market value.

- Terminal value = (Enterprise market/Book multiple) ∗ (Year-5 book value of debt + Equity)

- Terminal value = P/E ratio ∗ Year-5 profits + Year-5 book value of debt

- Terminal value = EBITDA ratio ∗ Year-5 anticipated EBITDA

  (EBITDA = Earnings before interest, taxes, depreciation, and amortization.)

3.5.2 The Treatment of Cash and Marketable Securities in the Valuation

We have added the initial cash balances back to the present value of the projected FCFs to get the enterprise value. This procedure assumes the following:

- Year-0 balances of cash and marketable securities are not needed to produce the FCFs in subsequent years.
- Year-0 balances of cash and marketable securities are "surpluses" that could be drawn down or paid out by shareholders without affecting the future economic performance of the firm.

A wholly equivalent assumption sometimes madc by investment bankers and equity analysts is to assume that initial cash balances are *negative debt.* If you made this assumption, you would value the equity in the following way:

	A	B	C	D
68	**Cash and marketable securities as negative debt**			
69	NPV of row 60 = enterprise value	1,231	<-- =B62	
70	Net year 0 debt: debt minus cash	(240)	<-- =-B36+B27	
71	Equity value	991	<-- =B69+B70	

3.5.3 Midyear Discounting

While the NPV formula assumes that all cash flows occur at the end of the year, it is more logical to assume that they occur smoothly throughout the year. For discounting purposes, we should therefore discount cash flows as if, on average, they occur in the middle of the year. Thus the enterprise value is more logically calculated as follows:

$$\text{Enterprise value} = \frac{FCF_1}{(1+WACC)^{0.5}} + \frac{FCF_2}{(1+WACC)^{1.5}} + \ldots + \frac{FCF_5}{(1+WACC)^{4.5}} + \frac{\text{Year-5 terminal value}}{(1+WACC)^{4.5}}$$

$$= \underbrace{\left[\frac{FCF_1}{(1+WACC)^{1}} + \frac{FCF_2}{(1+WACC)^{2}} + \ldots + \frac{FCF_5}{(1+WACC)^{5}} + \frac{\text{Year-5 terminal value}}{(1+WACC)^{5}}\right]}_{\text{This can be calculated using Excel's NPV function.}} * (1+WACC)^{0.5}$$

Incorporating this midyear discounting into our value calculations gives us the following:

	A	B	C	D	E	F	G	H	I	J
74	**Valuing the firm--using midyear discounting**									
75	Weighted average cost of capital	20%								
76	Long-term free cash flow growth rate	5%								
77										
78	**Year**	**0**	**1**	**2**	**3**	**4**	**5**			
79	FCF		176	188	201	214	228			
80	Terminal value						1,598	<-- =G79*(1+B76)/(B75-B76)		
81	Total		176	188	201	214	1,826			
82										
83	Enterprise value, NPV of row 81	1,348	<-- =NPV(B75,C81:G81)*(1+B75)^0.5							
84	Add in initial (year 0) cash and mkt. securities	80	<-- =B27							
85	Asset value in year 0	1,428	<-- =B84+B83							
86	Subtract out value of firm's debt today	(320)	<-- =B65							
87	Equity value	1,108	<-- =B85+B86							

3.6 Sensitivity Analysis

As in any Excel model, we can perform extensive sensitivity analysis on our valuation. Taking the last case as our base case, we can ask, for example, What is the effect of the sales growth rate on the equity value of the firm?

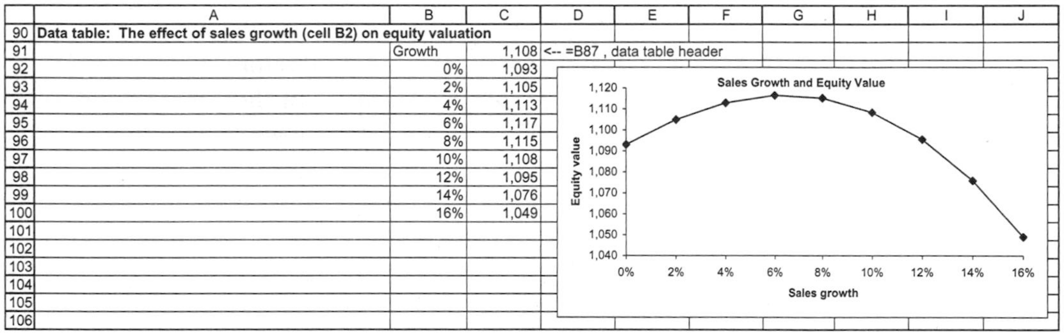

	A	B	C	D
90	**Data table: The effect of sales growth (cell B2) on equity valuation**			
91		Growth	1,108	<-- =B87 , data table header
92		0%	1,093	
93		2%	1,105	
94		4%	1,113	
95		6%	1,117	
96		8%	1,115	
97		10%	1,108	
98		12%	1,095	
99		14%	1,076	
100		16%	1,049	
101				
102				
103				
104				
105				
106				

Cells B91:C100 contain a data table (see Chapter 31 if you are unsure of how to construct these tables). While initial increases in sales growth increase the value of the firm, very high sales growth actually decreases firm value. We leave it to you to check that this result is due to the high fixed-assets-to-sales ratio.

Another variation is to calculate the effect on equity valuation of both the long-term FCF growth and the WACC. Here, however, you have to be careful: Examining the terminal value equation

$$\text{Terminal value} = \frac{FCF_5 * (1 + \text{Long-term FCF growth})}{WACC - \text{Long-term FCF growth}}$$

will show you that this calculation only makes sense if the WACC is greater than the growth rate.[7] To overcome this problem we define the data table cell B107 (the calculation on which the data table does its sensitivity analysis) in the following way:

	A	B	C	D	E	F	G	H	I	J	K
107			WACC								
108	=IF(B75<=B76,"nmf",B87) →	1,108.37	10%	12%	14%	16%	18%	20%	22%	24%	26%
109		0%	2,038.12	1,660.04	1,390.52	1,188.82	1,032.29	907.35	805.37	720.58	649.00
110	Long-term FCF growth rate -->	2%	2,447.00	1,915.96	1,562.34	1,310.08	1,121.12	974.36	857.11	761.31	681.59
111		4%	3,128.45	2,299.84	1,802.89	1,471.75	1,235.34	1,058.12	920.35	810.19	720.10
112		6%	4,491.36	2,939.65	2,163.72	1,698.09	1,387.62	1,165.81	999.40	869.93	766.32
113		8%	8,580.08	4,219.26	2,765.09	2,037.61	1,600.82	1,309.39	1,101.03	944.61	822.81
114		10%	nmf	8,058.09	3,967.84	2,603.47	1,920.62	1,510.41	1,236.55	1,040.62	893.42
115		12%	nmf	nmf	7,576.07	3,735.18	2,453.61	1,811.94	1,426.27	1,168.64	984.20
116		14%	nmf	nmf	nmf	7,130.34	3,519.60	2,314.48	1,710.85	1,347.86	1,105.25
117		16%	nmf	nmf	nmf	nmf	6,717.58	3,319.58	2,185.15	1,616.70	1,274.71

3.7 Debt as a Plug

In the model that we have shown, cash and marketable securities were the plug and debt was a constant. However, for some values of the model parameters, you can get *negative* cash and marketable securities. Consider the following example, which is still the same model, but—as indicated on the spreadsheet itself—with some different parameter values:

7. If the growth rate > WACC, then Terminal value $= \sum_{t=1}^{\infty} \frac{FCF_5 * (1 + \text{Long-term FCF growth})^t}{(1+WACC)^t} = \infty$. This problem was also discussed in Chapter 2 in the context of the Gordon dividend model.

	A	B	C	D	E	F	G
1	**NEGATIVE CASH BALANCES: ILLUSTRATION**						
2	Sales growth	20%	<-- Increased from 10%				
3	Current assets/Sales	20%	<-- Increased from 15%				
4	Current liabilities/Sales	8%					
5	Net fixed assets/Sales	80%	<-- Increased from 77%				
6	Costs of goods sold/Sales	50%					
7	Depreciation rate	10%					
8	Interest rate on debt	10.00%					
9	Interest paid on cash and marketable securities	8.00%					
10	Tax rate	40%					
11	Dividend payout ratio	50%	<-- Increased from 40%				
12							
13	**Year**	**0**	**1**	**2**	**3**	**4**	**5**
14	**Income statement**						
15	Sales	1,000	1,200	1,440	1,728	2,074	2,488
16	Costs of goods sold	(500)	(600)	(720)	(864)	(1,037)	(1,244)
17	Interest payments on debt	(40)	(40)	(40)	(40)	(40)	(40)
18	Interest earned on cash and marketable securities	6	4	(0)	(6)	(13)	(21)
19	Depreciation	(100)	(124)	(156)	(194)	(242)	(299)
20	Profit before tax	366	440	524	624	742	884
21	Taxes	(147)	(176)	(210)	(249)	(297)	(354)
22	Profit after tax	220	264	314	374	445	530
23	Dividends	(110)	(132)	(157)	(187)	(223)	(265)
24	Retained earnings	110	132	157	187	223	265
25							
26	**Balance sheet**						
27	Cash and marketable securities	80	28	(36)	(113)	(209)	(325)
28	Current assets	200	240	288	346	415	498
29	Fixed assets						
30	At cost	1,100	1,384	1,732	2,157	2,675	3,306
31	Depreciation	(300)	(424)	(580)	(774)	(1,016)	(1,315)
32	Net fixed assets	800	960	1,152	1,382	1,659	1,991
33	**Total assets**	1,080	1,228	1,404	1,615	1,865	2,163
34							
35	Current liabilities	80	96	115	138	166	199
36	Debt	400	400	400	400	400	400
37	Stock	450	450	450	450	450	450
38	Accumulated retained earnings	150	282	439	626	849	1,114
39	**Total liabilities and equity**	1,080	1,228	1,404	1,615	1,865	2,163

Given these changes, the cash and marketable securities account (row 27) turns negative by year 2, a result which is obviously illogical. However, the economic meaning of these negative numbers is clear: Given the increased sales growth, increased current-asset and fixed-asset requirements, and increased dividend payouts, the firm needs more financing.[8]

What we want is a model which recognizes that

- Cash cannot be less than zero.
- When the firm needs additional financing, it *borrows* money.

---

8. If you examine the model as it now stands, you will see that it implicitly assumes that this extra financing comes at the cost of the cash and marketable securities. If we consider this account a kind of checking account with interest, then the model implicitly assumes that the firm can finance overdrafts from this account at the same rate of interest as it is being paid on the account.

Here is the model:

	A	B	C	D	E	F	G	H
1		**NO NEGATIVE CASH BALANCES**						
2	Sales growth	20%	<-- Increased from 10%					
3	Current assets/Sales	20%	<-- Increased from 15%					
4	Current liabilities/Sales	8%						
5	Net fixed assets/Sales	80%	<-- Increased from 77%					
6	Costs of goods sold/Sales	50%						
7	Depreciation rate	10%						
8	Interest rate on debt	10.00%						
9	Interest paid on cash and marketable securities	8.00%						
10	Tax rate	40%						
11	Dividend payout ratio	50%	<-- Increased from 40%					
12								
13	**Year**	**0**	**1**	**2**	**3**	**4**	**5**	
14	**Income statement**							
15	Sales	1,000	1,200	1,440	1,728	2,074	2,488	
16	Costs of goods sold	(500)	(600)	(720)	(864)	(1,037)	(1,244)	
17	Interest payments on debt	(40)	(40)	(42)	(47)	(56)	(67)	
18	Interest earned on cash and marketable securities	6	4	1	-	-	-	
19	Depreciation	(100)	(124)	(156)	(194)	(242)	(299)	
20	Profit before tax	366	440	524	622	739	878	
21	Taxes	(147)	(176)	(209)	(249)	(296)	(351)	
22	Profit after tax	220	264	314	373	443	527	
23	Dividends	(110)	(132)	(157)	(187)	(222)	(263)	
24	Retained earnings	110	132	157	187	222	263	
25								
26	**Balance sheet**							
27	Cash and marketable securities	80	28	0	0	0	0	<-- =G39-G28-G32
28	Current assets	200	240	288	346	415	498	
29	Fixed assets							
30	At cost	1,100	1,384	1,732	2,157	2,675	3,306	
31	Depreciation	(300)	(424)	(580)	(774)	(1,016)	(1,315)	
32	Net fixed assets	800	960	1,152	1,382	1,659	1,991	
33	**Total assets**	1,080	1,228	1,440	1,728	2,074	2,488	
34								
35	Current liabilities	80	96	115	138	166	199	
36	Debt	400	400	436	514	610	728	<-- =MAX(G28+G32-G35-G37-G38,F36)
37	Stock	450	450	450	450	450	450	
38	Accumulated retained earnings	150	282	439	626	847	1,111	
39	**Total liabilities and equity**	1,080	1,228	1,440	1,728	2,074	2,488	

The equations for cash (row 27) and debt (row 36) are indicated for the year-5 entries. What they do, in accounting terms is the following:

Cash and marketable securities remains the plug in the model.

The debt on the balance sheet conforms to the following test:

- Current assets + Net fixed assets > Current liabilities + *Last year's debt* + stock + Accumulated retained earnings?

  In this case even if cash and marketable securities are equal to 0, we need to increase debt balances in order to finance the firm's productive activities.

- Current assets + Net fixed assets < Current liabilities + *Last year's debt* + Stock + Accumulated retained earnings?

  If this relation holds, then there is no need to increase debt, and, in fact, the firm has to have positive cash and marketable securities as a balancing item, and the fact that we have made cash the plug will take care of this concern.

• In Excel programming terms, this formula becomes (for the year 5, but each previous year has the same type of equation) Max (G28+G32-G35-G37-G38,F36).

As shown in the exercises to this chapter, the model can easily accommodate a situation in which there are minimum cash balances.

3.8 Incorporating a Target Debt/Equity Ratio into a Pro Forma

Another change we might want to make in our model relates to the plug. Suppose that the firm has a target ratio of debt to equity: In each of the years 1–5, it wants debt and equity on the balance sheet to conform to a certain ratio. This situation is illustrated in the following example:

	A	B	C	D	E	F	G	H
1	**TARGET DEBT-EQUITY RATIO** **Cash is fixed, ratio of debt/equity changes in each year**							
2	Sales growth	10%						
3	Current assets/Sales	15%						
4	Current liabilities/Sales	8%						
5	Net fixed assets/Sales	77%						
6	Costs of goods sold/Sales	50%						
7	Depreciation rate	10%						
8	Interest rate on debt	10.00%						
9	Interest paid on cash & marketable securities	8.00%						
10	Tax rate	40%						
11	Dividend payout ratio	60%						
12								
13	**Year**	**0**	**1**	**2**	**3**	**4**	**5**	
14	**Income statement**							
15	Sales	1,000	1,100	1,210	1,331	1,464	1,611	
16	Costs of goods sold	(500)	(550)	(605)	(666)	(732)	(805)	
17	Interest payments on debt	(32)	(30)	(29)	(28)	(29)	(32)	
18	Interest earned on cash & marketable securities	6	6	6	6	6	6	
19	Depreciation	(100)	(117)	(137)	(161)	(189)	(220)	
20	Profit before tax	374	409	445	483	521	560	
21	Taxes	(150)	(164)	(178)	(193)	(208)	(224)	
22	Profit after tax	225	246	267	290	313	336	
23	Dividends	(135)	(147)	(160)	(174)	(188)	(202)	
24	Retained earnings	90	98	107	116	125	134	
25								
26	**Balance sheet**							
27	Cash and marketable securities	80	80	80	80	80	80	
28	Current assets	150	165	182	200	220	242	
29	Fixed assets							
30	At cost	1,070	1,264	1,486	1,740	2,031	2,364	
31	Depreciation	(300)	(417)	(554)	(715)	(904)	(1,124)	
32	Net fixed assets	770	847	932	1,025	1,127	1,240	
33	**Total assets**	1,000	1,092	1,193	1,305	1,427	1,562	
34								
35	Current liabilities	80	88	97	106	117	129	
36	Debt	320	287	284	276	302	331	<-- =G41*(G37+G38)
37	Stock	450	469	457	451	412	372	<-- =G33-G35-G36-G38
38	Accumulated retained earnings	150	248	355	471	596	730	
39	**Total liabilities and equity**	1,000	1,092	1,193	1,305	1,427	1,562	
40								
41	**Target debt-equity ratio**	0.53	0.40	0.35	0.30	0.30	0.30	

Initial (year 0) debt/equity ratio: =B36/(B37+B38)

Row 41 of the spreadsheet shows the target debt/equity ratio in each of years 1–5. The firm wants to lower its current debt/equity ratio of 53 percent to 30 percent over the next two years. The relevant changes to the equations of our initial model are the following:

- Debt = **Target debt/equity ratio** * (Stock + Retained earnings)
- Stock = Total assets − Current liabilities − Debt − Accumulated retained earnings

Note that the firm will issue new debt years 4 and 5; in year 1 the stock account grows (indicating that new equity is issued), whereas in subsequent years stock decreases (indicating a repurchase of equity).

3.9 Project Finance: Debt Repayment Schedules

Here is another use for pro forma modeling: In a typical case of *project finance*, the firm borrows money in order to finance a project. The borrowing often comes with strings attached:

- The firm is not allowed to pay any dividends until the debt is paid off.
- The firm is not allowed to issue any new equity.
- The firm must pay back the debt over a specified period.

The following simplified example uses a variation of the version of our basic model with cash balances. A new firm or project is set up; in year 0,

- The firm has assets of 2,200, which are financed with 200 of current liabilities, 1,100 of equity, and 1,000 of debt.
- The debt must be paid off in equal installments of principal over the next five years. Until the debt is paid off, the firm is not allowed to pay dividends (if there is extra cash, this will go into a cash and marketable securities account).

	A	B	C	D	E	F	G	H
1	**PROJECT FINANCE** **No dividends, debt repayment schedule fixed, net fixed assets constant**							
2	Sales growth	15%						
3	Current assets/Sales	15%						
4	Current liabilities/Sales	8%						
5	Costs of goods sold/Sales	45%						
6	Depreciation rate	10%						
7	Interest rate on debt	10.00%						
8	Interest paid on cash and marketable securities	8.00%						
9	Tax rate	40%						
10	Dividend payout ratio	0%	<-- No dividends until all the debt is paid off					
11								
12	**Year**	**0**	**1**	**2**	**3**	**4**	**5**	
13	**Income statement**							
14	Sales		1,150	1,323	1,521	1,749	2,011	
15	Costs of goods sold		(518)	(595)	(684)	(787)	(905)	
16	Interest payments on debt		(90)	(70)	(50)	(30)	(10)	
17	Interest earned on cash and marketable securities		1	3	9	21	40	
18	Depreciation		(211)	(233)	(257)	(284)	(314)	
19	Profit before tax		333	428	539	669	822	
20	Taxes		(133)	(171)	(216)	(268)	(329)	
21	Profit after tax		200	257	323	401	493	
22	Dividends		0	0	0	0	0	
23	Retained earnings		200	257	323	401	493	
24								
25	**Balance sheet**							
26	Cash and marketable securities	0	19	64	173	359	633	<-- =G38-G27-G31
27	Current assets	200	173	198	228	262	302	
28	Fixed assets							
29	At cost	2,000	2,211	2,443	2,700	2,985	3,299	
30	Depreciation	0	(211)	(443)	(700)	(985)	(1,299)	<-- =F30-$B$6*(G29+F29)/2
31	Net fixed assets	2,000	2,000	2,000	2,000	2,000	2,000	<-- NFA don't change
32	**Total assets**	2,200	2,192	2,262	2,401	2,621	2,935	
33								
34	Current liabilities	100	92	106	122	140	161	
35	Debt	1,000	800	600	400	200	0	<-- =F35-$B$35/5
36	Stock	1,100	1,100	1,100	1,100	1,100	1,100	
37	Accumulated retained earnings	0	200	456	780	1,181	1,674	
38	**Total liabilities and equity**	2,200	2,192	2,262	2,401	2,621	2,935	

The debt repayment terms are incorporated into the model by simply specifying the debt balances at the end of each year. Since the firm is assumed to issue no new equity (in accordance with the covenants on the lending), it follows that the model's plug cannot be on the liabilities side of the balance sheet. In our model the plug is the cash and marketable securities account.

The model incorporates one other assumption often made about fixed assets: It assumes that the *net* fixed assets stay constant over the life of the project. Essentially this assumption means that the depreciation accurately reflects the capital maintenance of the fixed assets. As you can see from looking at rows 29–31, this means that the fixed assets at cost grow each year by the increase in asset depreciation. It also means that in there is no net cash flow from depreciation:

	A	B	C	D	E	F	G	H
41	**FREE CASH FLOW CALCULATION**							
42	**Year**	**0**	**1**	**2**	**3**	**4**	**5**	
43	Profit after tax		200	257	323	401	493	
44	Add back depreciation		211	233	257	284	314	Cash flow generated by depreciation equals capital expenditures.
45	Subtract increase in current assets		28	(26)	(30)	(34)	(39)	
46	Add back increase in current liabilities		(8)	14	16	18	21	
47	Subtract increase in fixed assets at cost		(211)	(233)	(257)	(284)	(314)	
48	Add back after-tax interest on debt		54	42	30	18	6	
49	Subtract after-tax interest on cash and mkt. securities		(0)	(2)	(6)	(13)	(24)	
50	**Free cash flow**		273	285	334	391	457	

In this example, the firm has no problem in making its debt principal repayments. As credit analysts, we might be interested in how the firm's ability to meet its payments is affected by the various parameter values. In the following example we have increased the ratio of costs of goods sold (COGS) to sales. With the new parameter values, the firm can no longer meet its debt repayments in years 1–3. This fact can be seen in the pro forma: In years 1–4 the balances of cash and marketable securities are negative, indicating that—in order to make the repayment of the loan principal—the firm had to borrow money.[9]

9. From the point of view of corporate finance, positive balances of cash are like *negative balances* of debt. Thus, when the cash is negative, it is equivalent to the firm having borrowed money.

	A	B	C	D	E	F	G	H
1	**PROJECT FINANCE** **With these parameters the project cannot pay off its debt**							
2	Sales growth	15%						
3	Current assets/Sales	15%						
4	Current liabilities/Sales	8%						
5	Costs of goods sold/Sales	55%						
6	Depreciation rate	10%						
7	Interest rate on debt	10.00%						
8	Interest paid on cash and marketable securities	8.00%						
9	Tax rate	40%						
10	Dividend payout ratio	0%	<-- No dividends until all the debt is paid off					
11								
12	**Year**	**0**	**1**	**2**	**3**	**4**	**5**	
13	**Income statement**							
14	Sales		1,150	1,323	1,521	1,749	2,011	
15	Costs of goods sold		(633)	(727)	(836)	(962)	(1,106)	
16	Interest payments on debt		(90)	(70)	(50)	(30)	(10)	
17	Interest earned on cash and marketable securities		(2)	(6)	(7)	(4)	4	
18	Depreciation		(211)	(233)	(257)	(284)	(314)	
19	Profit before tax		215	287	370	469	585	
20	Taxes		(86)	(115)	(148)	(187)	(234)	
21	Profit after tax		129	172	222	281	351	
22	Dividends		0	0	0	0	0	
23	Retained earnings		129	172	222	281	351	
24								
25	**Balance sheet**							
26	Cash and marketable securities	0	(52)	(92)	(83)	(18)	114	<-- =G38-G27-G31, the plug
27	Current assets	200	173	198	228	262	302	
28	Fixed assets							
29	At cost	2,000	2,211	2,443	2,700	2,985	3,299	
30	Depreciation	0	(211)	(443)	(700)	(985)	(1,299)	
31	Net fixed assets	2,000	2,000	2,000	2,000	2,000	2,000	<-- NFA don't change
32	**Total assets**	2,200	2,121	2,107	2,145	2,244	2,416	
33								
34	Current liabilities	100	92	106	122	140	161	
35	Debt	1,000	800	600	400	200	0	
36	Stock	1,100	1,100	1,100	1,100	1,100	1,100	
37	Accumulated retained earnings	0	129	301	523	804	1,155	
38	**Total liabilities and equity**	2,200	2,121	2,107	2,145	2,244	2,416	

3.10 Calculating the Return on Equity

We can use the pro forma models illustrated in this chapter to compute the anticipated return on equity. Look at the previous example: Equity owners in the project have to pay 1,100 in year 0. During years 1–4 they get no payoffs, but in year 5 they own the company. Suppose that the book value of the assets accurately reflects the market value. Then at the end of year 5 the equity in the firm is worth Stock + Accumulated retained earnings = 2,255. The return on the equity investment (ROE) is calculated as follows:

	A	B	C	D	E	F	G	H
56	**RETURN ON EQUITY (ROE)**							
57	**Year**	**0**	**1**	**2**	**3**	**4**	**5**	
58	Equity cash flow	-1,100	-	-	-	-	2,255	<-- =G22+G36+G37
59	RETURN ON EQUITY (ROE)	15.44%	<-- =IRR(B58:G58)					

Note that this equity return increases as the equity investment decreases.[10] Consider the case where the firm initially borrows 1,500 and the equity owners invest 600:

	A	B	C	D	E	F	G	H
56	**RETURN ON EQUITY (ROE)**							
57	**Year**	**0**	**1**	**2**	**3**	**4**	**5**	
58	Equity cash flow	-600	-	-	-	-	1,602	<-- =G22+G36+G37
59	RETURN ON EQUITY (ROE)	21.70%	<-- =IRR(B58:G58)					

As the following data table and graph show, the less the initial equity investment, the greater the equity return:

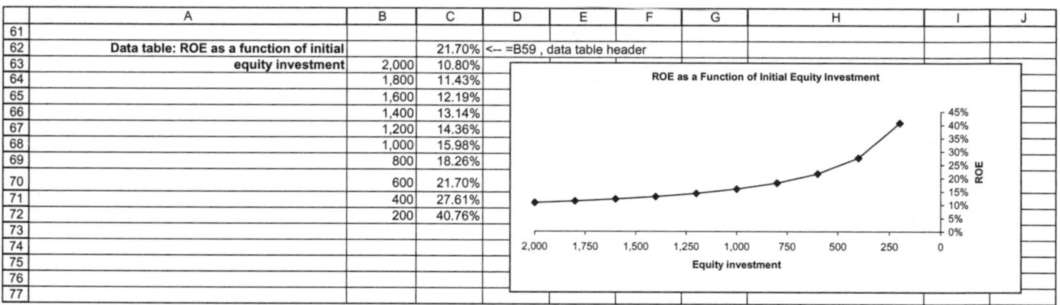

	A	B	C	D
61				
62	**Data table: ROE as a function of initial**		21.70%	<-- =B59 , data table header
63	**equity investment**	2,000	10.80%	
64		1,800	11.43%	
65		1,600	12.19%	
66		1,400	13.14%	
67		1,200	14.36%	
68		1,000	15.98%	
69		800	18.26%	
70		600	21.70%	
71		400	27.61%	
72		200	40.76%	
73				
74				
75				
76				
77				

3.10.1 The ROE in Our First Full Model

The model in sections 3.2–3.4 has annual dividends. If we use the midyear discounting explained in section 3.5.3 to value the firm, we can compute the return on equity (ROE) of an investor who purchases the firm at date 0 at its imputed equity valuation, gets five years of dividends, and sells it for the imputed terminal value of the equity:

10. Interesting but not surprising: As the equity investment goes down, the project becomes more leveraged and hence more risky for the equity investors. The increased return should compensate the equity holders for this extra risk. The really interesting question (not answered here) is whether the increased return is in fact a compensation for the riskiness.

	A	B	C	D	E	F	G	H
1	**COMPUTING THE ROE IN THE FIRST FINANCIAL MODEL**							
2	Sales growth	10%						
3	Current assets/Sales	15%						
4	Current liabilities/Sales	8%						
5	Net fixed assets/Sales	77%						
6	Costs of goods sold/Sales	50%						
7	Depreciation rate	10%						
8	Interest rate on debt	10.00%						
9	Interest paid on cash and marketable securities	8.00%						
10	Tax rate	40%						
11	Dividend payout ratio	40%						
12								
13	**Year**	**0**	**1**	**2**	**3**	**4**	**5**	
14	**Income statement**							
15	Sales	1,000	1,100	1,210	1,331	1,464	1,611	
51								
52								
53	**Valuing the firm (mid-year discounting)**							
54	Weighted average cost of capital	20%						
55	Long-term free cash flow growth rate	5%						
56								
57	**Year**	**0**	**1**	**2**	**3**	**4**	**5**	
58	FCF		176	188	201	214	228	
59	Terminal value						1,598	<-- =G58*(1+B55)/(B54-B55)
60	Total		176	188	201	214	1,826	
61								
62	Enterprise value, NPV of row 60	1,348	<-- =NPV(B54,C60:G60)*(1+B54)^0.5					
63	Add in initial (year 0) cash and mkt. securities	80	<-- =B27					
64	Asset value, year 0	1,428	<-- =B63+B62					
65	Subtract out value of firm's debt today	(320)	<-- =-B36					
66	Equity value	1,108	<-- =B64+B65					
67								
68								
69	**RETURN ON EQUITY (ROE)**							
70	**Year**	**0**	**1**	**2**	**3**	**4**	**5**	
71	Projected dividends	(1,108)	98	108	118	129	141	
72	Anticipated equity value, year 5						1,737	<-- Terminal value + year 5 cash - year 5 debt
73	Equity cash flow	(1,108)	98	108	118	129	1,878	<-- =SUM(G71:G72)
74	RETURN ON EQUITY (ROE)	18.29%	<-- =IRR(B73:G73)					

3.11 Conclusion

Pro forma modeling is one of the basic skills of corporate financial analysis—a devious combination of finance, the implementation of accounting rules, and spreadsheet skills. In order to be useful, financial models must match the situation at hand, but they must also be simple enough so that the user can easily understand *why* the results happen (be they valuations, creditworthiness, or simply commonsense predictions of how a firm or project might look several years down the road).

Exercises

1. Here's a basic exercise that will help you understand what's going on in the modeling of financial statements. Replicate the model in section 3.1. That is, enter the correct formulas for the cells and see that you get the same results as the book. (This turns out to be more of an exercise in accounting than in finance. If you're

like many financial modelers, you'll see that there are some aspects of accounting that you've forgotten!)

2. The model of section 3.1 includes costs of goods sold but not selling, general, and administrative (SG&A) expenses. Suppose that the firm has $200 of these expenses each year, irrespective of the level of sales.

   a. Change the model to accommodate this new assumption. Show the resulting profit and loss statements, balance sheets, the free cash flows, and valuation.

   b. Do a data table in which you show the sensitivity of the equity value to the level of SG&A. Let SG&A vary from $0 per year to $600 per year.

3. Suppose that in the model of section 3.1 the fixed assets *at cost* for years 1–5 are 100 percent of sales (in the current model, it is *net* fixed assets which are a function of sales). Change the model accordingly. Show the resulting profit and loss statements, balance sheets, and free cash flows for years 1–5. (Assume that in year 0, the fixed assets accounts are as shown in section 3.2. Note that since year 0 is given—it is the current situation of the firm, whereas years 1–5 are the predictions for the future—there is no need for the year-0 ratios to conform to the predicted ratios for years 1–5.)

4. Referring again to the model of section 3.2, suppose that the fixed assets at cost follow the following step function:

$$\text{Fixed assets as cost} = \begin{cases} 100\% * \text{Sales} & \text{if Sales} \le 1{,}200 \\ 1{,}200 + 90\% * (\text{Sales} - 1{,}200) & 1{,}200 < \text{Sales} \le 1{,}400 \\ 1{,}380 + 80\% * (\text{Sales} - 1{,}400) & \text{Sales} > 1{,}400 \end{cases}$$

   Incorporate this function into the model.

5. Consider the model in section 3.6 (where debt is the plug).

   a. Suppose that the firm has 1,000 shares and that it decides to pay, in year 1, a dividend per share of 15 cents. In addition, suppose that it wants this dividend per share to grow in subsequent years by 12 percent per year. Incorporate these changes into the pro forma model.

   b. Do a sensitivity analysis in which you show the effect on the debt/equity ratio of the annual growth rate of dividends. Vary this rate from 0 to 18 percent, in steps of 2 percent. For this exercise, define debt as net debt (i.e., debt minus cash and marketable securities). (Note that since the WACC is equal to 20 percent, the growth rate must be less than 20 percent.)

6. In the model of section 3.6, assume that the firm needs to have minimum cash balances of 25 at the end of each year. Introduce this constraint into the model.

7. In the valuation exercise of section 3.4, the terminal value is calculated using a Gordon dividend model on the cash flows. Replace this terminal value by the year-5 book value of debt plus equity. In making this change, you are essentially assuming that the book value correctly predicts the market value.

8. Repeat exercise 7, but this time replace the terminal value by an EBITDA ratio times year-5 anticipated EBITDA. Show a graph of the *equity value* of the firm as a function of the assumed year-5 EBITDA ratio, varying this ratio from 6–14.

9. In the project finance pro forma of section 3.9 it is assumed that the firm pays off its initial debt of $1,000 in equal installments of principal over five years. Change

this assumption and assume instead that the firm pays off its debt in equal payments of interest and principal over five years. Hint: You have to use the **PMT** function to find the annual payments; then set up a loan table (as in Chapter 1) to split the annual payments into an interest and repayment of principal. Alternatively you can use the functions **PPMT** and **IPMT** discussed in Chapter 33.

10. This problem introduces the concept of "sustainable dividends": The firm whose financials are illustrated in the following spreadsheet wishes to maintain cash balances of 80 over the next five years. It also desires neither to issue additional stock nor to make any changes in its current level of debt. As a result, dividends are the plug in the balance sheet. Model this situation (note that for some parameter levels you may get "negative dividends," indicating that there is no sustainable level of dividends).

	A	B	C	D	E	F	G
1	**SUSTAINABLE DIVIDENDS--Template**						
2	Sales growth	10%					
3	Current assets/Sales	15%					
4	Current liabilities/Sales	8%					
5	Net fixed assets/Sales	77%					
6	Costs of goods sold/Sales	50%					
7	Depreciation rate	10%					
8	Interest rate on debt	10.00%					
9	Interest paid on cash & marketable securities	8.00%					
10	Tax rate	40%					
11							
12	**Year**	**0**	**1**	**2**	**3**	**4**	**5**
13	**Income statement**						
14	Sales	1,000					
15	Costs of goods sold	(500)					
16	Interest payments on debt	(32)					
17	Interest earned on cash & marketable securities	6					
18	Depreciation	(100)					
19	Profit before tax	374					
20	Taxes	(150)					
21	Profit after tax	225					
22	Dividends	(90)					
23	Retained earnings	135					
24							
25	**Balance sheet**						
26	Cash and marketable securities	80	80	80	80	80	80
27	Current assets	150					
28	Fixed assets						
29	At cost	1,070					
30	Depreciation	(300)					
31	Net fixed assets	770					
32	**Total assets**	1,000					
33							
34	Current liabilities	80					
35	Debt	320	320	320	320	320	320
36	Stock	450	450	450	450	450	450
37	Accumulated retained earnings	150					
38	**Total liabilities and equity**	1,000					

Appendix 1: Calculating the Free Cash Flows When There Are Negative Profits

We start off with a simple example. A firm that has no depreciation, no changes in net working capital, and no capital expenditures has the following profits in two successive years:

	A	B	C	D
1	**PROFIT AND LOSS WITH CARRYFORWARD**			
2	**Year**	**1**	**2**	
3	Earnings before interest and taxes (EBIT)	-100	400	
4	Interest	-50	-80	
5	Profit before tax	-150	320	<-- =SUM(C3:C4)
6	Loss carryforward	0	-150	<-- =IF(B9<0,B9,0)
7	Taxable income	-150	170	<-- =SUM(C5:C6)
8	Taxes (30%)	0	-51	<-- =-MAX(0,0.3*C7)
9	Profit after tax	-150	119	<-- =C8+C7

Recall that the free cash flow (FCF) is the amount of cash generated by the firm under the assumption that it has no debt. Thus, to calculate the FCFs of the firm, we calculate the profit and loss statement that it would have had (including tax carryforwards) if it had no interest payments:

	A	B	C	D
12	**Free Cash Flow (FCF) with No Debt**			
13	**Year**	**1**	**2**	
14	Earnings before interest and taxes (EBIT)	-100	400	
15	Interest	0	0	
16	Profit before tax	-100	400	
17	Loss carryforward	0	-100	<-- =IF(B20<0,B20,0)
18	Taxable income	-100	300	<-- =SUM(C16:C17)
19	Taxes (30%)	0	-90	<-- =-MAX(0,0.3*C18)
20	Profit after tax	-100	210	<-- =C19+C18
21	Add back tax-loss carryforward	0	100	<-- =-C17
22	Free cash flow (FCF)	-100	310	<-- =C21+C20

The loss carryforward is added back to the profit after tax because it is a *noncash* charge against earnings (like depreciation). We can also do this calculation directly from the profit and loss statement. However, we have to recognize that the tax-loss carryforward includes an element of the interest charges, which needs to be netted out:

	A	B	C	D
24	**CALCULATING FCF FROM PROFIT AND LOSS STATEMENT**			
25	**Year**	**1**	**2**	
26	Earnings before interest and taxes (EBIT)	-100	400	
27	Interest	-50	-80	
28	Profit before tax	-150	320	<-- =C5
29	Loss carryforward	0	-150	<-- =C6
30	Taxable income	-150	170	<-- =C7
31	Taxes (30%)	0	-51	<-- =C8
32	Profit after tax	-150	119	<-- =C9
33				
34	**FCF Calculation**			
35	Profit after tax	-150	119	<-- =C32
36	Add back loss carryforward	0	150	<-- =-C29
37	Add back interest, net of tax	50	56	<-- =-(1-0.3)*C27
38	Subtract interest tax shield on carryforward	0	-15	<-- =0.3*B27
39	Free cash flow (FCF)	-100	310	<-- =SUM(C35:C38)

Appendix 2: Accelerated Depreciation in Pro Forma Models[11]

The models in the chapter all use straight-line depreciation. However, they can be adjusted to accommodate accelerated depreciation (whether this adjustment is worth the effort is another question, which is discussed at the end of this appendix).

As an example, consider a company that depreciates all of its assets using the five-year accelerated cost recovery system (ACRS) depreciation schedule that is part of the 1986 Tax Reduction Act in the United States.[12] The depreciation rates for an asset under this act are as shown in the following table:

	A	B	C
78	**Depreciation Table--Five-Year Asset Life**		
79	**Year**	**Depreciation rate**	**Cumulative depreciation**
80	1	20.00%	20%
81	2	32.00%	52%
82	3	19.20%	71%
83	4	11.52%	83%
84	5	11.52%	94%
85	6	5.76%	100%

11. This appendix contains an advanced topic that can be skipped on first reading.

12. For more information about the ACRS depreciation schedules, you are referred to standard U.S. finance texts (for example, Brealey, Myers, Allen (2005).

(Note that the "five-year" depreciation schedule actually depreciates the asset over six years.)

The following spreadsheet fragment shows the fixed-asset schedule over the next five years:

	A	B	C	D	E	F	G	H
54	**DEPRECIATION CALCULATION--year 0 assets assumed 3 years old**							
55	Sales growth	10%						
56	Net fixed assets/Sales	77%						
57	Sales	1,000	1,100	1,210	1,331	1,464	1,611	
58								
59	**Year**	**0**	**1**	**2**	**3**	**4**	**5**	
60	Fixed assets at cost, end of year	2,674	3,155	3,838	4,536	5,516	6,239	<-- =G62-G61
61	Accumulated depreciation	(1,904)	(2,308)	(2,907)	(3,511)	(4,389)	(4,999)	<-- =-G74
62	Net fixed assets required, end of year	770	847	932	1,025	1,127	1,240	<-- =$B$5*G57
63								
64	New assets acquired during year		481	683	698	980	723	
65								
66	Accumulated depreciation calculation							
67	Accumulated depreciation, end of previous year		1,904	2,308	2,907	3,511	4,389	
68	Depreciation of year 0 assets		308	308	154	154	154	
69	Depreciation of assets acquired year 1		96	154	92	55	55	
70	Depreciation of assets acquired year 2			137	219	131	79	
71	Depreciation of assets acquired y	=VLOOKUP(3+C$59,$A$80:$B$85,2)*$B$60			140	223	134	
72	Depreciation of assets acquired y					314	188	
73	Depreciation of assets acquired year 5						231	
74	**Accumulated depreciation**	1,904	2,308	2,907	3,511	4,389	4,999	<-- =SUM(G67:G72)
75								
76				=VLOOKUP(C$59,$A$80:$B$85,2)*$C$64				
77								
78	**Depreciation table--5-year asset life**				=VLOOKUP(D$59-1,$A$80:$B$85,2)*$D$64			
79	**Year**	**Depr. rate**	**Cum. depr.**					
80	1	20.00%	20%					
81	2	32.00%	52%			=VLOOKUP(E$59-2,$A$80:$B$85,2)*$E$64		
82	3	19.20%	71%					
83	4	11.52%	83%					
84	5	11.52%	94%					
85	6	5.76%	100%					

Here's an explanation of this schedule:

• In each of the years, the ratio of net fixed assets to sales is assumed to be 77 percent. With anticipated sales as in row 57, the required net fixed assets are given in row 62.

• At date 0, the firm's assets are assumed to be three years old. Therefore, the cumulative depreciation on the assets is 71 percent of their initial value (cell C82 $*$ 2,674 = 1,904).

• The cumulative depreciation in years 1–5 is calculated by summing the annual depreciation on each set of assets using the **VLookup** function (for a description of this function, see Chapter 34).

• The results from the cumulative depreciation calculated in the previous screen are then referenced in row 61. The fixed assets at cost are calculated in row 60.

Is the Modeling of Accelerated Depreciation Worth the Effort?

As you can see, writing pro forma models to account for accelerated depreciation is a fairly big mess! Modeling accelerated depreciation requires additional assumptions about the schedule in use for the assets (i.e., are assets depreciated on a three-year, five-year, seven-year, . . . schedule?). It also requires the modeler to make assumptions about the average age of existing assets; in the present example we have assumed that assets are all depreciated on a five-year schedule and that existing assets in place at date 0 are three years old. Accelerated depreciation also requires separate depreciation schedules for assets acquired in each year.

As a financial analyst, you have to ask yourself whether this is worth the effort. In our opinion the detailed analysis of accelerated depreciation is worthwhile only in cases where the firm has large amounts of fixed assets that generate significantly large accretions to the fixed-asset base (meaning that the cash-flow effect of doing an accelerated-fixed-asset calculation versus a straight-line calculation is large). In Chapter 4 we return to this topic when we model both straight-line depreciation and deferred taxes instead of modeling the accelerated depreciation.

4 Building a Financial Model: The Case of PPG Corporation

4.1 Overview

In this chapter we implement the ideas of Chapter 3 and build a financial model for PPG Corporation. PPG is a large diversified manufacturer of chemicals, paints, and glass (the initials stand for Pittsburgh Paint and Glass). The company is the world's largest manufacturer of auto glass. In 2000, PPG had sales of $8.6 billion and profits of $620 million. The company has more than 35,000 employees and has paid a dividend continuously for 103 years.

In this chapter we

- Analyze the financial statements of PPG for the years 1991–2000.
- Use our analysis to build a pro forma model for the company for the years 2001–2005.
- Calculate the cost of capital for PPG and use this cost of capital to value the company and its shares.
- Do some appropriate sensitivity analysis on our calculations.

WARNING! This Chapter May Be Deleterious to Your Mental Health![1]

The material in this chapter is irritating and complicated but *not difficult*. Why irritating? Because financial models require a lot of assumptions and analysis. Everything is related to almost everything else. And because they require you to recall some basic accounting concepts.

However, the case in this chapter illustrates one of the most important corporate finance applications: the valuation of a company in the framework of its accounting and financial parameters. Such valuations are the core of most business plans, corporate financial planning models, and (intelligent) analyst valuations.

1. It certainly affected the author's mental stability.

4.2 PPG Financial Statements, 1991–2000

The next pages contain historical information and analysis about the balance sheets and income statements of PPG Corporation from 1991 to 2000. In section 4.3 we analyze these statements with a view to developing parameters to use in our financial model for PPG. In this section we present the statements and make several comments about them.

Cash and short-term investments Some firms use this item to build up a "nest egg" of assets which can be used as needed (for acquisitions, to pay for a dividend, etc.), but PPG keeps relatively low balances of cash. In the balance sheets of other firms, this item is often called "cash and cash equivalents" or "cash and marketable securities."

Other assets and other liabilities These items are primarily the assets and liabilities of the pension plans of PPG. The "other assets" represent the market value of PPG's pension assets and the "other liabilities" represent the present value of PPG's future pension liabilities. Note that the gap between the two has increased over the last 10 years—PPG's promised benefits to its employees are growing faster than the assets from which these benefits are to be paid.

Intangibles This item covers goodwill (see appendix to this chapter for a discussion) and a variety of other methods. Starting in 2001, this item is no longer depreciated.[2] At the end of 2000, PPG had intangibles of $1,071 million on its books.

Accounts payable and accrued expenses Accounts payable are usually due to costs of goods sold that are unpaid, whereas accrued expenses results from other unpaid expenses of the company (wages, SG&A, etc.).

Deferred taxes As discussed in appendix A.1, this item is due to the difference in reported depreciation for shareholder purposes and the (accelerated) depreciation with which PPG pays its taxes.

Minority interest PPG's balance sheets include the full value of certain companies and subsidiaries that it does not fully own. The *minority interest* is the book value of the equity of these companies not owned by PPG. This topic is discussed in the appendix.

2. This treatment of goodwill amortization is contained in FASB 142. Note also that in any case the depreciation of this item was never an expense for tax purposes in the United States.

	A	B	C	D	E	F	G	H	I	J	K
1	**PPG CORPORATION BALANCE SHEETS, 1991-2000 (Million $)**										
2	**ASSETS**	**2000**	**1999**	**1998**	**1997**	**1996**	**1995**	**1994**	**1993**	**1992**	**1991**
3	Cash and short-term investments	111	158	128	129	70	106	62	112	61	38
4	Receivables	1,563	1,594	1,366	1,353	1,226	1,245	1,229	997	1,023	1,058
5	Inventories - total	1,121	1,016	917	863	797	738	686	683	742	875
6	Other current assets	298	294	249	239	205	187	191	234	124	203
7	Total current assets	3,093	3,062	2,660	2,584	2,296	2,276	2,168	2,026	1,951	2,173
8											
9	Property, plant, and equipment, gross	7,089	6,859	6,739	6,758	6,688	6,464	6,163	6,042	6,158	6,212
10	Depreciation, depletion, and amortization (accumulated)	4,148	3,926	3,834	3,903	3,775	3,629	3,420	3,255	3,186	3,029
11	Property, plant, and equipment, net	2,941	2,933	2,905	2,855	2,914	2,835	2,742	2,787	2,972	3,183
12											
13	Intangibles	1,700	1,685	632	370	23	0	0	0	0	0
14	Other assets	1,391	1,234	1,190	1,059	1,208	1,084	983	838	739	700
15	**TOTAL ASSETS**	9,125	8,914	7,387	6,868	6,441	6,194	5,894	5,652	5,662	6,056
16											
17											
18	**LIABILITIES**										
19	Accounts payable	764	755	630	646	602	583	518	436	447	520
20	Accrued expense	606	649	634	564	504	520	481	423	323	348
21	Other current liabilities	12	26	11	8	15	41	55	67	48	62
22											
23	Debt	2,971	2,790	1,718	1,701	1,482	1,221	1,144	1,129	1,307	1,574
24	Deferred taxes	543	520	440	406	419	355	303	269	472	476
25	Minority interest	128	98	87	82	76	68	70	52	60	76
26	Other liabilities	1,004	970	987	952	861	837	766	803	306	347
27											
28	**EQUITY**										
29	Common stock	484	484	484	484	484	484	484	242	242	242
30	Capital surplus	102	104	105	99	97	81	68	298	233	230
31	Retained earnings	6,019	5,786	5,489	4,916	4,569	4,063	3,494	3,158	3,424	3,369
32	Less: treasury stock - total dollar amount	3,508	3,268	3,198	2,990	2,667	2,060	1,489	1,225	1,200	1,186
33	Total stockholders equity	3,097	3,106	2,880	2,509	2,483	2,569	2,557	2,473	2,699	2,655
34	**TOTAL LIABILITIES AND EQUITY**	9,125	8,914	7,387	6,868	6,441	6,194	5,894	5,652	5,662	6,056

	A	B	C	D	E	F	G	H	I	J	K
1	PPG CORPORATION INCOME STATEMENTS, 1991-2000 (Million $)										
2		2000	1999	1998	1997	1996	1995	1994	1993	1992	1991
3	Sales	8,629	7,757	7,510	7,379	7,218	7,058	6,331	5,754	5,814	5,673
4	Cost of goods sold	5,334	4,696	4,476	4,397	4,340	4,212	3,866	3,633	3,695	3,676
5	Selling, general, and administrative expense	1,646	1,514	1,404	1,318	1,243	1,214	1,137	1,073	1,083	1,079
6	Operating income before depreciation	1,649	1,547	1,630	1,664	1,634	1,632	1,329	1,048	1,036	918
7	Depreciation and amortization	447	415	354	348	340	332	318	331	352	351
8	Interest expense	193	142	119	115	108	93	91	109	148	169
9	Nonoperating income (expense) and special items	8	-17	137	-26	.	.	-64	-63	.	-44
10	Pretax income	1,017	973	1,294	1,175	1,240	1,262	856	544	542	354
11	Income taxes - total	369	377	466	435	471	480	325	236	218	147
12	Minority interest	28	28	27	26	25	15	16	13	4	5
13	Income before extraordinary items	620	568	801	714	744	768	515	295	319	201
14	Extraordinary items and discontinued operations	0	0	0	0	0	0	0	-273	0	75
15	Net income (loss)	620	568	801	714	744	767.6	514.6	22.2	319.4	276.2
16	Cash dividends	276	264	252	239	237	239	238	221	200	183
17	Retained	344	304	549	475	507	529	277	-199	120	94

4.3 Analyzing the Financial Statements

We're going to build a set of financial statements with roughly the same format as the historical statements.[3] In order to do so, we have to analyze the statements and make some decisions about plausible predictions and projections for the future.

4.3.1 Sales Projections

The sales projection is one of the most critical elements in our model of PPG; it is central to determining the value of the company in the financial model we build. Before we start, here are some details of PPG's sales between 1990 and 2000:

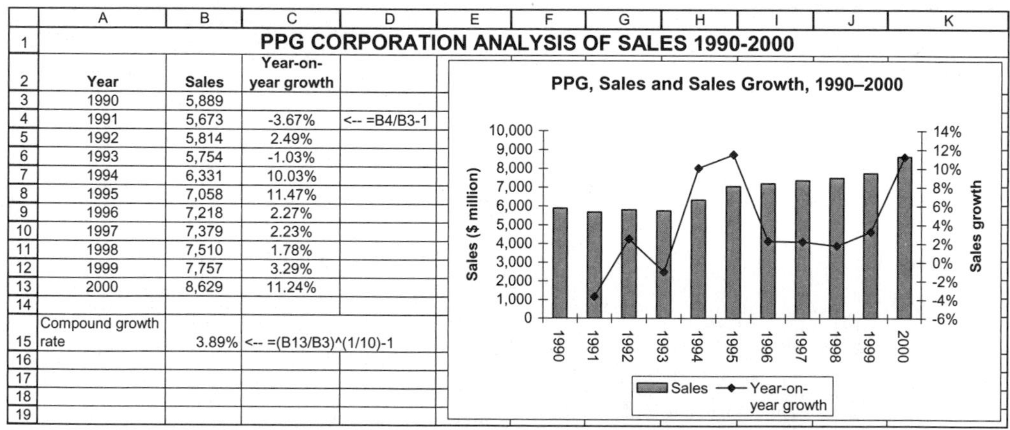

	A	B	C	D
1	PPG CORPORATION ANALYSIS OF SALES 1990-2000			
2	Year	Sales	Year-on-year growth	
3	1990	5,889		
4	1991	5,673	-3.67%	<-- =B4/B3-1
5	1992	5,814	2.49%	
6	1993	5,754	-1.03%	
7	1994	6,331	10.03%	
8	1995	7,058	11.47%	
9	1996	7,218	2.27%	
10	1997	7,379	2.23%	
11	1998	7,510	1.78%	
12	1999	7,757	3.29%	
13	2000	8,629	11.24%	
14				
15	Compound growth rate	3.89%	<-- =(B13/B3)^(1/10)-1	
16				
17				
18				
19				

3. We already made lots of judgment calls in the historical financial statements. For example, we combined all the debt items into one.

There are two things to notice about PPG's historic sales:

• Average sales growth is quite low (around 4 percent), as befits a company in a mature industry. In such an industry we would expect sales growth to be approximately the average growth of the economy as a whole.

• The growth pattern is very *cyclical*. This is typical of the chemicals industry. PPG's growth seems to fluctuate between low (and even negative) growth and high rates of growth.

Projection In our base-case projection (see section 4.6), we will assume that PPG's future sales growth is 4 percent. In the exercise at the end of the chapter we will let you use a variation where the growth is high for 2001 and 2002 and much lower afterward.

4.3.2 Profit and Loss Analysis

We analyze the ratios for the profit and loss statement. Our general approach is that the primary ratios are percentages of sales:

	A	B	C	D	E	F	G	H	I	J
28	**Profit and loss historical ratios**	**2000**	**1999**	**1998**	**1997**	**1996**	**1995**	**1994**	**1993**	**1992**
29	COGS/Sales	61.81%	60.54%	59.60%	59.59%	60.13%	59.68%	61.05%	63.14%	63.55%
30	SG&A/Sales	19.08%	19.52%	18.70%	17.86%	17.23%	17.19%	17.96%	18.65%	18.62%
31	Total costs/Sales (sum of above items)	80.89%	80.06%	78.30%	77.45%	77.36%	76.87%	79.02%	81.79%	82.18%
32										
33	Depreciation/Gross fixed assets	6.31%	6.05%	5.25%	5.15%	5.09%	5.13%	5.15%	5.48%	5.71%
34	Interest expense/Average debt	6.70%	6.30%	6.96%	7.23%	7.96%	7.88%	8.04%	8.96%	10.30%
35	Incomes taxes/Pretax income	36.28%	38.75%	36.01%	37.02%	38.00%	38.00%	38.00%	43.41%	40.31%
36	Minority Interest/(Pretax - Taxes)	4.32%	4.70%	3.26%	3.51%	3.20%	1.92%	3.00%	4.19%	1.24%
37	Dividends/Net income	44.52%	46.48%	31.46%	33.47%	31.80%	31.12%	46.21%	994.59%	62.49%
38										
39	**Profit and loss--model parameters**									
40	COGS/Sales	61.39%	<-- =AVERAGE(B29:K29)							
41	SG&A/Sales	18.38%	<-- =AVERAGE(B30:K30)							
42	Depreciation/Gross fixed assets	6.31%	<-- =B33							
43	Interest rate	6.70%	<-- =B34							
44	Tax rate	36.28%	<-- =B35							
45	Minority Interest/(Pretax - Taxes)	4.32%	<-- =B36							
46	Dividend growth	6.00%	<-- See explanation later on							

Model Parameters Our choice of model parameters (rows 40–46) may appear to be idiosyncratic. In some cases—for example in COGS/Sales and SG&A/Sales—we have decided to use the historical averages of the parameters. In other cases—for example, the depreciation rate, the firm's interest rate on future borrowings, and the percentage of earnings paid to minority interests—we have chosen to ignore historical information and to use only the last year's values. In the case of modeling the firm's future dividends, we have chosen another approach entirely—we will assume that the firm's total dividends will grow by 4.13 percent per year; an explanation for this assumption is given in section 4.9.

In every case we tried to make our parameter choice an *intelligent, informed* reflection of our knowledge of the firm.[4]

4.3.3 Balance Sheet Analysis

We analyze the balance sheet ratios as follows:

	A	B	C	D	E	F	G	H	I	J	K
39	**Balance sheet--historical ratios**										
40	**ASSETS**	**2000**	**1999**	**1998**	**1997**	**1996**	**1995**	**1994**	**1993**	**1992**	**1991**
41	Cash and short-term investments										
42	Receivables/Sales	18.11%	20.55%	18.19%	18.34%	16.98%	17.64%	19.41%	17.32%	17.60%	18.65%
43	Inventories/Sales	12.99%	13.10%	12.21%	11.70%	11.03%	10.45%	10.84%	11.88%	12.77%	15.43%
44	Other current assets/Sales	3.45%	3.79%	3.32%	3.24%	2.84%	2.65%	3.01%	4.07%	2.13%	3.57%
45	Operating CA/Sales	35.84%	39.47%	35.42%	35.02%	31.81%	32.24%	34.25%	35.21%	33.55%	38.31%
46											
47	Property, plant, equipment, gross/Sales	82.15%	88.42%	89.73%	91.58%	92.66%	91.59%	97.34%	105.01%	105.91%	109.52%
48	Annual depreciation/PPE	6.31%	6.05%	5.25%	5.15%	5.09%	5.13%	5.15%	5.48%	5.71%	5.65%
49	Property, Plant, equipment, net/Sales	34.08%	37.81%	38.68%	38.69%	40.36%	40.17%	43.31%	48.44%	51.11%	56.12%
50											
51	Other assets/Sales	16.12%	15.91%	15.85%	14.35%	16.74%	15.36%	15.53%	14.57%	12.72%	12.33%
52	Other assets, growth rate since 1991	7.93%	<-- =(B14/K14)^(1/9)-1								
53											
54	**LIABILITIES**										
55	Accounts payable/Sales	8.85%	9.73%	8.39%	8.75%	8.34%	8.27%	8.18%	7.58%	7.69%	9.17%
56	Accrued expense/Sales	7.02%	8.37%	8.44%	7.64%	6.98%	7.37%	7.60%	7.34%	5.56%	6.13%
57	Other Current liabilities/Sales	0.14%	0.34%	0.15%	0.11%	0.21%	0.58%	0.87%	1.17%	0.83%	1.09%
58	Operating CL/Sales	16.02%	18.43%	16.98%	16.51%	15.52%	16.21%	16.64%	16.09%	14.08%	16.40%
59											
60	Debt										
61	Debt/Equity	95.93%	89.83%	59.65%	67.80%	59.70%	47.52%	44.74%	45.66%	48.42%	59.28%
62	Debt/Assets	32.56%	31.30%	23.26%	24.77%	23.01%	19.71%	19.41%	19.98%	23.08%	25.98%
63											
64	Other liabilities/Sales	11.64%	12.50%	13.14%	12.90%	11.92%	11.86%	12.10%	13.95%	5.26%	6.12%
65	Other liabilities, growth rate since 1991	12.53%	<-- =(B26/K26)^(1/9)-1								

Model Parameters We use the historical ratios to project future anticipated ratios. As in the case of our parameter choice for the income statement, we make no claims for consistency, preferring instead to use our judgment (or lack of judgment). Following are our choices.

4. And just to make sure, we'll do sensitivity analysis on the parameters to test whether a different choice would have an impact.

	A	B	C	D	E	F	G
67	**Balance sheet--model parameters**						
68	**ASSETS**						
69	Cash and short-term investments	constant					
70	Receivables/Sales	18.28%	<-- =AVERAGE(B42:K42)				
71	Inventories/Sales	12.24%	<-- =AVERAGE(B43:K43)				
72	Other current assets/Sales	3.21%	<-- =AVERAGE(B44:K44)				
73	Operating CA/Sales	35.11%	<-- =AVERAGE(B45:K45)				
74							
75	Property, plant, equipment, gross	=accrued depreciation + net plant, property, equipment					
76	Accrued depreciation	=previous year's accrued + this year's depreciation from income					
77	Property, plant, equipment, net/Sales	34.08%	<-- =B49				
78							
79	Other assets, annual growth rate	7.93%	<-- =B52				
80							
81	**LIABILITIES**						
82	Accounts payable/Sales	8.50%					
83	Accrued expense/Sales	7.25%					
84	Other current liabilities/Sales	12	<-- constant at current level				
85							
86	Debt/Assets	32%	<-- approximately current level				
87	Deferred taxes	grows at sales growth					
88	Minority Interest	128	<-- constant at current level				
89	Other liabilities, annual growth rate	12.53%	<-- =B65				
90							
91	**EQUITY**						
92	Common stock	484					
93	Capital surplus	102					
94	Retained earnings	=previous year's retained + this year's retentions from income statement					
95	Treasury stock - total dollar amount	PLUG					

Net Fixed Assets/Sales PPG made great efforts over the 1991–2000 decade to become more efficient. These are reflected in the steady decline of the ratio of net plant, property, and equipment to sales.

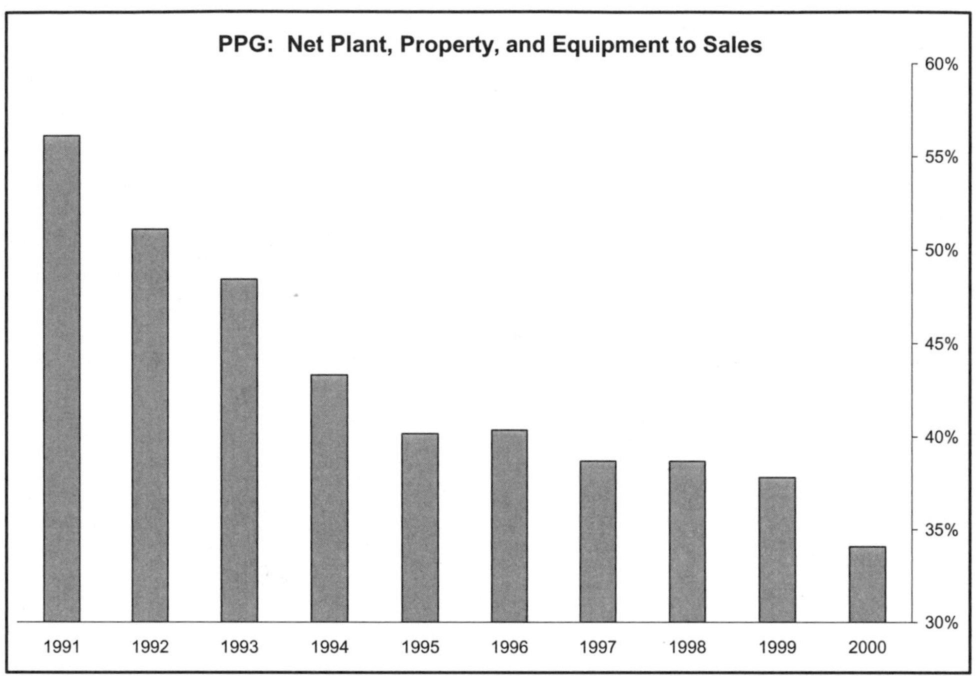

PPG became much more efficient during the 1990s: In 1991 it took about $560 of net fixed assets to produce $1,000 of sales; by 2000 it took only $340 of fixed assets to produce $1,000 of sales. The modeling question is whether this trend will continue. In our model we have assumed that it will not, and that PPG will maintain (but not improve) its current level of efficiency.[5]

4.4 A Model for PPG

We are now ready to model PPG's financial statements. We use the following model to project PPG's financial statements for 2001. The model uses the naming feature of Excel to name most of the cells. To name a cell, click on the **Name Box** and write in the name you choose for the cell:

5. This is an important parameter. In one of the exercises we ask you to perform some sensitivity analysis on PPE/Sales and judge its effect on the company's earnings and valuation.

cogs_sales | ='Income statements 1991-2000'!B40

	A	B	C
1		PPG, FINANCIAL MODEL first year only--2001	
2	**Profit and loss assumptions**		**Cell names**
3	Sales growth	3.89%	<-- =growth
4	COGS/Sales	61.39%	<-- =cogs_sales
5	SG&A/Sales	18.38%	<-- =sga_sales
6	Depreciation/Gross fixed assets	6.31%	<-- =depr_perc
7	Interest rate	6.70%	<-- =interest

4.4.1 What Is the Plug in the Model?

Our model assumes that PPG will have a debt/assets ratio of 32 percent and that treasury stock will be the plug. The basic assumption is that additional cash will be used to repurchase equity. We will discuss this issue further later on. For the moment, examine the following model and note that treasury stock is indeed the plug:

Treasury stock = −C62 + SUM(C66:C78)
= All current liabilities + Debt + Deferred taxes + Minority interest + Other liabilities + Common stock + Capital surplus + Retained earnings − Total assets

If you turn this equation around (putting Total assets on the left-hand side and Treasury stock on the right-hand side), then you see why we've correctly described the plug:

Total assets = All current liabilities + Debt + Deferred taxes
+ Minority interest + Other liabilities
+ Common stock + Capital surplus
+ Retained earnings − Treasury stock
= Total liabilities and equity

Here's the model:

	A	B	C	D
1	**PPG, FINANCIAL MODEL First year only--2001**			
2	**Profit and loss assumptions**		**Cell names**	
3	Sales growth	3.89%	<-- growth	
4	COGS/Sales	61.39%	<-- cogs_sales	
5	SG&A/Sales	18.38%	<-- sga_sales	
6	Depreciation/Gross fixed assets	6.31%	<-- depr_perc	
7	Interest rate	6.70%	<-- interest	
8	Minority interest as % of PAT	4.32%	<-- minority	
9	Growth rate of total dividends	4.13%	<-- divgrowth	
10	Tax rate	36.28%	<-- tax	
11				
12	**Balance sheet assumptions**			
13	**Assets**			
14	Cash and short-term investments	constant		
15	Receivables/Sales	18.28%	<-- ar_sales	
16	Inventories/Sales	12.24%	<-- inventory_sales	
17	Other current assets/Sales	3.21%	<-- otherca_sales	
18	Property, plant, equipment, net/Sales	34.08%	<-- ppe_sales	
19	Investments and advances	constant		
20	Other assets, annual growth rate	7.93%	<-- otherassets_growth	
21				
22	**Liabilities**			
23	Accounts payable/Sales	8.50%	<-- ap_sales	
24	Accrued expense/Sales	7.25%	<-- accruedexp_sales	
25	Other current liabilities/Sales	constant		
26				
27	Debt/Assets	32.00%	<-- debt_assets	
28	Deferred taxes	growth at sales growth		
29	Minority interest	constant		
30	Other liabilities, annual growth	12.53%	<-- otherliab_growth	
31	Treasury stock	plug		
32				
33	**PROFIT AND LOSS**	**2000**	**2001**	
34	Sales	8,629	8,965	<-- =B34*(1+growth)
35	Cost of goods sold	5,334	5,503	<-- =sales2001*cogs_sales
36	Selling, general, and administrative expense	1,646	1,648	<-- =sales2001*sga_sales
37	Operating income before depreciation	1,649	1,813	<-- =sales2001-C35-C36
38	Depreciation and amortization	447	465	<-- =depr_perc*AVERAGE(B55:C55)
39	Interest expense	193	200	<-- =interest*AVERAGE(B69:C69)
40	Nonoperating Income (expense) and special Items	8	8	<-- =B40
41	Pretax income	1,017	1,140	<-- =C37-C38-C39-C40
42	Income taxes - total	369	414	<-- =tax*C41
43	Minority interest	28	18	<-- =minority*C42
44	Net income	620	709	<-- =C41-C42-C43
45	Dividend	276	287	<-- =B45*(1+divgrowth)
46	Retained earnings	344	421	<-- =C44-C45

	A	B	C	D
48	**ASSETS**	**2000**	**2001**	
49	Cash and short-term investments	111	111	<-- =B49
50	Receivables	1,563	1,639	<-- =ar_sales*sales2001
51	Inventories - total	1,121	1,097	<-- =inventory_sales*sales2001
52	Other current assets	298	287	<-- =otherca_sales*sales2001
53	Total current assets	3,093	3,134	<-- =SUM(C49:C52)
54				
55	Property, plant, and equipment, gross	7,089	7,669	<-- =C56+C57
56	Depreciation, depletion, and amortization (accumulated)	4,148	4,613	<-- =B56+C38
57	Property, plant, and equipment, net	2,941	3,055	<-- =ppe_sales*sales2001
58				
59	Investments and advances	320	320	<-- =B59
60	Intangibles	1,700	1,700	<-- =B60
61	Other assets	1,071	1,156	<-- =B61*(1+otherassets_growth)
62	**TOTAL ASSETS**	9,125	9,366	<-- =SUM(C57:C61)+C53
63				
64	**LIABILITIES**	**2000**	**2001**	
65	Accounts payable	764	762	<-- =ap_sales*sales2001
66	Accrued expense	606	650	<-- =accruedexp_sales*sales2001
67	Other current liabilities	12	12	<-- =B67
68				
69	Debt	2,971	2,997	<-- =debt_assets*C62
70	Deferred taxes	543	564	<-- =B70*(1+growth)
71	Minority interest	128	128	<-- =B71
72	Other liabilities	1,004	1,130	<-- =B72*(1+otherliab_growth)
73				
74	**EQUITY**			
75	Common stock	484	484	<-- =B75
76	Capital surplus	102	102	<-- =B76
77	Retained earnings	6,019	6,440	<-- =B77+C46
78	Less: treasury stock	3,508	3,903	<-- =-C62+SUM(C65:C77)
79	Total stockholders equity	3,097	3,124	<-- =SUM(C75:C77)-C78
80	**TOTAL LIABILITIES AND EQUITY**	9,125	9,366	<-- =SUM(C65:C72)+C79

Here's the calculation of the free cash flow:

	A	B	C	D
83	**FREE CASH FLOW**		**2001**	
84	Profit after tax		709	<-- =C44
85	Add back depreciation		465	<-- =C38
86	Change in net working capital			
87	Increase in operating current assets		-41	<-- =+SUM(B50:B52)-SUM(C50:C52)
88	Add increase in operating current liabilities		41	<-- =SUM(C65:C67)-SUM(B65:B67)
89	Subtract capital expenditures		-580	<-- =-C55+B55
90	Subtract increase in other assets		-85	<-- =-C61+B61
91	Add back after-tax interest		127	<-- =(1-tax)*C39
92	FCF		636	<-- =SUM(C84:C91)

4.5 Back to Treasury Stock and the Dividend

Our model explains (1) how much money the firm pays to its shareholders and (2) how this amount was financed. In 2001 we predict that PPG will pay its shareholders \$682 million—\$287 million through dividends and a further \$395 million through share repurchases:

	A	B	C	D
95	**What's paid out to shareholders?**		**2001**	
96	Dividend		287	<-- =C45
97	Calculating the share repurchases			
98	New stock raised (*negative* equity payout)		0	<-- =SUM(C75:C76)-SUM(B75:B76)
99	Additional treasury stock (positive equity payout)		395	<-- =C78-B78
100	Paid out to shareholders = Dividend - New stock + Additional treasury		682	<-- =C96-C98+C99
101				
102	**How was this financed?**			
103	Free cash flow		636	<-- =C92
104	Additional debt financing		26	<-- =C69-B69
105	Increase in deferred taxes		21	<-- =C70-B70
106	Increase in minority interest		0	<-- =C71-B71
107	Increase in other liabilities		126	<-- =C72-B72
108	Interest after tax		127	<-- =(1-tax)*C39
109	Paid out to shareholders		682	<-- =SUM(C103:C107)-C108

4.6 The Whole Model

Here's the whole model:

	A	B	C	D	E	F	G
1	**PPG, FINANCIAL MODEL, 2001-2005**						
2	**Profit and loss assumptions**						
3	Sales growth	3.89%					
4	COGS/Sales	61.39%					
5	SG&A/Sales	18.38%					
6	Depreciation/Gross fixed assets	6.31%					
7	Interest rate	6.70%					
8	Minority interest as % of PAT	4.32%					
9	Growth rate of total dividends	4.13%					
10	Tax rate	36.28%					
11							
12	**Balance sheet assumptions**						
13	**Assets**						
14	Cash and short-term investments	constant					
15	Receivables/Sales	18.28%					
16	Inventories/Sales	12.24%					
17	Other Current Assets/Sales	3.21%					
18	Property, Plant, Equipment, Net/Sales	34.08%					
19	Investments and advances	constant					
20	Other Assets/Sales	7.93%					
21							
22	**Liabilities**						
23	Accounts Payable/Sales	8.50%					
24	Accrued Expense/Sales	7.25%					
25	Other Current Liabilities/Sales	constant					
26							
27	Debt/Assets	32.00%					
28	Deferred Taxes	growth at sales growth					
29	Minority Interest	assumed constant					
30	Other liabilities, annual growth	12.53%					
31	Treasury stock	plug					
32							
33	**PROFIT AND LOSS**	**2000**	**2001**	**2002**	**2003**	**2004**	**2005**
34	Sales	8,629	8,965	9,313	9,676	10,052	10,443
35	Cost of Goods Sold	5,334	5,503	5,718	5,940	6,171	6,411
36	Selling, General, and Administrative Expense	1,646	1,648	1,712	1,779	1,848	1,920
37	Operating Income Before Depreciation	1,649	1,813	1,884	1,957	2,033	2,112
38	Depreciation and Amortization	447	465	503	544	587	634
39	Interest Expense	193	200	204	212	219	227
40	Nonoperating Income (Expense) and Special Items	8	8	8	8	8	8
41	Pretax Income	1,017	1,156	1,184	1,210	1,235	1,259
42	Income Taxes - Total	369	419	430	439	448	457
43	Minority Interest	28	18	19	19	19	20
44	Net Income	620	718	736	752	767	783
45	Dividend	276	287	299	312	324	338
46	Accrued	344	431	437	440	443	445

	A	B	C	D	E	F	G
48	**ASSETS**	**2000**	**2001**	**2002**	**2003**	**2004**	**2005**
49	Cash and Short-Term Investments	111	111	111	111	111	111
50	Receivables	1,563	1,639	1,702	1,769	1,837	1,909
51	Inventories - Total	1,121	1,097	1,140	1,184	1,230	1,278
52	Other Current Assets	298	287	299	310	322	335
53	Total Current Assets	3,093	3,134	3,252	3,374	3,501	3,633
54							
55	Property, Plant, and Equipment, Gross	7,089	7,669	8,291	8,958	9,674	10,441
56	Depreciation, Depletion, and Amortization (Accumulated)	4,148	4,613	5,116	5,660	6,248	6,882
57	Property, Plant, and Equipment, Net	2,941	3,055	3,174	3,298	3,426	3,559
58							
59	Investments and Advances	320	320	320	320	320	320
60	Intangibles	1,700	1,700	1,700	1,700	1,700	1,700
61	Other Assets	1,071	1,156	1,248	1,347	1,454	1,569
62	**TOTAL ASSETS**	9,125	9,366	9,694	10,039	10,401	10,781
63							
64	**LIABILITIES**	**2000**	**2001**	**2002**	**2003**	**2004**	**2005**
65	Accounts Payable	764	762	791	822	854	887
66	Accrued Expense	606	650	675	701	728	757
67	Other Current Liabilities	12	12	12	12	12	12
68							
69	Debt	2,971	2,997	3,102	3,212	3,328	3,450
70	Deferred Taxes	543	564	586	609	633	657
71	Minority Interest	128	128	128	128	128	128
72	Other Liabilities	1,004	1,130	1,271	1,431	1,610	1,812
73							
74	**EQUITY**						
75	Common Stock	484	484	484	484	484	484
76	Capital Surplus	102	102	102	102	102	102
77	Retained Earnings	6,019	6,450	6,887	7,327	7,770	8,215
78	Less: Treasury Stock	3,508	3,912	4,345	4,790	5,248	5,722
79	Total Stockholders Equity	3,097	3,124	3,128	3,124	3,107	3,078
80	**TOTAL LIABILITIES AND EQUITY**	9,125	9,366	9,694	10,039	10,401	10,781

4.7 Free Cash Flows and Valuation

We haven't yet determined the cost of capital of this company (we do so in sections 4.10–4.12). Suppose it's 10 percent. Then here's a valuation:

	A	B	C	D	E	F	G	H	I	J
83	**FREE CASH FLOW (FCF)**		**2001**	**2002**	**2003**	**2004**	**2005**			
84	Profit after tax		718	736	752	767	783			
85	Add back depreciation		465	503	544	587	634			
86	Change in net working capital									
87	Increase in operating current assets		-41	-118	-122	-127	-132			
88	Add increase in operating current liabilities		41	55	57	59	62			
89	Subtract capital expenditures		-580	-622	-667	-716	-767			
90	Subtract increase in other assets		-85	-92	-99	-107	-115			
91	Add back after-tax interest		127	130	135	140	145			
92	**FCF**		646	593	599	604	608			
93										
94										
95	**Valuing PPG**									
96	WACC	10.00%								
97	Long-term free cash flow growth rate	5%								
98										
99	Year		**2001**	**2002**	**2003**	**2004**	**2005**			
100	FCF		646	593	599	604	608			
101	Terminal						12,774	<-- =G100*(1+B97)/(B96-B97)		
102	Total		646	593	599	604	13,382			
103										
104	Discounted value	10,750	<-- =NPV(B96,C102:G102)*(1+B96)^0.5							
105	Add back initial cash	111								
106	Firm value	10,861								
107	Subtract total debt value, Dec.00	4,646	<-- =SUM(B69:B72) -- this is controversial!							
108	Implied equity value	6,215								
109										
110	Number of shares outstanding, Dec.00	168.22								
111	Implied value per share	36.94								
112										
113	Market price per share, Dec. 00	46.31								
114	PPG over or under-valued?	overvalued	<-- =IF(B111>B113*1.1,"undervalued",IF(B111<B113/1.1,"overvalued","ok"))							

Following are some comments on our valuation.

4.7.1 Terminal Value

As discussed in Chapter 3, we've used a perpetuity model to arrive at the firm's terminal value:

$$\text{Terminal value} = \frac{FCF_{2005} * (1 + \text{Long-term growth rate})}{WACC - \text{Long-term growth rate}}$$

The estimate of the long-term growth rate (5% in this example) and the estimate of the difference between this long-term growth and the WACC (also 5% in our example) is critical for the valuation. Our 5 percent estimate for long-term growth is based on the assumption that in mature markets, such as those in which PPG operates, growth will be approximated by *real growth* of the economy (~2% per year) plus *inflation* (~2–4% per year). A small change in the long-term growth assumption can lead to significant differences in the valuation; for example, if we assume that long-term growth is equal to 6 percent, our valuation of PPG's stock increases to \$49.90, which leads us to conclude that the current market valuation is "ok." (In the spreadsheet cell B114 we've defined an "ok" valuation as one that is within 10% of the current market price. Otherwise the stock is either over- or undervalued.)

	A	B	C	D	E	F	G	H	I	J
95	**Valuing PPG**									
96	WACC	10.00%								
97	Long-term free cash flow growth rate	6%								
98										
99	Year		**2001**	**2002**	**2003**	**2004**	**2005**			
100	FCF		646	593	599	604	608			
101	Terminal						16,119	<-- =G100*(1+B97)/(B96-B97)		
102	Total		646	593	599	604	16,728			
103										
104	Discounted value	12,928	<-- =NPV(B96,C102:G102)*(1+B96)^0.5							
105	Add back initial cash	111								
106	Firm value	13,039								
107	Subtract total debt value, Dec.00	4,646	<-- =SUM(B69:B72) -- this is controversial!							
108	Implied equity value	8,393								
109										
110	Number of shares outstanding, Dec.00	168.22								
111	Implied value per share	49.90								
112										
113	Market price per share, Dec. 00	46.31								
114	PPG over or under-valued?	ok	<-- =IF(B111>B113*1.1,"undervalued",IF(B111<B113/1.1,"overvalued","ok"))							

4.7.2 Midyear Discounting

As discussed in Chapter 3, we assume that the FCFs and the terminal value occur *throughout the year* and not at year-end. As an approximation, we assume that they occur in midyear. This assumption requires that the Excel NPV formula in cell B104 be adjusted by a factor of $(1 + WACC)^{0.5}$.

4.7.3 Dealing with Initial Cash and Debt

In principle, the valuation format is as follows:

Valuation Schematic

Item	Why?
Enterprise value = PV of future FCFs and terminal value.	The enterprise value is the discounted value of the firm's future anticipated *business cash flows*, represented here by the free cash flow (FCF).
Add in initial cash.	The cash on the firm's balance sheet at end-year 2000 is assumed not to be needed for its business activities.

Subtract the current value of the firm's financial obligations.	Enterprise value + Initial cash = Firm's current market value. This value is split between its shareholders and its debt holders. In our model we approximate the *market* value of the firm's debt by the *book value* of the debt. Note that the firm's operating current liabilities are not included in the debt for valuation purposes—they've already been netted out of the FCF.
= Equity valuation of the firm.	This value has to be divided by the number of shares outstanding to arrive at a *per-share* valuation.

The implementation of this schematic is problematic, especially as it regards the firm's debt. The question is, Which of the liability items on the balance sheet are regarded by the market as financial obligations of the firm? In the preceding valuation we've chosen to include all of the following items as "financial debts" of PPG:

	A	B
69	Debt	2,971
70	Deferred taxes	543
71	Minority interest	128
72	Other liabilities	1,004

Many Wall Street analysts would consider this approach too conservative. They often argue that deferred taxes are not a financial obligation of the firm, and they might even take issue with our listing of other liabilities among the debts of PPG. Obviously, the fewer debts we list, the higher our valuation of PPG's equity.

4.7.4 Is PPG Overvalued? Undervalued?

In cell B114, we've used a "10 percent" rule: If PPG's computed stock price falls within a ±10% range of the current stock price of $46.31, we call our valuation "ok." The formula we use is =IF(B111>B113*1.1, "undervalued",IF(B111<B113/1.1,"overvalued","ok")).

4.8 What Is PPG's Dividend Policy?

PPG's dividend has increased consecutively for the past 31 years. In the following spreadsheet we show you two different aspects of this dividend history over the period 1992–2000.

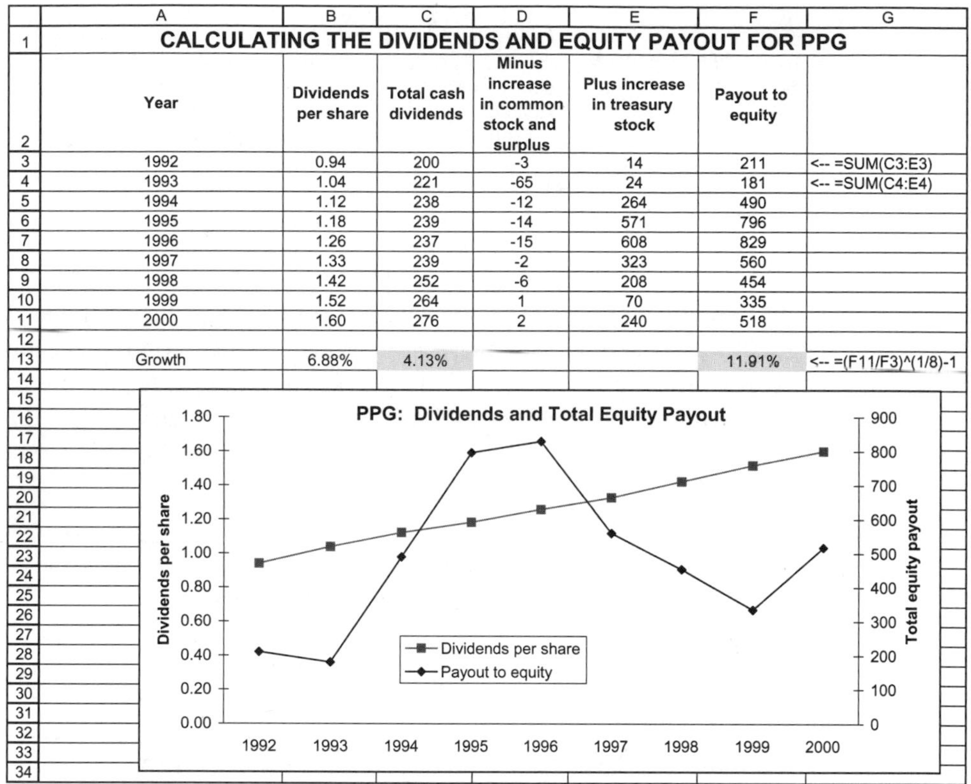

	A	B	C	D	E	F	G
1	CALCULATING THE DIVIDENDS AND EQUITY PAYOUT FOR PPG						
2	Year	Dividends per share	Total cash dividends	Minus increase in common stock and surplus	Plus increase in treasury stock	Payout to equity	
3	1992	0.94	200	-3	14	211	<-- =SUM(C3:E3)
4	1993	1.04	221	-65	24	181	<-- =SUM(C4:E4)
5	1994	1.12	238	-12	264	490	
6	1995	1.18	239	-14	571	796	
7	1996	1.26	237	-15	608	829	
8	1997	1.33	239	-2	323	560	
9	1998	1.42	252	-6	208	454	
10	1999	1.52	264	1	70	335	
11	2000	1.60	276	2	240	518	
12							
13	Growth	6.88%	4.13%			11.91%	<-- =(F11/F3)^(1/8)-1

In column B you can see PPG's dividends per share from 1992 to 2000. As you can see in the graph, this dividend has indeed increased continuously over this period. The compound growth rate of the dividends is 6.88 percent annually.

Columns C–F examine the *total payments* of PPG to its shareholders during this period—the sum of its cash dividends and its share repurchases. These columns tell a different (though no less compelling story):

Column C gives the *total dividend payout* by PPG.

Column D shows the *increases in common stock and surplus*—the additional cash directly paid into PPG by shareholders. This most often represents money paid in by those exercising employee stock options, but it can also represent additional funds directly raised from shareholders.

For PPG, this number is negative in most years (albeit only slightly), showing that shareholders paid in small amounts of capital to the firm.

Column E shows the *increase in treasury stock at cost*: This is the amount spent in each year by PPG to repurchase stock from its shareholders. Financial economists regard this as another form of dividend. When the firm pays out dividends, it pays out money to *all* of its shareholders. When it repurchases stock it directly pays out money to some of its shareholders (those that tender their stock); the remaining shareholders also benefit, since the future profits of the firm are now split among fewer shareholders, so that the proportional share of each individual non-bought-out shareholder is increased. An additional benefit of repurchases is their advantageous tax treatment: Shareholders have to pay an ordinary income tax rate on their cash dividends, but a "dividend" paid out as a repurchase is a capital gain and is thus taxed at a lower rate.[6]

Column F sums Columns C–E and computes the *total equity payout*. This is the total cash paid by PPG to shareholders. This total equity payout is larger than the dividend in all years except 1993. Note also the following:

- This payout is considerably more variable than the cash dividend alone (look at the graph of dividends versus total equity payout).
- The growth rate of the total equity payout—11.91 percent—is much larger than the growth rate of the dividends.

PPG is very proud of its dividend history—a document on its Web site brags that "dividends paid increased 31 consecutive years." PPG is also proud of its healthy growth in earnings per share; the same document includes the following graph:

6. One of the enduring mysteries of finance is why—given the tax superiority of repurchases over regular dividends—firms still pay dividends. The answer lies (we think) in two factors: (1) Many shareholders and analysts regard dividends as a strong signal about corporate health. (2) A firm paying out all its "dividends" as repurchases runs the risk of having the repurchases reclassified by the Internal Revenue Service as ordinary income. We should also stress that in many senses this is a peculiarly American story—the tax system in many European countries (and in Canada) essentially doesn't tax dividends as ordinary income.

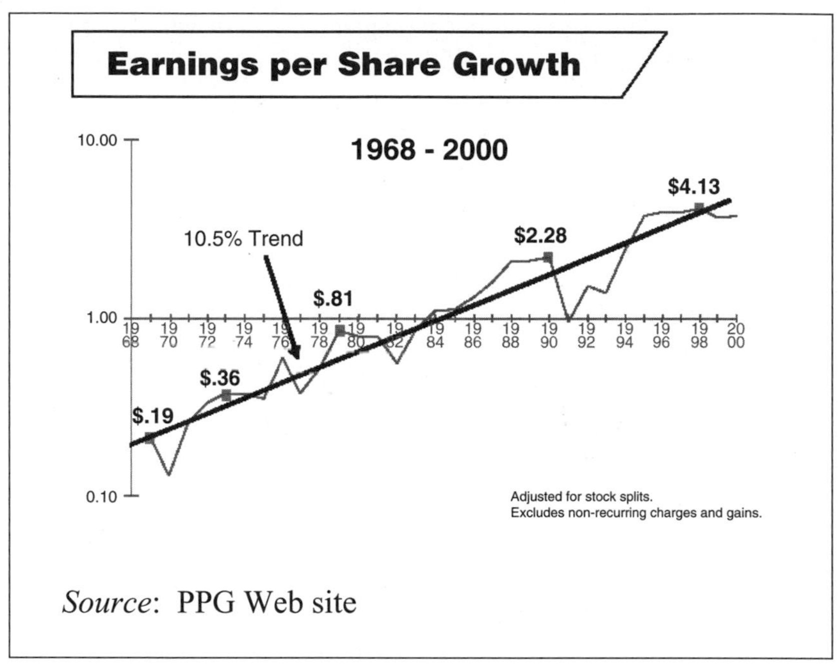

Source: PPG Web site

Earnings per share (EPS) have grown much faster than earnings. Why? Think about the EPS formula:

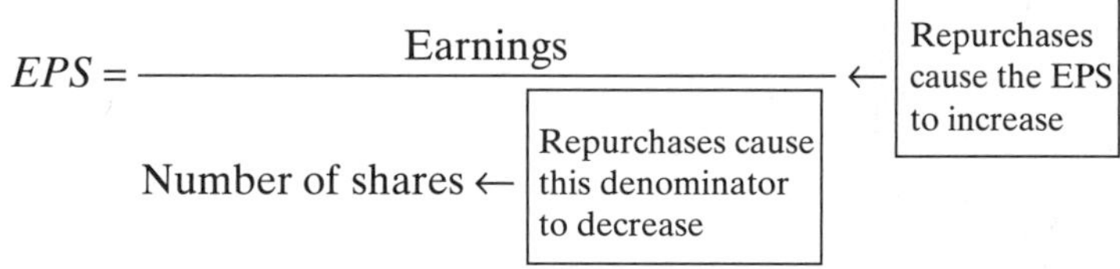

EPS = Earnings / Number of shares
Repurchases cause the EPS to increase
Repurchases cause this denominator to decrease

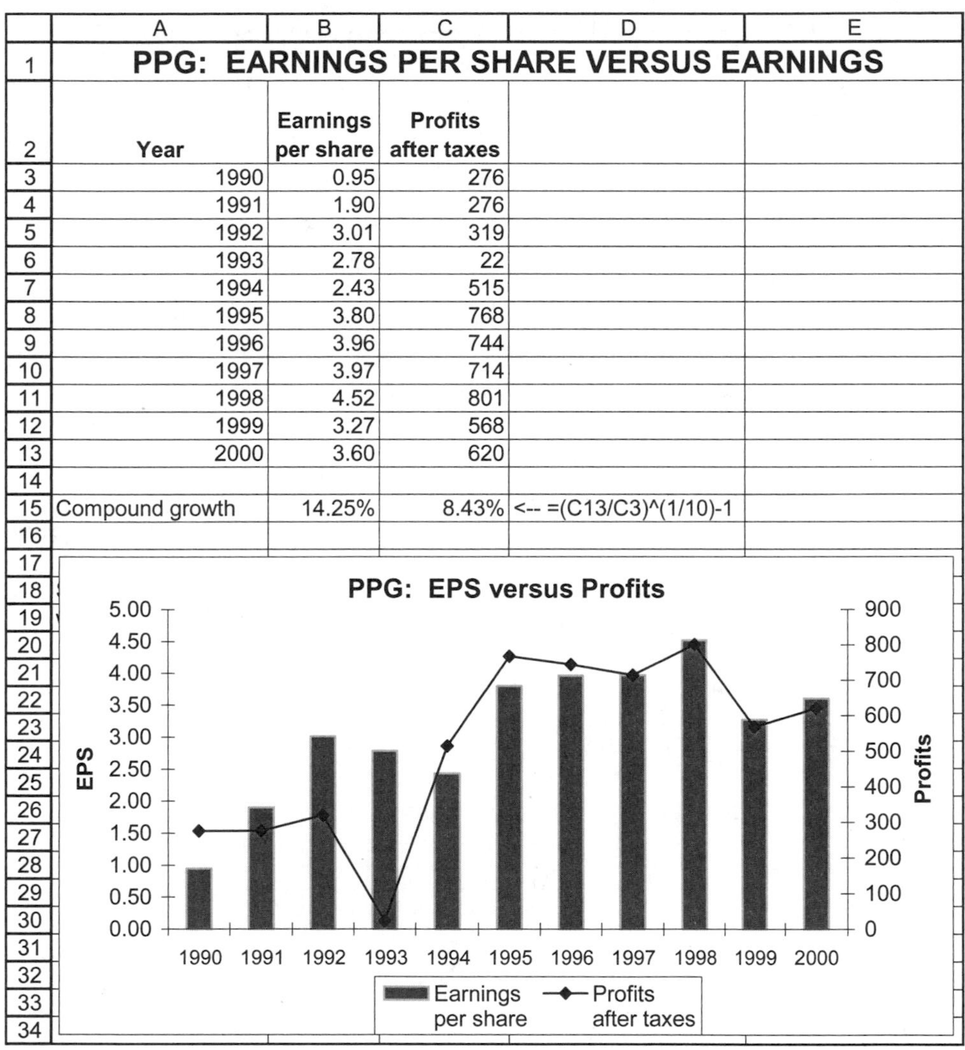

	A	B	C	D	E
1	**PPG: EARNINGS PER SHARE VERSUS EARNINGS**				
2	**Year**	**Earnings per share**	**Profits after taxes**		
3	1990	0.95	276		
4	1991	1.90	276		
5	1992	3.01	319		
6	1993	2.78	22		
7	1994	2.43	515		
8	1995	3.80	768		
9	1996	3.96	744		
10	1997	3.97	714		
11	1998	4.52	801		
12	1999	3.27	568		
13	2000	3.60	620		
14					
15	Compound growth	14.25%	8.43%	<-- =(C13/C3)^(1/10)-1	
16					

4.9 Modeling PPG's Dividend Policy

We think that PPG's dividend policy can be modeled most effectively by assuming the following:

- Total cash dividends exhibit a steady rate of growth. In the pro forma valuation model in this chapter we have chosen a dividend growth rate of 4.13 percent, equal to the historic compound growth rate of PPG's dividends.

- Debt equals 32 percent of total assets.
- Treasury stock (that is, the repurchases of stock from shareholders) is a plug.

Notice that the total equity payout by PPG to its stockholders depends on both its free cash flow *and* its financial policies—including the amount of debt the firm chooses.

4.10 Computing PPG's Cost of Equity r_E and Its Cost of Debt r_D

In this section we follow the format set out in sections 2.9–2.12 to compute the WACC for PPG. We compute the WACC based on four alternative models for the cost of equity r_E: Two of these methods use the Gordon dividend model, one on the dividends per share and the second on the total dividend payouts for PPG. Two additional methods use the CAPM, one the traditional CAPM and the other a tax-adjusted CAPM.

4.10.1 Using the Gordon Dividend Model to Determine the Cost of Equity r_E

We can apply this model, which was discussed in Chapter 2, using either the per-share dividends or the total equity payout. Each version of the model gives a different cost of equity for PPG:

	A	B	C
1	**CALCULATING THE GORDON MODEL r_E FOR PPG**		
2	Number of shares outstanding, Dec. 2000 (million)	168.22	
3	Share price, 31Dec00	46.31	
4	Equity value, Dec00	7,791	<-- =B2*B3
5			
6	**Method 1: r_E Gordon using only dividends**		
7	Stock price, 31dec00	46.31	
8	Dividend, 2000	1.60	
9	Anticipated dividend growth	6.88%	<-- =Dividends!$B$13
10	r_E, cost of equity using only dividends	10.57%	<-- =B8*(1+B9)/B7+B9
11			
12	**Method 2: r_E Gordon using equity payout**		
13	Total equity payout, 2000	518	<-- =Dividends!$F$11
14	Anticipated growth of this payout	11.91%	<-- =Dividends!$F$13
15	r_E, cost of equity using total equity payout	19.35%	<-- =B13*(1+B14)/B4+B14
16			
17	Using the two-stage Gordon model		
18	Number of high-growth years	3	
19	Normal growth after high-growth years	5.00%	
20	r_E, cost of equity using two-stage Gordon model	13.34%	<-- =twostagegordon(B4,B13,B14,B18,B19)

As noted in Chapter 2, method 1 uses *per-share* data, whereas method 2 uses *totals*—total equity value, total equity payout, and the growth rate of this payout. Given our estimate of 4 percent sales growth for PPG, we think it unlikely that the high total equity payout growth of 11.91 percent will continue ad infinitum. We therefore also use the two-stage Gordon model (section 2.4) to derive a third cost of equity (cell B20).

4.10.2 Which Method of Calculating r_E Is Better?

This is a trick question! The real question is, What do investors in PPG's stock *expect* when they're buying the stock. Savvy investors who understand the mechanics of finance (like the readers of this book!) will understand that method 2 represents the economic dividend of PPG. These investors will calculate PPG's cost of equity as r_E = 19.35 percent.

PPG's dividend policy—its pride in paying a continuously increasing dividend per share over such a long period—indicates that it thinks most investors do not understand the economics of firm payouts to shareholders. If PPG is right, then its cost of equity is considerably lower, $r_E = 10.57$ percent.

> This possible contradiction between dividends per share and total equity payouts completely disappears in a closely held firm or in a sole-ownership situation.
>
> Suppose you owned *all the shares* in PPG. You could then decide to pay yourself a "cash dividend per share" (to be taxed at your ordinary income tax rate) or to pay yourself a "share repurchase" (taxed at your capital gains rate). You'd immediately recognize that both payments are *economic dividends* (meaning: payouts to shareholders [you, in this case]). You'd also recognize that the only thing that's important is the *after-tax total payout.*

4.10.3 Applying the Security Market Line to Calculate PPG's Cost of Equity r_E

In Chapter 2 we presented two approaches to computing the cost of equity using the CAPM:

Classical SML	Tax-Adjusted SML
$r_E = r_f + \beta[E(r_M) - r_f]$	$r_E = r_f(1 - T_C) + \beta[E(r_M) - r_f(1 - T_C)]$
where	where
r_f = risk-free interest rate	r_f = risk-free interest rate
β = sensitivity of stock's returns to market return	β = sensitivity of stock's returns to market return
$= \dfrac{\text{Cov}(r_{PPG}, r_M)}{\text{Var}(r_M)}$	$= \dfrac{\text{Cov}(r_{PPG}, r_M)}{\text{Var}(r_M)}$
$E(r_M)$ = anticipated return on the market	$E(r_M)$ = anticipated return on the market
	T_C = firm's tax rate

Using monthly return data for PPG and the S&P 500 (the latter representing the stock market) can compute PPG's β as 0.8473. The following chart graphs S&P 500 returns (column C) on the x-axis against PPG returns (column G):

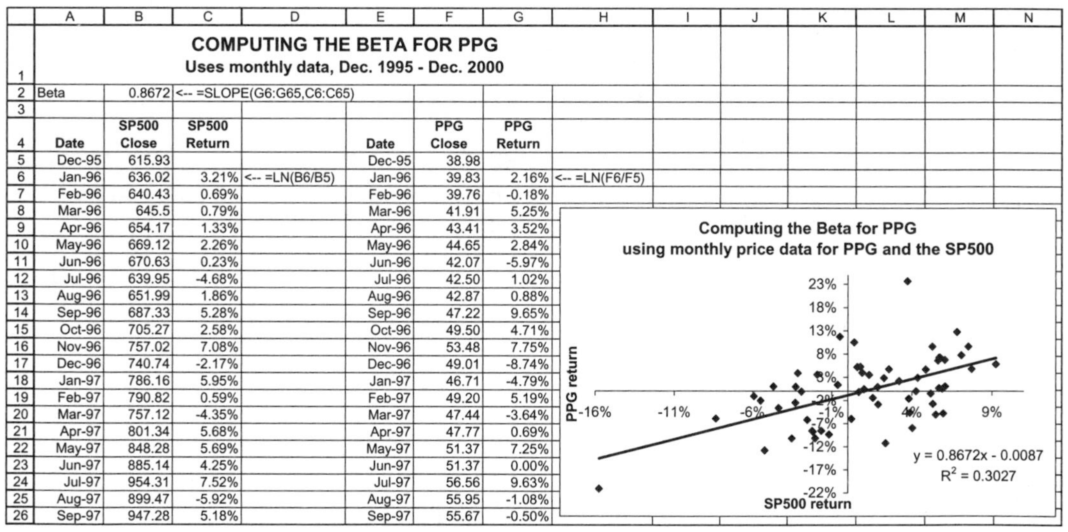

	A	B	C	D	E	F	G	H
1	COMPUTING THE BETA FOR PPG Uses monthly data, Dec. 1995 - Dec. 2000							
2	Beta	0.8672	<-- =SLOPE(G6:G65,C6:C65)					
3								
4	Date	SP500 Close	SP500 Return		Date	PPG Close	PPG Return	
5	Dec-95	615.93			Dec-95	38.98		
6	Jan-96	636.02	3.21%	<-- =LN(B6/B5)	Jan-96	39.83	2.16%	<-- =LN(F6/F5)
7	Feb-96	640.43	0.69%		Feb-96	39.76	-0.18%	
8	Mar-96	645.5	0.79%		Mar-96	41.91	5.25%	
9	Apr-96	654.17	1.33%		Apr-96	43.41	3.52%	
10	May-96	669.12	2.26%		May-96	44.65	2.84%	
11	Jun-96	670.63	0.23%		Jun-96	42.07	-5.97%	
12	Jul-96	639.95	-4.68%		Jul-96	42.50	1.02%	
13	Aug-96	651.99	1.86%		Aug-96	42.87	0.88%	
14	Sep-96	687.33	5.28%		Sep-96	47.22	9.65%	
15	Oct-96	705.27	2.58%		Oct-96	49.50	4.71%	
16	Nov-96	757.02	7.08%		Nov-96	53.48	7.75%	
17	Dec-96	740.74	-2.17%		Dec-96	49.01	-8.74%	
18	Jan-97	786.16	5.95%		Jan-97	46.71	-4.79%	
19	Feb-97	790.82	0.59%		Feb-97	49.20	5.19%	
20	Mar-97	757.12	-4.35%		Mar-97	47.44	-3.64%	
21	Apr-97	801.34	5.68%		Apr-97	47.77	0.69%	
22	May-97	848.28	5.69%		May-97	51.37	7.25%	
23	Jun-97	885.14	4.25%		Jun-97	51.37	0.00%	
24	Jul-97	954.31	7.52%		Jul-97	56.56	9.63%	
25	Aug-97	899.47	-5.92%		Aug-97	55.95	-1.08%	
26	Sep-97	947.28	5.18%		Sep-97	55.67	-0.50%	

We use the method outlined in section 2.7.3 to compute $E(r_M)$:

$$E(r_M) = \frac{a * EPS_0(1+g)}{P_0} + g = \frac{a*(1+g)}{P_0/EPS_0} + g = 7.66 \text{ percent}$$

where a is 50 percent (the payout ratio), g is 6 percent (the growth rate of market equity payouts), and P_0 / EPS_0 is equal to 32 (the market price-earnings ratio). Using this estimate, we find the following two (very close) estimates for the CAPM cost of equity:

	A	B	C
1	**USING THE CAPM TO COMPUTE PPG'S COST OF EQUITY**		
2	Market price/earnings multiple, December 2000	32	
3	Equity cash flow payout ratio	50.00%	
4	Anticipated growth of market equity cash flow	6.00%	
5	Expected market return, $E(r_M)$	7.66%	<-- =B3*(1+B4)/B2+B4
6	Treasury bill rate, December 2000	0.51%	
7	PPG's tax rate, T_C	36.28%	<-- ='Page 138, top and page 139'!B35
8			
9	**Method 3: r_E using the SML**		
10	Equity beta	0.8672	
11	r_E, cost of equity	6.71%	<-- =B6+B10*(B5-B6)
12			
13	**Method 4: r_E using the tax-adjusted SML**		
14	Equity beta	0.8672	
15	r_E, cost of equity	6.68%	<-- =B6*(1-B7)+B14*(B5-B6*(1-B7))

4.10.4 What Is PPG's Cost of Debt r_D?

The simplest way to calculate PPG's cost of debt r_D is to assume that r_D is the average current percentage cost of borrowing. This can be calculated from PPG's income statement and balance sheets:

	A	B	C
1	**COMPUTING PPG's COST OF DEBT, r_D**		
2	Year 2000 interest expense from PPG's income statement	193	
3	Year 2000 debt, from PPG's balance sheet	2,971	<-- ='Balance sheets 1991-2000'!B23
4	Year 1999 debt, from PPG's balance sheet	2,790	<-- ='Balance sheets 1991-2000'!C23
5	Average debt	2,881	<-- =AVERAGE(B3:B4)
6			
7	Cost of debt, r_D	6.70%	<-- =B2/B5

Note that we use only the financial debt of PPG to compute its cost of debt r_D.

There are, of course, other ways to calculate r_D for PPG: In principle we should ask what is the *firm's marginal cost of borrowing*—its cost for borrowing an extra dollar of debt. Implicitly our method assumes that PPG's current cost of borrowing is also its marginal cost.

4.11 What Is PPG's Weighted Average Cost of Capital?

A little review: In Chapter 2 we defined the weighted average cost of capital (WACC) as the *average return that the company has to pay to its equity and debt investors*. Another way of expressing this definition is that the WACC is the *average return that stakeholders (equity and bondholders)* expect *to make from the company*. If we let r_E denote the cost of equity (the return expected by equity holders) and r_D denote the cost of debt (the return expected by debt holders), then

$$WACC = r_E * \frac{E}{E+D} + r_D(1-T_C)\frac{D}{E+D}$$

where E is the market value of the firm's equity, D is the market value of the firm's debt, r_E is the cost of equity (rate of return demanded or required by shareholders), r_D is the cost of debt, and T_C is the firm's tax rate.

We use 6.70 percent as r_D, the cost of debt. As we showed in our analysis of PPG's income statement in section 4.5, this is PPG's current cost of debt.

	A	B	C
1	**COMPUTING THE WEIGHTED AVERAGE COST OF CAPITAL (WACC) FOR PPG**		
2	Shares outstanding (million)	168	<-- ='Page 137, 140, 141'!B36
3	Share price, end 2000	46.315	
4	Equity value, E	7,791	<-- =B2*B3
5	Net debt, D	4,535	<-- =SUM('Page 137, 140, 141'!B23:B26)-'Page 137, 140, 141'!B3
6	Cost of debt, r_D	6.70%	<-- ='Page 159, bottom'!B7
7	PPG's tax rate, T_C	36.28%	<-- ='Page 138, top and page 139'!B35
8	Market risk free rate, r_f	0.51%	<-- ='Page 159, top'!B6
9	Expected market return, $E(r_M)$	7.66%	<-- ='Page 159, top'!B5
10			
11	**WACC based on Gordon per-share dividends and interest from financial statements**		
12	Stock price, 31dec00	46.31	
13	Dividend, 2000	1.60	
14	Anticipated dividend growth	6.88%	
15	Cost of equity, r_E	10.57%	<-- =B13*(1+B14)/B12+B14
16	WACC	8.25%	<-- =$B$4/($B$4+$B$5)*B15+$B$5/($B$4+$B$5)*$B$6*(1-$B$7)
17			
18	**WACC based on Gordon equity payouts and interest from financial statements**		
19	Total equity payout, 2000	518	<-- ='Page 152'!$F$11
20	Anticipated growth of this payout	11.91%	<-- ='Page 152'!$F$13
21	Cost of equity, r_E	13.34%	<-- ='Page 156'!B20
22	WACC	10.00%	<-- =$B$4/($B$4+$B$5)*B21+$B$5/($B$4+$B$5)*$B$6*(1-$B$7)
23			
24	**WACC based on classic CAPM and interest from financial statements**		
25	PPG beta	0.8672	<-- ='Page 158'!B2
26	Cost of equity, r_E	6.71%	<-- =B8+B25*(B9-B8)
27	WACC	5.81%	<-- =$B$4/($B$4+$B$5)*B26+$B$5/($B$4+$B$5)*$B$6*(1-$B$7)
28			
29	**WACC based on tax-adjusted CAPM and interest from financial statements**		
30	PPG beta	0.8672	<-- ='Page 158'!B2
31	Cost of equity, r_E	6.68%	<-- =B8*(1-B7)+B30*(B9-B8*(1-B7))
32	WACC	5.79%	<-- =$B$4/($B$4+$B$5)*B31+$B$5/($B$4+$B$5)*$B$6*(1-$B$7)
33			
34	**Estimated WACC?**	7.47%	<-- =AVERAGE(B16,B22,B27,B32)

As you can see in cell B34, we've taken the easy way out of the WACC conundrum by choosing the average WACC of the four methods.[7]

4.12 Back to the Valuation—Sensitivity Analyses

As you've seen in this chapter, a valuation involves a tremendous amount of analysis and a bewildering array of assumptions about the firm's future. Hopefully you've done a good job of analysis and you've guessed

7. Our excuse: Between the two Gordon models, we definitely favor method 2, which uses the total equity payout (which gives a higher cost of equity). But we also "really like" the SML approach to the cost of capital, which gives a cost of equity more approaching that of method 1. So . . . we'll take the average and do some sensitivity analysis. Not heroic, but safe.

right, but prudence requires that you check whether alternative assumptions would make a difference in your valuation.

In this section we examine only two factors among the many that affect the valuation: the WACC and the long-run sales growth of the firm. Building a two-dimensional data table in Excel (see Chapter 31 for details) gives the following result:

	A	B	C	D	E	F	G	H	I	J
95	**Valuing PPG**									
96	WACC	7.47%								
97	Long-term free cash flow growth rate	4%								
98										
99	Year		**2001**	**2002**	**2003**	**2004**	**2005**			
100	FCF		646	593	599	604	608			
101	Terminal						18,231	<-- =G100*(1+B97)/(B96-B97)		
102	Total		646	593	599	604	18,839			
103										
104	Discounted value	15,748	<-- =NPV(B96,C102:G102)*(1+B96)^0.5							
105	Add back initial cash	111								
106	Firm value	15,859								
107	Subtract total debt value, Dec.00	4,646	<-- =SUM(B69:B72) -- this is controversial!							
108	Implied equity value	11,213								
109										
110	Number of shares outstanding, Dec.00	168.22								
111	Implied value per share	66.66								
112										
113	Market price per share, Dec.00	46.31								
114	PPG over or under-valued?	undervalued	<-- =IF(B111>B113*1.1,"undervalued",IF(B111<B113/1.1,"overvalued","ok"))							
115										
116	=IF(B96>B97,B111,"nmf")		**DATA TABLE: SENSITIVITY OF PPG'S STOCK VALUATION TO WACC AND LONG-TERM GROWTH RATE**							
117					**Long-term FCF growth ↓**					
118		66.66	**1%**	**3%**	**4%**	**5%**	**6%**	**7%**		
119		**6%**	44.99	84.30	133.45	280.89	nmf	nmf		
120		**7%**	33.34	57.12	80.90	128.46	271.13	nmf		
121	WACC →	**8%**	25.02	40.80	54.61	77.63	123.66	261.77		
122		**9%**	18.78	29.92	38.83	52.21	74.49	119.07		
123		**10%**	13.92	22.14	28.31	36.94	49.90	71.48		
124		**11%**	10.03	16.31	20.79	26.76	35.13	47.68		
125		**12%**	6.85	11.77	15.14	19.49	25.28	33.38		
126		**13%**	4.20	8.13	10.75	14.02	18.23	23.85		
127		**14%**	1.96	5.15	7.23	9.77	12.95	17.03		

The highlighted cells in the data table indicate those combinations of growth and WACC for which PPG is undervalued with respect to its current market value. Not surprisingly, this outcome occurs for combinations of high growth and low WACC.

An Excel note: The formula calculated by the data table (cell B118) is a slight variation of cell B111: If the long-term growth rate is less than the WACC, then the data table gives B111; otherwise it indicates that there is no meaningful figure ("nmf") for the valuation. This result relates to our terminal value calculation.

$$\text{Terminal value} = \frac{FCF_{2005} * (1 + \text{Long-term growth rate})}{WACC - \text{Long-term growth rate}}$$

This formula is only meaningful when *WACC* – Long-term growth rate > 0.

Exercises

1. Assume that in 2001 PPG sales will grow by 11 percent, in 2002, by 8 percent, in 2003 by –2 percent, and thereafter by 4 percent, which is also the long-term growth. Value the shares.

2. Using the data from the previous question, do a sensitivity analysis on the Net PPE/Sales ratio and the value of PPG shares. If PPG succeeds in improving its efficiency in this ratio by 1%, how will this impact the valuation of the shares?

3. At the end of 2000, PPG's stock was selling for a P/E multiple of 13. Re-examine the terminal value in the model of sections 4.5–4.6, and assume that it is

$$\text{terminal value} = \text{EPS}_{2005} * \underbrace{13}_{\substack{\text{the 2001} \\ \text{P/E multiple}}} + \begin{array}{l}\text{2005 projected} \\ \text{Book value} \\ \text{PPG debt}\end{array}$$

How is your valuation of PPG shares affected?

Appendix: Some Accounting Issues

Overview

This appendix covers a number of accounting issues that arise in the analysis of PPG's financial statements in this chapter. In each case we first try to explain the accounting issue and then show how we model the particular item in our firm financial model. Our explanations are informal and not "accounting based" (meaning that there are no T-accounts and everything is written directly onto the balance sheet and income statement).

Deferred Taxes and Accelerated Depreciation

The deferred tax account is often seen on the liabilities side of the balance sheet. Deferred taxes arise when companies report different depreciation figures to their shareholders and to the IRS.

Here's a very simple example. We assume that the firm has one fixed asset that is worth $500. This asset has a depreciable life of two years.

For reporting this asset's depreciation to the shareholders, the firm uses straight-line depreciation. For reporting the asset's depreciation to the tax authorities, the firm uses *accelerated depreciation*; it reports $300 of depreciation in year 1 and $200 depreciation in year 2.[8] Here's what the year-1 profit and loss (P&L) statements look like:

	A	B	C	D	E
1	**DEFERRED TAXES AND ACCELERATED DEPRECIATION An Example**				
2	**2006 P&L for tax purposes**			**2006 P&L for reporting purposes**	
3	Sales	1000		Sales	1000
4	Costs	500		Costs	500
5	Depreciation	300		Depreciation	250
6	PBT	200		PBT	250
7	Taxes (40%)	80		Taxes (40%)	100
8	PAT	120		PAT	150

Why?

Students and readers of accounting statements often ask why this double reporting should occur or even be allowed. The usual justification is as follows:

• The reporting of depreciation to shareholders should report the *economic essence* of the situation. In this example the managers of the firm may have thought that the asset had an economic life of two years and that its use was equally distributed between these two years.

• The reporting to the tax authorities should *utilize the tax system* to maximize shareholder cash flows. By reporting more depreciation earlier (which is what the accelerated depreciation schedule allows), the firm can pay less tax.

How Much Cash Is Generated?

In cells B11:B13 we calculate the cash generated by the firm in 2006. This cash flow of the firm is determined by its reporting to the tax authorities (since this reporting determines the actual taxes paid).

8. In order to simplify subsequent calculations in this section, we assume that (1) all costs of goods sold are in cash, (2) all sales are in cash, (3) the firm purchases no new fixed assets, (4) the firm has no debt, and (5) the firm pays no dividends and issues no new shares.

	A	B	C
10	**Cash flow**		
11	PAT	120	<-- =B8
12	Add back depreciation	300	<-- =B5
13	Cash flow	420	<-- =B12+B11

Changes in the Balance Sheet

We suppose that the firm's balance sheet at the end of 2005 (the year previous to these calculations) looks like the following:

	A	B
15	**Balance Sheet**	
16	**2005**	
17	**Assets**	
18	Cash	0
19	Other current assets	0
20		
21	FA at cost	500
22	Accumulated depreciation	0
23	Net fixed assets	500
24	**Total assets**	**500**
25		
26	**Liabilities and equity**	
27	Current liabilities	0
28	Deferred taxes	0
29	Debt	0
30	Equity	
31	Stock	200
32	Accumulated retained	300
33	**Total liabilities and equity**	**500**

Now think about the balance sheet at the end of 2006. This is where things get a bit more complicated:

• On the one hand, cash balances grow by the cash flow, which is determined by the tax P&L.

• On the other hand, depreciation and the change in accumulated retained earnings are determined by the shareholder P&L.

The result is that the asset side of the balance sheet grows by $170: An increase of $420 in cash balances from which is netted out an increase of $250 in depreciation. However, the liabilities side of the balance sheet grows by only $150 (the PAT reported to shareholders).

Since it's an immutable rule of accounting that the change in the right-hand side of the balance sheet must equal the change in the left-hand side, there must be a balancing item. This item—$20 in our example—is "Deferred taxes":

	A	B	C	D	E	F
15	**Balance Sheet**					
16	**2005**			**2006**		
17	**Assets**					
18	Cash	0		420	<-- =B18+B13	
19	Other current assets	0		0	<-- =B19	
20						
21	FA at cost	500		500		
22	Accumulated depreciation	0		250	<-- =B22+E5	
23	Net fixed assets	500		250		
24	**Total assets**	**500**		**670**		
25						
26	**Liabilities and equity**					
27	Current liabilities	0		0		
28	Deferred taxes	0		20	<-- =E7-B7+B28	
29	Debt	0		0		
30	Equity					
31	Stock	200		200		
32	Accumulated retained	300		450	<-- =B32+E8	
33	**Total liabilities and equity**	**500**		**670**		
34						
35	**Assumptions:**					
36	1. All COGS in cash					
37	2. All Sales in cash					
38	3. No new assets purchased					
39	4. No debt repaid or taken out					
40	5. No dividends paid or stock sold or repurchased					

Cash balances grow by the cash flow (determined by the tax P&L)

Depreciation is reported from the shareholder P&L

Accumulated retained earnings grow by the PAT from the shareholder P&L

The PLUG! Without this, the asset side of the balance sheet grows by 420 - 200= 220, whereas the liabilities/equity side grows by 180.

Why Call Them Deferred Taxes?

The justification for the name is that "deferred taxes" are taxes that the firm will have to pay at some point in the future. Suppose, for example, that the 2007 P&Ls for the firm are exactly the same as those for 2006, with the exception of the depreciation. This time, as you can see in the next spreadsheet, the situation is reversed: The firm pays more taxes to the IRS than it reports to its shareholders. This fact causes the deferred tax account to decrease.

	A	B	C	D	E	F
1	**DEFERRED TAXES AND ACCELERATED DEPRECIATION** **The next year--asset is fully depreciated**					
2	**2007 P&L for tax purposes**			**2007 P&L for reporting purposes**		
3	Sales	1000		Sales	1000	
4	Costs	500		Costs	500	
5	Depreciation	200		Depreciation	250	
6	PBT	300		PBT	250	
7	Taxes (40%)	120		Taxes (40%)	100	
8	PAT	180		PAT	150	
9						
10	**Cash flow**					
11	PAT	180	<-- =B8			
12	Add back depreciation	200	<-- =B5			
13	Cash flow	380	<-- =B12+B11			
14						
15	**Balance Sheet**					
16	**2003**			**2004**		
17	**Assets**					
18	Cash	420		800	<-- =B18+B13	
19	Other current assets	0		0	<-- =B19	
20						
21	FA at cost	500		500		
22	Accumulated depreciation	250		500	<-- =B22+E5	
23	Net fixed assets	250		0		
24	**Total assets**	**670**		**800**		
25						
26	**Liabilities and equity**					
27	Current liabilities	0		0		
28	Deferred taxes	20		0	<-- =E7-B7+B28	
29	Debt	0		0		
30	Equity					
31	Stock	200		200		
32	Accumulated retained	450		600	<-- =B32+E8	
33	**Total liabilities and equity**	**670**		**800**		
34						
35						
36						
37						
38						

Cash balances grow by the cash flow (determined by the tax P&L)

Depreciation is reported from the shareholder P&L

Accumulated retained earnings grow by the PAT from the shareholder P&L

Accumulated depreciation is zero in 2007--the firm's actual taxes paid are higher by $20 than taxes reported to shareholders.

Modeling Deferred Taxes

There are two possible ways to model deferred taxes. One way would be to model accelerated depreciation, as illustrated in appendix 2 to Chapter 3. Having modeled accelerated depreciation, we can then take the difference between an accelerated depreciation allowance and a straight-line depreciation allowance and derive the increment to deferred taxes.

We prefer a second method, which is illustrated in this chapter: Instead of modeling accelerated depreciation, we assume that depreciation is straight-line, both for reporting and tax purposes. We then allow the deferred depreciation line in the liabilities section of the balance sheet to grow by the rate of sales growth.

We realize that this is a "cheap out" to a complicated problem, but we think that the advantages of its simplicity outweigh the disadvantages of the misrepresentation of the actualities.

Taxes Payable versus Deferred Taxes

Taxes payable arise because of a *short-term* timing difference in the reporting of taxes and the payment of taxes, whereas the deferred taxes discussed in the previous section arise because of a *long-term* timing difference in the reporting and payment of taxes. Typically taxes payable occur because the end of the reporting year differs from the date of tax payments.

Here's an example: ABC Corporation (whose financial statements follow) has reported income of $200 for 2003. The company's tax rate is 40 percent, and therefore its taxes for the year are reported as $80. However, the company's actual tax payments for 2003 are only $60—the remaining $20 will be paid in January 2004, after the fiscal year ends.

The company reports this information as follows:

• On its profit and loss statement it reports taxes as $80. This gives it a PAT of $120, and since it pays no dividends, this PAT is added to the accumulated retained earnings in the balance sheet.

• The difference between the taxes reported and the taxes paid ($20) is put on the balance sheet as *taxes payable*. This is a current liability, meaning that the company anticipates that this liability will come due within a year.

• The company's cash flow includes an item for *increase in taxes payable*. The cash on the balance sheet grows by the cash flow.

	A	B	C	D	E	F	G	H
1				**TAXES PAYABLE**				
2				**2003 Profit & Loss**				
3				Sales	1000		Actual taxes paid	60
4				Costs	500			
5				Depreciation	300			
6				PBT	200			
7				Taxes (40%)	80			
8				PAT	120			
9								
10				**Cash flow**				
11				PAT	120	<-- =E8		
12				Add back depreciation	300	<-- =E5		
13				Increase in taxes payable	20			
14				Cash flow	440	<-- =SUM(E11:E13)		
15								
16	**Balance Sheet**					Cash balances grow by the cash flow		
17	**2002**			**2003**				
18	**Assets**							
19	Cash	0			440	<-- =B19+E14		
20	Other current assets	0			0	<-- =B20		
21							Depreciation is reported from the shareholder P&L	
22	FA at cost	500			500			
23	Accumulated depreciation	0			300	<-- =B23+E5		
24	Net fixed assets	500			200			
25	**Total assets**	**500**			**640**			
26								
27	**Liabilities and equity**							
28	Current liabilities	0			0			
29	Taxes payable	0			20	<-- =E7-H3		
30	Debt	0			0		Accumulated retained earnings grow by the PAT from the shareholder P&L (there are no dividends)	
31	Equity							
32	Stock	200			200			
33	Accumulated retained	300			420	<-- =B33+E8		
34	**Total liabilities and equity**	**500**			**640**			
35								
36								
37	**Assumptions:**			Taxes payable are the difference between taxes reported in the P&L and taxes actually paid.				
38	1. All COGS in cash							
39	2. All Sales in cash							
40	3. No new assets purchased							
41	4. No debt repaid or taken out							
42	5. No dividends paid or stock sold or repurchased							

Some companies report taxes payable and deferred taxes together; Northrop-Grumman is an example; even though deferred taxes are usually reported as long-term items, Northrop reports them as a current liability.

Goodwill

Goodwill is an accounting item that is created when assets of one company are bought by another company for an amount different from their book value. To understand this mysterious sentence, consider the balance sheets of Companies A and B:

	A	B	C	D	E
1	**GOODWILL ACCOUNTING**				
2	**Company A**			**Company B**	
3	**Assets**			**Assets**	
4	Cash	10,000		Cash	500
5	Current assets	12,000		Current assets	1,000
6					
7	Plant property and equipment			Plant property and equipment	
8	At cost	10,000		At cost	1,600
9	Accumulated depreciation	-3,000		Accumulated depreciation	-250
10	Net PP&E	7,000		Net PP&E	1,350
11	**Total Assets**	29,000		**Total Assets**	2,850
12					
13	**Liabilities and equity**			**Liabilities and equity**	
14	Current liabilities	10,000		Current liabilities	800
15	Debt	3,000		Debt	1,000
16	Equity			Equity	
17	Common stock	2,000		Common stock	1,000
18	Accumulated retained earnings	14,000		Accumulated retained earnings	50
19	**Total liabilities**	29,000		**Total liabilities**	2,850

Now suppose that Company A buys all of Company B's stock. We'll consider several scenarios.

Scenario 1

Company A buys B's assets for their book value and assumes the debts of B. The purchase price is equal to the book value of equity. There is no revaluation of any assets (you may have to read on to scenario 2 to understand this sentence). In this case, Company A pays the shareholders of Company B $1,050 for their shares. In return, Company A acquires all the assets of B and assumes responsibility for the current liabilities and debt of B.

Here's the resulting balance sheet of Company A after the acquisition:

	A	B	C	D
22	**Company A buys assets of Company B and assumes B's debt. Price = Book value of equity**			
23	Purchase price	1,050		
24				
25	**Assets**			
26	Cash	9,450	<-- =B4+E4-B23	
27	Current assets	13,000	<-- =B5+E5	
28				
29	Plant property and equipment			
30	At cost	11,350	<-- =B8+E10	
31	Accumulated depreciation	-3,000	<-- =B9	
32	Net PP&E	8,350	<-- =B30+B31	
33	**Total Assets**	30,800	<-- =B32+B27+B26	
34				
35	**Liabilities and equity**			
36	Current liabilities	10,800	<-- =B14+E14	
37	Debt	4,000	<-- =B15+E15	
38	Equity			
39	Common stock	2,000	<-- =B17	
40	Accumulated retained earnings	14,000	<-- =B18	
41	**Total liabilities**	30,800	<-- =SUM(B36:B40)	

Here are some points to note:

• Cash of A after purchase = Cash of A + Cash of B – Purchase price. Before the acquisition, A had $10,000 of cash and B had $500. In acquiring B, Company A gets all of B's cash, but pays $1,050. The total cash left after the acquistion is $10,000 + $500 – $1,050 = $9,450.

• Current liabilities, Current assets, Debt of A after purchase = sum of A + B debt before purchase. The acquiring company takes over the debts and assets of the acquired company. In this scenario there is no revaluation of the assets—meaning that A values B's current assets at their book value of $1,000 and values B's fixed assets at their book value of $1,350.

• At-cost value of fixed assets = prepurchase of A + Net fixed assets of B. The book value, $1,350, of B's fixed assets is their fair market value. However, in the acquisition this whole amount is booked as a "fixed asset at cost." This means that after their purchase the depreciation of B's assets is based on their prepurchase net value (and not on their prepurchase at-cost value).[9]

9. This is like a revaluation at the current book value.

• There is no change in equity accounts of A after purchase from A before purchase. A's equity before the purchase was $16,000; this number doesn't change in the purchase.

Scenario 2

Company A buys B's assets for more than their book value and assumes the debts of B. None of the assets is revalued—Company A considers that the current assets of B are worth $1,000 and that the fair market value of B's plant, property, and equipment is $1,350 (their preacquisition book value).

Suppose that Company A pays the shareholders of Company B $2,000 for their shares and in return acquires all the assets of B and assumes responsibility for the current liabilities and debt of B. In this case, the postacquisition balance sheet will show

• Cash balances of $10,000 + $500 – $2,000 = $8,500

• An item called Goodwill of $950. The goodwill is the excess of the price paid by A over the book value of B's equity.

	A	B	C	D
22	**Company A buys assets of Company B and assumes B's debt. Price > Book value of equity**			
23	Purchase price	2,000		
24				
25	**Assets**			
26	Cash	8,500	<-- =B4+E4-B23	
27	Current assets	13,000	<-- =B5+E5	Assumption: The book
28				value of B's assets is an
29	Plant property and equipment			accurate reflection of
30	At cost	11,350	<-- =B8+E10	their market value.
31	Accumulated depreciation	-3,000	<-- =B9	
32	Net PP&E	8,350	<-- =B30+B31	
33	Goodwill	950	<-- =B23-SUM(E17:E18)	
34				
35	**Total Assets**	30,800	<-- =B32+B27+B26+B33	
36				
37	**Liabilities and equity**			
38	Current liabilities	10,800	<-- =B14+E14	
39	Debt	4,000	<-- =B15+E15	
40	Equity			
41	Common stock	2,000	<-- =B17	
42	Accumulated retained earnings	14,000	<-- =B18	
43	**Total liabilities**	30,800	<-- =SUM(B38:B42)	

Scenario 3

Company A buys B's assets for more than their book value and assumes the debts of B. Some of the assets are revalued. In the following example Company A considers that the current assets of B are worth $1,200 in comparison to their preacquisition book value of $1,000 and that the fair market value of B's plant, property, and equipment is $1,500 (as opposed to their preacquisition value of $1,350).

Suppose that Company A pays the shareholders of Company B $2,000 for their shares and in return acquires all the assets of B and assumes responsibility for the current liabilities and debt of B. In this case, the postacquisition balance sheet will show

- Cash balances of $10,000 + $500 – $2,000 = $8,500
- Current assets of

$$\underbrace{\$12{,}000}_{\substack{\uparrow \\ \text{A's preacquisition} \\ \text{book value of current} \\ \text{assets}}} + \underbrace{\$1{,}200}_{\substack{\uparrow \\ \text{A's valuation} \\ \text{of the fair-market} \\ \text{value of B's current} \\ \text{assets}}} = \$13{,}200$$

- Fixed assets at cost of $11,500 and accumulated depreciation of $3,000:

	A	B	C	D	E
1	**COMPUTING THE FIXED-ASSET ACCOUNTS**				
2		**Preacquistion**	**Postacquistion fair-market value**	**Total on postacquisition balance sheet**	
3	Fixed assets at cost				
4	A	10,000	10,000		
5	B (revalued)	1,600	1,500	11,500	<-- =C5+C4
6	Accumulated depreciation				
7	A	-3,000	-3,000		
8	B (set to zero)	-250	0	-3,000	<-- =C8+C7
9	Net fixed assets				
10	A	7,000	7,000		
11	B	1,350	1,500	8,500	<-- =C11+C10

• An item called Goodwill of $600. The goodwill is the excess of the price paid by A over the book value of B's equity, *minus* the undervaluation of B's assets. In the case we're discussing:

	A	B	C
14	**COMPUTING THE GOODWILL**		
15	Acquisition price	2,000	
16	Book value of B's equity	1,050	
17			
18	B's current assets		
19	Fair-market value	1,200	
20	Book value	1,000	
21	Excess	200	<-- =B19-B20
22			
23	B's fixed assets		
24	Fair-market value	1,500	
25	Book value	1,350	
26	Excess	150	<-- =B24-B25
27			
28	Goodwill	600	<-- =B15-B16-B21-B26

Here's the whole balance sheet:

	A	B	C	D	E
1	**GOODWILL ACCOUNTING**				
2	**Company A**			**Company B**	
3	**Assets**			**Assets**	
4	Cash	10,000		Cash	500
5	Current assets	12,000		Current assets	1,000
6					
7	Plant property and equipment			Plant property and equipment	
8	At cost	10,000		At cost	1,600
9	Accumulated depreciation	-3,000		Accumulated depreciation	-250
10	Net PP&E	7,000		Net PP&E	1,350
11	**Total Assets**	29,000		**Total Assets**	2,850
12					
13	**Liabilities and equity**			**Liabilities and equity**	
14	Current liabilities	10,000		Current liabilities	800
15	Debt	3,000		Debt	1,000
16	Equity			Equity	
17	Common stock	2,000		Common stock	1,000
18	Accumulated retained earnings	14,000		Accumulated retained earnings	50
19	**Total liabilities**	29,000		**Total liabilities**	2,850
20					
21					
22	**Company A buys assets of Company B and assumes B's debt Price > Book value of equity**				
23	**B's assets are revalued**				
24	Purchase price	2,000			
25					
26	Revaluation of B's assets				
27	Current assets worth	1,200			
28	Fixed assets worth	1,500			
29					
30	**Assets**				
31	Cash	8,500	<-- =B4+E4-B24	Goodwill =	
32	Current assets	13,200	<-- =B5+B27	+ Excess of purchase price over	
33				B's BV of equity	
34	Plant property and equipment			- Excess of revaluation of B's	
35	At cost	11,500	<-- =B8+B28	assets over their BV	
36	Accumulated depreciation	-3,000	<-- =B9		
37	Net PP&E	8,500	<-- =B35+B36		
38	Goodwill	600	<-- =B24-SUM(E17:E18)-(B27-E5)-(B28-E10)		
39					
40	**Total Assets**	30,800	<-- =B37+B32+B31+B38		
41					
42	**Liabilities and equity**				
43	Current liabilities	10,800	<-- =B14+E14		
44	Debt	4,000	<-- =B15+E15		
45	Equity				
46	Common stock	2,000	<-- =B17		
47	Accumulated retained earnings	14,000	<-- =B18		
48	**Total liabilities**	30,800	<-- =SUM(B43:B47)		

Under new United States accounting rules adopted in 2002, Goodwill is not depreciated. It may, however, be decreased. A decrease would occur if the value of the acquired assets is subsequently "impaired." For example, suppose that subsequent to the acquisition, Company A decided that B's current assets are really worth $1,100. This asset impairment will cause a decrease in goodwill by $100.

Minority Interest

When a company owns more than a 50 percent stake in a subsidiary but does not fully own the subsidiary, the equity not owned is reported as minority interest. In the following example we compare the consequences of Company A buying all of Company B and Company A buying 90% of Company B. Neither company pays dividends.

	A	B	C	D	E	F	G	H	I
1				**MINORITY INTEREST**					
2		**Company A**					**Company B**		
3	**Profit and loss**					**Profit and loss**			
4	Sales	1000				Sales	100		
5	COGS	500				COGS	55		
6	Depreciation	100				Depreciation	8		
7	Interest	50				Interest	2		
8	PBT	350				PBT	35		
9	Taxes	140				Taxes	14		
10	PAT	210				PAT	21		
11	Retained	210				Retained	21		
12									
13	**Assets**		**Liabilities**			**Assets**		**Liabilities**	
14	Cash	100	CL	300		Cash	10	CL	30
15	CA	500	Debt	500		CA	50	Debt	20
16	NFA	1000	Equity	800		NFA	100	Equity	110
17	**Total assets**	**1600**	**Total liabilities**	**1600**		**Total assets**	**160**	**Total liabilities**	**160**
18									
19									
20				**Consolidation--100% ownership**					
21	**Profit and loss**			**Assets**		**Liabilities**			
22	Sales	1100		Cash	110	CL	330	<-- =D14+I14	
23	COGS	555		CA	550	Debt	520	<-- =D15+I15	
24	Depreciation	108		NFA	1100	Equity	910	<-- =D16+I16	
25	Interest	52		**Total assets**	**1760**	**Total liabilities**	**1760**	<-- =D17+I17	
26	PBT	385							
27	Taxes	154							
28	PAT	231							
29	Retained	231	<-- =B11+G11						
30									
31				**Consolidation--90% ownership**					
32	**Profit and loss**			**Assets**		**Liabilities**			
33	Sales	1100		Cash	110	CL	330		
34	COGS	555		CA	550	Debt	520		
35	Depreciation	108		NFA	1100	Minority interest	11	<-- =10%*I16	
36	Interest	52				Equity	899	<-- =D16+I16-G35	
37	PBT	385		**Total assets**	**1760**	**Total liabilities**	**1760**		
38	Taxes	154							
39	PAT	231	<-- =B10+G10						
40	Minority interest	2.1	<-- =10%*G10						
41	Retained	228.9	<-- =B39-B40						

5 Bank Valuation

5.1 Overview

This chapter applies pro forma techniques to the valuation of a bank. Many of the topics are similar to those in Chapters 3 and 4, which showed how to build a pro forma model of a firm and how to use this model for the valuation. As in our previous discussion, to do the valuation we will want to derive the bank's free cash flows (FCF) and discount them at an appropriate weighted average cost of capital (WACC).

However, banks have some peculiarities that warrant a separate discussion. The primary distinction has to do with the definition of the FCFs for a bank. Whereas the FCF for a nonfinancial company excludes all financial items, the FCF for a bank has to take explicit account of the financing of the bank's lending activities. To the extent that a bank borrows to finance its lending, this lending should be part of the bank's net working capital. The FCF for a bank therefore includes many of the financial items that we have excluded in the case of a nonfinancial company such as PPG (Chapter 4).

This chapter starts with a discussion of the financial statements of a bank and proceeds to show how to define a bank's free cash flows. We then illustrate several bank valuation techniques: using the FCFs, using the residual equity cash flows, and using P/E ratios.

5.2 Analyzing Bank Balance Sheets

In this section we analyze the balance sheets of banks using the enterprise valuation model of Chapters 3 and 4. Our main point is that many of the financial items on a bank's balance sheet should be included in the bank's working capital. This practice contrasts with our analysis of nonfinancial corporations, where we stressed the importance of excluding the financing items from the enterprise valuation.

5.2.1 The Enterprise Valuation Model for a Nonfinancial Company

We start by reviewing enterprise valuation for a nonfinancial company. As pointed out in the previous chapters, a good way of thinking about valuation is through the use of the accounting paradigm, but using market values. When we create a valuation model for a nonfinancial company, we rewrite the balance sheet by moving the current liabilities from the liabilities/equity side to the asset side of the balance sheet:

NONFINANCIAL FIRM: USING THE BALANCE SHEET AS AN ENTERPRISE VALUATION MODEL			
ORIGINAL BALANCE SHEET			
Assets		**Liabilities**	
Cash and marketable securities		Operating current liabilities	
Operating current assets		Debt	
Net fixed assets		Equity	
Goodwill			
Total assets		**Total liabilities and equity**	
THE ENTERPRISE VALUATION BALANCE SHEET			
Assets		**Liabilities**	
Cash and marketable securities			
Operating current assets		Debt	Enterprise value = PV (FCFs discounted at WACC)
- Operating current liabilities			
= Net working capital	←		
Net fixed assets		Equity	
Goodwill			
Market value		**Market value**	

The enterprise value is computed by taking the present value of the firm's free cash flows (FCF):

Enterprise value =

$$\begin{cases} \left[\sum_t \dfrac{FCF_t}{(1+WACC)^t}\right] * (1+WACC)^{0.5} & \text{Discounting all FCFs} \\ \left[\sum_{t=1}^{n} \dfrac{FCF_t}{(1+WACC)^t} + \dfrac{\text{Terminal value}}{(1+WACC)^n}\right] * (1+WACC)^{0.5} & \text{Terminal value proxies for PV of FCFs past date } n \end{cases}$$

The $(1 + WACC)^{0.5}$ term relates to midyear discounting (discussed in section 3.5.3). The most common terminal-value model (see section 3.5.1) is based on the assumption that the last projected free cash flow will continue to grow at a long-term growth rate. This growth rate, denoted by "LT growth rate" in the following formula, need not be the same as the short-term growth rate used to produce the projections of the bank's balance sheets and income statements:

$$\text{Terminal value} = \frac{FCF_n * (1 + \text{LT growth rate})}{WACC - \text{LT growth rate}}$$

To arrive at the market value of the firm's debt plus equity, we add the cash and marketable securities to the enterprise value:

$$\begin{aligned}
\text{Market value} &= \text{Cash and marketable securities} \\
&\quad + \left[\sum_t \frac{FCF_t}{(1+WACC)^t}\right] * (1+WACC)^{0.5} \\
&= \left[\sum_{t=1}^{n} \frac{FCF_t}{(1+WACC)^t} + \frac{\text{Terminal value}}{(1+WACC)^n}\right] * (1+WACC)^{0.5}
\end{aligned}$$

If we are valuing the equity of the firm, we subtract the value of the debt:

$$\begin{aligned}
\text{Equity value} &= \text{Market value} - \text{Debt} \\
&= \text{Cash and marketable securities} \\
&\quad + \left[\sum_{t=1}^{n} \frac{FCF_t}{(1+WACC)^t} + \frac{\text{Terminal value}}{(1+WACC)^n}\right] * (1+WACC)^{0.5} - \text{Debt} \\
&= \left[\sum_{t=1}^{n} \frac{FCF_t}{(1+WACC)^t} + \frac{\text{Terminal value}}{(1+WACC)^n}\right] * (1+WACC)^{0.5} \\
&\quad - (\text{Debt} - \text{Cash/Marketable securities})
\end{aligned}$$

Essentially we are writing the enterprise balance sheet in a slightly different form:

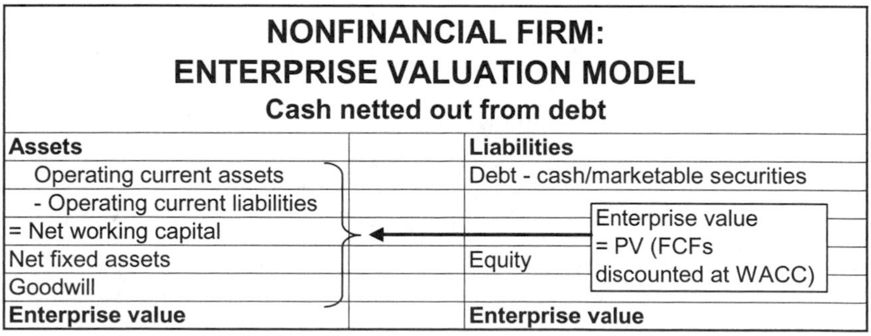

NONFINANCIAL FIRM:
ENTERPRISE VALUATION MODEL
Cash netted out from debt

Assets		**Liabilities**	
Operating current assets		Debt - cash/marketable securities	
- Operating current liabilities			
= Net working capital	←		Enterprise value = PV (FCFs discounted at WACC)
Net fixed assets		Equity	
Goodwill			
Enterprise value		**Enterprise value**	

5.2.2 Applying This Model to Banks

In the enterprise valuation model for nonfinancial firms, we lump together all financial liabilities (whether classified by accountants as current liabilities or as long-term liabilities) under the category of debt for a nonfinancial firm. Thus the net working capital in the preceding scheme represents only *operating* current assets. When this logic is applied to banks, a conceptual change is required: Banks borrow money (whether in the form of deposits or of loans from other financial institutions or markets) and then lend it out. It follows that when we are valuing or analyzing a bank, we should distinguish between the bank's borrowing *for the purpose of making loans* and the bank's *permanent debt.* (This is not to say that this distinction can always be made in practice.)[1]

Once we have made this conceptual distinction, we can apply the enterprise valuation model to banks. The distinction between funds used for the bank's lending activities and funds used as part of the bank's longer-term financing means that there are some important differences between banks and nonfinancial companies:

- **On the asset side**: For a nonfinancial company, cash and marketable securities are usually a store of value. For a bank, however, most marketable securities (and some of the cash) constitute an operating current asset.
- **On the liability side**: For a nonfinancial company, we put all debt items together, even if—from an accounting point of view—they are current liabilities. Thus,

Debt (nonfinancial company) = Long-term debt + Notes payable
+ Current portion of LTD + . . .

For a bank, most or all of the short-term debt items are *operating current liabilities* and are therefore part of the bank's working capital.

To stress this difference between nonfinancial companies and banks, we will analyze the balance sheets of two banks, Summit Bank and Cullen Frost Bankers.

5.2.3 Example 1: Summit Bank

Summit Bank is a small New Jersey bank. Following are the Summit Bank balance sheets for 1996 and 1997.

1. By permanent debt we mean essentially the same as Tier 2 capital (see box on p. 183).

SUMMIT BANK 1996 and 1997, (thousand $)		
ASSETS	**1997**	**1996**
Cash and due from banks	30,487	28,339
Federal funds sold	35,760	20,350
Investment securities		
Securities available-for-sale, at fair value	60,476	58,576
Securities held-to-maturity, at cost (fair value of $45,360,000 and $58,629,000 at December 31, 1997 and 1996, respectively)	45,151	58,437
Total investment securities	**141,387**	**137,363**
Loans, net of unearned discount	276,069	220,006
allowance for loan losses	-4,065	-2,972
Loans, net	**272,004**	**217,034**
Premises and equipment, net of depreciation	7,916	7,105
Accrued income receivable	3,442	3,189
Other real estate	151	166
Other assets	4,407	2,052
TOTAL ASSETS	**459,794**	**395,248**
LIABILITIES AND SHAREHOLDERS' EQUITY	**1997**	**1996**
Noninterest-bearing demand deposits	126,398	103,695
Interest-bearing deposits	275,326	241,328
Total deposits	**401,724**	**345,023**
Securities sold under agreement to repurchase	14,689	13,209
Accrued interest payable	678	638
Other liabilities	1,591	1,298
TOTAL LIABILITIES	**418,682**	**360,168**
Common Stock	8,127	4,041
Capital Surplus	6,251	6,136
Retained Earnings	26,491	24,675
Unrealized gain on investment securities available-for-sale, net of tax	243	228
Total shareholders equity	**41,112**	**35,080**
TOTAL LIABILITIES AND SHAREHOLDERS' EQUITY	**459,794**	**395,248**

A careful examination of these balance sheets leads to the conclusion that Summit Bank has no permanent debt. All the liabilities are funds that have been borrowed in order to finance the bank's lending and short-term investment activities and are therefore part of its working capital. Summit Bank has no permanent debt capital, so that it is effectively an all-equity enterprise. Rewriting the balance sheets to reflect this fact gives us the following:

SUMMIT BANK 1996 and 1997, (thousand $)			SUMMIT BANK'S BALANCE SHEETS IN ENTERPRISE VALUE FORM		
ASSETS	**1997**	**1996**	**ASSETS**	**1997**	**1996**
Cash and due from banks	30,487	28,339	Cash and due from banks	30,487	28,339
Federal funds sold	35,760	20,350	Total investment securities	141,387	137,363
Investment securities					
Securities available-for-sale, at fair value	60,476	58,576	Loans, Net	272,004	217,034
Securities held-to-mmaturity, at cost (fair value of $45,360,000 and $58,629,000 at December 31, 1997 and 1996, respectively)	45,151	58,437			
Total investment securities	**141,387**	**137,363**	Minus short-term liabilities	-418,682	-360,168
Loans, net of unearned discount	276,069	220,006			
Allowance for loan losses	-4,065	-2,972			
Loans, net	**272,004**	**217,034**			
Premises and equipment, net of depreciation	7,916	7,105			
Accrued income receivable	3,442	3,189			
Other real estate	151	166			
Other assets	4,407	2,052	Net fixed and other assets	15,916	12,512
TOTAL ASSETS	**459,794**	**395,248**	**ENTERPRISE VALUE**	**41,112**	**35,080**
LIABILITIES AND SHAREHOLDERS' EQUITY	**1997**	**1996**	**LIABILITIES AND SHAREHOLDERS' EQ**	**1997**	**1996**
Noninterest-bearing demand deposits	126,398	103,695			
Interest-bearing deposits	275,326	241,328			
Total deposits	**401,724**	**345,023**			
Securities sold under agreement to repurchase	14,689	13,209			
Accrued interest payable	678	638	"Permanent debt"	0	0
Other liabilities	1,591	1,298			
TOTAL LIABILITIES	**418,682**	**360,168**			
Common stock	8,127	4,041	Common Stock	8,127	4,041
Capital surplus	6,251	6,136	Capital Surplus	6,251	6,136
Retained earnings	26,491	24,675	Retained Earnings	26,491	24,675
Unrealized gain on investment securities available-for-sale, net of tax	243	228	Unrealized Gain on Investment Securities Available-for-Sale, Net of Tax	243	228
Total shareholders equity	**41,112**	**35,080**	**Total shareholders equity**	41,112	35,080
TOTAL LIABILITIES AND SHAREHOLDERS' EQUITY	**459,794**	**395,248**	**ENTERPRISE VALUE**	**41,112**	**35,080**

Capital Requirements for Banks: Basel I and Basel II

A series of international accords fixes standards of capital adequacy for banks by classifying a bank's capital according to its riskiness and the ease with which it can be redeemed at the option of the owner. A bank's core capital is the financing that is not readily redeemable by the owners and consists of Tier 1 and Tier 2 capital.

A bank's Tier 1 capital is essentially its common stock plus its irredeemable preferred stock. A bank's Tier 2 capital consists of some of the bank's debt: Nonredeemable subordinated-term debt (debt that will be paid out only after ordinary depositors of the bank have been paid) and intermediate-term preferred stock. Tier 2 capital does not include most debt that is used by the bank for financial intermediation and that is used for the short-term financing of a bank's commercial activities.

In our valuation examples equity can be thought of as corresponding to Tier 1 capital and debt as corresponding to Tier 2 capital.

5.2.4 Example 2: Cullen Frost

We do the same exercise for Cullen Frost Bankers, a much larger bank. The balance sheet for Cullen Frost is as follows:

	A	B	C	D
1	**CULLEN FROST BANKERS, INC. Balance Sheet**			
2	**Assets:**	**2005**	**2004**	
3	Cash and due from banks	873,015,000	545,602,000	
4	Interest-bearing deposits	6,438,000	3,512,000	
5	Federal funds sold and resell agreements	1,033,975,000	744,675,000	
6	Total cash and cash equivalents	1,913,428,000	1,293,789,000	
7				
8	Securities held to maturity	12,701,000	16,714,000	
9	Securities available for sale, fair value	3,059,111,000	2,957,296,000	
10	Trading account securities	6,217,000	4,671,000	
11				
12	Loans, net of unearned discounts	6,085,055,000	5,164,991,000	
13	Less: Allowance for possible loan losses	-80,325,000	-75,810,000	
14	Net loans	6,004,730,000	5,089,181,000	
15				
16	**Sum of cash, securities, and loans**	**10,996,187,000**	**9,361,651,000**	<-- =C14+C10+C9+C8+C6
17				
18	Premises and equipment, net	182,356,000	170,026,000	
19	Goodwill	168,983,000	102,367,000	
20	Other intangible assets, net	14,903,000	14,149,000	
21	Cash value of life insurance policies	102,604,000	105,223,000	
22	Accrued interest receivable	276,404,000	199,371,000	
23	**Total assets**	**11,741,437,000**	**9,952,787,000**	<-- =C16+SUM(C18:C22)
24				
25	**Liabilities:**	**2005**	**2004**	
26	**Deposits:**			
27	Non-interest-bearing demand deposits	3,484,932,000	2,969,387,000	
28	Interest-bearing deposits	5,661,462,000	5,136,291,000	
29	Total deposits	9,146,394,000	8,105,678,000	<-- =SUM(C27:C28)
30				
31	Federal funds purchased and repurchase agreements	740,529,000	506,342,000	
32	Subordinated notes payable and other borrowings	188,617,000	150,872,000	<-- Longer-term borrowing
33	Junior subordinated deferrable interest debentures	226,805,000	226,805,000	<-- Longer-term borrowing
34	Accrued interest payable and other liabilities	456,856,000	140,695,000	
35	**Total liabilities**	**10,759,201,000**	**9,130,392,000**	<-- =SUM(C31:C34)+C29
36				
37	**Shareholders Equity:**			
38	Common stock	550,000	536,000	
39	Additional paid-in capital	285,802,000	212,910,000	
40	Retained earnings	776,193,000	697,872,000	
41	Deferred compensation	-6,175,000	-5,567,000	
42	Accumulated other comprehensive loss, net of tax	-50,442,000	-10,784,000	
43	Treasury stock	-23,692,000	-72,572,000	
44	Total shareholders equity	982,236,000	822,395,000	<-- =SUM(C38:C43)
45	**Total liabilities and shareholders equity**	**11,741,437,000**	**9,952,787,000**	<-- =C44+C35

Notice that the liabilities of Cullen Frost are approximately equal to the firm's cash, securities, and loans (the two highlighted rows). Two items—subordinated notes and junior subordinated debentures—are essentially long-term borrowings of the company and should not be considered part of its working capital. Taking this fact into account, we get the following enterprise-value balance sheet for Cullen Frost:

	A	B	C	D
1	**CULLEN FROST BANKERS INC Enterprise Value Balance Sheet**			
2	**Assets:**	**2005**	**2004**	
3	Short-term assets	10,996,187,000	9,361,651,000	
4	Short-term liabilities	10,343,779,000	8,752,715,000	<-- ='Page 184'!C35-SUM('Page 184'!C32:C33)
5	Net working capital	652,408,000	608,936,000	<-- =C3-C4
6				
7	Other assets	745,250,000	591,136,000	<-- =SUM('Page 184'!C18:C22)
8	**Enterprise value**	**1,397,658,000**	**1,200,072,000**	<-- =SUM(C5:C7)
9				
10	Debt	415,422,000	377,677,000	<-- =SUM('Page 184'!C32:C33)
11	Equity	982,236,000	822,395,000	<-- ='Page 184'!C44
12	**Enterprise value**	**1,397,658,000**	**1,200,072,000**	<-- =C11+C10

Cullen Frost's short-term liabilities are calculated by subtracting its subordinated debt from the liabilities on the balance sheet. This longer-term debt, not directly related to the bank's lending activities—$415 million in 2005 and $377 million in 2004—is part of the firm's enterprise value.

5.3 The Bank's Free Cash Flow

The FCF calculations for an industrial company explained in Chapters 3 and 4 have to be modified somewhat when considering a financial company. Recall that the standard FCF calculation for an industrial company (see Chapter 3) is along the following lines:

Free Cash Flow Calculation for a Nonfinancial Company

Profit after taxes	The starting point for FCF
Add back depreciation	Depreciation is a noncash expense.
Subtract out increases in *operating net working capital*	NWC is a financial burden on the company that is not accounted for in the profit; the emphasis on *operating NWC* comes because we include only items like accounts receivable, accounts payable, inventories, etc. For purposes of calculating ΔNWC, we do not include changes in cash (assumed to be a store of value), notes payable, current portion of long-term debt, etc.
Subtract increases in fixed assets at cost	This item measures the cost of purchasing new productive assets for the company.
Add back after-tax interest	FCF is an *operating* concept; adding back after-tax interest costs neutralizes the effects of interest on the firm's profits.
= Free cash flow	

This calculation has to be modified for a bank. On the one hand, since cash, loans, deposits, short-term borrowings, and so forth are all part of a bank's productive working capital, we cannot add back the net interest on these items.[2] On the other hand, the bank's permanent capital includes both its equity and its long-term borrowing. The "free cash flow question"—for a bank as for an industrial company—is, How much *cash* would the company have produced were it an *unlevered entity*? What complicates things for a bank is that its productive assets are debts and loans. Our calculation for a bank's free cash flow is as follows:

Free Cash Flow Calculation for a Financial Company

Profit after taxes	
Add back depreciation	Depreciation is usually not a very significant item
Add back other noncash charges	In the case of Cullen Frost, for example, we add back loan loss provisions.
Subtract out increases in *operating NWC*	Since we define the NWC to include deposits, etc., this step effectively subtracts the *self-funded* part of the banks operations from the FCF. A bank's NWC includes all short-term liabilities used to fund the bank's lending and investment activities.
Subtract increases in fixed assets at cost	Note that fixed assets for banks are typically small relative to total assets.
Add back after-tax interest on *permanent debt items* (typically long-term debt)	This step leaves the net interest income on the bank's productive activities—its financial intermediation—in the FCF calculation.
= Free cash flow	For an all-equity bank, this figure is equal to the consolidated cash flow.

For Cullen Frost, the free cash flow can be most easily computed by making the necessary changes to the bank's consolidated statement of cash flows.

2. For an industrial company, cash is usually *not* part of operating working capital. (There are exceptions, of course: A supermarket needs some money in the till.) For a bank, however, a significant part of cash balances clearly constitutes a part of working capital. See the calculation of the bank's free cash flow that follows.

	A	B	C	D	E
1	**CULLEN FROST BANKERS, INC.** **Computing the Free Cash Flow from the Consolidated Statement of Cash Flows**				
2	**Operating activities:**	**2005**	**2004**	**2003**	
3	Net income	165,423,000	141,325,000	130,501,000	
4	Adjustments to reconcile net income to net cash from operating activities:				
5	Provision for possible loan losses	10,250,000	2,500,000	10,544,000	
6	Deferred tax expense (benefit)	555,000	5,319,000	-3,778,000	
7	Accretion of loan discounts	-10,124,000	-6,102,000	-4,127,000	
8	Securities premium amortization (discount accretion), net	329,000	1,815,000	1,167,000	
9	Net (gain) loss on securities transactions	-19,000	3,377,000	-40,000	
10	Depreciation and amortization	24,357,000	24,482,000	25,751,000	
11	Origination of loans held for sale, net of principal collected	-60,839,000	-61,035,000	-63,828,000	
12	Proceeds from sales of loans held for sale	76,431,000	58,139,000	50,813,000	
13	Net gain on sale of loans held for sale and other assets	-3,418,000	-2,274,000	-3,465,000	
14	Net proceeds from settlement of legal claims	-2,389,000	0	0	
15	Tax benefit from stock compensation	11,371,000	11,524,000	3,638,000	
16	Amortization of deferred compensation	1,986,000	1,377,000	833,000	
17	Earnings on life insurance policies	-3,934,000	-4,128,000	-4,624,000	
18	Net change in:				
19	Trading account securities	-1,546,000	918,000	-594,000	
20	Accrued interest receivable and other assets	-52,150,000	-30,480,000	25,334,000	
21	Accrued interest payable and other liabilities	-23,847,000	-17,976,000	34,237,000	
22	**Net cash from operating activities**	**132,436,000**	**128,781,000**	**202,362,000**	<-- =SUM(D3:D21)
23					
24	**Investing activities:**	**2005**	**2004**	**2003**	
25	Securities held to maturity:				
26	Purchases			-1,000,000	
27	Maturities, calls and principal payments	4,004,000	8,466,000	12,023,000	
28	Securities available for sale:				
29	Purchases	-10,763,788,000	-8,518,256,000	-8,603,817,000	
30	Sales	19,812,000	597,369,000	6,768,029,000	
31	Maturities, calls and principal payments	10,944,589,000	7,873,115,000	1,272,290,000	
32	Net change in loans	-605,415,000	-581,043,000	-65,555,000	
33	Net cash paid in acquisitions	-13,297,000	-7,063,000	-750,000	
34	Proceeds from sales of premises and equipment	465,000	276,000	1,070,000	
35	Purchases of premises and equipment	-18,098,000	-15,398,000	-12,512,000	
36	Benefits received on life insurance policies	6,553,000	4,883,000	3,296,000	
37	Proceeds from sales of repossessed properties	3,457,000	4,247,000	7,211,000	
38	**Net cash from investing activities**	**-421,718,000**	**-633,404,000**	**-619,715,000**	<-- =SUM(D26:D37)
39					
40	**Financing activities:**	**2005**	**2004**	**2003**	
41	Net change in deposits	721,655,000	36,821,000	440,714,000	
42	Net change in short-term borrowings	234,187,000	84,541,000	-389,417,000	
43	Principal payments on notes payable and other borrowings				
44	Proceeds from junior subordinated deferrable interest debentures				
45	Proceeds from stock option exercises				
46	Purchase of treasury stock				
47	Cash dividends paid				
48	**Net cash from financing activities**	**955,842,000**	**121,362,000**	**51,297,000**	<-- =SUM(D41:D47)
49					
50	**Free cash flow (FCF)**	**666,560,000**	**-383,261,000**	**-366,056,000**	<-- =D22+D38+D48

In this spreadsheet we have used the format of the consolidated statement of cash flows. The highlighted items relate to Cullen Frost's financing that we consider to be not directly related to its lending or other banking activities. The sum of the activities is the bank's free cash flow.

5.4 Large Bank Corporation Buys Small Bank: A Valuation Example

We implement the bank FCF valuation model by examining a possible purchase of Small Bank, Inc., by Large Bank Corporation. Our problem will be the valuation of Small Bank. In February 2007, Daniel Rogers, the CEO of Large Bank Corporation, was approached by an investment banker representing Small Bank, Inc. Small Bank's board had become convinced that there was no future for Small without its incorporation into a larger corporate structure. Small Bank was a very conservatively financed bank that had 350 offices throughout North and South Carolina. Its loan portfolio was about 70 percent consumer loans, 20 percent real estate lending, and 10 percent commercial loans. Small Bank was largely deposit driven: Of the $9 billion of total assets at year-end 1997, $7.6 billion were deposits, a significant percentage of which were non-interest-bearing. Large Bank, by contrast, had $31 billion of deposits out of total assets of $45 billion, but $23 billion of these deposits were interest-bearing. Small Bank's management was concerned that the cost of deposits would rise over the coming years, as their customers started to become more like the sophisticated customers of Large Bank. Furthermore, Small Bank's management knew that there were significant economies of scale in check processing and other "back office" activities that would stem from a merger with a large, efficient organization like Large Bank. Small Bank's current share price was $45.

Dan Rogers was interested in the deal: Under his leadership, Large Bank Corporation had been aggressive in purchasing numerous smaller banks. Its stock price rise had been very impressive, and Rogers was determined to keep purchasing banks. Large Bank had also branched out into securities dealership, having purchased one of the major mutual fund organizations. In the course of its expansions, Large Bank had learned some lessons the hard way:

- Engage only in share deals: Large Bank's preferred merger was an exchange of shares and a pooling of interest.
- Make purchases only where markets were mutually exclusive.
- Make purchases only where significant operational gains could be made.

5.4.1 Analysis

Rogers asked one of his financial analysts to perform a "quick and dirty" analysis of a possible merger between the two financial institutions. He wanted to come up with a range of possible values for Small Bank so that he could then discuss the merger with his chairman. If the chairman and some other leading members of the board's finance committee thought that the proposed merger should be brought to the full board of Large Bank, then an investment banking adviser would be brought in to work with the bank's staff to do a full-blown (and expensive) analysis of the merger.

5.4.2 The Model

Large Bank's financial analyst built a model, based only on publicly available information and some educated guesses. The critical assumptions of the model were as follows:

- Increasing cost of deposits over time: The market for "free" deposits—deposit accounts without interest paid to the depositor—was thought to be gradually phased out.
- A dividend payout ratio of 60 percent.
- Five percent of deposits held as non-interest-bearing cash.
- No increase in Small Bank's debt.
- A significant decrease in Small Bank's expense ratio (calculated by the analyst as the percentage of expenses out of net interest income). This represented savings in staffing and computerization—much of Small Bank's back office work could comfortably be accommodated by Large Bank with a significant decrease in costs.

	A	B	C	D	E	F	G	H
1				**SMALL BANK Pro forma model**				
2	Cash as percent of deposits	5.0%						
3	Interest on cash	0.0%						
4	Interest on other investment securities	6.19%						
5	Interest on mortgages	8.13%						
6	Interest on other earning assets	6.71%						
7	Interest on loans	8.77%						
8								
9	Interest on deposits	3.51%	3.60%	3.80%	3.90%	4.00%	4.20%	
10	Interest on short-term borrowing	4.72%						
11	Interest on long-term debt	6.38%						
12								
13	Loan loss as % of outstanding loans	0.30%						
14	Noninterest income as % of interest income	25.30%						
15	Noninterest expense as % of net interest income	70.00%	<-- was 74.35%, but Large Bank analyst thinks this will go down to 70%					
16								
17	Growth rate of net loans	6%						
18	Growth rate of deposits	5%						
19								
20	Depreciation rate	10%						
21	Income tax rate	35%						
22	Dividend payout ratio	60%						
23								
24								
25	**Balance sheets**	**2006 Financial statements**	**2007**	**2008**	**2009**	**2010**	**2011**	
26	Cash	386,832	400,042	420,044	441,046	463,098	486,253	<-- =$B$2*G40
27	Other investment securities, including money market instruments [balance sheet plug]	2,190,106	942,851	949,564	952,879	952,403	947,709	<-- =IF(G26+G28+G29+G30+G35+G37>G47, 0,G47-(G26+G28+G29+G30+G35+G37))
28	Mortgage loans held for sale	18,953	18,953	18,953	18,953	18,953	18,953	<-- =F28
29	Other earning assets	21,444	21,444	21,444	21,444	21,444	21,444	<-- =F29
30	Loans, net	5,869,914	6,222,109	6,595,435	6,991,161	7,410,631	7,855,269	<-- =F30*(1+$B$17)
31								
32	Land	38,099	38,099	38,099	38,099	38,099	38,099	
33	Other fixed assets	282,956	356,728	396,364	440,405	489,339	543,709	<-- =G34+G35
34	Accumulated depreciation	156,754	192,427	232,063	276,104	325,038	379,408	<-- =F34-G69
35	Net fixed assets and land	164,301	164,301	164,301	164,301	164,301	164,301	<-- =F35
36								
37	Other assets	360,087	360,087	360,087	360,087	360,087	360,087	<-- =F37
38	**Total Assets**	9,011,637	8,129,786	8,529,828	8,949,872	9,390,918	9,854,016	<-- =G37+G35+SUM(G26:G30)
39								
40	Deposits	7,619,842	8,000,834	8,400,876	8,820,920	9,261,966	9,725,064	<-- =F40*(1+$B$18)
41	Short-term borrowings [balance sheet plug]	251,687	0	0	0	0	0	<-- =IF(G38>G40+SUM(G42:G46),G38-G40-SUM(G42:G46),0)
42	Long-term indebtedness	2,826	2,826	2,826	2,826	2,826	2,826	<-- =F42
43	Other liabilities	126,126	126,126	126,126	126,126	126,126	126,126	<-- =F43
44	Shareholders' Equity							
45	Stock	489,322	489,322	489,322	489,322	489,322	489,322	
46	Accumulated retained earnings	521,834	585,807	646,865	709,962	775,863	844,684	<-- =F46+G74
47	**Total Liabilities and Shareholders' Equity**	9,011,637	8,129,786	8,529,828	8,949,872	9,390,918	9,854,016	<-- =SUM(G40:G44)
48								
49								
50	**Income statements**		**2007**	**2008**	**2009**	**2010**	**2011**	
51	Interest income							
52	Interest on cash balances		0	0	0	0	0	<-- =$B$3*(G26+F26)/2
53	Interest on other investment securities		96,965	58,570	58,881	58,968	58,808	<-- =$B$4*(G27+F27)/2
54	Interest on mortgage loans		1,541	1,541	1,541	1,541	1,541	<-- =$B$5*(G28+F28)/2
55	Interest on other earning assets		1,439	1,439	1,439	1,439	1,439	<-- =$B$6*(G29+F29)/2
56	Interest on net loans		530,235	562,049	595,772	631,519	669,410	<-- =$B$7*(G30+F30)/2
57	Total interest income		630,180	623,599	657,633	693,467	731,198	<-- =SUM(G52:G56)
58								
59	Interest expense							
60	Interest on deposits		-280,829	-302,432	-335,195	-361,217	-389,003	<-- =-F9*G40
61	Interest on short-term borrowings		0	0	0	0	0	<-- =-$B$10*G41
62	Interest on long-term borrowing		-180	-180	-180	-180	-180	<-- =-$B$11*G42
63	Total interest expense		-281,010	-302,612	-335,375	-361,397	-389,183	<-- =SUM(G60:G62)
64								
65	Net interest income		349,170	320,987	322,257	332,070	342,015	<-- =G57+G63
66	Provision for loan loss		-18,138	-19,226	-20,380	-21,603	-22,899	<-- =-$B$13*(G30+F30)/2
67	Noninterest income		159,436	157,771	166,381	175,447	184,993	<-- =$B$14*G57
68	Noninterest expenses		-244,419	-224,691	-225,580	-232,449	-239,411	<-- =-$B$15*G65
69	Depreciation and amortization		-35,673	-39,636	-44,040	-48,934	-54,371	<-- =-$B$20*G33
70	Income before income tax		246,049	234,841	242,678	253,465	264,699	<-- =SUM(G65:G68)
71	Provision for income tax		86,117	82,194	84,937	88,713	92,645	<-- =$B$21*G70
72	Net income		159,932	152,646	157,741	164,753	172,054	<-- =G70-G71
73	Dividends		95,959	91,588	94,645	98,852	103,233	<-- =$B$22*G72
74	Retained earnings		63,973	61,059	63,096	65,901	68,822	<-- =G72-G73

The balance sheet model is similar to the model of section 3.7. There are effectively two plugs:

• Cash balances are determined by the assumption that Small Bank requires balances of 5 percent of deposits in cash.

• If the bank's activities can be financed by using balances of other securities (row 27), then these will be used.

• If the bank's activities require further financing, then this will come from short-term borrowing (row 41).

Given the pro formas, the analyst derived Small Bank's anticipated cash flows:

	A	B	C	D	E	F	G	H
77	**Free Cash Flow Calculations**		**2007**	**2008**	**2009**	**2010**	**2011**	
78	Profit after taxes		159,932	152,646	157,741	164,753	172,054	<-- =G72
79	Add back depreciation		35,673	39,636	44,040	48,934	54,371	<-- =-G69
80	Add back after-tax interest on permanent debt		117	117	117	117	117	<-- =-(1-$B$21)*G62
81	Changes in operating Net Working Capital							
82	Subtract increases in Cash		-13,210	-20,002	-21,002	-22,052	-23,155	<-- =F26-G26
83	Subtract increases in Fixed Assets at Cost		-73,772	-39,636	-44,040	-48,934	-54,371	<-- =F33-G33
84	Free cash flow		108,740	132,761	136,856	142,817	149,016	<-- =SUM(G78:G83)

The β of Small Bank is estimated to be 0.9. Since Small Bank has very little permanent debt, the analyst assumes that it is essentially an all-equity firm. This assumption gives the following valuation:

	A	B	C	D	E	F	G	H
85	**Valuation of FCFs and terminal value**							
86	Equity beta	0.9						
87	Risk-free rate	5.80%						
88	Market risk premium	8.00%						
89	Cost of equity, r_E	10.97%	<-- =B87*(1-B21)+B86*B88					
90	Cost of debt, r_D	6.38%	<-- =B11					
91								
92	Current market value/share of Small Bank	51.00	<-- This is the current market value of Small Bank shares					
93	Number of shares of Small Bank	32,406,000						
94	Equity value	1,652,706,000	<-- =B92*B93					
95	Debt value	128,952						
96	Percentage of equity in capital structure	99.99%	<-- =B94/(B94+B95)					
97	Percentage of debt in capital structure	0.01%	<-- =1-B96					
98	Tax rate	35%	<-- =B21					
99								
100	Discount rate, WACC	10.97%	<-- =B89*B96+B97*(1-B98)*B90					
101	Terminal growth rate of FCF	5.00%						
102								
103			**2007**	**2008**	**2009**	**2010**	**2011**	
104	Free Cash Flow		112,401	136,423	140,517	146,479	152,678	<-- =G83
105	Terminal value						2,685,288	<-- =G104*(1+B101)/(B89-B101)
106	Total		112,401	136,423	140,517	146,479	2,837,966	<-- =G104+G105
107								
108	Value of Small Bank	2,210,090,780	<-- =NPV(B100,C106:G106)*(1+B100)^0.5*1000					
109	Long-term debt	128,952,000	<-- =B42*1000					
110	Implied equity value	2,081,138,780	<-- =B108-B109					
111	Number of Small Bank shares	32,406,000						
112	Imputed per-share value of Small Bank	64.22	<-- =B110/B111					

Here are several comments about this valuation:

• For generality, we have computed the WACC of Small Bank by taking the weighted average of its market equity value (cell B94) and its debt (B95). We could, of course, have just "eyeballed" the data and seen that Small Bank is essentially an all-equity operation. Neither deposits nor short-term debt are counted as debt for the purposes of computing the WACC.

• Because we have written Small Bank's financial statements in thousands of dollars, we multiply the valuations in rows 108 and following by 1,000.

• Although the current market value of a share of Small Bank is $51 (cell B92), the value per share imputed by the Large Bank analyst is significantly more (cell B112).

5.4.3 Sensitivity Analysis

By doing a **Data|Table** on the WACC and the long-term growth rate, the Large Bank analyst can judge the sensitivity of the valuation on its two main determinants:

	A	B	C	D	E	F	G
126	**Sensitivity analysis of Small Bank's value as function of its WACC and long-term growth** **Noninterest expense as % of net interest income (cell B15): 70.00%**						
127							
128	Data table header: =B112 -->	64.22	**0%**	**2%**	**3%**	**5%**	**6%**
129		**8.0%**	43.85	51.36	56.54	72.08	84.54
130		**8.5%**	43.02	50.39	55.45	70.68	82.88
131		**9.0%**	42.22	49.43	54.39	69.31	81.26
132		**9.5%**	41.44	48.50	53.36	67.97	79.68
133		**10.0%**	40.67	47.59	52.35	66.66	78.14
134		**10.5%**	39.92	46.70	51.37	65.39	76.63
135		**11.0%**	39.19	45.83	50.41	64.15	75.16
136		**11.5%**	38.47	44.99	49.47	62.93	73.73
137		**12.0%**	37.78	44.16	48.55	61.75	72.33

The efficiency ratio is an important determinant of the valuation. If Small Bank's noninterest expense ratio can be reduced by a further 5 percent, then the valuation rises significantly:

	A	B	C	D	E	F	G
126	**Sensitivity analysis of Small Bank's value as function of its WACC and long-term growth Noninterest expense as % of net interest income (cell B15): 65.00%**						
127							
128	Data table header: =B112 -->	69.18	**0%**	**2%**	**3%**	**5%**	**6%**
129		**8.0%**	47.36	55.41	60.95	77.60	90.95
130		**8.5%**	46.48	54.36	59.79	76.10	89.17
131		**9.0%**	45.62	53.34	58.66	74.63	87.43
132		**9.5%**	44.78	52.34	57.55	73.20	85.74
133		**10.0%**	43.95	51.37	56.47	71.80	84.09
134		**10.5%**	43.15	50.41	55.41	70.43	82.47
135		**11.0%**	42.37	49.48	54.38	69.10	80.90
136		**11.5%**	41.60	48.58	53.38	67.80	79.36
137		**12.0%**	40.85	47.69	52.39	66.53	77.86

5.5 Calculating the Exchange Ratio

At the time of the case, Large Bank had 294,330,960 shares worth $58 per share. Large Bank intended to do an exchange offer for Small Bank's shares, and the question about the proper exchange ratio was discussed. Assuming that the pro forma valuation of Large Bank is correct, this yields an exchange ratio of

$$x = \frac{\text{Calculated per-share valuation of Small Bank}}{\text{Current market price per share of Large Bank}}$$

Doing these calculations yields the following:

	A	B	C	D	E	F
108	Value of Small Bank	2,210,090,780	<-- =NPV(B100,C106:G106)*(1+B100)^0.5*1000			
109	Long-term debt	128,952,000	<-- =B42*1000			
110	Implied equity value	2,081,138,780	<-- =B108-B109			
111	Number of Small Bank shares	32,406,000				
112	Imputed per-share value of Small Bank	64.22	<-- =B110/B111			
113						
114	Number of Large Bank shares	294,330,960				
115	Value of Large Bank share	58.00				
116	Market value of Large Bank equity, before merger	17,071,195,680	<-- =B115*B114			
117	Exchange ratio (number of shares of Large Bank offered per share of Small Bank), x	1.11	<-- =B112/B115			
118						
119	**Check**					
120	Number of shares, new entity	330,212,663	<-- =B114+B117*B111			
121	Value of equity, new entity	19,152,334,460	<-- =B114*B115+B110			
122	Total value of Large Bank ex-shareholders	17,071,195,680	<-- =B115*B114			
123	Total value of Small Bank ex-shareholders	2,081,138,780	<-- =B115*B111*B117			

The exchange ratio of 1.11 (cell B117) is the maximum exchange ratio that Large Bank should offer for Small Bank. It could, of course, offer less: There is plenty of negotiating room between the current market value of Small Bank ($51 per share) and the imputed value from the

FCF valuation of $64.22. For example, if Large Bank offers an exchange ratio of 1, it is essentially valuing Small Bank at the same price as Large Bank and thus still offering the Small Bank shareholders a premium of $7 over their current market value.

5.6 Alternatives to Free Cash Flow Valuation of Financial Institutions

In the next two sections we show two variations on the bank valuation model. The first model assumes that the projected equity payouts of an institution are determined by the necessity to reserve a percentage of the retained earnings as reserves.

The second model assumes that the price/earnings (P/E) ratios are used to value a bank acquisition. This is a common practice in the banking industry.

5.7 Valuing a Bank by Using Capital Adequacy Ratios

An alternative way to value a bank is to back into the equity cash flows by modeling the bank's capital adequacy ratios.[3,4] Implementing this approach determines the maximum payout to equity as a residual determined by capital adequacy requirements:

Residual Approach to Bank Equity Cash Flow

Assets	Liabilities
Cash and marketable securities	Operating current liabilities—borrowed funds
Loan portfolio	Debt
Net fixed assets	Equity
Total assets	**Total liabilities and equity**

Next year's equity =
Year-t equity
+% reserve against increase in loan portfolio
+% margin for business expansion, prudence, etc.
⇒ Determines maximum payout to equity

3. I am indebted to Hernán Burde for sharing this idea with me. Hernán suggested that this particular form of bank valuation may be very appropriate to underbanked countries, where the growth rate of a financial institution is essentially determined by a bank's ability to maintain its capital adequacy. I suspect this approach also works well for many small banks in more sophisticated economies.

4. These valuations could be based either on BIS requirements or on a VaR approach.

Here is a simple example:

	A	B	C	D	E	F	G	H
1	**VALUING ROSARIO BANK** **A model using residual equity cash flows**							
2	Cash as percent of deposits	20%						
3	Deposit growth	10%						
4	Loan growth	12%						
5	Interest paid on deposits	1%						
6	Interest earned on loans	11%						
7	Interest paid on borrowing	6%						
8	General, selling, administrative expenses, growth	3%						
9	Fixed assets at cost, growth	10%						
10	Depreciation rate	8%						
11	Equity as percentage of loans	15%	<-- Capital adequacy ratio					
12								
13	**Balance sheet**							
14	**Assets**	**2006**	**2007**	**2008**	**2009**	**2010**	**2011**	
15	Cash	740,000	814,000	895,400	984,940	1,083,434	1,191,777	<-- =G24*$B$2
16	Loans	4,000,000	4,480,000	5,017,600	5,619,712	6,294,077	7,049,367	<-- =F16*(1+$B$4)
17								
18	Fixed assets at cost	400,000	440,000	484,000	532,400	585,640	644,204	<-- =F18*(1+$B$9)
19	Depreciation	100,000	133,600	170,560	211,216	255,938	305,131	<-- =F19+$B$10*AVERAGE(F18:G18)
20	Net fixed assets	300,000	306,400	313,440	321,184	329,702	339,073	<-- =G18-G19
21	**Total Assets**	5,040,000	5,600,400	6,226,440	6,925,836	7,707,214	8,580,217	<-- =G20+G16+G15
22								
23	**Liabilities and equity**	**2006**	**2007**	**2008**	**2009**	**2010**	**2011**	
24	Deposits	3,700,000	4,070,000	4,477,000	4,924,700	5,417,170	5,958,887	<-- =F24*(1+$B$3)
25	Borrowing	700,000	858,400	996,800	1,158,179	1,345,932	1,563,925	<-- =IF(G21>G24+SUM(G26:G28),G21-G24-SUM(G26:G28),0)
26	Shareholders' equity							
27	Stock	200,000	200,000	200,000	200,000	200,000	200,000	
28	Accumulated retained earnings	440,000	472,000	552,640	642,957	744,112	857,405	<-- =$B$11*G16-G27
29	**Total Liabilities and Shareholders' Equity**	5,040,000	5,600,400	6,226,440	6,925,836	7,707,214	8,580,217	<-- =SUM(G24:G28)

Rosario Bank is an all-equity bank that uses deposits and relatively modest borrowing to finance substantial cash reserves and a growing loan portfolio. The bank's accumulated retained earnings are determined by the necessity of maintaining a 15 percent ratio of equity to its loan portfolio (highlighted row 28). Therefore, the bank's borrowing is the plug in the balance sheet model.

Rosario Bank pays little on its deposits and earns well on its loans. Its income statement is as follows:

	A	B	C	D	E	F	G	H
31	**Income statement**	**2006**	**2007**	**2008**	**2009**	**2010**	**2011**	
32	Interest income	440,000	466,400	522,368	585,052	655,258	733,889	<-- =$B$6*AVERAGE(F16:G16)
33	Interest expense							<--
34	Paid on deposits	-37,000	-38,850	-42,735	-47,009	-51,709	-56,880	<-- =-$B$5*AVERAGE(F24:G24)
35	Paid on loans	-42,000	-46,752	-55,656	-64,649	-75,123	-87,296	<-- =-$B$7*AVERAGE(F25:G25)
36	GSA expense	-200,000	-200,000	-200,000	-200,000	-200,000	-200,000	
37	Depreciation	-30,000	-33,600	-36,960	-40,656	-44,722	-49,194	
38	Net income	131,000	147,198	187,017	232,738	283,704	340,520	<-- =SUM(G32:G37)

Rosario Bank's payouts to equity holders are determined by the capital adequacy ratio:

	A	B	C	D	E	F	G	H
40	**Cash flow to equity**		**2007**	**2008**	**2009**	**2010**	**2011**	
41	Net income		147,198	187,017	232,738	283,704	340,520	<-- =G38
42	Add back depreciation		33,600	36,960	40,656	44,722	49,194	<-- =-G37
43	Free cash flow		180,798	223,977	273,394	328,426	389,713	<-- =SUM(G41:G42)
44	Subtract increase in accumulated retained earnings		-32,000	-80,640	-90,317	-101,155	-113,293	<-- =F28-G28
45	Equity cash flow		329,596	367,314	456,472	555,697	666,133	<-- =SUM(G41:G44)

We now use the model of Chapter 3: We value Rosario Bank by discounting its equity cash flows at the cost of equity, modeling the terminal value by using an estimated long-term equity cash flow growth rate:

	A	B	C	D	E	F	G	H
47	**Valuing Rosario Bank**							
48	Cost of equity, r_E	16.00%						
49	Long-term equity cash flow growth	8.00%						
50								
51			**2007**	**2008**	**2009**	**2010**	**2011**	
52	Equity cash flow		329,596	367,314	456,472	555,697	666,133	<-- =G45
53	Bank terminal value						8,992,802	<-- =G52*(1+B49)/(B48-B49)
54	Total equity cash flow + terminal value		329,596	367,314	456,472	555,697	9,658,935	<-- =SUM(G52:G53)
55								
56	Valuation, using midyear discounting	6,198,542	<-- =NPV(B48,C54:G54)*(1+B48)^0.5					

5.8 Using P/Es to Value a Bank Acquisition: First Federal Savings Bank

We finish this chapter with a minicase that illustrates yet another approach to bank valuation. This time we use P/E ratios to value a bank.[5]

Here's the story: Your client, Fairmont National Bank, a $750 million community bank in Fairmont, West Virginia, has received an invitation to bid competitively to acquire First Federal Savings Bank, 20 miles away in Clarksburg, West Virginia. The invitation was sent out by First Federal's investment banker. Fairmont National has asked your firm to assist them in bidding for First Federal. Your assistance would include

- Evaluating First Federal as an acquisition considering Fairmont National's objectives.
- Predicting the actions of other potential bidders including Clarksburg National Bank, about the same size as Fairmont National, but headquartered 20 miles away, and a likely bidder.
- Preparing the client's bid including the price (i.e., the financial consideration) and a list of social undertakings (the nonfinancial consideration) including the probable number of First Federal's employees who would be terminated after the acquisition and the amount of termination compensation they would receive.

5. I want to thank David Martin and Jon Holtaway of Danielson Associates for helping me with this case.

5.8.1 Fairmont National Bank

Your client is a better-than-average performer, but it wasn't always. Ten years ago it was a poor performer: expenses were too high, fee income was too low, and it was relatively underlent—all measured in terms of its peers. After a change in management, Fairmont National began to improve steadily by controlling expenses more effectively, adjusting its fee schedules, and focusing more management attention on lending. But for the past two years, earnings have been flat, and loan growth has slowed. Meanwhile, equity has been growing in relation to assets, causing Fairmont's return on equity to fall slightly.

Fairmont's management concluded that it could no longer grow the bank's earnings by fixing its problems—it had to expand either by opening branches or by acquiring another bank. De novo branch openings offer a very slow payback, and in an industry that is already overbanked and overbranched, it usually makes more sense to acquire a bank and eliminate a competitor than to open a branch and add a competitor. Consequently, when Fairmont management heard about the opportunity to acquire First Federal, they were enthusiastic and determined to bid aggressively but sensibly. "Aggressively but sensibly" means they wanted to win and would be willing to suffer a short-term financial setback if it promised to pay off in the longer term. They hired you, their investment banker, to advise them on bidding for First Federal.

5.8.2 First Federal Savings Bank

First Federal is a traditional thrift. That is, it was organized under laws that effectively limited it to residential mortgage lending. Traditionally, thrifts funded their residential lending with passbook savings and certificates of deposit, and as passbook savings became a smaller and smaller part of thrifts' funding, their net interest margins grew very thin. In recent years, thrifts have been permitted to engage in virtually every business permitted to commercial banks, but most have found it difficult to develop the more profitable business enjoyed by commercial banks. The financial comparison of First Federal, Fairmont, and Clarksburg National Bank shows the typical differences between banks and thrifts.

First Federal's board and executives had felt they could "commercialize" the thrift, but they found the process was slow and began to doubt that they had the management to succeed. They felt, after talking with their investment bankers, that their franchise would be worth more to a commercial bank whose management could successfully commercialize First Federal. Moreover, prices being paid for both banks and thrift franchises were at all time highs, and First Federal's board believed the time was right to sell. First Federal's investment bankers told them that Fairmont and Clarksburg National Bank would be certain bidders and that others might bid as well.

First Federal has branches in both Fairmont's and Clarksburg's markets, but more in the latter's. First Federal expected that if Fairmont were the winning bidder at least two of its branches would be closed and consolidate with Fairmont's. If Clarksburg were the winner, as many as six of First Federal's branches would be closed. That difference meant two things—more First Federal employees would probably lose their jobs in a merger with Clarksburg, but First Federal's shareholders might receive more for their shares in a deal with Clarksburg. According to First Federal's investment bankers, however, Fairmont needed the deal for strategic reasons and for that reason might meet or beat a bid from Clarksburg.

5.8.3 Clarksburg National Bank

As the financial comparison shows, Clarksburg National Bank underperforms Fairmont, but enjoys a higher stock price (in relation to both book value and earnings). The reasons for this are not clear: Perhaps the reason is that Clarksburg's shares have been listed on the Nasdaq National Market for several years and Fairmont listed only recently. Also, Clarksburg has often been the subject of takeover rumors while Fairmont hasn't, and such rumors may add something to Clarksburg's stock price.

5.8.4 The Cities: Fairmont and Clarksburg

Although Fairmont, with 100,000 residents, is twice as large as Clarksburg, the two cities share many characteristics. Both are declining in population and commerce. Both have lost major manufacturing facilities. Their most prominent downtown structures are bank headquarter buildings, but most of those now house branches of large banks headquartered elsewhere. Both cities have prosperous suburbs served by busy shopping malls.

	A	B	C	D	E
1	**FIRST FEDERAL SAVINGS BANK** **Basic data about Fairmont National Bank (our client), First Federal Savings Bank (the target), and Clarksburg National Bank (the competitor)**				
2		**Fairmont**	**First Federal**	**Clarksburg**	
3	Assets	796,866,000	493,466,000	913,480,000	
4	Securities	245,767,000	194,792,000	280,010,000	
5	Residential loans	150,332,000	208,429,000	123,235,000	
6	Other loans	341,156,000	73,667,000	443,257,000	
7	Demand deposits	74,500,000	10,065,000	93,080,000	
8	Passbook savings accounts	195,446,000	69,644,000	155,127,000	
9	Certificates of deposit	195,473,000	239,247,000	390,263,000	
10	Total deposits	545,111,000	276,732,000	703,266,000	
11	Net income	12,941,000	3,538,000	9,510,000	
12	Shareholders' equity	86,579,000	37,329,000	79,428,000	
13					
14	Shares outstanding	6,300,000	869,364	6,900,000	
15					
16	Net interest income/Average assets	4.44%	2.71%	3.87%	
17	Non-interest income/Average assets	1.05%	0.37%	0.96%	
18	Non-interest expense/Average assets	2.66%	1.91%	3.09%	
19	Net income/Average assets	1.67%	0.74%	1.06%	
20					
21	Branch offices	24	7	25	
22					
23	Share price on February 2, 2007	35.00	-	37.25	
24					
25	Estimated cost savings from branch consolidations	450,000	nmf	1,000,000	
26					
27	Price/earnings (P/E) ratio	17.04		27.03	<-- =D23*D14/D11
28					
29					
30	**Valuation of First Federal using P/E ratios**	**Fairmont**		**Clarksburg**	
31	P/E ratio	17.04		27.03	
32	Value of First Federal at each bank's P/E ratio	60,283,518		95,620,868	<-- =D31*$C$11
33	Capitalized savings @ 10%	4,500,000		10,000,000	<-- =D25/0.1
34	**Valuation of First Federal**	64,783,518		105,620,868	<-- =D33+D32
35					
36	**Valuation using earnings/assets ratios**	**Fairmont**		**Clarksburg**	
37	Potential earnings on FF's assets at acquiror's ratio	8,240,882		5,230,740	<-- =$C$3*D19
38	**Valuation of First Federal**	140,415,310		141,370,226	<-- =D31*D37

5.8.5 Valuing First Federal Using P/E Ratios

The last rows of the preceding spreadsheet present a solution that is based on the P/E ratios of the two competing banks. This is a common practice in the banking industry; small bank boards basically understand only P/E ratios, and they are afraid of equity dilution—meaning that they will bid only slightly more than their existing P/E ratio. The P/E-based valuation assumes that each bank values First Federal at its own price/earnings ratio, with an addition for a capitalized savings from the merger.

It is clear that under this procedure Clarksburg can bid substantially more for First Federal than Fairmont Bank. The difference between the P/E ratios basically settles things: Fairmont will *never* be able to match

Clarksburg's bid! However, suppose we assume that First Federal can be made to earn at either Fairmont's or Clarkburg's earnings/assets ratio; then we get the following valuations:

	A	B	C	D	E
36	**Valuation using earnings/assets ratios**	**Fairmont**		**Clarksburg**	
37	Potential earnings on FF's assets at acquiror's ratio	8,240,882		5,230,740	<-- =$C$3*D19
38	**Valuation of First Federal**	140,415,310		141,370,226	<-- =D31*D37

Going back to the engagement terms, you, as Fairmont's investment banker, will have to advise your client how much to bid for First Federal. First Federal has stipulated that the transaction must be tax-free to its shareholders, and they would prefer to receive 100 percent common stock in the transaction. They would like the transaction price to be expressed as an exchange ratio; that is, they would want to know how many shares of the buyer's stock they would receive for each share of First Federal stock.

To solve for the exchange ratio, we have to solve the following equation:

$$\underbrace{\frac{x*N_{\text{FF}}}{x*N_{\text{FF}}+N_{\text{Acquirer}}}}_{\substack{\uparrow\\ \text{Percentage of}\\ \text{First Federal}\\ \text{shareholders in}\\ \text{combined firm}}} * \underbrace{\left(V_{\text{FF}}+V_{\text{Acquirer}}\right)}_{\substack{\uparrow\\ \text{Value of combined}\\ \text{firm}}} = \underbrace{V_{\text{FF}}}_{\substack{\uparrow\\ \text{Acquirer}\\ \text{valuation}\\ \text{of First Federal}}}$$

where x is the exchange ratio (number of shares of acquirer offered for each share of First Federal), N_{FF}, N_{Acquirer} is the number of shares of First Federal and acquirer, V_{FF} is the acquirer valuation of First Federal, and V_{A} is the market valuation of the acquirer.

This simple algebraic equation has the solution

$$x = \frac{N_{\text{Acquirer}} * V_{\text{FF}}}{N_{\text{FF}} * V_{\text{Acquirer}}}$$

Applying this in our spreadsheet gives us the following:

	A	B	C	D	E
42	**Computing the exchange ratio**				
43	**Based on valuation using P/E**	**Fairmont**		**Clarksburg**	
44	Acquirer's valuation of First Federal	64,783,518		105,620,868	<-- =D34
45	Acquirer's market value	220,500,000		257,025,000	<-- =D23*D14
46	Value of combined entity	285,283,518		362,645,868	<-- =D44+D45
47					
48	**Exchange ratio: Maximum shares of acquirer offered per share of First Federal**	2.13		3.26	<-- =D14*D44/($C$14*D45)
49	First Federal shareholders' portion of combined firm	22.71%		29.13%	<-- =$C$14*D48/($C$14*D48+D14)
50	Check: Valuation of First Federal in combined firm	64,783,518		105,620,868	<-- =D49*D46
51					
52	"Valuation" of First Federal shares at acquirer's preacquisition share price	74.52		121.49	<-- =D48*D23
53					
54					
55	**Based on valuation using earnings/assets ratios**	**Fairmont**		**Clarksburg**	
56	Acquirer's valuation of First Federal	140,415,310		141,370,226	<-- =D38
57	Acquirer's market value	220,500,000		257,025,000	<-- =D45
58	Value of combined entity	360,915,310		398,395,226	<-- =D56+D57
59					
60	**Exchange ratio: Maximum shares of acquirer offered per share of First Federal**	4.61		4.37	<-- =D14*D56/($C$14*D57)
61	First Federal shareholders' portion of combined firm	38.91%		35.48%	<-- =D60*$C$14/(D60*$C$14+D14)
62	Check: Valuation of First Federal in combined firm	140,415,310		141,370,226	<-- =D61*D58
63					
64	"Valuation" of First Federal shares at acquirer's preacquisition share price	161.51		162.61	<-- =D60*D23

Row 48 computes the exchange ratio when both Fairmont and Clarksburg value the target, First Federal, at their own P/E ratios. Row 60 repeats the exercise when both banks value First Federal based on their own earnings/assets ratios. Rows 52 and 64 are not strictly scientific, but they are indicative: Each row values the exchange offer at the preacquisition stock price of the acquirer.

6 The Financial Analysis of Leasing

6.1 Overview

A lease is a contractual arrangement by which the owner of an asset (the *lessor*) rents the assets to a *lessee*. In this chapter we analyze long-term leases, in which the asset spends most of its useful life with the lessee. In economic terms the leases we consider in this chapter are considered by the lessees as alternatives to purchasing an asset. Thus the analysis of this chapter fits many long-term equipment leases, but not short-term leasing (car rentals, for example). Financial theory regards such leases as being essentially debt contracts: For the lessee, the lease is an alternative to purchasing the asset with debt, and the lessor understands that it is essentially providing financing for the lessee.

In the example that follows we consider a company that is faced with the choice of either purchasing or leasing a piece of equipment. We assume that the operating inflows and outflows from the equipment are not affected by its ownership—irrespective of how the asset is held (whether owned or leased), the owner/lessee will have the same sales and must bear the responsibility for maintaining the equipment. In the words of Statement 13 of the Financial Accounting Standards Board, the lease we are considering is one that "transfers substantially all of the benefits and risks incident to the ownership of property" to the lessee.

The analysis in this chapter concentrates exclusively on the *cash flows* from the lease. It is assumed that the lessor pays taxes on the income from the lease rentals and gets a tax shield on the depreciation of the asset, and that the lessee can claim the rent as an expense. The analysis implicitly assumes that the tax authorities treat the lessor as the owner of the asset and the lessee as the user. As is explained in the appendix to this chapter, this assumption is not trivial. In addition to the cash-flow issues of leasing there are heavy accounting issues, which are also touched on briefly in the appendix.

6.2 A Simple Example

The essence of our analysis can be understood from the following simple example: A company has decided to acquire the use of a machine costing $600,000. If purchased, the machine will be depreciated on a straight-line basis to a residual value of zero. The machine's estimated life is six years, and the company's tax rate T_C is 40 percent.

The company's alternative to purchasing the machine is to lease it for six years. A lessor has offered to lease the machine to the company for $140,000 annually, with the first payment to be made today and with five additional payments to be made at the start of each of the next five years.

One way of analyzing this problem (a misleading way, as it turns out) is to compare the present values of the cash flows to the company of leasing and of buying the asset. The company feels that the lease payment and the tax shield from depreciation are riskless. Suppose, furthermore, that the risk-free rate is 12 percent. On the basis of the following calculation, the company should lease the asset.[1]

$$\text{NPV(leasing)} = \sum_{t=0}^{5} \frac{(1-T_c)*\text{Lease rental}}{(1+12\%)^t} = \sum_{t=0}^{5} \frac{(1-T_c)*140{,}000}{(1+12\%)^t} = 386{,}801$$

$$\text{NPV(buying)} = \text{Asset cost} - \text{PV(Tax shields on depreciation)}$$

$$= 600{,}000 - \sum_{t=1}^{6} \frac{0.40*100{,}000}{(1+12\%)^t} = 435{,}544$$

In a spreadsheet:

	A	B	C
1	**HOW NOT TO ANALYZE A LEASE**		
2	Asset cost	600,000	
3	Interest rate	12%	
4	Lease rental payment	140,000	
5	Annual depreciation	100,000	
6	Tax rate	40%	
7			
8	NPV(leasing)	386,801	<-- =-PV(B3,5,B4*(1-B6))+B4*(1-B6)
9	NPV(buying)	435,544	<-- =B2+PV(B3,6,B6*B5)

This analysis suggests that leasing the asset is preferable to buying it. However, it is misleading because it ignores the fact that leasing is very much like buying the asset with a loan. The financial risks are thus different when we compare a lease (implicitly a purchase with loan financ-

1. At this point we assume that the residual value of the asset at the end of its life is zero. In section 6.5 we drop this assumption.

ing) against a straightforward purchase without loan financing. If the company is willing to lease the asset, then perhaps it should also be willing to borrow money to buy the assets. This borrowing will change the cash-flow patterns and could also produce tax benefits. Hence, our decision about the leasing decision could change if we were to take the loan potential into account.

In the following section we present a method of analyzing leases that deals with this problem by imagining what kind of loan would produce cash flows (and hence financial risks) equivalent to those produced by the lease. This method of lease analysis is called the *equivalent-loan method.*

6.3 Leasing and Firm Financing: The Equivalent-Loan Method

The idea behind the equivalent-loan method is to devise a hypothetical loan that is somehow equivalent to the lease.[2] It then becomes easy to see whether the lease or the purchase of an asset is preferable.

The easiest way to understand the equivalent loan method is with an example. We return to the previous example:

	A	B	C	D	E	F	G	H
1	**EQUIVALENT LOAN METHOD**							
2	Asset cost	600,000						
3	Interest rate	12%						
4	Lease rental payment	140,000						
5	Annual depreciation	100,000						
6	Tax rate	40%						
7								
8	**Year**	**0**	**1**	**2**	**3**	**4**	**5**	**6**
9								
10	**After-tax cash flows from leasing**							
11	After-tax lease rental	-84,000	-84,000	-84,000	-84,000	-84,000	-84,000	
12								
13	**After-tax cash flows from buying the asset**							
14	Asset cost	-600,000						
15	Depreciation tax shield		40,000	40,000	40,000	40,000	40,000	40,000
16	Net cash from buying	-600,000	40,000	40,000	40,000	40,000	40,000	40,000
17								
18	**Differential cash flow: Lease saves lessor**							
19	Lease minus buy	516,000	-124,000	-124,000	-124,000	-124,000	-124,000	-40,000
20								
21	IRR of differential cash flow	8.30%	<-- =IRR(B19:H19,0)					
22								
23	Decision??	Buy	<-- =IF(B21<(1-B6)*B3,"Lease","Buy")					

2. This method is due to Myers, Dill, and Bautista (1976). A somewhat more accessible explanation can be found in Levy and Sarnat (1979).

Rows 2–6 give the various parameters of the problem. The spreadsheet then compares two *after-tax* cash flows, that of the lease and that of the buy; we write outflows with a minus sign and inflows (such as the tax shield from the depreciation) with a plus sign.

• The cash flow from leasing the asset is (1 – Tax rate) * Lease payment, in each of years 0–5.

• The cash flow from buying the asset is the asset cost in year 0 (an outflow, hence positive) and the tax shield on the asset's depreciation, *tax rate * depreciation*, in years 1–6 (an inflow, hence written here with a positive sign).

Line 19 of the spreadsheet shows the *differential cash flow* between the lease and the buy decision. This line shows that leasing the asset, instead of buying it, results in the following cash flows to the lessor:

• A cash inflow of $516,000 in year 0. This inflow is the *cash saved at time 0* by the lease: Purchasing the asset costs $600,000, whereas leasing the asset costs only $84,000 on an after-tax basis.

• A cash outflow of $124,000 in years 1–5 and an outflow of $40,000 in year 6. This outflow corresponds to the *marginal after-tax cost of the lease versus the buy* in these years. This marginal cost has two components: the after-tax lease payment ($84,000) and the fact that when we lease we do not get the tax shield on the asset's depreciation ($40,000).

Thus leasing instead of purchasing the asset is like getting a loan of $516,000 with after-tax repayments of $124,000 in years 1–5 and an after-tax repayment of $40,000 in year 6. The lease, in other words, can be viewed as an alternative method of financing the asset. *In order to compare the lease to the buy, we should compare the cost of this financing with the cost of alternative financing*. The internal rate of return of line 21—8.30 percent—gives us the cost of the financing implicit in the lease; this is larger than the after-tax cost of firm borrowing, since in this case (where the firm's tax rate is 40 percent and its borrowing cost is 12 percent), this cost is 7.20 percent. Thus our conclusion: Buying is preferable to leasing.

6.3.1 Why We Decided Against the Lease

Not everyone is fully convinced by the preceding argument. We therefore present an alternative argument in this subsection. We show that if the firm can borrow at 12 percent, it can borrow *more money* with the *same schedule of after-tax repayments* as that which resulted from the lease versus the buy. This hypothetical loan is shown in the following table:

	A	B	C	D	E	F	G
26				Split of loan repayment between:			
27	Year	Principal at beg. year	Loan payment, end year	Interest	Repayment of principal	After-tax loan repayment	Lease minus buy cash flows, years 1-6
28	1	532,070	149,539	63,848	85,691	124,000	124,000
29	2	446,379	145,426	53,565	91,861	124,000	124,000
30	3	354,518	141,017	42,542	98,475	124,000	124,000
31	4	256,044	136,290	30,725	105,565	124,000	124,000
32	5	150,479	131,223	18,057	113,166	124,000	124,000
33	6	37,313	41,791	4,478	37,313	40,000	40,000
34							
35	=NPV((1-$B$6)*$B$3,G28:$G$33)		=$B$3*B28	=B28-B29		=(1-$B$6)*D28+E28	
36		=D28+B28-B29					
37							

The table (a version of the loan tables discussed in Chapter 1) shows the principal of a hypothetical bank loan bearing a 12 percent interest rate. At the beginning of year 0 (that is, at the time when the firm either purchases or leases the asset), for example, the firm borrows $532,070 from the bank. At the end of the year, the firm repays $149,539 to the bank, of which $63,848 is interest (since $63,848 = 12 percent ∗ $532,070) and the remainder, $85,691, is repayment of principal. The net, after-tax, repayment in year 1—assuming full tax deductibility of the interest payment—is (1 – 40 percent) ∗ $63,848 + $85,691 = $124,000, which is, of course, the same after-tax differential cash flow calculated in our original spreadsheet.

Payments in subsequent years are calculated similarly to the illustration in the preceding paragraph. At the beginning of year 6, there is still $37,313 of principal outstanding; this is fully paid off at the end of the year with an after-tax payment of $40,000.

The point of this example? If the firm is considering leasing the asset in order to get the financing of $516,000 that the lease gives, it should instead borrow $532,070 from the bank at 12 percent; it can repay this larger loan with the same after-tax cash flows as are implicit in the lease. The bottom line: Purchasing is still preferable to leasing the asset.

The alternative loan table shown above was constructed in the following way:

The principal at the beginning of each of years 1–6 is the present value of the lease-versus-buy outflows, discounted at (1 – 38 percent) * 12 percent. Thus, for example,

$$532{,}070 = \sum_{t=1}^{5} \frac{124{,}000}{[1+(1-0.40)\cdot 0.12]^t} + \frac{40{,}000}{[1+(1-0.40)\cdot 0.12]^6}$$

$$446{,}379 = \sum_{t=1}^{4} \frac{124{,}000}{[1+(1-0.40)\cdot 0.12]^t} + \frac{40{,}000}{[1+(1-0.40)\cdot 0.12]^5}$$

$$\vdots$$

$$37{,}313 = \frac{40{,}000}{[1+(1-0.40)\cdot 0.12]}$$

Once the principal at the start of each year is known, it is an easy matter to construct the rest of the columns.

Interest = 12 percent * Principal, beginning of year
Total payment = Interest in year t + Repayment of principal in year t
After-tax payment, year t = (1 – Tax rate) * Interest + Repayment of principal

6.4 The Lessor's Problem: Calculating the Highest Acceptable Lease Rental

The lessor's problem is the opposite of that of the lessee:

- The lessee has to decided whether—given a rental rate on the leased asset—it is preferable to buy the asset or lease it.
- The lessor has to decide what *minimum rental rate* justifies the purchase of the asset in order to lease it out.

One way of solving the lessor's problem is to turn the preceding analysis around. We use the Excel Goal Seek (**Tools|Goal Seek**) to get $134,826 as the lessor's minimum acceptable rental:

	A	B	C	D	E	F	G	H
1		**THE LESSOR'S PROBLEM** **Calculating the lowest acceptable lease rate**						
2	Asset cost	600,000						
3	Interest rate	12%						
4	Lowest acceptable lease payment	134,826	<-- Computed either with **Goal Seek** or **Solver**					
5	Annual depreciation	100,000						
6	Tax rate	40%						
7								
8	**Year**	**0**	**1**	**2**	**3**	**4**	**5**	**6**
9								
10	**Lessor after-tax cash flows from leasing**							
11	After-tax lease rental	80,896	80,896	80,896	80,896	80,896	80,896	
12								
13	**Lessor after-tax cash flows from buying the asset**							
14	Asset cost	-600,000						
15	Depreciation tax shield		40,000	40,000	40,000	40,000	40,000	40,000
16	Net cash from buying	-600,000	40,000	40,000	40,000	40,000	40,000	40,000
17								
18	**Lessor cash flows**							
19	Lease + buy	-519,104	120,896	120,896	120,896	120,896	120,896	40,000
20								
21	IRR of differential cash flow	7.22%	<-- =IRR(B19:H19,0)					

Here's what the **Goal Seek** settings look like:

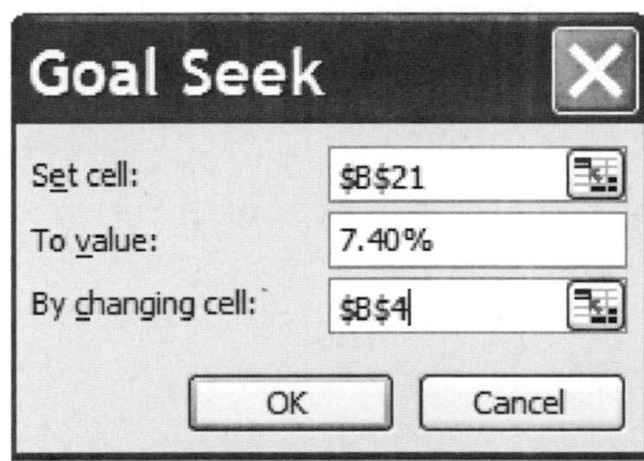

If you're using **Solver** to do this problem, it would look like:

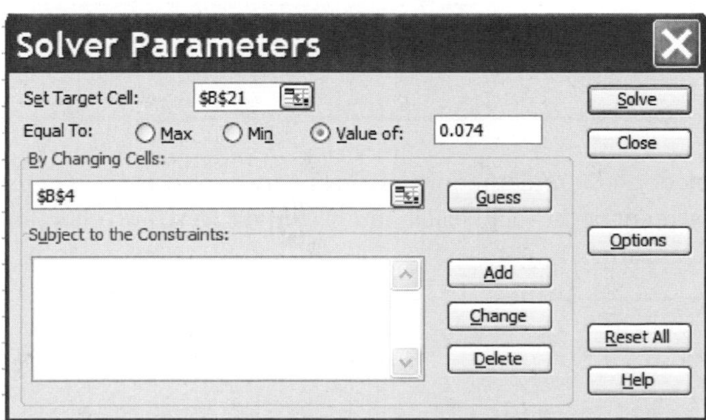

Some Peculiarities of the Excel Solver and Excel Goal Seek

1. Neither of these (otherwise wonderful) Excel tools will accept a formula in the box that specifies the target. Thus—in the present example—we would have liked to write the formula **=(1-B6)*B3** in the “To value” box of **Goal Seek**. But that technique won’t work: We have to specify a numerical value (in this case, the after-tax interest rate).

2. You may have to fiddle with **Tools|Options|Calculation** in order to specify enough accuracy to get cell B21 to be exactly 7.22 percent. If you do not get an acceptable answer, set a higher value for the option **Maximum change**.

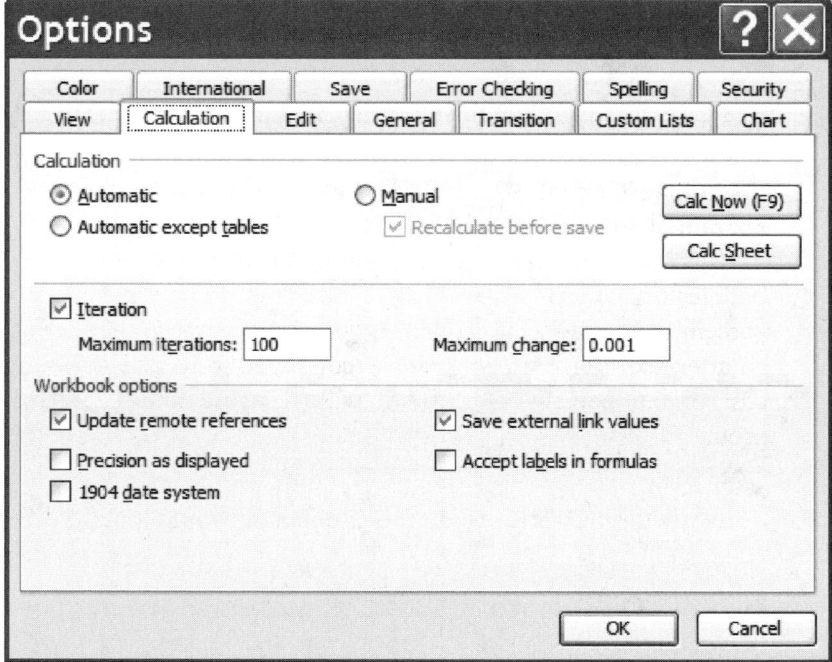

3. **Goal Seek** does not remember its settings between accesses. Therefore, you will have to reenter the data each time. (**Solver**, on the other hand, does remember its settings.)

6.4.1 Minicase: When Is Leasing Profitable for Both the Lessor and Lessee?

The symmetry between the lessee's problem and the lessor's problem suggests that if the lessee wants to lease, it will not be profitable for the lessor to purchase the asset in order to lease it out.

In some cases, however, it may be that the differences in tax rates between the lessee and the lessor make it profitable for both to enter into a leasing arrangement. Here is an example: Greenville Electric Corporation is a public utility that pays no taxes. Its credit rating is of the highest order, since all of Greenville's debts are guaranteed by the city of Greenville. Greenville Electric has decided that it requires a new turbine. The turbine costs $12 million and will be depreciated to zero salvage value over three years. Greenville Electric borrows at 6 percent.

Greenville can either lease or buy the plant. The lease offer it has is $2.3 million per year for six years (starting today); the lessee is a captive leasing subsidiary of United Turbine Corporation, the manufacturer of the turbine. United Turbine Leasing also borrows at 6 percent and has a tax rate of 40 percent.

As can be seen in the following spreadsheet, the lease is profitable to both lessor and lessee. Greenville Electric gets financing at a cost of 5.96 percent, compared to its borrowing cost of 6 percent; United Turbine gets an after-tax return of 3.96 percent, compared to its after-tax borrowing cost of 3.6 percent. Both Greenville Electric and United Turbine profit.[3]

3. Who loses? The government, of course! What makes the lease profitable is the utilization of otherwise unused depreciation tax shields.

	A	B	C	D	E	F	G
1	**GREENVILLE ELECTRIC CORPORATION**						
2	Turbine cost	12,000,000					
3	Greenville's borrowing rate	6.00%					
4	Lease payment	2,300,000					
5							
6	**Year**	**0**	**1**	**2**	**3**	**4**	**5**
7	**Lessee after-tax lease costs**						
8	After-tax lease rental	-2,300,000	-2,300,000	-2,300,000	-2,300,000	-2,300,000	-2,300,000
9							
10	**Lessee after-tax purchase costs**						
11	Asset cost	-12,000,000					
12	Depreciation tax shield (Greenville Electric's tax rate = 0)		0	0	0	0	0
13	Net cash from buying	-12,000,000	0	0	0	0	0
14							
15	**Cash saved by leasing**						
16	Lease - purchase cash flows	9,700,000	-2,300,000	-2,300,000	-2,300,000	-2,300,000	-2,300,000
17							
18	IRR of differential cash flow	5.96%	<-- =IRR(B16:G16,0)				
19	Greenville's after-tax borrowing cost	6.00%	<-- =B3				
20							
21	**UNITED TURBINE LEASING CORPORATION**						
22	Turbine cost	12,000,000					
23	Lease payment	2,300,000					
24	Depreciable life (years)	3					
25	Depreciation (straight line, 3 years)	4,000,000					
26	United Turbine's borrowing rate	6.00%					
27	United Turbine's corporate tax rate	40%					
28							
29	**Year**	**0**	**1**	**2**	**3**	**4**	**5**
30	**Lessor cash flows**						
31	Equipment cost	-12,000,000					
32	Lease payment, after tax	1,380,000	1,380,000	1,380,000	1,380,000	1,380,000	1,380,000
33	Depreciation tax shield		1,600,000	1,600,000	1,600,000	0	0
34	Total lessor cash flow	-10,620,000	2,980,000	2,980,000	2,980,000	1,380,000	1,380,000
35							
36	IRR of lessor cash flows	3.86%	<-- =IRR(B34:G34)				
37	United Turbine's after-tax borrowing cost	3.60%	<-- =B26*(1-B27)				

6.5 Asset Residual Value and Other Considerations

In the example of sections 6.3 and 6.4 we ignored the residual value of the asset—its anticipated market value at the end of the lease term. In a mechanical sense, it is easy to include the residual value in the calculations (but you have to be careful—see the warning after the numerical example). Suppose, for example, you think that the asset will have a market value of \$100,000 in year 7; assuming that this value is fully taxed (after all, we've depreciated the asset to zero value over the first six years), the after-tax residual value will be (1 – Tax rate) ∗ \$100,000 = \$60,000.

	A	B	C	D	E	F	G	H	I
1	**RESIDUAL VALUES IN LEASE ANALYSIS**								
2	Asset cost	600,000							
3	Interest rate	12%							
4	Lease rental payment	140,000							
5	Annual depreciation	100,000							
6	Tax rate	40%							
7	Residual value	100,000	<-- Anticipated to be realized in year 7; fully taxed						
8									
9	**Year**	**0**	**1**	**2**	**3**	**4**	**5**	**6**	**7**
10									
11	**After-tax cash flows from leasing**								
12	After-tax lease rental	-84,000	-84,000	-84,000	-84,000	-84,000	-84,000		
13									
14	**After-tax cash flows from buying the asset**								
15	Asset cost	-600,000							
16	Depreciation tax shield		40,000	40,000	40,000	40,000	40,000	40,000	
17	After-tax residual								60,000
18	Net cash from buying	-600,000	40,000	40,000	40,000	40,000	40,000	40,000	60,000
19									
20	**Differential cash flow**								
21	Lease minus buy	516,000	-124,000	-124,000	-124,000	-124,000	-124,000	-40,000	-60,000
22									
23	IRR of differential cash flow	10.49%	<-- =IRR(B21:I21,0)						
24									
25	Decision??	Buy	<-- =IF(B23<(1-B6)*B3,"Lease","Buy")						

Not surprisingly, the possibility of realizing an extra cash flow from asset ownership makes the lease even less attractive than before (you can see this difference by noting that the return rate in cell B23, the IRR of the differential cash flows, has increased from 8.30 percent in our original example to 10.49 percent).

Be a bit careful here, however; the spreadsheet treats the residual value as if it has the same certainty of realization as the depreciation tax shields and the lease rentals. This assumption can be far from the truth! There is no good practical solution to this problem; an ad hoc way of dealing with it might be to reduce the $100,000 by a factor that expresses the uncertainty about its realization. The finance technical jargon for this is "certainty-equivalence factor," and you can find it referenced in any basic finance text.[4] The last spreadsheet snapshot in this chapter (which follows) assumes that you've decided that the certainty-equivalence factor for the residual value is 0.7:

4. For further references on certainty equivalents, see Brealey, Myers, Allen (2005, chapter 9). However, note that neither this work nor the present text (nor anyone else) can tell you precisely how to calculate the certainty-equivalence factor. It depends on your attitudes toward risk.

	A	B	C	D	E	F	G	H	I	J
1	**RESIDUAL VALUES IN LEASE ANALYSIS** **Estimated residual value multiplied by certainty-equivalence factor which represents uncertainty about realizing residual**									
2	Asset cost	600,000								
3	Interest rate	12%								
4	Lease rental payment	140,000								
5	Annual depreciation	100,000								
6	Tax rate	40%								
7	Residual value	100,000	<-- Anticipated to be realized in year 7; fully taxed							
8	Certainty-equivalence factor	0.70								
9										
10	**Year**	**0**	**1**	**2**	**3**	**4**	**5**	**6**	**7**	
11										
12	**After-tax cash flows from leasing**									
13	After-tax lease rental	-84,000	-84,000	-84,000	-84,000	-84,000	-84,000			
14										
15	**After-tax cash flows from buying the asset**									
16	Asset cost	-600,000								
17	Depreciation tax shield		40,000	40,000	40,000	40,000	40,000	40,000		
18	After-tax residual								42,000	<-- =(1-B6)*B7*B8
19	Net cash from buying	-600,000	40,000	40,000	40,000	40,000	40,000	40,000	42,000	
20										
21	**Differential cash flow**									
22	Lease minus buy	516,000	-124,000	-124,000	-124,000	-124,000	-124,000	-40,000	-42,000	
23										
24	IRR of differential cash flow	9.88%	<-- =IRR(B22:I22,0)							

6.6 Summary

This chapter has looked at the lease-purchase decision. We have examined the decision to lease as a purely financing decision, assuming (1) that all operational factors between leasing and buying are equivalent, and (2) that the essential firm decision to acquire the use of the asset has already been made. On the basis of these assumptions, the lease-purchase decision can be made using the equivalent-loan method.

Exercises

1. Your company is considering either purchasing or leasing an asset that costs \$1,000,000. The asset, if purchased, will be depreciated on a straight-line basis over six years to a zero residual value. A leasing company is willing to lease the asset for \$300,000 per year; the first payment on the lease is due at the time the lease is undertaken (i.e., year 0), and the remaining five payments are due at the beginning of years 1–5. Your company has a tax rate t_C = 40 percent and can borrow at 10 percent from its bank.

   a. Should your company lease or purchase the asset?

   b. What is the maximum lease payment it will agree to pay?

2. ABC Corporation is considering leasing an asset from XYZ Corporation. Here are the relevant facts:

Asset cost	\$1,000,000
Depreciation schedule	Year 1: 20% Year 2: 32% Year 3: 19.20% Year 4: 11.52% Year 5: 11.52% Year 6: 5.76%
Lease term	6 years
Lease payment	\$200,000 per year, at the beginning of years 0, 1, . . . , 5
Asset residual value	Zero
Tax rates	ABC: $t_C = 0\%$ (ABC has tax-loss carryforwards that prevent it from utilizing any additional tax shields) XYZ: $t_C = 40\%$

ABC's interest costs are 10% and XYZ's interest costs are 7%. Show that it will be advantageous both for ABC to lease the asset and for XYZ to purchase the asset in order to lease it out to ABC.

3. Continuing with the same example: Find the *maximum rental* that ABC will pay and the *minimum rental* that XYZ will accept.

4. Perform a sensitivity analysis (using **Data|Table**, see Chapter 31) on the certainty-equivalence factor in section 6.5, showing how the IRR of the differential cash flows varies with the CE factor.

Appendix: The Tax and Accounting Treatment of Leases

This chapter discusses the case where the lessor retains the tax benefits of ownership; that is, the lessor is able to take the depreciation on the leased asset, and the lessee deducts the lease payments from his income as an expense. In order for these things to happen, it is critical that the Internal Revenue Service be willing to recognize the lease as a *true lease*.

Although the specific IRS rules change from time to time, the principle underlying the rules remains that the lessor should be accorded the benefits of ownership only if he bears some of the economic risks of ownership. This principle has led the IRS to develop a series of tests to determine whether or not the lessor has transferred essentially all of the ownership risks to the lessee. If this is the case, the IRS treats the "lease" arrangement as a sale of the asset by the "lessor" to the "lessee." If the ownership risks have not all been transferred to the lessee, then the lease is a true lease and the analysis of the chapter holds.

Revenue Ruling 55–540 sets out seven conditions under which a transaction will be found to be a sale rather than a lease for tax purposes:

1. Portions of the rental payments are specifically applicable to an equity interest to be acquired by the lessee.
2. The lessee will acquire title upon payment of a stated amount of rentals.
3. A substantial proportion of the asset's purchase price is paid in rentals in a relatively short period of time from the inception of the lease.
4. The rental payments exceed a "fair" rental value.
5. There is a bargain-purchase option; the option price is nominal in relation to the fair market value of the asset at the time when the option can be exercised.
6. Some part of the payments is designated as interest.
7. The lease may be renewed at nominal rentals over the useful life of the asset.

In addition to these conditions, Revenue Ruling 55–541 deals with the relation of the lease term to the useful life of the asset. The ruling would seem to suggest that the transaction will be classified as a conditional sale and not as a lease if the useful life of the asset is not in excess of the lease term.

One lease packager states that the IRS will generally classify a lease as a true lease if all the following criteria are met:

- The estimated fair market value of the leased asset at the end of the lease term will equal at least 20 percent of the original cost of the leased property.
- The lease term does not exceed 80 percent of the estimated useful life of the asset.
- There is no bargain-purchase option.
- The lessor's equity in the leased asset is at least 20 percent.

The Accounting Treatment of Leases

Accountants have found leases troublesome. Before the advent of Financial Accounting Standards Board Statement 13 (FASB 13) in 1976, it was common for firms to leave leases off their balance sheets altogether and to record only as footnotes to the financial statement the fact that some assets were leased. This practice created an asymmetry between the accounting treatment of a lease and the accounting treatment of a purchase of an asset with debt. Since the economic similarity between these two transactions is great, this asymmetric treatment is illogical.

FASB 13 attempts to solve this problem. The statement is long and complex, and it is beyond the purview of this book to fully present the statement's solutions. We will sketch here the solution to the problem as outlined in FASB 13; the next chapter deals with FASB 13's treatment of the leveraged leases.

The basic idea behind the FASB 13 treatment of leases is that *in some cases* the lessee should record a leased asset on his balance sheet, *even though legally the asset belongs to another party*. The cases in which this should happen are those in which the economic substance of the lease transaction (as opposed to the legal fiction) is that the lessee effectively owns the asset. An example would be a 10-year noncancelable lease of an automobile. By the time the car is returned to the lessor, it is likely to be practically worthless; hence, FASB 13 would require the lessee to record the asset on his balance sheet.

Formally, FASB 13 requires the lessee to put the lease on his balance sheet (the terminology is that in this case the lease is a *capital lease*) if one of four criteria applies:

1. The lease transfers ownership of the property to the lessee at the end of the lease term.
2. The lease contains a bargain-purchase option, which allows the lessee to purchase the leased asset at a very low price at the end of the lease term.
3. The lease term exceeds 75 percent of the life of the asset.
4. The present value of the lease payments (at the lessee's incremental borrowing rate) exceeds 90 percent of the asset's fair value.

If a lease is a capital lease under the FASB 13 rules, then the lessee records the capital lease as an asset and records a corresponding liability on his balance sheet. The asset is then depreciated, and the liability is amortized over the lease term. It is as if the asset in question has been bought with 100 percent loan financing.

What does the lessor do if the lessee has to record the lease on his balance sheet? If the lessee has (in an accounting sense) bought the asset with 100 percent loan financing, then the lessor must have (in the same sense) sold the asset with 100 percent loan financing. This is the essence of the FASB 13 treatment of the lessor.

Reconciling the Tax and Accounting Treatments of Leases

The tax treatment and the accounting treatment of leases are very similar in spirit. It is therefore logical to expect that whenever a lease is classified under the FASB 13 rules as a capital lease, it should be classified by the IRS as a sale. Thus, if the world were a rational place, lessees would put leases on their books only if the IRS decided to treat leases as sales.

However, the world is a funny place. It turns out to be fairly simple to keep a lease off the lessee's balance sheet, have the IRS treat it as a true lease, and still have all the parties involved feel as if they had transferred all of the economic benefits of ownership from the lessor to the lessee. See the references for further reading.

7 The Financial Analysis of Leveraged Leases

7.1 Overview

In Chapter 6 we analyzed the lease-versus-purchase decision from the points of view of both the lessee (the long-term user of the asset) and the lessor (the asset's owner, who rents it out to the lessee). In this chapter we analyze leveraged leasing: In a leveraged lease the lessor finances the purchase of the asset to be leased with debt. From the point of view of the lessee, there is no difference in the analysis of a leveraged or a nonleveraged lease. From the lessor's point of view, however, the cash flows of a leveraged lease present some interesting problems.

At least six parties are typically involved in a leveraged lease: the lessee, the equity partners in the lease, the lenders to the equity partners, an owner trustee, an indenture trustee, and the manufacturer of the asset. In most cases, a seventh party is also involved: a lease packager (a broker or leasing company). Figure 7.1 illustrates the arrangements among the six parties of a typical leveraged lease.

The two major problems related to the analysis of leveraged leases are these:

1. *The straightforward financial analysis of the lease from the point of view of the lessor*. This concerns the calculation of the cash flows obtained by the lessor, and a computation of these cash flows' net present value (NPV) or internal rate of return (IRR).

2. *The accounting analysis of the lease*. Accountants use a method called the *multiple phases method* (MPM) to calculate a rate of return on leveraged leases. The MPM rate of return is different from the internal rate of return (IRR). In an ordinary financial context this difference should be of no concern, since the efficient-markets hypothesis tells us that only cash flows matter. However, in a less than efficient world, people tend to get very concerned about how things look on their financial statements. Since the accounting rate of return on the lease is difficult to compute, we will use Excel to calculate it; then we will analyze the results.

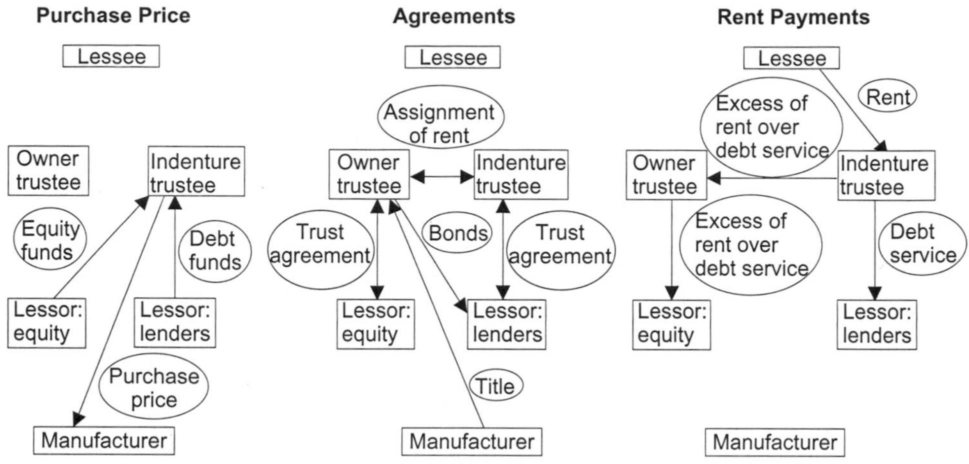

Figure 7.1
Leveraged leasing.

7.2 An Example

We can explore these issues by considering an example, roughly based on an example given in appendix E of FASB 13, the accounting profession's magnum opus on accounting for leases.

A leasing company is considering the purchase of an asset whose cost is $1,000,000. The asset will be purchased with $200,000 of the company's equity and with $800,000 of debt. The interest on the debt is 10 percent, so that the annual payment of interest and principal over the 15-year term of the debt is $105,179.[1]

The company will lease the asset out for $110,000 per year, payable at the end of each year. The lease term is 15 years. The asset will be depreciated over a period of eight years, using the standard IRS depreciation schedule for assets with a seven-year life.[2] The depreciation schedule for such assets is as follows:

1. Using Excel: **=PMT(10%,15,-800000)** gives 105,179.
2. The depreciation schedule we use is referred to as the modified cost recovery system (MACRS) depreciation. More information can be obtained from an introductory finance text or from many Web sites (one example: http://www.real-estate-owner.com/depreciation-chart.html).

Year	Depreciation (%)
1	14.28
2	24.49
3	17.49
4	12.5
5	8.92
6	8.92
7	8.92
8	4.48

Because the asset will be fully depreciated at the time it is sold (year 16), the whole anticipated residual value ($300,000) will be taxable. Since the company's tax rate is 40 percent, the after-tax cash flow from the residual is (1 – 40%) ∗ 300,000 = $180,000.

These facts are summarized in the following spreadsheet, which also derives the lessor's cash flows:

	A	B	C	D	E	F	G	H	I	J
1	BASIC LEVERAGED LEASE EXAMPLE									
2	Cost of asset	1,000,000								
3	Lease term	15								
4	Residual value	300,000	<-- Realized year 16							
5	Equity	200,000								
6	Debt	800,000	<-- 15-year term loan, equal payments of interest and principal							
7	Interest	10%								
8	Annual debt payment	105,179	<-- =PMT(B7,B3,-B6)							
9	Annual rent received	110,000								
10	Tax rate	40%								
11										
12	Year	Equity Invested	Rental or salvage	Depreciation	Principal at start of year	Loan payment	Interest	Repayment of principal	Cash flow to equity	
13		-200,000							-200,000	
14	1		110,000	142,800	800,000	105,179	80,000	25,179	49,941	<-- =(1-tax)*C14+tax*D14-(1-tax)*G14-H14
15	2		110,000	244,900	774,821	105,179	77,482	27,697	89,774	
16	3		110,000	174,900	747,124	105,179	74,712	30,467	60,666	
17	4		110,000	125,000	716,657	105,179	71,666	33,513	39,487	
18	5		110,000	89,200	683,144	105,179	68,314	36,865	23,827	
19	6		110,000	89,200	646,280	105,179	64,628	40,551	22,352	
20	7		110,000	89,200	605,728	105,179	60,573	44,606	20,730	
21	8		110,000	44,800	561,122	105,179	56,112	49,067	1,186	
22	9		110,000		512,056	105,179	51,206	53,973	-18,697	
23	10		110,000		458,082	105,179	45,808	59,371	-20,856	
24	11		110,000		398,711	105,179	39,871	65,308	-23,231	
25	12		110,000		333,403	105,179	33,340	71,839	-25,843	
26	13		110,000		261,565	105,179	26,156	79,023	-28,716	
27	14		110,000		182,542	105,179	18,254	86,925	-31,877	
28	15		110,000		95,617	105,179	9,562	95,617	-35,354	
29	16		300,000						180,000	
30										
31						IRR of cash flows			12.46%	<-- =IRR(I13:I29)

The last column gives the cash flow to the equity owners of the asset. A typical year's cash flow for the equity owner is calculated as follows:

$$\text{Cash flow }(t) = (1 - \text{Tax})\text{ Rent} + \text{Tax} * \text{Depreciation}(t) \\ - (1 - \text{Tax})\text{Interest}(t) - \text{Principal repayment}(t)$$

The explanation is as follows:

Item	Explanation
+ (1 − Tax) * Rent	Equity owners get the rental from the asset, net of any taxes.
+ Tax * Depreciation	Equity owners get the tax shield from the depreciation of the asset.
− (1 − Tax) * Interest	The interest on the debt is tax deductible.
− Repayment of debt principal	Repayment of debt principal is not tax deductible.
+ (1 − Tax) * Residual value	This item only occurs in the last year; the residual is usually fully taxed, since the depreciation has been taken on the whole value of the asset.
Cash flow (t) = (1 − Tax) * Rent + Tax * Depreciation(t) − (1 − Tax) * Interest(t) − Principal repayment(t)	The cash flow in a typical year (excluding the residual).

The cash flows of the typical long-lived leveraged lease are usually positive at the beginning of the lease term, and then decline over time, turning positive again at the end, when the residual value is received. There are three reasons for this phenomenon:

- The cash flow that stems from depreciation typically ends or falls off rapidly before the end of the lease term. The more accelerated the depreciation method is, the larger the depreciation allowances (and hence the larger the depreciation tax shields) will be at the beginning of the asset's life.

• In the later years of the lease, the portion of the annual debt payments devoted to interest (tax-deductible) falls, while the portion of the annual debt payments that constitutes a repayment of principal (not tax deductible) rises.

• Finally, of course, we anticipated a large cash flow from the realization of the asset's residual value at the end of the lease term.

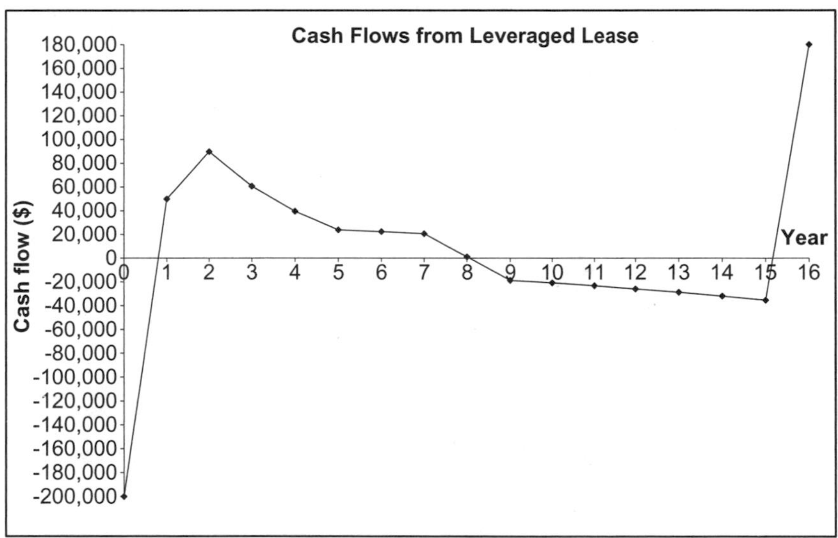

7.2.1 Digression: Computing the Interest Payments and Principal Repayments

In the preceding lease cash-flow spreadsheet, we computed the interest payments and principal repayments on the $800,000 debt by building a loan table (explained in Chapter 1, p. 12). We could also build this table by using the two Excel functions **IPMT** and **PPMT**, which compute the interest and principal payments on a term loan. An illustration is in the following spreadsheet:

	A	B	C	D	E
1	**COMPUTING THE LOAN PAYMENTS USING IPMT AND PPMT**				
2	Debt	800,000	=IPMT($B$4,A7,$B$3,-$B$2)		
3	Debt term (years)	15			
4	Interest	10%		=PPMT($B$4,A7,$B$3,-$B$2)	
5					
6	**Year**	**Interest payment on debt**	**Debt principal repayment**	**Total payment**	
7	1	80,000	25,179	105,179	<-- =B7+C7
8	2	77,482	27,697	105,179	
9	3	74,712	30,467	105,179	
10	4	71,666	33,513	105,179	
11	5	68,314	36,865	105,179	
12	6	64,628	40,551	105,179	
13	7	60,573	44,606	105,179	
14	8	56,112	49,067	105,179	
15	9	51,206	53,973	105,179	
16	10	45,808	59,371	105,179	
17	11	39,871	65,308	105,179	
18	12	33,340	71,839	105,179	
19	13	26,156	79,023	105,179	
20	14	18,254	86,925	105,179	
21	15	9,562	95,617	105,179	

7.3 Analyzing the Cash Flows by NPV or IRR

What do we make of the leveraged-lease cash flows? One way of viewing the cash flows (probably the best, at least in theory) is to take their net present value (NPV) at some appropriate risk-adjusted discount rate. If we analyze the cash-flow components, we see that the primary riskiness stems from three sources:

- The lessee may default on the rental.
- Tax rates can change, affecting the tax shields from depreciation and the cash flow from the interest payments.
- The residual value is highly uncertain.

The following graph shows the NPV of the cash flows at various interest rates:

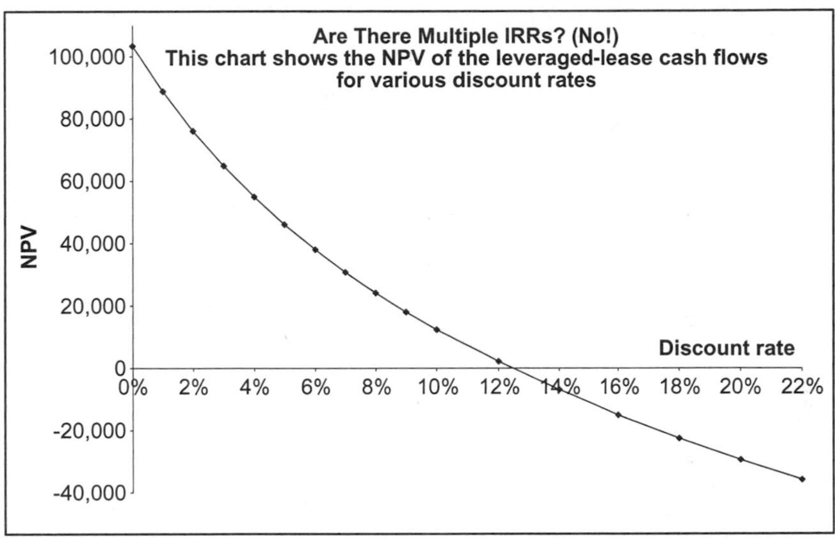

Note that since the cash flows are *after-tax*, the relevant basis for comparison is an after-tax interest rate. Suppose, for example, that the lessor feels highly certain about all the cash flows and therefore wants to compare the cash flows to his loan rate of 10 percent. Then, since the lessor's tax rate is 40 percent, the appropriate discount rate for comparison is (1 – 40 percent) ∗ 10 percent = 6 percent; at this rate the lease cash flows have an NPV of $38,068.

Lessors are often uncomfortable with net present value. They prefer internal rate of return as a measure of the acceptability of the lease. Since the cash flows of the leveraged lease have three changes in sign, it is—in principle—possible that they have three IRRs.[3] Since the IRR is the interest rate for which the net-present-value graph crosses the *x*-axis, we can use Excel to determine graphically how many IRRs there are. The graph shows that for a very large range of reasonable interest rates, there is only one IRR. We are thus safe in using **IRR(cash flows,0)** to determine that the internal rate of return of the lease cash flows is 12.46 percent.

3. Cash-flow sign changes: From negative in year 0 to positive in year 1; from positive in year 8 to negative in year 9; from negative in year 15 to positive in year 16.

7.4 What Does the IRR Mean?

Asking what the IRR means is relevant both to an economic understanding of the meaning of the internal rate of return and to the discussion in section 7.5 of the accounting determination of the income from a leveraged lease.

To illustrate the complexities, we stray for a moment from our original example to study a much simpler example. Consider an investment of $100,000 that has positive cash flows only for the next five years:

	A	B	C	D	E	F
1			UNDERSTANDING THE IRR			
2	Year	Cash flow				
3	0	-100,000				
4	1	31,000				
5	2	22,000				
6	3	16,000				
7	4	22,000				
8	5	35,000				
9						
10	IRR	8.097%	<-- =IRR(B3:B8,0)			
11						
12			CASH FLOW ATTRIBUTION TABLE			
13				Attribution of cash flow		
14	Year	Investment at beginning of period	Cash flow at end of year	Income	Repayment of investment	
15	1	100,000	31,000	8,097	22,903	<-- =C15-D15
16	2	77,097	22,000	6,242	15,758	
17	3	61,339	16,000	4,966	11,034	
18	4	50,305	22,000	4,073	17,927	
19	5	32,378	35,000	2,622	32,378	
20						
21	=B16-E16		=$B$10*B16			

What is the meaning of the IRR of 8.097 percent? If we think of the initial investment of $100,000 as a loan to the project, then each year's cash flow is attributable to

1. Income on the investment outstanding at the beginning of the year. In rows 15–19 we compute this by taking the project's IRR times the investment at the beginning of the period. This method parallels the computation of the annual interest on a loan illustrated on page 224.

2. Repayment of the investment. This is the remainder of the cash flow after the income and parallels the repayment of the loan in the same loan table.

Of course, at the end of the five years, all the principal must be repaid. *The IRR is the "rate of interest" that exactly repays the "loan" (that is, the investment) with its "interest payments"(the income) over the life of the project.*

Here is an example:

Investment at beginning of period 1 (i.e., the initial investment)	100,000
Cash flow for period	31,000
8.097 percent * Investment at beginning of period	8,097
Cash flow available for repayment of investment	22,903
Investment at beginning of period 2 = Investment at beginning of previous period – Cash flow available for repayment in period 1	100,000 – 22,903 = 77,097

Note the last line in our cash-flow attribution table: At the beginning of year 5, we still have $32,378 of investment left; the cash flow of $35,000 for year 5 suffices exactly to pay the income of $2,622 on this investment and to repay the investment itself. At the beginning of year 6, there is no investment left! (This result, of course, is not a miracle—it's the way we calculated the internal rate of return.)

There's another way to calculate the investment at the beginning of each period: As the following spreadsheet shows, the investment at the beginning of each period is the present value of all remaining future cash flows, where we use the project's IRR as the discount rate:

	A	B	C	D	E	F
24	THE INVESTMENT AT THE BEGINNING OF EACH PERIOD IS THE PRESENT VALUE (USING IRR AS DISCOUNT RATE) OF ALL FUTURE CASH FLOWS					
25	Year	Cash flow at end of year	Investment at beginning of period			
26	1	31,000	100,000	<-- =NPV($B$11,B26:$B$30)		
27	2	22,000	77,097	<-- =NPV($B$11,B27:$B$30)		
28	3	16,000	61,339			
29	4	22,000	50,305			
30	5	35,000	32,378			

7.4.1 Back to the Leveraged-Lease Example

We now apply this same logic to the cash flows of the leveraged lease.

	A	B	C	D	E	F
1	ATTRIBUTION OF LEVERAGED LEASE CASH FLOWS TO INCOME AND REPAYMENT OF INVESTMENT					
2	IRR	12.46%	<-- =IRR(C6:C22)		=$B$2*B7	
3						
4				Attribution of cash flow		
5	Year	Investment at beginning of period	Cash flow	Income	Repayment of investment	
6	0		-200,000			
7	1	200,000	49,941	24,913	25,028	<-- =C7-D7
8	2	174,972	89,774	21,796	67,978	
9	3	106,994	60,666	13,328	47,338	
10	4	59,656	39,487	7,431	32,056	
11	5	27,600	23,827	3,438	20,389	
12	6	7,212	22,352	898	21,454	
13	7	-14,242	20,730	-1,774	22,504	
14	8	-36,746	1,186	-4,577	5,763	
15	9	-42,510	-18,697	-5,295	-13,401	
16	10	-29,108	-20,856	-3,626	-17,230	
17	11	-11,878	-23,231	-1,480	-21,751	
18	12	9,873	-25,843	1,230	-27,073	
19	13	36,945	-28,716	4,602	-33,319	
20	14	70,264	-31,877	8,753	-40,630	
21	15	110,894	-35,354	13,814	-49,168	
22	16	160,062	180,000	19,938	160,062	

Note that—as in our simple example—the IRR of 12.46 percent successfully attributes income in such a way that the whole of the investment is accounted for at the end of the project's life (after 16 years, for the case of the leveraged lease). However, note that there are some unusual features of the table: five of the income figures are negative, as are seven of the "repayment of investment" terms. There are two ways to understand these features:

- In "mechanical" terms, the only way to make the table work is to have some negative income numbers. This interpretation, though true, is not very interesting.
- In economic terms, the negative income figures mean that in some years the project is not worth holding onto, but that it cannot be given away. As an example consider the lessor's position at the beginning of year 9. *Seven years* of negative cash flows lie ahead. Only in eight years, in year 16, will the lessor again see a positive cash flow from the lease. A rational lessor would like to give away the lease contract at this point; the present value of the cash flows at the beginning of year 9 at a 10 percent discount rate is –$39,333 (and this includes the realization of the residual value at the end of year 16!). But of course no rational investor would take over the contract at the beginning of year 9 *unless she were paid to do so*, or unless her discount rate were negative. It is this fact—that the lessor would have to pay someone to take the contract off her hands in year 9—that makes us attribute negative income to the project at this point.[4] In economic terms the lease at this point is worse than valueless; it is a burden.

Using our insight that the investment at the beginning of each period is the present value of all future cash flows discounted at the IRR, we can see this phenomenon in a different way.

4. Negative income attribution in fact starts in year 7, showing that already at this point the project has negative economic value.

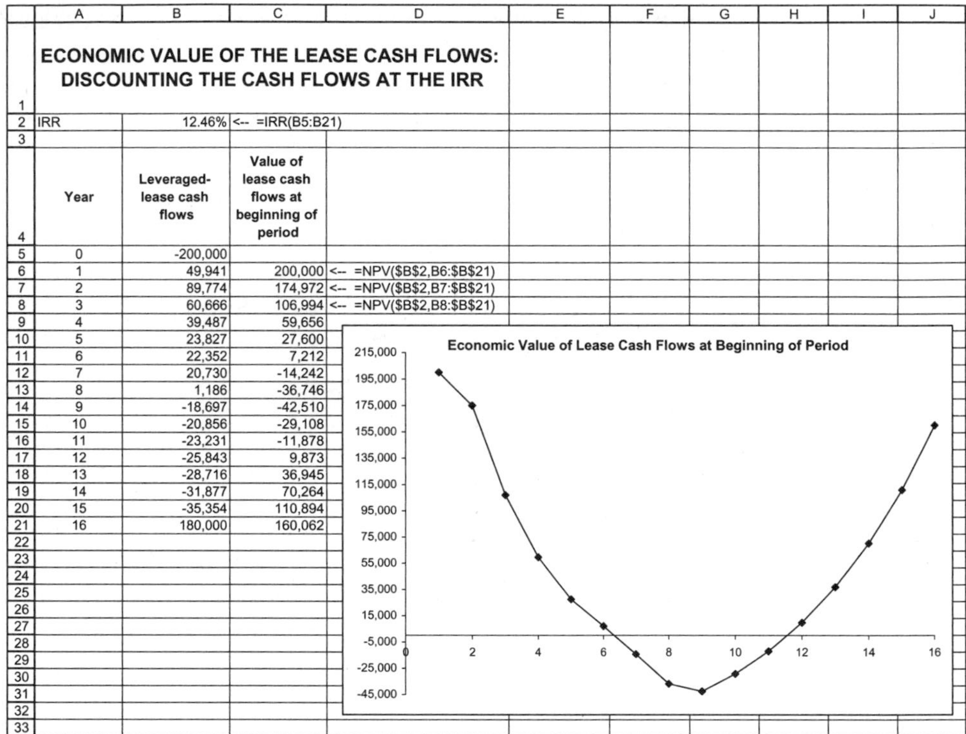

ECONOMIC VALUE OF THE LEASE CASH FLOWS: DISCOUNTING THE CASH FLOWS AT THE IRR

	A	B	C	D
2	IRR	12.46%	<-- =IRR(B5:B21)	
4	Year	Leveraged-lease cash flows	Value of lease cash flows at beginning of period	
5	0	-200,000		
6	1	49,941	200,000	<-- =NPV($B$2,B6:$B$21)
7	2	89,774	174,972	<-- =NPV($B$2,B7:$B$21)
8	3	60,666	106,994	<-- =NPV($B$2,B8:$B$21)
9	4	39,487	59,656	
10	5	23,827	27,600	
11	6	22,352	7,212	
12	7	20,730	-14,242	
13	8	1,186	-36,746	
14	9	-18,697	-42,510	
15	10	-20,856	-29,108	
16	11	-23,231	-11,878	
17	12	-25,843	9,873	
18	13	-28,716	36,945	
19	14	-31,877	70,264	
20	15	-35,354	110,894	
21	16	180,000	160,062	

As we shall see in the next section, the negative economic value of leveraged leases has caused the accounting profession a considerable headache.

7.5 Accounting for Leveraged Leases: The "Multiple Phases Method"

Financial Accounting Standards Board statement 13 (FASB 13) mandates that the lessor in a leveraged lease allocate the cash flow from the lease between income and investment. The logical way to do so would be to use the IRR of the lease's cash flows in the way illustrated in the preceding section. But here the promulgators of FASB 13 apparently ran up against the troublesome facet of human nature that hates to record a loss even if it is economically warranted. (The implausibility of the method for leveraged leases mandated in the statement is explained only by the assumption that lessors did not want, under any circumstances, to record economic losses that stemmed from the leases.)

The method that was devised to avoid the reporting of negative income is sometimes termed the multiple-phases method (MPM). A better term might have been "bastardized IRR method."

The fact that a somewhat silly method of recognizing income is used shouldn't bother us, since foolishness is rampant in this world. However, the complexity and the opaqueness of the method have lent it respectability. (There must be a lesson in this!) A little debunking, in the form of an explanation, is in order.

Suppose we let the multiple-phases rate of return Q (short for *quirky*) be defined as follows:

Year	MPM	Explanation
1	The lessor's investment in the lease at the beginning of year 1 is equal to her initial investment in the lease's equity. In our example, Investment(1) = \$200,000	This is the same as the calculation of the IRR.
t	The lessor's accounting income from the lease at the end of year t is $\begin{cases} Q * \text{Investment}(1) & \text{if this number} > 0 \\ 0 & \text{otherwise} \end{cases}$	If income is positive, MPM follows the attribution of income and investment of the standard IRR method. Otherwise, income is set to zero.
t	The lessor's investment in the lease at the beginning of any year $t > 1$ is defined as Investment(t) = Investment($t - 1$) −[Cash flow($t - 1$) − Income($t - 1$)]	Follows IRR method.
Last year	Cash flow(last year) = Investment(last year) ∗ (1 + Q)	Similar to IRR method.

Calculating the MPM *Q*: There is no formula to do this. However, it can be done in Excel by using an iterative method, **Solver** or **Goal Seek** (see next subsection).

7.5.1 Calculating the Multiple-Phases-Method Rate of Return

To calculate the MPM rate Q, we first set up a spreadsheet similar to the one we used to illustrate the IRR. The one difference is that we have extended the years to include year 17 (one year after the project ends). A solution Q should give a zero investment at the beginning of year 17. The following, for example is *not* a solution for Q:

	A	B	C	D	E	F	G	H
1	MPM METHOD: ATTRIBUTION OF LEVERAGED-LEASE CASH FLOWS TO INCOME AND REPAYMENT OF INVESTMENT							
2	Q	12.00%	<-- Possible MPM rate			=IF($B$2*B6>0,$B$2*B6,0)		
3								
4				MPM attribution of cash flows				
5	Year	Investment at beginning of period	Leveraged-lease cash flows	Income	Repayment of investment			
6	1	200,000	49,941	24,000	25,941	<-- =C6-D6		
7	2	174,059	89,774	20,887	68,887			
8	3	105,172	60,666	12,621	48,045			
9	4	57,127	39,487	6,855	32,632			
10	5	24,495	23,827	2,939	20,887			
11	6	3,608	22,352	433	21,919			
12	7	-18,312	20,730	0	20,730			
13	8	-39,042	1,186	0	1,186			
14	9	-40,228	-18,697	0	-18,697			
15	10	-21,531	-20,856	0	-20,856			
16	11	-675	-23,231	0	-23,231			
17	12	22,556	-25,843	2,707	-28,550			
18	13	51,105	-28,716	6,133	-34,849			
19	14	85,954	-31,877	10,314	-42,192			
20	15	128,146	-35,354	15,378	-50,732			
21	16	178,878	180,000	21,465	158,535			
22	17	20,343						

All the formulas in this table are the same as in the case of the IRR, with the exception of the formulas in the income column. For example, the income in year 1 has the following formula:

=IF($B$2*B6>0,$B$2*B6,0)

Using the Excel Solver, we find the solution for Q. The solver (**Tools|Solver**) dialog box looks like this:

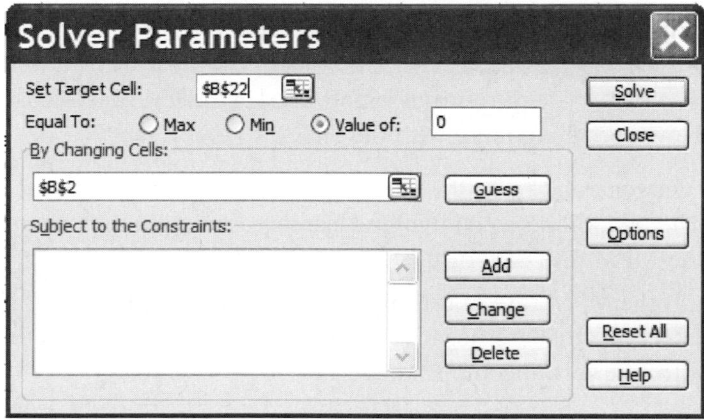

The **target cell** $B$22 is the investment at the beginning of year 17; since this is one year after the project ends, this investment should be zero. When this method is applied in our case, the solution is as follows:

	A	B	C	D	E	F
1	USING SOLVER TO FIND THE MULTIPLE-PHASES-METHOD (MPM) RETURN ON A LEVERAGED LEASE					
2	Q	10.91%	<-- Possible MPM rate			
3						
4				MPM attribution of cash flows		
5	Year	Investment at beginning of period	Leveraged-lease cash flows	Income	Repayment of investment	
6	1	200,000	49,941	21,822	28,119	<-- =C6-D6
7	2	171,881	89,774	18,754	71,019	
8	3	100,862	60,666	11,005	49,661	
9	4	51,201	39,487	5,587	33,901	
10	5	17,301	23,827	1,888	21,939	
11	6	-4,638	22,352	0	22,352	
12	7	-26,990	20,730	0	20,730	
13	8	-47,721	1,186	0	1,186	
14	9	-48,906	-18,697	0	-18,697	
15	10	-30,210	-20,856	0	-20,856	
16	11	-9,354	-23,231	0	-23,231	
17	12	13,877	-25,843	1,514	-27,357	
18	13	41,234	-28,716	4,499	-33,216	
19	14	74,449	-31,877	8,123	-40,001	
20	15	114,450	-35,354	12,488	-47,842	
21	16	162,292	180,000	17,708	162,292	
22	17	0				

7.6 Comparing the MPM Rate of Return with the IRR

The MPM rate of return is widely used in the leveraged-leasing industry. How does it compare with the IRR?

- In general, the MPM rate of return is less than or equal to the IRR. The two will be equal if all the lease's cash flows are positive. Otherwise the MPM rate of return is less than IRR.
- If the MPM rate of return is less than the IRR, then at some point the IRR will attribute negative income to the lease, whereas the MPM will attribute zero income to the lease.

Graphically, for the specific example of this chapter, we have

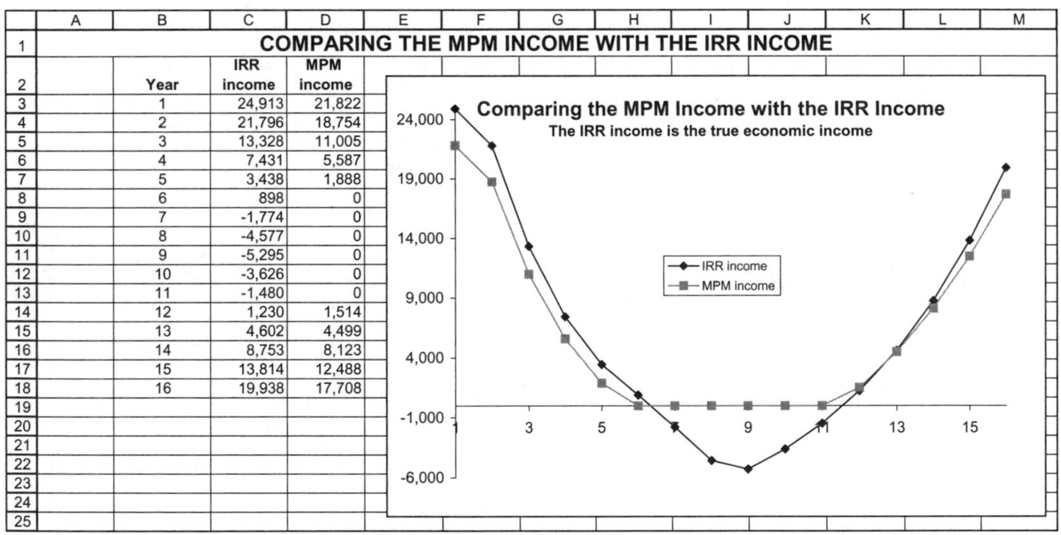

COMPARING THE MPM INCOME WITH THE IRR INCOME

Year	IRR income	MPM income
1	24,913	21,822
2	21,796	18,754
3	13,328	11,005
4	7,431	5,587
5	3,438	1,888
6	898	0
7	-1,774	0
8	-4,577	0
9	-5,295	0
10	-3,626	0
11	-1,480	0
12	1,230	1,514
13	4,602	4,499
14	8,753	8,123
15	13,814	12,488
16	19,938	17,708

7.7 Summary

A leveraged lease is an arrangement whereby the lessor—the owner of the asset—finances his investment with a combination of debt and equity. In this chapter we have analyzed the equity income of the lessor in a leveraged lease. The economic analysis of the lease cash flows shows that at some point in the lease life the equity owner has negative equity value. If properly reported, this negative equity should lead to negative accounting income. However, the MPM mandated by FASB 13 allows lessors to report only positive income. We explained the MPM method and showed how Excel can be used to compute the (otherwise meaningless) MPM rate of return.

Exercises

1. Reconsider the leveraged-leasing example in this chapter. Show that if depreciation is straight line over 15 years, then the MPM rate of return is equal to the IRR. Explain.

2. In the leveraged-lease example of section 7.6, find the lowest lease rental so that the MPM is equal to the IRR (assume the original depreciation schedule).

II Portfolio Models

Modern portfolio theory, which has its origins in the work of Harry Markowitz, John Lintner, Jan Mossin, and William Sharpe, represents one of the great advances in finance. Chapters 8–15 implement some of the ideas of these researchers and show you how to compute the standard portfolio problems in finance. In these chapters we make intensive use of Excel's matrix functions, array functions, and data tables, which are also discussed in Chapters 30, 31, and 34.

Chapter 8 reviews the basic mechanics of portfolio calculations. Starting with price data, we calculate asset and portfolio returns. While the bulk of the chapter deals with the simple two-asset portfolio problem, the case of multiple assets is discussed in sections 8.4 and 8.5.

Chapter 9 discusses both the theory and the mechanics of the calculation of efficient portfolios when there are no restrictions on short sales. Using Excel's matrix functions we can calculate two efficient portfolios, which can then be used to plot the whole efficient frontier.

The remaining chapters of this part of the book discuss computational and implementation issues:

- In Chapter 10 we show how to use return data to calculate the variance-covariance matrix. Excel's matrix-handling capabilities make it easy to do this calculation.
- In Chapter 11 we discuss the computation of beta, and we replicate a simple test of the capital asset pricing model (CAPM). We use some market data to derive the security market line (SML). We then relate the results to Roll's criticism of these tests. Excel makes it easy to do the regression analysis required for these tests. (Regressions are discussed in Chapter 33.)
- The preceding chapters have assumed that portfolio optimizers could sell securities short. In Chapter 12 we show how to use Excel's **Solver** to compute efficient portfolios when short sales are not allowed. We also show how to integrate other portfolio constraints into the optimization problem.
- Chapter 13 discusses the Black-Litterman model. This widely used model takes as its starting point the optimality of the benchmark portfolio and uses this assumption to derive the market's expected returns. The optimizer can then adjust the asset allocation to account for his or her own opinions.

- Chapter 14 shows how to do an event study. An event study is an attempt to determine whether a particular event in the capital market or in the life of a company affected a company's stock market performance. The event-study methodology aims to separate company-specific events from market- and/or industry-specific events, and has often been used as evidence for or against market efficiency.
- Finally, Chapter 15 is an introduction to value-at-risk (VaR) techniques in a portfolio context.

8 Portfolio Models—Introduction

8.1 Overview

In this chapter we review the basic mechanics of portfolio calculations. We start with a simple example of two assets, showing how to derive the return distributions from historical price data. We then discuss the general case of N assets; for this case it becomes convenient to use matrix notation and exploit Excel's matrix-handling capabilities.

It is useful before going on to review some basic notation: Each asset i (assets may be stocks, bonds, real estate, or whatever, although our numerical examples will be largely confined to stocks) is characterized by several statistics: $E(r_i)$, the expected return on asset i; $\text{Var}(r_i)$, the variance of asset i's return; and $\text{Cov}(r_i, r_j)$, the covariance of asset i's and asset j's returns. Occasionally we will use μ_i to denote the expected return on asset i. In addition, it will often be convenient to write $\text{Cov}(r_i, r_j)$ as σ_{ij} and $\text{Var}(r_i)$ as σ_{ii} (instead of σ_i^2, as usual). Since the covariance of an asset's returns with itself, $\text{Cov}(r_i, r_i)$, is in fact the variance of the asset's returns, this notation is not only economical but also logical.

8.2 Computing Returns for Walmart and Target

In this section we compute the return statistics for two stocks: Walmart (stock symbol WMT) and Target (TGT). We download the price and dividend data for each stock from Yahoo (see Chapter 2, appendix 2). With some slight massaging, we get the following spreadsheet:

	A	B	C	D	E	F	G
1	**PRICE AND RETURN DATA FOR WALMART (WMT) AND TARGET (TGT)** Yahoo adjusts prices for dividends						
2		Prices			Returns		
3	**Date**	**WMT**	**TGT**		**WMT**	**TGT**	
4	5-Jul-01	26.07	37.40				
5	1-Aug-01	22.00	33.53		-16.97%	-10.92%	<-- =LN(C5/C4)
6	4-Sep-01	20.07	30.73		-9.18%	-8.72%	<-- =LN(C6/C5)
7	1-Oct-01	20.02	30.15		-0.25%	-1.91%	<-- =LN(C7/C6)
8	1-Nov-01	23.35	36.38		15.39%	18.78%	
9	3-Dec-01	24.79	39.79		5.98%	8.96%	
10	2-Jan-02	23.03	43.04		-7.36%	7.85%	
11	4-Feb-02	18.09	40.66		-24.14%	-5.69%	
12	1-Mar-02	19.17	41.85		5.80%	2.88%	
13	1-Apr-02	20.25	42.36		5.48%	1.21%	
14	1-May-02	22.79	40.29		11.82%	-5.01%	
15	3-Jun-02	20.52	37.03		-10.49%	-8.44%	
55	3-Oct-05	50.93	55.37		7.95%	6.97%	
56	1-Nov-05	52.19	53.31		2.44%	-3.79%	
57	1-Dec-05	55.31	54.76		5.81%	2.68%	
58	3-Jan-06	55.63	54.54		0.58%	-0.40%	
59	1-Feb-06	58.46	54.29		4.96%	-0.46%	
60	1-Mar-06	60.23	51.90		2.98%	-4.50%	
61	3-Apr-06	65.46	52.99		8.33%	2.08%	
62	1-May-06	60.84	48.92		-7.32%	-7.99%	
63	1-Jun-06	67.51	48.87		10.40%	-0.10%	
64	3-Jul-06	67.65	49.17		0.21%	0.61%	

These data give the closing price at the end of each month for each stock and make an appropriate adjustment for dividends (see appendix 1 of this chapter). First we calculate the *monthly return* for each stock. This is the percentage return that would be earned by an investor who bought the stock at the end of a particular month $t-1$ and sold it at the end of the following month. For Walmart's stock in month t, the monthly return $r_{WMT,t}$ is defined as

$$r_{WMT,t} = \ln\left(\frac{P_{WMT,t}}{P_{WMT,t-1}}\right)$$

We note two things about this return calculation: First, we use the continuously compounded return on the stock. An alternative would have been to use the discrete return, $P_{WMT,t}/P_{WMT,t-1} - 1$. Appendix 2 at the end of this chapter discusses the reasons for our choice of the continuously compounded return. Second, the return data incorporate the dividends into the prices, in a manner explained in appendix 1.

We now make a heroic assumption: We assume that the return data for the 60 months represent the distribution of the returns for the coming month. We thus assume that the past gives us some information about the way returns will behave in the future. This assumption allows us to assume that the average of the historic data represents the *expected monthly return* from each stock. It also allows us to assume that we may learn from the historic data what is the variance of the future returns. Using the **Average, Varp**, and **Stdevp** functions in Excel, we calculate the statistics for the return distribution:

	D	E	F	G
66		WMT	TGT	
67	Monthly mean	1.59%	0.46%	<-- =AVERAGE(F5:F64)
68	Monthly variance	0.0093	0.0052	<-- =VARP(F5:F64)
69	Monthly standard deviation	9.63%	7.19%	<-- =STDEVP(F5:F64)
70				
71	Annual mean	19.07%	5.47%	<-- =12*F67
72	Annual variance	0.1114	0.0620	<-- =12*F68
73	Annual standard deviation	33.37%	24.90%	<-- =SQRT(F72)

Excel and Statistics Note

Note that we have used **Varp** instead of **Var** and **Stdevp** instead of **Stdev**. When the mean is defined by $E(r_{WMT}) = \frac{1}{M}\sum_{t=1}^{M} r_{WMT,t}$, then the definitions of these four functions are given by

$$\mathbf{Varp} = \text{Population variance} = \frac{1}{M}\sum_{t=1}^{M}[r_{WMT,t} - E(r_{WMT})]^2;\ \mathbf{Stdevp} = \sqrt{\mathbf{Varp}}$$

$$\mathbf{Var} = \text{Sample variance} = \frac{1}{M-1}\sum_{t=1}^{M}[r_{WMT,t} - E(r_{WMT})]^2;\ \mathbf{Stdev} = \sqrt{\mathbf{Var}}$$

There are two reasons why we choose **Varp** instead of **Var**: The first reason is that we implicitly assume that the historical data represent the distribution. The second reason for choosing **Varp** is that our choice makes the Excel **Slope** function consistent with the definition of β, $\beta_i = \frac{\text{Covariance}(r_{it}, r_{Mt})}{\text{Variance}(r_{Mt})}$.[1]

1. There's another point of view on this issue. As stated by Press et al. in their splendid book *Numerical Recipes*: "There is a long story about why the denominator is $M - 1$ instead of M. If you have never heard that story, you may consult any good statistics text. . . . We might also comment that if the difference between M and $M - 1$ ever matters to you, then you are up to no good anyway—e.g., trying to substantiate a questionable hypothesis with marginal data" (*Numerical Recipes*, 1st edition, page 456, slightly adapted).

Next we want to calculate the *covariance* of the returns. The covariance (and the correlation coefficient, which is derived from it) measures the degree to which the returns on the two assets move together. The definition is

$$Cov(r_{WMT}, r_{TGT}) = \frac{1}{M}\sum_{t}[r_{WMT,t} - E(r_{WMT})]\cdot[r_{TGT,t} - E(r_{TGT})]$$

where M is the number of points in the distribution (in our case, M = 60). This computation is easily set up in Excel:

	A	B	C	D	E	F	G	H	I	J	K
1	COMPUTING THE COVARIANCE FOR WALMART (WMT) AND TARGET (TGT)										
2	Date	WMT	Return	Return minus mean		TGT	Return	Return minus mean		Product	
3	5-Jul-01	26.07				37.40					
4	1-Aug-01	22.00	-16.97%	-18.56%		33.53	-10.92%	-11.38%	<-- =G4-$G$65	0.0211	<-- =D4*H4
5	4-Sep-01	20.07	-9.18%	-10.77%		30.73	-8.72%	-9.18%		0.0099	
6	1-Oct-01	20.02	-0.25%	-1.84%		30.15	-1.91%	-2.36%		0.0004	
7	1-Nov-01	23.35	15.39%	13.80%		36.38	18.78%	18.33%		0.0253	
8	3-Dec-01	24.79	5.98%	4.40%		39.79	8.96%	8.50%		0.0037	
9	2-Jan-02	23.03	-7.36%	-8.95%		43.04	7.85%	7.40%		-0.0066	
10	4-Feb-02	18.09	-24.14%	-25.73%		40.66	-5.69%	-6.14%		0.0158	
11	1-Mar-02	19.17	5.80%	4.21%		41.85	2.88%	2.43%		0.0010	
12	1-Apr-02	20.25	5.48%	3.89%		42.36	1.21%	0.76%		0.0003	
55	1-Nov-05	52.19	2.44%	0.85%		53.31	-3.79%	-4.25%		-0.0004	
56	1-Dec-05	55.31	5.81%	4.22%		54.76	2.68%	2.23%		0.0009	
57	3-Jan-06	55.63	0.58%	-1.01%		54.54	-0.40%	-0.86%		0.0001	
58	1-Feb-06	58.46	4.96%	3.37%		54.29	-0.46%	-0.92%		-0.0003	
59	1-Mar-06	60.23	2.98%	1.39%		51.90	-4.50%	-4.96%		-0.0007	
60	3-Apr-06	65.46	8.33%	6.74%		52.99	2.08%	1.62%		0.0011	
61	1-May-06	60.84	-7.32%	-8.91%		48.92	-7.99%	-8.45%		0.0075	
62	1-Jun-06	67.51	10.40%	8.81%		48.87	-0.10%	-0.56%		-0.0005	
63	3-Jul-06	67.65	0.21%	-1.38%		49.17	0.61%	0.16%		0.0000	
64											
65	Average		1.59%	<-- =AVERAGE(C4:C63)			0.46%		Covariance	0.0038	<-- =AVERAGE(J4:J63)
66	Standard deviation		9.63%	<-- =STDEVP(D4:D63)			7.19%			0.0038	<-- =COVAR(C3:C63,H4:H63)
67											
68									Correlation	0.5484	<-- =J65/(C66*G66)
69										0.5484	<-- =J65/(STDEVP(C4:C63)*STDEVP(G4:G63))
70										0.5484	<-- =CORREL(C4:C63,G4:G63)

The column **Product** contains the multiple of the deviation from the mean in each month, that is, the terms $[r_{WMT,t} - E(r_{WMT})]$ $[r_{TGM,t} - E(r_{TGT})]$, for $t = 1, \ldots, 12$. The covariance is **Average(product)** = 0.0038. While it is worthwhile calculating the covariance this way at least once, there is a shorter way, which is also illustrated: The Excel function **Covar(WMT returns,TGT returns)** calculates the covariance directly. To calculate the covariance using **Covar** there is no necessity to find the difference between the returns and the means. Simply use **Covar** directly on the columns, as illustrated in cell J66 of the spreadsheet.

The covariance is a hard number to interpret, since its size depends on the units in which we measure the returns. (If we were to write the returns in percentages—i.e., 4 instead of 0.04—then the covariance would be 38, which is 10,000 times the number we just calculated.) We can also calculate the *correlation coefficient* ρ_{AB}, which is defined as

$$\rho_{WMT,TGT} = \frac{\mathrm{Cov}(r_{WMT}, r_{TGT})}{\sigma_{WMT}\sigma_{TGT}}$$

The correlation coefficient is unit-free; calculating it for our example gives $\rho_{WMT,TGT} = 0.4415$. As illustrated in the preceding spreadsheet, the correlation coefficient can be calculated directly in Excel using the function **Correl(WMT returns,TGT returns)** (cell J70).

	A	B	C	D	E	F	G	H	I	J	K
1	COMPUTING THE COVARIANCE FOR WALMART (WMT) AND TARGET (TGT) All percentages expressed as whole numbers: the covariance grows by a factor of 10,000, but the correlation is unchanged										
2	**Date**	**WMT**	**Return**	**Return minus mean**		**TGT**	**Return**	**Return minus mean**		**Product**	
3	5-Jul-01	26.07				37.40					
4	1-Aug-01	22.00	-16.97	-18.56		33.53	-10.92	-11.38	<-- =G4-$G$65	211.24	<-- =D4*H4
5	4-Sep-01	20.07	-9.18	-10.77		30.73	-8.72	-9.18		98.84	
6	1-Oct-01	20.02	-0.25	-1.84		30.15	-1.91	-2.36		4.34	
7	1-Nov-01	23.35	15.39	13.80		36.38	18.78	18.33		252.87	
8	3-Dec-01	24.79	5.98	4.40		39.79	8.96	8.50		37.37	
9	2-Jan-02	23.03	-7.36	-8.95		43.04	7.85	7.40		-66.22	
10	4-Feb-02	18.09	-24.14	-25.73		40.66	-5.69	-6.14		158.12	
11	1-Mar-02	19.17	5.80	4.21		41.85	2.88	2.43		10.22	
12	1-Apr-02	20.25	5.48	3.89		42.36	1.21	0.76		2.94	
55	1-Nov-05	52.19	2.44	0.85		53.31	-3.79	-4.25		-3.63	
56	1-Dec-05	55.31	5.81	4.22		54.76	2.68	2.23		9.39	
57	3-Jan-06	55.63	0.58	-1.01		54.54	-0.40	-0.86		0.87	
58	1-Feb-06	58.46	4.96	3.37		54.29	-0.46	-0.92		-3.09	
59	1-Mar-06	60.23	2.98	1.39		51.90	-4.50	-4.96		-6.91	
60	3-Apr-06	65.46	8.33	6.74		52.99	2.08	1.62		10.93	
61	1-May-06	60.84	-7.32	-8.91		48.92	-7.99	-8.45		75.26	
62	1-Jun-06	67.51	10.40	8.81		48.87	-0.10	-0.56		-4.92	
63	3-Jul-06	67.65	0.21	-1.38		49.17	0.61	0.16		-0.22	
64											
65	Average		1.59	<-- =AVERAGE(C4:C63)			0.46		Covariance	37.9731	<-- =AVERAGE(J4:J63)
66	Standard deviation		9.63	<-- =STDEVP(D4:D63)			7.19			37.9731	<-- =COVAR(C4:C63,G4:G63)
67											
68									Correlation	0.5484	<-- =J65/(C66*G66)
69		=LN(B63/B62)*100								0.5484	<-- =J65/(STDEVP(C4:C63)*STDEVP(G4:G63))

The correlation coefficient measures the degree of linear relation between the returns of Stock A and Stock B. The following facts can be proven about the correlation coefficient:

- The correlation coefficient is always between +1 and −1: $-1 \le \rho_{AB} \le 1$.
- If the correlation coefficient is +1, then the returns on the two assets are linearly related with a positive slope; that is, if $\rho_{AB} = 1$, then

$$r_{At} = c + dr_{Bt}, \quad \text{where } d > 0$$

• If the correlation coefficient is −1, then the returns on the two assets are linearly related with a negative slope; that is, if $\rho_{AB} = -1$, then

$$r_{At} = c + dr_{Bt}, \quad \text{where } d < 0$$

• If the return distributions are independent, then the correlation coefficient will be zero. (The opposite is not true: If the correlation coefficient is zero, this fact does not necessarily mean that the returns are independent. See the exercises for an example.)

8.2.1 A Different View of the Correlation Coefficient

Another way to look at the correlation coefficient is to graph the Walmart and Target returns on the same axes and then use the Excel **Trendline** facility to regress the returns of TGT on those of WMT. (The use of Excel's **Trendline** function—used to calculate the regression equation—is explained in Chapter 33.) You can confirm from the previous calculations that the regression R^2 is the correlation squared:

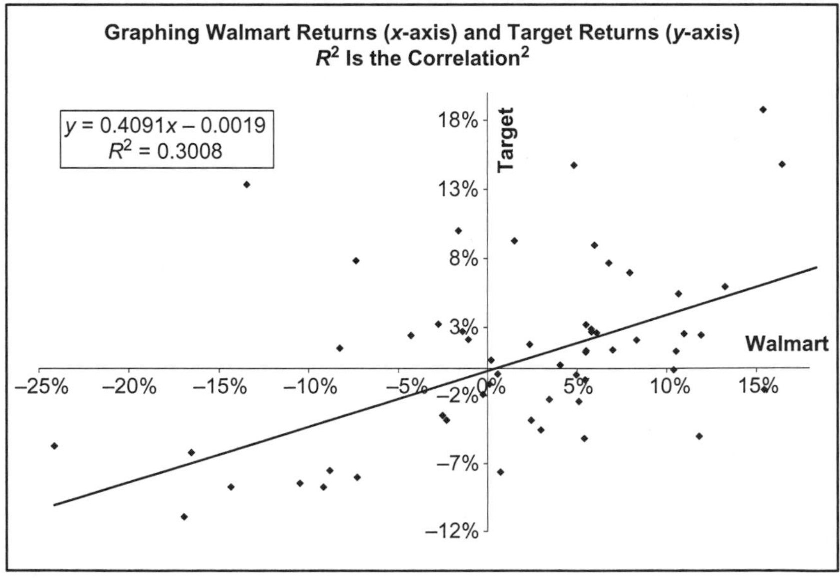

8.3 Calculating Portfolio Means and Variances

In this section we show how to do the basic calculations for a portfolio's mean and variance. Suppose we form a portfolio invested equally in WMT and TGT. What will be the mean and the variance of this portfolio? It is worth doing the brute force calculations at least once in Excel.

	A	B	C	D	E	F	G	H	I	J
1	**CALCULATING THE MEAN AND STANDARD DEVIATION OF A PORTFOLIO**									
2	Proportion of WMT	0.5								
3	Proportion of TGT	0.5	<-- =1-B2							
4										
5		**WMT return**	**TGT return**	**Portfolio return**						
6	1-Aug-01	-16.97%	-10.92%	-13.95%	<-- =$B$2*B6+$B$3*C6		Asset returns	WMT	TGT	
7	4-Sep-01	-9.18%	-8.72%	-8.95%	<-- =$B$2*B7+$B$3*C7		Mean return	1.59%	0.46%	<-- =AVERAGE(C6:C65)
8	1-Oct-01	-0.25%	-1.91%	-1.08%			Variance	0.0093	0.0052	<-- =VARP(C6:C65)
9	1-Nov-01	15.39%	18.78%	17.08%			Standard deviation	9.63%	7.19%	<-- =SQRT(I8)
10	3-Dec-01	5.98%	8.96%	7.47%			Covariance	0.0038		<-- =COVAR(B6:B65,C6:C65)
11	2-Jan-02	-7.36%	7.85%	0.24%						
12	4-Feb-02	-24.14%	-5.69%	-14.92%			Portfolio mean return			
13	1-Mar-02	5.80%	2.88%	4.34%				1.02%	<-- =AVERAGE(D6:D65)	
14	1-Apr-02	5.48%	1.21%	3.35%				1.02%	<-- =B2*H7+B3*I7	
15	1-May-02	11.82%	-5.01%	3.40%			Portfolio return variance			
16	3-Jun-02	-10.49%	-8.44%	-9.46%				0.0055	<-- =VARP(D6:D65)	
17	1-Jul-02	-21.80%	-13.33%	-17.57%				0.0055	<-- =B2^2*H8+B3^2*I8+2*B2*B3*H10	
18	1-Aug-02	-1.40%	2.71%	0.65%						
19	3-Sep-02	-8.66%	-14.73%	-11.69%			Portfolio return standard deviation	7.42%	<-- =STDEVP(D6:D65)	
20	1-Oct-02	18.82%	2.00%	10.41%						
21	1-Nov-02	21.95%	14.57%	18.26%						
22	2-Dec-02	-3.08%	-14.78%	-8.93%						
23	2-Jan-03	-16.56%	-6.17%	-11.37%						
24	3-Feb-03	2.36%	1.77%	2.06%						
25	3-Mar-03	-1.07%	2.12%	0.53%						

The mean portfolio return is exactly the average of the mean returns of the two assets:

$$\text{Expected portfolio return} = E(r_p) = 0.5E(r_{WMT}) + 0.5E(r_{TGT})$$
$$= 0.5 \cdot 1.59\% + 0.5 \cdot 0.46\% = 1.02\%$$

In general the mean return of the portfolio is the *weighted average return* of the component stocks. If we denote by x the proportion invested in WMT and $1-x$ the proportion invested in stock TGT, then the expected portfolio return is given by

$$E(r_p) = xE(r_{WMT}) + (1-x)E(r_{TGT})$$

However, the portfolio's variance is *not* the average of the two variances of the stocks! The formula for the variance is

$$\text{Var}(r_p) = x^2\text{Var}(r_{WMT}) + (1-x)^2\text{Var}(r_{TGT}) + 2x(1-x)\text{Cov}(r_{WMT}, r_{TGT})$$

Another way of writing this relation is as follows:

$$\sigma_p^2 = x^2\sigma_{WMT}^2 + (1-x)^2\sigma_{TGT}^2 + 2x(1-x)\rho_{WMT,TGT}\sigma_{WMT}\sigma_{TGT}$$

A frequently performed exercise is to plot the means and standard deviations for various portfolio proportions x. To do this we build a table using Excel's **Data|Table** command (see Chapter 30); cells B16 and C16 contain the data table's header, which refers to cells B12 and B10, respectively.

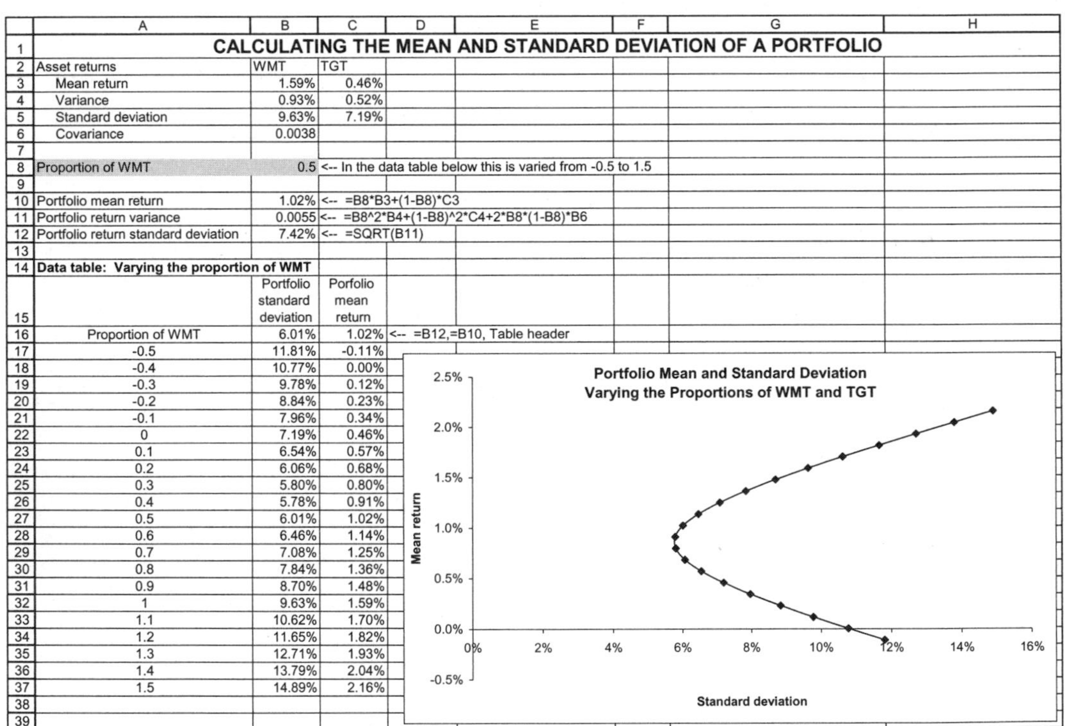

	A	B	C	D
1	CALCULATING THE MEAN AND STANDARD DEVIATION OF A PORTFOLIO			
2	Asset returns	WMT	TGT	
3	Mean return	1.59%	0.46%	
4	Variance	0.93%	0.52%	
5	Standard deviation	9.63%	7.19%	
6	Covariance	0.0038		
7				
8	Proportion of WMT	0.5	<-- In the data table below this is varied from -0.5 to 1.5	
9				
10	Portfolio mean return	1.02%	<-- =B8*B3+(1-B8)*C3	
11	Portfolio return variance	0.0055	<-- =B8^2*B4+(1-B8)^2*C4+2*B8*(1-B8)*B6	
12	Portfolio return standard deviation	7.42%	<-- =SQRT(B11)	
13				
14	Data table: Varying the proportion of WMT			
15		Portfolio standard deviation	Porfolio mean return	
16	Proportion of WMT	6.01%	1.02%	<-- =B12,=B10, Table header
17	-0.5	11.81%	-0.11%	
18	-0.4	10.77%	0.00%	
19	-0.3	9.78%	0.12%	
20	-0.2	8.84%	0.23%	
21	-0.1	7.96%	0.34%	
22	0	7.19%	0.46%	
23	0.1	6.54%	0.57%	
24	0.2	6.06%	0.68%	
25	0.3	5.80%	0.80%	
26	0.4	5.78%	0.91%	
27	0.5	6.01%	1.02%	
28	0.6	6.46%	1.14%	
29	0.7	7.08%	1.25%	
30	0.8	7.84%	1.36%	
31	0.9	8.70%	1.48%	
32	1	9.63%	1.59%	
33	1.1	10.62%	1.70%	
34	1.2	11.65%	1.82%	
35	1.3	12.71%	1.93%	
36	1.4	13.79%	2.04%	
37	1.5	14.89%	2.16%	
38				
39				

8.4 Portfolio Mean and Variance—The General Case

In the previous sections we discussed the computation of a portfolio's mean, variance, and standard deviation for a portfolio that is composed of only two assets. In this section we extend the discussion to portfolios of more than two assets. For this case, matrix notation greatly simplifies the writing of the portfolio problem.[2] In the general case of N assets, suppose that the proportion of asset i in the portfolio is denoted by x_i. We write the portfolio composition X and the vector of means $E(r)$ as column vectors:

$$x = \begin{bmatrix} x_1 \\ x_2 \\ x_3 \\ \vdots \\ x_N \end{bmatrix} \quad E(r) = \begin{bmatrix} E(r_1) \\ E(r_2) \\ E(r_3) \\ \\ E(r_N) \end{bmatrix}$$

We may then write X^T and $E(r)^T$ as the transpose of these two vectors:

$$x^T = [x_1, x_2, \ldots, x_N]$$
$$E(r)^T = [E(r_1), E(r_2), \ldots, E(r_N)]$$

The expected return of the portfolio whose proportions are given by X is the weighted average of the expected returns of the individual assets:

$$E(r_x) = \sum_{i=1}^{N} x_i E(r_i)$$

which, in matrix notation, can be written as

$$E(r_p) = \sum_{i=1}^{N} x_i E(r_i) = x^T E(r) = E(r)^T x$$

The portfolio's variance is given by

$$\text{Var}(r_X) = \sum_{i=1}^{N} (x_i)^2 \text{Var}(r_i) + 2\sum_{i=1}^{N} \sum_{j=i+1}^{N} x_i x_j \text{Cov}(r_i, r_j)$$

This looks bad, but it is really a straightforward extension of the expression for the variance of a portfolio of two assets that we had before: Each asset's variance appears once, multiplied by the square of the asset's

2. Chapter 31 gives an introduction to matrices sufficient to deal with all the problems encountered in this book. Since Excel has excellent matrix-handling capabilities, it is recommended that you study Chapter 31 before going on with the current chapter. The Excel matrix functions **MMult** and **MInverse** used in portfolio problems are discussed in this chapter.

proportion in the portfolio; the covariance of each pair of assets appears once, multiplied by twice the product of the individual assets' proportions. Another way of writing the variance is to use the notation

$$\text{Var}(r_i) = \sigma_{ii}, \quad \text{Cov}(r_i, r_j) = \sigma_{ij}$$

We may then write

$$\text{Var}(r_X) = \sum_i \sum_j x_i x_j \sigma_{ij}$$

The most economical representation of the portfolio variance uses matrix notation. It is also the easiest representation to implement for large portfolios in Excel. In this representation we call the matrix that has σ_{ij} in the ith row and the jth column the *variance-covariance matrix:*

$$S = \begin{bmatrix} \sigma_{11} & \sigma_{12} & \sigma_{13} & & \sigma_{1N} \\ \sigma_{21} & \sigma_{22} & \sigma_{23} & \cdots & \sigma_{2N} \\ \sigma_{31} & \sigma_{32} & \sigma_{33} & \cdots & \sigma_{3N} \\ \vdots & & & & \\ \sigma_{N1} & \sigma_{N2} & \sigma_{N3} & \cdots & \sigma_{NN} \end{bmatrix}.$$

Then the portfolio variance is given by $\text{Var}(r_p) = x^T S x$.

If we have two portfolios $x = [x_1, x_2, \ldots, x_N]$ and $y = [y_1, y_2, \ldots, y_N]$, then the covariance of the two portfolios is given by $\text{Cov}(x, y) = xSy^T = ySx^T$.

8.4.1 Portfolio Calculations Using Matrices—An Example

We implement the preceding formulas in a numerical example. Suppose that there are four risky assets that have the following expected returns and variance-covariance matrix:

	A	B	C	D	E	F
1	**A FOUR-ASSET PORTFOLIO PROBLEM**					
2	**Variance-covariance, S**					**Mean returns E(r)**
3	0.10	0.01	0.03	0.05		6%
4	0.01	0.30	0.06	-0.04		8%
5	0.03	0.06	0.40	0.02		10%
6	0.05	-0.04	0.02	0.50		15%

We consider two portfolios of risky assets:

	A	B	C	D	E
8	Portfolio x	0.2	0.3	0.4	0.1
9	Portfolio y	0.2	0.1	0.1	0.6

We calculate the means, variances, and covariance of the two portfolios. We use the Excel array function **Mmult** for all the calculations and the array function **Transpose** to make a row vector into a column vector.[3]

	A	B	C	D	E	F	G
11	**Portfolio x and y statistics: Mean, variance, covariance, correlation**						
12	Mean, $E(r_x)$	9.10%		Mean, $E(r_y)$	12.00%	<-- =MMULT(B9:E9,$F$3:$F$6)	
13	Variance, σ_x^2	0.1216		Variance, σ_y^2	0.2034	<-- =MMULT(B9:E9,MMULT(A3:D6,TRANSPOSE(B9:E9)))	
14	Covariance(x,y)	0.0714	<-- =MMULT(B8:E8,MMULT(A3:D6,TRANSPOSE(B9:E9)))				
15	Correlation, ρ_{xy}	0.4540	<-- =B14/SQRT(B13*E13)				

We can now calculate the standard deviation and return of combinations of portfolios *x* and *y*. Note that once we have calculated the means, variances, and the covariance of the returns of the two portfolios, the calculation of the mean and the variance of any portfolio is the same as for the two-asset case.

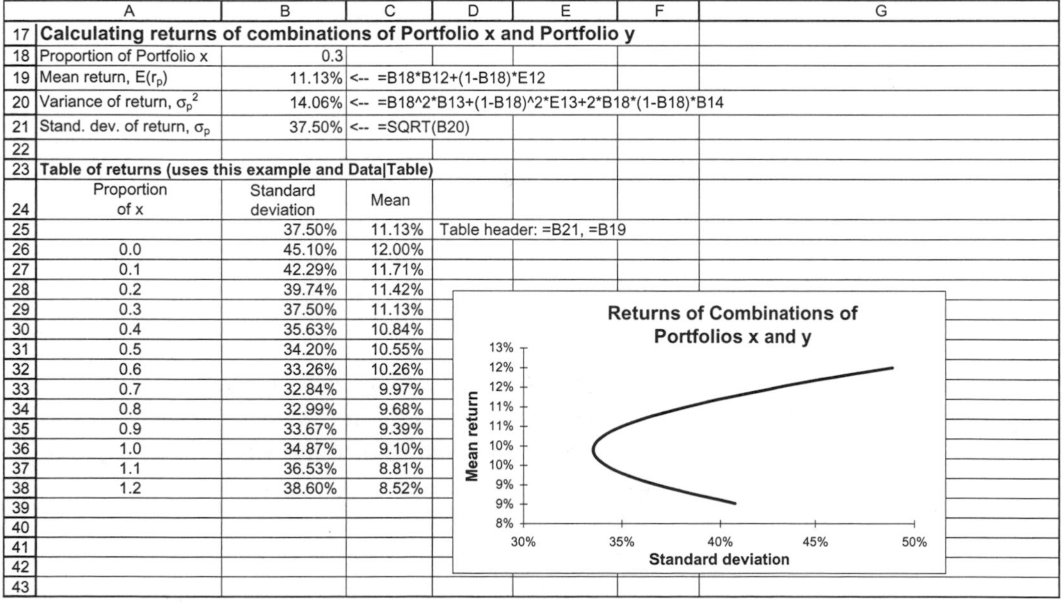

	A	B	C	D	E	F	G
17	**Calculating returns of combinations of Portfolio x and Portfolio y**						
18	Proportion of Portfolio x	0.3					
19	Mean return, $E(r_p)$	11.13%	<-- =B18*B12+(1-B18)*E12				
20	Variance of return, σ_p^2	14.06%	<-- =B18^2*B13+(1-B18)^2*E13+2*B18*(1-B18)*B14				
21	Stand. dev. of return, σ_p	37.50%	<-- =SQRT(B20)				
22							
23	**Table of returns (uses this example and Data|Table)**						
24	Proportion of x	Standard deviation	Mean				
25		37.50%	11.13%	Table header: =B21, =B19			
26	0.0	45.10%	12.00%				
27	0.1	42.29%	11.71%				
28	0.2	39.74%	11.42%				
29	0.3	37.50%	11.13%				
30	0.4	35.63%	10.84%				
31	0.5	34.20%	10.55%				
32	0.6	33.26%	10.26%				
33	0.7	32.84%	9.97%				
34	0.8	32.99%	9.68%				
35	0.9	33.67%	9.39%				
36	1.0	34.87%	9.10%				
37	1.1	36.53%	8.81%				
38	1.2	38.60%	8.52%				
39							
40							
41							
42							
43							

3. Remember that **MMult** and **Transpose** are array functions and must be entered by pushing [Ctrl]+[Shift]+[Enter] simultaneously.

8.5 Efficient Portfolios

An *efficient portfolio* is the portfolio of risky assets that gives the lowest variance of return of all portfolios having the same expected return. Alternatively, we may say that an efficient portfolio has the highest expected return of all portfolios having the same variance. Mathematically, we may define an efficient portfolio as follows: For a given return μ, an efficient portfolio $p = [x_1, x_2, \ldots, x_N]$ is one that solves

$$\min \sum_i \sum_j x_i x_j \sigma_{ij} = \mathrm{Var}(r_p)$$

subject to

$$\sum_i x_i r_i = \mu = E(r_p)$$

$$\sum_i x_i = 1$$

The *efficient frontier* is the set of all efficient portfolios. As shown by Black (1972), the efficient frontier is the set of all convex combinations of any two efficient portfolios. This statement means that if $x = [x_1, x_2, \ldots, x_N]$ and $y = [y_1, y_2, \ldots, y_N]$ are efficient portfolios and if a is a constant, then the portfolio Z defined by

$$z = ax + (1-a)y = \begin{bmatrix} ax_1 + (1-a)y_1 \\ ax_2 + (1-a)y_2 \\ \vdots \\ ax_N + (1-a)y_N \end{bmatrix}$$

is also efficient. Thus we can find the whole efficient frontier if we can find any two efficient portfolios.

By this theorem, once we have found two efficient portfolios x and y, we know that any other efficient portfolio is a convex combination of x and y. If we denote the mean and variance of x and y by $\{E(r_x), \sigma_x^2\}$ and $\{E(r_y), \sigma_y^2\}$, and if $z = ax + (1 - \mathrm{a})y$, then

$$\begin{aligned} E(r_z) &= aE(r_x) + (1-a)E(r_y) \\ \sigma_z^2 &= a^2\sigma_x^2 + (1-a)^2\sigma_y^2 + 2a(1-a)\mathrm{Cov}(x, y) \\ &= a^2\sigma_x^2 + (1-a)^2\sigma_y^2 + 2a(1-a)x^T S y \end{aligned}$$

Further details of the calculation of efficient portfolios are discussed in Chapter 9.

8.5.1 Showing That Portfolios *x* and *y* Are Not Efficient

To show that efficiency is a nontrivial concept, we show that the two portfolios whose combinations are graphed in the previous section are *not efficient*. This fact is easy to see if we extend the data table to include numbers for the individual stocks:

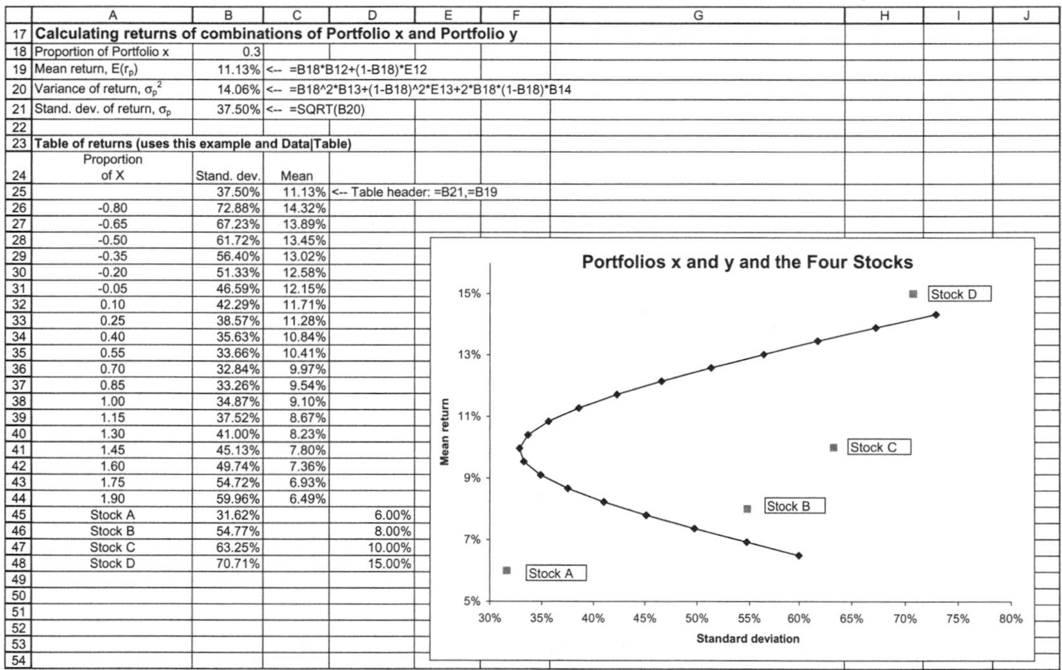

	A	B	C	D
17	**Calculating returns of combinations of Portfolio x and Portfolio y**			
18	Proportion of Portfolio x	0.3		
19	Mean return, $E(r_p)$	11.13%	<-- =B18*B12+(1-B18)*E12	
20	Variance of return, σ_p^2	14.06%	<-- =B18^2*B13+(1-B18)^2*E13+2*B18*(1-B18)*B14	
21	Stand. dev. of return, σ_p	37.50%	<-- =SQRT(B20)	
22				
23	**Table of returns (uses this example and Data|Table)**			
24	Proportion of X	Stand. dev.	Mean	
25		37.50%	11.13%	<-- Table header: =B21,=B19
26	-0.80	72.88%	14.32%	
27	-0.65	67.23%	13.89%	
28	-0.50	61.72%	13.45%	
29	-0.35	56.40%	13.02%	
30	-0.20	51.33%	12.58%	
31	-0.05	46.59%	12.15%	
32	0.10	42.29%	11.71%	
33	0.25	38.57%	11.28%	
34	0.40	35.63%	10.84%	
35	0.55	33.66%	10.41%	
36	0.70	32.84%	9.97%	
37	0.85	33.26%	9.54%	
38	1.00	34.87%	9.10%	
39	1.15	37.52%	8.67%	
40	1.30	41.00%	8.23%	
41	1.45	45.13%	7.80%	
42	1.60	49.74%	7.36%	
43	1.75	54.72%	6.93%	
44	1.90	59.96%	6.49%	
45	Stock A	31.62%		6.00%
46	Stock B	54.77%		8.00%
47	Stock C	63.25%		10.00%
48	Stock D	70.71%		15.00%
49				
50				
51				
52				
53				
54				

Were the two portfolios efficient, then all of the individual stocks would fall on or inside the graph of the combinations. In our case, two of the stock returns (stock A and stock D) fall outside the frontier created by combinations of portfolios *x* and *y*; thus *x* and *y* cannot be efficient portfolios. In Chapter 9 you will learn to compute efficient portfolios, and as you will see there, this task requires considerably more computation.

8.6 Conclusion

In this chapter we have reviewed the basic concepts and mathematics of portfolios. In succeeding chapters we shall describe how to compute the variance-covariance matrix from asset returns and how to calculate efficient portfolios.

Exercises

1. The attached spreadsheet **fm3_chapter08.xls** includes price data for the Dow-Jones 30 Industrials from July 1997 through July 2007. Isolating the data for Alcoa (AA) and Johnson & Johnson (JNJ), confirm the following statistics about the returns of these two stocks:

	A	B	C	D	E	F	G
1	**ALCOA (AA) AND JOHNSON & JOHNSON (JNJ)** **Return statistics, 1997-2007**						
2	**Monthly statistics**		**AA**			**JNJ**	
3	Average		0.68%			0.72%	<-- =AVERAGE(F16:F135)
4	Sigma		10.12%			5.84%	<-- =STDEVP(F16:F135)
5	Covariance		0.0002	<-- =COVAR(C16:C135,F16:F135)			
6							
7	Correlation		0.0398	<-- =CORREL(C16:C135,F16:F135)			
8			0.0398	<-- =C5/(C4*F4)			
9							
10	**Annual statistics**		**AA**			**JNJ**	
11	Average		8.11%			8.61%	<-- =12*F3
12	Sigma		35.07%			20.24%	<-- =SQRT(12)*F4

2. Using the data from the previous exercise, compute the statistics for each of the preceding two subperiods, July 1997–July 2002 and July 2002–July 2007.

3. Repeat exercise 2 for Merck (MRK) and Johnson & Johnson (JNJ). Merck had a big crisis in 2003–2004 related to Vioxx (http://en.wikipedia.org/wiki/Vioxx). Is this evident in the statistics?

4. Suppose that in July 1997 you bought and held through July 2007 a portfolio composed of 50% Alcoa (AA) and 50% Johnson & Johnson (JNJ) stock.

   a. Compute the average monthly return and standard deviation of returns for this portfolio.

   b. Vary the proportion of Alcoa from –1 to 1 and plot the portfolio average returns as a function of the standard deviation.

5. Following are annual return statistics for two mutual funds from the Vanguard family:

	A	B	C
1	**Vanguard's Windsor Fund and Index 500 Fund Returns**		
2	Source: http://www.vanguard.com		
3	The Index 500 fund mimics the SP500 index; the Windsor Fund is an "aggressive" growth fund		
4	**Year ended 31 December**	**Index 500 Fund**	**Windsor Fund**
5	1997	33.40%	22.00%
6	1996	23.00%	26.40%
7	1995	37.60%	30.10%
8	1994	1.30%	-0.10%
9	1993	10.10%	19.40%
10	1992	7.60%	16.50%
11	1991	30.50%	28.60%
12	1990	-3.10%	-15.50%
13	1989	31.70%	15.00%
14	1988	16.60%	28.70%
15	1987	5.30%	1.20%
16	1986	18.70%	20.30%
17	1985	31.80%	28.00%
18	1984	6.30%	19.50%

Use Excel to graph the combinations of standard deviation of return (x-axis) and expected return (y-axis) from varying the percentage of Index 500 Fund in the portfolio from 0% to 100%.

6. Using the database of the DJ Industrials (for 1997–2007), compute for General Electric (GE), Home Depot (HD), and Procter & Gamble (PG)

   a. Average monthly returns

   b. Covariances of the monthly returns

   c. Monthly expected return and monthly standard deviation of a portfolio that is equally invested in the three stocks

7. Suppose that X and Y are two random variables and that $Y = X^2$. Let X have values −5, −4, −2, 2, 4, 5 with equal probabilities. Show that the correlation coefficient between X and Y is zero. Does this fact mean that X and Y are independent random variables?

8. Consider two assets, A and B, that have the following means and variances:

   $E(r_A) = 0.03$, $E(r_B) = 0.05$

   $\text{Var}(r_A) = 0.0025$, $\text{Var}(r_B) = 0.0045$

Now consider three cases:

$\rho_{AB} = +1, \rho_{AB} = -1, \rho_{AB} = 0.$

Graph the combinations of portfolio means and variances for each case. (Graphs like these appear in virtually all elementary finance books. The standard deviation usually appears on the x-axis and the portfolio mean return on the y-axis. In this case, if you want to put all three graphs on the same set of axes, you will have to reverse this arrangement or use a trick.)

9. Consider a three-asset world with the following parameters:

$$\text{Mean returns} = \begin{pmatrix} 10\% \\ 12\% \\ 14\% \end{pmatrix}, \text{Variance-covariance matrix} = \begin{pmatrix} 0.3 & 0.02 & -0.05 \\ 0.02 & 0.4 & 0.06 \\ -0.05 & 0.06 & 0.6 \end{pmatrix}$$

Suppose you have two portfolios with the following portfolio weights:

$\text{Portfolio } 1 = (0.3 \quad 0.2 \quad 0.5)$

$\text{Portfolio } 2 = (0.5 \quad 0.4 \quad 0.1)$

a. Calculate the mean and variance of each portfolio's returns and the covariance and correlation coefficient of the portfolios' returns.

b. Create a graph of the means and variance of convex combinations of the portfolios.

10. In the following spreadsheet, implement the correct formula for cell B12 so that the portfolio gives the target return indicated in cell B10:

	A	B	C
1		**Mean return**	**Standard deviation of return**
2	Stock 1	12%	35%
3	Stock 2	18%	50%
4			
5	Covariance(r_1,r_2)	0.08350	

11. Using the data in the previous exercise, find two portfolios whose standard deviation of returns is 45%. (There's an analytical solution to this problem, but it can also be solved by **Solver**.)

Appendix 1: Adjusting for Dividends

When downloading data from Yahoo or other sources, the "adjusted price" includes an adjustment for dividends. In this appendix we discuss two ways of making this adjustment.[4] The first, and simplest, method of adjusting for dividends is to add them to the annual change in price. In the following example, if you purchased GM stock at the 1986 year-end price of $33 per share and held it for one year, you would, at the end of the year, have made 0.57 percent.

$$\text{Discretely compounded return, 1987} = \frac{30.69 + 2.50}{33.00} - 1 = 0.568 \text{ percent}$$

The continuously compounded return is calculated by

$$\begin{aligned}\text{Continuously compounded return, 1987} &= \ln\left[\frac{30.69 + 2.50}{33.00}\right] \\ &= 0.567 \text{ percent}\end{aligned}$$

(The choice between discrete and continuous compounding is discussed in appendix 2.)

4. It might be argued that since the free sources available on the Web make these adjustments automatically, the details in this appendix are superfluous. Nevertheless we think they offer some interesting insights. (If you disagree, turn the page!)

	A	B	C	D	E	F
1	GENERAL MOTORS (GM) STOCK ADJUSTING FOR DIVIDENDS					
2	Year	Share price at end year	Dividend per share	Discretely compounded return	Continuously compounded return	
3	1986	33.00				=(B4+C4)/B3-1
4	1987	30.69	2.50	0.57%	0.57%	
5	1988	41.75	2.50	44.20%	36.60%	
6	1989	42.25	3.00	8.38%	8.05%	<-- =LN((C4+B4)/B3)
7	1990	34.38	3.00	-11.54%	-12.26%	
8	1991	28.88	1.60	-11.35%	-12.04%	
9	1992	32.25	1.40	16.54%	15.30%	
10	1993	54.88	0.80	72.64%	54.60%	
11	1994	42.13	0.80	-21.78%	-24.56%	
12	1995	52.88	1.10	28.13%	24.79%	
13	1996	55.75	1.60	8.46%	8.12%	
14						
15	Arithmetic annual return			13.43%	9.92%	<-- =AVERAGE(E4:E13)
16	Standard deviation of returns			27.15%	22.84%	<-- =STDEVP(E4:E13)

Dividend Reinvestment

Another way of calculating returns is to assume that the dividends are reinvested in the stock:

	G	H	I	J	K	L	M	N
1	GM: REINVESTING THE DIVIDENDS IN SHARES							
2	Year	Effective shares held at beginning of year	Share price at end year	Dividend per share	Total dividends received	Number of shares at end of year	Value of shares at end of year	
3	1986		33.00				33.000	=H5+K5/I5
4	1987	1.00	30.69	2.500	2.500	1.081	33.188	
5	1988	1.08	41.75	2.500	2.704	1.146	47.855	<-- =L5*I5
6	1989	1.15	42.25	3.000	3.439	1.228	51.867	
7	1990	1.23	34.38	3.000	3.683	1.335	45.882	
8	1991	1.33	28.88	1.600	2.136	1.409	40.677	
9	1992	1.41	32.25	1.400	1.972	1.470	47.403	
10	1993	1.47	54.88	0.800	1.176	1.491	81.835	
11	1994	1.49	42.13	0.800	1.193	1.520	64.014	
12	1995	1.52	52.88	1.100	1.672	1.551	82.021	
13	1996	1.55	55.75	1.600	2.482	1.596	88.963	
14								
15		Annualized continous return					9.92%	<-- =LN(M13/M3)/10
16		Compound geometric return					10.43%	<-- =(M13/M3)^(1/10)-1
17								
18				=H5*J5				

Consider first 1987: Since we purchased the share at the end of 1986, we own one share at the end of 1987. If the 1987 dividend is turned into shares at the end of 1987 price, we can use it to buy 0.081 additional shares:

$$\text{New shares purchased at end of 1987} = \frac{2.50}{30.69} = 0.081$$

Thus we start 1988 with 1.081 shares. Since the 1988 dividend per share is \$2.50, the total dividend received on the shares is 1.081 * \$2.50 = \$2.704. Reinvesting these dividends in shares gives

$$\text{New shares purchased at end of 1988} = \frac{2.704}{41.75} = 0.065$$

Thus, at the end of 1988, the holder of GM shares will have accumulated 1 + 0.081 + 0.065 = 1.146 shares.

As the spreadsheet fragment shows, this reinvestment of dividends will produce a holding of 1.596 shares at the end of 1996, worth \$88.963.

We can calculate the return on this investment in one of two ways:

$$\text{Continuously compounded return} = \ln\left[\frac{\text{End-1996 value}}{\text{Beginning investment}}\right]\Big/10$$
$$= \ln\left[\frac{88.963}{33.00}\right]\Big/10 = 9.92 \text{ percent}$$

Note that this continuously compounded return (the method preferred in this book) is the same as that calculated in the first spreadsheet fragment in this appendix from the annual returns (cell E15).

An alternative is to calculate the geometric return:

$$\text{Compound geometric return} = \left[\frac{\text{End-1996 value}}{\text{Initial investment}}\right]^{1/10} - 1$$
$$= \left[\frac{88.963}{33.00}\right]^{1/10} - 1 = 10.43 \text{ percent}$$

Appendix 2: Continuously Compounded versus Geometric Returns

Using the continuously compounded return assumes that $P_t = P_{t-1}e^{r_t}$, where r_t is the rate of return during the period $(t-1, t)$. Suppose that $r_1, r_2, \ldots, r_{12}$ are the returns for 12 periods (a period could be a month or it could be a year), then the price of the stock at the end of the 12 periods will be

$$P_{12} = P_0 e^{r_1 + r_2 + \ldots + r_{12}}$$

This representation of prices and returns allows us to assume that the *average periodic return* is $r = (r_1 + r_2 + \ldots + r_{12})/12$. Since we wish to assume that the return data for the 12 periods represent the distribution of the returns for the coming period, it follows that the continuously compounded return is the appropriate return measure, and not the discretely compounded return

$$r_t = (P_{At} - P_{A,t-1}) / P_{A,t-1}$$

How Different Are Continuously Compounded and Discretely Compounded Returns?

The continuously compounded return will always be smaller than the discretely compounded return, but the difference is usually not large. The following table shows the differences for the example in section 8.2:

	A	B	C	D	E	F	G	H	I
1	COMPARING CONTINUOUS RETURNS TO DISCRETE RETURNS								
2	Date	WMT price	Continuous return	Discrete return		TGT price	Continuous return	Discrete return	
3	5-Jul-01	26.07				37.40			
4	1-Aug-01	22.00	-16.97%	-15.61%		33.53	-10.92%	-10.35%	<-- =F4/F3-1
5	4-Sep-01	20.07	-9.18%	-8.77%		30.73	-8.72%	-8.35%	
6	1-Oct-01	20.02	-0.25%	-0.25%		30.15	-1.91%	-1.89%	Cell G4 contains formula
7	1-Nov-01	23.35	15.39%	16.63%		36.38	18.78%	20.66%	=LN(F4/F3)
8	3-Dec-01	24.79	5.98%	6.17%		39.79	8.96%	9.37%	
9	2-Jan-02	23.03	-7.36%	-7.10%		43.04	7.85%	8.17%	
10	4-Feb-02	18.09	-24.14%	-21.45%		40.66	-5.69%	-5.53%	
11	1-Mar-02	19.17	5.80%	5.97%		41.85	2.88%	2.93%	
12	1-Apr-02	20.25	5.48%	5.63%		42.36	1.21%	1.22%	
55	1-Nov-05	52.19	2.44%	2.47%		53.31	-3.79%	-3.72%	
56	1-Dec-05	55.31	5.81%	5.98%		54.76	2.68%	2.72%	
57	3-Jan-06	55.63	0.58%	0.58%		54.54	-0.40%	-0.40%	
58	1-Feb-06	58.46	4.96%	5.09%		54.29	-0.46%	-0.46%	
59	1-Mar-06	60.23	2.98%	3.03%		51.90	-4.50%	-4.40%	
60	3-Apr-06	65.46	8.33%	8.68%		52.99	2.08%	2.10%	
61	1-May-06	60.84	-7.32%	-7.06%		48.92	-7.99%	-7.68%	
62	1-Jun-06	67.51	10.40%	10.96%		48.87	-0.10%	-0.10%	
63	3-Jul-06	67.65	0.21%	0.21%		49.17	0.61%	0.61%	
64									
65	Monthly average		1.59%	2.07%			0.46%	0.72%	<-- =AVERAGE(H4:H63)
66	Monthly standard deviation		9.61%	9.61%			7.30%	7.30%	<-- =STDEVP(H4:H63)

Calculating Annual Returns and Variances from Periodic Returns

Suppose we calculate a series of continuously compounded *monthly* rates of return $r_1, r_2, \ldots, r_n$ and we wish to then calculate the mean and the variance of the *annual* rate of return. Clearly the mean annual return is given by

$$\text{Mean annual return} = 12\left[\frac{1}{n}\sum_{t=1}^{n} r_t\right]$$

To calculate the variance of the annual rate of return, we assume that the monthly rates of return are independent identically distributed random variables. It then follows that $\mathrm{Var}(r) = 12\left[\frac{1}{n}\sum_{t=1}^{n}\mathrm{Var}(r_t)\right] = 12\sigma^2_{monthly}$ and that the standard deviation of the annual rate of return is given by $\sigma = \sqrt{12}\sigma_{monthly}$.

To return to our example: Given our monthly return data, here are the annual rates of return, their variance, and their standard deviation:

	A	B	C	D	E	F	G
1	**MONTHLY AND ANNUAL MEANS AND VARIANCES**						
2	**Date**	**WMT price**	**Continuous return**		**TGT price**	**Continuous return**	
3	5-Jul-01	26.07			37.40		
4	1-Aug-01	22.00	-16.97%		33.53	-10.92%	<-- =LN(E4/E3)
5	4-Sep-01	20.07	-9.18%		30.73	-8.72%	
6	1-Oct-01	20.02	-0.25%		30.15	-1.91%	
7	1-Nov-01	23.35	15.39%		36.38	18.78%	
8	3-Dec-01	24.79	5.98%		39.79	8.96%	
9	2-Jan-02	23.03	-7.36%		43.04	7.85%	
10	4-Feb-02	18.09	-24.14%		40.66	-5.69%	
11	1-Mar-02	19.17	5.80%		41.85	2.88%	
12	1-Apr-02	20.25	5.48%		42.36	1.21%	
55	1-Nov-05	52.19	2.44%		53.31	-3.79%	
56	1-Dec-05	55.31	5.81%		54.76	2.68%	
57	3-Jan-06	55.63	0.58%		54.54	-0.40%	
58	1-Feb-06	58.46	4.96%		54.29	-0.46%	
59	1-Mar-06	60.23	2.98%		51.90	-4.50%	
60	3-Apr-06	65.46	8.33%		52.99	2.08%	
61	1-May-06	60.84	-7.32%		48.92	-7.99%	
62	1-Jun-06	67.51	10.40%		48.87	-0.10%	
63	3-Jul-06	67.65	0.21%		49.17	0.61%	
64							
65	Monthly average		1.59%			0.46%	<-- =AVERAGE(F4:F63)
66	Monthly variance		0.93%			0.52%	<-- =VARP(F4:F63)
67	Monthly standard deviation		9.63%			7.19%	<-- =STDEVP(F4:F63)
68							
69	Annual average		19.07%			5.47%	<-- =12*F65
70	Annual variance		11.14%			6.20%	<-- =12*F66
71	Annual standard deviation		33.37%			24.90%	<-- =SQRT(12)*F67

9 Calculating Efficient Portfolios When There Are No Short-Sale Restrictions

9.1 Overview

This chapter covers the theory and calculations necessary for both versions of the classical capital asset pricing model (CAPM)—both that which is based on a risk-free asset (also known as the Sharpe-Lintner-Mossin model) and Black's (1972) zero-beta CAPM (which does not require the assumption of a risk-free asset). You will find that using a spreadsheet enables you to do the necessary calculations easily.

The structure of the chapter is as follows: We begin with some preliminary definitions and notation. We then state the major results (proofs are given in the appendix to the chapter). In succeeding sections we implement these results, showing you

- How to calculate efficient portfolios.
- How to calculate the efficient frontier.

This chapter includes more theoretical material than most chapters in this book: Section 9.3 contains the propositions on portfolios that underlie the calculations of both efficient portfolios and the security market line (SML) in Chapter 11. If you find the theoretical material in section 9.3 difficult, skip it at first and try to follow the illustrative calculations in section 9.4. This chapter assumes that the variance-covariance matrix is given; we delay a discussion of various methods of computing the variance-covariance matrix until Chapter 10.

9.2 Some Preliminary Definitions and Notation

Throughout this chapter we use the following notation: There are N risky assets, each of which has expected return $E(r_i)$. The matrix $E(r)$ is the column vector of expected returns of these assets:

$$E(r) = \begin{bmatrix} E(r_1) \\ E(r_2) \\ \vdots \\ E(r_N) \end{bmatrix}$$

and S is the $N \times N$ variance-covariance matrix:

$$S = \begin{bmatrix} \sigma_{11} & \sigma_{21} & \dots & \sigma_{N1} \\ \sigma_{12} & \sigma_{22} & \dots & \sigma_{N2} \\ \vdots & & & \\ \sigma_{1N} & \sigma_{2N} & \dots & \sigma_{NN} \end{bmatrix}$$

A *portfolio of risky assets* (when our intention is clear, we shall just use the word *portfolio*) is a column vector x whose coordinates sum to 1:

$$x = \begin{bmatrix} x_1 \\ x_2 \\ \vdots \\ x_N \end{bmatrix}, \quad \sum_{i=1}^{N} x_i = 1$$

Each coordinate x_i represents the proportion of the portfolio invested in risky asset i.

The *expected portfolio return* $E(r_x)$ of a portfolio x is given by the product of x and R:

$$E(r_x) = x^T * R \equiv \sum_{i=1}^{N} x_i E(r_i)$$

The *variance of portfolio x's return*, $\sigma_x^2 \equiv \sigma_{xx}$ is given by the product $x^T Sx = \sum_{i=1}^{N}\sum_{j=1}^{N} x_i x_j \sigma_{ij}$.

The *covariance between the return of two portfolios x and y*, Cov(r_x, r_y), is defined by the product $\sigma_{xy} = x^T Sy = \sum_{i=1}^{N}\sum_{j=1}^{N} x_i y_j \sigma_{ij}$. Note that $\sigma_{xy} = \sigma_{yx}$.

The following graph illustrates four concepts. A *feasible* portfolio is any portfolio whose proportions sum to one. The *feasible set* is the set of portfolio means and standard deviations generated by the feasible portfolios; this feasible set is the area inside and to the right of the curved line. A feasible portfolio is on the *envelope* of the feasible set if for a given mean return it has minimum variance. Finally, a portfolio x is *an efficient portfolio* if it maximizes the return given the portfolio variance (or standard deviation). That is, x is efficient if there is no other portfolio y such that $E(R_y) > E(R_x)$ and $\sigma_y \le \sigma_x$. The set of all efficient portfolios is called the *efficient frontier*; this frontier is the heavier line in the graph.

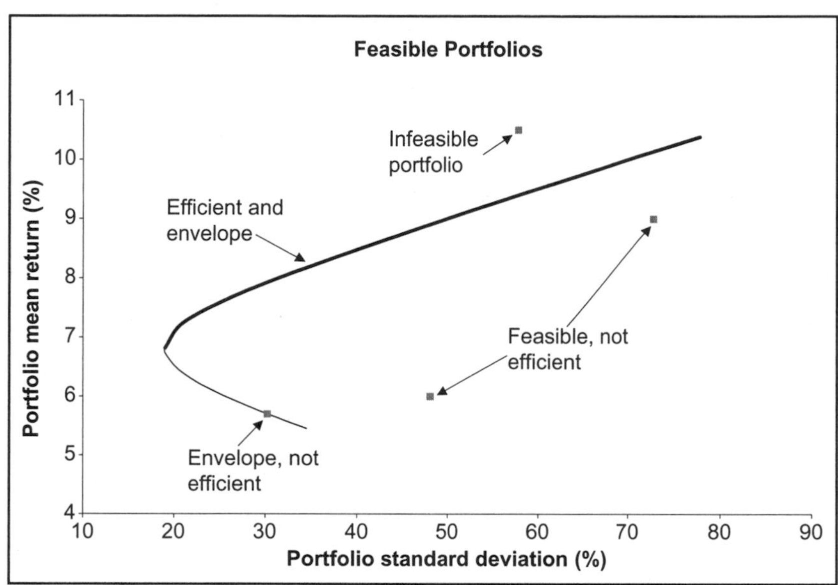

9.3 Some Theorems on Efficient Portfolios and the CAPM

In the appendix to this chapter we prove the following results, which are basic to the calculations of the CAPM. All these propositions are used in deriving the efficient frontier and the security market line; numerical illustrations are given in the next section and in succeeding chapters.

PROPOSITION 1 Let c be a constant. We use the notation $E(r) - c$ to denote the following column vector:

$$E(r)-c=\begin{bmatrix} E(r_1)-c \\ E(r_2)-c \\ E(r_N)-c \end{bmatrix}$$

Let the vector z solve the system of simultaneous linear equations $E(r) - c = Sz$. Then this solution produces a portfolio x on the envelope of the feasible set in the following manner:

$$z = S^{-1}\{E(r) - c\}$$
$$x = \{x_1, \ldots, x_N\}$$

where

$$x_i = \frac{z_i}{\sum_{j=1}^{N} z_j}$$

Furthermore, all envelope portfolios are of this form.

Intuition A formal proof of the proposition is given in the appendix to this chapter, but the intuition is simple and geometric. Suppose we pick a constant c and we try to find an efficient portfolio x for which there is a tangency between c and the feasible set:

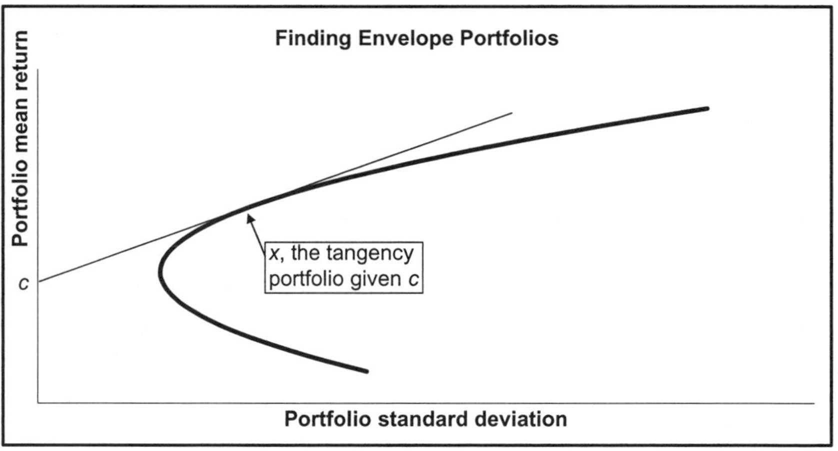

Proposition 1 gives a procedure for finding x; furthermore, the proposition states that all envelope portfolios (in particular: all efficient portfolios) are the result of the procedure outlined in the proposition. That is, if x is any envelope portfolio, then there exists a constant c and a vector z such that $Sz = E(r) - c$ and $x = z / \sum_i z_i$.

PROPOSITION 2 By a theorem first proved by Black (1972), any two envelope portfolios are enough to establish the whole envelope. Given any two envelope portfolios $x = \{x_1, \ldots, x_N\}$ and $y = \{y_1, \ldots, y_N\}$, all envelope portfolios are convex combinations of x and y. This means that given any constant a, the portfolio

$$ax + (1-a)y = \begin{bmatrix} ax_1 + (1-a)y_1 \\ ax_2 + (1-a)y_2 \\ \vdots \\ ax_N + (1-a)y_N \end{bmatrix}$$

is an envelope portfolio.

PROPOSITION 3 If y is any envelope portfolio, then for any other portfolio (envelope or not) x, we have the relationship

$$E(r_x) = c + \beta_x[E(r_y) - c]$$

where

$$\beta_x = \frac{\text{Cov}(x, y)}{\sigma_y^2}$$

Furthermore, c is the expected return of all portfolios z whose covariance with y is zero:

$$c = E(r_z)$$

where

$$\text{Cov}(y, z) = 0$$

Notes If y is on the envelope, the regression of any and all portfolios x on y gives a linear relationship. In this version of the CAPM (usually known as Black's zero-beta CAPM, in honor of Fisher Black, whose 1972 paper proved this result) the Sharpe-Lintner-Mossin security market line (SML) is replaced with an SML in which the role of the risk-free asset is played by a portfolio with a zero beta with respect to the particular envelope portfolio y. Note that this result is true for any envelope portfolio y.

The converse of Proposition 3 is also true:

PROPOSITION 4 Suppose that there exists a portfolio y such that for any portfolio x the following relation holds:

$$E(r_x) = c + \beta_x[E(r_y) - c]$$

where

$$\beta_x = \frac{\text{Cov}(x, y)}{\sigma_y^2}$$

Then the portfolio y is an envelope portfolio.

Propositions 3 and 4 show that *an SML relation holds if and only if we regress all portfolio returns on an envelope portfolio*. As Roll (1977, 1978) has forcefully pointed out, these propositions show that it is not enough to run a test of the CAPM by showing that the SML holds.[1] The only real test of the CAPM is *whether the true market portfolio is mean-variance efficient*. We shall return to this topic in Chapter 11.

THE MARKET PORTFOLIO The *market portfolio M* is a portfolio composed of *all the risky assets in the economy*, with each asset taken in proportion to its value. To make this definition more specific: Suppose that there are N risky assets and that the market value of asset i is V_i. Then the market portfolio has the following weights:

$$\text{Proportion of asset } i \text{ in } M = \frac{V_i}{\sum_{h=1}^{N} V_h}$$

If the market portfolio M is efficient (this is a big "if" as we shall see in Chapters 11 (testing the SML) and 13 (Black-Litterman), Proposition 3 is also true for the market portfolio. That is, the SML holds with $E(r_z)$ substituted for c:

$$E(r_x) = E(r_z) + \beta_x[E(r_M) - E(r_z)]$$

where

$$\beta_x = \frac{\text{Cov}(x, M)}{\sigma_M^2}$$

$$\text{Cov}(z, M) = 0$$

1. Roll's 1977 paper is more cited and more comprehensive, but his 1978 paper is much easier to read and intuitive. If you're interested in this literature, start there.

This version of the SML has received the most empirical attention of all of the CAPM results. In Chapter 11 we show how to calculate β and how to calculate the SML; we go on to examine Roll's criticism of these empirical tests. From the following graph, it is easy to see how to locate a zero-beta portfolio on the envelope of the feasible set:

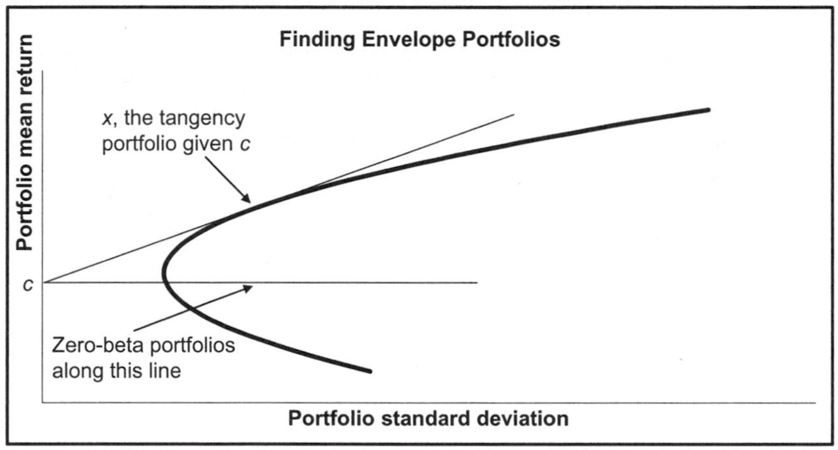

When there is a risk-free asset, Proposition 3 specializes to the security market line of the classic capital asset pricing model:

PROPOSITION 5 If there exists a risk-free asset with return r_f, then there exists an envelope portfolio M such that

$$E(r_x) = r_f + {}_x[E(r_M) - r_f]$$

where

$$\beta_x = \frac{\text{Cov}(x, M)}{\sigma_M^2}$$

As shown in the classic papers by Sharpe (1964), Lintner (1965), and Mossin (1966), if all investors choose their portfolios only on the basis of portfolio mean and standard deviation, then the portfolio x of Proposition 5 is the market portfolio M.

In the remainder of this chapter, we explore the meaning of these propositions using numerical examples worked out on Excel.

9.4 Calculating the Efficient Frontier: An Example

In this section we calculate the efficient frontier using Excel. We consider a world with four risky assets having the following expected returns and variance-covariance matrix:

	A	B	C	D	E	F	G	H
1	CALCULATING THE EFFICIENT FRONTIER							
2	Variance-covariance matrix					Expected returns E(r)	Expected minus constant E(r) - c	
3	0.40	0.03	0.02	0.00		0.06	0.02	<-- =F3-$B$8
4	0.03	0.20	0.00	-0.06		0.05	0.01	<-- =F4-$B$8
5	0.02	0.00	0.30	0.03		0.07	0.03	<-- =F5-$B$8
6	0.00	-0.06	0.03	0.10		0.08	0.04	<-- =F6-$B$8
7								
8	Constant	0.04						

Each cell of the column vector labeled **Expected minus constant** contains the mean return of the given asset minus the value of the constant c (in this case $c = 0.04$). We will use this column in finding the second envelope portfolio.

We separate our calculations into two parts: In section 9.4.1 we calculate two portfolios on the envelope of the feasible set. In section 9.4.2 we calculate the efficient frontier.

9.4.1 Calculating Two Envelope Portfolios

By Proposition 2, we have to find two efficient portfolios in order to identify the whole efficient frontier. By Proposition 1 each envelope portfolio solves the system $R - c = Sz$ for z. To identify two efficient portfolios, we use two different values for c. For each value of c, we solve for z and then set $x_i = z_i \Big/ \sum_h z_h$ to find an efficient portfolio.

The c's we solve for are arbitrary (see section 9.5), but to make life easy, we first solve this system for $c = 0$. This procedure gives the following results:

	A	B	C	D	E	F	G	H
10	**Computing an envelope portfolio with constant = 0**							
11	**z**					**Envelope portfolio x**		
12	0.1019	<-- {=MMULT(MINVERSE(A3:D6),F3:F6)}				0.0540	<-- =A12/SUM($A$12:$A$15)	
13	0.5657					0.2998		
14	0.1141					0.0605		
15	1.1052					0.5857		
16					Sum	1.0000	<-- =SUM(F12:F15)	

The formulas in the cells are as follows:

- For z we use the array function **MMult(MInverse(A3:D6),F3:F6)**. The range A3:D6 contains the variance-covariance matrix and the cells F3:F6 contain the expected returns of the assets.
- For x: Each cell contains the associated value of z divided by the sum of all the z's. Thus, for example, cell F12 contains the formula **=A12/SUM ($A$12:$A$15)**.

To find the second envelope portfolio we now solve this system for $c = 0.04$ (cell B8).

	A	B	C	D	E	F	G	H
18	**Computing an envelope portfolio with constant = 0.04**							
19	**z**					**Envelope portfolio y**		
20	0.0330	<-- {=MMULT(MINVERSE(A3:D6),G3:G6)}				0.0423	<-- =A20/SUM($A$20:$A$23)	
21	0.1959					0.2514		
22	0.0468					0.0601		
23	0.5035					0.6462		
24					Sum	1.0000	<-- =SUM(F20:F23)	

The portfolio y in cells F20:F23 is, by the results of Proposition 1, an envelope portfolio. This vector z associated with y is calculated in a manner similar to that of the first vector, except that the array function in the cells is **MMult(MInverse(A3:D6),G3:G6)**, where G3:G6 contains the vector of expected returns minus the constant 0.04.

To complete the basic calculations, we compute the means, standard deviations, and covariance of returns for portfolios x and y:

	A	B	C	D	E	F	G	H
26	**E(x)**	0.0693			**E(x)**	0.0710	<-- {=MMULT(TRANSPOSE(F20:F23),F3:F6)}	
27	**Var(x)**	0.0367			**Var(x)**	0.0398	<-- {=MMULT(MMULT(TRANSPOSE(F20:F23),A3:D6),F20:F23)}	
28	**Sigma(x)**	0.1917			**Sigma(x)**	0.1995	<-- =SQRT(F27)	
29								
30		**Cov(x,y)**	0.0376	<-- {=MMULT(MMULT(TRANSPOSE(F12:F15),A3:D6),F20:F23)}				
31		**Corr(x,y)**	0.9842	<-- =C30/(B28*F28)				

The transpose vectors of x and of y are inserted using the array function **Transpose** (see Chapter 35 for a discussion of array functions). This step now enables us to calculate the mean, variance, and covariance as follows:

E(x) uses the array formula **MMult(transpose_x,means)**. Note that we could have also used the function **SumProduct(x,means)**.

Var(x) uses the array formula **MMult(MMult(transpose_x,var_cov),x)**.

Sigma(x) uses the formula **Sqrt(var_x)**.

Cov(x,y) uses the array formula **MMult(MMult(transpose_x,var_cov),y)**.

Corr(x,y) uses the formula **cov(x,y)/(sigma_x*sigma_y)**.

The following spreadsheet illustrates everything that has been done in this subsection:

	A	B	C	D	E	F	G	H
1	**CALCULATING THE EFFICIENT FRONTIER**							
2	**Variance-covariance matrix**					**Expected returns E(r)**	**Expected minus constant E(r) - c**	
3	0.40	0.03	0.02	0.00		0.06	0.02	<-- =F3-$B$8
4	0.03	0.20	0.00	-0.06		0.05	0.01	<-- =F4-$B$8
5	0.02	0.00	0.30	0.03		0.07	0.03	<-- =F5-$B$8
6	0.00	-0.06	0.03	0.10		0.08	0.04	<-- =F6-$B$8
7								
8	Constant	0.04						
9								
10	**Computing an envelope portfolio with constant = 0**							
11	**z**					**Envelope portfolio x**		
12	0.1019	<-- {=MMULT(MINVERSE(A3:D6),F3:F6)}				0.0540	<-- =A12/SUM($A$12:$A$15)	
13	0.5657					0.2998		
14	0.1141					0.0605		
15	1.1052					0.5857		
16					Sum	1.0000	<-- =SUM(F12:F15)	
17								
18	**Computing an envelope portfolio with constant = 0.04**							
19	**z**					**Envelope portfolio y**		
20	0.0330	<-- {=MMULT(MINVERSE(A3:D6),G3:G6)}				0.0423	<-- =A20/SUM($A$20:$A$23)	
21	0.1959					0.2514		
22	0.0468					0.0601		
23	0.5035					0.6462		
24					Sum	1.0000	<-- =SUM(F20:F23)	
25								
26	**E(x)**	0.0693			**E(x)**	0.0710	<-- {=MMULT(TRANSPOSE(F20:F23),F3:F6)}	
27	**Var(x)**	0.0367			**Var(x)**	0.0398	<-- {=MMULT(MMULT(TRANSPOSE(F20:F23),A3:D6),F20:F23)}	
28	**Sigma(x)**	0.1917			**Sigma(x)**	0.1995	<-- =SQRT(F27)	
29								
30		**Cov(x,y)**	0.0376	<-- {=MMULT(MMULT(TRANSPOSE(F12:F15),A3:D6),F20:F23)}				
31		**Corr(x,y)**	0.9842	<-- =C30/(B28*F28)				

9.4.2 Calculating the Efficient Frontier

By Proposition 2 of section 9.3, convex combinations of the two portfolios calculated in the previous subsection allow us to calculate the whole envelope of the feasible set (which, of course, includes the efficient frontier). Suppose we let p be a portfolio that has proportion a invested in portfolio x and proportion $(1 - a)$ invested in y. Then—as discussed in Chapter 8—the mean and standard deviation of p's return are

$$E(r_p) = aE(r_x) + (1-a)E(r_y)$$

$$\sigma_p = \sqrt{a^2\sigma_x^2 + (1-a)^2\sigma_y^2 + 2a(1-a)\mathrm{Cov}(x, y)}$$

Here's a sample calculation for our two portfolios:

	A	B	C	D	E	F	G	H
34	**A single portfolio calculation**							
35	Proportion of x	0.3						
36	E(r$_p$)	7.05%	<-- =B35*B26+(1-B35)*F26					
37	σ$_p$	19.65%	<-- =SQRT(B35^2*B27+(1-B35)^2*F27+2*B35*(1-B35)*C30)					

We can turn this calculation into a data table (see Chapter 31) to get the following table:

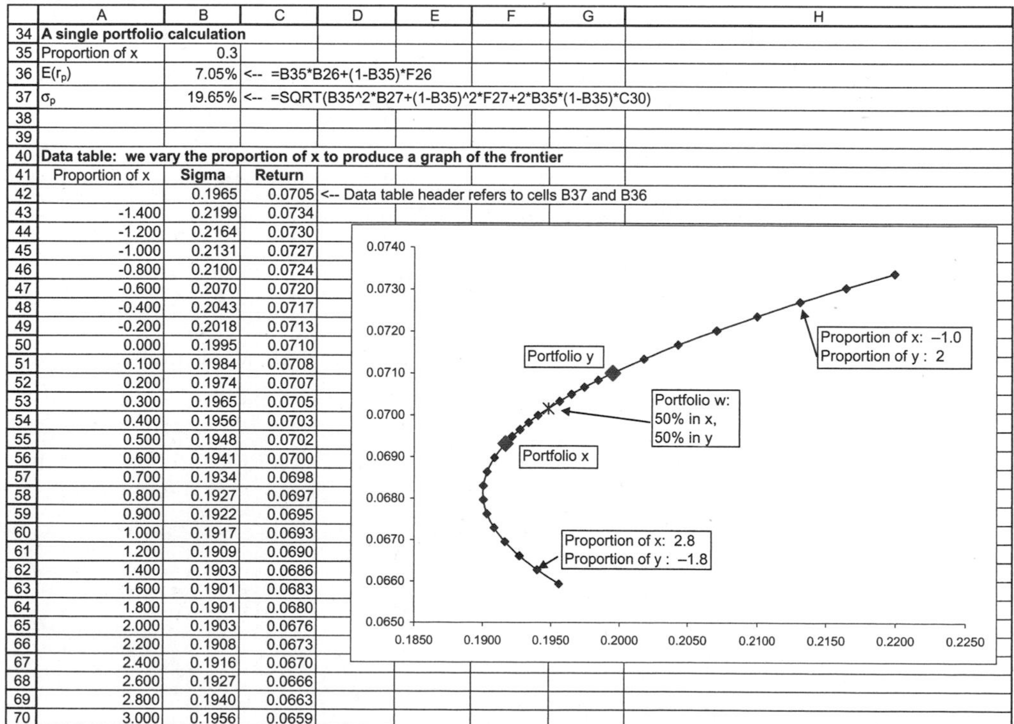

	A	B	C	D	E	F	G	H
34	**A single portfolio calculation**							
35	Proportion of x	0.3						
36	E(r$_p$)	7.05%	<-- =B35*B26+(1-B35)*F26					
37	σ$_p$	19.65%	<-- =SQRT(B35^2*B27+(1-B35)^2*F27+2*B35*(1-B35)*C30)					
38								
39								
40	**Data table: we vary the proportion of x to produce a graph of the frontier**							
41	Proportion of x	**Sigma**	**Return**					
42		0.1965	0.0705	<-- Data table header refers to cells B37 and B36				
43	-1.400	0.2199	0.0734					
44	-1.200	0.2164	0.0730					
45	-1.000	0.2131	0.0727					
46	-0.800	0.2100	0.0724					
47	-0.600	0.2070	0.0720					
48	-0.400	0.2043	0.0717					
49	-0.200	0.2018	0.0713					
50	0.000	0.1995	0.0710					
51	0.100	0.1984	0.0708					
52	0.200	0.1974	0.0707					
53	0.300	0.1965	0.0705					
54	0.400	0.1956	0.0703					
55	0.500	0.1948	0.0702					
56	0.600	0.1941	0.0700					
57	0.700	0.1934	0.0698					
58	0.800	0.1927	0.0697					
59	0.900	0.1922	0.0695					
60	1.000	0.1917	0.0693					
61	1.200	0.1909	0.0690					
62	1.400	0.1903	0.0686					
63	1.600	0.1901	0.0683					
64	1.800	0.1901	0.0680					
65	2.000	0.1903	0.0676					
66	2.200	0.1908	0.0673					
67	2.400	0.1916	0.0670					
68	2.600	0.1927	0.0666					
69	2.800	0.1940	0.0663					
70	3.000	0.1956	0.0659					

The two portfolios, x and y, whose convex combinations compose the envelope are marked, as well as other portfolios, some of which contain short positions of either x or y. Note that the convex combinations all lie on the envelope, but may not necessarily be efficient. For example, w is an efficient portfolio that is a convex combination of the two efficient portfolios x and y; in this particular case the proportion of x is 50 percent and that of y is 50 percent. Other envelope portfolios illustrated contain short positions in one of the two portfolios x and y, and may or may not be efficient. Thus, while every efficient portfolio is a convex combination of any two efficient portfolios, it is *not true* that every convex combination of any two efficient portfolios is efficient.

9.5 Three Notes on the Optimization Procedure

In this section we note three additional facts about the optimization procedure of Proposition 1 that leads to the computation of envelope portfolios.

NOTE 1: ALL ROADS LEAD TO ROME: THE PRECISE VALUES OF C ARE IRRELEVANT FOR DETERMINING THE ENVELOPE By Proposition 2, the envelope is determined by any two of its portfolios. Therefore, for the determination of the envelope it is irrelevant which two portfolios we use. To drive home this point, the following spreadsheet computes three envelope portfolios:

- The envelope portfolio x is computed with a constant $c = -0.03$.
- The envelope portfolio y is computed with a constant $c = 0.08$.
- A third envelope portfolio w is computed with a constant $c = 0.01$ (cells F29:F32). As shown in rows 36–44, portfolio w is composed of a convex combination of x and y. This statement is true for any x, y, and w: the constants c that determine the envelope are completely arbitrary.

	A	B	C	D	E	F	G
1	**CALCULATING THE ENVELOPE** **All constants *c* lead to the same envelope**						
2	**Variance-covariance matrix**					**Expected returns**	
3	0.40	0.03	0.02	0.00		0.06	
4	0.03	0.20	0.00	-0.06		0.05	
5	0.02	0.00	0.30	0.03		0.07	
6	0.00	-0.06	0.03	0.10		0.08	
7							
8	**Computing an envelope portfolio with constant = 0.03**						
9	**z**					**Envelope portfolio x**	
10	0.0502	<-- {=MMULT(MINVERSE(A3:D6),F3:F6-0.03)}				0.0475	<-- =A10/SUM($A$10:$A$13)
11	0.2883					0.2730	
12	0.0636					0.0603	
13	0.6539					0.6192	
14					Sum	1.0000	<-- =SUM(F10:F13)
15							
16	**Computing an envelope portfolio with constant = 0.08**						
17	**z**					**Envelope portfolio y**	
18	-0.0359	<-- {=MMULT(MINVERSE(A3:D6),F3:F6-0.08)}				0.1093	<-- =A18/SUM($A$18:$A$21)
19	-0.1740					0.5293	
20	-0.0205					0.0625	
21	-0.0982					0.2989	
22					Sum	1.0000	<-- =SUM(F18:F21)
23							
24	**Additional calculation: Fix another constant, and show that the resulting portfolio is a combination of the two above portfolios**						
25	Constant	0.01					
26							
27	**Computing an envelope portfolio with constant = 0.01**						
28	**z**					**Envelope portfolio w**	
29	0.0846	<-- {=MMULT(MINVERSE(A3:D6),F3:F6-B25)}				0.0526	<-- {=A29:A32/SUM(A29:A32)}
30	0.4732					0.2940	
31	0.0973					0.0604	
32	0.9548					0.5930	
33					Sum	1.0000	<-- =SUM(F29:F32)
34							
35							
36	**Proportions of x and y which determine w**						
37	Proportion of x	0.9183	<-- =(F29-F18)/(F10-F18)				
38	Proportion of y	0.0817	<-- =1-B37				
39							
40	**Check: Multiply the above proportions times portfolios x and y to get w**						
41		0.0526	<-- =$B$37*F10+$B$38*F18				
42		0.2940	<-- =$B$37*F11+$B$38*F19				
43		0.0604					
44		0.5930					

NOTE 2: CERTAIN VALUES OF C CAN ALSO LOCATE ENVELOPE PORTFOLIOS THAT ARE NONEFFICIENT, THOUGH THEY ARE ON THE ENVELOPE The optimization procedure of Proposition 1 locates a portfolio x that has proportions

$$x = \frac{S^{-1}\{E(r) - c\}}{\text{Sum}[S^{-1}\{E(r) - c\}]}$$

Although always on the envelope, this portfolio is not necessarily efficient, as is shown in the following example, where a constant $c = 0.11$ leads to an inefficient portfolio.

	A	B	C	D	E	F	G
1	**SOME c's CAN LEAD TO INEFFICIENT PORTFOLIOS** **The portfolio *x* determined by the constant c = 0.11 is inefficient**						
2	**Variance-covariance matrix**					**Expected returns E(r)**	
3	0.40	0.03	0.02	0.00		0.06	
4	0.03	0.20	0.00	-0.06		0.05	
5	0.02	0.00	0.30	0.03		0.07	
6	0.00	-0.06	0.03	0.10		0.08	
7							
8	Constant	0.11					
9							
10	**Computing an envelope portfolio with constant = 0.11**						
11	**z**					**Envelope portfolio x**	
12	-0.0876	<-- {=MMULT(MINVERSE(A3:D6),F3:F6-B8)}				0.0755	<-- {=A12:A15/SUM(A12:A15)}
13	-0.4514					0.3893	
14	-0.0710					0.0613	
15	-0.5495					0.4739	
16					Sum	1.0000	<-- =SUM(F12:F15)
17							
18							
19	$E(r_x)$	0.0662					
20	σ_x	0.1944					
21							
22							
23							
24							
25							
26							
27							
28							
29							
30							
31							

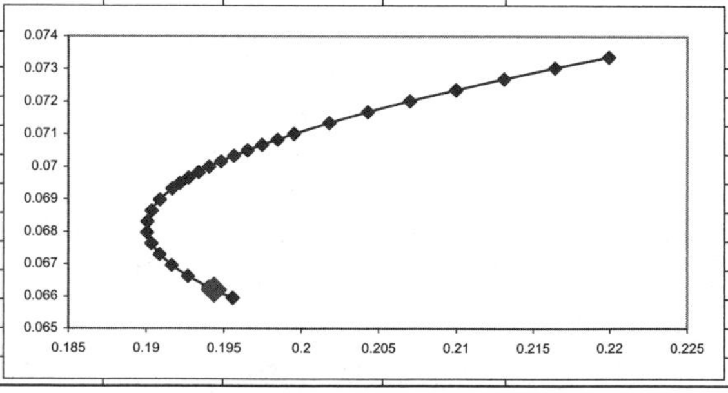

NOTE 3: IF C IS THE RISK-FREE RATE OF INTEREST AND IF THE PORTFOLIO ASSOCIATED WITH C,

$$x = \frac{S^{-1}\{E(r) - c\}}{\text{Sum}[S^{-1}\{E(r) - c\}]}$$

IS EFFICIENT, THEN THIS PORTFOLIO IS THE OPTIMAL PORTFOLIO We've said all this before in our discussion of Proposition 1, but it's worth repeating.[2] If we set c to be equal to the risk-free rate of interest, and if the resulting optimizing portfolio

$$x = \frac{S^{-1}\{E(r) - c\}}{\text{Sum}[S^{-1}\{E(r) - c\}]}$$

is efficient, then this portfolio is the optimal investment portfolio for an investor whose preferences are defined solely in terms of the mean and standard deviation of portfolio returns. In the following example we assume that r_f = 4 percent. Locating the optimizing portfolio

$$x = \frac{S^{-1}\{E(r) - c\}}{\text{Sum}[S^{-1}\{E(r) - c\}]}$$

on the envelope shows that it is efficient. Therefore the *optimal investment portfolio* for this case is given by x.

2. And it forms the basis of our discussion of the Black-Litterman model in Chapter 13.

	A	B	C	D	E	F	G
1	**IF c = r_f AND THE OPTIMIZING PORTFOLIO IS EFFICIENT, THEN THE ENVELOPE PORTFOLIO IS OPTIMAL** **The portfolio *x* determined by the constant c = 4% is optimal**						
2	**Variance-covariance matrix**					**Expected returns**	
3	0.40	0.03	0.02	0.00		0.06	
4	0.03	0.20	0.00	-0.06		0.05	
5	0.02	0.00	0.30	0.03		0.07	
6	0.00	-0.06	0.03	0.10		0.08	
7							
8	Constant	0.04					
9							
10	**Computing an envelope portfolio with constant = 0.04**						
11	**z**					**Envelope portfolio x**	
12	0.0330	<-- {=MMULT(MINVERSE(A3:D6),F3:F6-B8)}				0.0423	<-- {=A12:A15/SUM(A12:A15)}
13	0.1959					0.2514	
14	0.0468					0.0601	
15	0.5035					0.6462	
16					Sum	1.0000	<-- =SUM(F12:F15)
17							
18							
19	$E(r_x)$	0.0710					
20	σ_x	0.1995					
21							
22							
23							
24							
25							
26							
27							
28							
29							
30							

9.6 Finding Efficient Portfolios in One Step

The examples in section 9.4 find efficient portfolios by writing out most of the components of the portfolio separately on the spreadsheet. However, for some uses we will want to calculate the efficient portfolio in one step. Here's an example:

	A	B	C	D	E	F	G	H
1	**FINDING EFFICIENT PORTFOLIOS IN ONE STEP**							
2	**Variance-covariance matrix**					**Expected returns E(r)**		
3	0.40	0.03	0.02	0.00		0.06		
4	0.03	0.20	0.00	-0.06		0.05		
5	0.02	0.00	0.30	0.03		0.07		
6	0.00	-0.06	0.03	0.10		0.08		
7								
8	Constant	0.05						
9								
10	**Envelope portfolio**							
11	0.0314	<-- {=MMULT(MINVERSE(A3:D6),F3:F6-B8)/SUM(MMULT(MINVERSE(A3:D6),F3:F6-B8))}						
12	0.2059							
13	0.0597							
14	0.7031							
15								
16	Portfolio expected return, $E(r_x)$	7.26%	<-- =SUMPRODUCT(A11:A14,F3:F6)					
17	Portfolio standard devation, σ_x	21.21%	<-- {=SQRT(MMULT(MMULT(TRANSPOSE(A11:A14),A3:D6),A11:A14))}					

This approach requires a number of Excel tricks, most of which relate to the correct use of array functions. The end result is that we can write the Proposition 1 expression for an envelope portfolio,

$$x = \frac{S^{-1}\{E(r)-c\}}{\text{Sum}[S^{-1}\{E(r)-c\}]}$$

in one cell:

• In cells A11 : A14 we have used the array formula **F3:F6-B8** to indicate the expected returns minus the constant in cell B8.

• In these same cells we have used **SUM(MMULT(MINVERSE(A3:D6),F3:F6-B8))** to give the denominator of the expression

$$x = \frac{S^{-1}\{E(r)-c\}}{\text{Sum}[S^{-1}\{E(r)-c\}]}$$

9.7 Finding the Market Portfolio: The Capital Market Line

Suppose a risk-free asset exists, and suppose that this asset has expected return r_f. Let M be the efficient portfolio that is the solution to the system of equations

$$E(r) - r_f = Sz$$

$$M_i = \frac{z_i}{\sum_{i=1}^{N} z_i}$$

Now consider a convex combination of the portfolio M and the risk-free asset r_f; for example, suppose that the weight of the risk-free asset in such a portfolio is a. It follows from the standard equations for portfolio return and σ that

$$E(r_p) = ar_f + (1-a)E(r_M)$$

$$\sigma_p = \sqrt{a^2\sigma_{r_f}^2 + (1-a)^2\sigma_M^2 + 2a(1-a)\text{Cov}(r_f, r_y)} = (1-a)\sigma_M$$

The locus of all such combinations for $a \geq 0$ is known as the *capital market line* (CML). It appears along with the efficient frontier in the following graph:

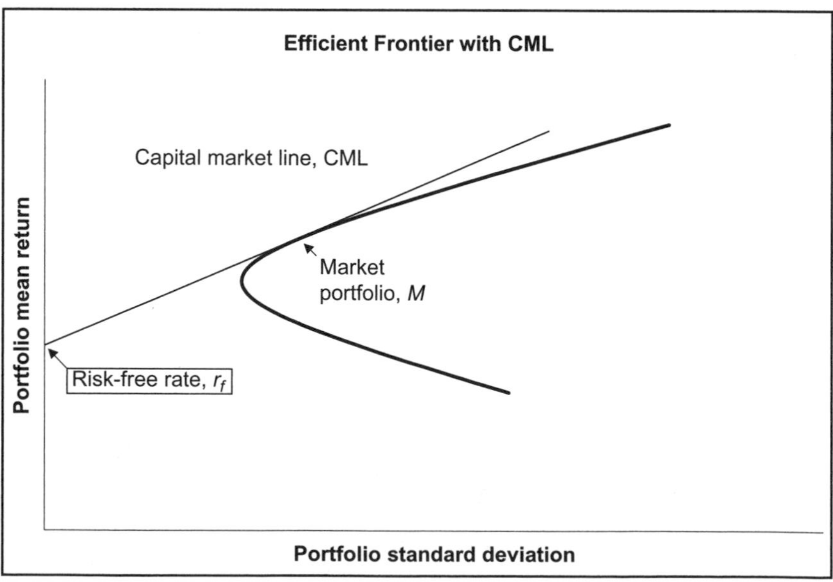

The portfolio M is called the *market portfolio* for several reasons:

- Suppose investors agree about the statistical portfolio information [i.e., the vector of expected returns $E(r)$ and the variance-covariance matrix S]. Suppose furthermore that investors are interested only in maximizing expected portfolio return given portfolio standard deviation σ. Then it follows that *all optimal portfolios will lie on the CML.*
- In this case, it further follows that *the portfolio M is the only portfolio of risky assets included in any optimal portfolio*. Portfolio M must therefore include *all the risky assets, with each asset weighted in proportion to its market value*. That is,

$$\text{Weight of risky asset } i \text{ in portfolio } M = \frac{V_i}{\sum_{i=1}^{N} V_i}$$

where V_i is the market value of asset i.

It is not difficult to find M when we know r_f: We merely have to solve for the efficient portfolio given that the constant $c = r_f$. When r_f changes, we get a different "market" portfolio—this is just the efficient portfolio given a constant of r_f. For example, in our numerical example, suppose that the risk-free rate is $r_f = 5$ percent. Then solving the system $E(r) - r_f = Sz$ gives

	A	B	C	D	E	F	G	H
1	**WHEN c = r$_f$, THE ENVELOPE PORTFOLIO IS THE MARKET PORTFOLIO M**							
2	**Variance-covariance matrix**					**Expected returns E(r)**		
3	0.40	0.03	0.02	0.00		0.06		
4	0.03	0.20	0.00	-0.06		0.05		
5	0.02	0.00	0.30	0.03		0.07		
6	0.00	-0.06	0.03	0.10		0.08		
7								
8	Constant	0.05						
9								
10	**Envelope portfolio is market portfolio M**							
11	0.0314	<-- {=MMULT(MINVERSE(A3:D6),F3:F6-B8)/SUM(MMULT(MINVERSE(A3:D6),F3:F6-B8))}						
12	0.2059							
13	0.0597							
14	0.7031							
15								
16	Portfolio expected return, E(r$_M$)	7.26%	<-- =SUMPRODUCT(A11:A14,F3:F6)					
17	Portfolio standard devation, σ$_M$	21.21%	<-- {=SQRT(MMULT(MMULT(TRANSPOSE(A11:A14),A3:D6),A11:A14))}					

9.8 Testing the SML: Implementing Propositions 3–5

To illustrate Propositions 3–5, consider the following data for four risky assets:

	A	B	C	D	E	F
1	**ILLUSTRATING PROPOSITIONS 3-5**					
2	**Dates**	**Asset 1**	**Asset 2**	**Asset 3**	**Asset 4**	
3	1	-6.63%	-2.49%	-4.27%	11.72%	
4	2	8.53%	2.44%	-3.15%	-8.33%	
5	3	1.79%	4.46%	1.92%	19.18%	
6	4	7.25%	17.90%	-6.53%	-7.41%	
7	5	0.75%	-8.22%	-1.76%	-1.44%	
8	6	-1.57%	0.83%	12.88%	-5.92%	
9	7	-2.10%	5.14%	13.41%	-0.46%	
10						
11	Mean	1.15%	2.87%	1.79%	1.05%	<-- =AVERAGE(E3:E9)

The asset returns on seven dates are given in rows 3–9, and the average return is given in row 11.

We use some sophisticated array functions to compute the variance-covariance matrix:

	A	B	C	D	E	F	G
13	**Variance-covariance matrix**						
14		Asset 1	Asset 2	Asset 3	Asset 4		
15	Asset 1	0.0024	0.0019	-0.0015	-0.0024		
16	Asset 2	0.0019	0.0056	-0.0007	-0.0016	cells B15:E18 contain the formula	
17	Asset 3	-0.0015	-0.0007	0.0057	-0.0005	{=MMULT(TRANSPOSE(B3:E9-B11:E11),B3:E9-	
18	Asset 4	-0.0024	-0.0016	-0.0005	0.0094	B11:E11)/7}	
19							
20	**Finding an efficient portfolio w**						
21	Constant	0.50%					
22							
23	Asset 1	0.3129					
24	Asset 2	0.2464		Cells B23:B26 contain the formula			
25	Asset 3	0.2690	<—	{=MMULT(MINVERSE(B15:E18),TRANSPOSE(B11:E11)-			
26	Asset 4	0.1717		B21)/SUM(MMULT(MINVERSE(B15:E18),TRANSPOSE(B11:E11)-B21))}			

The efficient portfolio given the constant $c = 0.5$ percent is given in cells B23:B26; we compute this portfolio using the method of Proposition 1.[3] We call this portfolio w. The returns of portfolio w on dates 1–7 are given in column G, as follows.

3. Following the discussion in section 9.5, a careful reader will recall that Proposition 1 only guarantees that this portfolio is on the envelope. But it is, in fact, efficient.

	A	B	C	D	E	F	G	H
2	Dates	Asset 1	Asset 2	Asset 3	Asset 4		Efficient portfolio w	
3	1	-6.63%	-2.49%	-4.27%	11.72%		-1.82%	<-- {=MMULT(B3:E9,B23:B26)}
4	2	8.53%	2.44%	-3.15%	-8.33%		0.99%	
5	3	1.79%	4.46%	1.92%	19.18%		5.47%	
6	4	7.25%	17.90%	-6.53%	-7.41%		3.65%	
7	5	0.75%	-8.22%	-1.76%	-1.44%		-2.51%	
8	6	-1.57%	0.83%	12.88%	-5.92%		2.16%	
9	7	-2.10%	5.14%	13.41%	-0.46%		4.14%	
10								
11	Mean	1.15%	2.87%	1.79%	1.05%	<-- =AVERAGE(E3:E9)	1.73%	

We illustrate Propositions 3–5 in two steps:

- *Step 1:* We regress the returns of each asset on the returns of the efficient portfolio: For $i = 1, \ldots, 4$ we run the regression $r_{it} = \alpha_i + \beta_i r_{wt} + \varepsilon_{it}$. This regression is often called the *first-pass regression*. The results are as follows:

	A	B	C	D	E	F
29	**Implementing propositions 3-5--finding the SML**					
30	Step 1: Regress each asset's returns on those of the efficient portfolio w					
31		Asset 1	Asset 2	Asset 3	Asset 4	
32	Alpha	0.0024	-0.0047	-0.0002	0.0028	<-- =INTERCEPT(E3:E9,$G$3:$G$9)
33	Beta	0.5284	1.9301	1.0490	0.4478	<-- =SLOPE(E3:E9,$G$3:$G$9)
34	R-squared	0.0897	0.5241	0.1505	0.0167	<-- =RSQ(E3:E9,$G$3:$G$9)

- *Step 2:* We now regress the mean returns of the assets on their betas. Running this regression, $\bar{r}_i = \gamma_0 + \gamma_1 \beta_i + \varepsilon_i$, gives

	A	B	C	D	E
36	Step 2: Regress the asset mean returns on their betas				
37	Intercept	0.005	<-- =INTERCEPT(B11:E11,B33:E33)		
38	Slope	0.0123	<-- =SLOPE(B11:E11,B33:E33)		
39	R-squared	1.0000	<-- =RSQ(B11:E11,B33:E33)		

To check the results of Propositions 3–5, we run a test:

	A	B	C	D	E
41	**Check Propositions 3 & 4: Step-2 coefficients should be Intercept = c, Slope = E(r$_w$) - c**				
42	Intercept = c ?	yes	<-- =IF(ROUND(B37-B21,10)=0,"yes","no"		
43	Slope = E(r$_w$) - c ?	yes	<-- =IF(B38=G11-B21,"yes","no")		

The "perfect" regression results (note the $R^2 = 1$ in cell B39) are the results promised us by Propositions 3–5:

- The second-pass regression intercept is equal to c, and the slope is equal to $E(r_w) - c$.
- If there is a riskless asset with return $c = r_f$, then Proposition 5 promises that in the second-pass regression $\bar{r}_i = \gamma_0 + \gamma_1\beta_i + \varepsilon_i$, $\gamma_0 = r_f$, and $\gamma_1 = E(r_w) - r_f$.
- If there is no riskless asset, then Proposition 3 states that in the second-pass regression $\gamma_0 = E(r_z)$ and $\gamma_1 = E(r_w) - E(r_z)$, where z is a portfolio whose covariance with w is zero.
- Finally, if we run a two-stage regression of the type described on *any portfolio w* and get a "perfect regression," then Proposition 4 guarantees that w is in fact efficient.

To drive home the point that this technique always works, we show you all the calculations using a different value for c (cell B21, highlighted in the following spreadsheet). As proved in Propositions 3–5, the result is still a perfect regression of the means on the betas.

	A	B	C	D	E	F	G	H
1	**ILLUSTRATING PROPOSITIONS 3-5** **This time the constant is 2% (cell B21)**							
2	**Dates**	**Asset 1**	**Asset 2**	**Asset 3**	**Asset 4**		Efficient portfolio w	
3	1	-6.63%	-2.49%	-4.27%	11.72%		-2.95%	<-- {=MMULT(B3:E9,B23:B26)}
4	2	8.53%	2.44%	-3.15%	-8.33%		3.64%	
5	3	1.79%	4.46%	1.92%	19.18%		5.16%	
6	4	7.25%	17.90%	-6.53%	-7.41%		-2.40%	
7	5	0.75%	-8.22%	-1.76%	-1.44%		2.24%	
8	6	-1.57%	0.83%	12.88%	-5.92%		0.01%	
9	7	-2.10%	5.14%	13.41%	-0.46%		-0.26%	
10								
11	Mean	1.15%	2.87%	1.79%	1.05%	<-- =AVERAGE(E3:E9)	0.78%	
12								
13	**Variance-covariance matrix**							
14		Asset 1	Asset 2	Asset 3	Asset 4			
15	Asset 1	0.0024	0.0019	-0.0015	-0.0024	<-- {=MMULT(TRANSPOSE(B3:E9-B11:E11),B3:E9-B11:E11)/7}		
16	Asset 2	0.0019	0.0056	-0.0007	-0.0016			
17	Asset 3	-0.0015	-0.0007	0.0057	-0.0005			
18	Asset 4	-0.0024	-0.0016	-0.0005	0.0094			
19								
20	**Finding an efficient portfolio w**							
21	Constant	2.00%						
22								
23	Asset 1	0.8234	<-- {=MMULT(MINVERSE(B15:E18),TRANSPOSE(B11:E11)-B21)/SUM(MMULT(MINVERSE(B15:E18),TRANSPOSE(B11:E11)-B21))}					
24	Asset 2	-0.2869						
25	Asset 3	0.2278						
26	Asset 4	0.2357						
27								
28								
29	**Implementing propositions 3-5--finding the SML**							
30	Step 1: Regress each asset's returns on those of the efficient portfolio w							
31		**Asset 1**	**Asset 2**	**Asset 3**	**Asset 4**			
32	Alpha	0.0061	0.0342	0.0165	0.0044	<-- =INTERCEPT(E3:E9,$G$3:$G$9)		
33	Beta	0.6968	-0.7075	0.1752	0.7776	<-- =SLOPE(E3:E9,$G$3:$G$9)		
34	R-squared	0.1570	0.0709	0.0042	0.0506	<-- =RSQ(E3:E9,$G$3:$G$9)		
35								
36	Step 2: Regress the asset mean returns on their betas							
37	Intercept	0.02	<-- =INTERCEPT(B11:E11,B33:E33)					
38	Slope	-0.0122	<-- =SLOPE(B11:E11,B33:E33)					
39	R-squared	1.0000	<-- =RSQ(B11:E11,B33:E33)					
40								
41	**Check Propositions 3 & 4: Step 2 coefficients should be:** **Intercept = c, Slope = $E(r_w)$ - c**							
42	Intercept = c ?	yes	<-- =IF(B36=B20,"yes","no")					
43	Slope = $E(r_w)$ - c ?	yes	<-- =IF(B38=G11-B21,"yes","no")					

9.9 Summary

In this chapter we have presented theorems relating to efficient portfolios and then showed how to implement these theorems to find the efficient frontier. Two basic propositions allow us to derive portfolios on the envelope of the feasible set of portfolios and the envelope itself. Three further propositions relate the expected returns of any asset or portfolio to the expected returns on any efficient portfolio. Under certain circumstances, these propositions allow us to derive the security market line (SML) and the capital market line (CML) of the classic capital asset pricing model (CAPM).

In subsequent chapters we discuss the implementation of the CAPM. We show how to compute the variance-covariance matrix (Chapter 10), how to test the SML (Chapter 11), how to optimize in the presence of short-sale constraints (Chapter 12), and how to derive useful portfolio optimization routines from our knowledge of efficient set mathematics (Chapter 13, which discusses the Black-Litterman model).

Exercises

1. Consider the following data for six furniture companies:

	A	B	C	D	E	F	G	H	I
2	**Variance-covariance matrix**	**La-Z-Boy**	**Kimball**	**Flexsteel**	**Leggett**	**Miller**	**Shaw**		**Means**
3	**La-Z-Boy**	0.1152	0.0398	0.1792	0.0492	0.0568	0.0989		29.24%
4	**Kimball**	0.0398	0.0649	0.0447	0.0062	0.0349	0.0269		20.68%
5	**Flexsteel**	0.1792	0.0447	0.3334	0.0775	0.0886	0.1487		25.02%
6	**Leggett**	0.0492	0.0062	0.0775	0.1033	0.0191	0.0597		31.64%
7	**Miller**	0.0568	0.0349	0.0886	0.0191	0.0594	0.0243		15.34%
8	**Shaw**	0.0989	0.0269	0.1487	0.0597	0.0243	0.1653		43.87%

a. Given this matrix, and assuming that the risk-free rate is 0 percent, calculate the efficient portfolio of these six firms.

b. Repeat, assuming that the risk-free rate is 10 percent.

c. Use these two portfolios to generate an efficient frontier for the six furniture companies. Plot this frontier.

d. Is there an efficient portfolio with only positive proportions of all the assets?[4]

4. The problem of when a portfolio contains only positive weights in nontrivial. See the articles by Green (1986) and Nielsen (1987).

2. A sufficient condition to produce positively weighted efficient portfolios is that the variance-covariance matrix be diagonal: That is, that $\sigma_{ij} = 0$, for $i \neq j$. By continuity, positively weighted portfolios will result if the off-diagonal elements of the variance-covariance matrix are sufficiently small compared to the diagonal. Consider a transformation of the preceding matrix in which

$$\sigma_{ij} = \begin{cases} \varepsilon \sigma_{ij}^{\text{Original}} & \text{if } i \neq j \\ \sigma_{ii}^{\text{Original}} \end{cases}$$

When $\varepsilon = 1$, this transformation will give the original variance-covariance matrix, and when $\varepsilon = 0$, the transformation will give a fully diagonal matrix.

For r = 10 percent, find the maximum ε for which all portfolio weights are positive.

3. In the following example, use Excel to find an envelope portfolio whose β with respect to the efficient portfolio y is zero. *Hint*: Notice that because the covariance is linear, so is β: Suppose that $z = \lambda x + (1 - \lambda)y$ is a convex combination of x and y, and that we are trying to find the β_z. Then

$$\beta_z = \frac{\text{Cov}(z, y)}{\sigma_y^2} = \frac{\text{Cov}[\lambda x + (1-\lambda)y, y]}{\sigma_y^2}$$
$$= \frac{\lambda \text{Cov}(x, y)}{\sigma_y^2} + \frac{(1-\lambda)\text{Cov}(y, y)}{\sigma_y^2} = \lambda \beta_x + (1-\lambda)$$

	A	B	C	D	E	F
1	**Variance-covariance matrix**					**Mean returns**
2	0.400	0.030	0.020	0.000		0.06
3	0.030	0.200	0.001	-0.060		0.05
4	0.020	0.001	0.300	0.030		0.07
5	0.000	-0.060	0.030	0.100		0.08

4. Calculate the envelope set for the following four assets and show that the individual assets all lie within this envelope set.

	A	B	C	D	E	F
1	**A FOUR-ASSET PORTFOLIO PROBLEM**					
2	Variance-covariance					Mean returns
3	0.10	0.01	0.03	0.05		6%
4	0.01	0.30	0.06	-0.04		8%
5	0.03	0.06	0.40	0.02		10%
6	0.05	-0.04	0.02	0.50		15%

You should get a graph which looks something like the following:

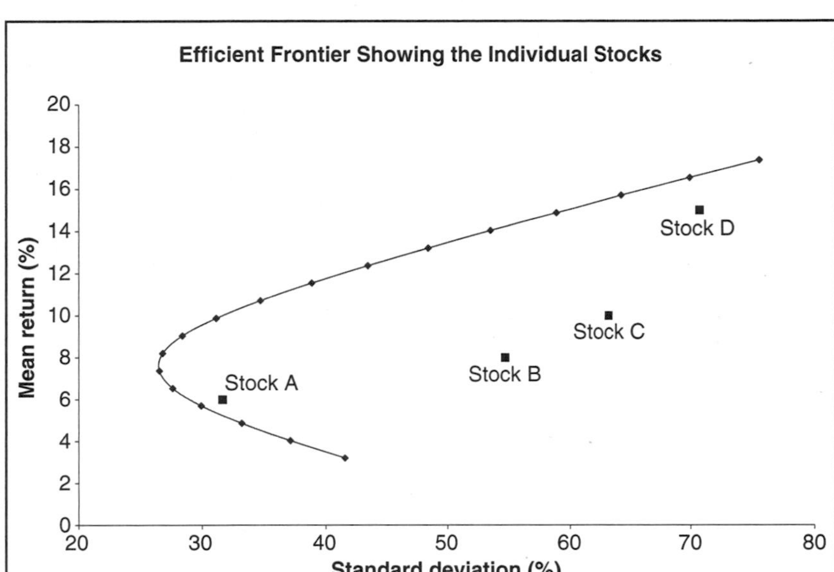

Appendix

In this appendix we collect the various proofs of statements made in the chapter. As in the chapter, we assume that we are examining data for N risky assets. It is important to note that all the definitions of "feasibility" and "optimality" are made relative to this set. Thus the phrase "efficient" really means "efficient relative to the set of the N assets being examined."

PROPOSITION 0 The set of all feasible portfolios of risky assets is convex.

Proof A portfolio x is feasible if and only if the proportions of the portfolio add up to 1; that is, $\sum_{i=1}^{N} x_i = 1$, where N is the number of risky assets. Suppose that x and y are feasible portfolios and suppose that λ is some number between 0 and 1. Then it is clear that $z = \lambda x + (1 - \lambda)y$ is also feasible.

PROPOSITION 1 Let c be a constant and denote by R the vector of mean returns. A portfolio x is on the envelope relative to the sample set of N assets if and only if it is the normalized solution of the system

$$R - c = Sz$$

$$x_i = \frac{z_i}{\sum_h z_h}$$

Proof A portfolio x is on the envelope of the feasible set of portfolios if and only if it lies on the tangency of a line connecting some point c on the y-axis to the feasible set. Such a portfolio must either maximize or minimize the ratio $\frac{x(R-c)}{\sigma^2(x)}$, where $x(R - c)$ is the vector product that gives the portfolio's expected excess return over c and $\sigma^2(x)$ is the portfolio's variance. Let this ratio's value when maximized (or minimized) be λ. Then our portfolio must satisfy

$$\frac{x(R-c)}{\sigma^2(x)} = \lambda$$

$$\Rightarrow x(R-c) = \sigma^2(x)\lambda = xSx^T\lambda$$

Let h be a particular asset, and differentiate this last expression with respect to x_h. This step gives $\bar{R}_h - c = Sx^T\lambda$. Writing $z_h = \lambda x_h$, we see that a portfolio is efficient if and only if it solves the system $R - c = Sz$. Normalizing z so that its coordinates add to 1 gives the desired result.

PROPOSITION 2 The convex combination of any two envelope portfolios is on the envelope of the feasible set.

Proof Let x and y be portfolios on the envelope. By Proposition 1, it follows that there exist two vectors, z_x and z_y, and two constants c_x and c_y, such that

- x is the normalized-to-unity vector of z_x, that is, $x_i = \frac{z_{xi}}{\sum_h z_{xh}}$, and y is the normalized-to-unity vector of z_y.
- $R - c_x = Sz_x$ and $R - c_y = Sz_y$.

Furthermore, since z maximizes the ratio $\frac{z(R-c)}{\sigma^2(z)}$, it follows that any normalization of z also maximizes this ratio. With no loss in generality, therefore, we can assume that z sums to 1.

It follows that for any real number a the portfolio $az_x + (1 - a)z_y$ solves the system $R - [ac_x + (1 - a)c_y] = Sz$. This result proves our claim.

PROPOSITION 3 Let y be any envelope portfolio of the set of N assets. Then for any other portfolio x (including, possibly, a portfolio composed of a single asset) there exists a constant c such that the following relation holds between the expected return on x and the expected return on portfolio y:

$$E(r_x) = c + \beta_x[E(r_y) - c]$$

where

$$\beta_x = \frac{\text{Cov}(x, y)}{\sigma_y^2}$$

Furthermore, $c = E(r_z)$, where z is any portfolio for which $\text{Cov}(z, y) = 0$.

Proof Let y be a particular envelope portfolio, and let x be any other portfolio. We assume that both portfolios x and y are column vectors. Note that

$$\beta_x \equiv \frac{\text{Cov}(x, y)}{\sigma_y^2} = \frac{x^T S y}{y^T S y}$$

Now since y is on the envelope, we know that there exist a vector w and a constant c that solve the system $Sw = R - c$ and that $y = w \Big/ \sum_i w_i = w / a$.

Substituting this equation in the expression for β_x, we get

$$\beta_x = \frac{\text{Cov}(x, y)}{\sigma_y^2} = \frac{x^T S y}{y^T S y} = \frac{x^T (R-c)/a}{y^T (R-c)/a} = \frac{x^T (R-c)}{y^T (R-c)}$$

Next note that since $\sum_i x_i = 1$, it follows that $x^T I(R - c) = E(r_x) - c$ and that $y^T I(R - c) = E(r_y) - c$. This relation shows that

$$\beta_x = \frac{E(r_x) - c}{E(r_y) - c}$$

which can be rewritten as

$$E(r_x) = c + \beta_x[E(r_y) - c]$$

To finish the proof, let z be a portfolio that has zero covariance with y. Then the preceding logic shows that $c = E(r_z)$. This result proves the claim.

PROPOSITION 4 If in addition to the N risky assets, there exists a risk-free asset with return r_f, then the standard *security market line* holds:

$$E(r_x) = r_f + \beta_x[E(r_M) - r_f]$$

where

$$\beta_x = \frac{\text{Cov}(x, M)}{\sigma_M^2}$$

Proof If there exists a risk-free security, then the tangent line from this security to the efficient frontier dominates all other feasible portfolios. Call the point of tangency on the efficient frontier M; then the result follows.

Note It is important to repeat again that the terminology "market portfolio" refers in this case to the "market portfolio relative to the sample set of N assets."

PROPOSITION 5 Suppose that there exists a portfolio y such that for any portfolio x the following relation holds:

$$E(r_x) = c + \beta_x[E(r_y) - c]$$

where

$$\beta_x = \frac{\text{Cov}(x, y)}{\sigma_y^2}$$

Then the portfolio y is on the envelope.

Proof Substituting in for the definition of β_x, it follows that for any portfolio x the following relation holds:

$$\frac{x^T S y}{\sigma_y^2} = \frac{x^T R - c}{y^T R - c}$$

Let x be the vector composed solely of the first risky asset: $x = \{1, 0, \ldots, 0\}$. Then the preceding equation becomes

$$S_1 y \frac{y^T R - c}{\sigma_y^2} = E(r_1) - c$$

which we write

$$S_1 a y = E(r_1) - c$$

where S_1 is the first row of the variance-covariance matrix S. Note that $a = \dfrac{y^T R - c}{\sigma_y^2}$ is a constant whose value is independent of the vector x. If we let x be a vector composed solely of the ith risky asset, we get

$$S_i a y = E(r_i) - c$$

This result proves that the vector $z = ay$ solves the system $Sz = R - c$; by Proposition 1, therefore, the normalization of z is on the envelope. But this normalization is simply the vector y.

10 Calculating the Variance-Covariance Matrix

10.1 Overview

In order to calculate efficient portfolios, we must be able to compute the variance-covariance matrix from return data for stocks. In this chapter we discuss this computation, showing how to do the calculations in Excel. The most obvious calculation is the *sample variance-covariance matrix*: This is the matrix computed directly from the historic returns. We illustrate several methods for calculating the sample variance-covariance matrix, including a direct calculation in the spreadsheet using the excess return matrix and an implementation of this method with Visual Basic for Applications (VBA).

While the sample variance-covariance matrix may appear to be an obvious choice, a large literature recognizes that it may not be the best estimate of variances and covariances. Disappointment with the sample variance-covariance matrix stems both from its often unrealistic parameters and from its inability to predict. These issues are discussed briefly in sections 10.5 and 10.6. As an alternative to the sample matrix, sections 10.9 and 10.10 discuss "shrinkage" methods for improving the estimate of the variance-covariance matrix.[1]

Before starting this chapter, you may want to peruse Chapter 34, which discusses array functions. These are Excel functions whose arguments are vectors and matrices; their implementation is slightly different from standard Excel functions. This chapter makes heavy use of the array functions **Transpose( )** and **MMult( )** as well as some other "homegrown" array functions.

10.2 Computing the Sample Variance-Covariance Matrix

Suppose we have return data for N assets over M periods. Writing the return of asset i in period t as r_{it}, we write the *mean return* of asset i as

$$\bar{r}_i = \frac{1}{M}\sum_{t=1}^{M} r_{it}, \quad i = 1, \ldots, N$$

Then the covariance of the return of asset i and asset j is calculated as

1. We return to the issue of prediction in Chapter 13, which discusses the Black-Litterman model of portfolio optimization.

$$\sigma_{ij} = \text{Cov}(i,j) = \frac{1}{M-1}\sum_{t=1}^{M}(r_{it} - \bar{r}_i) * (r_{jt} - \bar{r}_j), \quad i,j = 1,\ldots,N$$

The matrix of these covariances (which includes, of course, the variances when $i = j$) is the *sample variance-covariance matrix*. Our problem is to calculate these covariances efficiently. Define the *excess return matrix* to be

$$A = \text{Matrix of excess returns} = \begin{bmatrix} r_{11} - \bar{r}_1 & \cdots & r_{N1} - \bar{r}_N \\ r_{12} - \bar{r}_1 & \cdots & r_{N2} - \bar{r}_N \\ \vdots & & \vdots \\ r_{1M} - \bar{r}_1 & \cdots & r_{NM} - \bar{r}_N \end{bmatrix}$$

Columns of matrix A subtract the mean asset return from the individual asset returns. The transpose of this matrix is

$$A^T = \begin{bmatrix} r_{11} - \bar{r}_1 & r_{12} - \bar{r}_1 & \cdots & \cdots & r_{1M} - \bar{r}_1 \\ \vdots & \vdots & & & \vdots \\ r_{N1} - \bar{r}_N & r_{N2} - \bar{r}_N & \cdots & \cdots & r_{NM} - \bar{r}_N \end{bmatrix}$$

Multiplying A^T times A and dividing through by $M - 1$ gives the sample variance-covariance matrix:

$$S = [\sigma_{ij}] = \frac{A^T * A}{M-1}$$

To consider the computational aspects, we use $M = 11$ years of annual return data for $N = 6$ stocks. The following spreadsheet shows the price data (adjusted for dividends) and the computed returns:

	A	B	C	D	E	F	G	H
1	**ANNUAL STOCK PRICE AND RETURN DATA FOR SIX STOCKS** General Electric (GE), Microsoft (MSFT), Johnson & Johnson (JNJ), Kellogg (K), Boeing (BA), IBM							
2	**Price data**							
3	**Date**	**GE**	**MSFT**	**JNJ**	**K**	**BA**	**IBM**	
4	4-Jan-93	2.36	2.68	6.78	20.37	2.34	11.79	
5	3-Jan-94	4.15	2.64	7.20	18.47	4.21	14.62	
6	3-Jan-95	4.98	3.68	10.91	19.90	4.20	15.53	
7	2-Jan-96	8.80	5.73	19.43	29.03	8.09	20.41	
8	2-Jan-97	13.51	12.64	24.44	27.59	13.93	30.78	
9	2-Jan-98	21.64	18.49	29.15	38.01	20.19	31.60	
10	4-Jan-99	30.57	43.37	38.04	34.14	23.47	30.94	
11	3-Jan-00	40.51	48.51	39.36	20.93	36.27	39.24	
12	2-Jan-01	42.42	30.26	43.80	23.52	48.13	48.78	
13	2-Jan-02	34.82	31.58	55.19	28.70	41.39	51.05	
14	2-Jan-03	22.25	23.52	52.15	32.00	32.81	59.63	
15	2-Jan-04	31.86	28.16	51.49	37.36	48.86	81.95	
16								
17	Shares outstanding	10.56	10.86	2.97	0.41	0.84	0.79	
18	Market value	336.44	305.82	152.93	15.44	41.01	65.13	<-- =G15*G17
19	Percentage of portfolio	36.70%	33.36%	16.68%	1.68%	4.47%	7.10%	<-- =G18/SUM($B$18:$K$18)
20								
21	**Return data**							
22	**Date**	**GE**	**MSFT**	**JNJ**	**K**	**BA**	**IBM**	
23	3-Jan-94	56.44%	-1.50%	6.01%	-9.79%	58.73%	21.51%	<-- =LN(G5/G4)
24	3-Jan-95	18.23%	33.21%	41.56%	7.46%	-0.24%	6.04%	<-- =LN(G6/G5)
25	2-Jan-96	56.93%	44.28%	57.71%	37.76%	65.55%	27.33%	
26	2-Jan-97	42.87%	79.12%	22.94%	-5.09%	54.34%	41.08%	
27	2-Jan-98	47.11%	38.04%	17.62%	32.04%	37.11%	2.63%	
28	4-Jan-99	34.55%	85.25%	26.62%	-10.74%	15.05%	-2.11%	
29	3-Jan-00	28.15%	11.20%	3.41%	-48.93%	43.53%	23.76%	
30	2-Jan-01	4.61%	-47.19%	10.69%	11.67%	28.29%	21.76%	
31	2-Jan-02	-19.74%	4.27%	23.11%	19.90%	-15.09%	4.55%	
32	2-Jan-03	-44.78%	-29.47%	-5.67%	10.88%	-23.23%	15.54%	
33	2-Jan-04	35.90%	18.01%	-1.27%	15.49%	39.82%	31.80%	
34								
35	Average	23.66%	21.38%	18.43%	5.51%	27.63%	17.63%	<-- =AVERAGE(G23:G33)
36	Standard deviation	32.17%	40.71%	18.97%	23.86%	29.93%	13.56%	<-- =STDEV(G23:G33)
37	Variance	0.1035	0.1657	0.0360	0.0570	0.0896	0.0184	<-- =VAR(G23:G33)

We illustrate the matrix method of computing the variance-covariance matrix with our numerical example. Subtracting the mean return of each asset from its annual return, we create the matrix of excess returns (rows 42–52 in the following spreadsheet). In rows 55–61 we compute the sample variance-covariance matrix.

	A	B	C	D	E	F	G	H
40	**Excess returns**							
41	**Date**	**GE**	**MSFT**	**JNJ**	**K**	**BA**	**IBM**	
42	3-Jan-94	32.78%	-22.89%	-12.42%	-15.31%	31.11%	3.89%	<-- =G23-G$35
43	3-Jan-95	-5.43%	11.83%	23.13%	1.94%	-27.86%	-11.59%	<-- =G24-G$35
44	2-Jan-96	33.27%	22.90%	39.28%	32.25%	37.93%	9.70%	
45	2-Jan-97	19.21%	57.73%	4.51%	-10.60%	26.72%	23.46%	
46	2-Jan-98	23.45%	16.65%	-0.81%	26.53%	9.49%	-15.00%	
47	4-Jan-99	10.89%	63.87%	8.19%	-16.25%	-12.57%	-19.74%	
48	3-Jan-00	4.49%	-10.18%	-15.02%	-54.44%	15.90%	6.14%	
49	2-Jan-01	-19.05%	-68.58%	-7.74%	6.15%	0.67%	4.14%	
50	2-Jan-02	-43.40%	-17.11%	4.68%	14.39%	-42.71%	-13.08%	
51	2-Jan-03	-68.45%	-50.85%	-24.10%	5.37%	-50.86%	-2.09%	
52	2-Jan-04	12.24%	-3.38%	-19.70%	9.97%	12.20%	14.17%	
53								
54	**Uses the array formula {<-- {=MMULT(TRANSPOSE(B42:G52),B42:G52)/10}} to compute the sample var-cov matrix**							
55		**GE**	**MSFT**	**JNJ**	**K**	**BA**	**IBM**	
56	**GE**	0.1035	0.0758	0.0222	-0.0043	0.0857	0.0123	
57	**MSFT**	0.0758	0.1657	0.0412	-0.0052	0.0379	-0.0022	
58	**JNJ**	0.0222	0.0412	0.0360	0.0181	0.0101	-0.0039	
59	**K**	-0.0043	-0.0052	0.0181	0.0570	-0.0076	-0.0046	
60	**BA**	0.0857	0.0379	0.0101	-0.0076	0.0896	0.0248	
61	**IBM**	0.0123	-0.0022	-0.0039	-0.0046	0.0248	0.0184	
62								
63	**Note: To put the array formula into cells B56:G61:**							
64	1. Mark the whole area B56:G61							
65	2. Type <-- {=MMULT(TRANSPOSE(B42:G52),B42:G52)/10} into one of the cells.							
66	3. When finished typing, hit [Ctrl]+[Shift]+[Enter] to put in the formula as an array formula.							

10.2.1 A Slightly More Efficient Alternative Method

As you might expect, there are alternative methods for computing the variance-covariance matrix. The method illustrated here skips the computation of the excess return matrix and does the calculation directly inside the formula of cells B71:G76. It does so by using the array formula **= MMULT(TRANSPOSE(B23:G33-B35:G35),B23:G33-B35:G35)/10.** By writing B23:G33-B35 we directly subtract the means from each return to create the vector of excess returns:

	A	B	C	D	E	F	G	H
21	**Return data**							
22	**Date**	**GE**	**MSFT**	**JNJ**	**K**	**BA**	**IBM**	
23	3-Jan-94	56.44%	-1.50%	6.01%	-9.79%	58.73%	21.51%	<-- =LN(G5/G4)
24	3-Jan-95	18.23%	33.21%	41.56%	7.46%	-0.24%	6.04%	<-- =LN(G6/G5)
25	2-Jan-96	56.93%	44.28%	57.71%	37.76%	65.55%	27.33%	
26	2-Jan-97	42.87%	79.12%	22.94%	-5.09%	54.34%	41.08%	
27	2-Jan-98	47.11%	38.04%	17.62%	32.04%	37.11%	2.63%	
28	4-Jan-99	34.55%	85.25%	26.62%	-10.74%	15.05%	-2.11%	
29	3-Jan-00	28.15%	11.20%	3.41%	-48.93%	43.53%	23.76%	
30	2-Jan-01	4.61%	-47.19%	10.69%	11.67%	28.29%	21.76%	
31	2-Jan-02	-19.74%	4.27%	23.11%	19.90%	-15.09%	4.55%	
32	2-Jan-03	-44.78%	-29.47%	-5.67%	10.88%	-23.23%	15.54%	
33	2-Jan-04	35.90%	18.01%	-1.27%	15.49%	39.82%	31.80%	
34								
35	Average	23.66%	21.38%	18.43%	5.51%	27.63%	17.63%	<-- =AVERAGE(G23:G33)
36	Standard deviation	32.17%	40.71%	18.97%	23.86%	29.93%	13.56%	<-- =STDEV(G23:G33)
37	Variance	0.1035	0.1657	0.0360	0.0570	0.0896	0.0184	<-- =VAR(G23:G33)
38								
69	**Uses the array formula {<-- {=MMULT(TRANSPOSE(B23:G33-B35:G35),B23:G33-B35:G35)/10}} to compute the sample var-cov matrix**							
70		**GE**	**MSFT**	**JNJ**	**K**	**BA**	**IBM**	
71	**GE**	0.1035	0.0758	0.0222	-0.0043	0.0857	0.0123	
72	**MSFT**	0.0758	0.1657	0.0412	-0.0052	0.0379	-0.0022	
73	**JNJ**	0.0222	0.0412	0.0360	0.0181	0.0101	-0.0039	
74	**K**	-0.0043	-0.0052	0.0181	0.0570	-0.0076	-0.0046	
75	**BA**	0.0857	0.0379	0.0101	-0.0076	0.0896	0.0248	
76	**IBM**	0.0123	-0.0022	-0.0039	-0.0046	0.0248	0.0184	

10.3 Should We Divide by M or by $M - 1$? Excel versus Statistics?

In the foregoing calculations we divided by $M - 1$ instead of M in order to get the unbiased estimate of the variances and covariances. But perhaps this choice hardly matters. We quote from a major text: "There is a long story about why the denominator is $M - 1$ instead of M. If you have never heard that story, you may consult any good statistics text. Here we will be content to note that the $M - 1$ *should* be changed to M if you are ever in the situation of measuring the variance of a distribution whose mean is known *a priori* rather than being estimated from the data. (We might also comment that if the difference between M and $M - 1$ ever matters to you, then you are probably up to no good anyway—e.g., trying to substantiate a questionable hypothesis with marginal data.)"[2]

2. *Numerical Recipes: The Art of Scientific Computing* by William H. Press, Brian P. Flannery, Saul A. Teukolsky, and William T. Vetterling (Cambridge University Press, 1986). Slightly adapted from p. 456.

Excel itself is somewhat confused on this issue of dividing by M or by $M-1$. In the following spreadsheet we show several ways of computing the means, variances, standard deviations, and covariances:

	A	B	C	D	E	F	G	H
1	**SOME CONFUSION ABOUT M VERSUS M - 1 IN EXCEL?**							
2	**Date**	**GE**	**MSFT**	**JNJ**	**K**	**BA**	**IBM**	
3	3-Jan-94	56.44%	-1.50%	6.01%	-9.79%	58.73%	21.51%	
4	3-Jan-95	18.23%	33.21%	41.56%	7.46%	-0.24%	6.04%	
5	2-Jan-96	56.93%	44.28%	57.71%	37.76%	65.55%	27.33%	
6	2-Jan-97	42.87%	79.12%	22.94%	-5.09%	54.34%	41.08%	
7	2-Jan-98	47.11%	38.04%	17.62%	32.04%	37.11%	2.63%	
8	4-Jan-99	34.55%	85.25%	26.62%	-10.74%	15.05%	-2.11%	
9	3-Jan-00	28.15%	11.20%	3.41%	-48.93%	43.53%	23.76%	
10	2-Jan-01	4.61%	-47.19%	10.69%	11.67%	28.29%	21.76%	
11	2-Jan-02	-19.74%	4.27%	23.11%	19.90%	-15.09%	4.55%	
12	2-Jan-03	-44.78%	-29.47%	-5.67%	10.88%	-23.23%	15.54%	
13	2-Jan-04	35.90%	18.01%	-1.27%	15.49%	39.82%	31.80%	
14								
15	**Mean**	**GE**	**MSFT**	**JNJ**	**K**	**BA**	**IBM**	
16		23.66%	21.38%	18.43%	5.51%	27.63%	17.63%	<-- =AVERAGE(G3:G13)
17		23.66%	21.38%	18.43%	5.51%	27.63%	17.63%	<-- =SUM(G3:G13)/COUNT(G3:G13)
18								
19	**Variance**	**GE**	**MSFT**	**JNJ**	**K**	**BA**	**IBM**	
20		0.0941	0.1507	0.0327	0.0518	0.0814	0.0167	<-- =COVAR(G3:G13,G3:G13)
21		0.0941	0.1507	0.0327	0.0518	0.0814	0.0167	<-- =VARP(G3:G13)
22		0.1035	0.1657	0.0360	0.0570	0.0896	0.0184	<-- =VAR(G3:G13)
23								
24	**Standard deviation**	**GE**	**MSFT**	**JNJ**	**K**	**BA**	**IBM**	
25		0.3067	0.3882	0.1808	0.2275	0.2854	0.1293	<-- =SQRT(G20)
26		0.3067	0.3882	0.1808	0.2275	0.2854	0.1293	<-- =STDEVP(G3:G13)
27		0.3217	0.4071	0.1897	0.2386	0.2993	0.1356	<-- =STDEV(G3:G13)
28								
29	**Covariance(GE,MSFT)**							
30		0.0690	<-- =COVAR(B3:B13,C3:C13)					
31		0.0690	<-- {=MMULT(TRANSPOSE(B3:B13-B16),C3:C13-C16)/11}					
32		0.0758	<-- {=MMULT(TRANSPOSE(B3:B13-B16),C3:C13-C16)/10}					
33		0.0758	<-- =COVAR(B3:B13,C3:C13)*11/10					

Excel distinguishes between the *population variance* (**Varp**, which divides by M) and the *sample variance* (**Var**, which divides by $M-1$) and distinguishes between the population and sample standard deviation (**Stdevp** and **Stdev**, respectively). However, Excel does not make the same distinction for its covariance function **Covar**. As you can see in cell B30, **Covar** divides by M, in the same way that **Varp** divides by M. If you want to create a corresponding covariance function that divides by $M-1$, you either have to multiply **Covar** by $\frac{M}{M-1}$ as in cell B33 or you have to use the array function **=MMULT(TRANSPOSE(B3:B13-B16),C3:C13-C16)/10** as in cell B32. If Excel were completely logical, it would have two functions: **Covarp**, which divides by M (corresponding to **Varp** or **Stdevp**), and **Covar**, which divides by $M - 1$ (corresponding to **Var** or **Stdev**).

Confused? Don't worry! As the quote that starts this section indicates, perhaps it doesn't matter very much.

10.4 Alternative Methods for Computing the Sample Variance-Covariance Matrix

In this section we briefly discuss two alternatives to the techniques described in the previous section. The first alternative is a VBA array function that directly computes the sample variance-covariance matrix, and the second alternative makes use of Excel's **Offset** function.

10.4.1 A VBA Function to Compute the Variance-Covariance Matrix

Our first alternative uses a VBA function.[3,4]

```
Function VarCovar(rng As Range) As Variant
     Dim i As Integer
     Dim j As Integer
     Dim numCols As Integer
     numCols = rng.Columns.Count
     numRows = rng.Rows.Count
     Dim matrix() As Double
     ReDim matrix(numCols - 1, numCols - 1)

     For i = 1 To numCols
          For j = 1 To numCols
               matrix(i - 1, j - 1) = Application.
WorksheetFunction.Covar(rng.Columns(i), rng.Columns(j)) _
               * numRows / (numRows - 1)
          Next j
     Next i
     VarCovar = matrix
End Function
```

3. This section, which can be skipped on first reading, requires some knowledge of Excel's programming language Visual Basic for Applications (VBA), which is discussed in Chapters 37–43.
4. I thank Amir Kirsh for developing this function.

This function is an array function (meaning that it has to be applied using Ctrl-Shift-Enter). Here's an example:

	A	B	C	D	E	F	G	H
1	**USING A VBA FUNCTION TO COMPUTE THE COVARIANCE MATRIX** General Electric (GE), Microsoft (MSFT), Johnson & Johnson (JNJ), Kellogg (K), Boeing (BA), IBM							
21	**Return data**							
22	**Date**	**GE**	**MSFT**	**JNJ**	**K**	**BA**	**IBM**	
23	3-Jan-94	56.44%	-1.50%	6.01%	-9.79%	58.73%	21.51%	<-- =LN(G5/G4)
24	3-Jan-95	18.23%	33.21%	41.56%	7.46%	-0.24%	6.04%	<-- =LN(G6/G5)
25	2-Jan-96	56.93%	44.28%	57.71%	37.76%	65.55%	27.33%	
26	2-Jan-97	42.87%	79.12%	22.94%	-5.09%	54.34%	41.08%	
27	2-Jan-98	47.11%	38.04%	17.62%	32.04%	37.11%	2.63%	
28	4-Jan-99	34.55%	85.25%	26.62%	-10.74%	15.05%	-2.11%	
29	3-Jan-00	28.15%	11.20%	3.41%	-48.93%	43.53%	23.76%	
30	2-Jan-01	4.61%	-47.19%	10.69%	11.67%	28.29%	21.76%	
31	2-Jan-02	-19.74%	4.27%	23.11%	19.90%	-15.09%	4.55%	
32	2-Jan-03	-44.78%	-29.47%	-5.67%	10.88%	-23.23%	15.54%	
33	2-Jan-04	35.90%	18.01%	-1.27%	15.49%	39.82%	31.80%	
34								
38								
69	**Uses the homemade array formula {=varcovar(B23:G33)} to compute the sample varcov matrix**							
70		**GE**	**MSFT**	**JNJ**	**K**	**BA**	**IBM**	
71	**GE**	0.1035	0.0758	0.0222	-0.0043	0.0857	0.0123	
72	**MSFT**	0.0758	0.1657	0.0412	-0.0052	0.0379	-0.0022	
73	**JNJ**	0.0222	0.0412	0.0360	0.0181	0.0101	-0.0039	
74	**K**	-0.0043	-0.0052	0.0181	0.0570	-0.0076	-0.0046	
75	**BA**	0.0857	0.0379	0.0101	-0.0076	0.0896	0.0248	
76	**IBM**	0.0123	-0.0022	-0.0039	-0.0046	0.0248	0.0184	

VarCovar uses the Excel **Covar** function to compute the entries of the variance-covariance matrix. Because **Covar** divides by M, whereas we want to divide through by $M - 1$, the line

```
Application.WorksheetFunction.Covar(rng.
Columns(i), rng.Columns(j)) _
               * numRows / (numRows - 1)
```

adjusts by multiplying by $\frac{M}{M-1}$.

10.4.2 The Variance-Covariance Matrix Using Excel's Offset Function

Another way to calculate the variance-covariance function uses Excel's **Offset** function.[5] **Offset** takes a bit of getting used to: This function allows

5. Shay Zafrir, an MBA student at Tel-Aviv University, suggested using this function to define the var-cov matrix.

you to define a block of cells *relative* to some initial cell. Thus, for example, **Offset(initial cells, rows, columns)** refers to a block of cells of the same size as the initial cells, but **rows** and **columns** over from the initial cells. The technique is illustrated in the following spreadsheet. Note that the borders 0, 1, 2, 3, 4, 5 have been added to the variance-covariance matrix in the lower half of the spreadsheet:

	A	B	C	D	E	F	G
1	**USING OFFSET AND COVAR TO CREATE THE VARIANCE-COVARIANCE MATRIX**						
2	**Return data**						
3	**Date**	**GE**	**MSFT**	**JNJ**	**K**	**BA**	**IBM**
4	3-Jan-94	56.44%	-1.50%	6.01%	-9.79%	58.73%	21.51%
5	3-Jan-95	18.23%	33.21%	41.56%	7.46%	-0.24%	6.04%
6	2-Jan-96	56.93%	44.28%	57.71%	37.76%	65.55%	27.33%
7	2-Jan-97	42.87%	79.12%	22.94%	-5.09%	54.34%	41.08%
8	2-Jan-98	47.11%	38.04%	17.62%	32.04%	37.11%	2.63%
9	4-Jan-99	34.55%	85.25%	26.62%	-10.74%	15.05%	-2.11%
10	3-Jan-00	28.15%	11.20%	3.41%	-48.93%	43.53%	23.76%
11	2-Jan-01	4.61%	-47.19%	10.69%	11.67%	28.29%	21.76%
12	2-Jan-02	-19.74%	4.27%	23.11%	19.90%	-15.09%	4.55%
13	2-Jan-03	-44.78%	-29.47%	-5.67%	10.88%	-23.23%	15.54%
14	2-Jan-04	35.90%	18.01%	-1.27%	15.49%	39.82%	31.80%
15							
16	**Sample var-cov matrix, uses the formula =COVAR(OFFSET($B$4:$B$14,0,B$17),OFFSET($B$4:$B$14,0,$A18))*11/10 to compute the sample var-cov matrix. This formula is copied in each cell.**						
17		**0**	**1**	**2**	**3**	**4**	**5**
18	**0**	0.1035	0.0758	0.0222	-0.0043	0.0857	0.0123
19	**1**	0.0758	0.1657	0.0412	-0.0052	0.0379	-0.0022
20	**2**	0.0222	0.0412	0.0360	0.0181	0.0101	-0.0039
21	**3**	-0.0043	-0.0052	0.0181	0.0570	-0.0076	-0.0046
22	**4**	0.0857	0.0379	0.0101	-0.0076	0.0896	0.0248
23	**5**	0.0123	-0.0022	-0.0039	-0.0046	0.0248	0.0184

10.5 Computing the Global Minimum Variance Portfolio

The two most prominent uses of the variance-covariance matrix are to find the global minimum variance portfolio (GMVP) and to find efficient portfolios. Both uses illustrate the problematics of working with sample data and provide us with the introduction needed for sections 10.7–10.10, which discuss alternatives to the sample variance-covariance matrix. In this section we discuss the GMVP.

Suppose there are N assets having a variance-covariance matrix S. The GMVP is the portfolio $x = \{x_1, x_2, \ldots, x_N\}$ that has the lowest variance from among all feasible portfolios. The minimum variance portfolio is defined by

$$x_{GMVP} = \{x_{GMVP,1}, x_{GMVP,2}, \ldots, x_{GMVP,N}\} = \frac{1 \cdot S^{-1}}{1 \cdot S^{-1} \cdot 1^T}, \text{ where } 1 = \underbrace{\{1, 1, \ldots, 1\}}_{\uparrow \text{ N-dimensional}}$$

This formula is due to Merton.[6]

The particular fascination of the minimum variance portfolio is that it is the only portfolio on the efficient frontier whose computation does not require the asset expected returns. The mean μ_{GMVP} and the variance σ^2_{GMVP} of the minimum variance portfolio are given by

$$\mu_{GMVP} = x_{GMVP} \cdot E(r), \sigma^2_{GMVP} = x_{GMVP} \cdot S \cdot x^T_{GMVP}$$

Here's an implementation of these formulas for our particular example:

	A	B	C	D	E	F	G	H	I
1	**COMPUTING THE GLOBAL MINIMUM VARIANCE PORTFOLIO USING THE SAMPLE VARIANCE-COVARIANCE MATRIX**								
2	**Sample variance-covariance matrix**								
3		**GE**	**MSFT**	**JNJ**	**K**	**BA**	**IBM**		**One**
4	**GE**	0.1035	0.0758	0.0222	-0.0043	0.0857	0.0123		1
5	**MSFT**	0.0758	0.1657	0.0412	-0.0052	0.0379	-0.0022		1
6	**JNJ**	0.0222	0.0412	0.0360	0.0181	0.0101	-0.0039		1
7	**K**	-0.0043	-0.0052	0.0181	0.0570	-0.0076	-0.0046		1
8	**BA**	0.0857	0.0379	0.0101	-0.0076	0.0896	0.0248		1
9	**IBM**	0.0123	-0.0022	-0.0039	-0.0046	0.0248	0.0184		1
10									
11	**Mean**	23.66%	21.38%	18.43%	5.51%	27.63%	17.63%		
12									
13	**The global minimum variance portfolio (GMVP) is computed below with the formula {=MMULT(TRANSPOSE(I4:I9),MINVERSE(B4:G9))/MMULT(MMULT(TRANSPOSE(I4:I9),MINVERSE(B4:G9)),I4:I9)}**								
14		**GE**	**MSFT**	**JNJ**	**K**	**BA**	**IBM**		
15		0.6105	-0.1034	0.2074	0.0539	-0.7704	1.0019		
16									
17	**Sum**	1.0000	<-- =SUM(B15:G15)						
18									
19	**GMVP mean**	0.1273	<-- =SUMPRODUCT(B11:G11,B15:G15)						
20	**GMVP variance**	0.0060	<-- {=MMULT(MMULT(B15:G15,B4:G9),TRANSPOSE(B15:G15))}						
21	**GMVP standard deviation**	0.0773	<-- =SQRT(B20)						

6. Robert C. Merton 1973. "An Analytical Derivation of the Efficient Portfolio Frontier," *Journal of Financial and Quantitative Analysis* 7, pp. 1851–1872.

Note that the GMVP for our six stocks has two short positions (BA and MSFT) and that it has a very large positive position in GE and IBM. This is a potentially objectionable feature of computing the GMVP with the sample variance-covariance matrix: It is not credible that an investor seeking minimum variance would put 61 percent of his portfolio in GE and 100 percent of his portfolio in IBM, financing these positions with a short of 77 percent in BA and 10 percent in MSFT. The noncredible portfolios produced by the sample variance-covariance matrix have led to a variety of techniques for alternative methods of computing this matrix, which are discussed in sections 10.7–10.9. But before turning to this topic, we consider the computation of the efficient portfolio.

10.6 Computing an Efficient Portfolio

Following our discussion in Chapter 9, we can compute an efficient portfolio by solving the equation:

$$\text{Efficient portfolio} = \frac{S^{-1}[E(r)-c]}{\text{Sum}\{S^{-1}[E(r)-c]\}}$$

where S is the variance-covariance matrix, $E(r)$ is the vector of expected returns, and c is a constant. In the next spreadsheet we assume the $E(r)$ is the vector of historic asset means, and we set $c = 2$ percent. The efficient portfolio is given in row 14.

	A	B	C	D	E	F	G	H	I
1	**COMPUTING AN EFFICIENT PORTFOLIO**								
2		**GE**	**MSFT**	**JNJ**	**K**	**BA**	**IBM**		**Means**
3	**GE**	0.1035	0.0758	0.0222	-0.0043	0.0857	0.0123		23.66%
4	**MSFT**	0.0758	0.1657	0.0412	-0.0052	0.0379	-0.0022		21.38%
5	**JNJ**	0.0222	0.0412	0.0360	0.0181	0.0101	-0.0039		18.43%
6	**K**	-0.0043	-0.0052	0.0181	0.0570	-0.0076	-0.0046		5.51%
7	**BA**	0.0857	0.0379	0.0101	-0.0076	0.0896	0.0248		27.63%
8	**IBM**	0.0123	-0.0022	-0.0039	-0.0046	0.0248	0.0184		17.63%
9									
10	Risk-free rate	2%							
11									
12	**The efficient portfolio is computed by the array formula {=TRANSPOSE(MMULT(MINVERSE(B3:G8),I3:I8-B10)/SUM(MMULT(MINVERSE(B3:G8),I3:I8-B10)))} . The cells below use TRANSPOSE( ) to make this a row vector.**								
13		**GE**	**MSFT**	**JNJ**	**K**	**BA**	**IBM**		
14	Efficient portfolio	26.37%	-6.05%	36.98%	-4.81%	-33.87%	81.39%		
15									
16	Market value ($billion)	336.44	305.82	152.93	15.44	41.01	16.98		
17	Market proportions	38.73%	35.21%	17.61%	1.78%	4.72%	1.96%	<-- =G16/SUM($B$16:$G$16)	

Row 16 of the spreadsheet shows the market values of the individual stocks on the last date of the data (beginning of January 2004). Row 17 computes the proportions of a portfolio that is composed of the market weights of each asset. The difference between these market weights and the efficient-portfolio weights is striking.

The spreadsheet shows two additional problems associated with using the sample variance-covariance matrix for portfolio optimization.

The first problem is that the optimal portfolio exhibits a number of very significant short-sale positions and some equally unrealistically large long positions. Running a **Data Table** that calculates the envelope portfolios for various values of *c* shows that the whole efficient frontier contains portfolios with very large short and long positions. The highlights that follow indicate changes of sign that occur when *c* changes. Only JNJ has positive weights on the whole envelope of stocks.

	A	B	C	D	E	F	G	H	I
20	**Data table: Optimal portfolio for various c's: the table header (hidden) in row 22 refers to the computation of the efficient portfolio in row 14**								
21		**GE**	**MSFT**	**JNJ**	**K**	**BA**	**IBM**	**Largest long position**	**Smallest position**
22	c								
23	-10%	44.68%	-8.31%	28.41%	0.57%	-56.66%	91.32%	91.32%	-56.66%
24	-9%	43.92%	-8.22%	28.76%	0.35%	-55.72%	90.91%	90.91%	-55.72%
25	-8%	43.10%	-8.12%	29.15%	0.11%	-54.69%	90.46%	90.46%	-54.69%
26	-7%	42.19%	-8.01%	29.57%	-0.16%	-53.56%	89.97%	89.97%	-53.56%
27	-6%	41.18%	-7.88%	30.04%	-0.46%	-52.31%	89.42%	89.42%	-52.31%
28	-5%	40.06%	-7.74%	30.57%	-0.79%	-50.91%	88.81%	88.81%	-50.91%
29	-4%	38.80%	-7.59%	31.16%	-1.15%	-49.35%	88.13%	88.13%	-49.35%
30	-3%	37.39%	-7.41%	31.82%	-1.57%	-47.59%	87.37%	87.37%	-47.59%
31	-2%	35.78%	-7.21%	32.57%	-2.04%	-45.59%	86.50%	86.50%	-45.59%
32	-1%	33.94%	-6.98%	33.43%	-2.58%	-43.30%	85.50%	85.50%	-43.30%
33	0%	31.81%	-6.72%	34.43%	-3.21%	-40.65%	84.34%	84.34%	-40.65%
34	1%	29.32%	-6.41%	35.59%	-3.94%	-37.55%	82.99%	82.99%	-37.55%
35	2%	26.37%	-6.05%	36.98%	-4.81%	-33.87%	81.39%	81.39%	-33.87%
36	3%	22.80%	-5.61%	38.65%	-5.86%	-29.44%	79.46%	79.46%	-29.44%
37	4%	18.42%	-5.06%	40.70%	-7.15%	-23.99%	77.08%	77.08%	-23.99%
38	5%	12.91%	-4.38%	43.28%	-8.77%	-17.13%	74.10%	74.10%	-17.13%
39	7%	-3.89%	-2.30%	51.14%	-13.71%	3.77%	64.99%	64.99%	-13.71%
40	9%	-38.68%	2.00%	67.42%	-23.94%	47.07%	46.13%	67.42%	-38.68%
41	11%	-153.79%	16.25%	121.30%	-57.80%	190.31%	-16.27%	190.31%	-153.79%

If we think that the portfolio proportions derived in this way are unrealistic, then in terms of the optimization process, there must be something wrong with either the variance-covariance matrix or the vector of means (perhaps both). We will return to this topic both in sections 10.7–10.10 of this chapter and in Chapter 13 on the Black-Litterman model.

The second problem illustrated by this example relates to the implausible correlations implied by the sample variance-covariance matrix. In the next spreadsheet we show the matrix of correlations. For the period surveyed, the largest correlation (between General Electric and Boeing) is 0.89; examining the matrix shows that there are a number of other very large and implausible correlations: There are six correlation coefficients larger than 0.5. This is hard to believe! The smallest correlation (between Boeing and Kellogg), –0.10, is perhaps also a problem—could it be that when the returns on Boeing go up, the sales of cereals decrease?

	A	B	C	D	E	F	G	H
1	**THE CORRELATION MATRIX**							
2	**Variance-covariance matrix**							
3		**GE**	**MSFT**	**JNJ**	**K**	**BA**	**IBM**	
4	**GE**	**0.1035**	0.0758	0.0222	-0.0043	0.0857	0.0123	
5	**MSFT**	0.0758	**0.1657**	0.0412	-0.0052	0.0379	-0.0022	
6	**JNJ**	0.0222	0.0412	**0.0360**	0.0181	0.0101	-0.0039	
7	**K**	-0.0043	-0.0052	0.0181	**0.0570**	-0.0076	-0.0046	
8	**BA**	0.0857	0.0379	0.0101	-0.0076	**0.0896**	0.0248	
9	**IBM**	0.0123	-0.0022	-0.0039	-0.0046	0.0248	**0.0184**	
10								
11	**The range below computes the correlation coefficients based on the formula =C4/SQRT(INDEX($B$4:$G$9,C$13,C$13)*INDEX($B$4:$G$9,$A14,$A14)). The correlations on the diagonal (all = 1) are not shown. To make the formula work, we have labeled the rows and columns from 1 to 6.**							
12		**GE**	**MSFT**	**JNJ**	**K**	**BA**	**IBM**	
13		**1**	**2**	**3**	**4**	**5**	**6**	
14	**1**		0.5791	0.3632	-0.0560	0.8905	0.2819	**GE**
15	**2**			0.5340	-0.0532	0.3113	-0.0406	**MSFT**
16	**3**				0.4002	0.1780	-0.1529	**JNJ**
17	**4**					-0.1067	-0.1427	**K**
18	**5**						0.6116	**BA**
19								**IBM**
20	Largest correlation	0.8905	<-- =MAX(B14:G18)					
21	2nd largest correlation	0.6116	<-- =LARGE(B14:G18,2)					
22	3rd largest correlation	0.5791	<-- =LARGE(B14:G18,3)					
23	4th largest correlation	0.5340	<-- =LARGE(B14:G18,4)					
24	5th largest correlation	0.4002						
25	6th largest correlation	0.3632						
26	7th largest correlation	0.3113						
27	8th largest correlation	0.2819						
28	9th largest correlation	0.1780						
29	Smallest correlation	-0.1529	<-- =MIN(B14:G18)					
30	Average correlation	0.2398	<-- =AVERAGE(C14:G18)					
31								
32	Number of correlations greater than 0.5	4	<-- =COUNTIF(B14:G18,">0.5")					

10.7 Alternatives to the Sample Variance-Covariance: The Single-Index Model

The sample variance-covariance matrix is easily computable from historical data, but—as shown in the previous section—it has its problems. In particular, the sample matrix makes it difficult to predict the GMVP, and using it for portfolio optimization often leads to implausible asset positions (both long and short). In this section and the next we consider several alternatives to using the sample matrix. All these methods have two common features:

- They leave the variances alone—they compute them from the sample variance.
- They change the covariances (the off-diagonal) elements of the variance-covariance matrix.

10.7.1 The Single-Index Model

The single-index model (SIM) began as an attempt to simplify some of the computational complexities of calculating the variance-covariance matrix.[7] The basic assumption of the SIM is that the returns of each asset can be linearly regressed on a market index x:

$$\tilde{r}_i = \alpha_i + \beta_i \tilde{r}_x + \tilde{\varepsilon}_i$$

where the correlation between ε_i and ε_j is zero. Given this assumption, it is easy to establish the following two facts:

$$E = (\tilde{r}_i) = \alpha_i + \beta_i E(\tilde{r}_x)$$

$$\sigma_{ij} = \begin{cases} \beta_i \beta_j \sigma_x^2 & \text{when } i \neq j \\ \sigma_i^2 & \text{when } i = j \end{cases}$$

Essentially the SIM assumes involves changes in the estimates of the covariances, but not the sample variance. We illustrate the computation of the SIM with our six-asset example, adding a seventh column for the returns on the S&P 500. Regressing the returns of each asset on the Standard & Poor's 500 portfolio, we get the betas in row 20:

7. W. F. Sharpe 1963. "A Simplified Model for Portfolio Analysis," *Management Science* 9, pp. 277–293.

	A	B	C	D	E	F	G	H	I
1	**ESTIMATING THE VARIANCE-COVARIANCE MATRIX USING THE SINGLE-INDEX MODEL**								
2	**Return data**								
3	**Date**	**GE**	**MSFT**	**JNJ**	**K**	**BA**	**IBM**	**SP500**	
4	3-Jan-94	56.44%	-1.50%	6.01%	-9.79%	58.73%	21.51%	-2.35%	
5	3-Jan-95	18.23%	33.21%	41.56%	7.46%	-0.24%	6.04%	30.16%	
6	2-Jan-96	56.93%	44.28%	57.71%	37.76%	65.55%	27.33%	21.19%	
7	2-Jan-97	42.87%	79.12%	22.94%	-5.09%	54.34%	41.08%	22.07%	
8	2-Jan-98	47.11%	38.04%	17.62%	32.04%	37.11%	2.63%	26.65%	
9	4-Jan-99	34.55%	85.25%	26.62%	-10.74%	15.05%	-2.11%	8.59%	
10	3-Jan-00	28.15%	11.20%	3.41%	-48.93%	43.53%	23.76%	-2.06%	
11	2-Jan-01	4.61%	-47.19%	10.69%	11.67%	28.29%	21.76%	-18.95%	
12	2-Jan-02	-19.74%	4.27%	23.11%	19.90%	-15.09%	4.55%	-27.82%	
13	2-Jan-03	-44.78%	-29.47%	-5.67%	10.88%	-23.23%	15.54%	27.91%	
14	2-Jan-04	35.90%	18.01%	-1.27%	15.49%	39.82%	31.80%	4.34%	
15									
16	**Average**	23.66%	21.38%	18.43%	5.51%	27.63%	17.63%	8.16%	<-- =AVERAGE(H4:H14)
17	**Standard deviation**	32.17%	40.71%	18.97%	23.86%	29.93%	13.56%	19.59%	<-- =STDEV(H4:H14)
18	**Variance**	0.1035	0.1657	0.0360	0.0570	0.0896	0.0184	0.0384	<-- =VAR(H4:H14)
19									
20	**Beta**	0.3411	0.9185	0.2598	0.2344	0.1046	0.0186		<-- =SLOPE(G4:G14,$H$4:$H$14)

Using the wonders of Excel array functions (Chapter 35), we can compute the SIM variance-covariance function:

	A	B	C	D	E	F	G	H
23	**The SIM var-cov matrix uses the array formula {=IF(B24:G24=A25:A30,B18:G18,MMULT(TRANSPOSE(B20:G20),B20:G20)*H18)} to compute the sample var-cov matrix**							
24		**GE**	**MSFT**	**JNJ**	**K**	**BA**	**IBM**	
25	**GE**	0.1035	0.0120	0.0034	0.0031	0.0014	0.0002	
26	**MSFT**	0.0120	0.1657	0.0092	0.0083	0.0037	0.0007	
27	**JNJ**	0.0034	0.0092	0.0360	0.0023	0.0010	0.0002	
28	**K**	0.0031	0.0083	0.0023	0.0570	0.0009	0.0002	
29	**BA**	0.0014	0.0037	0.0010	0.0009	0.0896	0.0001	
30	**IBM**	0.0002	0.0007	0.0002	0.0002	0.0001	0.0184	

This array function needs to be picked apart:

- It contains an **If** function, which as we know has three parts: **If(condition, answer if condition is true, answer if condition is false)**
- The condition B24:G24=A25:A30 asks if the "cross entries" in the row B24:G24 (which contains the stock names as a row) are equal to the entries in the column vector A25:A30. To see this condition with greater clarity, we have inserted the formula **If(B24:G24=A25:A30,1,0)** into the following spreadsheet. As you can see this step creates a spreadsheet with 1 on the diagonal and zero elsewhere:

	A	B	C	D	E	F	G
1	**The SIM var-cov matrix uses the array formula {=IF(B2:G2=A3:A8,1,0)} to compute the sample var-cov matrix**						
2		**GE**	**MSFT**	**JNJ**	**K**	**BA**	**IBM**
3	**GE**	1	0	0	0	0	0
4	**MSFT**	0	1	0	0	0	0
5	**JNJ**	0	0	1	0	0	0
6	**K**	0	0	0	1	0	0
7	**BA**	0	0	0	0	1	0
8	**IBM**	0	0	0	0	0	1

- The first **If** condition in our SIM variance-covariance matrix is **IF(B24:G24=A25:A30, B18:G18, ...)**. This says that if we are on the diagonal, we should put in the asset's return variance.
- The second **If** condition says that if we are off-diagonal, we should put in **MMULT(TRANSPOSE(B20:G20),B20:G20)*H18)**. The formula **TRANSPOSE(B20:G20),B20:G20)** creates a matrix of $\beta_i\beta_j$. The formula multiplies this matrix by the variance of the S&P 500, given in column H.

10.8 Alternatives to the Sample Variance-Covariance: Constant Correlation

The constant-correlation model of Elton and Gruber (1973) computes the variance-covariance matrix by assuming that the variances of the asset returns are the sample returns, but that the covariances are all related by the same correlation coefficient, which is generally taken to be the average correlation coefficient of the assets in question. Since $\text{Cov}(r_i, r_j) = \sigma_{ij} = \rho_{ij}\sigma_i\sigma_j$, this assumption means that in the constant-correlation model

$$\sigma_{ij} = \begin{cases} \sigma_{ii} = \sigma_i^2 & \text{when } i = j \\ \sigma_{ij} = \rho\sigma_i\sigma_j & \text{when } i \neq j \end{cases}$$

Using our data for the six stocks, we can implement the constant-correlation model. We first compute the correlations of all the stocks:

	A	B	C	D	E	F	G	H
1	**ESTIMATING THE VARIANCE-COVARIANCE MATRIX USING THE CONSTANT-CORRELATION APPROACH**							
2	**Return data**							
3	**Date**	**GE**	**MSFT**	**JNJ**	**K**	**BA**	**IBM**	
4	3-Jan-94	56.44%	-1.50%	6.01%	-9.79%	58.73%	21.51%	
5	3-Jan-95	18.23%	33.21%	41.56%	7.46%	-0.24%	6.04%	
6	2-Jan-96	56.93%	44.28%	57.71%	37.76%	65.55%	27.33%	
7	2-Jan-97	42.87%	79.12%	22.94%	-5.09%	54.34%	41.08%	
8	2-Jan-98	47.11%	38.04%	17.62%	32.04%	37.11%	2.63%	
9	4-Jan-99	34.55%	85.25%	26.62%	-10.74%	15.05%	-2.11%	
10	3-Jan-00	28.15%	11.20%	3.41%	-48.93%	43.53%	23.76%	
11	2-Jan-01	4.61%	-47.19%	10.69%	11.67%	28.29%	21.76%	
12	2-Jan-02	-19.74%	4.27%	23.11%	19.90%	-15.09%	4.55%	
13	2-Jan-03	-44.78%	-29.47%	-5.67%	10.88%	-23.23%	15.54%	
14	2-Jan-04	35.90%	18.01%	-1.27%	15.49%	39.82%	31.80%	
15								
16	**Average**	23.66%	21.38%	18.43%	5.51%	27.63%	17.63%	<-- =AVERAGE(G4:G14)
17	**Standard deviation**	32.17%	40.71%	18.97%	23.86%	29.93%	13.56%	<-- =STDEV(G4:G14)
18	**Variance**	0.1035	0.1657	0.0360	0.0570	0.0896	0.0184	<-- =VAR(G4:G14)
19	**Average correlation**	0.2398	<-- =(AVERAGE(B23:G28)-1/6)*(36/30)					
20								
21	**Uses the array formula {=MMULT(TRANSPOSE(B4:G14-B16:G16),B4:G14-B16:G16)/10/MMULT(TRANSPOSE(B17:G17),B17:G17)} to compute the correlations.**							
22		**GE**	**MSFT**	**JNJ**	**K**	**BA**	**IBM**	
23	**GE**	1.0000	0.5791	0.3632	-0.0560	0.8905	0.2819	
24	**MSFT**	0.5791	1.0000	0.5340	-0.0532	0.3113	-0.0406	
25	**JNJ**	0.3632	0.5340	1.0000	0.4002	0.1780	-0.1529	
26	**K**	-0.0560	-0.0532	0.4002	1.0000	-0.1067	-0.1427	
27	**BA**	0.8905	0.3113	0.1780	-0.1067	1.0000	0.6116	
28	**IBM**	0.2819	-0.0406	-0.1529	-0.1427	0.6116	1.0000	

In the preceding spreadsheet we took our constant correlation to be the average correlation of our sample of the six stocks (cell B19). Of course this approach is open to variations: Suppose we feel that the average correlation of stocks in the future will be about 0.3. Then we can directly estimate the constant-correlation matrix from the return data.

	A	B	C	D	E	F	G	H
1	**ESTIMATING THE VARIANCE-COVARIANCE MATRIX USING THE CONSTANT-CORRELATION APPROACH** **The constant correlation is set as r = 0.3**							
2	**Return data**							
3	**Date**	**GE**	**MSFT**	**JNJ**	**K**	**BA**	**IBM**	
4	3-Jan-94	56.44%	-1.50%	6.01%	-9.79%	58.73%	21.51%	
5	3-Jan-95	18.23%	33.21%	41.56%	7.46%	-0.24%	6.04%	
6	2-Jan-96	56.93%	44.28%	57.71%	37.76%	65.55%	27.33%	
7	2-Jan-97	42.87%	79.12%	22.94%	-5.09%	54.34%	41.08%	
8	2-Jan-98	47.11%	38.04%	17.62%	32.04%	37.11%	2.63%	
9	4-Jan-99	34.55%	85.25%	26.62%	-10.74%	15.05%	-2.11%	
10	3-Jan-00	28.15%	11.20%	3.41%	-48.93%	43.53%	23.76%	
11	2-Jan-01	4.61%	-47.19%	10.69%	11.67%	28.29%	21.76%	
12	2-Jan-02	-19.74%	4.27%	23.11%	19.90%	-15.09%	4.55%	
13	2-Jan-03	-44.78%	-29.47%	-5.67%	10.88%	-23.23%	15.54%	
14	2-Jan-04	35.90%	18.01%	-1.27%	15.49%	39.82%	31.80%	
15								
16	Average	23.66%	21.38%	18.43%	5.51%	27.63%	17.63%	<-- =AVERAGE(G4:G14)
17	Standard deviation	32.17%	40.71%	18.97%	23.86%	29.93%	13.56%	<-- =STDEV(G4:G14)
18	Variance	0.1035	0.1657	0.0360	0.0570	0.0896	0.0184	<-- =VAR(G4:G14)
19	Constant correlation	0.3000	<-- This is an educated guesstimate					
20								
21	**Uses the array formula {=IF(A23:A28=B22:G22,B18:G18,MMULT(TRANSPOSE(B17:G17),B17:G17)*B19)} to compute the constant correlation matrix**							
22		**GE**	**MSFT**	**JNJ**	**K**	**BA**	**IBM**	
23	**GE**	0.1035	0.0393	0.0183	0.0230	0.0289	0.0131	
24	**MSFT**	0.0393	0.1657	0.0232	0.0291	0.0366	0.0166	
25	**JNJ**	0.0183	0.0232	0.0360	0.0136	0.0170	0.0077	
26	**K**	0.0230	0.0291	0.0136	0.0570	0.0214	0.0097	
27	**BA**	0.0289	0.0366	0.0170	0.0214	0.0896	0.0122	
28	**IBM**	0.0131	0.0166	0.0077	0.0097	0.0122	0.0184	

10.9 Shrinkage Methods

A third class of methods of estimating the variance-covariance matrix has recently achieved popularity. So-called *shrinkage methods* assume that the variance-covariance matrix is a convex combination of the sample covariance matrix and some other matrix:

$$\text{Shrinkage variance-covariance matrix} = \lambda * \text{Sample Var-Cov} + (1 - \lambda) * \text{Other matrix}$$

In the following example the "other" matrix is a diagonal matrix of only variances, with zeros elsewhere. The shrinkage estimator $\lambda = 0.3$ (cell B20).

	A	B	C	D	E	F	G	H
1	**ESTIMATING THE VARIANCE-COVARIANCE MATRIX USING THE SHRINKAGE APPROACH** **Gives weight 0.30 (the shrinkage factor) to sample var-cov and weight 0.70 to a diagonal matrix of only variances**							
2	**Return data**							
3	**Date**	**GE**	**MSFT**	**JNJ**	**K**	**BA**	**IBM**	
4	3-Jan-94	56.44%	-1.50%	6.01%	-9.79%	58.73%	21.51%	
5	3-Jan-95	18.23%	33.21%	41.56%	7.46%	-0.24%	6.04%	
6	2-Jan-96	56.93%	44.28%	57.71%	37.76%	65.55%	27.33%	
7	2-Jan-97	42.87%	79.12%	22.94%	-5.09%	54.34%	41.08%	
8	2-Jan-98	47.11%	38.04%	17.62%	32.04%	37.11%	2.63%	
9	4-Jan-99	34.55%	85.25%	26.62%	-10.74%	15.05%	-2.11%	
10	3-Jan-00	28.15%	11.20%	3.41%	-48.93%	43.53%	23.76%	
11	2-Jan-01	4.61%	-47.19%	10.69%	11.67%	28.29%	21.76%	
12	2-Jan-02	-19.74%	4.27%	23.11%	19.90%	-15.09%	4.55%	
13	2-Jan-03	-44.78%	-29.47%	-5.67%	10.88%	-23.23%	15.54%	
14	2-Jan-04	35.90%	18.01%	-1.27%	15.49%	39.82%	31.80%	
15								
16	**Average**	23.66%	21.38%	18.43%	5.51%	27.63%	17.63%	<-- =AVERAGE(G4:G14)
17	**Standard deviation**	32.17%	40.71%	18.97%	23.86%	29.93%	13.56%	<-- =STDEV(G4:G14)
18	**Variance**	0.1035	0.1657	0.0360	0.0570	0.0896	0.0184	<-- =VAR(G4:G14)
19								
20	**Shrinkage factor λ**	0.3	<-- This is the weight put on the sample var-cov					
21								
22	**Shrinkage matrix** **Uses the array formula {=B20*B34:G39+(1-B20)*B44:G49} to compute the shrinkage covariance matrix**							
23		**GE**	**MSFT**	**JNJ**	**K**	**BA**	**IBM**	
24	**GE**	0.1035	0.0228	0.0066	-0.0013	0.0257	0.0037	
25	**MSFT**	0.0228	0.1657	0.0124	-0.0016	0.0114	-0.0007	
26	**JNJ**	0.0066	0.0124	0.0360	0.0054	0.0030	-0.0012	
27	**K**	-0.0013	-0.0016	0.0054	0.0570	-0.0023	-0.0014	
28	**BA**	0.0257	0.0114	0.0030	-0.0023	0.0896	0.0074	
29	**IBM**	0.0037	-0.0007	-0.0012	-0.0014	0.0074	0.0184	
30								
31								
32	**Uses the array formula {=MMULT(TRANSPOSE(B4:G14-B16:G16),B4:G14-B16:G16)/10} to compute the constant sample covariance matrix. In the shrinkage var-cov, this matrix is given weight lambda.**							
33		**GE**	**MSFT**	**JNJ**	**K**	**BA**	**IBM**	
34	**GE**	0.1035	0.0758	0.0222	-0.0043	0.0857	0.0123	
35	**MSFT**	0.0758	0.1657	0.0412	-0.0052	0.0379	-0.0022	
36	**JNJ**	0.0222	0.0412	0.0360	0.0181	0.0101	-0.0039	
37	**K**	-0.0043	-0.0052	0.0181	0.0570	-0.0076	-0.0046	
38	**BA**	0.0857	0.0379	0.0101	-0.0076	0.0896	0.0248	
39	**IBM**	0.0123	-0.0022	-0.0039	-0.0046	0.0248	0.0184	
40								
41								
42	**Uses the array formula {=MMULT(TRANSPOSE(B4:G14-B16:G16),B4:G14-B16:G16)/10*IF(A44:A49=B43:G43,1,0)} to compute a matrix with only variances on diagonal and zeros elsewhere. In the shrinkage var-cov this matrix is given weight 1-lambda.**							
43		**GE**	**MSFT**	**JNJ**	**K**	**BA**	**IBM**	
44	**GE**	0.1035	0.0000	0.0000	0.0000	0.0000	0.0000	
45	**MSFT**	0.0000	0.1657	0.0000	0.0000	0.0000	0.0000	
46	**JNJ**	0.0000	0.0000	0.0360	0.0000	0.0000	0.0000	
47	**K**	0.0000	0.0000	0.0000	0.0570	0.0000	0.0000	
48	**BA**	0.0000	0.0000	0.0000	0.0000	0.0896	0.0000	
49	**IBM**	0.0000	0.0000	0.0000	0.0000	0.0000	0.0184	

There is little theory about choosing the proper shrinkage estimator.[8] Our suggestion is to choose a shrinkage operator λ so that the GMVP is wholly positive (see next section for details).

10.10 Alternatives to the Variance-Covariance Matrix: Impact on the Minimum-Variance Portfolio and the Optimal Portfolio

This chapter has given four alternatives to computing the variance-covariance matrix:

- The sample variance-covariance
- The single-index model
- The constant-correlation approach
- Shrinkage methods

How do we compare these alternatives? In this section we compare these four alternatives on two examples:

- First, we compute the minimum variance portfolio using each method.
- Second, we compute an optimal portfolio using each method.

10.10.1 Minimum Variance Portfolio Using the Sample Variance-Covariance

As its name indicates, the global minimum variance portfolio (GMVP) is the portfolio that gives the least variance of all portfolios of the assets under consideration. As shown in section 10.5, the formula for the GMVP is

$$\frac{1 \cdot S^{-1}}{1 \cdot S^{-1} \cdot 1^T}$$

where S is the variance-covariance portfolio and **1** is a column vector of 1's.

8. Three papers by Olivier Ledoit and Michael Wolf may offer some guidance: "Improved Estimation of the Covariance Matrix of Stock Returns with an Application to Portfolio Selection," *Journal of Empirical Finance*, 209, 10, 2003. "A Well-Conditioned Estimator for Large-Dimensional Covariance Matrices," *Journal of Multivariate Analysis*, 88, 2004. "Honey, I Shrunk the Sample Covariance Matrix." *Journal of Portfolio Management*, 30, 2004.

For our sample of six stocks and using the sample variance-covariance matrix, the GMVP is computed in the following spreadsheet:

	A	B	C	D	E	F	G	H
1	**COMPUTING THE GLOBAL MINIMUM VARIANCE PORTFOLIO USING THE SAMPLE VAR-COV MATRIX**							
2	**Sample variance-covariance matrix**							
3		**GE**	**MSFT**	**JNJ**	**K**	**BA**	**IBM**	
4	**GE**	0.1035	0.0758	0.0222	-0.0043	0.0857	0.0123	
5	**MSFT**	0.0758	0.1657	0.0412	-0.0052	0.0379	-0.0022	
6	**JNJ**	0.0222	0.0412	0.0360	0.0181	0.0101	-0.0039	
7	**K**	-0.0043	-0.0052	0.0181	0.0570	-0.0076	-0.0046	
8	**BA**	0.0857	0.0379	0.0101	-0.0076	0.0896	0.0248	
9	**IBM**	0.0123	-0.0022	-0.0039	-0.0046	0.0248	0.0184	
10								
11	Average	23.66%	21.38%	18.43%	5.51%	27.63%	17.63%	
12								
13	**Uses formula {=MMULT(MINVERSE(B4:G9),B22:B27)/SUM(MMULT(MINVERSE(B4:G9),B22:B27))} to compute the global minimum variance portfolio**							
14	**GE**	0.6105						
15	**MSFT**	-0.1034						
16	**JNJ**	0.2074			**GMVP statistics**			
17	**K**	0.0539			Mean return	12.73%	<-- {=MMULT(B11:G11,B14:B19)}	
18	**BA**	-0.7704			Variance	0.0060	<-- {=MMULT(MMULT(TRANSPOSE(B14:B19),B4:G9),B14:B19)}	
19	**IBM**	1.0019			Sigma	7.73%	<-- =SQRT(F18)	
20								
21	**Column vector of 1s**							
22	**GE**	1						
23	**MSFT**	1						
24	**JNJ**	1						
25	**K**	1						
26	**BA**	1						
27	**IBM**	1						

The GMVP has a mean return of 12.73 percent (cell F17) and standard deviation of 7.73 percent (cell F19).

There's a more compact way to do this calculation:

	A	B	C	D	E	F	G	H
1	**COMPUTING THE GLOBAL MINIMUM VARIANCE PORTFOLIO USING THE SAMPLE VAR-COV MATRIX** **More compact method: uses trick to compute vector of 1s**							
2	**Sample variance-covariance matrix**							
3		**GE**	**MSFT**	**JNJ**	**K**	**BA**	**IBM**	
4	**GE**	0.1035	0.0758	0.0222	-0.0043	0.0857	0.0123	
5	**MSFT**	0.0758	0.1657	0.0412	-0.0052	0.0379	-0.0022	
6	**JNJ**	0.0222	0.0412	0.0360	0.0181	0.0101	-0.0039	
7	**K**	-0.0043	-0.0052	0.0181	0.0570	-0.0076	-0.0046	
8	**BA**	0.0857	0.0379	0.0101	-0.0076	0.0896	0.0248	
9	**IBM**	0.0123	-0.0022	-0.0039	-0.0046	0.0248	0.0184	
10								
11	Average	23.66%	21.38%	18.43%	5.51%	27.63%	17.63%	
12								
13	**Uses formula {=MMULT(MINVERSE(B4:G9),IF(A14:A19=A14:A19,1,0))/SUM(MMULT(MINVERSE(B4:G9),IF(A14:A19=A14:A19,1,0)))} to compute the global minimum variance portfolio**							
14	**GE**	0.6105						
15	**MSFT**	-0.1034						
16	**JNJ**	0.2074			**GMVP statistics**			
17	**K**	0.0539			Mean return	12.73%	<-- {=MMULT(B11:G11,B14:B19)}	
18	**BA**	-0.7704			Variance	0.0060	<-- {=MMULT(MMULT(TRANSPOSE(B14:B19),B4:G9),B14:B19)}	
19	**IBM**	1.0019			Sigma	7.73%	<-- =SQRT(F18)	

This more compact method uses the array formula **If(A14:A19=A14: A19,1,0)** to compute the vector of 1s.

10.10.2 GMVP Using the Alternative Variance-Covariance Matrices

In this subsection we repeat the preceding exercise using three variations for the variance-covariance matrix. Using the single-index model (SIM) we get the following GMVP:

	A	B	C	D	E	F	G	H
1	**COMPUTING THE GLOBAL MINIMUM VARIANCE PORTFOLIO USING THE SINGLE-INDEX MODEL**							
2	**Sample variance-covariance matrix**							
3		**GE**	**MSFT**	**JNJ**	**K**	**BA**	**IBM**	
4	**GE**	0.1035	0.0120	0.0034	0.0031	0.0014	0.0002	
5	**MSFT**	0.0120	0.1657	0.0092	0.0083	0.0037	0.0007	
6	**JNJ**	0.0034	0.0092	0.0360	0.0023	0.0010	0.0002	
7	**K**	0.0031	0.0083	0.0023	0.0570	0.0009	0.0002	
8	**BA**	0.0014	0.0037	0.0010	0.0009	0.0896	0.0001	
9	**IBM**	0.0002	0.0007	0.0002	0.0002	0.0001	0.0184	
10								
11	Average	23.66%	21.38%	18.43%	5.51%	27.63%	17.63%	
12								
13	**Uses formula {=MMULT(MINVERSE(B4:G9),IF(A14:A19=A14:A19,1,0))/SUM(MMULT(MINVERSE(B4:G9),IF(A14:A19=A14:A19,1,0)))} to compute the global minimum variance portfolio**							
14	**GE**	0.0678						
15	**MSFT**	0.0251						
16	**JNJ**	0.2153			**GMVP statistics**			
17	**K**	0.1337			Mean return	17.59%	<-- {=MMULT(B11:G11,B14:B19)}	
18	**BA**	0.0907			Variance	0.0087	<-- {=MMULT(MMULT(TRANSPOSE(B14:B19),B4:G9),B14:B19)}	
19	**IBM**	0.4674			Sigma	9.33%	<-- =SQRT(F18)	

The remarkable change is not the GMVP statistics, but rather the composition of the GMVP, which is now composed solely of positive proportions of the stocks.

In the next spreadsheet we use the constant-correlation matrix:

	A	B	C	D	E	F	G	H
1	**COMPUTING THE GLOBAL MINIMUM VARIANCE PORTFOLIO USING CONSTANT CORRELATION MODEL**							
2	**Return data**							
3	**Date**	**GE**	**MSFT**	**JNJ**	**K**	**BA**	**IBM**	
4	3-Jan-94	56.44%	-1.50%	6.01%	-9.79%	58.73%	7.74%	
5	3-Jan-95	18.23%	33.21%	41.56%	7.46%	-0.24%	-12.16%	
6	2-Jan-96	56.93%	44.28%	57.71%	37.76%	65.55%	30.00%	
7	2-Jan-97	42.87%	79.12%	22.94%	-5.09%	54.34%	-41.78%	
8	2-Jan-98	47.11%	38.04%	17.62%	32.04%	37.11%	47.32%	
9	4-Jan-99	34.55%	85.25%	26.62%	-10.74%	15.05%	37.70%	
10	3-Jan-00	28.15%	11.20%	3.41%	-48.93%	43.53%	-13.32%	
11	2-Jan-01	4.61%	-47.19%	10.69%	11.67%	28.29%	-78.39%	
12	2-Jan-02	-19.74%	4.27%	23.11%	19.90%	-15.09%	-25.16%	
13	2-Jan-03	-44.78%	-29.47%	-5.67%	10.88%	-23.23%	-137.03%	
14	2-Jan-04	35.90%	18.01%	-1.27%	15.49%	39.82%	16.44%	
15								
16	Average	23.66%	21.38%	18.43%	5.51%	27.63%	-15.33%	<-- =AVERAGE(G4:G14)
17	Standard deviation	32.17%	40.71%	18.97%	23.86%	29.93%	54.71%	<-- =STDEV(G4:G14)
18	Variance	0.1035	0.1657	0.0360	0.0570	0.0896	0.2993	<-- =VAR(G4:G14)
19	Constant correlation	0.3000						
20								
21	**Uses the array formula {=IF(A23:A28=B22:G22,B18:G18,MMULT(TRANSPOSE(B17:G17),B17:G17)*B19)} to compute the constant correlation matrix**							
22		**GE**	**MSFT**	**JNJ**	**K**	**BA**	**IBM**	
23	**GE**	0.1035	0.0393	0.0183	0.0230	0.0289	0.0528	
24	**MSFT**	0.0393	0.1657	0.0232	0.0291	0.0366	0.0668	
25	**JNJ**	0.0183	0.0232	0.0360	0.0136	0.0170	0.0311	
26	**K**	0.0230	0.0291	0.0136	0.0570	0.0214	0.0392	
27	**BA**	0.0289	0.0366	0.0170	0.0214	0.0896	0.0491	
28	**IBM**	0.0528	0.0668	0.0311	0.0392	0.0491	0.2993	
29								
30	**Uses formula {=MMULT(MINVERSE(B23:G28),IF(A31:A36=A31:A36,1,0))/SUM(MMULT(MINVERSE(B23:G28),IF(A31:A36=A31:A36,1,0)))} to compute the global minimum variance portfolio**							
31	**GE**	0.0800						
32	**MSFT**	0.0030						
33	**JNJ**	0.5645			**GMVP statistics**			
34	**K**	0.2782			Mean return	17.71%	<-- =MMULT(B16:G16,B31:B36)	
35	**BA**	0.1152			Variance	0.4027	<-- {=MMULT(MMULT(TRANSPOSE(B31:B36),B4:G9),B31:B36)}	
36	**IBM**	0.0409			Sigma	63.46%	<-- =SQRT(F35)	

Using the shrinkage variance-covariance matrix, we get the following results:

	A	B	C	D	E	F	G	H
1	**COMPUTING THE GLOBAL MINIMUM VARIANCE PORTFOLIO USING A SHRINKAGE VARIANCE-COVARIANCE MATRIX**							
2	**Return data**							
3	**Date**	**GE**	**MSFT**	**JNJ**	**K**	**BA**	**IBM**	
4	3-Jan-94	56.44%	-1.50%	6.01%	-9.79%	58.73%	21.51%	
5	3-Jan-95	18.23%	33.21%	41.56%	7.46%	-0.24%	6.04%	
6	2-Jan-96	56.93%	44.28%	57.71%	37.76%	65.55%	27.33%	
7	2-Jan-97	42.87%	79.12%	22.94%	-5.09%	54.34%	41.08%	
8	2-Jan-98	47.11%	38.04%	17.62%	32.04%	37.11%	2.63%	
9	4-Jan-99	34.55%	85.25%	26.62%	-10.74%	15.05%	-2.11%	
10	3-Jan-00	28.15%	11.20%	3.41%	-48.93%	43.53%	23.76%	
11	2-Jan-01	4.61%	-47.19%	10.69%	11.67%	28.29%	21.76%	
12	2-Jan-02	-19.74%	4.27%	23.11%	19.90%	-15.09%	4.55%	
13	2-Jan-03	-44.78%	-29.47%	-5.67%	10.88%	-23.23%	15.54%	
14	2-Jan-04	35.90%	18.01%	-1.27%	15.49%	39.82%	31.80%	
15								
16	**Average**	23.66%	21.38%	18.43%	5.51%	27.63%	17.63%	<-- =AVERAGE(G4:G14)
17	**Standard deviation**	32.17%	40.71%	18.97%	23.86%	29.93%	13.56%	<-- =STDEV(G4:G14)
18	**Variance**	0.1035	0.1657	0.0360	0.0570	0.0896	0.0184	<-- =VAR(G4:G14)
19								
20	**Shrinkage factor λ**	0.3	<-- This is the weight put on the sample var-cov					
21								
22	**Shrinkage matrix** **Uses the array formula {=B20*MMULT(TRANSPOSE(B4:G14-B16:G16),B4:G14-B16:G16)/10+(1-B20)*MMULT(TRANSPOSE(B4:G14-B16:G16),B4:G14-B16:G16)/10*IF(A24:A29=B23:G23,1,0)}** **to compute the shrinkage covariance matrix**							
23		**GE**	**MSFT**	**JNJ**	**K**	**BA**	**IBM**	
24	**GE**	0.1035	0.0228	0.0066	-0.0013	0.0257	0.0037	
25	**MSFT**	0.0228	0.1657	0.0124	-0.0016	0.0114	-0.0007	
26	**JNJ**	0.0066	0.0124	0.0360	0.0054	0.0030	-0.0012	
27	**K**	-0.0013	-0.0016	0.0054	0.0570	-0.0023	-0.0014	
28	**BA**	0.0257	0.0114	0.0030	-0.0023	0.0896	0.0074	
29	**IBM**	0.0037	-0.0007	-0.0012	-0.0014	0.0074	0.0184	
30								
31	**Uses formula {=MMULT(MINVERSE(B24:G29),IF(A32:A37=A32:A37,1,0))/SUM(MMULT(MINVERSE(B24:G29),IF(A32:A37=A32:A37,1,0)))} to compute the global minimum variance portfolio**							
32	**GE**	0.0407						
33	**MSFT**	0.0337						
34	**JNJ**	0.2261			**GMVP statistics**			
35	**K**	0.1556			Mean return	16.71%	<-- {=MMULT(B16:G16,B32:B37)}	
36	**BA**	0.0412			Variance	0.0092	<-- {=MMULT(MMULT(TRANSPOSE(B32:B37),B24:G29),B32:B37)}	
37	**IBM**	0.5027			Sigma	9.59%	<-- =SQRT(F36)	

Changing the shrinkage factor alters the GMVP. In the following data table we vary λ from 0 to 1 (when $\lambda = 1$ the GMVP is the same as that achieved with the sample variance-covariance matrix):

	J	K	L	M	N	O	P	Q	R
2	**Data table: varying the shrinkage factor λ**								
3	**λ**	**GMVP mean**	**GMVP sigma**	**GE**	**MSFT**	**JNJ**	**K**	**BA**	**IBM**
4									
5	0	17.64%	8.89%	0.0763	0.0477	0.2196	0.1387	0.0882	0.4295
6	0.1	17.29%	9.19%	0.0630	0.0420	0.2216	0.1467	0.0726	0.4541
7	0.2	16.98%	9.42%	0.0511	0.0374	0.2238	0.1523	0.0571	0.4783
8	0.3	16.71%	9.59%	0.0407	0.0337	0.2261	0.1556	0.0412	0.5027
9	0.4	16.46%	9.71%	0.0319	0.0308	0.2287	0.1568	0.0243	0.5274
10	0.5	16.24%	9.77%	0.0251	0.0286	0.2316	0.1559	0.0055	0.5533
11	0.6	16.03%	9.79%	0.0214	0.0268	0.2349	0.1528	-0.0168	0.5811
12	0.7	15.81%	9.75%	0.0232	0.0247	0.2383	0.1470	-0.0457	0.6124
13	0.8	15.56%	9.63%	0.0379	0.0209	0.2415	0.1378	-0.0894	0.6513
14	0.9	15.15%	9.35%	0.0952	0.0087	0.2422	0.1217	-0.1807	0.7130
15	1	12.73%	7.73%	0.6105	-0.1034	0.2074	0.0539	-0.7704	1.0019

We have used Excel's **Conditional Formatting** feature to mark all the portfolios for which there are short sales.

10.11 Summary

In this chapter we considered how to compute the variance-covariance matrix, which is central to all portfolio optimization. Starting with the standard sample variance-covariance matrix, we also showed how to compute several alternatives that have appeared in the literature as perhaps improving portfolio computations.

Exercises

1. In the following table you will find annual return data for six furniture companies between the years 1982 and 1992. Use these data to calculate the variance-covariance matrix of the returns.

	A	B	C	D	E	F	G	H
1	**DATA FOR 6 FURNITURE COMPANIES**							
2		**La-Z-Boy**	**Kimball**	**Flexsteel**	**Leggett & Platt**	**Herman Miller**	**Shaw Industries**	
3	**1982**	36.67%	0.20%	41.54%	21.92%	26.13%	22.50%	
4	**1983**	122.82%	61.43%	195.09%	62.27%	73.38%	117.89%	
5	**1984**	14.44%	63.51%	-38.38%	-1.27%	45.15%	7.80%	
6	**1985**	21.39%	28.42%	1.30%	81.17%	24.27%	38.14%	
7	**1986**	45.36%	-7.44%	21.89%	19.83%	10.73%	54.48%	
8	**1987**	20.19%	48.27%	9.11%	-10.21%	-11.92%	26.82%	
9	**1988**	-8.94%	-11.28%	12.65%	13.77%	7.06%	-6.24%	
10	**1989**	27.02%	12.85%	12.08%	32.55%	-7.55%	123.03%	
11	**1990**	-11.64%	2.42%	-17.13%	-6.48%	1.31%	15.48%	
12	**1991**	20.29%	6.90%	3.62%	50.12%	-5.54%	19.92%	
13	**1992**	34.08%	22.21%	33.46%	84.40%	5.71%	62.76%	
14								
15	**Beta**	0.80	0.95	0.65	0.85	0.85	1.40	
16	**Mean returns**	29.24%	20.68%	25.02%	31.64%	15.34%	43.87%	<-- =AVERAGE(G3:G13)

2. For the firms from the previous example, calculate the variance-covariance matrix using the single-index model. Assume that the variance of the market portfolio is 18%.

3. In the Excel notebook **fm3_problems10.xls** on the disk accompanying this book, you will find monthly price data for the 30 stocks in the Dow-Jones Index of 30 Industrials for July 1997–July 2007. Use this data to compute the variance-covariance matrix of the DJ30.

4. The following chart shows the variance-covariance matrix and the mean returns for six stocks. All the data are for monthly data (raw data are on the disk with the book).

   a. Compute the global minimum variance portfolio (GMVP).
   b. Compute the efficient portfolio, assuming a monthly risk-free rate of 0.45%.
   c. Show the frontier as the expected return and standard deviation of convex combinations of the GMVP and the efficient portfolio.

	A	B	C	D	E	F	G	H	I
1		Kroger KR	Ford F	Target TGT	Juniper Networks JNPR	Ahold AHO	KeyCorp KEY		Mean returns
2	KR	0.0052	0.0033	0.0015	0.0039	0.0068	0.0010		0.24%
3	F	0.0033	0.0120	0.0034	0.0072	0.0063	0.0015		-0.89%
4	TGT	0.0015	0.0034	0.0046	0.0058	0.0039	0.0015		0.48%
5	JNPR	0.0039	0.0072	0.0058	0.0379	0.0073	0.0023		0.44%
6	AHO	0.0068	0.0063	0.0039	0.0073	0.0389	0.0023		-1.46%
7	KEY	0.0010	0.0015	0.0015	0.0023	0.0023	0.0018		1.04%

5. Repeat the preceding exercise when the variance-covariance matrix is an equally weighted combination of the sample matrix in exercise 4 and a pure diagonal matrix of only the variances.

11 Estimating Betas and the Security Market Line

11.1 Overview

The capital asset pricing model (CAPM) is one of the two most influential innovations in financial theory in the latter half of the twentieth century.[1] By integrating the portfolio decision with utility theory and the statistical behavior of asset prices, the formulators of the CAPM defined the paradigm that is now generally used for the analysis of stock prices.

What does the CAPM actually say? What are its empirical implications? Roughly speaking, we can differentiate between two kinds of implications of the CAPM. First, the capital market line (CML) defines the *individual optimal portfolios* for an investor interested in the mean and variance of her optimal portfolio. Second, given agreement between investors on the statistical properties of asset returns and on the importance of mean-variance optimization, the security market line (SML) defines the *risk-return* relation for *each individual asset.*

It is useful to differentiate between the case where a risk-free asset exists and the case where there is no risk-free asset.[2]

11.1.1 Case 1: A Risk-Free Asset Exists

Suppose a risk-free asset exists and has return r_f. We can differentiate between the individual optimization of investors and the general equilibrium implications of the CAPM:

- *Individual optimization*: Assuming that investors optimize based on the expected return and standard deviation of their portfolio returns (in the jargon of finance—they have "mean-variance" preferences), the CAPM states that each individual investor's optimal portfolio falls on the line $E(r_p) = r_f + \sigma_p[E(r_x) - r_f]$, where portfolio x is a portfolio that maximizes $\frac{E(r_y)-r_f}{\sigma_y}$ for all feasible portfolios y. Proposition 1 of Chapter 9 shows

1. The other remarkable innovation is option-pricing theory, which is discussed in Chapters 16–24. These two innovations together have accounted for a number of Nobel prizes in economics: Harry Markowitz (1990), William Sharpe (1990), Myron Scholes (1997), Robert Merton (1997). But for their untimely demise, others associated with these theories—Jan Mossin (1936–87) and Fisher Black (1938–95)—would doubtless also have received the Nobel.
2. The existence (or nonexistence) of a risk-free asset is closely related to the investment horizon. Assets that are risk-free over a short term may not be riskless over a longer term.

that x can be computed by $x=\{x_1, x_2, \ldots, x_N\}=\dfrac{S^{-1}[R-r_f]}{\sum S^{-1}[R-r_f]}$, where S is the variance-covariance matrix of risky asset returns and R is the vector of expected asset returns.

• *General equilibrium*: If all investors agree about the statistical assumptions of the model—the variance-covariance matrix S and the vector of expected asset returns R—and if a risk-free asset exists, then individual asset returns are defined by the security market line (SML):

$$E(r_i)=r_f+\frac{\text{Cov}(r_i, r_M)}{\sigma_M^2}[E(r_M)-r_f]$$

where M denotes the market portfolio—the value-weighted portfolio of all risky assets. The expression $\dfrac{\text{Cov}(r_i, r_M)}{\sigma_M^2}$ is generally termed the asset's *beta*: $\beta_i=\dfrac{\text{Cov}(r_i, r_M)}{\sigma_M^2}$.

11.1.2 Case 2: No Risk-Free Asset Exists

If there is no risk-free asset, then the implications of the CAPM for both individual optimization and for general equilibrium are defined by Black's (1972) zero-beta model (Proposition 3 of Chapter 9):

• *Individual optimization*: In the absence of a risk-free asset, individual optimal portfolios will fall along the *efficient frontier*. As shown in Proposition 3 of Chapter 9, this frontier is the upward-sloping portion of the mean-sigma combinations created by the convex combination of any two optimizing portfolios $x=\dfrac{S^{-1}[R-c_1]}{\sum S^{-1}[R-c_1]}$ and $y=\dfrac{S^{-1}[R-c_2]}{\sum S^{-1}[R-c_2]}$, where c_1 and c_2 are two arbitrary constants.

• *General equilibrium*: In the absence of a risk-free asset, if all investors agree about the statistical assumptions of the model—the variance-covariance matrix S and the vector of expected asset returns R—then individual asset returns are defined by the security market line (SML):

$$E(r_i)=E(r_z)+\frac{\text{Cov}(r_i, r_y)}{\sigma_y^2}[E(r_y)-E(r_z)]$$

where y is any efficient portfolio and z is a portfolio that has zero covariance with y (the "zero-beta portfolio").

The case of no risk-free asset is obviously weaker than the case of a risk-free asset. If there is a risk-free asset, the general equilibrium version of the CAPM says that all portfolios are situated on a single, agreed-upon line. If there is no risk-free asset, then all optimal portfolios are on the same frontier; but in this case asset betas can differ, since there are many portfolios y that fulfill the equation $E(r_i) = E(r_z) + \frac{\text{Cov}(r_i, r_y)}{\sigma_y^2}[E(r_y) - E(r_z)]$.

11.1.3 The CAPM as a Prescriptive and a Descriptive Tool

As you can see from the two bullets for cases 1 and 2, the CAPM is both *prescriptive* and *descriptive*.

As a prescriptive tool, the CAPM tells a mean-variance investor how to choose his optimal portfolio. By finding a portfolio of the form $\frac{S^{-1}[R - c_1]}{\sum S^{-1}[R - c_1]}$, the investor can identify an optimal portfolio from the data set.

As a descriptive tool, the CAPM gives conditions under which we can generalize about the structure of expected returns in the market. Whether or not a risk-free asset exists, these conditions assume that investors agree on the statistical structure of asset returns—the variance-covariance matrix and the expected returns. In this case all the returns are expected to lie on a security market line (SML) of the form $E(r_i) = r_f + \frac{\text{Cov}(r_i, r_M)}{\sigma_M^2}[E(r_M) - r_f]$ (if there is a risk-free asset) or of the form $E(r_i) = E(r_z) + \frac{\text{Cov}(r_i, r_y)}{\sigma_y^2}[E(r_y) - E(r_z)]$ if there is no risk-free asset.

11.1.4 This Chapter

In this chapter we look at some typical capital-market data and replicate a simple test of the descriptive part of the CAPM. To do so, we have to calculate the betas for a set of assets, and we then have to determine the equation of the security market line (SML). The test in this chapter is the simplest possible test of the CAPM. There is an enormous literature in which the possible statistical and methodological pitfalls of CAPM tests are discussed. Good places to begin are textbooks by Elton, Gruber, Brown, and Goetzmann (2006), and Bodie, Kane, and Marcus (2005).

11.2 Testing the Security Market Line

Typical tests of the security market line (SML) start with return data on a set of risky assets. The steps in the test are as follows:

1. Determine a candidate for the market portfolio M. In our example we will use the Standard & Poor's 500 Index (S&P 500) as a candidate for M. This is a critical step: In principle, the "true" market portfolio should—as pointed out in Chapter 8—contain all the market's risky assets in proportion to their value. It is clearly impossible to calculate this theoretical market portfolio, and we must therefore make do with a surrogate. As you will see in the next two sections, the propositions of Chapter 8 can shed much light on how the choice of the market surrogate affects the r-squared of our regression test of the CAPM.

2. For each of the assets in question, determine the asset beta, $\beta_i = \dfrac{\text{Cov}(r_i, r_M)}{\sigma_M^2}$. This is often called the *first-pass regression*.

3. Regress the mean returns of the assets on their respective betas (the *second-pass regression*):

$$\bar{r}_i = \gamma_0 + \gamma_1 \beta_i$$

If the CAPM in its descriptive format holds, then the second-pass regression should be the security market line.

We illustrate the tests of the CAPM with a simple numerical example that uses data for the 30 stocks in the Dow-Jones Industrials. We start with the prices of the S&P 500 (symbol ^SPX) and the stocks in the DJ30 (some of the rows and columns are not shown):

	A	B	C	D	E	F	G	H	I	J	K	L	M	N
1	**PRICE DATA FOR THE DOW-JONES INDUSTRIAL STOCKS AND THE STANDARD AND POOR'S 500** **July 2001 - July 2006**													
2	Date	S&P 500 Index SPX	Alcoa AA	American International Group AIG	American Express AXP	Boeing BA	Citigroup C	Caterpillar CAT	Du Pont DD	Disney DIS	General Electric GE	General Motors GM	Home Depot HD	Honeywell HON
3	3-Jul-01	1211.23	35.37	81.32	33.73	53.64	40.97	24.73	36.29	25.02	38.33	49.72	48.26	32.75
4	1-Aug-01	1133.58	34.50	76.43	30.46	47.06	37.49	22.45	35.01	24.14	36.04	43.14	44.06	33.27
5	4-Sep-01	1040.94	28.06	76.24	24.30	30.79	33.15	20.11	32.07	17.68	32.93	33.81	36.79	23.57
6	1-Oct-01	1059.78	29.34	76.82	24.68	29.97	37.26	20.23	34.18	17.65	32.23	32.56	36.66	26.38
7	1-Nov-01	1139.45	35.09	80.54	27.60	32.43	39.34	21.45	38.21	19.43	34.08	39.63	44.78	29.77
8	3-Dec-01	1148.08	32.32	77.64	29.93	35.83	41.46	23.63	36.63	19.88	35.63	38.75	48.97	30.38
9	2-Jan-02	1130.20	32.59	72.51	30.13	37.83	39.06	22.91	38.06	20.21	33.03	40.77	48.09	30.19
10	1-Feb-02	1106.73	34.31	72.38	30.64	42.64	37.29	25.29	40.68	22.07	34.39	42.67	48.00	34.43
51	1-Jul-05	1234.18	27.48	59.76	47.68	65.02	42.62	53.28	41.22	25.37	33.53	34.89	42.97	38.43
52	1-Aug-05	1220.33	26.38	58.92	47.89	66.26	42.89	54.85	38.55	24.93	32.66	32.86	39.92	37.66
53	1-Sep-05	1228.81	24.05	61.67	49.79	67.18	44.60	58.07	38.16	23.88	32.94	29.42	37.76	36.89
54	3-Oct-05	1207.01	23.92	64.49	49.41	63.91	44.86	52.22	40.62	24.11	33.17	26.33	40.63	33.65
55	1-Nov-05	1249.48	27.16	66.82	51.04	67.67	48.04	57.37	42.02	24.67	34.94	21.44	41.46	36.15
56	1-Dec-05	1248.29	29.30	67.91	51.08	69.71	48.02	57.36	41.77	23.97	34.53	19.01	40.17	36.85
57	3-Jan-06	1280.08	31.21	65.15	52.19	67.79	46.09	67.69	38.48	25.31	32.27	23.56	40.24	38.01
58	1-Feb-06	1280.66	29.19	66.05	53.61	72.44	46.37	72.85	39.91	27.99	32.63	20.11	41.83	40.74
59	1-Mar-06	1294.87	30.43	65.93	52.28	77.66	47.23	71.58	41.87	27.89	34.52	21.06	42.13	42.55
60	3-Apr-06	1310.61	33.63	65.09	53.66	83.17	49.95	75.74	43.74	27.96	34.33	22.66	39.77	42.28
61	1-May-06	1270.09	31.72	60.80	54.21	83.25	49.30	72.95	42.53	30.50	34.01	26.93	37.97	41.18
62	1-Jun-06	1270.20	32.36	59.05	53.07	81.91	48.25	74.48	41.60	30.00	32.96	29.79	35.79	40.30
63	3-Jul-06	1265.48	33.55	58.97	51.98	79.99	49.08	72.58	40.54	29.83	33.30	29.48	35.37	38.96

We first transform these price data to returns:

	A	B	C	D	E	F	G	H	I	J	K	L	M	N
1	**RETURN DATA FOR THE DOW-JONES INDUSTRIAL STOCKS AND THE STANDARD AND POOR'S 500** **July 2001 - July 2006**													
2	Date	S&P 500 Index SPX	Alcoa AA	American International Group AIG	American Express AXP	Boeing BA	Citigroup C	Caterpillar CAT	Du Pont DD	Disney DIS	General Electric GE	General Motors GM	Home Depot HD	Honeywell HON
3														
4	Average return	0.07%	-0.09%	[illegible]	[illegible]	0.67%	0.30%	1.79%	0.18%	0.29%	-0.23%	-0.87%	-0.52%	0.29%
5	Beta	1.00	1.90	[illegible]	[illegible]	[illegible]	[illegible]	1.39	1.00	1.28	0.84	1.41	1.55	1.66
6	Alpha	0	-0.23%	-0.61%	[illegible]	[illegible]	[illegible]	1.69%	0.11%	0.20%	-0.30%	-0.97%	-0.63%	0.17%
7	R-squared	1	0.6085	[illegible]	[illegible]	[illegible]	[illegible]	0.5158	0.4362	0.3845	0.3221	0.2607	0.5288	0.5473
8														
9	1-Aug-01	-6.63%	-2.49%	-6.20%	-10.20%	-13.09%	-8.88%	-9.67%	-3.59%	-3.58%	-6.16%	-14.20%	-9.11%	1.58%
10	4-Sep-01	-8.53%	-20.66%	[illegible]	[illegible]	[illegible]	-12.30%	-11.01%	-8.77%	-31.14%	-9.02%	-24.37%	-18.03%	-34.47%
11	1-Oct-01	1.79%	4.46%	[illegible]	[illegible]	[illegible]	11.69%	0.59%	6.37%	-0.17%	-2.15%	-3.77%	-0.35%	11.26%
12	1-Nov-01	7.25%	17.90%	4.73%	11.18%	7.89%	5.43%	5.86%	11.15%	9.61%	5.58%	19.65%	20.01%	12.09%
13	3-Dec-01	0.75%	-8.22%	-3.67%	8.10%	9.97%	5.25%	9.68%	-4.22%	2.29%	4.45%	-2.25%	8.94%	2.03%
14	2-Jan-02	-1.57%	0.83%	-6.84%	0.67%	5.43%	-5.96%	-3.09%	3.83%	1.65%	-7.58%	5.08%	-1.81%	-0.63%
15	1-Feb-02	-2.10%	5.14%	-0.18%	1.68%	11.97%	-4.64%	9.88%	6.66%	8.80%	4.03%	4.55%	-0.19%	13.14%
16	1-Mar-02	3.61%	0.47%	-2.52%	11.66%	4.85%	9.02%	2.38%	0.66%	0.36%	-2.89%	13.20%	-2.72%	0.41%
17	1-Apr-02	-6.34%	-10.35%	-4.27%	0.32%	-7.85%	-13.41%	-3.38%	-5.78%	0.41%	-17.02%	5.94%	-4.71%	-4.25%
18	1-May-02	-0.91%	3.20%	-3.15%	3.58%	-4.09%	0.11%	-4.41%	4.11%	-1.18%	-1.29%	-2.43%	-10.65%	7.13%
19	3-Jun-02	-7.52%	-5.38%	1.92%	-15.73%	5.37%	-10.81%	-6.55%	-3.56%	-19.26%	-6.34%	-15.08%	-12.54%	-10.67%
20	1-Jul-02	-8.23%	-19.75%	-6.53%	-2.75%	-8.07%	-14.43%	-8.26%	-5.75%	-6.38%	10.29%	-13.83%	-17.35%	-8.51%

=AVERAGE(C9:C68)
=SLOPE(C9:C68,$B$9:$B$68)
=INTERCEPT(C9:C68,$B$9:$B$68)
=RSQ(C9:C68,$B$9:$B$68)

11.2.1 The First-Pass Regression

Row 4 gives each asset's average monthly return over the 60-month period (to annualize these returns, we would multiply by 12). Rows 5–7 report the results of the *first-pass regression*. For each asset i we report the regression $r_{it} = \alpha_i + \beta_i r_{SP,t}$. We use the Excel function **Slope** to compute the β of each asset, and the functions **Intercept** and **Rsq** to compute the α and R^2 for each regression.

As a check, we also compute the α, β, and R^2 for the S&P 500 index (column B). Not surprisingly, $\alpha_{SP} = 0$, $\beta_{SP} = 1$, and $R^2 = 1$.

11.2.2 The Second-Pass Regression

The SML postulates that the mean return of each security should be linearly related to its beta. Assuming that the historic data provide an accurate description of the distribution of future returns, we postulate that $E(R_i) = \alpha + \beta_i \Pi + \varepsilon_i$. In the second step of our test of the CAPM, we examine this hypothesis by regressing the mean returns on the βs.

	A	B	C	D	E	F	G	H
1	THE SECOND-PASS REGRESSION							
2	**Stock**	**Average monthly return**	**Beta**	**Alpha**				
3	Alcoa AA	-0.09%	1.9028	-0.0023		**Second-pass regression, regressing monthly returns on Beta**		
4	American International Group AIG	-0.54%	0.9936	-0.0061		Intercept	0.0036	<-- =INTERCEPT(B3:B32,C3:C32)
5	American Express AXP	0.72%	1.3784	0.0062		Slope	-0.0020	<-- =SLOPE(B3:B32,C3:C32)
6	Boeing BA	0.67%	1.1515	0.0058		R-squared	0.0238	<-- =RSQ(B3:B32,C3:C32)
7	Citigroup C	0.30%	1.2952	0.0021				
8	Caterpillar CAT	1.79%	1.3903	0.0169		t-statistic, intercept	1.23813	<-- =tintercept(B3:B32,C3:C32)
9	Du Pont DD	0.18%	1.0009	0.0011		t-statistic, slope	-0.825378	<-- =tslope(B3:B32,C3:C32)
10	Disney DIS	0.29%	1.2805	0.0020				
11	General Electric GE	-0.23%	0.8420	-0.0030				
12	General Motors GM	-0.87%	1.4060	-0.0097				
13	Home Depot HD	-0.52%	1.5528	-0.0063				
14	Honeywell HON	0.29%	1.6640	0.0017				
15	Hewlitt Packard HPQ	0.61%	1.9594	0.0046				
16	IBM	-0.47%	1.5764	-0.0058				
17	Intel INTC	-0.73%	2.2648	-0.0089				
18	Johnson & Johnson JNJ	0.34%	0.2471	0.0032				
19	JP Morgan JPM	0.18%	1.7917	0.0005				
20	Coca Cola KO	0.12%	0.3590	0.0009				
21	McDonalds MCD	0.35%	1.2646	0.0025				
22	3M MMM	0.64%	0.6504	0.0059				
23	AltriaMO	1.30%	0.6633	0.0125				
24	Merck MRK	-0.63%	0.6099	-0.0068				
25	Microsoft MSFT	-0.35%	1.1219	-0.0043				
26	Pfizer PFE	-0.74%	0.5572	-0.0078				
27	Procter Gamble PG	0.94%	0.1687	0.0093				
28	AT&T T	-0.41%	1.1275	-0.0050				
29	United Technologies UTX	1.03%	1.0659	0.0095				
30	Verizon VZ	-0.49%	1.0231	-0.0057				
31	Walmart WMT	-0.25%	0.6000	-0.0030				
32	Exxon Mobil XOM	0.88%	0.6455	0.0083				

The results (cells F4:G6) are very disappointing. Our test yields the following SML:

$$E(r_i) = \underbrace{0.0036}_{\substack{\uparrow \\ \gamma_0}} - \underbrace{0.0020}_{\substack{\uparrow \\ \gamma_1}} \beta_i, \; R^2 = 0.0238$$

There is nothing about these numbers that inspires confidence:

- γ_0 should correspond to the risk-free rate over the period. In section 11.6 we will discuss this rate, which changed wildly over the 60 months surveyed. At this point it is enough to point out that the average monthly risk-free interest rate was 0.18 percent (or 0.0018, exactly half of γ_0).
- γ_1 should correspond to $E(r_M) - r_f$. The average monthly return of the S&P 500 over the period was –0.10 percent, and the average monthly risk-free interest rate was 0.18 percent, so that γ_1 should be approximated by –0.28 percent (or 0.0028).
- Both the *t*-statistics for the *i* (cell G8) and the slope (cell G9) indicate that they are not statistically different from zero.[3]

Our test of the SML has failed. The CAPM may have prescriptive validity, but it does not describe our data.

11.2.3 Why Are the Results So Bad?

The experiment we did—checking the CAPM by plotting the security market line—does not appear to have worked out very well. There does not appear to be much evidence in favor of the SML: neither the R^2 of the regression nor the *t*-statistics give much evidence that there is a relation between expected return and portfolio β.

There are a number of reasons why these disappointing results may hold:

1. One reason is that perhaps the CAPM itself does not hold. This assumption could be true for a variety of reasons:

a. Perhaps short sales of assets are restricted in the market. Our derivation of the CAPM (see Chapter 9 on efficient portfolios) assumes that there are no short-sale restrictions. Clearly this is an unrealistic assumption. The computation of efficient portfolios when short sales are restricted is considered in Chapter 12. In this case, however, there are no simple relations (such as those proven in Chapter 9) between the returns of assets and their betas. In particular, if short sales are restricted, there is no reason to expect the SML to hold.

b. Perhaps individuals do not have homogeneous probability assessments, or perhaps they do not have the same expectations of asset returns, variances, and covariances.

3. The functions **tintercept** and **tslope** were created by the author. They are attached to the spreadsheet for this chapter and are discussed in Chapter 2.

2. Perhaps the CAPM holds only for portfolios and not for single assets.

3. Perhaps our set of assets isn't large enough: After all, the CAPM talks about *all risky assets*, whereas we have chosen—for illustrative purposes—to do our test on a very small subset of these assets. The literature on CAPM testing records tests in which the set of risky assets has been expanded to include bonds, real estate, and even nondiversifiable assets such as human capital.

4. Perhaps the "market portfolio" isn't efficient. This possibility is suggested by the mathematics of Chapter 9 on efficient portfolios, and it is this suggestion that we further explore in the next section.

5. Perhaps the CAPM holds only if the market returns are positive (in the period surveyed they were, on average, negative).

11.3 Did We Learn Something?

The results of our exercise in section 11.2 are quite disappointing. Did we learn anything positive from this exercise? Absolutely. For example, the regression model does a pretty good job of describing individual asset returns in relation to the S&P 500:

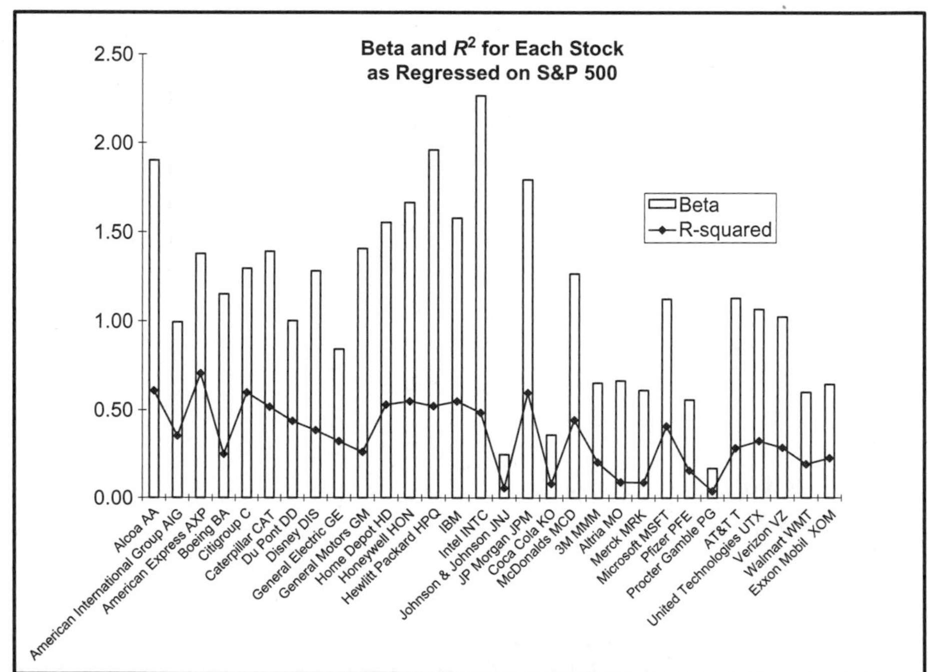

On average the S&P 500 describes about 35 percent of the variability of the DJ30 stocks, which have an average beta of 1.12. If we exclude the seven stocks with the lowest R^2, the S&P describes almost 43 percent of the variation in the stocks' returns:

	A	B	C	D	E	F	G	H	I
1	**OUR SML EXERCISE: WHAT DID WE LEARN?**								
2	Average alpha	0.06%	<-- =AVERAGE('DJ return data'!C6:AF6)						
3	Average beta	1.12	<-- =AVERAGE('DJ return data'!C5:AF5)						
4	Average r-squared	0.3510	<-- =AVERAGE('DJ return data'!C7:AF7)						
5									
6	**Average R² for best regressions**								
7	Cutoff for R²	0.2	<-- Below we count all R² which are greater than this number						
8		9.8258	<-- =SUMIF('DJ return data'!C7:AF7,">"&TEXT(B7,"0.00"))						
9		23	<-- =COUNTIF('DJ return data'!C7:AF7,">"&TEXT(B7,"0.00"))						
10	Average R²	0.4272	<-- =B8/B9						
11									
12	**t-statistics for intercept and slope**								
13		Alcoa AA	American International Group AIG	American Express AXP	Boeing BA	Citigroup C	Caterpillar CAT	Du Pont DD	Disney DIS
14	t-stat for intercept	0.3144	0.6324	-1.0525	-0.1584	-0.2013	-1.6120	-0.0192	-0.0371
15	t-stat for slope	9.4942	5.6112	11.7783	4.3815	9.2729	7.8607	6.6993	6.0199
16									
17	Average absolute t-stat for intercept	0.3998	<-- {=AVERAGE(ABS(B14:AE14))}						
18	Average t-stat for slope	5.7866	<-- =AVERAGE(B15:AE15)						

Cell B10 computes the average R^2 for regressions that had an $R^2 > 0.2$. These are 23 of the Dow-Jones 30. So, on average the first-pass regressions are very significant. The average R^2 of 35 percent that we got for our first-pass regressions of the basic SML is actually a respectable number in finance. Students—influenced by overenthusiastic statistics instructors and an overly linear view of the world—often feel that the R^2 of any convincing regression should be at least 90 percent. Finance does not appear to be a highly linear profession: A good rule of thumb is that any financial regression that gives an R^2 greater than 80 percent is possibly misspecified and misleading.[4]

Another way to look at the significance of our results is to compute the *t*-statistics for the intercept and slope of the first-pass regressions (rows 14–15). While the intercepts are not significantly different from zero (since their *t*-statistic is less than 2), the slopes are very significant.

4. If you look back at the appendix to Chapter 2, you will see that—had we run our regressions on diversified *portfolios* of stocks—the R^2 would increase dramatically.

11.3.1 An Excel Note: Computing the Absolute Value of an Array of Numbers

In the preceding computations we used a neat Excel trick related to array functions (see Chapter 34). By using **Abs** as an array function (that is, by entering the function using [Ctrl] + [Shift] + [Enter]), we can compute the average of the absolute values of a vector of numbers. Here is a simple example:

	A	B	C	D	E	F
1	**USING ABS FUNCTION IN ARRAY** **The Excel "Abs" function computes the absolute value** **If we use it as an array function, it can be applied to a range of numbers**					
2						
3	Numbers	1	-2	-3	-6	8
4						
5	Average number	-0.4000	<-- =AVERAGE(B3:F3)			
6	Average absolute number	4.0000	<-- {=AVERAGE(ABS(B3:F3))}			
7	The above, but not as array function	1.0000	<-- =AVERAGE(ABS(B3:F3))			

Notice cell B7: using the same function as a regular function does not produce the correct answer.

11.4 The Inefficiency of the "Market Portfolio"

When we calculated the SML in section 11.2, we regressed the mean return of each asset on the returns of the market portfolio. The propositions of Chapter 9 on efficient portfolios suggest that our failure to find adequate results may stem from the fact that the S&P 500 portfolio is not efficient relative to the set of the six assets that we have chosen. Proposition 3 of Chapter 9 states that if we had chosen to regress our asset returns on a portfolio that is efficient with respect to the asset set itself, we would get an *r*-squared of 100 percent. Proposition 4 of Chapter 9 shows that—if we get an *r*-squared of 100 percent—then the portfolio on which we regress the asset returns is necessarily efficient with respect to the set of assets. In this section we give a numerical illustration of these propositions.

In the following spreadsheet below we create a "mysterious portfolio" in column B. This portfolio (its construction is described in the next subsection) is efficient with respect to the Dow-Jones 30. As you can see in cells A10:B12, when we perform the second-pass regression—regressing the individual average returns of the assets on their betas computed with respect to the mysterious portfolio—the results are perfect. The resulting regression has an intercept of 0.0030 and a slope of 0.0425. Most important—it has an R^2 of 100 percent.

	A	B	C	D	E	F	G	H	I	J	K	L	M	N
1	RETURN DATA FOR THE DOW-JONES INDUSTRIAL STOCKS AND THE STANDARD & POOR'S 500 July 2001 - July 2006													
2	Date	Mysterious portfolio	Alcoa AA	American International Group AIG	American Express AXP	Boeing BA	Citigroup C	Caterpillar CAT	Du Pont DD	Disney DIS	General Electric GE	General Motors GM	Home Depot HD	Honeywell HON
3														
4	Average return	4.55%	-0.09%	-0.54%	0.72%	0.67%	0.30%	1.79%	0.18%	0.29%	-0.23%	-0.87%	-0.52%	0.29%
5	Beta		-0.09	-0.20	0.10	0.09	0.00	0.35	-0.03	0.00	-0.13	-0.28	-0.19	0.00
6	Alpha		0.33%	0.36%	0.27%	0.27%	0.30%	0.19%	0.31%	0.30%	0.34%	0.38%	0.36%	0.30%
7	R-squared		0.0025	0.0242	0.0064	0.0024	0.0000	0.0579	0.0006	0.0000	0.0126	0.0176	0.0143	0.0000
8														
9	**SML--regressing the average returns on the betas**													
10	Intercept	0.0030	<-- =INTERCEPT(C4:AF4,C5:AF5)											
11	Slope	0.0425	<-- =SLOPE(C4:AF4,C5:AF5)											
12	R-squared	1.0000	<-- =RSQ(C4:AF4,C5:AF5)											
13														
14														
15	1-Aug-01	-1.01%	-2.49%	-6.20%	-10.20%	-13.09%	-8.88%	-9.67%	-3.59%	-3.58%	-6.16%	-14.20%	-9.11%	1.58%
16	4-Sep-01	0.40%	-20.66%	-0.25%	-22.59%	-42.42%	-12.30%	-11.01%	-8.77%	-31.14%	-9.02%	-24.37%	-18.03%	-34.47%
17	1-Oct-01	4.71%	4.46%	0.76%	1.55%	-2.70%	11.69%	0.59%	6.37%	-0.17%	-2.15%	-3.77%	-0.35%	11.26%
18	1-Nov-01	-1.33%	17.90%	4.73%	11.18%	7.89%	5.43%	5.86%	11.15%	9.61%	5.58%	19.65%	20.01%	12.09%
19	3-Dec-01	8.11%	-8.22%	-3.67%	8.10%	9.97%	5.25%	9.68%	-4.22%	2.29%	4.45%	-2.25%	8.94%	2.03%
20	2-Jan-02	6.73%	0.83%	-6.84%	0.67%	5.43%	-5.96%	-3.09%	3.83%	1.65%	-7.58%	5.08%	-1.81%	-0.63%
21	1-Feb-02	9.38%	5.14%	-0.18%	1.68%	11.97%	-4.64%	9.88%	6.66%	8.80%	4.03%	4.55%	-0.19%	13.14%
22	1-Mar-02	6.93%	0.47%	-2.52%	11.66%	4.85%	9.02%	2.38%	0.66%	0.36%	-2.89%	13.20%	-2.72%	0.41%
23	1-Apr-02	9.47%	-10.35%	-4.27%	0.32%	-7.85%	-13.41%	-3.38%	-5.78%	0.41%	-17.02%	5.94%	-4.71%	-4.25%
24	1-May-02	3.54%	3.20%	-3.15%	3.58%	-4.09%	0.11%	-4.41%	4.11%	-1.18%	-1.29%	-2.43%	-10.65%	7.13%
25	3-Jun-02	-2.92%	-5.38%	1.92%	-15.73%	5.37%	-10.81%	-6.55%	-3.56%	-19.26%	-6.34%	-15.08%	-12.54%	-10.67%
26	1-Jul-02	3.38%	-19.75%	6.53%	-2.75%	-8.07%	-14.43%	-8.26%	-5.75%	-6.38%	10.29%	-13.83%	-17.35%	-8.51%
27	1-Aug-02	4.93%	-7.53%	-1.76%	2.26%	-10.86%	5.13%	-2.40%	-3.07%	-12.24%	-6.57%	3.92%	6.45%	-7.16%
28	3-Sep-02	4.85%	-26.22%	-13.73%	-14.54%	-8.26%	-9.96%	-15.93%	-11.11%	-3.52%	-19.45%	-20.72%	-23.11%	-32.37%

11.4.1 The Mysterious Portfolio Is Efficient

The propositions of Chapter 9 leave us with only one conclusion: the "mysterious portfolio" must be efficient with respect to the DJ30. And so it is. In the next spreadsheet we show the construction of this efficient portfolio, which follows the propositions of Chapter 9.

- We first construct the variance-covariance matrix S of the excess returns.
- We then compute the efficient portfolio by solving $\dfrac{S^{-1}[R-c]}{\sum S^{-1}[R-c]}$. In the

spreadsheet we use $c = 0.0030$, which then turns out to be the intercept of the second-pass regression.

	A	B	C	D	E	F	G	H	I	J	K	L	M	N
1	**RETURN DATA FOR THE DOW-JONES INDUSTRIAL STOCKS AND THE STANDARD & POOR'S 500** July 2001 - July 2006													
2	Date	S&P 500 Index SPX	Alcoa AA	American International Group AIG	American Express AXP	Boeing BA	Citigroup C	Caterpillar CAT	Du Pont DD	Disney DIS	General Electric GE	General Motors GM	Home Depot HD	Honeywell HON
3														
4	Average return	0.07%	-0.09%	[illegible]	[illegible]	0.67%	0.30%	1.79%	0.18%	0.29%	-0.23%	-0.87%	-0.52%	0.29%
5	Beta	1.00	1.90	[illegible]	[illegible]	[illegible]	[illegible]	1.39	1.00	1.28	0.84	1.41	1.55	1.66
6	Alpha	0	-0.23%	-0.61%	[illegible]	[illegible]	[illegible]	1.69%	0.11%	0.20%	-0.30%	-0.97%	-0.63%	0.17%
7	R-squared	1	0.6085	[illegible]	[illegible]	[illegible]	[illegible]	0.5158	0.4362	0.3845	0.3221	0.2607	0.5288	0.5473
8														
9	1-Aug-01	-6.63%	-2.49%	-6.20%	-10.20%	-13.09%	-8.88%	-9.67%	-3.59%	-3.58%	-6.16%	-14.20%	-9.11%	1.58%
10	4-Sep-01	-8.53%	-20.66%	[illegible]	[illegible]	[illegible]	-12.30%	-11.01%	-8.77%	-31.14%	-9.02%	-24.37%	-18.03%	-34.47%
11	1-Oct-01	1.79%	4.46%	[illegible]	[illegible]	[illegible]	11.69%	0.59%	6.37%	-0.17%	-2.15%	-3.77%	-0.35%	11.26%
12	1-Nov-01	7.25%	17.90%	4.73%	11.18%	7.89%	5.43%	5.86%	11.15%	9.61%	5.58%	19.65%	20.01%	12.09%
13	3-Dec-01	0.75%	-8.22%	-3.67%	8.10%	9.97%	5.25%	9.68%	-4.22%	2.29%	4.45%	-2.25%	8.94%	2.03%
14	2-Jan-02	-1.57%	0.83%	-6.84%	0.67%	5.43%	-5.96%	-3.09%	3.83%	1.65%	-7.58%	5.08%	-1.81%	-0.63%
15	1-Feb-02	-2.10%	5.14%	-0.18%	1.68%	11.97%	-4.64%	9.88%	6.66%	8.80%	4.03%	4.55%	-0.19%	13.14%
67	1-Jun-06	0.01%	2.00%	-2.92%	-2.13%	-1.62%	-2.15%	2.08%	-2.21%	-1.65%	-3.14%	10.09%	-5.91%	-2.16%
68	3-Jul-06	-0.37%	3.61%	-0.14%	-2.08%	-2.37%	1.71%	-2.58%	-2.58%	-0.57%	1.03%	-1.05%	-1.18%	-3.38%
69														
70														
71														
72	**The following cells compute the variance-covariance matrix for the DJ30 by using the formula {=MMULT(TRANSPOSE(C9:AF68-C4:AF4),C9:A F68-C4:AF4)/60}**													
73		AA	AIG	AXP	BA	C	CAT	DD	DIS	GE	GM	HD	HON	HPQ
74	AA	0.0091	0.0031	0.0037	0.0044	0.0033	0.0045	0.0040	0.0042	0.0024	0.0046	0.0045	0.0060	0.0059
75	AIG	0.0031	0.0043	0.0020	0.0010	0.0023	0.0022	0.0022	0.0015	0.0015	0.0018	0.0020	0.0026	0.0024
76	AXP	0.0037	0.0020	0.0041	0.0030	0.0030	0.0029	0.0020	0.0036	0.0019	0.0033	0.0032	0.0041	0.0049
102	WMT	0.0018	0.0014	0.0010	0.0003	0.0015	0.0011	0.0014	0.0008	0.0009	0.0012	0.0024	0.0008	0.0008
103	XOM	0.0024	0.0010	0.0010	0.0017	0.0008	0.0021	0.0012	0.0004	0.0007	0.0019	0.0007	0.0020	0.0011
104														
105	**Finding an efficient portfolio**													
106	Constant	0.30%												
107														
108	AA	5.5%	<-- {=MMULT(MINVERSE(varcov),TRANSPOSE(C4:AF4)-B106)/SUM(MMULT(MINVERSE(varcov),TRANSPOSE(C4:AF4)-B106))}											
109	AIG	-11.8%												
110	AXP	-5.8%												
111	BA	-13.9%												
112	C	-36.6%												
113	CAT	76.3%												
114	DD	-22.6%												
115	DIS	-17.0%												
116	GE	-8.8%												
117	GM	-37.7%												
118	HD	-37.2%												
119	HON	-17.4%												
120	HPQ	39.8%												
121	IBM	-26.4%												
122	INTC	-18.6%												
123	JNJ	65.1%												
124	JPM	53.6%												
125	KO	-13.0%												
126	MCD	-12.2%												
127	MMM	-2.1%												
128	MP	42.1%												
129	MRK	8.3%												
130	MSFT	3.6%												
131	PFE	-61.2%												
132	PG	54.7%												
133	T	-8.4%												
134	UTX	44.1%												
135	VZ	-36.6%												
136	WMT	64.8%												
137	XOM	29.4%												
138	Sum	100.0%												

=AVERAGE(C9:C68)

=SLOPE(C9:C68,$B$9:$B$68)

=INTERCEPT(C9:C68,$B$9:$B$68)

=RSQ(C9:C68,$B$9:$B$68)

Note that the "mysterious portfolio" is far from unique. In the next spreadsheet we show results using another constant c that gives another version of the SML.

	A	B	C	D	E	F	G	H	I	J	K	L	M	N
1	**RETURN DATA FOR THE DOW-JONES INDUSTRIAL STOCKS AND THE STANDARD & POOR'S 500 July 2001 - July 2006**													
2	Date	Mysterious portfolio	Alcoa AA	American International Group AIG	American Express AXP	Boeing BA	Citigroup C	Caterpillar CAT	Du Pont DD	Disney DIS	General Electric GE	General Motors GM	Home Depot HD	Honeywell HON
3														
4	Average return	8.88%	-0.09%	-0.54%	0.72%	0.67%	0.30%	1.79%	0.18%	0.29%	-0.23%	-0.87%	-0.52%	0.29%
5	Beta		-0.07	-0.12	0.03	0.02	-0.02	0.15	-0.04	-0.02	-0.09	-0.16	-0.12	-0.03
6	Alpha		0.54%	0.56%	0.49%	0.49%	0.51%	0.42%	0.52%	0.51%	0.54%	0.58%	0.56%	0.51%
7	R-squared		0.0061	0.0399	0.0019	0.0005	0.0015	0.0467	0.0045	0.0010	0.0256	0.0259	0.0237	0.0009
8														
9	**SML--regressing the average returns on the betas**													
10	Intercept	0.0050	<-- =INTERCEPT(C4:AF4,C5:AF5)											
11	Slope	0.0838	<-- =SLOPE(C4:AF4,C5:AF5)											
12	R-squared	1.0000	<-- =RSQ(C4:AF4,C5:AF5)											
13														

Note also that even though the R^2 of the second-pass regression is 100 percent (since the "mysterious portfolio" is efficient), the R^2's of the individual first-pass regressions are far from notable.

11.5 So What's the Real Market Portfolio? How Can We Test the CAPM?

A little reflection will reveal that although the "mysterious" portfolio of the previous section may be efficient with respect to the 30 stocks of the Dow-Jones, it could not be the *true market portfolio*, even if the DJ30 stocks represented the whole universe of risky securities. This statement is true because many of the stocks appear in the "mysterious portfolio" with negative weights. Surely a minimal characteristic of the market portfolio must be that all shares appear in it with *positive proportions*.

Roll (1977, 1978) suggests that the only test of the CAPM is to answer the question, *Is the true market portfolio mean-variance efficient?* If the answer to this question is yes, then it follows from Proposition 3 of Chapter 9 that a linear relation holds between the mean of each portfolio and its β. In our example, we can shed some light on this question by building a table of the asset proportions of portfolios on the efficient frontier.

In the following table we give some evidence that all efficient portfolios for the DJ30 contain significant short positions. Using the wonders of Excel's **Data|Table**, we compute the largest short and long positions for a series of efficient portfolios, each defined by its own constant c. All these portfolios contain large short positions (and, as you can see, also large long positions).

	A	B	C	D	E	F	G	H	I
105	**An efficient portfolio**			**Data table: computing the largest short and long position for a given constant c**					
106	Constant	0.30%			**Largest short**	**Largest long**			
107				**Constant c**			<-- Data table hidden: =B141		
108	AA	5.5%		0.00%	-32.64%	52.33%			
109	AIG	-11.8%		0.05%	-35.51%	53.58%			
110	AXP	-5.8%		0.10%	-38.87%	55.05%			
111	BA	-13.9%		0.15%	-42.86%	56.79%			
112	C	-36.6%		0.20%	-47.69%	59.70%			
113	CAT	76.3%		0.25%	-53.65%	67.01%			
114	DD	-22.6%		0.30%	-61.19%	76.26%			
115	DIS	-17.0%		0.35%	-71.01%	88.32%			
116	GE	-8.8%		0.40%	-84.36%	104.71%			
117	GM	-37.7%		0.45%	-103.56%	128.28%			
118	HD	-37.2%		0.50%	-133.51%	165.05%			
119	HON	-17.4%		0.55%	-186.77%	230.42%			
120	HPQ	39.8%		0.60%	-307.86%	379.08%			
121	IBM	-26.4%		0.65%	-853.66%	1049.09%			
122	INTC	-18.6%		0.70%	-1398.93%	1140.50%			
123	JNJ	65.1%		0.75%	-422.59%	345.18%			
124	JPM	53.6%		0.80%	-249.90%	204.50%			
125	KO	-13.0%							
126	MCD	-12.2%							
127	MMM	-2.1%							
128	MP	42.1%							
129	MRK	8.3%							
130	MSFT	3.6%							
131	PFE	-61.2%							
132	PG	54.7%							
133	T	-8.4%							
134	UTX	44.1%							
135	VZ	-36.6%							
136	WMT	64.8%							
137	XOM	29.4%							
138	Sum	100.0%							
139									
140	Largest short	-61.2%	<-- =MIN(B108:B137)						
141	Largest long	76.3%	<-- =MAX(B108:B137)						

Using the data for the DJ30, we can conclude that there is no way that the CAPM will work.[5]

11.6 Using Excess Returns

Perhaps we should have conducted our experiment on the CAPM in terms of excess returns—the difference between the stocks' monthly returns and the risk-free rates. In this section we perform this

5. In Chapter 13 we examine the Black-Litterman model, which is a more positivist approach to portfolio choice.

variation on the experiment and show that it does little to improve our analysis.

The next table shows the same Dow-Jones data, with an additional column appended for Treasury bill returns; these varied wildly over the period:

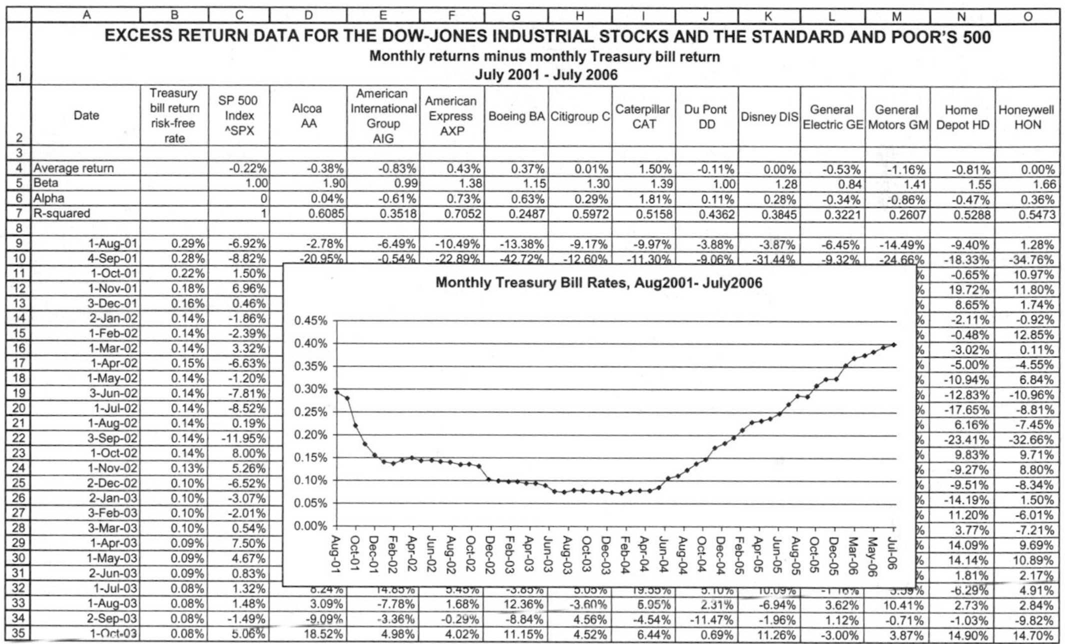

	A	B	C	D	E	F	G	H	I	J	K	L	M	N	O
1	**EXCESS RETURN DATA FOR THE DOW-JONES INDUSTRIAL STOCKS AND THE STANDARD AND POOR'S 500** **Monthly returns minus monthly Treasury bill return** **July 2001 - July 2006**														
2	Date	Treasury bill return risk-free rate	SP 500 Index ^SPX	Alcoa AA	American International Group AIG	American Express AXP	Boeing BA	Citigroup C	Caterpillar CAT	Du Pont DD	Disney DIS	General Electric GE	General Motors GM	Home Depot HD	Honeywell HON
3															
4	Average return		-0.22%	-0.38%	-0.83%	0.43%	0.37%	0.01%	1.50%	-0.11%	0.00%	-0.53%	-1.16%	-0.81%	0.00%
5	Beta		1.00	1.90	0.99	1.38	1.15	1.30	1.39	1.00	1.28	0.84	1.41	1.55	1.66
6	Alpha		0	0.04%	-0.61%	0.73%	0.63%	0.29%	1.81%	0.11%	0.28%	-0.34%	-0.86%	-0.47%	0.36%
7	R-squared		1	0.6085	0.3518	0.7052	0.2487	0.5972	0.5158	0.4362	0.3845	0.3221	0.2607	0.5288	0.5473
8															
9	1-Aug-01	0.29%	-6.92%	-2.78%	-6.49%	-10.49%	-13.38%	-9.17%	-9.97%	-3.88%	-3.87%	-6.45%	-14.49%	-9.40%	1.28%
10	4-Sep-01	0.28%	-8.82%	-20.95%	-0.54%	-22.89%	-42.72%	-12.60%	-11.30%	-9.06%	-31.44%	-9.32%	-24.66%	-18.33%	-34.76%
11	1-Oct-01	0.22%	1.50%											-0.65%	10.97%
12	1-Nov-01	0.18%	6.96%											19.72%	11.80%
13	3-Dec-01	0.16%	0.46%											8.65%	1.74%
14	2-Jan-02	0.14%	-1.86%											-2.11%	-0.92%
15	1-Feb-02	0.14%	-2.39%											-0.48%	12.85%
16	1-Mar-02	0.14%	3.32%											-3.02%	0.11%
17	1-Apr-02	0.15%	-6.63%											-5.00%	-4.55%
18	1-May-02	0.14%	-1.20%											-10.94%	6.84%
19	3-Jun-02	0.14%	-7.81%											-12.83%	-10.96%
20	1-Jul-02	0.14%	-8.52%											-17.65%	-8.81%
21	1-Aug-02	0.14%	0.19%											6.16%	-7.45%
22	3-Sep-02	0.14%	-11.95%											-23.41%	-32.66%
23	1-Oct-02	0.14%	8.00%											9.83%	9.71%
24	1-Nov-02	0.13%	5.26%											-9.27%	8.80%
25	2-Dec-02	0.10%	-6.52%											-9.51%	-8.34%
26	2-Jan-03	0.10%	-3.07%											-14.19%	1.50%
27	3-Feb-03	0.10%	-2.01%											11.20%	-6.01%
28	3-Mar-03	0.10%	0.54%											3.77%	-7.21%
29	1-Apr-03	0.09%	7.50%											14.09%	9.69%
30	1-May-03	0.09%	4.67%											14.14%	10.89%
31	2-Jun-03	0.09%	0.83%											1.81%	2.17%
32	1-Jul-03	0.08%	1.32%	[illegible]	[illegible]	[illegible]	[illegible]	[illegible]	[illegible]	[illegible]	[illegible]	[illegible]	[illegible]	-6.29%	4.91%
33	1-Aug-03	0.08%	1.48%	3.09%	-7.78%	1.68%	12.36%	-3.60%	6.95%	2.31%	-6.94%	3.62%	10.41%	2.73%	2.84%
34	2-Sep-03	0.08%	-1.49%	-9.09%	-3.36%	-0.29%	-8.84%	4.56%	-4.54%	-11.47%	-1.96%	1.12%	-0.71%	-1.03%	-9.82%
35	1-Oct-03	0.08%	5.06%	18.52%	4.98%	4.02%	11.15%	4.52%	6.44%	0.69%	11.26%	-3.00%	3.87%	14.90%	14.70%

Running the second-pass regression shows only minor changes from the results of section 11.2:

	A	B	C	D	E	F	G	H
1	**THE SECOND-PASS REGRESSION FOR EXCESS RETURNS**							
2	**Stock**	**Average monthly excess return**	**Beta**	**Alpha**				
3	Alcoa AA	-0.38%	1.9028	0.0004		**Second-pass regression, regressing monthly returns on Beta**		
4	American International Group AIG	-0.83%	0.9936	-0.0061		Intercept	0.0007	<-- =INTERCEPT(B3:B32,C3:C32)
5	American Express AXP	0.43%	1.3784	0.0073		Slope	-0.0020	<-- =SLOPE(B3:B32,C3:C32)
6	Boeing BA	0.37%	1.1515	0.0063		R-squared	0.0238	<-- =RSQ(B3:B32,C3:C32)
7	Citigroup C	0.01%	1.2952	0.0029				
8	Caterpillar CAT	1.50%	1.3903	0.0181		t-statistic, intercept	0.243911	<-- =tintercept(B3:B32,C3:C32)
9	Du Pont DD	-0.11%	1.0009	0.0011		t-statistic, slope	-0.825378	<-- =tslope(B3:B32,C3:C32)
10	Disney DIS	0.00%	1.2805	0.0028				
11	General Electric GE	-0.53%	0.8420	-0.0034				
12	General Motors GM	-1.16%	1.4060	-0.0086				
13	Home Depot HD	-0.81%	1.5528	-0.0047				
14	Honeywell HON	0.00%	1.6640	0.0036				
15	Hewlitt Packard HPQ	0.31%	1.9594	0.0074				
16	IBM	-0.76%	1.5764	-0.0041				
17	Intel INTC	-1.02%	2.2648	-0.0052				
18	Johnson & Johnson JNJ	0.04%	0.2471	0.0010				
19	JP Morgan JPM	-0.11%	1.7917	0.0029				
20	Coca Cola KO	-0.18%	0.3590	-0.0010				
21	McDonalds MCD	0.05%	1.2646	0.0033				
22	3M MMM	0.34%	0.6504	0.0049				
23	AltriaMO	1.01%	0.6633	0.0116				
24	Merck MRK	-0.92%	0.6099	-0.0079				
25	Microsoft MSFT	-0.64%	1.1219	-0.0040				
26	Pfizer PFE	-1.04%	0.5572	-0.0091				
27	Proctor Gamble PG	0.65%	0.1687	0.0068				
28	AT&T T	-0.71%	1.1275	-0.0046				
29	United Technologies UTX	0.74%	1.0659	0.0097				
30	Verizon VZ	-0.78%	1.0231	-0.0056				
31	Walmart WMT	-0.54%	0.6000	-0.0041				
32	Exxon Mobil XOM	0.59%	0.6455	0.0073				
33								
34	Average	-0.17%	1.13	0.07%				

11.7 Does the CAPM Have Any Uses?

Is the game lost? Do we have to give up on the CAPM? Not totally.

• First of all, it could be that the mean returns are approximately described by their regression on a market portfolio. In this alternative description of the CAPM, we claim (with some justification, see footnote) that the β of an asset (which measures the dependence of the asset's returns on the market returns) is an important measure of the asset's risk.

• Second, the CAPM might be a good normative description of how to choose portfolios. As we showed in the appendix of Chapter 2, larger diversified portfolios are quite well described by their betas, so that the average beta of a well-diversified portfolio may be a reasonable description of the portfolio's risk.

Exercises

1. This exercise asks you to repeat the computations of section 11.1 for a somewhat different percent. In the file **fm3_problems11.xls** you will find monthly returns for the Dow-Jones 30 Industrials and the S&P 500 for July 1997–July 2007.

   a. Regress the monthly returns of each of the stocks on the S&P 500, computing the slope, intercept, R^2, and t-statistics for the slope and intercept.

   b. Perform the second-pass regression: Regress the average monthly return of each stock on its beta. Analyze the results.

	A	B	C	D	E	F	G	H	I	J	K	L
1	PRICES FOR DOW-JONES 30 STOCKS, JULY 1997 - JULY 2007											
2	Date	S&P 500	DJ30	Alcoa AA	American International Group AIG	American Express AXP	Boeing BA	Citigroup C	Caterpillar CAT	Dupont DD	Disney DIS	General Electric GE
3	1-Jul-97	954.31	8222.61	18.38	36.31	22.38	50.44	17.87	22.22	49.92	24.71	18.97
4	1-Aug-97	899.47	7622.42	17.13	32.18	20.78	46.96	15.78	23.04	46.61	23.49	16.93
5	2-Sep-97	947.28	7945.26	17.08	35.21	21.88	46.91	16.97	21.41	46.05	24.65	18.49
6	1-Oct-97	914.62	7442.08	15.20	34.83	20.90	41.36	17.43	20.42	42.55	25.23	17.55
7	3-Nov-97	955.40	7823.13	14.05	34.40	21.14	45.92	19.00	19.10	45.54	29.08	20.06
8	1-Dec-97	970.43	7908.25	14.71	37.13	23.98	42.30	20.12	19.33	45.16	30.32	20.01
9	2-Jan-98	980.28	7906.50	15.96	37.67	22.49	41.16	18.51	19.23	42.58	32.77	21.14
10	2-Feb-98	1049.34	8545.72	15.41	41.04	24.20	47.02	20.83	21.86	46.33	34.33	21.21
11	2-Mar-98	1101.75	8799.81	14.45	43.03	24.67	45.18	22.46	22.06	51.39	32.74	23.60
12	1-Apr-98	1111.75	9063.37	16.27	44.95	27.52	43.39	22.95	22.91	55.02	38.25	23.33
13	1-May-98	1090.82	8899.95	14.61	42.30	27.63	41.50	22.98	22.11	58.59	34.78	22.83

2. In a well-known paper, Roll (1978), discusses tests of the SML in a four-asset context:

Variance-covariance matrix					Returns
0.10	0.02	0.04	0.05		0.06
0.02	0.20	0.04	0.01		0.07
0.04	0.04	0.40	0.10		0.08
0.05	0.01	0.10	0.60		0.09

   a. Derive two efficient portfolios in this four-asset model and draw a graph of the efficient frontier.

   b. Show that the following four portfolios are efficient by proving that each is a convex combination of the two portfolios you derived in part a:

Security 1	0.59600	0.40700	-0.04400	-0.49600
Security 2	0.27621	0.31909	0.42140	0.52395
Security 3	0.07695	0.13992	0.29017	0.44076
Security 4	0.05083	0.13399	0.33242	0.53129

c. Suppose that the market portfolio is composed of equal proportions of each asset (i.e., the market portfolio has proportions [0.25, 0.25, 0.25, 0.25]). Calculate the resulting SML. Is the portfolio [0.25, 0.25, 0.25, 0.25] efficient?

d. Repeat this exercise, but substitute one of the four portfolios from part b as the candidate for the market portfolio.

12 Efficient Portfolios without Short Sales

12.1 Overview

In Chapter 9 we discussed the problem of finding an efficient portfolio. As shown there, this problem can be written as finding a tangent portfolio on the envelope of the feasible set of portfolios:

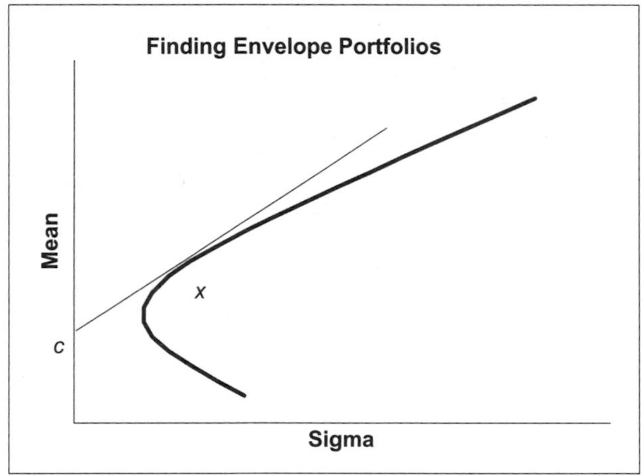

The proof in the appendix to Chapter 9 for solving for such an efficient portfolio involved finding the solution to the following problem:

$$\max \Theta = \frac{E(r_x) - c}{\sigma_p}$$

such that

$$\sum_{i=1}^{N} x_i = 1$$

where

$$E(r_x) = x^T * R = \sum_{i=1}^{N} x_i E(r_i)$$

$$\sigma_p = \sqrt{x^T S x} = \sqrt{\sum_{i=1}^{N} \sum_{j=1}^{N} x_i x_j \sigma_{ij}}$$

Proposition 1 of Chapter 9 gives a methodology for solving this problem. Solutions to the maximization problem allow *negative* portfolio proportions; when $x_i < 0$, this approach assumes that the ith security is sold short by the investor and that the proceeds from this short sale become immediately available to the investor. Reality is, of course, considerably more complicated than this academic model of short sales. In particular, it is rare for all of the short-sale proceeds to become available to the investor at the time of investment, since brokerage houses typically escrow some or even all of the proceeds. It may also be that the investor is completely prohibited from making any short sales (indeed, most small investors seem to proceed on the assumption that short sales are impossible).[1]

In this chapter we investigate these problems. We show how to use Excel's **Solver** to find efficient portfolios of assets when we restrict short sales.[2]

12.2 A Numerical Example

We start with the problem of finding an optimal portfolio when no short sales are allowed. The problem we solve is similar to the maximization problem stated previously, with the addition of the short-sales constraint:

$$\max \Theta = \frac{E(r_x) - c}{\sigma_p}$$

such that

$$\sum_{i=1}^{N} x_i = 1$$

$$x_i \geq 0, i = 1, \ldots, N$$

1. The actual procedures for implementing a short sale are not simple. A well-written academic survey is a recent paper by Gene D'Avolio, "The Market for Borrowing Stock," *Journal of Financial Economics*, 2003, pp. 271–306. There's also a wonderful article in the 1 December 2003 issue of the *New Yorker Magazine* by James Surowiecki entitled "Get Shorty."
2. We do not go into the efficient set mathematics when short sales of assets are restricted. This involves the Kuhn-Tucker conditions, a discussion of which can be found in Elton, Gruber, Brown, and Goetzmann (2002), *Modern Portfolio Theory and Investment Analysis*, 6th edition.

where

$$E(r_x) = x^T * R = \sum_{i=1}^{N} x_i E(r_i)$$

$$\sigma_p = \sqrt{x^T S x} = \sqrt{\sum_{i=1}^{N} \sum_{j=1}^{N} x_i x_j \sigma_{ij}}$$

12.2.1 Solving an Unconstrained Portfolio Problem

To set the scene, we consider the following optimization problem, which we solve without any short-sale constraints. The spreadsheet shows a four-asset variance-covariance matrix and associated expected returns. Given a constant $c = 8$ percent, the optimal portfolio is given in cells B11:B14. Notice θ in cell B19: This is the *Sharpe ratio* of the portfolio, the ratio of its excess return over the constant c to its standard deviation: $\theta = \frac{E(r_x) - c}{\sigma_x}$. The optimal portfolio maximizes the Sharpe ratio θ.

	A	B	C	D	E	F	G	H
1	PORTFOLIO OPTIMIZATION ALLOWING SHORT SALES Follows Proposition 1, Chapter 9							
2		**Variance-covariance matrix**					**Means**	
3		0.10	0.03	-0.08	0.05		8%	
4		0.03	0.20	0.02	0.03		9%	
5		-0.08	0.02	0.30	0.20		10%	
6		0.05	0.03	0.20	0.90		11%	
7								
8		c	3.0%	<-- This is the constant				
9								
10	**Optimal portfolio without short sale restrictions (Chapter 9, Proposition 1)**							
11	x_1	0.6219	<-- {=MMULT(MINVERSE(B3:E6),G3:G6-C8)/SUM(MMULT(MINVERSE(B3:E6),G3:G6-C8))}					
12	x_2	0.0804						
13	x_3	0.3542						
14	x_4	-0.0565						
15	Total	1	<-- =SUM(B11:B14)					
16								
17	Portfolio mean	8.62%	<-- {=MMULT(TRANSPOSE(B11:B14),G3:G6)}					
18	Portfolio sigma	19.39%	<-- {=SQRT(MMULT(TRANSPOSE(B11:B14),MMULT(B3:E6,B11:B14)))}					
19	θ = Theta = (mean-constant)/sigma	28.99%	<-- =(B17-C8)/B18					

There is another way to solve this unconstrained problem. Starting from an arbitrary portfolio (the spreadsheet below uses $x_1 = x_2 = x_3 = x_4 = 0.25$), we use **Solver** to find a solution:

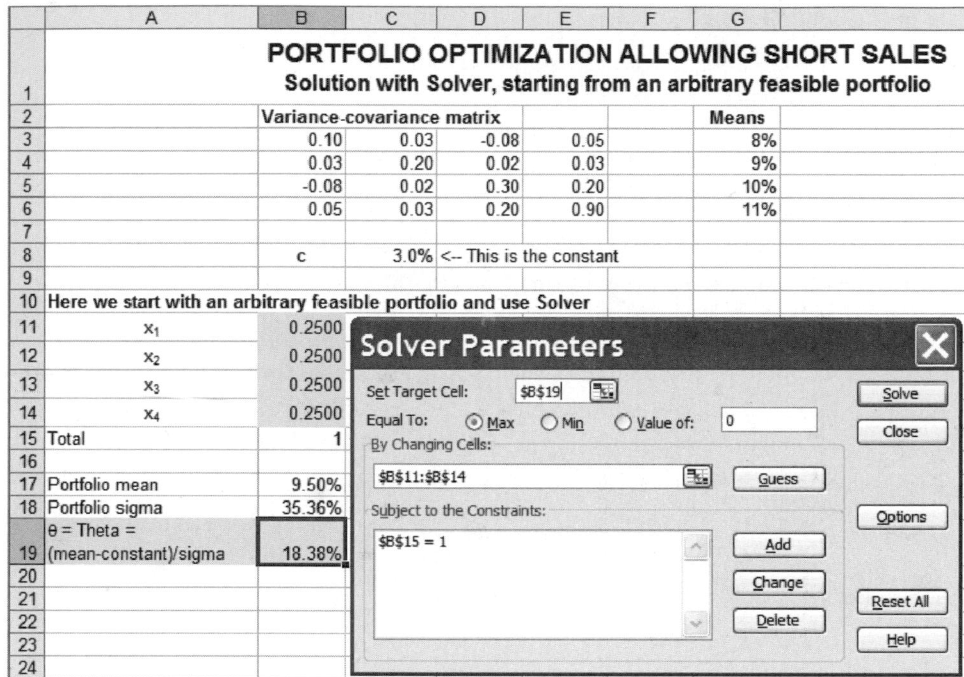

	A	B	C	D	E	F	G
1		PORTFOLIO OPTIMIZATION ALLOWING SHORT SALES Solution with Solver, starting from an arbitrary feasible portfolio					
2		Variance-covariance matrix					Means
3		0.10	0.03	-0.08	0.05		8%
4		0.03	0.20	0.02	0.03		9%
5		-0.08	0.02	0.30	0.20		10%
6		0.05	0.03	0.20	0.90		11%
7							
8		c	3.0%	<-- This is the constant			
9							
10	Here we start with an arbitrary feasible portfolio and use Solver						
11	x_1	0.2500					
12	x_2	0.2500					
13	x_3	0.2500					
14	x_4	0.2500					
15	Total	1					
16							
17	Portfolio mean	9.50%					
18	Portfolio sigma	35.36%					
19	θ = Theta = (mean-constant)/sigma	18.38%					

The **Solver** solution maximizes θ (cell B19) subject to the constraint that cell B15, which contains the sum of the portfolio positions, equal 1.[3] When we press **Solve** we get the solution we achieved before:

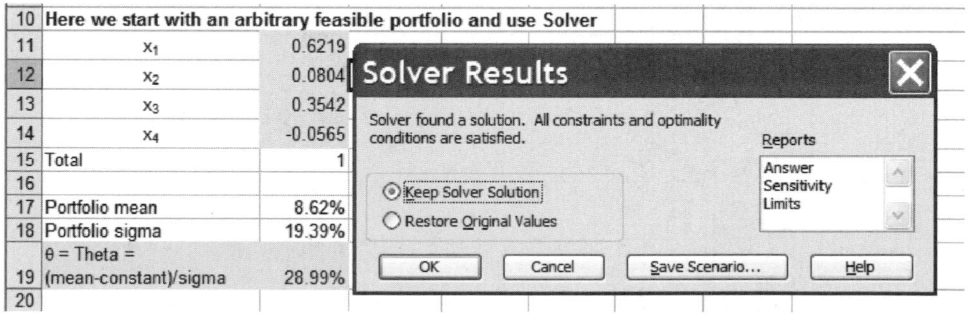

	A	B
10	Here we start with an arbitrary feasible portfolio and use Solver	
11	x_1	0.6219
12	x_2	0.0804
13	x_3	0.3542
14	x_4	-0.0565
15	Total	1
16		
17	Portfolio mean	8.62%
18	Portfolio sigma	19.39%
19	θ = Theta = (mean-constant)/sigma	28.99%

3. If **Tools|Solver** doesn't work, you may not have loaded the **Solver** add-in. To do so, go to **Tools|Add-ins** and click next to the **Solver Add-in**.

12.2.2 Solving a Constrained Portfolio Problem

The preceding optimal solution contains a short position in asset 4. To restrict the short selling, we add a no-short-sale constraint to **Tools|Solver**. Starting from an arbitrary solution, we bring up **Solver**, as follows:

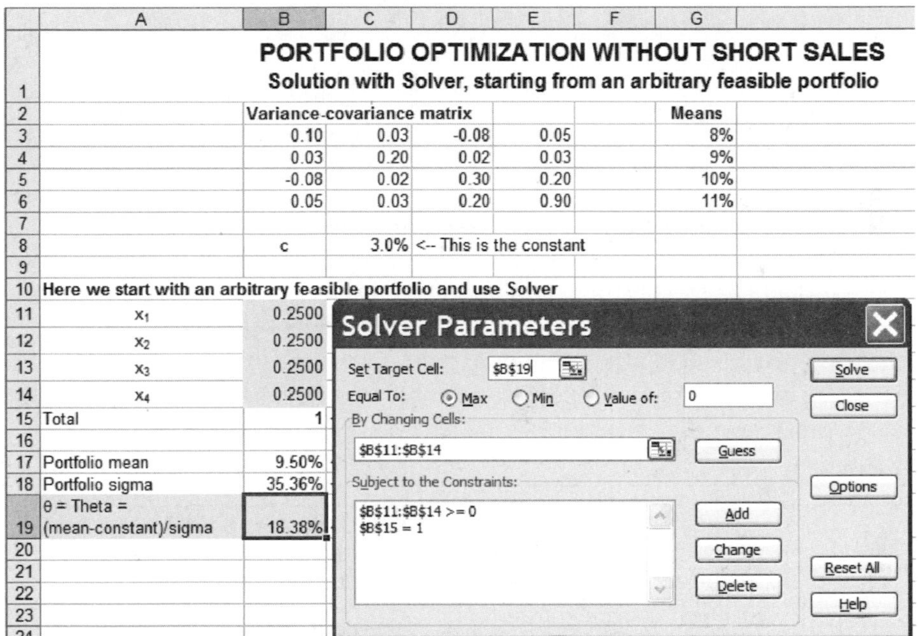

	A	B	C	D	E	F	G
1		PORTFOLIO OPTIMIZATION WITHOUT SHORT SALES Solution with Solver, starting from an arbitrary feasible portfolio					
2		Variance-covariance matrix					Means
3		0.10	0.03	-0.08	0.05		8%
4		0.03	0.20	0.02	0.03		9%
5		-0.08	0.02	0.30	0.20		10%
6		0.05	0.03	0.20	0.90		11%
7							
8		c	3.0%	<-- This is the constant			
9							
10	Here we start with an arbitrary feasible portfolio and use Solver						
11	x_1	0.2500					
12	x_2	0.2500					
13	x_3	0.2500					
14	x_4	0.2500					
15	Total	1					
16							
17	Portfolio mean	9.50%					
18	Portfolio sigma	35.36%					
19	θ = Theta = (mean-constant)/sigma	18.38%					

Pressing **Solve** yields the following solution:

	A	B	C	D	E	F	G	H
1		PORTFOLIO OPTIMIZATION WITHOUT SHORT SALES Solution with Solver, starting from an arbitrary feasible portfolio						
2		Variance-covariance matrix					Means	
3		0.10	0.03	-0.08	0.05		8%	
4		0.03	0.20	0.02	0.03		9%	
5		-0.08	0.02	0.30	0.20		10%	
6		0.05	0.03	0.20	0.90		11%	
7								
8		c	3.0%	<-- This is the constant				
9								
10	Here we start with an arbitrary feasible portfolio and use Solver							
11	x_1	0.5856						
12	x_2	0.0965						
13	x_3	0.3179						
14	x_4	0.0000						
15	Total	1	<-- =SUM(B11:B14)					
16								
17	Portfolio mean	8.73%	<-- {=MMULT(TRANSPOSE(B11:B14),G3:G6)}					
18	Portfolio sigma	20.32%	<-- {=SQRT(MMULT(TRANSPOSE(B11:B14),MMULT(B3:E6,B11:B14)))}					
19	θ = Theta = (mean-constant)/sigma	28.21%	<-- =(B17-C8)/B18					

The nonnegativity constraint is added by clicking on the **Add** button in the **Solver** dialogue box. This brings up the following window (shown here filled in):

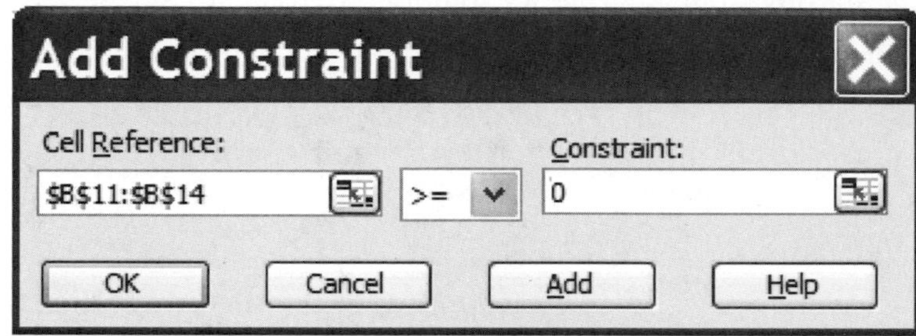

The second constraint (which constrains the portfolio proportions to sum to 1) is added in a similar fashion.

By changing the value of c in the spreadsheet, we can compute other portfolios; in the following example, we have set the constant $c = 8.5$ percent:

	A	B	C	D	E	F	G	H
1	**PORTFOLIO OPTIMIZATION WITHOUT SHORT SALES** **Solution with Solver, starting from an arbitrary feasible portfolio**							
2		**Variance-covariance matrix**					**Means**	
3		0.10	0.03	-0.08	0.05		8%	
4		0.03	0.20	0.02	0.03		9%	
5		-0.08	0.02	0.30	0.20		10%	
6		0.05	0.03	0.20	0.90		11%	
7								
8		c	8.5%	<-- This is the constant				
9								
10	**Here we start with an arbitrary feasible portfolio and use Solver**							
11	x_1	0.0000						
12	x_2	0.2515						
13	x_3	0.4885						
14	x_4	0.2601						
15	Total	1	<-- =SUM(B11:B14)					
16								
17	Portfolio mean	10.01%	<-- {=MMULT(TRANSPOSE(B11:B14),G3:G6)}					
18	Portfolio sigma	45.25%	<-- {=SQRT(MMULT(TRANSPOSE(B11:B14),MMULT(B3:E6,B11:B14)))}					
19	θ = Theta = (mean-constant)/sigma	3.33%	<-- =(B17-C8)/B18					

In both examples, the short-sale restriction is effective, with zero positions in some asset. However, not all values of c give portfolios in which the short-sale constraints are effective. For example, if the constant is 8 percent, we get this result:

	A	B	C	D	E	F	G	H
1	**PORTFOLIO OPTIMIZATION WITHOUT SHORT SALES** **Solution with Solver, starting from an arbitrary feasible portfolio**							
2		**Variance-covariance matrix**					**Means**	
3		0.10	0.03	-0.08	0.05		8%	
4		0.03	0.20	0.02	0.03		9%	
5		-0.08	0.02	0.30	0.20		10%	
6		0.05	0.03	0.20	0.90		11%	
7								
8		c	8.0%	<-- This is the constant				
9								
10	**Here we start with an arbitrary feasible portfolio and use Solver**							
11	x_1	0.2004						
12	x_2	0.2587						
13	x_3	0.4219						
14	x_4	0.1190						
15	Total	1	<-- =SUM(B11:B14)					
16								
17	Portfolio mean	9.46%	<-- {=MMULT(TRANSPOSE(B11:B14),G3:G6)}					
18	Portfolio sigma	31.91%	<-- {=SQRT(MMULT(TRANSPOSE(B11:B14),MMULT(B3:E6,B11:B14)))}					
19	θ = Theta = (mean-constant)/sigma	4.57%	<-- =(B17-C8)/B18					

As we saw for the example where $c = 3$ percent, as c gets lower, the short-sale constraint begins to be effective with respect to asset 4. For very high c's (the following case illustrates $c = 11$ percent) only asset 4 is included in the maximizing portfolio:

	A	B	C	D	E	F	G	H
8		c	11.0%	<-- This is the constant				
9								
10	**Here we start with an arbitrary feasible portfolio and use Solver**							
11	x_1	0.0000						
12	x_2	0.0000						
13	x_3	0.0000						
14	x_4	1.0000						
15	Total	1	<-- =SUM(B11:B14)					
16								
17	Portfolio mean	11.00%	<-- {=MMULT(TRANSPOSE(B11:B14),G3:G6)}					
18	Portfolio sigma	94.87%	<-- {=SQRT(MMULT(TRANSPOSE(B11:B14),MMULT(B3:E6,B11:B14)))}					
19	θ = Theta = (mean-constant)/sigma	0.00%	<-- =(B17-C8)/B18					

12.3 The Efficient Frontier with Short-Sale Restrictions

We want to graph the efficient frontier with short-sale restrictions. Recall that in the case of no short-sale restrictions discussed in Chapter 9, it was enough to find two efficient portfolios in order to determine the whole efficient frontier (this conclusion was proved in Proposition 2 of Chapter 9). When we impose short-sale restrictions, this statement is no longer true. In this case the determination of the efficient frontier requires the plotting of a large number of points. The only efficient (pardon the pun!) way of doing so is with a VBA program that repeatedly applies the **Solver** and puts the solutions in a table.

In this section we describe such a program. One aim of the program is to create a graph of the efficient frontier without short sales:

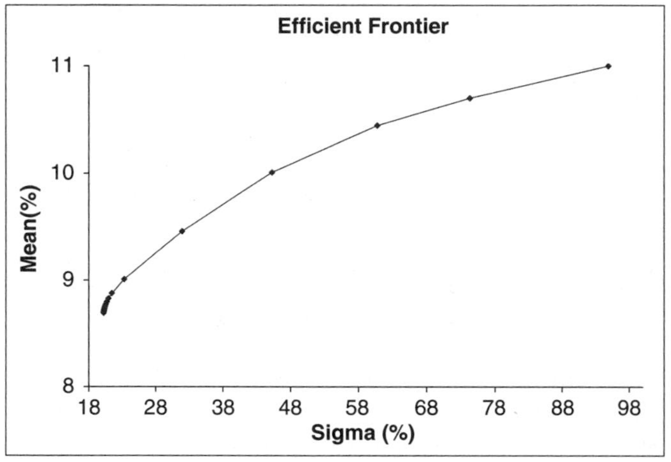

Once we have the program and the graph of the efficient frontier without short sales, we will also compare this efficient frontier to the efficient frontier *with* short sales allowed:

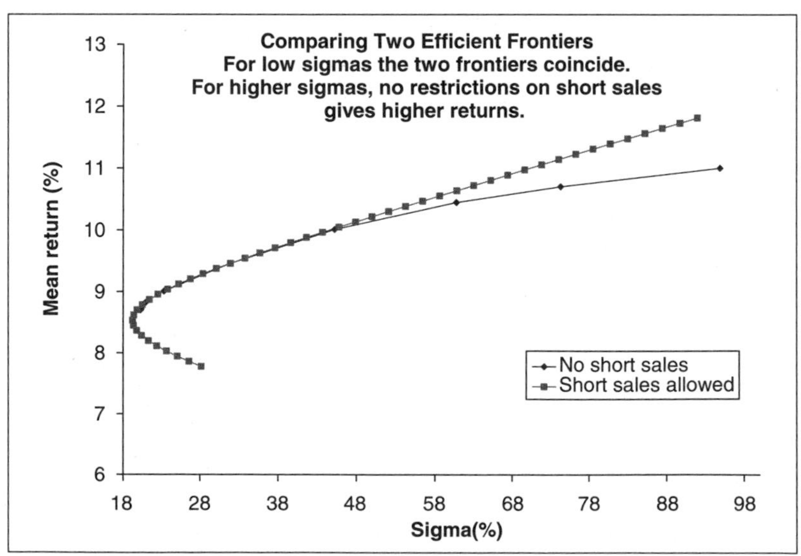

The relation between these two graphs is not all that surprising:

• In general, the efficient frontier with short sales dominates the efficient frontier without short sales. This statement must clearly be so, since the short-sales restriction imposes an extra constraint on the maximization problem.

• For some cases the two efficient frontiers coincide. One such point occurs, as we saw before, when $c = 8$ percent.

Putting these two graphs on one set of axes shows that the effect of the short-sale restrictions is mainly on portfolios with higher returns and sigmas.

12.4 A VBA Program to Create the Efficient Frontier

The output for the restricted short-sale case shown in section 12.3 was produced with the following VBA program:

```
Sub Solve()
        SolverOk SetCell:="$B$19", MaxMinVal:=1, ValueOf:="0",
ByChange:="$B$11:$B$14"
        SolverSolve UserFinish:=True
End Sub

Sub Doit()
     Range("Results").ClearContents
     For counter = 1 To 40
          Range("constant") = -0.04 + counter * 0.005
          Solve
          Application.SendKeys ("{Enter}")
          Range("Results").Cells(counter, 1) = ActiveSheet.
            Range("constant")
          Range("Results").Cells(counter, 2) = ActiveSheet.
            Range("portfolio_sigma")
          Range("Results").Cells(counter, 3) = ActiveSheet.
            Range("portfolio_mean")
          Range("Results").Cells(counter, 4) = ActiveSheet.
            Range("x_1")
```

```
            Range("Results").Cells(counter, 5) = ActiveSheet.
              Range("x_2")
            Range("Results").Cells(counter, 6) = ActiveSheet.
              Range("x_3")
            Range("Results").Cells(counter, 7) = ActiveSheet.
              Range("x_4")
        Next counter
    End Sub                ActiveSheet.Range("x_3")
            Range("Results").Cells(counter, 7) = _
                ActiveSheet.Range("x_4")
        Next counter
    End Sub
```

The program includes two subroutines: `Solve` calls the Excel Solver; and the subroutine `Doit` repeatedly calls the solver for different values of the range named `Constant` (this is cell C8 in the spreadsheet), putting the output in a range called Results.

The final output looks like this:

	A	B	C	D	E	F	G	H	I	J	K	L	M	N	O	P
1	**PORTFOLIO OPTIMIZATION WITHOUT SHORT SALES**									**RESULTS**						
2		**Variance-covariance matrix**					**Means**			**c**	**Sigma**	**Mean**	x_1	x_2	x_3	x_4
3		0.10	0.03	-0.08	0.05		8%		Ctrl+A works the VBA program	-0.035	20.24%	8.70%	0.6049	0.0885	0.3066	0.0000
4		0.03	0.20	0.02	0.03		9%		which calculates efficient	-0.03	20.25%	8.70%	0.6042	0.0887	0.3070	0.0000
5		-0.08	0.02	0.30	0.20		10%		portfolios for no-short sales.	-0.025	20.25%	8.70%	0.6035	0.0890	0.3075	0.0000
6		0.05	0.03	0.20	0.90		11%		This program iteratively	-0.02	20.25%	8.71%	0.6027	0.0893	0.3080	0.0000
7									substitutes a constant ranging	-0.015	20.25%	8.71%	0.6017	0.0897	0.3086	0.0000
8		c	16.0%	<-- This is the constant					from -3.5% 'till 16% (1/2%	-0.01	20.26%	8.71%	0.6007	0.0901	0.3092	0.0000
9									jumps) and calculates the	-0.005	20.26%	8.71%	0.5994	0.0908	0.3098	0.0000
10									optimal portfolio.	0	20.27%	8.71%	0.5982	0.0912	0.3106	0.0000
11	x_1	0.0000	0							0.005	20.27%	8.71%	0.5968	0.0917	0.3115	0.0000
12	x_2	0.0000	0							0.01	20.28%	8.72%	0.5950	0.0926	0.3123	0.0000
13	x_3	0.0000	0							0.015	20.29%	8.72%	0.5932	0.0934	0.3134	0.0000
14	x_4	1.0000	0							0.02	20.30%	8.72%	0.5910	0.0943	0.3147	0.0000
15	Total	1.0000	<-- =SUM(B11:B14)							0.025	20.31%	8.73%	0.5885	0.0953	0.3161	0.0000
16										0.03	20.32%	8.73%	0.5856	0.0965	0.3179	0.0000
17	Portfolio mean	11.00%	<-- {=MMULT(TRANSPOSE(B11:B14),G3:G6)}							0.035	20.34%	8.74%	0.5821	0.0980	0.3199	0.0000
18	Portfolio sigma	94.87%	<-- {=SQRT(MMULT(TRANSPOSE(B11:B14),MMULT(B3:E6,B11:B14)))}							0.04	20.37%	8.74%	0.5779	0.0998	0.3224	0.0000
19	Theta	-5.27%	<-- =(portfolio_mean-C8)/Portfolio_sigma							0.045	20.41%	8.75%	0.5726	0.1019	0.3255	0.0000
20										0.05	20.46%	8.76%	0.5659	0.1047	0.3294	0.0000
21										0.055	20.54%	8.78%	0.5572	0.1083	0.3345	0.0000
22										0.06	20.67%	8.80%	0.5452	0.1133	0.3415	0.0000
23										0.065	20.90%	8.82%	0.5277	0.1205	0.3518	0.0000
24										0.07	21.36%	8.87%	0.4992	0.1324	0.3684	0.0000
25										0.075	23.27%	9.01%	0.4267	0.1630	0.3856	0.0248

12.4.1 Adding a Reference to Solver in VBA

If the preceding routine does not work, you may need to add a reference to **Solver** in the VBA editor. Press [Alt] + F11 to get to the editor and check the reference.

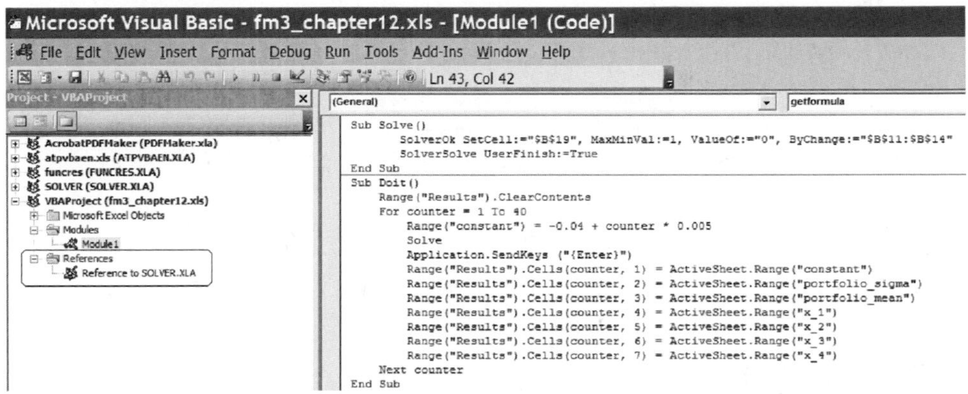

If this reference is missing, go to **Tools|References** on the VBA menu and make sure that **Solver** is indicated.

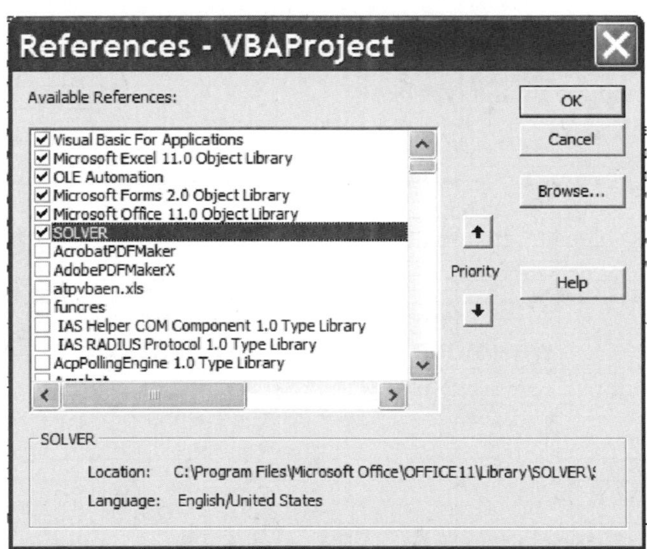

12.5 Other Position Restrictions

It goes without saying that Excel and **Solver** can accommodate other position limits. Suppose, for example, that the investor wants at least 5 percent of her portfolio invested in any asset and no more than 40 percent of the portfolio invested in any single asset. This portfolio problem is easily set up in **Solver**:

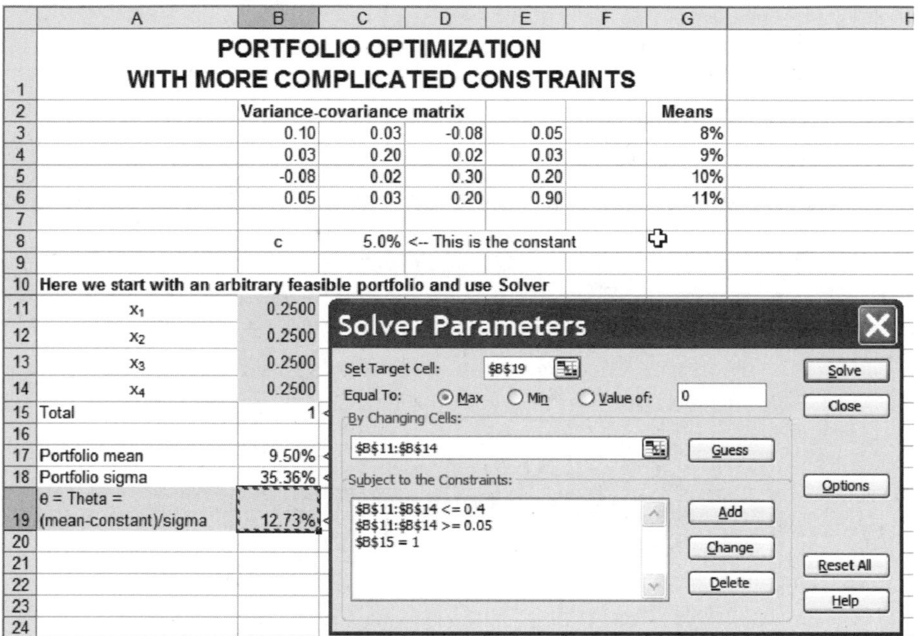

	A	B	C	D	E	F	G
1	**PORTFOLIO OPTIMIZATION WITH MORE COMPLICATED CONSTRAINTS**						
2		**Variance-covariance matrix**					**Means**
3		0.10	0.03	-0.08	0.05		8%
4		0.03	0.20	0.02	0.03		9%
5		-0.08	0.02	0.30	0.20		10%
6		0.05	0.03	0.20	0.90		11%
7							
8		c	5.0%	<-- This is the constant			
9							
10	**Here we start with an arbitrary feasible portfolio and use Solver**						
11	x_1	0.2500					
12	x_2	0.2500					
13	x_3	0.2500					
14	x_4	0.2500					
15	Total	1					
16							
17	Portfolio mean	9.50%					
18	Portfolio sigma	35.36%					
19	θ = Theta = (mean-constant)/sigma	12.73%					

This solves to give the following:

	A	B	C	D	E	F	G
1	**PORTFOLIO OPTIMIZATION WITH MORE COMPLICATED CONSTRAINTS**						
2		**Variance-covariance matrix**					**Means**
3		0.10	0.03	-0.08	0.05		8%
4		0.03	0.20	0.02	0.03		9%
5		-0.08	0.02	0.30	0.20		10%
6		0.05	0.03	0.20	0.90		11%
7							
8		c	5.0%	<-- This is the constant			
9							
10	**Here we start with an arbitrary feasible portfolio and use Solver**						
11	x_1	0.4000					
12	x_2	0.2270					
13	x_3	0.3230					
14	x_4	0.0500					
15	Total	1	<-- =SUM(B11:B14)				
16							
17	Portfolio mean	9.02%	<-- {=MMULT(TRANSPOSE(B11:B14),G3:G6)}				
18	Portfolio sigma	23.81%	<-- {=SQRT(MMULT(TRANSPOSE(B11:B14),MMULT(B3				
19	θ = Theta = (mean-constant)/sigma	16.89%	<-- =(B17-C8)/B18				

12.6 Conclusion

No one would claim that Excel offers a quick way to solve for portfolio maximization, with or without short-sale constraints. However, it can be used to illustrate the principles involved, and the Excel **Solver** provides an easy-to-use and intuitive interface for setting up these problems.

Exercises

Given the following data below

a. Calculate the efficient frontier assuming that no short sales are allowed.
b. Calculate the efficient frontier assuming that short sales are allowed.
c. Graph both frontiers on the same set of axes.

	A	B	C	D	E	F	G	H	I
3		A	B	C	D	E	F		Mean returns
4	A	0.0100	0.0000	0.0000	0.0000	0.0000	0.0000		0.0100
5	B	0.0000	0.0400	0.0000	0.0000	0.0000	0.0000		0.0200
6	C	0.0000	0.0000	0.0900	0.0000	0.0000	0.0000		0.0300
7	D	0.0000	0.0000	0.0000	0.1500	0.0000	0.0000		0.0400
8	E	0.0000	0.0000	0.0000	0.0000	0.2000	0.0000		0.0500
9	F	0.0000	0.0000	0.0000	0.0000	0.0000	0.3000		0.0550

13 The Black-Litterman Approach to Portfolio Optimization

13.1 Overview

Chapters 8–12 have set out the classic approach to portfolio optimization that was first explicated by Harry Markowitz in the 1950s and subsequently expanded by Sharpe (1964), Lintner (1965), and Mossin (1966). An enormous academic and practitioner literature (as well as several Nobel prizes in economics) testifies to the impact of this new point of view on asset valuation and portfolio choice. Today no conversation about a stock's risk is complete without mentioning its beta, and discussions of portfolio performance regularly invoke the alpha (both of these topics are discussed in Chapter 11).

It is not an exaggeration to say that Markowitz changed the paradigm of investment management. Well before Markowitz, individual investors knew that they should "diversify" and not "put all their eggs in one basket." But Markowitz and those who followed him gave statistical and implementational meaning to these clichés. Modern portfolio theory (MPT) changed the way intelligent investors discuss investment.

Nevertheless, MPT has disappointed. It is possible to come away from a standard textbook discussion of portfolio optimization with the impression that a fixed set of mechanical optimization rules, combined with a bit of knowledge about personal preferences, suffices to define an investor's optimal portfolio. Anyone who has tried to implement portfolio optimization using market data knows that the dream is often a nightmare. Implementations of portfolio theory produce wildly unrealistic portfolios with huge short positions and correspondingly imaginary long positions.[1]

The main problem with the mechanical implementation of portfolio optimization is that historical asset return data produce bad predictions for future asset returns. The estimation of the covariances between asset returns and the estimation of expected returns—the underpinnings of portfolio theory—from historical data often produces unbelievable numbers.

1. It might be thought that limiting short sales, as we have illustrated in Chapter 12, could solve some of these problems. However, short-sale limitations severely restrict the investible asset universe. In many cases short-sales are caused by bad historical returns that are not necessarily indicative of future anticipated returns; investors may want to purchase assets with these properties despite their "bad" histories.

In Chapter 10 we alluded to some of these problems in the context of estimating the variance-covariance matrix. There we showed that historical data may not be the best way to estimate this matrix; other methods—in particular the "shrinkage" methods—may produce more reliable estimates of the covariances. In this chapter we take things a step further. We illustrate the problems of standard portfolio optimization by using a 10-asset portfolio problem. The MPT optimization for our data produces an insane "optimal" portfolio, with many huge long and short positions. The problems of portfolio optimization illustrated in our example are, unfortunately, not unusual. Using the data in a mechanical way to derive "optimal" portfolios simply doesn't work.[2]

In 1991, Fisher Black and Robert Litterman of Goldman-Sachs published an approach that deals with many of the problematics of portfolio optimization. Black and Litterman start with the assumption that an investor chooses his optimal portfolio from among a given group of assets. This group of assets—it might be the Standard & Poor's 500 Index, the Russell 2000, or a mix of international indexes—defines the framework within which the investor chooses his portfolio. The investor's universe of assets defines a *benchmark* portfolio.

The Black-Litterman model takes as its starting point the assumption that, in the absence of additional information, the benchmark cannot be outperformed. This assumption is based on much research, which shows that it is very difficult to outperform a typical well-diversified benchmark.[3]

In effect the Black-Litterman model turns modern portfolio theory on its head—instead of inputting data and deriving an optimal portfolio, the

2. A recent paper by DeMiguel, Garlappi, and Uppal (2007), "Optimal versus Naive Diversification: How Inefficient Is the 1/N Portfolio Strategy?," forthcoming in *The Review of Financial Studies*, illustrates how badly mechanical optimization works. The authors examine optimal allocations among ten sector portfolios. They find that a naive portfolio allocation rule of investing equal proportions in each portfolio—irrespective of market values—outperforms more sophisticated data-based optimizations.

3. According to Lipper Analytical Services, "over the ten years ended in June 2000, more than 80% of 'general equity' mutual funds, meaning garden variety stock funds, underperformed the Standard and Poor's 500 Index—the major benchmark for stock mutual funds" (quoted in http://www.fool.com/Seminars/OLA/2001/Retire1_4C.htm). Or, from a well-known academic: "Professional investment managers, both in the U.S. and abroad, do not outperform their index benchmarks" Burton G. Malkiel, "Reflections on the Efficient Market Hypothesis: 30 Years Later." *The Francial Review*, Vol. 40, 2005, pp. 1–9.)

BL approach assumes that a given portfolio is optimal and from this assumption derives the expected returns of the benchmark components. The implied vector of expected benchmark returns is the starting point of the BL model.

The BL implied asset returns can be interpreted as the market's information about the future returns of each asset in the benchmark portfolio. If our investor agrees with this market assessment, he's finished: He can then buy the benchmark, knowing that it is optimal. But what if he disagrees with one or more of the implied returns? Black and Litterman show how the investor's opinions can be incorporated into the optimization problem to produce a portfolio that is better for the investor.

In this chapter we start with an illustration of the problematics of MPT. We then go on to illustrate the Black-Litterman approach.

13.2 A Naive Problem

We start with a naive, though representative, problem: The Super Duper Fund has set its benchmark portfolio to be a portfolio composed of 10 leading stocks. Joanna Roe, a new portfolio analyst for the Super Duper Fund, has decided to use portfolio theory to recommend optimal portfolio holdings based on this benchmark. The following screen gives five years of monthly price data on these stocks as of 1 July 2006 (note that some of the rows have been hidden):

	A	B	C	D	E	F	G	H	I	J	K	L
1	PRICE AND MARKET CAP DATA FOR 10 COMPANIES											
2		General Motors GM	Home Depot HD	International Paper IP	Hewlett-Packard HPQ	Altria MO	American Express AXP	Alcoa Aluminum AA	DuPont DD	Merck MRK	MMM	
3	Equity value	16.85	73.98	15.92	88.37	153.33	65.66	28.16	38.32	79.51	60.9	
4	Benchmark proportion	2.71%	11.91%	2.56%	14.23%	24.69%	10.57%	4.53%	6.17%	12.80%	9.81%	<-- =K3/SUM($B$3:$K$3)
5												
6	Monthly price data (includes dividends)											
7	1-Jun-01	50.31	45.26	31.22	26.47	38.74	32.47	36.06	40.88	50.74	51.56	
8	2-Jul-01	49.72	48.26	35.64	22.83	35.61	33.82	35.37	36.29	53.98	50.55	
9	1-Aug-01	43.14	44.06	35.32	21.48	37.10	30.54	34.50	35.01	51.96	47.30	
10	4-Sep-01	33.81	36.79	30.66	14.92	37.79	24.37	28.06	32.07	53.16	44.71	
11	1-Oct-01	32.56	36.66	31.50	15.65	36.63	24.75	29.34	34.18	50.93	47.43	
12	1-Nov-01	39.63	44.78	35.37	20.45	36.92	27.68	35.09	38.21	54.07	52.33	
13	3-Dec-01	38.75	48.97	35.73	19.17	36.34	30.02	32.32	36.63	47.18	53.99	
14	2-Jan-02	40.77	48.09	36.99	20.64	39.71	30.22	32.59	38.06	47.48	50.70	
15	1-Feb-02	42.67	48.00	38.96	18.78	41.73	30.72	34.31	40.68	49.21	54.16	
16	1-Mar-02	48.69	46.71	38.30	16.81	42.21	34.52	34.47	40.95	46.46	52.81	
17	1-Apr-02	51.67	44.56	36.90	16.02	43.62	34.64	31.08	38.65	43.85	57.77	
61	1-Dec-05	19.01	40.17	33.12	28.48	73.08	51.23	29.30	41.77	31.10	76.60	
62	3-Jan-06	23.56	40.24	32.15	31.02	70.75	52.33	31.21	38.48	33.73	71.91	
63	1-Feb-06	20.11	41.83	32.53	32.64	70.32	53.76	29.19	39.91	34.09	73.20	
64	1-Mar-06	21.06	42.13	34.32	32.81	70.06	52.43	30.43	41.87	34.83	75.29	
65	3-Apr-06	22.66	39.77	36.09	32.38	72.34	53.81	33.63	43.74	34.03	84.98	
66	1-May-06	26.93	37.97	33.98	32.29	71.54	54.36	31.72	42.53	33.29	83.66	
67	1-Jun-06	29.79	35.79	32.30	31.68	73.43	53.22	32.36	41.60	36.43	80.77	

Row 3 gives the current equity value of each of the benchmark stocks, and row 4 computes the benchmark proportions—the individual equity values divided by the total market capitalization of the benchmark.

Following the procedures described in Chapters 9 and 10, Joanna first transforms the price data to returns and then computes a variance-covariance matrix for these returns:

	A	B	C	D	E	F	G	H	I	J	K
1	RETURN DATA FOR THE SUPER DUPER BENCHMARK PORTFOLIO										
2		General Motors GM	Home Depot HD	International paper IP	Hewlett-Packard HPQ	Altria MO	American Express AXP	Alcoa Aluminum AA	DuPont DD	Merck MRK	MMM
3	Equity value (billion $)	16.85	73.98	15.92	88.37	153.33	65.66	28.16	38.32	79.51	60.9
4	Benchmark proportion	2.71%	11.91%	2.56%	14.23%	24.69%	10.57%	4.53%	6.17%	12.80%	9.81%
5											
6	Mean return	-0.87%	-0.39%	0.06%	0.30%	1.07%	0.82%	-0.18%	0.03%	-0.55%	0.75%
7	Return sigma	10.78%	8.41%	6.23%	10.80%	8.71%	6.43%	9.54%	6.12%	8.06%	5.54%
8											
9											
10	Date	GM	HD	IP	HPQ	MO	AXP	AA	DD	MRK	MMM
11	2-Jul-01	-1.18%	6.42%	13.24%	-14.79%	-8.42%	4.07%	-1.93%	-11.91%	6.19%	-1.98%
12	1-Aug-01	-14.20%	-9.11%	-0.90%	-6.10%	4.10%	-10.20%	-2.49%	-3.59%	-3.81%	-6.65%
13	4-Sep-01	-24.37%	-18.03%	-14.15%	-36.44%	1.84%	-22.57%	-20.66%	-8.77%	2.28%	-5.63%
14	1-Oct-01	-3.77%	-0.35%	2.70%	4.78%	-3.12%	1.55%	4.46%	6.37%	-4.29%	5.91%
15	1-Nov-01	19.65%	20.01%	11.59%	26.75%	0.79%	11.19%	17.90%	11.15%	5.98%	9.83%
16	3-Dec-01	-2.25%	8.94%	1.01%	-6.46%	-1.58%	8.12%	-8.22%	-4.22%	-13.63%	3.12%
17	2-Jan-02	5.08%	-1.81%	3.47%	7.39%	8.87%	0.66%	0.83%	3.83%	0.63%	-6.29%
61	1-Sep-05	-11.06%	-5.56%	-3.48%	5.32%	5.28%	3.90%	-9.25%	-1.02%	-3.66%	3.05%
62	3-Oct-05	-11.10%	7.33%	-2.08%	-4.05%	1.81%	-0.78%	-0.54%	6.25%	3.63%	3.50%
63	1-Nov-05	-20.55%	2.02%	8.56%	5.66%	-3.06%	3.28%	12.70%	3.39%	5.40%	3.77%
64	1-Dec-05	-12.03%	-3.16%	6.39%	-3.32%	3.67%	0.08%	7.58%	-0.60%	7.86%	-1.26%
65	3-Jan-06	21.46%	0.17%	-2.97%	8.54%	-3.24%	2.12%	6.32%	-8.20%	8.12%	-6.32%
66	1-Feb-06	-15.83%	3.88%	1.18%	5.09%	-0.61%	2.70%	-6.69%	3.65%	1.06%	1.78%
67	1-Mar-06	4.62%	0.71%	5.36%	0.52%	-0.37%	-2.51%	4.16%	4.79%	2.15%	2.82%
68	3-Apr-06	7.32%	-5.76%	5.03%	-1.32%	3.20%	2.60%	10.00%	4.37%	-2.32%	12.11%
69	1-May-06	17.26%	-4.63%	-6.02%	-0.28%	-1.11%	1.02%	-5.85%	-2.81%	-2.20%	-1.57%
70	1-Jun-06	10.09%	-5.91%	-5.07%	-1.91%	2.61%	-2.12%	2.00%	-2.21%	9.01%	-3.52%

13.2.1 Naive Optimization

Using the return data, Joanna computes the sample variance-covariance matrix of excess returns as illustrated in Chapter 10. To implement the portfolio optimization, she needs data on the T-bill rate: The 1 July 2006 T-bill rate is 4.83 percent annually, and 4.83 percent/12 = 0.40 percent monthly. Using the variance-covariance matrix, the T-bill rate, and the historical mean returns, she computes an "optimal" portfolio by solving the equation

$$\text{Optimal portfolio } \{x_1, x_2, \ldots, x_{10}\} = \frac{S^{-1}\begin{bmatrix} \bar{r}_{\text{GM}} - r_f \\ \bar{r}_{\text{HD}} - r_f \\ \vdots \\ \bar{r}_{\text{MMM}} - r_f \end{bmatrix}}{[1, 1, \ldots, 1] * S^{-1} * \begin{bmatrix} \bar{r}_{\text{GM}} - r_f \\ \bar{r}_{\text{HD}} - r_f \\ \vdots \\ \bar{r}_{\text{MMM}} - r_f \end{bmatrix}} = \frac{S^{-1}\begin{bmatrix} \bar{r}_{\text{GM}} - r_f \\ \bar{r}_{\text{HD}} - r_f \\ \vdots \\ \bar{r}_{\text{MMM}} - r_f \end{bmatrix}}{\text{Sum}\left[S^{-1} * \begin{bmatrix} \bar{r}_{\text{GM}} - r_f \\ \bar{r}_{\text{HD}} - r_f \\ \vdots \\ \bar{r}_{\text{MMM}} - r_f \end{bmatrix} \right]}$$

This portfolio is as follows (highlighted):

	A	B	C	D	E	F	G	H	I	J	K	L	M
1	SUPER DUPER BENCHMARK PORTFOLIO--NAIVE OPTIMIZATION												
2		General Motors GM	Home Depot HD	International paper IP	Hewlett-Packard HPQ	Altria MO	American Express AXP	Alcoa Aluminum AA	DuPont DD	Merck MRK	MMM		
3	Equity value	16.85	73.98	15.92	88.37	153.33	65.66	28.16	38.32	79.51	60.9		
4	Benchmark proportion	2.71%	11.91%	2.56%	14.23%	24.69%	10.57%	4.53%	6.17%	12.80%	9.81%		
5													
6	**Variance-covariance matrix of excess returns**												
7		GM	HD	IP	HPQ	MO	AXP	AA	DD	MRK	MMM		Mean return
8	GM	0.0116	0.0030	0.0023	0.0041	0.0013	0.0032	0.0046	0.0018	0.0010	0.0014		-0.87%
9	HD	0.0030	0.0071	0.0018	0.0042	0.0022	0.0033	0.0045	0.0020	0.0002	0.0018		-0.39%
10	IP	0.0023	0.0018	0.0039	0.0031	0.0001	0.0023	0.0043	0.0021	0.0012	0.0016		0.06%
11	HPQ	0.0041	0.0042	0.0031	0.0117	0.0025	0.0048	0.0060	0.0033	0.0019	0.0022		0.30%
12	MO	0.0013	0.0022	0.0001	0.0025	0.0076	0.0016	0.0018	0.0009	0.0007	0.0008		1.07%
13	AXP	0.0032	0.0033	0.0023	0.0048	0.0016	0.0041	0.0037	0.0019	0.0011	0.0014		0.82%
14	AA	0.0046	0.0045	0.0043	0.0060	0.0018	0.0037	0.0091	0.0040	0.0018	0.0024		-0.18%
15	DD	0.0018	0.0020	0.0021	0.0033	0.0009	0.0019	0.0040	0.0038	0.0016	0.0019		0.03%
16	MRK	0.0010	0.0002	0.0012	0.0019	0.0007	0.0011	0.0018	0.0016	0.0065	0.0005		-0.55%
17	MMM	0.0014	0.0018	0.0016	0.0022	0.0008	0.0014	0.0024	0.0019	0.0005	0.0031		0.75%
18													
19	Current t-bill rate	0.40%											
20													
21	"Optimal" portfolio												
22	GM	480.2%	<-- {=MMULT(MINVERSE(B8:K17),M8:M17-B19)/SUM(MMULT(MINVERSE(B8:K17),M8:M17-B19))}										
23	HD	981.8%											
24	IP	689.3%											
25	HPQ	221.3%											
26	MO	-263.7%											
27	AXP	-1763.7%											
28	AA	-324.5%											
29	DD	528.8%											
30	MRK	469.5%											
31	MMM	-918.9%											
32	Sum of proportions	1	<-- =SUM(B22:B31)										

The “optimal” portfolio shown in cells B22:B31 is clearly not practically implementable: It contains too many large positions (both negative and positive). Note, for example, the –1763.7 percent short position in AXP and the 528.8 percent position in DD. Most mutual funds are prevented from taking short positions, and even funds that sell short will find it difficult to short-sell 17.63 times the fund value in AXP or 9.19 times the fund value in MMM. The enormous long positions that result from these short-sale positions (for example 9.82 times fund value invested long in HD) are similarly impracticable.

13.2.2 Why Does Naive Optimization Fail?

In some sense the strange portfolio “optimization” positions were predictable. The spreadsheet that follows highlights some disturbing features of the data that can partially explain the odd “optimized” portfolio.

- A number of the historical mean returns are negative. If we ignore the effects of correlations, a negative expected return should imply a short position in the stock. There is, however, a deeper philosophical question about using past returns as proxies for future expected returns: Even though the past returns are negative, there is no reason to assume that the future, expected returns from a stock should be negative. This is one of the problems when we use historical data to extract anticipations about the future.
- The correlations between asset returns are in some cases very large. Large correlations for a particular stock can lead us to prefer other stocks with smaller returns but more moderate correlations.

The following spreadsheet highlights stocks with negative historical returns and stocks whose correlations are greater than 0.5:

	A	B	C	D	E	F	G	H	I	J	K	L
1	NEGATIVE RETURNS AND HIGH CORRELATIONS											
2		General Motors GM	Home Depot HD	International Paper IP	Hewlett-Packard HPQ	Altria MO	American Express AXP	Alcoa Aluminum AA	DuPont DD	Merck MRK	MMM	
3	Equity value	16.85	73.98	15.92	88.37	153.33	65.66	28.16	38.32	79.51	60.9	
4	Benchmark proportion	2.71%	11.91%	2.56%	14.23%	24.69%	10.57%	4.53%	6.17%	12.80%	9.81%	
5												
6	Mean return	-0.87%	-0.39%	0.06%	0.30%	1.07%	0.82%	-0.18%	0.03%	-0.55%	0.75%	
7	Return sigma	10.78%	8.41%	6.23%	10.80%	8.71%	6.43%	9.54%	6.12%	8.06%	5.54%	
8												
9												
10		GM	HD	IP	HPQ	MO	AXP	AA	DD	MRK	MMM	
11	GM	1.0000	0.3320	0.3459	0.3534	0.1428	0.4676	0.4430	0.2737	0.1109	0.2277	<-- =CORREL($B$24:$B$83,K24:K83)
12	HD		1.0000	0.3512	0.4618	0.3012	0.6061	0.5618	0.3891	0.0260	0.3800	<-- =CORREL($C$24:$C$83,K24:K83)
13	IP			1.0000	0.4580	0.0159	0.5772	0.7181	0.5400	0.2362	0.4575	<-- =CORREL($D$24:$D$83,K24:K83)
14	HPQ				1.0000	0.2682	0.6965	0.5770	0.4924	0.2232	0.3666	
15	MO					1.0000	0.2839	0.2145	0.1647	0.0955	0.1645	
16	AXP						1.0000	0.6034	0.4855	0.2038	0.3798	
17	AA							1.0000	0.6863	0.2294	0.4525	
18	DD								1.0000	0.3287	0.5606	
19	MRK									1.0000	0.1079	
20	MMM										1.0000	

13.2.3 What about Changing the Variance-Covariance Matrix?

In Chapter 10 we discussed various methods for shrinking the variance-covariance matrix. "Shrinkage," you will recall, is a bit of jargon for taking a convex combination of the sample var-cov matrix with a diagonal matrix of only the variances. Shrinkage methods have been shown to be effective at improving the performance of the global minimum variance portfolio (GMVP).

Will shrinkage help us solve the extreme positions of the naive portfolio optimization? We make this attempt in the next spreadsheet, where cells B11:K20 contain a weighted combination of the sample covariance matrix (B39:K48) and an all-diagonal matrix of only the variances (B52:K61). The weight λ put on the sample covariance matrix is given in cell B7.

For $\lambda = 0.3$, the "optimal" portfolio indeed contains fewer extreme long and short positions. But it is clear that shrinkage can never solve the fundamental problem of the data—using negative historical returns as proxies for expected returns will always produce some negative portfolio positions in an optimizer. It is this problem which Black and Litterman solve and which we discuss in the next section.

	A	B	C	D	E	F	G	H	I	J	K	L	M
1	**SUPER DUPER BENCHMARK PORTFOLIO--NAIVE OPTIMIZATION WITH SHRUNK VARIANCE-COVARIANCE MATRIX**												
2		General Motors GM	Home Depot HD	International paper IP	Hewlett-Packard HPQ	Altria MO	American Express AXP	Alcoa Aluminum AA	DuPont DD	Merck MRK	MMM		
3	Equity value	16.85	73.98	15.92	88.37	153.33	65.66	28.16	38.32	79.51	60.9		
4	Benchmark proportion	2.71%	11.91%	2.56%	14.23%	24.69%	10.57%	4.53%	6.17%	12.80%	9.81%		
5													
6	**Variance-covariance matrix of excess returns**												
7	Shrinkage factor, λ	0.3	<-- Weight on sample var-cov matrix										
8													
9	The following matrix is a weighted combination of the sample variance-covariance matrix and a pure diagonal matrix of only variances. {=B7*B39:K48+(1-B7)*B52:K61}												
10		GM	HD	IP	HPQ	MO	AXP	AA	DD	MRK	MMM		Mean return
11	GM	0.0116	0.0009	0.0007	0.0012	0.0004	0.0010	0.0014	0.0005	0.0003	0.0004		-0.87%
12	HD	0.0009	0.0071	0.0006	0.0013	0.0007	0.0010	0.0014	0.0006	0.0001	0.0005		-0.39%
13	IP	0.0007	0.0006	0.0039	0.0009	0.0000	0.0007	0.0013	0.0006	0.0004	0.0005		0.06%
14	HPQ	0.0012	0.0013	0.0009	0.0117	0.0008	0.0015	0.0018	0.0010	0.0006	0.0007		0.30%
15	MO	0.0004	0.0007	0.0000	0.0008	0.0076	0.0005	0.0005	0.0003	0.0002	0.0002		1.07%
16	AXP	0.0010	0.0010	0.0007	0.0015	0.0005	0.0041	0.0011	0.0006	0.0003	0.0004		0.82%
17	AA	0.0014	0.0014	0.0013	0.0018	0.0005	0.0011	0.0091	0.0012	0.0005	0.0007		-0.18%
18	DD	0.0005	0.0006	0.0006	0.0010	0.0003	0.0006	0.0012	0.0038	0.0005	0.0006		0.03%
19	MRK	0.0003	0.0001	0.0004	0.0006	0.0002	0.0003	0.0005	0.0005	0.0065	0.0001		-0.55%
20	MMM	0.0004	0.0005	0.0005	0.0007	0.0002	0.0004	0.0007	0.0006	0.0001	0.0031		0.75%
21													
22	Current T-bill rate	0.40%											
23													
24	"Optimal" portfolio												
25	GM	84.3%	<-- {=MMULT(MINVERSE(B11:K20),M11:M20-B22)/SUM(MMULT(MINVERSE(B11:K20),M11:M20-B22))}										
26	HD	96.4%											
27	IP	50.2%											
28	HPQ	-3.6%											
29	MO	-76.1%											
30	AXP	-134.6%											
31	AA	32.5%											
32	DD	62.5%											
33	MRK	112.1%											
34	MMM	-123.8%											
35	Sum of proportions	1	<-- =SUM(B25:B34)										
36													
37	**Variance-covariance matrix of excess returns**												
38		GM	HD	IP	HPQ	MO	AXP	AA	DD	MRK	MMM		
39	GM	0.0116	0.0030	0.0023	0.0041	0.0013	0.0032	0.0046	0.0018	0.0010	0.0014		
40	HD	0.0030	0.0071	0.0018	0.0042	0.0022	0.0033	0.0045	0.0020	0.0002	0.0018		
41	IP	0.0023	0.0018	0.0039	0.0031	0.0001	0.0023	0.0043	0.0021	0.0012	0.0016		
42	HPQ	0.0041	0.0042	0.0031	0.0117	0.0025	0.0048	0.0060	0.0033	0.0019	0.0022		
43	MO	0.0013	0.0022	0.0001	0.0025	0.0076	0.0016	0.0018	0.0009	0.0007	0.0008		
44	AXP	0.0032	0.0033	0.0023	0.0048	0.0016	0.0041	0.0037	0.0019	0.0011	0.0014		
45	AA	0.0046	0.0045	0.0043	0.0060	0.0018	0.0037	0.0091	0.0040	0.0018	0.0024		
46	DD	0.0018	0.0020	0.0021	0.0033	0.0009	0.0019	0.0040	0.0038	0.0016	0.0019		
47	MRK	0.0010	0.0002	0.0012	0.0019	0.0007	0.0011	0.0018	0.0016	0.0065	0.0005		
48	MMM	0.0014	0.0018	0.0016	0.0022	0.0008	0.0014	0.0024	0.0019	0.0005	0.0031		
49													
50	**Pure diagonal matrix. The array formula in the cells produces a matrix with only variances on the diagonal and zero elsewhere. {=IF(B51:K51=A52:A61,B39:K48,0)}**												
51		GM	HD	IP	HPQ	MO	AXP	AA	DD	MRK	MMM		
52	GM	0.0116	0.0000	0.0000	0.0000	0.0000	0.0000	0.0000	0.0000	0.0000	0.0000		
53	HD	0.0000	0.0071	0.0000	0.0000	0.0000	0.0000	0.0000	0.0000	0.0000	0.0000		
54	IP	0.0000	0.0000	0.0039	0.0000	0.0000	0.0000	0.0000	0.0000	0.0000	0.0000		
55	HPQ	0.0000	0.0000	0.0000	0.0117	0.0000	0.0000	0.0000	0.0000	0.0000	0.0000		
56	MO	0.0000	0.0000	0.0000	0.0000	0.0076	0.0000	0.0000	0.0000	0.0000	0.0000		
57	AXP	0.0000	0.0000	0.0000	0.0000	0.0000	0.0041	0.0000	0.0000	0.0000	0.0000		
58	AA	0.0000	0.0000	0.0000	0.0000	0.0000	0.0000	0.0091	0.0000	0.0000	0.0000		
59	DD	0.0000	0.0000	0.0000	0.0000	0.0000	0.0000	0.0000	0.0038	0.0000	0.0000		
60	MRK	0.0000	0.0000	0.0000	0.0000	0.0000	0.0000	0.0000	0.0000	0.0065	0.0000		
61	MMM	0.0000	0.0000	0.0000	0.0000	0.0000	0.0000	0.0000	0.0000	0.0000	0.0031		

13.3 Black and Litterman's Solution to the Optimization Problem

The Black-Litterman approach provides an initial solution to the optimization problem we have presented. The BL approach is composed of two parts:

Step 1: *What does the market think*? A vast amount of financial research shows that it is difficult to beat the returns of benchmark portfolios. The first step of the BL approach takes this research as a starting point. It assumes that the benchmark is optimal and derives the expected returns of each asset under this assumption. To put it another way, in Step 1 we compute the expected returns of the assets that would make the investor choose the benchmark using the optimization techniques in Chapters 9–11.

Step 2: *Incorporating investor opinions*. In Step 1, Black and Litterman show how to compute the benchmark asset returns based on the assumption of optimality. Suppose the investor has divergent opinions from these market-based expected returns. Step 2 shows how to incorporate these opinions into the optimization procedure. Note that—because of the correlations between asset returns—an investor's opinion about any particular asset's returns will affect all the other expected returns. A critical part in Step 2 is to adjust *all* asset returns for an investor's opinion about any return.

An investor who follows the Black-Litterman procedure starts off by seeing what the market weights imply for the expected returns. He can then adjust these weights by adding his own opinions about any asset's expected returns. In the next two sections we discuss these two steps in detail.

13.4 Black-Litterman Step 1: What Does the Market Think?

As shown in Chapter 9, an optimal portfolio must solve the equation

$$\begin{bmatrix} \text{Efficient} \\ \text{portfolio} \\ \text{proportions} \end{bmatrix} = \underbrace{\begin{bmatrix} \text{Variance-} \\ \text{covariance} \\ \text{matrix} \end{bmatrix}^{-1} * \left\{ \begin{bmatrix} \text{Expected} \\ \text{portfolio} \\ \text{returns} \end{bmatrix} - \text{Risk-free rate} \right\}}_{\uparrow \atop \text{Normalize to sum to 1}}$$

Solving the equation for the vector of expected portfolio returns, this expression means that an efficient portfolio must solve the following equation:

$$\begin{bmatrix}\text{Expected}\\ \text{portfolio}\\ \text{returns}\end{bmatrix} = \begin{bmatrix}\text{Variance-}\\ \text{covariance}\\ \text{matrix}\end{bmatrix}\begin{bmatrix}\text{Efficient}\\ \text{portfolio}\\ \text{proportions}\end{bmatrix} * \begin{matrix}\text{Normalizing}\\ \text{factor}\end{matrix} + \begin{matrix}\text{Risk-free}\\ \text{rate}\end{matrix}$$

Joanna assumes that, in the absence of any additional knowledge or opinions about the market, the current market weights of the portfolio indicate the efficiency weights. She estimates that the expected benchmark return over the next month will be 1 percent and uses this estimation to set the normalizing factor.[4]

Solving the first part of the latter equation (without the normalizing factor) gives the following:

	A	B	C	D	E	F	G	H	I	J	K	L	M
1	**SUPER DUPER BENCHMARK PORTFOLIO--WHAT DOES THE MARKET THINK?** **No normalizing factor**												
2	Anticipated benchmark return	1.00%	<-- =12%/12										
3	Current t-bill rate	0.40%											
4													
5		General Motors GM	Home Depot HD	International Paper IP	Hewlett-Packard HPQ	Altria MO	American Express AXP	Alcoa Aluminum AA	DuPont DD	Merck MRK	MMM		
6	Equity value	16.85	73.98	15.92	88.37	153.33	65.66	28.16	38.32	79.51	60.9		
7	Benchmark proportions	2.71%	11.91%	2.56%	14.23%	24.69%	10.57%	4.53%	6.17%	12.80%	9.81%		
8													
9	**Variance-covariance matrix**												
10		GM	HD	IP	HPQ	MO	AXP	AA	DD	MRK	MMM		Without normalizing factor
11	GM	0.0116	0.0030	0.0023	0.0041	0.0013	0.0032	0.0046	0.0018	0.0010	0.0014		0.27%
12	HD	0.0030	0.0071	0.0018	0.0042	0.0022	0.0033	0.0045	0.0020	0.0002	0.0018		0.31%
13	IP	0.0023	0.0018	0.0039	0.0031	0.0001	0.0023	0.0043	0.0021	0.0012	0.0016		0.18%
14	HPQ	0.0041	0.0042	0.0031	0.0117	0.0025	0.0048	0.0060	0.0033	0.0019	0.0022		0.46%
15	MO	0.0013	0.0022	0.0001	0.0025	0.0076	0.0016	0.0018	0.0009	0.0007	0.0008		0.31%
16	AXP	0.0032	0.0033	0.0023	0.0048	0.0016	0.0041	0.0037	0.0019	0.0011	0.0014		0.27%
17	AA	0.0046	0.0045	0.0043	0.0060	0.0018	0.0037	0.0091	0.0040	0.0018	0.0024		0.37%
18	DD	0.0018	0.0020	0.0021	0.0033	0.0009	0.0019	0.0040	0.0038	0.0016	0.0019		0.21%
19	MRK	0.0010	0.0002	0.0012	0.0019	0.0007	0.0011	0.0018	0.0016	0.0065	0.0005		0.18%
20	MMM	0.0014	0.0018	0.0016	0.0022	0.0008	0.0014	0.0024	0.0019	0.0005	0.0031		0.16%
21													
22	Check: The expected return of the benchmark?	0.29%	<-- {=MMULT(B7:K7,M11:M20)}					Cells M11:M20 contain the array formula					
23								{=MMULT(B11:K20,TRANSPOSE(B7:K7)+B3)}					
24													

Note that given the weights in row 7, the expected benchmark return is 0.29 percent per month as opposed to the 1 percent per month posited by Joanne (cell B2). To achieve this expected benchmark returns we multiply row 7 by a normalizing factor.

4. One percent per month is equivalent to estimating an annual expected benchmark return of 12 percent.

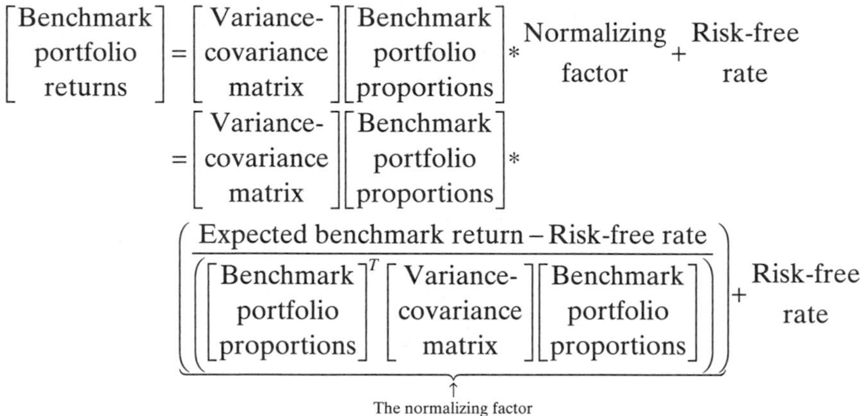

$$\begin{bmatrix}\text{Benchmark}\\\text{portfolio}\\\text{returns}\end{bmatrix}=\begin{bmatrix}\text{Variance-}\\\text{covariance}\\\text{matrix}\end{bmatrix}\begin{bmatrix}\text{Benchmark}\\\text{portfolio}\\\text{proportions}\end{bmatrix}*\begin{matrix}\text{Normalizing}\\\text{factor}\end{matrix}+\begin{matrix}\text{Risk-free}\\\text{rate}\end{matrix}$$

$$=\begin{bmatrix}\text{Variance-}\\\text{covariance}\\\text{matrix}\end{bmatrix}\begin{bmatrix}\text{Benchmark}\\\text{portfolio}\\\text{proportions}\end{bmatrix}*\underbrace{\left(\frac{\text{Expected benchmark return}-\text{Risk-free rate}}{\left(\begin{bmatrix}\text{Benchmark}\\\text{portfolio}\\\text{proportions}\end{bmatrix}^T\begin{bmatrix}\text{Variance-}\\\text{covariance}\\\text{matrix}\end{bmatrix}\begin{bmatrix}\text{Benchmark}\\\text{portfolio}\\\text{proportions}\end{bmatrix}\right)}\right)}_{\uparrow\ \text{The normalizing factor}}+\begin{matrix}\text{Risk-free}\\\text{rate}\end{matrix}$$

This procedure is illustrated in the next spreadsheet:

	A	B	C	D	E	F	G	H	I	J	K	L	M
1	**SUPER DUPER BENCHMARK PORTFOLIO--WHAT DOES THE MARKET THINK?** **We multiply row 7 by a normalizing factor** **The expected returns make the benchmark optimal**												
2	Anticipated benchmark return	1.00%	<-- =12%/12										
3	Current t-bill rate	0.40%											
4													
5		General Motors GM	Home Depot HD	International Paper IP	Hewlett-Packard HPQ	Altria MO	American Express AXP	Alcoa Aluminum AA	DuPont DD	Merck MRK	MMM		
6	Equity value	16.85	73.98	15.92	88.37	153.33	65.66	28.16	38.32	79.51	60.9		
7	Benchmark proportions	2.71%	11.91%	2.56%	14.23%	24.69%	10.57%	4.53%	6.17%	12.80%	9.81%		
8													
9	**Variance-covariance matrix**												
10		GM	HD	IP	HPQ	MO	AXP	AA	DD	MRK	MMM		With normalizing factor
11	GM	0.0116	0.0030	0.0023	0.0041	0.0013	0.0032	0.0046	0.0018	0.0010	0.0014		0.96%
12	HD	0.0030	0.0071	0.0018	0.0042	0.0022	0.0033	0.0045	0.0020	0.0002	0.0018		1.05%
13	IP	0.0023	0.0018	0.0039	0.0031	0.0001	0.0023	0.0043	0.0021	0.0012	0.0016		0.77%
14	HPQ	0.0041	0.0042	0.0031	0.0117	0.0025	0.0048	0.0060	0.0033	0.0019	0.0022		1.36%
15	MO	0.0013	0.0022	0.0001	0.0025	0.0076	0.0016	0.0018	0.0009	0.0007	0.0008		1.05%
16	AXP	0.0032	0.0033	0.0023	0.0048	0.0016	0.0041	0.0037	0.0019	0.0011	0.0014		0.97%
17	AA	0.0046	0.0045	0.0043	0.0060	0.0018	0.0037	0.0091	0.0040	0.0018	0.0024		1.17%
18	DD	0.0018	0.0020	0.0021	0.0033	0.0009	0.0019	0.0040	0.0038	0.0016	0.0019		0.84%
19	MRK	0.0010	0.0002	0.0012	0.0019	0.0007	0.0011	0.0018	0.0016	0.0065	0.0005		0.77%
20	MMM	0.0014	0.0018	0.0016	0.0022	0.0008	0.0014	0.0024	0.0019	0.0005	0.0031		0.73%
21													
22	Check: The expected return of the benchmark?	1.00%	<-- {=MMULT(B7:K7,M11:M20)}					Cells M11:M20 contain the array formula {=(MMULT(B11:K20,TRANSPOSE(B7:K7))*(B2-B3)/MMULT(B7:K7,MMULT(B11:K20,TRANSPOSE(B7:K7))))+B3}					
23													
24													
25													
26	Additional check: Optimal portfolio												
27	GM	2.71%	<-- {=MMULT(MINVERSE(B11:K20),M11:M20-B3)/SUM(MMULT(MINVERSE(B11:K20),M11:M20-B3))}										
28	HD	11.91%											
29	IP	2.56%											
30	HPQ	14.23%		Note that Chapter 9 optimization on the expected returns in cells M11:M20 and the variance-covariance matrix produces the market weights as the optimal portfolio.									
31	MO	24.69%											
32	AXP	10.57%											
33	AA	4.53%											
34	DD	6.17%											
35	MRK	12.80%											
36	MMM	9.81%											
37	Sum of proportions	100.0%	<-- =SUM(B27:B36)										

We have performed an additional check in the spreadsheet by deriving the optimal portfolio given the current T-bill rate of 0.40 percent and the expected returns in M11:M20. This should give us back the benchmark proportions in row 7—and it does!

13.5 Black-Litterman Step 2: Introducing Opinions—What Does Joanna Think?

Having made two assumptions—(1) that the benchmark is efficient and (2) that the expected benchmark return is 1 percent per month—Joanna has derived the expected returns for each of the benchmark components (cells M11:M20). We are now ready to introduce Joanna's opinions about asset returns. The rough idea is that if she disagrees with a market return, she can use the optimization procedure from Chapter 9 to derive a portfolio whose proportions differ from those of the benchmark.

We have to be careful, however: Because asset returns are correlated, any opinion Joanna has about one asset's returns will translate to an opinion about all other asset returns. To illustrate this point, suppose that Joanna thinks that the return on GM will be 1.1 percent over the next month instead of the market opinion of 0.96 percent. Then this assumption translates to the following picture:

	A	B	C	D	E	F	G	H	I	J	K	L
1	**ADJUSTING THE BENCHMARK FOR AN ANALYST'S OPINION** In this example the only opinion is about GM											
2	Anticipated benchmark return	1.00%	<-- =12%/12									
3	Current t-bill rate	0.40%										
4												
5		General Motors GM	Home Depot HD	International Paper IP	Hewlett-Packard HPQ	Altria MO	American Express AXP	Alcoa Aluminum AA	DuPont DD	Merck MRK	MMM	
6	Market cap (billion $)	16.85	73.98	15.92	88.37	153.33	65.66	28.16	38.32	79.51	60.9	
7	Benchmark proportions	2.71%	11.91%	2.56%	14.23%	24.69%	10.57%	4.53%	6.17%	12.80%	9.81%	
8												
9	**Variance-covariance matrix**											
10		GM	HD	IP	HPQ	MO	AXP	AA	DD	MRK	MMM	
11	GM	0.0116	0.0030	0.0023	0.0041	0.0013	0.0032	0.0046	0.0018	0.0010	0.0014	
12	HD	0.0030	0.0071	0.0018	0.0042	0.0022	0.0033	0.0045	0.0020	0.0002	0.0018	
13	IP	0.0023	0.0018	0.0039	0.0031	0.0001	0.0023	0.0043	0.0021	0.0012	0.0016	
14	HPQ	0.0041	0.0042	0.0031	0.0117	0.0025	0.0048	0.0060	0.0033	0.0019	0.0022	
15	MO	0.0013	0.0022	0.0001	0.0025	0.0076	0.0016	0.0018	0.0009	0.0007	0.0008	
16	AXP	0.0032	0.0033	0.0023	0.0048	0.0016	0.0041	0.0037	0.0019	0.0011	0.0014	
17	AA	0.0046	0.0045	0.0043	0.0060	0.0018	0.0037	0.0091	0.0040	0.0018	0.0024	
18	DD	0.0018	0.0020	0.0021	0.0033	0.0009	0.0019	0.0040	0.0038	0.0016	0.0019	
19	MRK	0.0010	0.0002	0.0012	0.0019	0.0007	0.0011	0.0018	0.0016	0.0065	0.0005	
20	MMM	0.0014	0.0018	0.0016	0.0022	0.0008	0.0014	0.0024	0.0019	0.0005	0.0031	
21												
22												
23	Expected benchmark returns, no opinions	Analyst opinion, delta		Returns adjusted for opinions						Optimized benchmark proportions		Portfolio benchmark, no opinions
24	0.96%	0.14%	GM	1.10%	<--					7.85%	GM	2.71%
25	1.05%	0.00%	HD	1.08%	{=A24:A33+MMULT(TRANSPOS					11.28%	HD	11.91%
26	0.77%	0.00%	IP	0.80%	E(B38:K47),B24:B33)}					2.43%	IP	2.56%
27	1.36%	0.00%	HPQ	1.41%						13.48%	HPQ	14.23%
28	1.05%	0.00%	MO	1.07%		Cells J24:J33 contain the array formula {=MMULT(MINVERSE(B11:K20),D24:D33-B3)/SUM(MMULT(MINVERSE(B11:K20),D24:D33-B3))}				23.39%	MO	24.69%
29	0.97%	0.00%	AXP	1.00%						10.01%	AXP	10.57%
30	1.17%	0.00%	AA	1.23%						4.30%	AA	4.53%
31	0.84%	0.00%	DD	0.86%						5.84%	DD	6.17%
32	0.77%	0.00%	MRK	0.78%						12.13%	MRK	12.80%
33	0.73%	0.00%	MMM	0.75%						9.29%	MMM	9.81%
34												
35												
36	**Tracking factors: in each row i Cov(r_i,r_j) is divided by Var(r_i)**											
37		GM	HD	IP	HPQ	MO	AXP	AA	DD	MRK	MMM	
38	GM	1.0000	0.2589	0.1999	0.3540	0.1153	0.2788	0.3920	0.1555	0.0829	0.1169	
39	HD	0.4257	1.0000	0.2603	0.5934	0.3119	0.4635	0.6376	0.2834	0.0250	0.2501	
40	IP	0.5985	0.4738	1.0000	0.7940	0.0222	0.5954	1.0994	0.5306	0.3056	0.4063	
41	HPQ	0.3527	0.3594	0.2642	1.0000	0.2162	0.4145	0.5097	0.2791	0.1665	0.1878	
42	MO	0.1769	0.2909	0.0114	0.3328	1.0000	0.2096	0.2351	0.1158	0.0884	0.1046	
43	AXP	0.7843	0.7927	0.5595	1.1704	0.3845	1.0000	0.8956	0.4624	0.2556	0.3270	
44	AA	0.5006	0.4950	0.4690	0.6533	0.1957	0.4066	1.0000	0.4404	0.1938	0.2625	
45	DD	0.4820	0.5343	0.5496	0.8687	0.2342	0.5097	1.0694	1.0000	0.4327	0.5067	
46	MRK	0.1483	0.0272	0.1826	0.2991	0.1032	0.1626	0.2715	0.2497	1.0000	0.0741	
47	MMM	0.4437	0.5772	0.5151	0.7156	0.2588	0.4412	0.7802	0.6202	0.1571	1.0000	

The δ introduced in column B of the preceding figure indicates Joanna's deviation from the Black-Litterman base case. In this example, Joanna thinks that GM will have a monthly return 0.14 percent higher than the market's return of 0.96 percent (cell B24). Because of the covariance between asset returns, this change means that the HD return she expects is 1.11 percent:

$$r_{\text{HD, opinion adjusted}} = r_{\text{HD, market}} + \frac{\text{Cov}(r_{\text{HD}}, r_{\text{GM}})}{\text{Var}(r_{\text{HD}})}\delta_{\text{GM}} = 1.11\%$$

$$r_{\text{IP, opinion adjusted}} = r_{\text{IP, market}} + \frac{\text{Cov}(r_{\text{IP,}} r_{\text{GM}})}{\text{Var}(r_{\text{IP}})} \delta_{\text{GM}} = 0.86\%$$

and so on.

The newly optimized portfolio is given in cells J24:J33. Joanna's opinion about GM has dramatically changed the portfolio composition from its benchmark weights (L24:L33):

	J	K	L
23	Optimized benchmark proportions		Portfolio benchmark, no opinions
24	7.85%	GM	2.71%
25	11.28%	HD	11.91%
26	2.43%	IP	2.56%
27	13.48%	HPQ	14.23%
28	23.39%	MO	24.69%
29	10.01%	AXP	10.57%
30	4.30%	AA	4.53%
31	5.84%	DD	6.17%
32	12.13%	MRK	12.80%
33	9.29%	MMM	9.81%

Notice that Joanna's positive opinion about GM returns has, predictably, increased the proportion of GM in her portfolio. But the opinion about GM has also affected all the other portfolio weights—increasing the weight on AXP, decreasing the weight on AA, ...

13.5.1 Two or More Opinions

If Joanna has two or more opinions, the situation becomes more difficult. Suppose, for example, that she believes the GM return will be 1.10 percent instead of its market return of 0.96 percent and the HD return will be 1 percent instead of its market return of 1.05 percent. Using **Solver** we can find a solution for δ_{GM} and δ_{HD} that gives an opinion-adjusted return of 1.10 percent for GM and 1.00 percent for HD:

We achieved this result by using **Solver**:

	B	C	D	E	F	G	H	I	J	K	L
9			Solver Parameters								
10	GM	HD							MRK	MMM	
11	0.0116	0.0030							0.0010	0.0014	
12	0.0030	0.0071	Set Objective:		$D$24				0.0002	0.0018	
13	0.0023	0.0018							0.0012	0.0016	
14	0.0041	0.0042	To: Max		Min	Value Of:		0.011	0.0019	0.0022	
15	0.0013	0.0022							0.0007	0.0008	
16	0.0032	0.0033	By Changing Variable Cells:						0.0011	0.0014	
17	0.0046	0.0045	$B$24:$B$25						0.0018	0.0024	
18	0.0018	0.0020							0.0016	0.0019	
19	0.0010	0.0002	Subject to the Constraints:						0.0065	0.0005	
20	0.0014	0.0018	$D$25 = 0.01						0.0005	0.0031	
21											
22											
23	Analyst opinion, delta		Returns adjusted for opinions						Optimized benchmark proportions		Portfolio benchmark, no opinions
24	0.18%	GM	1.10%	<--					9.89%	GM	2.71%
25	-0.09%	HD	1.00%	{=A24:A33+MMULT(TRANSPOS					5.70%	HD	11.91%
26	0.00%	IP	0.78%	E(B38:K47),B24:B33)}					2.53%	IP	2.56%
27	0.00%	HPQ	1.37%						14.07%	HPQ	14.23%
28	0.00%	MO	1.04%		Cells J24:J33 contain the array formula {=MMULT(MINVERSE(B11:K20),D24:D33-B3)/SUM(MMULT(MINVERSE(B11:K20),D24:D33-B3))}				24.41%	MO	24.69%
29	0.00%	AXP	0.97%						10.45%	AXP	10.57%
30	0.00%	AA	1.18%						4.48%	AA	4.53%
31	0.00%	DD	0.84%						6.10%	DD	6.17%
32	0.00%	MRK	0.78%						12.66%	MRK	12.80%
33	0.00%	MMM	0.73%						9.70%	MMM	9.81%

Note The philosophically inclined reader might well ask what an "opinion" really is. In this example we have limited the deltas to be only about GM and HD. However, suppose we allow deltas for other assets; then we get a whole class of "opinions" that fit the bill of having $E(r_{GM})$ = 1.10 percent and $E(r_{HD})$ = 1.00 percent. For example, if we are willing to allow δs for all the assets, we could ask **Solver** for a minimal set of divergent opinions ( ) that gives Joanna's two expected returns for GM and HD:

	A	B	C	D	E	F	G	H	I	J
23	Expected benchmark returns, no opinions	Analyst opinion, delta		Returns adjusted for opinions						Optimized benchmark proportions
24	0.96%	0.14%	GM	1.10%	<--					7.74%
25	1.05%	-0.13%	HD	1.00%	{=A24:A33+MMULT(TRANSPOS					2.92%
26	0.77%	0.04%	IP	0.84%	E(B38:K47),B24:B33)}					6.73%
27	1.36%	0.01%	HPQ	1.42%						13.70%
28	1.05%	-0.01%	MO	1.03%		Cells J24:J33 contain the array formula {=MMULT(MINVERSE(B11:K20),D24:D33-B3)/SUM(MMULT(MINVERSE(B11:K20),D24:D33-B3))}				22.45%
29	0.97%	0.03%	AXP	1.01%						12.56%
30	1.17%	0.02%	AA	1.24%						5.09%
31	0.84%	0.01%	DD	0.88%						6.78%
32	0.77%	0.02%	MRK	0.82%						13.49%
33	0.73%	0.00%	MMM	0.75%						8.53%

In the preceding spreadsheet clip, we have solved for the minimal squared deltas that give the requisite opinions about GM and HD.[5]

13.5.2 Do You Believe Your Opinions?

Do we really believe our own opinions? Do we actually have confidence in what we believe? There is a whole theory of Bayesian adjustments to our beliefs, which is adumbrated in Theil (1971).[6] An application to portfolio modeling can be found in Black and Litterman (1991) and other associated papers. This author finds these papers dauntingly complicated and difficult to implement. A simpler approach to the confidence question is to form a portfolio based on a convex combination of the market weights and the opinion-adjusted weights:

$$\text{Portfolio proportions} = (1-\gamma)*\text{Market weights} + \gamma*\text{Opinion-adjusted weights}$$

where γ is our degree of confidence in our opinions. Here is an application to our last example:

	A	B	C	D	E	F	G	H	I	J
23	Expected benchmark returns, no opinions	Analyst opinion, delta		Returns adjusted for opinions						Optimized benchmark weights
24	0.96%	0.18%		1.10%	<-- {=A24:A33+MMULT(TRANSPOSE(B56:K65),B24:B3					9.76%
25	1.05%	-0.09%		1.00%						5.94%
26	0.77%	0.00%		0.79%						2.53%
27	1.36%	0.00%		1.37%		Cells J24:J33 contain the array formula {=MMULT(MINVERSE(B11:K20),D24:D33-B3)/SUM(MMULT(MINVERSE(B11:K20),D24:D33-B3))}				14.05%
28	1.05%	0.00%		1.04%						24.38%
29	0.97%	0.00%		0.97%						10.44%
30	1.17%	0.00%		1.19%						4.48%
31	0.84%	0.00%		0.84%						6.09%
32	0.77%	0.00%		0.78%						12.64%
33	0.73%	0.00%		0.73%						9.68%
34										
35	γ, opinion confidence	0.60	<-- Weight attached to analyst opinion							
36										
37	**Opinion and confidence-adjusted portfolio**									
38	GM	6.94%	<-- =(1-$B$35)*L24+$B$35*J24							
39	HD	8.33%								
40	IP	2.54%								
41	HPQ	14.12%								
42	MO	24.50%								
43	AXP	10.49%								
44	AA	4.50%								
45	DD	6.12%								
46	MRK	12.71%								
47	MMM	9.73%								
48	Sum of weights	100.00%								

5. Note that this vector of deltas is not unique. If we replace cell B35 by the sum of the absolute values of delta, we will get a different set of deltas (see exercises to this chapter).

6. Theil, Henri. 1971. *Principles of Econometrics*. New York: Wiley and Sons.

13.6 Implementing Black-Litterman on an International Portfolio

We end this chapter by implementing the BL model on data for five international indices.[7] The spreadsheet that follows gives data on five major world stock market indices:

1. The S&P 500, a value-weighted index of the 500 largest U.S. stocks.
2. The MSCI World ex-US index: The Morgan Stanley Capital International (MSCI) World ex-US index comprises 21 developed countries based on GDP per capita.
3. The Russell 2000 index: The Russell 3000 Index is market cap weighted and captures about 98 percent of the investable U.S. marketplace. The Russell 2000 Index consists of the 2,000 smallest companies in the Russell 3000 Index.
4. The MSCI Emerging Markets index: The Morgan Stanley Capital International (MSCI) Emerging Markets index consists of indexes for 26 emerging economies.
5. The LB Global Aggregate index: This Lehman Brothers index covers the most liquid portion of the global investment-grade fixed-rate bond market, including government, credit, and collateralized securities.

	A	B	C	D	E	F	G	H	I
1		INDEX DATA, 2001-2005							
2	5 YEARS ENDING DEC05								
3	Correlation	S&P 500	MSCI World ex-US	Russell 2000	MSCI Emerging	LB Global Aggregate		Weight	Standard deviation
4	S&P 500	1.0000	0.8800	0.8400	0.8100	-0.1600		24%	14.90%
5	MSCI World ex-US	0.8800	1.0000	0.8300	0.8700	0.0700		26%	15.60%
6	Russell 2000	0.8400	0.8300	1.0000	0.8300	-0.1400		3%	19.20%
7	MSCI Emerging	0.8100	0.8700	0.8300	1.0000	-0.0500		3%	21.00%
8	LB Global Aggregate	-0.1600	0.0700	-0.1400	-0.0500	1.0000		44%	5.80%
9								100%	

Column H gives the weights on the index in a composite portfolio as of the end of December 2005, and column I gives the standard deviation of each index component.

7. I thank Steven Schoenfeld of Northern Trust for providing me with the data and some suggestions.

13.6.1 The Variance-Covariance Matrix

We first use the wonders of the Excel array functions (see Chapter 34) to compute the variance-covariance matrix for the five indexes:

	A	B	C	D	E	F	G	H
12	Variance-covariance matrix: cells contain formula {=I4:I8*TRANSPOSE(I4:I8)*B4:F8}							
13	**Variance-covariance matrix**	**S&P 500**	**MSCI World ex-US**	**Russell 2000**	**MSCI Emerging**	**LB Global Aggregate**		
14	**S&P 500**	0.0222	0.0205	0.0240	0.0253	-0.0014		
15	**MSCI World ex-US**	0.0205	0.0243	0.0249	0.0285	0.0006		
16	**Russell 2000**	0.0240	0.0249	0.0369	0.0335	-0.0016		
17	**MSCI Emerging**	0.0253	0.0285	0.0335	0.0441	-0.0006		
18	**LB Global Aggregate**	-0.0014	0.0006	-0.0016	-0.0006	0.0034		
19								
20	**Checks**							
21	First row of var-cov	0.0222	0.0205	0.0240	0.0253	-0.0014	<-- =I4*I8*F4	
22	Standard deviation of composite	8.72%	<-- {=SQRT(MMULT(MMULT(TRANSPOSE(H4:H8),B14:F18),H4:H8))}					

The strange formula, I4:I8*TRANSPOSE(I4:I8)*B4:F8, in the cells B14:F19 is composed of two parts:

• I4:I8*TRANSPOSE(I4:I8) multiplies the column vector I4:I8 times its transpose. This is equivalent to multiplying

$$\begin{bmatrix} \sigma_{\text{SP500}} \\ \sigma_{\text{MSCI World}} \\ \sigma_{\text{Russell 2000}} \\ \sigma_{\text{MSCI Emerging}} \\ \sigma_{\text{LB Global}} \end{bmatrix} * \begin{bmatrix} \sigma_{\text{SP500}} & \sigma_{\text{MSCI World}} & \sigma_{\text{Russell 2000}} & \sigma_{\text{MSCI Emerging}} & \sigma_{\text{LB Global}} \end{bmatrix}$$

Which—in the wonderful world of array functions—gives a matrix of the covariances:

$$\begin{bmatrix} \sigma^2_{\text{SP500}} & \sigma_{\text{SP500}}\sigma_{\text{MSCI World}} & \sigma_{\text{SP500}}\sigma_{\text{Russell 2000}} & \sigma_{\text{SP500}}\sigma_{\text{LB Global}} \\ \sigma_{\text{MSCI World}}\sigma_{\text{SP500}} & \sigma^2_{\text{MSCI World}} & \cdots & \\ \vdots & & & \\ \vdots & & & \\ \sigma_{\text{LB Global}}\sigma_{\text{SP500}} & \sigma_{\text{LB Global}}\sigma_{\text{MSCI World}} & \cdots & \cdots\ \sigma^2_{\text{LB Global}} \end{bmatrix}$$

• Multiplying the preceding by the matrix of correlations B4:F8 gives the variance-covariance matrix.

• Of course the whole array formula I4:I8*TRANSPOSE(I4:I8)*B4:F8 is entered with [Ctrl] + [Shift] + [Enter].

In rows 21 and 22 we perform two checks on our computation: Row 21 contains brute-force computations of the first row of the variance-covariance matrix—just to make sure our array formula works as advertised. In cell B22 we compute the standard deviation of the five-index portfolio using their relative weights.

	A	B	C	D	E	F
25	Risk-free rate	5.00%				
26	Expected return on S&P 500	12.00%				
27						
28	**Black-Litterman implied returns**					
29	**S&P 500**	12.00%	<-- {=MMULT(B14:F18,H4:H8)*(B26-			
30	**MSCI World ex-US**	13.66%	B25)/INDEX((MMULT(B14:F18,H4:H8)),1,1)+B25}			
31	**Russell 2000**	14.22%				
32	**MSCI Emerging**	16.20%				
33	**LB Global aggregate**	1.30%				

The Black-Litterman implied expected returns are based on three assumptions:

• The weighted portfolio of the five indexes is mean-variance optimal.

• The anticipated risk-free rate is 5 percent.

• The expected return of the S&P 500 index is 12 percent.

Given these assumptions, the expected returns on the five-index portfolio are given in cells B29:B33. Note the array formula given in these cells:

=MMULT(B14:F18,H4:H8)*(B26-B25)/INDEX
((MMULT(B14:F18,H4:H8)),1,1)+B25

This formula uses the expected return on the S&P 500 to normalize the returns. It is equivalent to

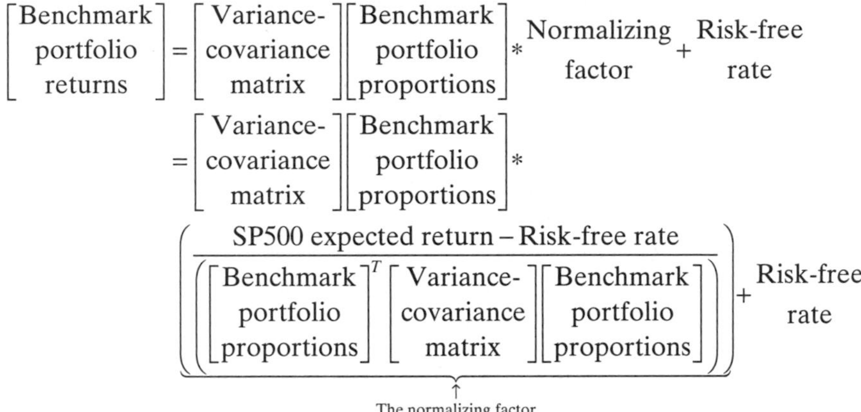

13.6.2 What's the Upshot?

If we believe that the world portfolio is efficient (and in the absence of further information, there is little reason to believe otherwise), then the anticipated returns from each of its components are given by the Black-Litterman model, by the risk-free rate, and by an additional assumption on expected returns (in our case, the expected return of the S&P 500 index). The exercises for this chapter explore some other variations to the latter assumption.

13.7 Summary

Applying portfolio theory is not merely a matter of using historical market data to derive covariances and expected returns. Blindly applying sample data to derive optimal portfolios (as in section 13.2) usually leads to absurd results. The Black-Litterman approach gets around these absurdities by first assuming that—in the absence of analyst opinions and other information—the benchmark market weights and current risk-free interest rate correctly predict the future asset returns. The resulting asset returns can then be adjusted for opinions and confidence in opinions to derive an optimal portfolio.

Exercises

1. You have decided to create your own index of high-beta components of the Dow-Jones 30 Industrials. Using Yahoo's stock screener, you come up with the following data.

	A	B	C	D	E	F	G	H	I	J	K	L	M	N	O
1	HIGH-BETA INDEX FROM DOW-JONES 30 COMPONENTS														
2		3M Company MMM	Alcoa AA	American Express AXP	American International Group AIG	Caterpillar CAT	Dupont DD	Exxon XOM	Hewlett Packard HPQ	Home Depot HD	Honeywell HON	Intel INTC	IBM	McDonalds MCD	Merck MRK
3	Market cap ($B)	65.66	39.11	77.91	180.72	55.7	49.08	519.89	126.75	78.37	47.55	146.76	172.03	62.88	106.93
4	Beta	1.07	1.37	1.06	1.17	1.98	1.06	1.13	1.6	1.2	1.3	1.9	1.81	1.37	1.16
5															
6	**Stock prices**														
7	2-Jul-02	56.69	24.41	29.46	61.98	20.21	35.54	32.85	13.22	29.07	28.77	17.76	67.04	22.57	38.95
8	1-Aug-02	56.56	22.64	30.12	60.89	19.73	34.46	31.88	12.54	31.00	26.78	15.78	71.94	21.67	39.67
9	3-Sep-02	49.78	17.41	26.05	53.08	16.83	30.84	28.69	10.96	24.61	19.37	13.14	55.65	16.11	36.16
10	1-Oct-02	57.47	19.91	30.46	60.70	18.64	35.27	30.27	14.84	27.23	21.41	16.37	75.34	16.52	42.91
64	2-Apr-07	82.31	35.32	60.52	69.75	72.32	48.81	79.04	42.07	37.66	53.95	21.39	101.81	48.28	51.06
65	1-May-07	87.96	41.28	64.82	72.34	78.25	52.32	83.17	45.63	38.65	57.91	22.18	106.60	50.55	52.06
66	1-Jun-07	86.79	40.53	61.03	70.03	77.97	50.84	83.88	44.62	39.35	56.28	23.74	105.25	50.76	49.80
67	2-Jul-07	90.21	43.08	64.51	69.04	83.20	52.62	91.94	48.54	39.39	60.96	24.55	114.81	52.09	49.02

a. Compute the variance-covariance matrix of returns.

b. Assuming that the risk-free rate is 5.25% annually (=5.25%/12=0.44% monthly), and that the expected high-beta index annual return is 12% (= 1% monthly), compute the Black-Litterman monthly expected returns for each stock.

2. You are an analyst investing in the high-beta DJ30 portfolio from the previous exercise. You believe that the monthly return of MMM will be 1%. What are your recommended optimal portfolio proportions?

3. Another analyst believes that HD will return only 0.5% per month over the next year. What are her recommended portfolio proportions?

14 Event Studies[1]

14.1 Overview

Event studies are one of the most powerful and widely used applications of the capital asset pricing model (CAPM) discussed in Chapters 8–11. An event study is an attempt to determine whether a particular event in the capital market or in the life of a company has affected a company's stock market performance. The event-study methodology aims to separate company-specific events from market- and industry-specific events, and has often been used as evidence for or against market efficiency.

An event study aims to determine whether an event or announcement caused an abnormal movement in a company's stock price. The *abnormal returns* (AR) are calculated as the difference between a stock's actual return and its expected return, where the stock's expected return is typically measured using the market model, which relies only on a stock's market index to estimate its expected return.[2] Using the market model can measure the correlation between an individual stock's return and its corresponding market returns. In some cases, we sum the abnormal returns to arrive at the *cumulative abnormal return* (CAR), which measures the total impact of an event through a particular time period, also called the event window.

14.2 Outline of an Event Study

In this section we outline the methodology of an event study. In succeeding sections we apply the methodology to a number of different cases.

An event study is composed of three time frames: the *estimation window* (sometimes referred to as the control period), the *event window*, and the *postevent window*. The following chart illustrates these time frames:

1. This chapter was coauthored with Torben Voetmann (tvoetmann@cornerstone.com) of Cornerstone Research.

2. Abnormal returns are also referred to as residual returns, and both terms are used interchangeably throughout the chapter.

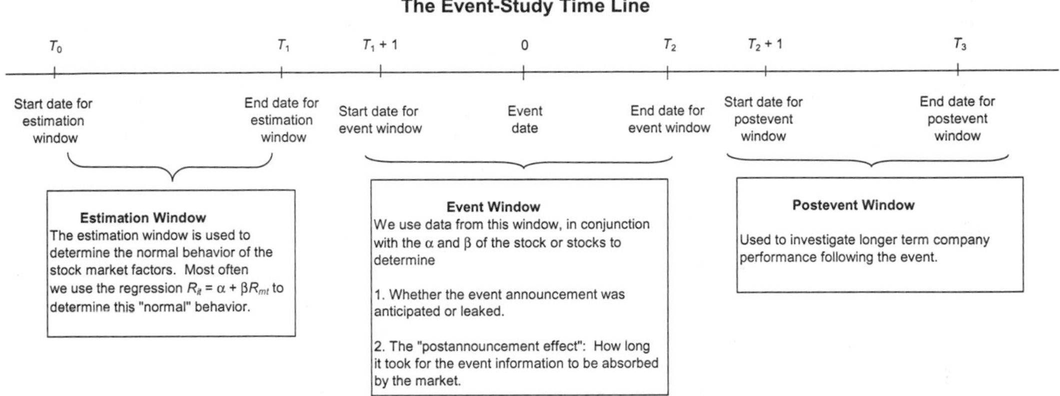
The Event-Study Time Line
T_0
T_1
$T_1 + 1$
0
T_2
$T_2 + 1$
T_3
Start date for estimation window
End date for estimation window
Start date for event window
Event date
End date for event window
Start date for postevent window
End date for postevent window
Estimation Window
The estimation window is used to determine the normal behavior of the stock market factors. Most often we use the regression $R_{it} = \alpha + \beta R_{mt}$ to determine this "normal" behavior.
Event Window
We use data from this window, in conjunction with the α and β of the stock or stocks to determine
1. Whether the event announcement was anticipated or leaked.
2. The "postannouncement effect": How long it took for the event information to be absorbed by the market.
Postevent Window
Used to investigate longer term company performance following the event.

The time line illustrates the timing sequence of an event. The length of the estimation window (also referred to as the control period) is represented as T_0 to T_1. The event occurs at time 0, and the event window is represented as $T_1 + 1$ to T_2. The length of the postevent window is represented as $T_2 + 1$ to T_3.

An event is defined as a point in time when a company makes an announcement or when a significant market event occurs. For example, if we are studying the impact of mergers and acquisitions on the stock market, the announcement date is normally the point of interest. If we are examining how the market reacts to earnings restatements, the event window begins on the date when a company announces its restatements. A common practice is to expand the event date to two trading days, the event date and the following trading day. This is done to capture the market movement if the event was announced immediately before the market closed or after market closing.

The *event window* often starts a few trading days before the actual event day. The length of the event window is centered on the announcement and is normally three, five, or ten days. This procedure enables us to investigate preevent leakage of information. The *postevent window* is most often used to investigate the performance of a company following announcements such as a major acquisition or an IPO.

The *estimation window* is also used to determine the normal behavior of a stock's return with respect to a market or industry index. The estimation of the stock's return in the estimation window requires us to define a model of "normal" behavior: Most often we use a regression model for this purpose.[3]

The usual length of the estimation window is 252 trading days (or one calendar year), but you may not always have this many days in your sample. If not, you need to determine whether the number of observations you do have is sufficient to produce robust results. As a guideline, you should have a minimum of 126 observations; if you have less than 126 observations in the estimation window, it is possible that the parameters of the market model will not indicate the true stock price movements, and thus the relationship between the stock returns and the market returns. The estimation window that you select is supposedly a period that was free of any problems—that is, a period that reflects the stock's normal price movements.

The *postevent window* allows us to measure the longer term impact of the event. The postevent window can be as short as one month and as long as several years depending on the event.

14.2.1 Measuring the Stock's Behavior in the Estimation Window and the Event Window

As its name implies, the *estimation window* is used to estimate a model of the stock's returns under "normal" circumstances. The most common model used for this purpose is the market model, which is essentially a regression of the stock returns and the returns of the market index.[4] The market model for a stock i can be expressed as

$$r_{it} = \alpha_i + \beta_i r_{Mt}$$

Here r_{it} and r_{Mt} represent the stock and the market return on day t. The coefficients α_i and β_i are estimated by running an ordinary least-square regression over the estimation window.

The most common criteria for selecting market and industry indexes are whether the company is listed on NYSE/AMEX or Nasdaq and whether any restrictions are imposed by data availability. In general, the market index should be a broad-based value-weighted index or a float-

3. The regression model is similar to the first-pass regression discussed in Chapter 11. See further discussion that follows.

4. Financial economists most often use the market model to estimate the expected return of a security, although they sometimes use the market-adjusted model or the two-factor market model. An example of the two-factor model will be presented in section 14.5.

weighted index. The industry index should be specific to the company being analyzed. For litigation purposes, it is common to construct the industry index instead of using alternative S&P 500 or MSCI indexes (most industry indexes are available from Yahoo).[5]

Given the equation $r_{it} = \alpha_i + \beta_i r_{Mt}$ in the estimation window, we can now measure the impact of an event on the stock's return in the event window. For a particular day t in the event window, we define the stock's *abnormal return* (AR) as the difference between its actual return and the return that would be predicted by the equation

$$AR_{it} = \underbrace{r_{it}}_{\substack{\uparrow \\ \text{Actual stock} \\ \text{return in event} \\ \text{window day } t}} - \underbrace{(\alpha_i + \beta_i r_{Mt})}_{\substack{\uparrow \\ \text{Return predicted} \\ \text{by the stock's } \alpha, \\ \beta, \text{ and market return}}}$$

We interpret the abnormal return during the event window as a measure of the impact the event had on the market value of the security. This interpretation assumes that the event is exogenous with respect to the change in the security's market value.

The *cumulative abnormal return* (CAR) is a measure of the total abnormal returns during the event window. The variable CAR_t is the sum of all the abnormal returns from the beginning of the event window T_1 until a particular day t in the window:

$$CAR_t = \sum_{j=1}^{t} AR_{T_1+j}$$

14.2.2 Market-Adjusted and Two-Factor Models

As mentioned previously, you can use several alternative models to calculate a security's expected return. The market-adjusted model is simplest in design and is often used to get a first impression of stock price movements. When using the market-adjusted model, you calculate the abnormal return by taking the difference between the actual return of

5. Yahoo is probably not the best source for index data (though it is free!). A widely used source for industry data is Bloomberg. A wonderful free source of industry portfolio data is available from Fama-French at http://mba.tuck.dartmouth.edu/pages/faculty/ken.french/data_library.html.

the security and the actual return of the market index. Thus there is no need to run OLS regressions to estimate parameters. In fact, all you need is the returns at the time of the event. However, when testing the abnormal returns for statistical significance, you still need to gather returns for the estimation period.

The two-factor model compares the returns from the market and the industry. You calculate a stock's expected return using parameters from a regression of the actual returns against the market and industry returns during the estimation period. The industry returns are included primarily to account for industry-specific information in addition to the market-specific information. To calculate the abnormal return you subtract from the actual return the portion that can be explained by the market and the portion that can be explained by the industry. The two-factor model is illustrated in detail in section 14.5.

As Brown and Warner (1985) showed, the results in a large sample of events are not especially sensitive to your choice of estimation model. However, if you are dealing with a small sample, you should explore alternative models.

14.3 An Initial Event Study: Procter & Gamble Buys Gillette

On 28 January 2005, Procter & Gamble announced a bid for Gillette Company. As can be seen from the press release on page 379, the bid valued Gillette at a premium of 18 percent over its market price. As might be expected, the bid had a dramatic effect on Gillette's stock price:

From the graph it appears that there might have also been a decrease in the price of Procter & Gamble.

14.3.1 The Estimation Window

We will attempt an event study to judge the impact of the takeover announcement on the returns of Gillette and Procter & Gamble. We first determine the event window as the 252 trading days preceding the two days before the announcement on 28 January 2005:

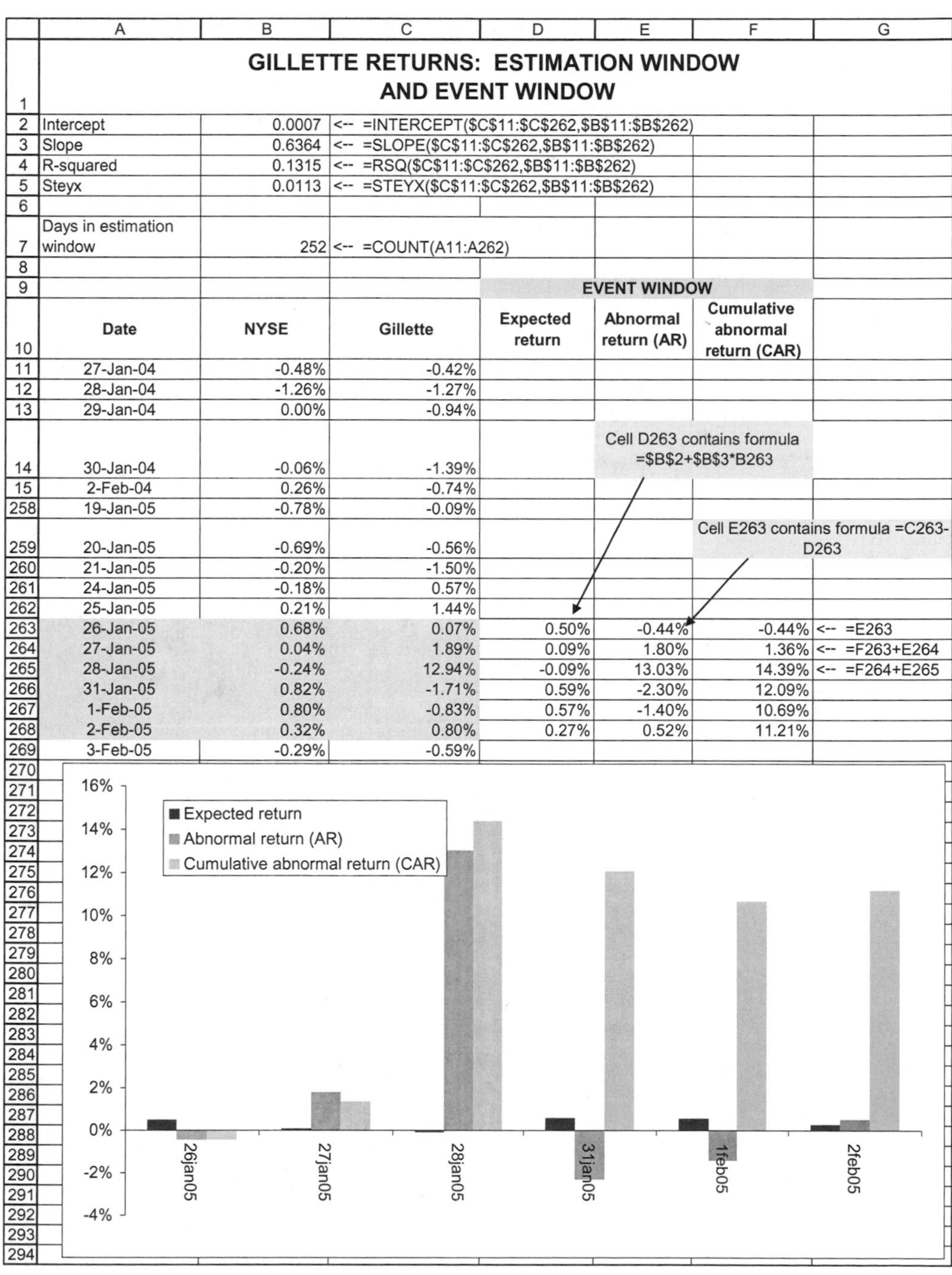

	A	B	C	D	E	F	G
1	**GILLETTE RETURNS: ESTIMATION WINDOW AND EVENT WINDOW**						
2	Intercept	0.0007	<-- =INTERCEPT($C$11:$C$262,$B$11:$B$262)				
3	Slope	0.6364	<-- =SLOPE($C$11:$C$262,$B$11:$B$262)				
4	R-squared	0.1315	<-- =RSQ($C$11:$C$262,$B$11:$B$262)				
5	Steyx	0.0113	<-- =STEYX($C$11:$C$262,$B$11:$B$262)				
6							
7	Days in estimation window	252	<-- =COUNT(A11:A262)				
8							
9					**EVENT WINDOW**		
10	**Date**	**NYSE**	**Gillette**	**Expected return**	**Abnormal return (AR)**	**Cumulative abnormal return (CAR)**	
11	27-Jan-04	-0.48%	-0.42%				
12	28-Jan-04	-1.26%	-1.27%				
13	29-Jan-04	0.00%	-0.94%				
14	30-Jan-04	-0.06%	-1.39%		Cell D263 contains formula =$B$2+$B$3*B263		
15	2-Feb-04	0.26%	-0.74%				
258	19-Jan-05	-0.78%	-0.09%				
259	20-Jan-05	-0.69%	-0.56%			Cell E263 contains formula =C263-D263	
260	21-Jan-05	-0.20%	-1.50%				
261	24-Jan-05	-0.18%	0.57%				
262	25-Jan-05	0.21%	1.44%				
263	26-Jan-05	0.68%	0.07%	0.50%	-0.44%	-0.44%	<-- =E263
264	27-Jan-05	0.04%	1.89%	0.09%	1.80%	1.36%	<-- =F263+E264
265	28-Jan-05	-0.24%	12.94%	-0.09%	13.03%	14.39%	<-- =F264+E265
266	31-Jan-05	0.82%	-1.71%	0.59%	-2.30%	12.09%	
267	1-Feb-05	0.80%	-0.83%	0.57%	-1.40%	10.69%	
268	2-Feb-05	0.32%	0.80%	0.27%	0.52%	11.21%	
269	3-Feb-05	-0.29%	-0.59%				

The regression results indicate the normal behavior of Gillette in the estimation window:

$r_{\text{Gillette},t} = 0.0007 + 0.6364 r_{\text{NYSE},t}$

The **Steyx** function measures the standard error of the regression-predicted y-values. In the next subsection we show how to use this value to measure the significance of the event's abnormal returns.

14.3.2 The Event Window

We define the event window as two days before and three days after the announcement. To measure the impact of the announcement effect in the event window we use the market model $r_{\text{Gillette},t} = 0.0007 + 0.6356 r_{\text{NYSE},t}$. The formulas in the event window are in the preceding spreadsheet. As you can see, the announcement of the acquisition of Gillette by Procter & Gamble led to several large abnormal Gillette returns in the event window.

We can use **Steyx**, the standard error of the regression prediction, to measure the significance of the abnormal returns. Only two of the abnormal returns—on the event date 28 January and the day following—are actually significant at the 5 percent level:

	A	B	C	D	E	F	G	H	I
1		GILLETTE RETURNS: THE SIGNIFICANCE OF THE ABNORMAL RETURNS							
2	Intercept	0.0007	<-- =INTERCEPT($C$11:$C$262,$B$11:$B$262)						
3	Slope	0.6364	<-- =SLOPE($C$11:$C$262,$B$11:$B$262)						
4	R-squared	0.1315	<-- =RSQ($C$11:$C$262,$B$11:$B$262)						
5	Steyx	0.0113	<-- =STEYX($C$11:$C$262,$B$11:$B$262)						
6									
7	Days in estimation window	252	<-- =COUNT(A11:A262)						
8									
9				EVENT WINDOW					
10	Date	NYSE	Gillette	Abnormal return (AR)	AR t-test	AR signicant?			
11	27-Jan-04	-0.48%	-0.42%						
12	28-Jan-04	-1.26%	-1.27%						
13	29-Jan-04	0.00%	-0.94%						
14	30-Jan-04	-0.06%	-1.39%						
15	2-Feb-04	0.26%	-0.74%						
258	19-Jan-05	-0.78%	-0.09%						
259	20-Jan-05	-0.69%	-0.56%						
260	21-Jan-05	-0.20%	-1.50%						
261	24-Jan-05	-0.18%	0.57%						
262	25-Jan-05	0.21%	1.44%						
263	26-Jan-05	0.68%	0.07%	-0.44%	-0.39	no			
264	27-Jan-05	0.04%	1.89%	1.80%	1.59	no			
265	28-Jan-05	-0.24%	12.94%	13.03%	11.56	yes			
266	31-Jan-05	0.82%	-1.71%	-2.30%	-2.04	yes			
267	1-Feb-05	0.80%	-0.83%	-1.40%	-1.24	no			
268	2-Feb-05	0.32%	0.80%	0.52%	0.46	no			
269	3-Feb-05	-0.29%	-0.59%						

Cell D263 contains formula =C263-($B$2+$B$3*B263)

Cell E263 contains formula =D263/$B$5

Cell F263 contains formula =IF(ABS(E263)<1.96,"no","yes")

We define the test statistic for the abnormal return AR by dividing AR by the **Steyx** in cell B5. Assuming that the regression residuals are normally distributed, if the absolute value of the test statistic is larger than 1.96, then the abnormal return is significant at the 95 percent level (meaning that the chances that the abnormal return is random and insignificant is less than 5 percent). If the test statistic is larger than 2.58, its significance level is 1 percent. As can be seen from rows 263–268, at the 1 percent level, only the announcement itself has a significant abnormal return.[6]

14.3.3 What about Procter & Gamble?

Thus far we have concentrated on the event influence on the takeover target, Gillette. Applying the same methodology to Procter & Gamble's stock returns shows that the announcement had a negative impact on its stock returns. There may also have been some leakage of the information prior to the announcement on 28 January 2005:

6. One limitation of **Steyx** is that the variance is slightly understated. The true variance of the market model is the estimation variance from **Steyx** and the additional variance due to the sampling error in α_i and β_i. However, the sampling error approaches zero as the length of the estimation window increases. Since we suggest using 252 trading days in the estimation window, the effect of the sampling error is minimal, and it is, therefore, often disregarded when calculating the variance of the abnormal returns.

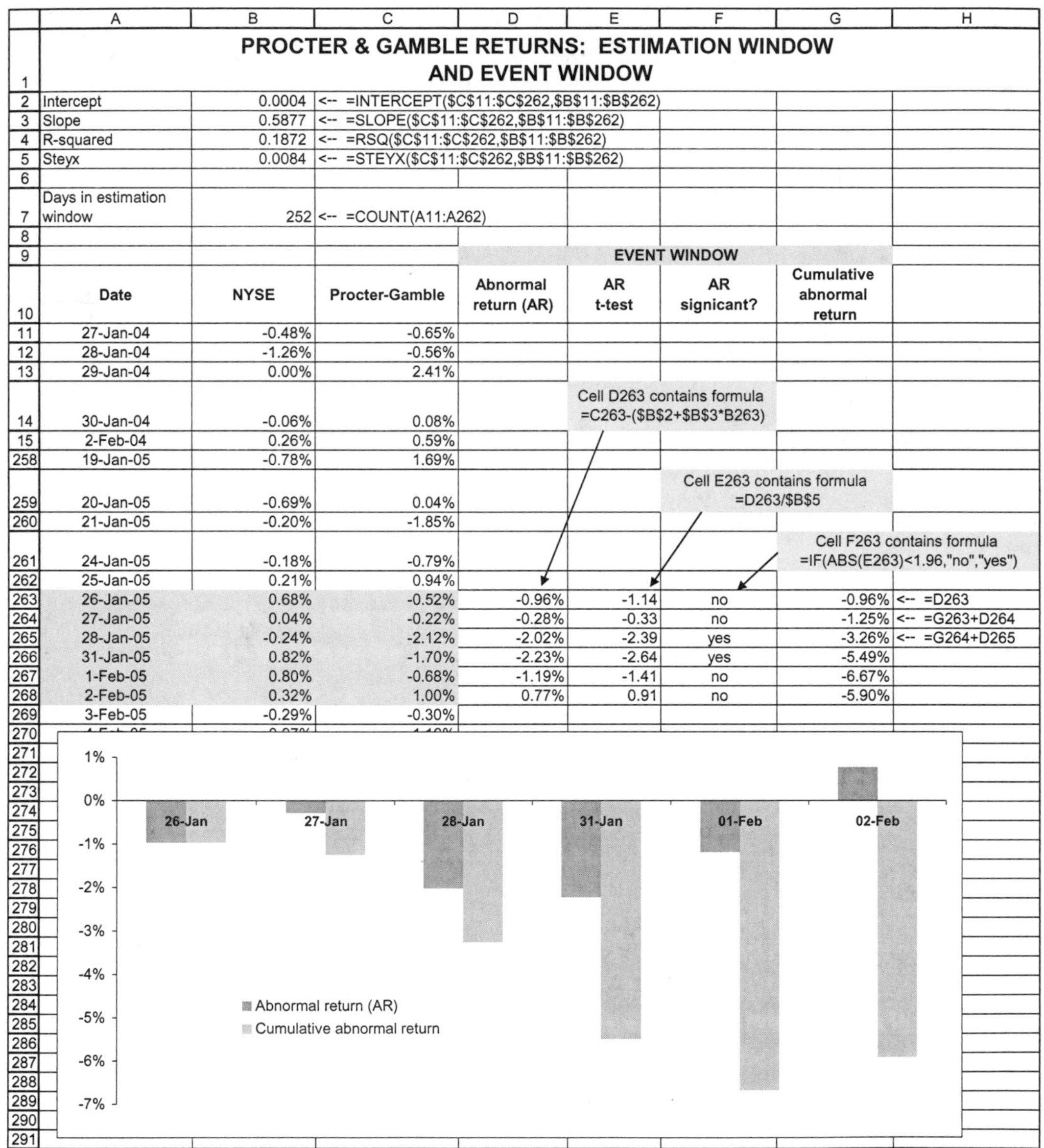

	A	B	C	D	E	F	G	H
1	**PROCTER & GAMBLE RETURNS: ESTIMATION WINDOW AND EVENT WINDOW**							
2	Intercept	0.0004	<-- =INTERCEPT($C$11:$C$262,$B$11:$B$262)					
3	Slope	0.5877	<-- =SLOPE($C$11:$C$262,$B$11:$B$262)					
4	R-squared	0.1872	<-- =RSQ($C$11:$C$262,$B$11:$B$262)					
5	Steyx	0.0084	<-- =STEYX($C$11:$C$262,$B$11:$B$262)					
6								
7	Days in estimation window	252	<-- =COUNT(A11:A262)					
8								
9				**EVENT WINDOW**				
10	**Date**	**NYSE**	**Procter-Gamble**	**Abnormal return (AR)**	**AR t-test**	**AR signicant?**	**Cumulative abnormal return**	
11	27-Jan-04	-0.48%	-0.65%					
12	28-Jan-04	-1.26%	-0.56%					
13	29-Jan-04	0.00%	2.41%					
14	30-Jan-04	-0.06%	0.08%		Cell D263 contains formula =C263-($B$2+$B$3*B263)			
15	2-Feb-04	0.26%	0.59%					
258	19-Jan-05	-0.78%	1.69%					
259	20-Jan-05	-0.69%	0.04%			Cell E263 contains formula =D263/$B$5		
260	21-Jan-05	-0.20%	-1.85%					
261	24-Jan-05	-0.18%	-0.79%				Cell F263 contains formula =IF(ABS(E263)<1.96,"no","yes")	
262	25-Jan-05	0.21%	0.94%					
263	26-Jan-05	0.68%	-0.52%	-0.96%	-1.14	no	-0.96%	<-- =D263
264	27-Jan-05	0.04%	-0.22%	-0.28%	-0.33	no	-1.25%	<-- =G263+D264
265	28-Jan-05	-0.24%	-2.12%	-2.02%	-2.39	yes	-3.26%	<-- =G264+D265
266	31-Jan-05	0.82%	-1.70%	-2.23%	-2.64	yes	-5.49%	
267	1-Feb-05	0.80%	-0.68%	-1.19%	-1.41	no	-6.67%	
268	2-Feb-05	0.32%	1.00%	0.77%	0.91	no	-5.90%	
269	3-Feb-05	-0.29%	-0.30%					

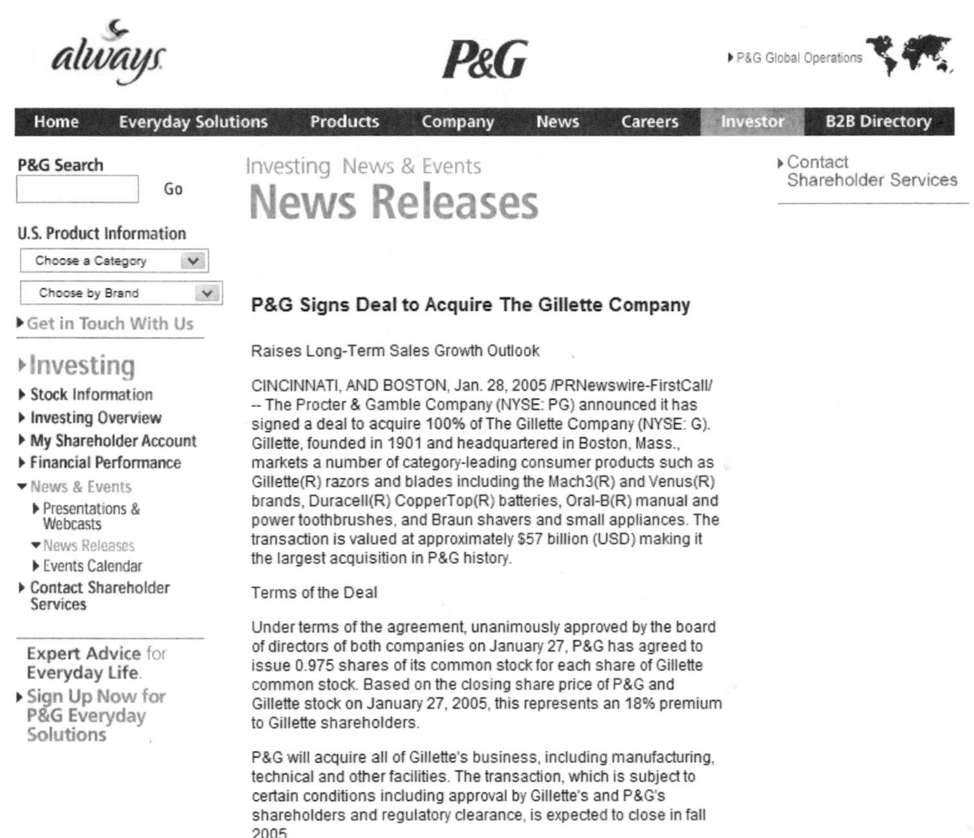

always P&G ▸ P&G Global Operations

Home | Everyday Solutions | Products | Company | News | Careers | Investor | B2B Directory

P&G Search Go

U.S. Product Information

Choose a Category

Choose by Brand

▸ Get in Touch With Us

▸ Investing

▸ Stock Information

▸ Investing Overview

▸ My Shareholder Account

▸ Financial Performance

▾ News & Events

▸ Presentations & Webcasts

▾ News Releases

▸ Events Calendar

▸ Contact Shareholder Services

Expert Advice for Everyday Life.

▸ Sign Up Now for P&G Everyday Solutions

Investing News & Events

News Releases

▸ Contact Shareholder Services

P&G Signs Deal to Acquire The Gillette Company

Raises Long-Term Sales Growth Outlook

CINCINNATI, AND BOSTON, Jan. 28, 2005 /PRNewswire-FirstCall/ -- The Procter & Gamble Company (NYSE: PG) announced it has signed a deal to acquire 100% of The Gillette Company (NYSE: G). Gillette, founded in 1901 and headquartered in Boston, Mass., markets a number of category-leading consumer products such as Gillette(R) razors and blades including the Mach3(R) and Venus(R) brands, Duracell(R) CopperTop(R) batteries, Oral-B(R) manual and power toothbrushes, and Braun shavers and small appliances. The transaction is valued at approximately $57 billion (USD) making it the largest acquisition in P&G history.

Terms of the Deal

Under terms of the agreement, unanimously approved by the board of directors of both companies on January 27, P&G has agreed to issue 0.975 shares of its common stock for each share of Gillette common stock. Based on the closing share price of P&G and Gillette stock on January 27, 2005, this represents an 18% premium to Gillette shareholders.

P&G will acquire all of Gillette's business, including manufacturing, technical and other facilities. The transaction, which is subject to certain conditions including approval by Gillette's and P&G's shareholders and regulatory clearance, is expected to close in fall 2005.

14.3.4 Summary: What Happened on the Announcement Date?

On 28 January 2005, Procter & Gamble announced the purchase of Gillette. Each share of Gillette was purchased for 0.975 shares of Procter & Gamble. At the 5 percent significance level, the acquisition announcement had significant effects on the stock prices of Gillette and Procter & Gamble only on the announcement date and the day after. After an initial positive impact on Gillette (a 13.03 percent increase in the normally anticipated stock return on the event date 28 January and a further –2.30 percent on 31 January) and an initial negative impact on Procter & Gamble (–2.02 percent on 28 January and –2.23 percent on 31 January), there were no additional significant effects on the stock prices. The cumulative effects are as follows:

	A	B	C	D	E	F	G	H	I
1	**GILLETTE PURCHASED BY PROCTER & GAMBLE Measuring the synergies in event window**								
2		**Shares outstanding (thousands)**	**Share price, 25jan05**	**Market value, 25jan05 (billion $)**					
3	Gillette	1,000,000	44.53	44.53					
4	P&G	2,741,000	53.49	146.62					
5					Cell F12 contains formula				
6					=$D$3*SUM($B$12:B12)/1000				
7									
8							Cell G12 contains formula		
9							=$D$4*SUM($C$12:C12)/1000		
10	**Date**	**Abnormal returns (AR)**				**Cumulative abnormal valuations (billion $)**			
11		Gillette	P&G	Sum		Gillette	P&G	Sum	
12	26-Jan-05	-0.44%	-0.96%	-1.40%		-0.19	-1.41	-1.61	<-- =F12+G12
13	27-Jan-05	1.80%	-0.28%	1.52%		0.61	-1.83	-1.22	
14	28-Jan-05	13.03%	-2.02%	11.01%		6.41	-4.78	1.63	
15	31-Jan-05	-2.30%	-2.23%	-4.52%		5.38	-8.04	-2.66	
16	1-Feb-05	-1.40%	-1.19%	-2.59%		4.76	-9.78	-5.02	
17	2-Feb-05	0.52%	0.77%	1.29%		4.99	-8.66	-3.66	

The preceding table attempts to measure the short-term synergies of the announcement by multiplying the CAR for Gillette and P&G times their market value on the day before the event window. In the short period of time measured by this event window, the cumulative surgery appears to be negative, with the positive value creation for Gillette shareholders outweighted by the negative impact on P&G.[7]

14.4 A Fuller Event Study: Impact of Earnings Announcements on Stock Prices

In the previous section we used the event-study methodology to explore the impact of a merger announcement on the returns of both the takeover target (Gillette) and acquirer (Procter & Gamble). In this section we show how to aggregate the returns of an event in order to evaluate the market response to a particular type of event. We consider the effect of earning announcements on a set of stores in the grocery industry.

7. A study commissioned by the Massachusetts Secretary of the Commonwealth William F. Galvin after the merger offer suggests that the synergies of the merger, between $22–$28 billion, were largely captured by Procter & Gamble. See http://www.sec.state.ma.us/sct/sctpdf/Gillettefairnessreport.pdf (on the disk with this book) and http://www.businessweek.com/bwdaily/dnflash/jun2005/nf20050616_1121_db016.htm.

14.4.1 An Initial Example: Safeway's Positive Earnings Surprise on 20 July 2006

To set the stage, consider the earnings announcement made by Safeway on 20 July 2006. On this date Safeway announced earnings per share (EPS) of \$0.42, a number which exceeded by 6 cents the market consensus estimate of \$0.36.[8] On the same day, the S&P 500 declined by 0.85 percent, and Safeway stock rose by 8.39 percent. The following spreadsheet shows the example of Safeway's earnings announcement on 20 July 2006. We use the event-study methodology to gauge the market reaction to this earnings surprise:

	A	B	C
1	**THE MARKET REACTION TO A POSITIVE EARNINGS SURPRISE BY SAFEWAY, 20 July 2006**		
2	Announcement date	20-Jul-06	
3	Earnings per share	\$0.42	
4	Consensus earnings estimate	\$0.36	
5	Earnings surprise (forecast error)	\$0.06	
6			
7	**How did the market interpret the earnings surprise? Using the market model**		
8	Safeway	8.39%	
9	S&P 500	-0.85%	
10			
11	**Regressing Safeway returns on the S&P returns: Safeway = 0.0001 + 0.9289*SP**		
12	Intercept	0.0001	
13	Slope	0.9289	
14	Steyx	0.0118	
15			
16	**The residual return: Expected stock returns versus actual returns**		
17	Expected return	-0.78%	<-- =B13*B9+B12
18	Residual return	9.17%	<-- =B8-B17
19	t-statistic	7.75	<-- =B18/B14

In cells B12:B14 we have regressed Safeway daily returns on those of the S&P 500 for the 252 trading days preceding the announcement. The regression shows that $r_{Safeway} = 0.0001 + 0.9289 * r_{SP500}$ and that the standard error of the estimate is 0.0118.

Given these data, we can see that on the day of the announcement the anticipated return of Safeway, given the negative 0.85 percent return of

8. Yahoo is the source of our earnings surprise data (see p. 384).

the S&P and absent the earnings surprise, should have been –0.78 percent. This means that the abnormal return, measuring the impact of the earnings announcement, was 9.17 percent (cell B18). The *t*-statistic for the return was 7.75, showing that it is highly significant.

14.4.2 The Earnings Surprise Numbers

Our earnings surprise numbers are drawn from Yahoo, as shown in the following picture. While Yahoo is an admirable source of data, it does not provide a database of historical analyst estimates and actual earnings numbers; such data are available from Bloomberg's Best Consensus Earnings Estimates and other commercial sources.

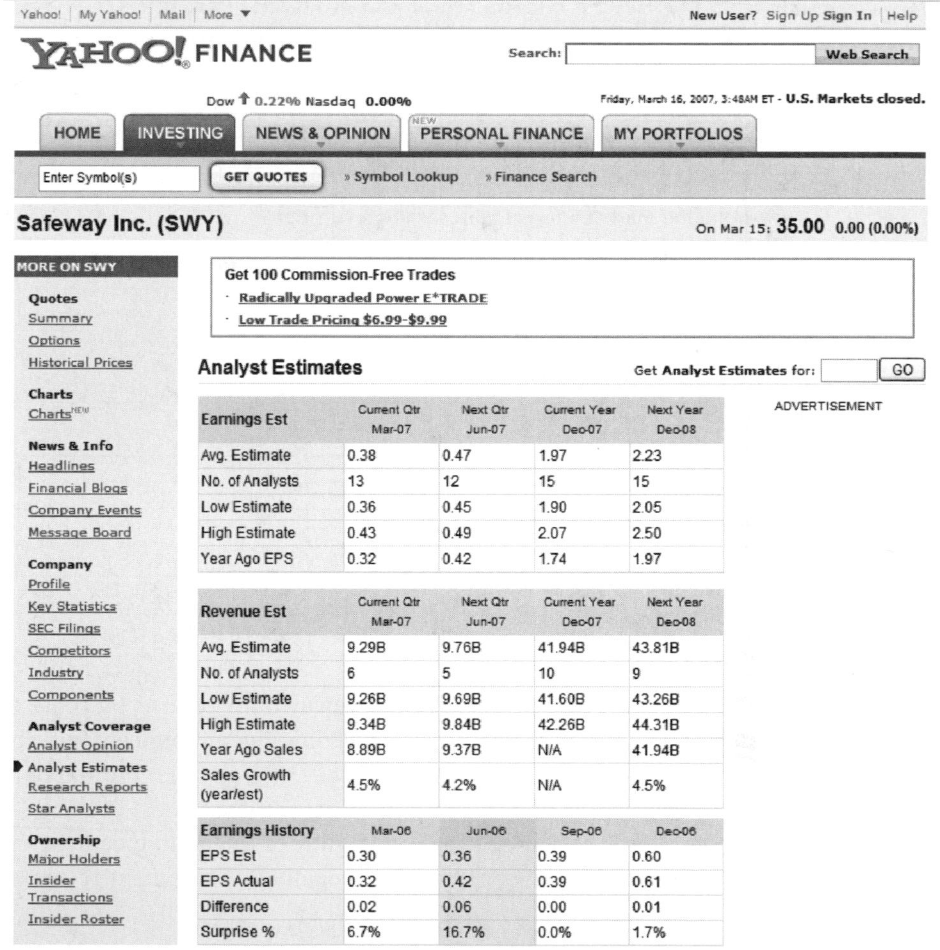

Yahoo! | My Yahoo! | Mail | More ▼ New User? Sign Up Sign In | Help

YAHOO! FINANCE Search: [ ] Web Search

Dow ↑ 0.22% Nasdaq 0.00% Friday, March 16, 2007, 3:48AM ET - U.S. Markets closed.

HOME | INVESTING | NEWS & OPINION | NEW PERSONAL FINANCE | MY PORTFOLIOS

Enter Symbol(s) GET QUOTES » Symbol Lookup » Finance Search

Safeway Inc. (SWY) On Mar 15: **35.00** 0.00 (0.00%)

MORE ON SWY

Quotes
Summary
Options
Historical Prices

Charts
Charts NEW

News & Info
Headlines
Financial Blogs
Company Events
Message Board

Company
Profile
Key Statistics
SEC Filings
Competitors
Industry
Components

Analyst Coverage
Analyst Opinion
Analyst Estimates
Research Reports
Star Analysts

Ownership
Major Holders
Insider Transactions
Insider Roster

Get 100 Commission-Free Trades
· Radically Upgraded Power E*TRADE
· Low Trade Pricing $6.99-$9.99

Analyst Estimates Get Analyst Estimates for: [ ] GO

ADVERTISEMENT

Earnings Est	Current Qtr Mar-07	Next Qtr Jun-07	Current Year Dec-07	Next Year Dec-08
Avg. Estimate	0.38	0.47	1.97	2.23
No. of Analysts	13	12	15	15
Low Estimate	0.36	0.45	1.90	2.05
High Estimate	0.43	0.49	2.07	2.50
Year Ago EPS	0.32	0.42	1.74	1.97

Revenue Est	Current Qtr Mar-07	Next Qtr Jun-07	Current Year Dec-07	Next Year Dec-08
Avg. Estimate	9.29B	9.76B	41.94B	43.81B
No. of Analysts	6	5	10	9
Low Estimate	9.26B	9.69B	41.60B	43.26B
High Estimate	9.34B	9.84B	42.26B	44.31B
Year Ago Sales	8.89B	9.37B	N/A	41.94B
Sales Growth (year/est)	4.5%	4.2%	N/A	4.5%

Earnings History	Mar-06	Jun-06	Sep-06	Dec-06
EPS Est	0.30	0.36	0.39	0.60
EPS Actual	0.32	0.42	0.39	0.61
Difference	0.02	0.06	0.00	0.01
Surprise %	6.7%	16.7%	0.0%	1.7%

14.4.3 An Event Study: The Grocery Industry

We extend our Safeway study by considering 16 quarterly earnings announcements by four grocery companies for fiscal year 2006.[9]

EARNINGS ANNOUNCEMENT IN 2006-07 FOR KROGER (KR), SUPERVALU (SVU), SAFEWAY (SWY), AND WHOLE FOODS (WFMI)

	Calendar Date	Ticker	Consensus	Actual	Surprise: =D3-C3	Starting Point	Intercept	Slope	STEXY	Actual Return	S&P 500 Return	Expected Return: =H3+I3*M3	Abnormal Return: =L3-N3	T-stat	
3	7-Mar-06	KR	0.36	0.39	0.03	44	0.0003	0.6662	0.0123	1.36%	-0.19%	-0.09%	1.46%	1.1808	<-- =O3/J3
4	20-Jun-06	KR	0.42	0.42	0.00	117	0.0004	0.6063	0.0113	5.05%	0.00%	0.04%	5.01%	**4.4355**	<-- =O4/J4
5	12-Sep-06	KR	0.29	0.29	0.00	175	0.0006	0.5628	0.0108	-5.67%	1.03%	0.64%	-6.31%	**-5.8201**	<-- =O5/J5
6	5-Dec-06	KR	0.28	0.30	0.02	234	0.0003	0.4483	0.0118	5.08%	0.40%	0.21%	4.87%	**4.1297**	
7	18-Apr-06	SVU	0.56	0.55	-0.01	73	-0.0008	0.7049	0.0123	-0.28%	1.69%	1.11%	-1.39%	-1.1313	
8	26-Jul-06	SVU	0.57	0.53	-0.04	142	-0.0003	0.5416	0.0122	-7.09%	-0.04%	-0.05%	-7.03%	**-5.7632**	
9	10-Oct-06	SVU	0.53	0.61	0.08	195	-0.0002	0.6014	0.0128	4.36%	0.20%	0.10%	4.26%	**3.3170**	
10	9-Jan-07	SVU	0.56	0.54	-0.02	256	0.0003	0.5238	0.0130	-1.70%	-0.05%	0.00%	-1.70%	-1.3061	
11	27-Apr-06	SWY	0.30	0.32	0.02	80	0.0001	1.0139	0.0130	2.88%	0.33%	0.34%	2.54%	**1.9473**	
12	20-Jul-06	SWY	0.36	0.42	0.06	138	0.0001	0.9289	0.0118	8.39%	-0.85%	-0.78%	9.17%	**7.7519**	
13	12-Oct-06	SWY	0.39	0.39	0.00	197	0.0003	0.7533	0.0134	-1.43%	0.95%	0.75%	-2.18%	-1.6265	
14	27-Feb-07	SWY	0.60	0.61	0.01	289	0.0012	0.7505	0.0131	-3.95%	-3.53%	-2.54%	-1.41%	-1.0814	
15	4-May-06	WFMI	0.35	0.36	0.01	85	0.0006	0.8345	0.0175	12.50%	0.32%	0.33%	12.17%	**6.9434**	
16	1-Aug-06	WFMI	0.34	0.35	0.01	146	-0.0007	1.2329	0.0164	-12.51%	-0.45%	-0.63%	-11.88%	**-7.2345**	
17	3-Nov-06	WFMI	0.29	0.29	0.00	213	-0.0014	1.3199	0.0195	-26.21%	-0.22%	-0.43%	-25.78%	**-13.2186**	
18	22-Feb-07	WFMI	0.40	0.38	-0.02	286	-0.0020	1.5321	0.0243	13.13%	-0.09%	-0.33%	13.46%	**5.5465**	
20												Positive surprise	2.65%	<-- =SUMIF($E$3:$E$18,">0",$O$3:$O$18)/COUNTIF(E3:E18,">0")	
21												None-positive surprise	-3.24%	<-- =SUMIF($E$3:$E$18,"<=0",$O$3:$O$18)/COUNTIF(E3:E18,"<=0")	

Cell G18 contains formula:
=COUNTIF('Stock Prices'!$A$3:$A$551,"<="&TEXT(A18,"0"))-252

Cell H18 contains formula:
=INTERCEPT(OFFSET('Stock Prices'!$A$2,$G18,10,252,1),OFFSET('Stock Prices'!$A$2,$G18,2,252,1))

Cell I18 contains formula:
=SLOPE(OFFSET('Stock Prices'!$A$2,$G18,10,252,1),OFFSET('Stock Prices'!$A$2,$G18,2,252,1))

Cell J18 contains formula:
=STEYX(OFFSET('Stock Prices'!$A$2,$G18,10,252,1),OFFSET('Stock Prices'!$A$2,$G18,2,252,1))

For each announcement we have determined the intercept and slope of the market-response regression for the 252 days preceding the announcement.[10] Following is a specific example from the spreadsheet.

9. We only included Kroger, Supervalu, Safeway, and Whole Foods in the sample. This is obviously an incomplete sample, both in terms of the firms covered and the number of announcements. However, this extended example is meant to impart the flavor of a full-bodied event study.

10. The event window is defined in column G by the "Starting Point," which uses **Countif** to locate a date 252 business days before the event date in the database of stock returns. Notice that the "Starting Point" is used in the **Intercept**, **Slope**, **Rsq** formulas in columns H, I, and J.

	A	B	C	D	E	F	G	H	I	J	K	L	M	N	O	P
2	**Calendar Date**	**Ticker**	**Consensus**	**Actual**	**Surprise: =D3-C3**		**Starting Point**	**Intercept**	**Slope**	**STEXY**		**Actual Return**	**S&P 500 Return**	**Expected Return: =H3+I3*M3**	**Abnormal Return: =L3-N3**	**T-stat**
3	7-Mar-06	KR	0.36	0.39	0.03		44	0.0003	0.6662	0.0123		1.36%	-0.19%	-0.09%	1.46%	1.1808
18	22-Feb-07	WFMI	0.40	0.38	-0.02		286	-0.0020	1.5321	0.0243		13.13%	-0.09%	-0.33%	13.46%	**5.5465**

Row 3 tracks the market model of Kroger stock to the S&P 500 in the 252 trading days before the earnings announcement on 7 March 2006. The market model is $r_{\text{Kroger},t} = 0.003 + 0.662 {*} r_{\text{SP},t}$. Kroger's actual return on the announcement date, 1.36 percent, is 1.46 percent higher than the return that would have been predicted by its market model. However, dividing this 1.46 percent by the standard deviation of the abnormal returns (the regression residuals) (**Steyx** = 0.0123) gives a *t*-statistic of 1.1808, which is not significant at the 5 percent level.

Row 18 tracks the market model of Whole Foods stock to the S&P 500 in the year before the earnings announcement after market close on 21 February 2007. The market model is $r_{\text{Whole food},t} = -0.0020 + 1.5321 {*} r_{\text{SP},t}$, with **Steyx** = 0.0243. The abnormal return on the day of the announcement, 13.46 percent, is significant at the 1 percent level (hence the boldface in cell P18). To temper this interpretation, note that on the day of the earnings announcement, Whole Foods announced the merger with Wild Oats Markets; this second announcement makes it difficult to interpret the true market reaction to the earnings release. In general, we have to be careful interpreting abnormal returns when an event is announced with confounding information.

14.4.4 Cumulative Abnormal Returns

We restate the data in slightly different form in the next spreadsheet—using the **OFFSET** function—and then compute the abnormal returns in an event window which goes from −10 to +10 days around the earnings announcements:

	A	B	C	D	E	F	G	H	I	J	K	L	M	N	O	P	Q
1	CUMULATIVE ABNORMAL RETURNS IN THE WINDOW -10 TO +10																
2	Calendar Date	7-Mar-06	20-Jun-06	12-Sep-06	5-Dec-06	18-Apr-06	26-Jul-06	10-Oct-06	9-Jan-07	27-Apr-06	20-Jul-06	12-Oct-06	27-Feb-07	4-May-06	1-Aug-06	3-Nov-06	22-Feb-07
3	Ticker	KR	KR	KR	KR	SVU	SVU	SVU	SVU	SWY	SWY	SWY	SWY	WFMI	WFMI	WFMI	WFMI
4	Consensus	0.36	0.42	0.29	0.28	0.56	0.57	0.53	0.56	0.3	0.36	0.39	0.6	0.35	0.34	0.29	0.4
5	Actual	0.39	0.42	0.29	0.3	0.55	0.53	0.61	0.54	0.32	0.42	0.39	0.61	0.36	0.35	0.29	0.38
6	**Surprise**	0.03	0.00	0.00	0.02	-0.01	-0.04	0.08	-0.02	0.02	0.06	0.00	0.01	0.01	0.01	0.00	-0.02
7																	
8	Starting Point	44	117	175	234	73	142	195	256	80	138	197	289	85	146	213	286
9	Intercept	0.0003	0.0004	0.0006	0.0003	-0.0008	-0.0003	-0.0002	0.0003	0.0001	0.0001	0.0003	0.0012	0.0006	-0.0007	-0.0014	-0.0020
10	Slope	0.6662	0.6063	0.5628	0.4483	0.7049	0.5416	0.6014	0.5238	1.0139	0.9289	0.7533	0.7505	0.8345	1.2329	1.3199	1.5321
11	STEXY	0.0123	0.0113	0.0108	0.0118	0.0123	0.0122	0.0128	0.0130	0.0130	0.0118	0.0134	0.0131	0.0175	0.0164	0.0195	0.0243
12																	
13																	
14	**Day relative to event**	**ABNORMAL RETURN**															
15	-10	0.59%	-0.07%	0.72%	-0.46%	-0.68%	-1.81%	-1.04%	0.47%	0.32%	-0.01%	0.36%	0.46%	-0.52%	-3.87%	0.05%	0.26%
16	-9	-1.19%	0.89%	0.38%	-1.20%	-1.06%	0.33%	-0.43%	0.36%	0.65%	-0.96%	-0.94%	0.29%	-1.94%	0.93%	-0.06%	0.94%
17	-8	1.08%	0.58%	-0.32%	0.00%	0.25%	-0.35%	0.29%	-0.92%	-0.65%	0.21%	0.22%	0.60%	-1.20%	-0.33%	-0.98%	1.82%
18	-7	-0.67%	-1.34%	0.85%	-0.23%	-0.86%	1.30%	0.05%	0.66%	0.90%	-0.78%	-0.16%	-0.96%	-1.27%	-0.18%	0.53%	-0.87%
19	-6	0.98%	-0.35%	-0.59%	-0.67%	-0.55%	1.24%	-0.66%	-0.48%	-2.40%	0.20%	-3.61%	0.33%	-0.59%	-1.79%	0.10%	-0.11%
20	-5	-0.34%	1.41%	-0.84%	0.42%	0.29%	0.13%	2.44%	-1.05%	-0.66%	0.19%	-4.99%	0.68%	-1.35%	-0.97%	0.25%	0.35%
21	-4	-0.23%	0.11%	0.49%	0.62%	-0.71%	0.79%	-0.63%	0.71%	-0.57%	0.93%	0.88%	0.21%	0.09%	-1.88%	0.31%	0.35%
22	-3	-1.55%	-1.16%	-0.39%	-1.92%	-1.01%	-0.64%	-0.11%	-0.46%	-0.80%	0.92%	1.21%	-3.80%	0.41%	0.85%	-1.52%	1.22%
23	-2	0.93%	-0.59%	1.97%	0.98%	0.34%	0.49%	-0.05%	0.68%	0.61%	1.79%	2.36%	-1.12%	-0.28%	1.38%	0.03%	-1.01%
24	-1	0.03%	-0.26%	0.29%	2.63%	0.29%	-0.60%	2.95%	-0.79%	0.82%	-1.33%	0.30%	0.60%	1.08%	0.01%	-4.74%	-0.39%
25	0	1.46%	5.01%	-6.31%	4.87%	-1.39%	-7.03%	4.26%	-1.70%	2.54%	9.17%	-2.18%	-1.41%	12.17%	-11.88%	-25.78%	13.46%
26	1	1.43%	-0.63%	0.38%	-1.35%	-1.12%	-4.37%	0.58%	-1.57%	-0.12%	0.83%	-2.34%	1.01%	1.42%	-0.14%	-0.94%	-2.45%
27	2	-1.15%	-0.56%	0.93%	-0.15%	1.43%	-2.64%	0.99%	1.59%	1.33%	-1.44%	0.34%	0.37%	0.37%	-0.19%	2.02%	0.06%
28	3	1.08%	1.15%	-2.90%	-0.24%	-0.82%	0.87%	0.20%	-0.91%	-3.28%	-0.24%	0.35%	-1.44%	-1.78%	0.67%	3.11%	0.94%
29	4	0.03%	1.37%	0.27%	2.61%	0.36%	0.20%	-0.71%	-0.56%	-1.34%	-0.23%	1.26%	-0.06%	-0.40%	0.24%	0.14%	-1.13%
30	5	0.11%	-0.31%	-0.31%	1.19%	-0.99%	0.62%	-0.47%	-0.53%	0.58%	0.76%	-1.94%	-0.59%	0.04%	-4.00%	0.44%	-1.13%
31	6	-0.12%	2.70%	0.50%	-0.42%	-0.23%	-0.76%	0.83%	0.04%	1.02%	-1.13%	0.93%	-0.40%	-0.76%	-1.24%	0.84%	0.41%
32	7	-0.20%	0.35%	-0.96%	0.75%	0.63%	0.11%	0.27%	1.26%	-0.45%	-0.09%	0.13%	1.20%	1.25%	-0.02%	0.25%	1.97%
33	8	-0.18%	0.73%	1.90%	0.33%	0.46%	-0.41%	-0.02%	1.75%	-1.43%	0.26%	-2.28%	-0.12%	-0.46%	-1.25%	-0.34%	-0.63%
34	9	-1.34%	-0.52%	0.14%	-2.86%	0.23%	-1.15%	-0.23%	0.04%	-0.82%	1.04%	0.13%	-0.12%	-1.59%	7.14%	-0.99%	-1.50%
35	10	0.86%	0.08%	-0.14%	-1.19%	-0.88%	-1.27%	0.00%	0.48%	0.46%	-0.33%	0.92%	-0.12%	-0.85%	2.10%	-0.12%	-0.63%

We can compute the average abnormal return (AAR) and cumulative abnormal return (CAR) for each of the days in the event window. In the following table we perform this computation separately for positive versus nonpositive earnings announcements:

Cell U11 contains formula
{=SQRT(SUMPRODUCT(IF($B$6:$Q$6>0,$B$11:$Q$11),IF($B$6:$Q$6>0,$B$11:$Q$11))*(1/COUNTIF($B$6:$Q$6,">0")^2))}

	S	T	U	V	W	X	Y	Z	AA	AB
9		**Unadjusted cross-sectional errors - Positive**				**Unadjusted cross-sectional errors - Nonpositive**				
11			0.49%				0.54%			
13		**Positive-Earnings Announcements**				**Nonpositive Earnings Announcements**				
14	**Day relative to event**	**AAR**	**T-stat**	**Cumulative Abnormal Returns**		**AAR**	**T-stat**	**Cumulative Abnormal Returns**		
15	-10	-0.57%	-1.1615	-0.57%		-0.09%	-0.1632	-0.09%		
16	-9	-0.48%	-0.9931	-1.05%		0.10%	0.1944	0.02%		
17	-8	0.00%	0.0026	-1.05%		0.04%	0.0670	0.05%		
18	-7	-0.39%	-0.8046	-1.44%		0.01%	0.0251	0.07%		
19	-6	-0.57%	-1.1777	-2.01%		-0.54%	-1.0058	-0.48%		
20	-5	0.05%	0.1043	-1.96%		-0.55%	-1.0278	-1.03%		
21	-4	-0.18%	-0.3753	-2.14%		0.37%	0.6774	-0.67%		
22	-3	-0.75%	-1.5410	-2.89%		-0.34%	-0.6376	-1.01%		
23	-2	0.53%	1.0900	-2.36%		0.54%	0.9917	-0.47%		
24	-1	0.85%	1.7437	-1.51%		-0.74%	-1.3685	-1.21%		
25	0	2.65%	**5.4406**	1.13%		-3.24%	**-6.0062**	-4.46%		
26	1	0.46%	0.9409	1.59%		-1.63%	**-3.0190**	-6.08%		
27	2	0.02%	0.0335	1.61%		0.40%	0.7356	-5.69%		
28	3	-0.63%	-1.2939	0.98%		0.22%	0.4121	-5.47%		
29	4	0.02%	0.0355	0.99%		0.24%	0.4434	-5.23%		
30	5	-0.30%	-0.6087	0.70%		-0.52%	-0.9620	-5.75%		
31	6	-0.28%	-0.5690	0.42%		0.55%	1.0269	-5.19%		
32	7	0.34%	0.6998	0.76%		0.47%	0.8643	-4.72%		
33	8	-0.36%	-0.7326	0.41%		0.14%	0.2680	-4.58%		
34	9	0.15%	0.3154	0.56%		-0.45%	-0.8382	-5.03%		
35	10	0.12%	0.2425	0.68%		-0.20%	-0.3614	-5.23%		

Cell T35 contains formula
=SUMIF($B$6:$Q$6,">0",B35:Q35)/COUNTIF($B$6:$Q$6,">0")

Cell X35 contains formula
=SUMIF($B$6:$Q$6,"<=0",B35:Q35)/COUNTIF($B$6:$Q$6,"<=0")

Cell U35 contains formula =T35/$U$11

Cell Y35 contains formula =X35/$Y$11

Cell V35 contains formula =T35+V34

Cell Z35 contains formula =X35+Z34

The test statistics for the positive and nonpositive announcements have been computed by dividing the AAR for each day by the appropriate cross-sectional error for the specific type of return (cells U11 and Y11):

$$\text{Cell U11: } \sqrt{\frac{\text{Sum}^2 \text{ of Steyx for positive announcements}}{\text{Number of positive announcements}}}$$

$$\text{Cell Y11: } \sqrt{\frac{\text{Sum}^2 \text{ of Steyx for negative announcements}}{\text{Number of negative announcements}}}$$

Graphing the CARs gives this graph:

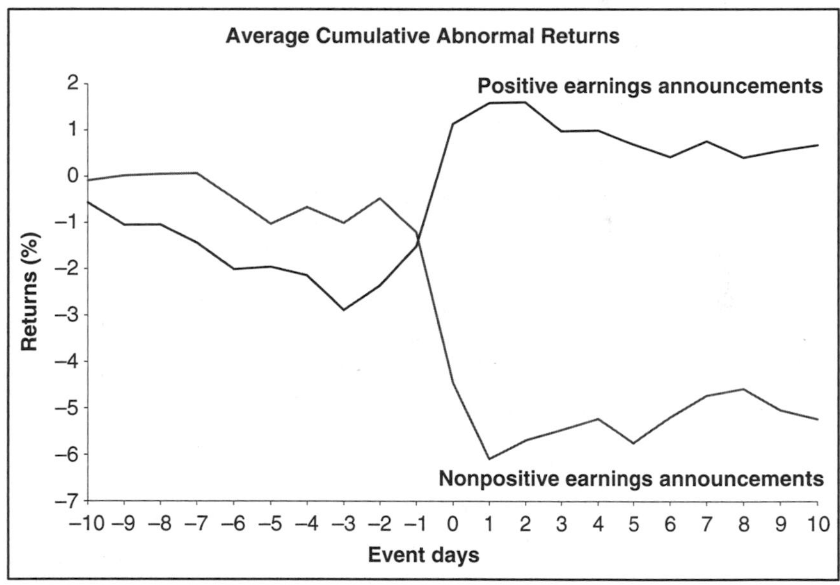

On average, there appears to have been little leakage prior to the announcement date of either the good news announcements or the bad news. The market appears to have absorbed the information in the announcements rapidly: following the announcement date ("event day 0"), there appears to have been little additional response.

14.5 Using a Two-Factor Model of Returns for an Event Study

The model used in section 14.4 assumes an equilibrium model $r_{it} = \alpha_i + \beta_i r_{Mt}$. This "one-factor" model assumes that the returns on the stocks in question are driven only by one market index. In this section we illustrate a two-factor model. We assume that returns are a function of both a market and an industry factor: $r_{it} = \alpha_i + \beta_{i,\text{Market}} r_{Mt} + \beta_{i,\text{Industry}} r_{\text{Industry},t}$. We then use this model to determine whether a specific event influenced the returns and in which direction.

Our event: On 16 November 2006, Wendy's announced the purchase by tender of 22,418,000 shares at a price of $35.75 per share. This share purchase represented approximately 19 percent of the firm's equity. Wendy's stock closed on 16 November at $35.66.

Wendy's Announces Final Results of Its Modified "Dutch Auction" Tender Offer

DUBLIN, Ohio (November 22, 2006) – Wendy's International, Inc. (NYSE:WEN) today announced the final results of its modified "Dutch Auction" tender offer, which expired at 5:00 p.m., Eastern Time, on November 16, 2006.

The Company has accepted for purchase 22,413,278 of its common shares at a purchase price of $35.75 per share, for a total cost of $801.3 million.

Shareholders who deposited common shares in the tender offer at or below the purchase price will have all of their tendered common shares purchased, subject to certain limited exceptions.

American Stock Transfer & Trust Company, the depositary for the tender offer, will promptly issue payment for the shares validly tendered and accepted for purchase under the tender offer.

The number of shares the Company accepted for purchase in the tender offer represents approximately 19% of its currently outstanding common shares.

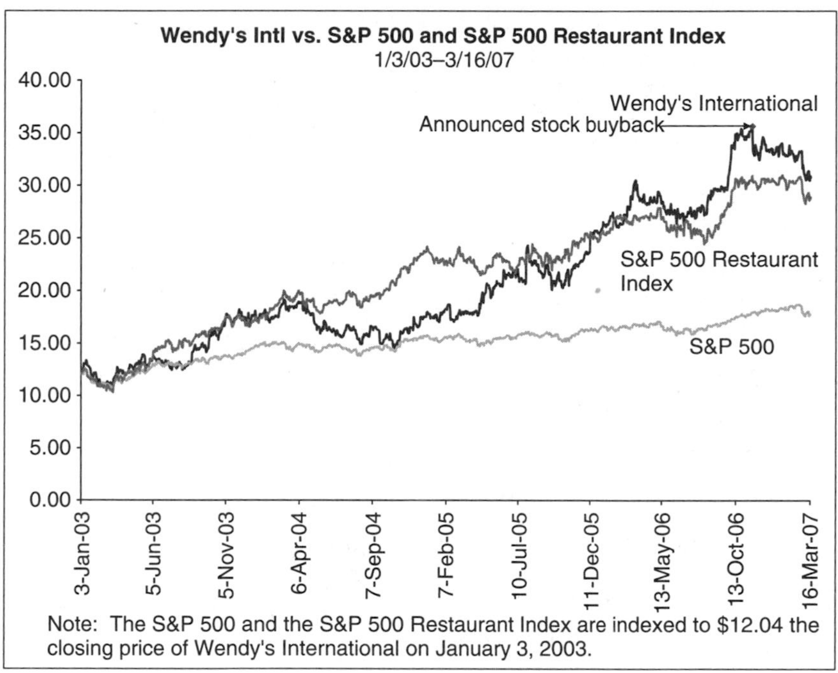

14.5.1 Did the Repurchase Affect Wendy's Returns?

We start by regressing the daily returns on Wendy's on the S&P 500 and the S&P 500 Restaurant Index for the 252 days preceding the tender date of 16 November 2006. We use the array function **Linest** to do this computation.[11] The **Linest** box looks like this:

	A	B	C	D
2		Industry	Market	Intercept
3	Slope -->	0.4157	0.5095	0.0012
4	Standard Error -->	0.0851	0.1410	0.0007
5	R^2 -->	0.3140	0.0103	#N/A
6	F statistic -->	56.9738	249	#N/A
7	SS_{xy} -->	0.0122	0.0266	#N/A

11. The use of **Linest** to perform multiple regressions is discussed in Chapter 33. It is not the most user friendly of all Excel functions.

From this box we can conclude that Wendy's return is sensitive to both the market and the industry.

$$r_{\text{Wendys},t} = 0.0012 + \underbrace{0.5095}_{\substack{\uparrow \\ \text{Market reaction} \\ \text{coefficient.} \\ \text{Standard error:} \\ 0.1410}} * r_{Mt} + \underbrace{0.4157}_{\substack{\uparrow \\ \text{Industry reaction} \\ \text{coefficient.} \\ \text{Standard error:} \\ 0.0851}} * r_{\text{Industry},t}$$

This **Linest** box is shown again in the next spreadsheet. Dividing the coefficients by their respective standard errors (row 9) shows that they are both significant at the 1 percent level. Note that cell C5 gives the standard error of the y-estimate; we use this in the analysis to determine the significance of the abnormal returns. Further analysis follows the spreadsheet.

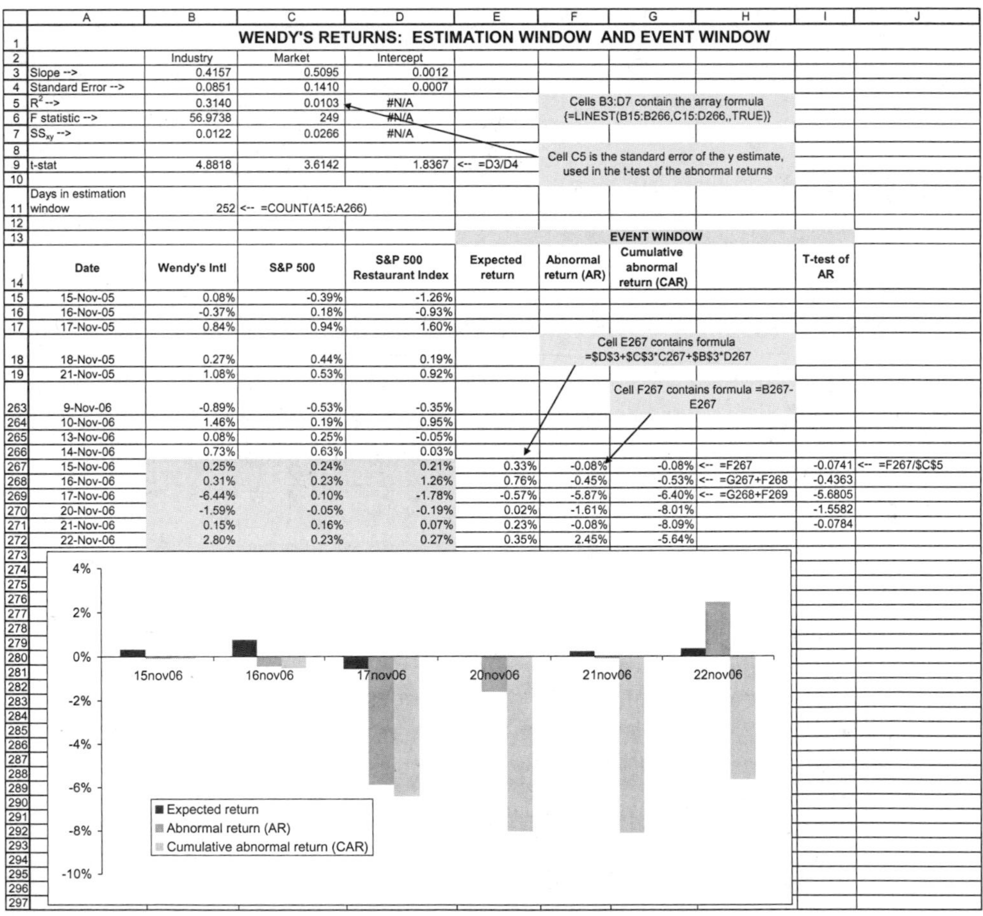

	A	B	C	D	E	F	G	H	I	J
1	WENDY'S RETURNS: ESTIMATION WINDOW AND EVENT WINDOW									
2		Industry	Market	Intercept						
3	Slope -->	0.4157	0.5095	0.0012						
4	Standard Error -->	0.0851	0.1410	0.0007						
5	R^2-->	0.3140	0.0103	#N/A		Cells B3:D7 contain the array formula {=LINEST(B15:B266,C15:D266,,TRUE)}				
6	F statistic -->	56.9738	249	#N/A						
7	SS_{xy} -->	0.0122	0.0266	#N/A						
8										
9	t-stat	4.8818	3.6142	1.8367	<-- =D3/D4	Cell C5 is the standard error of the y estimate, used in the t-test of the abnormal returns				
10										
11	Days in estimation window	252	<-- =COUNT(A15:A266)							
12										
13					EVENT WINDOW					
14	Date	Wendy's Intl	S&P 500	S&P 500 Restaurant Index	Expected return	Abnormal return (AR)	Cumulative abnormal return (CAR)		T-test of AR	
15	15-Nov-05	0.08%	-0.39%	-1.26%						
16	16-Nov-05	-0.37%	0.18%	-0.93%						
17	17-Nov-05	0.84%	0.94%	1.60%						
18	18-Nov-05	0.27%	0.44%	0.19%		Cell E267 contains formula =$D$3+$C$3*C267+$B$3*D267				
19	21-Nov-05	1.08%	0.53%	0.92%						
263	9-Nov-06	-0.89%	-0.53%	-0.35%			Cell F267 contains formula =B267-E267			
264	10-Nov-06	1.46%	0.19%	0.95%						
265	13-Nov-06	0.08%	0.25%	-0.05%						
266	14-Nov-06	0.73%	0.63%	0.03%						
267	15-Nov-06	0.25%	0.24%	0.21%	0.33%	-0.08%	-0.08%	<-- =F267	-0.0741	<-- =F267/$C$5
268	16-Nov-06	0.31%	0.23%	1.26%	0.76%	-0.45%	-0.53%	<-- =G267+F268	-0.4363	
269	17-Nov-06	-6.44%	0.10%	-1.78%	-0.57%	-5.87%	-6.40%	<-- =G268+F269	-5.6805	
270	20-Nov-06	-1.59%	-0.05%	-0.19%	0.02%	-1.61%	-8.01%		-1.5582	
271	21-Nov-06	0.15%	0.16%	0.07%	0.23%	-0.08%	-8.09%		-0.0784	
272	22-Nov-06	2.80%	0.23%	0.27%	0.35%	2.45%	-5.64%			

In rows 267–272 of the spreadsheet we use the two-factor model to analyze the abnormal returns (AR) and the cumulative abnormal returns (CAR) of the Wendy's announcement. While there is little AR or CAR on the days before the announcement, it is clear that the announcement on 16 November had a considerable impact on Wendy's returns on the day following (–5.87% abnormal return on 17 November) and on the next day (–1.63% AR on 20 November). Dividing the abnormal return by the standard error in C5 shows that only the AR on the event day is significant at the 5 percent level.

Furthermore, an analysis of the announcement broken down into the market and the industry factors shows that on both of the two days after the 16 November announcement date the effects of the market index on Wendy's returns were slight. On 17 November, however, there was a significant impact of the S&P 500 Restaurant Index on Wendy's that was lacking on 20 November.

To see this point, we first discuss the day after the event, 17 November 2006:

	A	B	C	D	E	F	G	H
13					EVENT WINDOW			
14	Date	Wendy's Intl	S&P 500	S&P 500 Restaurant Index	Expected return	Abnormal return (AR)	Cumulative abnormal return (CAR)	
266	14-Nov-06	0.73%	0.63%	0.03%				
267	15-Nov-06	0.25%	0.24%	0.21%	0.33%	-0.08%	-0.08%	<-- =F267
268	16-Nov-06	0.31%	0.23%	1.26%	0.76%	-0.45%	-0.53%	<-- =F267+F268
269	17-Nov-06	-6.44%	0.10%	-1.78%	-0.57%	-5.87%	-6.32%	<-- =F268+F269
270	20-Nov-06	-1.59%	-0.05%	-0.19%	0.02%	-1.61%	-7.48%	
271	21-Nov-06	0.15%	0.16%	0.07%	0.23%	-0.08%	-1.69%	
272	22-Nov-06	2.80%	0.23%	0.27%	0.35%	2.45%	2.37%	

On 17 November, the S&P 500 rose by 0.10 percent and the S&P 500 Restaurant Index fell by 1.78 percent. Given the regression $r_{\text{Wendy's},t} = 0.0012 + 0.5095 * r_{Mt} + 0.4157 * r_{\text{Industry},t}$, the change in the S&P 500 would have affected Wendy's returns by approximately +0.05 percent, and the change in the industry index would have affected Wendy's returns by approximately –0.74 percent. But Wendy's decreased by –6.44 percent on the same day, well in excess of the impact of either of the two factors.

Here are the data for 20 November:

	A	B	C	D	E	F	G	H
13					EVENT WINDOW			
14	Date	Wendy's Intl	S&P 500	S&P 500 Restaurant Index	Expected return	Abnormal return (AR)	Cumulative abnormal return (CAR)	
266	14-Nov-06	0.73%	0.63%	0.03%				
267	15-Nov-06	0.25%	0.24%	0.21%	0.33%	-0.08%	-0.08%	<-- =F267
268	16-Nov-06	0.31%	0.23%	1.26%	0.76%	-0.45%	-0.53%	<-- =F267+F268
269	17-Nov-06	-6.44%	0.10%	-1.78%	-0.57%	-5.87%	-6.32%	<-- =F268+F269
270	20-Nov-06	-1.59%	-0.05%	-0.19%	0.02%	-1.61%	-7.48%	
271	21-Nov-06	0.15%	0.16%	0.07%	0.23%	-0.08%	-1.69%	
272	22-Nov-06	2.80%	0.23%	0.27%	0.35%	2.45%	2.37%	

On 20 November, the S&P 500 fell by 0.05 percent and the S&P 500 Restaurant Index fell by 0.19 percent. Given the regression $r_{\text{Wendy's},t} = 0.0012 + 0.5095 * r_{Mt} + 0.4157 * r_{\text{Industry},t}$, the change in the S&P 500 would have affected Wendy's returns by approximately –0.08 percent, and the change in the industry index would have affected Wendy's returns by approximately –0.03 percent. But Wendy's decreased by –1.59 percent on the same day, which is again well in excess of the impact of either of the two factors.

The impact of the announcement was felt even in the third day after the event, but we leave this analysis to the reader.

14.6 Using Excel's Offset Function to Locate a Regression in a Data Set

The analysis in section 14.4 requires us to do a regression of a specific stock's returns on the returns of the S&P 500, where the starting point of the regression is the 252 trading days before a specific date. The technique in section 14.4 uses a number of Excel functions:

- The functions **Intercept**, **Slope**, **Rsq** give the regression intercept, slope, and r-squared. These functions have been illustrated in Chapter 2 and in the previous portfolio chapters. The function **Steyx** gives the standard deviation of the regression residuals.
- The function **Countif** counts the number of cells in a range that meet a specific condition. **Countif** has the syntax **Countif(data,condition)**. *However*, the **condition** must be a text condition (which means that in this example we will use the Excel function **Text** to translate a date to a text number—more later).
- The function **Offset** (see also Chapter 34) allows us to specify a cell or a block of cells in an array.

To illustrate the problem, consider the following data of returns for General Mills (GIS) and the S&P 500. We want to run a regression of the GIS returns on the S&P 500 returns for 10 dates before 29 January 1997:

	A	B	C	D	E	F	G
1	**USING OFFSET, COUNTIF, AND TEXT TO LOCATE A REGRESSION IN A DATA SET**						
2	**Date**	**General Mills GIS**	**Return**		**SP500**	**Return**	
3	3-Jan-97	57.96			748.03		
4	6-Jan-97	58.19	0.0040	<-- =LN(B4/B3)	747.65	-0.0005	<-- =LN(E4/E3)
5	7-Jan-97	59.33	0.0194		753.23	0.0074	
6	8-Jan-97	59.33	0.0000		748.41	-0.0064	
7	9-Jan-97	59.91	0.0097		754.85	0.0086	
8	10-Jan-97	59.91	0.0000		759.5	0.0061	
9	13-Jan-97	59.68	-0.0038		759.51	0.0000	
10	14-Jan-97	59.91	0.0038		768.86	0.0122	
11	15-Jan-97	59.56	-0.0059		767.2	-0.0022	
12	16-Jan-97	59.56	0.0000		769.75	0.0033	
13	17-Jan-97	59.56	0.0000		776.17	0.0083	
14	20-Jan-97	59.44	-0.0020		776.7	0.0007	
15	21-Jan-97	60.71	0.0211		782.72	0.0077	
16	22-Jan-97	61.4	0.0113		786.23	0.0045	
17	23-Jan-97	62.09	0.0112		777.56	-0.0111	
18	24-Jan-97	61.63	-0.0074		770.52	-0.0091	
19	27-Jan-97	61.29	-0.0055		765.02	-0.0072	
20	28-Jan-97	61.06	-0.0038		765.02	0.0000	
21	29-Jan-97	62.09	0.0167		772.5	0.0097	
22	30-Jan-97	62.21	0.0019		784.17	0.0150	
23	31-Jan-97	62.44	0.0037		786.16	0.0025	
24	3-Feb-97	62.09	-0.0056		786.73	0.0007	
25							
26	Starting date	29-Jan-97					
27	Rows from top of data to starting date	19	<-- =COUNTIF(A3:A24,"<="&TEXT(B26,"0"))				
28	**Regression**						
29	Intercept	0.0022	<-- =INTERCEPT(OFFSET(A3:F24,B27-11,2,10,1),OFFSET(A3:F24,B27-11,5,10,1))				
30	Slope	0.5198	<-- =SLOPE(OFFSET(A3:F24,B27-11,2,10,1),OFFSET(A3:F24,B27-11,5,10,1))				
31	R-squared	0.1413	<-- =RSQ(OFFSET(A3:F24,B27-11,2,10,1),OFFSET(A3:F24,B27-11,5,10,1))				
32							
33							
34	**Check**						
35	Intercept	0.0022	<-- =INTERCEPT(C11:C20,F11:F20)				
36	Slope	0.5198	<-- =SLOPE(C11:C20,F11:F20)				
37	R-squared	0.1413	<-- =RSQ(C11:C20,F11:F20)				

To run this regression, we first use **Countif(data,condition)** to count the row number of the data on which the starting date falls. Since **condition** must be a text entry, we translate the date in cell B26 to a text by using **Text(b26,″0″)**. The Excel function **=Countif(A3:A24,″<= ″&Text(B26,″0″))** now counts the number of cells in the column A3:A24 that are less than or equal to the date in cell B26. The answer, as you can see in cell B27, is 19.

Next, we use **Offset(A3:F24,B27-11,2,10,1)** to locate the 10 rows of GIS returns before the 19th row indicated by the starting date. This is a tricky function!

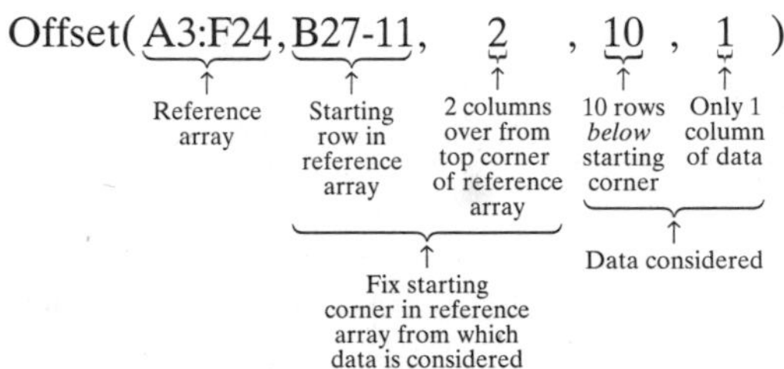

The functions **Intercept**, **Slope**, **Rsq** can now be used with **Offset(A3:F24,B27-11,2,10,1)** and **Offset(A3:F24,B27-11,5,10,1)**:

= Intercept(Offset(A3:F24,B27-11,2,10,1),Offset(A3:F24,B27-11,5,10,1))

(first argument: *y*-data; second argument: *x*-data)

14.7 Conclusion

Event studies, used to determine the impact of a particular market effect on a specific stock or a generic market effect on a set of stocks, are one of the most widely used technologies in practical finance. While Excel may not be the optimal tool for performing an event study, we have used it in this chapter to illustrate both uses of the event study. We have shown that Excel can readily be used to perform either a one-factor or a two-factor event study. The Excel techniques employed are easily acquired by a sophisticated user.

15 Value at Risk[1]

15.1 Overview

Value at risk (VaR) measures the worst expected loss under normal market conditions over a specific time interval at a given confidence level. As one of our references states, "VaR answers the question: how much can I lose with x% probability over a pre-set horizon" (J. P. Morgan, *RiskMetrics—Technical Document*).[2] Another way of expressing this definition is that VaR is the lowest quantile of the potential losses that can occur within a given portfolio during a specified time period. The basic time period T and the confidence level (the quantile) q are the two major parameters that should be chosen in a way appropriate to the overall goal of risk measurement. The time horizon can differ from a few hours for an active trading desk to a year for a pension fund. When the primary goal is to satisfy external regulatory requirements, such as bank capital requirements, the quantile is typically very small (for example, 1 percent of worst outcomes). However, for an internal risk-management model used by a company to control the risk exposure, the typical number is around 5 percent (visit the Internet sites in the references for more details). A general introduction to VaR can be found in Linsmeier and Pearson (1996) and Jorion (1997).

In the jargon of VaR, suppose that a portfolio manager has a daily VaR equal to $1 million at 1 percent. This statement means that there is only one chance in 100 that a daily loss bigger than $1 million occurs under normal market conditions.

15.2 A Really Simple Example

Suppose a manager has a portfolio that consists of a single asset. The return of the asset is normally distributed with a mean return of 20 percent and standard deviation of 30 percent. The value of the portfolio today is $100 million. We want to answer various simple questions about the end-of-year distribution of portfolio value:

1. This chapter is based on an article written with Zvi Wiener, "Value-at-Risk (VaR)," which first appeared in *Mathematica in Education and Research*, Vol. 7, 1998, pp. 39–45.

2. This and other valuable documents initially produced by J. P. Morgan can be found at the site of the successor company, RiskMetrics, http://www.riskmetrics.com/techdoc.html.

1. What is the distribution of the end-of-year portfolio value?
2. What is the probability of a loss of more than $20 million by year-end (i.e., what is the probability that the end-of-year value is less than $80 million)?
3. With 1 percent probability what is the maximum loss at the end of the year? This is the VaR at 1 percent.

The probability that the end-of-year portfolio value is less than $80 million is about 9 percent. ("Million" is omitted in the example.)

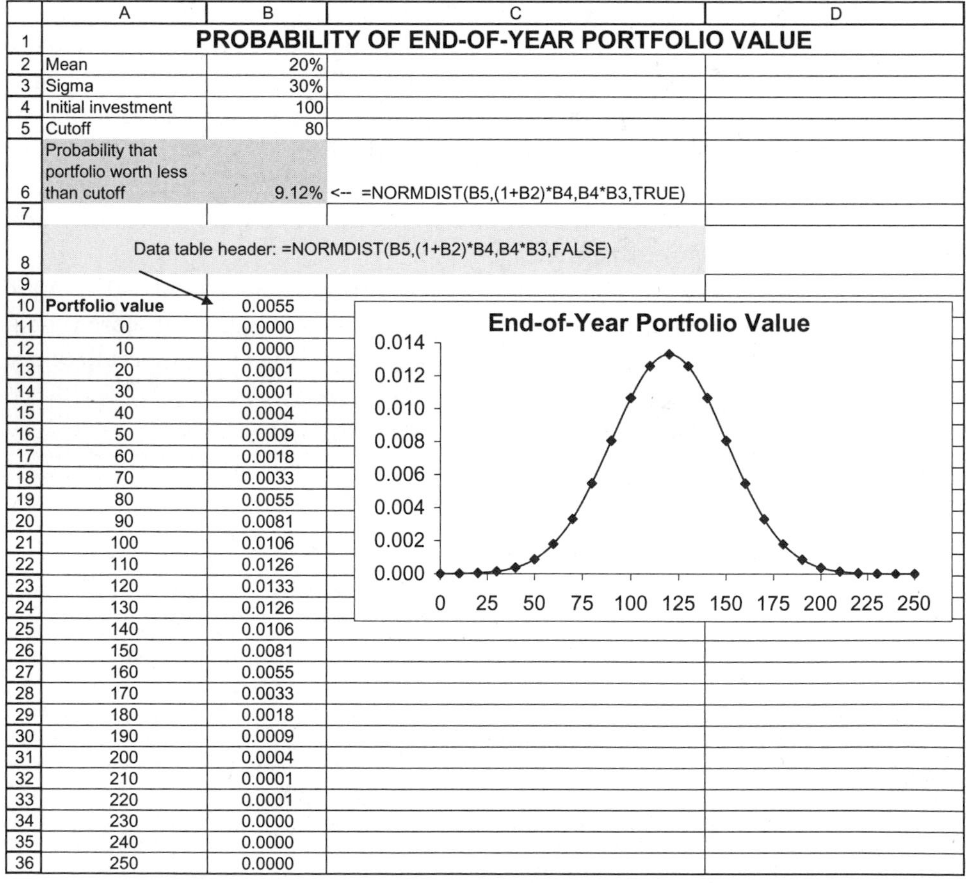

	A	B	C	D
1	**PROBABILITY OF END-OF-YEAR PORTFOLIO VALUE**			
2	Mean	20%		
3	Sigma	30%		
4	Initial investment	100		
5	Cutoff	80		
6	Probability that portfolio worth less than cutoff	9.12%	<-- =NORMDIST(B5,(1+B2)*B4,B4*B3,TRUE)	
7				
8	Data table header: =NORMDIST(B5,(1+B2)*B4,B4*B3,FALSE)			
9				
10	**Portfolio value**	0.0055		
11	0	0.0000		
12	10	0.0000		
13	20	0.0001		
14	30	0.0001		
15	40	0.0004		
16	50	0.0009		
17	60	0.0018		
18	70	0.0033		
19	80	0.0055		
20	90	0.0081		
21	100	0.0106		
22	110	0.0126		
23	120	0.0133		
24	130	0.0126		
25	140	0.0106		
26	150	0.0081		
27	160	0.0055		
28	170	0.0033		
29	180	0.0018		
30	190	0.0009		
31	200	0.0004		
32	210	0.0001		
33	220	0.0001		
34	230	0.0000		
35	240	0.0000		
36	250	0.0000		

Excel's **NormDist** function can return both the cumulative distribution and the probability mass function. Here's the way the screen looks when we apply the **NormDist** function in cell B6:

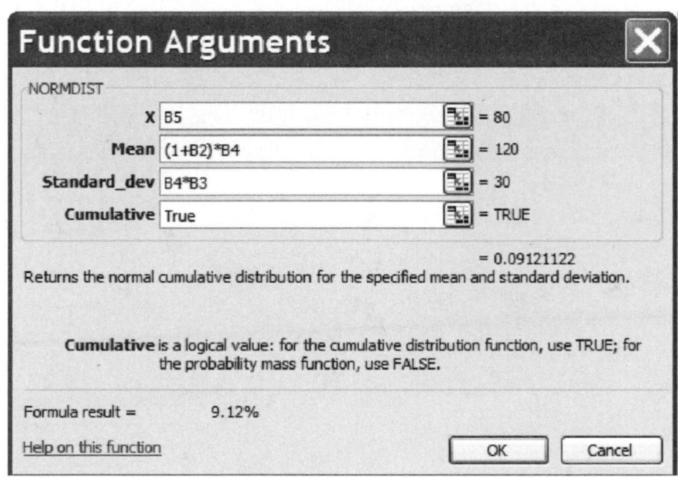

The spreadsheet uses two versions of **NormDist**: First we use the function in cell B6 to determine the probability that the end-year value of the portfolio is less than 80. In this version of the function we use the value TRUE for the last entry in **NormDist**; when we write =NORM DIST(B5,(1+B2)*B4,B4*B3,TRUE), **NormDist** returns values of the cumulative normal distribution. In the data table we set this value to FALSE to plot the probability mass function of the end-year portfolio value.

15.3 Defining Quantiles in Excel

By using Excel's **Solver**, we can determine that with a probability of 1 percent, the end-of-year portfolio value will be less than 50.209. Recall that the value at risk is the worst expected loss under normal market conditions over a specific time interval at a given confidence level. Therefore, the value 50.210 means that the VaR of the portfolio at the 1 percent level is 100 – 50.210 = 49.790.

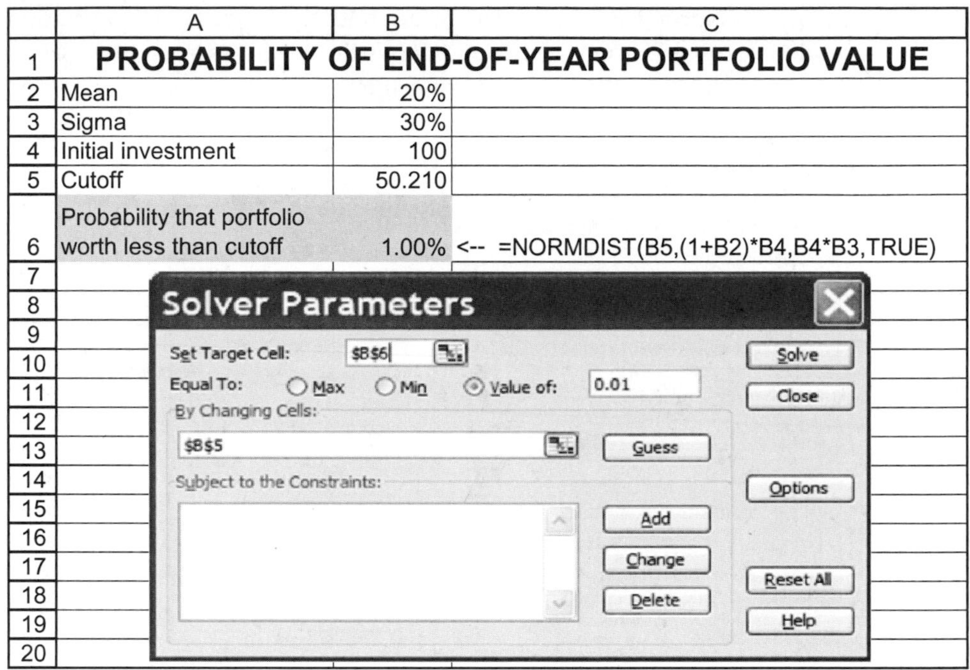

The cutoff is known as the quantile of the distribution. In Excel it can be determined by using **Solver**, as illustrated here. For two distributions we use—the normal and the lognormal distribution—Excel has built-in functions that find the quintile. These functions—**Norminv**, **Normsinv**, and **Loginv**—find the inverse for the normal, standard normal, and lognormal distributions.

Here's an example for the numbers that we've been using; this time we have written the function **=NORMINV(0.01,(1+B3)*B5,B5*B4)** in cell B6. This function finds the cutoff point for which the normal distribution with a mean of 120 and a standard deviation of 30 has probability of 1 percent. You can see this point on the following graph, which shows part of the cumulative distribution:

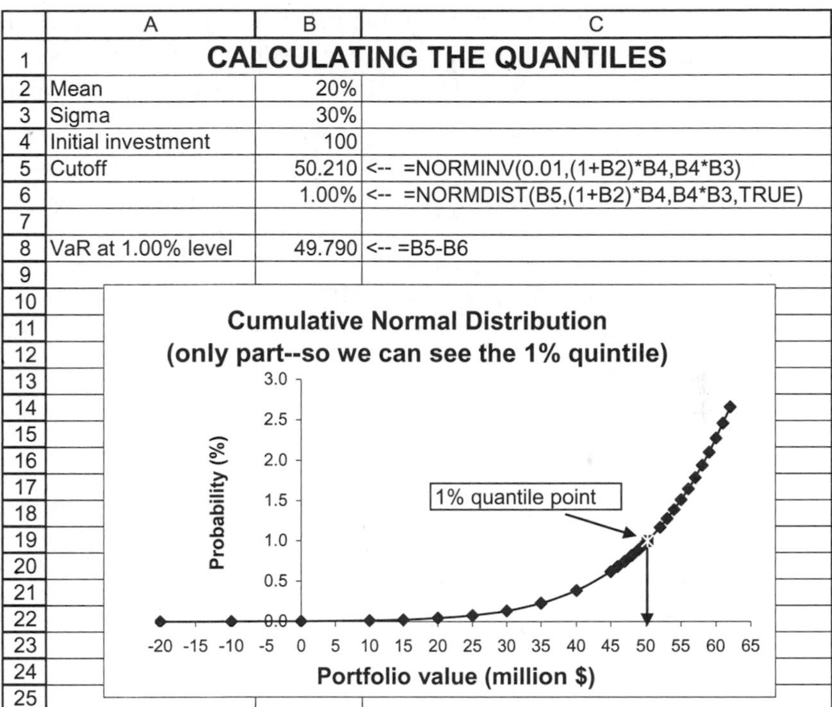

	A	B	C
1	CALCULATING THE QUANTILES		
2	Mean	20%	
3	Sigma	30%	
4	Initial investment	100	
5	Cutoff	50.210	<-- =NORMINV(0.01,(1+B2)*B4,B4*B3)
6		1.00%	<-- =NORMDIST(B5,(1+B2)*B4,B4*B3,TRUE)
7			
8	VaR at 1.00% level	49.790	<-- =B5-B6

15.3.1 The Lognormal Distribution

The lognormal distribution is a more reasonable distribution for many asset prices (which cannot become negative) than the normal distribution. Suppose that the return [return = log(price relative)] on the portfolio is normally distributed with annual mean μ and annual standard deviation σ. Furthermore, suppose that the current value of the portfolio is given by V_0. Then it follows (see Hull 2006, Chapter 11) that the logarithm of the portfolio value at time T, V_T, is normally distributed:

$$\ln(V_T) \sim \text{Normal}\left[\ln(V_0) + \left(\mu - \frac{\sigma^2}{2}\right)T, \sigma\sqrt{T}\right]$$

Suppose, for example, that $V_0 = 100$, $\mu = 10$ percent, and $\sigma = 30$ percent. Thus the end-of-year log of the portfolio value is distributed normally:

$$\ln(V_1) \sim \text{Normal}\left[\ln(100) + \left(0.10 - \frac{0.3^2}{2}\right), 0.3\right] = \text{Normal}[4.666017, 0.3]$$

Thus a portfolio whose initial value is \$100 million and whose annual returns are lognormally distributed with parameters $\mu = 10$ percent and $\sigma = 30$ percent has an annual VaR equal to \$47.42 million at 1 percent:

	A	B	C
1	**QUANTILES FOR LOGNORMAL DISTRIBUTION**		
2	Initial value, V_0	100	
3	Mean, μ	10%	
4	Sigma, σ	30%	
5	Time period, T	1	<-- in years
6			
7	**Parameters of normal distribution of ln(V_T)**		
8	Mean	4.6602	<-- =LN(B2)+(B3-B4^2/2)*B5
9	Sigma	0.3000	<-- =B4*SQRT(B5)
10			
11	Cutoff	52.576	<-- =LOGINV(0.01,B8,B9)
12	VaR at 1% level	47.424	<-- =B2-B11

Most VaR calculations are not concerned with annual value at risk. The main regulatory and management concern is with loss of portfolio value over a much shorter time period (typically several days or perhaps weeks). It is clear that the distribution formula

$$\ln(V_T) \sim \text{Normal}\left[\ln(V_0) + \left(\mu - \frac{\sigma^2}{2}\right)T, \sigma\sqrt{T}\right]$$

can be used to calculate the VaR over any horizon. Recall that T is measured in annual terms; if there are 250 business days in a year, then the daily VaR corresponds to $T = 1/250$ (for many fixed-income instruments one should use 1/360, 1/365, or 1/365.25 depending on the market convention).

15.4 A Three-Asset Problem: The Importance of the Variance-Covariance Matrix

As can be seen from the preceding examples, VaR is not—in principle, at least—a very complicated concept. In the implementation of VaR, however, there are two big practical problems (both problems are discussed in much greater detail in the material available on the RiskMetrics Web site cited in footnote 2):

1. The first problem is the estimation of the parameters of asset return distributions. In "real-world" applications of VaR, it is necessary to estimate means, variances, and correlations of returns. This is a not-inconsiderable problem! In this section we illustrate the importance of the correlations between asset returns. In the following section we give a highly simplified example of the estimation of return distributions from market data. For example, you can imagine that a long position in euros and a short position in U.S. dollars is less risky than a position in only one of the currencies, because of a high probability that profits of one position will be mainly offset by losses of another.
2. The second problem is the actual calculation of position sizes. A large financial institution may have thousands of loans outstanding. The database of these loans may not classify them by their riskiness, nor even by their term to maturity. Or—to give a second example—a bank may have offsetting positions in foreign currencies at different branches in different locations. A long position in Deutschmarks in New York may be offset by a short position in Deutschmarks in Geneva; the bank's risk—which we intend to measure by VaR—is based on the net position.

We start with the problem of correlations between asset returns. We continue the previous example, but assume that there are three risky assets. As before, the parameters of the distributions of the asset returns are known: all the means, μ_1, μ_2, μ_3, as well as the variance-covariance matrix of the returns:

$$S = \begin{pmatrix} \sigma_{11} & \sigma_{12} & \sigma_{13} \\ \sigma_{21} & \sigma_{22} & \sigma_{23} \\ \sigma_{31} & \sigma_{32} & \sigma_{33} \end{pmatrix}$$

The matrix S is of course symmetric; σ_{ii} is the variance of the ith asset's return, and σ_{ij} is the covariance of the returns of assets i and j (if $i = j$, σ_{ij} is the variance of asset i's return).

Suppose that the total portfolio value today is \$100 million, with \$30 million invested in asset 1, \$25 million in asset 2, and \$45 million in asset 3. Then the return distribution of the portfolio is given by

$$\text{Mean return} = \{x_1, x_2, x_3\}\begin{Bmatrix}\mu_1 \\ \mu_2 \\ \mu_3\end{Bmatrix} = x_1\mu_1 + x_2\mu_2 + x_3\mu_3$$

$$\text{Variance of return} = \{x_1, x_2, x_3\}S\{x_1, x_2, x_3\}^T$$

where $x = \{x_1, x_2, x_3\} = \{0.3, 0.25, 0.45\}$ is the vector of proportions invested in each of the three assets. Assuming that the returns are normally distributed (meaning that prices are lognormally distributed), we may calculate the VaR as in the following spreadsheet fragment:

	A	B	C	D	E	F	G	H
1		VaR FOR THREE-ASSET PROBLEM						
2		Mean returns		Variance-covariance matrix				Portfolio proportions
3	Asset 1	10%		0.10	0.04	0.03		0.30
4	Asset 2	12%		0.04	0.20	-0.04		0.25
5	Asset 3	13%		0.03	-0.04	0.60		0.45
6								
7	Initial investment	100						
8	Mean return	0.1185	<-- {=MMULT(TRANSPOSE(B3:B5),H3:H5)}					
9	Portfolio sigma	0.3848	<-- {=SQRT(MMULT(MMULT(TRANSPOSE(H3:H5),D3:F5),H3:H5))}					
10								
11	Mean investment value	111.8500						
12	Sigma of investment value	38.4838						
13								
14	Cutoff	22.3234	<-- =NORMINV(0.01,(1+B8)*B7,B9*B7)					
15	Cumulative PDF	0.01	<-- =NORMDIST(B16,B13,B14,TRUE)					
16	VaR at 1.00% level	77.6766	<-- =B7-B14					
17								
18		Note that the functions in cells B8 and B9 are array functions: You must press [Ctrl]+[Shift]+[Enter] after you write the function in the cell. The curly brackets {} are not written--they appear automatically.						

15.5 Simulating Data—Bootstrapping

Sometimes it helps to simulate data. In this section we give an example. We suppose that the current date is 10 February, 1997, and we consider a firm that has an investment in two assets:

• It is long two units of an index fund. The fund's current market price is 293, so that the investment in the index fund is worth $2 * 293 = 586$.

• It is short a foreign bond denominated in rubles. The bond is a zero-coupon bond (i.e., pays no interest), has face value of 100 rubles and maturity of 8 May, 2000. If the current ruble interest rate is 5.30 percent, then the 10 February, 1997, ruble value of the bond is

$$-100 * \exp[-5.30 \text{ percent} * (\text{May } 8, 2000 - \text{Feb. } 10, 1997)/365] = -84.2166$$

In dollars, the value of the bond is –84.2166 ∗ 3.40 = –286.3365, so that the net portfolio value is 586 – 286.3365 = 299.66.

This example is illustrated in the following display:

	A	B	C	D	E	F	G	H	I
1	**BOOTSTRAPPING DATA--INITIAL POSITION**								
2	Units of Index held	2							
3	Bond maturity	May 8, 2000							
4									
5	**Date**	**Index value**	**Ruble interest rate**	**Ruble exchange rate**		**Total index value**	**Ruble bond value**	**Dollar bond value**	**Portfolio value**
6	2/10/1997	293	5.30%	3.40		586.00	-84.2166	-286.3365	299.66
7									
8						=B2*B6			
9								=G6*D6	=F6+H6
10									
11						=-100*EXP(-(B3-A6)/365*C6)			

Now suppose we have exchange-rate and index data. We illustrate data for 40 days (the middle of the data has been hidden, but you will see that the rows go from 8 to 45):

	A	B	C	D	E	F
1	**EXCHANGE-RATE AND INDEX DATA**					
2	Units of Index held	2				
3	Bond maturity	May 8, 2000				
4						
5	**Day**	**Index**	**Foreign interest rate**	**Exchange rate**		**Portfolio value**
6	1/2/1997	462.71	5.28%	3.50		632.13
7	1/3/1997	514.71	5.26%	3.47		738.41
8	1/4/1997	456.5	5.23%	3.46		622.49
9	1/5/1997	487.39	5.24%	3.45		685.17
10	1/6/1997	470.42	5.25%	3.45		651.28
43	2/8/1997	467.14	5.31%	3.44		644.75
44	2/9/1997	562.06	5.32%	3.41		837.17
45	2/10/1997	481.61	5.30%	3.40		676.88

We want to use these data as a basis for generating “random” return data. We illustrate one technique for doing so, called *bootstrapping*: This term refers to random reshufflings of the data. For each iteration, we reorder the series of index prices, interest rates, and exchange rates and calculate the return on the portfolio.[3]

	A	B	C	D	E	F	G	H
1	**BOOTSTRAPPING RETURN DISTRIBUTIONS**							
2	Units of Index held	2			Iterations	5,000	Start time	11:45:50
3	Bond maturity	May 8, 2000			Return	0.15	Elapsed	0:16:41
4	Number of data points	40						
5							=H46/H7-1	
6	**Day**	**Index**	**Index rand**	**Foreign interest rate**	**Interest rand**	**Exchange rate**	**Exchange rand**	**Portfolio value**
7	1/2/1997	615.93	0.0029	5.31%	0.0148	3.40	0.0202	947.24
8	1/3/1997	757.02	0.0447	5.24%	0.0179	3.41	0.0456	1,227.87
9	1/4/1997	581.50	0.0452	5.32%	0.0377	3.44	0.0620	875.04
10	1/5/1997	651.99	0.0742	5.28%	0.0383	3.42	0.0846	1,017.27
11	1/6/1997	605.37	0.1027	5.28%	0.0634	3.50	0.1070	917.28
12	1/7/1997	514.71	0.1455	5.28%	0.0640	3.43	0.1321	741.79
13	1/8/1997	640.43	0.1574	5.28%	0.0652	3.48	0.1522	988.99
14	1/9/1997	645.50	0.2020	5.25%	0.0789	3.43	0.1532	1,003.00
15	1/10/1997	450.91	0.2049	5.34%	0.0884	3.46	0.1994	612.12
16	1/11/1997	475.49	0.2075	5.26%	0.1111	3.46	0.2074	660.47
17	1/12/1997	654.17	0.3184	5.36%	0.3611	3.42	0.2156	1,022.10
18	1/13/1997	445.77	0.3308	5.31%	0.3662	3.37	0.2309	608.98
19	1/14/1997	669.12	0.3799	5.28%	0.4016	3.44	0.2428	1,049.48
20	1/15/1997	500.71	0.3878	5.31%	0.4112	3.44	0.2469	712.65
21	1/16/1997	705.27	0.3951	5.35%	0.4387	3.46	0.2963	1,120.69
22	1/17/1997	533.40	0.4201	5.28%	0.4603	3.46	0.3266	776.23
23	1/18/1997	639.95	0.4465	5.32%	0.4751	3.42	0.3454	993.03
24	1/19/1997	444.27	0.4551	5.30%	0.4763	3.39	0.4183	603.96
25	1/20/1997	670.63	0.4654	5.25%	0.4797	3.45	0.5154	1,051.12
26	1/21/1997	470.42	0.4655	5.25%	0.4952	3.42	0.5357	653.18
27	1/22/1997	458.26	0.5114	5.26%	0.5059	3.45	0.5883	626.39
28	1/23/1997	466.45	0.5386	5.27%	0.5217	3.47	0.6197	641.14
29	1/24/1997	462.71	0.5456	5.27%	0.5596	3.48	0.6813	632.78
30	1/25/1997	459.27	0.5682	5.24%	0.5798	3.42	0.7240	630.62
31	1/26/1997	740.74	0.6100	5.23%	0.6026	3.41	0.7321	1,194.27
32	1/27/1997	790.82	0.6245	5.28%	0.6068	3.41	0.7507	1,294.86
33	1/28/1997	487.39	0.6405	5.34%	0.6384	3.44	0.7987	686.00
34	1/29/1997	456.50	0.6795	5.29%	0.6583	3.52	0.8033	616.98
35	1/30/1997	467.14	0.6922	5.24%	0.6601	3.40	0.8047	647.84
36	1/31/1997	481.61	0.7349	5.27%	0.6699	3.41	0.8337	676.18
37	2/1/1997	544.75	0.7357	5.26%	0.6836	3.42	0.8501	801.48
38	2/2/1997	453.69	0.7423	5.24%	0.7388	3.68	0.8512	597.22
39	2/3/1997	786.16	0.7436	5.27%	0.7867	3.49	0.8553	1,278.42
40	2/4/1997	561.88	0.7944	5.29%	0.8107	3.41	0.8797	836.74
41	2/5/1997	562.06	0.9345	5.32%	0.8328	3.45	0.8811	833.97
42	2/6/1997	472.35	0.9353	5.23%	0.8759	3.42	0.9045	656.19
43	2/7/1997	636.02	0.9406	5.35%	0.8899	3.42	0.9336	984.61
44	2/8/1997	461.79	0.9630	5.30%	0.9238	3.49	0.9662	629.75
45	2/9/1997	584.41	0.9688	5.26%	0.9403	3.47	0.9878	876.25
46	2/10/1997	687.33	0.9713	5.25%	0.9585	3.41	0.9990	1,087.02

The distribution of the bootstrapped return data looks like the following.

3. The bootstrapping technique is illustrated in the appendix to this chapter.

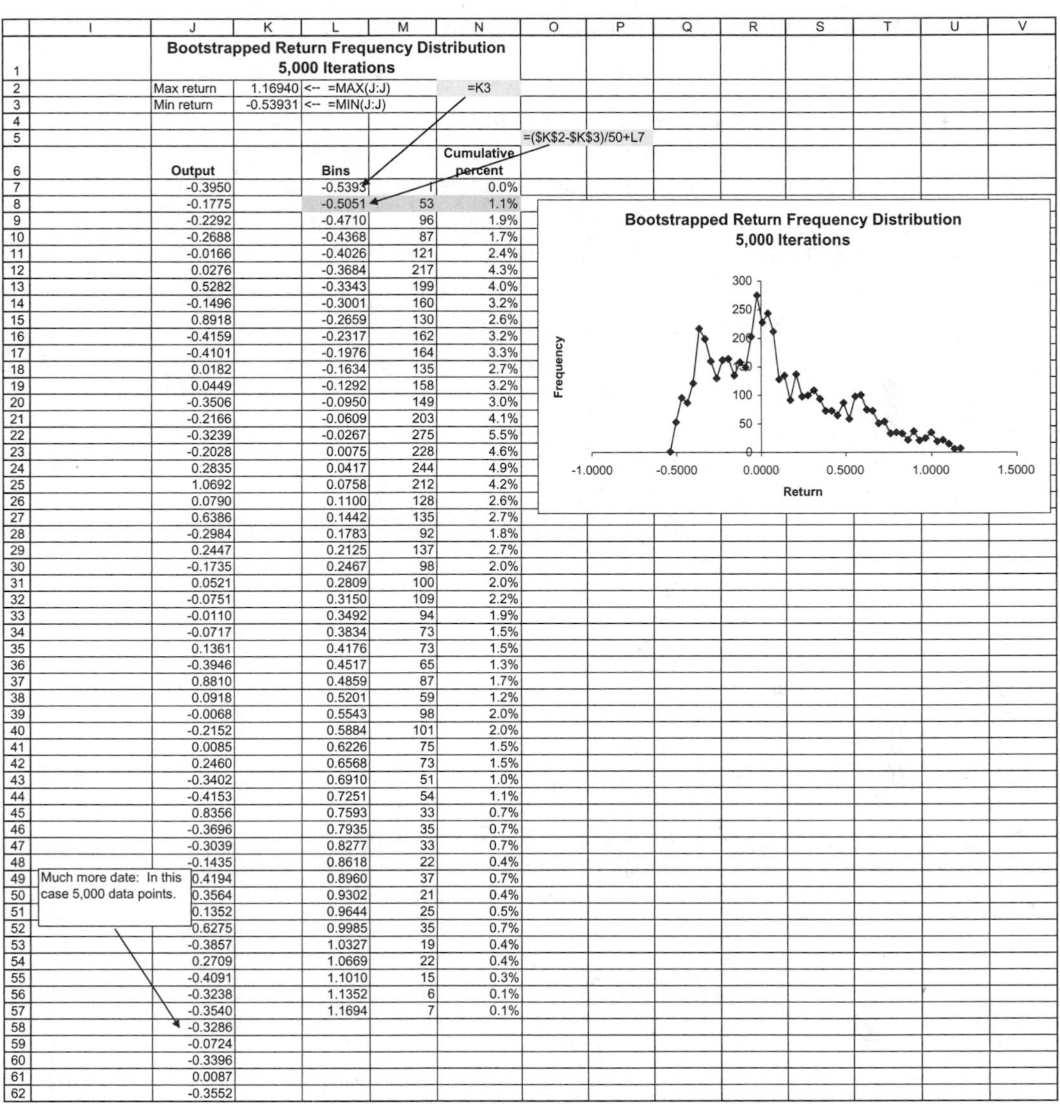

	I	J	K	L	M	N	O
1		**Bootstrapped Return Frequency Distribution 5,000 Iterations**					
2		Max return	1.16940	<-- =MAX(J:J)		=K3	
3		Min return	-0.53931	<-- =MIN(J:J)			
4							
5							=($K$2-$K$3)/50+L7
6		**Output**		**Bins**		**Cumulative percent**	
7		-0.3950		-0.5393	1	0.0%	
8		-0.1775		-0.5051	53	1.1%	
9		-0.2292		-0.4710	96	1.9%	
10		-0.2688		-0.4368	87	1.7%	
11		-0.0166		-0.4026	121	2.4%	
12		0.0276		-0.3684	217	4.3%	
13		0.5282		-0.3343	199	4.0%	
14		-0.1496		-0.3001	160	3.2%	
15		0.8918		-0.2659	130	2.6%	
16		-0.4159		-0.2317	162	3.2%	
17		-0.4101		-0.1976	164	3.3%	
18		0.0182		-0.1634	135	2.7%	
19		0.0449		-0.1292	158	3.2%	
20		-0.3506		-0.0950	149	3.0%	
21		-0.2166		-0.0609	203	4.1%	
22		-0.3239		-0.0267	275	5.5%	
23		-0.2028		0.0075	228	4.6%	
24		0.2835		0.0417	244	4.9%	
25		1.0692		0.0758	212	4.2%	
26		0.0790		0.1100	128	2.6%	
27		0.6386		0.1442	135	2.7%	
28		-0.2984		0.1783	92	1.8%	
29		0.2447		0.2125	137	2.7%	
30		-0.1735		0.2467	98	2.0%	
31		0.0521		0.2809	100	2.0%	
32		-0.0751		0.3150	109	2.2%	
33		-0.0110		0.3492	94	1.9%	
34		-0.0717		0.3834	73	1.5%	
35		0.1361		0.4176	73	1.5%	
36		-0.3946		0.4517	65	1.3%	
37		0.8810		0.4859	87	1.7%	
38		0.0918		0.5201	59	1.2%	
39		-0.0068		0.5543	98	2.0%	
40		-0.2152		0.5884	101	2.0%	
41		0.0085		0.6226	75	1.5%	
42		0.2460		0.6568	73	1.5%	
43		-0.3402		0.6910	51	1.0%	
44		-0.4153		0.7251	54	1.1%	
45		0.8356		0.7593	33	0.7%	
46		-0.3696		0.7935	35	0.7%	
47		-0.3039		0.8277	33	0.7%	
48		-0.1435		0.8618	22	0.4%	
49	Much more date: In this	0.4194		0.8960	37	0.7%	
50	case 5,000 data points.	0.3564		0.9302	21	0.4%	
51		0.1352		0.9644	25	0.5%	
52		0.6275		0.9985	35	0.7%	
53		-0.3857		1.0327	19	0.4%	
54		0.2709		1.0669	22	0.4%	
55		-0.4091		1.1010	15	0.3%	
56		-0.3238		1.1352	6	0.1%	
57		-0.3540		1.1694	7	0.1%	
58		-0.3286					
59		-0.0724					
60		-0.3396					
61		0.0087					
62		-0.3552					

The graph on the right indicates the return distribution, which is far from normal. From columns L, M, and N, you can tell that the 1 percent VaR is about −50 percent, meaning that with a probability of 1 percent, the firm could lose 50 percent of its investment.

15.5.1 How Did We Produce the Bootstrapped Data?

Bootstrapping basically consists of reshuffling the data randomly, and then viewing each reshuffle as a point in a distribution. In the preceding spreadsheet, columns C, E, and G contain random numbers. The VBA program that follows (which is operated on the spreadsheet fm3_chapter15.xls by pressing [Ctrl] + a) contains three **For** loops that insert three columns of random numbers into the spreadsheet.

Having inserted the random numbers, the spreadsheet then uses Excel's **Sort** function to sort the index prices (column B), the foreign interest rates (column D), and the exchange rate (column F). This procedure produces random combinations of the three portfolio pricing factors, which give the resulting portfolio values in column H and the portfolio return in cell F3).

```
'My thanks to Marek Jochec for cleaning up
this code!
Sub randomizeit()
  Range("starttime") = Time
  Range("J7:J15000").ClearContents
  Application.ScreenUpdating = False

  For Iteration = 1 To Range("iterations")
  For Row = 1 To 40
  Range("IndexRand").Cells(Row, 1) = Rnd
  Next Row

  For Row = 1 To 40
  Range("InterestRand").Cells(Row, 1) = Rnd
  Next Row

  For Row = 1 To 40
  Range("ExchangeRand").Cells(Row, 1) = Rnd
  Next Row
```

```
   Range("B7:C46").Sort Key1:=Range("C6"),
    Order1:=xlAscending, _
     Header:=xlNo
   Range("D7:E46").Sort Key1:=Range("E6"),
    Order1:=xlAscending, _
     Header:=xlNo
   Range("F7:G46").Sort Key1:=Range("G6"),
    Order1:=xlAscending, _
     Header:=xlNo

   Range("returndata").Cells(Iteration, 1) =
    Range("meanreturn")
   Next Iteration

   Range("elapsed") = Time - Range("starttime")

End Sub
```

Having produced the bootstrapped data, we use the array function **Frequency** (see Chapter 35) to produce a distribution of the simulated data.

Notice that this simulation takes a very long time! On the author's laptop 5,000 simulations took almost 17 minutes.

Appendix: How to Bootstrap: Making a Bingo Card in Excel

Bootstrapping refers to a technique of random shuffling of data to create more "data." This appendix gives a simple illustration of bootstrapping. It is based on the "birthday bingo" game created for Helena Benninga's 85th birthday. The game goes like this:

• Everyone gets a "Helen Bingo Card," which has five columns of five numbers each. The first column has five numbers from 1 to 17, the second column five numbers between 18 and 34, and so on. A typical card looks like this:

HELEN'S 85TH BIRTHDAY BINGO GAME!!!

H	E	L	E	N
3	23	51	52	75
15	26	40	57	70
9	21	50	68	82
7	22	49	56	71
8	20	45	55	69

• We made up 85 questions with answers from 1 to 85. When a card with a question was drawn, someone had to give the correct answer, and then everyone who had the number on his or her card could cross it out. For example, if we asked, "How many grandchildren does Helen have?" and someone answered, "Thirteen," then everyone with a 13 in the first column could cross it out.

• The first person with five numbers in a line (a column, a row, or a diagonal) won the prize. (Note that it didn't take any talent to win—all you had to do was hear the right answers.)

We wanted to use Excel to create the cards, but it wasn't initially clear how to go about this task. Finally, the requisite trick, which is that we want to model the selection of balls from an urn without replacement, was discovered. (We will discuss this topic in greater detail later.)

The Trick

The trick is very simple. As an illustration, suppose we want to make a random draw of five numbers between 1 and 17. (These will be the five numbers that will appear in the first column of a particular Helen Bingo card.) Here's how we go about it:

• First create a list of numbers from 1 to 17 and an adjoining column of random numbers. This step will give something that looks like the following:

	A	B
1	EXPLAINING THE TRICK	
2	1	0.653152
3	2	0.425876
4	3	0.743173
5	4	0.911709
6	5	0.104356
7	6	0.09228
8	7	0.49608
9	8	0.210725
10	9	0.740506
11	10	0.724376
12	11	0.310175
13	12	0.437225
14	13	0.197224
15	14	0.145462
16	15	0.797405
17	16	0.52166
18	17	0.438188

The list of numbers was itself created in two stages: In the first stage **=Rand()** was entered into each of the cells B2:B18. In the second stage B2:B18 were copied and were then pasted special back into their locations using **Edit|Paste Special|Values**. This procedure gets rid of the formulas behind the numbers (else **Rand()** will change its values every time we hit [Enter]).

• Next, sort both columns using the second column as a sorting key. First mark off the relevant data, and then use the Excel command **Data|Sort**. This will bring up the following screen, in which I've chosen to sort the data by Column B.

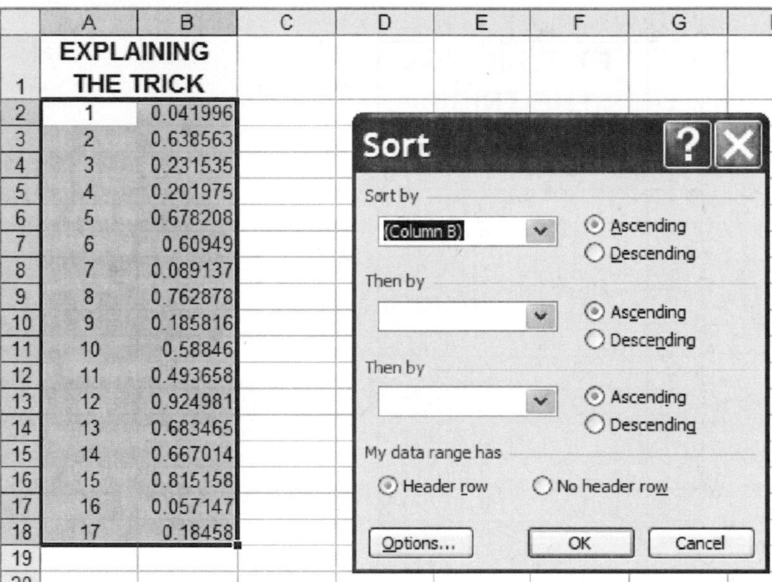

- In this case the sort command will give

	A	B
1	EXPLAINING THE TRICK	
2	1	0.041996
3	16	0.057147
4	7	0.089137
5	17	0.18458
6	9	0.185816
7	4	0.201975
8	3	0.231535
9	11	0.493658
10	10	0.58846
11	6	0.60949
12	2	0.638563
13	14	0.667014
14	5	0.678208
15	13	0.683465
16	8	0.762878
17	15	0.815158
18	12	0.924981

• Finally, pick the first five numbers from the first column (in this example, 1, 16, 7, 17, 9). You could, of course, equally well pick the last five, the middle five, or any other five numbers from the column.

The Probabilistic Model

What we're doing here is just like picking random numbers out of an urn *without replacement.* This model, standard in all introductory probability books, imagines an urn filled with balls. Each ball has a different number—in our case, there are 17 balls with numbers between 1 and 17. The urn is shaken to mix up the balls, and then five balls are drawn out. Each ball, once drawn, is not placed back in the urn.

This model is somewhat different from the standard random-number generators, which pick random numbers with replacement (i.e., once the ball's number is recorded, it is placed back in the urn, so that it could possibly be drawn again).[4]

Writing a VBA Program

The next obvious step was to write a program in VBA to automate the procedure. Here is the spreadsheet:

4. Excel has a function **Randbetween(low,high)** which lets you create random integers between **low** and **high**. Thus, to create five numbers between 1 and 17, you just copy **=Randbetween(1,17)** into five adjacent cells. However, this is like drawing numbers from the urn with replacement and hence can give you multiple draws of the same number—a bingo no-no!

	B	C	D	E	F	G	H	I
1		HELEN'S						
2		85TH BIRTHDAY					Ctrl + b runs the macro	
3		BINGO GAME!						
4								
5		H	E	L	E	N		
6		2	20	47	63	73		
7		15	18	39	68	78		
8		5	31	43	58	80		
9		11	19	44	65	69		
10		17	26	51	64	76		
11								

The code that produced this spreadsheet is as follows:[5]

5. I thank Paul Legerer for vastly improving the code for this program from the previous edition of *Financial Modeling*. An astute reader will note that Paul's program internalizes the sorting of the random numbers in the VBA code, so that only the printing of the card is done in the spreadsheet.

```
Public Const NperR = 17
Public Const BingoRows = 5
Public Const BingoColumns = 5
Public Const BingoCard = "C6:G10"

Option Base 1

Sub DoIt()
'loop 5 time (1 loop for each
'column on the bingo card)

For iii = 1 To BingoColumns
  Dim ArraySort(NperR, 2)
  For i = 1 To NperR

'first dimension of the array:
'random number between 0 and 1
  ArraySort(i, 1) = Rnd

'second dimension of the array:
'position in the array (1-17 in the first loop,
'18 to 34 in the second loop, etc...)
  ArraySort(i, 2) = i + (iii - 1) * NperR
  Next i

  For ii = 1 To NperR

'look for the minimum value in the array
'and keep also the value of the position (1
to 17)
  MinNum = ArraySort(ii, 1)
  MinIndex = ArraySort(ii, 2)
  RealIndex = ii
  For i = ii To NperR
    If ArraySort(i, 1) < MinNum Then
    MinNum = ArraySort(i, 1)
    MinIndex = ArraySort(i, 2)
    RealIndex = i
    End If
```

```
    Next i

'Replace the first number in the array by the
'minimum value and...
   TempNum = ArraySort(ii, 1)
   TempIndex = ArraySort(ii, 2)
   ArraySort(ii, 1) = MinNum
   ArraySort(ii, 2) = MinIndex
   ArraySort(RealIndex, 1) = TempNum
   ArraySort(RealIndex, 2) = TempIndex

'start again with the remaining numbers: once
the
'the last loop is completed, all numbers are
sorted
   Next ii

'write the first 5 numbers (number of rows on
the
'bingo card) of the results into the
spreadsheet

   With ActiveSheet.Range(BingoCard)
      For ii = 1 To BingoRows
           .Cells(ii, iii) = ArraySort(ii, 2)
      Next ii
      End With
   Next iii
End Sub
```

Another Way to Do the Bingo Cards

There's another way to design the bingo cards, using the Excel **Rank** function:[6]

6. I thank A. C. M. de Bakker for the suggestion in this subsection.

	A	B	C	D	E	F	G
1							
2		**H**	**E**	**L**	**E**	**N**	
3		1	31	36	63	83	<-- =(F$9-1)*17+RANK(F10,F$10:F$26)
4		3	27	38	58	84	<-- =(F$9-1)*17+RANK(F11,F$10:F$26)
5		11	32	44	55	78	
6		2	23	35	68	75	
7		6	19	45	61	76	
8							
9		1	2	3	4	5	
10		0.9562	0.2730	0.8788	0.2574	0.0735	<-- =RAND()
11		0.8333	0.5145	0.7366	0.5556	0.0702	<-- =RAND()
12		0.4827	0.2727	0.4318	0.8825	0.5355	<-- =RAND()
13		0.8475	0.6533	0.9783	0.0103	0.6092	
14		0.7706	0.9582	0.3832	0.3485	0.6019	
15		0.4284	0.6652	0.2587	0.6039	0.9998	
16		0.2066	0.3386	0.0672	0.0924	0.5632	
17		0.6735	0.1244	0.3091	0.8998	0.8532	
18		0.2589	0.6032	0.0847	0.4665	0.4054	
19		0.6858	0.9602	0.4834	0.6650	0.8638	
20		0.3187	0.6513	0.2867	0.8896	0.0098	
21		0.3953	0.1872	0.3402	0.1919	0.7563	
22		0.8029	0.3386	0.5020	0.2635	0.8696	
23		0.8241	0.5994	0.7240	0.0538	0.9613	
24		0.5427	0.9184	0.7793	0.4888	0.2180	
25		0.7136	0.4916	0.4389	0.9486	0.1391	
26		0.0453	0.8367	0.5422	0.2381	0.5272	

The entries in rows 10–26 are created with **Rand()**. The entries of the bingo card are computed with the formula:

$$= \underbrace{(F\$9-1)*17}_{\uparrow} + \underbrace{RANK(F10,F\$10:F\$26)}_{\uparrow}$$

Guarantees that all numbers in column F are more than 68 (and likewise for other columns)

What is the rank of F10 among F10:F26? When copied down one cell: What is the rank of F11 among F10:F26? etc.

The only disadvantage of this very clever implementation of bootstrapping is that the entries on the card change with each recomputation of the spreadsheet.

III Option-Pricing Models

Chapters 16–24 deal with option pricing and applications. Chapter 16 is an introduction to options. After defining the option terminology, Chapter 16 discusses option payoffs and basic option pricing propositions. In Chapter 17 we discuss the binomial option pricing model and its implementation in Excel. After showing how these binomial models work, we use Visual Basic for Applications (VBA; see Chapters 37–40) to build binomial option-pricing functions for both European and American options. One of the applications discussed is the pricing of employee stock options.

Chapter 18 discusses the lognormality of stock prices. The assumption of lognormality underlies the Black-Scholes pricing formulas; in Chapter 18 we use Excel to simulate lognormal price processes.

Chapter 19 discusses the Black-Scholes pricing formulas for European calls and puts. These formulas can be implemented either by direct calculation in the spreadsheet or by using VBA to build new spreadsheet functions. An extension of the Black-Scholes model to the pricing of dividend-paying stocks (the so-called Merton model) is implemented. We show how to apply the option pricing models to the valuation of structured securities. Chapter 20 discusses the computation of "Greeks"—the derivatives of the option-pricing formula that show the sensitivities of the option valuation to its various parameters.

In Chapter 21 we discuss an application of the Black-Scholes model—portfolio insurance. We use Excel to simulate the performance of portfolio insurance strategies; these simulations use the lognormal simulations developed in Chapter 18.

Many options cannot be priced by the closed-form formulas discussed in Chapter 19. Chapters 22 and 23 show how to implement Monte Carlo techniques for the pricing of Asian and barrier options. VBA and Excel lend themselves readily to Monte Carlo.

Real options are illustrated in Chapter 24. Real options are an application of option-like concepts to the capital budgeting and valuation problems discussed in Chapters 1–4. We show an application of the real-option technique to the valuation of a bio-med startup.

16 An Introduction to Options

16.1 Overview

In this chapter we give a brief introduction to options. The chapter can, at best, serve as an introduction to the already informed. If you know nothing whatsoever about options, read an introduction to the topic in a basic finance text.[1] We start with the basic definitions and options terminology, go on to discuss graphs of option payoffs and "profit diagrams," and finally discuss some of the more important option arbitrage propositions (sometimes referred to as linear pricing restrictions). In subsequent chapters we discuss two methods of pricing options: The binomial option-pricing model (Chapter 17) and the Black-Scholes option-pricing model (Chapter 19).

16.2 Basic Option Definitions and Terminology

An *option on a stock* is a security that gives the holder the right to buy or to sell one share of the stock on or before a particular date for a predetermined price. Here is a brief glossary of terms and notation used in the field of options:

- *Call, C:* An option that gives the holder the right to buy a share of stock on or before a given date at a predetermined price.
- *Put, P:* An option that gives the holder the right to sell a share of stock on or before a given date at a predetermined price.
- *Exercise price, X:* The price at which the holder can buy or sell the underlying stock; sometimes also referred to as the *strike price.*
- *Expiration date, T:* The date on or before which the holder can buy or sell the underlying stock.
- *Stock price, S_t:* The price at which the underlying stock is selling at date t. The current stock price is denoted S_0.
- *Option price:* The price at which the option is sold or bought.

1. Good chapters can be found in the following books: John Hull, *Options, Futures, and Other Derivatives* (6th edition, 2006, Upper Saddle River, NJ: Prentice Hall); Bodie, Kane, and Marcus, *Investments* (6th edition, 2004, New York: McGraw Hill Higher Education).

American versus European options In the jargon of options markets, an American option is an option that can be exercised on or before the expiration date T, whereas a European option is one that can be exercised only on the expiration date T. This terminology is confusing for two reasons:

1. The options sold on both European and American options exchanges are almost invariably American options.

2. The simplest option-pricing formulas (including the famous Black-Scholes option-pricing formula discussed in Chapter 19) are for *European options*. As we show in section 16.6, in many cases we can price American options as if they were European options.

We use C_t to denote the price of a European call on date t, and P_t to denote the European put price. If it is clear that the option price refers to today's price, we often drop the subscript, writing C or P instead of C_0 or P_0. When we need fuller notation, we write $C_t(S_t, X, T)$ for the price of a call on date t when the price of the underlying stock is S_t, the exercise price is X, and the expiration date is T. If we wish to specify that our option-pricing formula relates to an American option, we use the superscript A: C_t^A, $C_t^A(S_t, X, T)$ or $P_t^A(S_t, X, T)$. When written without superscripts, the symbols refer to European options.

At the Money, in the Money, out of the Money If the exercise price X of a call or a put is equal to the current price of the stock S_0, then the option is *at the money*. If a positive cash flow could be made by immediately exercising an American option (that is, $S_0 - X > 0$ for a call and $X - S_0 > 0$ for a put), then the option is *in the money*.[2]

16.2.1 Writing Options versus Purchasing Options: Cash Flows

The purchaser of a call option acquires the right to buy a share of stock for a given price on or before date T and pays for this right at the time of purchase. The *writer* or seller of this call option is the seller of this right: The writer collects the option price today in return for obligating herself to deliver one share of stock in the future for the exercise price,

2. It is of course not logical that you can ever make an immediate profit by buying an American option and immediately exercising it. Thus, for American calls, $C_0 > S_0 - X$, and for American puts, $P_0 > X - S_0$. Thus *in the money* and *out of the money* refer only to the relation between S_0 and X without taking into account the option price.

if the purchaser of the call demands. In terms of cash flows, the purchaser of an option always has an initial negative cash flow (the price of the option) and a future cash flow that is at worst zero (if it is not worthwhile exercising the option) and otherwise positive (if the option is exercised). The cash-flow position of the writer of the option is reversed: An initial positive cash flow is followed by a terminal cash flow that is at best zero.

Call Option Payoff Patterns

Time 0	Between times 0 and T	Time T	
Purchase call option, cash flow < 0	Cash flow = 0 for European option Cash flow ≥ 0 for American option	Terminal call payoff, $\text{Max}[S_T - X, 0] \geq 0$	Cash flows of call buyer
Write (i.e., issue) call option, cash flow > 0	Cash flow = 0 for European option Cash flow ≤ 0 for American option	Pay terminal call payoff $= -\text{Max}[S_T - X, 0] \leq 0$	Cash flows of call writer

A similar payoff pattern holds for the cash flows of the purchaser and writer of a put option on a stock:

Put Option Payoff Patterns

Time 0	Between times 0 and T	Time T	
Purchase put option, cash flow < 0	Cash flow = 0 for European option Cash flow ≥ 0 for American option	Terminal put payoff, $\text{Max}[X - S_T, 0] \geq 0$	Cash flows of put buyer
Write (i.e., issue) call option, cash flow > 0	Cash flow = 0 for European option Cash flow ≤ 0 for American option	Pay terminal call payoff $= -\text{Max}[X - S_T, 0] \leq 0$	Cash flows of put writer

16.3 Some Examples

The following spreadsheet shows the most actively traded options on 3 October 2006:

	A	B	C	D	E	F	G	H	I	J
1	MOST ACTIVE OPTIONS, 3 OCTOBER 2006									
2		Stock								
3	Rank	Symbol	Name	Option expiration	Option exercise price	Put or call?	Stock closing price	Option closing price	Volume	Open Interest
4	1	HAL	Halliburton	20-Apr-07	27.5	Put	26.75	3.025	60,945	7,305
5	2	HAL	Halliburton	19-Jan-07	27.5	Put	26.75	2.450	59,767	61,121
6	3	HAL	Halliburton	19-Jan-07	30.0	Put	26.75	4.100	59,131	68,782
7	4	QQQQ	Nasdaq 100 Index	20-Oct-06	40.0	Put	40.31	0.475	57,073	262,601
8	5	HAL	Halliburton	20-Apr-07	22.5	Put	26.75	1.025	53,901	5,530
9	6	IWM	Russell 2000 Index	17-Nov-06	70.0	Put	71.22	1.650	49,387	203,975
10	7	QQQQ	Nasdaq 100 Index	17-Nov-06	39.0	Put	40.31	0.575	45,666	93,169
11	8	IWM	Russell 2000 Index	20-Oct-06	72.0	Put	71.22	1.650	43,432	154,148
12	9	SPY	S&P Depository Receipts ("Spider")	15-Dec-06	120.0	Put	133.36	0.400	40,125	32,090
13	10	SPY	S&P Depository Receipts ("Spider")	15-Dec-06	139.0	Call	133.36	0.850	40,116	21,036
14	11	SPY	S&P Depository Receipts ("Spider")	15-Dec-06	126.0	Put	133.36	0.925	40,082	32,249
15	12	IWM	Russell 2000 Index	20-Oct-06	71.0	Put	71.22	1.200	39,015	168,035
16	13	QQQQ	Nasdaq 100 Index	20-Oct-06	40.0	Call	40.31	0.875	37,502	196,355
17	14	BMY	Bristol-Myers Squibb	20-Oct-06	22.5	Call	24.82	2.325	31,989	10,934
18	15	SPY	S&P Depository Receipts ("Spider")	20-Oct-06	125.0	Put	133.36	0.075	31,964	25,569
19	16	S	Sprint Nextel	17-Nov-06	17.5	Call	16.97	0.525	31,350	9,078
20	17	IWM	Russell 2000 Index	20-Oct-06	69.0	Put	71.22	0.600	30,777	111,620
21	18	SPY	S&P Depository Receipts ("Spider")	20-Oct-06	137.0	Call	133.36	0.125	30,199	6,261
22	19	QQQQ	Nasdaq 100 Index	20-Oct-06	41.0	Put	40.31	0.975	29,881	94,955
23	20	MMM	MMM	20-Oct-06	85.0	Put	74.03	11.000	25,732	6,364
24										
25	Volume: Number of options traded on 4 Oct. 2006. Each option is for 100 shares, but price quotes are per share.									
26	Open interest: Number of open positions at end of day. A position is closed out (i.e., not open) if the option has been sold by day end.									

Here are some comments on this list:

Out of the 20 most active options, 14 are on exchange-traded funds (ETFs) and 6 are on stocks. For purposes of analysis, we can regard the ETFs as if they are stocks.

- QQQQ is an index of the 100 largest nonfinancial companies traded on Nasdaq.
- SPY tracks the Standard & Poor's 500 index.
- IMW tracks the Russell 2000 index.

Out of the 20 most active options, 5 are calls and 15 are puts. On 3 October 2006, U.S. markets closed at or near their seven-year highs, so the preponderance of puts is perhaps indicative of a tendency to bet on market declines.

Of the 20 most active options, 10 are for the closest option expiration date—20 October 2006. The most active options are often the closest-term options.

In many cases the volume of trading exceeds the open interest at the end of the day. This fact indicates that option positions opened during the day were closed out by the day's end. An option position is closed out if the holder has sold her options.

We examine the January 2007 options of Halliburton (HAL) somewhat more closely.[3]

	A	B	C	D	E	F	G	H
1	HALLIBURTON JAN 07 OPTIONS, PRICES ON 3 OCT 06 Closing price of stock: 26.75, down 1.29							
2		Calls				Puts		
3	Exercise price	Closing option price	Volume	Open interest		Closing option price	Volume	Open interest
4	15.0	11.90	20	1,724		0.05	50	1,153
5	17.5	12.70	23	9,449		0.05	140	3,312
6	20.0	7.17	5	13,801		0.20	50	18,277
7	22.5	5.00	339	4,595		0.60	49	15,247
8	25.0	3.20	200	3,306		1.25	423	21,793
9	27.5	1.85	571	3,918		2.50	53,267	61,121
10	30.0	0.95	2,140	12,008		4.10	52,631	68,782
11	32.5	0.55	810	10,527		6.00	216	21,562
12	33.8	0.40	78	2,276		6.90	168	3,378
13	35.0	0.30	231	69,727		8.10	142	20,258
14	36.3	0.20	460	5,989		8.00	2	1,280
15	37.5	0.15	1,249	78,762		9.10	5	5,530
16	40.0	0.10	32	85,037		11.01	16	322
17	42.5	0.05	170	24,439		15.70	135	1,920
18	45.0	0.05	6	8,509		17.10	76	0
19	47.5	0.05	10	6,591		14.60	76	0
20	50.0	0.05	20	10,528		17.00	52	0
21	55.0	0.05	12	694		22.10	28	0

Note the imbalance in trading volume between the calls and the puts. Note also that most of the put trading volume is concentrated on the at-the-money puts.

3. Why were four Halliburton put options among the most active? On 3 October 2006 the stock itself traded at twice its average daily volume (29 million shares as opposed to 14 million daily for the three months previously). Strong rumors were circulating about a possible cover-up at the company related to bribes paid to government officials in Nigeria.

16.4 Option Payoff and Profit Patterns

One of the attractions of options is that they allow their owners to change the payoff patterns of the underlying assets. In this section we consider

- The basic payoff and profit patterns of a call and a put option and a share.
- The payoff patterns of various combinations of options and shares.

16.4.1 Stock Profit Patterns

16.4.1.1 Payoff Pattern from a Purchased Stock

Suppose you buy a share of General Pills stock in July at its then-current market price of $40. If in September the price of the stock is $70, you will have made a $30 profit; if its price is $30, you will have a loss (or a negative profit) of $10.[4] Generalize this pattern by writing the price of the stock in September as S_T and its price in July by S_0. Then we write the profit function from the stock as

$$\text{Profit from stock} = S_T - S_0$$

16.4.1.2 Payoff from the Short Sale of a Stock

Suppose we had sold one share of GP stock short in July, when its market price was $40. If in September the market price of GP was $70, and if at that point we undid the short sale (i.e., we purchase a share at the market price in order to return the share to the lender of the original short), then our profit would be –$30:

$$\begin{aligned}\text{Profit from short sale of stock} &= S_0 - S_T \\ &= -\text{ (Profit from purchase of stock)}\end{aligned}$$

Notice that the profit from the short sale is the *negative* of the profit from the purchase; this is always the case (also for options, considered in section 16.4.2).

4. Our use of the word *profit* in this section constitutes a slight abuse of the English language and the standard finance concept of the word, since we are ignoring the interest costs associated with buying the asset. In the case at hand, this abuse of language is both traditional and harmless.

16.4.1.3 Graphing Stock Profit Patterns

The following Excel figure graphs the profit patterns from both a purchase and a short sale of the GP stock:

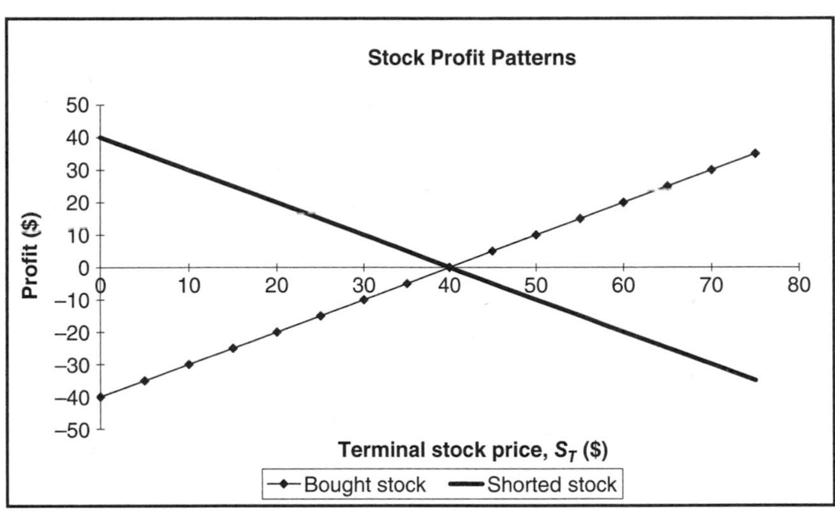

16.4.2 Call Option Profit Patterns

16.4.2.1 Payoff Pattern from a Purchased Call

We return to the General Pills (GP) options of the previous section. Suppose that in July you bought one GP September 40 call for \$4.[5] In September you will exercise the call only if the market price of GP is higher than \$40. If we write the initial (July) call price as C_0, we can write the profit function from the call in September as follows:

$$\begin{aligned}\text{Call profit in September} &= \max(0, S_T - X) - C_0 \\ &= \max(0, S_T - 40) - 4 \\ &= \begin{cases} -4 & \text{if } S_T \le 40 \\ S_T - 44 & \text{if } S_T > 40 \end{cases}\end{aligned}$$

5. Because the exercise price of this call is equal to the current market price of the stock, it is called an *at-the-money* call. When the exercise price of the call is higher than the current market price, it is called an *out-of-the-money* call, and when the exercise price is lower than the current market price, the call is an *in-the-money* call.

16.4.2.2 Payoff Pattern from a Written Call

In options markets the purchaser of a call buys the call from a counterparty who issues the call. In the jargon of options, the issuer of the call is called the *call writer*. It is worthwhile to spend a few minutes considering the difference between the security bought by the call purchaser and the call writer:

• The call purchaser buys a security that *gives the right to buy a share of stock on or before date T for price X*. The cost of this privilege is the *call price* C_0, which is paid at the time of the call purchase. Thus the call purchaser has an initial negative cash flow (the purchase price C_0); however, his cash flow at date T is always nonnegative: $\max(S_T - X, 0)$.

• The call writer gets C_0 at the date of the call purchase. In return for this price, the writer of the call *agrees to sell a share of the stock for price X on or before date T*. Notice that whereas the call purchaser has an option, the call writer has undertaken an obligation. Furthermore, note that the cash flow pattern of the call writer is opposite to that of the call purchaser: The writer's initial cash flow is positive ($+C_0$), and her cash flow at date T is always nonpositive: $-\max(S_T - X, 0)$.

The profit of a call writer is the opposite of that of the call purchaser. For the case of the GP options,

$$\begin{aligned}\text{Call writer's profit in September} &= C_0 - \max(0, S_T - X) \\ &= 4 - \max(0, S_T - 40) \\ &= \begin{cases} +4 & \text{if } S_T \leq 40 \\ 44 - S_T & \text{if } S_T > 40 \end{cases}\end{aligned}$$

Graphing the profit patterns of the bought and the written call gives:

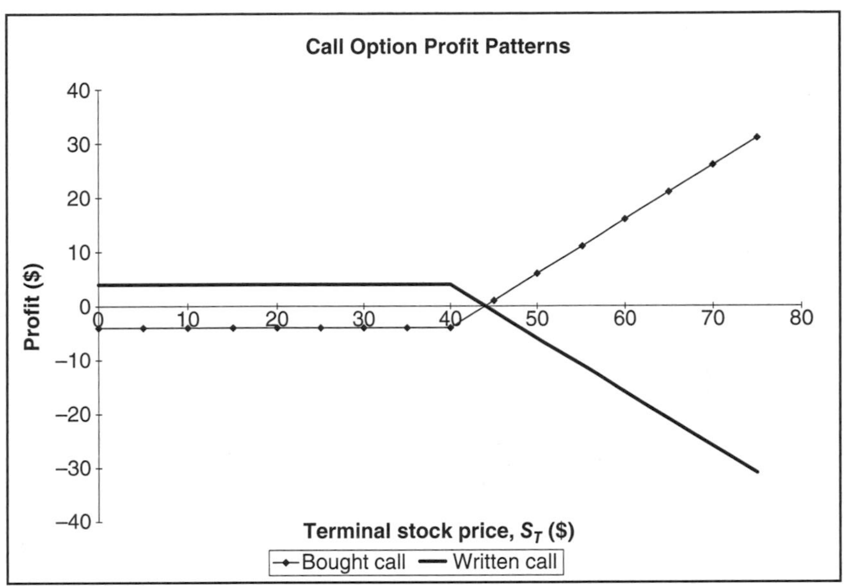

16.4.3 Put Option Profit Patterns

16.4.3.1 Payoff Pattern from a Purchased Put

If in July you bought one GP September 40 put for \$2, then in September you will exercise the put only if the market price of GP is lower than \$40. If we write the initial (July) put price as P_0, we can write the profit function from the put in September as follows:

$$
\begin{aligned}
\text{Put profit in September} &= \max(0, X - S_T) - P_0 \\
&= \max(0, 40 - S_T) - 2 \\
&= \begin{cases} 38 - S_T & \text{if } S_T \leq 40 \\ -2 & \text{if } S_T > 40 \end{cases}
\end{aligned}
$$

16.4.3.2 Payoff Pattern from a Written Put

The *put writer* obligates herself to purchase one share of GP stock on or before date T for the put exercise price of X. For putting herself in this invidious position, the writer of the put receives, at the time the put is written, the put price P_0. The payoff pattern from writing the GP September 40 put is therefore

$$
\begin{aligned}
\text{Put writer's profit in September} &= P_0 - \max(0, X - S_T) \\
&= 2 - \max(0, 40 - S_T) \\
&= \begin{cases} -38 + S_T & \text{if } S_T \le 40 \\ 2 & \text{if } S_T > 40 \end{cases}
\end{aligned}
$$

Graphing the profit patterns of the bought and the written put gives the following:

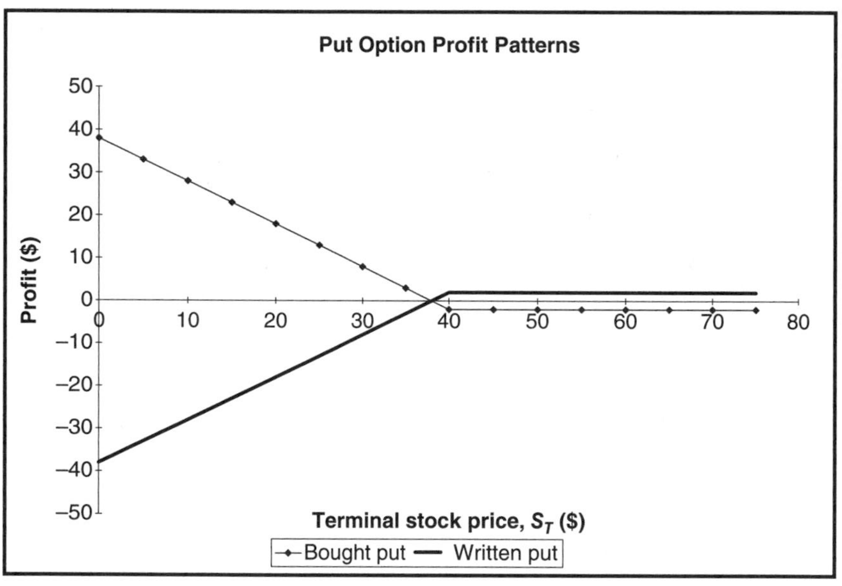

16.5 Option Strategies: Payoffs from Portfolios of Options and Stocks

There is some interest in graphing the combined profit pattern from a portfolio of options and stocks. These patterns give an indication of how options can be used to *change the payoff patterns* of "standard" securities such as stocks and bonds. Here are a few examples.

16.5.1 The Protective Put

Consider the following combination:

- One share of stock, purchased for S_0.
- One put, purchased for P with exercise price X.

This option strategy is often called a "protective put" strategy or "portfolio insurance"; in Chapter 21 we return to this topic, exploring it in much further detail. The payoff pattern of the protective put is given by

$$\text{Stock profit} + \text{Put profit} = S_T - S_0 + \max(X - S_T, 0) - P_0$$
$$= \begin{cases} S_T - S_0 + X - S_T - P_0 & \text{if } S_T \le X \\ S_T - S_0 - P_0 & \text{if } S_T > X \end{cases}$$
$$= \begin{cases} X - S_0 - P_0 & \text{if } S_T \le X \\ S_T - S_0 - P_0 & \text{if } S_T > X \end{cases}$$

When applied to the GP example (that is, buying a share at \$40 and a put with X = \$40 for \$2) this strategy gives the following graph:

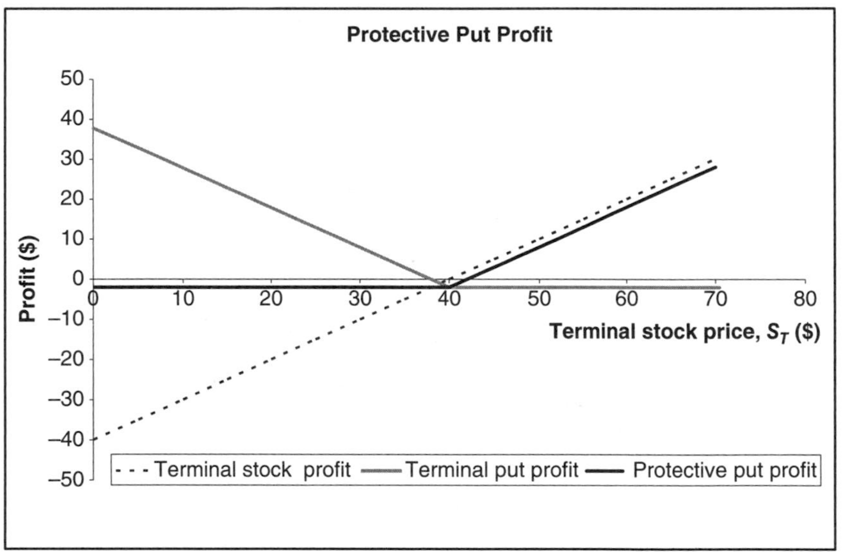

This pattern looks very much like the payoff patterns from a call.[6]

6. In section 16.6 we prove and illustrate the *put-call parity theorem*. It follows from this theorem that a call must be priced at a price C such that $C = P + S_0 - Xe^{-rT}$. Thus, when calls are correctly priced according to this theorem, the payoff from a put + stock combination is the same as that from a call + bond combination.

16.5.2 Spreads

Another combination involves buying and writing calls with different exercise prices. When the bought call has a low exercise price and the written call has a higher exercise price, the combination is called a *bull spread*. As an example, suppose you bought a call (for \$4) with an exercise price of \$40 and wrote a call (for \$2) with an exercise price of \$50. This bull spread gives a profit of

$$\max(S_T - 40, 0) - 4 - [\max(S_T - 50, 0) - 2]$$
$$= \begin{cases} -4 + 2 & \text{if } S_T \le 40 \\ S_T - 40 - 4 + 2 = S_T - 42 & \text{if } 40 \le S_T \le 50 \\ S_T - 40 - 4 - (S_T - 50 - 2) = 8 & \text{if } S_T \ge 50 \end{cases}$$

The following Excel graph shows each of the two calls and the resulting spread profit:

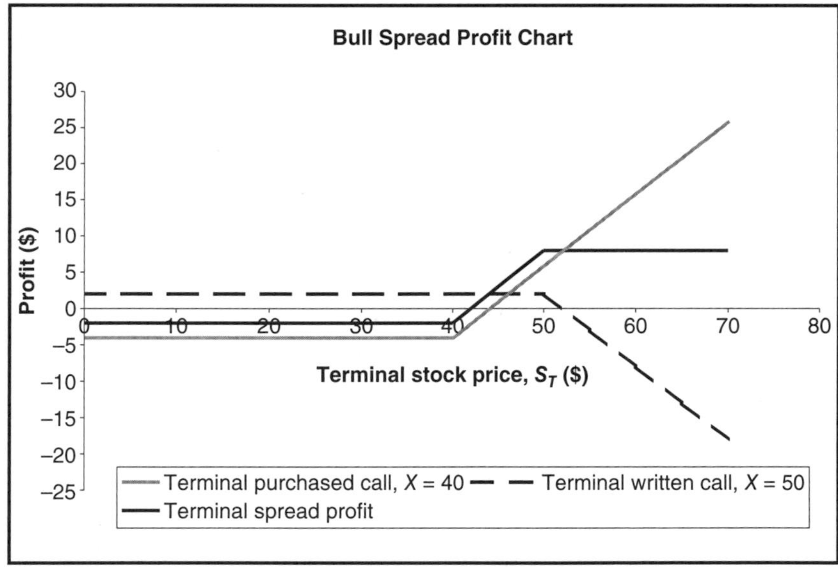

16.6 Option Arbitrage Propositions

In succeeding chapters we price options given specific assumptions about the probability distribution of the underlying asset (usually the stock) on which the option is written. However, there is much that can be learned about the pricing of options without making these specific probability assumptions. In this section we consider a number of these *arbitrage restrictions* on option pricing. Our list is by no means exhaustive, and we have concentrated on those propositions which provide insight into the pricing of options or that will be used in later sections.

Throughout we assume that there is a single risk-free interest rate that prices bonds; we also assume that this risk-free rate is continuously compounded, so that the present value of a riskless security that pays off X at time T is given by $e^{-rT}X$.

PROPOSITION 1 Consider a call option written on a stock that pays no dividends before the option's expiration date T. Then the lower bound on a call option price is given by

$$C_0 \geq \max\left(S_0 - Xe^{-rT}, 0\right)$$

Comment Before proving this proposition, it will be helpful to consider its meaning: Suppose that the riskless interest rate is 10 percent, and suppose we have an American call option with maturity $T = 1/2$ (i.e., the expiration date of the option is one-half year from today) with $X = 80$ written on a stock whose current stock price $S_0 = 83$. A naive approach to determining a lower bound on this option's price would be to state that it is worth at least \$3, since it could be exercised immediately with a profit of \$3. Proposition 1 shows that the option's value is *at least* $83 - e^{-0.10*0.5}80 = 6.90$. Furthermore, a careful examination of the following proof will show that this fact *does not* depend on the option being an American option—it is also true for a European option.

	A	B	C
1	**Proposition 1--Higher Lower Bounds for Call Prices**		
2	Current stock price, S_0	83	
3	Option time to maturity, T	0.5	
4	Option exercise price, X	80	
5	Interest rate, r	10%	
6			
7	Naive minimum option price, Max(S_0-X,0)	3	<-- =MAX(B2-B4,0)
8	Proposition 1 lower bound on option price, Max(S_0 - Exp(-rT)X,0)	6.902	<-- =MAX(B2-EXP(-B5*B3)*B4,0)

Proof Standard arbitrage proofs are built on the consideration of the cash flows from a particular strategy. In this case the strategy is the following:

At time 0 (today):

- Buy one share of the stock.
- Borrow the present value (PV) of the option exercise price X.
- Write a call on the option.

***At time* T:**

- Exercise the option if it is profitable to do so.
- Repay the borrowed funds.

This strategy produces the following cash flow table:

Today		At Time T	
Action	Cash Flow	$S_T < X$	$S_T \geq X$
Buy stock	$-S_0$	$+S_T$	$+S_T$
Borrow PV of X	$+Xe^{-rT}$	$-X$	$-X$
Write call	$+C_0$	0	$-(S_T - X)$
Total	$-S_0 + Xe^{-rT} + C_0$	$S_T - X \leq 0$	0

Note that at time T, the cash flow resulting from this option is either negative (if the call is not exercised) or zero (when $S_T \geq X$). Now a financial asset (in this case, the combination of purchasing a stock, borrowing X, and writing a call) that has only nonpositive payoffs in the future must have a positive initial cash flow; therefore,

$$C_0 - S_0 + Xe^{-rT} > 0 \qquad \text{or} \qquad C_0 > S_0 - Xe^{-rT}$$

To finish the proof, we note that in no case can the value of a call be less than zero. Thus we have that $C_0 \geq \max(S_0 - Xe^{-rT}, 0)$, which proves the proposition.

Proposition 1 has an immediate and very interesting consequence: In many cases the early-exercise feature of an American call option is worthless; therefore, an American call option can be valued as if it were a European call. The precise conditions are the following:

PROPOSITION 2 Consider an American call option written on a stock that will not pay any dividends before the option's expiration date T. Then it is never optimal to exercise the option before its maturity.

Proof Suppose the holder of the option is considering exercising it early, at some date $t < T$. The only reason to consider such early exercise is that $S_t - X > 0$, where S_t is the price of the underlying stock at time t. However, by Proposition 1 the market value of the option at time t is at least $S_t - Xe^{-r(T-t)}$, where r is the risk-free rate of interest. Since $S_t - Xe^{-r(T-t)} > S_t - X$, it follows that the option's holder is better off selling the option in the market than exercising it.

Proposition 2 means that many American call options can be priced as if they were European calls. Note that this statement is not true for American puts, even if the underlying stock pays no dividends (we give an example in Chapter 19).

PROPOSITION 3 (PUT BOUNDS) The lower bound on the value of a put option is

$$P_0 \geq \max(0, Xe^{-rT} - S_0)$$

Proof The proof of this proposition has the same form as the proof of the previous theorem. We set up a table of strategies:

Today		At Time T	
Action	Cash Flow	$S_T < X$	$S_T \geq X$
Short stock	$+S_0$	$-S_T$	$-S_T$
Lend PV of X	$-Xe^{-rT}$	$+X$	$+X$
Write put	$+P_0$	$-(X - S_T)$	0
Total	$P_0 + S_0 - Xe^{rT}$	0	$X - S_T \leq 0$

Since the strategy has only negative or zero payoffs in the future, it must have a positive cash flow today, so that we can conclude that

$$P_0 - Xe^{-rT} + S_0 \geq 0$$

Combined with the fact that in no case can a put value be negative, this proves the proposition.

PROPOSITION 4 (PUT-CALL PARITY) Let C_0 be the price of a European call with exercise price X written on a stock whose current price is S_0. Let P_0 be the price of a European put on the same stock with the same exercise price X. Suppose both put and call have exercise date T, and suppose that the continuously compounded interest rate is r. Then,

$$C_0 + Xe^{-rT} = P_0 + S_0$$

Proof The proof is similar in style to that of the two previous propositions. We consider a combination of the four assets (the put, the call, the stock, and a bond), and show that the pricing relation must hold.

Today		At Time T	
Action	Cash Flow	$S_T < X$	$S_T \geq X$
Buy call	$-C_0$	0	$+S_T - X$
Buy a bond with payoff X at time T	$-Xe^{-rT}$	X	X
Write a put	$+P_0$	$-(X - S_T)$	0
Short one share of the stock	$+S_0$	$-S_T$	$-S_T$
Total	$-C_0 - Xe^{-rT} + P_0 + S_0$	0	0

Since the strategy has future payoffs that are zero no matter what happens to the price of the stock, it follows that the initial cash flow of the strategy must also be zero.[7] Therefore,

$$C_0 + Xe^{-rT} - P_0 - S_0 = 0$$

which proves the proposition.

Put-call parity states that the stock price S_0, the price of a call C_0 with exercise price X and the price of a put P_0 with exercise price X, are simultaneously determined with the interest rate r. Following is an illustration which uses the call price C_0, the option exercise price X, the current stock price S_0, and the interest rate r to compute the price of a put with exercise price X and time to maturity T:

7. This is a fundamental fact of finance: If a financial strategy has future payoffs that are identically zero, then its current cost must also be zero. Likewise, if a financial strategy has future payoffs that are nonnegative, then its time-zero payoff must be negative (that is, it must cost something).

	A	B	C
1	**Put-Call Parity**		
2	Current stock price, S_0	55	
3	Option time to maturity, T	0.5	
4	Option exercise price, X	60	
5	Interest rate, r	10%	
6	Call price, C_0	3	
7	Put price, P_0	5.0738	<-- =B6+B4*EXP(-B5*B3)-B2
8			
9	This spreadsheet uses put-call parity to derive the put price P_0 from the call price C_0, the interest rate r, the time to maturityT, and the exercise price X.		

PROPOSITION 5 (CALL OPTION PRICE CONVEXITY) Consider three European calls, all written on the same non-dividend-paying stock and with the same expiration date T. We suppose that the exercise prices on the calls are X_1, X_2, and X_3, and denote the associated call prices by C_1, C_2, and C_3. We further assume that $X_2 = \frac{X_1 + X_3}{2}$. Then,

$$C_2 < \frac{C_1 + C_3}{2}$$

It follows that the call option price is a convex function of the exercise price.

Proof To prove the proposition, we consider the following strategy:

At Time 0		At Time T			
Action	Cash Flow	$S_T < X_1$	$X_1 \le S_T < X_2$	$X_2 \le S_T < X_3$	$X_3 \le S_T$
Buy call with exercise price X_1	$-C_1$	0	$S_T - X_1$	$S_T - X_1$	$S_T - X_1$
Buy call with exercise price X_3	$-C_3$	0	0	0	$S_T - X_3$
Write two calls with exercise price X_2	$+2C_2$	0	0	$-2(S_T - X_2)$	$-2(S_T - X_2)$
Total	$2C_2 - C_1 - C_3$	0	$S_T - X_1 \ge 0$	$2X_2 - X_1 - S_T = X_3 - S_T > 0$	0

Since the payoffs in the future are all nonnegative (with a positive probability of being positive), it follows that the initial cash flow from the position must be negative:

$$2C_2 - C_1 - C_3 < 0 \Rightarrow C_2 < \frac{C_1 + C_3}{2}$$

This proves the proposition. (Note that the assumption that $X_2 = \frac{X_1 + X_3}{2}$ is made for convenience and does not affect the generality of the argument.)

Without proof we state a similar proposition for puts:

PROPOSITION 6 (PUT PRICE CONVEXITY) Consider three European puts, all written on the same non-dividend-paying stock and with the same expiration date T. We suppose that the exercise prices on the calls are X_1, X_2, and X_3, and denote the associated put prices by P_1, P_2, and P_3. We further assume that $X_2 = \frac{X_1 + X_3}{2}$. Then the put price is a convex function of the exercise price:

$$P_2 < \frac{P_1 + P_3}{2}$$

Finally, we state the following proposition, whose proof involves only a minor modification of the proof of Proposition 1:

PROPOSITION 7 (CALL OPTION BOUNDS WITH A KNOWN FUTURE DIVIDEND) Consider a call with exercise price X and maturity date T. Suppose that at some time $t < T$, the stock will, with certainty, pay a dividend D. Then the lower bound on the call option price is given by

$$C_0 \geq \max\,(S_0 - De^{-rt} - Xe^{-rT}, 0)$$

Proof The proof involves only a minor modification of the proof of Proposition 1.

Today		Time t	At Time T	
Action	Cash Flow		$S_T < X$	$S_T \geq X$
Buy stock	$-S_0$	$+D$	$+S_T$	$+S_T$
Borrow the PV of the dividend D	$+De^{-rt}$	$-D$		
Borrow PV of X	$+Xe^{-rT}$		$-X$	$-X$
Write call	$+C_0$		0	$-(S_T - X)$
Total	$-S_0 + De^{-rt} + Xe^{-rT} + C_0$	0	$S_T - X \leq 0$	0

This proves the proposition.

16.7 Summary

This chapter summarizes the basic definitions and features of options. It is, however, by no means an adequate introduction to these complex securities for those with no preknowledge. To decipher the mysteries of options, we recommend the introductory chapters of a good option text.

Exercises

1. When you looked at the newspaper quotes for options on ABC stock, you saw that a February call option with $X = 37.5$ is priced at 6.375, whereas the April call option with the same exercise price is priced at 6. Can you devise an arbitrage out of these prices? Do you have an explanation for the newspaper quotes?

2. An American call option is written on a stock whose price today is $S = 50$. The exercise price of the call is $X = 45$.

   a. If the call price is 2, explain how you would use arbitrage to make an immediate profit.

   b. If the option is exercisable at time $T = 1$ year and if the interest rate is 10%, what is the minimum price of the option? Use Proposition 1.

3. A European call option is written on a stock whose current price $S = 80$. The exercise price $X = 80$, the interest rate $r = 8\%$, and the time to option exercise $T = 1$. The stock is assumed to pay a dividend of 3 at time $t = 1/2$. Use Proposition 7 to determine the minimum price of the call option.

4. A put with an exercise price of 50 has a price of 6, and a call on the same stock with an exercise price of 60 has a price of 10. Both put and call have the same expiration date.

 a. On the same set of axes, draw the "profit" diagram for

 - One put bought and one call bought.
 - Two puts bought and one call bought.
 - Three puts bought and one call bought.

 b. All three lines cross each other for the same value of S_T. Derive this value.

5. Consider the following two calls:

 - Both calls are written on shares of ABC Corporation, whose current share price is \$100. ABC does not pay any dividends.
 - Both calls have one year to maturity.
 - One call has $X_1 = 90$ and has price of 30; the second call has $X_2 = 100$ and has price of 20.
 - The riskless, continuously compounded interest rate is 10 percent.

 By designing a spread position (i.e., buying one call and writing another), show that the difference between the two call prices is *too large* and that a riskless arbitrage exists.

6. A share of ABC Corporation sells for \$95. A call on the share with exercise price \$90 sells for \$8.

 a. Graph the profit pattern from buying one share and one call on the share.

 b. Graph the profit pattern from buying one share and two calls.

 c. Consider the profit pattern from buying one share and N calls. At which share price do all the profit lines cross?

7. A European call with a maturity of six months and exercise price $X = 80$, written on a stock whose current price is 85, is selling for \$12.00; a European put written on the same stock with the same maturity and with the same exercise price is selling for \$5.00. If the annual interest rate (continuously compounded) is 10 percent, construct an arbitrage from this situation.

8. Prove Proposition 6. Then solve the following problem:

 Three puts on shares of XYZ with the same expiration date are selling at the following prices:

 Exercise price 40: 6

 Exercise price 50: 4

 Exercise price 60: 1

 Show an arbitrage strategy that allows you to profit from these prices and prove that it works.

9. The current stock price of ABC Corporation is 50. Prices for six-month calls on ABC are given in the following table:

Call	Price
40	16.5
50	9.5
60	4.5
70	2

Draw a profit diagram of the following strategy: Buy one 40 call, write two 50 calls, buy one 60 call, and write two 70 calls.

10. Consider the following option strategy, which consists only of calls:

Exercise Price	Bought/Written? Number?	Price per Call Option
20	1 written	45
30	2 bought	33
40	1 written	22
50	1 bought	18
60	2 written	17
70	1 bought	16

a. Draw the profit diagram for this strategy.

b. The prices given include one violation of an arbitrage condition. Identify this violation and explain.

11. A share of Formila Corporation is currently trading at \$38.50, and a one-year call option on Formila with X = \$40 is trading at \$3. The risk-free interest rate is 4.5%.

a. What should be the price of a one-year put option on the stock with X = \$40? Why?

b. If the price of a put is \$2, construct an arbitrage strategy.

c. If the price of a put is \$4, construct an arbitrage strategy.

17 The Binomial Option-Pricing Model

17.1 Overview

Next to the Black-Scholes model (discussed in Chapter 19), the binomial option-pricing model is the most widely used option-pricing model. It has many advantages: It is a simple model, which—in addition to giving many insights into option pricing—is easily programmed and adapted to numerous, and often quite complicated, option-pricing problems. When extended to many periods, the binomial model becomes one of the most powerful ways of valuing securities like options whose payoffs are contingent on the market prices of other assets.

The binomial model depends on using state prices to compute the values of risky assets. When the state-pricing principles underlying the model are understood, we gain deeper insight into the economics of contingent asset pricing. In this chapter, which illustrates the simple uses of the binomial model, we devote a considerable amount of space to deriving and using state prices. In Chapters 22 and 23 we return to the binomial model and use it in the Monte Carlo pricing of contingent securities.

17.2 Two-Date Binomial Pricing

To illustrate the use of the binomial model, we start with the following very simple example:

- There is one period and two dates; date 0 represents today and date 1 is one year from now.
- There are two "fundamental" assets: a stock and a bond. There is also a derivative asset, a call option written on the stock.
- The stock price today is $50. At date 1 it will either go up by 10 percent or go down by 3 percent.
- The one-period interest rate is 6 percent.
- The call option matures at date 1 and has exercise price $X = \$50$.

Here is a picture from a spreadsheet that incorporates this model. Notice that in cells B2, B3, and B6 we have used values for 1 plus the 10 percent up move, 1 plus the –3 percent down move, and 1 plus the

6 percent interest. We use capital letters U, D, and R to denote these values.[1]

	A	B	C	D	E	F	G	H	I	J
1	**BINOMIAL OPTION PRICING IN A ONE-PERIOD MODEL**									
2	Up, U	1.10								
3	Down, D	0.97								
4										
5	Initial stock price	50.00								
6	Interest rate, R	1.06								
7	Exercise price	50.00								
8										
9		**Stock price**					**Bond price**			
10				55.00	<-- =$B$11*B2				1.06	<-- =$G$11*$B$6
11		50.00					1.00			
12				48.50	<-- =$B$11*B3				1.06	<-- =$G$11*$B$6
13										
14		**Call option**								
15				5.00	<-- =MAX(D10-$B$7,0)					
16		???								
17				0.00	<-- =MAX(D12-$B$7,0)					

We wish to price the call option. We do so by showing that there is a *combination of the bonds and stocks that exactly replicates the call option's payoffs*. To show this fact, we use some basic linear algebra; suppose we find A shares of the stock and B bonds such that

$$55A + 1.06B = 5$$
$$48.5A + 1.06B = 0$$

This system of equations solves to give

$$A = \frac{5}{55 - 48.5} = 0.7692$$

$$B = \frac{0 - 48.5A}{1.06} = -35.1959$$

Thus purchasing 0.77 of a share of the stock and borrowing \$35.20 at 6 percent for one period will give payoffs of \$5 if the stock price goes up and \$0 if the stock price goes down—the payoffs of the call option. It follows that the price of the option must be equal to the cost of replicating its payoffs; that is,

1. Should there be a need to distinguish between 1.10 (1 plus the 10 percent up move of the stock) and 10 percent (the up move itself), we will use U for the former and lowercase u for the latter.

Call option price = 0.7692∗$50 – $35.1959 = $3.2656

This logic is called "pricing by arbitrage": If two assets or sets of assets (in our case—the call option and the portfolio of 0.77 of the stock and –$35.20 of the bonds) have the same payoffs, they must have the same market price.

	A	B	C	D	E	F	G
19	**Solving the portfolio problem: A shares + B bonds combine to give option payoffs**						
20	A	0.7692	<-- =D15/(D10-D12)				
21	B	-35.1959	<-- =-D12*B20/B6				
22							
23	Call price	3.2656	<-- =B20*B5+B21				

In succeeding sections we show that this simple arbitrage argument can be extended to multiple periods. But in the meantime we confine ourselves in the next section to generalizing the logic.

17.3 State Prices

There is actually a simpler (and more general) way to solve this problem: Viewed from today, there are only two possibilities for next period: Either the stock price goes up or it goes down. Think about the market determining a price q_U for $1 in the "up" state of the world and a price q_D for $1 in the "down" state of the world. Then both the bond and the stock have to be priced using these *state prices*:

$$q_U * S * U + q_D * S * D = S \Rightarrow q_U U + q_D D = 1$$
$$q_U * R + q_D * R = 1$$

The state prices are thus an illustration of the linear pricing principle: If the stock price can move up in one period by a factor U and down by a factor R, and if 1 plus the one-period interest rate is R, then any other asset will be priced by discounting its payoff in the "up" state by q_U and by discounting its payoff in the "down" state by q_D.

The two preceding equations solve to give

$$q_U = \frac{R-D}{R(U-D)}, \quad q_D = \frac{U-R}{R(U-D)}$$

In our case these state prices are given by

	A	B	C
1	**DERIVING THE STATE PRICES**		
2	Up, U	1.10	
3	Down, D	0.97	
4	Interest rate, R	1.06	
5			
6	**State prices**		
7	q_U	0.6531	<-- =(B4-B3)/(B4*(B2-B3))
8	q_D	0.2903	<-- =(B2-B4)/(B4*(B2-B3))
9			
10	**Check: Confirm that state prices actually price the stock and the bond**		
11	Pricing the stock: 1 = q_U*U+q_D*D?	1	<-- =B7*B2+B8*B3
12	Pricing the bond: 1/R = q_U+q_D ?	1.06	<-- =1/(B7+B8)

In rows 11 and 12 we check that the state prices indeed give back the interest rate and the stock price.

We can now use the state prices to price the call and the put on the stock and also to establish that put-call parity holds. The call and the put options should be priced by

$$C = q_U \max(S*U - X, 0) + q_D \max(S*D - X, 0)$$
$$P = q_U \max(X - S*U, 0) + q_D \max(X - S*D, 0)$$

or, if priced by put-call parity,

$$P = C + PV(X) - S$$

We can present these relations in a spreadsheet:

	A	B	C
1	**BINOMIAL OPTION PRICING WITH STATE PRICES IN A ONE-PERIOD (TWO-DATE) MODEL**		
2	Up, U	1.10	
3	Down, D	0.97	
4	Interest rate, R	1.06	
5	Initial stock price, S	50.00	
6	Option exercise price, X	50.00	
7			
8	**State prices**		
9	q_U	0.6531	<-- =(B4-B3)/(B4*(B2-B3))
10	q_D	0.2903	<-- =(B2-B4)/(B4*(B2-B3))
11			
12	**Pricing the call and the put**		
13	Call price	3.2656	<-- =B9*MAX(B5*B2-B6,0)+B10*MAX(B5*B3-B6,0)
14	Put price	0.4354	<-- =B9*MAX(B6-B5*B2,0)+B10*MAX(B6-B5*B3,0)
15			
16	**Put-call parity**		
17	Stock + put	50.4354	<-- =B5+B14
18	Call + PV(X)	50.4354	<-- =B13+B6/B4
19			
20	**Note about PV(X) in put-call parity:** In the continuous-time framework (the standard Black-Scholes framework), PV(X) = X*Exp(-r*T). Because the framework here is discrete time, PV(X) is also discrete-time: PV(X)=X/(1+r)=X/R.		

The formulas we use (with $S = 50$, $X = 50$, $U = 1.10$, $D = 0.97$, $R = 1.06$) are

$$C = q_U \max(S*U - X, 0) + q_D \max(S*D - X, 0) = 0.6531*5 + 0.2903*0$$
$$= 3.2657$$

for the call, and

$$P = q_U \max(X - S*U, 0) + q_D \max(X - S*D, 0)$$
$$= 0.6531*\max(50 - 55, 0) + 0.2903*\max(50 - 48.5, 0) = 0.4354$$

for the put. As expected—the put-call parity theorem holds for this particular put and call (cells B17:B18):

$$P + S = 0.4354 + 50 = C + \frac{X}{R} = 3.27 + \frac{50}{1.06}$$

17.3.1 State Prices or Risk-Neutral Prices?

Multiplying the state prices by 1 plus the interest rate R gives the *risk-neutral prices:* $\pi_U = q_U R$, $\pi_D = q_D R$. The risk-neutral prices look like a probability distribution of the states, since they sum to 1:

$$\pi_U + \pi_D = q_U R + q_D R = \frac{R - D}{R(U - D)} R + \frac{U - R}{R(U - D)} R = 1$$

Furthermore, there is a fundamental equivalence of pricing by the risk-neutral prices and pricing by the state prices. Suppose an asset has state-dependent payoffs X_U in the "up" state and X_D in the "down" state of a two-date model. Then the date-0 price of the asset using the state prices is $q_U X_U + q_D X_D$, and the date-0 price of the asset using the risk-neutral prices is the discounted expected asset payoff, where the expectation is computed using the risk-neutral prices as if they are the actual state probabilities:

$$\frac{\pi_U X_U + \pi_D X_D}{R} = \frac{\text{“Expected” asset payoff using risk-neutral prices}}{1 + r}$$
$$= q_U X_U + q_D X_D$$

These two computations are, of course equal. This author prefers to use state prices, but many researchers are more comfortable using the pseudoprobabilities of the risk-neutral prices and then discounting the "expected" payoffs.

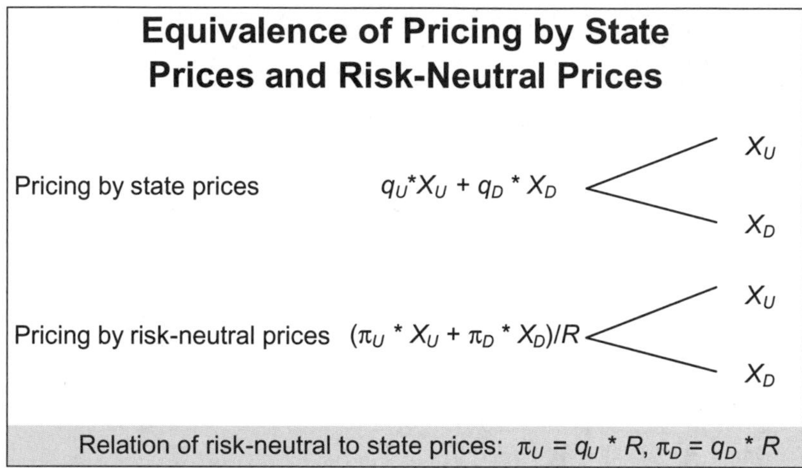

To drive home the equivalence between state prices and risk-neutral prices, we close this subsection with a numerical example:

	A	B	C
1	**RISK-NEUTRAL PRICES OR STATE PRICES?**		
2	Up, U	1.10	
3	Down, D	0.97	
4	Interest rate, R	1.06	
5	Initial stock price, S	50.00	
6	Option exercise price, X	50.00	
7			
8	**State prices**		
9	q_U	0.6531	<-- =(B4-B3)/(B4*(B2-B3))
10	q_D	0.2903	<-- =(B2-B4)/(B4*(B2-B3))
11			
12	**Risk-neutral prices**		
13	$\pi_U = q_U*R$	0.6923	<-- =B9*$B$4
14	$\pi_D = q_D*R$	0.3077	<-- =B10*$B$4
15			
16	**Pricing the call and the put using state prices**		
17	Call price	3.2656	<-- =B9*MAX(B5*B2-B6,0)+B10*MAX(B5*B3-B6,0)
18	Put price	0.4354	<-- =B9*MAX(B6-B5*B2,0)+B10*MAX(B6-B5*B3,0)
19			
20	**Pricing the call and the put using risk-neutral prices**		
21	Call price	3.2656	<-- =(B13*MAX(B5*B2-B6,0)+B14*MAX(B5*B3-B6,0))/B4
22	Put price	0.4354	<-- =(B13*MAX(B6-B5*B2,0)+B14*MAX(B6-B5*B3,0))/B4

17.4 The Multiperiod Binomial Model

The binomial model can easily be extended to more than one period. Consider, for example, a two-period (three-date) binomial model that has the following characteristics:

- In each period the stock price goes up by 10 percent or down by 3 percent from what it was in the previous period. Therefore, $U = 1.10$, $D = 0.97$.
- In each period the interest rate is 6 percent, so that $R = 1.06$.

Because U, D, and R are the same in each period,

$$q_U = \frac{R-D}{R(U-D)} = 0.6531, \quad q_D = \frac{U-R}{R(U-D)} = 0.2903$$

We can now use these state prices to price a call option written on the stock after two periods. As before, we assume that the stock price is \$50 initially and that the call exercise price is $X = 50$ after two periods. These assumptions give the following picture:

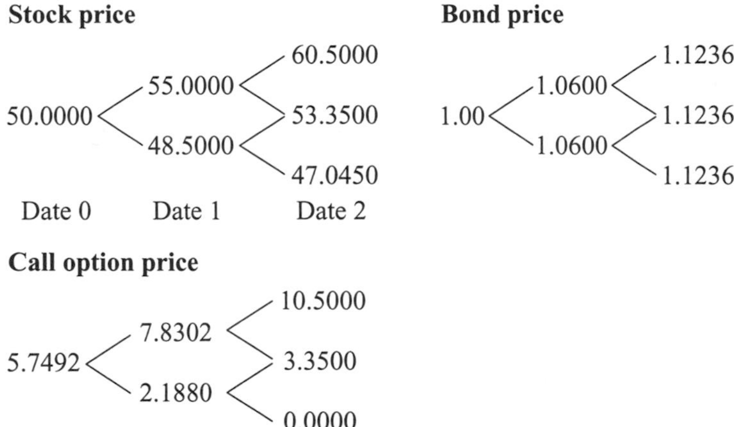

How was the call option price of 5.7492 determined? To make this determination, we go backward, starting at period 2:

At date 2: At the end of two periods the stock price is either \$60.50 (corresponding to two "up" movements in the price), \$53.35 (one "up" and one "down" movement), or \$47.05 (two "down" movements in the price).

Given the exercise price of $X = 50$, therefore, the terminal option payoff in period 2 is either \$10.50, \$3.35, or \$0.

At date 1: At date 1, there are two possibilities: Either we have reached an "up" state, in which case the current stock price is \$55 and the option will pay off \$10.50 or \$3.35 in the next period:

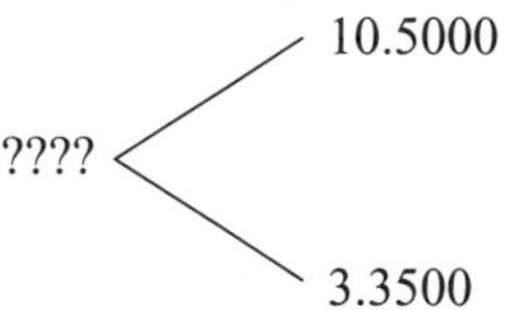

We use the state prices of $q_u = 0.6531$, $q_d = 0.2903$ to price the option at this state:

$$\text{Option price at "up" state, date } 1 = 0.6531*10.50 + 0.2903*3.35 = 7.8302$$

The alternative possibility is that we're in the "down" state of period 1:

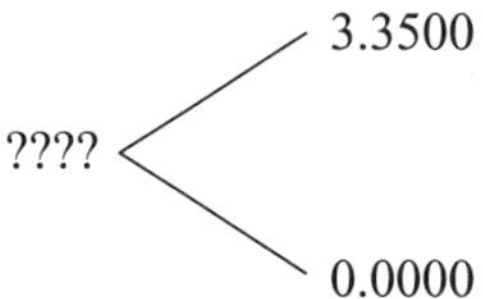

Using the same state prices (which, after all, depend only on the "up" and "down" movements of the stock price and the interest rate), we get

$$\text{Option price at "down" state, date } 1 = 0.6531*3.35 + 0.2903*0 = 2.1880$$

At date 0: Going backward in this way, we've now filled in the following picture:

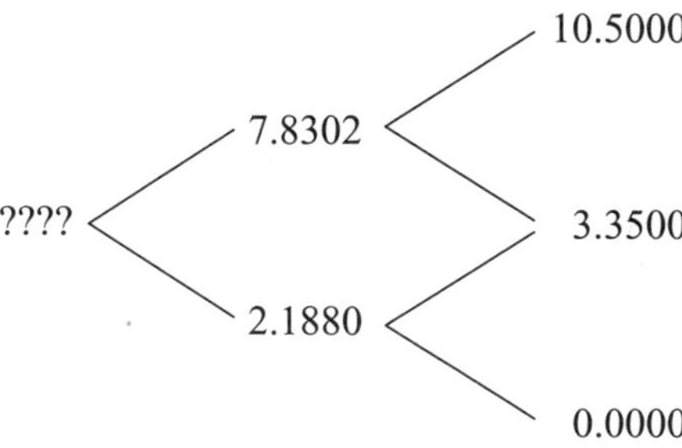

Thus at period 0 the buyer of an option owns a security that will be worth \$7.83 if the underlying stock has an "up" movement in its return and \$2.19 if the stock has a "down" movement in its return. We can again use the state prices to value this option:

$$\text{Option price at date } 0 = 0.6531*7.830 + 0.2903*2.188 = 5.749$$

	A	B	C	D	E	F	G	H	I	J	K
1	BINOMIAL OPTION PRICING WITH STATE PRICES IN A TWO-PERIOD (THREE-DATE) MODEL										
2	Up, U	1.10									
3	Down, D	0.97		State prices							
4	Interest rate, R	1.06		q_U	0.6531	<-- =(B4-B3)/(B4*(B2-B3))					
5	Initial stock price, S	50.00		q_D	0.2903	<-- =(B2-B4)/(B4*(B2-B3))					
6	Option exercise price, X	50.00									
7											
8	Stock price						Bond price				
9					60.5000						1.1236
10			55.0000						1.0600		
11		50.0000			53.3500		1.00				1.1236
12			48.5000						1.0600		
13					47.0450						1.1236
14											
15											
16	Call option price										
17			=qU*E18+qD*E20								
18					10.5000	<-- =MAX(E9-\$B\$5,0)					
19			7.8302								
20		5.7492			3.3500	<-- =MAX(E11-\$B\$5,0)					
21			2.1880								
22	=qU*C19+qD*C21				0.0000	<-- =MAX(E13-\$B\$5,0)					
23			=qU*E20+qD*E22								
24											

17.4.1 Extending the Binomial Pricing Model to Many Periods

It is clear that the logic of the example can be extended to many periods. Here's another Excel graphic showing a five-date model using the same "up" and "down" parameters as before:

Stock price

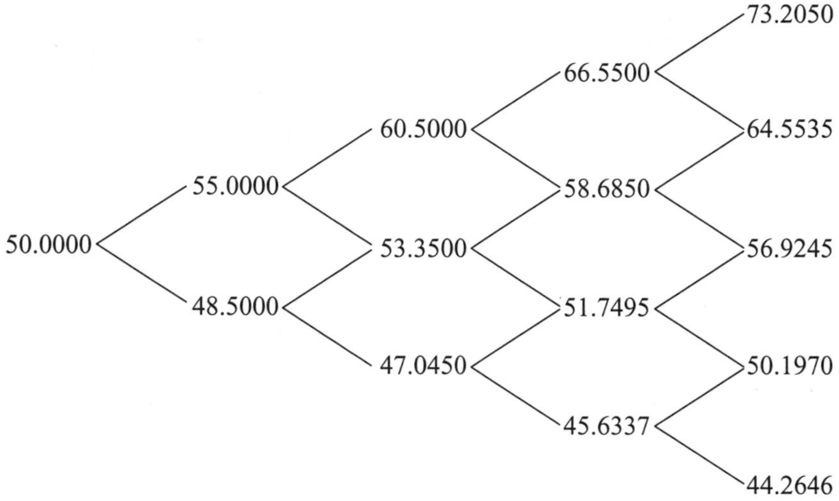

73.2050

66.5500

60.5000 64.5535

55.0000 58.6850

50.0000 53.3500 56.9245

48.5000 51.7495

47.0450 50.1970

45.6337

44.2646

Bond price

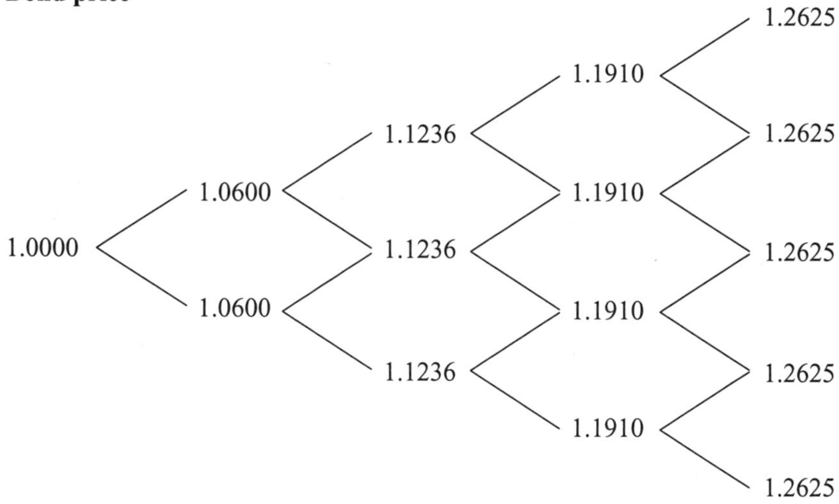

1.2625

1.1910

1.1236 1.2625

1.0600 1.1910

1.0000 1.1236 1.2625

1.0600 1.1910

1.1236 1.2625

1.1910

1.2625

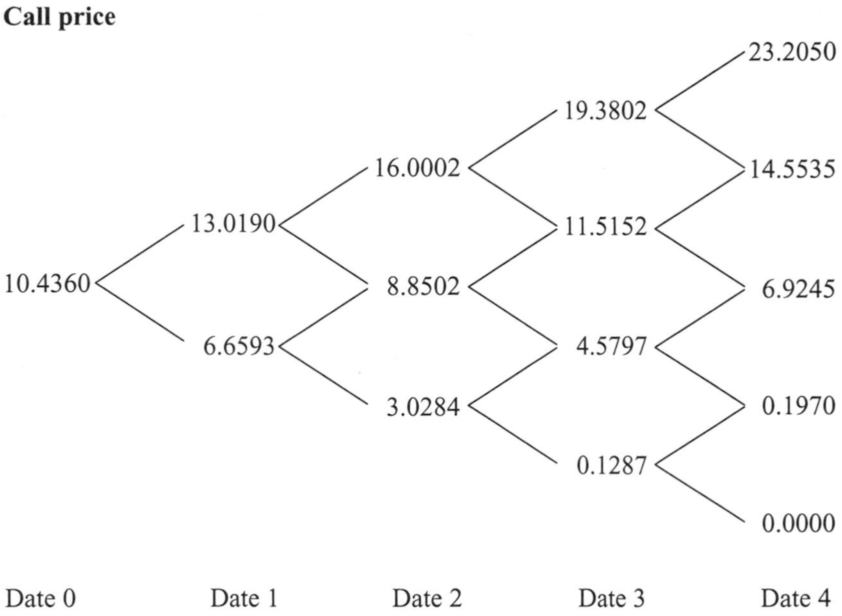

17.4.2 Do You Really Have to Price Everything Backward?

The answer is no. There's no necessity to price the call price payoffs "backward" at each node back from the terminal date, *as long as the call is European*.[2] It is enough to price each of the terminal payoffs by the state prices, providing you count properly the number of paths to each terminal node. Here's an illustration, using the same example:

2. When we discuss American options in section 17.5, we will see that backward pricing is critical.

	A	B	C	D	E	F	G	H
1	**BINOMIAL OPTION PRICING WITH STATE PRICES IN A FOUR-PERIOD (FIVE-DATE) MODEL**							
2	Up, U	1.10						
3	Down, D	0.97		**State prices**				
4	Interest rate, R	1.06		q_U	0.6531	<-- =(B4-B3)/(B4*(B2-B3))		
5	Initial stock price, S	50.00		q_D	0.2903	<-- =(B2-B4)/(B4*(B2-B3))		
6	Option exercise price, X	50.00						
7								
8								
9	**Number of "up" steps at terminal date**	**Number of "down" steps at terminal date**	**Terminal stock price = S*U^(# up) *D^(# down)**	**Option payoff at terminal state**	**State price for terminal date = q_U^(# up) *q_D^(# down)**	**Number of paths to terminal state**	**Value =payoff*state price*#paths**	
10	4	0	73.2050	23.2050	0.1820	1	4.2224	
11	3	1	64.5535	14.5535	0.0809	4	4.7078	
12	2	2	56.9245	6.9245	0.0359	6	1.4933	
13	1	3	50.1970	0.1970	0.0160	4	0.0126	
14	0	4	44.2646	0.0000	0.0071	1	0.0000	
15						Call price	10.4360	<-- =SUM(G10:G14)
16						Put price	0.0407	<-- =G15+B6/B4^4-B5
17								
18	**Notes**							
19	There are 5 dates in this model (0, 1, ... , 5) but only 4 periods and thus only 4 possible "up" or "down" steps.							
20	The put price in cell G16 is computed using put-call parity: put = call + PV(X) - stock							

An explanation for the preceding spreadsheet follows. For each terminal option payoff, we consider these questions:

How was this terminal payoff reached? How many "up" steps did the stock make, and how many "down" steps did it make?		Example: The terminal payoff of 14.5535 arises when the stock price is 64.5535. This result occurs when the stock price goes up three times and down once.
What is the price per dollar of the payoff in the particular state?	State price = $q_U^{\#up\ steps} q_D^{\#down\ steps}$	Example: The value at time 0 of the terminal payoff considered in the same example is $0.6531^3 * 0.2903^1 = 0.0809$
How many paths are there with the same terminal payoff?	The answer is given by the binomial coefficient $\binom{\text{Number of periods}}{\text{Number of "up" steps}}$	Example: There are $\binom{4}{3} = 4$ paths which give the terminal stock price of 64.5535. The Excel function **Combin(4,3)** gives this binomial coefficient.
What is the value at time 0 of a particular terminal payoff?	The answer is the product of the payoff times the price times the number of paths.	Example: $14.5535 * 0.0809 * 4 = 4.7078$
What is the value at time 0 of the option?	The sum of the values of each payoff.	Total value: 10.4360. This is the multiperiod call option value in the five-date (four-period) binomial model.

European puts can be priced either by using the preceding logic or—as in cell G16—by using put-call parity.

To recapitulate: The price of a European call option in a binomial model with n periods is given by

$$\text{Call price} = \sum_{i=0}^{n} \binom{n}{i} q_U^i q_D^{n-i} \max(S*U^i D^{n-i} - X, 0)$$

$$\text{Put price} = \begin{cases} \sum_{i=0}^{n} \binom{n}{i} q_U^i q_D^{n-i} \max(X - S*U^i D^{n-i}, 0) & \text{Direct pricing} \\ \text{Call price} + \dfrac{X}{R^n} - S & \text{Using put-call parity} \end{cases}$$

In section 17.6 of this chapter we implement these formulas in VBA.

17.5 Pricing American Options Using the Binomial Pricing Model

We can use the binomial pricing model to calculate the prices of American options as well as European options.[3] We reconsider the same basic model, in which Up = 1.10, Down = 0.97, R = 1.06, S = 50, X = 50. We examine the three-date version of the model. The payoff patterns for the stock and the bond have been given previously, and it remains only to consider the payoff patterns for a put option with $X = 50$. We reference the states of the world by using the following labels:

State labels

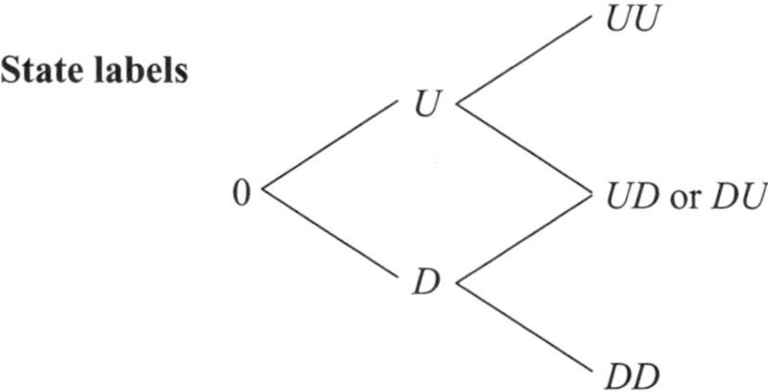

Put payoffs at date 3

Here are the values of the stock and the date 3 put payoffs:

3. Recall from Chapter 16 that an American call option on a non-dividend-paying stock has the same value as a European call option. We return to calls at the end of this section.

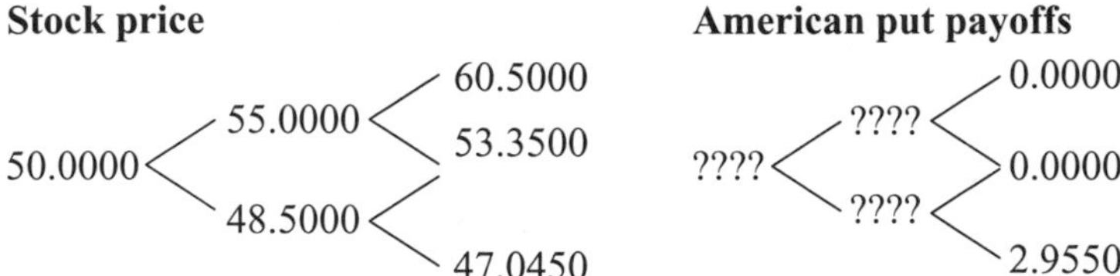

At date 2, the holder of an American put can choose whether to hold the put or to exercise it. We now have the following value function:

$$\begin{array}{l}\text{Put value}\\ \text{at date 2}\\ \text{state U}\end{array} = \max\begin{cases}\text{Put value if exercised} = \max(X - S_U, 0)\\ q_U * \text{Put payoff in state } UU + q_D * \text{Put payoff in state UD}\end{cases}$$

A similar function holds for the put value in state D at date 2. The resulting tree now looks like this:

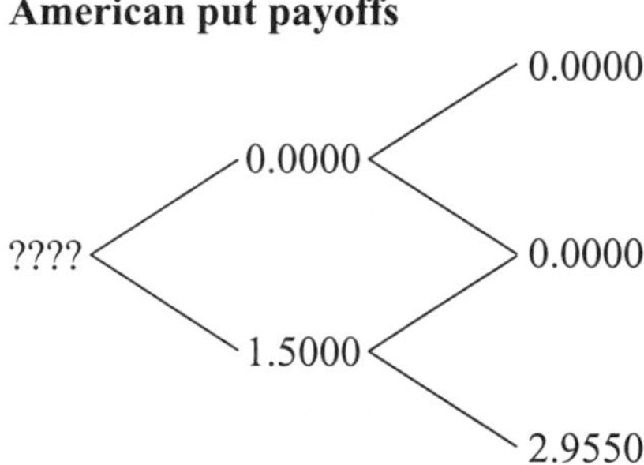

Here's the explanation:

- In state U, the put is valueless. When the stock price is \$55, it is not worthwhile to early-exercise the put, since $\max(X - S_U, 0) = \max(50 - 55, 0) = 0$. However, since the future put payoffs from state U are zero, the state-dependent present value of these future payoffs (the second line in the previous formula) is also zero.
- In state D, however, the holder of the put gets $\max(50 - 48.5, 0) = 1.5$ if he exercises the put; however, if he holds the put without exercise, its market value is the state-dependent value of the future payoffs:

$$q_U * 0 + q_D * 2.9550 = 0.6531 * 0 + 0.2903 * 2.9550 = 0.8578$$

It is clearly preferable to exercise the put in this state rather than hold onto it.

At date 0, a similar value function recurs:

$$\begin{matrix}\text{Put value} \\ \text{at date 0}\end{matrix} = \max\begin{cases}\text{Put value if exercised} = \max(X - S_0, 0) \\ q_U * \text{Put payoff in state } U + q_D * \text{Put payoff in state D}\end{cases}$$

Here is the spreadsheet:

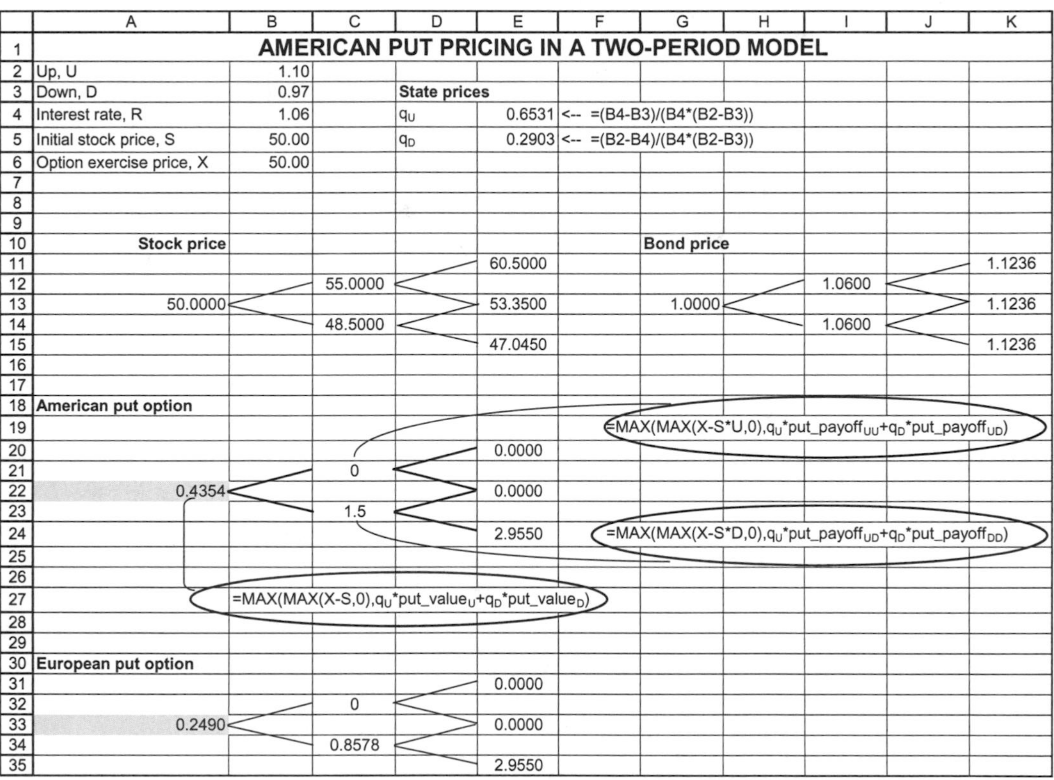

	A	B	C	D	E	F	G	H	I	J	K
1	**AMERICAN PUT PRICING IN A TWO-PERIOD MODEL**										
2	Up, U	1.10									
3	Down, D	0.97		**State prices**							
4	Interest rate, R	1.06		q_U	0.6531	<-- =(B4-B3)/(B4*(B2-B3))					
5	Initial stock price, S	50.00		q_D	0.2903	<-- =(B2-B4)/(B4*(B2-B3))					
6	Option exercise price, X	50.00									
7											
8											
9											
10	**Stock price**						**Bond price**				
11					60.5000						1.1236
12			55.0000						1.0600		
13		50.0000			53.3500		1.0000				1.1236
14			48.5000						1.0600		
15					47.0450						1.1236
16											
17											
18	**American put option**										
19						=MAX(MAX(X-S*U,0),q_U*put_payoff$_{UU}$+q_D*put_payoff$_{UD}$)					
20					0.0000						
21			0								
22		0.4354			0.0000						
23			1.5								
24					2.9550	=MAX(MAX(X-S*D,0),q_U*put_payoff$_{UD}$+q_D*put_payoff$_{DD}$)					
25											
26											
27		=MAX(MAX(X-S,0),q_U*put_value$_U$+q_D*put_value$_D$)									
28											
29											
30	**European put option**										
31					0.0000						
32			0								
33		0.2490			0.0000						
34			0.8578								
35					2.9550						

We can use the same logic to price an American call option, though—following Proposition 2 of Chapter 16—we know that the value of an American and a European call should coincide. And so they do:

	A	B	C	D	E	F	G	H	I	J	K
1	AMERICAN CALL PRICING IN A TWO-PERIOD MODEL										
2	Up, U	1.10									
3	Down, D	0.97		**State prices**							
4	Interest rate, R	1.06		q_U	0.6531	<-- =(B4-B3)/(B4*(B2-B3))					
5	Initial stock price, S	50.00		q_D	0.2903	<-- =(B2-B4)/(B4*(B2-B3))					
6	Option exercise price, X	50.00									
7											
8											
9											
10	**Stock price**						**Bond price**				
11					60.5000						1.1236
12			55.0000						1.0600		
13	50.0000				53.3500		1.0000				1.1236
14			48.5000						1.0600		
15					47.0450						1.1236
16											
17											
18	**American call option**										
19						=MAX(MAX(S*U-X,0),q_U*call_payoff$_{UU}$+q_D*call_payoff$_{UD}$)					
20					10.5000						
21			7.8302								
22	5.7492				3.3500						
23			2.1880								
24					0.0000	=MAX(MAX(S*D-X,0),q_U*call_payoff$_{UD}$+q_D*call_payoff$_{DD}$)					
25											
26											
27		=MAX(MAX(S-X,0),q_U*call_value$_U$+q_D*call_value$_D$)									
28											
29											
30	**European call option**										
31					10.5000						
32			7.8302								
33	5.7492				3.3500						
34			2.1880								
35					0.0000						

17.6 Programming the Binomial Option-Pricing Model in VBA

The pricing procedure used in the preceding examples can easily be programmed using Excel's VBA programming language. In the binomial model the price can move *up* or *down* in any time period. If q_U is the state price associated with an up move and if q_D is the state price associated with a down move, then the binomial European option prices are given by

$$\text{Binomial European call} = \sum_{i=0}^{n} \binom{n}{i} q_U^i q_D^{n-i} \max(S * U^i D^{n-i} - X, 0)$$

$$\text{Binomial European put} = \begin{cases} \sum_{i=0}^{n} \binom{n}{i} q_U^i q_D^{n-i} \max(X - S * U^i D^{n-i}, 0) \\ \text{or by put-call parity} \end{cases}$$

where U is an up move, R is a down move in the stock price, and $\binom{n}{i}$ is the binomial coefficient (the number of up moves in n total moves):

$$\binom{n}{i} = \frac{n!}{i!(n-i)!}$$

We use Excel's **Combin(n,i)** to give values for the binomial coefficients.

Following are two VBA functions that compute the value of binomial European calls and puts. The function **Binomial_eur_put** uses put-call parity to price the put.

```
Function Binomial_eur_call(Up, Down, Interest, Stock, _
  Exercise, Periods)
  q_up = (Interest - Down) / (Interest * (Up - Down))
  q_down = 1 / Interest - q_up
  Binomial_eur_call = 0
  For Index = 0 To Periods
     Binomial_eur_call = Binomial_eur_call _
       + Application.Combin(Periods, Index) * _
       q_up ^ Index * _
       q_down ^ (Periods - Index) * _
       Application.Max(Stock * Up ^ Index * Down ^ _
       (Periods - Index) - Exercise, 0)
    Next Index
End Function

Function Binomial_eur_put(Up, Down, Interest, Stock, _
  Exercise, Periods)
  Binomial_eur_put = Binomial_eur_call(Up, Down, _
  Interest, _ Stock, Exercise, Periods) _
  + Exercise / Interest ^ Periods - Stock
End Function
```

Implementing this procedure in a spreadsheet, we get for the four-period example of section 17.4:

	A	B	C
1	**VBA FUNCTIONS FOR CALLS AND PUTS**		
2	Up, U	1.10	
3	Down, D	0.97	
4	Interest rate, R	1.06	
5	Initial stock price, S	50.00	
6	Option exercise price, X	50.00	
7	Number of periods, n	4	
8			
9	European call	10.4360	<-- =binomial_eur_call(B2,B3,B4,B5,B6,B7)
10	European put	0.0407	<-- =binomial_eur_put(B2,B3,B4,B5,B6,B7)

17.6.1 American Put Pricing

As discussed in Chapter 16, a well-known theorem states that the price of an American call on a non-dividend-paying stock is the same as that of a European option. The pricing of American put, however, can be different. The following VBA function uses a binomial option-pricing model like the one from section 17.5 to price American puts:

```
Function Binomial_amer_put(Up, Down, Interest, Stock, _
     Exercise, Periods)
     q_up = (Interest - Down) / (Interest *
     (Up - Down))
     q_down = 1 / Interest - q_up
     Dim OptionReturnEnd() As Double
     Dim OptionReturnMiddle() As Double
     ReDim OptionReturnEnd(Periods + 1)
     For State = 0 To Periods
           OptionReturnEnd(State) = _
           Application.Max(Exercise - Stock * Up ^ _
           State * Down ^ _
           (Periods - State), 0)
     Next State

     For Index = Periods - 1 To 0 Step -1
          ReDim OptionReturnMiddle(Index)
          For State = 0 To Index
              OptionReturnMiddle(State) = _
              Application.Max(Exercise - Stock * Up ^ _
              State * Down ^ _
```

```
                (Index - State), q_down * _
                OptionReturnEnd(State) + q_up * _
                OptionReturnEnd(State + 1))
            Next State
            ReDim OptionReturnEnd(Index)
            For State = 0 To Index
                OptionReturnEnd(State) = _
                OptionReturnMiddle(State)
            Next State
        Next Index
        Binomial_amer_put = OptionReturnMiddle(0)
End Function
```

In this function we use two arrays, called **OptionReturnEnd** and **OptionReturnMiddle**. At each date t, these arrays store the option values for the date itself and the next date—$t + 1$.

Here's an implementation in a spreadsheet, using the two-period, three-date example from section 17.5:

	A	B	C
1	**VBA FUNCTIONS FOR CALLS AND PUTS**		
2	Up, U	1.10	
3	Down, D	0.97	
4	Interest rate, R	1.06	
5	Initial stock price, S	50.00	
6	Option exercise price, X	50.00	
7	Number of periods, n	2	
8			
9	American put	0.4354	<-- =binomial_amer_put(B2,B3,B4,B5,B6,B7)
10	European put	0.2490	<-- =binomial_eur_put(B2,B3,B4,B5,B6,B7)
11	American call	5.7492	<-- =binomial_amer_call(B2,B3,B4,B5,B6,B7)
12	European call	5.7492	<-- =binomial_eur_call(B2,B3,B4,B5,B6,B7)

The values in cells B9 and B10 are for an American and a European put; these values correspond to those given in section 17.5. In cell B11 we use a function similar to the American put function to price American calls. Unsurprisingly—given Proposition 2 of Chapter 16—this function gives the same value as the binomial European call-pricing function.

The VBA function works well for many more periods.[4] In the example that follows we calculate the value of an American put and call for options that expire at T = 0.75 of a year. The stochastic process that defines the stock returns has mean $\mu = 15$ percent and standard deviation $\sigma = 35$ percent. The annual continuously compounded interest rate r is 6 percent, and each year is divided into 25 subperiods, so that a single period has length $\Delta t = 1/25 = 0.04$. Given these numbers, Up, Down, and R are defined by $\text{Up} = e^{\mu\Delta t+\sigma\sqrt{\Delta t}}$, $\text{Down} = e^{\mu\Delta t-\sigma\sqrt{\Delta t}}$, $R = e^{r\Delta t}$.

Here is the pricing of an American and European call and put:

	A	B	C
1	**VBA FUNCTIONS FOR CALLS AND PUTS** **n divisions per year, Δt = 1/n** **Up=exp(μ*Δt + σ*sqrt(Δt)), Down = exp(μ*Δt - σ*sqrt(Δt))**		
2	Mean return per year, μ	15%	
3	Standard deviation of annual return, σ	35%	
4	Annual interest rate, r	6%	
5			
6	Initial stock price, S	50.00	
7	Option exercise price, X	50.00	
8	Option exercise date (years)	0.75	
9	Number of divisions of 1 year	25	<-- each year divided into 25 subperiods
10	Δt, the length of one division	0.04	<-- =1/B9
11	Up move per Δt	1.078963	<-- =EXP(B2*B10+B3*SQRT(B10))
12	Down move per Δt	0.938005	<-- =EXP(B2*B10-B3*SQRT(B10))
13	Interest rate per Δt	1.002403	<-- =EXP(B4*B10)
14			
15	Number of periods until maturity, n	19	<-- =ROUND(B8*B9,0)
16			
17	American put	5.1311	<-- =binomial_amer_put(B11,B12,B13,B6,B7,B15)
18	European put	4.9213	<-- =binomial_eur_put(B11,B12,B13,B6,B7,B15)
19	American call	7.1501	<-- =binomial_amer_call(B11,B12,B13,B6,B7,B15)
20	European call	7.1501	<-- =binomial_eur_call(B11,B12,B13,B6,B7,B15)

Notice that we have compromised on the number of periods, by using Excel's **Round** function—since there are 25 divisions of one year and the option's maturity is T = 0.75, the actual number of periods to maturity is $25 * 0.75$, which is not a round number.

This procedure works well even for a very large number of periods. In the next example, the option has a maturity T = 0.5, and the basic one-year period is divided into 400 subperiods. Excel easily computes the

4. The discussion that follows is perhaps best read after Chapters 18 and 19.

value of the American put and call, even though a considerable amount of computation is involved.

	A	B	C
1	**VBA FUNCTIONS FOR CALLS AND PUTS** **n divisions per year, Δt = 1/n** **Up=exp(μ*Δt + σ*sqrt(Δt)), Down = exp(μ*Δt - σ*sqrt(Δt))**		
2	Mean return per year, μ	15%	
3	Standard deviation of annual return, σ	35%	
4	Annual interest rate, r	6%	
5			
6	Initial stock price, S	50.00	
7	Option exercise price, X	50.00	
8	Option exercise date (years)	0.50	
9	Number of divisions of 1 year	400	<-- each year divided into 400 subperiods
10	Δt, the length of one division	0.0025	<-- =1/B9
11	Up move per Δt	1.018036	<-- =EXP(B2*B10+B3*SQRT(B10))
12	Down move per Δt	0.983021	<-- =EXP(B2*B10-B3*SQRT(B10))
13	Interest rate per Δt	1.00015	<-- =EXP(B4*B10)
14			
15	Number of periods until maturity, n	200	<-- =ROUND(B8*B9,0)
16			
17	American put	4.2882	<-- =binomial_amer_put(B11,B12,B13,B6,B7,B15)
18	European put	4.1471	<-- =binomial_eur_put(B11,B12,B13,B6,B7,B15)
19	American call	5.6248	<-- =binomial_amer_call(B11,B12,B13,B6,B7,B15)
20	European call	5.6248	<-- =binomial_eur_call(B11,B12,B13,B6,B7,B15)

17.7 Convergence of Binomial Pricing to the Black-Scholes Price

In this section we discuss the convergence of the binomial model to the Black-Scholes pricing formula. The discussion assumes some understanding of lognormality (discussed in Chapter 18) and the Black-Scholes option-pricing formula (discussed in Chapter 19). So you may want to skip this section and come back to it later.

Whenever we consider a finite approximation to the option-pricing formulas, we have to use an approximation to the up and the down movements. One widespread translation of the interest rate r and the stock's volatility σ to an "up" or "down" move necessary for the binomial model is

$$\Delta t = T/n \qquad R = e^{r\Delta t}$$

$$U = 1 + \text{Up} = e^{\sigma\sqrt{\Delta t}} \qquad D = 1 + \text{Down} = e^{-\sigma\sqrt{\Delta t}}$$

This approximation guarantees that as $\Delta t \to 0$ (i.e., as $n \to \infty$), the resulting distribution of the stock returns approaches the lognormal distribution.[5]

An implementation of this methodology in a spreadsheet follows. The function **Binomial_Eur_call** is the same as that defined previously; the function **BSCall** is the Black-Scholes formula, defined and discussed in Chapter 19:

	A	B	C
1	**BLACK-SCHOLES AND BINOMIAL PRICING**		
2	S	60	Current stock price
3	X	50	Option exercise price
4	T	0.5000	Time to option exercise (in years)
5	r	8%	Annual interest rate
6	Sigma	30%	Riskiness of stock
7	n	20	Number of subdivisions of T
8			
9	Δt = T/n	0.0250	<-- =B4/B7
10	Up, U	1.0486	<-- =EXP(B6*SQRT(B9))
11	Down, D	0.9537	<-- =EXP(-B6*SQRT(B9))
12	Interest rate, R	1.0020	<-- =EXP(B5*B9)
13			
14	Binomial European call	12.8055	<-- =binomial_eur_call(B10,B11,B12,B2,B3,B7)
15	Black-Scholes call	12.8226	<-- =BSCall(B2,B3,B4,B5,B6)

The binomial model gives a good approximation to the Black-Scholes (cells B14:B15). As the n gets larger, this approximation gets better, though the convergence to the Black-Scholes price is not smooth:

5. An alternative approximation that converges to a lognormal price process is given in section 17.7.1. See also Omberg (1987), Hull (2006), and Benninga, Steinmetz, and Stroughair (1993).

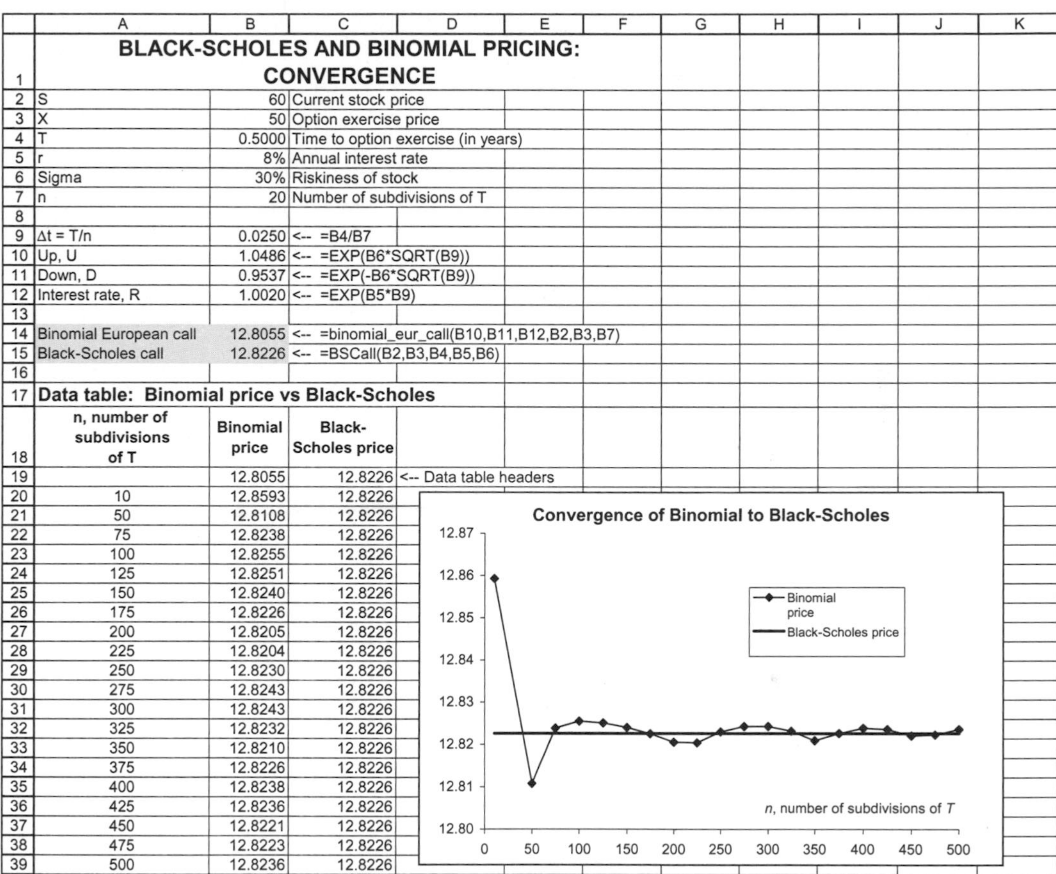

	A	B	C	D
1	**BLACK-SCHOLES AND BINOMIAL PRICING: CONVERGENCE**			
2	S	60	Current stock price	
3	X	50	Option exercise price	
4	T	0.5000	Time to option exercise (in years)	
5	r	8%	Annual interest rate	
6	Sigma	30%	Riskiness of stock	
7	n	20	Number of subdivisions of T	
8				
9	Δt = T/n	0.0250	<-- =B4/B7	
10	Up, U	1.0486	<-- =EXP(B6*SQRT(B9))	
11	Down, D	0.9537	<-- =EXP(-B6*SQRT(B9))	
12	Interest rate, R	1.0020	<-- =EXP(B5*B9)	
13				
14	Binomial European call	12.8055	<-- =binomial_eur_call(B10,B11,B12,B2,B3,B7)	
15	Black-Scholes call	12.8226	<-- =BSCall(B2,B3,B4,B5,B6)	
16				
17	**Data table: Binomial price vs Black-Scholes**			
18	**n, number of subdivisions of T**	**Binomial price**	**Black-Scholes price**	
19		12.8055	12.8226	<-- Data table headers
20	10	12.8593	12.8226	
21	50	12.8108	12.8226	
22	75	12.8238	12.8226	
23	100	12.8255	12.8226	
24	125	12.8251	12.8226	
25	150	12.8240	12.8226	
26	175	12.8226	12.8226	
27	200	12.8205	12.8226	
28	225	12.8204	12.8226	
29	250	12.8230	12.8226	
30	275	12.8243	12.8226	
31	300	12.8243	12.8226	
32	325	12.8232	12.8226	
33	350	12.8210	12.8226	
34	375	12.8226	12.8226	
35	400	12.8238	12.8226	
36	425	12.8236	12.8226	
37	450	12.8221	12.8226	
38	475	12.8223	12.8226	
39	500	12.8236	12.8226	

17.7.1 An Alternative Approximation to the Lognormal

The approximation of the first part of this section is not the only approximation that works. If the stock price is lognormally distributed with mean μ and standard deviation σ, we can also use the following approximation:

$$\Delta t = T/n \qquad R = e^{r\Delta t}$$

$$U = 1 + \text{Up} = e^{\mu\Delta t + \sigma\sqrt{\Delta t}} \qquad D = 1 + \text{Down} = e^{\mu\Delta t - \sigma\sqrt{\Delta t}}$$

Implementing this in our spreadsheet gives

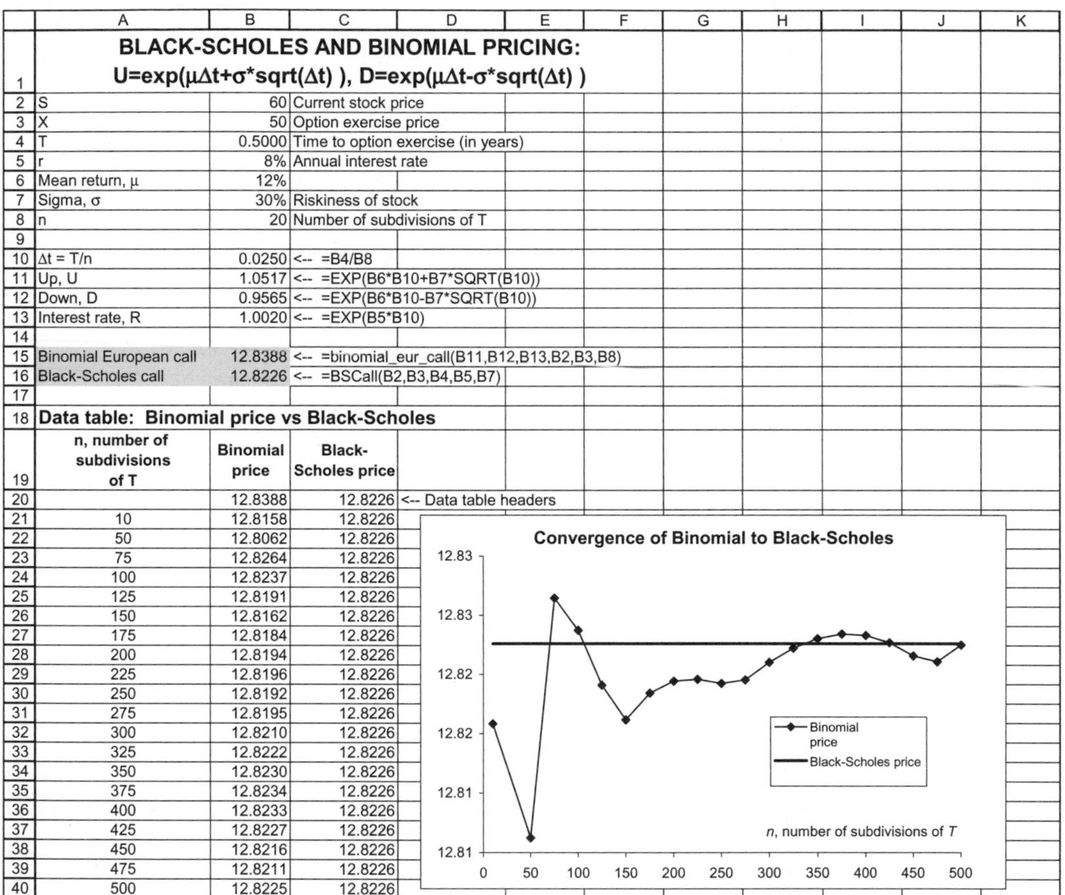

	A	B	C	D
1	**BLACK-SCHOLES AND BINOMIAL PRICING: U=exp(μΔt+σ*sqrt(Δt)), D=exp(μΔt-σ*sqrt(Δt))**			
2	S	60	Current stock price	
3	X	50	Option exercise price	
4	T	0.5000	Time to option exercise (in years)	
5	r	8%	Annual interest rate	
6	Mean return, μ	12%		
7	Sigma, σ	30%	Riskiness of stock	
8	n	20	Number of subdivisions of T	
9				
10	Δt = T/n	0.0250	<-- =B4/B8	
11	Up, U	1.0517	<-- =EXP(B6*B10+B7*SQRT(B10))	
12	Down, D	0.9565	<-- =EXP(B6*B10-B7*SQRT(B10))	
13	Interest rate, R	1.0020	<-- =EXP(B5*B10)	
14				
15	Binomial European call	12.8388	<-- =binomial_eur_call(B11,B12,B13,B2,B3,B8)	
16	Black-Scholes call	12.8226	<-- =BSCall(B2,B3,B4,B5,B7)	
17				
18	**Data table: Binomial price vs Black-Scholes**			
19	**n, number of subdivisions of T**	**Binomial price**	**Black-Scholes price**	
20		12.8388	12.8226	<-- Data table headers
21	10	12.8158	12.8226	
22	50	12.8062	12.8226	
23	75	12.8264	12.8226	
24	100	12.8237	12.8226	
25	125	12.8191	12.8226	
26	150	12.8162	12.8226	
27	175	12.8184	12.8226	
28	200	12.8194	12.8226	
29	225	12.8196	12.8226	
30	250	12.8192	12.8226	
31	275	12.8195	12.8226	
32	300	12.8210	12.8226	
33	325	12.8222	12.8226	
34	350	12.8230	12.8226	
35	375	12.8234	12.8226	
36	400	12.8233	12.8226	
37	425	12.8227	12.8226	
38	450	12.8216	12.8226	
39	475	12.8211	12.8226	
40	500	12.8225	12.8226	

The convergence of this parameterization to Black-Scholes is somewhat less smooth, though the ultimate result is the same.[6]

17.8 Using the Binomial Model to Price Employee Stock Options[7]

An employee stock option (ESO) is a call option given by a company to its employees as part of their remuneration package. Like all call options,

6. Note that both methods actually converge quite quickly—within several dozen steps the binomial is within 0.01 of the Black-Scholes price.

7. This section has benefited from discussions with Torben Voetmann of Cornerstone Research and Zvi Wiener of Hebrew University, Jerusalem.

the value of an ESO depends on the current price of the stock, the option's exercise price, and the time until exercise. However, ESOs typically have several special conditions:

- The option has a vesting period. During this period, the employee is not allowed to exercise the option. An employee leaving the company before the vesting period forfeits his option. In the model of this section we assume that a typical employee of the company leaves at exit rate *e* per year.
- An employee leaving the company after the vesting period is forced to exercise his option immediately.
- For tax reasons, almost all ESOs have exercise prices equal to the stock price on the date of issue.

In the model that follows, adapted from a paper by Hull and White (2004), we assume that an employee will choose to exercise his option when the price of the stock is greater than some multiple *m* of the ESOs exercise price X. We first present the model's implementation and results and then discuss the VBA program that gives us these results:

	A	B	C
1	**A BINOMIAL EMPLOYEE STOCK-OPTION-PRICING MODEL** **Based on Hull and White (2004)**		
2	S	50	Current stock price
3	X	50	Option exercise price
4	T	10.00	Time to option exercise (in years)
5	Vesting period (years)	3.00	
6	Interest	5.00%	Annual interest rate
7	Sigma	35%	Riskiness of stock
8	Stock dividend rate	2.50%	Annual dividend rate on stock
9	Exit rate, e	10.00%	
10	Option exercise multiple, m	3.00	
11	n	50	Number of subdivisions of one year
12			
13	Employee stock option value	13.56	<-- =ESO(B2,B3,B4,B5,B6,B7,B8,B9,B10,B11)
14	Black-Scholes call	19.18	<-- =BSCall(B2*EXP(-B8*B4),B3,B4,B6,B7)

The **ESO** function in cell B13 depends on the 10 variables listed in cells B2:B11. The screen for this function looks like this:

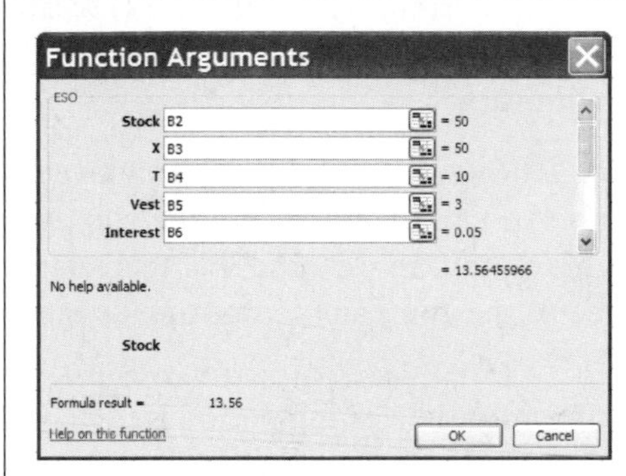

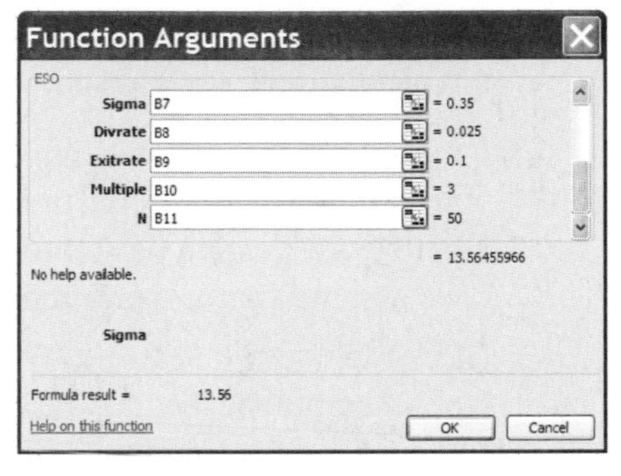

In this example, the employee stock option is given when the stock price is \$50. The ESO has exercise price X = \$50. The option has a 10-year maturity and a three-year vesting period. The interest rate is 5 percent annually, and the stock pays an annual dividend of 2.5 percent of its stock value. The rate at which employees leave the company is 10 percent per year. The model assumes that after the vesting period, the employee will choose to exercise his option if the stock price is three or more times the option's exercise price.[8] The binomial model with which the computations in cell B13 were done divides each year into 50 subdivisions.

Given these assumptions, the employee stock option is valued at \$13.56 (cell B13). A comparable Black-Scholes option on a dividend-paying stock would be valued at \$19.18.[9]

17.8.1 The ESO Valuation and FASB 123

The American Financial Accounting Standards Board (FASB) and the International Accounting Standards Board (IASB) agree that executive stock options should be priced using a model of the type explored here and that the value of options awarded should be accounted for in a firm's net income. If, for example, a firm had issued 1 million options of the

8. Research cited by Hull and White (2004) shows that the average stock-price-to-exercise-price ratio at which ESO owners exercise their options is between 2.2 and 2.8.

9. We're getting way ahead of ourselves here! The adaptation of Black-Scholes for dividend-paying stock is given in section 19.6.

type that appears in the previous spreadsheet, we would value these options at $13,564,600.

17.8.2 The VBA Code for the ESO Model

In this subsection we give the VBA code for this model. A short discussion follows the code.

```
Function ESO(Stock As Double, X As Double, T
As Double, Vest As Double, _
     Interest As Double, Sigma As Double, _
       Divrate As Double, _
     Exitrate As Double, Multiple As Double, _
       n As Single)

     Dim Up As Double, Down As Double, R As _
       Double, Div As Double, _
     piUp As Double, piDown As Double, Delta _
       As Double, _
     i As Integer, j As Integer

   ReDim Opt(T * n, T * n)
   ReDim S(T * n, T * n)

   Up = Exp(Sigma * Sqr(1 / n))
   Down = Exp(-Sigma * Sqr(1 / n))
   R = Exp(Interest / n)
   Div = Exp(-Divrate / n)
   piUp = (R * Div - Down) / (Up - Down)
     'Risk-neutral up probability
   piDown = (Up - R * Div) / (Up - Down)
     'Risk-neutral down probability

   'Defining the stock price
   For i = 0 To T * n
        For j = 0 To i ' j is the number of
        'Up steps
        S(i, j) = Stock * Up ^ j * Down ^ _
          (i - j)
        Next j
   Next i
```

```
    'Defining the option value on the last
    'nodes of tree
    For i = 0 To T * n
        Opt(T * n, i) = Application.Max(S(T _
          * n, i) - X, 0)
    Next i

    'Early exercise when stock price >
    'multiple * exercise after vesting
    For i = T * n - 1 To 0 Step -1
    For j = 0 To i
    If i > Vest * n And S(i, j) >= Multiple _
      * X Then _
        Opt(i, j) = Application.Max _
          (S(i, j) - X, 0)
    If i > Vest * n And S(i, j) < Multiple * _
      X Then _
        Opt(i, j) = ((1 - Exitrate / n) * _
        (piUp * Opt(i + 1, j + 1) + _
        piDown * Opt(i + 1, j)) / R + _
          Exitrate / n * _
        Application.Max(S(i, j) - X, 0))
    If i <= Vest * n Then Opt(i, j) = _
      (1 - Exitrate / n) * _
    (piUp * Opt(i + 1, j + 1) + piDown * _
      Opt(i + 1, j)) / R

    Next j
    Next i

    ESO = Opt(0, 0)
End Function
```

17.8.3 Explaining the VBA Code[10]

The VBA code has several parts. The first part defines the variables, adjusting the Up, Down, and 1 + interest R for the n divisions of each year. Having made this adjustment, the code defines the risk-neutral probabilities π_{Up} and π_{Down}:

10. This subsection is tedious and can be skipped. But take a look at the next subsection, where we use **Data|Table** to do sensitivity analysis.

```
Up = Exp(Sigma * Sqr(1 / n))
Down = Exp(-Sigma * Sqr(1 / n))
R = Exp(Interest / n)
Div = Exp(-Divrate / n)
piUp = (R * Div - Down) / (Up - Down)
  'Risk-neutral up probability
piDown = (Up - R * Div) / (Up - Down)
  'Risk-neutral down probability
```

The stock price is defined as an array $S(i, j)$, where i defines the periods, $i = 0, 1, \ldots, T*n$, and j defines the number of Up steps at each period, $j = 0, 1, \ldots, i$. The next part of the code defines the stock price

```
'Defining the stock price
 For i = 0 To T * n
      For j = 0 To i ' j is the number of
        Up steps
      S(i, j) = Stock * Up ^ j * Down ^ _
        (i - j)
      Next j
Next i
```

The option values are defined in the next piece of code, which is the heart of our employee-stock-option function. Option value is defined as an array opt(i, j):

```
'Defining the option value on the last nodes of
'tree
For i = 0 To T * n
   Opt(T * n, i) = Application.Max(S(T * n, i) _
   - X, 0)
Next i

'Early exercise when stock price > multiple *
'exercise after vesting
For i = T * n - 1 To 0 Step -1
For j = 0 To i
```

```
If i > Vest * n And S(i, j) >= Multiple * X
Then _
   Opt(i, j) = Application.Max(S(i, j) - X, 0)
If i > Vest * n And S(i, j) < Multiple * X
Then _
   Opt(i, j) = ((1 - Exitrate / n) * (piUp * _
Opt(i + 1, j + 1) + _
   piDown * Opt(i + 1, j)) / R + Exitrate / n _
     * _
   Application.Max(S(i, j) - X, 0))
If i <= Vest * n Then Opt(i, j) = (1 - _
Exitrate / n) * _
   (piUp * Opt(i + 1, j + 1) + piDown * Opt(i _
     + 1, j)) / R

Next j
Next i
```

Here's what this piece of code says:

$$\text{opt}(i,j)=\begin{cases}\max[S(T*n,j)-X,0] & \text{terminal nodes}\\ \max[S(i,j)-X,0] & \text{after vesting, } S(i,j)\geq m*X\\ (1-\text{Exitrate}/n)*\dfrac{\pi_{\text{Up}}\,\text{opt}(i+1,j+1)+\pi_{\text{Down}}\,\text{opt}(i+1,j)}{R} & \\ & \text{after vesting, } S(i,j)<m*X\\ \quad+\text{Exitrate}/n*\text{Max}[S(i,j)-X,0] & \\ (1-\text{Exitrate}/n)*\dfrac{\pi_{\text{Up}}\,\text{opt}(i+1,j+1)+\pi_{\text{Down}}\,\text{opt}(i+1,j)}{R} & \\ & \text{before vesting}\end{cases}$$

At the terminal nodes, we simply exercise the option. Before the terminal nodes and after vesting, we check to see whether the stock price is greater than the desired multiple m of the exercise price. If it is, we exercise the option. If $S(i, j) < m*X$ the ESO's payoff depends on whether the employee exits the firm or not. With a probability (1 – Exitrate/n) the employee does not exit the firm, in which case the option payoff is the discounted expected next-period payoff:

$$(1-\text{Exitrate}/n)*\frac{\pi_{\text{Up}}\,\text{opt}(i+1,j+1)+\pi_{\text{Down}}\,\text{opt}(i+1,j)}{R}$$

However, if the employee exits the firm and the vesting period has passed, he will try to see if he can exercise the option, giving the expected payoff

$$\text{Exitrate}/n * \max[S(i, j) - X, 0]$$

Finally, before vesting, the ESO is simply worth the expected payoff, discounted (by the risk-neutral probabilities), of the next-period values:

$$(1 - \text{Exitrate}/n) * \frac{\pi_{\text{Up}} \operatorname{opt}(i+1, j+1) + \pi_{\text{Down}} \operatorname{opt}(t+1, j)}{R}$$

The final step in the code is to define the value of the function ESO: $ESO = \operatorname{opt}(0, 0)$.

17.8.4 Some Sensitivity Analysis

We can use data tables to perform sensitivity analysis on our **ESO** function.

	A	B	C	D	E	F
1	**ESO FUNCTION SENSITIVITY TO NUMBER OF SUBDIVISIONS n OF ONE YEAR**					
2	S	50	Current stock price			
3	X	50	Option exercise price			
4	T	10.0000	Time to option exercise (in years)			
5	Vesting period (years)	3.00				
6	Interest	5.00%	Annual interest rate			
7	Sigma	35%	Riskiness of stock			
8	Stock dividend rate	2.50%	Annual dividend rate on stock			
9	Exit rate, e	10.00%				
10	Option exercise multiple, m	3.00				
11	n	25	Number of subdivisions of one year			
12						
13	Employee stock option value	13.5275	<-- =ESO(B2,B3,B4,B5,B6,B7,B8,B9,B10,B11)			
14	Black-Scholes call	19.1842	<-- =BSCall(B2*EXP(-B8*B4),B3,B4,B6,B7)			
15						
16	**Sensitivity of ESO value to number of subdivisions n**					
17	n	13.5275	<-- =B13, data table header			
18	2	12.8213				
19	5	13.2870				
20	10	13.4312				
21	25	13.5275				
22	50	13.5646				
23	75	13.5733				
24	100	13.5753				
25	200	13.5810				
26						
27						
28						
29						
30						
31						
32						
33						
34						
35						

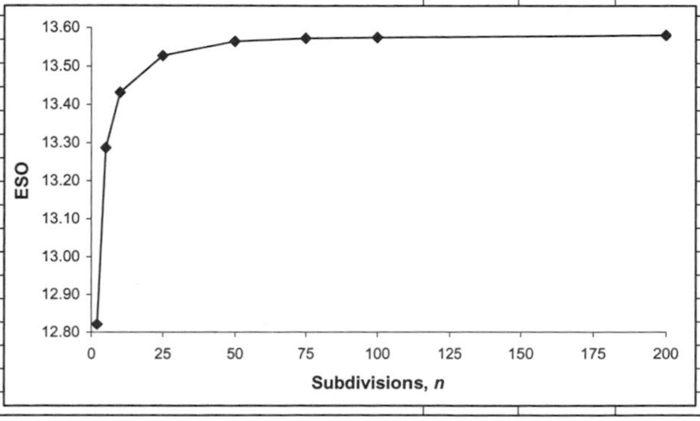

The graph gives ample evidence that $n = 25$ or 50 does well enough for valuing ESOs. Since larger values of n become time-consuming, we recommend lower numbers.

In the next graph we show the sensitivity of the ESO value to the employee exit rate e, the rate at which employees leave the firm each year:

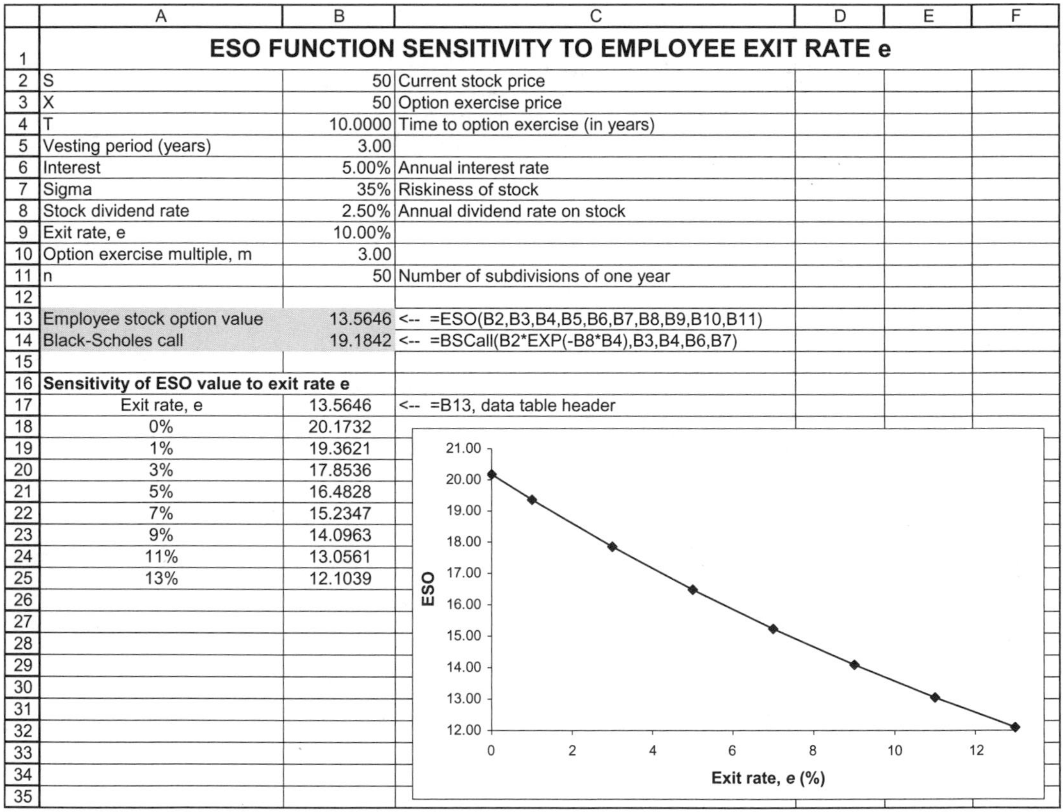

	A	B	C	D	E	F
1	**ESO FUNCTION SENSITIVITY TO EMPLOYEE EXIT RATE e**					
2	S	50	Current stock price			
3	X	50	Option exercise price			
4	T	10.0000	Time to option exercise (in years)			
5	Vesting period (years)	3.00				
6	Interest	5.00%	Annual interest rate			
7	Sigma	35%	Riskiness of stock			
8	Stock dividend rate	2.50%	Annual dividend rate on stock			
9	Exit rate, e	10.00%				
10	Option exercise multiple, m	3.00				
11	n	50	Number of subdivisions of one year			
12						
13	Employee stock option value	13.5646	<-- =ESO(B2,B3,B4,B5,B6,B7,B8,B9,B10,B11)			
14	Black-Scholes call	19.1842	<-- =BSCall(B2*EXP(-B8*B4),B3,B4,B6,B7)			
15						
16	**Sensitivity of ESO value to exit rate e**					
17	Exit rate, e	13.5646	<-- =B13, data table header			
18	0%	20.1732				
19	1%	19.3621				
20	3%	17.8536				
21	5%	16.4828				
22	7%	15.2347				
23	9%	14.0963				
24	11%	13.0561				
25	13%	12.1039				
26						
27						
28						
29						
30						
31						
32						
33						
34						
35						

The exit rate has a major effect on the value of the ESO: The higher the turnover of employees, the lower the value of the employee stock options. In terms of FASB 123 valuation, the exit rate e is an important valuation factor.

Finally we do a sensitivity analysis of the ESO value on the exit multiple m. Recall that the Hull-White model assumes that an employee holding an ESO exercises her option when the stock price is a multiple m of the option exercise price X. Basically this assumption locks the employee into a suboptimal strategy, since in general call options should be held to maturity (though note that in this case the option is written on a stock that pays a dividend, which may in some cases make early exercise optimal). In the next example we clearly see the suboptimality of early ESO exercise: The higher the multiple m, the higher the value of the ESO.

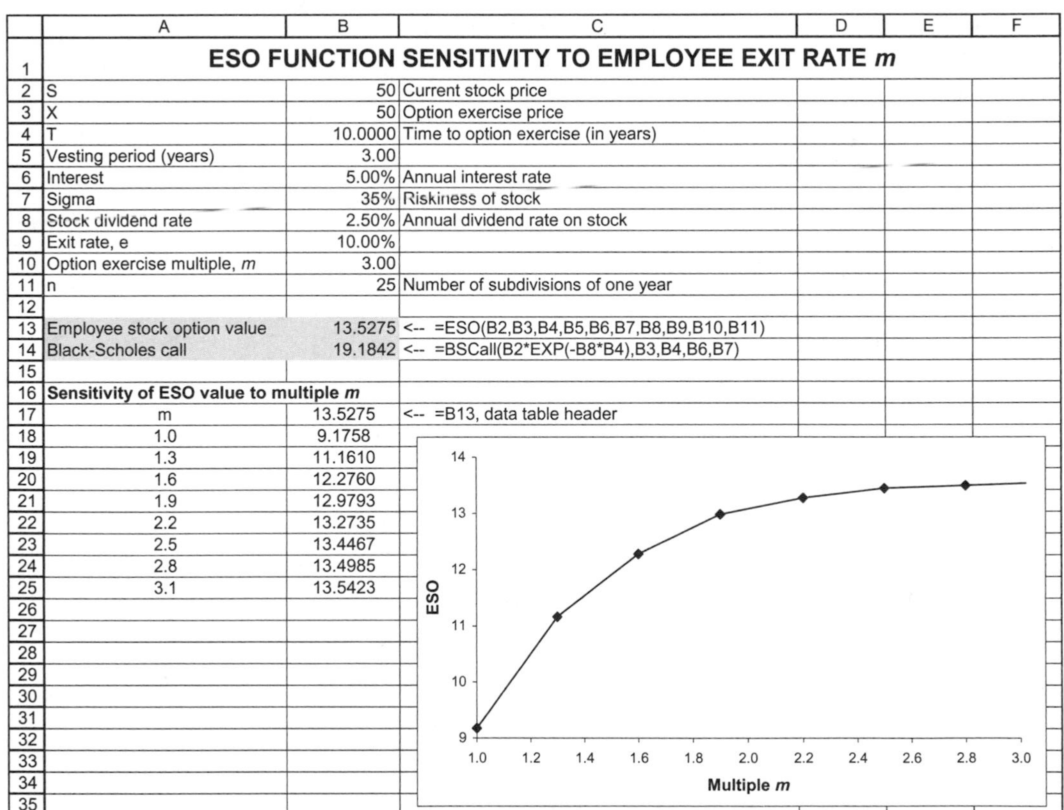

	A	B	C
1	**ESO FUNCTION SENSITIVITY TO EMPLOYEE EXIT RATE *m***		
2	S	50	Current stock price
3	X	50	Option exercise price
4	T	10.0000	Time to option exercise (in years)
5	Vesting period (years)	3.00	
6	Interest	5.00%	Annual interest rate
7	Sigma	35%	Riskiness of stock
8	Stock dividend rate	2.50%	Annual dividend rate on stock
9	Exit rate, e	10.00%	
10	Option exercise multiple, *m*	3.00	
11	n	25	Number of subdivisions of one year
12			
13	Employee stock option value	13.5275	<-- =ESO(B2,B3,B4,B5,B6,B7,B8,B9,B10,B11)
14	Black-Scholes call	19.1842	<-- =BSCall(B2*EXP(-B8*B4),B3,B4,B6,B7)
15			
16	**Sensitivity of ESO value to multiple *m***		
17	m	13.5275	<-- =B13, data table header
18	1.0	9.1758	
19	1.3	11.1610	
20	1.6	12.2760	
21	1.9	12.9793	
22	2.2	13.2735	
23	2.5	13.4467	
24	2.8	13.4985	
25	3.1	13.5423	

17.8.5 Last but Not Least

The Hull-White model is a numerical approximation of the ESO option valuation, but it is not a closed-form formula. A recent paper by Cvitanić, Wiener, and Zapatero (2006) gives an analytical derivation of the value of employee stock options. The formula stretches over 16 pages of typescript and will not be given here. However, an Excel implementation of the formula exists and can be downloaded at http://pluto.mscc.huji.ac.il/~mswiener/research/ESO.htm.

17.9 Using the Binomial Model to Price Nonstandard Options: An Example

The binomial model can also be used to price nonstandard options. Consider the following example: You hold an option to buy a share of a company. The option allows for early exercise, but the exercise price varies with the time at which you choose to exercise. For the case we consider, the option has the following conditions:

- There are n possible exercise dates *only* (i.e., the option is only exercisable on these dates).
- Exercise at date t precludes exercise at all dates $s > t$. However, if you don't exercise at date s, you may still exercise at date $t > s$.
- The exercise price at date t is X_t. In other words, the exercise price can vary with time.

We want to value this option using a binomial framework. To do so, we recognize that basically this is just an American option with three separate exercise prices.

Here's how we set this problem up in a spreadsheet, using the logic of the American option valuation described in section 17.5:

	A	B	C	D	E	F	G	H	I
1				**TIME-DEPENDENT EXERCISE PRICES**					
2	Initial stock price	100		**Exercise prices**					
3	Up	10%		Date 1	100				
4	Down	-5%		Date 2	105				
5	Interest rate	6%		Date 3	112				
6									
7	**State prices**								
8	q_u	0.6918	<-- =(B5-B4)/((1+B5)*(B3-B4))						
9	q_d	0.2516	<-- =(B3-B5)/((1+B5)*(B3-B4))						
10									
11	**Check**								
12	$1/(q_u+q_d)$	1.06	<-- =1/(B8+B9)						
13	q_u*(1+up)+q_d*(1+down)	1	<-- =B8*(1+B3)+B9*(1+B4)						
14									
15		**Stock price**						133.100	
16						121.000			
17				110.000				114.950	
18		100.000				104.500			
19				95.000				99.275	
20						90.250			
21								85.738	
22									=MAX(q_U*H25+q_D*H27,MAX(F16-E4,0))
23		**Date 0**		**Date 1**		**Date 2**		**Date 3**	
24									
25		**Value at each node**						21.100	<-- =MAX(H16-E6,0)
26						16.000			
27				11.583				2.950	<-- =MAX(H18-E6,0)
28		8.368				2.041			
29				1.412				0.000	
30						0.000			
31	=MAX(q_U*F28+q_D*F30,MAX(D19-E3,0))							0.000	
32									
33		**Early exercise?**							
34						yes			
35				no					
36						no			=IF(q_U*H25+q_D*H27>= MAX(F16-E4,0),"no","yes")
37				no					
38						no			
39									

Most of this spreadsheet follows section 17.5. Cells B15:H21 describe the stock price over time, which follows a binomial process with the Up = 1.10 and Down = 0.95 (cells B3 and B4). Where things get interesting is in the valuation:

	A	B	C	D	E	F	G	H	I
22									=MAX(q_U*H25+q_D*H27,MAX(F16-E4,0))
23		**Date 0**		**Date 1**		**Date 2**		**Date 3**	
24									
25		**Value at each node**						21.100	<-- =MAX(H16-E6,0)
26						16.000			
27				11.583				2.950	<-- =MAX(H18-E6,0)
28		8.368				2.041			
29				1.412				0.000	
30						0.000			
31	=MAX(q_U*F28+q_D*F30,MAX(D19-E3,0))							0.000	
32									

As is usual for an American option, at each node of the tree we consider whether the option is worth more whether exercised or whether held. But note that in this picture, the exercise price varies with the date, so that the exercise price at date 3 is E5, that of date 2 is E4, and that of date 1 is E3. As you can see in cell B28, the value of the American call option is 8.368.

17.10 Summary

The binomial model is intuitive and easy to implement. As a widespread alternative to Black-Scholes pricing, the model can easily be put into a spreadsheet and programmed in VBA. This chapter has explored both the basic uses of the binomial model and its implementation to price American and other nonstandard options. A section on employee stock options has shown how to implement the Hull and White (2004) model for valuing these options. Throughout, we have laid special stress on the role of state prices in implementing the model.

Exercises

1. A stock selling for $25 today will, in one year, be worth either $35 or $20. If the interest rate is 8 percent, what is the value today of a one-year call option on the stock with exercise price $30? Use the simultaneous equation approach of section 17.2 to price the option.

2. In exercise 1, compute the state prices q_U and q_D, and use these prices to calculate the value today of a one-year put option on the stock with exercise price $30. Show that put-call parity holds: That is, using your answer from this problem and the previous problem, show that

$$\text{Call price} + \frac{X}{1+r} = \text{Stock price today} + \text{Put price}.$$

3. In a binomial model, a call option and a put option are both written on the same stock. The exercise price of the call option is 30, and the exercise price of the put option is 40. The call option's payoffs are 0 and 5, and the put option's payoffs are 20 and 5. The price of the call is 2.25 and the price of the put is 12.25.

   a. What is the riskless interest rate? Assume that the basic period is one year.

   b. What is the price of the stock today?

4. All reliable analysts agree that a share of ABC Corporation, selling today for $50, will be priced at either $65 or $45 one year from now. They further agree that the probabilities of these events are 0.6 and 0.4, respectively. The market risk-free rate is 6 percent. What is the value of a call option on ABC whose exercise price is $50 and that matures in one year?

5. A stock is currently selling for \$60. The price of the stock at the end of the year is expected either to increase by 25 percent or to decrease by 20 percent. The riskless interest rate is 5 percent. Calculate the price of a European put on the stock with exercise price \$55. Use the binomial option-pricing model.

6. Fill in all the cells labeled ??? in the following spreadsheet. Why is there no additional pricing tree for an American call option?

	A	B	C	D	E	F	G	H	I	J	K
1				THREE-DATE BINOMIAL OPTION PRICING							
2	Up, U	1.35									
3	Down, D	0.95		state prices							
4				q_u							
5	Initial stock price	40		q_d							
6	Interest rate, R	1.25									
7	Exercise price	40									
8											
9	**Stock price**						**Bond price**				
10											???
11			???						???		
12		40					1				???
13			???						???		
14											???
15											
16	**European call option**						**European put option**				
17											
18					???						???
19			???						???		
20	???				???		???				???
21			???						???		
22					???						???
23											
24							**American put option**				
25											
26											???
27									???		
28											???
29									???		
30											???

7. Consider the following two-period binomial model, in which the annual interest rate is 9 percent and in which the stock price goes up by 15 percent per period or down by 10 percent:

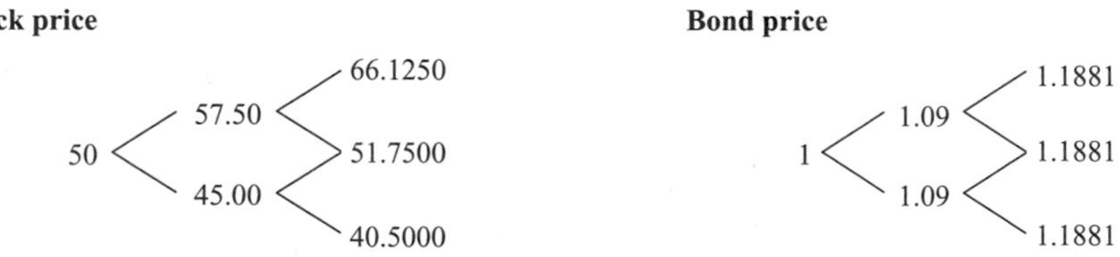

a. Price a European call on the stock with exercise price 60.

b. Price a European put on the stock with exercise price 60.

c. Price an American call on the stock with exercise price 60.

d. Price an American put on the stock with exercise price 60.

8. Consider the following three-date binomial model:

- In each period the stock price either goes up by 30 percent or decreases by 10 percent.
- The one-period interest rate is 25 percent.

Stock price

30
39.00
27.00
50.70
35.10
24.30

Bond price

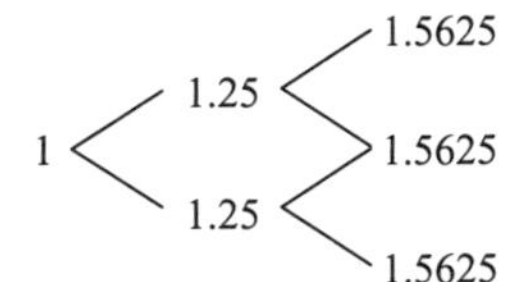

a. Consider a European call with $X = 30$ and $T = 2$. Fill in the blanks in the tree:

Call option price

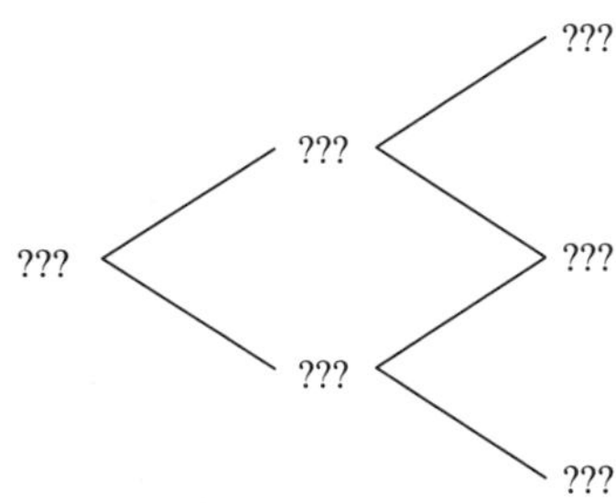

b. Price a European put with $X = 30$ and $T = 2$.

c. Now consider an American put with $X = 30$ and $T = 2$. Fill in the blanks in the tree:

American put option price

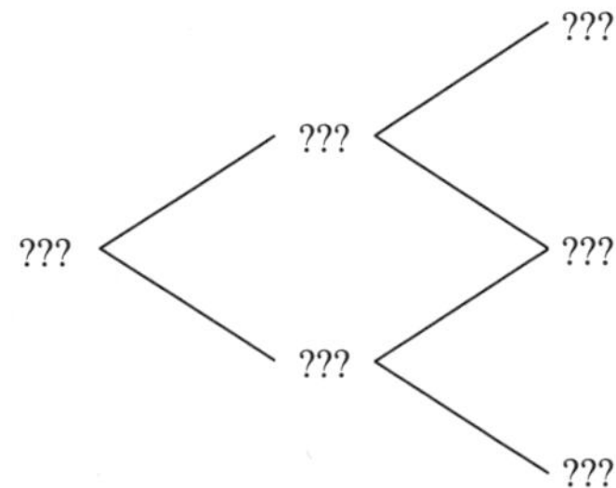

9. A prominent securities firm recently introduced a new financial product. This product, called the Best of Both Worlds (BOBOW for short), costs $10. It matures in five years, at which point it repays the investor the $10 cost *plus* 120 percent of any positive return in the S&P 500 index. There are no payments before maturity.

For example, if the S&P 500 is currently at 1500, and if it is at 1800 in five years, a BOBOW owner will receive back \$12.40 = \$10 ∗ [1 + 1.2 ∗ (1800/1500 – 1)]. If the S&P is at or below 1500 in five years, the BOBOW owner will receive back \$10.

Suppose that the annual interest rate on a five-year, continuously compounded, pure-discount bond is 6 percent. Suppose further that the S&P 500 is currently at 1500 and that you believe that in five years it will be at either 2500 or 1200. Use the binomial option-pricing model to show that BOBOWs are underpriced.

10. This problem is a continuation of the discussion of section 17.6.1. Show that as $n \to \infty$, the binomial European put price converges to the Black-Scholes put price. (Note that, as part of the spreadsheet **fm3_chapter17.xls**, we have included a function called **BSPut** that computes the Black-Scholes put price.)

11. Here's an advanced version of exercise 10. Consider an alternative parameterization of the binomial:

$$\Delta t = T/n \qquad R = e^{r\Delta t}$$

$$\text{Up} = e^{(r-\sigma^2/2)\Delta t+\sigma\sqrt{\Delta t}} \qquad q_U = \frac{R-\text{Down}}{R*(\text{Up}-\text{Down})}$$

$$\text{Down} = e^{(r-\sigma^2/2)\Delta t \ \ \sigma\sqrt{\Delta t}} \qquad q_D = \frac{1}{R} - q_U$$

Construct binomial European call and put option-pricing functions in VBA for this parameterization, and show that they also converge to the Black-Scholes formula. (The message here is that the parameterization of the binomial σ is not unique.)

12. A call option is written on a stock whose current price is \$50. The option has maturity of three years, and during this time the annual stock price is expected to increase by 25 percent or to decrease by 10 percent. The annual interest rate is constant at 6 percent. The option is exercisable at date 1 at a price of \$55, at date 2 for a price of \$60, and at date 3 for a price of \$65. What is its value today? Will you ever exercise the option early?

13. Reconsider exercise 12. Show that if the date-1 exercise price is X, the date-2 exercise price is $X*(1 + r)$, and the date-3 exercise price is $X*(1 + r)^2$, you will not exercise the option early.[11]

14. An investment bank is offering a security linked to the price two years from today of Bisco stock, which is currently at \$3 per share. Denote Bisco's stock price in two periods by S_2. The security being offered pays off $\text{Max}(S_2^3 - 40,0)$. You estimate that in each of the next two periods, Bisco stock will increase by either 50 percent or decrease by 20 percent. The annual interest rate is 8 percent. Price the security.

11. It can also be shown that this property holds if the exercise prices grow more slowly than the interest rate. Thus for the problem considered in section 17.7, there will be early exercise of the American call only when the exercise prices grow at a rate faster than the interest rate.

18 The Lognormal Distribution

18.1 Overview

In the previous chapter we discussed the pricing of options using the binomial option-pricing model. The binomial model—besides being an attractive and intuitive way to price options and other derivative securities—also has a deeper message for derivative asset pricing: It shows us that, given some assumptions about the uncertainty governing the stock price and given a risk-free interest rate, we can price options and other assets whose prices are dependent on the price of an underlying stock.

A problem with the binomial option-pricing approach is that we were not able to give simple formulas for the pricing of options. The pricing approach developed in the previous chapter is computational, not analytic. In order to develop a *formula* for the pricing of options (such as the Black-Scholes formula, discussed in Chapter 19), we need to make some assumptions about the statistical properties of the underlying stock price.

A central assumption of the Black-Scholes (BS) pricing model is that stock prices are distributed lognormally. An alternative statement of this assumption is that stock returns are distributed normally. In this chapter we attempt to give this assumption enough content so that you will be happy using it. Our method is as follows: We shall not, in this book, prove the Black-Scholes option-pricing formula. Instead, we shall try to convince you in this chapter that the basic assumption made by the BS model with regard to stock prices—the lognormality of stock prices—is reasonable. If we can convince you that it is, then we will leave the technical details of the BS proof to other, more advanced, texts.

The structure of this chapter is as follows:

- We start with a discussion of what constitutes "reasonable" assumptions about stock prices.
- We then discuss why the lognormal distribution is a reasonable distribution for stock prices.
- Next, we show how to simulate lognormal price paths.
- Finally, we show you how to derive the parameters of the lognormal distribution—the mean and standard deviation of the stock returns—from historical stock price data.

18.2 What Do Stock Prices Look Like?

What are reasonable assumptions about the way stock prices behave over time? Clearly the price of a stock (or any other risky financial asset) is uncertain. What is its distribution? This is a perplexing question. One way to answer this question is to ask what are reasonable statistical properties of a stock price. Here are five reasonable properties:

1. The stock price is uncertain. Given the price today, we do not know the price tomorrow.

2. Changes in the stock's price are continuous. Over short periods of time, changes in a stock's price are very small, and the change goes to zero as the time span goes to zero.[1]

3. The stock price is never zero. This property means that we exclude the stocks of "dead" companies.

4. The average return from holding a stock tends to increase over time. Notice the word "tends": We do not *know* that holding a stock for a longer time will lead to a higher return; however, we *expect* that holding a risky asset over a longer term will lead to a higher *average* return.

5. The *uncertainty* associated with the return from holding a stock also tends to increase the longer the stock is held. Thus, given the stock's price today, the variance of the stock price tomorrow is small; however, the price variance in one month is larger, and the variance in one year is larger still.

18.2.1 Reasonable Stock Properties and Stock Price Paths

One way of viewing these five "reasonable properties" of stock prices is to think about *price paths*. A stock price path is a graph of a stock price over a period of time. Here, for example, is the price path of several actual stocks:

---

1. If you have watched stock prices, you know that continuity is usually not a bad assumption. Sometimes, however, it can be disastrous (look at the way stock market prices behaved in October 1987, for a dramatic example of price *discontinuities*). It is possible to build a stock-price model that assumes that prices are usually continuous but have occasional (and random) jumps. See Cox and Ross (1976), Merton (1976), and Jarrow and Rudd (1983).

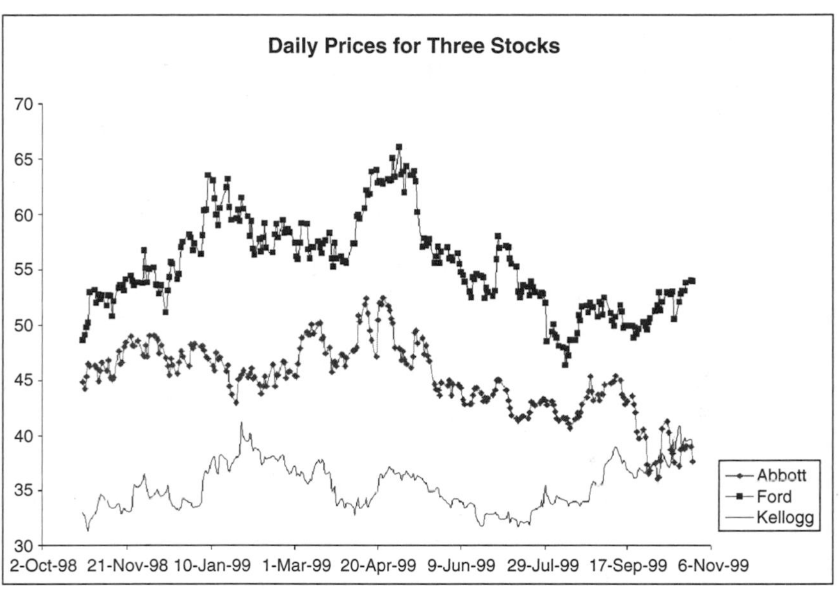

If we simulated stock price paths (something we will do using the lognormal model later on in this chapter), how would we expect them to look? Our five properties imply that we would expect

1. Wiggly lines.
2. Lines that are continuous (solid), with no jumps.
3. Lines that are always positive and never cross zero, no matter how low they get.
4. That at a given point in time, the average over all plausible lines is greater than the initial price of the stock. The farther out we go, the higher this average becomes.
5. That the standard deviation over all plausible lines is greater the farther out we go.

Here's another way of thinking about stock prices. Suppose we take the daily returns on the Standard & Poor's 500 index (we only show the start of the data):

	A	B	C	D
1	**S&P 500 DAILY PRICES 1950-2006**			
2	Date	Price	Return	
3	3-Jan-50	16.66		
4	4-Jan-50	16.85	1.13%	<-- =LN(B4/B3)
5	5-Jan-50	16.93	0.47%	
6	6-Jan-50	16.98	0.29%	
7	9-Jan-50	17.08	0.59%	
8	10-Jan-50	17.03	-0.29%	
9	11-Jan-50	17.09	0.35%	
10	12-Jan-50	16.76	-1.95%	
11	13-Jan-50	16.67	-0.54%	
12	16-Jan-50	16.72	0.30%	
13	17-Jan-50	16.86	0.83%	
14	18-Jan-50	16.85	-0.06%	
15	19-Jan-50	16.87	0.12%	
16	20-Jan-50	16.9	0.18%	
17	23-Jan-50	16.92	0.12%	
18	24-Jan-50	16.86	-0.36%	
19	25-Jan-50	16.74	-0.71%	
20	26-Jan-50	16.73	-0.06%	
21	27-Jan-50	16.82	0.54%	
22	30-Jan-50	17.02	1.18%	
23	31-Jan-50	17.05	0.18%	
24	1-Feb-50	17.05	0.00%	
25	2-Feb-50	17.23	1.05%	
26	3-Feb-50	17.29	0.35%	

If we graph these returns over any given period, we get a mess of dots that is difficult to interpret:

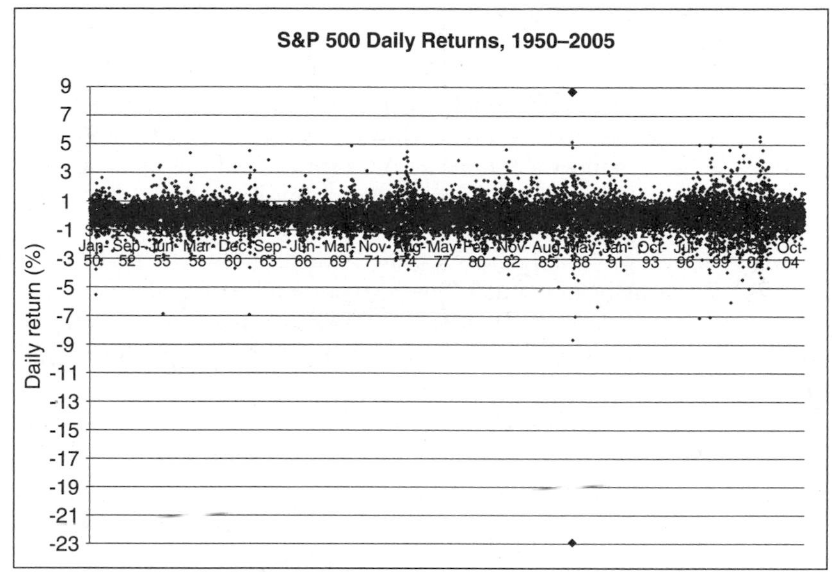

Three extreme returns for the S&P 500 occurred on the day of the 1987 stock market crash (19 October 1987, a decline of 22.9 percent in the S&P) and in the two days following (increases of 5.20 percent and 8.71 percent on 20 and 21 October 1987, respectively). The decline of 19 October and the increase on 21 October are marked on the chart with large diamonds.

This smear of dots on a graph is difficult to interpret. Excel can help us make some sense of the data:

	A	B	C	D	E	F	G	H
1	**S&P 500 DAILY PRICES AND RETURNS, 1950-2005** **Some distributional details**							
2	**Date**	**Price**	**Return**					
3	3-Jan-50	16.66						
4	4-Jan-50	16.85	1.13%	<-- =LN(B4/B3)		Count	14,094	<-- =COUNT(C4:C14097)
5	5-Jan-50	16.93	0.47%					
6	6-Jan-50	16.98	0.29%			Maximum daily return	8.71%	<-- =MAX(C4:C14097)
7	9-Jan-50	17.08	0.59%			Minimum daily return	-22.90%	<-- =MIN(C4:C14097)
8	10-Jan-50	17.03	-0.29%					
9	11-Jan-50	17.09	0.35%			Number of returns between -1% and +1%	11,436	<-- =SUMPRODUCT((C4:C14097>-1%)*(C4:C14097<1%),(C4:C14097>-1%)*(C4:C14097<1%))
10	12-Jan-50	16.76	-1.95%					
11	13-Jan-50	16.67	-0.54%			Daily mean return	0.0309%	<-- =AVERAGE(C4:C14097)
12	16-Jan-50	16.72	0.30%			Daily standard deviation	0.899%	<-- =STDEV(C4:C14097)
13	17-Jan-50	16.86	0.83%					
14	18-Jan-50	16.85	-0.06%			Annual return	7.78%	<-- =G11*252
15	19-Jan-50	16.87	0.12%			Annual standard deviation	14.27%	<-- =G12*SQRT(252)
16	20-Jan-50	16.9	0.18%					

> ### An Excel Note
>
> In cell G9 we used **Sumproduct** to count the number of daily returns between –1 percent and +1 percent. The Boolean formula (C4:C14097>–1%)*(C4:C14097<1%) produces a column of ones for cells in the interval (–1%, +1%) and zeros elsewhere. Using **Sumproduct** to multiply and add the product of two such columns produces the result we want.
>
> Why didn't we use Excel's **CountIf** function (see Chapter 34) for this purpose? **CountIf** can count a "one-directional" sort of the data, but not the data in an interval. Thus **CountIf (C4:C14097,"<1%")** will count the number of data points less than 1%, but there is no way to use **CountIf** to count the data points between –1 percent and +1 percent.

If we use the Excel function **Frequency** (see Chapter 35) to do a frequency distribution of these returns, we see that they look normally distributed:

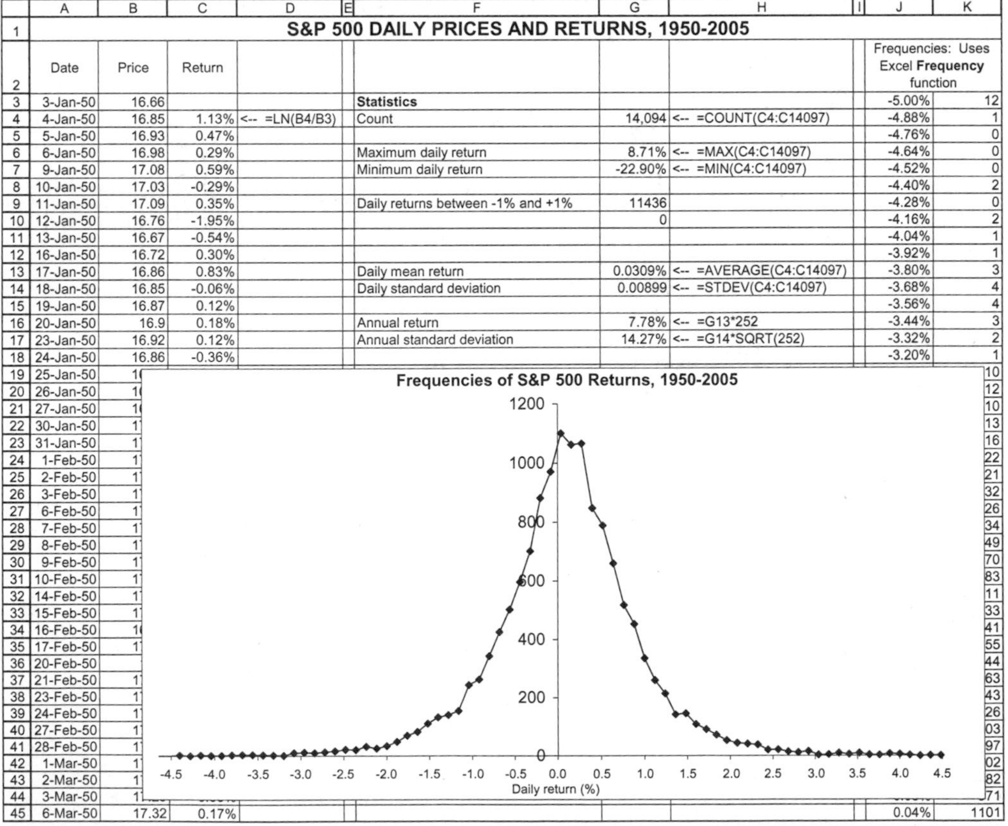

	A	B	C	D	E	F	G	H	I	J	K
1	S&P 500 DAILY PRICES AND RETURNS, 1950-2005										
2	Date	Price	Return							Frequencies: Uses Excel **Frequency** function	
3	3-Jan-50	16.66				**Statistics**				-5.00%	12
4	4-Jan-50	16.85	1.13%	<-- =LN(B4/B3)		Count	14,094	<-- =COUNT(C4:C14097)		-4.88%	1
5	5-Jan-50	16.93	0.47%							-4.76%	0
6	6-Jan-50	16.98	0.29%			Maximum daily return	8.71%	<-- =MAX(C4:C14097)		-4.64%	0
7	9-Jan-50	17.08	0.59%			Minimum daily return	-22.90%	<-- =MIN(C4:C14097)		-4.52%	0
8	10-Jan-50	17.03	-0.29%							-4.40%	2
9	11-Jan-50	17.09	0.35%			Daily returns between -1% and +1%	11436			-4.28%	0
10	12-Jan-50	16.76	-1.95%				0			-4.16%	2
11	13-Jan-50	16.67	-0.54%							-4.04%	1
12	16-Jan-50	16.72	0.30%							-3.92%	1
13	17-Jan-50	16.86	0.83%			Daily mean return	0.0309%	<-- =AVERAGE(C4:C14097)		-3.80%	3
14	18-Jan-50	16.85	-0.06%			Daily standard deviation	0.00899	<-- =STDEV(C4:C14097)		-3.68%	4
15	19-Jan-50	16.87	0.12%							-3.56%	4
16	20-Jan-50	16.9	0.18%			Annual return	7.78%	<-- =G13*252		-3.44%	3
17	23-Jan-50	16.92	0.12%			Annual standard deviation	14.27%	<-- =G14*SQRT(252)		-3.32%	2
18	24-Jan-50	16.86	-0.36%							-3.20%	1
19	25-Jan-50	1									10
20	26-Jan-50	1									12
21	27-Jan-50	1									10
22	30-Jan-50	1									13
23	31-Jan-50	1									16
24	1-Feb-50	1									22
25	2-Feb-50	1									21
26	3-Feb-50	1									32
27	6-Feb-50	1									26
28	7-Feb-50	1									34
29	8-Feb-50	1									49
30	9-Feb-50	1									70
31	10-Feb-50	1									83
32	14-Feb-50	1									11
33	15-Feb-50	1									33
34	16-Feb-50	1									41
35	17-Feb-50	1									55
36	20-Feb-50										44
37	21-Feb-50	1									63
38	23-Feb-50	1									43
39	24-Feb-50	1									26
40	27-Feb-50	1									03
41	28-Feb-50	1									97
42	1-Mar-50	1									02
43	2-Mar-50	1									82
44	3-Mar-50	1									71
45	6-Mar-50	17.32	0.17%							0.04%	1101

18.2.2 Computing Returns and Their Distribution for a Continuous-Return-Generating Process[2]

The return statistics in cells G9:G13 assume that the return-generating process has a normal distribution. Given this assumption, we can compute the return over a period by taking the natural logarithm of the price relatives, defined as $\ln\left(\frac{\text{Price}_t}{\text{Price}_{t-1}}\right)$. Furthermore, if $\{r_1, r_2, \ldots, r_M\}$ is a series of periodic returns, we can compute the mean, variance, and standard deviation of the returns as

$$\text{Periodic mean} = \mu_{\text{Periodic}} = \underbrace{\frac{1}{M}\sum_{t=1}^{M} r_t}_{\substack{\uparrow \\ \text{Use Excel} \\ \textbf{Average} \\ \text{function}}}$$

$$\text{Periodic variance} = \sigma^2_{\text{Periodic}} = \underbrace{\frac{1}{M}\sum_{t=1}^{M} (r_t - \mu_{\text{Periodic}})^2}_{\substack{\uparrow \\ \text{Use Excel} \\ \textbf{Stdev}\text{ function}}}$$

Assuming that there are n periods per year, we can compute the annualized returns by

$$\text{Annualized mean} = n\mu_{\text{Periodic}}$$

$$\text{Annualized variance} = n\sigma^2_{\text{Periodic}}$$

$$\text{Annualized standard deviation} = \sigma\sqrt{n}$$

We can do another interesting exercise on these data. In the following graph we plot the mean and standard deviation of each year's returns:

2. This subsection anticipates section 18.7.

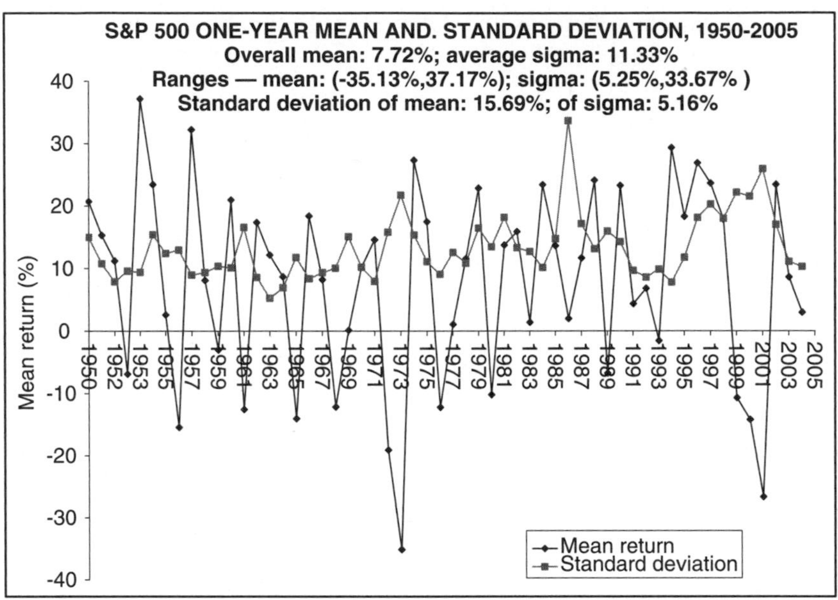

Over the time period from 1950 to 2005, both the means and standard deviations vary widely. However, the variation of the standard deviation is much less than that of the means. Almost 60 percent of the standard deviations are between 10 and 20 percent:

Number of sigmas between		
Lower bound	Upper bound	
10%	20%	58.93%
8%	22%	85.71%
6%	10%	28.57%
20%	34%	10.71%
13%	26%	41.07%

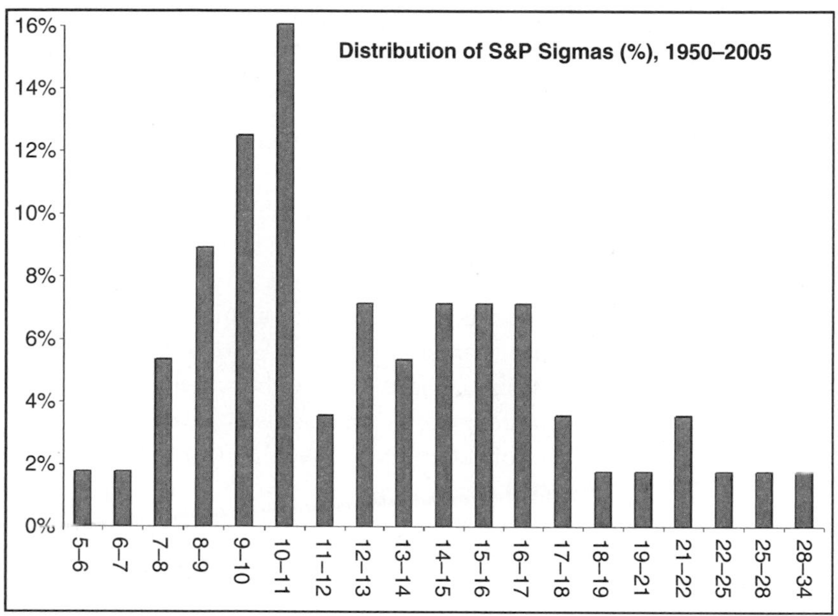

Compare this graph to the distribution of the means, which is more spread out:

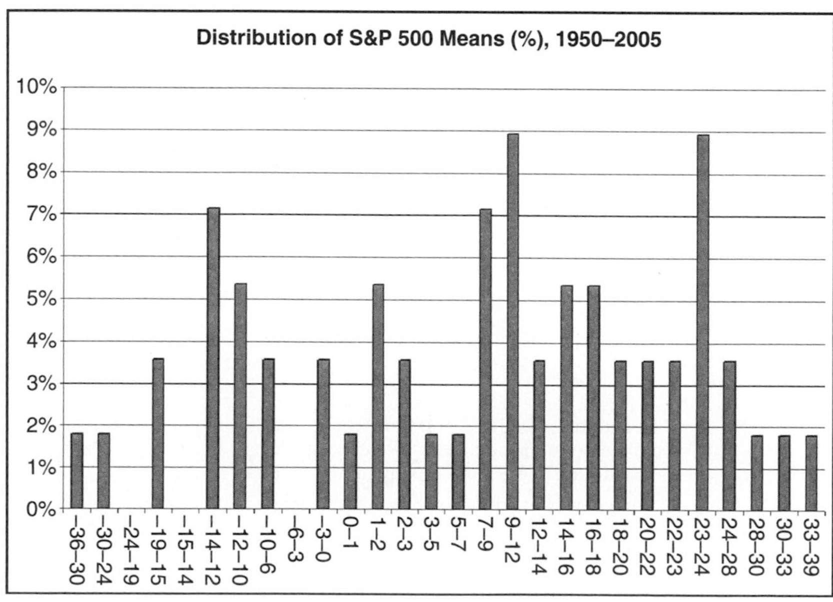

As we will see in the next section, the assumption that stock returns are normally distributed underlies the lognormal distribution.[3]

18.3 Lognormal Price Distributions and Geometric Diffusions

In this section we get a bit more formal and describe what we mean by a lognormal price distribution. We then relate the lognormal price process to a geometric diffusion.

Suppose we denote by S_t the price at time t of a share of stock. The lognormal distribution assumes that *the natural logarithm of 1 plus the return* from holding a share of stock between time t and time $t + \Delta t$ is normally distributed with mean μ and standard deviation σ. Denote the (uncertain) rate of return over an interval Δt by $\tilde{r}_{\Delta t}$. Then we can write $S_{t+\Delta t} = S_t \exp[\tilde{r}_{\Delta t}\Delta t]$. In the lognormal distribution, we assume that the rate of return $\tilde{r}_{\Delta t}$ over a short period Δt is normally distributed with mean $\mu\Delta t$ and variance $\sigma^2\Delta t$.

Another way of writing this relation is to write the stock price $S_{t+\Delta t}$ at time $t + \Delta t$ in the following way:

$$\frac{S_{t+\Delta t}}{S_t} = \exp[\mu\Delta t + \sigma Z\sqrt{\Delta t}]$$

where Z is a standard normal variable (mean = 0, standard deviation = 1).[4]

To see what this assumption means, suppose first that $\sigma = 0$. In this case we have

$$S_{t+\Delta t} = S_t \exp[\mu\Delta t]$$

which simply says that the stock price grows at an exponential rate with certainty. In this case the stock is like a riskless bond that bears interest rate μ, continuously compounded.

3. The counting of returns and standard deviations in specific intervals uses the same trick employing **Sumproduct** that was discussed in the Excel box on page 488. Details can be found in the files accompanying this book.

4. If you know about diffusion processes, then the lognormal price process is a *geometric diffusion*: $\frac{dS}{S} = \left(\mu + \frac{\sigma^2}{2}\right)dt + \sigma dB$, where dB is a Wiener process ("white noise"): $dB = Z\sqrt{dt}$, where Z is a standard random variable.

Now suppose that $\sigma > 0$. In this case, the lognormal assumption says that, although the tendency is for the stock price to increase, there is an uncertain element (normally distributed) that must be taken into account. The best way to think about this process is in terms of a simulation.

Suppose, for example, that we're trying to simulate a lognormal price process in which $\mu = 15$ percent, $\sigma = 30$ percent, and $\Delta t = 0.004$. Suppose the price at time 0 is $S_0 = 35$. To simulate the possible stock prices at time Δt we first have to pick (at random) a number Z from a standard normal distribution.[5] Suppose that this number is 0.1165. Then the stock price $S_{\Delta t}$ at time Δt will be

$$S_{\Delta t} = S_0 * \exp[\mu\Delta t + \sigma Z\sqrt{\Delta t}] = 35 * \exp[0.15 * 0.004 + 0.3 * 0.1165 * \sqrt{0.004}]$$
$$= 35.0985$$

Of course we could have drawn a different random number. If, for example, our random number Z had been –0.9102, then we would have

$$S_{\Delta t} = S_0 * \exp[\mu\Delta t + \sigma Z\sqrt{\Delta t}]$$
$$= 35 * \exp[0.15 * 0.004 - 0.3 * (-0.9102) * \sqrt{0.004}] = 34.4214$$

This process is illustrated in the following spreadsheet picture, where we generated a list of 250 numbers picked from a standard-normal distribution (the technical nomenclature is "standard normal deviates").[6] Each is an equally likely potential candidate to be Z. Having picked Z for a particular time interval Δt, the price $S_{t+\Delta t}$ follows.

---

5. See Chapter 30 for some techniques (using both Excel and VBA) for generating random numbers.

6. The number of business days in a year is approximately 250. Thus when we define $\Delta t = 1/250 = 0.004$, we are simulating the stock price on a daily basis over the course of a year.

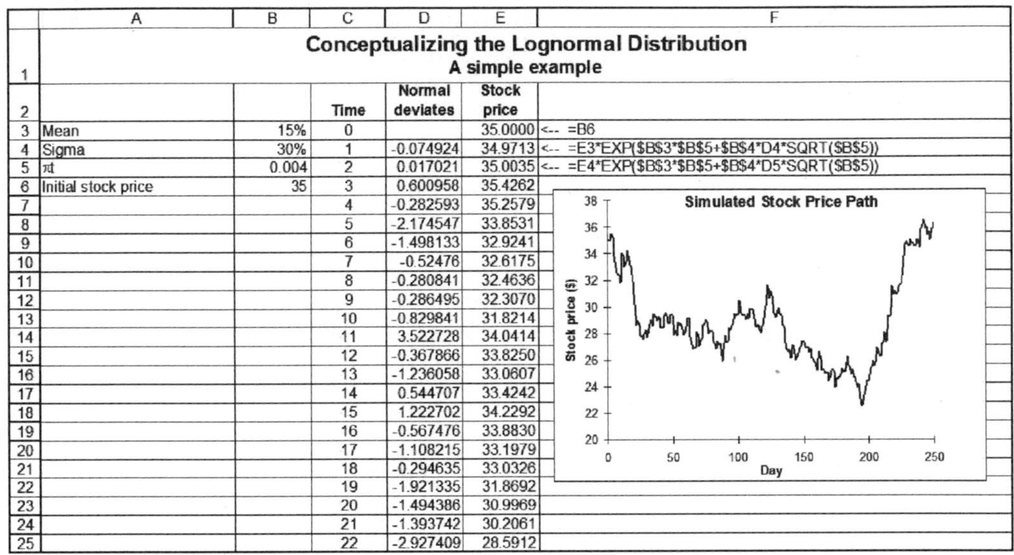

	A	B	C	D	E	F
1	**Conceptualizing the Lognormal Distribution** **A simple example**					
2			Time	Normal deviates	Stock price	
3	Mean	15%	0		35.0000	<-- =B6
4	Sigma	30%	1	-0.074924	34.9713	<-- =E3*EXP($B$3*$B$5+$B$4*D4*SQRT($B$5))
5	Δt	0.004	2	0.017021	35.0035	<-- =E4*EXP($B$3*$B$5+$B$4*D5*SQRT($B$5))
6	Initial stock price	35	3	0.600958	35.4262	
7			4	-0.282593	35.2579	
8			5	-2.174547	33.8531	
9			6	-1.498133	32.9241	
10			7	-0.52476	32.6175	
11			8	-0.280841	32.4636	
12			9	-0.286495	32.3070	
13			10	-0.829841	31.8214	
14			11	3.522728	34.0414	
15			12	-0.367866	33.8250	
16			13	-1.236058	33.0607	
17			14	0.544707	33.4242	
18			15	1.222702	34.2292	
19			16	-0.567476	33.8830	
20			17	-1.108215	33.1979	
21			18	-0.294635	33.0326	
22			19	-1.921335	31.8692	
23			20	-1.494386	30.9969	
24			21	-1.393742	30.2061	
25			22	-2.927409	28.5912	

The spreadsheet uses **Tools|Data Analysis|Random Number Generation** to generate a list of 250 standard-normal deviates. The command looks like this:

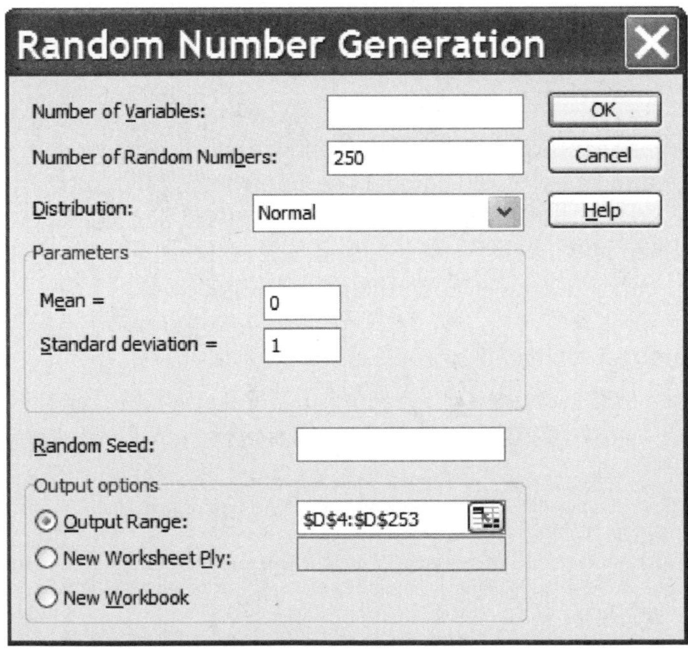

To summarize: In order to simulate *the growth of the stock price*, when the price follows a lognormal price distribution,

- Multiply Δt (the elapsed time interval) by μ (the average rate of growth). This gives the certain portion of the return.
- Take a draw Z from a random variable that is standard normal, and multiply this draw by $\sigma\sqrt{\Delta t}$. This step gives the uncertain portion of the return. (The square root implies that the variance of the stock's return is linear in time. See the next section.)
- Add the two results and exponentiate. The daily return is $\exp[\mu\Delta t + \sigma Z\sqrt{\Delta t}]$. If the price on date t is S_t, then the price on date t + 1 is $S_{t+1} = S_t \exp[\mu\Delta t + \sigma Z\sqrt{\Delta t}]$.

18.4 What Does the Lognormal Distribution Look Like?

We know that the normal distribution produces a bell curve. What about the lognormal distribution? In the following experiment we simulate 1,000 random end-of-year stock prices. The experiment is a continuation of the experiment performed in the previous section; since we are simulating end-of-year prices, we set $\Delta t = 1$. To perform this experiment,

- We produce a list of 1,000 normal deviates.
- We use each normal deviate to produce an end-of-period stock price

$$S_1 = S_0 * \exp[\mu\Delta t + \sigma Z\sqrt{\Delta t}] = S_0 * \exp[\mu + \sigma Z], \quad \text{since } \Delta t = 1$$

- We put the stock prices into bins and produce a histogram.

Here's what the spreadsheet for this experiment looks like:

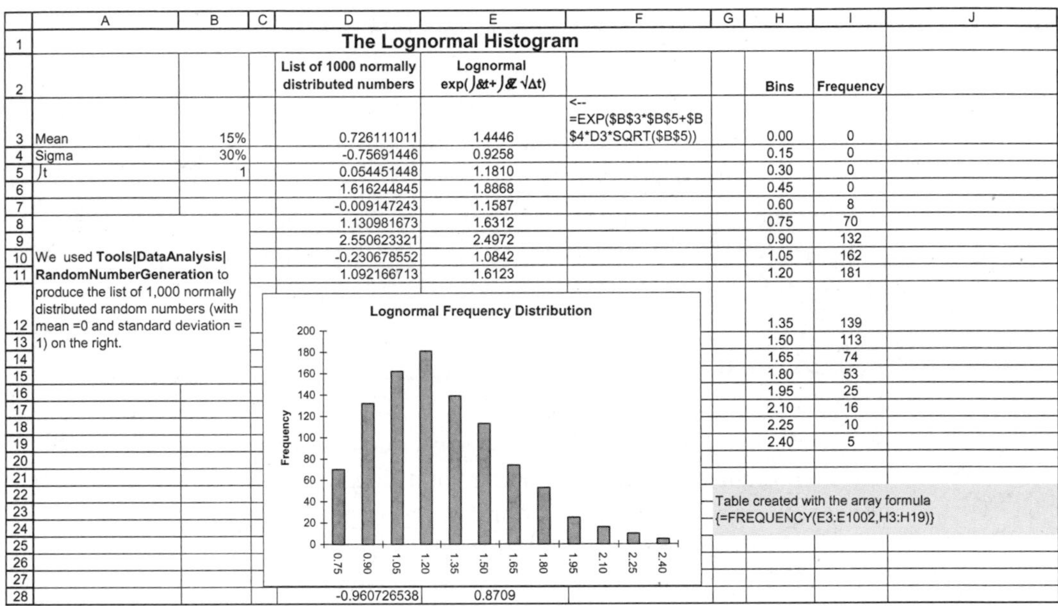

	A	B	C	D	E	F	G	H	I	J
1	**The Lognormal Histogram**									
2				**List of 1000 normally distributed numbers**	**Lognormal exp()&t+)& √Δt)**			**Bins**	**Frequency**	
3	Mean	15%		0.726111011	1.4446	<-- =EXP($B$3*$B$5+$B$4*D3*SQRT($B$5))		0.00	0	
4	Sigma	30%		-0.75691446	0.9258			0.15	0	
5	)t	1		0.054451448	1.1810			0.30	0	
6				1.616244845	1.8868			0.45	0	
7				-0.009147243	1.1587			0.60	8	
8				1.130981673	1.6312			0.75	70	
9				2.550623321	2.4972			0.90	132	
10	We used **Tools|DataAnalysis|**			-0.230678552	1.0842			1.05	162	
11	**RandomNumberGeneration** to			1.092166713	1.6123			1.20	181	
12	produce the list of 1,000 normally distributed random numbers (with mean =0 and standard deviation =							1.35	139	
13	1) on the right.							1.50	113	
14								1.65	74	
15								1.80	53	
16								1.95	25	
17								2.10	16	
18								2.25	10	
19								2.40	5	
20										
21										
22								Table created with the array formula		
23								{=FREQUENCY(E3:E1002,H3:H19)}		
24										
25										
26										
27										
28				-0.960726538	0.8709					

Having produced 1,000 lognormal price relatives $\exp[\mu\Delta t + \sigma Z\sqrt{\Delta t}]$, we can use the array function **Frequency( )** (this function is discussed in Chapter 35) to put them into bins (cells H3:I19).

When we do this simulation for a large number of points, the resulting density curve becomes smooth. Here, for example, is the frequency distribution of 100,000 trials with μ = 10 percent, σ = 20 percent, and $\Delta t = 1$:

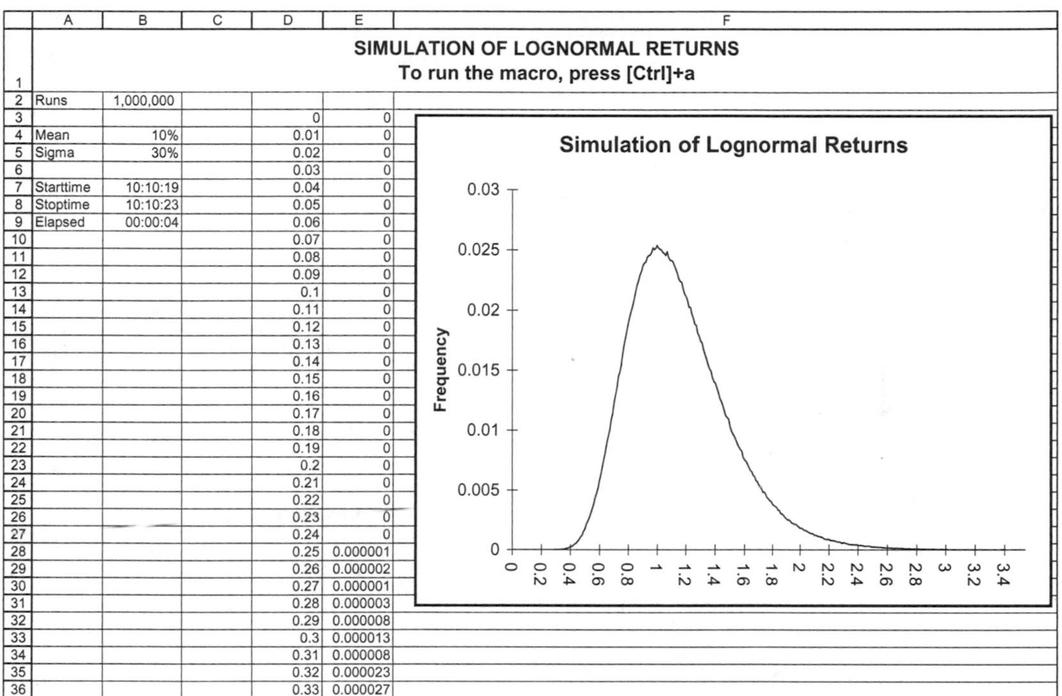

	A	B	C	D	E	F
1	SIMULATION OF LOGNORMAL RETURNS To run the macro, press [Ctrl]+a					
2	Runs	1,000,000				
3				0	0	
4	Mean	10%		0.01	0	
5	Sigma	30%		0.02	0	
6				0.03	0	
7	Starttime	10:10:19		0.04	0	
8	Stoptime	10:10:23		0.05	0	
9	Elapsed	00:00:04		0.06	0	
10				0.07	0	
11				0.08	0	
12				0.09	0	
13				0.1	0	
14				0.11	0	
15				0.12	0	
16				0.13	0	
17				0.14	0	
18				0.15	0	
19				0.16	0	
20				0.17	0	
21				0.18	0	
22				0.19	0	
23				0.2	0	
24				0.21	0	
25				0.22	0	
26				0.23	0	
27				0.24	0	
28				0.25	0.000001	
29				0.26	0.000002	
30				0.27	0.000001	
31				0.28	0.000003	
32				0.29	0.000008	
33				0.3	0.000013	
34				0.31	0.000008	
35				0.32	0.000023	
36				0.33	0.000027	

The VBA program that produced this output follows:

```
'Simulating the lognormal distribution
'Note that I take delta = 1!
Sub RandomNumberSimulation()
Application.ScreenUpdating = False
Range("starttime") = Time
N = Range("runs").Value
mean = Range("mean")
sigma = Range("sigma")
ReDim Frequency(0 To 1000) As Integer

For Index = 1 To N
start:
   Static rand1, rand2, S1, S2, X1, X2
   rand1 = 2 * Rnd - 1
```

```
    rand2 = 2 * Rnd - 1
    S1 = rand1 ^ 2 + rand2 ^ 2
    If S1 > 1 Then GoTo start
    S2 = Sqr(-2 * Log(S1) / S1)
    X1 = rand1 * S2
    X2 = rand2 * S2

    Return1 = Exp(mean + sigma * X1)
    Return2 = Exp(mean + sigma * X2)

    Frequency(Int(Return1 / 0.01)) = Frequency _
       (Int(Return1 / 0.01)) + 1
    Frequency(Int(Return2 / 0.01)) = Frequency _
       (Int(Return2 / 0.01)) + 1
Next Index

For Index = 0 To 400
    Range("output").Cells(Index + 1, 1) =
       Frequency(Index) / N
Next Index

Range("stoptime") = Time
Range("elapsed") = Range("stoptime") - _
    Range("starttime")
Range("elapsed").NumberFormat = "hh:mm:ss"

End Sub
```

The routine that produces randomly distributed standard normal deviates is contained in the eight lines following the word `start`; this routine is further explained in Chapter 30.

18.5 Simulating Lognormal Price Paths

We now return to the problem of simulating lognormal price paths that we started to discuss in section 18.3. We shall try to understand, through a simulation written in VBA, the meaning of the following sentences: “The price of a stock today is $25. The price of the stock is distributed lognormally, with an annual log mean return of 10 percent and an annual log standard deviation of 20 percent." We want to know how the price of the stock might behave on a daily basis throughout the next year. There are an infinite number of price paths for the stock. What we will do is simulate (randomly) one of these paths. If we want another price path, we can merely rerun the simulation.

There are about 250 business days in a year. Therefore, the daily price movement of the stock between day t and day $t+1$ can be simulation by setting $\Delta t = 1/250 = 0.004$, $\mu = 10$ percent, and $\sigma = 20$ percent. If the initial price of the stock $S_0 = \$25$, then the price after one day will be

$$S_{\Delta t} = S_0 * \exp[\mu\Delta t + \sigma Z\sqrt{\Delta t}] = 25 * \exp[0.15 * 0.004 + 0.20 * Z\sqrt{0.004}]$$

and the price after two days will be

$$S_{0.008} = S_{0.004} * \exp[0.15 * 0.004 + 0.20 * Z\sqrt{0.004}]$$

and so on. At each step the random normal deviate Z is the uncertain factor in the price return. Because of this uncertainty, all paths produced will be different.

Here is a VBA program **PricePathSimulation** that reproduces a typical price path:

```
Sub PricePathSimulation()
Range("starttime") = Time

N = Range("runs").Value
mean = Range("mean")
sigma = Range("sigma")
delta_t = 1 / (2 * N)

ReDim price(0 To 2 * N) As Double

price(0) = Range("initial_price")

For Index = 1 To N
start:
   Static rand1, rand2, S1, S2, X1, X2
   rand1 = 2 * Rnd - 1
```

```
    rand2 = 2 * Rnd - 1
    S1 = rand1 ^ 2 + rand2 ^ 2
    If S1 > 1 Then GoTo start
    S2 = Sqr(-2 * Log(S1) / S1)
    X1 = rand1 * S2
    X2 = rand2 * S2

    price(2 * Index - 1) = price(2 * Index - 2) _
      * Exp(mean * delta_t + _
        sigma * Sqr(delta_t) * X1)
    price(2 * Index) = price(2 * Index - 1) * _
      Exp(mean * delta_t + _
        sigma * Sqr(delta_t) * X2)
Next Index

For Index = 0 To 2 * N
    Range("output").Cells(Index + 1, 1) = Index
    Range("output").Cells(Index + 1, 2) =
price(Index)
Next Index

Range("stoptime") = Time
Range("elapsed") = Range("stoptime") - _
    Range("starttime")
Range("elapsed").NumberFormat = "hh:mm:ss"

End Sub
```

The output from this program looks like this on the spreadsheet:

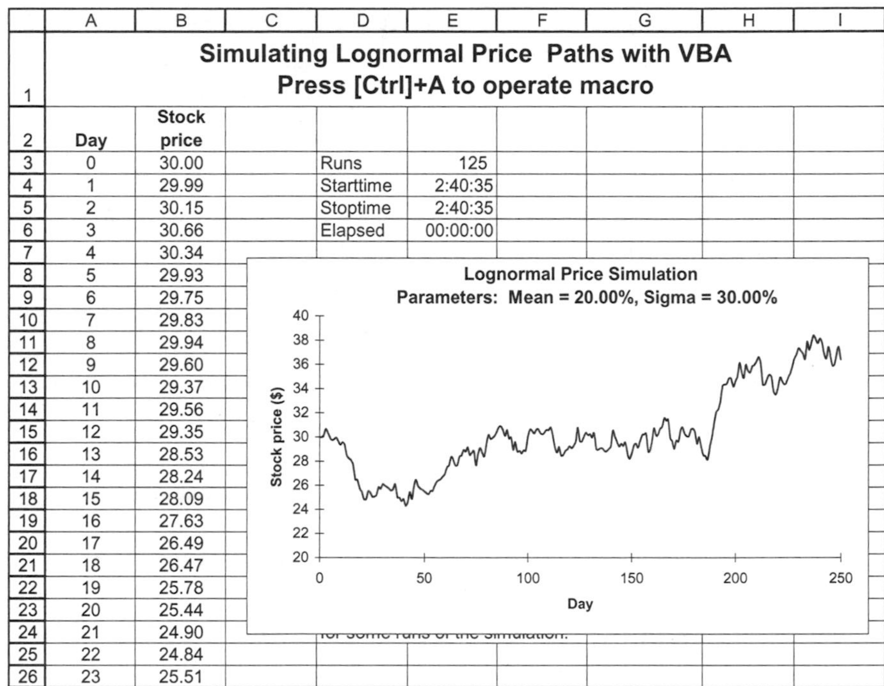

Simulating Lognormal Price Paths with VBA
Press [Ctrl]+A to operate macro

Day	Stock price			
0	30.00		Runs	125
1	29.99		Starttime	2:40:35
2	30.15		Stoptime	2:40:35
3	30.66		Elapsed	00:00:00
4	30.34			
5	29.93			
6	29.75			
7	29.83			
8	29.94			
9	29.60			
10	29.37			
11	29.56			
12	29.35			
13	28.53			
14	28.24			
15	28.09			
16	27.63			
17	26.49			
18	26.47			
19	25.78			
20	25.44			
21	24.90			
22	24.84			
23	25.51			

We can modify the program slightly to produce many lognormal price paths (see exercise 1). The output from this program looks like this:

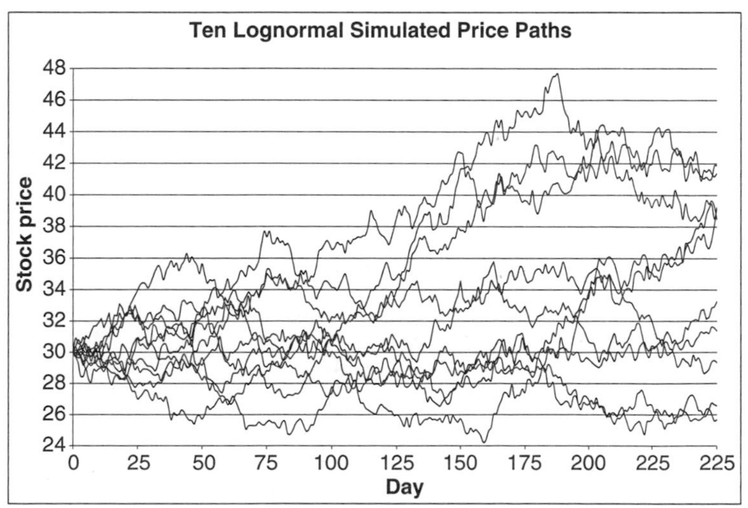

As you can see, on average the price of the asset increases over time, as does the variance of the returns. These results accord with properties 4 and 5 of stock prices in section 18.2.1—we expect both the return on an asset and the uncertainty associated with this return to increase over time.

18.6 Technical Analysis

Security analysts are divided into "fundamentalists" and "technicians." This division has nothing to do with their outlook on the Creator of the Universe, but rather with the way they regard stock prices. Fundamentalists believe that the value of a stock is ultimately determined by underlying economic variables. Thus, when a fundamentalist analyzes a company, she will look at its earnings, its debt/equity ratio, its markets, and so forth.

Technicians, in contrast, think that stock prices are determined by patterns. They believe that, by examining the pattern of past prices of a stock, they can predict (or at least make sensible statements about) the stock's future prices. A technician may tell you that "we're currently in a head-and-shoulders pattern," by which he means that a graph of the stock price looks like the following figure:

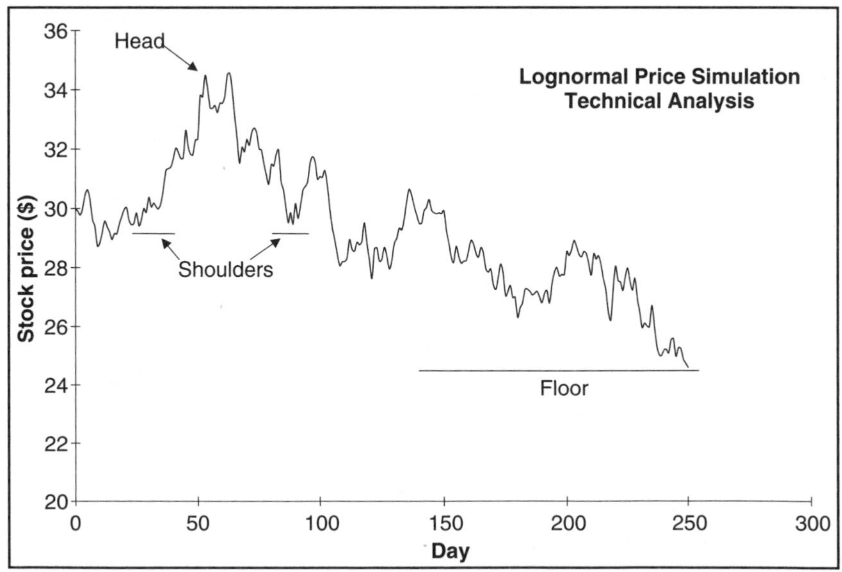

Other terms used by technicians include "floors" (there's one in the graph), "rebound levels," and "pennants."[7]

The orthodox (some would say ivory-tower) view of technical analysis is that it is worthless. A basic theory of finance says that markets efficiently incorporate the information known about the securities traded on them. There are several versions of this theory; one of them, the *weak efficient markets hypothesis*, says that at the very least all information about past prices is incorporated into the current price. The weak efficient markets hypothesis means that technical analysis cannot make predictions about futures prices, since technical analysis is based solely on past price information.[8]

Nevertheless, a lot of people believe in technical analysis. (This belief in itself may give technical analysis some validity.) The simulations we are running in this chapter will allow us to generate a myriad of patterns which, when analyzed, will yield "good" predictions of future prices. For example, in the preceding figure it appears that $24 is a floor for the stock price, since it never goes any lower. A perspicacious analyst can detect a clear head-and-shoulders pattern between days 40 and 100. There appears to be a ceiling of $35. Thus a technician might predict that the stock price will stay below $35 unless it rises above that level. (If you are going to be a technician, you have to learn to say these things with a straight face.)

18.7 Calculating the Parameters of the Lognormal Distribution from Stock Prices

The main purpose of this section is to show you how stock price data can be used to compute the μ and σ needed in the lognormal simulations (and—in the next chapter—the σ needed as an input to the Black-Scholes formula). Before doing so, note that the mean and variance of the logarithm of the stock return over an interval Δt are

$$E\left[\ln\left(\frac{S_{t+\Delta t}}{S_t}\right)\right] = E[\mu\Delta t + \sigma Z\sqrt{\Delta t}] = \mu\Delta t$$

7. A good compendium of technical analysis nomenclature can be found at http://www.sstfutures.com/futures_chart_patterns.htm.

8. For a discussion of this point, see Chapter 13 of Brealey, Myers, Allen (2005); for a more advanced treatment, see Chapters 10–11 of Copeland, Weston, Shastri (2003).

$$\mathrm{Var}\left[\ln\left(\frac{S_{t+\Delta t}}{S_t}\right)\right] = \mathrm{Var}[\mu\Delta t + \sigma Z\sqrt{\Delta t}] = \sigma^2\Delta t$$

These expressions indicate that both the expected log return and the variance of the log return are linear in time.

Now suppose we want to estimate the lognormal μ and σ from data on historical prices. It follows that

$$\mu = \frac{\mathrm{Mean}\left[\ln\left(S_{t+\Delta t}/S_t\right)\right]}{\Delta t}, \quad \sigma^2 = \frac{\mathrm{Var}\left[\ln\left(S_{t+\Delta t}/S_t\right)\right]}{\Delta t}$$

To make things specific, the following spreadsheet gives monthly prices for a particular stock. From these prices we calculate the log returns and the *annualized* mean and standard deviation. Note that we have used the function **Stdevp** to calculate σ; it is assumed that the data represent the actual distribution.

	A	B	C	D
1	**Calculating Lognormal Mean and Sigma from Stock Price Data for Halliburton Corporation**			
2	**Month**	**Price**	**Monthly return**	
3	31-Aug-05	30.74		
4	1-Sep-05	33.97	9.99%	<-- =LN(B4/B3)
5	3-Oct-05	29.3	-14.79%	<-- =LN(B5/B4)
6	1-Nov-05	31.62	7.62%	<-- =LN(B6/B5)
7	1-Dec-05	30.78	-2.69%	
8	3-Jan-06	39.55	25.07%	
9	1-Feb-06	33.86	-15.53%	
10	1-Mar-06	36.35	7.10%	
11	3-Apr-06	38.91	6.81%	
12	1-May-06	37.21	-4.47%	
13	1-Jun-06	37.02	-0.51%	
14	3-Jul-06	33.29	-10.62%	
15	1-Aug-06	32.62	-2.03%	
16	1-Sep-06	28.45	-13.68%	
17	2-Oct-06	28.78	1.15%	
18				
19	Monthly average		-0.47%	<-- =AVERAGE(C4:C17)
20	Monthly standard deviation		10.93%	<-- =STDEVP(C4:C17)
21				
22	Annual average		-5.65%	<-- =C19*12
23	Annual standard deviation		37.87%	<-- =C20*SQRT(12)

Note that the annual average log return is 12 times the monthly average log return, whereas the annual standard deviation is $\sqrt{12}$ the monthly standard deviation. In general, if the return data are generated for n periods per year, then

$$\text{Mean}_{\text{Annual return}} = n \cdot \text{Mean}_{\text{Periodic return}}, \quad \sigma_{\text{Annual return}} = \sqrt{n} \cdot \sigma_{\text{Periodic return}}$$

Of course, this is not the only way to calculate the parameters of the lognormal distribution. We should mention at least two other methods:

- We can use some other procedure to extrapolate the mean and standard deviation of *future* returns from the past history of returns. One example of this would be to use a moving average.
- We can use the Black-Scholes formula to find the *implied volatility*: the σ of the stock's log returns that fits the price of an option on the stock. This method is illustrated in section 19.4.

18.8 Summary

The lognormal distribution is one of the foundations of the Black-Scholes formula for option pricing discussed in the next chapter. In this chapter we have explored the meaning of lognormality for stock prices. We have shown how lognormality—the assumption that the returns on an asset are normally distributed—can be justified visually for the S&P 500 portfolio. We have also shown how to simulate price paths that are lognormally distributed. Finally, we have shown how to compute the mean and the standard deviation of a lognormal distribution from the historic returns of an asset.

Exercises

1. Use **NormSInv(Rand())** to produce a simulation of monthly stock prices, as in the following illustration.[9]

9. The use of **NormSInv** for this purpose is discussed in Chapter 29, section 4.

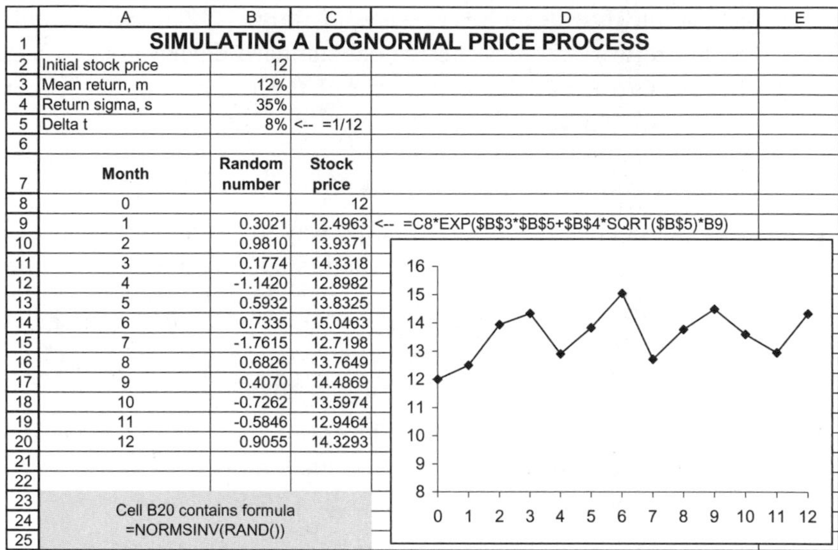

	A	B	C	D
1	SIMULATING A LOGNORMAL PRICE PROCESS			
2	Initial stock price	12		
3	Mean return, m	12%		
4	Return sigma, s	35%		
5	Delta t	8%	<-- =1/12	
6				
7	Month	Random number	Stock price	
8	0		12	
9	1	0.3021	12.4963	<-- =C8*EXP($B$3*$B$5+$B$4*SQRT($B$5)*B9)
10	2	0.9810	13.9371	
11	3	0.1774	14.3318	
12	4	-1.1420	12.8982	
13	5	0.5932	13.8325	
14	6	0.7335	15.0463	
15	7	-1.7615	12.7198	
16	8	0.6826	13.7649	
17	9	0.4070	14.4869	
18	10	-0.7262	13.5974	
19	11	-0.5846	12.9464	
20	12	0.9055	14.3293	

Cell B20 contains formula =NORMSINV(RAND())

2. Expand the previous exercise and use **NormSInv(Rand())** to produce a simulation of daily stock prices.

3. Re-create the following spreadsheet. Play with the spreadsheet (each press of **F9** will recompute the numbers) to convince yourself that higher σ means a more volatile price path for the stock.

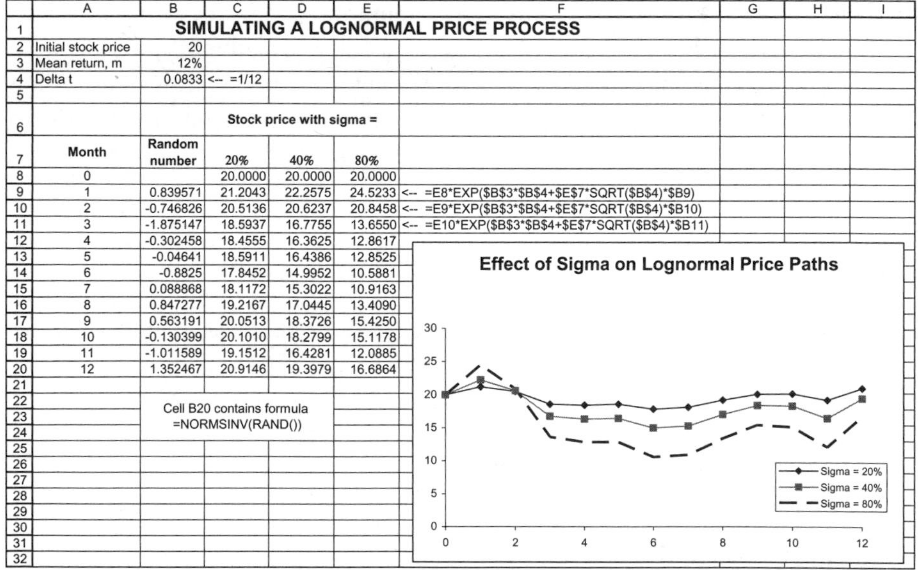

	A	B	C	D	E	F
1	SIMULATING A LOGNORMAL PRICE PROCESS					
2	Initial stock price	20				
3	Mean return, m	12%				
4	Delta t	0.0833	<-- =1/12			
5						
6			Stock price with sigma =			
7	Month	Random number	20%	40%	80%	
8	0		20.0000	20.0000	20.0000	
9	1	0.839571	21.2043	22.2575	24.5233	<-- =E8*EXP($B$3*$B$4+$E$7*SQRT($B$4)*$B9)
10	2	-0.746826	20.5136	20.6237	20.8458	<-- =E9*EXP($B$3*$B$4+$E$7*SQRT($B$4)*$B10)
11	3	-1.875147	18.5937	16.7755	13.6550	<-- =E10*EXP($B$3*$B$4+$E$7*SQRT($B$4)*$B11)
12	4	-0.302458	18.4555	16.3625	12.8617	
13	5	-0.04641	18.5911	16.4386	12.8525	
14	6	-0.8825	17.8452	14.9952	10.5881	
15	7	0.088868	18.1172	15.3022	10.9163	
16	8	0.847277	19.2167	17.0445	13.4090	
17	9	0.563191	20.0513	18.3726	15.4250	
18	10	-0.130399	20.1010	18.2799	15.1178	
19	11	-1.011589	19.1512	16.4281	12.0885	
20	12	1.352467	20.9146	19.3979	16.6864	

Cell B20 contains formula =NORMSINV(RAND())

4. Write a VBA program that reproduces the lognormal frequency distribution for an arbitrary number of runs. That is, this program should do the following:

   - Produce N normal random deviates.
   - Produce a lognormal price relative $\exp[\mu\Delta t + \sigma Z\sqrt{\Delta t}]$ for each deviate.
   - Classify each price relative into a set of bins running from 0, 0.1, . . . , 3.
   - Put the frequencies on the spreadsheet and produce a frequency graph such as the one in section 18.5.

5. Run a few of the lognormal price path simulations. Examine the price pattern for trends. Find one or more of the following technical patterns:

   Support area
   Resistance area
   Uptrend/downtrend
   Head and shoulders
   Inverted head and shoulders
   Double top/bottom
   Rounded top/bottom
   Triangle (ascending, symmetrical, descending)
   Flag

6. The Excel notebook **fm3_problems18.xls** contains daily price data for the S&P 500 index and for Abbott Laboratories for the three months April–June 2007. Use this data to compute the annual average, variance, and standard deviation of the logarithmic returns for the S&P and for Abbott. What is the correlation between the returns of the S&P 500 and Abbott?

19 The Black-Scholes Model

19.1 Overview

In a pathbreaking paper published in 1973, Fisher Black and Myron Scholes proved a formula for pricing European call and put options on non-dividend-paying stocks. Their model is probably the most famous model of modern finance. The Black-Scholes formula is relatively easy to use, and it is often an adequate approximation to the price of more complicated options.

In this chapter we make no pretense at a full-blown development of the model; this requires a knowledge of stochastic processes and a not-inconsiderable mathematical investment. Instead, we shall describe the mechanics of the model and show how to implement it in Excel. We also illustrate several uses of the Black-Scholes formula in the valuation of structured assets.

19.2 The Black-Scholes Model

Consider a stock whose price is lognormally distributed.[1] The Black-Scholes model uses the following formula to price European calls on a stock:

$$C = SN(d_1) - Xe^{-rT}N(d_2)$$

where

$$d_1 = \frac{\ln(S/X) + (r + \sigma^2/2)T}{\sigma\sqrt{T}}$$

$$d_2 = d_1 - \sigma\sqrt{T}$$

Here C denotes the price of a call, S is the price of the underlying stock, X is the exercise price of the call, T is the call's time to exercise, r is the interest rate, and σ is the standard deviation of the logarithm of the stock's return. $N(\ )$ denotes a value of the standard normal distribution. It is assumed that the stock will pay no dividends before date T.

By the put-call parity theorem (see Chapter 16), a put with the same exercise date T and exercise price X written on the same stock will have

1. The lognormal distribution is discussed in Chapter 18.

price $P = C - S + Xe^{-rT}$. Substituting for C in this equation and doing some algebra gives the Black-Scholes European-put-pricing formula:

$$P = Xe^{-rT}N(-d_2) - SN(-d_1)$$

We note that in Chapter 17 we hinted at one form of the proof of the Black-Scholes formula. There it was shown numerically that the Black-Scholes formula coincides with the binomial option-pricing model formula when (1) the length of a typical period approaches 0, (2) the "up" and "down" moves in the binomial model converge to a lognormal price process, and (3) the term structure of interest rates is flat.

19.2.1 Implementing the Black-Scholes Formulas in a Spreadsheet

The Black-Scholes formulas for call and put pricing are easily implemented in a spreadsheet. The following example shows how to calculate the price of a call option written on a stock whose current price $S = 50$, when the exercise price $X = 45$, the annualized interest rate $r = 4$ percent, and $\sigma = 30$ percent. The option has $T = 0.75$ years to exercise. All three of the parameters T, r, and σ are assumed to be in annual terms.[2]

	A	B	C
1	**Black-Scholes Option-Pricing Formula**		
2	S	50	Current stock price
3	X	45	Exercise price
4	r	4.00%	Risk-free rate of interest
5	T	0.75	Time to maturity of option (in years)
6	Sigma	30%	Stock volatility, σ
7			
8	d_1	0.6509	<-- (LN(S/X)+(r+0.5*sigma^2)*T)/(sigma*SQRT(T))
9	d_2	0.3911	<-- d_1-sigma*SQRT(T)
10			
11	N(d_1)	0.7424	<-- Uses formula NormSDist(d_1)
12	N(d_2)	0.6521	<-- Uses formula NormSDist(d_2)
13			
14	Call price	8.64	<-- S*N(d_1)-X*exp(-r*T)*N(d_2)
15	Put price	2.31	<-- call price - S + X*Exp(-r*T): by Put-Call parity
16		2.31	<-- X*exp(-r*T)*N(-d_2) - S*N(-d_1): direct formula

2. Section 18.7 discusses how to calculate the annualized σ of the lognormal process given nonannual data.

The spreadsheet calculates the put price twice: In cell B15 the put price is computed by using put-call parity, and in cell B16 it is calculated by using the direct Black-Scholes formula.

We can use this spreadsheet to do the usual sensitivity analysis. For example, the following **Data|Table** (see Chapter 31) gives—as the stock price S varies—the Black-Scholes value of the call compared to its intrinsic value [i.e., $\max(S - X, 0)$].

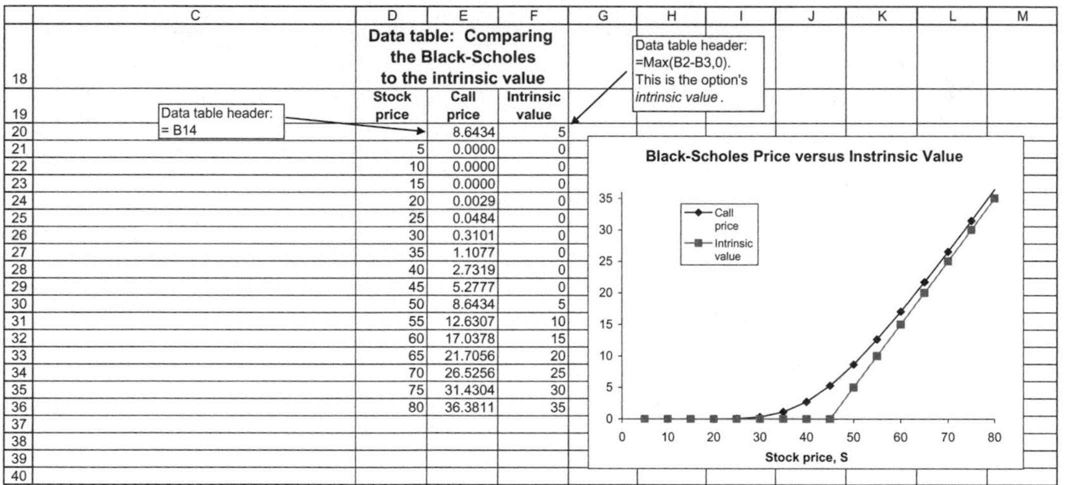

	D	E	F
18	Data table: Comparing the Black-Scholes to the intrinsic value		
19	Stock price	Call price	Intrinsic value
20		8.6434	5
21	5	0.0000	0
22	10	0.0000	0
23	15	0.0000	0
24	20	0.0029	0
25	25	0.0484	0
26	30	0.3101	0
27	35	1.1077	0
28	40	2.7319	0
29	45	5.2777	0
30	50	8.6434	5
31	55	12.6307	10
32	60	17.0378	15
33	65	21.7056	20
34	70	26.5256	25
35	75	31.4304	30
36	80	36.3811	35

19.3 Using VBA to Define a Black-Scholes Pricing Function

Although the spreadsheet implementation of the Black-Scholes formulas illustrated in the previous section is sufficient for some purposes, we are sometimes interested in having a closed-form function that we can use directly in Excel. We can do so with Visual Basic for Applications. In the following program we define functions **dOne**, **dTwo**, and **BSCall**:

```
Function dOne(Stock, Exercise, Time, Interest, sigma)
    dOne = (Log(Stock / Exercise) + Interest * _
      Time) / (sigma * Sqr(Time)) _
      + 0.5 * sigma * Sqr(Time)
End Function
```

```
Function dTwo(Stock, Exercise, Time, Interest, sigma)
     dTwo = dOne(Stock, Exercise, Time, Interest, _
       sigma) - sigma * Sqr(Time)
End Function

Function BSCall(Stock, Exercise, Time, Interest, sigma)
     BSCall = Stock * Application.NormSDist(dOne(Stock, _
     Exercise, Time, Interest, sigma)) - _
     Exercise * Exp(-Time * Interest) * _
      Application.NormSDist(dTwo(Stock, Exercise, _
      Time, Interest, sigma))
End Function
```

Note the use of the Excel function **NormSDist**, which gives the standard normal distribution; in order to use this function in VBA, we must write **Application.NormSDist**.

19.3.1 Pricing Puts

By the put-call parity theorem we know that a put is priced by the formula $P = C - S + Xe^{-rT}$. We can implement this in another VBA function, **BSPut**:

```
Function BSPut(Stock, Exercise, Time, Interest, sigma)
     BSPut = BSCall(Stock, Exercise, Time, Interest, _
     sigma) + Exercise * Exp(-Interest * Time) - Stock
End Function
```

19.3.2 Using These Functions in an Excel Spreadsheet

Here's an example of these functions used in Excel. The graph was created by a data table. (In presentations we usually hide the first row of such a table; here we have shown it.)

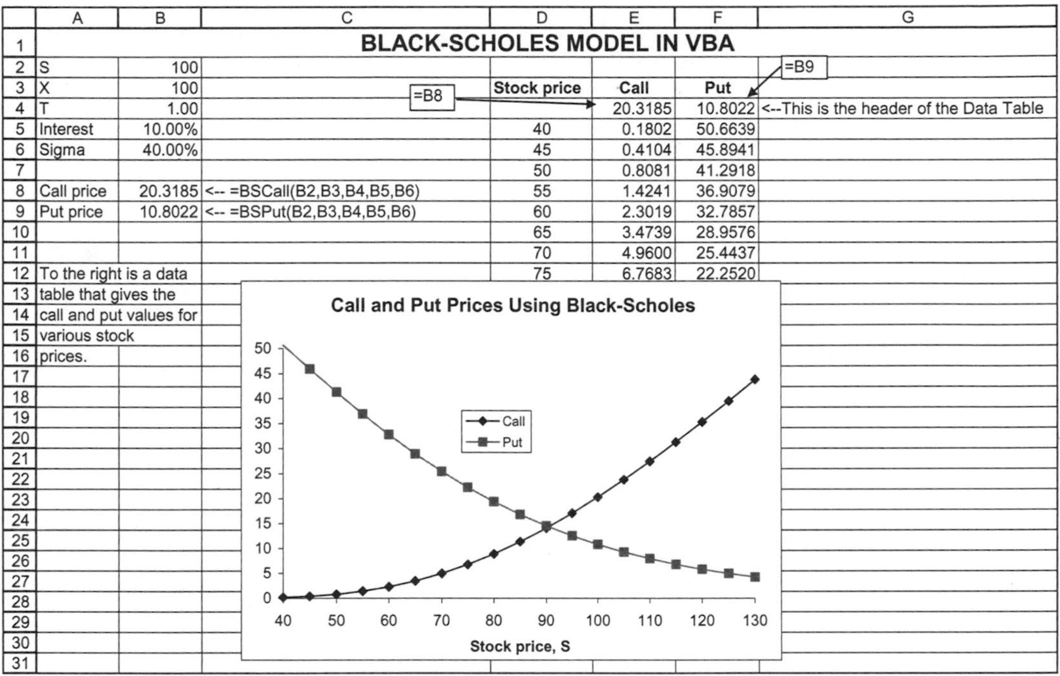

	A	B	C	D	E	F	G
1	BLACK-SCHOLES MODEL IN VBA						
2	S	100					=B9
3	X	100	=B8	Stock price	Call	Put	
4	T	1.00			20.3185	10.8022	<--This is the header of the Data Table
5	Interest	10.00%		40	0.1802	50.6639	
6	Sigma	40.00%		45	0.4104	45.8941	
7				50	0.8081	41.2918	
8	Call price	20.3185	<-- =BSCall(B2,B3,B4,B5,B6)	55	1.4241	36.9079	
9	Put price	10.8022	<-- =BSPut(B2,B3,B4,B5,B6)	60	2.3019	32.7857	
10				65	3.4739	28.9576	
11				70	4.9600	25.4437	
12	To the right is a data			75	6.7683	22.2520	
13	table that gives the						
14	call and put values for						
15	various stock						
16	prices.						

19.4 Calculating the Implied Volatility

The Black-Scholes formula depends on five parameters: The stock price S, the option exercise price X, the option's time to maturity T, the interest rate r, and the standard deviation of the returns of the stock underlying the option σ (sigma). Four of these five parameters are straightforward, but the fifth parameter, σ, is problematic. There are two common ways of computing σ:

- σ can be computed based on the *historical returns* of the stock.
- σ can be computed based on the *implied volatility* of the stock.

In the two subsections that follow, we illustrate both methods of computing σ.

19.4.1 The Sigma of Historical Returns

We examine the option prices on the Nasdaq index QQQQ on 28 July 2006. A complete listing of these prices (from Yahoo) is given in Figure 19.1.

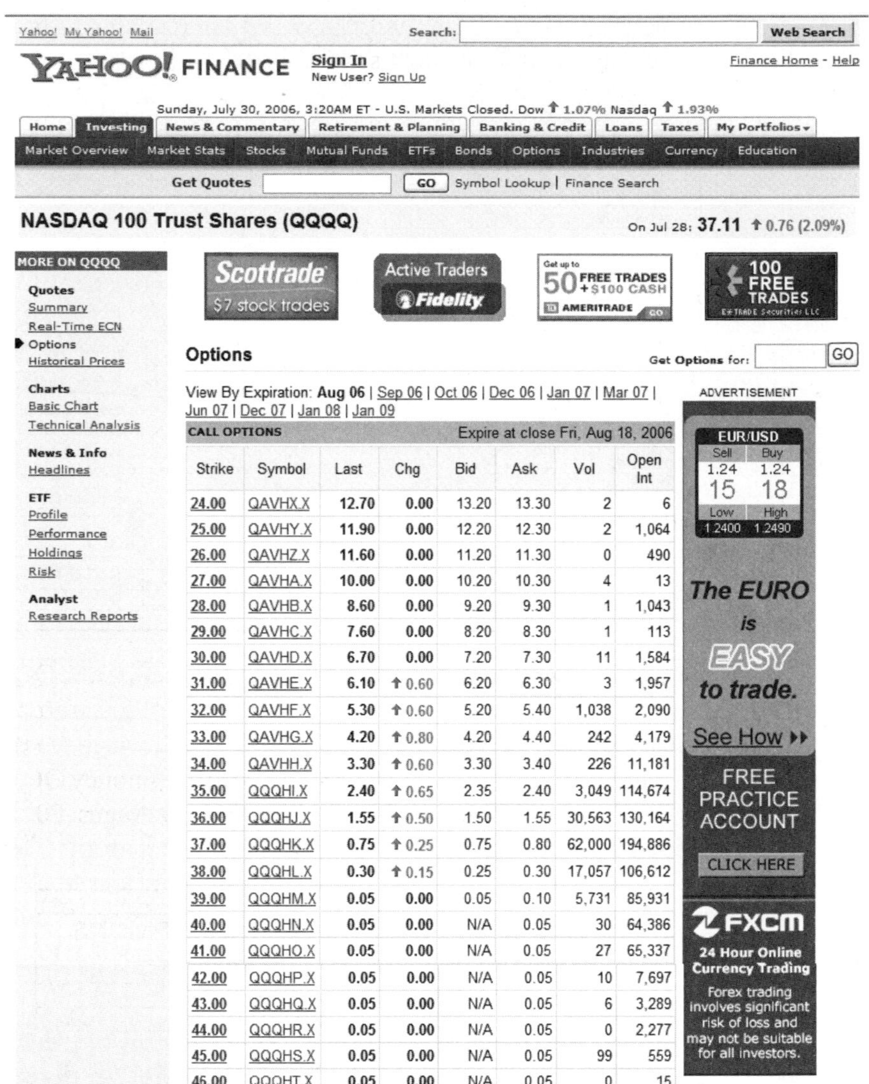

Yahoo! My Yahoo! Mail Search: Web Search

YAHOO! FINANCE Sign In New User? Sign Up Finance Home - Help

Sunday, July 30, 2006, 3:20AM ET - U.S. Markets Closed. Dow ↑ 1.07% Nasdaq ↑ 1.93%

Home | Investing | News & Commentary | Retirement & Planning | Banking & Credit | Loans | Taxes | My Portfolios

Market Overview | Market Stats | Stocks | Mutual Funds | ETFs | Bonds | Options | Industries | Currency | Education

Get Quotes GO Symbol Lookup | Finance Search

NASDAQ 100 Trust Shares (QQQQ) On Jul 28: **37.11** ↑ 0.76 (2.09%)

MORE ON QQQQ
Quotes: Summary, Real-Time ECN, Options, Historical Prices
Charts: Basic Chart, Technical Analysis
News & Info: Headlines
ETF: Profile, Performance, Holdings, Risk
Analyst: Research Reports

Options Get Options for: GO

View By Expiration: **Aug 06** | Sep 06 | Oct 06 | Dec 06 | Jan 07 | Mar 07 | Jun 07 | Dec 07 | Jan 08 | Jan 09

CALL OPTIONS — Expire at close Fri, Aug 18, 2006

Strike	Symbol	Last	Chg	Bid	Ask	Vol	Open Int
24.00	QAVHX.X	12.70	0.00	13.20	13.30	2	6
25.00	QAVHY.X	11.90	0.00	12.20	12.30	2	1,064
26.00	QAVHZ.X	11.60	0.00	11.20	11.30	0	490
27.00	QAVHA.X	10.00	0.00	10.20	10.30	4	13
28.00	QAVHB.X	8.60	0.00	9.20	9.30	1	1,043
29.00	QAVHC.X	7.60	0.00	8.20	8.30	1	113
30.00	QAVHD.X	6.70	0.00	7.20	7.30	11	1,584
31.00	QAVHE.X	6.10	↑ 0.60	6.20	6.30	3	1,957
32.00	QAVHF.X	5.30	↑ 0.60	5.20	5.40	1,038	2,090
33.00	QAVHG.X	4.20	↑ 0.80	4.20	4.40	242	4,179
34.00	QAVHH.X	3.30	↑ 0.60	3.30	3.40	226	11,181
35.00	QQQHI.X	2.40	↑ 0.65	2.35	2.40	3,049	114,674
36.00	QQQHJ.X	1.55	↑ 0.50	1.50	1.55	30,563	130,164
37.00	QQQHK.X	0.75	↑ 0.25	0.75	0.80	62,000	194,886
38.00	QQQHL.X	0.30	↑ 0.15	0.25	0.30	17,057	106,612
39.00	QQQHM.X	0.05	0.00	0.05	0.10	5,731	85,931
40.00	QQQHN.X	0.05	0.00	N/A	0.05	30	64,386
41.00	QQQHO.X	0.05	0.00	N/A	0.05	27	65,337
42.00	QQQHP.X	0.05	0.00	N/A	0.05	10	7,697
43.00	QQQHQ.X	0.05	0.00	N/A	0.05	6	3,289
44.00	QQQHR.X	0.05	0.00	N/A	0.05	0	2,277
45.00	QQQHS.X	0.05	0.00	N/A	0.05	99	559
46.00	QQQHT.X	0.05	0.00	N/A	0.05	0	15

Figure 19.1
QQQQ index call prices, 28 July 2006. The highlighted prices are for in-the-money options.

The historical prices of the QQQQ and the resulting historical volatility are computed in the next spreadsheet:

	A	B	C	D	E	F	G	H
1	**QQQQ HISTORICAL PRICES, DAILY DATA and resulting statistics**							
2	**Date**	**Closing price**	**Return**					
3	30-May-06	38.61						
4	31-May-06	38.79	0.47%	<-- =LN(B4/B3)		**Return statistics**		
5	1-Jun-06	39.71	2.34%	<-- =LN(B5/B4)		Average daily return	-0.09%	<-- =AVERAGE(C4:C45)
6	2-Jun-06	39.61	-0.25%	<-- =LN(B6/B5)		Standard deviation of daily return	1.31%	<-- =STDEVP(C4:C45)
7	5-Jun-06	38.75	-2.20%	<-- =LN(B7/B6)				
8	6-Jun-06	38.72	-0.08%			Annualized mean return	-23.59%	<-- =250*G5
9	7-Jun-06	38.43	-0.75%			Annualized sigma	20.66%	<-- =G6*SQRT(250)
10	8-Jun-06	38.37	-0.16%					
11	9-Jun-06	38.12	-0.65%					
12	12-Jun-06	37.37	-1.99%					
13	13-Jun-06	37.22	-0.40%					
14	14-Jun-06	37.6	1.02%					
38	19-Jul-06	36.62	1.29%					
39	20-Jul-06	36.08	-1.49%					
40	21-Jul-06	35.7	-1.06%					
41	24-Jul-06	36.41	1.97%					
42	25-Jul-06	36.62	0.58%					
43	26-Jul-06	36.59	-0.08%					
44	27-Jul-06	36.35	-0.66%					
45	28-Jul-06	37.11	2.07%					

Based on two months of daily data, the annualized QQQQ sigma is 20.66 percent. Note that this result is based on the assumption of 250 trading days per year; many traders use 365 days, which would of course give a higher σ. Based on this volatility, the at-the-money QQQQ August 2006 call would be priced at 0.85 and the QQQQ August 2006 put would be priced at 0.63 (cell B12):

	A	B	C
1	**PRICING THE AUGUST 2006 QQQQ OPTIONS Using the Historical Volatility σ**		
2	Current date	28-Jul-06	
3	Option expiration date	18-Aug-06	
4			
5	S	37.11	
6	X	37	
7	T	0.06	<-- =(B3-B2)/365
8	Interest	5.00%	
9	Sigma	20.66%	
10			
11	Call price	0.8447	<-- =BSCall(B5,B6,B7,B8,B9)
12	Put price	0.6284	<-- =BSPut(B5,B6,B7,B8,B9)
13			
14	Actual prices		
15	Call	0.75	
16	Put	0.55	

Compared to the actual prices, this picture seems to indicate that the historical volatility somewhat overstates the volatility at which the options are actually priced. Note, however, that it is not clear which data are the correct historical data. If, for example, we were to use two years of monthly data to determine the historical volatility for the QQQQ, we would arrive at a much lower number:

	A	B	C	D	E	F	G
1	QQQQ HISTORICAL PRICES, MONTHLY DATA and resulting statistics						
2	Date	Closing price	Return				
3	30-Jul-04	34.40					
4	2-Aug-04	33.54	-2.53%		**Return statistics**		
5	1-Sep-04	34.64	3.23%		Average monthly return	0.18%	<-- =AVERAGE(C4:C45)
6	1-Oct-04	36.38	4.90%		Standard deviation of monthly return	3.31%	<-- =STDEVP(C4:C45)
7	1-Nov-04	38.57	5.85%				
8	1-Dec-04	39.73	2.96%		Annualized mean return	2.17%	<-- =12*F5
9	3-Jan-05	37.22	-6.53%		Annualized sigma	11.48%	<-- =F6*SQRT(12)
10	1-Feb-05	37.05	-0.46%				
11	1-Mar-05	36.40	-1.77%				
12	1-Apr-05	34.82	-4.44%				
13	2-May-05	37.90	8.48%				
14	1-Jun-05	36.64	-3.38%				
38	19-Jul-06	36.62	1.29%				
39	20-Jul-06	36.08	-1.49%				
40	21-Jul-06	35.70	-1.06%				
41	24-Jul-06	36.41	1.97%				
42	25-Jul-06	36.62	0.58%				
43	26-Jul-06	36.59	-0.08%				
44	27-Jul-06	36.35	-0.66%				
45	28-Jul-06	37.11	2.07%				

19.4.2 The Implied Volatility

The implied volatility ignores history; instead it determines the option σ based on actual option prices. Whereas the historical volatility is a backward-looking volatility, the implied volatility is a forward-looking estimate.[3]

To estimate the implied volatility for the August 2006 QQQQ calls, we solve the Black-Scholes formula for the sigma that gives the current market price:

3. The nomenclature "forward-looking" versus "backward-looking" makes it sound as if the implied volatility is always better than the historical. This is, of course, not the intention.

	A	B	C
1	**IMPLIED VOLATILITY FOR THE AUGUST 2006 QQQQ OPTIONS**		
2	Current date	28-Jul-06	
3	Option expiration date	18-Aug-06	
4			
5	S	37.11	
6	X	37	
7	T	0.06	<-- =(B3-B2)/365
8	Interest	5.00%	
9	Implied volatility, σ	17.96%	
10			
11	Call price	0.7500	<-- =BSCall(B5,B6,B7,B8,B9)
12	Put price	0.5337	<-- =BSPut(B5,B6,B7,B8,B9)
13			
14	Actual prices		
15	Call	0.75	
16	Put	0.55	

The implied volatility is 17.96 percent. This exactly gives the market call price of $0.75 (cell B15) and almost gives the market put price of $0.55 (cell B16). We solved the problem by using **Solver**:

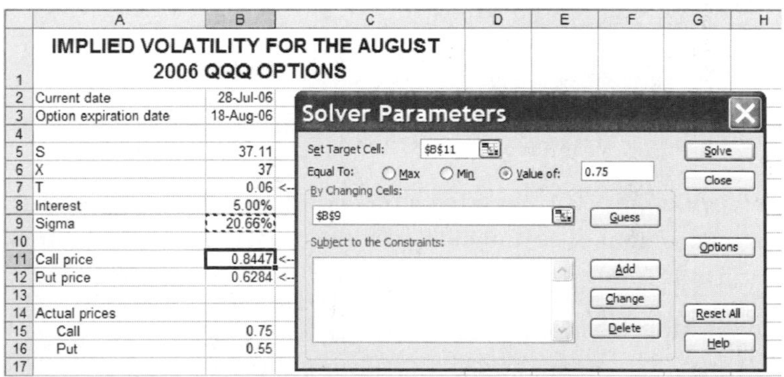

19.5 A VBA Function to Find the Implied Variance

We want to design a Visual Basic for Applications function that computes the implied volatility. To do so, we first note that the option price is a monotonic function of the sigma. Here's a **Data|Table** from our basic Black-Scholes spreadsheet:

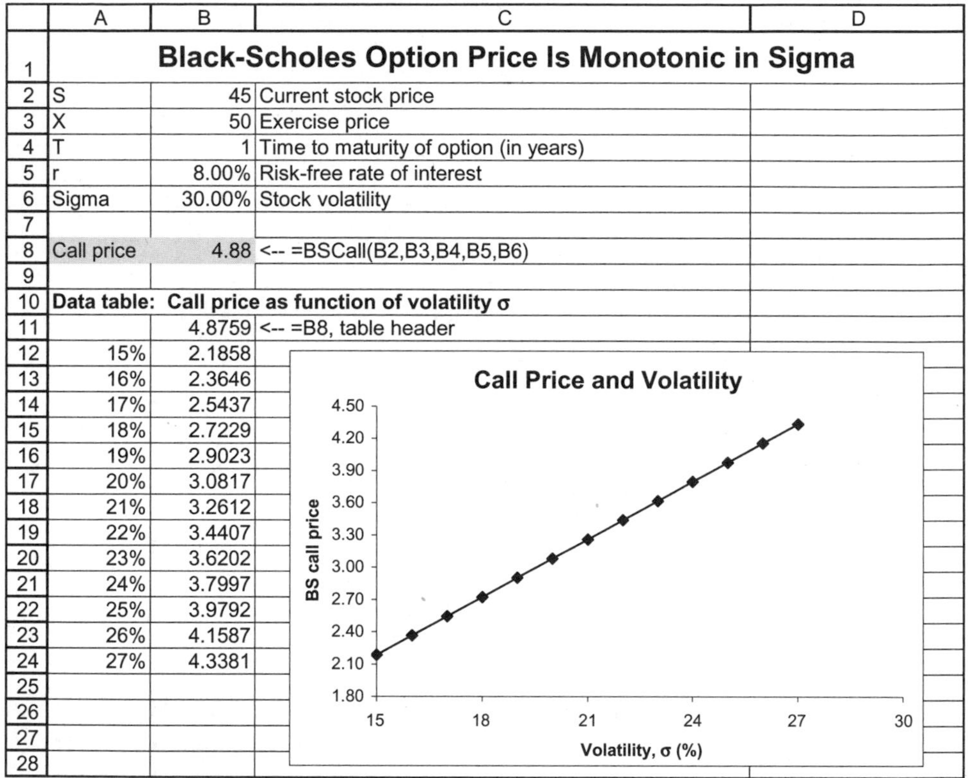

	A	B	C	D
1	**Black-Scholes Option Price Is Monotonic in Sigma**			
2	S	45	Current stock price	
3	X	50	Exercise price	
4	T	1	Time to maturity of option (in years)	
5	r	8.00%	Risk-free rate of interest	
6	Sigma	30.00%	Stock volatility	
7				
8	Call price	4.88	<-- =BSCall(B2,B3,B4,B5,B6)	
9				
10	**Data table: Call price as function of volatility σ**			
11		4.8759	<-- =B8, table header	
12	15%	2.1858		
13	16%	2.3646		
14	17%	2.5437		
15	18%	2.7229		
16	19%	2.9023		
17	20%	3.0817		
18	21%	3.2612		
19	22%	3.4407		
20	23%	3.6202		
21	24%	3.7997		
22	25%	3.9792		
23	26%	4.1587		
24	27%	4.3381		
25				
26				
27				
28				

We use VBA to define a function **CallVolatility** that finds the σ for a call option. The function is defined as **CallVolatility(Stock, Exercise, Time, Interest, Target)**, where the definitions are as follows:

Stock is the stock price S.

Exercise is the option's exercise price X.

Time is the time to the option's maturity T.

Interest is the interest rate r.

Target is the call price C.

The function finds σ for which the Black-Scholes formula is equal to C.

```
Function CallVolatility(Stock, Exercise, Time,
Interest, Target)
     High = 1
     Low = 0
     Do While (High - Low) > 0.0001
     If BSCall(Stock, Exercise, Time,
        Interest, (High + Low) / 2) > Target
           Then
                  High = (High + Low) / 2
                  Else Low = (High + Low) / 2
     End If
     Loop
     CallVolatility = (High + Low) / 2
End Function
```

The technique used by the function is very similar to the technique used in trial and error: We start with two estimates for the possible σ: a **High** estimate of 100 percent and a **Low** estimate of 0 percent. We now do the following:

• Plug the average of the **High** and the **Low** into the Black-Scholes formula. This gives us **CallOption(Stock, Exercise, Time, Interest, (High + Low) / 2)**. (Note that the function **CallVolatility** assumes that the function **CallOption** is available to the spreadsheet.)

• If **CallOption(Stock, Exercise, Time, Interest, (High + Low) / 2) > Target**, then the current σ estimate of **(High + Low) / 2** is too high, and we replace **High** by **(High + Low) / 2**.

• If **CallOption(Stock, Exercise, Time, Interest, (High + Low) / 2) < Target**, then the current σ estimate of **(High + Low) / 2** is too low and we replace **Low** by **(High + Low) / 2**.

We repeat this procedure until the difference **High-Low** is less than 0.0001 (or some other arbitrary constant).

Here's an example of this function, including a data table and a graph that show the implied volatility as a function of the call price:

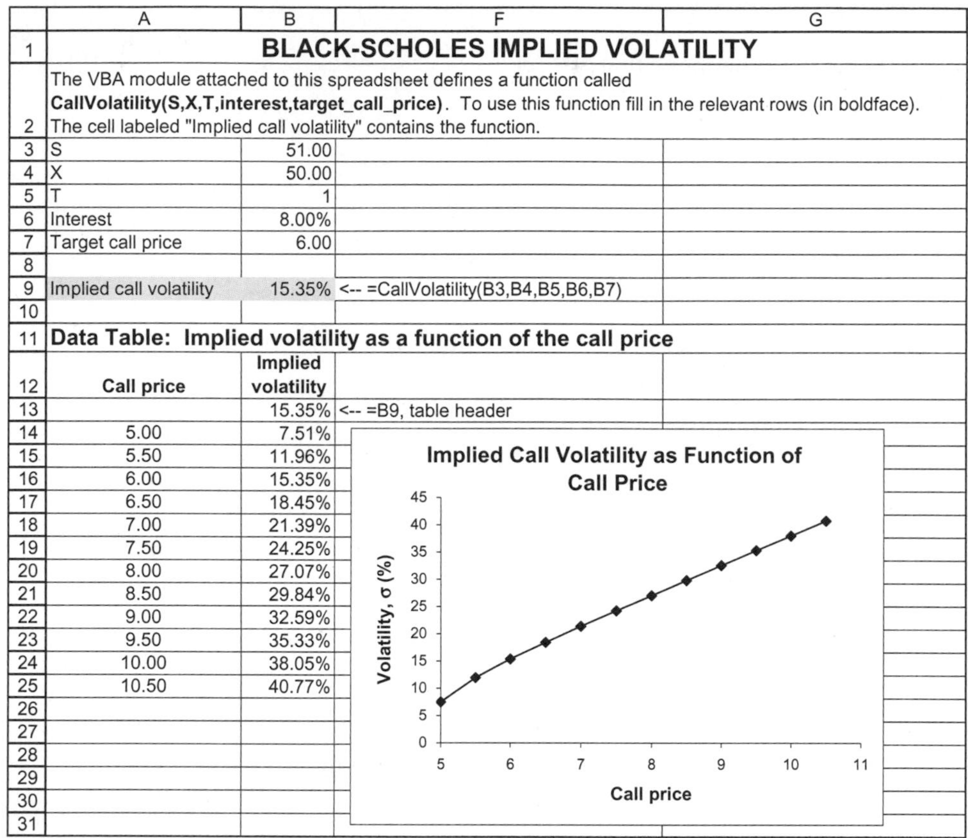

	A	B	F	G
1	**BLACK-SCHOLES IMPLIED VOLATILITY**			
2	The VBA module attached to this spreadsheet defines a function called **CallVolatility(S,X,T,interest,target_call_price)**. To use this function fill in the relevant rows (in boldface). The cell labeled "Implied call volatility" contains the function.			
3	S	51.00		
4	X	50.00		
5	T	1		
6	Interest	8.00%		
7	Target call price	6.00		
8				
9	Implied call volatility	15.35%	<-- =CallVolatility(B3,B4,B5,B6,B7)	
10				
11	**Data Table: Implied volatility as a function of the call price**			
12	**Call price**	**Implied volatility**		
13		15.35%	<-- =B9, table header	
14	5.00	7.51%		
15	5.50	11.96%		
16	6.00	15.35%		
17	6.50	18.45%		
18	7.00	21.39%		
19	7.50	24.25%		
20	8.00	27.07%		
21	8.50	29.84%		
22	9.00	32.59%		
23	9.50	35.33%		
24	10.00	38.05%		
25	10.50	40.77%		
26				
27				
28				
29				
30				
31				

19.6 Dividend Adjustments to the Black-Scholes

The Black-Scholes formula assumes that the option's underlying security pays no dividends prior to the exercise date T. In certain cases it is easy to make an adjustment to the model for dividends. This section surveys two such adjustments: We first look at option pricing when future dividends are known with certainty, and we then examine option pricing when the underlying security pays out a continuous dividend. The principle underlying both cases is the same: The options are priced on an adjusted underlying value that nets out the present value of dividends paid between the option purchase date and the option exercise date.

19.6.1 A Known Dividend to Be Paid before the Option Expiration

It often happens that a stock's future dividend is known at the time the option is traded. This is most commonly the case when a dividend has already been announced, but it can also happen because many stocks pay quite regular and relatively inflexible dividends. In this case the option should be priced not on the current stock price S but on the stock price minus the present value of the dividend or dividends anticipated before the option expiration date T:

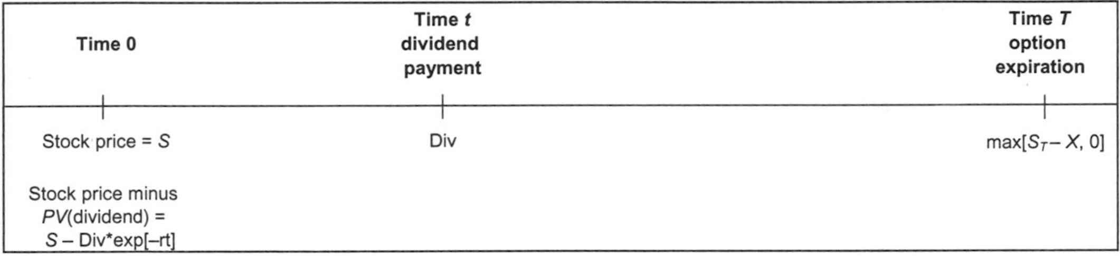

Here's an example: Coca-Cola (stock symbol KO) pays quarterly dividends in March, June, September, and November of each year. Dividends (Figure 19.2) seem quite stable; on 28 July 2006, the last two dividends were \$0.31 per share.

Computing the implied volatility for the January 2007 calls and puts on Coca-Cola shows that taking account of anticipated dividends makes a significant difference in the pricing. We can also deduce from the proximity of the prices that take dividends into account (cells B19:B20) versus the distance between the prices that do not take the dividends into account (cells B22:B23) that the former are correct.

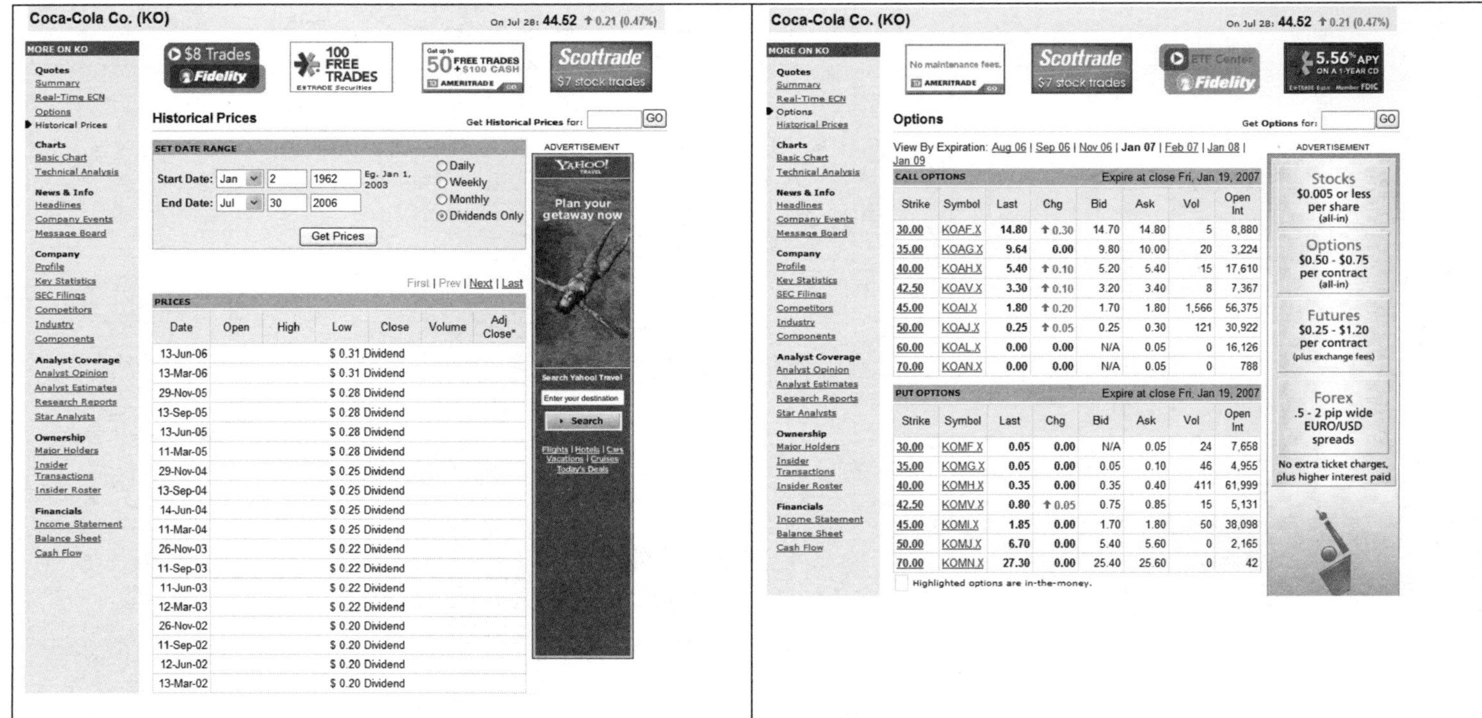

Coca-Cola Co. (KO) — On Jul 28: **44.52** ↑ 0.21 (0.47%)

MORE ON KO
Quotes: Summary, Real-Time ECN, Options, Historical Prices
Charts: Basic Chart, Technical Analysis
News & Info: Headlines, Company Events, Message Board
Company: Profile, Key Statistics, SEC Filings, Competitors, Industry, Components
Analyst Coverage: Analyst Opinion, Analyst Estimates, Research Reports, Star Analysts
Ownership: Major Holders, Insider Transactions, Insider Roster
Financials: Income Statement, Balance Sheet, Cash Flow

Historical Prices — Get Historical Prices for: GO

SET DATE RANGE
Start Date: Jan 2 1962 (Eg. Jan 1, 2003)
End Date: Jul 30 2006
Daily / Weekly / Monthly / ⊙ Dividends Only
Get Prices

First | Prev | Next | Last

PRICES

Date	Open	High	Low	Close	Volume	Adj Close*
13-Jun-06	$ 0.31 Dividend					
13-Mar-06	$ 0.31 Dividend					
29-Nov-05	$ 0.28 Dividend					
13-Sep-05	$ 0.28 Dividend					
13-Jun-05	$ 0.28 Dividend					
11-Mar-05	$ 0.28 Dividend					
29-Nov-04	$ 0.25 Dividend					
13-Sep-04	$ 0.25 Dividend					
14-Jun-04	$ 0.25 Dividend					
11-Mar-04	$ 0.25 Dividend					
26-Nov-03	$ 0.22 Dividend					
11-Sep-03	$ 0.22 Dividend					
11-Jun-03	$ 0.22 Dividend					
12-Mar-03	$ 0.22 Dividend					
26-Nov-02	$ 0.20 Dividend					
11-Sep-02	$ 0.20 Dividend					
12-Jun-02	$ 0.20 Dividend					
13-Mar-02	$ 0.20 Dividend					

Coca-Cola Co. (KO) — On Jul 28: **44.52** ↑ 0.21 (0.47%)

Options — Get Options for: GO

View By Expiration: Aug 06 | Sep 06 | Nov 06 | **Jan 07** | Feb 07 | Jan 08 | Jan 09

CALL OPTIONS — Expire at close Fri, Jan 19, 2007

Strike	Symbol	Last	Chg	Bid	Ask	Vol	Open Int
30.00	KOAF.X	14.80	↑ 0.30	14.70	14.80	5	8,880
35.00	KOAG.X	9.64	0.00	9.80	10.00	20	3,224
40.00	KOAH.X	5.40	↑ 0.10	5.20	5.40	15	17,610
42.50	KOAV.X	3.30	↑ 0.10	3.20	3.40	8	7,367
45.00	KOAI.X	1.80	↑ 0.20	1.70	1.80	1,566	56,375
50.00	KOAJ.X	0.25	↑ 0.05	0.25	0.30	121	30,922
60.00	KOAL.X	0.00	0.00	N/A	0.05	0	16,126
70.00	KOAN.X	0.00	0.00	N/A	0.05	0	788

PUT OPTIONS — Expire at close Fri, Jan 19, 2007

Strike	Symbol	Last	Chg	Bid	Ask	Vol	Open Int
30.00	KOMF.X	0.05	0.00	N/A	0.05	24	7,658
35.00	KOMG.X	0.05	0.00	0.05	0.10	46	4,955
40.00	KOMH.X	0.35	0.00	0.35	0.40	411	61,999
42.50	KOMV.X	0.80	↑ 0.05	0.75	0.85	15	5,131
45.00	KOMI.X	1.85	0.00	1.70	1.80	50	38,098
50.00	KOMJ.X	6.70	0.00	5.40	5.60	0	2,165
70.00	KOMN.X	27.30	0.00	25.40	25.60	0	42

Highlighted options are in-the-money.

Figure 19.2
Yahoo data for Coca-Cola. Note the stability of the dividends. On 28 July 2006, the closing stock price was $44.52.

	A	B	C	D	E
1	**PRICING THE COCA-COLA JAN07 CALLS AND PUTS**				
2	Current date	28-Jul-06			
3	Option expiration date	19-Jan-07			
4	Current stock price	44.52			
5	Interest rate	5.00%			
6					
7		Date	Anticipated dividend	Present value	
8	Mid September	13-Sep-06	0.31	0.31	<-- =C8*EXP(-$B$5*((B8-$B$2)/365))
9	End November	29-Nov-06	0.31	0.30	<-- =C9*EXP(-$B$5*((B9-$B$2)/365))
10					
11	Stock price net of PV(dividends)	43.91	<-- =B4-SUM(D8:D9)		
12	Exercise price, X	45.00	<-- Approximately at the money		
13	Time to maturity, T	0.4795	<-- =(B3-B2)/365		
14	Interest rate, r	5.00%	Risk-free rate of interest		
15	Call price	1.80	<-- Call price on 28jul06		
16	Put price	1.85	<-- Put price on 28jul06		
17					
18	**Implied volatility**				
19	Call, S net of dividends	14.95%	<-- =CallVolatility(B11,B12,B13,B14,B15)		
20	Put, S net of dividends	15.15%	<-- =PutVolatility(B11,B12,B13,B14,B16)		
21					
22	Call, S with dividends	12.19%	<-- =CallVolatility(B4,B12,B13,B14,B15)		
23	Put, S with dividends	17.45%	<-- =PutVolatility(B4,B12,B13,B14,B16)		

19.6.2 Dividend Adjustments for Continuous Dividend Payouts: The Merton Model

In the preceding subsection we looked at the case of known future dividends. This subsection discusses a model due to Merton (1973) for pricing options on a stock that pays continuous dividends. Continuous dividends may seem an odd assumption. But a basket of stocks such as the S&P 500 index or the Dow-Jones 30 can best be approximated by the assumption of a continuous dividend payout, since there are many stocks and since the index components more or less pay out their dividends throughout the year.

Assuming the continuous dividend yield of k, Merton proved the following call-option-pricing formula:

$$C = Se^{-kT}N(d_1) - Xe^{-rT}N(d_2)$$

where

$$d_1 = \frac{\ln(S/X) + (r - k + \sigma^2/2)T}{\sigma\sqrt{T}}$$

$$d_2 = d_1 - \sigma\sqrt{T}$$

This model is used in the next spreadsheet to price the exchange-traded fund that tracks the S&P 500 index:

	A	B	C
1	**Merton's Dividend-Adjusted Option-Pricing Model Used Here to Price S&P 500 Spiders (symbol: SPY)**		
2	S	127.98	Current stock price
3	X	127.00	Exercise price
4	T	0.6329	<-- Option expires 16-Mar-07, today's date 28-Jul-06
5	r	5.00%	Risk-free rate of interest
6	k	1.70%	Dividend yield
7	Sigma	14%	Stock volatility
8	d_1	0.3122	<-- =(LN(B2/B3)+(B5-B6+0.5*B7^2)*B4)/(B7*SQRT(B4))
9	d_2	0.2008	<-- =B8-B7*SQRT(B4)
10			
11	$N(d_1)$	0.6226	<--- Uses formula NormSDist(d_1)
12	$N(d_2)$	0.5796	<--- Uses formula NormSDist(d_2)
13			
14	Call price	7.51	<-- S*Exp(-k*T)*N(d_1)-X*exp(-r*T)*N(d_2)
15	Put price	3.94	<-- call price - S*Exp(-k*T) + X*Exp(-r*T): by Put-Call parity
16		3.94	<-- X*exp(-r*T)*N(-d_2)-S*Exp(-k*T)*N(-d_1): direct formula

The Merton model is often used to price currency options. Suppose we take an option on the euro. The option specifies a dollar exchange rate for euros (in the following example, the call option lets us buy 10,000 euros in 0.0575 years for $1.285 per euro). The asset underlying the option is a euro interest-bearing security with interest rate $r_{€}$.

	A	B	C	D
1	**Pricing Currency Options**			
2	S	1.276	Current exchange rate: U.S. dollar price of one Euro	Intuition: The underlying asset of the currency option is a euro. The euro pays a dividend, which is the euro interest rate. Therefore the Merton model applies, with the underlying asset price being S*exp(-$r_{€}$*T), where $r_{€}$ is the interest rate on euros. Note also the change in d_1, where r_{US} -$r_{€}$ appears instead of r_{US} as in the regular Black-Scholes formula.
3	X	1.285	Exercise price	
4	r_{US}	5.00%	U.S. interest rate	
5	$r_{€}$	5.50%	Euro interest rate	
6	T	0.0575	Time to maturity of option (in years)	
7	Sigma	4.70%	Euro volatility in dollars	
8	d_1	-0.6095	<--(LN(S/X)+(r_{US}-$r_{€}$+0.5*sigma^2)*T)/(sigma*SQRT(T))	
9	d_2	-0.6208	<-- d_1 - sigma*SQRT(T)	
10				
11	Number of Euros per call contract	10,000		
12				
13	$N(d_1)$	0.2711	<--- Uses formula NormSDist(d_1)	
14	$N(d_2)$	0.2674	<--- Uses formula NormSDist(d_2)	
15				
16	Call price	23.69	<-- (S*Exp(-$r_{€}$*T)*N(d_1)-X*exp(-r_{US}*T)*N(d_2))*B11	
17	Put price	112.23	<-- (X*exp(-r_{US}*T)*N(-d_2)-S*Exp(-$r_{€}$*T)*N(-d_1))*B11: direct formula	

19.7 Using the Black-Scholes Formula to Price Structured Securities

A "structured security" is Wall Street parlance for securities that incorporate combinations of stocks, options, and bonds. In this section we give three examples of such securities and show how to price them using the Black-Scholes model.[4] In the process we also return to the discussion of Chapter 16, showing how the profit diagrams of option strategies can help us understand such securities.

19.7.1 A Simple Structured Security: Principal Protection plus Participation in Market Upside Moves

A simple and popular structured offers guaranteed return of the investor's principal plus some participation in the upside moves of the market. Here's an example: Homeside Bank offers its customers the following "principal-protected, upside potential" security (PPUP).

- Initial investment in the security: \$1,000.
- No interest paid on the security.
- In five years the PPUP pays back the \$1,000 plus 50 percent of the increase in the S&P 500 index. Writing the index price today as S_0 and the index price in five years as S_T, the payoff on the PPUP can be written as

$$\$1{,}000\left[1+50\%*\max\left(\frac{S_T}{S_0}-1,0\right)\right]$$

To analyze the PPUP, we first rewrite the maturity payment as

$$\$1{,}000\left[1+50\%*\max\left(\frac{S_T}{S_0}-1,0\right)\right]=\underbrace{\$1{,}000}_{\substack{\uparrow\\ \text{Payoff on}\\ \text{zero coupon}\\ \text{bond}}}+\$1{,}000*\frac{50\%}{S_0}*\underbrace{\max\left(S_T-S_0,0\right)}_{\substack{\uparrow\\ \text{Payoff on at-the-money}\\ \text{call option}}}$$

This shows that the PPUP payoff is composed of two parts:

- A \$1,000 return of principal. Since no interest is paid on this principal, its value today is the present value of the payment at the risk-free

4. Not all structureds can be priced using Black-Scholes; more complicated, path-dependent securities often need to be priced using the Monte Carlo methods discussed in Chapters 22 and 23.

interest rate, $1,000*e^{-rT}$, where r is the interest rate and $T = 5$ is the maturity of the PPUP.

- $\$1,000*\frac{50\%}{S_0}$ times the value today of an at-the-money call on the S&P 500.

We can use the following spreadsheet to price this security:

	A	B	C
1	**ANALYZING A SIMPLE STRUCTURED PRODUCT** **$1,000 Deposit with 50% Participation in S&P Increase over 5 Years**		
2	Initial S&P 500 price, S_0	950	<-- The price of the S&P 500 at PPUP issuance
3	Structured exercise price, X	950	
4	Risk-free interest rate for 5 years, r	5.00%	
5	Time to maturity, T	5	
6	Volatility of S&P 500, σ_{SP}	25%	
7	Participation rate	50%	<-- Percentage of increase in the S&P going to PPUP owner
8			
9	Strutured components, value today		
10	Bond paying $1,000 at maturity	778.80	<-- =EXP(-B4*B5)*1000
11	Participation rate /S_0*at-the-money call on S&P 500	162.52	<-- =1000*B7/B2*BSCall(B2,B3,B5,B4,B6)
12	Value of structured security today	941.32	<-- =SUM(B10:B11)

The value of the structured security (cell B12) is $941.42. This valuation has two parts:

- The present value of the bond part of the PPUP is $778.80 (cell B10).
- The value of $\$1,000*\frac{50\%}{950}$ at-the-money calls on the S&P is $162.52.

Given the parameters in cells B2:B7, the PPUP is *overpriced*—it sells for $1,000, whereas its market value ought to be $941.32. Another way to think about the structured is to compute its implied volatility: What σ_{SP} (cell B6) will give the market valuation (cell B12) of the PPUP to equal the $1,000 price being asked by the Homeside Bank? Either **GoalSeek** or **Solver** will solve this problem:

	A	B	C
1	**ANALYZING A SIMPLE STRUCTURED PRODUCT** **$1,000 Deposit with 50% Participation in S&P Increase over 5 Years**		
2	Initial S&P 500 price, S_0	950	<-- The price of the S&P 500 at PPUP issuance
3	Structured exercise price, X	950	
4	Risk-free interest rate for 5 years, r	5.00%	
5	Time to maturity, T	5	
6	Volatility of S&P 500, σ_{SP}	42.00%	
7	Participation rate	50%	<-- Percentage of increase in the S&P going to PPUP owner
8			
9	Strutured components, value today		
10	Bond paying $1000 at maturity	778.80	<-- =EXP(-B4*B5)*1000
11	Participation rate /S_0*At-the-money call on S&P 500	221.20	<-- =1000*B7/B2*BSCall(B2,B3,B5,B4,B6)
12	Value of structured security today	1000.00	<-- =SUM(B10:B11)

19.7.2 More Complicated Structured Products

Suppose you want to create a security with the following payoff pattern:

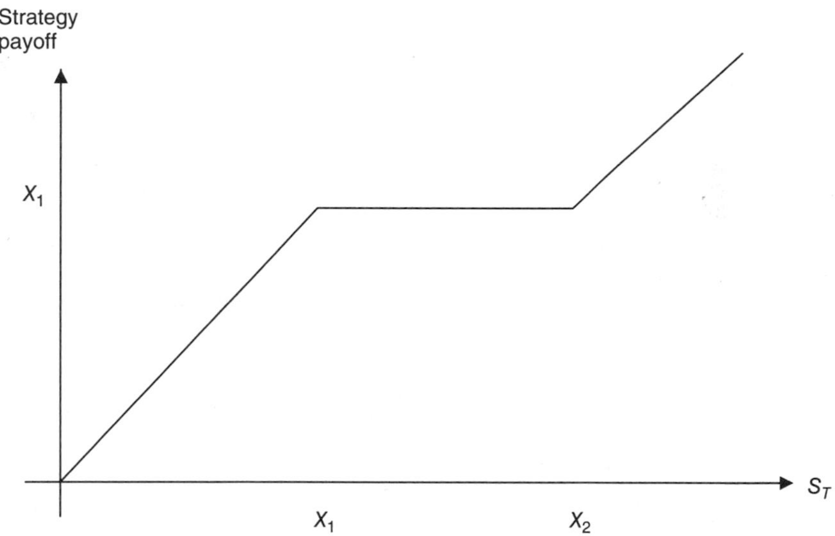

The payoff pattern increases (dollar for dollar) as the terminal price of the underlying asset increases from $0 \le S_T \le X_1$. Between X_1 and X_2, the payoff pattern is flat, and for $X_2 \le S_T$, the payoff again increases dollar for dollar with the price of the underlying. The algebraic formula for this payoff pattern is

$$X_1 - \max(X_1 - S_T, 0) + \max(S_T - X_2, 0)$$

To prove that this formula creates the graph,

$$\underbrace{X_1 - \max(X_1 - S_T, 0)}_{\substack{\uparrow \\ \text{Payoff of written} \\ \text{put}}} + \underbrace{\max(S_T - X_2, 0)}_{\substack{\uparrow \\ \text{Payoff of bought} \\ \text{call}}} = \begin{cases} X_1 - X_1 + S_T = S_T & S_T < X_1 \\ X_1 & X_1 \le S_T < X_2 \\ X_1 + S_T - X_2 & X_2 \le S_T \end{cases}$$

A slightly more complicated payoff pattern is the following:

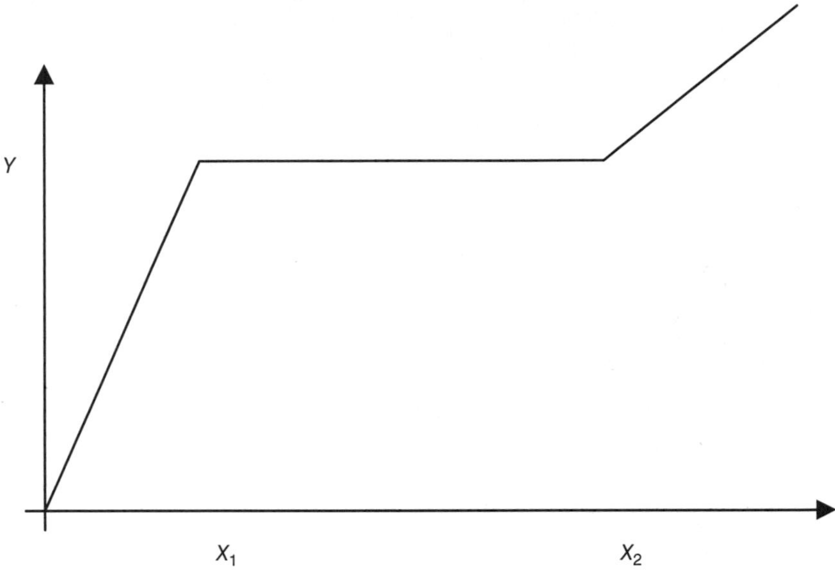

The initial part of the payoff has slope Y/X_1, and the second increasing part of the payoff pattern has slope Y/X_2. This payoff pattern is created by the following formula:

$$\underbrace{Y - \frac{Y}{X_1}\max(X_1 - S_T, 0)}_{\substack{\uparrow \\ \text{Payoff of } \frac{Y}{X_1} \\ \text{written puts}}} + \underbrace{\frac{Y}{X_2}\max(S_T - X_2, 0)}_{\substack{\uparrow \\ \text{Payoff of } \frac{Y}{X_2} \\ \text{bought calls}}}$$

To prove that this is indeed the payoff,

$$\underbrace{Y - \frac{Y}{X_1}\max(X_1 - S_T, 0)}_{\substack{\uparrow \\ \text{Payoff of } \frac{Y}{X_1} \\ \text{written puts}}} + \underbrace{\frac{Y}{X_2}\max(S_T - X_2, 0)}_{\substack{\uparrow \\ \text{Payoff of } \frac{Y}{X_2} \\ \text{bought calls}}}$$

$$= \begin{cases} Y - \frac{Y}{X_1}(X_1 - S_T) = \frac{Y}{X_1}S_T & S_T < X_1 \\ Y & X_1 \le S_T < X_2 \\ Y + \frac{Y}{X_2}(S_T - X_2) = \frac{Y}{X_2}S_T & X_2 \le S_T \end{cases}$$

As an example of this kind of structured payoff security, Figure 19.3 shows the term sheet for a structured product issued by ABN-AMRO bank. The payment on this "Airbag" security depends on the value of the Stoxx50—an index of European stocks. Here are the details:

- Issuance date: 24 March 2003
- Terminal date: 24 March 2008
- Cost: €1,020
- Payment at terminal date:

$$\text{Payment at maturity} = \begin{cases} 1{,}000 * 1.33 * \left(\dfrac{\text{Stoxx50}_{\text{Maturity}}}{\text{Stoxx50}_{\text{Initial}}} \right) & \text{If Stoxx50}_{\text{Maturity}} < 1{,}618.50 \\ 1{,}000 & 1{,}618.50 < \text{Stoxx50}_{\text{Maturity}} < 2{,}158 \\ 1{,}000 * \left(\dfrac{\text{Stoxx50}_{\text{Maturity}}}{\text{Stoxx50}_{\text{Initial}}} \right) & \text{If Stoxx50}_{\text{Maturity}} > 2{,}158 \end{cases}$$

We recognize this security as one whose payoff has the form discussed earlier:

$$\underbrace{Y}_{\text{Bond payoff}} \underbrace{-\frac{Y}{X_1}\max(X_1 - S_T, 0)}_{\frac{Y}{X_1} \text{ written puts with exercise price } X_1} + \underbrace{\frac{Y}{X_2}\max(S_T - X_2, 0)}_{\frac{Y}{X_2} \text{ purchased call with exercise price } X_2}$$

where $X_1 = 1{,}618.50$, $X_2 = 2{,}158$, and $Y = 1{,}000$.

Here's the spreadsheet for the payoff. Cell B7 shows the payoff definition given by the Airbag issuer, and cell B8 shows the payoff in the option terms defined in the preceding formulas. The data table in cells A13:B29 shows that these two definitions are equivalent:

AirBag on the Euro STOXX 50

17 March 2003

FINAL TERMS AND CONDITIONS

We are pleased to present for your consideration the transaction described below. We are willing to negotiate a transaction with you because we understand that you have sufficient knowledge, experience and professional advice to make your own evaluation of the merits and risks of a transaction of this type and you are not relying on ABN AMRO Bank N.V. nor any of the companies in the ABN AMRO group for information, advice or recommendations of any sort other than the factual terms of the transaction. This term sheet does not identify all the risks (direct or indirect) or other considerations which might be material to you when entering into the transaction. You should consult your own business, tax, legal and accounting advisors with respect to this proposed transaction and you should refrain from entering into a transaction with us unless you have fully understood the associated risks and have independently determined that the transaction is appropriate for you. Due to the proprietary nature of this proposal please understand that it is confidential.

SUMMARY	**Issuer & Lead Manager:**	ABN AMRO Bank N.V. (Senior Long Term Debt Rating: Moody's Aa3, S&P AA-)
	Issue:	AirBag on the Euro STOXX 50
	Underlying:	Euro STOXX 50 (Bloomberg: SX5E)
	Spot Reference (SX5E(t)):	2158.00
	Issue Price:	**EUR 1,020**
	Entitlement:	1
	Issue Size:	5,000 Certificates
	AirBag Start:	100% of the Spot Reference (2158.00)
	AirBag Stop:	75% of the Spot Reference (1618.50)
	Percentage drop without any loss:	25%
	SX5E(t1):	Official closing level of the Underlying on the Valuation Date
	Redemption:	1. If SX5E(t1) is less than or equal to the AirBag Stop: EUR 1,000 x 1.33 x $\left(\frac{\text{SX5E(t1)}}{\text{SX5E(t)}}\right)$ 2. If SX5E(t1) is greater than the AirBag Stop but less than or equal to the AirBag Start: EUR 1,000 x 100% 3. If SX5E(t1) is greater than the AirBag Start: EUR 1,000 x $\left(\frac{\text{SX5E(t1)}}{\text{SX5E(t)}}\right)$
	Form:	Global bearer (permanent)
	Clearing:	Euroclear Bank SA, Clearstream Banking SA
	ISIN Code:	XS0165647966
	Valoren Code:	1578781
	Common Code:	16564796
	Minimum Trading Size:	1 AirBag Certificate
	Quoted on:	Reuters page: ABNPB15, Bloomberg page: AAPB, Internet: www.abnamro-sp.com
	Listing:	None
	Applicable Law:	English
	Selling Restrictions:	No sales to US persons or into the US, standard Dutch and UK selling restrictions apply.
TIMETABLE	**Launch Date:**	17/03/03
	Pricing Date:	17/03/03
	Issue & Payment Date:	24/03/03
	Valuation & Expiration Date:	14/03/08
	Final Settlement Date:	21/03/08

This term sheet is for information purposes only and does not constitute an offer to sell or a solicitation to buy any security or other financial instrument. All prices are indicative and dependent upon market conditions and the terms are liable to change and completion in the final documentation.

Figure 19.3
The ABN-AMRO term sheet for its Euro Stoxx50 Airbag security.

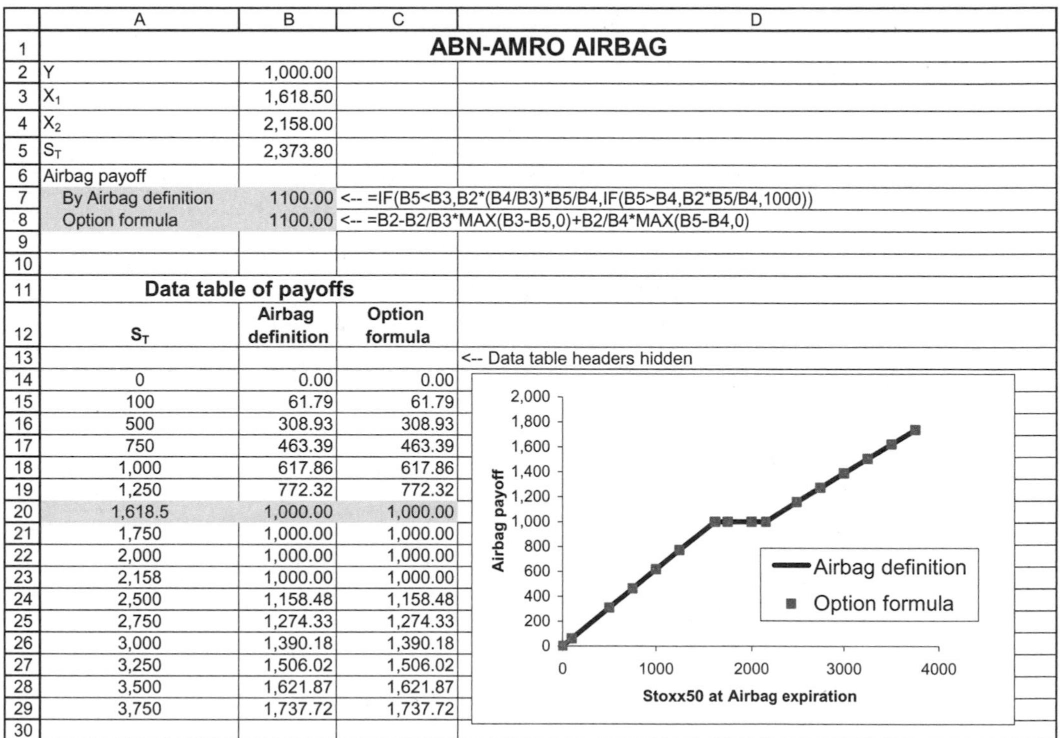

	A	B	C	D
1	**ABN-AMRO AIRBAG**			
2	Y	1,000.00		
3	X_1	1,618.50		
4	X_2	2,158.00		
5	S_T	2,373.80		
6	Airbag payoff			
7	By Airbag definition	1100.00	<-- =IF(B5<B3,B2*(B4/B3)*B5/B4,IF(B5>B4,B2*B5/B4,1000))	
8	Option formula	1100.00	<-- =B2-B2/B3*MAX(B3-B5,0)+B2/B4*MAX(B5-B4,0)	
9				
10				
11	**Data table of payoffs**			
12	**S_T**	**Airbag definition**	**Option formula**	
13				<-- Data table headers hidden
14	0	0.00	0.00	
15	100	61.79	61.79	
16	500	308.93	308.93	
17	750	463.39	463.39	
18	1,000	617.86	617.86	
19	1,250	772.32	772.32	
20	1,618.5	1,000.00	1,000.00	
21	1,750	1,000.00	1,000.00	
22	2,000	1,000.00	1,000.00	
23	2,158	1,000.00	1,000.00	
24	2,500	1,158.48	1,158.48	
25	2,750	1,274.33	1,274.33	
26	3,000	1,390.18	1,390.18	
27	3,250	1,506.02	1,506.02	
28	3,500	1,621.87	1,621.87	
29	3,750	1,737.72	1,737.72	
30				

To see how the Airbag is priced, we use the Black-Scholes model and find the Stoxx50 volatility implied by the Airbag price:

	A	B	C
1	**PRICING THE ABN-AIRBAG** **Find the Implied Volatility**		
2	Stoxx50 price today, S_0	2,158.0	
3	X_1	1,618.50	
4	X_2	2,158.0	
5	Y	1,000.0	
6	Risk-free interest rate for 5 years, r	7.00%	
7	Time to maturity, T	5	
8	Volatility of the Stoxx50, sigma	15.75%	
9			
10	Airbag components, value today		
11	Bond paying X_1 at maturity	704.69	<-- =EXP(-B6*B7)*B5
12	Y/X_1 * written puts with exercise X_1	-4.69	<-- =-B5/B3*BSPut(B2,B3,B7,B6,B8)
13	Purchased call with exercise X_2	320.01	<-- =B5/B4*BSCall(B2,B4,B7,B6,B8)
14	Value of structured security today	1,020.00	<-- =SUM(B11:B13)
15			
16			
17	**Table: Sensitivity of Airbag to Sigma**	1,020.00	<-- =B14, data table header
18	0%	1,000.00	
19	1%	1,000.00	
20	3%	1,000.00	
21	6%	1,000.16	
22	9%	1,002.76	
23	10%	1,004.57	
24	11%	1,006.80	
25	12%	1,009.34	
26	13%	1,012.09	
27	14%	1,014.95	
28	15%	1,017.84	
29	16%	1,020.70	
30	17%	1,023.49	
31	18%	1,026.16	
32	19%	1,028.70	
33	20%	1,031.11	
34	21%	1,033.35	
35	22%	1,035.45	
36	23%	1,037.39	
37	24%	1,039.19	
38	25%	1,040.84	

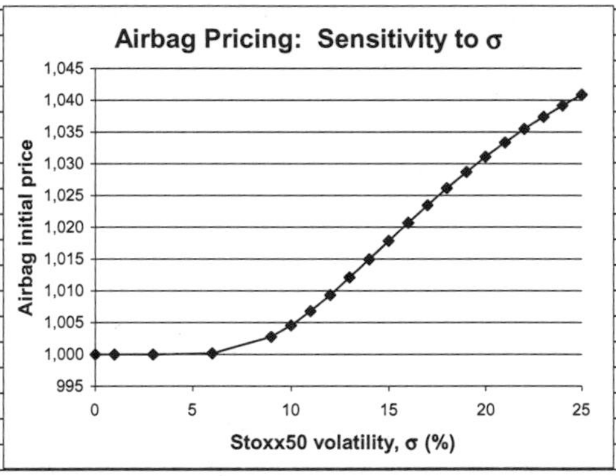

When the Stoxx50 σ is 15.75 percent (cell B8), the Airbag's price is €1,020 (cell B14). The table shows the sensitivity of this price to the σ. Notice that Airbag values are not very sensitive to σ. Doubling the sigma from 10 percent to 20 percent increases the Airbag value by about €17. This result occurs because of the offsetting values of the short put and the long call in the Airbag.

We can do one more exercise on the Airbag. Using a two-dimensional **Data Table**, we examine the Airbag's price sensitivity to both time to maturity T and the Stoxx50 volatility σ.

	A	B	C	D	E	F	G	H
1	**ABN-AMRO AIRBAG SENSITIVITY TO TIME TO MATURITY AND SIGMA**							
2	Stoxx50 price today, S_0	2,158.0						
3	X_1	1,618.50						
4	X_2	2,158.0						
5	Y	1,000.0						
6	Risk-free interest rate for 5 years, r	7.00%						
7	Time to maturity, T	5						
8	Volatility of the Stoxx50, sigma	15.75%						
9								
10	Airbag components, value today							
11	Bond paying X_1 at maturity	704.69	<-- =EXP(-B6*B7)*B5					
12	Y/X_1 * written puts with exercise X_1	-4.69	<-- =-B5/B3*BSPut(B2,B3,B7,B6,B8)					
13	Purchased call with exercise X_2	320.01	<-- =B5/B4*BSCall(B2,B4,B7,B6,B8)					
14	Value of structured security today	1,020.00	<-- =SUM(B11:B13)					
15								
16			**Time to maturity, T**					
17	Data table	1,020.00	**5**	**4**	**3**	**2**	**1**	**0.0001**
18	header:	**5%**	1,000.02	1,000.07	1,000.20	1,000.59	1,001.77	1,000.20
19	=B14	**10%**	1,004.57	1,006.22	1,008.40	1,011.13	1,013.78	1,000.40
20		**15%**	1,017.84	1,021.09	1,024.72	1,028.28	1,029.65	1,000.59
21		**20%**	1,031.11	1,035.21	1,039.61	1,043.69	1,044.54	1,000.79
22	**Volatility of the Stoxx50, sigma -->**	**25%**	1,040.84	1,045.48	1,050.44	1,055.14	1,056.54	1,000.99
23		**30%**	1,047.16	1,052.22	1,057.69	1,063.09	1,065.58	1,001.19
24		**35%**	1,050.86	1,056.29	1,062.26	1,068.39	1,072.19	1,001.39
25		**40%**	1,052.66	1,058.44	1,064.88	1,071.75	1,076.95	1,001.59
26		**45%**	1,053.10	1,059.19	1,066.10	1,073.70	1,080.28	1,001.79
27		**50%**	1,052.55	1,058.94	1,066.29	1,074.59	1,082.53	1,001.99

The Airbag is a fairly stable security—its price varies no more than 10 percent for a wide variety of σs and for nearly all times to maturity.

19.7.3 A Reverse Convertible: Analyzing the UBS "Goals"

The Swiss bank UBS has issued a series of stock-linked securities called Goals. All the Goals pay interest on the initial price; the final repayment depends on the market price of the underlying stock: If the stock price is high, the Goals investor gets back her initial investment, and if the stock price is low, the Goals investor is paid out in a package of shares whose value is less than her initial investment.

An example of such a security is the Cisco-linked Goals issued by UBS on 17 January 2001 (Figure 19.4). The main details of this security are as follow:

The purchaser pays UBS $1,000 on 23 January 2001. In return, she gets three payments of $\$97.50\left(=\dfrac{19.50 \text{ percent}}{2}*1{,}000\right)$ on 23 July 2001, 23 January 2002, and 23 July 2002.

THE SEC FILING FOR UBS AG $60,000,000 GOALS

UBS AG
$60,000,000
19.5% GOALs DUE JULY 23, 2002

Each note being offered has the terms described beginning on page S-14, including the following:

- - Issuer: UBS AG
- - Issue: $60,000,000 USD principal amount of GOALs due July 23, 2002 linked to shares in the common stock of Cisco Systems, Inc.
- - Coupon: 19.5% per annum, payable semi-annually in arrears on each January 23 and July 23 which shall be composed of (1) an interest coupon representing a rate of 5.2% per annum and (2) a coupon representing an option premium of 14.3% per annum
- - Initial price of underlying stock (strike price): $39.00 per share, subject to antidilution adjustments
- - Key dates: Trade: January 17, 2001
Settlement: January 23, 2001
Determination: July 18, 2002
Maturity: July 23, 2002
- - Booking branch: The GOALs will be booked in UBS AG, Jersey Branch

- - Proceeds at maturity are based on the closing price of Cisco Systems, Inc. common stock three business days before maturity:

If the closing price of Cisco Systems, Inc. common stock is at or above the initial price per share of $39.00, holders will receive a cash payment equal to the principal amount of their GOALs.

If the closing price of Cisco Systems, Inc. is lower than the initial price per share of $39.00, holders will receive 25.641 shares of Cisco Systems, Inc. common stock for each $1,000 principal amount of their GOALs (the stock redemption amount). Fractional shares will be paid in cash. The number of shares received for each $1,000 invested will be calculated by dividing the initial price per share of $39.00 into $1,000. The stock redemption amount and the initial price per share of $39.00 (strike price) may change due to stock splits or other corporate actions.

Figure 19.4
From the SEC filing for the UBS Cisco-linked Goals.

On 23 July 2002, in addition to the \$97.50 payment,

• If the price of Cisco stock ≥ \$39 per share, the purchaser of the security gets \$1,000.

• If the price of Cisco stock < \$39 per share, the purchaser gets $\frac{1,000}{39} = 25.641$ shares of Cisco.

The closing stock price of Cisco on 23 January 2001 was 42.625.

The continuously compounded risk-free interest rate at the time of the Goals issuance was 5.2 percent annually (2.6 percent semiannually).

To analyze the Cisco-linked Goals, we start by noting that the cash flow can be written as follows:

Time	0	1	2	3
	−1,000	97.50	97.50	97.50 $1{,}000 - 25.641 * \max(39 - S_T, 0)$

To prove that this definition is equivalent, we write a short spreadsheet that compares the Goals payoff according to the UBS definition with its payoff as we have described it:

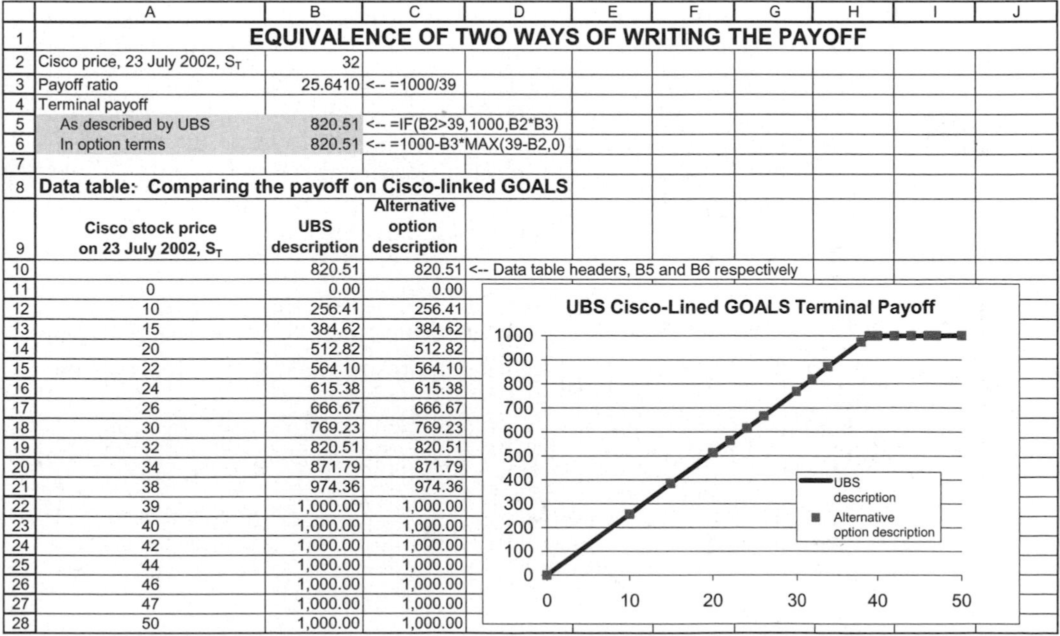

	A	B	C	D
1	**EQUIVALENCE OF TWO WAYS OF WRITING THE PAYOFF**			
2	Cisco price, 23 July 2002, S_T	32		
3	Payoff ratio	25.6410	<-- =1000/39	
4	Terminal payoff			
5	As described by UBS	820.51	<-- =IF(B2>39,1000,B2*B3)	
6	In option terms	820.51	<-- =1000-B3*MAX(39-B2,0)	
7				
8	**Data table: Comparing the payoff on Cisco-linked GOALS**			
9	**Cisco stock price on 23 July 2002, S_T**	**UBS description**	**Alternative option description**	
10		820.51	820.51	<-- Data table headers, B5 and B6 respectively
11	0	0.00	0.00	
12	10	256.41	256.41	
13	15	384.62	384.62	
14	20	512.82	512.82	
15	22	564.10	564.10	
16	24	615.38	615.38	
17	26	666.67	666.67	
18	30	769.23	769.23	
19	32	820.51	820.51	
20	34	871.79	871.79	
21	38	974.36	974.36	
22	39	1,000.00	1,000.00	
23	40	1,000.00	1,000.00	
24	42	1,000.00	1,000.00	
25	44	1,000.00	1,000.00	
26	46	1,000.00	1,000.00	
27	47	1,000.00	1,000.00	
28	50	1,000.00	1,000.00	

The equivalence of these two definitions means that the purchaser of the Cisco-linked Goals

- Acquires a $1,000 bond paying 9.75 percent interest semiannually.
- Writes UBS 25.641 puts with exercise $X = 39$ and with time to maturity $T = 1.5$.

At the time the Goals were issued, the semiannual interest rate was around 2.6 percent, far below 9.75 percent. Thus the bond component of the Goals was worth much more than $1,000. However, the purchaser of the Goals was *giving* UBS 25.641 puts. The value of this "gift" should be accounted for in any analysis of the Goals.

We illustrate two ways to value the Goals. The first method assumes that the equilibrium net present value of any security should be zero. Applying this method for the UBS security gives

$$\underbrace{-1{,}000+\frac{97.50}{(1+r)^{0.5}}+\frac{97.50}{(1+r)^{1.0}}+\frac{1{,}097.50}{(1+r)^{1.5}}}_{\substack{\uparrow \\ \text{Value=\$205.11} \\ \text{at } r=2.6\%}}-25.641*\text{Puts on Cisco }(X=39, T=1.5)=0$$

In the next spreadsheet, we use this logic to price the puts embedded in the UBS security, and we compare this price to the Black-Scholes price.

$$\begin{aligned}\text{Implicit put valuation} &= \frac{1}{25.641}\left[-1{,}000+\frac{97.50}{(1+2.6\%)^{0.5}}+\frac{97.50}{(1+2.6\%)^{1.0}}+\frac{1{,}097.50}{(1+2.6\%)^{1.5}}\right] \\ &= \frac{\$205.11}{25.641}=\$8.00\end{aligned}$$

UBS is implicitly paying the Goals purchaser $8.00 per Cisco put. However, as shown in the spreadsheet, the Black-Scholes price of such a put is $11.71 if σ = 80 percent.[5] This result makes the Goals a bad buy.

5. The Cisco-linked Goals was issued during the Nasdaq crash of the early 2000s. The implied volatility of Cisco stock during this period varied between 80 and 120 percent.

	A	B	C
1	**PRICING THE UBS GOALS IMPLICIT PUT**		
2	Annual risk-free rate	5.20%	
3	Coupon rate	19.50%	
4	Initial cost	1,000	
5	Conversion ratio: number of shares of Cisco received if share price is low	25.641	<-- =1000/39
6			
7	**Valuing the fixed payments at 5.20%**		
8	Fixed payments		
9	**Date**	**Cash flow**	
10	23-Jan-01	(1,000.00)	
11	23-Jul-01	97.50	<-- =$B$3*B4/2
12	23-Jan-02	97.50	
13	23-Jul-02	1,097.50	
14	**PV of Goals bond component**	**205.11**	<-- =XNPV(B2,B10:B13,A10:A13)
15			
16	Value of 25.641 puts embedded in Goals	205.11	<-- =B14
17	**Value per put**	**8.00**	<-- =B16/25.641
18	This is what UBS is *paying* the Goals purchaser for the embedded puts.		
19			
20	**Valuing the puts with Black-Scholes**		
21	S	42.625	Current stock price
22	X	39	Exercise price
23	r	5.20%	Risk-free interest rate
24	T	1.5	Time to maturity of option (in years)
25	Sigma	80%	Stock volatility
26	**Put price**	**11.71**	<-- =BSPut(B21,B22,B24,B23,B25)
27			
28	Is the Goals a good buy?	No	<-- =IF(B17>B26,"Yes","No")
29			
30	**Technical note**: For didactic clarity, the computations use 5.2% as the interest rate for valuing both the bond component of the Goals (rows 10-14) and for the option valuation. Given a 2.6% semiannual discrete interest rate, it would be technically more correct to use an equivalent continuously compounded interest rate of **LN((1.026)^2)** in the option computations. The reader can confirm that the effect of this correction is negligible.		

There is another way to look at the Goals. Consider a Goals purchaser who buys the Goals and also buys 25.641 puts on Cisco with $T = 1.5$, $X = 39$. This "engineered" combination of a Goals + 25.641 puts creates a risk-free security:

$$\text{Payoff Goals} + 25.641 \text{ puts} = \begin{cases} \$1{,}000 \underbrace{-25.641*(39-S_T)}_{\substack{\uparrow \\ \text{Payment on Goals} \\ \text{embedded puts}}} \\ +\underbrace{25.641*(39-S_T)}_{\substack{\uparrow \\ \text{Payment on puts} \\ \text{purchased}}} = \$1{,}000 & S_T < 39 \\ \$1{,}000 & S_T \geq 39 \end{cases}$$

In the following spreadsheet, we assume that the bought puts are priced using Black-Scholes and compare the rate of return on this "engineered" security to the risk-free rate:

	A	B	C
1	**CREATING A RISKLESS SECURITY WITH THE UBS GOALS AND 25.641 PUTS**		
2	**Initial cash flows**		
3	Buy UBS security	-1,000.00	
4	Buy 25.641 puts	-300.21	<-- =-25.641*BSPut(B16,B17,B19,B18,B20)
5			
6	**Cash flow of "engineered" security: GOALS + 25.641 bought puts**		
7	**Date**	**Cash flow**	
8	23-Jan-01	(1,300.21)	<-- =SUM(B3:B4)
9	23-Jul-01	97.50	
10	23-Jan-02	97.50	
11	23-Jul-02	1,097.50	
12			
13	IRR of above	-0.43%	<-- =XIRR(B8:B11,A8:A11)
14			
15	**Inputs for Black-Scholes formula in cell B4**		
16	S	42.625	Current stock price
17	X	39	Exercise price
18	r	5.20%	Risk-free rate of interest
19	T	1.5	Time to maturity of option (in years)
20	Sigma	80%	Stock volatility

Cell B13 uses the Excel function **XIRR** (see Chapter 34) to compute the annualized internal rate of return on the engineered security. Clearly this return is less than the alternative risk-free rate of return (5.2 percent) that can be earned in the market. This is an alternative confirmation of the fact that the Goals are a bad buy.

19.8 Bang for the Buck with Options

This section presents another application of the Black-Scholes formula. Suppose that you are convinced that a given stock will go up in a very short period of time. You want to buy calls on the stock that have a maximum "bang for the buck"—that is, you want the percentage profit on your option investment to be maximal. Using the Black-Scholes formula, it is easy to show that you should

- Buy calls with the shortest possible maturity.
- Buy calls that are most highly out of the money (i.e., with the highest exercise price possible).

Here's a spreadsheet illustration:

	A	B	C
1	"BANG FOR THE BUCK" WITH OPTIONS		
2	S	25	Current stock price
3	X	25	Exercise price
4	r	6.00%	Risk-free rate of interest
5	T	0.5	Time to maturity of option (in years)
6	Sigma	30%	Stock volatility
7			
8	d_1	0.2475	<-- (LN(S/X)+(r+0.5*sigma^2)*T)/(sigma*SQRT(T))
9	d_2	0.0354	<-- d_1-sigma*SQRT(T)
10			
11	N(d_1)	0.5977	<-- Uses formula NormSDist(d_1)
12	N(d_2)	0.5141	<-- Uses formula NormSDist(d_2)
13			
14	Call price	2.47	<-- S*N(d_1)-X*exp(-r*T)*N(d_2)
15	Put price	1.73	<-- call price - S + X*Exp(-r*T): by put-call parity
16			
17	Call bang	6.0483	<-- =B11*B2/B14
18	Put bang	5.8070	<-- =NORMSDIST(-B8)*B2/B15

The "call bang" defined in cell B17 is simply the percentage change in the call price dividend by the percentage change in the stock price (in economics this is known as the *price elasticity*):

$$\text{Call bang} = \frac{\partial C/C}{\partial S/S} = \frac{\partial C}{\partial S}\frac{S}{C} = N(d_1)\frac{S}{C}$$

Similarly, for a put, the "bang for the buck" is defined by the following formula (of course, the story behind the put "bang for the buck" is that you are convinced that the stock price will go down):

$$\text{Put bang} = \frac{\partial P/P}{\partial S/S} = \frac{\partial P}{\partial S}\frac{S}{P} = -N(-d_1)\frac{S}{P}$$

This is defined in cell B18. To make the numbers easier to understand, we have dropped the minus sign, making the "put bang" $= N(-d_1)\dfrac{S}{P}$.

The following graph shows the "bang for the buck" for both calls and puts:

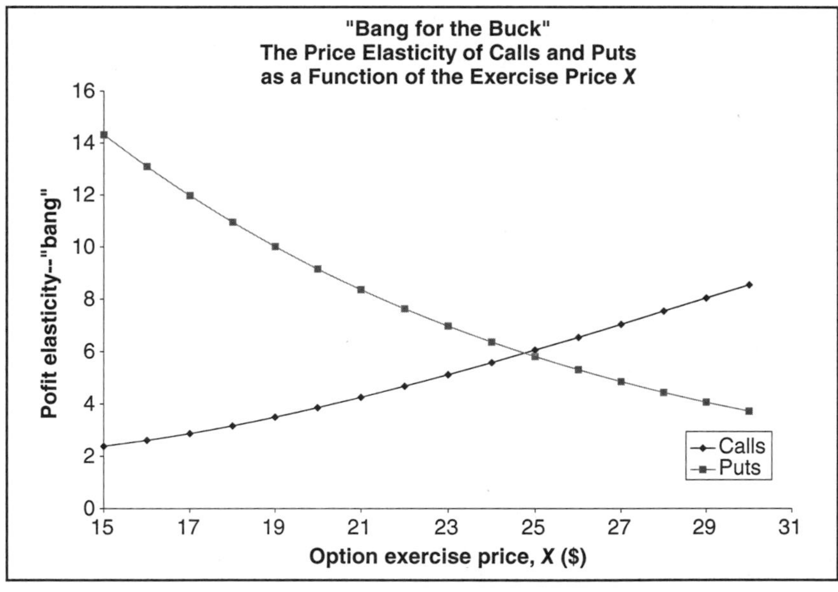

If you play with the spreadsheet, you will see that the longer the time to maturity, the less the bang for the buck. (Another way of saying all this is that the most risky options are the most out-of-the-money and the shortest-term options.)

	D	E	F	G	H	I
23		Data table: Effect of S and T on "call bang"				
24	Data table header: =B17					
25			T--option time to exercise			
26		6.0483	**0.25**	**0.5**	**0.75**	**1**
27		**15**	25.8856	14.1771	10.1696	8.1112
28		**16**	23.3305	12.9884	9.4123	7.5625
29		**17**	20.9954	11.9033	8.7218	7.0623
30		**18**	18.8590	10.9121	8.0914	6.6057
31		**19**	16.9052	10.0067	7.5154	6.1882
32		**20**	15.1222	9.1805	6.9891	5.8062
33		**21**	13.5007	8.4274	6.5082	5.4565
34		**22**	12.0334	7.7424	6.0691	5.1362
35		**23**	10.7137	7.1205	5.6682	4.8426
36		**24**	9.5347	6.5572	5.3025	4.5737
37		**25**	8.4893	6.0483	4.9691	4.3272
38		**26**	7.5694	5.5896	4.6655	4.1012
39		**27**	6.7664	5.1773	4.3892	3.8941
40		**28**	6.0706	4.8074	4.1379	3.7043
41		**29**	5.4720	4.4764	3.9094	3.5303
42		**30**	4.9598	4.1807	3.7019	3.3708

19.9 The Black (1976) Model for Bond Option Valuation[6]

Black (1976) suggested an adaptation of the Black-Scholes model, which is often used for simple valuation of options on bonds or forwards. Letting F stand for the forward price of an asset, the Black-Scholes equation given in section 19.2 is replaced by

$$C = e^{-rT}[FN(d_1) - XN(d_2)],$$

where

$$d_1 = \frac{\ln(F/X) + \sigma^2 T/2}{\sigma\sqrt{T}}$$

$$d_2 = d_1 - \sigma\sqrt{T}$$

6. This section is advanced and can be skipped on first reading. A full discussion of the pricing of bond options is beyond the scope of the current edition of this book. However, this very useful and often-used adaptation of the Black model is simple enough to attach to this chapter.

The corresponding put price is given by

$$P = e^{-rT}[XN(-d_2) - FN(-d_1)]$$

To use the Black (1976) model, consider the case of an option on a zero coupon bond, where the option maturity is $T = 0.5$. The option gives the holder the opportunity to buy the bond at time T for exercise price $X = 130$. Suppose that the risk-free interest rate is $r = 4$ percent. If the forward price of the bond to the exercise date is $F = 133$ and the volatility of the forward price is $\sigma = 6$ percent, then the pricing of the bond option using the Black (1976) model is as follows:

	A	B	C
1	USING THE BLACK (1976) MODEL TO PRICE A BOND OPTION		
2	F	133.011	<-- Bond forward price
3	X	130.000	<-- Exercise price
4	r	4.00%	<--Risk-free rate of interest
5	T	0.5	
6	Sigma	6%	<-- Bond forward price volatility, σ
7			
8	d_1	0.5609	<-- =(LN(B2/B3)+B6^2*B5/2)/(B6*SQRT(B5))
9	d_2	0.5185	<-- =B8-SQRT(B5)*B6
10			
11	Call price	3.97	<-- =EXP(--B4*B5)*(B2*NORMSDIST(B8)-B3*NORMSDIST(B9))
12	Put price	1.02	<-- =EXP(-B4*B5)*(B3*NORMSDIST(-B9)-B2*NORMSDIST(-B8))

Thus a call on the bond is worth 3.97 and a put is worth 1.02.

19.9.1 Determining the Bond's Forward Price

The forward interest rate is the interest rate that can be locked in today for a loan in the future. In the next example, the current 7-year rate is 6 percent and the 4-year rate is 5 percent. By simultaneously creating a deposit in one maturity and a loan in the other maturity, we create a security that has zero cash flows everywhere except at years 4 and 7:

	A	B	C	D	E	F	G	H	I	J
1	**THE FORWARD INTEREST RATE**									
2	Bond maturity, W	7								
3	Option maturity, T	4								
4	Year W pure discount rate	6%								
5	Year T pure discount rate	5%								
6										
7	**Discretely-compounded interest rates**									
8		**0**	**1**	**2**	**3**	**4**	**5**	**6**	**7**	**8**
9	7-year deposit at 6.00%	100.00							-150.36	
10	4-year loan at 5.00%	-100.00				121.55				
11	**Sum of above: A 3-year deposit at year 4**	0.00				121.55			-150.36	
12										
13	Discretely-compounded forward interest rate from year 4 to year 7	7.35%	<-- =(-I11/F11)^(1/(B2-B3))-1							
14										
15	**Continuously-compounded interest rates**									
16		**0**	**1**	**2**	**3**	**4**	**5**	**6**	**7**	**8**
17	7-year deposit at 6.00%	100.00							-152.20	
18	4-year loan at 5.00%	-100.00				122.14				
19	**Sum of above: A 3-year deposit at year 4**	0.00				122.14			-152.20	
20										
21	Continuously-compounded forward interest rate from year 4 to year 7	7.33%	<-- =LN(-I19/F19)/(B2-B3)							

The preceding spreadsheet shows two forward rate computations. If the interest rates are discretely compounded, then the forward rate from year 4 to year 7 is given by

$$\begin{aligned}\text{Discretely compounded forward rate, year 4 to 7} &= \left[\frac{(1+r_7)^7}{(1+r_4)^4}\right]^{(1/3)} - 1 \\ &= \left[\frac{(1+6\%)^7}{(1+5\%)^4}\right]^{(1/3)} - 1 = \left(\frac{1.5036}{1.2155}\right)^{(1/3)} - 1 = 7.35\%\end{aligned}$$

If the rates are continuously compounded (as in the Black model and most option calculations) then the forward rate from year 4 to 7 is given by

$$\begin{aligned}\text{Continously compounded forward rate, year 4 to 7} &= \left(\frac{1}{3}\right)\text{Ln}\left[\frac{e^{r_7*7}}{e^{r_4*4}}\right] \\ &= \left(\frac{1}{3}\right)\text{Ln}\left[\frac{e^{r_7*7}}{e^{r_4*4}}\right] = \left(\frac{1}{3}\right)\left(\frac{1.5220}{1.2214}\right) = 7.33\%\end{aligned}$$

To apply the forward interest rate to the example in the previous subsection, assume that the bond in question has a maturity of two years and a face value at maturity of 147. Then if the 2-year interest rate is $r_2 = 6$ percent and the interest rate to the option's maturity is $r_{0.5} = 4$ percent, the forward price of the bond is $F = 133.011$, as shown here:

	A	B	C
1	**DETERMINING THE FORWARD PRICE OF THE BOND**		
2	Bond's maturity, N	2	
3	Option maturity, T	0.5	
4	Bond maturity value	147	
5			
6	Interest rate to N	6%	
7	Interest rate to T	4%	
8			
9	Bond forward price to T	133.011	<-- =B4*EXP(-B6*B2)*EXP(B7*B3)

19.10 Summary

The Black-Scholes formula for pricing options is one of the most powerful innovations in finance. The formula is widely used both to price options and as a conceptual framework for analyzing complex securities. In this chapter we have explored the implementation of the Black-Scholes formula. Using "plain vanilla" Excel allows us to price Black-Scholes options; using VBA we are able to define both the Black-Scholes price and the implied volatility for options. Finally, we showed how to use Black-Scholes to price structured products—combinations of options, stocks, and bonds.

Exercises

1. Use the Black-Scholes model to price the following:

   a. A call option on a stock whose current price is 50, with exercise price $X = 50$, $T = 0.5$, $r = 10$ percent, $\sigma = 25$ percent.

   b. A put option with the same parameters.

2. Use the data from exercise 1 and **Data|Table** to produce graphs that show

   a. The sensitivity of the Black-Scholes call price to changes in the initial stock price S.

   b. The sensitivity of the Black-Scholes put price to changes in σ.

   c. The sensitivity of the Black-Scholes call price to changes in the time to maturity T.

   d. The sensitivity of the Black-Scholes call price to changes in the interest rate r.

   e. The sensitivity of the put price to changes in the exercise price X.

3. Produce a graph comparing a call's *intrinsic value* [defined as max($S - X$, 0)] and its Black-Scholes price. From this graph you should be able to deduce that it is never optimal to exercise a call priced by the Black-Scholes early.

4. Produce a graph comparing a put's intrinsic value [max($X - S$, 0)] and its Black-Scholes price. From this graph you should be able to deduce that it may be optimal to exercise a put priced by the Black-Scholes formula early.

5. The following table gives prices for American Airlines (AMR) options on 12 July 2007. The option with exercise price X = \$27.50 is assumed to be the at-the-money option.

   a. Compute the implied volatility of each option (use the functions **CallVolatility** and **PutVolatility** defined in the chapter).

   b. Graph these volatilities. Is there a volatility "smile"?

	A	B	C	D	E	F	G
1			AMR OPTIONS				
2	Stock price	27.82					
3	Current date	12-Jul-07					
4	Expiration date	16-Nov-07					
5	Time to maturity,	0.35	<-- =(B4-B3)/365				
6	Interest	5%					
7							
8	Strike	Call option price	Implied volatility		Strike	Put option price	Implied volatility
9	15.0	13.50			15.0	0.15	
10	17.5	10.40			17.5	0.25	
11	20.0	8.40			20.0	0.55	
12	22.5	7.20			22.5	1.06	
13	25.0	4.90			25.0	1.90	
14	27.5	3.30			27.5	2.95	
15	30.0	2.30			30.0	4.30	
16	32.5	1.65			32.5	6.10	
17	35.0	1.00			35.0	7.40	
18	37.5	0.70			37.5	9.60	
19	40.0	0.45			40.0	12.70	
20	45.0	0.25					
21	50.0	0.05					

6. Re-examine the X = 17.50 call for AMR in the previous exercise.

   a. Is the call correctly priced?

   b. What price would be necessary for this call in order for the implied volatility to be 60%?

7. Use the Excel **Solver** to find the stock price for which there is the maximum difference between the Black-Scholes call option price and the option's intrinsic value. Use the following values: $S = 45$, $X = 45$, $T = 1$, $\sigma = 40$ percent, $r = 8$ percent.

8. As shown in this chapter, Merton (1973) shows that for the case of an asset with price S paying a continuously compounded dividend yield k, leads to the following call option pricing formula:

$$C = Se^{-kT} N(d_1) - Xe^{-rT} N(d_2),$$

where

$$d_1 = \frac{\ln(S/X) + (r - k + \sigma^2/2)T}{\sigma\sqrt{T}}$$

$$d_2 = d_1 - \sigma\sqrt{T}$$

a. Modify the **BSCall** and **BSPut** functions defined in this chapter to fit the Merton model.

b. Use the function to price an at-the-money option on an index whose current price is $S = 1{,}500$, when the option's maturity $T = 1$, the dividend yield is $k = 2.2$ percent, its standard deviation $\sigma = 20$ percent, and the interest rate $r = 7$ percent.

9. On 12 July 2007, call and put options to purchase and sell 10,000 euros at $1.37 per euro are traded on the Philadelphia options exchange. The options' expiration date is 20 December 2007. If the dollar interest rate is 5 percent, the euro interest rate is 4.5 percent and the volatility of the euro is 6 percent, what should be the price of a call and a put?

10. Note that you can use the Black-Scholes formula to calculate the call option premium as a percentage of the exercise price in terms of S/X:

$$C = SN(d_1) - Xe^{-rT} N(d_2) \Rightarrow \frac{C}{X} = \frac{S}{X} N(d_1) - e^{-rT} N(d_2)$$

where

$$d_1 = \frac{\ln(S/X) + (r + \sigma^2/2)T}{\sigma\sqrt{T}}$$

$$d_2 = d_1 - \sigma\sqrt{T}$$

Implement this formula in a spreadsheet.

11. Note that you can also calculate the Black-Scholes put option premium as a percentage of the exercise price in terms of S/X:

$$P = -SN(-d_1) + Xe^{-rT} N(-d_2) \Rightarrow \frac{P}{X} = e^{-rT} N(-d_2) - \frac{S}{X} N(-d_1)$$

where

$$d_1 = \frac{\ln(S/X) + (r + \sigma^2/2)T}{\sigma\sqrt{T}}$$

$$d_2 = d_1 - \sigma\sqrt{T}$$

Implement this formula in a spreadsheet. Find the ratio of S/X for which C/X and P/X cross when $T = 0.5$, $\sigma = 25$ percent, $r = 10$ percent. (You can use a graph or you can use Excel's **Solver**.) Note that this crossing point is affected by the interest rate and the option maturity, but not by σ.

12. Consider a structured security of the following type: The purchaser invests $1,000 and in three years gets back the initial investment, plus 95 percent of the increase in a market index whose current price is 100. The interest rate is 6 percent per year, continuously compounded. Assuming the security is fairly priced, what is the implied volatility of the market index?

20 Option Greeks

20.1 Overview

In this chapter we discuss the sensitivities of the Black-Scholes formula to its various parameters. The "Greeks," as they are called (because of the Greek letters used to denote most of them), are the partial derivatives of the Black-Scholes formula with respect to its arguments. They can be thought of as giving a measure of the riskiness of an option:

- Delta, denoted by Δ, is the partial derivative of the option price with respect to the price of the underlying stock:

$$\Delta_{\text{Call}} = \frac{\partial \text{Call}}{\partial S}, \quad \Delta_{\text{Put}} = \frac{\partial \text{Put}}{\partial S}$$

Delta can be thought of as a measure of the variability of the option's price when the price of the underlying stock changes.[1]

- Gamma, Γ, is the second derivative of the option's price with respect to the underlying stock. Gamma gives the convexity of the option price with respect to the stock price. For options priced by the Black-Scholes formula, the call and put have the same gamma:

$$\Gamma_{\text{Call}} = \frac{\partial^2 \text{Call}}{\partial S^2} = \Gamma_{\text{Put}} = \frac{\partial^2 \text{Put}}{\partial S^2}$$

- Vega is the sensitivity of the option price to the standard deviation of the underlying stock's return σ. For no obvious reason, the Greek letter kappa, κ, is sometimes used to denote vega. Given the Black-Scholes formula, calls and puts have the same vega:

$$\kappa = \frac{\partial \text{Call}}{\partial \sigma} = \frac{\partial \text{Put}}{\partial \sigma}$$

- Theta, θ, is change in the option's value as the time to maturity decreases. We generally expect that options will become less valuable with the passage of time (though this assumption turns out not to be always true). Writing T as the option's remaining time to maturity, we set theta equal to the negative of the derivative of the option price with respect to T:

1. Table 20.1, page 551, gives the formulas for all the Greeks.

$$\theta_{\text{Call}} = -\frac{\partial \text{Call}}{\partial T}, \quad \theta_{\text{Put}} = -\frac{\partial \text{Put}}{\partial T}$$

• Rho, ρ, measures the interest rate sensitivity of an option:

$$\rho_{\text{Call}} = -\frac{\partial \text{Call}}{\partial r}, \quad \rho_{\text{Put}} = -\frac{\partial \text{Put}}{\partial r}$$

In this chapter we show you how to measure an option's Greeks and how to use them in hedging. For generality we illustrate using the Merton model (section 19.6.2), an extended version of the Black-Scholes formula that applies either to stocks paying a continuous dividend or to currencies.

20.2 Defining and Computing the Greeks

The "Greeks" are the sensitivities of an option price with respect to certain of its variables. In Table 20.1 we set out the Greeks for options defined on an underlying stock that pays a continuous dividend. As discussed in section 19.6.2, such options are priced using the Merton model. Of course, the standard Black-Scholes model is obtained from the Merton model by setting the dividend yield $k = 0$. Currency options can be priced by the Merton formula by setting S equal to the current exchange rate, X equal to the option exercise exchange rate, r equal to the domestic interest rate, and k equal to the foreign interest rate.

The Merton version of the Black-Scholes formula is given by

$$C = Se^{-kT}N(d_1) - Xe^{-rT}N(d_2)$$

$$P = -Se^{-kT}N(-d_1) + Xe^{-rT}N(-d_2)$$

where

$$d_1 = \frac{\ln\left(\frac{S}{X}\right) + (r - k + \sigma^2/2)T}{\sigma\sqrt{T}}$$

$$d_2 = d_1 - \sigma\sqrt{T}$$

Table 20.1 gives the Greeks for this formula.

Table 20.1
Black-Scholes Greeks

	Measures	Call	Put
Delta, written as either Δ or δ	Price sensitivity of option $\frac{\partial V}{\partial S}$	$\Delta_{Call} = e^{-kT}N(d_1)$	$\Delta_{Put} = e^{-kT}[N(d_1) - 1] = -e^{-kT}N(-d_1)$
Gamma, written as Γ	Second-order price sensitivity $\frac{\partial^2 V}{\partial S^2}$. The option's convexity with respect to underlying price.	$\frac{e^{-kT}N'(d_1)}{S\sigma\sqrt{T}} = \frac{e^{(d_1)^2/2-kT}}{S\sigma\sqrt{2T\pi}}$	
Vega, no Greek letter, though sometimes the Greek kappa κ is used	Sensitivity to volatility $\frac{\partial V}{\partial \sigma}$	$Se^{-kT}N'(d_1)\sqrt{T} = \frac{S\sqrt{T}e^{(d_1)^2/2-kT}}{\sqrt{2\pi}}$	
Theta, written as θ	Time sensitivity $-\frac{\partial V}{\partial T}$	$-\frac{Se^{-kT}N'(d_1)\sigma}{2\sqrt{T}} + kSe^{-kT}N(d_1) - rXe^{-rT}N(d_2)$	$-\frac{Se^{-kT}N'(d_1)\sigma}{2\sqrt{T}} - kSe^{-kT}N(-d_1) + rXe^{-rT}N(-d_2)$
Rho, ρ	Interest rate sensitivity	$XTe^{-rT}N(d_2)$	$-XTe^{-rT}N(-d_2)$

Reminders:

$$d_1 = \frac{\ln(S/X) + \left(r - k + \frac{\sigma^2}{2}\right)T}{\sigma T}, \quad d_2 = d_1 - \sigma\sqrt{T}$$

$$N'(x) = \frac{1}{\sqrt{2\pi}}e^{\left(-x^2/2\right)}$$

VBA Implementation of Black-Scholes Greeks

```
Function dOne(stock, exercise, time, interest, _
     divyield, sigma)
     dOne = (Log (stock / exercise) + _
     (interest - divyield) _
     * time) / (sigma * Sqr(time)) + 0.5 * _
     sigma * Sqr(time)
End Function

Function dTwo(stock, exercise, time, interest, _
     divyield, sigma)
```

```
    dTwo = dOne(stock, exercise, time, _
    interest, divyield, sigma) - sigma _
    * Sqr(time)
End Function

'The standard normal probability density, this is
'N′ (x)
Function normaldf(x)
    normaldf = Exp(-x ^ 2 / 2) / _
    (Sqr(2 * Application.Pi()))
End Function

Function BSMertonCall(stock, exercise, time, _
    interest, divyield, sigma)
    BSMertonCall = stock * Exp(-divyield * time) * _
    Application.NormSDist(dOne(stock, exercise, _
    time, interest, divyield, sigma)) - exercise * _
    Exp(-time * interest) * Application.NormSDist _
    (dTwo (stock, exercise, time, interest, _
    divyield, sigma))
End Function

'Put pricing function uses put-call parity theorem
Function BSMertonPut(stock, exercise, time, _
    interest, divyield, sigma)
    BSMertonPut = BSMertonCall(stock, exercise, _
    time, interest, divyield, sigma) + exercise * _
    Exp(-interest * time) - stock * Exp(-divyield _
    * time)
End Function

Function DeltaCall(stock, exercise, time, interest, _
    divyield, sigma)
    DeltaCall = Exp(-divyield * time) * _
    Application.NormSDist(dOne(stock, exercise, _
    time, interest, divyield, sigma))
End Function
```

```
Function DeltaPut(stock, exercise, time, interest, _
    divyield, sigma)
    DeltaPut = -Exp(-divyield * time) * _
    Application.NormSDist (-dOne(stock, exercise, _
    time, interest, divyield, sigma))
End Function

Function Gamma(stock, exercise, time, interest, _
    divyield, sigma)
    Gamma = (Exp(dOne(stock, exercise, time, _
    interest, divyield, sigma) ^ 2 / 2 - _
    divyield * time)) / (stock * sigma * _
    Sqr(2 * time * Application.Pi()))
End Function

Function Vega(stock, exercise, time, interest, _
    divyield, sigma)
    Vega = stock * Sqr(time) * normaldf(dOne(stock, _
    * Exp(-divyield * time)
End Function

Function ThetaCall(stock, exercise, time, interest, _
    divyield, sigma)
    ThetaCall = -stock * normaldf(dOne(stock, _
    exercise, time, interest, divyield, sigma)) * _
    sigma * Exp(-divyield * time) / _
    (2 * Sqr(time)) + divyield * stock * _
    Application.NormSDist(dOne(stock, exercise, _
    time, interest, divyield, sigma)) * _
    Exp(-divyield * time) _
    - interest * exercise * Exp(-interest * time) _
    * Application.NormSDist(dTwo(stock, exercise, _
    time, interest, divyield, sigma))
End Function
```

```
Function ThetaPut(stock, exercise, time, interest, _
    divyield, sigma)
    ThetaPut = -stock * normaldf(dOne(stock, _
    exercise, time, interest, divyield, sigma)) _
    * sigma * Exp(-divyield * time) / _
    (2 * Sqr(time)) - divyield * _
    stock * Application.NormSDist(-dOne(stock,
    exercise, time, interest, divyield, _
    sigma)) * Exp(-divyield * time) + interest _
    * exercise * Exp(-interest * time) * _
    Application.NormSDist (-dTwo(stock, exercise, _
    time, interest, divyield, sigma))
End Function

Function RhoCall(stock, exercise, time, interest, _
    divyield, sigma)
    RhoCall = exercise * time * Exp(-interest * _
    time) * Application.NormSDist(dTwo(stock, _
    exercise, time, interest, divyield, sigma))
End Function

Function RhoPut(stock, exercise, time, interest, _
    divyield, sigma)
    RhoPut = -exercise * time * Exp(-interest * _
    time) * Application.NormSDist(-dTwo(stock, _
    exercise, time, interest, divyield, sigma))
End Function
```

The Greeks are implemented in the following spreadsheet, which shows both the brute-force calculation of each Greek and a VBA function implementation.

	A	B	C	D	E
1	**Black-Scholes Greeks** **This spreadsheet uses the Merton model for a continuously dividend-paying stock**				
2	S	100	Current stock price		
3	X	90	Exercise price		
4	T	0.5	Time to maturity of option (in years)		
5	r	6.00%	Risk-free rate of interest		
6	k	2.00%	Dividend yield		
7	Sigma	35%	Stock volatility		
8					
9	d_1	0.6303	<-- =(LN(B2/B3)+(B5-B6+0.5*B7^2)*B4)/(B7*SQRT(B4))		
10	d_2	0.3828	<-- d_1-sigma*SQRT(T)		
11					
12	N(d_1)	0.7357	<-- Uses formula NormSDist(d_1)		
13	N(d_2)	0.6491	<-- Uses formula NormSDist(d_2)		
14					
15	Call price	16.1531	<-- =B2*EXP(-B6*B4)*B12-B3*EXP(-B5*B4)*B13		
16		16.1531	<-- =bsmertoncall(B2,B3,B4,B5,B6,B7)		
17	Put price	4.4882	<-- =B3*EXP(-B5*B4)*NORMSDIST(-B10)-B2*EXP(-B6*B4)*NORMSDIST(-B9)		
18		4.4882	<-- =bsmertonput(B2,B3,B4,B5,B6,B7)		
19					
20	**Greeks: Brute force**				
21		**Call**		**Put**	
22	Delta	0.7284	<-- =EXP(-B6*B4)*NORMSDIST(B9)	-0.2616	<-- =-EXP(-B6*B4)*NORMSDIST(-B9)
23	Gamma	0.0195	<-- =EXP(B9^2/2-B6*B4)/(B2*B7*SQRT(2*B4*PI()))	0.0195	<-- =EXP((B9^2)/2-B6*B4)/(B2*B7*SQRT(2*B4*PI()))
24	Vega	22.8976	<-- =B2*SQRT(B4)*EXP(-(B9^2)/2)*EXP(-B6*B4)/SQRT(2*PI())	22.8976	<-- =B2*EXP(-(B9^2)/2-B6*B4)*SQRT(B4)/SQRT(2*PI())
25	Theta	-9.9587	<-- =-B2*EXP(-(B9^2)/2-B6*B4)*B7/SQRT(8*B4*PI())+B6*B2*EXP(-B6*B4)*B12-B5*B3*EXP(-B5*B4)*B13	-6.6984	<-- =-B2*EXP(-(B9^2)/2-B6*B4)*B7/SQRT(8*B4*PI())-B6*B2*EXP(-B6*B4)*(1-B12)+B5*B3*EXP(-B5*B4)*(1-B13)
26	Rho	28.3446	<-- =B3*B4*EXP(-B5*B4)*NORMSDIST(B10)	-15.3255	<-- =-B3*B4*EXP(-B5*B4)*NORMSDIST(-B10)
27					
28	**Greeks: VBA functions**				
29		**Call**		**Put**	
30	Delta	0.7284	<-- =deltacall(B2,B3,B4,B5,B6,B7)	-0.2616	<-- =deltaput(B2,B3,B4,B5,B6,B7)
31	Gamma	0.0195	<-- =gamma(B2,B3,B4,B5,B6,B7)	0.0195	<-- =gamma(B2,B3,B4,B5,B6,B7)
32	Vega	22.8976	<-- =vega(B2,B3,B4,B5,B6,B7)	22.8976	<-- =vega(B2,B3,B4,B5,B6,B7)
33	Theta	-9.9587	<-- =Thetacall(B2,B3,B4,B5,B6,B7)	-6.6984	<-- =Thetaput(B2,B3,B4,B5,B6,B7)
34	Rho	28.3446	<-- =rhocall(B2,B3,B4,B5,B6,B7)	-15.3255	<-- =rhoput(B2,B3,B4,B5,B6,B7)

Excel can be used to examine the sensitivities of the Greeks to various parameters. For example, Figure 20.1 shows the deltas as functions of the stock price, and Figure 20.2 shows them as functions of the moneyness of the call option.

Figure 20.3 shows the theta of a call as a function of the stock price, and Figure 20.4 shows it as a function of the time to option expiration.

20.3 Delta Hedging a Call

Delta hedging is a fundamental technique in option pricing. The idea is to replicate an option by a portfolio of stocks and bonds, with the portfolio proportions determined by the Black-Scholes formula.

Suppose we decide to replicate an at-the-money European call option that has 12 weeks to run until expiration. The stock on which the option is written has $S_0 = \$40$ and exercise price $X = \$45$, the interest rate is

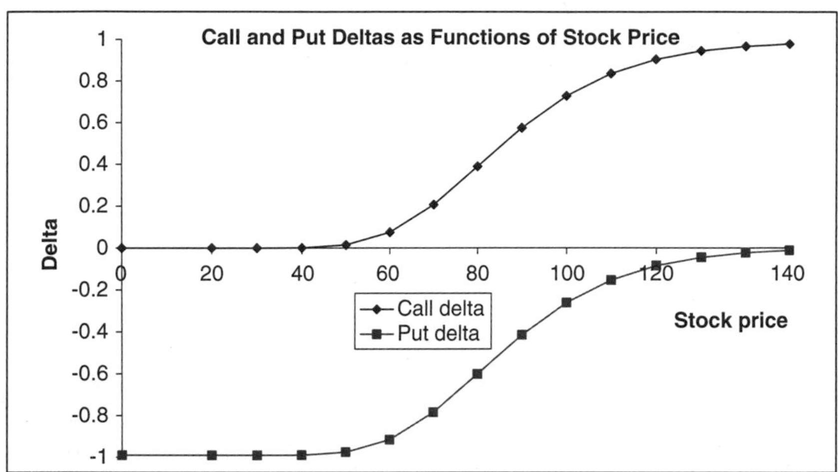

Figure 20.1
As a call or a put becomes more in-the-money, the delta tends toward +1 for a call and –1 for a put. Essentially the call or put price moves in tandem with the underlying stock price. An extremely out-of-the-money put or call has a delta equal to 0.

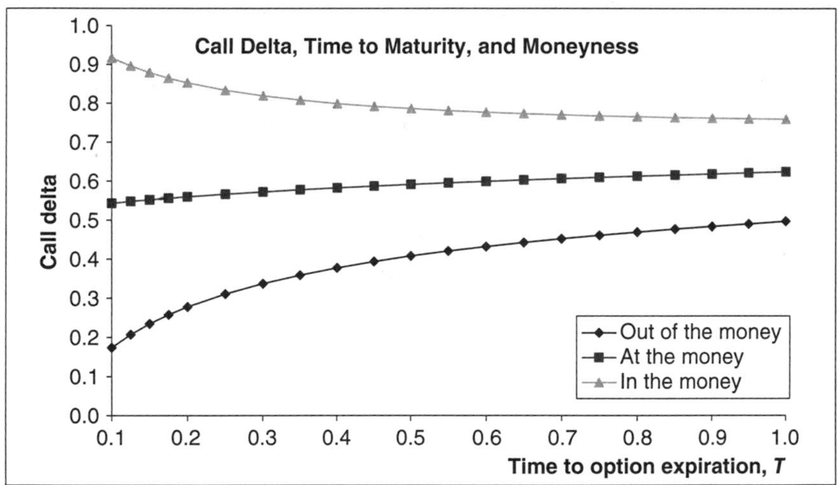

Figure 20.2
As the option's maturity T increases, the delta of an at-the-money or an out-of-the-money call increases, whereas the delta of an in-the-money call decreases.

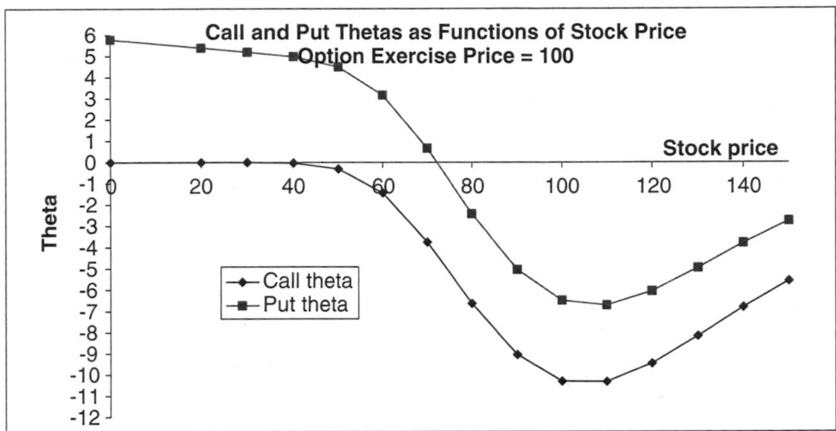

Figure 20.3
Very in-the-money puts can have a positive theta, meaning that as the time to maturity gets shorter, the put gains in value. Other than this case, options generally have a negative theta, meaning that they lose value as the time to maturity decreases.

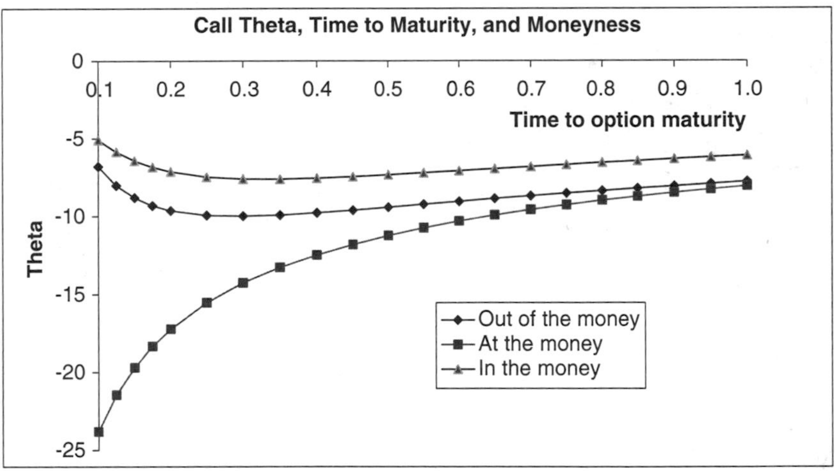

Figure 20.4
Calls always have negative theta (meaning that they lose value as the time to maturity decreases). However, the rate at which they lose value varies with the moneyness of the call.

r = 4 percent, and the stock's volatility is σ = 25 percent. The Black-Scholes price of this option is \$0.51:

	A	B	C	D	
2	S, current stock price	40.00			
3	X, exercise	45.00			
4	r, interest rate	4.00%			
5	k, dividend yield	0.00%			
6	T, expiration	0.2308	<-- =12/52		Initial
7	Sigma	25%			
8					
9	BS value	0.51	<-- =bsmertoncall(B2,B3,B6,B4,B5,B7)		

Note that we use the formula **BSMertoncall** but with the dividend yield k = 0 percent, so that this is in effect a regular BS call option.

We decide to create this option by replicating, on a week-to-week basis, the BS option-pricing formula using delta hedging.

- At the beginning, 12 weeks before the option's expiration, we determine our stock/bond portfolio according to the formula Call = $SN(d_1) - Xe^{-rT}N(d_2)$, so that we have a dollar amount $SN(d_1)$ of shares in the portfolio and have borrowing of $Xe^{-rT}N(d_2)$. Having determined the portfolio holdings at the beginning of the 12-week period, we now determine our portfolio holdings for each of the successive weeks as in the following steps.
- In each successive week we set the stock holdings in the portfolio according to the formula $SN(d_1)$, but we set the portfolio borrowing so that the *net cash flow of the portfolio* is zero. Note that $SN(d_1) = S\Delta_{Call}$, hence the name "delta hedging."
- At the end of the 12-week period, we liquidate the portfolio.

The stock and the bond positions for each of the 12 weeks are computed in the following spreadsheet:

	A	B	C	D	E	F	G	H
1				DELTA HEDGING A CALL				
2	S, current stock price	40.00						
3	X, exercise	45.00						
4	r, interest rate	4.00%						
5	k, dividend yield	0.00%						
6	T, expiration	0.2308	<-- =12/52	Initial pricing of call using BS formula				
7	Sigma	25%						
8								
9	BS value	0.51	<-- =bsmertoncall(B2,B3,B6,B4,B5,B7)					
10								
11				Hedging portfolio				
12	Weeks until expiration	Time until expiration	Stock price	Stock = <-- =C13*deltacall(C13,$B$3, B13,$B$4,0,$B$7)	Bond	Porfolio value	Portfolio cash flow	
13	12	0.2308	40.000	7.98	-7.47	0.51	0.51	
14	11	0.2115	39.615	6.51	-6.13	0.38	0.05	<-- =(D13*C14/C13-D14)+E13*EXP($B$4*(B13-B14))-E14
15	10	0.1923	40.607	8.46	-7.96	0.50	0.04	<-- =(D14*C15/C14-D15)+E14*EXP($B$4*(B14-B15))-E15
16	9	0.1731	38.963	4.00	-3.81	0.19	-0.04	<-- =(D15*C16/C15-D16)+E15*EXP($B$4*(B15-B16))-E16
17	8	0.1538	38.813	3.15	-3.02	0.14	0.04	
18	7	0.1346	40.563	6.17	-5.89	0.28	-0.01	
19	6	0.1154	41.377	7.71	-7.37	0.34	0.06	
20	5	0.0962	43.321	14.89	-14.15	0.74	-0.04	
21	4	0.0769	42.791	11.08	-10.63	0.45	0.10	
22	3	0.0577	43.509	13.53	-13.03	0.51	0.12	
23	2	0.0385	45.547	28.18	-26.95	1.23	-0.10	
24	1	0.0192	46.943	42.06	-40.00	2.06	0.01	
25	0	0.0000	47.101			2.17		<-- =D24*C25/C24+E24*EXP($B$4*(B24-B25))
26								
27	Hedged position payoff	2.17	<-- =F25					
28	Actual call payoff	2.10	<-- =MAX(C25-B3,0)					
29								
30				At initial date, the stock and bond positions are set using the Black-Scholes				
31				formula: Stock = SN(d_1), Bond = -X*exp(-rT)N(d_2).				
32								
33				At each subsequent date t, the stock position is adjusted to S_t*Δ_{call} . The bond				
34				position is adjusted so that the net cash flow of the portfolio is zero.				
35								
36				At the final date, the stock and bond portfolios are liquidated.				
37								
38								

The delta hedge would be perfect if we rebalanced our portfolio continuously. However, here we have rebalanced only weekly. Had we a perfect hedge, the portfolio would have paid off $\max[S_{\text{Terminal}} - X, 0]$ (cell B27); the actual hedge payoff (cell B28) is slightly different.

Pressing [Ctrl] + a works a macro that puts in a new set of random numbers and runs a different simulation of the stock prices:

	A	B	C	D	E	F	G
11				Hedging Portfolio			
12	Weeks until expiration	Time until expiration	Stock price	Stock = <-- =C13*deltacall(C13,$B$3, B13,$B$4,0,$B$7)	Bond	Porfolio value	Portfolio cash flow
13	12	0.2308	40.000	7.98	-7.47	0.51	0.51
14	11	0.2115	38.989	5.15	-4.87	0.28	0.01
15	10	0.1923	41.125	10.00	-9.38	0.61	-0.05
16	9	0.1731	39.905	5.98	-5.67	0.31	0.00
17	8	0.1538	40.264	6.17	-5.87	0.30	0.06
18	7	0.1346	40.158	5.14	-4.91	0.23	0.06
19	6	0.1154	42.966	14.06	-13.31	0.75	-0.17
20	5	0.0962	43.185	14.21	-13.51	0.69	0.12
21	4	0.0769	41.125	4.58	-4.43	0.15	-0.14
22	3	0.0577	40.246	1.47	-1.44	0.03	0.01
23	2	0.0385	40.765	1.02	-1.00	0.02	0.03
24	1	0.0192	40.573	0.06	-0.06	0.00	0.01
25	0	0.0000	40.709			0.00	
26							
27	Hedged position payoff	0.00	<-- =F25				
28	Actual call payoff	0.00	<-- =MAX(C25-B3,0)				

20.3.1 Simulating the Stock Prices

To simulate the stock prices we use a technique explained in Chapter 18. **Tools|Data Analysis|Random Number Generation**. We use this Excel tool to produce 12 random numbers that are distributed normally with mean equal to 0 and standard deviation equal to 1.

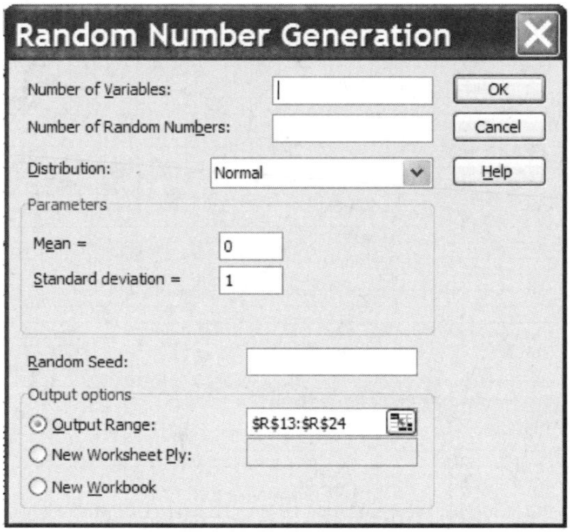

Random Number Generation

Number of Variables:

Number of Random Numbers:

Distribution: Normal

Parameters

Mean = 0

Standard deviation = 1

Random Seed:

Output options

Output Range: $R$13:$R$24

New Worksheet Ply:

New Workbook

OK

Cancel

Help

In the spreadsheet simulation of delta hedging, the random numbers appear in column R. The stock price $40 in cell C12 is the initial stock price; each subsequent stock price is computed by

$$S_{\text{Previous}} * \exp[\mu * \Delta t + \sigma * \sqrt{\Delta t} * Z]$$

where μ (in our example, 20 percent) is the stock's mean return, σ (25 percent) is the standard deviation of the stock's returns, and Z is the random number generated by our simulation.

	A	B	C	D	Q	R	S	T	U
11	Weeks until expiration	Time until expiration	Stock price			Standard normal random numbers			
12	12	0.2308	40.000						
13	11	0.2115	41.710	<-- =C12*EXP($U$13*(B12-B13)+$U$14*SQRT(B12-B13)*R13)		1.096416		mu	20%
14	10	0.1923	42.093	<-- =C13*EXP($U$13*(B13-B14)+$U$14*SQRT(B13-B14)*R14)		0.152941		sigma	25%
15	9	0.1731	43.380	<-- =C14*EXP($U$13*(B14-B15)+$U$14*SQRT(B14-B15)*R15)		0.757611			
16	8	0.1538	45.231			1.094604			
17	7	0.1346	48.050			1.632943			
18	6	0.1154	48.296			0.035924			
19	5	0.0962	47.363			-0.67341			
20	4	0.0769	47.728			0.110728			
21	3	0.0577	46.838			-0.653959			
22	2	0.0385	47.186			0.102266			
23	1	0.0192	46.586			-0.480061			
24	0	0.0000	49.257			1.497197			

By recording the keystrokes of the random number generator (see the next subsection) and making a few changes, we are able to do this simulation many times:

```
Sub run_random()
' Keyboard Shortcut: Ctrl+a
     ActiveSheet.Range("$R$13:$R$24"). _
       ClearContents
     Application.Run "ATPVBAEN.XLA!Random", _
          ActiveSheet.Range("$r$13:$r$24") _
            , , , 2, , 0, 1
End Sub
```

Note that we assigned the keystrokes [Ctrl] + a to run the macro.

20.3.2 Recording Keystrokes to Create VBA Program

We briefly review the simple technique of recording a macro in Excel. The previous spreadsheet has a column of random normal deviates in column R. These numbers, generated by **Tools|Data Analysis|Random Number Generation**, give us a series of random stock prices in column C. Each stock price S_t is defined by $S_t = S_{t-1} \exp[\mu\Delta t + \sigma\sqrt{\Delta t} Z]$, where μ and σ are given in cells T14 and T15:

	R	S	T	U
12	**Standard normal random numbers**			
13	1.385106			
14	-0.389564		mu	20%
15	0.601965		sigma	25%
16	-1.302831			
17	-0.222169			
18	1.16092			
19	0.462537			
20	1.212907			
21	-0.465775			
22	0.368848			
23	1.209403			
24	0.759856			
25	-0.014038			

To record the macro, push **Tools|Macro|Record New Macro:**

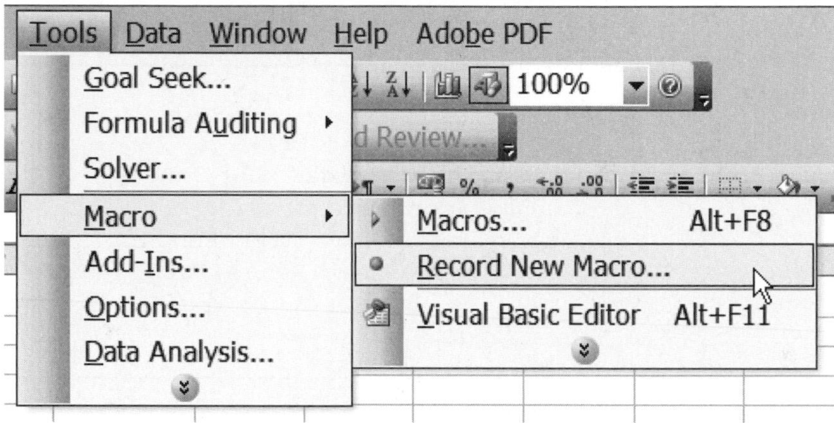

This brings up the following screen.

After pressing **OK**, a **Stop recording** button will appear on the spreadsheet:

Now push the correct buttons to create the column of random numbers, using **Tools|Data Analysis|Random Number Generation**, with the screen as indicated in the previous subsection. This procedure replaces the numbers in cells R13:R24. When you are finished, push the **Stop recording** button. Now go to the VBA editor ([Alt]+F11) and see what you've recorded:

```
Sub run_random()
'
' Sub Macro1()
'
' Macro1 Macro
' Macro recorded 4/20/2007 by Simon Benninga
'
' Keyboard Shortcut: Ctrl+a
'
    Range("R13:R24").Select
    Selection.ClearContents
     Application.Run "ATPVBAEN.XLA! _
      Random", , , , 2, , 0, 1
End Sub
```

(Note that before we ran **Tools|Data Analysis|Random Number Generation**, we actually cleared range R13:R24. This step prevents the message asking if we want to replace the data. The deletion of the range was faithfully recorded by Excel.)

This macro can be edited. Here's the way the final version appears. We have renamed the macro **run_random** and used Tools|Macro|Options to assign a shortcut key to the macro:

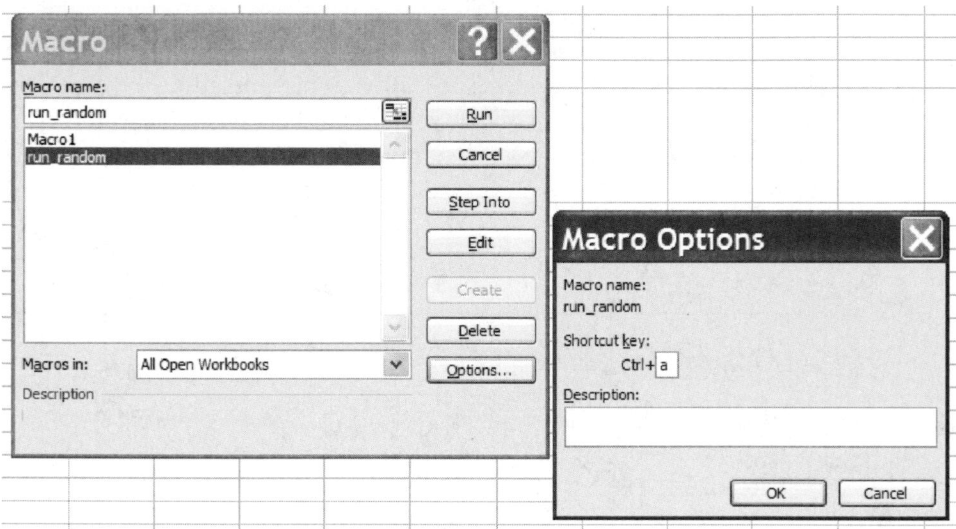

Here's the final product:

```
Sub run_random()
' Keyboard Shortcut: Ctrl+a
     ActiveSheet.Range("$R$13:$R$24").
ClearContents
     Application.Run "ATPVBAEN.XLA!Random", _
         ActiveSheet.Range("$r$13:$r$24"), , _
           , 2, , 0, 1
End Sub
```

This macro can now be run repeatedly by pressing [Ctrl] + a.

20.4 Hedging a Collar

A collar is an option strategy designed to protect the holder of a package of shares against possible price losses. The usual collar is a combination of a written call plus a purchased put, designed so that the net cost of the position is zero. Thus the collar provides costless protection to its holder. Here's an example: On January 1, 2008, a bank's client holds 5,000,000 shares of XYZ Corporation. Each share is currently worth $55. Because the stock is currently restricted, the client cannot sell the shares until one year from now. However, he is worried that the stock price will decline, and hence he desires to purchase a collar.

The client asks an investment bank to design the following package:

- He wants to buy a put on the shares with $T = 1$ year and exercise price $X_{Put} = \$49.04$.
- He wants to write a call on the shares with $T = 1$ year and exercise price $X_{Call} = \$70.00$.

The exercise prices have been set so that the Black-Scholes value of the call and the put are equal:

	A	B	C	D
1	**COLLAR: THE PURCHASER OWNS A WRITTEN CALL AND A BOUGHT PUT**			
2		**Call**	**Put**	
3	S	55.00	55.00	
4	X	70.00	49.04	
5	T	1	1	
6	r, interest	4.00%	4.00%	
7	k, dividend yield	0.00%	0.00%	
8	Sigma	40%	40%	
9				
10	BS option value	4.74	4.74	<-- =bsmertonput(C3,C4,C5,C6,C7,C8)
11				
12	Call minus put	0.00	<-- =B10-C10	
13				
14				
15				=bsmertoncall(B3,B4,B5,B6,B7,B8)

Given $X_{call} = 70$ for the call, the put exercise price was determined using **Solver**:

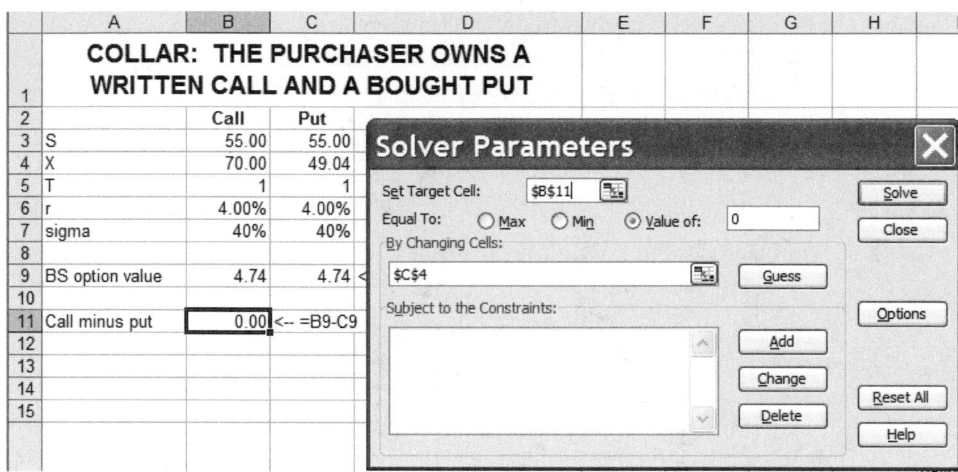

	A	B	C	D
1	COLLAR: THE PURCHASER OWNS A WRITTEN CALL AND A BOUGHT PUT			
2		Call	Put	
3	S	55.00	55.00	
4	X	70.00	49.04	
5	T	1	1	
6	r	4.00%	4.00%	
7	sigma	40%	40%	
8				
9	BS option value	4.74	4.74	<
10				
11	Call minus put	0.00	<-- =B9-C9	

The point of the collar is to give the purchaser upside potential with limited downside risk. In this example, the terminal payoffs are given by

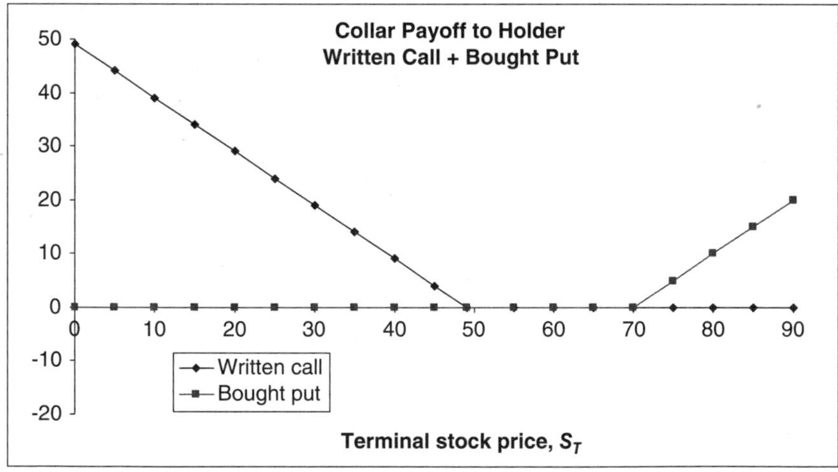

In addition to his collar, the client has a portfolio of the shares. The payoffs to the holder of the collar plus the shares are never less than $49. This is, of course, the protection that the client was seeking.

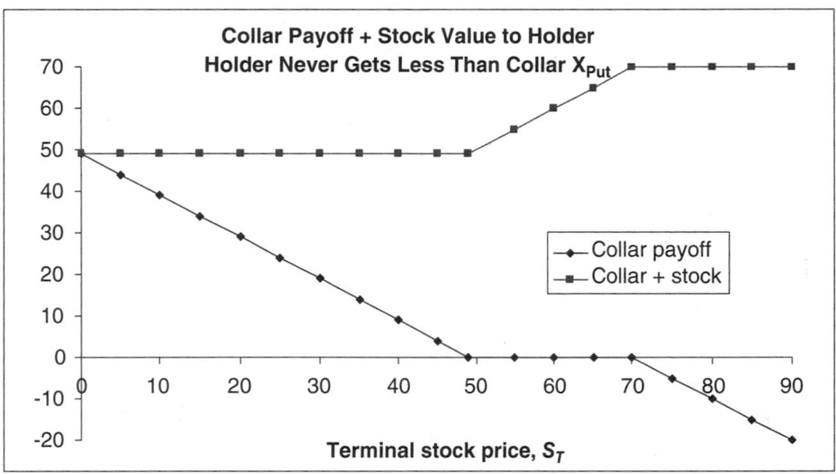

20.4.1 A Slightly Longer Story

Even though the Black-Scholes value of the collar is initially zero, actually the investment bank sold the collar to the client for \$5. There are several reasons why the client might want to pay this amount:

• Perhaps there is low liquidity in the options (this is often the case in longer-term options), so that the bank is actually supplying a valuable liquidity service.

• It might be that the options do not actually exist—either because the particular long-term options in question are not marketed or perhaps because there are no options on the particular underlying stock (this is often the case for specific portfolios). In this case the bank is actually creating the options underlying the collar by creating an appropriate portfolio of stocks and bonds and by changing the portfolio proportions over time (see next subsection). The creation and constant monitoring of this portfolio is a service worth paying for.

20.4.2 Delta Hedging the Collar: The Bank's Problem

The client for the collar is short a call and long a put. The bank wants to make a similar investment, so that it will parallel the client's portfolio and have the money to pay off the client at the maturity of his collar. In terms of the Black-Scholes formula, this situation turns out to mean that the net position of the bank is a short stock financed by a bond investment:

$$\underbrace{-[SN(d_1[X_{\text{Call}}]) - X_{\text{Call}}e^{-rT}N(d_2[X_{\text{Call}}])]}_{\substack{\uparrow \\ \text{Short call}}} \underbrace{-SN(-d_1[X_{\text{Put}}]) + X_{\text{Put}}e^{-rT}N(-d_2[X_{\text{Put}}])}_{\substack{\uparrow \\ \text{Long put}}}$$

$$= \underbrace{-S(N(d_1[X_{\text{Call}}]) + N(-d_1[X_{\text{Put}}]))}_{\substack{\uparrow \\ \text{Short stock position}}} \underbrace{+e^{-rT}[X_{\text{Call}}N(d_2[X_{\text{Call}}]) + X_{\text{Put}}N(-d_2[X_{\text{Put}}])]}_{\substack{\uparrow \\ \text{Long bond position}}}$$

We rewrite this expression in terms of Greeks:

$$\underbrace{-S[N(d_1[X_{\text{Call}}]) + N(-d_1[X_{\text{Put}}])]}_{\substack{\uparrow \\ \text{Short stock position}}} \underbrace{-e^{-rT}[X_{\text{Call}}N(d_2[X_{\text{Call}}]) + X_{\text{Put}}N(-d_2[X_{\text{Put}}])]}_{\substack{\uparrow \\ \text{Long bond position}}}$$

$$= S[-\Delta_{\text{Call}}(X_{\text{Call}}) - \Delta_{\text{Put}}(X_{\text{Put}})] + e^{-rT}[X_{\text{Call}}N(d_2[X_{\text{Call}}]) + X_{\text{Put}}N(-d_2[X_{\text{Put}}])]$$

Here's a run of a simulated position over the course of a year. In this simulation the position is updated every $\Delta t = 0.05$; assuming 250 trading days in a year, this is approximately every 12 days.

	A	B	C	D	E	F	G
1			**DELTA HEDGING A COLLAR**				
2	S	55.00					
3	X_{Call}	70.00					
4	X_{Put}	49.04					
5	r	4.00%					
6	Sigma	40%					
7							
8	**Time until expiration**	**Stock price**	**Stock =-B9*(calldelta(B9,$B$3,A9,$B$5,$B$6)-putdelta(B9,$B$4,A9,$B$5,$B$6))**	**Bond**	**Porfolio value**	**Portfolio cash flow**	
9	1.00	55.00	-36.28	36.28	0.00	0.00	
10	0.95	53.57	-34.75	35.77	1.02	0.00	<-- =(C9*B10/B9-C10)-(D10-D9*EXP($B$5*(A9-A10)))
11	0.90	52.39	-33.49	35.34	1.85	0.00	<-- =(C10*B11/B10-C11)-(D11-D10*EXP($B$5*(A10-A11)))
12	0.85	48.07	-30.81	35.49	4.68	0.00	<-- =(C11*B12/B11-C12)-(D12-D11*EXP($B$5*(A11-A12)))
13	0.80	49.46	-30.98	34.84	3.86	0.00	
14	0.75	50.33	-30.86	34.25	3.39	0.00	
15	0.70	50.54	-30.40	33.73	3.33	0.00	
16	0.65	58.10	-34.27	33.12	-1.15	0.00	
17	0.60	55.71	-31.57	31.90	0.32	0.00	
18	0.55	67.93	-43.58	37.04	-6.54	0.00	
19	0.50	66.69	-40.90	35.23	-5.67	0.00	
20	0.45	73.10	-50.24	40.71	-9.53	0.00	
21	0.40	78.79	-60.20	46.84	-13.36	0.00	
22	0.35	72.21	-47.38	39.15	-8.23	0.00	
23	0.30	77.20	-57.29	45.86	-11.43	0.00	
24	0.25	73.30	-48.65	40.20	-8.45	0.00	
25	0.20	85.78	-77.08	60.44	-16.65	0.00	
26	0.15	80.97	-69.22	57.01	-12.20	0.00	
27	0.10	82.00	-74.69	61.72	-12.97	0.00	
28	0.05	99.59	-99.59	70.72	-28.87	0.00	<-- =(C27*B28/B27-C28)-(D28-D27*EXP($B$5*(A27-A28)))
29	0.00	89.31			-18.44	<-- =C28*B29/B28+D28*EXP($B$5*(A28-A29))	
30							
31	**Check: Collar payoff to client at time 0**						
32	Short call payoff	-19.31	<-- =-MAX(B29-B3,0)				
33	Long put payoff	0.00	<-- =MAX(B4-B29,0)				
34	Total	-19.31	<-- =SUM(B32:B33)				
35							
36	**Payoff to bank from delta hedge**						
37		-18.44	<-- =E29				
38							
39	**Terminal cash flow to bank**	0.86	<-- =-B34+B37				

Here's what happens in this spreadsheet:

• The initial (row 9) stock and bond positions are determined by the Black-Scholes formula. The stock position is $-S[\Delta_{Call}(X_{Call}) - \Delta_{Put}(X_{Put})]$, and the bond position is $e^{-rT}[X_{Call}N(d_2[X_{Call}]) + X_{Put}N(-d_2[X_{Put}])]$. Not surprisingly, the net value of this portfolio is zero—this is the way we determined the collar X_{Call} and X_{Put}.

• In each of the subsequent rows, the stock position is determined by the Black-Scholes formula, and the bond position is determined so that the net cash flow of the position is zero:

$$\text{Bonds} = \underbrace{\text{Stock\_position}_{t-1} * \frac{\text{Stock\_price}_t}{\text{Stock\_price}_{t-1}} - \underbrace{\text{Stock\_position}_t}_{\substack{\uparrow \\ \text{Determined by} \\ \text{Black-Scholes}}}}_{\substack{\uparrow \\ \text{Cash flow into stocks}}} + \underbrace{\text{Bond\_position}_{t-1} * \exp(r * \Delta t)}_{\substack{\uparrow \\ \text{Value today of } t-1 \text{ bond position}}}$$

• At the terminal date (row 29), the portfolio is liquidated:

$$\text{Stock\_position}_{\text{Terminal}} = \text{Stock\_position}_{\text{Previous}} * \frac{\text{Stock\_price}_{\text{Terminal}}}{\text{Stock\_price}_{\text{Previous}}} + \text{Bond\_position}_{\text{Previous}} * \exp(r * \Delta t)$$

• At the terminal date, the purchaser of the collar collects on his short position in the call and his long position in the put (cell B34). The bank collects its position value (cell E29 or B37). The bank's net cash flow on termination is the difference between these two (cell B39). To understand this last cell, consider that the client's collar payoff is the bank's income: In the particular example shown here, the client has a negative cash flow of $19.31, which he pays to the bank. The bank's position shows a negative payoff of $18.44, so that the bank makes $0.86 on the collar.[2]

Here's another run of this same simulation. This time the client's put pays off and the bank has to cover the loss.

2. Of course, if the hedge were adjusted continuously, it would be perfect. This is the essence of the proof of the Black-Scholes theorem (for details, see Jarrow and Rudd, *Option Pricing*, Irwin, 1983, Chapter 8).

	A	B	C	D	E	F	G
1	**The Collar Gamma** **Press [Ctrl]+q to run simulation**						
2	S	55.00					
3	X_{call}	70.00					
4	X_{put}	49.04					
5	r	4.00%					
6	k, dividend yield	0.00%					
7	Sigma	40%					
8							
9	**Time until expiration**	**Stock price**	**Stock =-B10*(deltacall(B10,$B$3,A10,$B$5,$B$6,$B$7)-deltaput(B10,$B$4,A10,$B$5,$B$6,$B$7))**	**Bond**	**Porfolio value**		**Porfolio cash flow**
10	1.00	55.00	-36.28	36.28	0.00		0.00
11	0.95	49.33	-32.15	35.97	3.81		0.00
12	0.90	53.08	-33.93	35.37	1.44		0.00
13	0.85	56.16	-35.60	35.15	-0.46		0.00
14	0.80	56.82	-35.50	34.70	-0.81		0.00
15	0.75	55.68	-33.95	33.93	-0.02		0.00
16	0.70	64.54	-41.65	36.29	-5.36		0.00
17	0.65	60.82	-36.78	33.89	-2.89		0.00
18	0.60	62.63	-37.77	33.86	-3.91		0.00
19	0.55	68.04	-43.74	36.63	-7.11		0.00
20	0.50	79.78	-61.96	47.38	-14.58		0.00
21	0.45	81.13	-64.30	48.77	-15.53		0.00
22	0.40	93.35	-85.04	59.92	-25.12		0.00
23	0.35	107.30	-104.78	67.07	-37.71		0.00
24	0.30	97.33	-92.75	64.91	-27.84		0.00
25	0.25	92.03	-86.14	63.48	-22.66		0.00
26	0.20	95.90	-93.11	66.96	-26.15		0.00
27	0.15	91.52	-88.56	66.79	-21.77		0.00
28	0.10	78.27	-65.43	56.62	-8.81		0.00
29	0.05	83.46	-81.71	68.67	-13.04		0.00
30	0.00	80.42					-9.92
31							
32	**Check: Collar payoff to client at time 0**						
33	Call	-10.42	<-- =-MAX(B30-B3,0)				
34	Put	0.00	<-- =MAX(B4-B30,0)				
35	Total	-10.42	<-- =SUM(B33:B34)				
36							
37	**Payoff to bank from delta hedge**						
38		-9.92	<-- =G30				
39							
40	**Terminal cash flow to bank**	0.50	<-- =-B35+B38				

20.4.3 Making the Collar Gamma Neutral

As the option gets closer to expiration, the hedge position can become extremely sensitive to small changes in the stock price, meaning that the gamma of the collar can grow enormously. In the following example, the gamma explodes toward the end of the hedging period:

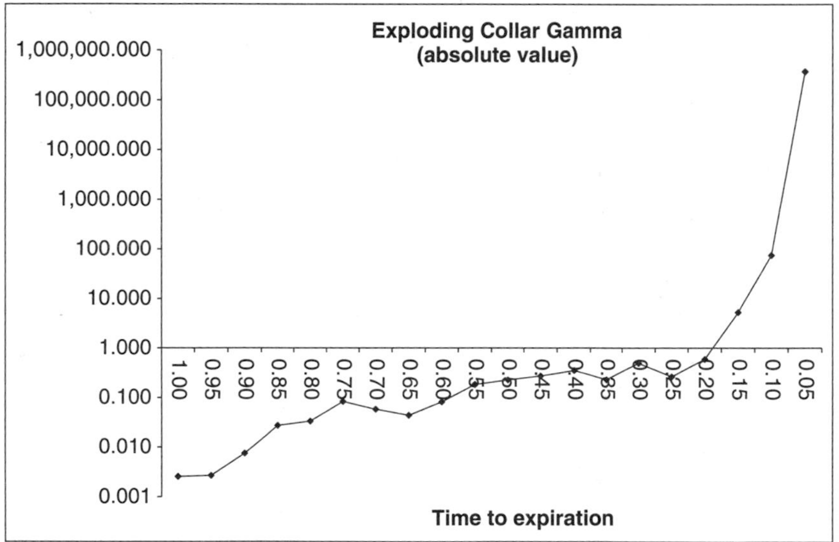

This need not always be the case—here's another simulation of the price path without an exploding gamma:

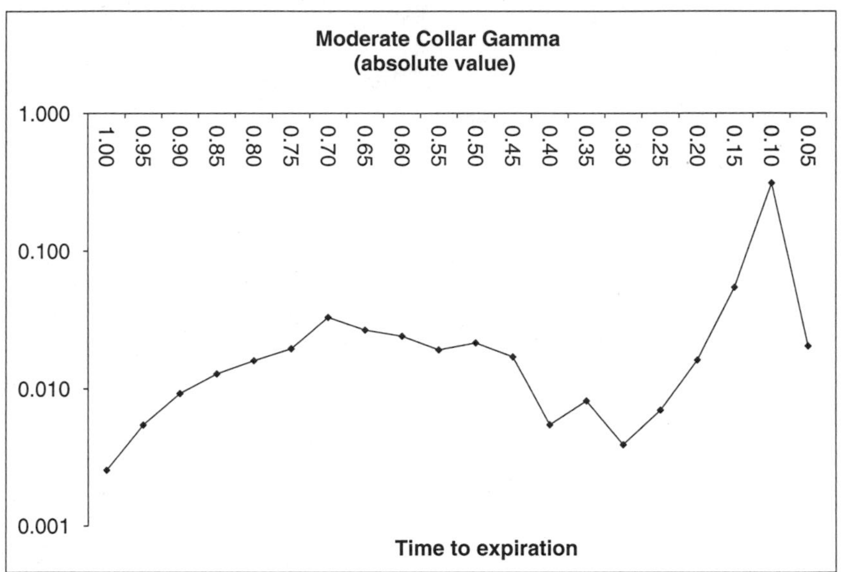

There are two solutions to this problem:

• We could (should?) increase our hedging frequency as we get closer to the collar expiration date.

• We could (should?) change our hedge strategy in order to temper the hedge gamma, as we get closer to the option maturity.

We explore both solutions in the following subsections.

20.4.4 Increasing the Hedge Frequency

The main problem of the hedge seems to be for the last 10–15 percent of the expiration period. Since the initial options have maturity $T = 1$, we have to be very careful during the one or two months of the hedging period. Delta hedging the position more often may work, though it is easy to come up with counterexamples:

	A	B	C	D	E	F
1	**MODERATING THE COLLAR GAMMA This example starts with T = 0.20 and hedges every Delta_t = 0.01**					
2	S	55.00				
3	X_{Call}	70.00				
4	X_{Put}	49.04				
5	r	4.00%				
6	k, dividend yield	2.00%				
7	Sigma	40%				
8						
9	**Time until expiration**	**Stock price**	**Stock =-B10*(deltacall(B10,$B$3,A10,$B$5,$B$6,$B$7)-deltaput(B10,$B$4,A10,$B$5,$B$6,$B$7))**	**Bond**	**Porfolio value**	**Portfolio cash flow**
10	0.20	55.00	-18.29	18.29	0.00	0.00
11	0.19	53.62	-18.43	18.90	0.47	0.00
12	0.18	54.12	-17.55	17.85	0.30	0.00
13	0.17	54.65	-16.60	16.74	0.14	0.00
14	0.16	50.15	-21.44	22.96	1.51	0.00
15	0.15	51.18	-19.49	20.58	1.08	0.00
16	0.14	50.05	-21.20	22.72	1.52	0.00
17	0.13	51.20	-18.76	19.80	1.04	0.00
18	0.12	50.71	-19.42	20.65	1.23	0.00
19	0.11	48.61	-24.11	26.15	2.04	0.00
20	0.10	50.83	-18.55	19.49	0.95	0.00
21	0.09	47.75	-26.65	28.73	2.08	0.00
22	0.08	44.94	-34.04	37.70	3.66	0.00
23	0.07	45.97	-32.46	35.36	2.90	0.00
24	0.06	41.06	-39.37	45.75	6.38	0.00
25	0.05	40.60	-39.75	46.59	6.84	0.00
26	0.04	38.35	-38.27	47.33	9.06	0.00
27	0.03	36.60	-36.58	47.40	10.82	0.00
28	0.02	36.28	-36.27	47.43	11.16	0.00
29	0.01	35.73	-35.72	47.45	11.73	0.00
30	0.00	36.36			11.11	<-- =C29*I
31						
32	**Check: Collar payoff to client at time 0**					
33	Short call payoff	0.00	<-- =-MAX(B30-B3,0)			
34	Long put payoff	12.68	<-- =MAX(B4-B30,0)			
35	Total	12.68	<-- =SUM(B33:B34)			
36						
37	**Payoff to bank from delta hedge**					
38		11.11	<-- =E30			
39						
40	**Terminal cash flow to bank**	-1.56	<-- =-B35+B38			

Repeated simulation of this hedge shows that it works quite well.

20.4.5 Making the Hedge Gamma Neutral

Another strategy is to add another asset to the hedge position, in an effort to neutralize the Gamma. In this example we have added an out-of-the-money put to the position to neutralize the large call gamma:

	A	B	C	D	E
1	**COLLAR HEDGE: DELTA AND GAMMA in this example we costlessly neutralize a large call gamma**				
2		**Call**	**Put**	**Another put**	
3	S	48.00	48.00	48.00	
4	X	70.00	49.04	35.00	
5	r	5.00%	5.00%	5.00%	
6	k, dividend yiel	0.00%	0.00%	0.00%	
7	T	0.0200	0.0200	0.0200	
8	Sigma	40.00%	40.00%	40.00%	
9					
10	Option prices	0.00	1.66	0.00	
11					
12	Delta	0.0000	-0.6304	0.0000	<-- =deltaput(D3,D4,D7,D5,D6,D8)
13	Gamma	494,472,087	0	1,118,872	<-- =gamma(D3,D4,D7,D5,D6,D8)
14					
15					
16	**Bank position: short call with X = 70.00 + long put with X = 49.04 + put with X = 35.00**				
17	Call, X = 70.00	-1			
18	Put, X = 49.04	1			
19	Put, X = 35.00	441.938			
20					
21	Position delta	-0.6304	<-- {=SUMPRODUCT(TRANSPOSE(B17:B19),B12:D12)}		
22	Position gamma	0.1553	<-- {=SUMPRODUCT(TRANSPOSE(B17:B19),B13:D13)}		
23					
24	Position cost				
25	Without second put	1.6604	<-- =B17*B10+B18*C10		
26	With second put	1.6604	<-- =B17*B10+B18*C10+B19*D10		
27					
28	Traditional collar delta	-0.6304	<-- =-B12+C12		

This strategy can be carried out at very little cost, since the put in question is almost costless (cell D10). Of course, it may not always be possible to neutralize the gamma costlessly. In this case we would have to make some compromises.

20.5 Summary

In this chapter we have explored the sensitivities of the option-pricing formula to its various parameters. Using these Greeks, we have delved into the intricacies of delta hedging, a useful technique for replicating an option position with a combination of stocks and bonds. The interested reader should know that there is much more that can be said about this topic. Good starting places for further reading are Hull (2006) and Taleb (1997). An extensive collection of option-pricing formulas including Greeks can be found in Haug (2006).

Exercises

1. Produce a graph similar to Figure 20.2 for puts.
2. Figure 20.3 shows the call theta as a function of time to maturity. Produce a similar graph for puts.
3. Although θ is generally negative, there are cases (typically of high interest rates) where it can be positive:

    - An in-the-money put with a high interest rate
    - An in-the-money call on a currency that has a high interest rate (or—equivalently—an in-the-money call on a stock with a very high dividend payout rate).

    Find two examples.

21 Portfolio Insurance

21.1 Overview

Options can be used to guarantee minimum returns from stock investments. As we showed in our discussion of option strategies in Chapter 16, when you purchase a stock (or a portfolio of stocks) and simultaneously purchase a put on the stock (on the portfolio), you are assured that the dollar return from the purchase will never be lower than the exercise price on the put. However, it is not always possible to find marketed puts on all portfolios; in this case the Black-Scholes option-pricing formula can show us how to *replicate* a put by a dynamic strategy in which the investment in a risky asset (be it a single stock or a portfolio) and the investment in riskless bonds changes over time to mimic the returns of a put option. Such *replication strategies* are at the heart of the portfolio insurance strategies discussed here.

We start by considering the following simple example: You decide to invest in one share of General Pills stock, which currently costs \$56. The stock pays no dividends. You hope for a large capital gain at the end of the year, but you worry that the stock's price may decline. To guard against a decline in the stock's price, you decide to purchase a European put on the stock. The put you purchase allows you to sell the stock at the end of one year for \$50. The cost of the put, \$2.38, is derived from the Black-Scholes model (see Chapter 19) using the following data: $S_0 =$ \$56, $X =$ \$50, $\sigma = 30$ percent, and $r = 8$ percent:

	A	B	C
1	**Black-Scholes Option-Pricing Formula Applied to General Pills Put**		
2	S	56	Stock price
3	X	50	Exercise price
4	T	1	Time remaining
5	r	8.00%	Risk-free rate of interest
6	Sigma	30%	Stock volatility
7			
8	d_1	0.7944	<-- (LN(S/X)+(r+0.5*sigma^2)*T)/(sigma*SQRT(T))
9	d_2	0.4944	<-- d_1-Sigma*SQRT(T)
10			
11	N(d_1)	0.7865	<-- Uses formula NormSDist(d_1)
12	N(d_2)	0.6895	<-- Uses formula NormSDist(d_2)
13			
14	Call price	12.22	<-- S*N(d_1)-X*exp(-r*T)*N(d_2)
15	Put price	2.38	<-- call price - S + X*Exp(-r*T): by Put-Call parity

This *protective put* or *portfolio insurance* strategy guarantees that you will lose no more than \$6 on your share of General Pills stock. If the stock's price at the end of the year is more than \$50, you will simply let the put expire without exercising it. However, if the stock's price at the end of the year is less than \$50, you will exercise the put and collect \$50. It is as if you had purchased an insurance policy on the stock with a \$6 deductible.

Of course this protection doesn't come for free: Instead of investing \$56 in your single share of stock, you have invested \$58.38. You could have deposited the additional \$2.38 in the bank and earned interest of 8 percent $*$ \$2.38 = \$0.19 in the course of the year; alternatively, you could have used the \$2.38 to buy more shares.

21.2 Portfolio Insurance on More Complicated Assets

In the example, we have implemented a portfolio insurance strategy by purchasing a put whose underlying asset exactly corresponds to our share portfolio. But this technique may not always be possible:

- It could be that there is no traded put option on the shares we wish to insure.
- It could also happen that we want to purchase portfolio insurance on a more complicated basket of assets, such as a portfolio of shares. Puts on portfolios do exist (for example, there are traded puts on the S&P 100 and S&P 500 portfolios), but there are no traded puts on most portfolios.

It is here that the Black-Scholes option-pricing model comes to our aid. From this formula it follows that a put option on a stock (from here on, "stock" will be used to refer to a portfolio of stocks as well as a single stock) is simply a portfolio consisting of a short position in the stock and a long position in the risk-free asset, with both positions being adjusted continuously. For example, consider the Black-Scholes formula for a put with expiration date $T = 1$ and exercise price X. At time t, $0 \le t < 1$, the put has value

$$P_t = -S_t N(-d_1) + Xe^{-r(1-t)} N(-d_2)$$

where

$$d_1 = \frac{\ln\left(S_t/X\right) + (r + \sigma^2/2)(1-t)}{\sigma\sqrt{1-t}}, \quad d_2 = d_1 - \sigma\sqrt{1-t}$$

where $1 - t$ is time remaining to maturity and S_t is the price of the stock at time t.

Thus buying a put is equivalent to investing $Xe^{-r(1-t)}N(-d_2)$ in a risk-free bond that matures at time 1 and investing $-S_tN(-d_1)$ in the stock. Since the investment in the stock is negative, a put is equivalent to a short position in the stock and a long position in the risk-free asset.

The total investment required to buy one share of the stock plus a put on the stock is $S_t + P_t$. Writing this out and substituting in the Black-Scholes put formula gives

$$\begin{aligned}\text{Total investment, protective put} &= S_t + P_t \\ &= S_t - S_tN(-d_1) + Xe^{-r(1-t)}N(-d_2) \\ &= S_t[1 - N(-d_1)] + Xe^{-r(1-t)}N(-d_2) \\ &= S_tN(d_1) + Xe^{-r(1-t)}N(-d_2)\end{aligned}$$

where the last equality uses the fact that for the standard normal distribution $N(x) + N(-x) = 1$. An even more useful way of looking at this problem is to regard the total investment $S_t + P_t$ at time t as a portfolio of a stock and a bond; we can then ask what is the proportion ω_t of this portfolio invested in the stock at time t. Rewriting the preceding formula in terms of portfolio proportions gives

$$\begin{aligned}\text{Proportion invested in stock} &= \omega_t \\ &= \frac{S_tN(d_1)}{S_tN(d_1) + Xe^{-r(1-t)}N(-d_2)}\end{aligned}$$

$$\begin{aligned}\text{Proportion invested in risk-free asset} &= 1 - \omega_t \\ &= \frac{Xe^{-r(1-t)}N(-d_2)}{S_tN(d_1) + Xe^{-r(1-t)}N(-d_2)}\end{aligned}$$

In summary, if you want to buy a specific portfolio of assets *and* an insurance policy guaranteeing that at $t = 1$ your total investment will not be worth less than X, then at each point in time, t, you should invest a proportion ω_t of your wealth in the specific portfolio you have chosen, and a proportion $1 - \omega_t$ in riskless, pure-discount bonds that mature at

$t = 1$. The Black-Scholes put-pricing formula can be used to determine these proportions.

21.3 An Example

Suppose you decide to invest \$1,000 in General Pills (GP) stock (currently selling at \$56) and in protective puts on the shares with an exercise price of \$50 and an expiration date one year from now. This method insures that your dollar value per share at the end of one year will be no less than \$50. Suppose that there is no traded put on GP, so that you will have to create your own put by investing in the share and in riskless discount bonds. The riskless rate of interest is 8 percent, and the standard deviation of GP's log return is 30 percent. We will construct a series of portfolios that implements this strategy on a week-by-week basis.[1]

21.3.1 Week 0

At the beginning of week 0, the initial investment in shares of GP should be

$$\omega_0 = \frac{S_0 N(d_1)}{S_0 + P_0} = \frac{56 * 0.7865}{56 + 2.38} = 75.45 \text{ percent}$$

with the remaining proportion, $1 - \omega_0 = 24.55$ percent, invested in riskless discount bonds maturing in one year. If traded European puts on GP existed and if these puts had an exercise price of 50 with an exercise date one year from now, these would be trading at \$2.38. Your strategy would consist of buying 17.13 shares of GP (cost = \$959.23) and 17.13 puts (cost = \$40.77). Buying \$754.40 of shares and \$245.60 of bonds exactly duplicates the initial investment in 17.13 shares and 17.13 puts. This equivalence is guaranteed by Black and Scholes. The calculations of the option price and the appropriate portfolio proportions are shown in the following spreadsheet picture:

1. There's an implicit contradiction here between the finite updating strategy and the continuous rebalancing that underlies the Black-Scholes model. This is discussed at the end of this section.

	A	B	C
1	**Black-Scholes Option-Pricing Formula Applied to General Pills Put**		
2	S	56	Stock price
3	X	50	Exercise price
4	T	1	Time remaining
5	r	8.00%	Risk-free rate of interest
6	Sigma	30%	Stock volatility
7			
8	d_1	0.7944	<-- (LN(S/X)+(r+0.5*sigma^2)*T)/(sigma*SQRT(T))
9	d_2	0.4944	<-- d_1-Sigma*SQRT(T)
10			
11	N(d_1)	0.7865	<-- Uses formula NormSDist(d_1)
12	N(d_2)	0.6895	<-- Uses formula NormSDist(d_2)
13			
14	Call price	12.22	<-- S*N(d_1)-X*exp(-r*T)*N(d_2)
15	Put price	2.38	<-- call price - S + X*Exp(-r*T): by Put-Call parity
16			
17	**Calculating the portfolio insurance proportions**		
18	Omega	75.45%	<-- =B2*B11/(B2+B15), proportion in shares
19	1-omega	24.55%	<-- =1-B18, proportion in bonds

We now turn to the end of week 0. You started at $t = 0$ with an initial investment of $1,000; now suppose that by the end of the first week the price of GP shares had increased to $60. Then your portfolio value at the beginning and end of the first week would look like this:

						Portfolio value, beginning of week				Portfolio value, end of week		
Week	Stock price at begin. of week	Stock price at end of week	d_1, beginning of week	Omega, beginning of week		Stocks	Bonds	Portfolio value		Stocks	Bonds	Portfolio value
0	56.00	60.00	0.7944	0.7545		754.50	245.50	1000.00		808.39	245.88	1054.27

Note that the value of your bonds at the end of the week is known in advance; this value grows by a factor of $1.00154 = e^{(1/52)0.08}$ per week.[2] The

2. Throughout we assume that the interest rate does not change. As an approximation to reality, this assumption is acceptable in this situation (meaning that the effect of interest rate changes is much smaller than the effect of changes in the stock price). If we wished to account for interest-rate changes, then this would add another source of uncertainty to the model.

value of your shares, however, depends on the rate of growth in the price of GP stock. During week 0, this rate of growth was 60/56 = 1.0714.

21.3.2 Week 1

At the beginning of week 1 you rebalance your portfolio, increasing the proportion of equity and decreasing the amount invested in the bonds. The new portfolio proportions reflect the time to maturity (time after one week is $t = 1/52 = 0.0192$), the stock price at the beginning of the week ($60), and the total portfolio value at the beginning of the week ($1,054.27). As the next spreadsheet picture shows, you should now *rebalance* your portfolio, investing

$$\omega_{0.0192} = \frac{SN(d_1)}{S+P} = \frac{60*0.8476}{60+1.63} = 82.53 \text{ percent}$$

in shares of GP and the remainder, 17.47 percent in bonds. Here $1.63 is the Black-Scholes cost of a European put, calculated with the correct parameters:

	A	B	C
1	**Black-Scholes Option-Pricing Formula Applied to General Pills Put**		
2	S	60	Stock price
3	X	50	Exercise price
4	T	0.9808	<-- =1-1/52 , time remaining
5	r	8.00%	Risk-free rate of interest
6	Sigma	30%	Stock volatility
7			
8	d_1	1.0263	<-- (LN(S/X)+(r+0.5*sigma^2)*T)/(sigma*SQRT(T))
9	d_2	0.7292	<-- d_1-Sigma*SQRT(T)
10			
11	$N(d_1)$	0.8476	<-- Uses formula NormSDist(d_1)
12	$N(d_2)$	0.7671	<-- Uses formula NormSDist(d_2)
13			
14	Call price	15.40	<-- S*$N(d_1)$-X*exp(-r*T)*$N(d_2)$
15	Put price	1.63	<-- call price - S + X*Exp(-r*T): by Put-Call parity
16			
17	**Calculating the portfolio insurance proportions**		
18	Omega	82.53%	<-- =B2*B11/(B2+B15), proportion in shares
19	1-omega	17.47%	<-- =1-B18, proportion in bonds

Suppose that at the end of week 1, the price of a share of GP tumbled to 52. Your position now would look like this:

						Portfolio value, beginning of week				Portfolio value, end of week		
Week	Stock price at begin. of week	Stock price at end of week	d_1, beginning of week	Omega, beginning of week		Stocks	Bonds	Portfolio value		Stocks	Bonds	Portfolio value
0	56.00	60.00	0.7944	0.7545		754.50	245.50	1000.00		808.39	245.88	1054.27
1	60.00	52.00	1.0263	0.8253		870.06	184.22	1054.27		754.05	184.50	938.55

21.3.3 Week 2

Since another week has passed, the proportion of your investment in GP should now be

$$\omega_{0.0385} = \frac{S * N(d_1)}{S+P} = \frac{52 * 0.7061}{52+3.33} = 66.35 \text{ percent}$$

This gives

						Portfolio value, beginning of week				Portfolio value, end of week		
Week	Stock price at begin. of week	Stock price at end of week	d_1, beginning of week	Omega, beginning of week		Stocks	Bonds	Portfolio value		Stocks	Bonds	Portfolio value
0	56.00	60.00	0.7944	0.7545		754.50	245.50	1000.00		808.39	245.88	1054.27
1	60.00	52.00	1.0263	0.8253		870.06	184.22	1054.27		754.05	184.50	938.55
2	52.00	???	0.5419	0.6635		622.73	315.82	938.55		???	316.30	???

The uncertainty will be resolved only when we know the value of the shares at the end of the week.

Of course this example is somewhat misleading because the Black-Scholes model assumes that portfolio proportions are continuously adjusted, whereas we have waited a whole week to readjust our proportions. In the background lurks a pious hope that finite (but short) adjustment intervals will approximate the Black-Scholes continuous-readjustment scheme. (Since we are only human, we can't in fact make continuous adjustments to our portfolio. Moreover, since readjustment of the portfolio involves transaction costs to the investor, only finite adjustment is possible.)

21.4 Some Properties of Portfolio Insurance

The preceding example illustrates some of the typical properties of portfolio insurance. Three important properties are the following:

PROPERTY 1 When the stock price is above the exercise price X, then the proportion ω invested in the risky asset is greater than 50 percent.

Proof The proof of this property requires a little manipulation of our formula for ω. Rewrite ω as

$$\omega=\frac{SN(d_1)}{SN(d_1)+Xe^{-r(1-t)}N(-d_2)}=\frac{1}{1+\dfrac{Xe^{-r(1-t)}N(-d_2)}{SN(d_1)}}$$

We will show that when $S \geq X$, the denominator of ω is < 2, which will prove the proposition: First note that when $S \geq X$, $X/S \leq 1$. Next note that $e^{-r(1-t)} < 1$ for all $0 \leq t \leq 1$. Finally, examine the expression

$$\frac{N(-d_2)}{N(d_1)}=\frac{N(\sigma\sqrt{1-t}-d_1)}{N(d_1)}=\frac{N(0.5\sigma\sqrt{1-t}-[\ln(S/X)+r(1-t)]/\sigma(1-t))}{N(0.5\sigma\sqrt{1-t}+[\ln(S/X)+r(1-t)]/\sigma(1-t))}<1$$

This proves the property.

PROPERTY 2 When the stock's price increases, the proportion ω invested in the stock increases and vice versa.

Proof To see this property, it is enough to see that when S increases, the value of the put decreases and $N(-d_1)$ decreases. Rewrite the original definition of ω as

$$\omega=\frac{S[1-N(-d_1)]}{S+P}=\frac{[1-N(-d_1)]}{1+P/S}$$

Thus, when S increases, the denominator of ω decreases and the numerator increases, which proves Property 2.

PROPERTY 3 As $t \to 1$, one of two things happens: If $S_t > X$, then $\omega_t \to 1$. If $S_t < X$, then $\omega_t \to 0$.

Proof To see this property, note that when $S_t > X$ and $t \to 1$, $N(d_1) \to 1$ and $N(-d_1) \to 0$; thus for this case $\omega_t \to 1$. Conversely, when $S_t < X$ and

$t \to 1$, $N(d_1) \to 0$ and $N(-d_1) \to 1$ and thus $\omega_t \to 0$. (Strictly speaking these statements are only true as "probability limits"—see Billingsley, 1968. What about the case when, as $t \to 1$, $S_t/X \to 1$? In this case $\omega_t \to$ $^1/_2$. However, the probability of this occurring is zero.)

21.5 What Do Portfolio Insurance Strategies Look Like? A Simulation

What do portfolio insurance strategies look like? In this section we consider this question by simulating such a strategy. Throughout we assume that the interest rate is constant and that the stock price is lognormally distributed. Here is a sample from the output of a simulation:

	A	B	C	D	E	F	G	H	I	J	K	L	M	N	O
8							Portfolio value, beginning of week				Portfolio value, end of week				
9	Week	Stock price at begin. of week	Stock price at end of week	d_1, beginning of week	Omega, beginning of week		Stocks	Bonds	Portfolio value		Stocks	Bonds	Portfolio value		Standard normal deviates
10	0	56.00	53.61	0.7944	0.7545		754.50	245.50	1000.00		722.24	245.88	968.12		-1.119738
11	1	53.61	50.96	0.6470	0.7029		680.53	287.58	968.12		646.97	288.02	935.00		-1.2849841
12	2	50.96	50.51	0.4734	0.6364		595.04	339.96	935.00		589.75	340.48	930.23		-0.2841057
13	3	50.51	47.70	0.4392	0.6232		579.68	350.55	930.23		547.40	351.09	898.48		-1.4467969
14	4	47.70	47.68	0.2366	0.5394		484.61	413.87	898.48		484.45	414.51	898.96		-0.0774548
15	5	47.68	45.33	0.2295	0.5370		482.71	416.25	898.96		458.87	416.89	875.77		-1.2863848
16	6	45.33	46.71	0.0440	0.4588		401.77	474.00	875.77		414.00	474.73	888.73		0.65187578
17	7	46.71	48.31	0.1434	0.5016		445.83	442.90	888.73		461.15	443.59	904.73		0.7427127
18	8	48.31	49.11	0.2587	0.5512		498.68	406.06	904.73		506.97	406.68	913.65		0.32723278
19	9	49.11	48.02	0.3134	0.5747		525.10	388.56	913.65		513.39	389.15	902.54		-0.6115295
20	10	48.02	45.45	0.2245	0.5380		485.59	416.95	902.54		459.59	417.60	877.19		-1.3919225
21	11	45.45	47.19	0.0117	0.4486		393.51	483.68	877.19		408.57	484.42	892.99		0.83319264
22	12	47.19	47.85	0.1454	0.5059		451.73	441.26	892.99		458.11	441.94	900.05		0.26805196
23	13	47.85	48.50	0.1920	0.5263		473.68	426.37	900.05		480.05	427.03	907.08		0.25198915
24	14	48.50	44.49	0.2373	0.5460		495.30	411.78	907.08		454.40	412.42	866.82		-2.1408232
25	15	44.49	42.46	-0.1096	0.4012		347.79	519.03	866.82		331.88	519.83	851.71		-1.194594
26	16	42.46	43.19	-0.3083	0.3234		275.45	576.27	851.71		280.17	577.15	857.32		0.3392006
27	17	43.19	43.46	-0.2534	0.3453		296.04	561.28	857.32		297.92	562.15	860.07		0.08344159
28	18	43.46	42.55	-0.2408	0.3510		301.91	558.17	860.07		295.56	559.02	854.58		-0.5803736
29	19	42.55	44.13	-0.3434	0.3126		267.14	587.44	854.58		277.05	588.35	865.40		0.80632162
30	20	44.13	42.79	-0.2042	0.3671		317.70	547.70	865.40		308.08	548.54	856.63		-0.8078064
31	21	42.79	38.00	-0.3504	0.3116		266.96	589.67	856.63		237.09	590.58	827.66		-2.9218791
32	22	38.00	37.27	-0.8876	0.1467		121.40	706.26	827.66		119.07	707.35	826.41		-0.5369145
33	23	37.27	37.11	-1.0003	0.1220		100.82	725.59	826.41		100.39	726.71	827.10		-0.1717774
34	24	37.11	36.76	-1.0483	0.1128		93.28	733.82	827.10		92.40	734.95	827.35		-0.296393
35	25	36.76	37.72	-1.1223	0.0993		82.17	745.19	827.35		84.30	746.34	830.63		0.54612656
36	26	37.72	40.11	-1.0343	0.1168		96.99	733.64	830.63		103.13	734.77	837.91		1.40720203
37	27	40.11	37.71	-0.7711	0.1801		150.89	687.02	837.91		141.88	688.07	829.96		-1.5486603
38	28	37.71	39.18	-1.1007	0.1050		87.14	742.82	829.96		90.54	743.96	834.50		0.85074817
39	29	39.18	37.16	-0.9446	0.1381		115.25	719.25	834.50		109.28	720.36	829.65		-1.3460431
40	30	37.16	35.92	-1.2504	0.0806		66.87	762.78	829.65		64.65	763.95	828.60		-0.8818097
41	31	35.92	33.18	-1.4697	0.0523		43.37	785.23	828.60		40.05	786.44	826.49		-1.9797517
42	32	33.18	33.54	-1.9461	0.0176		14.59	811.91	826.49		14.75	813.16	827.90		0.19301183
43	33	33.54	35.22	-1.9497	0.0177		14.63	813.28	827.90		15.36	814.53	829.89		1.10285782
44	34	35.22	34.58	-1.7405	0.0296		24.52	805.36	829.89		24.08	806.60	830.68		-0.5111133
45	35	34.58	33.14	-1.9121	0.0198		16.45	814.23	830.68		15.77	815.48	831.25		-1.0873919
46	36	33.14	33.15	-2.2399	0.0085		7.08	824.17	831.25		7.09	825.44	832.52		-0.0628847
47	37	33.15	33.47	-2.3266	0.0068		5.64	826.88	832.52		5.70	828.15	833.85		0.1581293
48	38	33.47	34.20	-2.3629	0.0062		5.17	828.68	833.85		5.28	829.96	835.24		0.45234401
49	39	34.20	35.10	-2.3234	0.0070		5.87	829.37	835.24		6.03	830.64	836.67		0.55609917
50	40	35.10	35.18	-2.2544	0.0086		7.23	829.44	836.67		7.24	830.72	837.97		-0.0135788
51	41	35.18	37.68	-2.3553	0.0066		5.55	832.42	837.97		5.94	833.70	839.64		1.57773229
52	42	37.68	36.82	-1.9677	0.0188		15.76	823.88	839.64		15.40	825.15	840.55		-0.6214282
53	43	36.82	37.28	-2.2774	0.0085		7.14	833.41	840.55		7.23	834.69	841.92		0.22663926
54	44	37.28	36.70	-2.3313	0.0074		6.27	835.65	841.92		6.17	836.94	843.11		-0.4465892
55	45	36.70	37.70	-2.6567	0.0029		2.47	840.64	843.11		2.53	841.94	844.47		0.57648549
56	46	37.70	35.60	-2.6295	0.0033		2.75	841.73	844.47		2.59	843.02	845.62		-1.4459283
57	47	35.60	37.72	-3.5220	0.0002		0.13	845.49	845.62		0.14	846.79	846.93		1.31853994
58	48	37.72	38.96	-3.2727	0.0004		0.34	846.58	846.93		0.35	847.89	848.24		0.70896249
59	49	38.96	38.99	-3.3629	0.0003		0.26	847.98	848.24		0.26	849.29	849.55		-0.0466423
60	50	38.99	41.97	-4.1436	0.0000		0.01	849.53	849.55		0.01	850.84	850.85		1.69782197
61	51	41.97	42.84	-4.1505	0.0000		0.01	850.84	850.85		0.01	852.15	852.17		0.42271154
62	52	42.84							852.17						

All the columns of the simulation have already been explained except column O: This column contains a series of random numbers drawn from a standard normal distribution. The price of the stock at the end of each week is determined by these random numbers. In this example the stock price of 56.87 at the end of week 0 is—as explained in Chapter 18—determined by the lognormal assumption $S_t = S_{t-1} * e^{\mu\Delta t + \sigma Z\sqrt{\Delta t}}$, which for this particular case becomes $56.59 = 50 * e^{0.15*\frac{1}{52}+0.30*0.183745\sqrt{\frac{1}{52}}}$. As explained in Chapter 18, these standard normal deviates were created with the Excel command **Tools|Data Analysis|Random Number Generation**.

When graphed, the results look like this:

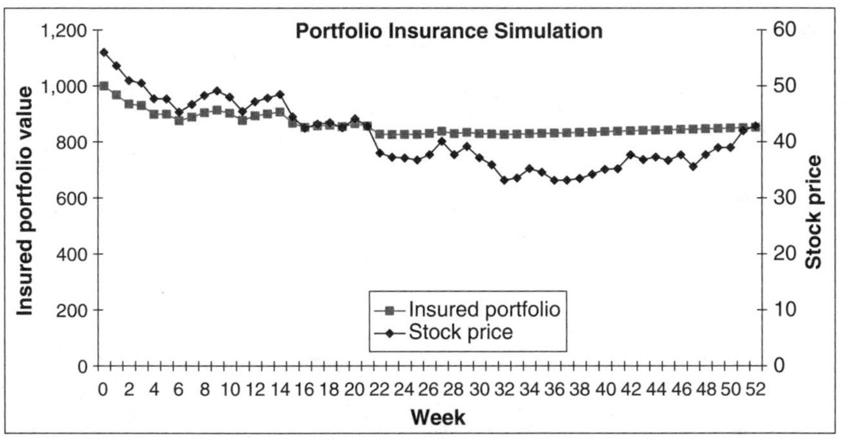

In this particular graph the stock price (graphed on the right axis) declined over the year, so that the portfolio insurance strategy pays off more than a straight stock strategy would have. In effect, we have used the puts that are implicit in this strategy.

In this example, the stock price declines below \$50 per share. As we pointed out in section 21.3, at date 0 the portfolio insurance strategy involved the equivalent of purchasing 17.13 shares of the stock and a put on each of these shares. If our simulation were continuously updated, the portfolio value would never dip below \$856.50 (= 17.13 * \$50). In this case, because the updating of the portfolio positions is weekly and not continuous, the terminal value of the portfolio is close to \$856. As suggested by Property 3 of section 21.4, by the end of the year, the portfolio insurance strategy is wholly invested in bonds. By week 47 there is no investment in stocks whatsoever.

We can rerun the simulation and graph the output, tracking both the stock price and the total portfolio value over the course of the year:

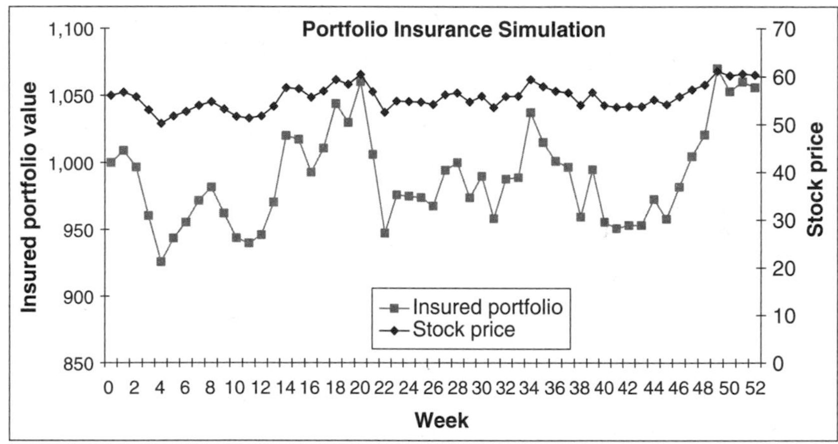

In this example, by the end of the year the portfolio insurance strategy will be wholly invested in stocks (again this result follows from Property 3 of section 21.4). In this example the portfolio insurance proves more expensive than an uninsured investment—ex post, we would have been better off not following an insurance policy.

We can use the **Tools|Record Macro** feature of Excel to produce a macro that automates the simulation procedure.

```
Sub Simulation()
' Simulation Macro
' key assigned:  [Ctrl]+a
'
  Application.SendKeys ("{Enter}")
  Application.Run "ATPVBAEN.XLA!Random", _
  ActiveSheet.Range("$O$11:$O$61"), , _
      , 2, , 0, 1
End Sub
```

The first line of the macro `Application.SendKeys ("{Enter}")` was added because each run of the random number generator brings up the following dialogue box:

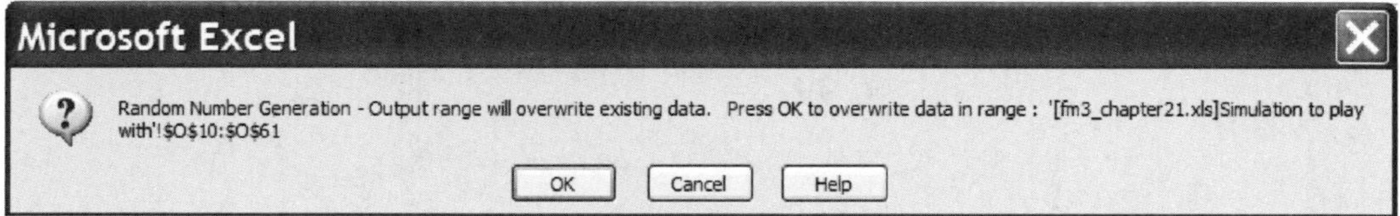

The first line of the macro sends an Enter to answer this dialogue box, so that the macro automatically enters the data into the range.

21.6 Insuring Total Portfolio Returns

So far we have considered only the problem of constructing artificial puts, one per share. A slightly different version of this problem involves constructing a portfolio of puts and shares that guarantees the *total* dollar returns on the *total* initial investment. A typical story goes like this:

You have \$1,000 to invest, and you want to guarantee that a year from now you will have at least \$1,000z. Here z is some number, generally between 0 and 1; for example, a z equal to 0.93, would mean that you want your final wealth to be at least \$930.[3] You want to invest in a stock whose current price is S_0 and in a put on the stock with an exercise price X. You want the number of puts to be equal to the number of shares. Given X and S_0, the put price is $P(S_0, X)$. To implement the strategy, you must therefore buy α shares, where

$$\alpha = \frac{1{,}000}{S_0 + P(S_0, X)}$$

Since you have bought α shares and α puts with an exercise price of X, the minimum dollar return from your portfolio is αX. You want this

3. As we will show in section 21.6.1, it is possible to insure (up to a point) even with $z > 1$.

to be equal to 1,000z, and therefore you solve to get $\alpha = 1{,}000z/X$. Thus you can guarantee your minimum return if

$$S_0 + P(S_0, X) = X/z$$

A spreadsheet implementation of this equation follows. The data table shows the graph of the left-hand side of the preceding equation; where this graph crosses the x-axis is the solution for the synthetic put exercise price X when $S_0 = 56$, $\sigma = 30$ percent, $r = 6$ percent, $T = 1$, and $z = 93$ percent.

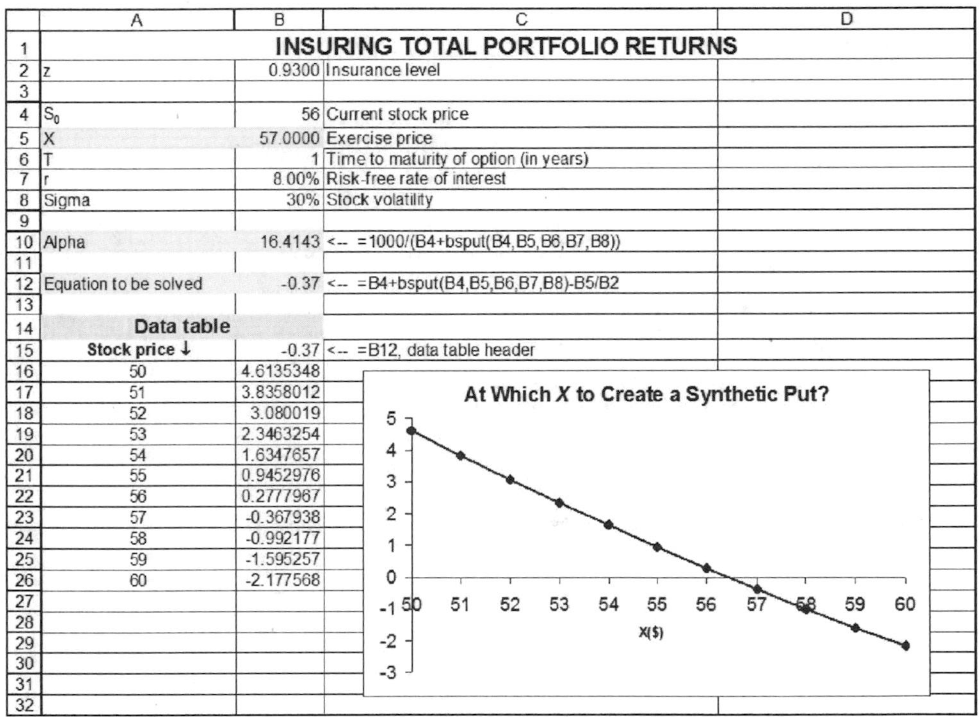

	A	B	C	D
1		INSURING TOTAL PORTFOLIO RETURNS		
2	z	0.9300	Insurance level	
3				
4	S_0	56	Current stock price	
5	X	57.0000	Exercise price	
6	T	1	Time to maturity of option (in years)	
7	r	8.00%	Risk-free rate of interest	
8	Sigma	30%	Stock volatility	
9				
10	Alpha	16.4143	<-- =1000/(B4+bsput(B4,B5,B6,B7,B8))	
11				
12	Equation to be solved	-0.37	<-- =B4+bsput(B4,B5,B6,B7,B8)-B5/B2	
13				
14	Data table			
15	Stock price ↓	-0.37	<-- =B12, data table header	
16	50	4.6135348		
17	51	3.8358012		
18	52	3.080019		
19	53	2.3463254		
20	54	1.6347657		
21	55	0.9452976		
22	56	0.2777967		
23	57	-0.367938		
24	58	-0.992177		
25	59	-1.595257		
26	60	-2.177568		
27				
28				
29				
30				
31				
32				

Solver gives the solution to the equation $S_0 + \text{Put}(S_0, X) - X/z = 0$. The solution is indicated in the next picture:

	A	B	C
1	**INSURING TOTAL PORTFOLIO RETURNS**		
2	z	0.9300	Insurance level
3			
4	S_0	56	Current stock price
5	X	56.4261	Exercise price
6	T	1	Time to maturity of option (in years)
7	r	8.00%	Risk-free rate of interest
8	Sigma	30%	Stock volatility
9			
10	Alpha	16.4817	<-- =1000/(B4+bsput(B4,B5,B6,B7,B8))
11			
12	Equation to be solved	0.00	<-- =B4+bsput(B4,B5,B6,B7,B8)-B5/B2
13			
14	Check		
15	Cost of shares	922.98	
16	Cost of puts	77.02	
17	Total cost	1000.00	
18			
19	Minimum portfolio return	930.00	<-- =B10*B5

The solution is to buy $\alpha = 16.4817$ puts and shares (the cost of which is $1,000, as you can see in cell B17). The minimum return of this portfolio is $16.4817 * X = \$930$ (cell B19).

21.6.1 What Is the Effect of Raising the Insurance Level? Can You Insure for More Than Your Initial Investment?

When we raise the insurance level, the implied exercise price of the put must go up. Therefore, as we buy more insurance, we spend relatively more of our $1,000 on puts (insurance) and relatively less on the stocks (which have the upside potential).

Can we insure for more than our current level of investment? To put it another way, can we set $z > 1$? We would be picking an insurance level that guarantees that we end up with *more* than our initial investment. A little thought and some calculations reveal that we can indeed choose $z > 1$ as long as $z \leq 1 + r$. That is, we cannot guarantee ourselves a return greater than the riskless interest rate! To demonstrate this point, we offer two examples. In the first example, we solve for $z = 1.08 = 1 + r$. This has a solution (note that the value of cell B12 is zero):

	A	B	C
1	**INSURING TOTAL PORTFOLIO RETURNS**		
2	z	1.0800	Insurance level
3			
4	S_0	56	Current stock price
5	X	104.8368	Exercise price
6	T	1	Time to maturity of option (in years)
7	r	8.00%	Risk-free rate of interest
8	Sigma	30%	Stock volatility
9			
10	Alpha	10.3017	<-- =1000/(B4+bsput(B4,B5,B6,B7,B8))
11			
12	Equation to be solved	0.00	<-- =B4+bsput(B4,B5,B6,B7,B8)-B5/B2
13			
14	Check		
15	Cost of shares	576.90	
16	Cost of puts	423.10	
17	Total cost	1,000.00	
18			
19	Minimum portfolio return	1,080.00	<-- =B10*B5

When $z > 1.08$, however, there is no solution. Even the best efforts of **Solver** do not give zero in cell B12, as you can see in the following example:

	A	B	C
1	**INSURING TOTAL PORTFOLIO RETURNS**		
2	z	1.0900	Insurance level
3			
4	S_0	56	Current stock price
5	X	122.8824	Exercise price
6	T	1	Time to maturity of option (in years)
7	r	8.00%	Risk-free rate of interest
8	Sigma	30%	Stock volatility
9			
10	Alpha	8.8099	<-- =1000/(B4+bsput(B4,B5,B6,B7,B8))
11			
12	Equation to be solved	0.77	<-- =B4+bsput(B4,B5,B6,B7,B8)-B5/B2
13			
14	Check		
15	Cost of shares	493.35	
16	Cost of puts	506.65	
17	Total cost	1,000.00	
18			
19	Minimum portfolio return	1,082.58	<-- =B10*B5

21.7 Implicit Puts and Asset Values

Up to this point in the chapter, we have been discussing the construction of puts in order to construct portfolio insurance. We will now reverse the logic and consider situations in which we are offered a package that includes an implicit put. The problem is how to deduce the true value of the underlying asset that is part of the package.

Many commonly encountered situations include implicit puts. Consider the situation in which you are offered an asset plus an option to have the seller repurchase the asset. Some examples that come to mind are irrevocable tender offers, "satisfaction guaranteed or your money back" offers, and computer sales where you get to return the item but have to pay a 15 percent "restocking charge." (See Bhagat, Brickley, and Loewenstein, 1987, for an application of these ideas to cash tender offers.)

Were you in possession of the asset's variance, you could deduce from the offer the true value of the asset. Without this information, you can deduce the locus of the asset's standard deviation and its true value. To do so, let V_a denote the true value of the asset stripped of any puts or repurchase offers. Let V_p denote the value of the put. Let Y denote the purchase price (which, of course, includes the put), and let X denote the price at which you can get your money back. Then it follows that

$$Y = V_a + V_p$$

If we assume that the put option can be priced by the Black-Scholes formula, we will have

$$V_p = -V_a N(-d_1) + Xe^{-rT} N(\sigma\sqrt{T} - d_1)$$

where

$$d_1 = \frac{\ln(V_a/X) + \left(rT + \frac{\sigma}{2}\sqrt{T}\right)}{\sigma\sqrt{T}}$$

Thus, to solve this problem, we must find a σ and V_a that simultaneously solve

$$Y = V_a N(d_1) + Xe^{-rT} N(\sigma\sqrt{T} - d_1)$$

The right-hand side of this equation is increasing in σ and in V_a.

Here is an example: You are offered a risky asset for $100. If not satisfied with the asset, you may return it within one year and get back $85 (the remaining $15 is a "restocking charge"). How much is the asset worth? If you think that the asset's σ is 30 percent, then we have to solve

$$Y = V_a N(d_1) + Xe^{-rT} N(\sigma\sqrt{T} - d_1)$$

where $Y = 100$, $\sigma = 30$ percent, $T = 1$, $r = 10$ percent, and $X = 85$.

The answer, calculated in the following spreadsheet using **Tools|Solver**, is that the underlying asset value $V_a = \$96.71$:

	A	B	C
1	**IMPLICIT PUTS AND ASSET VALUES**		
2	V_a	96.70586	Actual asset value
3	X	85	Money-back guarantee
4	r	10.00%	Risk-free rate of interest
5	T	1	Time to maturity of option (in years)
6	Sigma	30%	Stock volatility
7	d_1	0.9134	<-- (LN(S/X)+(r+0.5*sigma^2)*T)/(sigma*SQRT(T))
8	d_2	0.6134	<-- d_1 - sigma*SQRT(T)
9			
10	$N(d_1)$	0.8195	<-- Uses formula NormSDist(d_1)
11	$N(d_2)$	0.7302	<-- Uses formula NormSDist(d_2)
12			
13	Put price	3.29	<-- =-B3*(1-B11)+B4*EXP(-B5*B6)*(1-B12)
14	Put + asset value	100.00	<-- =B3+B14

21.8 Summary

This chapter has concentrated mainly on implementing the classic portfolio insurance strategies by which we delta hedge a put on a portfolio. In many ways these strategies are no different from the delta hedging discussed in Chapter 20, though the implementation to portfolio insurance is important enough to warrant a chapter of its own.

Portfolio insurance strategies simulate a put on the stock, with the result that the total minimal return is less than what is implied by the ratio X/S_0. What if we want to insure the total portfolio value? This question is discussed in section 21.6. A final discussion on this topic is the implied put value in a money-back guarantee, section 21.7.

Exercises

1. You are a portfolio manager, and you want to invest in an asset having $\sigma = 40$ percent. You want to create a put on the investment so that at the end of the year you have losses no greater than 5 percent. Since there is no put on this specific asset, you plan to create a synthetic put by engaging in a dynamic investment strategy—purchasing a portfolio composed of dynamically changing proportions of the risky asset and riskless bonds. If the interest rate is 6 percent, how much should your initial investment be in the portfolio and in the riskless bond?

2. Simulate the strategy of exercise 1, assuming weekly rebalancing of the portfolio.

3. Go back to the numerical example of section 21.7. Write a VBA function that solves for the implied asset value V_a. (Hint: Use the bisection method.) Then use this function to create a graph showing the trade-off between the implied asset value and the asset volatility.

4. You have been offered the chance to purchase stock in a firm. The seller wants \$55 per share, but offers to repurchase the stock at the end of one-half year for \$50 per share. If the σ of the share's log returns is 80 percent, determine the true value per share. Assume that the interest rate is 10 percent.

5. A covered call is a long stock and short call. The pattern of payoffs is as follows:

	A	B	C
1	**COVERED CALL PROFIT PATTERN**		
2	Future stock price, S_T	50	
3	Call exercise price, X	45	
4	Call price	6	
5			
6	Payoffs at T		
7	Long stock, $+S_T$	50	<-- =B2
8	Short call payoff, $-\text{Max}[S_T\text{-}X,0]$	-5	<-- =-MAX(B2-B3,0)
9	Total payoff	45	<-- =B7+B8
10			
11			
12	**Data table of payoffs**		
13	Future stock price, S_T	45	
14	0	0	
15	5	5	
16	10	10	
17	15	15	
18	20	20	
19	25	25	
20	30	30	
21	35	35	
22	40	40	
23	45	45	
24	50	45	
25	55	45	
26	60	45	
27	65	45	
28	70	45	
29	75	45	
30			

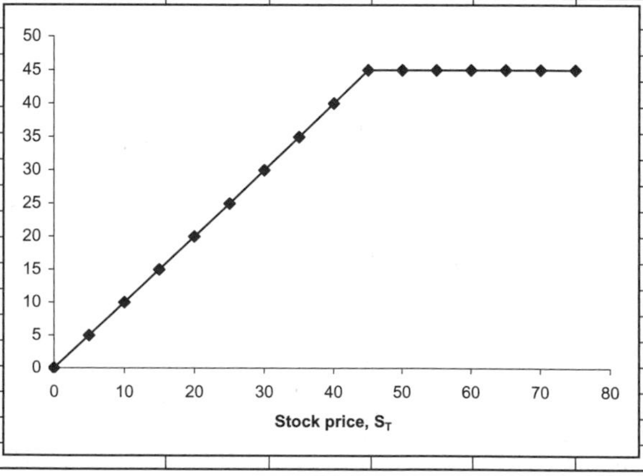

Simulate the payoffs of a covered call over 52 weeks, with weekly updating of the positions. Start by deriving the formula for the covered call—add together the Black-Scholes price and the stock price:

$$\underbrace{S_0}_{\substack{\uparrow \\ \text{Long stock}}} \quad \underbrace{-S_0N(d_1)+Xe^{-rT}N(d_2)}_{\substack{\uparrow \\ \text{Short call}}} = \underbrace{S_0(1-N(d_1))}_{\substack{\uparrow \\ \text{Long position} \\ \text{in stock}}} + \underbrace{Xe^{-rT}N(d_2)}_{\substack{\uparrow \\ \text{Long position} \\ \text{in bond}}}$$

Thus we see that a covered call is a long position in the stock and a long position in the bond. Now implement the following spreadsheet to test the effectiveness of a simulated covered call strategy:

	A	B	C	D	E	F	G	H	I	J	K
1				**COVERED CALL SIMULATION**							
2	Initial stock price, S_0	50									
3	X	45									
4	Mean stock return	12%									
5	Sigma	40%									
6	Interest rate, r	6%									
7											
8	Initial call price	11.7393	<-- =bscall(B2,B3,1,B6,B5)								
9	Initial investment in covered call	38.2607	<-- =B2-B8								
10											
11	Simulated payoff of strategy	????									
12	Payoff of covered call strategy	????									
13											
14											
15	**Week**	**Time**	**Stock price**	**d_1**	**Invested in stock**	**Invested in bond**	**Total investment at beginning of week**		**Random Z at end of week**	**Stock price at end of week**	**Investment at the end of week**
16	0	0.0000	50.00	0.6134	13.4903	24.7705	38.2607		0.0035	50.1253	38.3232
17	1	0.0192	50.13	0.6189	13.4330	24.8902	38.3232				
18	2	0.0385									
64	48	0.9231									
65	49	0.9423									
66	50	0.9615									
67	51	0.9808									

22 An Introduction to Monte Carlo Methods

22.1 Overview

Monte Carlo (MC) methods are a variety of random simulations used to determine the values of parameters. In this introductory chapter we use MC to determine the value of π. In the next chapter we will use MC to determine the values of various kinds of options that cannot be readily priced using closed-form formulas. The MC method has its source in physics, where it is often used to determine model values for which there is no analytical solution.[1] The use of MC in finance is similar: MC methods use simulation to price assets whose prices are not readily determined by analytical means. In short, if there is no formula for computing the value of an asset, maybe we can determine its value with a simulation. Clearly the category of options for which there exist no analytical solutions does not include "plain vanilla" European calls and puts, which can be priced by the Black-Scholes formula. However, many options are more complicated than these. In Chapter 23 we will illustrate MC methods for Asian options (where the terminal payoff of the option is *path dependent*) and American options.

In this chapter we give a laywoman's introduction to MC pricing.[2] As a precursor you might want to read Chapter 30, which discusses random-number generators.

22.2 Computing π Using Monte Carlo

All MC methods involve random simulation. We illustrate how to use Monte Carlo to calculate the value of π, a number with which you are presumably familiar.

Here's our method: We know that the area of the unit circle (circle with radius 1) is π. It follows that the area of a quarter circle is $\pi/4$. We inscribe a quarter circle into a unit square, as seen in the following illustration. We then proceed to "shoot" random points at the unit square. Each random point has an x component and a y component. We generate such points by using the Excel function **Rand**.

1. Two good Web sites with introductions to MC methods are http://www.phy.ornl.gov/csep/CSEP/MC/NODE1.html and http://www.puc-rio.br/marco.ind/monte-carlo.html.

2. An excellent nonintroductory text is Glasserman (2005).

The picture shows the quarter circle inscribed in the unit square and a single random point, which happened to land inside the circle.

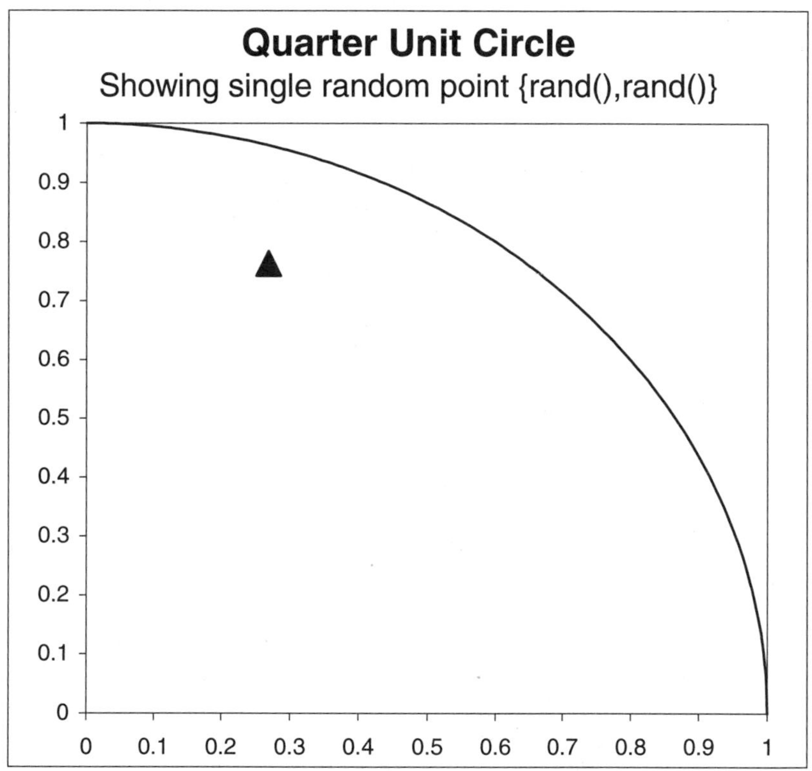

By pressing **F9** in the spreadsheet **fm3_chapter22.xls**, you can generate different values of the random point. In some cases, the point will be outside the unit circle:

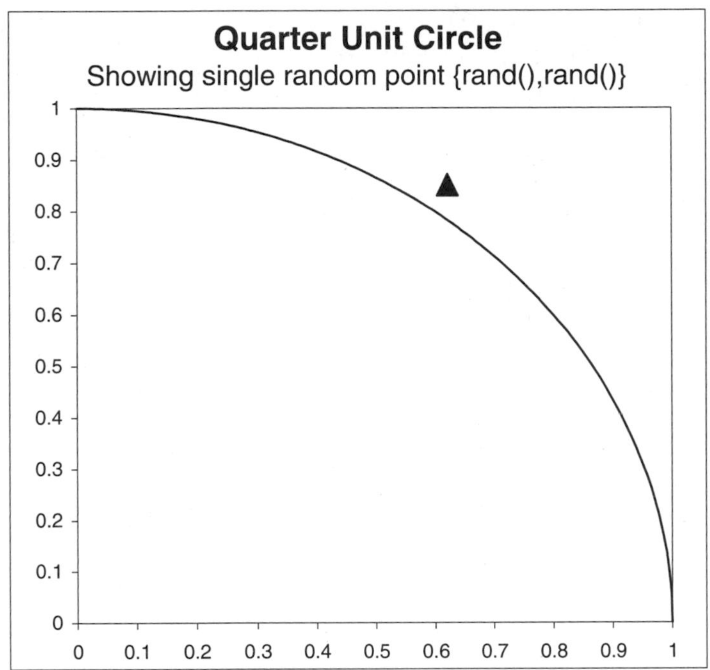

We can easily do a calculation of the probability that the point will be inside the circle:

• The area of the whole unit circle is $\pi * r^2 = \pi$. Thus the area of the quarter unit circle is $\pi/4$.

• The random point—generated by **{Rand(), Rand()}**—is always inside the unit square, whose area is 1.

• Thus the probability of the random point being inside the unit circle is

$$\frac{\text{Area unit circle}}{\text{Area unit square}} = \frac{\pi/4}{1} = \pi/4$$

22.2.1 Monte Carlo Computation of π

If we count the relative number of points that fall inside the unit circle, we should approximate $\pi/4$. Thus

$$\begin{aligned}\text{Monte Carlo approximation of } \pi &= 4 * \text{Relative number points inside unit circle} \\ &= 4 * \frac{\text{Number points inside unit circle}}{\text{Total number of points}}\end{aligned}$$

In the following spreadsheet we generate a list of random numbers (columns B and C) and then use a Boolean function to test whether the numbers are in or out of the unit circle. In row 8, for example, the function = (B8^2 + C8^2 <= 1) returns TRUE if the sum of the squares of B8 and C8 is less than or equal to 1 and 0 otherwise. In cells B2 and B3 we use **Count** to count the total number of points generated and **CountIf** to determine the number of data points that fall inside the unit circle.[3]

	A	B	C	D	E
1	**COMPUTING PI USING MONTE CARLO METHODS INITIAL EXPERIMENT**				
2	Number of data points	30	<-- =COUNT(A:A)		
3	Inside circle	22	<-- =COUNTIF(D:D,TRUE)		
4	Pi?	2.933333333	<-- =B3/B2*4		
5					
6		Each cell in these columns contains the Excel function **=Rand()**			
7	**Experiment**	**Random1**	**Random2**	**In unit circle?**	
8	1	0.93377	0.14390	TRUE	<-- =(B8^2+C8^2<=1)
9	2	0.28866	0.68112	TRUE	
10	3	0.53592	0.60165	TRUE	
11	4	0.38665	0.27952	TRUE	
12	5	0.02396	0.62680	TRUE	
13	6	0.98093	0.02753	TRUE	
14	7	0.57770	0.34427	TRUE	
15	8	0.58922	0.26317	TRUE	
16	9	0.34752	0.77355	TRUE	
17	10	0.96858	0.08618	TRUE	
18	11	0.32394	0.66268	TRUE	
19	12	0.04574	0.69957	TRUE	
20	13	0.53216	0.99862	FALSE	
21	14	0.88861	0.60825	FALSE	
22	15	0.65561	0.39199	TRUE	
23	16	0.79978	0.21315	TRUE	
24	17	0.65605	0.99905	FALSE	
25	18	0.23636	0.95164	TRUE	
26	19	0.75541	0.17700	TRUE	
27	20	0.29197	0.01494	TRUE	
28	21	0.56781	0.40796	TRUE	
29	22	0.25891	0.04545	TRUE	
30	23	0.61585	0.88576	FALSE	
31	24	0.32830	0.43645	TRUE	
32	25	0.52969	0.47640	TRUE	
33	26	0.60362	0.85435	FALSE	
34	27	0.97880	0.20737	FALSE	
35	28	0.62883	0.84034	FALSE	
36	29	0.13787	0.66466	TRUE	
37	30	0.98497	0.36433	FALSE	

3. All the functions in this paragraph—Boolean functions, **Count** and **CountIF**—are discussed in Chapter 34.

Each time we press **F9** to recalculate the spreadsheet, we get different values for the = **Rand** and hence a different Monte Carlo value for π. Here is an example:

	A	B	C	D	E
1	**COMPUTING PI USING MONTE CARLO METHODS INITIAL EXPERIMENT**				
2	Number of data points	30	<-- =COUNT(A:A)		
3	Inside circle	24	<-- =COUNTIF(D:D,TRUE)		
4	Pi?	3.2	<-- =B3/B2*4		
5					
6		Each cell in these columns contains the Excel function **=Rand()**			
7	**Experiment**	**Random1**	**Random2**	**In unit circle?**	
8	1	0.19891	0.21584	TRUE	<-- =(B8^2+C8^2<=1)
9	2	0.60485	0.39918	TRUE	
10	3	0.54090	0.50887	TRUE	
11	4	0.01367	0.82935	TRUE	
12	5	0.29872	0.02460	TRUE	
13	6	0.98014	0.75186	FALSE	
14	7	0.01627	0.34278	TRUE	

Pressing **F9** again:

	A	B	C	D	E
1	**COMPUTING PI USING MONTE CARLO METHODS INITIAL EXPERIMENT**				
2	Number of data points	30	<-- =COUNT(A:A)		
3	Inside circle	25	<-- =COUNTIF(D:D,TRUE)		
4	Pi?	3.333333333	<-- =B3/B2*4		
5					
6		Each cell in these columns contains the Excel function **=Rand()**			
7	**Experiment**	**Random1**	**Random2**	**In unit circle?**	
8	1	0.95610	0.35792	FALSE	<-- =(B8^2+C8^2<=1)
9	2	0.65874	0.62250	TRUE	
10	3	0.67164	0.23791	TRUE	
11	4	0.81134	0.46254	TRUE	
12	5	0.06633	0.01178	TRUE	
13	6	0.70038	0.91783	FALSE	
14	7	0.22334	0.19309	TRUE	

Now it's clear that the values we get for π are experimental, but if we applied this method for a lot of points we would get closer to the actual value of π. In the following example we fill the whole of columns B and C with random values:

	A	B	C	D	E
1	**COMPUTING PI USING MONTE CARLO METHODS All of columns B and C filled with random numbers**				
2	Number of data points	65,529	<-- =COUNT(A:A)		
3	Inside circle	51,676	<-- =COUNTIF(D:D,TRUE)		
4	Pi?	3.15438966	<-- =B3/B2*4		
5					
6		Each cell in these columns contains the Excel function **=Rand()**			
7	**List**	**Random1**	**Random2**	**In unit circle?**	
8	1	0.47482	0.76071	TRUE	<-- =(B8^2+C8^2<=1)
9	2	0.81690	0.85186	FALSE	
10	3	0.21643	0.90968	TRUE	
11	4	0.47165	0.50493	TRUE	
12	5	0.89530	0.12251	TRUE	
13	6	0.72624	0.37979	TRUE	
14	7	0.60837	0.23161	TRUE	

When we've filled columns B and C with random numbers, you can see that there are 65,529 random pairs. Pressing **F9** gives much more accurate values for π. A few more presses of **F9** produced the following Monte Carlo values for π:

3.150544034, 3.144256741, 3.139556532, 3.149872576, 3.138213615, 3.132780906

Using more data points makes our MC value for π more accurate, though none of these values is very close to the actual value of π.[4]

22.3 Writing a VBA Program

This Monte Carlo business requires some VBA. Here's a program:

```
Sub MonteCarlo()
    n = Worksheets("MC").Range("Number")
    Hits = 0
    For Index = 1 To n
        If Rnd ^ 2 + Rnd ^ 2 < 1 Then Hits = Hits + 1
   Next Index
   Range("Estimate") = 4 * Hits / n
End Sub
```

4. The actual value of π, correct to 50 digits, is 3.1415926535897932384626433832795028841971693993751. One of the end-of-chapter problems shows you a quick way of computing this value using several remarkable functions due to the Indian mathematician Srinivasa Ramanujan (1887–1920).

The next spreadsheet shows this program and two other VBA programs. The program **MonteCarloTimer** computes both the **StartTime** and the **StopTime**, so that we can compute the elapsed time for the computations. You can see that 50 million iterations of the program took 33 seconds on the author's Lenovo T60 laptop.

The program **MonteCarloTimeRecord** records each iteration of the program on the screen. This VBA routine allows you to see how the values of π in cell B3 develop. You can stop this or any VBA routine in midstream by pressing [Ctrl] + [Break]. This macro is incredibly time wasteful. It took us 103 seconds to run 5,000 iterations of the routine (compare this figure to running the 50 million iterations without the screen updating).

	A	B	C	D	E
1	**COMPUTING PI USING VBA**				
2	Number of data points	50,000,000	<-- This cell called "Number"		
3	Pi?	3.14158984	<-- This cell called "Estimate"		Sub MonteCarlo()
4					n = Range("Number")
5					Hits = 0
6	StartTime	9:35:41	<-- This cell called "StartTime"		For Index = 1 To n
7	StopTime	9:36:14	<-- This cell called "StopTime"		If Rnd ^ 2 + Rnd ^ 2 < 1 Then Hits = Hits + 1
8	Elapsed	0:00:33	<-- =Stoptime-StartTime		Next Index
9					Range("Estimate") = 4 * Hits / n
10					End Sub
11	**Note**				
12	[Ctrl]+a runs the macro "MonteCarlo"				Sub MonteCarloTime()
13	[Ctrl]+q runs the macro "MonteCarloTime" which also records the time				'Includes timer
14	[Ctrl]+t runs the macro "MonteCarloTimeRecord" which records the results as they are generated. For large number of points, this takes a *very long* time!				n = Range("Number")
15					Range("StartTime") = Time
16					
17					n = Range("Number")
18					Hits = 0
19					For Index = 1 To n
20					If Rnd ^ 2 + Rnd ^ 2 < 1 Then Hits = Hits + 1
21					Next Index
22					Range("Estimate") = 4 * Hits / n
23					Range("StopTime") = Time
24					End Sub
25					
26					
27					Sub MonteCarloTimeRecord()
28					'Records everything (takes a long time)
29					n = Range("Number")
30					Range("StartTime") = Time
31					n = Range("Number")
32					Hits = 0
33					For Index = 1 To n
34					Range("Number") = Index
35					If Rnd ^ 2 + Rnd ^ 2 < 1 Then Hits = Hits + 1
36					Range("Estimate") = 4 * Hits / Index
37					Range("StopTime") = Time
38					Next Index
39					End Sub

22.4 Another Monte Carlo Problem: Investment and Retirement

The problem: You are 65 years old and you have $1,000,000. You are trying to decide on a mix of investments: There is a riskless bond with an annual return of 6 percent and a risky stock portfolio with an expected log return of 12 percent and a standard deviation of return of 30 percent. Your limitations: You want to take $150,000 out of the account every year and have something left over at age 75.

To get a better handle on this situation, you plot out a spreadsheet:

	A	B	C	D	E	F	G	H	I
1				**PLANNING YOUR RETIREMENT**					
2	Current wealth	1,000,000							
3	Risk-free rate	6%							
4	Parameters of risky investment								
5	Expected annual return	8%							
6	Standard deviation of return	20%							
7	Proportion invested in risky	70%							
8	Annual drawdown	150,000							
9									
10	**Year**	**Wealth at beginning of year**	**Invested in risky**	**Invested in bonds**	**Random number, normally distributed**	**1+return on risky investment**	**Wealth at end of year**	**Drawdown**	**Left at end of 10 years**
11	1	1,000,000	700,000	300,000	0.5450	1.2080	1,164,185	150,000	
12	2	1,014,185	709,930	304,256	-0.1724	1.0466	1,066,069	150,000	
13	3	916,069	641,248	274,821	-0.3924	1.0015	934,036	150,000	
14	4	784,036	548,825	235,211	-0.3179	1.0166	807,665	150,000	
15	5	657,665	460,366	197,300	-0.0825	1.0656	700,044	150,000	
16	6	550,044	385,030	165,013	0.9566	1.3117	680,264	150,000	
17	7	530,264	371,185	159,079	0.2509	1.1390	591,712	150,000	
18	8	441,712	309,198	132,514	0.8803	1.2918	540,143	150,000	
19	9	390,143	273,100	117,043	0.7485	1.2582	467,904	150,000	
20	10	317,904	222,533	95,371	-1.4671	0.8078	281,032	150,000	131,032
21									
22		Normally-distributed random numbers generated by =NORMSINV(RAND())					=C20*F20+D20*EXP($B$3)		
23									
24	Wealth at beginning of year =G19-H19			1+return on risky investment =EXP($B$5+$B$6*E20)					
25									
26									
27		Investment in risky asset =B20*$B$7							

In this spreadsheet column B shows the wealth at the beginning of every year. The wealth is divided between risky and riskless investments according to the proportions in cell B7. The riskless investment earns a continuously compounded return of 6 percent (meaning that $100 invested in the riskless investment grows to $100*e^{6\%}$ at the end of the year). The risky part of the investment grows by a factor of $e^{\mu+\sigma*Z}$ =

$e^{8\%+20\%*Z}$, where Z is a random number that is normally distributed with mean 0 and standard deviation 1. As explained in Chapter 30, one way of generating these numbers is to use the Excel function **NormSInv(Rand())**. With each press of **F9**, this function recomputes and produces another normally distributed random number.

In the preceding simulation the investor has money left at the end of the 10-year period. But it is clear that not every simulation will leave the investor with spare cash at the end of year 10. A few presses of **F9** to recalculate the spreadsheet will produce something like this:

	A	B	C	D	E	F	G	H	I
1	PLANNING YOUR RETIREMENT								
2	Current wealth	1,000,000							
3	Risk-free rate	6%							
4	Parameters of risky investment								
5	Expected annual return	8%							
6	Standard deviation of return	20%							
7	Proportion invested in risky	70%							
8	Annual drawdown	150,000							
9									
10	Year	Wealth at beginning of year	Invested in risky	Invested in bonds	Random number, normally distributed	1+return on risky investment	Wealth at end of year	Drawdown	Left at end of 10 years
11	1	1,000,000	700,000	300,000	-1.2459	0.8444	909,604	150,000	
12	2	759,604	531,723	227,881	0.8373	1.2808	922,985	150,000	
13	3	772,985	541,090	231,896	0.2468	1.1381	862,046	150,000	
14	4	712,046	498,432	213,614	-0.1490	1.0515	750,918	150,000	
15	5	600,918	420,643	180,276	-0.4724	0.9856	606,022	150,000	
16	6	456,022	319,215	136,807	-1.1769	0.8561	418,543	150,000	
17	7	268,543	187,980	80,563	1.3347	1.4147	351,485	150,000	
18	8	201,485	141,040	60,446	-0.0254	1.0778	216,195	150,000	
19	9	66,195	46,337	19,859	1.0822	1.3451	83,412	150,000	
20	10	-66,588	-46,611	-19,976	-0.9549	0.8950	-62,927	150,000	-212,927
21									
22		Normally-distributed random numbers generated by =NORMSINV(RAND())					=C20*F20+D20*EXP($B$3)		
23									
24	Wealth at beginning of year =G19-H19			1+return on risky investment =EXP($B$5+$B$6*E20)					
25									
26									
27		Investment in risky asset =B20*$B$7							

What interests us is *what percentage of the investment-consumption paths will end with a positive remainder*? We will use Monte Carlo techniques to answer this question. But before we do, we consider a few questions.

22.4.1 Should We Apply the 70 Percent Rule Blindly?

In the preceding simulations we have split our investment between the risky and the riskless investments mechanically. We have also continued to draw down funds irrespective of whether there are funds in the account.

In the following spreadsheet we correct this mechanical approach. We assume that the investor defines a "safety cushion." The cushion in cell B8 is 3, which is taken to mean that the annual drawdown is \$150,000 if the investor's portfolio is worth at least 3 ∗ \$150,000 at the end of the year. If it is not, then the investor takes one-third of her portfolio value as a drawdown:

	A	B	C	D	E	F	G	H	I
1	**PLANNING YOUR RETIREMENT Using a safety cushion of 3 Investor takes 150,000 if end-year wealth > 3*150,000, else takes end-year wealth/3**								
2	Current wealth	1,000,000							
3	Risk-free rate	6%							
4	Parameters of risky investment								
5	Expected annual return	8%							
6	Standard deviation of return	20%							
7	Proportion invested in risky	70%							
8	Safety cushion	3							
9	Annual drawdown	150,000							
10									
11	**Year**	**Wealth at beginning of year**	**Invested in risky**	**Invested in bonds**	**Random number, normally distributed**	**1+return on risky investment**	**Wealth at end of year**	**Drawdown**	**Left at end of 10 years**
12	1	1,000,000	700,000	300,000	-0.5471	0.9710	998,253	150,000	
13	2	848,253	593,777	254,476	0.4716	1.1904	977,072	150,000	
14	3	827,072	578,950	248,121	-0.8906	0.9065	788,306	150,000	
15	4	638,306	446,814	191,492	0.4212	1.1785	729,907	150,000	
16	5	579,907	405,935	173,972	0.9129	1.3003	712,560	150,000	
17	6	562,560	393,792	168,768	0.0895	1.1029	613,500	150,000	
18	7	463,500	324,450	139,050	-0.3590	1.0082	474,770	150,000	
19	8	324,770	227,339	97,431	-0.9809	0.8903	305,860	101,953	
20	9	203,906	142,734	61,172	-1.1469	0.8612	187,882	62,627	
21	10	125,255	87,678	37,576	-0.2989	1.0204	129,369	43,123	86,246
22									
23		Normally-distributed random numbers generated by =NORMSINV(RAND())					=C21*F21+D21*EXP(\$B\$3)		
24									
25	Wealth at beginning of year =G20-H20			1+return on risky investment =EXP(\$B\$5+\$B\$6*E21)					
26									
27							Drawdown calculated as =IF(G21>\$B\$8*\$B\$9,\$B\$9,G21/\$B\$8)		
28		Investment in risky asset =B21*\$B\$7							

Many rules like this can be devised. The problem here—phrased as investment and payouts over retirement—is substantially the same as that faced by any endowment manager struggling with the problem of how to determine simultaneously the investment and the drawdown policy of the endowment. As far as we know there is no analytical solution to this problem, though, as can be seen, it is not difficult to simulate the problem.

22.5 A Monte Carlo Simulation of the Investment Problem

We will write a VBA function **Successfulruns** that resembles the earlier problem (the one without the cushion). Given an investment policy, the function **Successfulruns** determines the percentage of investment/drawdown trajectories that will leave the retiree with positive wealth at the end of his investment horizon.

Here is some output from this function:

	A	B	C	D	E
1	HOW WELL DO WE DO? PERCENTAGE OF POSITIVE OUTCOMES				
2	Current wealth	1,000,000			
3	Risk-free rate	8%			
4	Parameters of risky investment				
5	Expected annual return	10%			
6	Standard deviation of return	40%			
7	Proportion invested in risky	40%			
8	Annual drawdown	100,000			
9	Years of investment	10			
10					
11	Runs	1,000			
12					
13	Successful runs	87.60%	<-- =successfulruns(B2,B8,B3,B5,B6,B7,B9,B11)		

The function result in cell B13 considers a retiree starting with $1 million, making an investment decision between a risk-free asset with return 8 percent and a risky asset with stochastic returns $\mu = 10$ percent and $\sigma = 40$ percent, and desiring to draw down $100,000 per year. Simulating 1,000 returns, we determine that in 87.6 percent of the cases the investor will finish with positive wealth at the end of 10 years.

To see if this outcome is reasonable, we do some "brute force" simulations. In the next spreadsheet, we examine 100 investment trajectories. In each cell of the table we consider a function of the following type:

Wealth, end year t =

$$\begin{cases} \text{Wealth}(t-1) * \text{Percent in risky} * \text{Up} \\ + \text{Wealth}(t-1) * (1 - \text{Percent in risky}) * R - \text{Drawdown} & \text{if } \mathbf{Rand()} > \pi_D \\ \text{Wealth}(t-1) * \text{Percent in risky} * \text{Down} \\ + \text{Wealth}(t-1) * (1 - \text{Percent in risky}) * R - \text{Drawdown} & \text{if } \mathbf{Rand()} \le \pi_D \end{cases}$$

where $R = \exp(r)$, $\text{Up} = \exp(\mu + \sigma)$, $\text{Down} = \exp(\mu - \sigma)$,

$$\pi_U = \frac{R - \text{Down}}{\text{Up} - \text{Down}}, \quad \text{and} \quad \pi_D = \frac{\text{Up} - R}{\text{Up} - \text{Down}}.$$

This simulation—like those in Chapter 18—simulates a lognormal return for the risky asset, taking out the drawdown desired by the investor in each period. Here's the output:

	A	B	C	D	E	F	G	H	I	J
1	**HOW WELL DO WE DO? PERCENTAGE OF POSITIVE OUTCOMES**									
2	Current wealth	1,000,000								
3	Risk-free rate	8%								
4	Parameters of risky investment									
5	Expected annual return	10%								
6	Standard deviation of return	40%								
7	Proportion invested in risky	40%								
8	Annual drawdown	100,000								
9	Years of investment	10								
10										
11	Runs	1,000								
12										
13	Successful runs	87.60%	<-- =successfulruns(B2,B8,B3,B5,B6,B7,B9,B11)							
14										
15										
16	**SIMULATION OF 100 PATHS**									
17	R	1.0833	<-- =EXP(B3)							
18	Up	1.6487	<-- =EXP(B5+B6)							
19	Down	0.7408	<-- =EXP(B5-B6)							
20										
21	PiUp (risk-neutral prob. of Up)	0.3772	<-- =(B17-B19)/(B18-B19)							
22	PiDown (risk-neutral prob. of Down)	0.6228	<-- =(B18-B17)/(B18-B19)							
23										
24										
25	Number of year 10 wealth > 0	85	<-- =COUNTIF(C40:CX40,">0")							
26	Percentage of successful simulations	85.00%	<-- =B25/100							
27										
28			**Wealth at end of year**							
29		**Year**	Simulation 1	Simulation 2	Simulation 3	Simulation 4	Simulation 5	Simulation 6	Simulation 7	Simulation 8
30		0	1,000,000	1,000,000	1,000,000	1,000,000	1,000,000	1,000,000	1,000,000	1,000,000
31		1	1,209,461	846,300	846,300	1,209,461	846,300	846,300	846,300	846,300
32		2	1,483,741	700,853	700,853	1,044,512	700,853	700,853	700,853	1,008,196
33		3	1,842,901	817,739	563,217	888,421	563,217	817,739	817,739	854,055
34		4	1,643,936	970,798	432,972	1,063,353	432,972	673,826	970,798	708,192
35		5	1,455,656	818,665	309,721	1,292,419	309,721	537,642	818,665	827,350
36		6	1,277,487	674,703	305,567	1,123,015	193,089	408,770	674,703	983,382
37		7	1,108,885	538,471	189,158	962,709	152,842	435,268	538,471	830,574
38		8	949,338	409,555	79,000	811,011	44,634	311,894	409,555	987,604
39		9	1,143,120	436,296	3,448	961,987	-41,553	308,413	287,561	834,569
40		10	981,734	312,866	-96,737	1,159,684	-139,322	191,851	276,550	689,753

Cell C31 contains formula =IF(RAND()>$B$22,$B$7*C30*$B$18+(1-$B$7)*C30*$B$17-$B$8,$B$7*C30*$B$19+(1-$B$7)*C30*$B$17-$B$8)

In this particular simulation (the results change with every press on **F9** to recalculate the spreadsheet), 85 percent of all the simulated paths ended with positive wealth—substantially in agreement with the results of the function **Successfulruns**.

22.5.1 The VBA Code for Successfulruns

We almost forgot! Here it is:

```
Function SuccessfulRuns(Initial, Drawdown, Interest,
Mean, _
   Sigma, PercentRisky, Years, Runs)
   Dim PortfolioValue() As Double
   ReDim PortfolioValue(Years + 1)
   Dim Success As Integer

   Up = Exp(Mean + Sigma)
   Down = Exp(Mean - Sigma)

   PiUp = (Exp(Interest) - Down) / (Up - Down)
   PiDown = 1 - PiUp

   For Index = 1 To Runs
   For j = 1 To Years
   Randomize

   PortfolioValue(0) = Initial
   If Rnd > PiDown Then
      PortfolioValue(j) = _
      PortfolioValue(j - 1) * PercentRisky * Up + _
      PortfolioValue(j - 1) * (1 - PercentRisky) * _
      Exp(Interest) - Drawdown
   Else
      PortfolioValue(j) = PortfolioValue(j - 1) * _
      PercentRisky * Down + _
      PortfolioValue(j - 1) * (1 - PercentRisky) *
Exp(Interest) _
      - Drawdown
   End If

   Next j
      If PortfolioValue(Years) > 0 Then Success = _
      Success + 1
   Next Index
   SuccessfulRuns = Success / Runs
End Function
```

22.6 Summary

Monte Carlo methods are experimental techniques for determining the numerical value of a function or a procedure. In general these methods are to be avoided when there is another, closed-form, way of determining the value. In cases where no such method exists, however, you can use Monte Carlo to approximate the value. In this chapter we have used the example of π to illustrate how Monte Carlo might be applied. In Chapter 23 we use Monte Carlo to price various kinds of options.

Exercises

1. In section 22.3 we designed a macro that calculates the value of π using Monte Carlo and that updates the screen every iteration. Modify the macro so that it updates the screen only every 1,000 iterations.

   Hints:

   - Use the VBA function **Mod**. From the VBA help menu, note that this function has syntax **a Mod b**. (A similar Excel function has syntax **Mod(a,b)**, but cannot be used in VBA.)
   - Use the VBA commands **Application.ScreenUpdating = True** and **Application.ScreenUpdating = False** to control the updating of the screen.

2. Put a "switch" on the spreadsheet itself from exercise 1 that controls the updating of the macro (whether to update, yes or no, and how often to update).

3. Use Monte Carlo to calculate the integral of the function exp(x) for $0 < x < 3$. Here's the graph of this function:

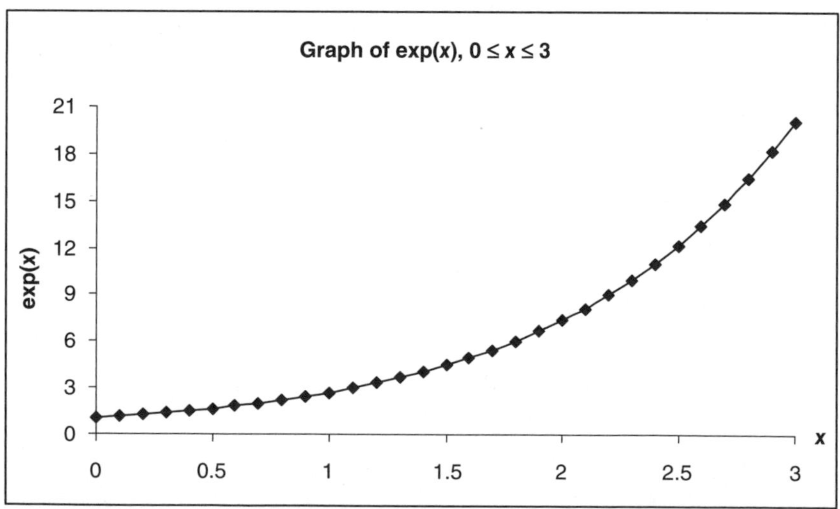

4. One of the messages of this chapter is that while Monte Carlo is a clever method of calculation, it shouldn't be used when a better method exists. The MC valuation of π in section 22.2.1, for example, converges very slowly. It's a crummy way to compute π, since well-known methods exist. To see this point, answer the following questions:

   a. Approximately how many runs are required until you get four-decimal accuracy for π using our MC simulation?
   b. Approximately how many runs are required until you get eight-decimal accuracy for π using our MC simulation?
   c. Approximately how many runs are required until you get 16-decimal accuracy for π using our MC simulation?

   Note that in exercises 5 and 6 we show you several alternative ways to compute the value of π. All are substantially better than Monte Carlo!

5. The first method for computing π is

$$\frac{\pi^2}{6} = 1 + \frac{1}{2^2} + \frac{1}{3^2} + \ldots$$

   Use this series to construct a VBA function to value π, where n is the number of terms in the series. What value of n gives you four-decimal-place accuracy? Eight-decimal-place?

6. The great Indian mathematical genius Ramanujan showed that

$$\frac{1}{\pi} = \frac{\sqrt{8}}{9{,}801} \sum_{n=0}^{\infty} \frac{(4n)!}{(n!)^4} \frac{(1{,}103 + 26{,}390n)}{396^{4n}}$$

   The $n!$ indicates the factorial:

$$n! = n*(n-1)*(n-2)*\ldots*2*1$$
$$0! = 1$$

   Excel's function **Fact** computes the factorial.

   Use this series to construct a VBA function to value π, where n is the number of terms in the series. Show that two iterations give you more than 15 digits of accuracy.

Some Comments on the Value of π

Exercise 6 is based on an article by D. H. Bailey, J. M. Borwein, and P. B. Borwein: "Ramanujan, Modular Equations, and Approximations to π Or How to Compute One Billion Digits of Pi." The article originally appeared in the *American Mathematical Monthly*, 1987, volume 96, number 3, pages 201–219. It can be downloaded at http://www.cecm.sfu.ca/organics/papers/borwein/index.html. Ramanujan's method in exercise 6 adds roughly eight digits with each iteration. Ramanujan developed an even faster method, where only 13 iterations provide more than *one billion* digits of π. (Excel's maximal accuracy is only 15 digits, but there is a nice Excel add-in that extends the precision to 32,767 digits: http://precisioncalc.com/).

Srinivasan Ramanujan (1887–1920) was one of the great mathematical geniuses of all time. Read a biography of this unique individual: *The Man Who Knew Infinity: A Life of the Genius Ramanujan* by Robert Kanigel, published by Charles Scribner, 1991 (paperback edition, Washington Square Press, 1992).

Finally: So what's the value of π? *Mathematica*—a very sophisticated mathematical programming language (http://www.wolfram.com)—gives the following values for π:

Number of Significant Digits	Value of π
25	3.141592653589793238462643
50	3.1415926535897932384626433832795028841971693993751
75	3.141592653589793238462643383279502884197169399375105 8209749445923078164062 9
500	3.1415926535897932384626433832795028841971693993751058 2097494459230781640628620899862803482534211706798214808 6513282306647093844609550582231725359408128481117450284 1027019385211055596446229489549303819644288109756659 3344612847564823378678316527120190914564856692346034861 0454326648213393607260249141273724587006606315588174881 5209209628292540917153643678925903600113305305488204 6652138414695194151160943305727036575959195309218611738 1932611793105118548074462379962749567351885752724891227 9381830119491

23 Using Monte Carlo Methods for Option Pricing

23.1 Overview

This chapter continues the discussion of the previous chapter and shows how to implement Monte Carlo methods for pricing options. The main object of the chapter is to show how to price Asian options and barrier options. An Asian option has a payoff that depends on the average price of the underlying asset for some period before option maturity, and a barrier option's payoff depends on the underlying price reaching a particular level at some point before maturity. In sections 23.5–23.7 we will make these general statements more explicit.

Both Asian and barrier options are *path-dependent* options—options whose price depends not only on the terminal price of the asset, but also on the path of the prices by which the terminal price was reached. In general a path-dependent option does not have an analytic price solution. Monte Carlo provides us with a handy numerical tool for pricing such options.

Monte Carlo pricing of options depends on a simulation of the price path of the underlying asset. In order to clarify the Monte Carlo pricing algorithms, we start in section 23.2 with a brief review of state prices and risk neutrality. We then show, in section 23.3, how to price a plain-vanilla option with a Monte Carlo algorithm. Since plain-vanilla options—jargon by which we simply mean European calls and puts on a stock whose price process is lognormal—are accurately priced using the Black-Scholes formula, this exercise allows us to check our pricing method against a known result and also allows us to develop the proper intuitions about the Monte Carlo pricing of more complicated options.

23.2 State Prices, Probabilities, and Risk Neutrality

We start with a brief recapitulation of the basic facts about state prices and risk-neutral pricing discussed in Chapter 17.

Suppose we have binomial framework with stock price S that grows at U or D in every period. Suppose the interest rate is R.[1] Risk neutrality is a property of every set of state prices: Given state prices

1. Properly speaking, U, D, and R are *one plus* the growth and interest rates. For the sake of linguistic parsimony, we will use "up growth," "down growth," and "interest rate" even though we mean something slightly different.

$\left\{q_U = \dfrac{R-D}{R(U-D)}, q_D = \dfrac{U-R}{R(U-D)}\right\}$, the risk-neutral probabilities are defined by $\{\pi_U = Rq_U, \pi_D = Rq_D\}$. The risk-neutral probabilities can be used to price assets by taking the *discounted expected value* of the asset payoffs.[2] An asset with payoffs one period hence of $\{\text{Payoff}_U, \text{Payoff}_D\}$ in states U and D, respectively, has value today of

$$\text{Asset value today} = q_U \text{Payoff}_U + q_D \text{Payoff}_D = \underbrace{\frac{\pi_U \text{Payoff}_U + \pi_D \text{Payoff}_D}{R}}_{\substack{\uparrow \\ \text{The risk-neutral expected payoff} \\ \text{(expectation computed} \\ \text{with the risk-neutral probabilities)} \\ \text{discounted at the risk-free interest} \\ \text{rate}}}$$

The $\{\text{Payoff}_U, \text{Payoff}_D\}$ are usually functions of the underlying asset price. For an ordinary call, for example, $\{\text{Payoff}_U = \max(S^*U - X,0), \text{Payoff}_D = \max(S^*D - X,0)\}$.

We can extend the risk-neutral pricing scheme to multiperiod frameworks. Consider a multiperiod binomial setting where U and D do not change over time, and indicate the date-n state payoffs by $\text{Payoff}_{n,j}$, $j = 0, \ldots, n$. The notation $\text{Payoff}_{n,j}$ indicates the date-n payoff of the asset in a state where there are j up moves on the binomial tree; for a call in a binomial framework, $\text{Payoff}_{n,j} = \max(S^*U^jD^{n-j} - X,0)$ Then the value of this asset is given by

$$\text{Asset value today} = \sum_{j=0}^{n} \binom{n}{j} q_U^j q_D^{n-j} \text{Payoff}_{n,j} = \underbrace{\frac{1}{R^n} \sum_{j=0}^{n} \binom{n}{j} \pi_U^j \pi_D^{n-j} \text{Payoff}_{n,j}}_{\substack{\uparrow \\ \text{The risk-neutral expected} \\ \text{discounted value}}}$$

This particular notation assumes that the tree is *recombining*. It assumes, in other words, that the date-n payoffs are *path independent*—the option payoff is a function only of the terminal stock price and does not depend on the path by which this price is reached (Fig. 23.1). We will return to this topic later in this chapter.

2. As discussed in Chapter 17, the risk-neutral probabilities are not the actual probabilities of the state occurrences. They are in fact "pseudoprobabilities" that derive from the state prices.

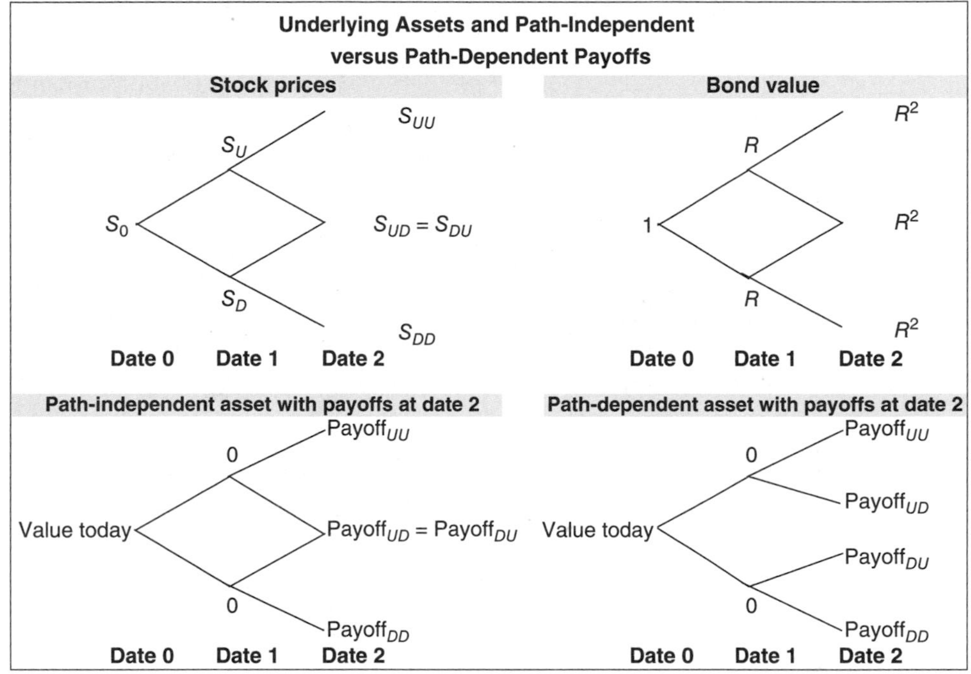

Figure 23.1
Recombining versus nonrecombining binomial models.

23.3 Pricing a Plain-Vanilla Call Using Monte Carlo Methods

In this section we explore the pricing of a European call using Monte Carlo. In one sense, of course, this is an immense waste of time—the Black-Scholes formula (Chapter 19) gives a wonderful pricing solution for European calls and puts. However, like the example of estimating the value of π discussed in Chapter 22, the exercise of pricing a plain-vanilla call using Monte Carlo methods gives us considerable insight into the application of Monte Carlo methods.

23.3.1 A Really Simple Example

We start with a ridiculously simple example. We use Monte Carlo to price a European call in a two-period setting in which the stock price goes either up or down each period. In the following spreadsheet we use Monte Carlo methods to price an at-the-money option on a stock whose price today is $S_0 = 50$. There are two periods, and in each period the stock

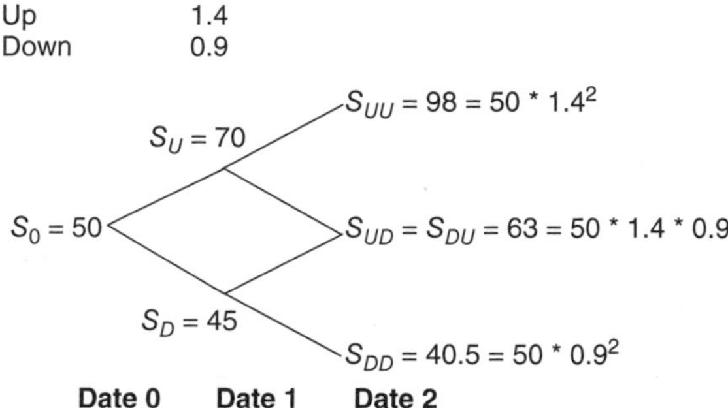

Figure 23.2
Stock-price tree in a standard recombining binomial model.

price goes either Up = 1.4 or Down = 0.9; the interest rate is $R = 1.05$. Given Up and Down, the stock-price tree looks like Figure 23.2.

The following spreadsheet shows two random price paths and their pricing:

	A	B	C	D
1	**SIMPLE SIMULATION: TWO PATHS IN A TWO-DATE MODEL**			
2	Initial stock price	50		
3	X	50		
4				
5	Up	1.4		
6	Down	0.9		
7	R	1.05		
8				
9	**State prices**			
10	q_u	0.2857	<-- =(B7-B6)/(B7*(B5-B6))	
11	q_d	0.6667	<-- =(B7-B6)/(B7*(B5-B6))	
12				
13	**Risk-neutral probabilities**			
14	π_u	0.3000	<-- =B10*$B$7	
15	π_d	0.7000	<-- =B11*$B$7	
16				
17	**Random paths and the Monte Carlo price**			
18	First period, up (1) or down (0)?	0	0	<-- =IF(RAND()>$B$15,1,0)
19	Second period, up (1) or down (0)?	0	1	<-- =IF(RAND()>$B$15,1,0)
20				
21	**Total ups**	0	1	<-- =SUM(C18:C19)
22	**Terminal stock price**	40.5	63	<-- =$B$2*up^C21*down^(2-C21)
23	**Option payoff**	0	13	<-- =MAX(C22-$B$3,0)
24				
25	**Average discounted payoff**	5.8957	<-- =AVERAGE(23:23)/R_^2	
26				
27	**Computing the actual option price with state prices**			
28	**Payoffs**			
29	top	48	<-- =MAX(B2*up^2-B3,0)	
30	middle	13	<-- =MAX(B2*up*down-B3,0)	
31	bottom	0	<-- =MAX(B2*down^2-B3,0)	
32	Actual option price	8.8707	<-- =q_up^2*B29+2*q_up*q_down*B30+q_down^2*B31	

The state prices and risk-neutral probabilities are computed in cells B10:B11 and B14:B15. Cells B18:B29 and C18:C19 show two random price paths. In each period we use a random number from Excel generated by the function **Rand**. If **Rand()** > π_D, then the stock price goes up, and if **Rand()** ≤ π_D then the stock price goes down.

- In the first price path (cells B18:B19), the stock price goes down in both periods. The terminal stock price is 40.5, and the option's payoff is 0 (cell B23).
- In the second price path (cells C18:C19), the stock price goes up in the first period and down in the second period. The terminal stock price is 63 and the option's payoff is 13 (cell C23).

If these were the only two random price paths, the Monte Carlo option price would be the discounted average 5.8957 (cell B25). Notice that we have also computed the *actual call price* using the state prices; cell B32 shows this price to be 8.8707.

Risk-Neutral Probabilities in Monte Carlo

Notice the role of the risk-neutral probabilities in the Monte Carlo simulation: The price path is determined *not by the actual probabilities*, but by the risk-neutral probabilities π_U and π_D. There is no role for the actual probabilities in Monte Carlo pricing.

23.3.2 Extending the Two-Period Model

You can't, of course, run a Monte Carlo simulation by using only two price paths. In the next spreadsheet we've extended our price paths to all the columns in the spreadsheet. Excel's spreadsheet is 256 columns wide; therefore, the computation in cell B25 is the average of the option value over 255 simulated price paths.

	A	B	C	D	E	F	G	H	I
1	**SIMPLE SIMULATION: A TWO-DATE MODEL** **As many price paths as there are columns** **Pressing F9 runs the simulation and will change the value in cell B25** **This value should be compared to the actual option price in cell B32**								
2	Initial stock price	50							
3	X	50							
4									
5	Up	1.4							
6	Down	0.9							
7	R	1.05							
8									
9	**State prices**								
10	q_u	0.2857	<-- =(B7-B6)/(B7*(B5-B6))						
11	q_d	0.6667	<-- =(B7-B6)/(B7*(B5-B6))						
12									
13	**Risk-neutral probabilities**								
14	π_u	0.3000	<-- =B10*$B$7						
15	π_d	0.7000	<-- =B11*$B$7						
16									
17	**Random paths and the Monte Carlo price**								
18	First period, up (1) or down (0)?	0	0	1	0	1	0	0	0
19	Second period, up (1) or down (0)?	0	0	1	1	0	1	0	1
20									
21	**Total ups**	0	0	2	1	1	1	0	1
22	**Terminal stock price**	40.5	40.5	98	63	63	63	40.5	63
23	**Option payoff**	0	0	48	13	13	13	0	13
24									
25	**Average discounted payoff**	**8.3055**	<-- =AVERAGE(23:23)/R_^2						
26									
27	**Computing the actual option price with state prices**								
28	**Payoffs**								
29	top	48	<-- =MAX(B2*up^2-B3,0)						
30	middle	13	<-- =MAX(B2*up*down-B3,0)						
31	bottom	0	<-- =MAX(B2*down^2-B3,0)						
32	**Actual option price**	**8.8707**	<-- =q_up^2*B29+2*q_up*q_down*B30+q_down^2*B31						

The average discounted payoff (cell B25) is 8.3055. This value is random, meaning it will change each time we press F9 to produce a new set of random paths. Monte Carlo methods imply that for even more paths we would converge to the actual option price of 8.8707. In the next section we show that the Monte Carlo method eventually produces convergence to this price.

23.4 Monte Carlo Plain-Vanilla Call Pricing Converges to Black-Scholes

Now that we understand the principles, we extend our logic. We write a VBA routine that prices a plain-vanilla call using Monte Carlo methods under conditions that converge to Black-Scholes pricing.

Our basic setup is as follows: We price a European call on a stock whose current price is S_0. The option's exercise price is X, and the time to maturity of the option is T. We assume that the stock price is lognormally distributed with mean μ and standard deviation σ.

To price the call using Monte Carlo,

- We divide the unit time interval into n divisions. Therefore, $\Delta t = 1/n$.
- For each Δt, we define $\text{Up}_{\Delta t} = \exp[\mu\Delta t + \sigma\sqrt{\Delta t}]$ and $\text{Down}_{\Delta t} = \exp[\mu\Delta t - \sigma\sqrt{\Delta t}]$. The interest rate on the interval Δt is $R_{\Delta t} = \exp[r\Delta t]$.
- Therefore, the state prices and risk-neutral probabilities are given by

$$q_u = \frac{R_{\Delta t} - \text{Down}_{\Delta t}}{R_{\Delta t}(\text{Up}_{\Delta t} - \text{Down}_{\Delta t})}, \quad q_d = \frac{\text{Up}_{\Delta t} - R_{\Delta t}}{R_{\Delta t}(\text{Up}_{\Delta t} - \text{Down}_{\Delta t})}$$

$$\pi_u = \frac{R_{\Delta t} - \text{Down}_{\Delta t}}{\text{Up}_{\Delta t} - \text{Down}_{\Delta t}}, \quad \pi_d = \frac{\text{Up}_{\Delta t} - R_{\Delta t}}{\text{Up}_{\Delta t} - \text{Down}_{\Delta t}} = 1 - \pi_u$$

- Since the time to maturity of the option is T, the price path to T requires $m = T/\Delta t$ periods. A price path of length m is created by determining the Up or Down move of the stock as a function of a random number between 0 and 1 and the risk-neutral probability π_d. As discussed in the example of section 23.3, if the random number is greater than π_d, the stock makes an Up move; otherwise it makes a Down move.

23.4.1 A VBA Routine

The VBA routine that follows defines a function **VanillaCall**. This function requires as inputs the variables mentioned previously. The variable **Runs** is the number of random price paths created; these paths are averaged to determine the Monte Carlo value of the call:

```
Function VanillaCall(S0, Exercise, Mean, Sigma,
Interest, _
  Time, Divisions, Runs)

  deltat = 1 / Divisions
  interestdelta = Exp(Interest * deltat)

  up = Exp(Mean * deltat + Sigma * Sqr(deltat))
  down = Exp(Mean * deltat - Sigma * Sqr(deltat))
```

```
    pathlength = Int(Time / deltat)

    'Risk-neutral probabilities
    piup = (interestdelta - down) / (up - down)
    pidown = 1 - piup

    Temp = 0

    For Index = 1 To Runs
    Upcounter = 0
        'Generate terminal price
        For j = 1 To pathlength
            If Rnd > pidown Then Upcounter = _
              Upcounter + 1
        Next j
             callvalue = Application.Max(S0 * _
              (up ^ Upcounter) * _
              (down ^ (pathlength - Upcounter)) _
              - Exercise, 0) / (interestdelta ^ _
              pathlength)
             Temp = Temp + callvalue
    Next Index

    VanillaCall = Temp / Runs
End Function
```

The number of Up moves is stored in a counter called **Upcounter**, and the value of the call for each **Run** is the discounted value of the call payoff for a particular terminal price S_0*Up^{Upcounter} Down$^{\text{Pathlength–Upcounter}}$, where `pathlength = Int(Time / deltat)` is the integer part of $T/\Delta t$:

```
callvalue = Application.Max(S0 * (up ^ Upcounter) * _
   (down ^ (pathlength - Upcounter)) _
   - Exercise, 0) / (interestdelta ^ pathlength)
```

The Monte Carlo value of the call is given by **`VanillaCall = Temp / Runs`**.

23.4.2 Understanding the Principles of the Monte Carlo Simulation

For future reference we state the principles of the Monte Carlo simulation. These principles hold not only for the plain-vanilla options of this section but also for the Asian options treated later in this chapter:

- Price paths are generated by using the risk-neutral probabilities. In the program **Vanillacall**, for example, the price of the stock moves Up if the random-number generator is greater than π_D and moves Down if the random-number generator is less than or equal to π_D. Effectively, therefore, the risk-neutral probabilities $\{\pi_U = 1 - \pi_D, \pi_D\}$ of each price path are incorporated into the price path itself.
- The value of the option using Monte Carlo is determined by the discounted value of the simple average of all results over the price paths generated.

23.4.3 Implementing the MC Function VanillaCall in a Spreadsheet

The following spreadsheet shows the implementation of **VanillaCall**. The value in cell B14 is the option value as computed by the Black-Scholes formula; the function **BSCall** was defined in Chapter 19.

	A	B	C
1	MONTE CARLO PRICING OF PLAIN-VANILLA CALLS		
2	S_0 , current stock price	50	
3	X, exercise price	50	
4	r, interest rate	10%	
5	T, time	0.8	
6	μ, mean stock return	33%	
7	σ, sigma--standard deviation of stock return	30%	
8			
9	n, divisions of unit time	200	
10	Runs	3,000	
11			
12	VanillaCall	7.4417	<-- =vanillacall(B2,B3,B6,B7,B4,B5,B9,B10)
13			
14	BS call	7.2782	<-- =BSCall(B2,B3,B5,B4,B7)

The function divides the time to option expiration $T = 0.8$ (cell B5) into 200 divisions (cell B9), so that $\Delta t = 1/200$. Each time the function is called, it runs 3,000 price paths (cell B10). A particular call of this function produced the value 7.4417 (cell B12), whereas the Black-Scholes call value—computed with the function **BSCall** defined in Chapter 19—is 7.2782 (cell B14).

How good is this MC routine? One way to test it is to run it many times. In the next spreadsheet, we've run 40 instances of the function **VanillaCall**.

	A	B	C	D	E
1	**RUNNING THE MONTE CARLO FUNCTION MANY TIMES**				
2	S_0 , current stock price	50			
3	X, exercise price	50			
4	r, interest rate	10%			
5	T, time	0.8			
6	μ, mean stock return	33%			
7	σ, sigma--standard deviation of stock return	30%			
8					
9	n, divisions	100			
10	Runs	3,000			
11					
12	VanillaCall	7.1404	<-- =vanillacall(B2,B3,B6,B7,B4,B5,B9,B10)		
13					
14	BS call	7.2782	<-- =BSCall(B2,B3,B5,B4,B7)		
15					
16		**Multiple runs of the function**			
17	7.0727	7.4166	7.4725	6.8758	<-- =vanillacall(B2,B3,B6,B7,B4,B5,B9,B10)
18	7.2110	7.4123	7.0760	7.4490	<-- =vanillacall(B2,B3,B6,B7,B4,B5,B9,B10)
19	7.3331	7.5241	7.3272	7.2245	<-- =vanillacall(B2,B3,B6,B7,B4,B5,B9,B10)
20	7.2895	7.6088	7.4434	7.4520	
21	7.4052	7.2947	7.1995	7.4959	
22	7.0948	7.2209	7.2246	7.3204	
23	7.1768	7.3582	7.4190	7.2144	
24	7.1601	7.1392	7.0774	7.2948	
25	7.0564	7.3033	7.2096	7.2723	
26	7.1043	7.1631	7.6564	7.0906	
27					
28	7.2785	<-- =AVERAGE(A17:D26)			
29	0.1673	<-- =STDEV(A17:D26)			

The average value (cell B28) has a relatively low standard deviation (cell B29). The Monte Carlo routine works pretty well.

23.4.4 Improving the Efficiency of the MC Routine

Monte Carlo routines are inherently very wasteful—you have to run them many times to get a reasonable approximation to the true value. Thus there is a lot of mileage in making a particular routine more efficient. Continuing with our **VanillaCall** example, we show one example of such an efficiency gain.

Suppose that after j random numbers the random price is such that there is no chance that the call option will be in the money. Denote the number of Ups after j random coin tosses by Upcounter(j). Then the call option cannot be in the money after n random numbers if $S_0 \text{Up}^{\text{Upcounter}(j)+(n-j)}\text{Down}^{j-\text{Upcounter}(j)} < X$. This formula assumes that all the remaining random numbers (there will be $n - j$ such numbers) will give an Up stock-price movement.

For this case, we should stop choosing random numbers after j and let the call value be zero. The following VBA routine implements this logic:

```
Function BetterVanillaCall(S0, Exercise, Mean, _
  Sigma, Interest, Time, Divisions, Runs)
  deltat = Time / Divisions
  interestdelta = Exp(Interest * deltat)

up = Exp(Mean * deltat + Sigma * Sqr(deltat))
down = Exp(Mean * deltat - Sigma * Sqr(deltat))

pathlength = Int(Time / deltat)

'Risk-neutral probabilities
piup = (interestdelta - down) / (up - down)
pidown = 1 - piup

Temp = 0

For Index = 1 To Runs
  Upcounter = 0
  'Generate terminal price
  For j = 1 To pathlength
  If Rnd > pidown Then Upcounter = Upcounter + 1
    If S0 * up ^ (Upcounter + pathlength - j) * _
   down ^ (j - Upcounter) < X then Goto Compute
```

```
   Next j
Compute:
   callvalue = Application.Max(S0 * (up ^ _
   Upcounter) * (down ^ (pathlength - Upcounter)) _
   - Exercise, 0) / (interestdelta ^ pathlength)
   Temp = Temp + callvalue
Next Index

BetterVanillaCall = Temp / Runs
End Function
```

The highlighted portions of the code show the changes. The lines called **Compute** simply calculate the **Callvalue**.

The following spreadsheet shows the implementation:

	A	B	C
1	**MONTE CARLO PRICING OF PLAIN-VANILLA CALLS** **BetterVanillaCall: A somewhat more efficient function: If, after *j* random numbers that produce *k* Up moves, S_0*Up$^{(k+n-j)}$*Down$^{(j-k)}$<X, then we abort the random price path and let the call value = 0**		
2	S_0 , current stock price	50	
3	X, exercise price	45	
4	r, interest rate	6%	
5	T, time	0.8	
6	μ, mean stock return	12%	
7	σ, sigma--standard deviation of stock return	30%	
8			
9	n, divisions	100	
10	Runs	2,000	
11			
12	VanillaCall	9.2110	<-- =bettervanillacall(B2,B3,B6,B7,B4,B5,B9,B10)
13			
14	BS call	9.2931	<-- =BSCall(B2,B3,B5,B4,B7)

23.4.5 Where Do We Go from Here?

Now that we understand the Monte Carlo technology and its implementation in VBA, we can extend our examples in two directions. In the next two sections we discuss the pricing of Asian options—options in which the option's terminal payoff depends on the average price over the path. In section 23.7 we discuss the pricing of barrier options.

23.5 Pricing Asian Options

An Asian option is an option whose payoff depends in some way on the average price of the asset over a period of time prior to option expiration.[3] Asian options are sometimes called "average price options." There are two common kinds of Asian options:

- In the first kind of Asian option, the option's payoff is based on difference between the average price of the underlying asset and the strike price: max[Average underlying – Strike, 0]. The examples in Figures 23.3 and 23.4 of the oil contract traded on the NYMEX and the traded average price option (TAPO) traded on the London Metals Exchange are this kind of option.
- In the second kind of Asian option, the option's exercise price is the average of the underlying asset's price over a period preceding option maturity: max[Terminal underlying – Average underlying, 0]. Such *average strike* options are common in markets for electric energy. They assist hedgers whose primary risks are related to the average price of the underlying.

Asian options are particularly useful when the user sells the underlying during the period and is therefore exposed to the average price and when there is danger of price manipulation in the underlying. The Asian option mitigates the effect of manipulation, since it is based not on a single price, but on a sequence of prices.

3. See http://www.riskglossary.com/articles/asian_option.htm and http://www.global-derivatives.com/options/asian-options.php for some definitions and a discussion of the literature. A list of references is also given in the bibliography section of this book.

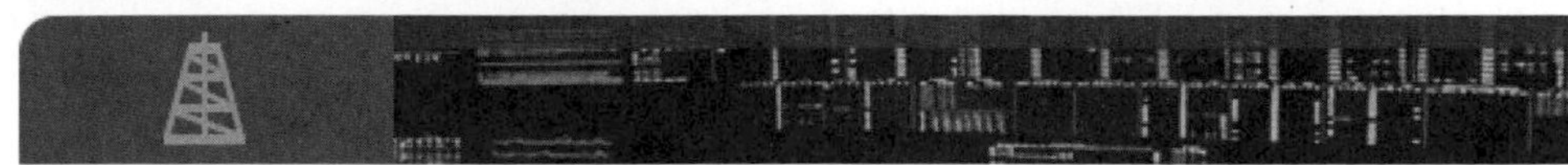

Crude Oil Average Price Options

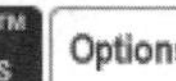

Options

Market Data

Current Session Overview
Current Session Calls
Current Session Puts
Previous Session Calls
Previous Session Puts

Contract Detail

Description
Specifications
Expiration Schedule
Request for Information

Light Sweet Crude Oil Average Price Options

Type

An Asian-style options contract that is cash-settled on expiration day.

Trading Unit

Upon expiration of a call options contract, the value will be the difference between the average front month settlement price over the calendar month of the underlying NYMEX Division West Texas Intermediate crude oil calendar swap futures contract and the strike price multiplied by 1,000 barrels or zero, whichever is greater. Upon expiration of a put options contract, the value will be the difference between the strike price and average front month settlement price over the calendar month of the underlying WTI crude oil calendar swap futures contract multiplied by 1,000 barrels or zero, whichever is greater.

Figure 23.3
Average price crude oil options traded on NYMEX. http://www.nymex.com/AO_spec.aspx

Copper

Where would we be without copper? Well in theory probably still in the stone age, as we would not have had the Bronze Age yet. Copper was the first mineral man extracted from the earth to make utensils, weapons and tools and since the early days it has become invaluable.

LME Traded Average Price Options Specification

Contract date:	The business day on which the contract is traded
Contract period:	Calendar months up to 15, 27 or 63 months forward (in line with the underlying futures contracts). The inclusive period between the first business day and the last business day of the traded month.
Option type:	Calls & puts based on the monthly average settlement price (MASP)
Currency & strike price:	US dollars :$1 gradations
Premium tick size:	0.01 USD (one cent)
Premium payment:	Next business day after contract is traded
Settlement date:	Settlement is two business days after exercise The futures trades settle as per LME rules & regulations

Figure 23.4

Asian options on copper traded on the London Metals Exchange (LME). http://www.basemetals.com/html/cuinfo.htm

23.5.1 An Initial Example of an Asian Option

We start by considering an Asian option on a stock whose price either increases by 40 percent or decreases by 20 percent each period. We look at five dates, starting with date 0:

	A	B	C	D	E	F	G	H	I	J
1					**ASIAN OPTION PICTURE**					
2	Initial stock price	30								
3	Up	1.4								
4	Down	0.8								
5	R, 1+interest rate	1.08								
6	Exercise price	50								
7										
8	**State prices**									
9	q_u	0.4321	<-- =(B5-B4)/(B5*(B3-B4))							
10	q_d	0.4938	<-- =(B3-B5)/(B5*(B3-B4))							
11										
12	**Risk-neutral probabilities**									
13	π_u	0.4667	<-- =B9*$B$5							
14	π_d	0.5333	<-- =B10*$B$5							
15										
16										
17									115.25	<-- =G18*B3
18	**Stock price**						82.32			
19					58.80				65.86	<-- =G18*B4
20			42.00				47.04			
21	30.00				33.60				37.63	<-- =G20*B4
22			24.00				26.88			
23					19.20				21.50	<-- =G22*B4
24							15.36			
25									12.29	<-- =G24*B4
26										
27										
28									1.3605	<-- =G29*$B$5
29		**Bond price**					1.2597			
30					1.1664				1.3605	<-- =G31*$B$5
31			1.0800				1.2597			
32	1.0000				1.1664				1.3605	
33			1.0800				1.2597			
34					1.1664				1.3605	
35							1.2597			
36									1.3605	

To compute the value of the option, we first compute each *price path*. There are 16 such paths. The following spreadsheet shows each path, the average stock price over the path, the option payoff, and the path's risk-neutral probability:

	A	B	C	D	E	G	H	I	J	K	M	N	O
1	**PRICING AN ASIAN OPTION BY PRICING ALL THE PATHS**												
2	Initial stock price	30											
3	Up	1.40											
4	Down	0.80											
5	Interest	1.08											
6	Option exercise price	30											
7											Formula in cell O16: =$B$11^4		
8	State price, Up: q_U	0.4321	<-- =(B5-B4)/(B5*(B3-B4))								Formula in cell O18: =$B$11^3*$B$12		
9	State price, Down, q_D	0.4938	<-- =(B3-B5)/(B5*(B3-B4))										
10							Formula in cell M16 =AVERAGE(G16:K16)						
11	Risk-neutral prob., Up	0.4667	<-- =B8*B5										
12	Risk-neutral prob., Down	0.5333	<-- =B9*B5								Formula in cell N16 =MAX(M16-$B$6,0)		
13													
14								**STOCK PRICE**					
15	**Paths**	**Period 1**	**Period 2**	**Period 3**	**Period 4**	**Period 0**	**Period 1**	**Period 2**	**Period 3**	**Period 4**	**Average stock price**	**Option payoff**	**Path risk-neutral probability**
16	All up (1 path)	up	up	up	up	30.00	42.00	58.80	82.32	115.25	65.67	35.67	0.0474
17													
18	One down (4 paths)	down	up	up	up	30.00	24.00	33.60	47.04	65.86	40.10	10.10	0.0542
19		up	down	up	up	30.00	42.00	33.60	47.04	65.86	43.70	13.70	0.0542
20		up	up	down	up	30.00	42.00	58.80	47.04	65.86	48.74	18.74	0.0542
21		up	up	up	down	30.00	42.00	58.80	82.32	65.86	55.80	25.80	0.0542
22													
23	Two down (6 paths)	down	down	up	up	30.00	24.00	19.20	26.88	37.63	27.54	0.00	0.0619
24		down	up	down	up	30.00	24.00	33.60	26.88	37.63	30.42	0.42	0.0619
25		down	up	up	down	30.00	24.00	33.60	47.04	37.63	34.45	4.45	0.0619
26		up	down	down	up	30.00	42.00	33.60	26.88	37.63	34.02	4.02	0.0619
27		up	up	down	down	30.00	42.00	58.80	47.04	37.63	43.09	13.09	0.0619
28		up	down	up	down	30.00	42.00	33.60	47.04	37.63	38.05	8.05	0.0619
29													
30	Three down (4 paths)	up	down	down	down	30.00	42.00	33.60	26.88	21.50	30.80	0.80	0.0708
31		down	up	down	down	30.00	24.00	33.60	26.88	21.50	27.20	0.00	0.0708
32		down	down	up	down	30.00	24.00	19.20	26.88	21.50	24.32	0.00	0.0708
33		down	down	down	up	30.00	24.00	19.20	15.36	21.50	22.01	0.00	0.0708
34													
35	Four down (1 path)	down	down	down	down	30.00	24.00	19.20	15.36	12.29	20.17	0.00	0.0809
36													
37											Option value	5.3756	
38													
39													
40								Formula in cell N37 =SUMPRODUCT(N16:N35,O16:O35)/B5^4					
41													

The paths are determined by number and sequence of the up and down movements of the stock. For explanatory purposes we have highlighted two price paths:

• Along the path {up, down, up, up} the terminal stock price is 65.856, the average price is 43.699, the option payoff is 13.699, and the discounted expected value using the risk-neutral prices is 0.546:

	A	B	C
1	PATH PRICE EXAMPLE: {Up, Down, Up, Up}		
2	Initial stock price	30	
3	Up	1.40	
4	Down	0.80	
5	Interest	1.08	
6	Option exercise price	30	
7			
8	State price, Up: q_U	0.4321	<-- =(B5-B4)/(B5*(B3-B4))
9	State price, Down, q_D	0.4938	<-- =(B3-B5)/(B5*(B3-B4))
10			
11	Risk-neutral prob., Up	0.4667	<-- =B8*B5
12	Risk-neutral prob., Down	0.5333	<-- =B9*B5
13			
14	**Date**	**Price at beginning of period**	**Price movement: Up or Down**
15	0	30.000	
16	1	42.000	Up
17	2	33.600	Down
18	3	47.040	Up
19	4	65.856	Up
20	Average price along path	43.699	<-- =AVERAGE(B15:B19)
21	Option payoff at path end	13.699	<-- =MAX(B20-$B$6,0)
22	Path risk-neutral price	0.0542	<-- =B11^COUNTIF(C16:C19,"Up")*B12^COUNTIF(C16:C19,"Down")
23	Value of path: Payoff * Risk-neutral price * Discount factor	0.546	<-- =B21*B22/B5^4

The average stock price along this path is 43.699, so that the option pays off max[43.699 – 30, 0] = 13.699.

• Along the path {up, up, down, up} the terminal stock price is the same as before: 65.856. However, the average price and thus the option payoff and value are different:

	A	B	C
1	**PATH PRICE EXAMPLE: {Up, Up, Down, Up}**		
2	Initial stock price	30	
3	Up	1.40	
4	Down	0.80	
5	Interest	1.08	
6	Option exercise price	30	
7			
8	State price, Up: q_U	0.4321	<-- =(B5-B4)/(B5*(B3-B4))
9	State price, Down, q_D	0.4938	<-- =(B3-B5)/(B5*(B3-B4))
10			
11	Risk-neutral prob., Up	0.4667	<-- =B8*B5
12	Risk-neutral prob., Down	0.5333	<-- =B9*B5
13			
14	**Date**	**Price at beginning of period**	**Price movement: Up or Down**
15	0	30.000	
16	1	42.000	Up
17	2	58.800	Up
18	3	47.040	Down
19	4	65.856	Up
20	Average price along path	48.739	<-- =AVERAGE(B15:B19)
21	Option payoff at path end	18.739	<-- =MAX(B20-$B$6,0)
22	Path risk-neutral price	0.0542	<-- =B11^COUNTIF(C16:C19,"Up")*B12^COUNTIF(C16:C19,"Down")
23	Value of path: Payoff * Risk-neutral price * Discount factor	0.747	<-- =B21*B22/B5^4

These two paths illustrate what we mean when we say that an Asian option price is *path dependent*: Two paths—both starting at the initial stock price of 30 and ending at 65.856—have different option payoffs because the stock-price average along the path is different.

This example, which we've not yet concluded, also illustrates the difficulty of pricing Asian options: Each single path must be dealt with—16 separate paths. This fact distinguishes Asian options from the case of ordinary options ("plain vanilla," in the jargon of option pricers); for the particular example we're considering here, a plain-vanilla option requires dealing only with five ending prices.

To price the Asian option, we attach a risk-neutral probability to each price path:

	M	N	O	P
15	**Average stock price**	**Option payoff**	**Path risk-neutral probability**	
16	65.67	35.67	0.0474	<-- =B11^4
17				
18	40.10	10.10	0.0542	<-- =$B$11^3*$B$12
19	43.70	13.70	0.0542	
20	48.74	18.74	0.0542	
21	55.80	25.80	0.0542	
22				
23	27.54	0.00	0.0619	<-- =$B$11^2*$B$12^2
24	30.42	0.42	0.0619	
25	34.45	4.45	0.0619	
26	34.02	4.02	0.0619	
27	43.09	13.09	0.0619	
28	38.05	8.05	0.0619	
29				
30	30.80	0.80	0.0708	<-- =$B$11*$B$12^3
31	27.20	0.00	0.0708	
32	24.32	0.00	0.0708	
33	22.01	0.00	0.0708	
34				
35	20.17	0.00	0.0809	<-- =$B$12^4
36				
37	Option value	5.3756	<-- =SUMPRODUCT(N16:N35,O16:O35)/B5^4	

The option price is the discounted expected payoff value, where the expectations are computed with the risk-neutral probabilities:

$$\frac{\sum_{\text{All paths}} \pi_{\text{Path}} * \text{Option payoff on path}}{R^n} = 5.3756$$

Risk-Neutral Probabilities—Again

We repeat our earlier comments (p. 617) about the role of risk-neutral probabilities: Each path is priced by its discounted risk-neutral probability, which is a function of the Up, Down, and *R*. The actual state probabilities are not relevant.

23.6 Pricing Asian Options with a VBA Program

Our spreadsheet example in the previous section illustrated both the principle of Monte Carlo pricing of options and the problematics of pricing the options directly in a spreadsheet. For four periods, we require the computation of $2^4 = 16$ paths. For a more general problem with n periods, there are 2^n paths to consider; this number rapidly becomes too large for even a very powerful computer. In order to price the options accurately, you would need hundreds or thousands of simulations. Doing these in a spreadsheet directly would be cumbersome. The obvious answer is to write some VBA code to automate the process and allow us to run an arbitrarily large number of simulations.

In this section we write VBA code to do a Monte Carlo simulation of Asian pricing options. We generate price paths by simulating a sequence of Up and Down movements of the underlying stock price; the probability of Up or Down depends on the risk-neutral probabilities—in this sense our Monte Carlo simulation for Asian options is similar to that illustrated in section 23.4 for plain-vanilla options. For each price path generated, we calculate the option payoff, and after generating a large number of price paths, we compute the option price by discounting and averaging these payoffs. The VBA function **MCAsian**, which prices the Asian options, follows:

VBA Asian-Option-Pricing Function

```
Function FCAsian(initial, Exercise, Up, _
     Down, Interest, Periods, Runs)
   Dim PricePath() As Double
   ReDim PricePath (Periods + 1)

   'Risk-neutral probabilities
   piup = (Interest - Down) - (Up - Down)
   pidown = 1 - piup

   Temp = 0
```

```
    For Index = 1 To Runs
       'Generate path
       For i = 1 To Periods
       Pricepath(0) = initial
       pathprob = 1
       If Rnd > pidown Then
            PricePath(i) = PricePath(i - 1) * Up

            Else:
            PricePath(i) = PricePath(i - 1) * Down
       End If
    Next i

          PriceAverage = Application.Sum _
          (PricePath) / (Periods + 1)
          callpayoff = Application.Max _
          (PriceAverage - Exercise, 0)
          Temp = Temp + callpayoff

    Next Index

    MCAsian = (Temp / Interests ^ Periods) _
    / Runs

End Function
```

Here's the implementation of the function in a spreadsheet:

	A	B	C
1	**PRICING AN ASIAN OPTION BY MONTE CARLO**		
2	Up	1.4	
3	Down	0.8	
4	Interest	1.08	
5	Initial price	30	
6	Periods	20	
7	Exercise	30	
8	Runs	500	
9	Asian call value	9.7253	<-- =MCAsian(B5,B7,B2,B3,B4,B6,B8)

The function in cell B9 is our Monte Carlo valuation of the option—the simulated value. Any recalculation of the spreadsheet will cause the function to rerun and recompute the option value.

In the next spreadsheet we show a block of replications of the function. Each of the cells A10:F17 contains **=MCAsian(Initialprice,exercise,Up, Down,Interest,Periods,Runs)**, so that we calculate 48 simulations of the option value.

	A	B	C	D	E	F	G
1	**PRICING AN ASIAN OPTION--VBA FUNCTION** **Prices an Asian option with four periods and 100 runs for each simulation**						
2	Up	1.4					
3	Down	0.8					
4	Interest	1.08					
5	Initial price	30					
6	Periods	4					
7	Exercise	30					
8	Runs	100					
9							
10	6.1553	4.2242	6.5765	4.8856	5.0011	5.3158	<-- =MCAsian($B$5,$B$7,$B$2,$B$3,$B$4,$B$6,$B$8)
11	5.6501	6.0547	5.3120	5.1381	5.0030	3.9862	
12	4.3910	5.5588	5.3586	5.4741	5.4985	6.3849	
13	6.2332	4.9783	4.2952	4.7955	5.1351	3.8102	
14	5.6826	5.3159	5.5378	6.3488	6.3157	5.3347	
15	5.5535	5.6785	5.0737	6.2634	5.8400	5.1982	
16	5.6582	6.0569	6.1157	5.3885	5.0708	5.7090	
17	5.5615	5.4652	5.1437	5.4799	5.7300	4.9654	
18							
19	Average of MC simulations	5.4105	<-- =AVERAGE(A10:F17)				
20	True value	5.3756	<-- From Section 23.5				
21							
22		3.8102	<-- =MIN(A10:F17)				
23		6.5765	<-- =MAX(A10:F17)				
24		0.6227	<-- =STDEV(A10:F17)				

We have deliberately priced the Asian option for which we know the true value—as we showed in section 23.5, the value of an Asian option in a four-period model with the parameters for Up, Down, and Interest illustrated here is 5.3756. The average of our Monte Carlo simulations is 5.4105, with a standard deviation of 0.6227.

When we increase the number of runs (cell B8), we will usually decrease the standard deviation of our estimates (cell B24); this decrease is equivalent to increasing the accuracy of the simulation. In the next example, we have run the 48 simulations 500 runs each:

	A	B	C	D	E	F	G
1	**PRICING AN ASIAN OPTION--VBA FUNCTION** **Pricing an Asian option with four periods and 500 runs for each simulation**						
2	Up	1.4					
3	Down	0.8					
4	Interest	1.08					
5	Initial price	30					
6	Periods	4					
7	Exercise	30					
8	Runs	500					
9							
10	5.2446	5.3915	5.5127	4.7900	5.7154	5.4045	<-- =MCAsian($B$5,$B$7,$B$2,$B$3,$B$4,$B$6,$B$8)
11	5.5467	5.8816	5.1299	5.4879	5.5207	5.1372	
12	5.7815	5.0557	5.3597	5.6537	4.9744	5.1238	
13	5.0642	4.9823	5.4147	5.5262	5.3900	5.3530	
14	4.9365	5.2247	5.3370	5.2451	4.9379	5.6638	
15	5.5245	5.1445	5.1902	5.9107	5.9324	5.3908	
16	5.6054	5.1735	5.6206	4.9663	5.8997	5.0975	
17	4.9088	4.9482	5.3003	4.9104	4.9713	5.5325	
18							
19	Average of MC simulations	5.3295	<-- =AVERAGE(A10:F17)				
20	True value	5.3756	<-- From Section 23.5				
21							
22		4.7900	<-- =MIN(A10:F17)				
23		5.9324	<-- =MAX(A10:F17)				
24		0.3051	<-- =STDEV(A10:F17)				

As you can see, the standard deviation is much reduced—about half of the standard deviation with 100 runs.[4]

23.6.1 Asian Options with More Periods

In the following spreadsheet we divide the unit time interval into n subperiods. We follow the procedure of section 23.4 for defining the returns, state prices, and risk-neutral probabilities over the subperiod Δt. Following is the resulting spreadsheet.

4. The bad news, of course, is that we have to increase the number of runs by a factor of 5 to reduce the standard deviation by one-half.

	A	B	C	D	E	F	G	H
1	**PRICING AN ASIAN OPTION--VBA FUNCTION** **Each time interval is divided into n subintervals. In this simulation the initial stock price = 50.00, the exercise price = 45.00, the time to maturity = 0.40, and the unit time interval is divided into 80 subintervals. The stock price process has mean return = 15.00% and standard deviation = 1.25%, and the interest rate = 8.00%.** **There are 100 runs in each Monte Carlo simulation**							
2	S_0, current stock price	50						
3	X, exercise price	45						
4	T, time to option exercise	0.4						
5	r, interest rate	8%						
6	μ, mean stock return	15%						
7	σ, standard deviation of stock return	22%						
8								
9	n, number of sub-intervals of T	80						
10	Delta t	0.0125	<-- =1/B9					
11								
12	Up over 1 sub-interval	1.0268	<-- =EXP(B6*B10+B7*SQRT(B10))					
13	Down over 1 sub-interval	0.9775	<-- =EXP(B6*B10-B7*SQRT(B10))					
14	Interest over 1 sub-interval	1.0010	<-- =EXP(B5*B10)					
15								
16	Runs	100						
17								
18	6.2475	5.9146	6.0242	5.5575	6.5308	5.0464	<-- =MCAsian($B$2,$B$3,$B$12,$B$13,$B$14,$B$4*$B$9,$B$16)	
19	5.3977	5.6106	5.6373	6.7208	5.4349	5.2232		
20	4.8632	5.7098	5.3437	5.6366	5.1776	5.1993		
21	5.7539	5.4739	6.3559	5.9198	5.9364	5.2982		
22	6.1369	5.4303	4.9872	5.3160	5.4158	5.3885		
23	5.9276	5.5548	5.7701	5.8524	5.4137	5.6423		
24	5.4583	5.4490	5.4570	5.3789	5.6247	5.2845		
25	5.5649	5.6722	5.9362	5.4512	5.5657	5.4095		
26								
27	Average of above	5.6063	<-- =AVERAGE(A18:F25)					
28	Minimum	4.8632	<-- =MIN(A18:F25)					
29	Maxmimum	6.7208	<-- =MAX(A18:F25)					
30	Standard deviation	0.3775	<-- =STDEV(A18:F25)					

The block of results in cells A18:F25 gives 48 results for running the function **MCAsian**. Following this block we give the statistics for these simulations.

These simulations use 100 price paths per iteration of the function **MCAsian**; this is the number contained in cell B16. We can use **Data|Table** to see the effect of changing the number of runs:

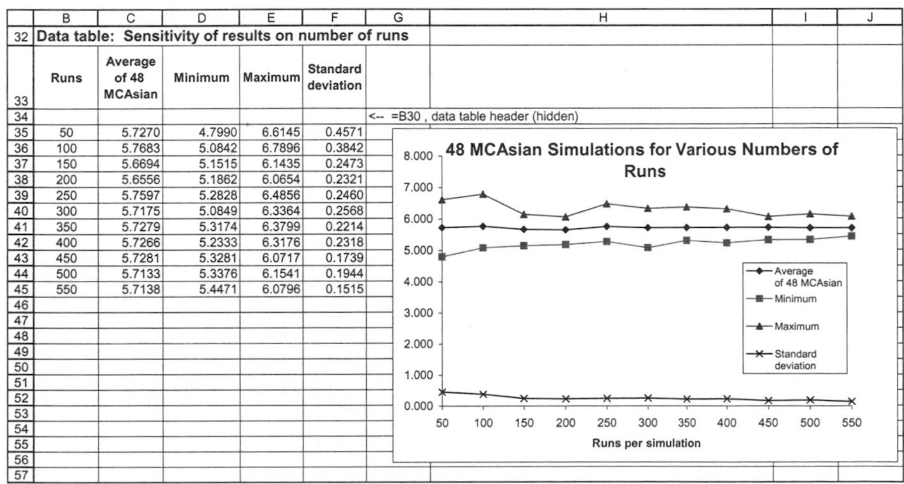

	B	C	D	E	F	G
32	**Data table: Sensitivity of results on number of runs**					
33	**Runs**	**Average of 48 MCAsian**	**Minimum**	**Maximum**	**Standard deviation**	
34						<-- =B30 , data table header (hidden)
35	50	5.7270	4.7990	6.6145	0.4571	
36	100	5.7683	5.0842	6.7896	0.3842	
37	150	5.6694	5.1515	6.1435	0.2473	
38	200	5.6556	5.1862	6.0654	0.2321	
39	250	5.7597	5.2828	6.4856	0.2460	
40	300	5.7175	5.0849	6.3364	0.2568	
41	350	5.7279	5.3174	6.3799	0.2214	
42	400	5.7266	5.2333	6.3176	0.2318	
43	450	5.7281	5.3281	6.0717	0.1739	
44	500	5.7133	5.3376	6.1541	0.1944	
45	550	5.7138	5.4471	6.0796	0.1515	

It is clear that increasing the number of runs narrows the bounds on the simulation.

23.7 Pricing Barrier Options with Monte Carlo[5]

A barrier option's payoff depends on whether the price reaches a specific level during the life of the option:

- A *knockin* barrier call option has payoff $\max(S_T - X, 0)$ only if at some time $t < T$, $S_t > K$. A knockin put has the same condition but pays off $\max(X - S_T, 0)$.
- A *knockout* barrier call or put option has these payoffs provided that at no time before T does the stock price reach the barrier.

Imposing a barrier makes it more difficult for an option to be in the money at expiration; thus barrier options have lower value than regular options.

23.7.1 A Simple Example of a Barrier Call Option

In this section we show an extended example for a knockout barrier option that is similar to the example for an Asian option given in section 23.5.

5. Pricing barrier options with Monte Carlo isn't necessarily a good idea, but it's a good exercise. See Broadie, Glaserman, and Kou (1997) for a complete discussion.

	A	B	C	D	E	F	G	H	I	J	K	L	M	N	O	P
1	PRICING A KNOCKOUT BARRIER OPTION															
2	Initial stock price	30														
3	Up	1.40														
4	Down	0.80														
5	Interest	1.08														
6	Option exercise price	30														
7	Barrier	50.00														
8																
9	q_U	0.4321	<-- =(B5-B4)/(B5*(B3-B4))													
10	q_D	0.4938	<-- =(B3-B5)/(B5*(B3-B4))													
11																
12	Risk-neutral probability, up	0.4667	<-- =B9*B5										Formula in cell M17: =MAX(G17:K17)<$B$7			
13	Risk-neutral probability, down	0.5333	<-- =B10*B5													
14																
15							STOCK PRICE									
16	Paths	Period 1	Period 2	Period 3	Period 4		Period 0	Period 1	Period 2	Period 3	Period 4		Max(S_t)< Barrier?	Path risk-neutral probability	Knockout option payoff	
17	All up (1 path)	up	up	up	up		30.00	42.00	58.80	82.32	115.25		FALSE	0.0474	0.00	
18																
19	One down (4 paths)	down	up	up	up		30.00	24.00	33.60	47.04	65.86		FALSE	0.0542	0.00	
20		up	down	up	up		30.00	42.00	33.60	47.04	65.86		FALSE	0.0542	0.00	
21		up	up	down	up		30.00	42.00	58.80	47.04	65.86		FALSE	0.0542	0.00	
22		up	up	up	down		30.00	42.00	58.80	82.32	65.86		FALSE	0.0542	0.00	
23																
24	Two down (6 paths)	down	down	up	up		30.00	24.00	19.20	26.88	37.63		TRUE	0.0619	7.63	
25		down	up	down	up		30.00	24.00	33.60	26.88	37.63		TRUE	0.0619	7.63	
26		down	up	up	down		30.00	24.00	33.60	47.04	37.63		TRUE	0.0619	7.63	
27		up	down	down	up		30.00	42.00	33.60	26.88	37.63		TRUE	0.0619	7.63	
28		up	up	down	down		30.00	42.00	58.80	47.04	37.63		FALSE	0.0619	0.00	
29		up	down	up	down		30.00	42.00	33.60	47.04	37.63		TRUE	0.0619	7.63	
30																
31	Three down (4 paths)	up	down	down	down		30.00	42.00	33.60	26.88	21.50		TRUE	0.0708	0.00	
32		down	up	down	down		30.00	24.00	33.60	26.88	21.50		TRUE	0.0708	0.00	
33		down	down	up	down		30.00	24.00	19.20	26.88	21.50		TRUE	0.0708	0.00	
34		down	down	down	up		30.00	24.00	19.20	15.36	21.50		TRUE	0.0708	0.00	
35																
36	Four down (1 path)	down	down	down	down		30.00	24.00	19.20	15.36	12.29		TRUE	0.0809	0.00	
37																
38													Knockout value	1.7375		
39																
40													Formula in cell N38: =SUMPRODUCT(O17:O36,N17:N36)/B5^4			
41																
42													Formula in cell O36: =M36*MAX(K36-$B$6,0)			

In this example, we model a five-date, four-period barrier call option. The barrier is 50 (cell B7). A knockout option pays off only if the price never goes through this barrier, and a knockin option pays off only if the stock price goes through the barrier. In an equation,

$$\text{Barrier knockin call payoff} = \begin{cases} \max[S_T - X, 0] & \text{if } S_t > \text{Barrier for } t < T \\ 0 & \text{otherwise} \end{cases}$$

$$\text{Barrier knockout call payoff} = \begin{cases} \max[S_T - X, 0] & \text{if } S_t < \text{Barrier for } t < T \\ 0 & \text{otherwise} \end{cases}$$

The knockout barrier call illustrated here pays off only when two things happen simultaneously:

1. The stock price does not exceed the barrier. This result occurs for all the paths labeled TRUE in column M. To check this condition in cell M17 we use the Boolean function (=MAX(G17:K17)<$B$7).[6] This function evaluates to TRUE or FALSE, depending on whether the condition is met. Other cells in column M use a similar condition. When used in a formula as in item 2, the Boolean function evaluates to 1 if TRUE and to 0 if FALSE.

2. The terminal stock price S_T is greater than the option exercise price of 30. In cell O17 we use the condition M17*MAX(K17-$B$6,0) to evaluate the option payoff.

a. If M17 equals 0 (meaning that $S_t > 50$ somewhere along the path and the option was "knocked out"), then the option doesn't pay off.

b. If M17 equals 1 (so that $S_t < 50$ throughout the path), then the option has a standard call payoff of $\max(S_T - X, 0)$.

As in all previous cases discussed in this chapter, the barrier call's value is the discounted expected payoff of the option, where the probabilities are the risk-neutral probabilities:

$$\text{Option value} = \frac{\sum_{\substack{\text{All states} \\ j}} \pi_j \text{Payoff}_j}{R^4} = 1.7375$$

23.7.2 The Knockin Barrier Call

By changing the condition in column O we can price the knockin barrier call. This time we write (in cell O17, for example) the function =(1-M17)*MAX(K17-$B$6,0). The value in M17 tests whether the barrier has never been passed; if this is FALSE (i.e., has a value of zero), then the option is "knocked in" and the payoff is like that of a regular call. If M17 is TRUE, then the barrier has not been passed and the option does not pay off:

6. Boolean functions are discussed in Chapter 34.

	A	B	C	D	E	F	G	H	I	J	K	L	M	N	O	P
1							PRICING A KNOCKIN BARRIER OPTION									
2	Initial stock price	30														
3	Up	1.40														
4	Down	0.80														
5	Interest	1.08														
6	Option exercise price	30														
7	Barrier	50.00														
8																
9	q_U	0.4321	<-- =(B5-B4)/(B5*(B3-B4))													
10	q_D	0.4938	<-- =(B3-B5)/(B5*(B3-B4))													
11																
12	Risk-neutral probability, up	0.4667	<-- =B9*B5								Formula in cell M17: =MAX(G17:K17)<$B$7					
13	Risk-neutral probability, down	0.5333	<-- =B10*B5													
14																
15								STOCK PRICE								
16	Paths	Period 1	Period 2	Period 3	Period 4		Period 0	Period 1	Period 2	Period 3	Period 4		Max(S_t)< Barrier?	Path risk-neutral probability	Option payoff	
17	All up (1 path)	up	up	up	up		30.00	42.00	58.80	82.32	115.25		FALSE	0.0474	85.25	
18																
19	One down (4 paths)	down	up	up	up		30.00	24.00	33.60	47.04	65.86		FALSE	0.0542	35.86	
20		up	down	up	up		30.00	42.00	33.60	47.04	65.86		FALSE	0.0542	35.86	
21		up	up	down	up		30.00	42.00	58.80	47.04	65.86		FALSE	0.0542	35.86	
22		up	up	up	down		30.00	42.00	58.80	82.32	65.86		FALSE	0.0542	35.86	
23																
24	Two down (6 paths)	down	down	up	up		30.00	24.00	19.20	26.88	37.63		TRUE	0.0619	0.00	
25		down	up	down	up		30.00	24.00	33.60	26.88	37.63		TRUE	0.0619	0.00	
26		down	up	up	down		30.00	24.00	33.60	47.04	37.63		TRUE	0.0619	0.00	
27		up	down	down	up		30.00	42.00	33.60	26.88	37.63		TRUE	0.0619	0.00	
28		up	up	down	down		30.00	42.00	58.80	47.04	37.63		FALSE	0.0619	7.63	
29		up	down	up	down		30.00	42.00	33.60	47.04	37.63		TRUE	0.0619	0.00	
30																
31	Three down (4 paths)	up	down	down	down		30.00	42.00	33.60	26.88	21.50		TRUE	0.0708	0.00	
32		down	up	down	down		30.00	24.00	33.60	26.88	21.50		TRUE	0.0708	0.00	
33		down	down	up	down		30.00	24.00	19.20	26.88	21.50		TRUE	0.0708	0.00	
34		down	down	down	up		30.00	24.00	19.20	15.36	21.50		TRUE	0.0708	0.00	
35																
36	Four down (1 path)	down	down	down	down		30.00	24.00	19.20	15.36	12.29		TRUE	0.0809	0.00	
37																
38													Knockin value	9.0334		
39																
40													Formula in cell N38: =SUMPRODUCT(O17:O36,N17:N36)/B5^4			
41																
42													Formula in cell O36: =(1-M36)*MAX(K36-$B$6,0)			
43																

The spreadsheets for the knockout and knockin barriers illustrate another principle of pricing barrier options: The price of a knockin plus a knockout call equals the price of a regular plain-vanilla call:

	A	B	C	D	E	F	G	H	I	J	K	L	M	N	O	P	Q
1							**KNOCKIN + KNOCKOUT = PLAIN VANILLA**										
2	Initial stock price	30															
3	Up	1.40															
4	Down	0.80															
5	Interest	1.08															
6	Option exercise price	30															
7	Barrier	50.00															
8																	
9	q_U	0.4321	<-- =(B5-B4)/(B5*(B3-B4))														
10	q_D	0.4938	<-- =(B3-B5)/(B5*(B3-B4))									Formula in cell M17: =MAX(G17:K17)<$B$7					
11																	
12	Risk-neutral probability, up	0.4667	<-- =B9*B5														
13	Risk-neutral probability, down	0.5333	<-- =B10*B5														
14																	
15								**STOCK PRICE**									
16	**Paths**	**Period 1**	**Period 2**	**Period 3**	**Period 4**		**Period 0**	**Period 1**	**Period 2**	**Period 3**	**Period 4**		**Max(S_t)< Barrier?**	**Path risk-neutral probability**	**Knockout payoff**	**Knockin payoff**	**Plain vanilla**
17	All up (1 path)	up	up	up	up		30.00	42.00	58.80	82.32	115.25		FALSE	0.0474	0	85.2480	85.2480
18																	
19	One down (4 paths)	down	up	up	up		30.00	24.00	33.60	47.04	65.86		FALSE	0.0542	0	35.8560	35.8560
20		up	down	up	up		30.00	42.00	33.60	47.04	65.86		FALSE	0.0542	0	35.8560	35.8560
21		up	up	down	up		30.00	42.00	58.80	47.04	65.86		FALSE	0.0542	0	35.8560	35.8560
22		up	up	up	down		30.00	42.00	58.80	82.32	65.86		FALSE	0.0542	0	35.8560	35.8560
23																	
24	Two down (6 paths)	down	down	up	up		30.00	24.00	19.20	26.88	37.63		TRUE	0.0619	7.632	0.0000	7.6320
25		down	up	down	up		30.00	24.00	33.60	26.88	37.63		TRUE	0.0619	7.632	0.0000	7.6320
26		down	up	up	down		30.00	24.00	33.60	47.04	37.63		TRUE	0.0619	7.632	0.0000	7.6320
27		up	down	down	up		30.00	42.00	33.60	26.88	37.63		TRUE	0.0619	7.632	0.0000	7.6320
28		up	up	down	down		30.00	42.00	58.80	47.04	37.63		FALSE	0.0619	0	7.6320	7.6320
29		up	down	up	down		30.00	42.00	33.60	47.04	37.63		TRUE	0.0619	7.632	0.0000	7.6320
30																	
31	Three down (4 paths)	up	down	down	down		30.00	42.00	33.60	26.88	21.50		TRUE	0.0708	0	0.0000	0.0000
32		down	up	down	down		30.00	24.00	33.60	26.88	21.50		TRUE	0.0708	0	0.0000	0.0000
33		down	down	up	down		30.00	24.00	19.20	26.88	21.50		TRUE	0.0708	0	0.0000	0.0000
34		down	down	down	up		30.00	24.00	19.20	15.36	21.50		TRUE	0.0708	0	0.0000	0.0000
35																	
36	Four down (1 path)	down	down	down	down		30.00	24.00	19.20	15.36	12.29		TRUE	0.0809	0	0.0000	0.0000
37																	
38											Knockin	9.0334	<-- =SUMPRODUCT(N17:N36,P17:P36)/B5^4				
39											Knockout	1.7375	<-- =SUMPRODUCT(N17:N36,O17:O36)/B5^4				
40											Sum	10.7708	<-- =L38+L39				
41											Plain vanilla	10.7708	<-- =SUMPRODUCT(N17:N36,Q17:Q36)/B5^4				
42																	
43													Formula in cell P36: =(1-M36)*MAX(K36-$B$6,0)				
44																	
45														Formula in cell O36: =M36*MAX(K36-$B$6,0)			
46																	

23.8 Using VBA and Monte Carlo to Price a Barrier Option

We write two VBA functions to price knockin and knockout barrier options. Here is the function for knockout options:

```
Function MCBarrierOut(Initial, Exercise, Barrier, Up, _
   Down, Interest, Periods, Runs)
   Dim PricePath() As Double
   ReDim PricePath(Periods + 1)

   'Risk-neutral probabilities
   piup = (Interest - Down) / (Up - Down)
   pidown = 1 - piup
```

```
  Temp = 0

  For Index = 1 To Runs
    'Generate path
    For i = 1 To Periods
      PricePath(0) = Initial
      pathprob = 1
      If Rnd > pidown Then
        PricePath(i) = PricePath(i - 1) * Up

        Else:
        PricePath(i) = PricePath(i - 1) * Down
      End If
     Next i

      If Application.Max(PricePath) < Barrier Then
        Callpayoff = _
        Application.Max(PricePath(Periods) - _
        Exercise, 0) _
        Else Callpayoff = 0
      Temp = Temp + Callpayoff

  Next Index

  MCBarrierOut = (Temp / Interest ^ Periods) / Runs

End Function
```

Since this function is very similar to the function **MCAsian** of section 23.6, we will not discuss it, except to point out that the operative part for the “knockin” option is contained in the following lines (note the use of Excel’s **Max** function—in the form of **Application.Max**; VBA does not have its own maximum function):

```
If Application.Max(PricePath) < Barrier Then
Callpayoff = _
   Application.Max(PricePath(Periods) - Exercise, 0) _
   Else Callpayoff = 0
```

In the next spreadsheet we use this function and its associated function **MCBarrierOut** to price the options previously priced in our extensive example:

	A	B	C	D	E	F
1	PRICING BARRIER OPTIONS BY MONTE CARLO					
2	Up	1.4				
3	Down	0.8				
4	Interest	1.08				
5						
6	Initial price	30				
7	Periods	4				
8	Exercise	30				
9	Barrier	50				
10						
11	Runs	100				
12						
13	Knockin option value	7.0810	<-- =mcbarrierin(B6,B8,B9,B2,B3,B4,B7,B11)			
14	Actual value	9.0334	<-- ='Initial knockin'!N38			
15						
16	Knockout option value	1.6829	<-- =mcbarrierout(B6,B8,B9,B2,B3,B4,B7,B11)			
17	Actual value	1.7375	<-- Determined from fully-worked out example			
18						
19	**48 iterations of MCBarrierIn**					
20	7.7944	7.2408	8.4210	9.2159	6.8481	13.1353
21	11.6143	8.3860	9.5916	9.1598	7.6430	11.3200
22	9.3154	6.7095	7.2673	9.2593	9.7948	8.9174
23	11.0269	10.1018	7.4959	7.5435	9.3069	9.3799
24	11.7265	8.4210	6.5369	10.6289	8.8613	8.6327
25	9.5016	9.6350	9.1037	7.9066	8.2262	8.9565
26	10.9358	7.4440	9.2550	12.1806	8.1056	8.9216
27	6.3771	7.4440	9.4318	9.3323	9.5831	9.1428
28						
29	Average of simulations	9.0162	<-- =AVERAGE(A20:F27)			
30	True value	9.0334	<-- =B14			
31						
32		6.3771	<-- =MIN(A20:F27)			
33		13.1353	<-- =MAX(A20:F27)			
34		1.5066	<-- =STDEV(A20:F27)			

Finally, we can also show the implementation of the functions **MCBarrierIn** and **MCBarrierOut** for the case where the unit period is divided into n subperiods:

	A	B	C	D	E	F	G	H
1	**PRICING BARRIER OPTIONS--VBA FUNCTION** **Each time interval is divided into n subintervals. In this simulation the initial stock price = 50.00, the exercise price = 45.00, the time to maturity = 0.40, and the unit time interval is divided into 80 subintervals. The stock price process has mean return = 15.00% and standard deviation = 1.25%, and the interest rate = 8.00%.** **There are 100 runs in each Monte Carlo simulation**							
2	S_0, current stock price	50						
3	X, exercise price	45						
4	Barrier	50						
5	T, time to option exercise	0.4						
6	r, interest rate	8%						
7	μ, mean stock return	15%						
8	σ, standard deviation of stock return	22%						
9								
10	n, number of subintervals of 1 period	80						
11	Delta t	0.0125	<-- =1/B10					
12								
13	Up over 1 subinterval	1.0268	<-- =EXP(B7*B11+B8*SQRT(B11))					
14	Down over 1 subinterval	0.9775	<-- =EXP(B7*B11-B8*SQRT(B11))					
15	Interest over 1 subinterval	1.0010	<-- =EXP(B6*B11)					
16								
17	Runs	100						
18								
19	6.9666	7.8251	6.0301	7.5631	6.2022	6.0205	<-- =mcbarrierin($B$2,$B$3,$B$4,$B$13,$B$14,$B$15,INT($B$10*$B$5),$B$17)	
20	6.2149	7.2956	7.0748	7.7456	6.4665	7.3994		
21	7.2747	7.8567	7.4531	7.4395	7.5946	6.8954		
22	6.6258	6.8220	6.2379	6.7264	6.9056	6.4062		
23	6.8421	8.4597	7.2974	7.6032	6.3056	6.5011		
24	8.4227	6.6866	7.3832	6.6680	7.6663	6.8732		
25	7.5956	7.6050	6.9231	6.7689	7.1278	8.7135		
26	7.5495	7.1480	6.4259	7.5199	6.1428	6.7183		
27								
28	Average of above	7.0831	<-- =AVERAGE(A19:F26)					
29	Minimum	6.0205	<-- =MIN(A19:F26)					
30	Maxmimum	8.7135	<-- =MAX(A19:F26)					
31	Standard deviation	0.6412	<-- =STDEV(A19:F26)					

As for the case discussed in section 23.6 for Asian options, as the number of runs (cell B17) gets larger, the approximations become better, although the improvement is not dramatic:

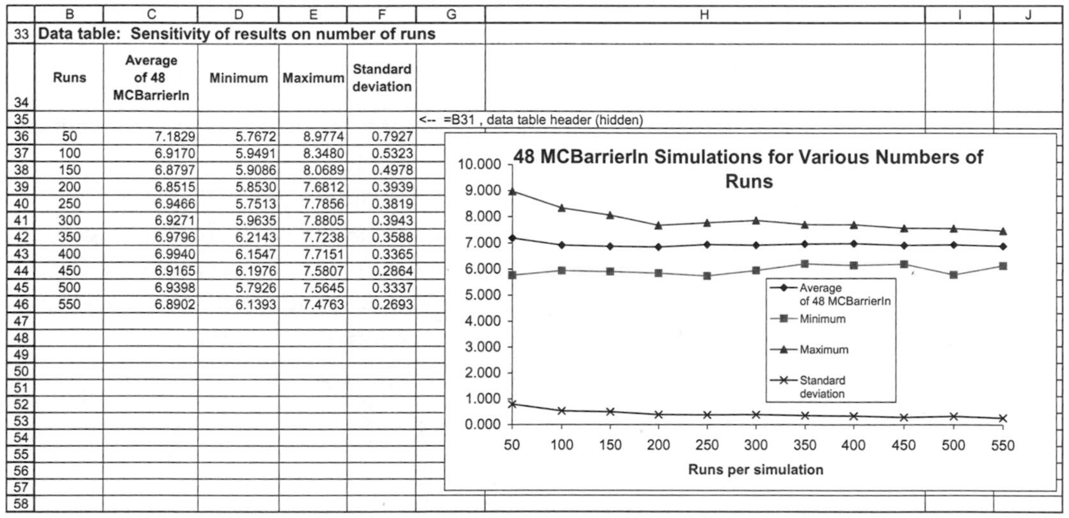

	B	C	D	E	F	G
33	**Data table: Sensitivity of results on number of runs**					
34	**Runs**	**Average of 48 MCBarrierIn**	**Minimum**	**Maximum**	**Standard deviation**	
35						<-- =B31 , data table header (hidden)
36	50	7.1829	5.7672	8.9774	0.7927	
37	100	6.9170	5.9491	8.3480	0.5323	
38	150	6.8797	5.9086	8.0689	0.4978	
39	200	6.8515	5.8530	7.6812	0.3939	
40	250	6.9466	5.7513	7.7856	0.3819	
41	300	6.9271	5.9635	7.8805	0.3943	
42	350	6.9796	6.2143	7.7238	0.3588	
43	400	6.9940	6.1547	7.7151	0.3365	
44	450	6.9165	6.1976	7.5807	0.2864	
45	500	6.9398	5.7926	7.5645	0.3337	
46	550	6.8902	6.1393	7.4763	0.2693	

Finally, we can show that the sum of the knockin plus knockout is approximately equal to the Black-Scholes call when *n*, the number of divisions of the unit time interval, is very large:

	A	B	C
1	**KNOCKIN + KNOCKOUT = CALL** **The almost-continuous case**		
2	S_0, current stock price	30	
3	X, exercise price	30	
4	Barrier	40	
5	T, time to option exercise	0.4	
6	r, interest rate	8%	
7	μ, mean stock return	15%	
8	σ, standard deviation of stock return	22%	
9			
10	n, number of subintervals of 1 period	200	
11	Delta t	0.0050	<-- =1/B10
12			
13	Up over 1 subinterval	1.0164	<-- =EXP(B7*B11+B8*SQRT(B11))
14	Down over 1 subinterval	0.9853	<-- =EXP(B7*B11-B8*SQRT(B11))
15	Interest over 1 subinterval	1.0004	<-- =EXP(B6*B11)
16			
17	Runs	700	
18			
19	Knockout barrier	1.653148	<-- =mcbarrierout(B2,B3,B4,B13,B14,B15,INT(B10*B5),B17)
20	Knockin barrier	0.504321	<-- =mcbarrierin(B2,B3,B4,B13,B14,B15,INT(B10*B5),B17)
21	Sum of knockout + knockin	2.157468	<-- =B19+B20
22	Black-Scholes call price	2.153173	<-- =BSCall(B2,B3,B5,B6,B8)

23.9 Summary

Monte Carlo methods—simulations of option pricing by tracing out many paths of the stock price—are at best a "second best" method of pricing. But in cases where no analytical formulas are available, Monte Carlo is easy to program in VBA and easy to see in Excel. In this chapter we have illustrated Monte Carlo methods for plain-vanilla options, Asian options, and barrier options. Other variations of path-dependent options and their Monte Carlo solutions are considered in the exercises.

Exercises

1. Create a VBA subroutine [call it **Exercise1( )**] that generates a random number and prints it on the screen in a message box that looks like this:

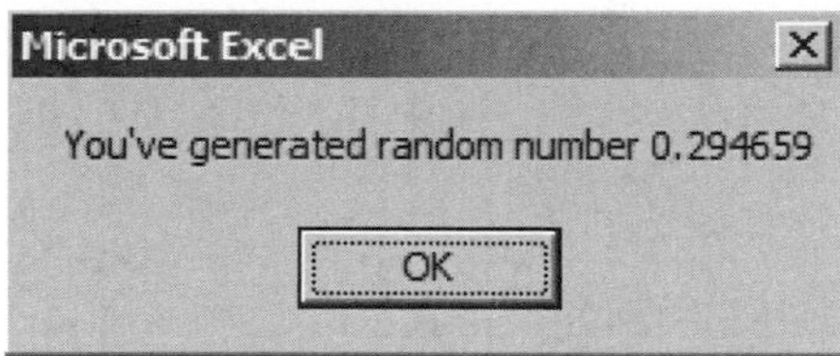

Note Use the VBA keyword **Rnd**.

2. Create a VBA subroutine [call it **Exercise2( )**] that generates five random numbers and prints them out on the screen in a message box like the following:

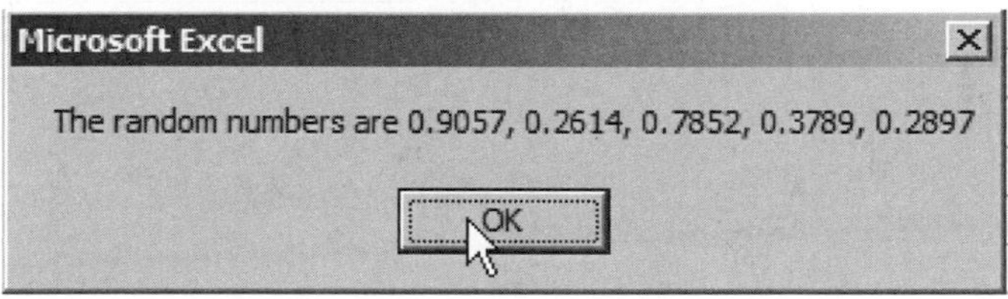

Note Use **FormatNumber**(*Expression*,*NumDigitsAfterDecimal*) to print out only four digits.

3. Create a VBA subroutine [call it **Exercise3( )**] that generates five random digits of either 1 or 0 and prints them out on the screen in a message box like the following:

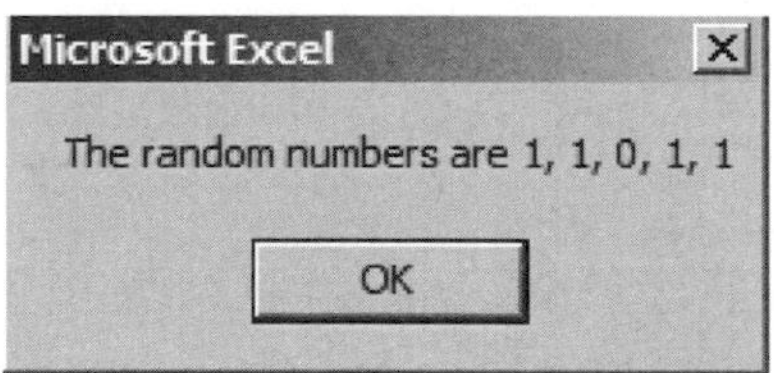

4. Suppose a stock price follows a binomial distribution. We want to create *random price path* for the stock in a VBA macro. The picture shows the input with some sample output. Write an appropriate VBA subroutine.

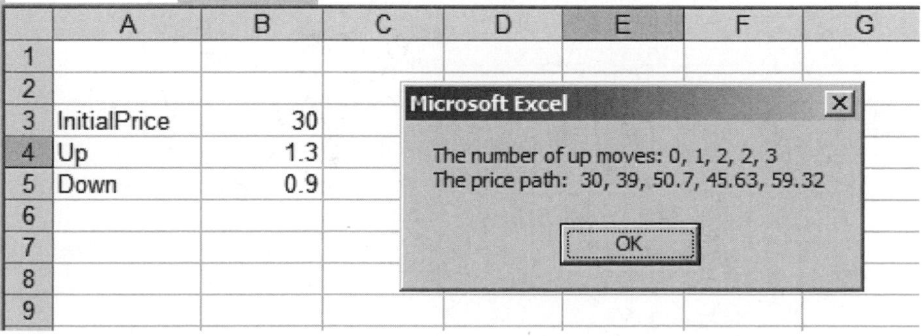

Notes

- In the VBA message box, use **Chr(13)** to start a new line.
- Use range names in the spreadsheet to transfer values from the spreadsheet to the VBA routine.

5. Repeat the last exercise. This time compute the average price of a path:

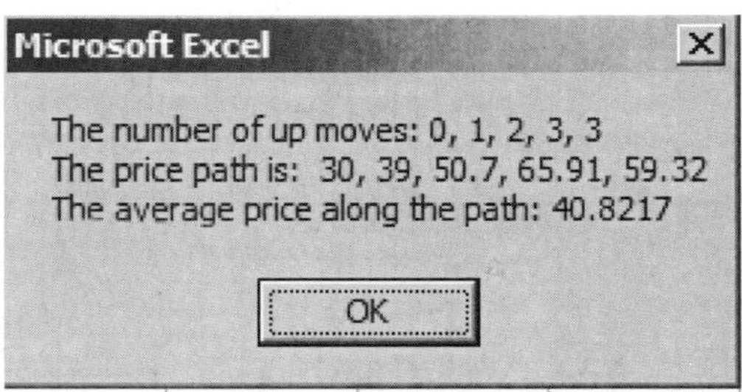
Microsoft Excel
The number of up moves: 0, 1, 2, 3, 3
The price path is: 30, 39, 50.7, 65.91, 59.32
The average price along the path: 40.8217
OK

6. Use the function **VanillaCall** defined in the chapter to create a **Data table** in which you can see the relation between the number of runs incorporated in the function and the Black-Scholes value of a call. Your result should look something like the following:

	A	B	C
1	**MONTE CARLO PRICING OF PLAIN VANILLA CALLS**		
2	S_0 , current stock price	50	
3	X, exercise price	50	
4	r, interest rate	10%	
5	T, time	0.8	
6	μ, mean stock return	33%	
7	σ, sigma--standard deviation of stock return	30%	
8			
9	n, divisions of unit time	100	<-- Try playing around with this
10	Runs	200	<-- This is what's altered in the data table
11			
12	VanillaCall	8.6676	<-- =vanillacall(B2,B3,B6,B7,B4,B5,B9,B10)
13			
14	BS call	7.2782	<-- =BSCall(B2,B3,B5,B4,B7)
15			
16			
17	Data table: the effect of runs on the MC Vanilla call value		
18		Monte Carlo	Black-Scholes
19	**Runs**	8.6676	7.2782
20	100	7.2390	7.2782
21	500	7.6714	7.2782
22	1,000	6.9776	7.2782
23	1,500	7.1376	7.2782
24	2,000	7.1541	7.2782
25	2,500	6.9955	7.2782
26	3,000	7.2497	7.2782
27	3,500	7.2132	7.2782
28	4,000	7.4493	7.2782
29	4,500	7.2588	7.2782
30	5,000	7.1575	7.2782
31	5,500	7.2380	7.2782
32	6,000	7.4882	7.2782
33	6,500	7.4087	7.2782
34			
35			
36			
37			

24 Real Options

24.1 Overview

The standard net present value (NPV) analysis of capital budgeting values a project by discounting its expected cash flows at a risk-adjusted cost of capital. This *discounted cash flow* (DCF) technique is by far the most widely used practice for evaluating capital projects, be they acquisitions of companies or the purchases of machines. However, standard NPV analysis does not take account of the *flexibility* inherent in the capital budgeting process: Part of the complexity of the capital budgeting process is that the firm can change its decision dynamically, depending on the circumstances.

Here are two examples:

1. A firm is considering replacing some of its machines with a new type of machine. Instead of replacing all the machines together, it can first replace one machine. Based on the performance of the first machine replaced, the firm can then decide whether to replace the rest of the machines. This "option to wait" (or perhaps the "option to expand") is not valued in the standard NPV process. It is essentially a call option.
2. A firm is considering investing in a project that will produce (uncertain) cash flows over time. One option—not valued in the standard NPV framework—is to *abandon* the project if its performance is not satisfactory. The *abandonment option*, as we will see, is a put option that is implicit in many projects. It is also sometimes called the *option to contract scale*.

There are many other real options. In the leading book on the valuation of real options, Trigeorgis (1996) lists the following common ones:

- The option to defer or to wait when developing a natural resource or build a plant.
- The time-to-build option (staged investment): At each stage the investment can be reevaluated and (possibly) abandoned or expanded.
- The option to alter operating scale (expand, contract, shut down, or restart).
- The option to abandon.
- The option to switch inputs or outputs.
- The growth option—an early investment in a project constitutes an option to "get into the market" at a later date.

The recognition of real options is an important extension of the NPV techniques. However, modeling and valuing real options is more difficult than modeling and valuing standard cash flows by the DCF method. Our examples in this chapter illustrate these difficulties. Often it is best to implement real options by recognizing that the DCF technique misjudges the value of a project because it ignores the project's real options. Our usual conclusion will be that real options add to the value of a project, and that the NPV thus underestimates the true value.

24.2 A Simple Example of the Option to Expand

In this section we give a simple example of the option to expand. Consider ABC Corporation, which has six widget machines. ABC is considering replacing each of the old machines with a new machine that costs $1,000. The new machines have a five-year life. The anticipated cash flows for the new machine are as follows:[1]

	A	B	C	D	E	F	G
1	THE OPTION TO EXPAND						
2	Year	0	1	2	3	4	5
3	CF of single machine	-1,000	220	300	400	200	150
4							
5	Discount rate for machine cash flows (risk-adjusted)	12%					
6	Riskless discount rate	6%					
7	Present value of machine's future cash flows	932.52	<-- =NPV(B5,C3:G3)				
8	NPV of single machine	-67.48	<-- =NPV(B5,C3:G3)+B3				

The financial analyst working on the replacement project has estimated a cost of capital for the project of 12 percent. Using these anticipated cash flows and the 12 percent cost of capital, the analyst has concluded that the replacement of a single old machine by a new machine is unprofitable, since the NPV is negative:

$$-1000+\underbrace{\frac{220}{1.12}+\frac{300}{(1.12)^2}+\frac{400}{(1.12)^3}+\frac{200}{(1.12)^4}+\frac{150}{(1.12)^5}}_{\substack{\uparrow \\ \text{The present value of the machine's future} \\ \text{cash flow is \$932.52}}}=-67.48$$

1. These cash flows are the incremental cash flow of replacing a single old machine by a new machine. The computations include taxes, incremental depreciation, and the sale of the old machine.

Now comes the (real options) twist. The line manager in charge of the widget line says, "I want to try one of the new machines for a year. At the end of the year, if the experiment is successful, I want to replace five other similar machines on the line with the new machines."

Does this plan change our previously negative conclusion about replacing a single machine? The answer is yes. To see this point, we now realize that what we have is a package:

- Replacing a single machine today. This has an NPV of –67.48.
- The *option* of replacing five more machines in one year. Suppose that the risk-free rate is 6 percent. Then we view each such option as a call option on an asset that has current value S equal to the present value of the machine's future cash flows. As can be seen in cell B7, this present value is S = 932.52. The exercise price of this option is X = 1,000. Of course these call options can be exercised only if we purchase the first machine now.[2]

Suppose we assume that the Black-Scholes option-pricing model can price this option. In this case we have the following:

	A	B	C	D	E	F	G
1	**THE OPTION TO EXPAND**						
2	Year	0	1	2	3	4	5
3	CF of single machine	-1,000	220	300	400	200	150
4							
5	Discount rate for machine cash flows (risk-adjusted)	12%					
6	Riskless discount rate	6%					
7	Present value of machine's future cash flows	932.52	<-- =NPV(B5,C3:G3)				
8	NPV of single machine	-67.48	<-- =NPV(B5,C3:G3)+B3				
9							
10	Number of machines bought next year	5					
11	Option value of single machine purchased in one more year	143.98	<-- =B24				
12	NPV of total project	652.39	<-- =B8+B10*B11				
13							
14	**Black-Scholes Option-Pricing Formula**						
15	S	932.52	PV of machine CFs				
16	X	1,000.00	Exercise price = Machine cost				
17	r	6.00%	Risk-free rate of interest				
18	T	1	Time to maturity of option (in years)				
19	Sigma	40%	<-- Volatility				
20	d_1	0.1753	<-- (LN(S/X)+(r+0.5*sigma^2)*T)/(sigma*SQRT(T))				
21	d_2	-0.2247	<-- d_1 - sigma*SQRT(T)				
22	N(d_1)	0.5696	<--- Uses formula NormSDist(d_1)				
23	N(d_2)	0.4111	<--- Uses formula NormSDist(d_2)				
24	Option value = BS call price	143.98	<-- S*N(d_1)-X*exp(-r*T)*N(d_2)				

2. What we're really doing is pricing the cost of learning!

As cell B12 shows, the value of the whole project is 652.39.

Our conclusion: Buying one machine today, and knowing that we have the option to purchase five more machines in one year is a worthwhile project. One critical element here is the volatility. The lower the volatility (i.e., the lower the uncertainty), the less worthwhile this project is:

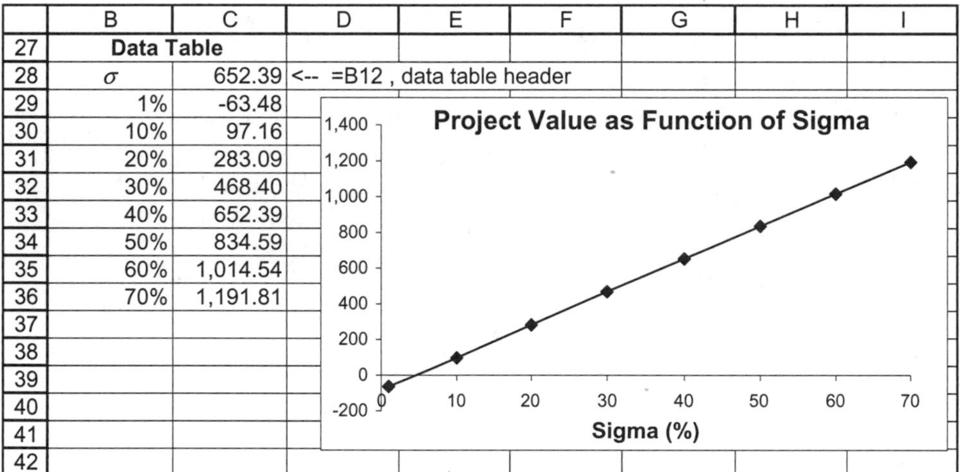

	B	C	D
27	**Data Table**		
28	σ	652.39	<-- =B12 , data table header
29	1%	-63.48	
30	10%	97.16	
31	20%	283.09	
32	30%	468.40	
33	40%	652.39	
34	50%	834.59	
35	60%	1,014.54	
36	70%	1,191.81	
37			
38			
39			
40			
41			
42			

This outcome is not very surprising: The value of the project as a whole comes from our uncertainty about the actual cash flows one year from now. The less is this uncertainty (measured by σ), the less valuable is the project.

24.2.1 Sidebar: Is Black-Scholes the Appropriate Valuation Tool for Real Options?

The answer is almost certainly no: Black-Scholes is not the appropriate tool. However, the Black-Scholes model is by far the most numerically tractable (i.e., easiest) model we have for valuing options of any kind. In valuing real options we often use the Black-Scholes model, realizing that at best it can give an approximation to the actual option value. Such is life.

Nevertheless, you should realize that the assumptions of the Black-Scholes option valuation model—continuous trading, constant interest rate, no exercise before final option maturity—are not really appropriate to the real options considered in this chapter. In many cases real options involve what, in a securities option context, would be considered dividend-paying securities and/or early exercise. Here are two examples:

- The staged-investment real option, when we have the opportunity to expand or contract the investment over time, is intrinsically an option with early exercise.
- When an option to abandon an investment exists, as long as the investment is still in place and not abandoned, it continues to pay "dividends," in the form of cash flows.

We can only hope is that the Black-Scholes model gives an *approximation* to the option value intrinsic in the real options.

24.3 The Abandonment Option

Consider the following capital budgeting project:

	A	B	C	D	E
7	**Project cash flows**				
8					
9					150
10			100		
11					80
12	-50				
13					80
14			-50		
15					-60

As you can see, the initial cost of this project is \$50. In one period the project will produce cash flows of either \$100 or –\$50; that is, under certain circumstances, it will lose money. Two periods hence the project again has chances of either losing money (in the worst case) or making money.

24.3.1 Valuing the Project

In order to value the project, we use the state prices from option pricing.[3] The state price q_u is the price today of $1 to be paid in the succeeding period in the "up" state; and the price q_d is the price today of $1 to be paid in the "down" state. The following spreadsheet fragment shows all the relevant details, leading to a project valuation of –$29.38 (implying rejection of the project):

	A	B	C	D	E	F	G	H	I	J	K	L
1				PRICING AN ABANDONMENT OPTION								
2	**Market data**			**State prices**								
3	Expected market return	12%		q_U	0.3087	<-- =(1+B5-B9)/((1+B5)*(B8-B9))						
4	Sigma of market return	30%		q_D	0.6347	<-- =(B8-1-B5)/((1+B5)*(B8-B9))						
5	Risk-free rate	6%										
6												
7	**One-period "up" and "down" of market**											
8	Up	1.521962	<-- =EXP(B3+B4) , note that a valid alternative is 'Up' = EXP(B4)									
9	Down	0.83527	<-- =EXP(B3-B4) , note that a valid alternative is 'Down' = EXP(-B4)									
10												
11												
12	**Project cash flows**						**State-dependent present value factors**					
13												
14					150						0.0953	<-- =E3^2
15			100						0.3087			
16					80						0.1959	<-- =E3*E4
17		-50					1					
18					80						0.1959	<-- =E3*E4
19			-50						0.6347			
20					-60						0.4028	<-- =E4^2
21			=C15*I15									
22	**State-by-state present value**											
23					14.2981	<-- =E14*K14						
24			30.8740									
25					15.6755	<-- =E16*K16						
26		-50										
27					15.6755	<-- =E18*K18						
28			-31.7328									
29					-24.1673	<-- =E20*K20						
30												
31	**Net present value**		-29.38	<-- =SUM(A23:E29)								

The methodology is to calculate state-dependent present value factors (discussed later) and to multiply these factors times the individual state-dependent cash flows. Each node of the tree is discounted by the relevant state price for the node; for example, the cash flow of 80 that occurs at date 2 is discounted by $q_U q_D$. The NPV of the project is the sum of all the discounted cash flows plus the initial cost (cell B31).

3. See section 24.3.4 on how to calculate these state prices.

24.3.2 The Abandonment Option Can Enhance Value

Now suppose that we can abandon the project at date 1 if its cash flow "threatens" to be –50; suppose, furthermore, that this abandonment means that all subsequent cash flows will also be zero. As the next picture shows, this *option to abandon the project* enhances its value:

	A	B	C	D	E	F	G	H	I	J	K	L
34	Cash flows with abandonment						Present value with abandonment					
35												
36					150						14.2981	<-- =E36*K14
37			100						30.8740			
38					80						15.6755	<-- =E38*K16
39	-50						-50					
40					0						0	
41			0						0			
42					0						0	
43												
44												
45							Present value with abandonment				10.85	<-- =SUM(G36:K42)

Thinking about this topic further, it is clear that it might even be worthwhile to *pay to abandon the project*. Here's what the project looks like when we pay $10 to abandon it in the troublesome state (this payment can be thought of as representing the cost of closing down a facility, for example):

	A	B	C	D	E	F	G	H	I	J	K	L
34	Cash flows with abandonment						Present value with abandonment					
35												
36					150						14.2981	<-- =E36*K14
37			100						30.8740			
38					80						15.6755	<-- =E38*K16
39	-50						-50					
40					0						0	
41			-10						-6.3466			
42					0						0	
43												
44												
45							Present value with abandonment				4.50	<-- =SUM(G36:K42)

24.3.3 Abandonment When We Sell the Equipment

Another possibility is, of course, that "abandonment" means selling the equipment. In this case there might even be a positive cash flow from abandonment. As an example, suppose that we can sell the asset for $15:

	A	B	C	D	E	F	G	H	I	J	K	L
34	Cash flows with abandonment						Present value with abandonment					
35												
36					150						14.2981	<-- =E36*K14
37			100						30.8740			
38					80						15.6755	<-- =E38*K16
39	-50						-50					
40					0						0	
41			15						9.5198			
42					0						0	
43												
44												
45							Present value with abandonment				20.37	<-- =SUM(G36:K42)

24.3.4 Determining the State Prices

The method we have used to determine the state prices was explained in greater detail in Chapter 17. We assume that in each period the market portfolio (by which we mean some large, diversified stock market portfolio such as the S&P 500) either moves "up" or "down"; the size of these moves is determined by the mean return μ of the market portfolio and by the standard deviation σ of the market portfolio's returns. Assuming that the returns on the market portfolio have mean $\mu = 12$ percent and standard deviation of returns $\sigma = 30$ percent, we have—in the preceding examples—calculated

$$\text{Up} = \exp[\mu + \sigma] = 1.53, \quad \text{Down} = \exp[\mu - \sigma] = 0.84$$

Denote by q_U the price today for one dollar in the up state in one period, and denote by q_D the price today for one dollar in the down state in one period. Then—as explained in Chapter 17—the state prices are calculated by solving the following system of linear equations:

$$1 = q_U * \text{Up} + q_D * \text{Down}$$
$$\frac{1}{1+r} = q_U + q_D$$

The solution to this system of equations is

$$q_U = \frac{R - \text{Down}}{R * (\text{Up} - \text{Down})}, \quad q_D = \frac{\text{Up} - R}{R * (\text{Up} - \text{Down})}$$

This method is illustrated in the spreadsheet from section 24.3.1:

	A	B	C	D	E	F	G	H	I
2	**Market data**			**State prices**					
3	Expected market return	12%		q_U	0.3087	<-- =(1+B5-B9)/((1+B5)*(B8-B9))			
4	Sigma of market return	30%		q_D	0.6347	<-- =(B8-1-B5)/((1+B5)*(B8-B9))			
5	Risk-free rate	6%							
6									
7	**One-period "up" and "down" of market**								
8	Up	1.521962	<-- =EXP(B3+B4) , note that a valid alternative is 'Up' = EXP(B4)						
9	Down	0.83527	<-- =EXP(B3-B4) , note that a valid alternative is 'Down' = EXP(-B4)						

24.3.5 Alternative State-Price Determinations

An alternative method of calculating the state prices is to try to match them to the project's cost of capital. Reconsider the project discussed previously, and suppose that the actual probability of each state's occurrence is $^1/_2$. Furthermore, suppose that the risk-free rate is 6 percent. Finally, assume that the project's discount rate—if it has no options whatsoever—is 22 percent. Then we can calculate the project's NPV without real options as 12.48:

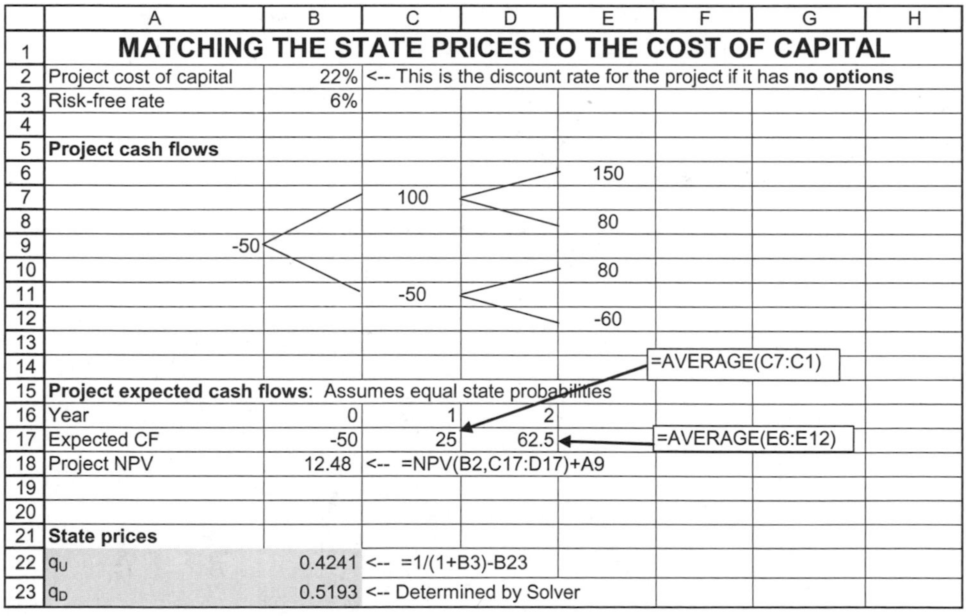

	A	B	C	D	E	F	G	H
1	**MATCHING THE STATE PRICES TO THE COST OF CAPITAL**							
2	Project cost of capital	22%	<-- This is the discount rate for the project if it has **no options**					
3	Risk-free rate	6%						
4								
5	**Project cash flows**							
6					150			
7			100					
8					80			
9		-50						
10					80			
11			-50					
12					-60			
13								
14						=AVERAGE(C7:C1)		
15	**Project expected cash flows**: Assumes equal state probabilities							
16	Year	0	1	2				
17	Expected CF	-50	25	62.5		=AVERAGE(E6:E12)		
18	Project NPV	12.48	<-- =NPV(B2,C17:D17)+A9					
19								
20								
21	**State prices**							
22	q_U	0.4241	<-- =1/(1+B3)-B23					
23	q_D	0.5193	<-- Determined by Solver					

In cells B22 and B23 we look for state prices q_U and q_D that have two properties:

1. They are consistent with the risk-free interest rate; therefore,

$$q_U + q_D = \frac{1}{R} = \frac{1}{1.06}$$

2. The state prices give the same NPV for the project as that calculated by the cost of capital.

The second requirement means that we have to use the Excel Solver to determine the state prices. Here's what the solution looks like (the discussion of how Solver was used follows this spreadsheet picture):

	A	B	C	D	E	F	G
21	**State prices**						
22	q_U	0.4241	<-- =1/(1+B3)-B23				
23	q_D	0.5193	<-- Determined by Solver				
24							
25					=C7*B22		
26	**Project state-by-state discounting**						
27					26.9797	<-- =E6*B22^2	
28			42.4105				
29					17.6187	<-- =E8*B22*B23	
30		-50					
31					17.6187	<-- =E10*B22*B23	
32			-25.9646				
33					-16.1798	<-- =E12*B23^2	
34							
35			=C11*B23				
36							
37							
38	State-by-state NPV	12.48	<-- =SUM(A27:E33)				
39							
40	Target cell	(0.00)	<-- =B38-B18				

To determine the state prices, we use the Solver (**Tools|Solver**):

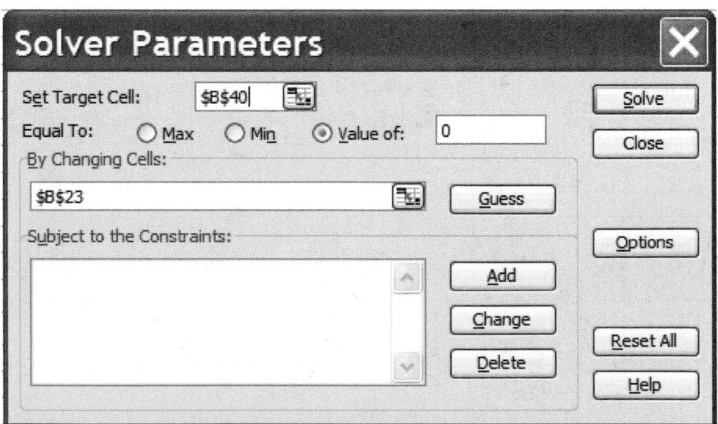

You can also use Goal Seek (**Tools|Goal Seek**) to get the same result. However, Excel's Goal Seek does not remember its previous settings, meaning that each time you repeat this calculation you will have to reset the cell references. Here's what the Goal Seek dialogue box looks like:

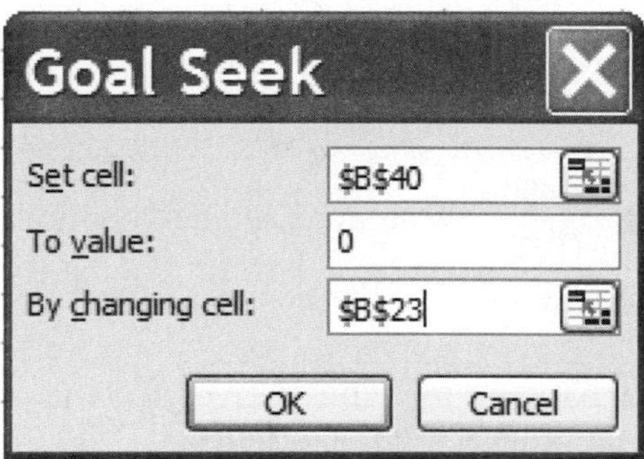

24.4 Valuing the Abandonment Option as a Series of Puts

The preceding example shows how and why the abandonment option can have value. It also illustrates another, more troublesome, feature of the abandonment option, namely, that it may be very difficult to value. While it is difficult enough to project expected cash flows, it is even more difficult to project state-by-state cash flows and state prices for a complex project.

A possible compromise in the valuation of an abandonment option is to value a project as a series of cash flows *plus* a series of Black-Scholes put options. Consider the following example: You are valuing a four-year project with the expected cash flows given in the following spreadsheet and with a risk-adjusted discount rate of 12 percent. As you can see, the project has a negative NPV:

	A	B	C	D	E	F
1	**STANDARD DCF PROJECT VALUATION**					
2	**Project cash flows**					
3	Year	**0**	**1**	**2**	**3**	**4**
4	Cash flow	-750	100	200	300	400
5						
6	Risk-adjusted discount rate	12%	The project's cost of capital			
7	NPV without options	-33.53	<-- =B4+NPV(B6,C4:F4)			

Suppose that we can abandon the project at the end of any of the next four years, selling the equipment for 300. Although this abandonment option is an American option and not a Black-Scholes option, we value it as a series of Black-Scholes put options. In each case we suppose that we first get the year-end cash flow; we then value the abandonment option on the remaining project value.

- *End of year 1:* The asset's expected value at the end of year 1 will be the discounted value of its future expected cash flows: $702.44 = \frac{200}{1.12} + \frac{300}{(1.12)^2} + \frac{400}{(1.12)^3}$. The abandonment option means that we can get \$300 for the asset during the next three years. Suppose that the value has a volatility of 50 percent; then valuing this option as a Black-Scholes put with one year to maturity gives its value as 19.53. The following spreadsheet uses the VBA function **BSPut** defined in Chapter 19:

	A	B	C	D	E	F
1	**ABANDONMENT VALUE--DETAILS OF YEAR-1 CALCULATION**					
2	**Project cash flows**					
3	Year	**0**	**1**	**2**	**3**	**4**
4	Cash flow	-750	100	200	300	400
5						
6	Risk-adjusted discount rate	12%	The project's cost of capital			
7	NPV without options	-33.53	<-- =B4+NPV(B6,C4:F4)			
8						
9	**Valuing the year-1 abandonment put**					
10	Value of project, end year 1	702.44	<-- =NPV(B6,D4:F4)			
11	Abandonment value	300	Like strike price in put formula			
12	Time to option maturity (years)	3				
13	Risk-free rate	6%				
14	Sigma	50%				
15						
16	Put value	19.53	<-- =bsput(B10,B11,B12,B13,B14)			

- *End of year 2:* We have a put option with exercise price \$300 on an asset worth $586.73 = \frac{300}{1.12} + \frac{400}{(1.12)^2}$. Valuing the abandonment option as a Black-Scholes put with two years to exercise gives its value (when $\sigma = 50$ percent) as 17.74.

• *End of year 3:* We have a put option with exercise price \$300 on an asset worth $357.14 = \frac{400}{1.12}$. The option has one more year remaining to its life and is worth 32.47.

• *End of year 4:* The asset is worthless in terms of future anticipated cash flows, but it can be abandoned for \$300 (this is thus its scrap or salvage value). The abandonment option is worth \$300.

In the next spreadsheet the asset has been valued as the sum of

• The present value of the future expected cash flows. As we showed, this is –\$33.53.

• The present value (at the risk-free rate) of a series of Black-Scholes puts. This value is \$299.10.

The total value of the project is –\$33.53 + \$299.10 = \$265.57.

	A	B	C	D	E	F	G
1	**PRICING AN ABANDONMENT OPTION AS A SERIES OF PUTS**						
2	**Project cash flows**						
3	Year	**0**	**1**	**2**	**3**	**4**	
4	Cash flow	-750	100	200	300	400	
5							
6	Risk-adjusted discount rate	12%	The project's cost of capital				
7							
8	NPV without options	-33.53	<-- =NPV(B6,C4:F4)+B4				
9							
10	Sigma	50%					
11	Risk-free rate	6%					
12	Abandonment value	300	Project can be abandoned at end of any year for this amount				
13							
14	NPV of cash flows at RADR	-33.53	<-- =B8				
15	Value of abandonment option	299.10	<-- =NPV(B11,C20:F20)				
16	Adjusted present value	265.57	<-- =B15+B14				
17					Function in cell D19: =NPV($B$6,E4:$F$4)		
18							
19	End-year value of remaining cash flows		702.44	586.73	357.14	0.00	
20	Put option value		19.53	17.74	32.47	300.00	
21							
22					Function in cell D20: =bsput(D19,$B$12,$F$3-D3,$B$11,$B$10)		

24.5 Valuing a Biotechnology Project[4]

One of the interesting features of the biotech industry is the existence of highly valued firms that have no revenues. It is common understanding that the value of those firms is in their future cash flow opportunities. Therefore, understanding the translation of qualitative investment opportunities into quantitative valuation is of great importance when valuating those firms. In this section we use the real-option method to value a biotechnology project and to illustrate the application of the real-option approaches.

Consider the following story.[5] A firm is considering the initiation of research into a new drug. It knows that there are three stages to the drug's development:

1. In the *discovery phase* the firm does preliminary research about the viability of the idea. This research takes one year and costs $1,000 at the beginning of the year, with 50 percent probability that the results will be positive enough to proceed to the next stage of research.
2. If the discovery phase yields success, then the drug goes into the *clinical phase*, in which the drug is tested. This stage lasts one year, costs $2,000 at the beginning of the year, and with a probability of 30 percent yields enough positive results to proceed to the next stage.
3. If the drug passes the clinical phase successfully, then it goes into the *market stage*, in which it is sold. This phase costs $15,000 per year (at the beginning of each year) and on average lasts five years. On average, a successful drug can be expected to start the marketing phase with income of $20,000. This income grows with annual mean 10 percent and standard deviation $\sigma = 100$ percent.

The expected return on a project of this type is 25 percent. We assume that this is the cost of capital of the project in the case of a discounted-cash-flow (DCF) valuation.

4. A version of this example originally appeared in Benninga and Tolkowsky (2002).
5. We have made the story simple enough to fit an understandable spreadsheet. For a somewhat more complicated story in the same spirit, see Kellogg and Charnes (2000).

24.5.1 The Expected Value of the Project Using Traditional Discounted-Cash-Flow Analysis

If we estimate the value of this project using traditional discounted-cash-flow analysis, we get a negative net present value for the project:

	A	B	C	D	E	F	G	H
1	BIOTECH PROJECT EXPECTED CASH FLOWS							
2	Discount rate	25%						
3	Growth	10%						
4								
5	Year	Stage	Cost	Income	Net	Probability	Expected cash flow	
6	0	Discovery	-1,000	0	-1,000	1	-1,000	<-- =F6*E6
7	1	Clinical	-2,000	0	-2,000	0.5	-1,000	<-- =F7*E7
8	2	Clinical	-2,000	0	-2,000	0.5	-1,000	
9	3	Marketing	-15,000	20,000	5,000	0.15	750	
10	4	Marketing	-15,000	22,000	7,000	0.15	1,050	
11	5	Marketing	-15,000	24,200	9,200	0.15	1,380	
12	6	Marketing	-15,000	26,620	11,620	0.15	1,743	
13	7	Marketing	-15,000	29,282	14,282	0.15	2,142	
14								
15	Project NPV	-268	<-- =G6+NPV(B2,G7:G13)					

Since the project's net present value is negative, the DCF approach indicates that it should not be undertaken.

24.5.2 Using a Real-Options Approach

An alternative method for estimating the present value of proceeds is to plot the project's cash flows on a binomial tree. This is done in the following spreadsheet:

	A	B	C	D	E	F	G	H	I	J	K
1	**BIOTECH PROJECT, BINOMIAL TREE FOR THE CASH FLOWS**										
2	Marketing phase, Initial revenue	20,000					The expected return and variance of return				
3	Marketing, annual cost	15,000					is given by:				
4	Clinical annual cost	2,000					Expected	10%			
5	Initial, annual cost	1,000					Sigma	100%			
6											
7	Up	300%	<-- =EXP(H4+H5)								
8	Down	41%	<-- =EXP(H4-H5)								
9											
10	State prices										
11	q_u	0.2816									
12	q_d	0.6618	<-- =1/1.06-B11								
13											
14		**Net cash flows**								1,614,017	<-- =B2*B7^4-B3
15								527,253			
16							165,500			205,464	<-- =B2*B7^3*B8-B3
17						45,083		58,386			
18					5,000		9,428			14,836	<-- =B2*B7^2*B8^2-B3
19						-6,869		-5,068			
20							-11,694			-10,962	<-- =B2*B7*B8^3-B3
21				-2,000				-13,656			
22										-14,454	<-- =B2*B8^4-B3
23			-2,000								
24											
25		-1,000									
26											
27	**Time line**		**1**	**2**	**3**	**4**	**5**	**6**		**7**	
28											
29											
30		**State prices (to start of market phase)**								0.0001	<-- =B11^J27
31								0.0005			
32							0.0018			0.0013	<-- =B11^6*B12*COMBIN(4,3)
33						0.0063		0.0035			
34					0.0223		0.0083			0.0141	<-- =B11^5*B12^2*COMBIN(4,2)
35						0.0148		0.0083			
36							0.0098			0.0073	<-- =B11^4*B12^3*COMBIN(4,1)
37				0.079316				0.0065			
38										0.0043	<-- =B11^3*B12^4*COMBIN(4,0)
39			0.2816								
40											
41		1									
42											
43											
44	Binomial tree valuation	-268	<-- =SUMPRODUCT(B14:J25,B30:J41)								
45	Target										
46	DCF valuation	-268									
47	**DCF valuation - binomial tree value**	0	<-- Should be zero for correct state prices								

We use the Excel function **Sumproduct** to do this computation.

24.5.3 A Note about the State Prices

The net present value of the proceeds from this project is the product of the net cash flows and the appropriate state prices:

$$NPV = \sum_{t=0}^{7} \sum_{j=0}^{t} CF_{jt} * (q_U)^j * (q_D)^{t-j} * \binom{\text{Number of}}{\text{paths to node}},$$

where CF_{jt} denotes the proceeds from the project at date t and state j, and where j is the number of up moves. As explained in Chapter 17, in the standard binomial model, the state price for a node is $(q_U)^j * (q_D)^{n-j}\binom{t}{j}$, where n is the time at which the node occurs, j is the number of Up steps needed to get to the node, and $\binom{t}{j}$ is the number of paths to reach the node. The latter expression is computed in Excel by using the function **Combin(n,j)**. However, for the preceding real-options model, the number of paths to each node is slightly different, since the beginning of the tree (the initial and clinical states) are accessible via only one path.

In the preceding spreadsheet, the prices q_U and q_D were computed (using **Solver**) so that the present value of the project on the binomial tree equals that of the DCF valuation and that the equilibrium condition, $q_U + q_D = \frac{1}{1.06}$ holds. Here's the **Solver** screen:

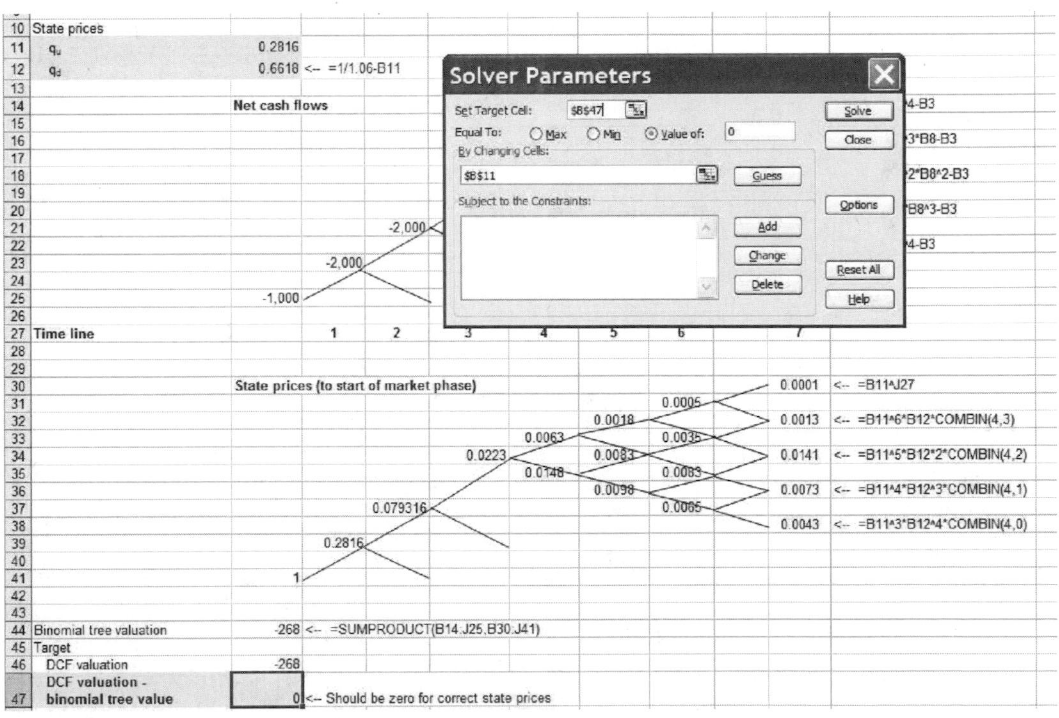

24.5.4 The Real-Options Approach

The real-options approach to R&D recognizes that at each stage in the project the managers can choose whether to continue the project or not. They do this by comparing the value and costs of continuation. In option terminology, at each stage, the manager exercises her continuation option if the value from exercising the option exceeds the exercise price. In the following spreadsheet, we have eliminated obvious negative cash flows from the marketing stage, taking care to also eliminate the subsequent cash flows and to make an adjustment to the state prices:

	A	B	C	D	E	F	G	H	I	J	K
1	**BIOTECH PROJECT, OPTION-ADJUSTED BINOMIAL TREE FOR THE CASH FLOWS**										
2	Marketing phase, Initial revenue	20,000					The expected return and variance of return				
3	Marketing, annual cost	15,000					is given by:				
4	Clinical annual cost	2,000					Expected	10%			
5	Initial, annual cost	1,000					Sigma	100%			
6											
7	Up	300%									
8	Down	41%									
9											
10	State prices										
11	q_u	0.2816									
12	q_d	0.6618									
13											
14		**Net cash flows**								1,614,017	<-- =B2*B7^4-B3
15								527,253			
16							165,500			205,464	<-- =B2*B7^3*B8-B3
17						45,083		58,386			
18					5,000		9,428			14,836	<-- =B2*B7^2*B8^2-B3
19											
20											
21				-2,000							
22											
23			-2,000								
24											
25		-1,000									
26											
27	**Time line**		**1**	**2**	**3**	**4**	**5**	**6**		**7**	
28											
29											
30		**State prices (to start of market phase)**								0.0001	<-- =B11^J27
31								0.0005			
32							0.0018			0.0010	<-- =B11^6*B12*(COMBIN(4,3)-1)
33						0.0063		0.0059			
34					0.0223		0.0167			0.0047	<-- =B11^5*B12^2*(COMBIN(4,1)-2)
35											
36											
37				0.079316							
38											
39			0.2816								
40											
41		1									
42											
43											
44	**Binomial tree valuation**	**229**	<-- =SUMPRODUCT(B14:J25,B30:J41)								

24.5.5 Another Note about State Prices

When we eliminate states in the real-option approach, we must also adjust the number of paths to each node to account for the fact that some states are no longer reachable. This has been done in the preceding spreadsheet. For example, the state in cell J7 (highlighted) is now reachable by one fewer path.

24.6 Conclusion

Recognizing that capital budgeting should include option aspects of projects is clear and obvious. Valuing these options is often difficult. In this chapter we have tried to emphasize the intuitions and—insofar as is possible—to give some implementation of the valuation.

Exercises

1. Your company is considering purchasing 10 machines, each of which has the following expected cash flows (the entry in B4 of –$550 is the cost of the machine):

	A	B	C	D	E	F
3	Year	0	1	2	3	4
4	CF of single machine	-550	100	200	300	400

You estimate the appropriate discount rate for the machines as 25 percent.

a. Would you recommend buying just one machine, if there are no options effects?

b. Your purchase manager recommends buying one machine today and then—after seeing how the machine operates—reconsidering the purchase of the other nine machines in six months. Assuming that the cash flows from the machines have a standard deviation of 30 percent and that the risk-free rate is 10 percent, value this strategy.

2. Your company is considering the purchase of a new piece of equipment. The equipment costs $50,000, and your analysis indicates that the PV of the future cash flows from the equipment is $45,000. Thus the NPV of the equipment is –$5,000. This estimated NPV is based on some initial numbers provided by the manufacturer plus some creative thinking on the part of your financial analyst.

The seller of the new piece of equipment is offering a course on how it works. The course costs $1,500. You estimate that

- The σ of the equipment's cash flows is 30 percent.
- The risk-free rate is 6 percent.
- You will have another half year after the course to purchase the equipment at the price of $50,000.

Is it worth taking the course?

3. Consider the project whose cash flows are as follows:

	A	B	C	D	E	F	G	H
1	**Project cash flows**							
2								
3					169		**State prices**	
4			130				q_U	0.3000
5					91		q_D	0.5000
6		-100						
7					91			
8			70					
9					-90			

a. Using the state prices, value the project.

b. Suppose that at date 2 the project can be abandoned at no cost. What does this fact do to its value?

c. Suppose that at any time the project can be sold for $100. Show the tree of cash flows and value the project.

4. Suppose that the market portfolio has mean $\mu = 15$ percent and standard deviation $\sigma = 20$ percent.

a. If the risk-free rate of interest is 8 percent, calculate the one-period state prices for an up and a down state.

b. Show the effect (in a data table) of the risk-free rate on the state prices.

c. Show the effect of the σ on the state prices.

5. Consider the following cash flows:

	A	B	C	D	E
6	**Project cash flows**				
7					180
8			130		
9					90
10		-50			
11					60
12			-50		
13					-100

a. If the cost of capital is 30 percent and the risk-free rate is 5 percent, find the state prices that match the project's NPV.

b. If there exists an abandonment option so that we can change all negative cash flows to zero, value the project.

IV Bonds

Chapters 25–28 cover topics related to bonds and term structure. Chapters 25 and 26 concentrate on the classic duration and immunization formulations. In Chapter 25 we develop the basic Macauley duration concept. Excel's **Duration( )** formula is somewhat cumbersome to use; we use VBA to build a new, easier-to-use formula. Chapter 26 discusses the use of duration to immunize bond portfolios. Chapter 27 shows how to model the term structure using a polynomial approximation. These approximations are in wide use and appear to work well for certain purposes. Chapter 28 uses a Markov process and much information about default probabilities and bond recovery ratios to model the expected rate of return on a risky corporate bond.

25 Duration

25.1 Overview

Duration is a measure of the sensitivity of the price of a bond to changes in the interest rate at which the bond is discounted. It is widely used as a risk measure for bonds—the higher a bond's duration, the more risky it is. In this chapter we consider a basic duration measure—Macauley duration—which is defined for the case when the term structure is flat. In Chapter 26 we examine the uses of duration in immunization strategies.

Consider a bond with payments C_t, where $t = 1, \ldots, N$. Ordinarily, the first $N - 1$ payments will be interest payments, and C_N will be the sum of the repayment of principal and the last interest payment. If the term structure is flat and the discount rate for all of the payments is r, then the bond's market price today will be

$$P = \sum_{t=1}^{N} \frac{C_t}{(1+r)^t}$$

The Macauley duration measure (throughout this chapter and the next, when we use the word "duration" we shall always refer to this measure) is defined as

$$D = \frac{1}{P} \sum_{t=1}^{N} \frac{t\,C_t}{(1+r)^t}$$

In section 25.4 we will consider the meaning of this formula. Before doing so, however, we show how to calculate the duration in Excel.

25.2 Two Examples

Consider two bonds. Bond A has just been issued. Its face value is $1,000, it bears the current market interest rate of 7 percent, and it will mature in 10 years. Bond B was issued five years ago, when interest rates were higher. This bond has $1,000 face value and bears a 13 percent coupon rate. When issued, this bond had a 15-year maturity, so its remaining maturity is 10 years. Since the current market rate of interest is 7 percent, Bond B's market price is given by

$$\$1{,}421.41 = \sum_{t=1}^{10} \frac{\$130}{(1.07)^t} + \frac{\$1{,}000}{(1.07)^{10}}$$

It is worthwhile calculating the duration of each of the two bonds (just once!) the long way. We set up a table in Excel:

	A	B	C	D	E	F	G
1			**BASIC DURATION CALCULATION**				
2	YTM	7%					
3							
4	**Year**	**$C_{t,A}$**	**$t*C_{t,A}$ / $Price_A*(1+YTM)^t$**		**$C_{t,B}$**	**$t*C_{t,B}$ / $Price_B*(1+YTM)^t$**	
5	1	70	0.0654		130	0.0855	<-- =$A5*E5/(E$16*(1+$B$2)^$A5)
6	2	70	0.1223		130	0.1598	<-- =$A6*E6/(E$16*(1+$B$2)^$A6)
7	3	70	0.1714		130	0.2240	
8	4	70	0.2136		130	0.2791	
9	5	70	0.2495		130	0.3260	
10	6	70	0.2799		130	0.3657	
11	7	70	0.3051		130	0.3987	
12	8	70	0.3259		130	0.4258	
13	9	70	0.3427		130	0.4477	
14	10	1,070	5.4393		1,130	4.0413	
15							
16	Bond price	1,000.00	<-- =NPV(B2,B5:B14)		1,421.41	<-- =NPV(B2,E5:E14)	
17	Duration	7.5152	<-- =SUM(C5:C14)		6.7535	<-- =SUM(F5:F14)	
18							
19	Using the Excel function **Duration** and the "home-made" function **Dduration**						
20	Bond A	7.5152	<-- =DURATION(DATE(1996,12,3),DATE(2006,12,3),7%,B2,1)				
21		7.5152	<-- =dduration(A14,7%,B2,1)				
22							
23	Bond B	6.7535	<-- =DURATION(DATE(1996,12,3),DATE(2006,12,3),13%,B2,1)				
24		6.7535	<-- =dduration(A14,13%,7%,1)				

As might be expected, the duration of bond A is longer than that of bond B, since the average payoff of bond A takes longer than that of bond B. To look at this another way, the net present value of bond A's first-year payoff ($70) represents 6.54 percent of the bond's price, whereas the net present value of bond B's first-year payoff ($130) is 8.55 percent of its price. The figures for the second-year payoffs are 6.11 percent and 7.99 percent, respectively. (For the second-year figures, you have to divide the appropriate line of the spreadsheet by 2, since in the duration formula each payoff is weighted by the period in which it is received.)

25.2.1 Using the Excel Duration Formula

Excel has two duration formulas, **Duration( )** and **MDuration( )**. **MDuration**—somewhat inaccurately termed Macauley duration by Excel—is defined as

$$\text{MDuration} = \frac{\text{Duration}}{\left(1 + \dfrac{\text{Yield to maturity}}{\text{Number of coupon payments per year}}\right)}$$

Both formulas have the same syntax; for example, for **Duration( )** the syntax is as follows:

Duration(settlement, maturity, coupon, yield, frequency, basis)

where

settlement is the settlement date (i.e., the purchase date) of the bond.
maturity is the bond's maturity date.
coupon is the bond's coupon.
yield is the bond's yield to maturity.
frequency is the number of coupon payments per year.
basis is the "day count basis" (i.e., the number of days in a year). This is a code between 0 and 4:

0 or omitted	US (NASD) 30/360
1	Actual/actual
2	Actual/360
3	Actual/365
4	European 30/360

The **Duration** formula gives the standard Macauley duration. The **MDuration** formula can be used in calculating the price elasticity of the bond (see section 25.3.2). These two duration formulas may require a bit of trickery to implement, because they demand a date serial number for both the settlement and the maturity. In the preceding spreadsheet picture, the Excel formula is implemented in cell C20 by assuming that bond A's settlement date (for our purposes, the current date) is December 3, 1996, and that the bond's maturity date is December 3, 2006. The choice of dates is arbitrary. The last parameter of the Excel duration formula, which gives the basis, is optional and could be omitted.

The insertion of serial date formats in the Excel **Duration** formula is often unhandy. Later in this chapter we use VBA to define a simpler duration formula that overcomes this problem and that also computes the duration of a bond when bond payments are unevenly spaced. This "homemade" duration formula is called **Dduration**. The programming aspects of this function are discussed in section 25.5.1. The previous spreadsheet illustrates this function in cells B21 and B24. The dialogue box for **Dduration**'s computation of the duration of bond B follows:

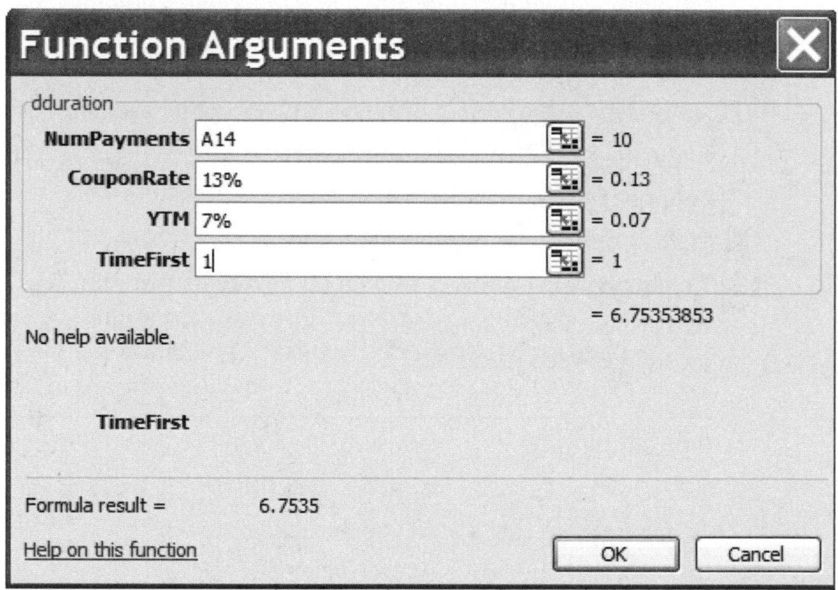

The parameter **TimeFirst** is the time from the bond purchase date until the first payment. For the examples of bond A and bond B this parameter is 1.

25.3 What Does Duration Mean?

In this section we present three different meanings of duration. Each is interesting and important in its own right.

25.3.1 Duration as the Time-Weighted Average of the Bond's Payments

As originally defined by Macauley (1938), duration is the time-weighted average of the bond's payments. Rewrite the duration formula as follows:

$$D = \frac{1}{P}\sum_{t=1}^{N}\frac{t\,C_t}{(1+r)^t} = \sum_{t=1}^{N}\left[\frac{C_t/P}{(1+r)^t}\right]*t$$

The bracketed terms $\left[\frac{C_t/P}{(1+r)^t}\right]$ sum to 1. This fact follows from the definition of the bond price; each of these terms is the proportion of the bond's price represented by the payment at time *t*. In the duration formula, each of the terms $\left[\frac{C_t/P}{(1+r)^t}\right]$ is multiplied by its time of occurrence: Thus *the duration is the time-weighted average of the bond's discounted payments as a proportion of the bond's price.*

25.3.2 Duration as the Bond's Price Elasticity with Respect to Its Discount Rate

Viewing duration as the bond's price elasticity with respect to its discount rate explains why the duration measure can be used to measure the bond's price volatility; it also shows why duration is often used as a risk measure for bonds. To derive this interpretation, we take the derivative of the bond's price with respect to the current interest rate:

$$\frac{dP}{dr} = \sum_{t=1}^{N}\frac{-t\,C_t}{(1+r)^{t+1}}$$

A little algebra shows that

$$\frac{dP}{dr} = \sum_{t=1}^{N}\frac{-t\,C_t}{(1+r)^{t+1}} = -\frac{DP}{1+r}$$

This formula transforms into two useful interpretations of duration:

• First, duration can be regarded as the *elasticity of the bond price with respect to the discount factor*, where by "discount factor" we mean $1 + r$:

$$\frac{dP/P}{dr/(1+r)} = \frac{\text{Percent change in bond price}}{\text{Percent change in discount factor}} = -D$$

• Second, we can use duration to measure the *price volatility* of a bond by rewriting the previous equation as

$$\frac{dP}{P} = -D\frac{dr}{1+r}$$

To show this interpretation of duration in a spreadsheet, we go back to the examples of the previous section. Suppose that the market interest rate rises by 10 percent, from 7 percent to 7.7 percent. What will happen to the bond prices? The price of bond A will be

$$\$952.39 = \sum_{t=1}^{10} \frac{\$70}{(1.077)^t} + \frac{\$1{,}000}{(1.077)^{10}}$$

A similar calculation shows the price of bond B to be

$$\$1{,}360.50 = \sum_{t=1}^{10} \frac{\$130}{(1.077)^t} + \frac{\$1{,}000}{(1.077)^{10}}$$

As predicted by the price-volatility formula, the changes in the bond prices are approximated by $\Delta P \cong -DP\Delta r/(1+r)$. To see this relationship, work out the numbers for each bond:

	A	B	C	D	E	F
1	**DURATION AS PRICE ELASTICITY** **The change in the bond price can be approximated by** **ΔP ≈ - Duration*Price*Δr/(1+r)**					
2	Discount rate	7%				
3						
4	**Bond A**			**Bond B**		
5	Coupon rate	7%		Coupon	13%	
6	Face value	1,000		Face value	1,000	
7	Maturity	10		Maturity	10	
8						
9	Price	1,000.00		Price	1,421.41	<-- =PV($B$2,E7,-E5*E6)+E6/(1+$B$2)^E7
10	Duration	7.5152		Duration	6.7535	<-- =DURATION(DATE(1996,1,1),DATE(2006,1,1),E5,B2,1)
11						
12	New discount rate	7.70%				
13	New price	952.39			1,360.50	<-- =PV($B$12,E7,-E5*E6)+E6/(1+$B$12)^E7
14						
15	**Change in price**					
16	Actual	47.61			60.92	<-- =E9-E13
17	Using duration as approximation DP ≈ - Duration *Price*Δr/(1+r)	49.17			62.80	<-- =-E10*E9*($B$2-$B$12)/(1+$B$2)
18						
19	Using **MDuration**	49.17			62.80	<-- =-($B$2-$B$12)*E9*MDURATION(DATE(1996,1,1),DATE(2006,1,1),E5,$B$2,1)

Note row 19 of the spreadsheet: Instead of using the Excel **Duration** function and multiplying by $\Delta r/(1+r)$, we could have used the **MDuration** function and multiplied by Δr.

25.3.3 Babcock's Formula: Duration as the Convex Combination of Bond Yields

A third interpretation of duration is Babcock's (1985) formula, which shows that duration is a weighted average of two factors:

$$D = N\left(1-\frac{y}{r}\right)+\frac{y}{r}PVIF(r,N)*(1+r),$$

where the "current yield" of the bond is

$$y=\frac{\text{Bond coupon}}{\text{Bond price}}$$

and the present value of an N-period annuity is

$$PVIF(r,N)=\sum_{i=1}^{N}\frac{1}{(1+r)^i}$$

Babcock's formula gives two useful insights into the duration measure:

• Duration is a weighted average of the maturity of the bond and of (1 + r) times the PVIF associated with the bond. (Note that the PVIF is given by the Excel formula **PV(r,N,–1)**.)

• In many cases the current yield of the bond, y, is not greatly different from its yield to maturity r. In these cases, duration is not very different from $(1 + r)PVIF$.

Unlike the two previous interpretations, Babcock's formula holds only for the case of a bond with constant coupon payments and single repayment of principal at time N; that is, the formula does not extend to the case where the payments C_t differ over time.

Here's an implementation of Babcock's formula for bond B:

	A	B	C
1	**BABCOCK'S FORMULA FOR DURATION** **Duration is convex combination of current-yield and present-value factors:** **D = N*y/r + (1 - y/r) * PVIF(N,r,-1)*(1+r)**		
2	N, bond maturity	10	
3	r,	7%	
4	C, bond coupon	13%	
5	Face value	1,000	
6	Price	1,421.41	<-- =PV(B3,B2,-B4*B5)+B5/(1+B3)^B2
7	Current yield	9.15%	<-- =B4*B5/B6
8	PVIF(r,N)	7.0236	<-- =PV(B3,B2,-1)
9			
10	**Two duration formulas**		
11	Babcock's formula	6.7535	<-- =B2*(1-B7/B3)+B7/B3*B8*(1+B3)
12	Standard formula	6.7535	<-- =DURATION(DATE(1995,1,1),DATE(2005,1,1),B4,B3,1)

25.4 Duration Patterns

Intuitively we would expect duration to be a decreasing function of a bond's coupon and an increasing function of a bond's maturity. The first of these intuitions is correct, but the second is not.

The following spreadsheet shows the effect of increasing the coupon on a bond's duration, which—as our intuition indicated—indeed declines as the coupon increases:

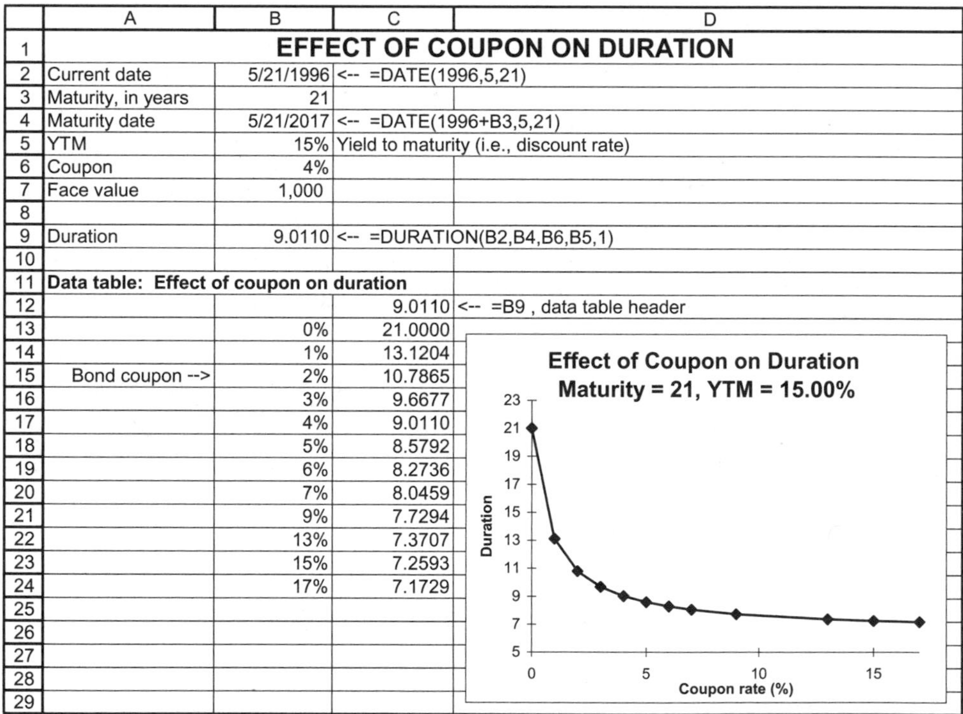

	A	B	C	D
1	EFFECT OF COUPON ON DURATION			
2	Current date	5/21/1996	<-- =DATE(1996,5,21)	
3	Maturity, in years	21		
4	Maturity date	5/21/2017	<-- =DATE(1996+B3,5,21)	
5	YTM	15%	Yield to maturity (i.e., discount rate)	
6	Coupon	4%		
7	Face value	1,000		
8				
9	Duration	9.0110	<-- =DURATION(B2,B4,B6,B5,1)	
10				
11	**Data table: Effect of coupon on duration**			
12			9.0110	<-- =B9 , data table header
13		0%	21.0000	
14		1%	13.1204	
15	Bond coupon -->	2%	10.7865	
16		3%	9.6677	
17		4%	9.0110	
18		5%	8.5792	
19		6%	8.2736	
20		7%	8.0459	
21		9%	7.7294	
22		13%	7.3707	
23		15%	7.2593	
24		17%	7.1729	
25				
26				
27				
28				
29				

It is not true, however, that the duration is always an increasing function of the bond maturity:

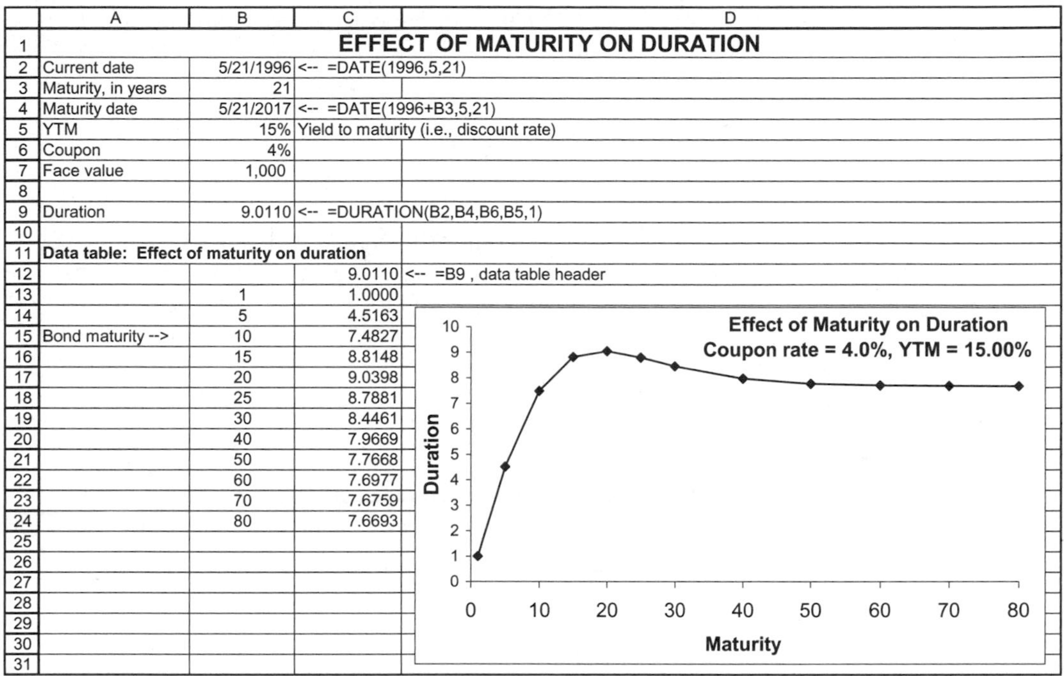

	A	B	C	D
1	**EFFECT OF MATURITY ON DURATION**			
2	Current date	5/21/1996	<-- =DATE(1996,5,21)	
3	Maturity, in years	21		
4	Maturity date	5/21/2017	<-- =DATE(1996+B3,5,21)	
5	YTM	15%	Yield to maturity (i.e., discount rate)	
6	Coupon	4%		
7	Face value	1,000		
8				
9	Duration	9.0110	<-- =DURATION(B2,B4,B6,B5,1)	
10				
11	**Data table: Effect of maturity on duration**			
12			9.0110	<-- =B9 , data table header
13		1	1.0000	
14		5	4.5163	
15	Bond maturity -->	10	7.4827	
16		15	8.8148	
17		20	9.0398	
18		25	8.7881	
19		30	8.4461	
20		40	7.9669	
21		50	7.7668	
22		60	7.6977	
23		70	7.6759	
24		80	7.6693	
25				
26				
27				
28				
29				
30				
31				

25.5 The Duration of a Bond with Uneven Payments

The duration formulas that we have discussed assume that bond payments are evenly spaced. This is almost invariably the case for bonds, *except for the first payment*. For example, consider a bond that pays interest on May 1 of each of the years 1997, 1998, . . . , 2010, with repayment of its face value on the last date. All the payments are spaced one year apart; however, if this bond is purchased on September 1, 1996, then the time to the first payment is eight months, not one year. We shall refer to such a bond as a *bond with uneven payments*. In this section we discuss two aspects of this (extremely common) problem:

• The calculation of the duration of such a bond, when the YTM is known. We show that the duration has a very simple formula, related to the duration of a bond with even payments (i.e., the standard duration formula). In the process of the discussion we develop a simpler duration formula in Excel.

- The calculation of the YTM of a bond with uneven payments. This requires a bit of trickery, and ultimately leads us to another VBA function.

25.5.1 Duration of a Bond with Uneven Payments

Consider a bond with N payments, the first of which occurs at time $\alpha < 1$, and the rest of which are evenly spaced. In the derivation that follows we show that the duration of such a bond is given by the sum of two terms:

- The duration of a bond with N payments spaced at even intervals (i.e., the standard duration discussed previously).
- $\alpha - 1$

The derivation is relatively simple. Denote the payments on the bond by $C_\alpha, C_{\alpha+1}, C_{\alpha+2}, \ldots, C_{\alpha+N-1}$, where $0 < \alpha < 1$. The price of the bond is given by

$$P = \sum_{t=1}^{N} \frac{C_{\alpha+t-1}}{(1+r)^{\alpha+t-1}} = (1+r)^{1-\alpha} \sum_{t=1}^{N} \frac{C_{\alpha+t-1}}{(1+r)^t}$$

The duration of this bond is given by

$$D = \frac{1}{P} \sum_{t=1}^{N} \frac{(\alpha+t-1)C_{\alpha+t-1}}{(1+r)^{\alpha+t-1}}$$

Rewrite this last expression as follows:

$$\begin{aligned}
D &= \frac{1}{P}(1+r)^{1-\alpha} \left\{ \sum_{t=1}^{N} \frac{tC_{t+\alpha-1}}{(1+r)^t} + \sum_{t=1}^{N} \frac{(\alpha-1)C_{t+\alpha-1}}{(1+r)^t} \right\} \\
&= \frac{1}{(1+r)^{1-\alpha} \sum_{t=1}^{N} \frac{C_{t+\alpha-1}}{(1+r)^t}} (1+r)^{1-\alpha} \left\{ \sum_{t=1}^{N} \frac{tC_{t+\alpha-1}}{(1+r)^t} + (\alpha-1) \sum_{t=1}^{N} \frac{C_{t+\alpha-1}}{(1+r)^t} \right\} \\
&= \frac{1}{\sum_{t=1}^{N} \frac{C_{t+\alpha-1}}{(1+r)^t}} \left\{ \sum_{t=1}^{N} \frac{tC_{t+\alpha-1}}{(1+r)^t} \right\} + \alpha - 1
\end{aligned}$$

Here is an example of the calculation of the duration of a bond with uneven periods. Recall that when there is α until the first payment, the duration formula is given by

$$D=\sum_{t=1}^{N}\frac{1}{P}\frac{(\alpha+t-1)C_{\alpha+t-1}}{(1+r)^{\alpha+t-1}}$$

Here is an example of the calculation of the duration of a bond with uneven periods. Each of the cells D10:D14 calculates the value of a term of this formula:

	A	B	C	D
1	**DURATION OF BOND WITH UNEVEN PERIODS** **Brute Force Calculation and Dduration function**			
2	Alpha	0.3	Time until first coupon payment (in years)	
3	N	5	Number of payments	
4	YTM	6%		
5	Coupon	100		
6	Face	1,000		
7	Bond price	1,217	<-- =NPV(B4,B10:B14)*(1+B4)^(1-B2)	
8				
9	**Period**	**Payment**	**t^*C_t /Price*(1+YTM)^t**	
10	0.3	100	0.0242	<-- =(B10*A10)/(1+$B$4)^A10/$B$7
11	1.3	100	0.0990	
12	2.3	100	0.1653	
13	3.3	100	0.2237	
14	4.3	1,100	3.0249	
15	Duration		3.5371	<-- =SUM(C10:C14)
16				
17	Newly defined VBA function		3.5371	<-- =dduration(B3,B5/B6,B4,B2)

As noted in section 25.2.1, the built-in Excel formula **Duration( )** is somewhat difficult to use, because of the insertion of the dates. We therefore write a simpler duration formula using VBA; the syntax of this formula is **DDuration(numPayments, couponRate, YTM, timeFirst)**:

```
Function dduration(numPayments, couponRate,
YTM, timeFirst)
   price = 1 / (1 + YTM) ^ numPayments
   dduration = numPayments / (1 + YTM) ^ _
     numPayments

   For Index = 1 To numPayments
       price = couponRate / (1 + YTM) ^ _
         Index + price
   Next Index
```

```
    For Index = 1 To numPayments
      dduration = couponRate * Index / _
        (1 + YTM) ^ Index + dduration
    Next Index

    dduration = dduration / price + timeFirst
      - 1

End Function
```

Our homemade formula **DDuration** requires only the number of payments on the bond, the coupon rate, and the time to the first payment α. The use of the formula is illustrated in the previous spreadsheet picture, in cell C17.

25.5.2 Calculating the YTM for Uneven Periods

As the preceding discussion shows, the calculation of duration requires us to know the bond's yield to maturity (YTM); this YTM is just the internal rate of return of the bond's payments and its initial price. Often the YTM is given, but when it is not, we cannot use Excel's **IRR** function but must instead use the **XIRR** function.

Consider a bond that currently costs $1,123 and that pays a coupon of $89 on January 1 of each year. On January 1, 2001, the bond will pay $1,089, the sum of its annual coupon and its face value. The current date is October 3, 1996. The problem in finding the YTM of this bond is that while most of the bond payments are spaced one year apart, there is only 0.2466 of a year until the first coupon payment: 0.2466 = [Date(1997,1,1) – Date(1996,10,3)/365]. Thus we wish to use Excel to solve the following equation:

$$-1{,}123+\sum_{t=0}^{3}\frac{89}{(1+YTM)^{t+0.2466}}+\frac{1{,}089}{(1+YTM)^{4.2466}}=0$$

To solve this problem, we can use the Excel function **XIRR**:

	A	B	C	D
1	**USING XIRR TO CALCULATE THE IRR WITH UNEVEN PAYMENTS**			
2	Current date	3-Oct-96		
3	Annual coupon	89	Paid January 1 for each of next 5 years	
4	Maturity date	1-Jan-01		
5	Face value	1,000		
6	Price of bond	1,123		
7				
8	Time to first payment	0.2466	<-- =(B12-B11)/365	
9				
10		**Date**	**Payment**	
11		3-Oct-96	-1,123	
12		1-Jan-97	89	
13		1-Jan-98	89	
14		1-Jan-99	89	
15		1-Jan-00	89	
16		1-Jan-01	1,089	
17				
18		YTM	7.300%	<-- =XIRR(C11:C16,B11:B16)

To use the **XIRR** function, you first have to make sure that the Analysis ToolPak is loaded into Excel. Go to **Tools|Add-Ins**. This brings up the following menu, in which you have to make sure that **Analysis ToolPak** is checked:

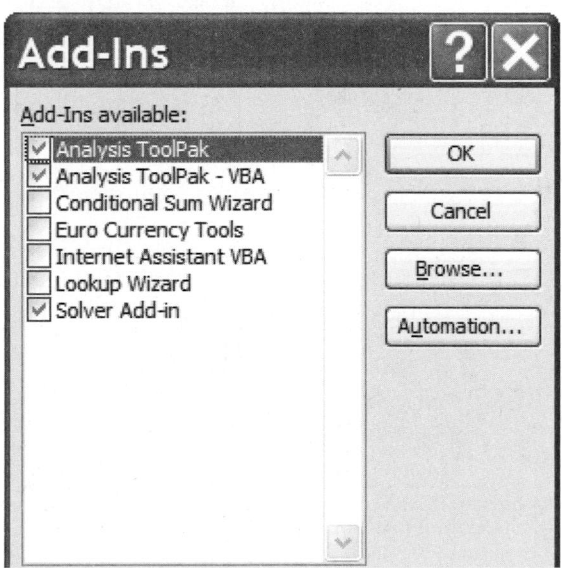

You can now use **XIRR**, which returns the internal rate of return for a schedule of cash flows that is not necessarily periodic. To use this function you have to specify the list of cash flows and the list of dates. As in the case of the Excel function **IRR**, you can also provide a guess for the IRR, although this may be left out.[1]

25.5.3 Calculating the YTM for Uneven Payments Using a VBA Program

If you do not know the payment dates, you can use VBA to calculate the YTM for a series of uneven payments. The following program is composed of two functions. The first function, **annuityvalue**, calculates the value $\sum_{t=1}^{N} \frac{1}{(1+r)^t}$. The second function, **unevenYTM**, uses the simple bisection technique to calculate the YTM of a series of uneven payments, leaving you to choose the accuracy **epsilon** of the desired result.

```
Function annuityvalue(interest, numberPeriods)
   annuityvalue = 0

   For Index = 1 To numberPeriods
      annuityvalue = annuityvalue + 1 / _
        (1 + interest) ^ Index
   Next Index
End Function

Function unevenYTM(couponRate, faceValue,
bondPrice, _
      numberPayments, timeToFirstPayment, _
        epsilon)
   Dim YTM As Double
   high = 1
   low = 0
```

1. There is also a function **XNPV** for finding the present value of a series of payments made at uneven dates. This function is discussed in Chapter 34.

```
   While Abs(annuityvalue(YTM, numberPayments) _
   * couponRate * _
         faceValue + faceValue / (1 + YTM) ^
           numberPayments - _
         bondPrice / (1 + YTM) ^ (1 - _
           timeToFirstPayment)) >= epsilon

      YTM = (high + low) / 2

      If annuityvalue(YTM, numberPayments) _
      * couponRate * _
         faceValue + faceValue / (1 + YTM) ^ _
           numberPayments - _
         bondPrice / (1 + YTM) ^ (1 - _
           timeToFirstPayment) > 0 Then _
            low = YTM
      Else
            high = YTM
      End If

      Wend

   unevenYTM = (high + low) / 2

End Function
```

An illustration of the use of this function follows:

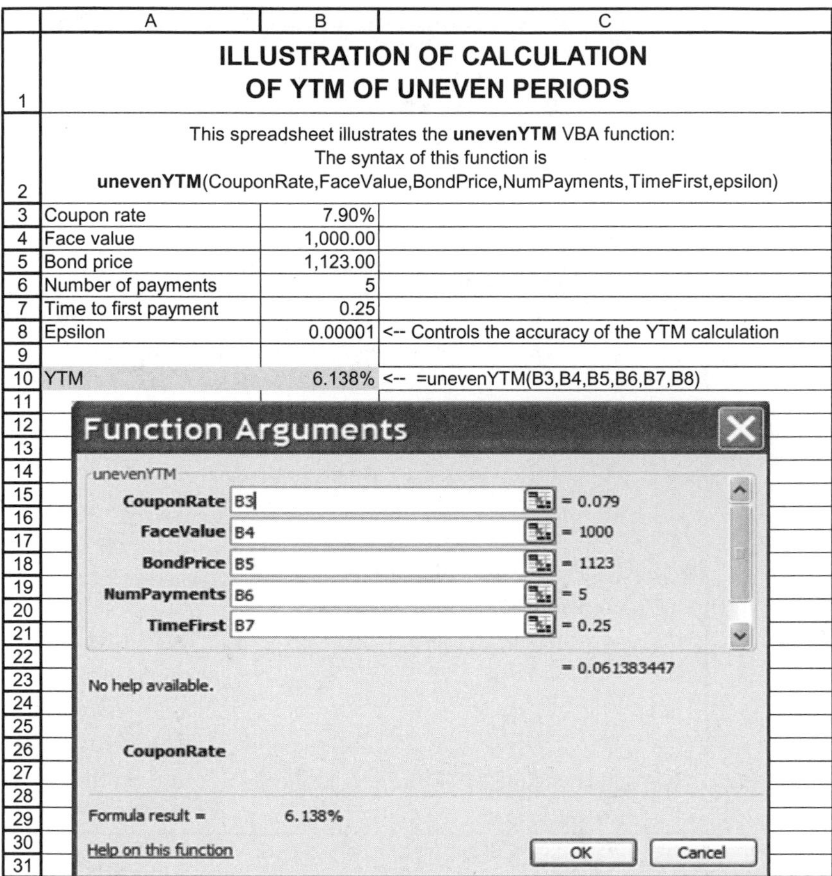

	A	B	C
1	**ILLUSTRATION OF CALCULATION OF YTM OF UNEVEN PERIODS**		
2	This spreadsheet illustrates the **unevenYTM** VBA function: The syntax of this function is **unevenYTM**(CouponRate,FaceValue,BondPrice,NumPayments,TimeFirst,epsilon)		
3	Coupon rate	7.90%	
4	Face value	1,000.00	
5	Bond price	1,123.00	
6	Number of payments	5	
7	Time to first payment	0.25	
8	Epsilon	0.00001	<-- Controls the accuracy of the YTM calculation
9			
10	YTM	6.138%	<-- =unevenYTM(B3,B4,B5,B6,B7,B8)

We can, of course, use the **Dduration** function in conjunction with **unevenYTM** to compute the duration:

	A	B	C
1	**USING DDURATION AND UNEVENYTM TOGETHER**		
2	Coupon rate	7.90%	
3	Face value	1,000.00	
4	Bond price	1,123.00	
5	Number of payments	5	
6	Time to first payment	0.25	
7	Epsilon	0.00001	<-- Controls the accuracy of the YTM calculation
8			
9	YTM	6.138%	<-- =unevenYTM(B2,B3,B4,B5,B6,B7)
10			
11	Duration	3.5959	<-- =dduration(B5,B2,B9,B6)

25.6 Nonflat Term Structures and Duration

In a general model of the term structure, payments at time t are discounted by rate r_t, so that the value of a bond is given by

$$P = \sum_{t=1}^{N} \frac{C_t}{(1+r_t)^t}$$

The duration measure discussed in this chapter assumes either a flat term structure (i.e., $r_t = r$ for all t) or a term structure that shifts in a parallel fashion. When the term structure exhibits parallel shifts, we can write the bond price as

$$P = \sum_{t=1}^{N} \frac{C_t}{(1+r_t+\Delta t)^t}$$

and then derive a measure of duration by taking the derivative with respect to Δt.

A general model of the term structure should explain how the discount rate r_t for time-t payments comes about and how the rates at time t change. This is a difficult problem, one aspect of which we discuss in Chapter 28. A somewhat simpler problem, discussed in Chapter 27, is the construction of a polynomial approximation to the term structure.

Does the difficulty of the problem mean that the simple duration measure we present in this chapter is useless? Not necessarily. It may be that the Macauley duration measure gives a good approximation for changes in bond value as a result of changes in the term structure, even for the case when the term structure itself is relatively complex and not flat.[2] In this section, we explore this possibility, using data from the file **McCulloch_term_structures.xls**, which is on the disk that accompanies this book.[3] The file contains monthly information on the term structure of interest rates in the United States for the period 12.1946–2.87 (i.e., December 1946–February 1987). A typical row of this file looks like this:

2. A paper by Gultekin and Rogalski (1984) seems to confirm that it does.

3. The data are from McCulloch (1990). A second file on the disk with this book, **Daily treasury yields, 1961–2006.xls** gives the daily term structures.

	0mo	1mo	2mo	3mo	4mo	5mo	6mo
12.1946	0.18	0.32	0.42	0.48	0.52	0.55	0.58

9mo	1yr	2 yr	3yr	4yr	5yr	10yr	15yr	20yr
0.65	0.72	0.95	1.15	1.3	1.41	1.82	2.16	2.32

This particular row gives the term structure of interest rates in December 1946. Interest rates are given in *annual percentage terms*; that is, 0.32 means 0.32 percent per year. The next two graphs are pictures of term structures, taken from the file.[4] Each line in the graphs represents the term structure in a particular month. In 1948 the term structures were very closely correlated, and all were upward sloping:

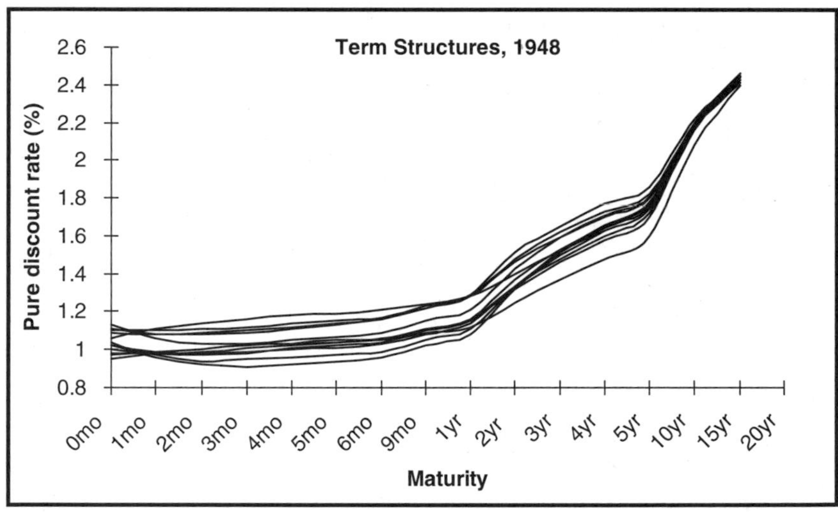

4. The interest rates are pure discount rates, calculated so that the value of a bond with price P and with N payments, $C_1, C_2, \ldots, C_N$ is $P = \sum_{t=1}^{N} \frac{C_t}{(1+r_t)^t}$. The column marked "0mo" gives the *instantaneous interest rate*—the shortest-term interest rate in the market. You can think of this as the rate paid by a money-market fund on a one-day deposit.

Contrast this graph with the term structures in 1981: Here there were upward and downward sloping term structures, as well as term structures with "humps":

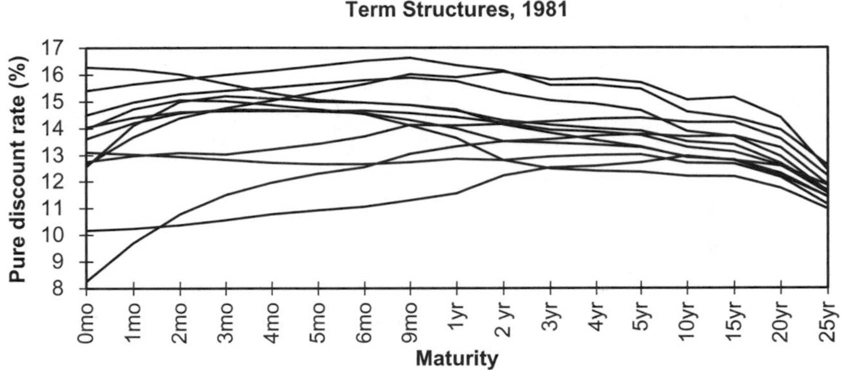

Despite this great variety of term structure shapes, you will see in exercise 7 that the Macauley duration can give an adequate approximation to the change in bond value over short periods.

25.7 Summary

In this chapter we have summarized the basics of duration, a commonly used risk measure for bonds. The duration measure was originally developed by Macauley (1938) to measure the time-weighted average of a bond's payments. It can also represent the bond's price elasticity to a change in its discount rate. This chapter has explored duration computation basics; in the next chapter we use duration to describe the immunization of a bond portfolio.

Exercises

1. In the following spreadsheet, create a **Data Table** in which the duration is computed as a function of the coupon rate (coupon = 0%, 1%, . . . , 11%). Comment on the relationship between the coupon rate and the duration.

	A	B	C
1	**CHANGING THE COUPON RATE** **Effect on Duration**		
2	Current date	21-May-07	
3	Maturity, in years	21	
4	Maturity date	21-May-27	
5	YTM	15%	
6	Coupon	4%	
7	Face value	1,000	
8			
9	Duration	9.03982	<-- =DURATION(B2,B4,B6,B5,1)

2. What is the effect on a bond's duration of increasing the bond's maturity? As in exercise 1, use a numerical example and plot the answer. Note that as $N \to \infty$, the bond becomes a consol (a bond that has no repayment of principal but an infinite stream of coupon payments). The duration of a consol is given by $(1 + YTM)/YTM$. Show that your numerical answers converge to this formula.

3. "Duration can be viewed as a proxy for the riskiness of a bond. All other things being equal, the riskier of two bonds should have lower duration." Check this claim with an example. What is its economic logic?

4. A pure discount bond with maturity N is a bond with *no payments* at times $t = 1, \ldots,$ $N - 1$; at time $t = N$, a pure discount bond has a single terminal payment of both principal and interest. What is the duration of such a bond?

5. Replicate the two graphs in section 25.4.

6. On January 23, 1987, the market price of a West Jefferson Development Bond was $1,122.32. The bond pays $59 in interest on March 1 and September 1 of each of the years 1987–1993. On September 1, 1993, the bond is redeemed at its face value of $1,000. Calculate the yield to maturity of the bond and then calculate its duration.

7. The file **fm3_problem25-7.xls** contains a term structure data set constructed by Professor J. Huston McCulloch. Use this set to answer the following questions:

   a. Produce at least three graphs of six term structures each for 10 typical subperiods. For example, the term structures from January to June 1953, July to December 1980, and so on.

   b. For January 1980, what would have been the coupon rate on a five-year bond with annual coupons? A 10-year bond? To answer this question you have to solve the following equation:

$$1{,}000 = \sum_{t=1}^{5} \frac{c * 1{,}000}{(1+r_t)^t} + \frac{1{,}000}{(1+r_5)^5}$$

where c is the coupon rate on the bond and r_t is the pure discount rate for period t. Note that for a 10-year bond you will have to *interpolate* the data.

c. Calculate the coupon rate on five-year bonds *for all the data*. Graph the results.

d. Now for duration: Return to exercise 7b. Suppose that you have calculated $c_{\text{Jan.80}}$ and that immediately following this calculation, the term structure changes to that of February 1980. What will be the effect on the price of the bond? How well is this change approximated by the Macauley duration measure? (Assume that the change in the interest rate Δr is the change in the short-term rate.)

e. Repeat the calculation of exercise 7c for at least 10 periods. Report on the results in an attractive and understandable way.

8. Rewrite the formula **DDuration** in section 25.5.1 so that if the **timeToFirstPayment** α is not inserted, then α automatically defaults to 1.

26 Immunization Strategies

26.1 Overview

A bond portfolio's value in the future depends on the interest-rate structure prevailing up to and including the date at which the portfolio is liquidated. If a portfolio has the same payoff at some specific future date, no matter what interest-rate structure prevails, then it is said to be *immunized*. This chapter discusses immunization strategies, which are closely related to the conception of duration discussed in Chapter 25. Immunization strategies have been discussed for many concepts of duration, but this chapter is restricted to the simplest duration concept, that of Macauley.

26.2 A Basic Simple Immunization Model

Consider the following situation: A firm has a known future obligation, Q. (A good example would be an insurance firm, which knows that it has to make a payment in the future.) The discounted value of this obligation is

$$V_0 = \frac{Q}{(1+r)^N}$$

where r is the appropriate discount rate.

Suppose that this future obligation is hedged by a bond held by the firm. That is, the firm currently holds a bond whose value V_B is equal to the discounted value of the future obligation V_0. If $P_1, P_2, \ldots, P_M$ is the stream of anticipated payments made by the bond, then the bond's present value is given by

$$V_B = \sum_{t=1}^{M} \frac{P_t}{(1+r)^t}$$

Now suppose that the underlying interest rate, r, changes to $r + \Delta r$. Using a first-order linear approximation, we find that the new value of the future obligation is given by

$$V_0 + \Delta V_0 \approx V_0 + \frac{dV_0}{dr}\Delta r = V_0 + \Delta r\left[\frac{-NQ}{(1+r)^{N+1}}\right]$$

However, the new value of the bond is given by

$$V_B + \Delta V_B \approx V_B + \frac{dV_B}{dr}\Delta r = V_B + \Delta r \sum_{t=1}^{N} \frac{-tP_t}{(1+r)^{t+1}}$$

If these two expressions are equal, a change in r will not affect the hedging properties of the company's portfolio. Setting the expressions equal gives us the condition

$$V_B + \Delta r \sum_{t=1}^{N} \frac{-tP_t}{(1+r)^{t+1}} = V_0 + \Delta r \left[\frac{-NQ}{(1+r)^{N+1}} \right]$$

Recalling that

$$V_B = V_0 = \frac{Q}{(1+r)^N}$$

we can simplify this expression to get

$$\frac{1}{V_B} \sum_{t=1}^{M} \frac{tP_t}{(1+r)^t} = N$$

The last equation is worth restating as a formal proposition: Suppose that the term structure of interest rates is always flat (that is, the discount rate for a cash flows occurring at all future times is the same) or that the term structure moves up or down in parallel movements. Then a necessary and sufficient condition that the market value of an asset be equal under all changes of the discount rate r to the market value of a future obligation Q is that the duration of the asset equal the duration of the obligation. Here we understand the word "equal" to mean equal in the sense of a first-order approximation.

An obligation against which an asset of this type is held is said to be *immunized*.

The preceding statement has two critical limitations:

• The immunization discussed applies only to first-order approximations. When we get to a numerical example in the succeeding sections, we shall see that there is a big difference between first-order equality and "true" equality. In *Animal Farm*, George Orwell made the same observation about the barnyard: "All animals are equal, but some animals are more equal than others."

• We have assumed either that the term structure is flat or that the term structure moves up or down in parallel movements. At best, this assumption might be considered to be a poor approximation of reality (recall the term structure graphs in section 25.6). Alternative theories of the term structure lead to alternative definitions of duration and immunization (for alternatives, see Bierwag et al., 1981, 1983a, 1983b; Cox, Ingersoll, and Ross, 1985; Vasicek, 1977). In an empirical investigation of these alternatives, Gultekin and Rogalski (1984) found that the simple Macauley duration we use in this chapter works at least as well as any of the alternatives.

26.3 A Numerical Example

In this section we consider a basic numerical immunization example. Suppose you are trying to immunize a year-10 obligation whose present value is \$1,000; that is, at the current interest rate of 6 percent, its future value is $\$1{,}000 * (1.06)^{10} = \$1{,}790.85$. You intend to immunize the obligation by purchasing \$1,000 worth of a bond or a combination of bonds. You consider three bonds:

• Bond 1 has 10 years remaining until maturity, a coupon rate of 6.7 percent, and a face value of \$1,000.

• Bond 2 has 15 years until maturity, a coupon rate of 6.988 percent, and a face value of \$1,000.

• Bond 3 has 30 years until maturity, a coupon rate of 5.9 percent and a face value of \$1,000.

At the existing yield to maturity of 6 percent, the prices of the bonds differ. Bond 1, for example, is worth $\$1{,}051.52 = \sum_{t}^{10} \frac{67}{(1.06)^t} + \frac{1{,}000}{(1.06)^{10}}$; thus, in order to purchase \$1,000 worth of this bond, you have to purchase \$951 = \$1,000/\$1,051.52 of *face value* of the bond.

Bond 3, however, is currently worth \$986.24, so that in order to buy \$1,000 of market value of this bond, you will have to buy \$1,013.96 of face value. If you intend to use this bond to finance a \$1,790.85 obligation 10 years from now, here's a schematic of the problem you face:

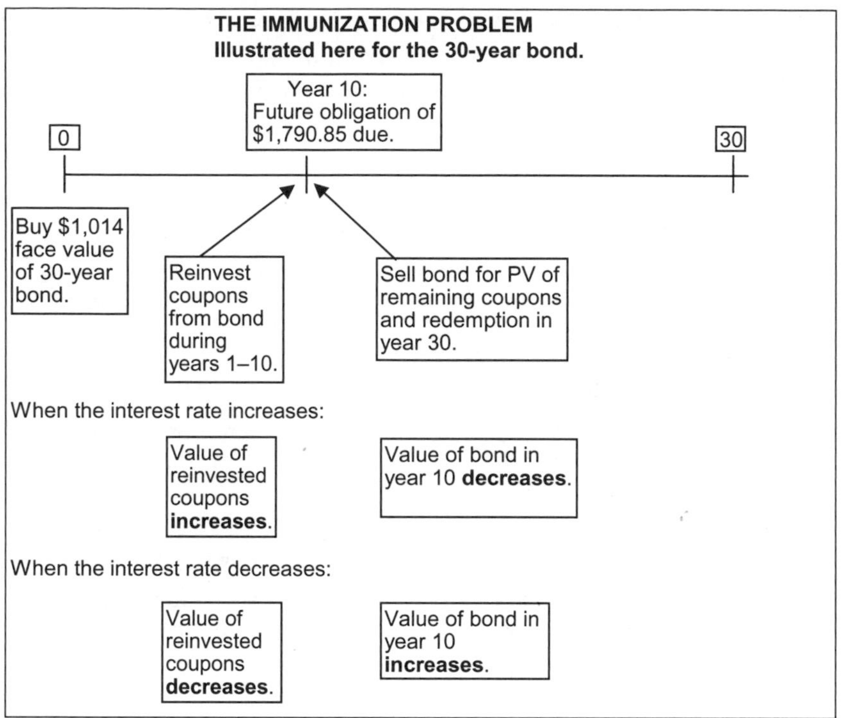

As we will see, the 30-year bond will exactly finance the future obligation of $1,790.85 only for the case in which the current market interest rate of 6 percent remains unchanged.

Here is a summary of price and duration information for the three bonds:

	A	B	C	D	E
1	**BASIC IMMUNIZATION EXAMPLE WITH 3 BONDS**				
2	Yield to maturity	6%			
3					
4		**Bond 1**	**Bond 2**	**Bond 3**	
5	Coupon rate	6.70%	6.988%	5.90%	
6	Maturity	10	15	30	
7	Face value	1,000	1,000	1,000	
8					
9	Bond price	$1,051.52	$1,095.96	$986.24	<-- =-PV($B$2,D6,D5*D7)+D7/(1+$B$2)^D6
10	Face value equal to $1,000 of market value	$ 951.00	$ 912.44	$ 1,013.96	<-- =D7/D9*D7
11					
12	Duration	7.6655	10.0000	14.6361	<-- =dduration(D6,D5,$B$2,1)

Note that to calculate the duration, we have used the “homemade” **DDuration** function defined in Chapter 25.

If the yield to maturity doesn't change, then you will be able to reinvest each coupon at 6 percent. Bond 2, for example, will give a terminal wealth at the end of 10 years of

$$\sum_{t=0}^{9} 69.88 \cdot (1.06)^t + \left[\sum_{t=1}^{5} \frac{69.88}{(1.06)^t} + \frac{1{,}000}{(1.06)^5} \right] = 921.07 + 1{,}041.62 = 1{,}962.69$$

The first term in this expression, $\sum_{t=0}^{9} 69.88 \cdot (1.06)^t$, is the sum of the reinvested coupons. The second and third terms, $\sum_{t=1}^{5} \frac{69.88}{(1.06)^t} + \frac{1{,}000}{(1.06)^5}$, represent the market value of the bond in year 10, when the bond has five more years until maturity. Since we will be buying only \$912.44 of face value of this bond, we have, at the end of 10 years, $0.91244 * \$1{,}962.69 = \$1{,}790.85$. This is exactly the amount we wanted to have at this date. The results of this calculation for all three bonds, provided there is no change in the yield to maturity, are as shown in the following table:

	A	B	C	D	E
14	New yield to maturity	6%			
15					
16		**Bond 1**	**Bond 2**	**Bond 3**	
17	Bond price	$1,000.00	$1,041.62	$988.53	<-- =-PV($B$14,D6-10,D5*D7)+D7/(1+$B$14)^(D6-10)
18	Reinvested coupons	$883.11	$921.07	$777.67	=-FV($B$14,10,D5*D7)
19	**Total**	$1,883.11	$1,962.69	$1,766.20	<-- =D17+D18
20					
21	Multiply by percent of face value bought	95.10%	91.24%	101.40%	<-- =D10/1000
22	**Product**	$ 1,790.85	$ 1,790.85	$ 1,790.85	<-- =D21*D19

The upshot of this table is that purchasing \$1,000 of any of the three bonds will provide—10 years from now—funding for your future obligation of \$1,790.85, *provided the market interest rate of 6 percent doesn't change.*

Now suppose that, immediately after you purchase the bonds, the yield to maturity changes to some new value and stays there. This change will obviously affect the calculation we just did. For example, if the yield falls to 5 percent, the table will now look as follows:

	A	B	C	D	E
14	New yield to maturity	5%			
15					
16		**Bond 1**	**Bond 2**	**Bond 3**	
17	Bond price	$1,000.00	$1,086.07	$1,112.16	<-- =-PV($B$14,D6-10,D5*D7)+D7/(1+$B$14)^(D6-10)
18	Reinvested coupons	$842.72	$878.94	$742.10	=-FV($B$14,10,D5*D7)
19	**Total**	$1,842.72	$1,965.01	$1,854.26	<-- =D17+D18
20					
21	Multiply by percent of face value bought	95.10%	91.24%	101.40%	<-- =D10/1000
22	**Product**	$ 1,752.43	$ 1,792.97	$ 1,880.14	<-- =D21*D19

Thus, if the yield falls, bond 1 will no longer fund our obligation, whereas bond 3 will overfund it. Bond 2's ability to fund the obligation—not surprisingly, in view of the fact that its duration is exactly 10 years—hardly changes. We can repeat this calculation for any new yield to maturity. The results are shown in the following figure, which was produced by running a **Data|Table** (see Chapter 31):

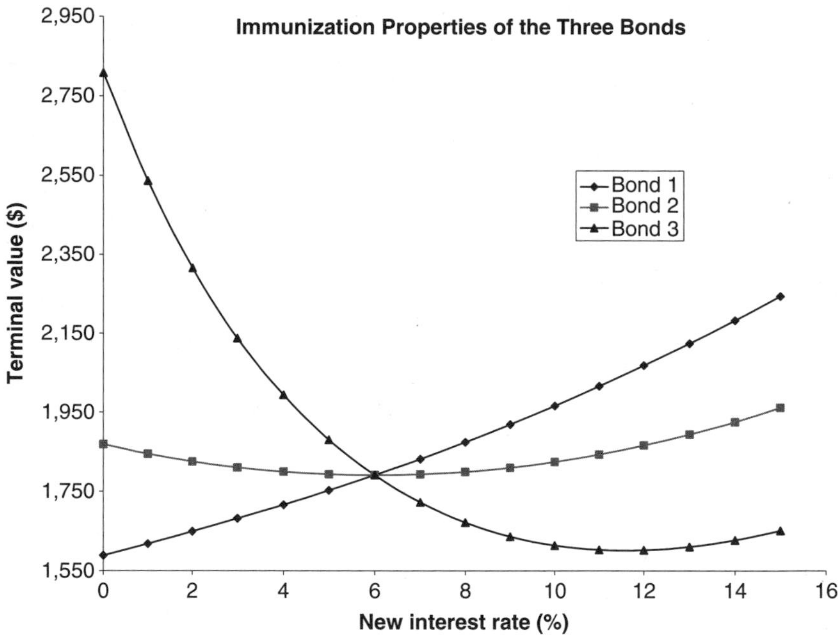

Clearly, if you want an immunized strategy, you should buy bond 2!

26.4 Convexity: A Continuation of Our Immunization Experiment

The duration of a portfolio is the weighted average duration of the assets in the portfolio. Therefore, there is another way to get a bond investment with a duration of 10: If we invest \$665.09 in bond 1 and \$344.91 in bond 3, the resulting portfolio also has a duration of 10. These weights are calculated as follows:

$$\lambda * Duration_{Bond1} + (1-\lambda) * Duration_{Bond3} = 7.6655\lambda + 14.6361(1-\lambda) = 10$$

Suppose we repeat our experiment with this portfolio of bonds. Starting in row 15 of the following spreadsheet, we repeat the experiment of the previous section (varying the YTM), but add in the portfolio of bond 1 and bond 3. The results show that the future value in row 23 does not vary for the portfolio.

	A	B	C	D	E	F	G
1	**EXPERIMENTING WITH BOND PORTFOLIOS AND CONVEXITY**						
2	Yield to maturity (YTM)	6%					
3							
4		**bond 1**	**bond 2**	**bond 3**			
5	Coupon rate	6.70%	6.988%	5.90%			
6	Maturity	10	15	30			
7	Face value	1,000	1,000	1,000			
8							
9	Bond price	$1,051.52	$1,095.96	$986.24	<-- =-PV($B$2,D6,D5*D7)+D7/(1+$B$2)^D6		
10	Face value equal to $1,000 of market value	$ 951.00	$ 912.44	$ 1,013.96	<-- =D7/D9*D7		
11							
12	Duration	7.6655	10.0000	14.6361	<-- =dduration(D6,D5,$B$2,1)		
13							
14							
15	New YTM	7%					
16							
17		**Bond 1**	**Bond 2**	**Bond 3**		**Bond 1 & 3 portfolio**	
18	Bond price	$1,000.00	$999.51	$883.47			
19	Reinvested coupons	$925.70	$965.49	$815.17			
20	**Total**	$1,925.70	$1,965.00	$1,698.64			
21							
22	Multiply by percent of face value bought	95.10%	91.24%	101.40%			
23	**Product**	$ 1,831.35	$ 1,792.95	$ 1,722.34		$ 1,794.84	<-- =B26*B23+(1-B26)*D23
24							
25	Portfolio of bonds 1 and 3						
26	Proportion of bond 1	0.6651	<-- =(10-D12)/(B12-D12)				
27	Proportion of bond 3	0.3349	<-- =1-B26				

Building a data table based on this experiment and graphing the results shows that the portfolio's performance is better than that of bond 2 by itself:

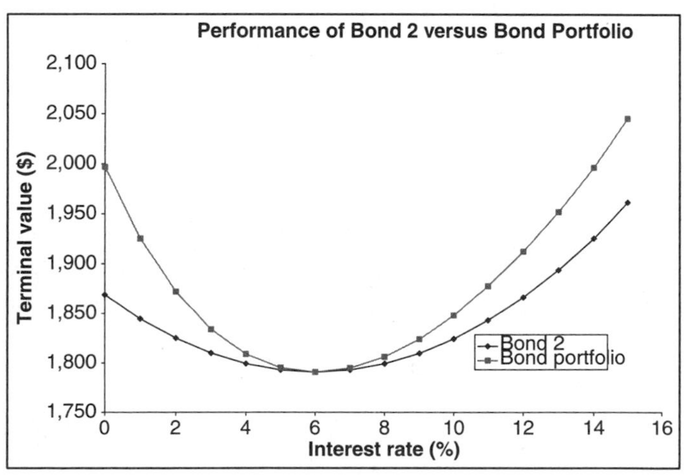

Look again at the graph: Notice that, while for both bond 2 and the bond portfolio, the terminal value is somewhat convex in the yield to maturity, the terminal value of the portfolio is *more convex* than that of the single bond. Redington (1952), one of the influential propagators of the concept of duration and immunization, thought this convexity very desirable, and we can see why: No matter what the change in the yield to maturity, the portfolio of bonds provides *more overfunding* of the future obligation than the single bond. This is obviously a desirable property for an immunized portfolio, and it leads us to formulate the following rule:

In a comparison between two immunized portfolios, both of which are to fund a known future obligation, the portfolio whose terminal value is more convex with respect to changes in the yield to maturity is preferable.[1]

26.5 Building a Better Mousetrap

Despite what was said in the preceding section, there is some interest in deriving the characteristics of a bond portfolio whose terminal value is as insensitive to changes in the yield as possible. One way of improving the performance (when so defined) of the bond portfolio is not only to match the first derivatives of the change in value (which, as we saw in section 26.2, leads to the duration concept), but also to match the second derivatives.

A direct extension of the analysis of section 26.2 leads us to the conclusion that matching the second derivatives requires

$$N(N+1) = \frac{1}{V_B} \sum_{t=1}^{M} \frac{t(t+1)P_t}{(1+r)^t}$$

The following example illustrates the kind of improvement that can be made in a portfolio where the second derivatives are also matched. Consider four bonds, one of which, bond 2, is our old friend from the

1. There is another interpretation of the convexity shown in this example: It shows the impossibility of parallel changes in the term structure! If such changes describe the uncertainty relating to the term structure, a bond position can be chosen that always benefits from changes in the term structure. This is an arbitrage, and therefore impossible. I thank Zvi Wiener for pointing this fact out to me.

previous example, whose duration is exactly 10. The bonds are described in the following table:

	A	B	C	D	E	F
1			BOND CONVEXITY			
2	Yield to maturity	6%				
3						
4		**Bond 1**	**Bond 2**	**Bond 3**	**Bond 4**	
5	Coupon rate	4.50%	6.988%	3.50%	11.00%	
6	Maturity	20	15	14	10	
7	Face value	1,000	1,000	1,000	1,000	
8						
9	Bond price	$827.95	$1,095.96	$767.63	$1,368.00	<-- =-PV($B$2,E6,E5*E7)+E7/(1+$B$2)^E6
10	Face value equal to $1,000 of market value	$ 1,207.80	$ 912.44	$ 1,302.72	$ 730.99	<-- =E7/E9*E7
11						
12	Duration	12.8964	10.0000	10.8484	7.0539	<-- =dduration(E6,E5,$B$2,1)
13	Second derivative of duration	229.0873	136.4996	148.7023	67.5980	<-- =secondDur(E6,E5,$B$2)/bondprice(E6,E5,$B$2)

Here `secondDur(numberPayments, couponRate, YTM)` is a VBA function we have defined to calculate $\sum_{t=1}^{M} \frac{t(t+1)P_t}{(1+r)^t}$.

```
Function secondDur(numberPayments, _
  couponRate, YTM)

  For Index = 1 To numberPayments
   If Index < numberPayments Then
    secondDur = couponRate * Index * _
      (Index + 1) / (1 + YTM) ^ Index + _
      secondDur
   Else
    secondDur = (couponRate + 1) * Index * _
      (Index + 1) / (1 + YTM) ^ Index + _
      secondDur
   End If

    secondDur = secondDur
  Next Index

End Function
```

We need three bonds in order to calculate a portfolio of bonds whose duration and whose second duration derivative are exactly equal to those of the liability. The proportions of a portfolio that sets both the duration and its second derivative equal to those of the liability are as follows:

bond 1 = –0.5619, bond 3 = 1.6415, bond 4 = –0.0797.[2] As the following figure shows, this portfolio provides a better hedge against the terminal value than even bond 2:

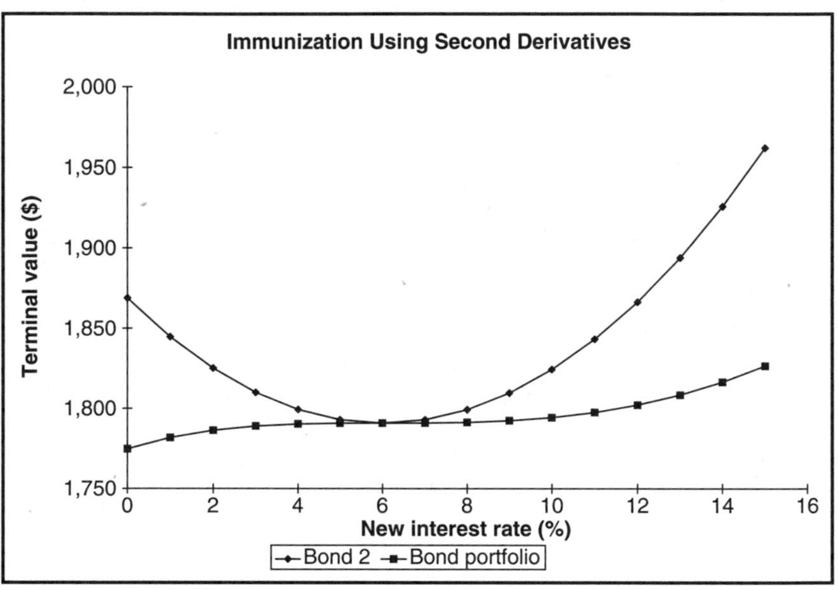

26.5.1 Computing the Bond Portfolio

We want to invest proportions x_1, x_3, x_4 in bonds 1, 3, and 4 so that

- The portfolio is totally invested: $x_1 + x_3 + x_4 = 1$.
- The portfolio duration is matched to that of bond 2: $x_1D_1 + x_3D_3 + x_4D_4 = D_2$, where D_i is the duration of bond i.
- The second derivative of the portfolio duration is matched to that of bond 2: $x_1D_1^2 + x_3D_3^2 + x_4D_4^2 = D_2^2$, where D_i^2 is the duration derivative.

Writing this problem in matrix form, we get

$$\begin{bmatrix} 1 & 1 & 1 \\ D_1 & D_3 & D_4 \\ D_1^2 & D_3^2 & D_4^2 \end{bmatrix} \begin{bmatrix} x_1 \\ x_3 \\ x_4 \end{bmatrix} = \begin{bmatrix} 1 \\ D_2 \\ D_2^2 \end{bmatrix}$$

2. See next subsection for the details of this computation.

whose solution is given by

$$\begin{bmatrix} x_1 \\ x_3 \\ x_4 \end{bmatrix} = \begin{bmatrix} 1 & 1 & 1 \\ D_1 & D_3 & D_4 \\ D_1^2 & D_3^2 & D_4^2 \end{bmatrix}^{-1} \begin{bmatrix} 1 \\ D_2 \\ D_2^2 \end{bmatrix}$$

This matrix can easily be set up in Excel:

	I	J	K	L	M	N
15	**Calculating the bond portfolio:**					
16					Vector of	
17	Matrix of coefficients				constants	
18	1	1	1		1	
19	12.8964	10.8484	7.0539		10.0000	
20	229.0873	148.7023	67.5980		110.0000	
21						
22	Solution					
23	-0.5619					
24	1.6415	<-- {=MMULT(MINVERSE(I18:K20),M18:M20)}				
25	-0.0797					
26						
27						
28	Explanation: We want to invest proportions					
29	x1, x3, and x4 in bonds 1, 3, and 4, respectively, in order that					
30	(a) The total investment is $1,000; this means x1+x2+x4=1.					
31	(b) Portfolio duration is matched to that of bond 2; this means					
32	that x1*D1+x3*D3+x4*D4 = D2, where Di is the duration					
33	of bond I.					
34	(c) The weighted average duration derivatives are equal					
35	to that of bond 2.					
36						
37	These three conditions give us the matrix system in					
38	cells I18:K20 and the corresponding solution in					
39	cells I23:I25.					

Given this solution, the last chart is produced by the following data table:

	A	B	C	D	E	F
26	**Data table: Sensitivity of Bond 2 and bond portfolio terminal values to interest rate**		**Bond 2**	**Bond portfolio**		
27					<-- =I23*B23+I24*D23+I25*E23 , data table header (hidden)	
28		0%	$ 1,868.87	$ 1,774.63		
29		1%	$ 1,844.71	$ 1,781.79		
30		2%	$ 1,825.14	$ 1,786.37		
31		3%	$ 1,810.05	$ 1,789.02		
32		4%	$ 1,799.35	$ 1,790.32		
33		5%	$ 1,792.97	$ 1,790.78		
34		6%	$ 1,790.85	$ 1,790.85		
35		7%	$ 1,792.95	$ 1,790.91		
36		8%	$ 1,799.26	$ 1,791.31		
37		9%	$ 1,809.76	$ 1,792.38		
38		10%	$ 1,824.46	$ 1,794.38		
39		11%	$ 1,843.37	$ 1,797.58		
40		12%	$ 1,866.53	$ 1,802.21		
41		13%	$ 1,893.98	$ 1,808.46		
42		14%	$ 1,925.77	$ 1,816.55		
43		15%	$ 1,961.98	$ 1,826.65		

26.6 Summary

The value of an immunized portfolio of bonds is insensitive to small changes in the underlying yield to maturity of the bonds. Immunization involves setting the bond portfolio's duration equal to the duration of the underlying liability against which the portfolio is held. This chapter shows how to effect the immunization of the portfolio. Needless to say, Excel is an excellent tool for immunization calculations.

Exercises

1. Prove that the duration of a portfolio is the weighted average duration of the portfolio assets.

2. Set up a spreadsheet that enables you to duplicate the calculations of section 26.5 of this chapter.

3. Follow the example of section 26.3 for this exercise.

   a. Find a combination of bonds 1 and 3 with a duration of 8.

   b. Find a combination of bonds 1 and 2 with a duration of 8.

4. In exercise 3, which portfolio (a or b) would you prefer to immunize an obligation with a duration of 8?

5. In exercise 3, recalculate the portfolio proportions assuming that you need a target duration of 12. Which portfolio would you prefer now?

27 Modeling the Term Structure

27.1 Overview

In this chapter we model the term structure using polynomial and other regression models. The object of this exercise is to fit a curve to an existing data set of bond yields. In many cases this technique works remarkably well. Its use has already been illustrated in section 2.8, where we used a fitted yield curve to estimate the cost of capital for Kraft.

27.2 An Initial Example

The following example shows data for BBB corporate bonds downloaded from Yahoo on 11 August 2006.[1] The data have been graphed using an Excel XY Scatter Chart.

1. A description of how to download and massage the data is given in section 27.3.

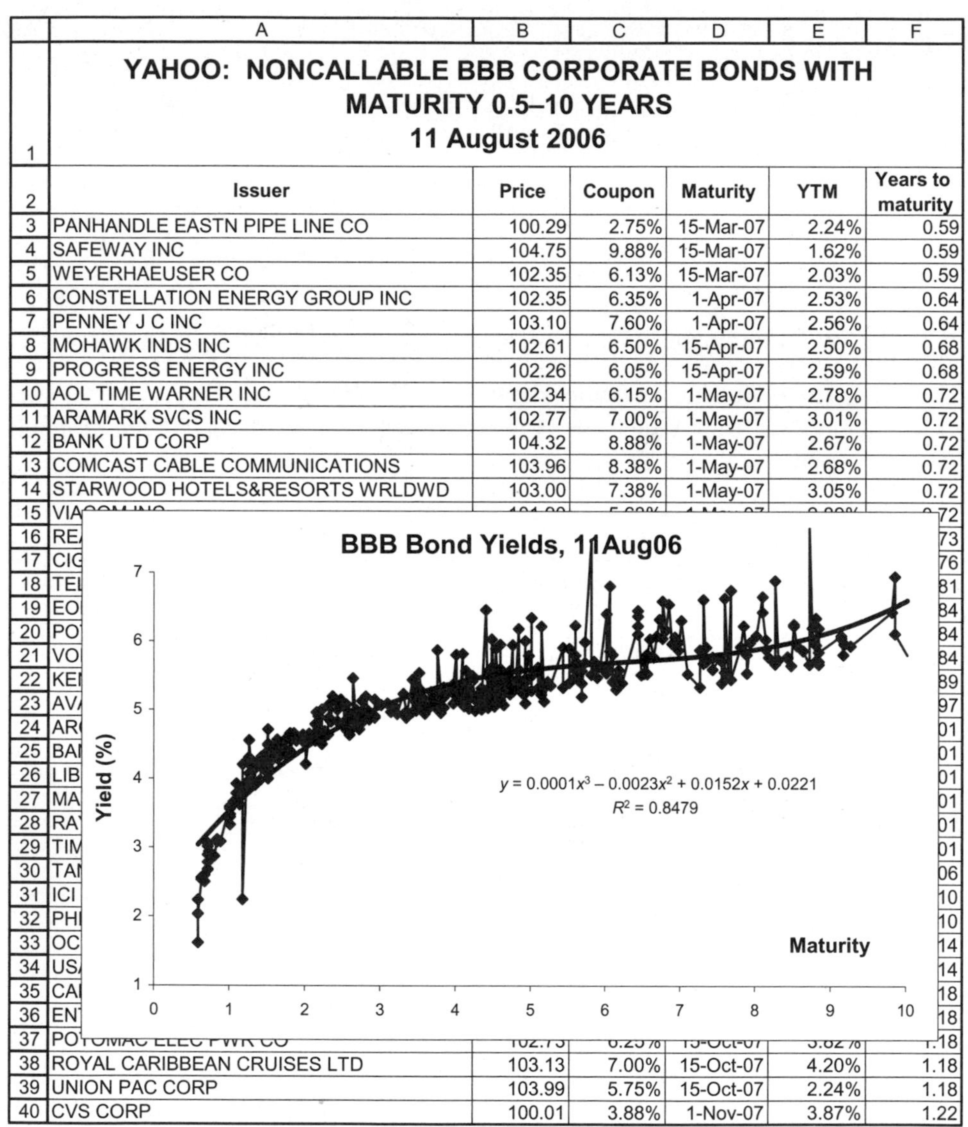

	A	B	C	D	E	F
1	**YAHOO: NONCALLABLE BBB CORPORATE BONDS WITH MATURITY 0.5–10 YEARS 11 August 2006**					
2	**Issuer**	**Price**	**Coupon**	**Maturity**	**YTM**	**Years to maturity**
3	PANHANDLE EASTN PIPE LINE CO	100.29	2.75%	15-Mar-07	2.24%	0.59
4	SAFEWAY INC	104.75	9.88%	15-Mar-07	1.62%	0.59
5	WEYERHAEUSER CO	102.35	6.13%	15-Mar-07	2.03%	0.59
6	CONSTELLATION ENERGY GROUP INC	102.35	6.35%	1-Apr-07	2.53%	0.64
7	PENNEY J C INC	103.10	7.60%	1-Apr-07	2.56%	0.64
8	MOHAWK INDS INC	102.61	6.50%	15-Apr-07	2.50%	0.68
9	PROGRESS ENERGY INC	102.26	6.05%	15-Apr-07	2.59%	0.68
10	AOL TIME WARNER INC	102.34	6.15%	1-May-07	2.78%	0.72
11	ARAMARK SVCS INC	102.77	7.00%	1-May-07	3.01%	0.72
12	BANK UTD CORP	104.32	8.88%	1-May-07	2.67%	0.72
13	COMCAST CABLE COMMUNICATIONS	103.96	8.38%	1-May-07	2.68%	0.72
14	STARWOOD HOTELS&RESORTS WRLDWD	103.00	7.38%	1-May-07	3.05%	0.72
15	VIA					72
16	RE					73
17	CIG					76
18	TEL					81
19	EO					84
20	PO					84
21	VO					84
22	KE					89
23	AV					97
24	AR					01
25	BA					01
26	LIB					01
27	MA					01
28	RA					01
29	TIM					01
30	TA					06
31	ICI					10
32	PH					10
33	OC					14
34	US					14
35	CA					18
36	EN					18
37	PO					.18
38	ROYAL CARIBBEAN CRUISES LTD	103.13	7.00%	15-Oct-07	4.20%	1.18
39	UNION PAC CORP	103.99	5.75%	15-Oct-07	2.24%	1.18
40	CVS CORP	100.01	3.88%	1-Nov-07	3.87%	1.22

The polynomial regression shows that 85 percent of the variability of the yields to maturity is explained by the curve

$$\text{YTM} = 0.0221 + 0.0152 * \text{Time} + 0.0023 * \text{Time}^2 + 0.0001 * \text{Time}^3$$

This simple model for the yield curve can be very useful. In Chapter 2, for example, we used this model to estimate the cost of debt for Kraft. Assuming that Kraft's average debt maturity is five years, its cost of debt is estimated to be 5.31 percent:

	A	B	C
1	**COMPUTING KRAFT'S r_D FROM A YIELD CURVE** **YTM=0.0001*time^3-0.0023*time^2+0.0152*time+0.0221**		
2	Average time to maturity (years)	5	
3	Yield	5.31%	<-- =0.0001*B2^3-0.0023*B2^2+0.0152*B2+0.0221

The same regression relation can be used to attempt to spot mispriced bonds. For example, the Union Pacific bond in row 39 appears to be overpriced (its yield is significantly below the regression line).

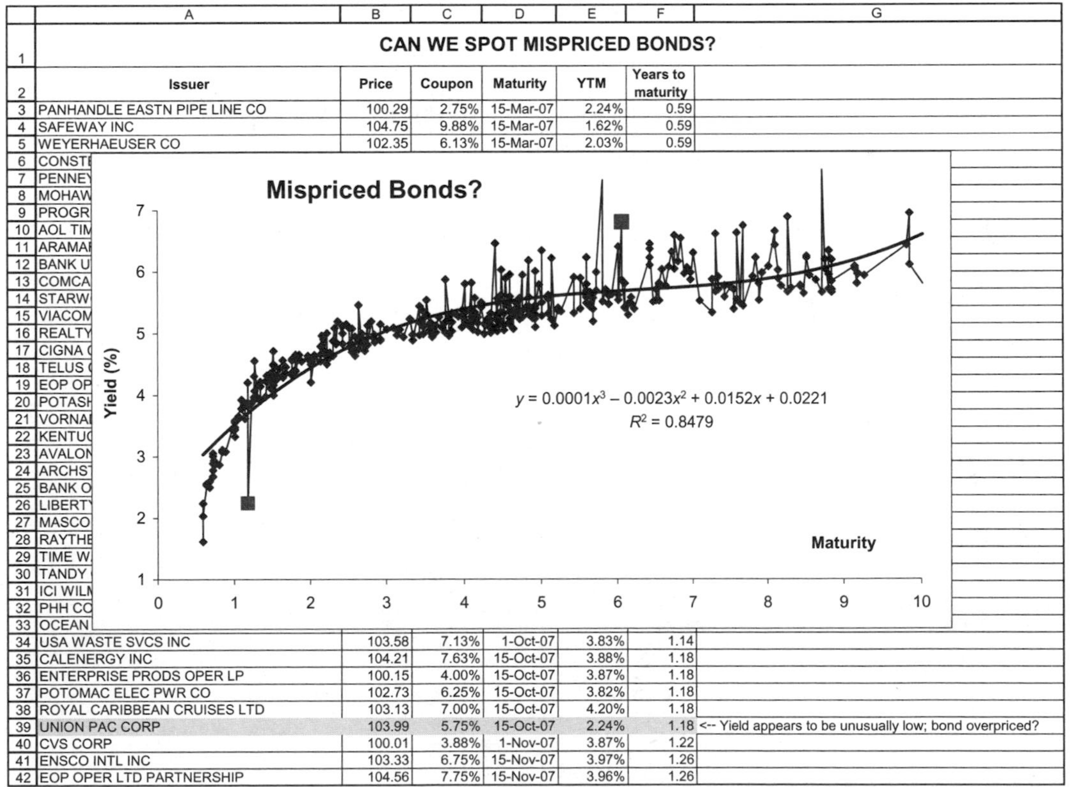

	A	B	C	D	E	F	G
1	**CAN WE SPOT MISPRICED BONDS?**						
2	**Issuer**	**Price**	**Coupon**	**Maturity**	**YTM**	**Years to maturity**	
3	PANHANDLE EASTN PIPE LINE CO	100.29	2.75%	15-Mar-07	2.24%	0.59	
4	SAFEWAY INC	104.75	9.88%	15-Mar-07	1.62%	0.59	
5	WEYERHAEUSER CO	102.35	6.13%	15-Mar-07	2.03%	0.59	
6	CONST						
7	PENNE						
8	MOHAW						
9	PROGR						
10	AOL TIM						
11	ARAMA						
12	BANK U						
13	COMCA						
14	STARW						
15	VIACOM						
16	REALTY						
17	CIGNA						
18	TELUS						
19	EOP OP						
20	POTASH						
21	VORNA						
22	KENTU						
23	AVALON						
24	ARCHS						
25	BANK O						
26	LIBERT						
27	MASCO						
28	RAYTHE						
29	TIME W						
30	TANDY						
31	ICI WIL						
32	PHH CO						
33	OCEAN						
34	USA WASTE SVCS INC	103.58	7.13%	1-Oct-07	3.83%	1.14	
35	CALENERGY INC	104.21	7.63%	15-Oct-07	3.88%	1.18	
36	ENTERPRISE PRODS OPER LP	100.15	4.00%	15-Oct-07	3.87%	1.18	
37	POTOMAC ELEC PWR CO	102.73	6.25%	15-Oct-07	3.82%	1.18	
38	ROYAL CARIBBEAN CRUISES LTD	103.13	7.00%	15-Oct-07	4.20%	1.18	
39	UNION PAC CORP	103.99	5.75%	15-Oct-07	2.24%	1.18	<-- Yield appears to be unusually low; bond overpriced?
40	CVS CORP	100.01	3.88%	1-Nov-07	3.87%	1.22	
41	ENSCO INTL INC	103.33	6.75%	15-Nov-07	3.97%	1.26	
42	EOP OPER LTD PARTNERSHIP	104.56	7.75%	15-Nov-07	3.96%	1.26	

Another possibly mispriced bond is the Kinder Morgan bond maturing 1 September 2012, whose yield appears to be significantly above the regression curve, indicating that the bond may be underpriced:

	A	B	C	D	E	F	G
327	CONTINENTAL CORP	109.71	8.38%	15-Aug-12	6.40%	6.02	
328	PEPCO HOLDINGS INC	104.2	6.45%	15-Aug-12	5.62%	6.02	
329	VIACOM INC	100.47	5.63%	15-Aug-12	5.53%	6.02	
330	KINDER MORGAN INC	98.52	6.50%	1-Sep-12	6.80%	6.06	<-- Yield is significantly above curve. Bond underpriced?
331	SAFECO CORP	107	7.25%	1-Sep-12	5.86%	6.06	
332	ALCAN INC	97.28	4.88%	15-Sep-12	5.41%	6.10	
333	AMERISOURCEBERGEN CORP	99.08	5.63%	15-Sep-12	5.81%	6.10	
334	CINCINNATI GAS & ELEC CO	101.45	5.70%	15-Sep-12	5.42%	6.10	

27.2.1 Very Short-Term Bonds May Not Fit the Model

The preceding is a valuable example of when the yield curve can be described well by a polynomial regression. Unfortunately this technique does not always work if we include very short-term bonds. Here's a negative example drawn from the same data source but a different date. This time we have included data for all corporate bond maturities:

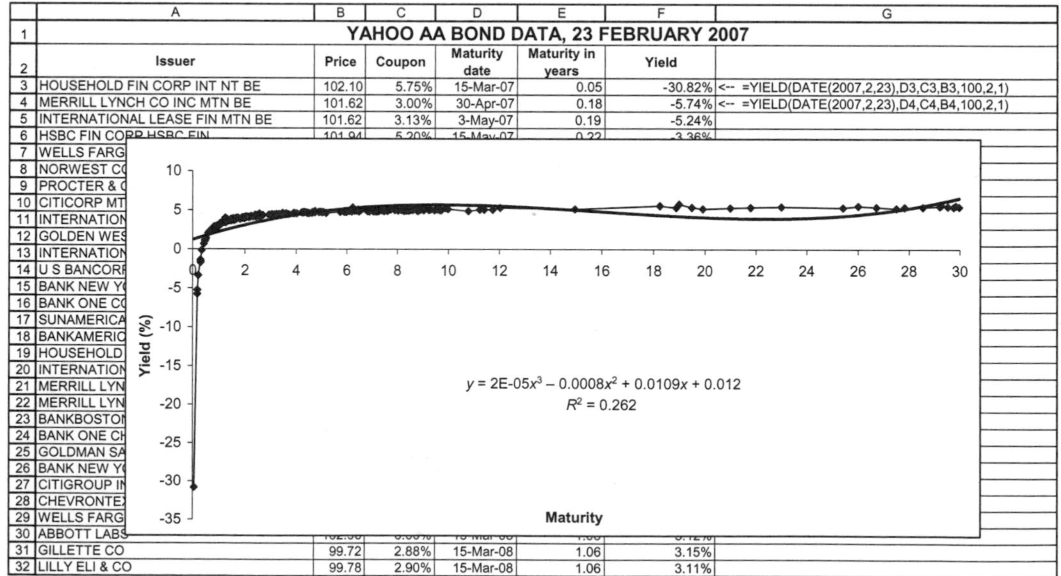

	A	B	C	D	E	F	G
1	YAHOO AA BOND DATA, 23 FEBRUARY 2007						
2	Issuer	Price	Coupon	Maturity date	Maturity in years	Yield	
3	HOUSEHOLD FIN CORP INT NT BE	102.10	5.75%	15-Mar-07	0.05	-30.82%	<-- =YIELD(DATE(2007,2,23),D3,C3,B3,100,2,1)
4	MERRILL LYNCH CO INC MTN BE	101.62	3.00%	30-Apr-07	0.18	-5.74%	<-- =YIELD(DATE(2007,2,23),D4,C4,B4,100,2,1)
5	INTERNATIONAL LEASE FIN MTN BE	101.62	3.13%	3-May-07	0.19	-5.24%	
6	HSBC FIN CO						
7	WELLS FARG						
8	NORWEST C						
9	PROCTER &						
10	CITICORP MT						
11	INTERNATION						
12	GOLDEN WES						
13	INTERNATION						
14	U S BANCOR						
15	BANK NEW Y						
16	BANK ONE C						
17	SUNAMERICA						
18	BANKAMERIC						
19	HOUSEHOLD						
20	INTERNATION						
21	MERRILL LYN						
22	MERRILL LYN						
23	BANKBOSTO						
24	BANK ONE CH						
25	GOLDMAN SA						
26	BANK NEW Y						
27	CITIGROUP I						
28	CHEVRONTE						
29	WELLS FARG						
30	ABBOTT LAB						
31	GILLETTE CO	99.72	2.88%	15-Mar-08	1.06	3.15%	
32	LILLY ELI & CO	99.78	2.90%	15-Mar-08	1.06	3.11%	

The data include some odd points, such as the highly negative yields on the Household Finance bonds (row 3) and even the –5.74 percent on the Merrill Lynch bonds. If we are willing to make some judgment calls and throw out some of the data as inexplicable, we can improve our prediction of the term structure.

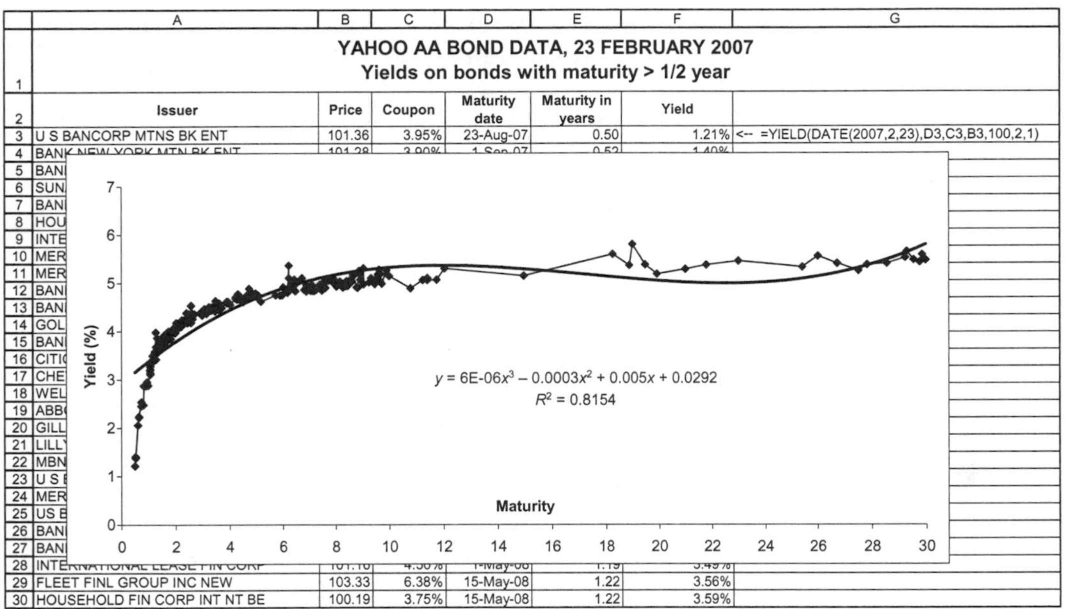

YAHOO AA BOND DATA, 23 FEBRUARY 2007
Yields on bonds with maturity > 1/2 year
Issuer
Price
Coupon
Maturity date
Maturity in years
Yield
U S BANCORP MTNS BK ENT
101.36
3.95%
23-Aug-07
0.50
1.21%
<-- =YIELD(DATE(2007,2,23),D3,C3,B3,100,2,1)
FLEET FINL GROUP INC NEW
103.33
6.38%
15-May-08
1.22
3.56%
HOUSEHOLD FIN CORP INT NT BE
100.19
3.75%
15-May-08
1.22
3.59%
Yield (%)
Maturity
y = 6E-06x³ – 0.0003x² + 0.005x + 0.0292
R² = 0.8154

It is clear that the regression provides an even better explanation for yields of bonds with maturities greater than two years. Examining the regression shows that the contribution of the two nonlinear terms is quite marginal: The coefficient of Time^3 is 0.000006 and the coefficient of Time^2 is –0.0003. The term structure is, in fact, more or less linear.

27.2.2 Doing the Regressions with Linest

Excel's **Linest** function (discussed in Chapter 34) can be used to estimate the regression, as follows:

	A	B	C	D	E	F	G	H	I	J	K	L	M	N
1	USING LINEST TO ESTIMATE THE REGRESSION													
2	Issuer	Price	Coupon	Maturity date	Maturity in years	Maturity^2	Maturity^3	Yield		The cells K4:N8 below contain the array equation {=LINEST(H3:H238,E3:G238,,TRUE)}				
3	U S BANCORP MTNS BK E	101.36	3.95%	23-Aug-07	0.50	0.25	0.12	1.21%			time^3	time^2	time	intercept
4	BANK NEW YORK MTN BK	101.28	3.90%	1-Sep-07	0.52	0.27	0.14	1.40%		Slope	0.000006	-0.00032	0.005	0.02918
5	BANK ONE CORP	101.41	4.13%	1-Sep-07	0.52	0.27	0.14	1.38%		Standard error	0.00000	0.00002	0.00024	0.00059
6	SUNAMERICA INC	102.79	6.75%	1-Oct-07	0.60	0.36	0.22	2.06%		R^2	0.81539	0.00347	#N/A	#N/A
7	BANKAMERICA CORP	102.77	6.63%	15-Oct-07	0.64	0.41	0.26	2.24%		F statistic	341.57800	232.00000	#N/A	#N/A
8	HOUSEHOLD FIN CORP IN	103.65	8.00%	15-Oct-07	0.64	0.41	0.26	2.22%		SS_{xy}	0.01234	0.00279	#N/A	#N/A

Note that we have added two additional columns to our data—in columns F and G we added the maturity squared and the maturity to the power three, both factors in our regression.

By using the function **Index**, also discussed in Chapter 34, we can pick out individual items from the **Linest** array. In the following cells we show the regression intercept and coefficients, and also the *t*-statistics for the coefficients:

	J	K	L	M	N	O	P
11	**Coefficients**						
12	Time	0.000006	<-- =INDEX(LINEST(H3:H238,E3:G238,,TRUE),1,1)				
13	Time^2	-0.000320	<-- =INDEX(LINEST(H3:H238,E3:G238,,TRUE),1,2)				
14	Time^3	0.004991	<-- =INDEX(LINEST(H3:H238,E3:G238,,TRUE),1,3)				
15							
16	Intercept	0.02918	<-- =INDEX(LINEST(H3:H238,E3:G238,,TRUE),1,4)				
17	R-squared	81.54%	<-- =INDEX(LINEST(H3:H238,E3:G238,,TRUE),3,1)				
18							
19	**Coefficient t-statistic**						
20	Time	10.351011	<-- =INDEX(LINEST(H3:H238,E3:G238,,TRUE),1,1)/INDEX(LINEST(H3:H238,E3:G238,,TRUE),2,1)				
21	Time^2	-13.250878	<-- =INDEX(LINEST(H3:H238,E3:G238,,TRUE),1,2)/INDEX(LINEST(H3:H238,E3:G238,,TRUE),2,2)				
22	Time^3	20.763478	<-- =INDEX(LINEST(H3:H238,E3:G238,,TRUE),1,3)/INDEX(LINEST(H3:H238,E3:G238,,TRUE),2,3)				

27.3 Description of the Data

Bond data are much more difficult to access than stock price data. The data for the regression illustrated in the previous section come from Yahoo's bond screener (http://screen.yahoo.com/bonds.html), the data for which are supplied by ValuBond. The following screen finds corporate bonds with a Fitch AA rating:

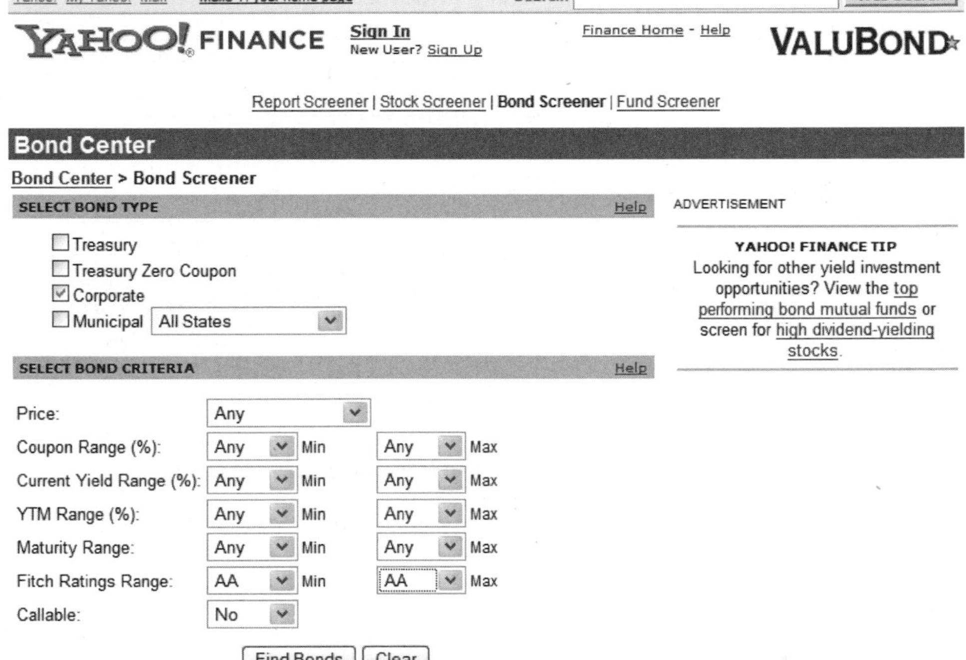

A typical screen of data looks like this:

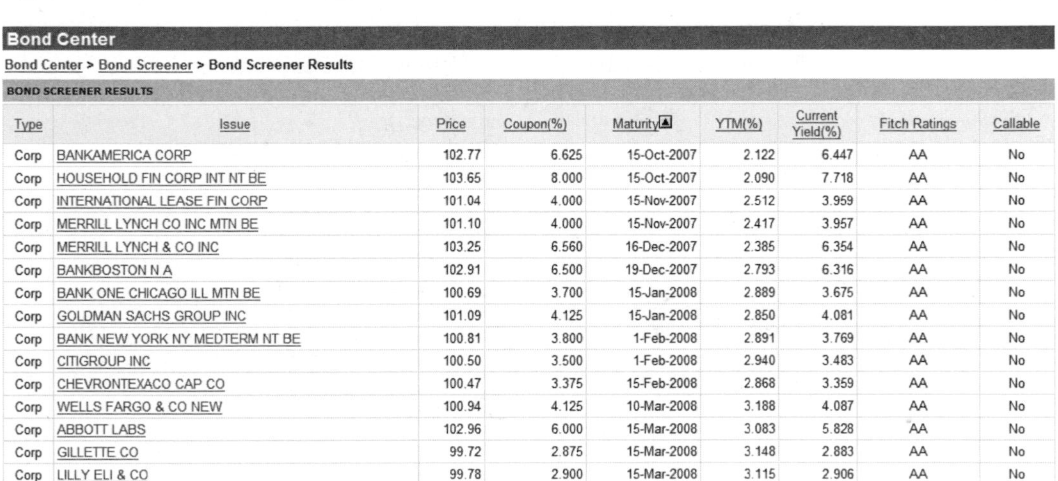

Type	Issue	Price	Coupon(%)	Maturity	YTM(%)	Current Yield(%)	Fitch Ratings	Callable
Corp	BANKAMERICA CORP	102.77	6.625	15-Oct-2007	2.122	6.447	AA	No
Corp	HOUSEHOLD FIN CORP INT NT BE	103.65	8.000	15-Oct-2007	2.090	7.718	AA	No
Corp	INTERNATIONAL LEASE FIN CORP	101.04	4.000	15-Nov-2007	2.512	3.959	AA	No
Corp	MERRILL LYNCH CO INC MTN BE	101.10	4.000	15-Nov-2007	2.417	3.957	AA	No
Corp	MERRILL LYNCH & CO INC	103.25	6.560	16-Dec-2007	2.385	6.354	AA	No
Corp	BANKBOSTON N A	102.91	6.500	19-Dec-2007	2.793	6.316	AA	No
Corp	BANK ONE CHICAGO ILL MTN BE	100.69	3.700	15-Jan-2008	2.889	3.675	AA	No
Corp	GOLDMAN SACHS GROUP INC	101.09	4.125	15-Jan-2008	2.850	4.081	AA	No
Corp	BANK NEW YORK NY MEDTERM NT BE	100.81	3.800	1-Feb-2008	2.891	3.769	AA	No
Corp	CITIGROUP INC	100.50	3.500	1-Feb-2008	2.940	3.483	AA	No
Corp	CHEVRONTEXACO CAP CO	100.47	3.375	15-Feb-2008	2.868	3.359	AA	No
Corp	WELLS FARGO & CO NEW	100.94	4.125	10-Mar-2008	3.188	4.087	AA	No
Corp	ABBOTT LABS	102.96	6.000	15-Mar-2008	3.083	5.828	AA	No
Corp	GILLETTE CO	99.72	2.875	15-Mar-2008	3.148	2.883	AA	No
Corp	LILLY ELI & CO	99.78	2.900	15-Mar-2008	3.115	2.906	AA	No

We can copy/paste this screen into Excel. Cleaning up the page somewhat gives the following Excel spreadsheet:

	A	B	C	D	E	F	G	H
1	**YAHOO'S BOND SCREENER--TYPICAL PAGE** **Data from 23 February 2007** **Comparing the Yahoo YTM with Excel's Yield function**							
2	**Issue**	**Price**	**Coupon**	**Maturity**	**YTM**		**Excel Yield function**	
3	BANKAMERICA CORP	102.77	6.63%	15-Oct-07	2.12%		2.24%	<-- =YIELD(DATE(2007,2,23),D3,C3,B3,100,2,1)
4	HOUSEHOLD FIN CORP INT NT BE	103.65	8.00%	15-Oct-07	2.09%		2.22%	<-- =YIELD(DATE(2007,2,23),D4,C4,B4,100,2,1)
5	INTERNATIONAL LEASE FIN CORP	101.04	4.00%	15-Nov-07	2.51%		2.54%	<-- =YIELD(DATE(2007,2,23),D5,C5,B5,100,2,1)
6	MERRILL LYNCH CO INC MTN BE	101.10	4.00%	15-Nov-07	2.42%		2.45%	<-- =YIELD(DATE(2007,2,23),D6,C6,B6,100,2,1)
7	MERRILL LYNCH & CO INC	103.25	6.56%	16-Dec-07	2.39%		2.48%	
8	BANKBOSTON N A	102.91	6.50%	19-Dec-07	2.79%		2.87%	
9	BANK ONE CHICAGO ILL MTN BE	100.69	3.70%	15-Jan-08	2.89%		2.91%	
10	GOLDMAN SACHS GROUP INC	101.09	4.13%	15-Jan-08	2.85%		2.88%	
11	BANK NEW YORK NY MEDTERM NT BE	100.81	3.80%	1-Feb-08	2.89%		2.92%	
12	CITIGROUP INC	100.50	3.50%	1-Feb-08	2.94%		2.95%	
13	CHEVRONTEXACO CAP CO	100.47	3.38%	15-Feb-08	2.87%		2.88%	
14	WELLS FARGO & CO NEW	100.94	4.13%	10-Mar-08	3.19%		3.20%	
15	ABBOTT LABS	102.96	6.00%	15-Mar-08	3.08%		3.12%	
16	GILLETTE CO	99.72	2.88%	15-Mar-08	3.15%		3.15%	
17	LILLY ELI & CO	99.78	2.90%	15-Mar-08	3.12%		3.11%	

In this spreadsheet we have used Excel's **Yield** function to recompute the Yahoo reported yield (column E). The differences between the reported Yahoo yields and those computed by Excel's **Yield** function are not large.

The Excel **Yield** function looks like this:

Two Screens from Excel's Yield Function

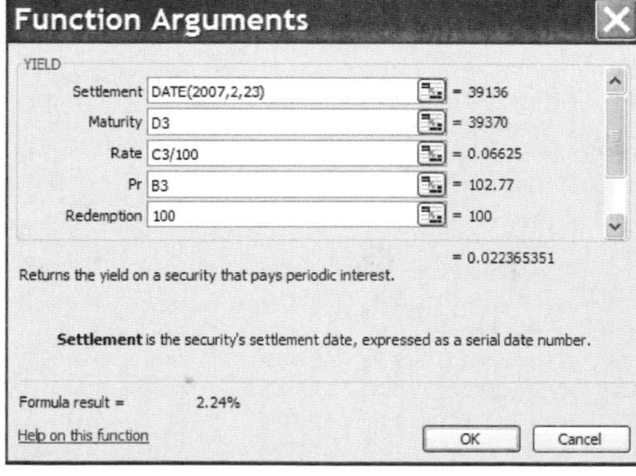

Some notes on the **Yield** function's inputs:

- The **Settlement** date is the transaction date. The data were recorded on 23 February 2007, and we have used Excel's **Date** function to enter this date in the serial number form required by the function.
- **Rate** refers to the bond's coupon. Yahoo reports this coupon as a whole number; we have divided by 100 to make it into a percentage.
- **Pr** refers to the bond's price.
- **Redemption** is the bond's face value.
- **Frequency** is set to 2; this assumes the bond pays interest semiannually.
- **Basis** is set to 1, indicating that the computation is based on actual days to maturity and a 365-day year.

27.4 The Treasury Yield Curve

The discussion in this chapter has thus far concentrated on corporate bonds. The largest and most efficient bond market in the world is, of course, the market for United States Treasury securities. A wonderful paper by Gürkaynak, Sack, and Wright computes the daily term structure for U.S. Treasuries from 1961 to 2006.[2] Here is a snapshot from the data; note that in the early part of the period covered by this paper, not all currently available long-term Treasury securities existed, so that it is impossible to compute a longer-term term structure. Notice also that the interest rates are given in whole numbers, not percentages.

2. "The U.S. Treasury Yield Curve: 1961 to the Present," by Refet S. Gürkaynak, Brian Sack, and Jonathan H. Wright. http://www.federalreserve.gov/Pubs/feds/2006/ (this site also has the data file for this paper). The version of this data set used for this chapter is on the disk that comes with this book.

	A	B	C	D	E	F	G	H	I	J	K	L	M	N
1	**DAILY TERM STRUCTURES, 1961-2006** **Source: "The U.S. Treasury Yield Curve: 1961 to Present"** **by Gürkaynak, Sack, Wright** **http://www.federalreserve.gov/pubs/FEDS/2006/200628/feds200628.xls**													
2	**Maturity (years) -->**													
3		1	2	3	4	5	6	7	8	9	10	11	12	13
4	Date													
5	14-Jun-61	2.9825	3.3771	3.553	3.6439	3.6987	3.7351	3.7612						
6	15-Jun-61	2.9941	3.4137	3.5981	3.693	3.7501	3.7882	3.8154						
7	16-Jun-61	3.0012	3.4142	3.5994	3.6953	3.7531	3.7917	3.8192						
8	19-Jun-61	2.9949	3.4386	3.6252	3.7199	3.7768	3.8147	3.8418						
9	20-Jun-61	2.9833	3.4101	3.5986	3.6952	3.7533	3.7921	3.8198						
10	21-Jun-61	2.9993	3.4236	3.6132	3.7107	3.7694	3.8085	3.8364						
11	22-Jun-61	2.9837	3.4036	3.5976	3.6981	3.7587	3.799	3.8279						
12	23-Jun-61	2.9749	3.3706	3.5725	3.6816	3.7478	3.7921	3.8237						
13	26-Jun-61	2.9563	3.3623	3.5678	3.6784	3.7455	3.7903	3.8224						
10926	20-Apr-05	3.2856	3.5096	3.635	3.7329	3.8289	3.9296	4.0338	4.1382	4.2395	4.3349	4.4224	4.501	4.5699
10927	21-Apr-05	3.3738	3.6294	3.7571	3.8484	3.9366	4.0306	4.1294	4.2295	4.3272	4.4194	4.5041	4.5799	4.646
10928	22-Apr-05	3.3584	3.606	3.7261	3.811	3.8939	3.9834	4.0788	4.1763	4.2721	4.363	4.4469	4.5223	4.5885
10929	25-Apr-05	3.3711	3.6236	3.7436	3.8254	3.9038	3.9884	4.0789	4.1718	4.2633	4.3505	4.431	4.5034	4.567
10930	26-Apr-05	3.3877	3.6503	3.7687	3.8478	3.9248	4.0094	4.1006	4.1944	4.2868	4.3745	4.4552	4.5274	4.5903
10931	27-Apr-05	3.3664	3.614	3.73	3.8097	3.8874	3.9722	4.0633	4.1571	4.2496	4.3377	4.4191	4.4923	4.5565
10932	28-Apr-05	3.329	3.5593	3.6647	3.7391	3.8153	3.9008	3.9936	4.0895	4.1844	4.2747	4.3583	4.4336	4.4999
10933	29-Apr-05	3.3855	3.6232	3.725	3.7923	3.8608	3.9392	4.026	4.1169	4.2076	4.2946	4.3755	4.4487	4.5132
10934	2-May-05	3.3729	3.6039	3.7057	3.7751	3.8462	3.9271	4.0161	4.1089	4.2012	4.2895	4.3716	4.4457	4.5111
10935	3-May-05	3.3987	3.636	3.7331	3.7963	3.8622	3.9392	4.0253	4.1159	4.2064	4.2932	4.3738	4.4465	4.5105
10936	4-May-05	3.3656	3.5984	3.6955	3.7618	3.8325	3.9151	4.0074	4.1043	4.2013	4.2945	4.3814	4.4604	4.5305
10937	5-May-05	3.3197	3.5398	3.6399	3.7134	3.7917	3.881	3.9789	4.0805	4.1814	4.278	4.3678	4.4495	4.522

A few term structures from this data set are shown in the following graph:

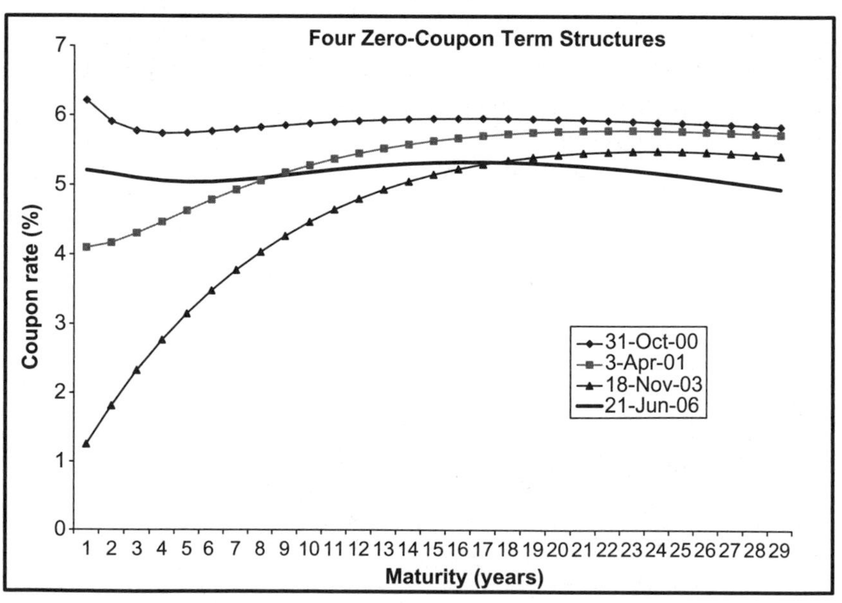

27.5 Computing Par Yields from a Zero-Coupon Yield Curve

One of the interesting details on the Federal Reserve data set is the computation of the *par yield*. This is defined as the yield X on a coupon bond computed so that the price of the bond on a given date is 1.

$$\sum_{t=1}^{N} \frac{X}{(1+r_t)^t} + \frac{1}{(1+r_N)^N} = 1$$

A little fiddling shows that the solution for X is

$$X = \frac{1 - \dfrac{1}{(1+r_N)^N}}{\displaystyle\sum_{t=1}^{N} \frac{1}{(1+r_t)^t}}$$

Computing these yields is simple if we recognize that the denominator needs to be computed using an Excel array function. (This specific array function is described in the following subsection; for a general description of array functions, see Chapter 35.)

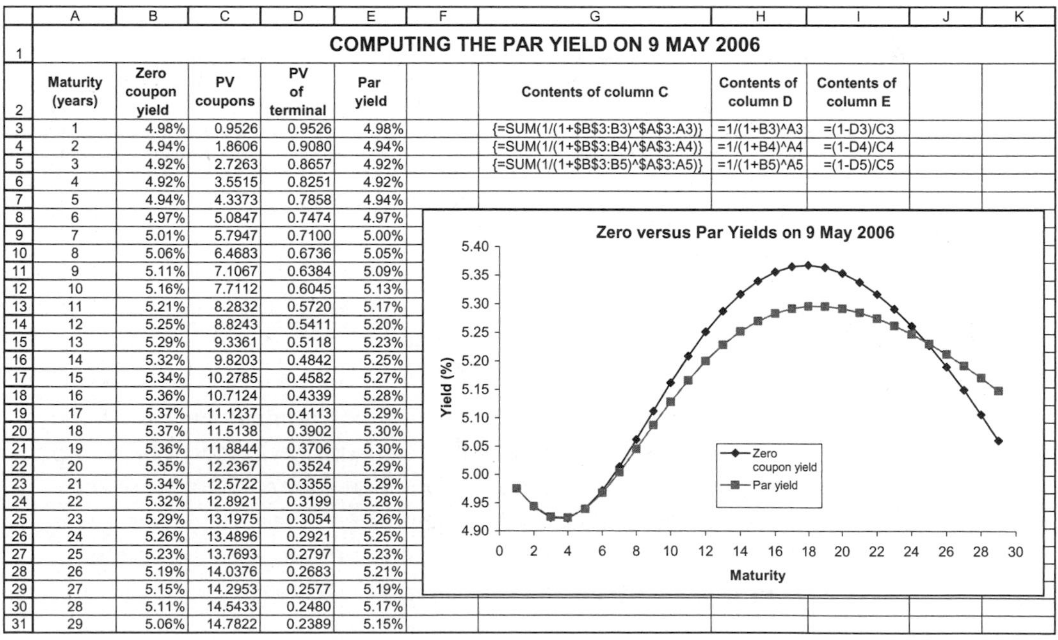

	A	B	C	D	E	F	G	H	I	J	K
1	COMPUTING THE PAR YIELD ON 9 MAY 2006										
2	Maturity (years)	Zero coupon yield	PV coupons	PV of terminal	Par yield		Contents of column C	Contents of column D	Contents of column E		
3	1	4.98%	0.9526	0.9526	4.98%		{=SUM(1/(1+$B$3:B3)^$A$3:A3)}	=1/(1+B3)^A3	=(1-D3)/C3		
4	2	4.94%	1.8606	0.9080	4.94%		{=SUM(1/(1+$B$3:B4)^$A$3:A4)}	=1/(1+B4)^A4	=(1-D4)/C4		
5	3	4.92%	2.7263	0.8657	4.92%		{=SUM(1/(1+$B$3:B5)^$A$3:A5)}	=1/(1+B5)^A5	=(1-D5)/C5		
6	4	4.92%	3.5515	0.8251	4.92%						
7	5	4.94%	4.3373	0.7858	4.94%						
8	6	4.97%	5.0847	0.7474	4.97%						
9	7	5.01%	5.7947	0.7100	5.00%						
10	8	5.06%	6.4683	0.6736	5.05%						
11	9	5.11%	7.1067	0.6384	5.09%						
12	10	5.16%	7.7112	0.6045	5.13%						
13	11	5.21%	8.2832	0.5720	5.17%						
14	12	5.25%	8.8243	0.5411	5.20%						
15	13	5.29%	9.3361	0.5118	5.23%						
16	14	5.32%	9.8203	0.4842	5.25%						
17	15	5.34%	10.2785	0.4582	5.27%						
18	16	5.36%	10.7124	0.4339	5.28%						
19	17	5.37%	11.1237	0.4113	5.29%						
20	18	5.37%	11.5138	0.3902	5.30%						
21	19	5.36%	11.8844	0.3706	5.30%						
22	20	5.35%	12.2367	0.3524	5.29%						
23	21	5.34%	12.5722	0.3355	5.29%						
24	22	5.32%	12.8921	0.3199	5.28%						
25	23	5.29%	13.1975	0.3054	5.26%						
26	24	5.26%	13.4896	0.2921	5.25%						
27	25	5.23%	13.7693	0.2797	5.23%						
28	26	5.19%	14.0376	0.2683	5.21%						
29	27	5.15%	14.2953	0.2577	5.19%						
30	28	5.11%	14.5433	0.2480	5.17%						
31	29	5.06%	14.7822	0.2389	5.15%						

27.5.1 Excel Sidebar: Computing $\sum_{t=1}^{N} \frac{1}{(1+r_t)^t}$ Using an Array Function

The expression $\sum_{t=1}^{N} \frac{1}{(1+r_t)^t}$ requires that each interest rate r_t in the zero-coupon term structure be raised to the power t. There is no built-in Excel financial function that performs this task. However, if we write =SUM(1/(1+$B$3:B3)^$A$3:A3), then Excel knows that each term in column B should be raised to the power given in the corresponding cell of column A. This is an array function: It has to be inserted by pressing [Ctrl]+[Shift]+[Enter].

Because we are suspicious, we always check to see if the array function indeed works. Here's a test; this time we use a recursive function in column C. The results are the same as before—the Excel array function is correct.

	A	B	C	D	E	F	G	H	I
1	**CHECKING THE ARRAY FUNCTION COMPUTATION OF THE PAR YIELD** **Instead of an array function in column C, we've used a recursive function:** **Cell C3 = 1/(1+r$_1$)^1; Cell C2 = C3 + 1/(1+r$_2$)^2, etc.**								
2	**Maturity (years)**	**Zero coupon yield in %**	**PV coupons**	**PV of terminal**	**Par yield**		**Contents of column C**	**Contents of column D**	**Contents of column E**
3	1	4.98%	0.9526	0.9526	4.98%		=1/(1+B3)^A3	=1/(1+B3)^A3	=(1-D3)/C3
4	2	4.94%	1.8606	0.9080	4.94%		=C3+1/(1+B4)^A4	=1/(1+B4)^A4	=(1-D4)/C4
5	3	4.92%	2.7263	0.8657	4.92%		=C4+1/(1+B5)^A5	=1/(1+B5)^A5	=(1-D5)/C5
6	4	4.92%	3.5515	0.8251	4.92%		=C5+1/(1+B6)^A6		
7	5	4.94%	4.3373	0.7858	4.94%				
8	6	4.97%	5.0847	0.7474	4.97%				
9	7	5.01%	5.7947	0.7100	5.00%				
10	8	5.06%	6.4683	0.6736	5.05%				
11	9	5.11%	7.1067	0.6384	5.09%				
12	10	5.16%	7.7112	0.6045	5.13%				

27.6 Summary

We can use Excel efficiently to compute a polynomial curve to fit the term structure. This chapter has illustrated this technique using both corporate bond yields and using a U.S. Federal Reserve data set of zero-coupon bond rates. As illustrated in Chapter 2, curve-fitting technique is useful for computing the firm's cost of debt; it may also be helpful in spotting mispriced bonds.

Exercises

1. The Excel notebook **fm3_problems27.xls** includes data for noncallable CCC-rated bonds. The data were reported on Yahoo on 20 July 2007.

   a. Graph the bond yield to maturity (YTM) on the *x*-axis of an XY-scatter plot, with the bond maturity in years on the *x*-axis.

   b. Use a polynomial regression to determine the relation between the YTM and the bond maturity.

	A	B	C	D	E	F
1	**CCC CORPORATE BONDS, NONCALLABLE, 20 JULY 2007**					
2	**Type**	**Price**	**Coupon(%)**	**Maturity**	**YTM(%)**	**Fitch Rating**
3	LEVEL 3 COMMUNICATIONS INC	105.50	11.00	15-Mar-08	3.134	CCC
4	FORD MTR CO DEL	102.50	7.25	1-Oct-08	5.163	CCC
5	USEC INC	101.75	6.75	20-Jan-09	5.561	CCC
6	XM SATELLITE RADIO HLDGS INC	88.75	1.75	1-Dec-09	6.864	CCC
7	LEVEL 3 COMMUNICATIONS INC	98.75	6.00	15-Mar-10	6.505	CCC
8	VISTEON CORP	102.75	8.25	1-Aug-10	7.237	CCC
9	TEMBEC INDS INC	59.00	8.50	1-Feb-11	27.020	CCC
10	TOYS R US INC	97.00	7.63	1-Aug-11	8.505	CCC
11	TENET HEALTHCARE CORP	94.00	6.38	1-Dec-11	8.010	CCC
12	TEMBEC INDS INC	58.00	7.75	15-Mar-12	22.696	CCC
13	TENET HEALTHCARE CORP	93.50	6.50	1-Jun-12	8.126	CCC
14	AMR CORP	106.00	9.00	1-Aug-12	7.556	CCC
15	TENET HEALTHCARE CORP	93.50	7.38	1-Feb-13	8.872	CCC
16	TOYS R US INC	93.50	7.88	15-Apr-13	9.348	CCC
17	POPE & TALBOT INC	86.00	8.38	1-Jun-13	11.714	CCC
18	POPE & TALBOT INC	86.00	8.38	1-Jun-13	11.714	CCC
19	RITE AID CORP	91.00	6.88	15-Aug-13	8.803	CCC
20	Scotia Pacific Co LLC	95.50	7.11	20-Jan-14	8.003	CCC
21	VISTEON CORP	89.25	7.00	10-Mar-14	9.180	CCC
22	TENET HEALTHCARE CORP	102.00	9.88	1-Jul-14	9.478	CCC
23	TENET HEALTHCARE CORP	99.00	9.25	1-Feb-15	9.434	CCC
24	AMR CORP	102.49	9.00	15-Sep-16	8.600	CCC
25	TOYS R US INC	90.00	7.38	15-Oct-18	8.786	CCC
26	BORDEN CHEMICAL INC	102.50	9.20	15-Mar-21	8.878	CCC
27	BORDEN CHEMICAL INC	92.62	7.88	15-Feb-23	8.748	CCC
28	RITE AID CORP	89.00	7.70	15-Feb-27	8.893	CCC
29	TENET HEALTHCARE CORP	83.00	6.88	15-Nov-31	8.543	CCC
30	FORD MTR CO DEL	96.25	9.98	15-Feb-47	10.374	CCC

2. Clean up the data in exercise 1 by eliminating obviously problematic points. Repeat the regression exercise.

3. The Excel notebook **fm3_problems27.xls** includes data for 249 noncallable BB-rated bonds. The data were reported on Yahoo on 20 July 2007.

   a. Graph the bond yield to maturity (YTM) on the *x*-axis of an XY-scatter plot, with the bond maturity in years on the *x*-axis.

b. Use a polynomial regression to determine the relation between the YTM and the bond maturity.

	A	B	C	D	E	F
1	**BB CORPORATE BONDS, NONCALLABLE, 20 JULY 2007**					
2	**Type**	**Price**	**Coupon(%)**	**Maturity**	**YTM(%)**	**Fitch Rating**
3	DILLARDS INC	102.50	6.690	1-Aug-07	-19.559	BB
4	GENERAL MTRS ACCEP CORP	101.75	3.800	15-Aug-07	-9.400	BB
5	GAP INC DEL	102.31	6.900	15-Sep-07	-3.732	BB
6	GENERAL MTRS ACCEP CPSMARTNBE	101.95	5.600	15-Sep-07	-3.493	BB
7	SEARS ROEBUCK ACCEP CORP	102.14	6.700	18-Sep-07	-2.817	BB
8	DELUXE CORP	101.38	3.500	1-Oct-07	-1.783	BB
9	SONAT INC	102.50	6.750	1-Oct-07	-2.811	BB
10	CMS ENERGY CORP	103.50	9.875	15-Oct-07	-1.802	BB
11	GENERAL MTRS ACCEP CPSMARTNBE	101.94	5.600	15-Oct-07	-0.909	BB
12	CASE CR CORP	103.00	6.750	21-Oct-07	-2.693	BB
13	GENERAL MTRS ACCEP CPSMARTNBE	101.98	6.000	15-Nov-07	0.768	BB
14	NORTHWEST PIPELINE CORP	102.50	6.625	1-Dec-07	0.721	BB
15	EL PASO ENERGY CORP MTN BE	102.46	6.950	15-Dec-07	1.595	BB
16	BROWNING FERRIS INDS	102.75	6.375	15-Jan-08	1.313	BB
17	PANAMSAT CORP NEW	102.50	6.375	15-Jan-08	1.739	BB
18	SPIEKER PPTYS L P	102.70	6.750	15-Jan-08	1.748	BB
19	MIRAGE RESORTS INC	103.25	6.750	1-Feb-08	1.193	BB
20	CONSTELLATION BRANDS INC	104.00	8.000	15-Feb-08	1.567	BB
21	DILLARDS INC	103.50	6.300	15-Feb-08	0.701	BB
22	GENERAL MTRS ACCEP CPSMARTNBE	101.54	5.250	15-Feb-08	2.767	BB
23	PSEG ENERGY HLDGS INC	103.75	8.625	15-Feb-08	2.557	BB
24	SEARS ROEBUCK ACCEP CORP INTER	102.00	6.200	15-Feb-08	2.954	BB
25	SEARS ROEBUCK ACCEP CORP INTER	101.80	6.100	15-Feb-08	3.174	BB
26	SEARS ROEBUCK ACCEP CORP INTER	102.39	6.650	15-Feb-08	2.784	BB
27	SMITHFIELD FOODS INC	103.50	7.625	15-Feb-08	1.982	BB
28	EOP OPER LTD PARTNERSHIP EOP	100.65	4.400	15-Mar-08	3.464	BB

4. Clean up the data in exercise 3 by eliminating obviously problematic points. Repeat the regression exercise.

5. Graph the cleaned-up data for the CCC and BB bonds on one set of axes.

6. Graph the spread between the CCC and BB bonds using the polynomial regressions from exercises 2 and 4.

28 Calculating Default-Adjusted Expected Bond Returns

28.1 Overview

In this chapter we discuss the effects of default risk on the returns from holding bonds to maturity. The *expected return* on a bond that may possibly default is different from the bond's *promised return*. The latter is defined as the bond's *yield to maturity*, the internal rate of return calculated from the bond's current market price, and its *promised* coupon payments and *promised eventual return* of principal in the future. The bond's expected return is less easily calculated: We need to take into account both the bond's probability of future default and the *recovery rate*, the percentage of its principal that holders can expect to recover in the case of default. To complicate matters still further, default can happen in stages, through the gradual degradation of the issuing company's creditworthiness.[1]

In this chapter we use a Markov model to solve for the expected return on a risky bond. Our adjustment procedure takes into account all three of the factors mentioned: the probability of default, the transition of the issuer from one state of creditworthiness to another, and the percentage recovery of face value when the bond defaults. In sections 28.3–28.5 we first use Excel to solve a relatively small-scale problem. We then use some publicly available statistics to program a fuller spreadsheet model. Finally, we show that this model can be used to derive bond betas, the CAPM's risk measure for securities (discussed previously in Chapters 8–11).

28.1.1 Some Preliminaries

Before proceeding, we define a number of terms:

• A bond is issued with a given amount of *principal* or *face value*. When the bond matures, the bondholder is promised the return of this principal. If the bond is issued *at par*, then it is sold for the principal amount.

1. Besides default risk, bonds are also subject to term-structure risk: The prices of bonds may show significant variations over time as a result of changing term structure. This statement will be especially true for long-term bonds. In this chapter we abstract from term-structure risk, confining ourselves only to a discussion of the effects of default risk on bond expected returns.

• A bond bears an interest rate called the *coupon rate*. The periodic payment promised to the bondholders is the product of the coupon rate times the bond's face value.

• At any given moment, a bond will be sold in the market for a *market price*. This price may differ from the bond's coupon rate.[2]

• The bond's *yield to maturity* (YTM) is the internal rate of return of the bond, assuming that it is held to maturity and that it does not default.

American corporate bonds are rated by various agencies on the basis of the bond issuer's ability to make repayment on the bonds. The classification scheme for two of the major rating agencies, Standard & Poor's (S&P) and Moody's, is given in the following table:

Long-Term Senior Debt Ratings

Investment-Grade Ratings			Speculative-Grade Ratings		
S&P	Moody's	Interpretation	S&P	Moody's	Interpretation
AAA	Aaa	Highest quality	BB+	Ba1	Likely to fulfill
			BB	Ba2	obligations; ongoing
			BB–	Ba3	uncertainty
AA+	Aa1	High quality	B+	B1	High-risk obligations
AA	Aa2		B	B2	
AA–	Aa3		B–	B3	
A+	A1	Strong payment	CCC+	Caa	Current vulnerability
A	A2	capacity	CCC		to default
A–	A3		CCC–		
BBB+	Baa1	Adequate payment	C	Ca	In bankruptcy or
BBB	Baa2	capacity	D	D	default, or other
BBB–	Baa3				marked shortcomings

When a bond defaults, its holders will typically receive some payoff, though less than the promised bond coupon rate and return of principal.

2. Just to complicate matters, in the United States the convention is to add to a bond's listed price the *prorated coupon* (the accrued interest) between the time of the last coupon payment and the purchase date. The sum of these two is termed the *invoice price* of the bond; the invoice price is the actual cost at any moment to a purchaser of buying the bond. In our discussion in this chapter we use the term *market price* to denote the invoice price. The computation of the accrued interest is illustrated in section 28.6.

We refer to the percent of face value paid off in default as the *recovery percentage*.[3]

28.2 Calculating the Expected Bond Return in a One-Period Framework

The bond's yield to maturity is *not* its expected return: It is clear that both a bond's rating and the anticipated payoff to bondholders in the case of bond default should affect its expected return. All other things being equal, we would expect that if two newly issued bonds have the same term to maturity, then the lower-rated bond (having the higher default probability) should have a higher coupon rate. Similarly, we would expect that an issued and traded bond whose rating has been lowered would experience a decrease in price. We might also expect that the lower the anticipated payoff in the case of default, the lower will be the bond's expected return.

As a simple illustration, we calculate the expected return of a one-year bond that can default at maturity. We use the following symbols:

F = face value of the bond

P = price of bond

Q = annual coupon rate of the bond

π = probability that the bond will *not* default at end of year

π = fraction of bond's value that bondholders collect upon default

The bond's expected end-of-year cash flow is $\pi * (1 + Q) * F + (1 - \pi) * \lambda * F$, and its *expected return* is given by

$$\text{One-year bond expected return} = \frac{\text{Expected year-end cash flow}}{\text{Initial bond price, } P} - 1$$

$$= \frac{\pi * (1+Q) * F + (1-\pi) * \lambda * F}{P} - 1$$

This calculation is illustrated in the following spreadsheet:

3. The bond's recovery percentage is not, as you might think, the payoff to the bondholders in the final settlement of a bankruptcy. Instead it is usually computed as the price of the bond in the period immediately following a financial distress event.

	A	B	C
1	EXPECTED RETURN ON A ONE-YEAR BOND WITH AN ADJUSTMENT FOR DEFAULT PROBABILITY		
2	Face value, F	100	
3	Price, P	90	
4	Annual coupon rate, Q	8%	
5	Default probability	20%	
6	Recovery percentage	40%	
7			
8	Expected period 1 cash flow	94.4	<-- =B2*(1+B4)*(1-B5)+B2*B6*B5
9	Expected return	4.89%	<-- =B8/B3-1

28.3 Calculating the Expected Bond Return in a Multiperiod Framework

We now introduce multiple periods into the problem. In this section we define a basic Markov model that uses a ratings transition matrix to compute a bond's expected return. The model is illustrated using a very simple set of ratings, much simpler than the complex rating system illustrated in section 28.1. Section 28.6 will use more realistic data.

We suppose that at any date there are four possible bond "ratings":

A, B, C — Bond ratings of solvent bonds in decreasing order of creditworthiness.

D — The bond is in default for the first time and pays off recovery rate λ of the face value.

E — The bond was in default in the previous period; it therefore pays off 0 in the current period and in any future periods.

The *transition probability* matrix Π is given by

$$\Pi = \begin{bmatrix} \pi_{AA} & \pi_{AB} & \pi_{AC} & \pi_{AD} & 0 \\ \pi_{BA} & \pi_{BB} & \pi_{BC} & \pi_{BD} & 0 \\ \pi_{CA} & \pi_{CB} & \pi_{CC} & \pi_{CD} & 0 \\ 0 & 0 & 0 & 0 & 1 \\ 0 & 0 & 0 & 0 & 1 \end{bmatrix}$$

The probabilities π_{ij} indicate the probability that in *one period* the bond will go from a rating of i to a rating of j. In the numerical examples in this and the following two sections, we use the following Π:

	A	B	C	D	E	F
2		**A**	**B**	**C**	**D**	**E**
3	**A**	0.9700	0.0200	0.0100	0.0000	0.0000
4	**B**	0.0500	0.8000	0.1500	0.0000	0.0000
5	**C**	0.0100	0.0200	0.7500	0.2200	0.0000
6	**D**	0.0000	0.0000	0.0000	0.0000	1.0000
7	**E**	0.0000	0.0000	0.0000	0.0000	1.0000

What does this matrix Π mean?

• If a bond is rated A in the current period, there is a probability of 0.97 that it will still be rated A in the next period. There is a probability 0.02 that it will be rated B in the next period and a probability of 0.01 that it will be rated C. It is impossible for the bond to be rated A today and D or E in the subsequent period.

• A bond that starts off with a rating of B can—in a subsequent period—be rated A (with a probability of 0.05), be rated B (with a probability of 0.8) or be rated C (probability 0.15). Bonds rated B in the current period do not default (rating D) in the next period. The transition probabilities from state C to states A, B, C, and D are 0.01, 0.02, 0.75, and 0.22, respectively.

• While it is possible to go from rating A, B, or C to any of ratings A, B, C, or D, it is *not* possible to go from A, B, or C to E. This statement is true because E denotes that default took place in the *previous period*.

• A bond that is currently in state D (i.e., first-time default), will necessarily be in E in the next period. Thus the fourth row of our matrix Π will always be $[0 \quad 0 \quad 0 \quad 0 \quad 1]$.

• Once the rating is in E, it remains there permanently. Therefore, the fifth row of the matrix Π will also always be $[0 \quad 0 \quad 0 \quad 0 \quad 1]$.

28.3.1 The Multiperiod Transition Matrix

The matrix Π defines the transition probabilities over one period. The two-period transition probabilities are given by the matrix product $\Pi * \Pi$. The following spreadsheet uses the array function **MMult**.[4] It shows that the product $\Pi * \Pi$ is

4. See discussion of matrix products and array functions in Chapter 34.

Two-period transition probability $= \Pi * \Pi =$

$$\begin{bmatrix} 0.9420 & 0.0356 & 0.0202 & 0.0022 & 0.0000 \\ 0.0900 & 0.6440 & 0.2330 & 0.0330 & 0.0000 \\ 0.0182 & 0.0312 & 0.5656 & 0.1650 & 0.2200 \\ 0.0000 & 0.0000 & 0.0000 & 0.0000 & 1.0000 \\ 0.0000 & 0.0000 & 0.0000 & 0.0000 & 1.0000 \end{bmatrix}$$

Thus if a bond is rated B today, there is a probability of 9 percent that in two periods it will be rated A, a probability of 64.4 percent that in two periods it will be rated B, a probability of 23.3 percent that in two periods it will be rated C, and a probability of 3.3 percent that in two periods it will default (and hence be rated D).

Here is the spreadsheet:

	A	B	C	D	E	F
1	**USING THE MMULT FUNCTION To Compute Multiperiod Transition Matrices**					
2	**One-period transition matrix**					
3		**A**	**B**	**C**	**D**	**E**
4	**A**	0.9700	0.0200	0.0100	0.0000	0.0000
5	**B**	0.0500	0.8000	0.1500	0.0000	0.0000
6	**C**	0.0100	0.0200	0.7500	0.2200	0.0000
7	**D**	0.0000	0.0000	0.0000	0.0000	1.0000
8	**E**	0.0000	0.0000	0.0000	0.0000	1.0000
9						
10	**Two-period transition matrix**					
11		**A**	**B**	**C**	**D**	**E**
12	**A**	0.9420	0.0356	0.0202	0.0022	0.0000
13	**B**	0.0900	0.6440	0.2330	0.0330	0.0000
14	**C**	0.0182	0.0312	0.5656	0.1650	0.2200
15	**D**	0.0000	0.0000	0.0000	0.0000	1.0000
16	**E**	0.0000	0.0000	0.0000	0.0000	1.0000
17	**Cells B12:F16 contain the array formula =MMULT(B4:F8,B4:F8)**					
18						
19	**Three-period transition matrix**					
20		**A**	**B**	**C**	**D**	**E**
21	**A**	0.9157	0.0477	0.0299	0.0044	0.0022
22	**B**	0.1218	0.5217	0.2723	0.0513	0.0330
23	**C**	0.0249	0.0366	0.4291	0.1244	0.3850
24	**D**	0.0000	0.0000	0.0000	0.0000	1.0000
25	**E**	0.0000	0.0000	0.0000	0.0000	1.0000
26	**Cells B21:F25 contain the array formula =MMULT(B4:F8,B12:F16)**					

In general, the year-t transition matrix is given by the matrix power Π^t. Calculating these matrix powers by the procedure that we have illustrated is cumbersome, so we define a VBA function **MatrixPower** to compute powers of matrices:

```
Function matrixpower(matrix, n)
  If n = 1 Then
     matrixpower = matrix
     Else: matrixpower = Application.MMult _
       (matrixpower(matrix, n - 1), matrix)
  End If
End Function
```

The use of this function is illustrated in the following spreadsheet. The function **Matrixpower** allows a one-step computation of the power of any transition matrix:

	A	B	C	D	E	F
1	**USING THE FUNCTION MATRIXPOWER To Compute Multiperiod Transition Matrices**					
2	**One-period transition matrix**					
3		**A**	**B**	**C**	**D**	**E**
4	**A**	0.9700	0.0200	0.0100	0.0000	0.0000
5	**B**	0.0500	0.8000	0.1500	0.0000	0.0000
6	**C**	0.0100	0.0200	0.7500	0.2200	0.0000
7	**D**	0.0000	0.0000	0.0000	0.0000	1.0000
8	**E**	0.0000	0.0000	0.0000	0.0000	1.0000
9						
10	**t**	**10**				
11						
12	**t-period transition matrix**					
13		**A**	**B**	**C**	**D**	**E**
14	**A**	0.7648	0.0799	0.0699	0.0148	0.0706
15	**B**	0.2123	0.1429	0.1747	0.0432	0.4269
16	**C**	0.0450	0.0250	0.0755	0.0208	0.8338
17	**D**	0.0000	0.0000	0.0000	0.0000	1.0000
18	**E**	0.0000	0.0000	0.0000	0.0000	1.0000
19	**Cells B14:F18 contain the array formula =matrixpower(B4:F8,B10)**					

From this example it follows that if a bond started out with an A rating, there is a probability of 1.48 percent that the bond will be in default at the end of ten periods and a 7.06 percent probability that it will have defaulted in a previous period (rating E).

28.3.2 The Bond Payoff Vector

Recall that Q denotes the bond's coupon rate and λ denotes the recovery percentage payoff of face value if the bond defaults. The payoff vector of the bond depends on whether the bond is currently in its last period N or whether $t < N$:

$$\text{Payoff }(t, t<N) = \begin{cases} Q \\ Q \\ Q \\ \lambda \\ 0 \end{cases} \quad \text{Payoff }(t, t=N) = \begin{cases} 1+Q \\ 1+Q \\ 1+Q \\ \lambda \\ 0 \end{cases}$$

The first three elements of each vector denote the payoff in nondefaulted states, the fourth element λ is the payoff if the rating is D, and the fifth element 0 is the payoff if the bond rating is E. (Recall that E is the rating for the period *after* the bond defaults—in our model the payoff in rating E is always zero.) The distinction between the two vectors depends, of course, on the repayment of principal in the terminal period.

Before we can define the expected payoffs, we need to define one further vector, which will denote the *initial state of the bond*. This current state vector is a vector with a 1 for the current rating of the bond and zeros elsewhere. Thus, for example, if the bond has rating A at date 0, then Initial = [1 0 0 0 0]; if it has date-0 rating of B, then Initial = [0 1 0 0 0].

We can now define the expected bond payoff in period t:

$$E[\text{Payoff }(t)] = \text{Initial} * \Pi^t * \text{Payoff }(t)$$

28.4 A Numerical Example

We continue using the numerical Π from the previous section to price a bond with the following characteristics:

- The bond is currently rated B.
- Its coupon rate $Q = 7$ percent.
- The bond has five more years to maturity.
- The bond's current market price is 100 percent of its face value.
- The bond's recovery percentage $\lambda = 50$ percent.

The following spreadsheet shows the facts in the preceding list as well as the payoff vectors of the bond at dates before maturity (in cells F3:F7) and on the maturity date (cells I3:I7). The transition matrix is given in cells C10:G14, and the initial vector is given in C16:G16.

The expected bond payoffs are given in cells B20:I20. Before we explain how they were calculated, we note the important economic fact that—if the expected payoffs are as given—then the *bond's expected return* is calculated by the Excel **IRR** function. As Cell B21 shows, this expected return is 4.61 percent. The actual formula in cell B21 is **IRR(B20:AN20)**. This allows the calculation of the IRR of bonds of maturity up to 40 years.

	A	B	C	D	E	F	G	H	I
1	**CALCULATING THE EXPECTED BOND RETURN**								
2	Bond price	100.00%				**Payoff (t<N)**			**Payoff (N)**
3	Coupon rate, Q	7%			Cells to right	7%		Cells to right	107%
4	Recovery rate,	50%			are called	7%		are called	107%
5	Bond term, N	5			"payoff1"	7%		"payoff2"	107%
6	Initial rating	B			in row 20	50%		in row 20	50%
7						0%			0%
8									
9			**A**	**B**	**C**	**D**	**E**		
10	**Transition matrix ?**	**A**	0.9700	0.0200	0.0100	0.0000	0.0000		
11		**B**	0.0500	0.8000	0.1500	0.0000	0.0000		
12		**C**	0.0100	0.0200	0.7500	0.2200	0.0000		
13		**D**	0.0000	0.0000	0.0000	0.0000	1.0000		
14		**E**	0.0000	0.0000	0.0000	0.0000	1.0000		
15									
16	**Initial vector**		0	1	0	0	0		
17	Formula in cell C16: =IF(UPPER(B6)="A",1,0)								
18									
19	**Year**	**0**	**1**	**2**	**3**	**4**	**5**	**6**	**7**
20	Expected payoffs	-1.0000	0.0700	0.0842	0.0897	0.0899	0.8802	0.0000	0.0000
21	Expected yield	4.61%	<-- =IRR(B20:AN20,0)						
22									
23			=IF(year>bondterm,0,						
24	IRR of expected		IF(year=bondterm,MMULT(initial,MMULT(matrixpower(transition,year),payoff2)),						
25	payoffs		MMULT(initial,MMULT(matrixpower(transition,year),payoff1))))						
26									

Note the use of the **IF** statement in translating the bond's initial rating (cell B6) to the initial vector given in row 16. To avoid confusion, we write this as **IF(Upper(B6)="A",1,0)**, etc. This method guarantees that even if the bond's rating is entered as a lowercase letter, the initial vector will come out correctly.

28.4.1 How to Calculate the Expected Bond Payoffs

As indicated in the previous section, the period-t expected bond payoff is given by the following formula $E[\text{Payoff}(t)] = \text{Initial} * \Pi^t * \text{Payoff}(t)$. The formula in row 20 uses two **IF** statements to implement this formula:

=IF(year>bondterm,0,
IF(year=bondterm,MMUL(initial,MMULT(matrixpower(transition,
year),payoff2)),
MMULT(initial,MMULT(matrixpower(transition,year),payoff1)
)))

Here's what these statements mean:

• First **IF**: If the current year is greater than the bond term N (in our example $N = 5$), then the payoff on the bond is 0.

• Second **IF**: If the current year is equal to the bond term N, then the expected payoff on the bond is **MMULT(initial,MMULT(matrixpower (transition,year),payoff2))**. Here **transition** is the name for the transition matrix in cells C10:G14 and **payoff2** is the name for cells I3:I7.

• If the current year n is less than the bond term, then the expected payoff on the bond is **MMULT(initial,MMULT(matrixpower(transition, C19),payoff1)**, where **payoff1** is the name for cells F3:F7.

Copying this formula gives the whole vector of expected bond payoffs.

28.5 Experimenting with the Example

We can gain some insight into the relation between a bond's expected return, its coupon rate, and its yield to maturity (YTM) by constructing some data tables. In the following data table we compute the bond's expected return as a function of its recovery percentage λ:

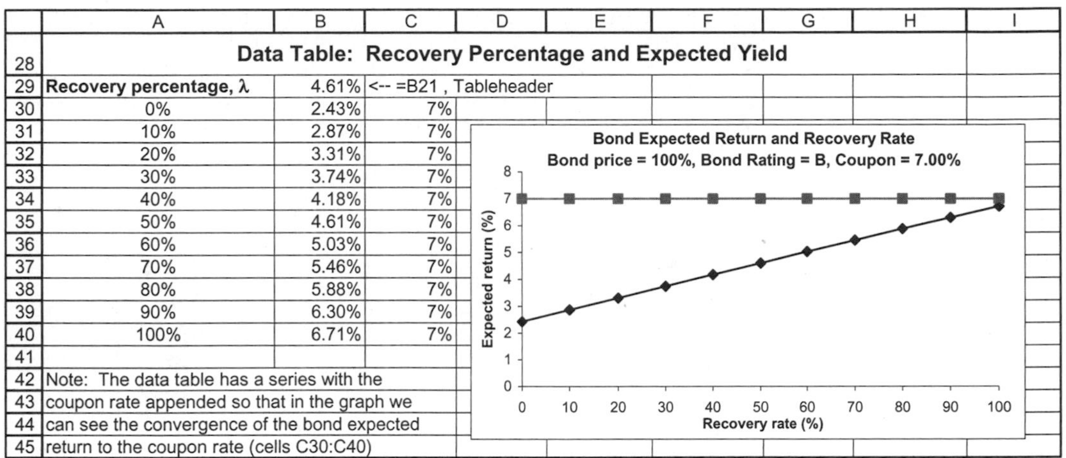

	A	B	C
28	**Data Table: Recovery Percentage and Expected Yield**		
29	**Recovery percentage, λ**	4.61%	<-- =B21 , Tableheader
30	0%	2.43%	7%
31	10%	2.87%	7%
32	20%	3.31%	7%
33	30%	3.74%	7%
34	40%	4.18%	7%
35	50%	4.61%	7%
36	60%	5.03%	7%
37	70%	5.46%	7%
38	80%	5.88%	7%
39	90%	6.30%	7%
40	100%	6.71%	7%
41			
42	Note: The data table has a series with the		
43	coupon rate appended so that in the graph we		
44	can see the convergence of the bond expected		
45	return to the coupon rate (cells C30:C40)		

We conclude that a bond selling at par will, for every recovery percentage λ, have expected return less than the coupon rate. If the bond's initial rating is lower, then the expected return is less for every λ:

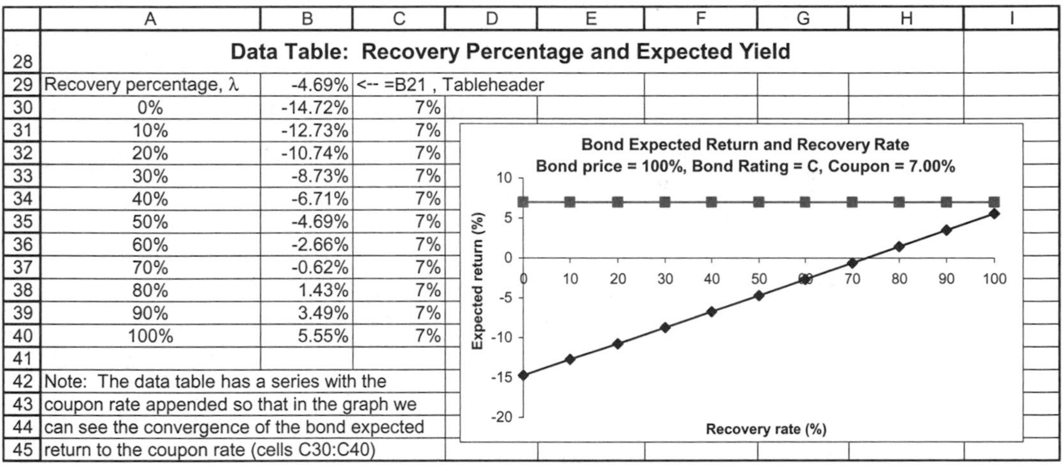

	A	B	C
28	**Data Table: Recovery Percentage and Expected Yield**		
29	Recovery percentage, λ	-4.69%	<-- =B21 , Tableheader
30	0%	-14.72%	7%
31	10%	-12.73%	7%
32	20%	-10.74%	7%
33	30%	-8.73%	7%
34	40%	-6.71%	7%
35	50%	-4.69%	7%
36	60%	-2.66%	7%
37	70%	-0.62%	7%
38	80%	1.43%	7%
39	90%	3.49%	7%
40	100%	5.55%	7%
41			
42	Note: The data table has a series with the		
43	coupon rate appended so that in the graph we		
44	can see the convergence of the bond expected		
45	return to the coupon rate (cells C30:C40)		

As shown in the next example, when the bond price is below par (meaning that the bond is sold at less than 100 percent of its face value), the bond's expected return can be both below and above its coupon rate.

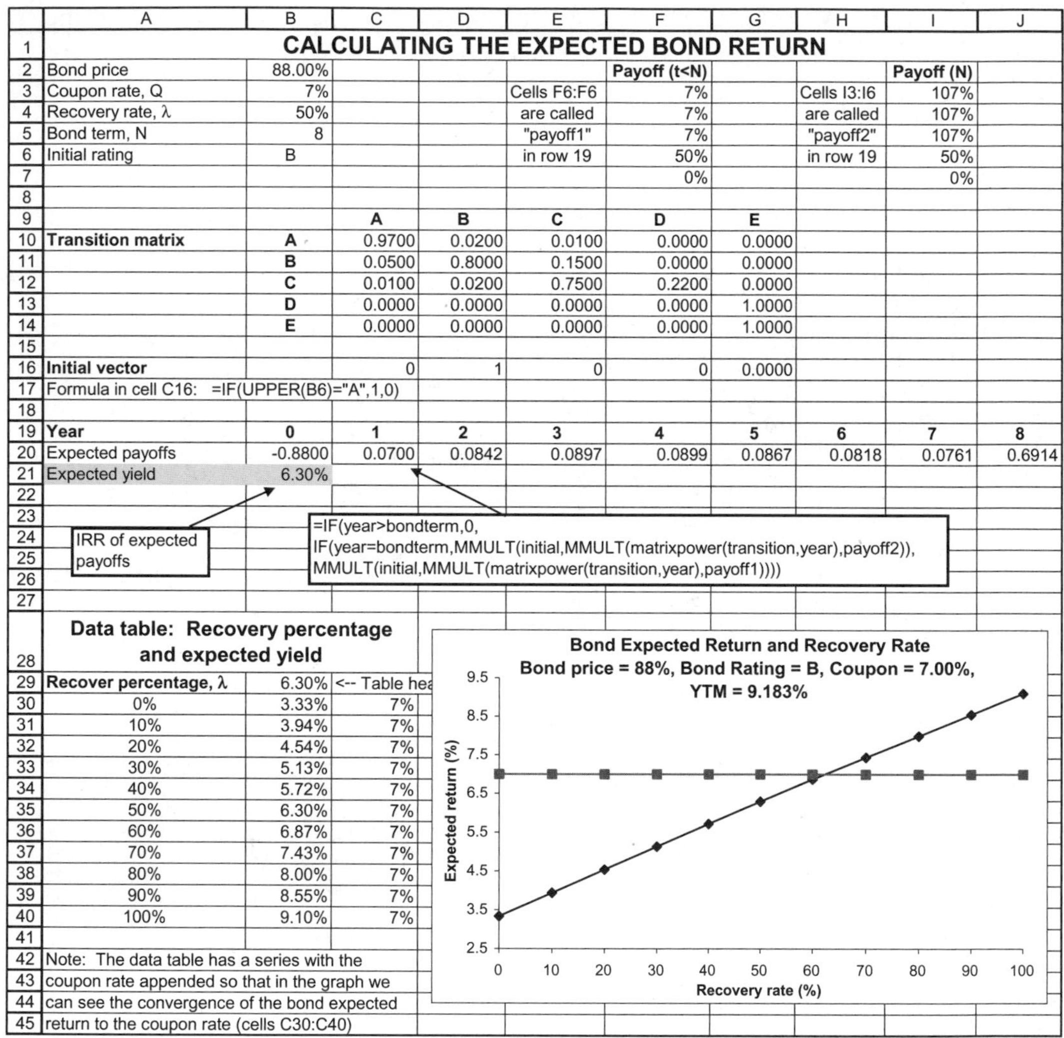

	A	B	C	D	E	F	G	H	I	J
1	CALCULATING THE EXPECTED BOND RETURN									
2	Bond price	88.00%				Payoff (t<N)			Payoff (N)	
3	Coupon rate, Q	7%			Cells F6:F6	7%		Cells I3:I6	107%	
4	Recovery rate, λ	50%			are called	7%		are called	107%	
5	Bond term, N	8			"payoff1"	7%		"payoff2"	107%	
6	Initial rating	B			in row 19	50%		in row 19	50%	
7						0%			0%	
8										
9			A	B	C	D	E			
10	Transition matrix	A	0.9700	0.0200	0.0100	0.0000	0.0000			
11		B	0.0500	0.8000	0.1500	0.0000	0.0000			
12		C	0.0100	0.0200	0.7500	0.2200	0.0000			
13		D	0.0000	0.0000	0.0000	0.0000	1.0000			
14		E	0.0000	0.0000	0.0000	0.0000	1.0000			
15										
16	Initial vector		0	1	0	0	0.0000			
17	Formula in cell C16: =IF(UPPER(B6)="A",1,0)									
18										
19	Year	0	1	2	3	4	5	6	7	8
20	Expected payoffs	-0.8800	0.0700	0.0842	0.0897	0.0899	0.0867	0.0818	0.0761	0.6914
21	Expected yield	6.30%								
28	Data table: Recovery percentage and expected yield									
29	Recover percentage, λ	6.30%	<-- Table hea							
30	0%	3.33%	7%							
31	10%	3.94%	7%							
32	20%	4.54%	7%							
33	30%	5.13%	7%							
34	40%	5.72%	7%							
35	50%	6.30%	7%							
36	60%	6.87%	7%							
37	70%	7.43%	7%							
38	80%	8.00%	7%							
39	90%	8.55%	7%							
40	100%	9.10%	7%							
42	Note: The data table has a series with the									
43	coupon rate appended so that in the graph we									
44	can see the convergence of the bond expected									
45	return to the coupon rate (cells C30:C40)									

28.6 Computing the Bond Expected Return for an Actual Bond

In this section we illustrate the computation of a bond expected return for an actual bond. Although the principles used are the same as those discussed earlier, we introduce three innovations:

1. We compute the bond's actual price using its quoted price and the accrued interest. The *accrued interest* is jargon for the unpaid part of the bond coupon since the last interest payment. In U.S. bond markets, the accrued interest is added to the quoted bond price to compute the amount actually paid for the bond. In most European bond markets, the quoted bond price is the actual price paid for the bond and there is no separate accrued interest calculation. The accrued interest is defined as follows:

$$\text{Accrued interest} = \frac{\text{Current date} - \text{Last interest date}}{\text{Next interest date} - \text{Last interest date}} * \text{Periodic interest}$$

2. We use actual payment dates for the bond and use the **XIRR** function to compute the bond's expected yield.
3. We use an actual transition matrix for bond ratings.

The bond we analyze is a CCC-rated bond issued by AMR (the parent company of American Airlines). Originally issued on 15 May 1991 and maturing on 12 March 2021, the AMR bond has a coupon of 10.55 percent payable semiannually on 15 May and 15 November.

When we looked up the bond on Yahoo on 20 July 2005, its price was 76.75 percent of par:

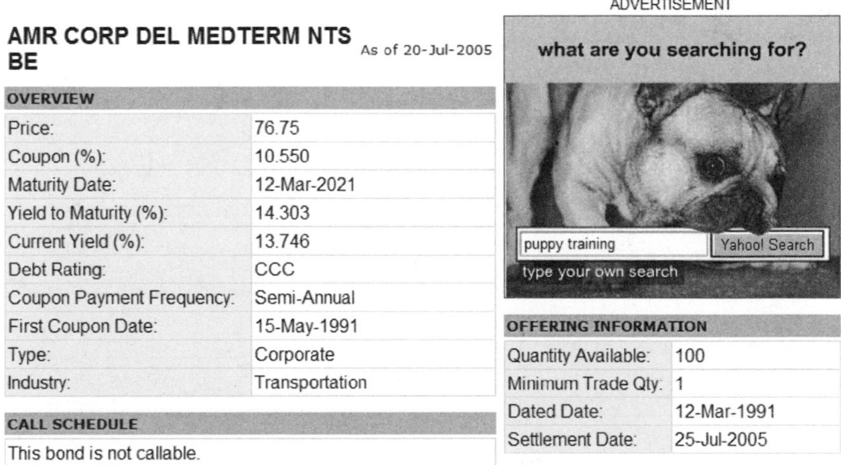

AMR CORP DEL MEDTERM NTS BE As of 20-Jul-2005

OVERVIEW	
Price:	76.75
Coupon (%):	10.550
Maturity Date:	12-Mar-2021
Yield to Maturity (%):	14.303
Current Yield (%):	13.746
Debt Rating:	CCC
Coupon Payment Frequency:	Semi-Annual
First Coupon Date:	15-May-1991
Type:	Corporate
Industry:	Transportation

CALL SCHEDULE
This bond is not callable.

OFFERING INFORMATION	
Quantity Available:	100
Minimum Trade Qty:	1
Dated Date:	12-Mar-1991
Settlement Date:	25-Jul-2005

To the quoted price of 76.75 percent we must add the bond's accrued interest:

	M	N
3	**Accrued interest calculation**	
4	Last payment date	15-Mar-05
5	Next payment date	15-Sep-05
6	Current date	20-Jul-05
7	Percentage of period	0.69
8	Accrued interest	0.0364

It follows that the actual price paid for the bond is 76.75 percent + 3.64 percent = 80.39 percent.

In the following spreadsheet we compute the AMR expected return:

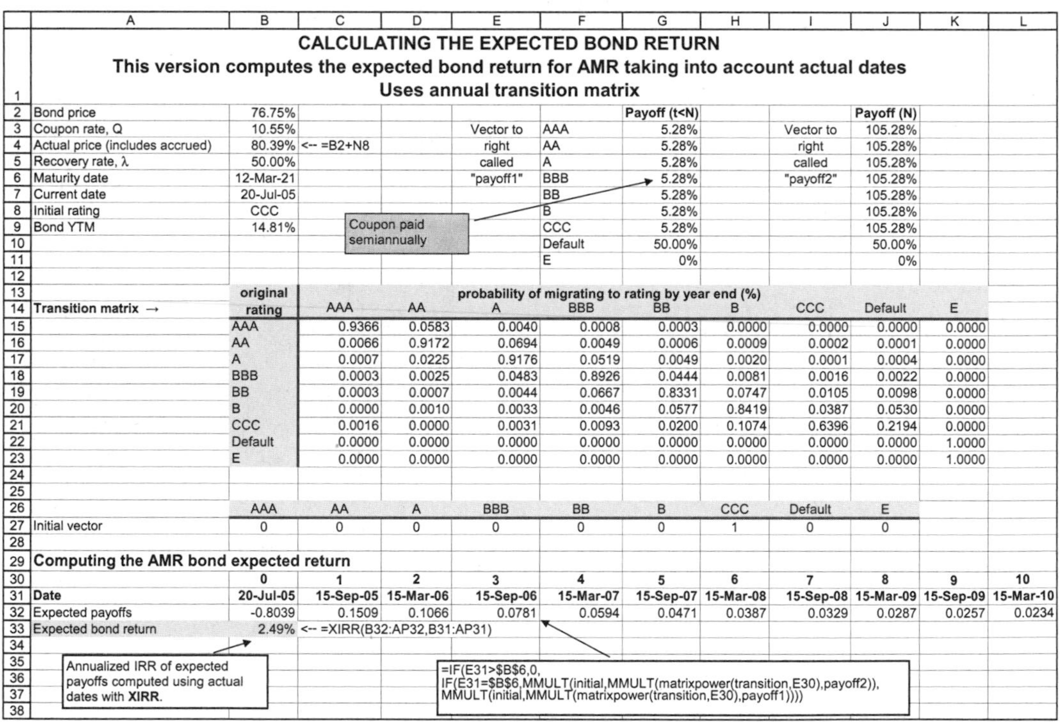

	A	B	C	D	E	F	G	H	I	J	K	L
1	**CALCULATING THE EXPECTED BOND RETURN** **This version computes the expected bond return for AMR taking into account actual dates** **Uses annual transition matrix**											
2	Bond price	76.75%					**Payoff (t<N)**			**Payoff (N)**		
3	Coupon rate, Q	10.55%			Vector to	AAA	5.28%		Vector to	105.28%		
4	Actual price (includes accrued)	80.39%	<-- =B2+N8		right	AA	5.28%		right	105.28%		
5	Recovery rate, λ	50.00%			called	A	5.28%		called	105.28%		
6	Maturity date	12-Mar-21			"payoff1"	BBB	5.28%		"payoff2"	105.28%		
7	Current date	20-Jul-05				BB	5.28%			105.28%		
8	Initial rating	CCC				B	5.28%			105.28%		
9	Bond YTM	14.81%				CCC	5.28%			105.28%		
10						Default	50.00%			50.00%		
11						E	0%			0%		
12												
13		**original**	**probability of migrating to rating by year end (%)**									
14	**Transition matrix →**	**rating**	AAA	AA	A	BBB	BB	B	CCC	Default	E	
15		AAA	0.9366	0.0583	0.0040	0.0008	0.0003	0.0000	0.0000	0.0000	0.0000	
16		AA	0.0066	0.9172	0.0694	0.0049	0.0006	0.0009	0.0002	0.0001	0.0000	
17		A	0.0007	0.0225	0.9176	0.0519	0.0049	0.0020	0.0001	0.0004	0.0000	
18		BBB	0.0003	0.0025	0.0483	0.8926	0.0444	0.0081	0.0016	0.0022	0.0000	
19		BB	0.0003	0.0007	0.0044	0.0667	0.8331	0.0747	0.0105	0.0098	0.0000	
20		B	0.0000	0.0010	0.0033	0.0046	0.0577	0.8419	0.0387	0.0530	0.0000	
21		CCC	0.0016	0.0000	0.0031	0.0093	0.0200	0.1074	0.6396	0.2194	0.0000	
22		Default	0.0000	0.0000	0.0000	0.0000	0.0000	0.0000	0.0000	0.0000	1.0000	
23		E	0.0000	0.0000	0.0000	0.0000	0.0000	0.0000	0.0000	0.0000	1.0000	
24												
25												
26		AAA	AA	A	BBB	BB	B	CCC	Default	E		
27	Initial vector	0	0	0	0	0	0	1	0	0		
28												
29	**Computing the AMR bond expected return**											
30		**0**	**1**	**2**	**3**	**4**	**5**	**6**	**7**	**8**	**9**	**10**
31	**Date**	**20-Jul-05**	**15-Sep-05**	**15-Mar-06**	**15-Sep-06**	**15-Mar-07**	**15-Sep-07**	**15-Mar-08**	**15-Sep-08**	**15-Mar-09**	**15-Sep-09**	**15-Mar-10**
32	Expected payoffs	-0.8039	0.1509	0.1066	0.0781	0.0594	0.0471	0.0387	0.0329	0.0287	0.0257	0.0234
33	Expected bond return	2.49%	<-- =XIRR(B32:AP32,B31:AP31)									
34												
35												
36												
37												
38												

Assuming a recovery rate of 50 percent, the bond has an expected return of 2.47 percent.

28.6.1 What Are the Recovery Rates?

The recovery rate is obviously a critical factor in computing the bond's expected return. Considerable information exists on the recovery rates in bankruptcy from various industries. A table from an article by Edward Altman and Velore M. Kishore follows; from this table we can see that the average recovery rate from a variety of industries was 41 percent.

Recovery Rates by Industry: Defaulted Bonds by Three-Digit SIC Code, 1971–1995

			Recovery Rate			
Industry	SIC Code	Number of Observations	Average	Weighted Observation	Median Average	Standard Deviation Weighted
Public utilities	490	56	70.47	65.48	79.07	19.46
Chemicals, petroleum, rubber and plastic products	280,290,300	35	62.73	80.39	71.88	27.10
Machinery, instruments, and related products	350,360,380	36	48.74	44.75	47.50	20.13
Services–business and personal	470,632,720,730	14	46.23	50.01	41.50	25.03
Food and kindred products	200	18	45.28	37.40	41.50	21.67
Wholesale and retail trade	500,510,520	12	44.00	48.90	37.32	22.14
Diversified manufacturing	390,998	20	42.29	29.49	33.88	24.98
Casino, hotel, and recreation	770,790	21	40.15	39.74	28.00	25.66
Building materials, metals, and fabricated products	320,330,340	68	38.76	29.64	37.75	22.86
Transportation and transportation equipment	370,410,420,450	52	38.42	41.12	37.13	27.98
Communication, broadcasting, movies, printing, publishing	270,480,780	65	37.08	39.34	34.50	20.79
Financial institutions	600,610,620,630, 670	66	35.69	35.44	32.15	25.72
Construction and real estate	150,650	35	35.27	28.58	24.00	28.69
General merchandise stores	530,540,560,570, 580,000	89	33.16	29.35	30.00	20.47
Mining and petroleum drilling	100,103	45	33.02	31.83	32.00	18.01
Textile and apparel products	220,230	31	31.66	33.72	31.13	15.24
Wood, paper, and leather products	240,250,260,310	11	29.77	24.30	18.25	24.38
Lodging, hospitals, and nursing facilities	700 through 890	22	26.49	19.61	16.00	22.65
Total		**696**	**41.00**	**39.11**	**36.25**	**25.56**

Source: E. Altman and V. M. Kishore, "Almost Everything You Wanted to Know about Recoveries on Defaulted Bonds," Table 3, *Financial Analysts Journal*, November/December 1996, pp. 57–64.

Using the Altman and Kishore numbers, the average recovery percentage for transportation companies is 38.42 percent, with a standard deviation of 27.98 percent. Taking one standard deviation on either side of the average, we can conclude that the recovery percentage for a transportation company is somewhere around (38.42 percent – 27.98 percent, 38.42 percent + 27.98 percent) = (~10 percent, ~66 percent).

In the next spreadsheet we have "backward engineered" a plausible set of recovery ratios, from 55 to 65 percent, for the AMR bond. These "guesstimates" for the AMR recovery are based on two assumptions:

- The AMR bond should not have an expected return significantly more than the riskless rate of return, which at the time of our calculations was around 4 percent.
- The AMR bond expected return should be significantly less than its YTM of ~15 percent. The YTM is based on promised payments, and we find it implausible that these should correspond to the expected returns.

This calculation gives an expected bond yield of between 3.85 and 6.86 percent for the AMR bond (highlighted area):

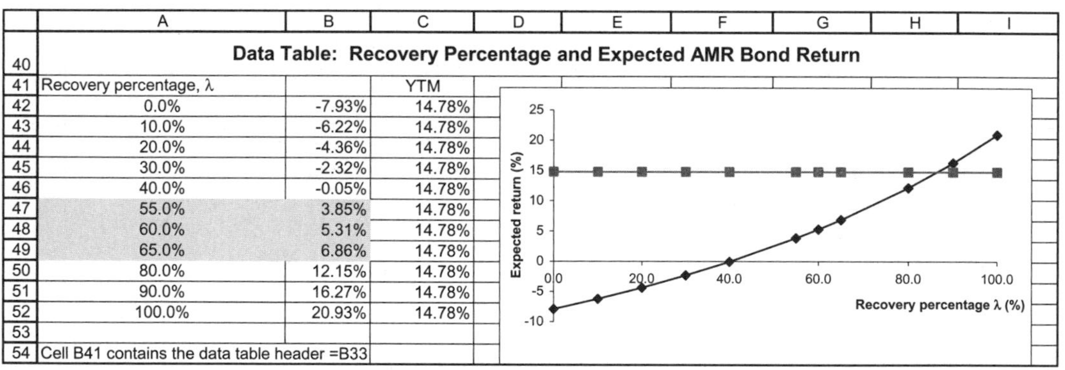

	A	B	C
40	**Data Table: Recovery Percentage and Expected AMR Bond Return**		
41	Recovery percentage, λ		YTM
42	0.0%	-7.93%	14.78%
43	10.0%	-6.22%	14.78%
44	20.0%	-4.36%	14.78%
45	30.0%	-2.32%	14.78%
46	40.0%	-0.05%	14.78%
47	55.0%	3.85%	14.78%
48	60.0%	5.31%	14.78%
49	65.0%	6.86%	14.78%
50	80.0%	12.15%	14.78%
51	90.0%	16.27%	14.78%
52	100.0%	20.93%	14.78%
53			
54	Cell B41 contains the data table header =B33		

28.7 Semiannual Transition Matrices

The analysis of the AMR bond in the previous section assumes that the annual transition probabilities are also valid for bonds paying semiannual coupons. We could refine this assumption by computing a semiannual transition matrix from the S&P data. Such a matrix would be the square root of the Π matrix. This calculation cannot be easily done in

Excel. In the following spreadsheet we have used a computation from *Mathematica* to find the semiannual transition matrix.[5]

COMPUTING THE SQUARE ROOT OF THE TRANSITION MATRIX

The one-year transition matrix

Original rating	Probability of migrating to rating by year end (%)								
	AAA	AA	A	BBB	BB	B	CCC	Default	E
AAA	0.9366	0.0583	0.0040	0.0008	0.0003	0.0000	0.0000	0.0000	0.0000
AA	0.0066	0.9172	0.0694	0.0049	0.0006	0.0009	0.0002	0.0001	0.0000
A	0.0007	0.0225	0.9176	0.0519	0.0049	0.0020	0.0001	0.0004	0.0000
BBB	0.0003	0.0025	0.0483	0.8926	0.0444	0.0081	0.0016	0.0022	0.0000
BB	0.0003	0.0007	0.0044	0.0667	0.8331	0.0747	0.0105	0.0098	0.0000
B	0.0000	0.0010	0.0033	0.0046	0.0577	0.8419	0.0387	0.0530	0.0000
CCC	0.0016	0.0000	0.0031	0.0093	0.0200	0.1074	0.6396	0.2194	0.0000
Default	0.0000	0.0000	0.0000	0.0000	0.0000	0.0000	0.0000	0.0000	1.0000
E	0.0000	0.0000	0.0000	0.0000	0.0000	0.0000	0.0000	0.0000	1.0000

The square root of the one-year transition matrix as computed by *Mathematica*
Note the negative entries

Original rating	Probability of migrating to rating by year end (%)								
	AAA	AA	A	BBB	BB	B	CCC	Default	E
AAA	0.9677	0.0303	0.0015	0.0004	0.0001	0.0000	0.0000	0.0000	0.0000
AA	0.0034	0.9574	0.0362	0.0021	0.0002	0.0004	0.0001	0.0000	0.0000
A	0.0003	0.0117	0.9573	0.0272	0.0023	0.0010	0.0000	0.0003	-0.0001
BBB	0.0001	0.0012	0.0254	0.9439	0.0238	0.0038	0.0008	0.0017	-0.0007
BB	0.0002	0.0003	0.0018	0.0359	0.9115	0.0406	0.0056	0.0068	-0.0026
B	0.0000	0.0005	0.0017	0.0018	0.0314	0.9161	0.0225	0.0510	-0.0248
CCC	0.0009	-0.0001	0.0016	0.0050	0.0105	0.0624	0.7988	0.2706	-0.1495
Default	0.0000	0.0000	0.0000	0.0000	0.0000	0.0000	0.0000	0.0000	1.0000
E	0.0000	0.0000	0.0000	0.0000	0.0000	0.0000	0.0000	0.0000	1.0000

The semiannual transition matrix. To eliminate the negative entries in the *Mathematica* matrix:
a. We assume that a transition from AAA, . . . , CCC --> E is impossible (i.e., last column is zero except for last two entries).
b. We set all other negative entries to zero.
c. We set default probability so that each row sums to 1.

Original rating	Probability of migrating to rating by year end (%)								
	AAA	AA	A	BBB	BB	B	CCC	Default	E
AAA	0.9677	0.0303	0.0015	0.0004	0.0001	0.0000	0.0000	0.0000	0.0000
AA	0.0034	0.9574	0.0362	0.0021	0.0002	0.0004	0.0001	0.0001	0.0000
A	0.0003	0.0117	0.9573	0.0272	0.0023	0.0010	0.0000	0.0001	0.0000
BBB	0.0001	0.0012	0.0254	0.9439	0.0238	0.0038	0.0008	0.0010	0.0000
BB	0.0002	0.0003	0.0018	0.0359	0.9115	0.0406	0.0056	0.0041	0.0000
B	0.0000	0.0005	0.0017	0.0018	0.0314	0.9161	0.0225	0.0261	0.0000
CCC	0.0009	0.0000	0.0016	0.0050	0.0105	0.0624	0.7988	0.1208	0.0000
Default	0.0000	0.0000	0.0000	0.0000	0.0000	0.0000	0.0000	0.0000	1.0000
E	0.0000	0.0000	0.0000	0.0000	0.0000	0.0000	0.0000	0.0000	1.0000

5. *Mathematica* is a high-powered computational program. See http://www.wolfram.com.

If we use the semiannual transition matrix to compute the expected bond returns, we get the following results:

	A	B	C	D	E	F	G	H	I	J	K
1	**CALCULATING THE EXPECTED BOND RETURN** **This version computes the expected bond return for AMR taking into account actual dates** **Uses semiannual transition matrix**										
2	Bond price	76.75%					**Payoff (t<N)**			**Payoff (N)**	
3	Coupon rate, Q	10.55%			Vector to	AAA	5.28%		Vector to	105.28%	
4	Actual price (includes accrued)	80.39%	<-- =B2+N8		right	AA	5.28%		right	105.28%	
5	Recovery rate, λ	50.00%			called	A	5.28%		called	105.28%	
6	Maturity date	12-Mar-21			"payoff1"	BBB	5.28%		"payoff2"	105.28%	
7	Current date	20-Jul-05				BB	5.28%			105.28%	
8	Maturity (years)	15.65				B	5.28%			105.28%	
9	Number of semiannual payments	30.00	Coupon paid semiannually			CCC	5.28%			105.28%	
10	Initial rating	CCC				Default	50.00%			50.00%	
11	Bond YTM	14.81%				E	0%			0%	
12											
13		**Original**	**Probability of migrating to rating by year end (%)**								
14	**Transition matrix →**	**rating**	AAA	AA	A	BBB	BB	B	CCC	Default	E
15		AAA	0.9677	0.0303	0.0015	0.0004	0.0001	0.0000	0.0000	0.0000	0.0000
16		AA	0.0034	0.9574	0.0362	0.0021	0.0002	0.0004	0.0001	0.0001	0.0000
17		A	0.0003	0.0117	0.9573	0.0272	0.0023	0.0010	0.0000	0.0001	0.0000
18		BBB	0.0001	0.0012	0.0254	0.9439	0.0238	0.0038	0.0008	0.0010	0.0000
19		BB	0.0002	0.0003	0.0018	0.0359	0.9115	0.0406	0.0056	0.0041	0.0000
20		B	0.0000	0.0005	0.0017	0.0018	0.0314	0.9161	0.0225	0.0261	0.0000
21		CCC	0.0009	-0.0001	0.0016	0.0050	0.0105	0.0624	0.7988	0.1208	0.0000
22		Default	0.0000	0.0000	0.0000	0.0000	0.0000	0.0000	0.0000	0.0000	1.0000
23		E	0.0000	0.0000	0.0000	0.0000	0.0000	0.0000	0.0000	0.0000	1.0000
24											
25											
26		AAA	AA	A	BBB	BB	B	CCC	Default	E	
27	Initial vector	0	0	0	0	0	0	1	0	0	
28											
29	**Period**	**0**	**1**	**2**	**3**	**4**	**5**	**6**	**7**	**8**	**9**
30	**Date**	**20-Jul-05**	**15-Sep-05**	**15-Mar-06**	**15-Sep-06**	**15-Mar-07**	**15-Sep-07**	**15-Mar-08**	**15-Sep-08**	**15-Mar-09**	**15-Sep-09**
31	Expected payoffs	-0.8039	0.1068	0.0903	0.0771	0.0664	0.0578	0.0508	0.0451	0.0405	0.0367
32	Expected yield	8.07%	<-- =XIRR(B31:AP31,B30:AP30)								

The semiannual transition matrix gives expected bond returns that are, in general, higher than those given by the annual transition matrix:

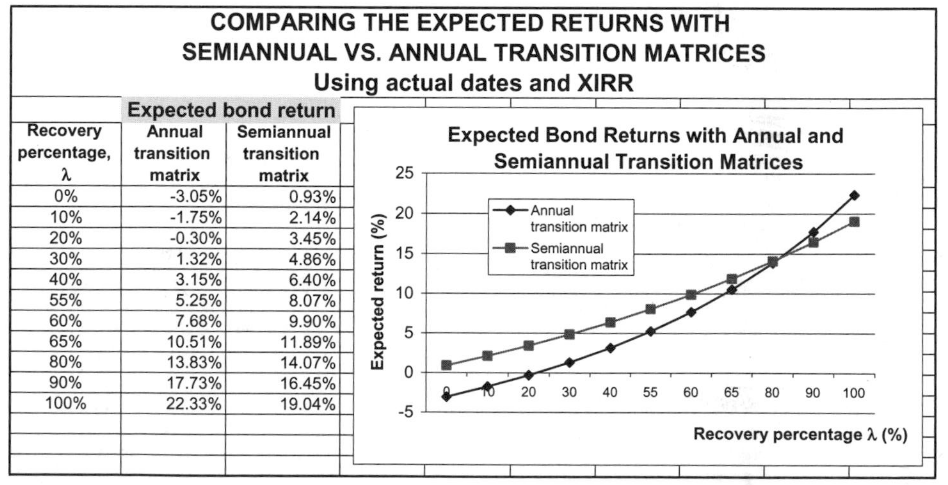

COMPARING THE EXPECTED RETURNS WITH SEMIANNUAL VS. ANNUAL TRANSITION MATRICES
Using actual dates and XIRR

	Expected bond return	
Recovery percentage, λ	**Annual transition matrix**	**Semiannual transition matrix**
0%	-3.05%	0.93%
10%	-1.75%	2.14%
20%	-0.30%	3.45%
30%	1.32%	4.86%
40%	3.15%	6.40%
55%	5.25%	8.07%
60%	7.68%	9.90%
65%	10.51%	11.89%
80%	13.83%	14.07%
90%	17.73%	16.45%
100%	22.33%	19.04%

28.8 Computing Bond Beta

A vexatious problem in corporate finance is the computation of bond betas. The model presented in this chapter can easily be used to compute the beta of a bond. Recall from Chapter 2 that the capital asset pricing model's *security market line* (SML) is given by

$$E(r_d) = r_f + \beta_d[E(r_m) - r_f]$$

where $E(r_d)$ is the expected return on debt, r_f is the return on riskless debt, and $E(r_m)$ is the return on equity market portfolio.

If we know the expected return on debt, we can calculate the debt β, provided we know the risk-free rate r_f and the expected rate of return on the market $E(r_m)$. Suppose, for example, that the market risk premium $E(r_m) - r_f = 8.4$ percent and that $r_f = 7$ percent. Then a bond having an expected return of 8 percent will have a β of 0.119:

	A	B	C
1	**CALCULATING A BOND'S BETA**		
2	Market risk premium, $E(r_m) - r_f$	8.40%	
3	r_f	7%	
4	Expected bond return	8.00%	
5	Implied bond beta	0.119	<-- =(B4-B3)/B2

If we use the tax-adjusted version of the SML (see section 2.6), then the bond SML becomes r_D = Cost of debt = $r_f + \beta_{Debt}[E(r_M) - r_f(1 - T_C)]$. This formula gives the bond beta as

	A	B	C
7	**Tax-adjusted SML (see section 2.6)**		
8	Market risk premium, $E(r_m) - r_f$	8.40%	
9	r_f	7%	
10	Corporate tax rate, T_C	40%	
11	Expected bond return	8.00%	
12	Implied bond beta	0.089	<-- =(B11-B9)/(B8+B9*B10)

Using our data for AMR, we get the following results for the classical SML model:

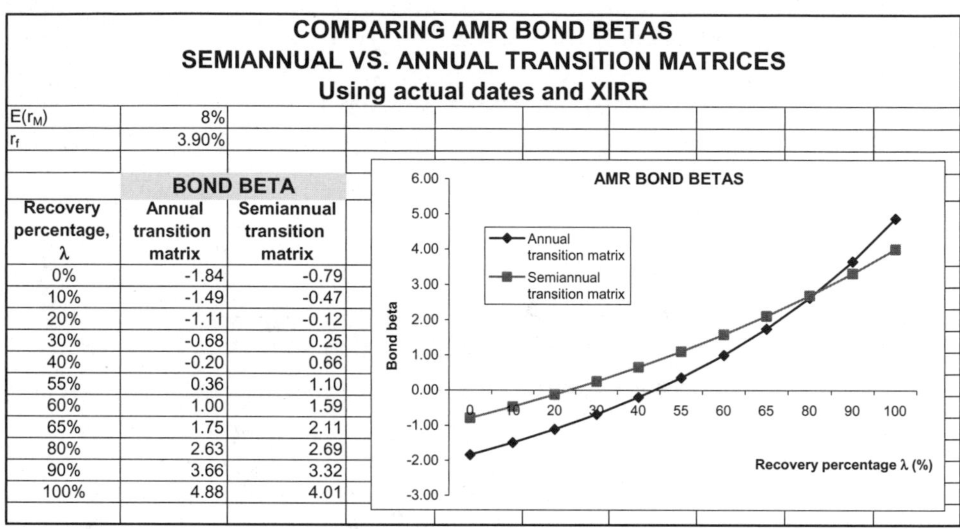

COMPARING AMR BOND BETAS
SEMIANNUAL VS. ANNUAL TRANSITION MATRICES
Using actual dates and XIRR

$E(r_M)$	8%
r_f	3.90%

	BOND BETA	
Recovery percentage, λ	Annual transition matrix	Semiannual transition matrix
0%	-1.84	-0.79
10%	-1.49	-0.47
20%	-1.11	-0.12
30%	-0.68	0.25
40%	-0.20	0.66
55%	0.36	1.10
60%	1.00	1.59
65%	1.75	2.11
80%	2.63	2.69
90%	3.66	3.32
100%	4.88	4.01

If we assume that the corporate tax rate is $T_C = 40$ percent, then the tax-adjusted CAPM gives the following betas:

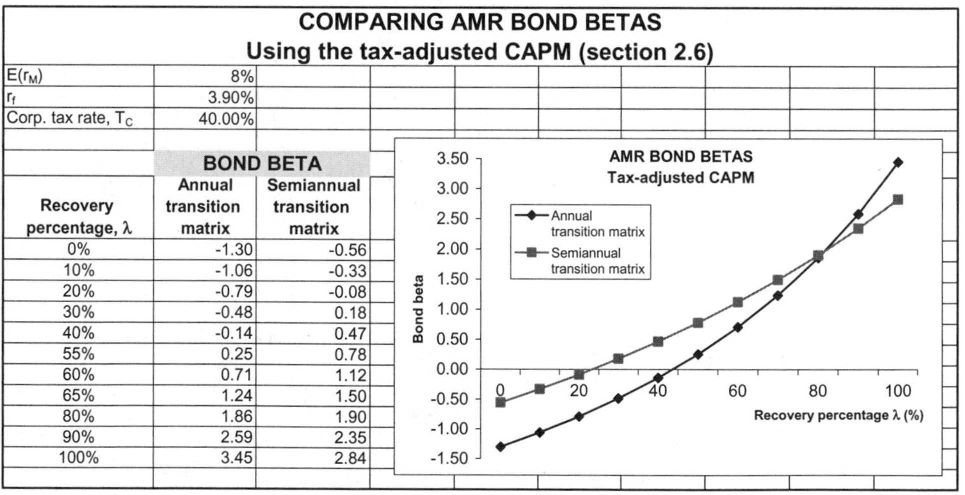

COMPARING AMR BOND BETAS
Using the tax-adjusted CAPM (section 2.6)

$E(r_M)$	8%
r_f	3.90%
Corp. tax rate, T_C	40.00%

	BOND BETA	
Recovery percentage, λ	Annual transition matrix	Semiannual transition matrix
0%	-1.30	-0.56
10%	-1.06	-0.33
20%	-0.79	-0.08
30%	-0.48	0.18
40%	-0.14	0.47
55%	0.25	0.78
60%	0.71	1.12
65%	1.24	1.50
80%	1.86	1.90
90%	2.59	2.35
100%	3.45	2.84

If these bond betas seem large, note that the AMR bond has a maturity comparable to these long-term Treasury bonds and has in addition considerable default risk. Another fact that helps place the AMR bond beta into context is AMR's stock beta. According to Yahoo this beta is 3.617:

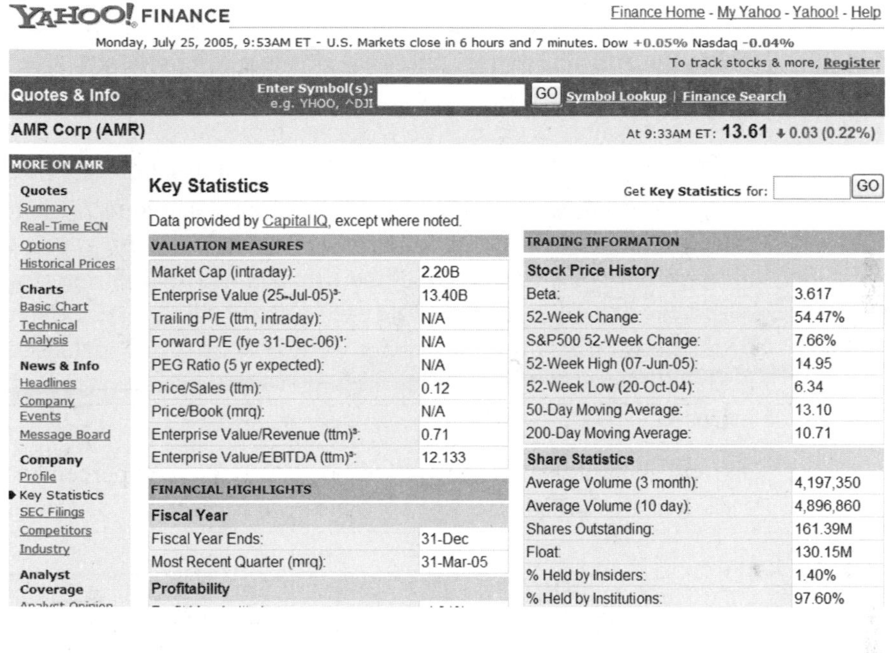

YAHOO! FINANCE

Finance Home - My Yahoo - Yahoo! - Help

Monday, July 25, 2005, 9:53AM ET - U.S. Markets close in 6 hours and 7 minutes. Dow +0.05% Nasdaq -0.04%

To track stocks & more, Register

Quotes & Info | Enter Symbol(s): e.g. YHOO, ^DJI | GO | Symbol Lookup | Finance Search

AMR Corp (AMR) At 9:33AM ET: 13.61 0.03 (0.22%)

MORE ON AMR
Quotes: Summary, Real-Time ECN, Options, Historical Prices
Charts: Basic Chart, Technical Analysis
News & Info: Headlines, Company Events, Message Board
Company: Profile, Key Statistics, SEC Filings, Competitors, Industry
Analyst Coverage

Key Statistics

Get Key Statistics for: GO

Data provided by Capital IQ, except where noted.

VALUATION MEASURES	
Market Cap (intraday):	2.20B
Enterprise Value (25-Jul-05)³:	13.40B
Trailing P/E (ttm, intraday):	N/A
Forward P/E (fye 31-Dec-06)¹:	N/A
PEG Ratio (5 yr expected):	N/A
Price/Sales (ttm):	0.12
Price/Book (mrq):	N/A
Enterprise Value/Revenue (ttm)³:	0.71
Enterprise Value/EBITDA (ttm)³:	12.133

FINANCIAL HIGHLIGHTS	
Fiscal Year	
Fiscal Year Ends:	31-Dec
Most Recent Quarter (mrq):	31-Mar-05
Profitability	

TRADING INFORMATION	
Stock Price History	
Beta:	3.617
52-Week Change:	54.47%
S&P500 52-Week Change:	7.66%
52-Week High (07-Jun-05):	14.95
52-Week Low (20-Oct-04):	6.34
50-Day Moving Average:	13.10
200-Day Moving Average:	10.71
Share Statistics	
Average Volume (3 month):	4,197,350
Average Volume (10 day):	4,896,860
Shares Outstanding:	161.39M
Float:	130.15M
% Held by Insiders:	1.40%
% Held by Institutions:	97.60%

28.9 Summary

In this chapter we have shown how to compute the expected return on a risky bond using a simple technique involving rating transitions. Computing a bond's expected returns puts the bond analysis on the same footing as the analysis of stocks. Expected returns—common in the analysis of stocks—are rarely computed for bonds, where the common analysis is in terms of yields to maturity. But the yield to maturity of a bond, essentially the bond's IRR based on its promised future payments, includes an ill-defined premium for the bond's default.

Having computed a bond's expected return, we can then compute its beta using the security market line (SML). Compared to the vast efforts to compute and calibrate stock betas, relatively little research energy has been expended on bond betas. The technique illustrated in this chapter, based on the transition matrix of the bond ratings, is relatively new. This technique still has to be refined and thoroughly tested by academic research. Several refinements to the rating-based technique for computing expected bond returns still need to be explored. These include

- *Better transition matrices.* Transition matrices need to be refined, and perhaps made industry specific. (The problem with industry-specific data is that the number of observations drops dramatically. Nevertheless, there are examples of such data [for example, an S&P study from 2004 on real-estate–backed loans; see the citation in the bibliography].)
- *Time-dependent transition matrices.* Our technique assumes that transition matrices are stationary—constant through time. Perhaps better techniques can be developed that allow for matrices to change with time. For example, we would expect that in difficult economic conditions the ratings transition matrix would "shift to the right"—that the probabilities of a given rating getting worse over any period would increase.
- *More data on recovery ratios.*

Exercises

1. A newly issued bond with one year to maturity has a price of 100, which equals its face value. The coupon rate on the bond is 15 percent; the probability of default in one year is 35 percent; and the bond's payoff in default will be 65 percent of its face value. Calculate the bond's expected return.

2. Consider a case of five possible rating states, A, B, C, D, and E. States A, B, and C are initial bond ratings, D symbolizes first-time default, and E indicates default in the previous period. Assume that the transition matrix Π is given by

$$\Pi = \begin{bmatrix} 1 & 0 & 0 & 0 & 0 \\ 0.06 & 0.90 & 0.03 & 0.01 & 0 \\ 0.02 & 0.05 & 0.88 & 0.05 & 0 \\ 0 & 0 & 0 & 0 & 1 \\ 0 & 0 & 0 & 0 & 1 \end{bmatrix}$$

A 10-year bond issued today at par with an A rating is assumed to bear a coupon rate of 7 percent.

a. If a bond is issued today at par with a B rating and with a recovery percentage of 50 percent, what should its coupon rate be so that its expected return will also be 7 percent?

b. If a bond is issued today at par with a C rating and with a recovery percentage of 50 percent, what should its coupon rate be so that its expected return will be 7 percent?

3. Using the transition matrix from exercise 2: A C-rated bond is selling at par on 18 July 2007. The bond's maturity is 17 July 2017, it has a coupon (paid annually on 17 July) of 11 percent, and it has a recovery percentage of $\lambda = 67$ percent. What is the bond's expected return?

4. An underwriter issues a new seven-year B bond with a coupon rate of 9 percent. If the expected rate of return on the bond is 8 percent, what is the bond's implied recovery percentage λ? Assume the transition matrix given in section 28.5.

5. An underwriter issues a new seven-year C-rated bond at par. The anticipated recovery rate in default of the bond is expected to be 55 percent. What should the coupon rate on the bond be so that its expected return is 9 percent? Assume the transition matrix from exercise 2.

V Technical Considerations

Chapters 29–35 cover a variety of technical subjects that are used in *Financial Modeling*. Chapter 29 discusses the generation of random numbers. The book uses random number generation extensively in Chapter 18 (simulating stock prices), Chapter 21 (simulating portfolio insurance), and Chapters 22 and 23 (Monte Carlo methods). Chapter 30 considers data tables. This is a basic Excel tool that allows us to build sophisticated sensitivity tables. It is used throughout *Financial Modeling*. Chapter 31 deals with matrices, used in the book to do portfolio optimization (Chapters 8–13). Chapter 32 discusses the Gauss-Seidel iterative method for solving simultaneous equations. This method, though never explicitly used in *Financial Modeling*, underlies the pro forma models of Chapters 3 and 4. Chapter 33 is a compendium of Excel functions used in the book. Chapter 34 discusses the use of array functions, with a special emphasis on homemade array functions. Chapter 35 discusses a grab-bag of Excel tricks that are used in various places in this book: Fast copying; graph titles that update automatically; creating multiline cells; putting Greek symbols, subscripts, and superscripts into Excel text; naming cells; hiding cells; some formatting tricks; and formula auditing. This chapter also shows how to add our auditing tool **Getformula** to your spreadsheets.

29 Generating Random Numbers

29.1 Overview

In several of the option chapters of this book we have used randomly generated stock prices to simulate and price options (see in particular Chapter 18 on the lognormal distribution, Chapter 20 on option Greeks, Chapter 21 on portfolio insurance, and Chapters 22–23 on Monte Carlo methods). In all these chapters, the stock price simulations are based on the generation of random numbers. In this chapter we discuss techniques for computing these numbers.

A random-number generator on a computer is a function that produces a seemingly unrelated set of numbers. The question of *what is* a random number is a philosophical one.[1] In this chapter we will ignore philosophy and concentrate on some simple random-number generators—primarily the Excel random-number generator **Rand( )** and the VBA random-number generator **Rnd**.[2]

To imagine a set of uniformly distributed random numbers, think of an urn filled with 1,000 little balls, numbered 000, 001, 002, . . . , 999. Suppose we perform the following experiment: Having shaken the urn to mix up the balls, we draw one ball out of the urn and record the ball's number. Next we put the ball back into the urn, shake the urn thoroughly so that the balls are mixed up again, and then draw out a new ball. The series of numbers produced by repeating this procedure many times should be *uniformly distributed* between 000 and 999.

A random number generator on a computer is a function that imitates this procedure. The random-number generators considered in this chapter are sometimes termed *pseudo-random-number generators*, since they are actually deterministic functions whose values are indistinguishable from random numbers. All pseudo-random-number generators have cycles (that is, they eventually start to repeat themselves). The trick is to find a random-number generator with a long cycle. The Excel **Rand( )** function has very long cycles and is a respectable random-number generator.

1. Knuth (1981, p. 142) gives the following quote: "A random sequence is a vague notion embodying the idea of a sequence in which each term is unpredictable to the uninitiated and whose digits pass a certain number of tests, traditional with statisticians and depending somewhat on the uses to which the sequence is to be put" (attributed to D. H. Lehmer, 1951).

2. In this book we usually write Excel functions in boldface without the parentheses. In this chapter we generally write **Rand( )** with the parentheses to emphasize (a) that the parentheses are necessary and (b) that they are empty.

If you've never used a random-number generator, open an Excel spreadsheet and type **=Rand( )** in any cell. You will see a 15-digit number between 0.000000000000000 and 0.999999999999999. Every time you recalculate the spreadsheet (for example, by hitting the **F9** button), the number changes. We leave the technical details of how **Rand( )** works for the exercises to this chapter, where we show you how to design your own random-number generator. Suffice it to say, however, that the series of numbers produced by the function should be (to use Lehmer's terminology from footnote 1) "unpredictable to the unitiated."

In this chapter we shall deal with several kinds of random-number generators: We first examine the uniform random-number generators that come with Excel and VBA. Subsequently we generate normally distributed random numbers.[3]

29.2 Rand( ) and Rnd: The Excel and VBA Random-Number Generators

Suppose you simply wanted to generate a list of random numbers. One way to do so would be to copy the Excel function **Rand( )** to a range of cells:

	A	B	C	D	E
1	USING EXCEL'S RAND( ) FUNCTION				
2	0.6337	0.7903	0.9283	0.0302	<-- =RAND()
3	0.5041	0.6606	0.1293	0.1976	
4	0.9407	0.9486	0.8677	0.4154	
5	0.9351	0.2060	0.9635	0.1074	
6	0.8297	0.4525	0.6394	0.8085	
7	0.5973	0.5655	0.8531	0.2139	
8	0.6800	0.7932	0.9045	0.9724	
9	0.7789	0.4750	0.7291	0.8122	
10	0.0466	0.7387	0.2422	0.8827	
11					
12	Each cell contains the function Rand( ). Each time you update the spreadsheet or press F9 the block of cells will produce a new set of random numbers.				

3. A common nomenclature speaks of "random deviates." Only in financial engineering can one find "normal deviates!"

In section 30.3 we will develop a crude test of how well **Rand( )** works.

29.2.1 Using VBA's Rnd Function

VBA contains its own function **Rnd** which is equivalent to the Excel **Rand** function.[4] Here's a small VBA program that illustrates a basic use of the **Rnd** function:

```
Sub RandomList()
'Produces a simple list of random numbers
    For Index = 1 To 10
         Range("A4").Cells(Index, 1) = Rnd
    Next Index
End Sub
```

In the next spreadsheet, the VBA program has been assigned to a button, so that each time we click on the button, it runs a VBA program that produces 10 random numbers:

```
Sub RandomList()
'Produces a simple list of random numbers
    For Index = 1 To 10
         Range("A3").Cells(Index, 1) = Rnd
    Next Index
End Sub
```

On the spreadsheet **fm3_chapter29.xls**, which comes with this chapter, you can push a button to operate this particular macro:

4. Confusing, no? Two different functions in the same computer package that do the same thing.

	A	B	C	D	E
1	**USING VBA'S RND FUNCTION TO PRODUCE A LIST OF RANDOM NUMBERS**				
2	List				
3	0.50972		RandomList Macro		
4	0.40606				
5	0.10613				
6	0.27612				
7	0.64305				
8	0.84910				
9	0.49797				
10	0.18778				
11	0.89662				
12	0.37281				

Assigning a Macro to a Button or to a Control Sequence

In the preceding spreadsheet, we have assigned the macro **RandomList** to the button marked "RandomList Macro." As explained in Chapter 38, any drawing shape in Excel can be assigned a VBA program. In this case we have created a rectangle; right-clicking on this rectangle, we have assigned it a macro:

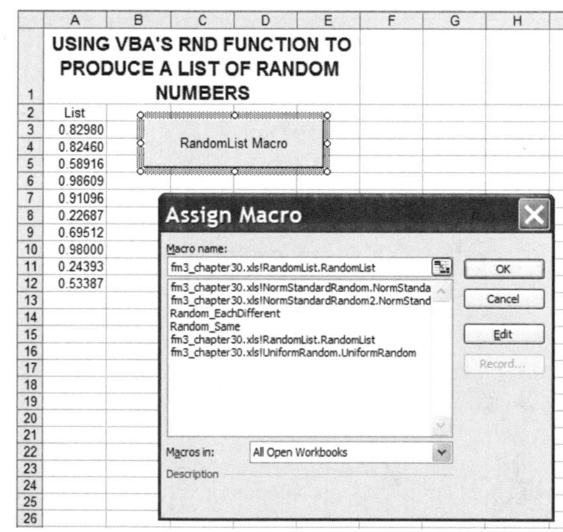

Elsewhere in this book, we usually assign macros a control sequence. After clicking on **Tools|Macro|Macros**, this particular macro **RandomList** has been assigned the sequence [Ctrl]+a:

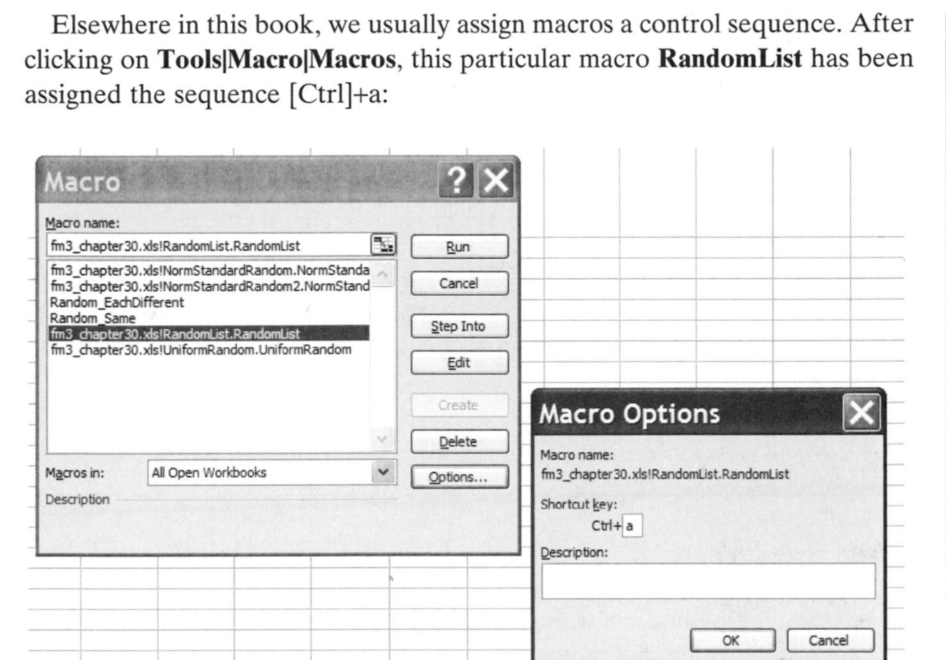

29.3 Testing Random-Number Generators

Producing lists of random numbers is interesting, though a bit uninformative. Is the list of numbers thus produced really uniformly distributed? A simple test is to generate each number and determine whether it falls into the interval $[0, 0.1), [0.1, 0.2), \ldots, [0.9, 1)$. The notation $[a, b)$ denotes the *half-open* interval between a and b; a number x is in this interval if $a \le x < b$. If the list of numbers is really uniformly distributed, we would expect roughly an even number of the "random" numbers to be in each of the ten intervals.

One way to test uniformity is to generate a list of random numbers on the spreadsheet by copying **Rand( )** to many cells and then using the Excel array function **Frequency(data_array,bins_array)**.[5] This procedure is illustrated in the following spreadsheet picture:

5. Array functions are explained in Chapter 34.

	A	B	C	D	E	F
1	**USING EXCEL'S FREQUENCY FUNCTION TO TEST THE DISTRIBUTION OF RAND( )**					
2	**Random numbers**			**Bin**	**Frequency**	
3	0.8978	<-- =RAND( )		0.1	0	
4	0.8354			0.2	1	
5	0.5188			0.3	1	
6	0.7317			0.4	0	
7	0.5067			0.5	0	<-- =FREQUENCY(A3:A12,D3:D12)
8	0.2418			0.6	4	
9	0.6406			0.7	1	
10	0.1228			0.8	1	
11	0.5611			0.9	2	
12	0.5543			1	0	
13						
14	Each cell in the range A3:A12 contains the formula **Rand( )**. Pressing F9 will produce a new set of random numbers and frequencies.					

This method is obviously not efficient (or even feasible) when we want to test the random-number generator for large numbers of random draws. The following program uses VBA to generate many random numbers and puts them into the bins in range A3:A12:

```
Sub UniformRandom()
'Puts random numbers into bins

    Range("E3") = Time
    N = Range("B2").Value 'the number of
    random draws

    Dim distribution(10) As Long 'bins

    For k = 1 To N
        draw = Rnd
        distribution(Int(draw * 10) + 1) = _
        distribution(Int(draw * 10) + 1) + 1
    Next k
```

```
        For Index = 1 To 10
            Range("B5").Cells(Index, 1) = _
              distribution(Index)
        Next Index

        Range("E4") = Time

End Sub
```

The output from this program produces the following spreadsheet:

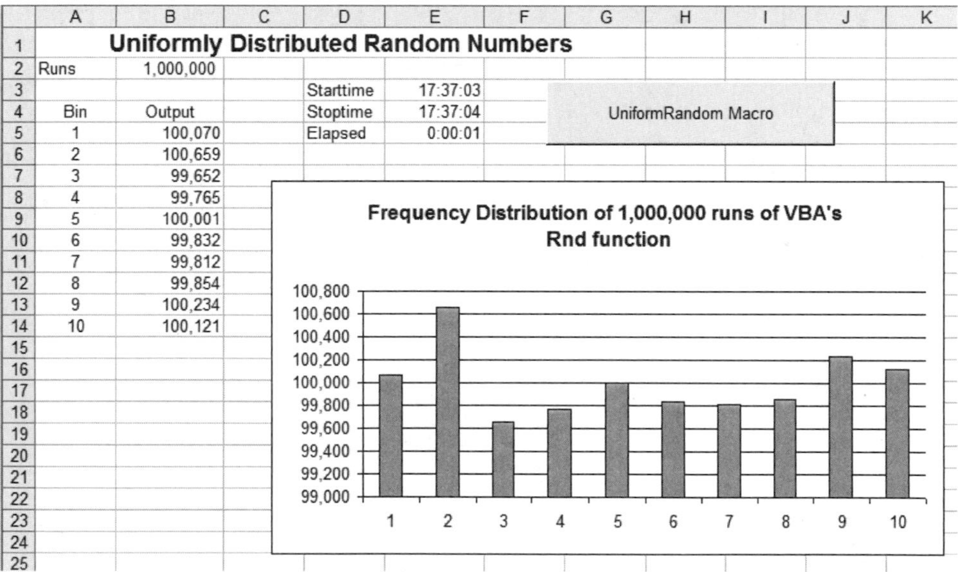

Uniformly Distributed Random Numbers

	A	B	C	D	E
2	Runs	1,000,000			
3				Starttime	17:37:03
4	Bin	Output		Stoptime	17:37:04
5	1	100,070		Elapsed	0:00:01
6	2	100,659			
7	3	99,652			
8	4	99,765			
9	5	100,001			
10	6	99,832			
11	7	99,812			
12	8	99,854			
13	9	100,234			
14	10	100,121			

Here are some things to note about **UniformRandom**:

• The program has a "clock" to measure the amount of time it takes to run. At the start of the program, we **use Range("E3")=Time** to put the current time into cell E3. At the end of the program, **Range("E4")=Time** puts in the ending time. The cell **elapsed** contains the formula =**stoptime-starttime**. Note that in order for the cells to read correctly, you have to use the command **Format|Cells|Number|Time** on the relevant cells.

• The heart of the program uses the function `Int(draw * 10) + 1`. Multiplying the random draw by 10 produces a number whose first digit is 0, 1, . . . , or 9. The VBA function **Int** gives this integer. **Distribution** is a VBA array numbered 1 to 10, with **Distribution(1)** being the number of random numbers in [0, 0.1), **Distribution(2)** the number of random numbers in [0.1, 0.2), etc. Thus `Int(draw * 10) + 1` is the proper place in **Distribution** to which the current random draw belongs.

29.3.1 Using Randomize to Produce the Same List (or Not) of Random Numbers

Most random-number generators use the last generated "random" number to produce the next.[6] The first number used in a particular sequence is controlled by the "seed," which is typically taken from the computer's clock. VBA's **Rnd** is no exception, but it allows you to control the seed by using the command **Randomize**. The two small programs that follow illustrate two uses of this command.

• Using **Randomize** without any numeric argument resets the seed (meaning that it breaks the connection between the next random number and the current random number). This approach is illustrated in the macro **Random_EachDifferent**, though it is difficult to see the effect.

```
Sub Random_EachDifferent()
'Produces a list of random numbers
Randomize
'Initializes the VBA random-number generator
   For Index = 1 To 10
       Range("A5").Cells(Index, 1) = Rnd()
   Next Index
End Sub
```

• Using **Randomize(seed)** uses a particular number as the seed.

• Using the sequence of commands **Rnd(negative number)** and **Randomize(seed)** guarantees the same sequence of random numbers. This approach is illustrated in the macro **Random_Same**.

6. There are more examples in the exercises at the end of the chapter.

```
Sub Random_Same()
'Produces the same list of random numbers
'which is always the same
Rnd (-4)
Randomize (Range("seed")) 'Initializes the VBA
'random-number generator
    For Index = 1 To 10
        Range("B5").Cells(Index, 1) = Rnd()
    Next Index
End Sub
```

In the following spreadsheet, pushing the top button produces a random set of random numbers. Pushing the bottom button activates the macro **Random_Same** and produces the same set of random numbers each time—provided the **Seed** (cell B2) is not changed.

	A	B	C
1	**PRODUCING LISTS OF RANDOM NUMBERS**		
2	Seed	334	
3			
4	**Output: Each run different**	**Output: Each run same**	Run Random_EachDifferent
5	0.85013	0.29708	
6	0.80044	0.70653	
7	0.23875	0.65463	
8	0.24357	0.96848	
9	0.70731	0.48999	
10	0.56897	0.72373	Run Random_Same
11	0.16289	0.06518	
12	0.03194	0.60034	
13	0.90985	0.25382	
14	0.50846	0.70398	
15			
16	**Note**: to see the effect of the "Run Random_Same" button, erase the cells B5:B14. Changing the seed in cell B2 changes the output in column B.		

29.4 Generating Normally Distributed Random Numbers

In the preceding sections we have generated numbers that are uniformly distributed. In this section we explore four ways to produce normally distributed random numbers using Excel.

29.4.1 Method 1: Normally Distributed Numbers Using Tools|Data Analysis|Random Number Generation

One way to generate normally distributed random numbers is to use the Excel command **Tools|Data Analysis|Random Number Generation**. Here's how we get Excel to produce 1,000 random numbers that are normally distributed (with $\mu = 0$ and $\sigma = 1$) in column G of the spreadsheet:

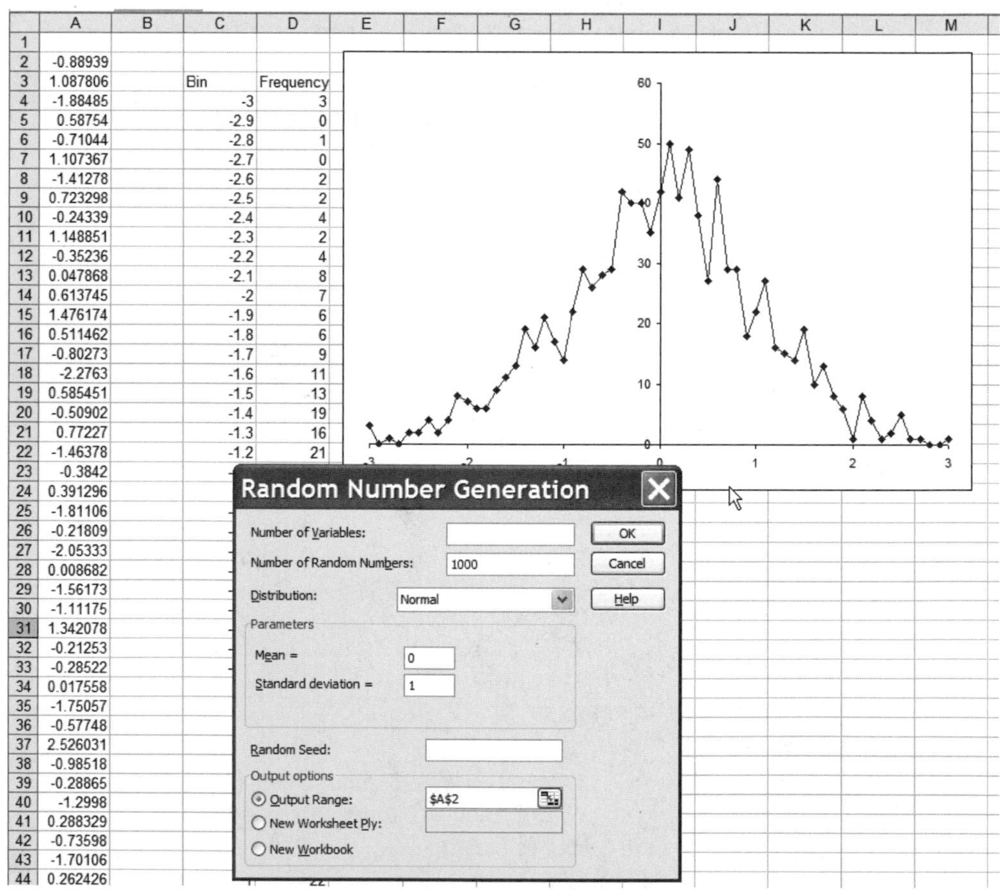

	A	C	D
1			
2	-0.88939		
3	1.087806	Bin	Frequency
4	-1.88485	-3	3
5	0.58754	-2.9	0
6	-0.71044	-2.8	1
7	1.107367	-2.7	0
8	-1.41278	-2.6	2
9	0.723298	-2.5	2
10	-0.24339	-2.4	4
11	1.148851	-2.3	2
12	-0.35236	-2.2	4
13	0.047868	-2.1	8
14	0.613745	-2	7
15	1.476174	-1.9	6
16	0.511462	-1.8	6
17	-0.80273	-1.7	9
18	-2.2763	-1.6	11
19	0.585451	-1.5	13
20	-0.50902	-1.4	19
21	0.77227	-1.3	16
22	-1.46378	-1.2	21
23	-0.3842		
24	0.391296		
25	-1.81106		
26	-0.21809		
27	-2.05333		
28	0.008682		
29	-1.56173		
30	-1.11175		
31	1.342078		
32	-0.21253		
33	-0.28522		
34	0.017558		
35	-1.75057		
36	-0.57748		
37	2.526031		
38	-0.98518		
39	-0.28865		
40	-1.2998		
41	0.288329		
42	-0.73598		
43	-1.70106		
44	0.262426		22

If we want to see whether the output is distributed normally, we can have Excel do a frequency distribution (either by using the array function **Frequency** or by using **Tools|Data Analysis|Histogram**). As the preceding graph shows, the output appears to be normally distributed.

29.4.2 Method 2: Normally Distributed Numbers Using NormInvS( )

Excel's **NormSInv( )** function inverts the function **NormSDist**. Given a number **x** between 0 and 1, **NormSInv(x)** produces number **y** such that **NormSDist(y) = x**. The function **NormSDist(Rand( ))** should produce a set of random numbers that is distributed standard normal:

	A	B	C
1	**NORMALLY DISTRIBUTED RANDOM NUMBERS USING NORMSINV( )**		
2	Any number between 0 and 1	0.6	
3	Normal number	0.2533471	<-- =NORMSINV(B2)
4	Check:	0.6	<-- =NORMSDIST(B3)
5			
6	Random normal number	0.56005094	<-- =NORMSDIST(RAND( ))

In the following spreadsheet we produce 114 iterations of **NormSInv(Rand( ))** and graph the resulting frequencies. They look normally distributed:

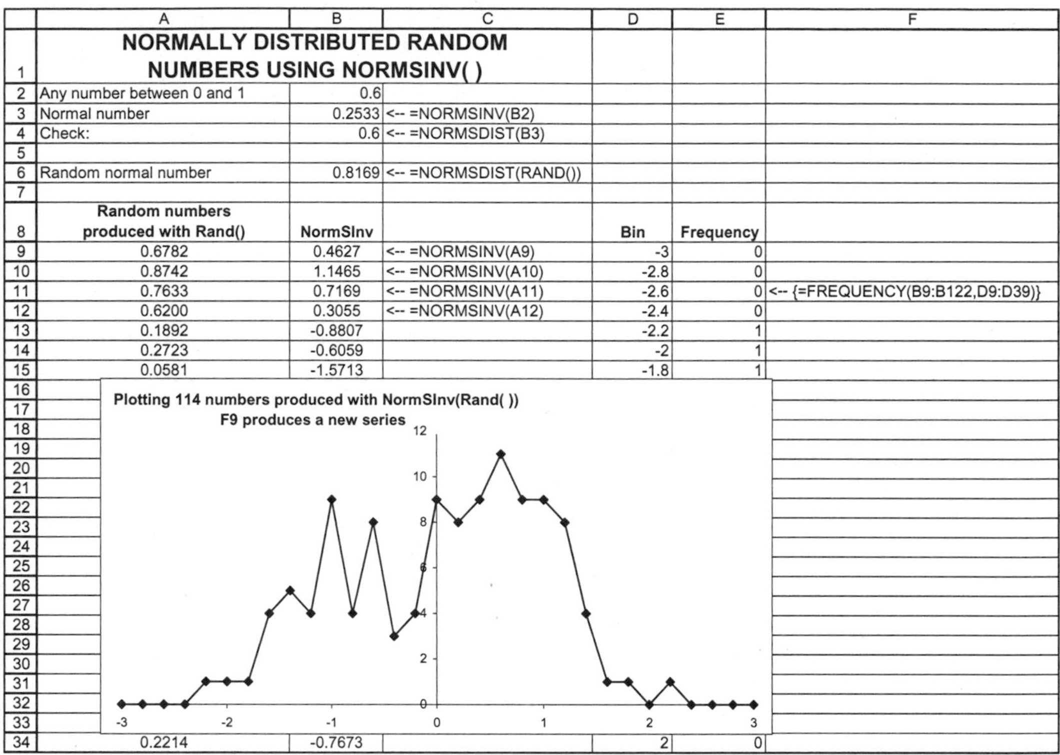

	A	B	C	D	E	F
1	**NORMALLY DISTRIBUTED RANDOM NUMBERS USING NORMSINV( )**					
2	Any number between 0 and 1	0.6				
3	Normal number	0.2533	<-- =NORMSINV(B2)			
4	Check:	0.6	<-- =NORMSDIST(B3)			
5						
6	Random normal number	0.8169	<-- =NORMSDIST(RAND())			
7						
8	**Random numbers produced with Rand()**	**NormSInv**		**Bin**	**Frequency**	
9	0.6782	0.4627	<-- =NORMSINV(A9)	-3	0	
10	0.8742	1.1465	<-- =NORMSINV(A10)	-2.8	0	
11	0.7633	0.7169	<-- =NORMSINV(A11)	-2.6	0	<-- {=FREQUENCY(B9:B122,D9:D39)}
12	0.6200	0.3055	<-- =NORMSINV(A12)	-2.4	0	
13	0.1892	-0.8807		-2.2	1	
14	0.2723	-0.6059		-2	1	
15	0.0581	-1.5713		-1.8	1	
16						
17						
18						
19						
20						
21						
22						
23						
24						
25						
26						
27						
28						
29						
30						
31						
32						
33						
34	0.2214	-0.7673		2	0	

29.4.3 Method 3: Incorporating NormSInv( ) into VBA

We can incorporate **NormSInv( )** into a VBA program. The VBA program **NormStandardRandom** uses **NormSInv** to produce random deviates. Here are the program, a comment, and the output it produces:

```
Sub NormStandardRandom()
'Produces a list of normally distributed
'random numbers
Randomize 'Initializes the VBA random-number
'generator
Application.ScreenUpdating = False
Range("E2") = Time
```

```
    Range("A8").Range(Cells(1, 1), _
      Cells(64000, 1)).Clear
    N = Range("B2").Value

    For Index = 1 To N
        Range("A8").Cells(Index, 1) _
          = Application.NormSInv(Rnd())
    Next Index
Range("E3") = Time
End Sub
```

The program **NormStandardRandom** includes two lines that measure the time taken for the whole simulation to run. The program is very slow, largely because of repeated calls on the spreadsheet function. As you will see in the sample screen that follows, 10,000 runs of the program take almost seven minutes (the button operates the macro):

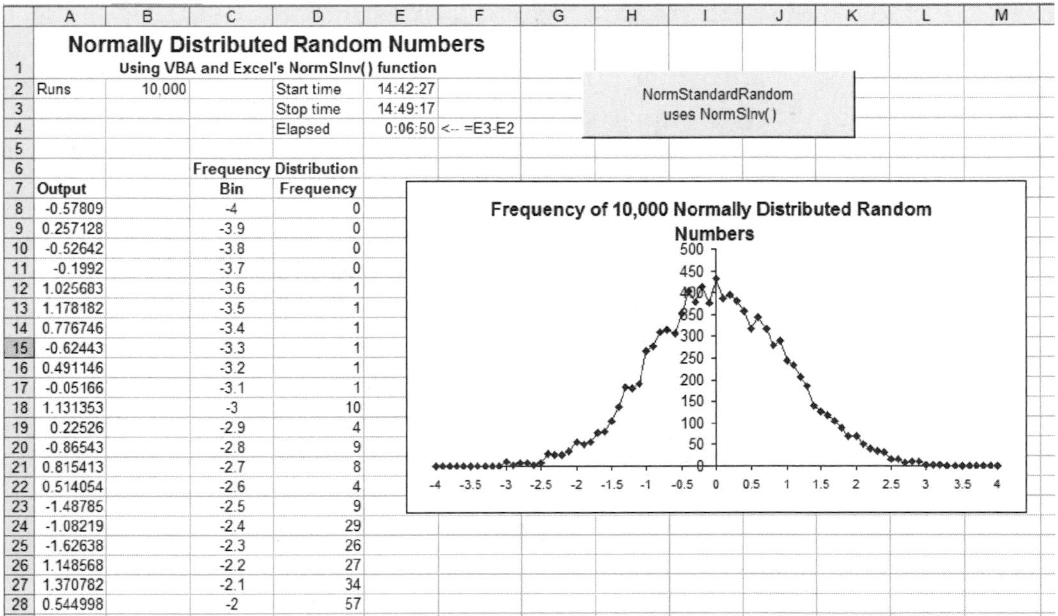

	A	B	C	D	E	F
1	Normally Distributed Random Numbers Using VBA and Excel's NormSInv( ) function					
2	Runs	10,000		Start time	14:42:27	
3				Stop time	14:49:17	
4				Elapsed	0:06:50	<-- =E3-E2
5						
6			Frequency Distribution			
7	Output		Bin	Frequency		
8	-0.57809		-4	0		
9	0.257128		-3.9	0		
10	-0.52642		-3.8	0		
11	-0.1992		-3.7	0		
12	1.025683		-3.6	1		
13	1.178182		-3.5	1		
14	0.776746		-3.4	1		
15	-0.62443		-3.3	1		
16	0.491146		-3.2	1		
17	-0.05166		-3.1	1		
18	1.131353		-3	10		
19	0.22526		-2.9	4		
20	-0.86543		-2.8	9		
21	0.815413		-2.7	8		
22	0.514054		-2.6	4		
23	-1.48785		-2.5	9		
24	-1.08219		-2.4	29		
25	-1.62638		-2.3	26		
26	1.148568		-2.2	27		
27	1.370782		-2.1	34		
28	0.544998		-2	57		

29.4.3.1 A Faster Version of Method 3

We can make Method 3 much faster by storing all the data in VBA and only writing the final frequency distribution on the screen:

```
Sub NormStandardRandom2()
Randomize 'Initializes the VBA random number
'generator
Dim distribution(-40 To 40) As Double
Application.ScreenUpdating = False
Range("E2") = Time
    N = Range("B2").Value

    For Index = 1 To N
        X = Application.NormSInv(Rnd())

    If X < -4 Then
        distribution(-40) = distribution(-40) + 1
     ElseIf X > 4 Then
        distribution(40) = distribution(40) + 1
     Else: distribution(Int(X / 0.1)) = _
       distribution(Int(X / 0.1)) + 1
     End If

    Next Index

For Index = -40 To 40
    Range("B7").Cells(Index + 41, 1) = _
      distribution(Index) / (2 * N)
Next Index

Range("E3") = Time
End Sub
```

Here's the output for 100,000 iterations. Note the time in cell E4.

	A	B	C	D	E	F
1		**Normally Distributed Random Numbers** This sheet saves time by not recording the random numbers on the screen				
2	Runs	100,000		Starttime	14:54:57	
3				Stoptime	14:55:34	
4				Elapsed	0:00:37	<-- =E3-E2
5						
6	**Bin**	**Output**				
7	-4	0.0000100				
8	-3.9	0.0000150				
9	-3.8	0.0000150				
10	-3.7	0.0000200				
11	-3.6	0.0000250				
12	-3.5	0.0000650				
13	-3.4	0.0000950				
14	-3.3	0.0001050				
15	-3.2	0.0001250				
16	-3.1	0.0001650				
17	-3	0.0003000				
18	-2.9	0.0003750				
19	-2.8	0.0004250				
20	-2.7	0.0006600				
21	-2.6	0.0008650				
22	-2.5	0.0010700				
23	-2.4	0.0012700				
24	-2.3	0.0016150				

NormStandardRandom2
Does all calculations internally to VBA

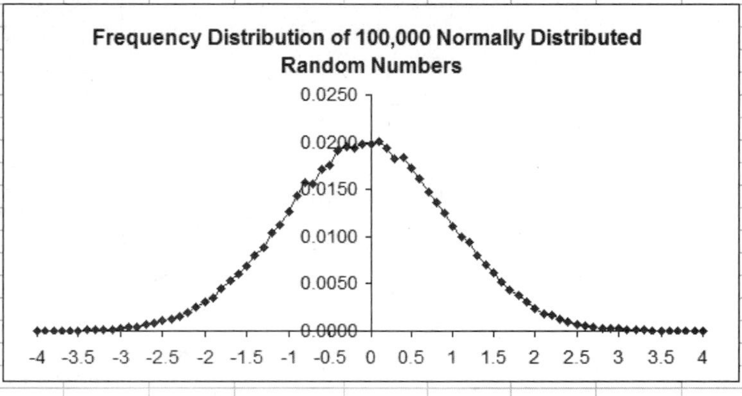

Frequency Distribution of 100,000 Normally Distributed Random Numbers

There are a few things to note about this program:

- Most of the results of the normal distribution are between –4 and +4. When, in **NormStandardRandom2**, we classify the output into bins, we want these bins to be $(-\infty, -3.9], (-2.9, -2.8], \ldots, (-3.9, \infty)$. We first define an array `distribution(-40 To 40)`; this array has 81 indices. To classify a particular random number (say X) into the bins of this array, we use the following function:

```
If X < -4 Then
   distribution(-40) = distribution(-40) + 1
 ElseIf X > 4 Then
   distribution(40) = distribution(40) + 1
 Else: distribution(Int(X / 0.1)) = _
  distribution(Int(X / 0.1)) + 1
 End If
```

• **NormStandardRandom2** produces not a histogram (which is a *count* of how many times a number falls into a particular bin), but a *frequency distribution*. We produce this by dividing by twice the number of runs (remember that each successful run produces two random numbers), $2N$, before we output the data to the spreadsheet:

```
For Index = -40 To 40
    Range("output").Cells(Index + 41, 1) = _
         distribution(Index) / (2 * N)
Next Index
```

• Finally, note that the command `Application.ScreenUpdating = False` makes a big difference! This command prevents both the updating of the output in the cells and the Excel chart. Try running the program with and without this command to see the effect.

29.4.4 Method 4: The Box-Muller Method

The Box-Muller method for creating randomly distributed normal deviates is the fastest method of the four.[7] The eight lines that follow `Start` in the VBA program define a routine, which in each successful iteration creates two numbers that are drawn from a standard normal distribution. The routine creates two random numbers, rand_1 and rand_2, between –1 and +1. If the sum of the squares of these numbers is within the unit circle, then the two normal deviates are defined by

$$\{X_1, X_2\} = \left\{\text{rand}_1 * \sqrt{\frac{-2\ln(S_1)}{S_1}}, \text{rand}_2 * \sqrt{\frac{-2\ln(S_1)}{S_1}}\right\}$$

where $S_1 = \text{rand}_1^2 + \text{rand}_2^2$.

Here's the VBA program:

7. See Box-Muller (1958) or Knuth (1981).

```
Sub NormStandardRandom3()
'Box-Muller for producing standard normal deviates

Dim distribution(-40 To 40) As Long

Range("E2") = Time
N = Range("B2").Value

Application.ScreenUpdating = False
For Index = 1 To N

start:
     Static rand1, rand2, S1, S2, X1, X2
     rand1 = 2 * Rnd - 1
     rand2 = 2 * Rnd - 1
     S1 = rand1 ^ 2 + rand2 ^ 2
     If S1 > 1 Then GoTo start
     S2 = Sqr(-2 * Log(S1) / S1)
     X1 = rand1 * S2
     X2 = rand2 * S2

     If X1 < -4 Then
          distribution(-40) = distribution(-40) + 1
     ElseIf X1 > 4 Then
          distribution(40) = distribution(40) + 1
     Else: distribution(Int(X1 / 0.1)) = _
       distribution(Int(X1 / 0.1)) + 1
     End If

     If X2 < -4 Then
          distribution(-40) = distribution(-40) + 1
     ElseIf X2 > 4 Then
          distribution(40) = distribution(40) + 1
     Else: distribution(Int(X2 / 0.1)) = _
       distribution(Int(X2 / 0.1)) + 1
     End If

Next Index

For Index = -40 To 40
    Range("B7").Cells(Index + 41, 1) = _
      distribution(Index) / (2 * N)
Next Index

Range("E3") = Time
End Sub
```

This routine is very fast. In the following spreadsheet we produce 10 million normal variates in 38 seconds:

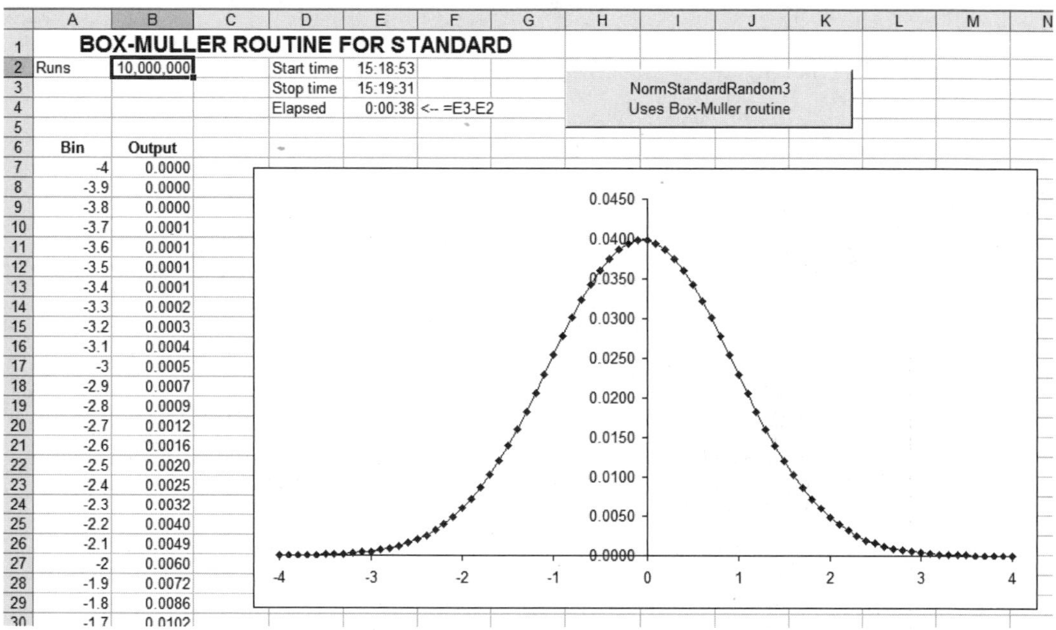

BOX-MULLER ROUTINE FOR STANDARD

Runs	10,000,000	Start time	15:18:53
		Stop time	15:19:31
		Elapsed	0:00:38 <-- =E3-E2

Bin	Output
-4	0.0000
-3.9	0.0000
-3.8	0.0000
-3.7	0.0001
-3.6	0.0001
-3.5	0.0001
-3.4	0.0001
-3.3	0.0002
-3.2	0.0003
-3.1	0.0004
-3	0.0005
-2.9	0.0007
-2.8	0.0009
-2.7	0.0012
-2.6	0.0016
-2.5	0.0020
-2.4	0.0025
-2.3	0.0032
-2.2	0.0040
-2.1	0.0049
-2	0.0060
-1.9	0.0072
-1.8	0.0086
-1.7	0.0102

29.5 Summary

Random numbers are widely used in financial engineering, especially in option pricing. This chapter has introduced you to the Excel and VBA random-number generators and has shown a number of techniques for producing normally distributed random numbers.

Exercises

1. Use the program **RandomList** from section 29.2.1 to produce a list of 200 random numbers. Use the Excel function **Frequency** to produce a histogram of the results.

2. Here is a random-number generator you can make yourself:

   a. Start with some number, *Seed*.

   b. Let $X_1 = Seed + \pi$. Let $X_2 = e^{5+\ln(X_1)}$.

c. The first random number is $Random = X_2 - Integer(X_2)$, where $Integer(X_2)$ is the integer part of X_2.

d. Repeat the process, letting $Seed = Random$.

Implement this random-number generator in a VBA program similar to **RandomList**, and produce a list of 50 random numbers.

3. Define *AmodB* as the *remainder* when *A* is divided by *B*. For example, 36mod25 = 11. Excel has this function; it is written **Mod(A,B)**. Now here is another random-number generator:

a. Let $X_0 = 1$.

b. Let $X_{n+1} = (7 * X_n)\text{mod}10^8$.

c. Let $U_{n+1} = X_{n+1}/10^8$.

The list of numbers $U_1, U_2, \ldots$ contains the pseudo-random numbers generated by this random-number generator. (This is one of the many random-number generators given in Abramowitz and Stegun, 1972).

Use VBA to produce this random number generator, and use it in a program similar to **UniformRandom**.

4. Many states have daily lotteries, which are played as follows: Sometime during the day, you buy a lottery ticket, on which the seller inscribes a number you choose, between 000 and 999. That night there is a drawing on television in which a three-digit number is drawn. If the number on your ticket matches the number drawn, you win and collect $500 (for a $1 wager). If you lose, you get nothing.

a. Write an Excel function that produces a random number between 000 and 999. (Hint: Use **Rand( )** and **Int( )**.)

b. Write a VBA program that reproduces 250 random draws of the daily lottery (about one year's worth, if there are no drawings on weekends). Assuming that each ticket costs $1, and assuming that you choose the same number each day, how much would you have won during the year?

5. Program **normalSimulation** but put the output into more bins (can you make the number of bins and their size controllable from the spreadsheet?). Does this get rid of the "fat tails" in the distribution graph?

6. It is well-known that if Z is a standard normal random variable (i.e., with mean $\mu = 0$ and standard deviation $\sigma = 1$) then $X = aZ + b$ is normally distributed with $\mu = \text{b}$ and $\sigma = \text{a}$. Modify **normalSimulation** to produce normal, nonstandard, distributions, with the mean and the standard deviation inputted from the spreadsheet.

7. a. Use **NormSInv** to produce a list of 1,000 random numbers and use **Frequency** to see whether they are indeed normally distributed with mean $\mu = 0$ and standard deviation $\sigma = 1$.

b. Following exercise 6, modify the numbers so that they are distributed with $\mu = b$ and $\sigma = a$.

30 Data Tables

30.1 Overview

Data table commands are powerful commands that make it possible to do complex sensitivity analyses. Excel offers the opportunity to build a table in which only one variable is changed, or one in which two variables are changed. Excel data tables are array functions and thus change dynamically when related spreadsheet cells are changed. In this chapter you will learn how to build both one-dimensional and two-dimensional Excel data tables.

30.2 An Example

Consider a project that has an initial cost of $1,150 and seven subsequent cash flows. The cash flows in years 1–7 grow at rate g, so that the cash flow in year t is $CF_t = CF_{t-1} * (1 + g)$. Given a discount rate r, the net present value (NPV) of the project is

$$NPV = -1{,}150 + \frac{CF_1}{(1+r)^1} + \frac{CF_1(1+g)}{(1+r)^2} + \frac{CF_1(1+g)^2}{(1+r)^3} + \ldots + \frac{CF_1(1+g)^6}{(1+r)^7}$$

The internal rate of return (IRR), i, is the rate at which the NPV equals zero:

$$0 = 1{,}150 + \frac{CF_1}{(1+i)^1} + \frac{CF_1(1+g)}{(1+i)^2} + \frac{CF_1(1+g)^2}{(1+i)^3} + \ldots + \frac{CF_1(1+g)^6}{(1+i)^7}$$

These calculations are easily done in Excel. In the following example the initial cash flow is 234, the growth rate g = 10 percent, and the discount rate r = 15 percent:

	A	B	C	D	E	F	G	H	I
1	CF_1	234							
2	Growth rate	10%							
3	Discount rate	15%							
4									
5	Year	0	1	2	3	4	5	6	7
6	Cash flow	-1,150.00	234.00	257.40	283.14	311.45	342.60	376.86	414.55
7									
8	NPV	101.46	<-- =+B6+NPV(B3,C6:I6)						
9	IRR	17.60%	<-- =IRR(B6:I6,0)						

Note the cell addresses for the growth rate, the discount rate, the NPV, and the IRR. They will be needed in this chapter.

30.3 Setting Up a Data Table

Suppose we want to know how the NPV and IRR are affected by a change in the growth rate. The command **Data Table** allows us to find this information simply. The first step is to set up the table's structure. In the next example, we put the formulas for the NPV and IRR on the top row, and we put the variable we wish to vary (in this case the growth rate) in the first column. At this point the table looks like this:

	F	G	H	I	J
10					
11		=B8			=B9
12					
13			NPV	IRR	
14			101.46	17.6%	
15		0			
16	Growth	5%			
17	rate	10%			
18		15%			
19					

The actual table (as opposed to the labels for the columns and the rows) is outlined in the dark border. The numbers directly under the labels "NPV" and "IRR" refer to the corresponding formulas in the previous picture. Thus, if cell B8 contains the calculation for the NPV, then the cell under the letters "NPV" contains the formula "=B8." Similarly, if cell B9 contains the original calculation for the IRR, then the cell under "IRR" in the table contains the formula "=B9."

We like to think of a data table spreadsheet as having two parts:

1. A basic example.
2. A table that does a sensitivity analysis on the basic example. In our example, the first row of the table contains references to calculations done in our basic example. While there are other ways to do data tables, this structure is both typical and easy to understand.

Now do the following:

- Highlight the table area (outlined in the dark border).
- Activate the command **Data|Table**. You will get a dialogue box that asks you to indicate a **Row Input Cell** and/or a **Column Input Cell**.

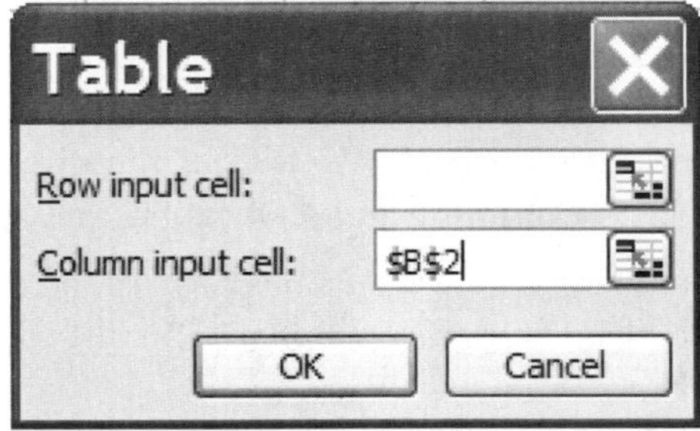

In this case, the variable we wish to change is in the left-hand column of our table, so we leave the Row Input Cell blank and indicate cell B2 (this cell contains the growth rate in our basic example) in the Column Input Cell box. Here's the result:

	F	G	H	I	J
10					
11		=B8			=B9
12					
13			NPV	IRR	
14			101.46	17.6%	
15		0	-176.46	9.71%	
16	Growth	5%	-47.82	13.67%	
17	rate	10%	101.46	17.60%	
18		15%	274.35	21.50%	
19					

30.4 Building a Two-Dimensional Data Table

We can also use the **Data Table** command to vary *one* formula while changing *two* parameters. Suppose, for example, that we want to calculate the net present value (NPV) of the cash flows for different growth rates and different discount rates. We create a new table that looks like this:

	E	F	G	H	I	J	K
19							
20	=B8						
21				Discount rate			
22			101.46	7%	10%	12%	
23		Growth	0				
24		rate	5%				
25			10%				
26			15%				
27							

The upper left-hand corner of the table contains the formula "=B8" as a reference to the basic example.

We now use the **Data Table** command again. This time we fill in both the **Row Input Cell** (indicating cell B3, the site of the discount rate in our basic example) and the **Column Input Cell** (indicating B2).

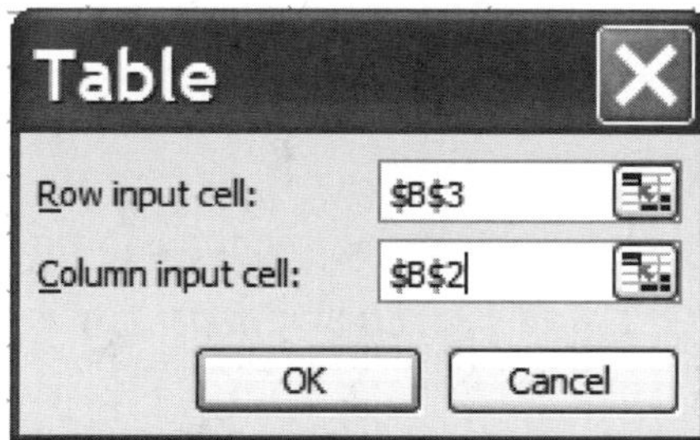

Here's the result:

	E	F	G	H	I	J	K
19							
20	=B8						
21				Discount rate			
22			101.46	7%	10%	12%	
23		Growth	0	111.09	-10.79	-82.08	
24		rate	5%	297.62	150.74	65.13	
25			10%	515.79	339.09	236.44	
26			15%	770.34	558.25	435.41	
27							

30.5 An Aesthetic Note: Hiding the Formula Cells

Data tables tend to look a bit strange, because the formula being calculated shows up in the data table (in our examples: in the top row of the first data table and in the left-hand top corner of the second data table). You can make your tables look nicer by *hiding* the formula cells. To do this, mark the offending cells and use the **Format Cells** command (or press the right mouse button and go to the **Number|Custom**). In the dialogue box go to the box marked **Type** and insert a semicolon into the box. Here's the way this screen looks for the previous example:

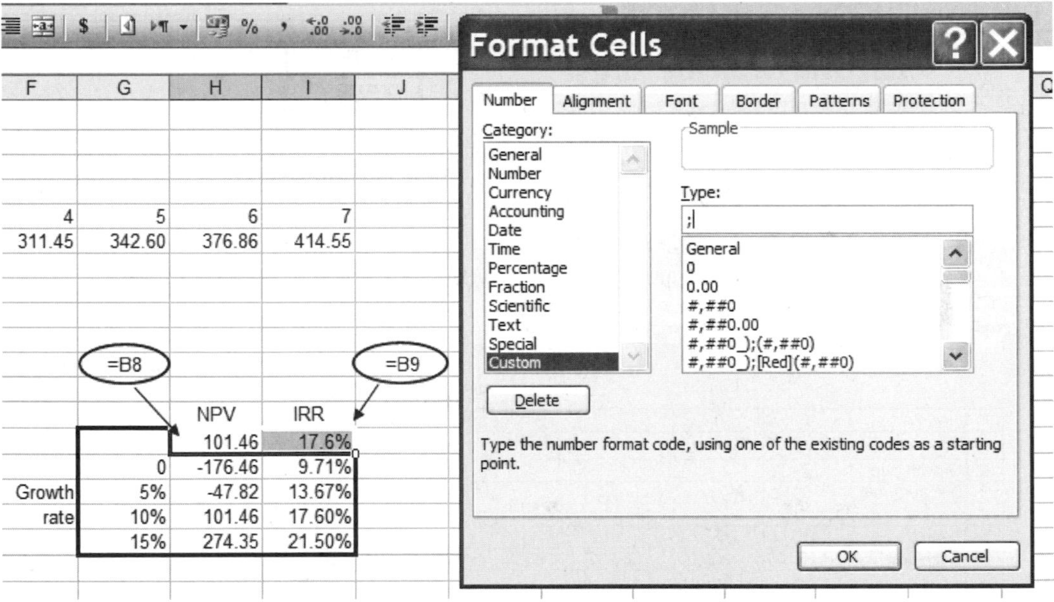

The cell contents will now be hidden. The result looks like the following:

	F	G	H	I	J
10					
11		=B8			=B9
12					
13			NPV	IRR	
14					
15		0	-176.46	9.71%	
16	Growth	5%	-47.82	13.67%	
17	rate	10%	101.46	17.60%	
18		15%	274.35	21.50%	
19					

30.6 Excel Data Tables Are Arrays

When we say that Excel data tables are arrays, we mean that they are dynamically linked to the initial example. When we change a parameter in the original example, the corresponding column or row of the data table changes. For example, if we change the initial cash flow from 234 to 300, here's what will happen in the preceding data table:

	A	B	C	D	E	F	G	H	I	J
1	CF_1	300								
2	Growth rate	10%								
3	Discount rate	15%								
4										
5	Year	0	1	2	3	4	5	6	7	
6	Cash flow	-1150.00	300.00	330.00	363.00	399.30	439.23	483.15	531.47	
7										
8	NPV	454.43	<-- =+B6+NPV(B3,C6:I6)							
9	IRR	26.01%	<-- =IRR(B6:I6,0)							
10										
11							=B8			=B9
12										
13								NPV	IRR	
14										
15							0	98.13	17.80%	
16						Growth	5%	263.06	21.92%	
17						rate	10%	454.43	26.01%	
18							15%	676.09	30.07%	
19										

Exercises

1. a. Use **Data|Table** to graph the function $f(x) = 3x^2 - 2x - 15$, as illustrated in this spreadsheet:

	A	B	C	D	E	F	G	H	I
1	USING DATA TABLE TO GRAPH A FUNCTION								
2	x	3							
3	f(x)	6	<-- =3*B2^2-2*B2-15						
4									
5									
6		x	6	<-- =B3, data table header					
7		-6	105						
8		-5	70						
9		-4	41						
10		-3	18						
11		-2	1						
12		-1	-10						
13		0	-15						
14		1	-14						
15		2	-7						
16		3	6						
17		4	25						
18		5	50						
19		6	81						
20		7	118						

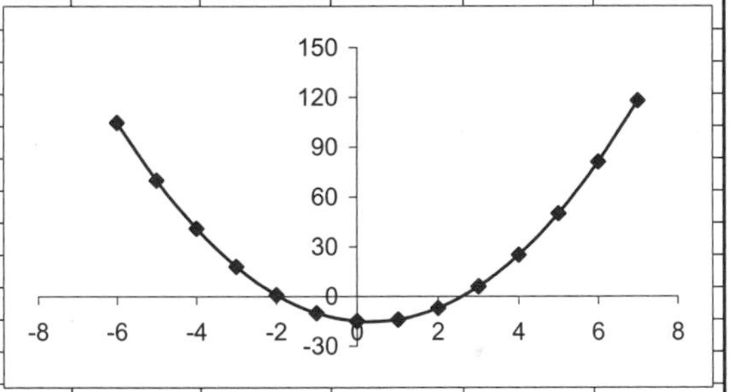

b. Use **Solver** or **Goal|Seek** to find two values of x, for which $f(x) = 0$.

2. The Excel function **PV(rate, number_periods, payment)** calculates the present value of a constant payment. Thus in the following spreadsheet example,

$$\text{PV}(15\text{ percent}, 15, -10) = \sum_{t=1}^{15} \frac{10}{(1.15)^t} = 58.47$$

(Note that we have put the payment as a negative number, since otherwise Excel returns a negative value! This little irritation is discussed in Chapters 1 and 33.)

Use **Data Table** to graph the present value as a function of the discount rate, as follows:

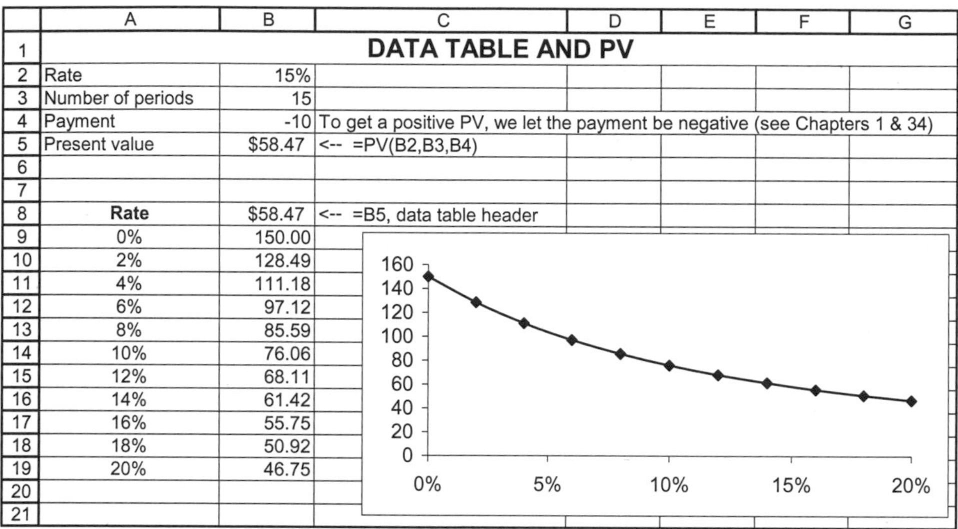

	A	B	C	D	E	F	G
1	DATA TABLE AND PV						
2	Rate	15%					
3	Number of periods	15					
4	Payment	-10	To get a positive PV, we let the payment be negative (see Chapters 1 & 34)				
5	Present value	$58.47	<-- =PV(B2,B3,B4)				
6							
7							
8	**Rate**	$58.47	<-- =B5, data table header				
9	0%	150.00					
10	2%	128.49					
11	4%	111.18					
12	6%	97.12					
13	8%	85.59					
14	10%	76.06					
15	12%	68.11					
16	14%	61.42					
17	16%	55.75					
18	18%	50.92					
19	20%	46.75					
20							
21							

3. The following spreadsheet fragment shows a net present value and internal rate of return calculation for a project:

	A	B	C	D	E	F	G	H
1	**NPV, DISCOUNT AND GROWTH RATES**							
2	Growth rate	10%						
3	Discount rate	15%						
4	Cost	500						
5	Year 1 cash flow	100						
6								
7	Year	0	1	2	3	4	5	
8	Cash flow	-500.00	100.00	110.00	121.00	133.10	146.41	
9								
10	NPV	(101.42)	<-- =NPV(B3,C8:G8)+B8					
11	IRR	6.60%	<-- =IRR(B8:G8)			Cell B15 contains the data table function =B10		
12								
13								
14			**Growth**					
15		($101.42)	0%	3%	6%	9%	12%	
16		0%	0.00	30.91	63.71	98.47	135.28	
17	**Discount rate**	3%	-42.03	-14.56	14.55	45.38	78.01	
18		6%	-78.76	-54.26	-28.30	-0.84	28.21	
19		9%	-111.03	-89.08	-65.85	-41.28	-15.33	
20		12%	-139.52	-119.78	-98.91	-76.86	-53.57	
21		15%	-164.78	-146.97	-128.15	-108.28	-87.32	
22		18%	-187.28	-171.15	-154.13	-136.16	-117.23	
23		21%	-207.40	-192.75	-177.30	-161.01	-143.84	
24		24%	-225.46	-212.11	-198.04	-183.22	-167.62	

Use **Data Table** to do a sensitivity analysis on the NPV of the project for discount rates 0, 3, 6, . . . , 21 percent and growth rates 0, 3, . . . , 12 percent.

4. Using **Data Table**, graph the function $\sin(x * y)$ for $x = 0, 0.2, 0.4, \ldots, 1.8, 2$ and $y = 0, 0.2, 0.4, \ldots, 1.8, 2$. Use the "Surface" graph option to make a three-dimensional graph of the function.

31 Matrices

31.1 Overview

The portfolio optimization chapters of *Financial Modeling* (Chapters 8–15) make extensive use of matrices to find efficient portfolios. This chapter contains enough information about matrices to make it possible for you to follow the discussion (and do the calculations!) required for portfolio mathematics.

A matrix is a rectangular array of numbers. All of the following are matrices:

	A	B	C	D	E	F	G	H	I
1	MATRICES IN EXCEL								
2	Matrix A (a row vector)				Matrix B (square 3 x 3 matrix)				Matrix C (column vector)
3	2	3	4		13	-8	-3		13
4					-8	10	-1		-8
5					-3	-1	11		-3
6									
7	Matrix D (a 4 x 3 matrix)								
8	13	-8	-3						
9	-8	10	-1						
10	-3	-1	11						
11	0	13	3						

A matrix with only one row is also called a *row vector*; a matrix with only one column is also called a *column vector*. A matrix with an equal number of rows and columns is called a *square matrix*.

A single letter is often used to denote a matrix or a vector. In this case we often write, for example, $\mathbf{B} = [b_{ij}]$, where b_{ij} stands for the entry in row i and column j of the matrix. For a vector we might write $\mathbf{A} = [a_i]$ or $\mathbf{C} = [c_i]$. Thus, for the examples given,

$$a_3 = 4 \qquad b_{22} = 10 \qquad c_1 = 13 \qquad d_{41} = 10$$

The matrix $\mathbf{B}$ is *symmetric*, meaning that $b_{ij} = b_{ji}$. (The variance-covariance matrices used in the portfolio discussion of Chapters 8–13 are symmetric.)

31.2 Matrix Operations

In this section we briefly review the basic operations on a matrix: multiplying a matrix by a scalar, adding matrices, transposition of matrices, and matrix multiplication.

31.2.1 Multiplication by a Scalar

Multiplying a matrix by a scalar multiplies every entry in the matrix by the scalar, as in this example:

	A	B	C	D	E
1	MULTIPLYING A MATRIX BY A SCALAR				
2	Scalar	6			
3					
4	Matrix B	13	-8	-3	
5		-8	10	-1	
6		-3	-1	11	
7					
8	Scalar * Matrix B				
9		78	-48	-18	<-- =D4*$B$2
10		-48	60	-6	
11		-18	-6	66	

31.2.2 Matrix Addition

Matrices may be added together provided they have the same number of rows and columns. Adding two vectors or matrices is accomplished by adding their corresponding entries. Thus if $\mathbf{A} = [a_{ij}]$ and $\mathbf{B} = [b_{ij}]$, $\mathbf{A} + \mathbf{B} = [a_{ij} + b_{ij}]$:

	A	B	C	D	E	F	G	H	I
1	ADDITION OF MATRICES								
2	Matrix A			Matrix B			Sum of A + B		
3	1	3		0.1	0		1.1	3	<-- =B3+E3
4	3	0		23	0		26	0	
5	6	-9		8	-33.4		14	-42.4	
6	5	11		-15	0		-10	11	
7	7	12		2.33	1.2		9.33	13.2	

31.2.3 Matrix Transposition

Transposition is an operation by which the rows of a matrix are turned into columns and vice versa. Thus for the matrix **E**:

	A	B	C	D	E	F	G	H	I
1	**TRANSPOSITION OF MATRICES**								
2	**Matrix E**					**Transpose of E: E^T**			
3	1	2	3	4		1	0	16	<-- {=TRANSPOSE(A3:D5)}
4	0	3	77	-9		2	3	7	
5	16	7	7	2		3	77	7	
6						4	-9	2	
7									
8	Cells F3:H6 are generated with the array function Transpose(A3:D5). This function is inserted by marking off the target area, typing the formula, and then finishing by pressing [Ctrl]+[Shift]+[Enter] . See Chapter 34 for more details.								

This illustration uses the array function **Transpose**. More details on the use of array functions are given in Chapter 34.

31.2.4 Multiplication of Matrices

You can multiply matrix **A** by matrix **B** to get product **AB**. However, you can only do so if the number of columns in **A** equals the number of rows in **B**. The resulting product **AB** is a matrix with the number of rows as **A** and the number of columns of **B**.

Confused? A couple of examples will help. Suppose that **X** is a row vector and that **Y** is a column vector, both with n coordinates:

$$\mathbf{X} = [x_1 \quad \dots \quad x_n], \qquad \mathbf{Y} = \begin{bmatrix} y_1 \\ \vdots \\ y_n \end{bmatrix}$$

Then the *product of* **X** *and* **Y** is defined by

$$\mathbf{XY} = [x_1 \quad \dots \quad x_n] \begin{bmatrix} y_1 \\ \vdots \\ y_n \end{bmatrix} = \sum_{i=1}^{n} x_i y_i$$

Now suppose that **A** and **B** are two matrices, and that **A** has n columns and p rows and **B** has n rows and m columns:

$$\mathbf{A} = \begin{bmatrix} a_{11} & a_{12} & \cdots & a_{1n} \\ \vdots & & & \\ a_{p1} & a_{p2} & \cdots & a_{pn} \end{bmatrix} \qquad \mathbf{B} = \begin{bmatrix} b_{11} & \cdots & b_{1m} \\ b_{21} & \cdots & b_{2m} \\ \vdots & & \\ b_{n1} & \cdots & b_{nm} \end{bmatrix}$$

Then the product of **A** and **B**, written **AB**, is defined by the matrix

$$\mathbf{AB} = \begin{bmatrix} \sum_{h=1}^{n} a_{1h} b_{h1} & \sum_{h=1}^{n} a_{1h} b_{h2} & \cdots & \sum_{h=1}^{n} a_{1h} b_{hm} \\ \vdots & & & \\ \vdots & & & \\ \sum_{h=1}^{n} a_{ph} b_{h1} & \cdots & \cdots & \sum_{h=1}^{n} a_{ph} b_{hm} \end{bmatrix}$$

with ij^{th} element $= \sum_{h=1}^{n} a_{ih} b_{hj}$.

Note that the ij^{th} coordinate of **AB** is the product of the *i*th row of **A** times the *j*th column of **B**. For example, if

$$\mathbf{A} = \begin{bmatrix} 2 & -6 \\ -9 & 3 \end{bmatrix}, \qquad \mathbf{B} = \begin{bmatrix} 6 & 9 & -12 \\ -5 & 2 & 4 \end{bmatrix}$$

then

$$\mathbf{AB} = \begin{bmatrix} 42 & 6 & -48 \\ -69 & -75 & 120 \end{bmatrix}$$

The order of matrix multiplication is critical. Multiplication of matrices is not commutative; that is, $\mathbf{AB} \neq \mathbf{BA}$. As the preceding example shows, the fact that it is possible to multiply **A** times **B** does not always imply that the multiplication **BA** is even defined.

In order to multiply matrices in Excel, we use the array function **MMult**:

	A	B	C	D	E	F
1	**MULTIPLYING MATRICES**					
2	**Matrix A**			**Matrix B**		
3	2	-7		6	9	-12
4	0	3		-5	2	4
5						
6	**Product AB**					
7	47	4	-52	<-- {=MMULT(A3:B4,D3:F4)}		
8	-15	6	12			

To multiply two matrices together, the number of columns in the first matrix must equal the number of rows in the second. Thus we can multiply **A** times **B**, but we cannot multiply **B** times **A**. If you try to do so in Excel, the function **MMult** will give you an error message:

	A	B	C	D	E	F
1	**MATRIX MULTIPLICATION: Number of columns of first matrix must equal number of rows of second matrix**					
2	**Matrix A**			**Matrix B**		
3	2	-7		6	9	-12
4	0	3		-5	2	4
5						
6	**Product BA**					
7	#VALUE!	#VALUE!	#VALUE!	<-- {=MMULT(D3:F4,A3:B4)}		
8	#VALUE!	#VALUE!	#VALUE!			

31.3 Matrix Inverses

A square matrix **I** is called the *identity matrix* if all its off-diagonal entries are 0 and all its diagonal entries are 1. Thus

$$\mathbf{I} = \begin{bmatrix} 1 & 0 & \cdots & 0 & 0 \\ 0 & 1 & \cdots & 0 & 0 \\ \vdots & \vdots & & \vdots & \vdots \\ 0 & 0 & & 1 & 0 \\ 0 & 0 & \cdots & 0 & 1 \end{bmatrix}$$

It is easy to confirm that multiplying any matrix **A** by the identity matrix of the proper dimension leaves that **A** unchanged. Thus, if $\mathbf{I}_n$ is an $n \times n$ identity matrix and **A** is an $n \times m$ matrix, $\mathbf{IA} = \mathbf{A}$. Similarly, if $\mathbf{I}_m$ is an $m \times m$ identity matrix, $\mathbf{AI} = \mathbf{A}$.

Now suppose we are given a *square* matrix **A** of dimension n. The $n \times n$ matrix $\mathbf{A}^{-1}$ is called the *inverse* of **A** if $\mathbf{A}^{-1}\mathbf{A} = \mathbf{AA}^{-1} = \mathbf{I}$. The computation of an inverse matrix can be a lot of work; fortunately, however, Excel has the array function **MInverse** which does the calculations for us. Here's an example:

	A	B	C	D	E	F	G	H	I	J
1	MATRIX INVERSE Use array function MInverse to compute the inverse of a square matrix									
2	Matrix A					Inverse of A				
3	1	-9	16	1		-0.0217	1.8913	0.5362	-1.1449	<-- {=MINVERSE(A3:D6)}
4	3	3	2	3		0.0000	-1.0000	-0.1667	0.6667	
5	2	4	0	-2		0.0652	-0.6739	-0.1087	0.4348	
6	5	7	3	4		-0.0217	-0.1087	-0.2971	0.1884	
7										
8	Verifying the inverse									
9	We multiply A*Inverse A: cells below contain array function {=MMULT(A3:D6,F3:I6)}									
10	1	1.07E-15	-2.22045E-16	-9.4369E-16						
11	0	1	-1.11022E-16	2.22045E-16						
12	6.94E-18	8.33E-17	1	5.55112E-16						
13	1.39E-17	1.17E-15	-4.44089E-16	1						

As the spreadsheet shows, you can use **MMult** to verify that the product of the matrix and its inverse indeed give the identity matrix. An expression like 1.07E-15 means $1.07 * 10^{-15}$, and such expressions are thus essentially zero; you can use **Format|Cells|Number** to specify the number of decimal places and get rid of these ugly expressions:

	A	B	C	D
9	We multiply A*Inverse A: cells below contain array function {=MMULT(A3:D6,F3:I6)}			
10	1.0000	0.0000	0.0000	0.0000
11	0.0000	1.0000	0.0000	0.0000
12	0.0000	0.0000	1.0000	0.0000
13	0.0000	0.0000	0.0000	1.0000

A square matrix that has an inverse is called a *nonsingular matrix*. The conditions for a matrix to be nonsingular are the following: Consider a square matrix **A** of dimension n. It can be shown that $\mathbf{A} = [a_{ij}]$ is nonsingular if and only if the only solution to the n equations

$$\sum_i a_{ij} x_i = 0, \quad j = 1, \ldots, n$$

is $x_i = 0$, $i = 1, \ldots, n$. Matrix inversion is a tricky business. If there exists a vector **X** whose components are almost zero and which solves the above system, then the matrix is *ill-conditioned*, and it may be very difficult to find an accurate inverse.

31.4 Solving Systems of Simultaneous Linear Equations

A system of n linear equations in m unknown is written as

$$\begin{aligned} &a_{11}x_1 + a_{12}x_2 + \cdots + a_{1n}x_n = y_1 \\ &a_{21}x_1 + a_{22}x_1 + \cdots + a_{2n}x_1 = y_2 \\ &\;\vdots \\ &a_{n1}x_1 + a_{n2}x_1 + \cdots + a_{nn}x_1 = y_n \end{aligned}$$

Writing the matrix of coefficients as $\mathbf{A} = [a_{ij}]$, the column vector of unknowns as $\mathbf{X} = [x_j]$, and the column vector of constants as $\mathbf{Y} = [y_j]$, we may write this system in matrix notation as $\mathbf{AX} = \mathbf{Y}$.

Not every system of linear equations has a solution, and not every solution of such a system is unique. The system $\mathbf{AX} = \mathbf{Y}$ *always* has a unique solution, however, if the matrix **A** is square and nonsingular. In this case the solution is found by premultiplying both sides of the equation $\mathbf{AX} = \mathbf{Y}$ by the inverse of **A**:

$$\text{since } \mathbf{AX} = \mathbf{Y} \Rightarrow \mathbf{A}^{-1}\mathbf{AX} = \mathbf{A}^{-1}\mathbf{Y} \Rightarrow \mathbf{X} = \mathbf{A}^{-1}\mathbf{Y}$$

Here is an example. Suppose we want to solve the following 3 × 3 system of equations:

$$\begin{aligned} 3x_1 + 4x_2 + 66x_3 &= 16 \\ -33x_2 + x_3 &= 77 \\ 42x_1 + 3x_2 + 2x_3 &= 12 \end{aligned}$$

We set this up and solve it in Excel as follows:

	A	B	C	D	E	F	G	H
1	**SOLVING SIMULTANEOUS EQUATIONS**							
2	**Matrix A of coefficients**				**Column vector y**		**Solution $A^{-1}Y$**	
3	3	4	66		16		0.4343	
4	0	-33	1		77		-2.3223	<-- {=MMULT(MINVERSE(A3:C5),E3:E5)}
5	42	3	2		12		0.3634	
6								
7	**Checking that the solution works**							
8		16						
9		77	<-- {=MMULT(A3:C5,G3:G5)}					
10		12						

In cells B8:B10 we check that the solution indeed solves the system by multiplying the matrix **A** times the column vector G3:G5.

Exercises

1. Use Excel to perform the following matrix operations:

a. $\begin{bmatrix} 2 & 12 & 6 \\ 4 & 8 & 7 \\ 1 & 0 & -9 \end{bmatrix} + \begin{bmatrix} 1 & 1 & 2 \\ 8 & 0 & -23 \\ 1 & 7 & 3 \end{bmatrix}$

b. $\begin{bmatrix} 2 & -9 \\ 5 & 0 \\ 6 & -6 \end{bmatrix} \begin{bmatrix} 3 & 1 & 1 \\ 2 & 3 & 2 \end{bmatrix}$

c. $\begin{bmatrix} 2 & 0 & 6 \\ 4 & 8 & 7 \\ 1 & 0 & -9 \end{bmatrix} \begin{bmatrix} 1 & 1 & 2 \\ 8 & 0 & -2 \\ 1 & 7 & 3 \end{bmatrix}$

2. Find the inverses of the following matrices:

a. $\begin{bmatrix} 1 & 2 & 8 & 9 \\ 2 & 5 & 3 & 0 \\ 4 & 4 & 2 & 7 \\ 5 & -2 & 1 & 6 \end{bmatrix}$

b. $\begin{bmatrix} 3 & 2 & 1 \\ 6 & -1 & 3 \\ 7 & 4 & 3 \end{bmatrix}$

c. $\begin{bmatrix} 20 & 2 & 3 & -3 \\ 2 & 10 & 2 & -2 \\ 3 & 2 & 40 & 9 \\ -3 & -2 & 9 & 33 \end{bmatrix}$

3. Transpose the following matrices using the Excel array function **Transpose**:

a. $\mathbf{A} = \begin{bmatrix} 3 & 2 & 1 \\ -15 & 4 & 1 \\ 6 & -9 & 1 \end{bmatrix}$

b. $\mathbf{B} = \begin{bmatrix} 1 & 2 & 3 & 4 & 5 \\ -2 & 7 & -9 & 0 & 0 \\ 3 & -3 & 11 & 12 & 1 \end{bmatrix}$

4. Solve the following system of equations by using matrices:

$$\begin{aligned} 3x \; +4y \; -6z \; -9w &= 15 \\ 2x \; - y \qquad\quad +w &= 2 \\ y \; +z \; +w &= 3 \\ x \; +y \; -z \qquad &= 1 \end{aligned}$$

5. Solve the equations $\mathbf{AX} = \mathbf{Y}$, where

$$\mathbf{A} = \begin{bmatrix} 13 & -8 & -3 \\ -8 & 10 & -1 \\ -3 & -1 & 11 \end{bmatrix}, \quad \mathbf{Y} = \begin{bmatrix} 20 \\ -5 \\ 0 \end{bmatrix}, \quad \mathbf{X} = \begin{bmatrix} x_1 \\ x_2 \\ x_3 \end{bmatrix}$$

6. An ill-conditioned matrix is a matrix that "almost doesn't have" an inverse. A set of examples of such matrices are Hilbert matrices. An n-dimensional Hilbert matrix looks like this:

$$\mathbf{H}_n = \begin{bmatrix} 1 & 1/2 & \cdots & 1/n \\ 1/2 & 1/3 & \cdots & 1/(n+1) \\ \vdots & & & \\ 1/n & 1/(n+1) & & 1/(2n-1) \end{bmatrix}$$

a. Calculate the inverses of $\mathbf{H}_2$, $\mathbf{H}_3$, and $\mathbf{H}_8$.

b. Consider the following system of equations:

$$\mathbf{H}_n \begin{bmatrix} x_1 \\ x_2 \\ \vdots \\ x_n \end{bmatrix} = \begin{bmatrix} 1 + 1/2 + \cdots + 1/n \\ 1/2 + 1/3 + \cdots + 1/(n+1) \\ \vdots \\ 1/n + 1/(n+1) + \cdots + 1/(2n-1) \end{bmatrix}$$

Find the answers to these problems by inspection.

c. Now solve $\mathbf{H}_n * \mathbf{X} = \mathbf{Y}$ for $n = 2, 8, 14$. How do you explain the differences?

32 The Gauss-Seidel Method

32.1 Overview

Many simultaneous equations can be solved by *recursive iteration*. In these methods we successively substitute a solution for one equation into another of the simultaneous equations until a solution is reached. These *Gauss-Seidel* methods are often efficient in solving complicated systems of equations. In this book we use them in Chapters 3–4 in solving for the solutions of pro forma financial statements (though we let Excel do the work!). With some further perspective, this chapter illustrates a widespread and useful computational technique for numerically solving complex systems.

32.2 A Simple Example

Suppose we are trying to solve the simultaneous linear equations

$$2x + 3y = 10$$
$$x - 4y = 2$$

The first equation solves to give $x = (10 - 3y)/2$, and from the second equation we obtain $y = (x - 2)/4$. To use the Gauss-Seidel method, we set some initial value for y; for example, we can let $y = 0$. If $y = 0$, then $x = (10 - 3*0)/2 = 5$. But if $x = 5$, then $y = (x - 2)/4 = (5 - 2)/4 = 0.75$. If we keep going, we will see that ultimately the values of x and y converge to a solution to the equations. Here is the problem, set up as an Excel table:

	A	B	C	D
1	GAUSS-SEIDEL METHOD: SOLUTION BY ITERATIVE SUBSTITUTION			
2		y	x	
3		0	5	
4	=(C3-2)/4 -->	0.75	3.875	<-- =(10-3*B4)/2
5	=(C4-2)/4 -->	0.46875	4.296875	<-- =(10-3*B5)/2
6	=(C5-2)/4 -->	0.574219	4.138672	<-- =(10-3*B6)/2
7		0.534668	4.197998	
8		0.5495	4.175751	
9		0.543938	4.184093	
10		0.546023	4.180965	
11		0.545241	4.182138	
12		0.545535	4.181698	
13		0.545425	4.181863	
14		0.545466	4.181801	

As you can see, the values converge. It follows from the way we have constructed the values that the limits of the two sequences are the solutions to the equations.

32.3 A More Concise Solution

A neater way of solving the same problem is to set up the following spreadsheet:

	A	B	C
1	GAUSS-SEIDEL METHOD--SHORTCUT		
2	Marker	5	
3	y	5	<-- =IF(B2<>0,B2,(B4-2)/4)
4	x	-2.5	<-- =(10-3*B3)/2

How does this implementation of recursive solutions work? If you set **Marker** equal to some nonzero value, c, then you see, as in the spreadsheet picture, that $y = c$ and $x = (10 - 3c)/2$. Once you let **Marker** equal zero, then the iterative process starts, and if there is a solution, Excel will find it. To make sure your spreadsheet recalculates, you have to go to the **Tools|Options|Calculation** box and click **Iteration**. See the note on this topic in section 3.2. Here's the solution:

	A	B	C
1	**GAUSS-SEIDEL METHOD--SHORTCUT**		
2	Marker	0	
3	y	0.545301	<-- =IF(B2<>0,B2,(B4-2)/4)
4	x	4.182049	<-- =(10-3*B3)/2

32.4 Conclusion

The Gauss-Seidel method is a somewhat untidy way of solving simultaneous equations. The solution may not always converge, and convergence may depend on whether x or y is solved for first. The advantage of the method is that it assures us that what we do in many financial models makes sense by allowing us to construct a model in which we set up the relations between the variables without asking how the equations are to be solved. If we observe convergence, then we have a solution. The financial statement models of Chapters 3 and 4 are examples of how powerful the Gauss-Seidel method can be.

Exercises

Solve the following system using the Gauss-Seidel method:

$$13x - 8y - 3z = 20$$
$$-8x + 10y - z = -5$$
$$-3x - y + 11z = 0$$

Note that in order to get a solution, you may have to hit the **F9** (recalculate spreadsheet) key a few times. You will have gotten a solution if the numbers on the screen stop changing.

33 Excel Functions

33.1 Overview

Excel contains several hundred functions. This chapter surveys only those functions used in the book. The following functions are discussed:

- Financial functions: **NPV**, **IRR**, **PV**, **PMT**, **XIRR**, **XNPV**
- Date functions: **Now**, **Today**, **Date**, **Weekday**, **Month**, **Datedif**
- Statistical functions: **Average**, **Var**, **Varp**, **Stdev**, **Stdevp**, **Correl**, **Covar**
- Regression functions: **Slope**, **Intercept**, **Rsq**, **Linest**
- Conditional functions: **If**, **VLookup**, **HLookup**
- **Large**, **Rank**, **Percentile**, **Percentrank**
- **Count**, **CountA**, **CountIf**
- **Offset**

A separate chapter, Chapter 34, is devoted to the important topic of array functions.

33.2 Financial Functions

33.2.1 NPV

The Excel definition of **NPV** differs somewhat from the standard finance definition. In the finance literature, the net present value of a sequence of cash flows $C_0, C_1, C_2, \ldots, C_n$ at a discount rate r refers to the expression

$$\sum_{t=0}^{n} \frac{C_t}{(1+r)^t} \quad \text{or} \quad C_0 + \sum_{t=1}^{n} \frac{C_t}{(1+r)^t}$$

In many cases C_0 represents the cost of the asset purchased and is therefore negative.

The Excel definition of **NPV** always assumes that the first cash flow occurs after one period. The user who wants the standard finance expression must therefore calculate **NPV(r,{C**$_1$**, . . . , C**$_n$**})** + **C**$_0$. Here is an example:

	A	B	C	D	E	F	G
1	EXCEL'S NPV FUNCTION						
2	Discount rate	10%					
3	Year	0	1	2	3	4	5
4	Cash flow	-100	35	33	34	25	16
5							
6	NPV	$11.65	<-- =NPV(B2,C4:G4)+B4				

The **NPV** function has a potential bug: It differentiates between blank cells and cells containing zeros. This can cause some confusion, as can be seen in the following example. The present value of the cash flows in B4:B6 is 65.75, which corresponds to $\frac{100}{1.15^3}$. But in the otherwise similar example of the cash flows in B11:B13, Excel's NPV function regards the first cash flow as being 100, and returns the answer $\frac{100}{1.15} = 86.96$. So—in using **NPV** you have to be explicit in putting in zeros for zero cash flows.

	A	B	C
1	NPV POTENTIAL PROBLEM		
2	Discount rate	15%	
3	Year	Cash flow	
4	1	0	
5	2	0	
6	3	100	
7			
8	Present value	65.75	<-- =NPV(B2,B4:B6)
9			
10	Year	Cash flow	
11	1		
12	2		
13	3	100	
14			
15	Present value	86.96	<-- =NPV(B2,B11:B13)

33.2.2 IRR

The internal rate of return (IRR) of a sequence of cash flows C_0, C_1, $C_2, \ldots, C_n$ is an interest rate r such that the net present value of the cash flows is zero:

$$\sum_{t=0}^{n} \frac{C_t}{(1+r)^t} = 0$$

The Excel syntax for the **IRR** function is **IRR(cash flows**, **guess**). Here **cash flows** represents the whole sequence of cash flows, including the first cash flow C_0, and **guess** is a starting point for the algorithm that calculates the IRR.

First a simple example—consider the cash flows given in the NPV example:

	A	B	C	D	E	F	G
1	EXCEL'S IRR FUNCTION						
2	Year	0	1	2	3	4	5
3	Cash flow	-100	35	33	34	25	16
4							
5	IRR	15.00%	<-- =IRR(B3:G3,0)				
6		15.00%	<-- =IRR(B3:G3)				

Note (see cell B6) that **guess** is not necessary when there is only one IRR. However, the choice of **guess** can make a difference when there is more than one IRR. Consider, for example, the following cash flows:

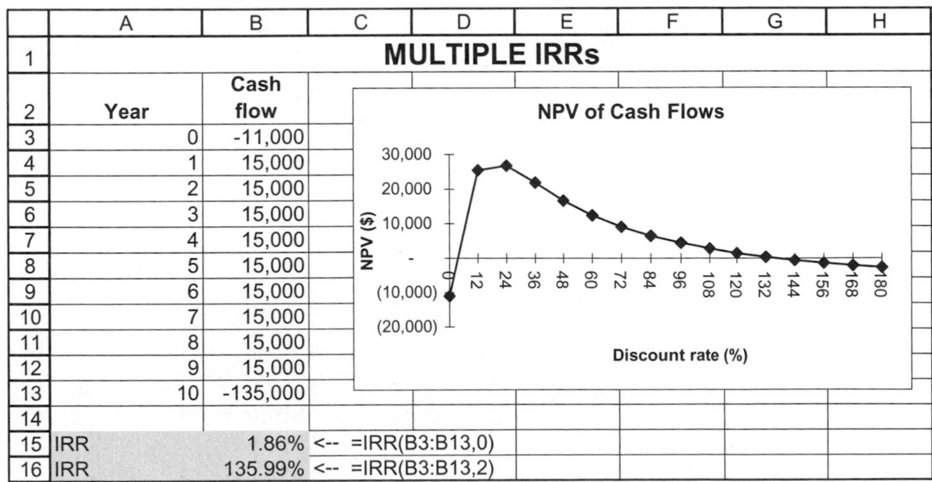

	A	B	C
1	MULTIPLE IRRs		
2	Year	Cash flow	
3	0	-11,000	
4	1	15,000	
5	2	15,000	
6	3	15,000	
7	4	15,000	
8	5	15,000	
9	6	15,000	
10	7	15,000	
11	8	15,000	
12	9	15,000	
13	10	-135,000	
14			
15	IRR	1.86%	<-- =IRR(B3:B13,0)
16	IRR	135.99%	<-- =IRR(B3:B13,2)

The graph (created from a **Data|Table** that is not shown) shows that there are two IRRs, since the NPV curve crosses the *x*-axis twice. To find both these IRRs, we have to change the **guess** (though the precise value of guess is still not critical). In the next example we have changed both guesses, but still get the same answer:

	A	B	C	D
15	IRR	1.86%	<-- =IRR(B3:B13,0.1)	
16	IRR	135.99%	<-- =IRR(B3:B13,0.8)	

Note A given set of cash flows typically has more than one IRR if there is more than one change of sign in the cash flows. In this example, the initial cash flow is negative, and CF_1–CF_9 are positive (this fact accounts for one change of sign); but then CF_{10} is negative—making a second change of sign. If you suspect that a set of cash flows has more than one IRR, the first thing to do is to use Excel to make a graph of the NPVs, as we did. The number of times that the NPV graph crosses the *x*-axis identifies the number of IRRs (and also their approximate values).

33.2.3 PV Function

This function calculates the present value of an annuity (a series of fixed periodic payments). For example:

	A	B	C
1	**THE PV FUNCTION**		
2	**Payments made at the end of the period**		
3	Rate	10%	
4	Number of periods	10	
5	Payment	100	
6	Present value	(614.46)	<-- =PV(B3,B4,B5)

Thus $\$614.46 = \sum_{t=1}^{10} \frac{100}{(1.10)^t}$. Here are two things to note about the **PV** function:

• Writing **PV(B3,B4,B5)** assumes that payments are made at dates 1, 2, . . . , 10. If the payments are made at dates 0, 1, 2, . . . , 9, you should write the following:

	A	B	C
8	**Payments made at the beginning of the period**		
9	Rate	10%	
10	Number of periods	10	
11	Payment	100	
12	Present value	(675.90)	<-- =PV(B9,B10,B11,,1)

The formula **PV(B9,B10,B11,,1)** can also be generated from the dialogue box:

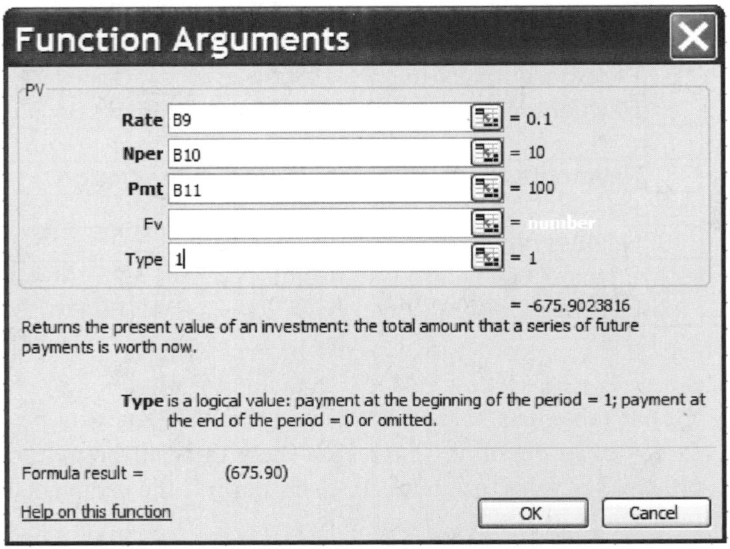

• Irritatingly, the **PV** function (and the **PMT**, **IPMT**, and **PPMT** functions—see next two subsections) produces a negative number (there is a logic here, but it's not worth explaining). The solution is obvious: Either write **-PV(B3,B4,B5)** or let the payment be negative by writing **PV(B3,B4,-B5)**.

33.2.4 PMT

The **PMT** function calculates the payment necessary to pay off a loan with equal payments over a fixed number of periods. For example, the first calculation in the following spreadsheet shows that a loan of $1,000 to be paid off over 10 years at an interest rate of 8 percent will require equal annual payments of interest and principal of $149.03. The calculation performed is the solution of the following equation:

$$\sum_{t=1}^{n} \frac{X}{(1+r)^t} = \text{Initial loan principal}$$

	A	B	C
1	**THE PMT FUNCTION**		
2	**Payments made at the end of the period**		
3	Rate	8%	
4	Number of periods	10	
5	Principal	1000	
6	Payment	-149.03	<-- =PMT(B3,B4,B5)
7			
8	**Payments made at the beginning of the period**		
9	Rate	8%	
10	Number of periods	10	
11	Principal	1000	
12	Payment	-137.99	<-- =PMT(B9,B10,B11,,1)

Loan tables can be calculated using the **PMT** function. These tables—explained in detail in Chapter 1—show the split between interest and principal of each payment. In each period, the payment on the loan (calculated with **PMT**) is split:

- We first calculate the interest owing for that period on the principal outstanding at the beginning of the period. In the following table, at the end of year 1 we owe $80 (= 8 percent * $1,000) of interest on the loan principal outstanding at the beginning of the year.
- The remainder of the payment (for year 1: $69.03) goes to reduce the principal outstanding.

	A	B	C	D	E	F
1	Loan Table					
2	Interest	8%				
3	Number of periods	10				
4	Principal	1,000			=-PMT(B2,B3,B4)	
5	Annual payment	149.03	<-- =-PMT(B2,B3,B4)			
6						
7				Split of payment between		
8	**Year**	**Principal at beginning of year**	**Payment**	**Interest**	**Repayment of principal**	
9	1	1,000.00	149.03	80.00	69.03	<-- =C9-D9
10	2	930.97	149.03	74.48	74.55	
11	3	856.42	149.03	68.51	80.52	
12	4	775.90	149.03	62.07	86.96	
13	5	688.95	149.03	55.12	93.91	
14	6	595.03	149.03	47.60	101.43	
15	7	493.60	149.03	39.49	109.54	
16	8	384.06	149.03	30.73	118.30	
17	9	265.76	149.03	21.26	127.77	
18	10	137.99	149.03	11.04	137.99	
19	=B9-E9				=$B$2*B9	
20						

Note that at the end of the 10 years the repayment of principal is exactly equal to the principal outstanding at the beginning of the year (i.e., the loan has been paid off).

33.2.5 The Functions IPMT and PPMT

As we have seen, a loan table shows the split of a loan's flat payments (computed with **PMT**) between interest and principal. In the loan table of the previous subsection, we computed this split by first computing the flat payment per period (column C), then taking the interest on the principal at the beginning of the period (column D) and finally subtracting this interest from the period's total payment (column E).

IPMT and **PPMT** perform this calculation without the necessity of relying on the total payment. Here's an example:

	A	B	C	D	E
1			IPMT AND PPMT		
2	Interest	8%			
3	Number of periods	10			
4	Principal	1,000			
5					
6	Year	Principal payment at end year		Interest payment at end year	
7	1	$69.03	<-- =PPMT($B$2,A7,$B$3,-$B$4)	$80.00	<-- =IPMT($B$2,A7,$B$3,-$B$4)
8	2	$74.55	<-- =PPMT($B$2,A8,$B$3,-$B$4)	$74.48	<-- =IPMT($B$2,A8,$B$3,-$B$4)
9	3	$80.52		$68.51	
10	4	$86.96		$62.07	
11	5	$93.91		$55.12	
12	6	$101.43		$47.60	
13	7	$109.54		$39.49	
14	8	$118.30		$30.73	
15	9	$127.77		$21.26	
16	10	$137.99		$11.04	

As you can see, the payments computed are the same as in the loan table of the previous subsection.

33.3 Dates and Date Functions

Read the quote from the Excel help that follows and you will know almost everything you need to know about entering dates into your spreadsheet:

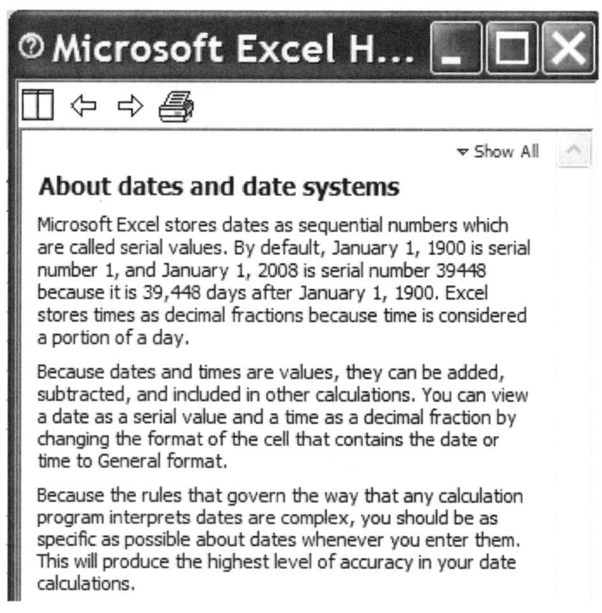

Microsoft Excel H...

Show All

About dates and date systems

Microsoft Excel stores dates as sequential numbers which are called serial values. By default, January 1, 1900 is serial number 1, and January 1, 2008 is serial number 39448 because it is 39,448 days after January 1, 1900. Excel stores times as decimal fractions because time is considered a portion of a day.

Because dates and times are values, they can be added, subtracted, and included in other calculations. You can view a date as a serial value and a time as a decimal fraction by changing the format of the cell that contains the date or time to General format.

Because the rules that govern the way that any calculation program interprets dates are complex, you should be as specific as possible about dates whenever you enter them. This will produce the highest level of accuracy in your date calculations.

The basic fact you need to know is that Excel translates dates into a number: Here's an example: Suppose you decide to type a date into a cell:

A2 ▾ X ✓ = 3Feb2001

	A	B	C	D
1				
2	3Feb2001			
3				
4				

When you hit **Enter**, Excel decides that you've entered a date. Here's the way it appears:

A2 ▾ = 2/3/2001

	A	B	C	D
1				
2	3-Feb-01			
3				

Note that in the formula bar (indicated by the arrow above), Excel interprets the date entered as **2/3/2001**.[1] When you reformat the cell as **Format|Cells|Number|General**, you see that Excel interprets this date as the number 36925, the number 1 being January 1, 1900.

	A	B
1		
2	36925	
3		

Spreadsheet dates can be subtracted: In the next spreadsheet we've entered two dates and subtracted them to find the number of days between the dates:

1. The way these dates appear and are interpreted depends on the Regional Settings entered in the Windows Control Panel. Our settings in this book follow the U.S. conventions.

	B	C	D	E
5		2-Dec-00		
6		8-Mar-99		
7	Days between	635	<-- =C5-C6	

(Cell C7 initially showed a date, but was then reformatted with **Format|Cells|Number|General**.)

You can also add a number to a date to find another date. What, for example, was the date 165 days after November 16, 1947?

	C	D	E
11	16-Nov-47		
12	29-Apr-48	<-- =C11+165	

33.3.1 Stretching Out Dates

In the two cells that follow we've put in two dates and then "stretched" the cells out to add more dates with the same difference between them:

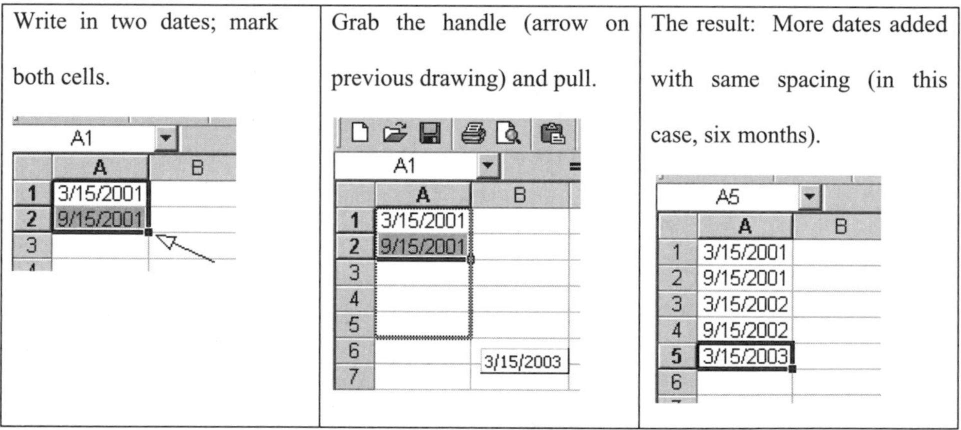

Write in two dates; mark both cells. | Grab the handle (arrow on previous drawing) and pull. | The result: More dates added with same spacing (in this case, six months).

33.3.2 Times in a Spreadsheet

Hours, minutes, and the like can also be typed into a cell. In the next cell we've typed in 8:22:

When we hit **Enter**, Excel interprets this entry as 8:22 A.M.:

Excel recognizes 24-hour times and also recognizes the symbol **a** for A.M. and **p** for P.M.:

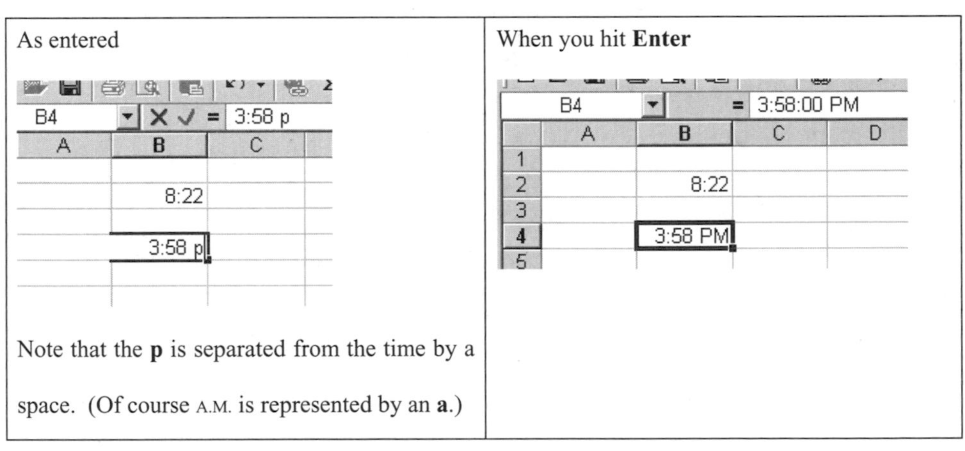

As entered	When you hit **Enter**
Note that the **p** is separated from the time by a space. (Of course A.M. is represented by an **a**.)	

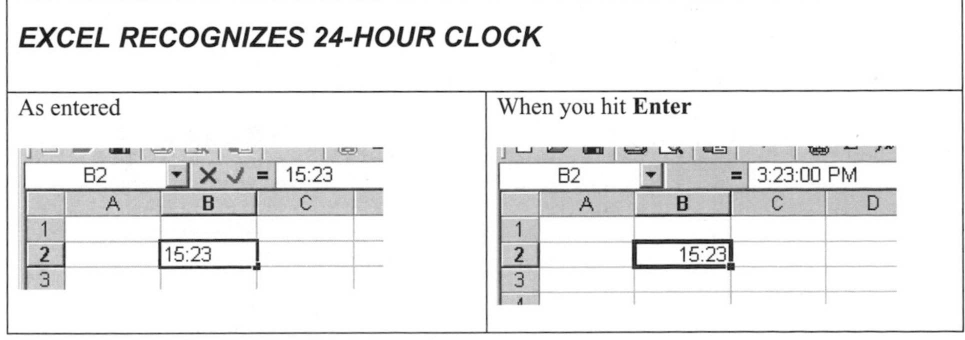

EXCEL RECOGNIZES 24-HOUR CLOCK	
As entered	When you hit **Enter**

You can subtract times just as you subtract dates; cell B5 tells you that 7 hours and 32 minutes have elapsed between the two times (ignore the "AM" in B5):

	B	C	D
3	3:48 PM		
4	8:16 AM		
5	7:32 AM	<-- =B3-B4	

When you reformat these cells with **Format|Cells|Number|General**, you can see that times are represented in Excel as fractions of a day:

	B	C	D
3	0.658333		
4	0.344444		
5	0.313889	<-- =B3-B4	

If you type in a date and a time and reformat, you can see the same thing:

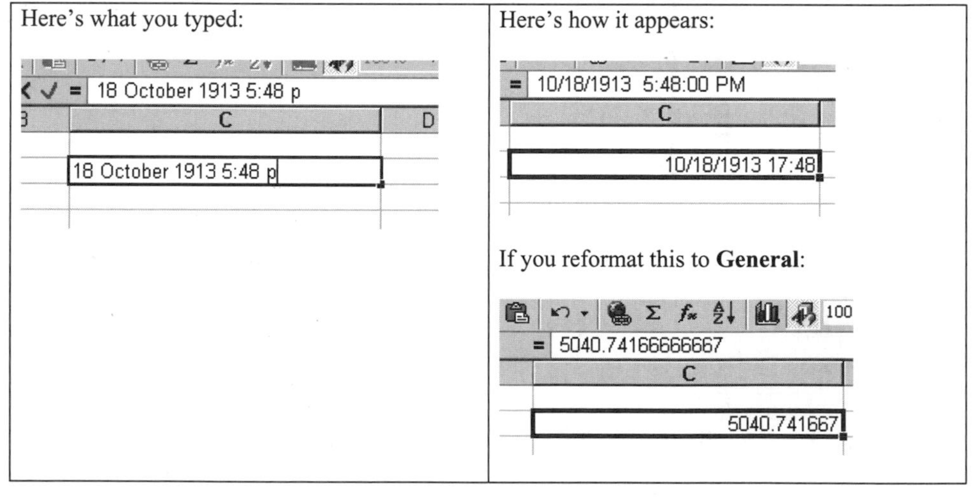

33.3.3 Time and Date Functions in Excel

Excel has a whole set of time and date functions. Here are several functions that we find useful:

- **Now** reads the computer clock and represents the date and the time. **Now** takes no arguments and is written with empty parentheses: **Now( )**.
- **Today** reads the computer's clock and prints the date. This function, like **Now** is written with empty parentheses: **Today( )**.
- **Date(yyyy,mm,dd)** gives the date entered.
- **Weekday** gives the day of the week.
- **Month** gives the month.

Here are the first three functions in a spreadsheet:

	A	B	C
1	**FORMATTING NOW(), TODAY(), DATE()**		
2	**Serial representation**	**Date/time format**	
3	39339.48933	9/14/2007 11:44	<-- =NOW()
4	39339	9/14/2007	<-- =TODAY()
5	36245	3/26/1999	<-- =DATE(1999,3,26)
6			
7	**Different formatting of Now()**		
8		September 14, 2007	<-- =NOW()
9		9/14/2007 11:44	<-- =NOW()
10		11:44 AM	<-- =NOW()
11			
12	**When was day 1?**		
13	1	<-- =DATE(1900,1,1)	

The use of **Weekday** and **Month** is self-explanatory:

	A	B	C
3	3-Nov-01	7	<-- =WEEKDAY(A3)
4		7	<-- =WEEKDAY("3nov2001")
5	In **Weekday**, 1=Sunday, 2=Monday, etc.		
6			
7		11	<-- =MONTH(A3)
8		12	<-- =MONTH("22dec2003")

33.3.4 Calculating the Diference between Two Dates: The Function Datedif

The Excel function **Datedif** computes the difference between two dates in various useful ways:

	A	B	C
1	DATEDIF COMPUTES DIFFERENCE BETWEEN TWO DATES		
2	Date1	3-Apr-47	
3	Date2	22-Dec-02	
4			
5			**Explanation**
6	55	<-- =DATEDIF(B2,B3,"y")	Number of years between dates
7	668	<-- =DATEDIF(B2,B3,"m")	Number of months between dates
8	20352	<-- =DATEDIF(B2,B3,"d")	Number of days between dates
9	19	<-- =DATEDIF(B2,B3,"md")	Number of days in excess of full number of months
10	8	<-- =DATEDIF(B2,B3,"ym")	Number of months in excess of full number of years
11	263	<-- =DATEDIF(B2,B3,"yd")	Number of days in excess of full number of years

If Date1 is the author's birth date and Date2 is today, then the author is currently 55 years and 263 days old (cells A6 and A11).

33.4 The Functions XIRR and XNPV

The functions **XIRR** and **XNPV** calculate the internal rate of return and the net present value for a series of cash flows received on specific dates. They are especially useful for calculating IRR and NPV when the dates are unevenly spaced.[2] If you do not have these functions, you will have to activate **Tools|Add-ins** and then click on **Analysis ToolPak:**

2. Excel's IRR function assumes that the first cash flow occurs today, the next cash flow occurs one period hence, the following cash flow two periods hence, and so on. Excel's NPV function assumes that the first cash flow occurs one period from now, the next cash flow in two periods, and so on. We call this pattern "even spacing of cash flows." When this is not the case, you'll need the **XIRR** and **XNPV** functions.

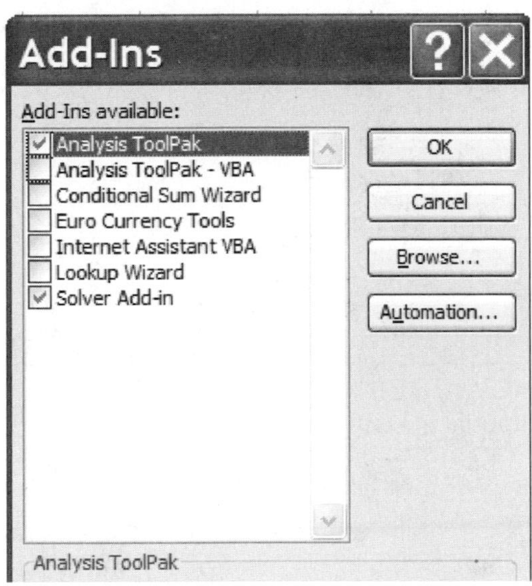

33.4.1 XIRR

Here's an example: You pay $600 on 16 February 2001 for an asset that repays $100 on 5 April 2001, $100 on 15 July 2001, and then $100 on every 22 September from 2001 until 2009. The dates are not evenly spaced, so that you cannot use **IRR**. With **XIRR** (cell B16 in the next spreadsheet), you can compute the *annualized IRR*.

	A	B	C
1	**THE EXCEL FUNCTION XIRR**		
2	**Date**	**Payment**	
3	16-Feb-01	-600	
4	5-Apr-01	100	
5	15-Jul-01	100	
6	22-Sep-01	100	
7	22-Sep-02	100	
8	22-Sep-03	100	
9	22-Sep-04	100	
10	22-Sep-05	100	
11	22-Sep-06	100	
12	22-Sep-07	100	
13	22-Sep-08	100	
14	22-Sep-09	100	
15			
16	**XIRR**	21.97%	<-- =XIRR(B3:B14,A3:A14)

The **XIRR** works by discounting each cash flow at the daily rate. In our example the first cash flow of $100 occurs 48 days from now, the second in 149 days, ... The XIRR transforms 21.97 percent to a daily rate and uses it to discount the cash flows:

$$-600+\frac{100}{(1.2197)^{48/365}}+\frac{100}{(1.2197)^{149/365}}+\ldots+\frac{100}{(1.2197)^{3140/365}}=0$$

	A	B	C	D	E
1	**HOW DOES XIRR WORK?** **XIRR computes the daily internal rate of return**				
2	**Date**	**Payment**	**Days from initial date**	**Present value**	
3	16-Feb-01	-600		-600.00	
4	5-Apr-01	100	48	97.42	<-- =B4/(1+$B$16)^(C4/365)
5	15-Jul-01	100	149	92.21	<-- =B5/(1+$B$16)^(C5/365)
6	22-Sep-01	100	218	88.81	<-- =B6/(1+$B$16)^(C6/365)
7	22-Sep-02	100	583	72.81	
8	22-Sep-03	100	948	59.70	
9	22-Sep-04	100	1,314	48.91	
10	22-Sep-05	100	1,679	40.10	
11	22-Sep-06	100	2,044	32.88	
12	22-Sep-07	100	2,409	26.96	
13	22-Sep-08	100	2,775	22.09	
14	22-Sep-09	100	3,140	18.11	
15					
16	**XIRR**	21.97%	<-- =XIRR(B3:B14,A3:A14)	0.00	<-- =SUM(D3:D14)
17					
18	Cell C4 contains the				
19	formula=A4-$A$3				

33.4.2 XNPV

The function **XNPV** computes the NPV for unevenly spaced cash flows. In the next example we use the function to compute the NPV on the same example we used for **XIRR**.

	A	B	C
1	**THE EXCEL FUNCTION XNPV**		
2	**Date**	**Payment**	
3	16-Feb-01	-600	
4	5-Apr-01	100	
5	15-Jul-01	100	
6	22-Sep-01	100	
7	22-Sep-02	100	
8	22-Sep-03	100	
9	22-Sep-04	100	
10	22-Sep-05	100	
11	22-Sep-06	100	
12	22-Sep-07	100	
13	22-Sep-08	100	
14	22-Sep-09	100	
15			
16	Discount rate	15%	
17	XNPV	97.29	<-- =XNPV(B16,B3:B14,A3:A14)

Notice that **XNPV** requires you to indicate all the cash flows (starting with the initial cash flow), as opposed to **NPV**, which starts from the first cash flow.

33.5 Statistical Functions

Excel contains a number of statistical functions. We illustrate these functions using the following data set:

	A	B	C	D
1	**BASIC STATISTICAL FUNCTIONS**			
2	**Observation**	**X**	**Y**	
3	1	35.30	10.98	
4	2	29.70	11.13	
5	3	30.80	12.51	
6	4	58.80	8.40	
7	5	61.40	9.27	
8	6	71.30	8.73	
9	7	74.40	6.36	
10	8	76.70	8.50	
11	9	70.70	7.82	
12	10	57.50	9.14	
13				
14	Average	56.6600	9.2840	<-- =AVERAGE(C3:C12)
15	Sample variance	334.1493	3.2342	<-- =VAR(C3:C12)
16	Population variance	300.7344	2.9108	<-- =VARP(C3:C12)
17	Sample standard deviation	18.2798	1.7984	<-- =STDEV(C3:C12)
18	Population standard deviation	17.3417	1.7061	<-- =STDEVP(C3:C12)
19				
20	Correlation	-0.9049	<-- =CORREL(C3:C12,B3:B12)	
21	Covariance	-26.7746	<-- =COVAR(C3:C12,B3:B12)	
22				
23	Regression intercept	14.3285	<-- =INTERCEPT(C3:C12,B3:B12)	
24	Regression slope	-0.0890	<-- =SLOPE(C3:C12,B3:B12)	
25	Regression r-squared	0.8189	<-- =RSQ(C3:C12,B3:B12)	

The functions **Varp** and **Stdevp** calculate the population variance and standard deviation, whereas the functions **Var** and **Stdev** calculate the sample variance and standard deviation. The difference between these two functions is that **Varp** assumes that your data include the whole population and thus divides by the number of data points, whereas **Var** assumes that the data are a sample from the distribution:[3]

$$\text{Varp}(x_1,\ldots,x_N)=\frac{1}{N}\sum_{i=1}^{N}[x_i-\text{Average}(x_1,\ldots,x_N)]^2$$

$$\text{Stdevp}(x_1,\ldots,x_N)=\sqrt{\text{Varp}(x_1,\ldots,x_N)}$$

3. We cannot resist a quote from *Numerical Recipes*, a wonderful book by W. H. Press, B. P. Flannery, S. A. Teukolsky, and W. T. Vetterling (Cambridge University Press, 1986): "There is a long story about why the denominator [of **Var**] is $N-1$ instead of N. If you have never heard that story, you may consult any good statistics text. Here we will be content to note that the $N-1$ *should* be changed to N if you are ever in the situation of measuring the variance of a distribution whose mean $\bar{x}$ is known *a priori* rather than being estimated from the data. (We might also comment that if the difference between N and $N-1$ ever matters to you, then you are probably up to no good anyway—e.g., trying to substantiate a questionable hypothesis with marginal data.)"

$$\text{Var}(x_1, \ldots, x_N) = \frac{1}{N-1}\sum_{i=1}^{N}[x_i - \text{Average}(x_1, \ldots, x_N)]^2$$

$$\text{Stdev}(x_1, \ldots, x_N) = \sqrt{\text{Var}(x_1, \ldots, x_N)}$$

Here's an example, showing both the brute-force calculations and the Excel functions **Var** and **Varp**.

	A	B	C	D
1	VAR VERSUS VARP			
2	Observation	X	$(X_i$ - average$)^2$	
3	1	35.30	456.2496	<-- =(B3-$B$14)^2
4	2	29.70	726.8416	
5	3	30.80	668.7396	
6	4	58.80	4.5796	
7	5	61.40	22.4676	
8	6	71.30	214.3296	
9	7	74.40	314.7076	
10	8	76.70	401.6016	
11	9	70.70	197.1216	
12	10	57.50	0.7056	
13				
14	Average	56.66	<-- =AVERAGE(B3:B12)	
15				
16	Var	334.1493	<-- =VAR(B3:B12)	
17		334.1493	<-- =SUM(C3:C12)/9	
18				
19	Varp	300.7344	<-- =VARP(B3:B12)	
20		300.7344	<-- =SUM(C3:C12)/10	

33.5.1 Covar and Correl

These two functions—used extensively in the portfolio chapters, 8–13—are used to compute the covariance and correlation of two series of numbers. For the definitions, we refer you to section 8.2. See the following example, in which we compute the covariance and correlation for returns on McDonald's stock and Wendy's stock. Note the two computations for the correlation. In the first (cell B33) we use the Excel **Correl** function; in cell B34 we use the definition correlation = Correlation(MCD,WEN) = Covar(MCD,WEN)/($\sigma_{MCD} * \sigma_{WEN}$). Because Excel's **Covar** is the population covariance (that is, divides by $1/M$, where

M is the population size), this definition can only be implemented if you use the Excel function **Stdevp** for the standard deviation.[4]

	A	B	C	D	E	F	G
1	**COMPUTING COVARIANCE AND CORRELATION FOR MCDONALD'S (MCD) AND WENDY'S (WEN)**						
2		**MCD**			**WEN**		
3	Date	Stock price	Return		Stock price	Return	
4	25-Jul-05	29.82			23.66		
5	1-Aug-05	31.04	4.01%		21.63	-8.97%	<-- =LN(E5/E4)
6	1-Sep-05	32.03	3.14%		20.72	-4.30%	
7	3-Oct-05	30.23	-5.78%		21.44	3.42%	
8	1-Nov-05	33.04	8.89%		23.39	8.71%	
9	1-Dec-05	32.92	-0.36%		25.45	8.44%	
10	3-Jan-06	34.18	3.76%		27.15	6.47%	
11	1-Feb-06	34.08	-0.29%		26.74	-1.52%	
12	1-Mar-06	33.54	-1.60%		28.67	6.97%	
13	3-Apr-06	33.75	0.62%		28.54	-0.45%	
14	1-May-06	32.38	-4.14%		27.92	-2.20%	
15	1-Jun-06	32.8	1.29%		27	-3.35%	
16	3-Jul-06	34.55	5.20%		27.87	3.17%	
17	1-Aug-06	35.04	1.41%		29.68	6.29%	
18	1-Sep-06	38.19	8.61%		31.12	4.74%	
19	2-Oct-06	40.92	6.90%		34.31	9.76%	
20	1-Nov-06	41.97	2.53%		32.38	-5.79%	
21	1-Dec-06	44.33	5.47%		32.9	1.59%	
22	3-Jan-07	44.35	0.05%		33.76	2.58%	
23	1-Feb-07	43.69	-1.50%		31.95	-5.51%	
24	1-Mar-07	45.05	3.07%		31.2	-2.38%	
25	2-Apr-07	48.28	6.92%		37.58	18.61%	
26	1-May-07	50.55	4.59%		40.13	6.57%	
27	1-Jun-07	50.76	0.41%		36.75	-8.80%	
28	2-Jul-07	52.5	3.37%		37.16	1.11%	
29							
30	Covariance	0.0009	<-- =COVAR(C5:C28,F5:F28)				
31							
32	Correlation						
33	Using Excel **Correl** function	0.3620	<-- =CORREL(C5:C28,F5:F28)				
34	Correlation = Covar(MCD,WEN)/(σ_{MCD}*σ_{WEN})	0.3620	<-- =COVAR(C5:C28,F5:F28)/(STDEVP(C5:C28)*STDEVP(F5:F28))				

33.6 Doing Regressions with Excel

There are several techniques to produce an ordinary least-squares regression with Excel. We illustrate two techniques using the data from the previous section.

4. If this sentence confuses you, either ignore it altogether or refer back to section 8.2.

The first technique involves the functions **Slope**, **Intercept**, and **Rsq**; these functions give the parameters for a simple regression of the data in column C on column B.

	A	B	C	D
1	**REGRESSIONS WITH EXCEL**			
2	**Observation**	**X**	**Y**	
3	1	35.3	10.98	
4	2	29.7	11.13	
5	3	30.8	12.51	
6	4	58.8	8.4	
7	5	61.4	9.27	
8	6	71.3	8.73	
9	7	74.4	6.36	
10	8	76.7	8.5	
11	9	70.7	7.82	
12	10	57.5	9.14	
13				
14	Regression intercept		14.3285	<-- =INTERCEPT(C3:C12,B3:B12)
15	Regression slope		-0.0890	<-- =SLOPE(C3:C12,B3:B12)
16	Regression r-squared		0.8189	<-- =RSQ(C3:C12,B3:B12)

Using these numbers, the best linear explanation of the relation between y and x is

$$y = 14.3285 - 0.0890x$$

About 82 percent of the variation in the data is explained by this linear relation.

Another way that we can produce a simple regression is to graph the data and let Excel calculate the ordinarily least squares (OLS) regression coefficients. To do so:

- First plot the data using an **XY Scatter Plot**.
- Double-click on the data and then go to **Insert|Trendline**. As the following picture shows, this function allows us to choose several types of regressions.

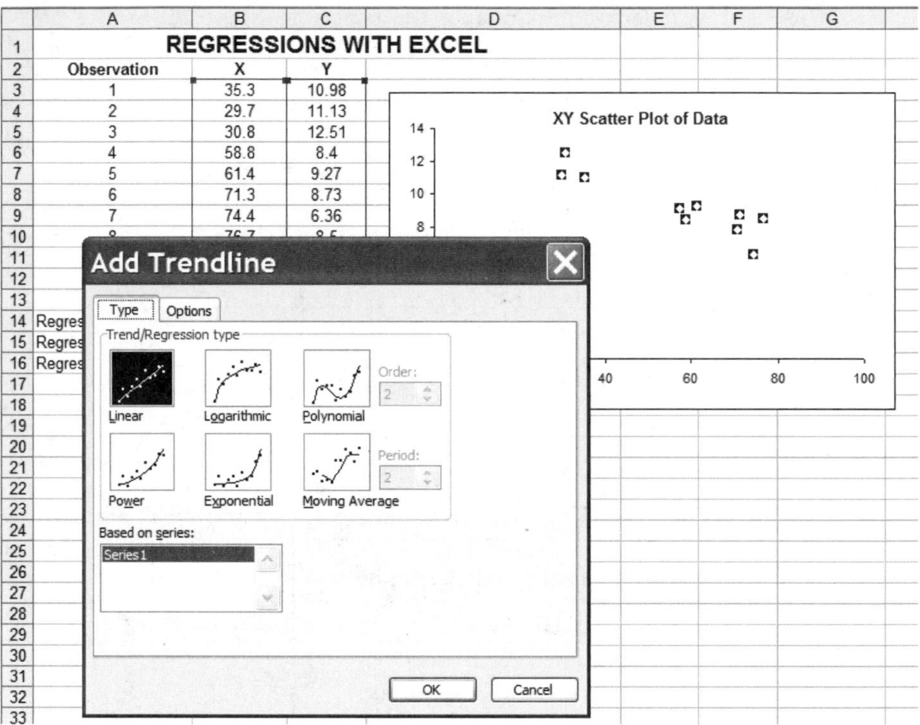

Choosing **Linear** produces the following plot (the equation and the R^2 are displayed on the chart by clicking the appropriate boxes on the **Options** tab of the dialogue box):

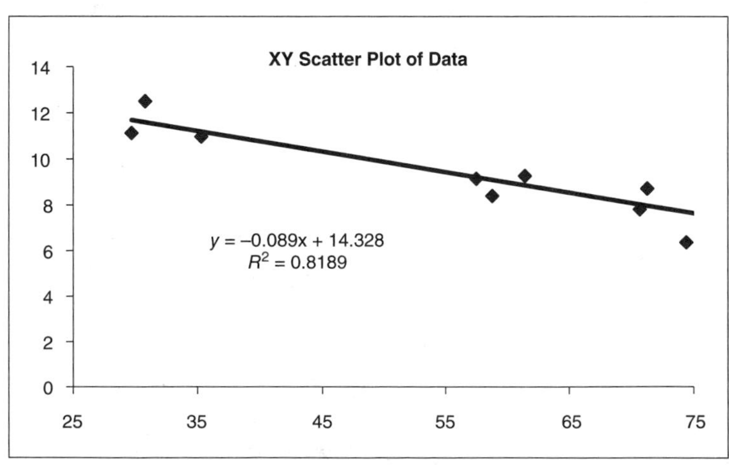

33.6.1 Index

The discussion of the **Index** function belongs in the section on statistics only because we want to use it in our next subsection. We sometimes want to pick an individual value out of an array. In the following example, the range of cells A2:C4 contains a mixture of numbers and names. To pick out an individual item from this range, we use **=Index(A2:C4,row,column)**, where **row** and **column** are relative to the range itself. Thus "Howie" appears in row 2 and column 3 of the range A2:C4.

	A	B	C
1	**USING THE INDEX FUNCTION**		
2	a	b	3
3	Simon	6	Howie
4	q	7	Jack
5			
6	Howie	<-- =INDEX(A2:C4,2,3)	

In the next subsection we use the **Index** function to pick out a single item in the **Linest** array.

33.6.2 Using Linest

Excel has an array function **Linest** whose output consists of a number of regression statistics for an ordinary least-squares regression.[5] Here is a picture of the spreadsheet and the **Linest** dialogue box:

5. There is also an Excel function **Logest**, whose syntax is exactly the same as that of **Linest**. **Logest** calculates the parameters to fit an exponential curve.

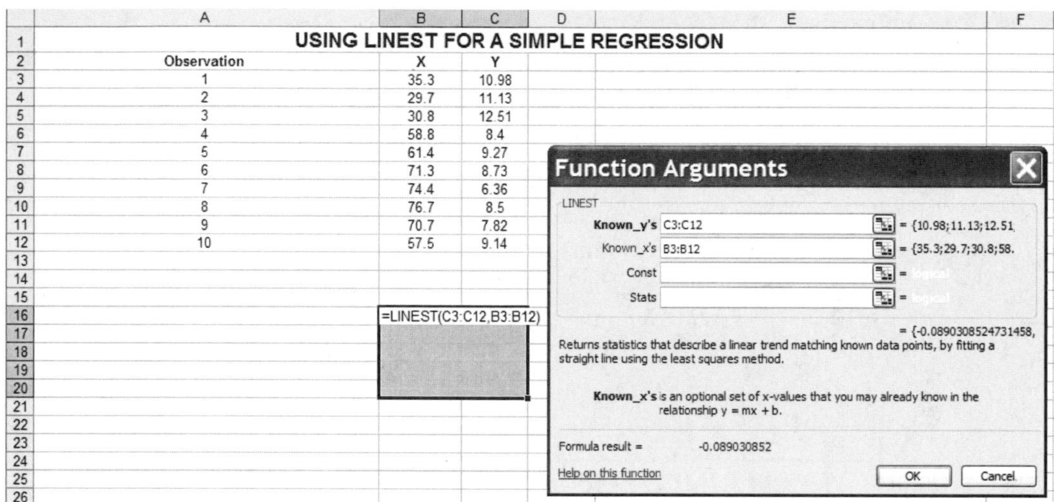

Linest is an array function (see next chapter); therefore, instead of **[Enter]**, we press [Control] + [Shift] + [Enter] at the same time. With the data from this example, we can use **Linest** to produce the following output:

	A	B	C	D
1	USING LINEST FOR A SIMPLE REGRESSION			
2	**Observation**	**X**	**Y**	
3	1	35.3	10.98	
4	2	29.7	11.13	
5	3	30.8	12.51	
6	4	58.8	8.4	
7	5	61.4	9.27	
8	6	71.3	8.73	
9	7	74.4	6.36	
10	8	76.7	8.5	
11	9	70.7	7.82	
12	10	57.5	9.14	
13				
14		**Linest output**		
15		**slope**	**intercept**	
16	Slope (also **=slope(C3:C12,B3:B12)**)-->	-0.0890	14.3285	<-- Intercept
17	Standard error of slope -->	0.0148	0.8770	<-- Standard error of intercept
18	R^2 (also **=Rsq(C3:C12,B3:B12)**) -->	0.8189	0.8117	<-- Standard error of y values (also **=Steyx(C3:C12,B3:B12)**)
19	F statistic -->	36.1825	8	<-- Degrees of freedom
20	SS_{xy} = Slope*(summed product of observations from means) -->	23.8377	5.2705	<-- SSE = Residual sum of squares
21				
22		Slope	-0.0890	<-- =INDEX(LINEST(C3:C12,B3:B12,,1),1,1)
23		Intercept	14.3285	<-- =INDEX(LINEST(C3:C12,B3:B12,,1),1,2)
24		R^2	0.8189	<-- =INDEX(LINEST(C3:C12,B3:B12,,1),3,1)
25		t-statistic	16.3376	<-- =C23/INDEX(LINEST(C3:C12,B3:B12,,1),2,2)
26				
27		Slope	-0.0890	<-- =INDEX(LINEST(C3:C12,B3:B12,,TRUE),1,1)
28		Standard error of slope	0.0148	<-- =INDEX(LINEST(C3:C12,B3:B12,,TRUE),2,1)
29		t-statistic	-6.0152	<-- =C27/C28

Linest produces a block of output without column headers or row labels that identify the output. Excel's Help provides a good explanation of the meaning of the output; in the preceding picture, we have added in the explanations.

Note the syntax of this function: **Linest(y-range,x-range,constant,statistics)**. The **y-range** is the range of dependent variables, and the **x-range** is the range of the independent variables. If **constant** is omitted (as in this case) or set to **True**, then the regression is calculated normally; if **constant** is set to **False**, then the intercept is forced to be zero. If **statistics** is set to **True** (as in this case), then the range of statistics is calculated; otherwise only the slope and intercept are calculated.

Individual items of this output can be accessed by using the function **Index** discussed earlier. Suppose, for example, that we want to do a simple *t*-test on the slope; this task requires us to divide the slope value by its standard error.

	A	B	C	D	E	F	G	H	I	J
19			**Linest output**							
20			**slope**	**intercept**						
21		Slope (also **=slope(D4:D13,C4:C13)**)-->	-0.0890	14.3285	<-- Intercept					
22		Standard error of slope -->	0.0148	0.8770	<-- Standard error of intercept					
23		R^2 (also **=Rsq(D4:D13,C4:C13)**) -->	0.8189	0.8117	<-- Standard error of y values (also **=Steyx(D4:D13,C4:C13)**)					
24		F statistic -->	36.1825	8	<-- Degrees of freedom					
25		SS_{xy} = Slope*(summed product of observations from means) -->	23.8377	5.2705	<-- SSE = Residual sum of squares					
26										
27		Slope	-0.0890	<-- =INDEX(LINEST(D4:D13,C4:C13,,1),1,1)						
28		Intercept	14.3285	<-- =INDEX(LINEST(D4:D13,C4:C13,,1),1,2)						
29		R^2	0.8189	<-- =INDEX(LINEST(D4:D13,C4:C13,,1),3,1)						
30										
31		Slope	-0.0890	<-- =INDEX(LINEST(D4:D13,C4:C13,,TRUE),1,1)						
32		S.e. of slope	0.0148	<-- =INDEX(LINEST(D4:D13,C4:C13,,TRUE),2,1)						
33		t-statistic	-6.0152	<-- =C31/C32						

33.6.3 Multiple Regressions

Linest can also be used to do a multiple regression, as in the following illustration:

	A	B	C	D	E	F
1	**USING LINEST TO DO A MULTIPLE REGRESSION**					
2		**Observation**	**X_1**	**X_2**	**Y**	
3		1	35.3	81.2	10.98	
4		2	29.7	22.5	11.13	
5		3	30.8	77.3	12.51	
6		4	58.8	34.8	8.4	
7		5	61.4	55.1	9.27	
8		6	71.3	124.8	8.73	
9		7	74.4	18.5	6.36	
10		8	76.7	234.6	8.5	
11		9	70.7	22.5	7.82	
12		10	57.5	123.3	9.14	
13						
14			**x_2 coeff.**	**x_1 coeff.**	**intercept**	
15		Slope -->	0.0089	-0.0987	14.1705	<-- Intercept
16	Standard error -->		0.0030	0.0110	0.6271	
17		R^2 -->	0.9196	0.5783	#N/A	
18		F statistic -->	40.0228	7.0000	#N/A	
19		SS_{xy} -->	26.7674	2.3408	#N/A	
20						
21						
22						
23			{=LINEST(E3:E12,C3:D12,,TRUE)}			
24						

The predicted versus the actual y's are as follows:

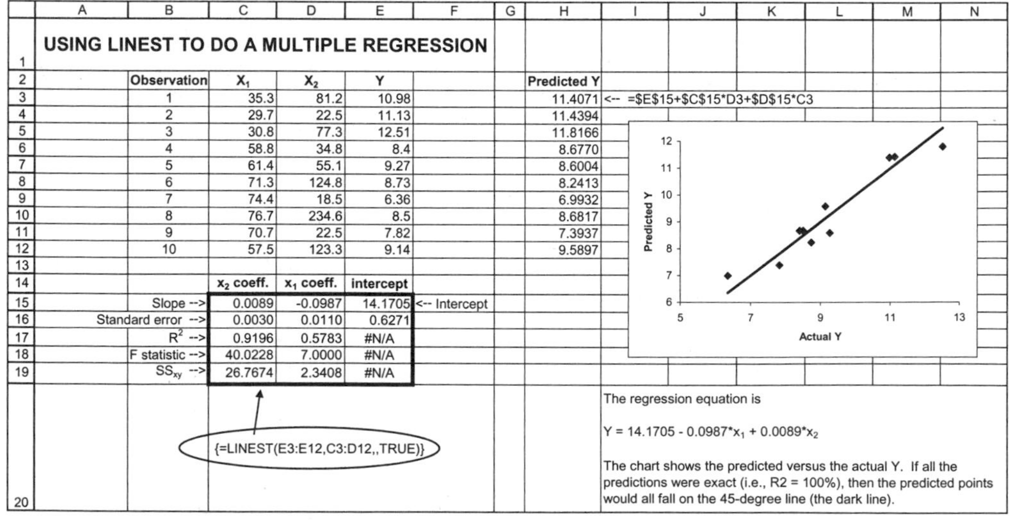

	B	C	D	E	F	H	I
1	**USING LINEST TO DO A MULTIPLE REGRESSION**						
2	**Observation**	**X_1**	**X_2**	**Y**		**Predicted Y**	
3	1	35.3	81.2	10.98		11.4071	<-- =$E$15+$C$15*D3+$D$15*C3
4	2	29.7	22.5	11.13		11.4394	
5	3	30.8	77.3	12.51		11.8166	
6	4	58.8	34.8	8.4		8.6770	
7	5	61.4	55.1	9.27		8.6004	
8	6	71.3	124.8	8.73		8.2413	
9	7	74.4	18.5	6.36		6.9932	
10	8	76.7	234.6	8.5		8.6817	
11	9	70.7	22.5	7.82		7.3937	
12	10	57.5	123.3	9.14		9.5897	
14		**x_2 coeff.**	**x_1 coeff.**	**intercept**			
15	Slope -->	0.0089	-0.0987	14.1705	<-- Intercept		
16	Standard error -->	0.0030	0.0110	0.6271			
17	R^2 -->	0.9196	0.5783	#N/A			
18	F statistic -->	40.0228	7.0000	#N/A			
19	SS_{xy} -->	26.7674	2.3408	#N/A			
20		{=LINEST(E3:E12,C3:D12,,TRUE)}					The regression equation is $Y = 14.1705 - 0.0987*x_1 + 0.0089*x_2$ The chart shows the predicted versus the actual Y. If all the predictions were exact (i.e., R2 = 100%), then the predicted points would all fall on the 45-degree line (the dark line).

33.7 Conditional Functions

If, **VLookup**, and **HLookup** are three functions that allow you to put in conditional statements.

The syntax of Excel's **If** statement is **If(condition, output if condition is true, output if condition is false)**. In the following example, if the initial number in B3 is less than or equal to 3, then the desired output is 15. If B3 is greater than 3, then the output is 0:

	A	B	C
1	THE IF FUNCTION		
2	Initial number	2	
3	If statement	15	<-- =IF(B2<=3,15,0)
4			
5	Initial number	2	
6	If statement	Less than or equal to 3	<-- =IF(B5<=3,"Less than or equal to 3","More than 3")

As you can see in row 6, you can make **If** print text also, by enclosing the desired text in double quotes.

Since **VLookup** and **HLookup** both have the same structure, we will concentrate on **VLookup** and leave you to figure out **HLookup** for yourself. **VLookup** is a way to introduce a table search in your spreadsheet. Here is an example: Suppose the marginal tax rates on income are given by the following table (i.e., for income less than $8,000, the marginal tax rate is 0 percent; for income above $8,000, the marginal tax rate is 15 percent; etc.). Cell B9 illustrates how the function **VLookup** is used to look up the marginal tax rate.

	A	B	C
1	VLOOKUP FUNCTION		
2	**Income**	**Tax rate**	
3	0	0%	
4	8,000	15%	
5	14,000	25%	
6	25,000	38%	
7			
8	Income	15,000	
9	Tax rate	25%	<-- =VLOOKUP(B8,A3:B6,2)

The syntax of this function is **VLookup(lookup_value,table,column)**. The first column of the lookup table, A3:A6, must be arranged in ascending (increasing) order. The **lookup_value**, in this case the income of 15,000, is used to determine the applicable row of the **table**. The row is the first row whose value is less than or equal to the **lookup_value**; in this case, this is the row that starts with 14,000. The **column** entry determines from which column of the applicable row the answer is taken; in this case the marginal tax rates are in column 2.

33.8 Large and Rank, Percentile, and Percentrank

Large(array, k) returns the *k*th largest number of the **array**, and **Rank(number, array)** returns the rank in **array** of **number**.

Here is an example of each function:

	A	B	C
1	**LARGE, RANK, PERCENTILE, PERCENTRANK**		
2	**Data**		
3	10.98		
4	11.13		
5	12.51		
6	8.40		
7	9.27		
8	8.73		
9	6.36		
10	8.50		
11	7.82		
12	9.14		
13			
14	Ranking, k	3	
15	K-th largest	10.98	<-- =LARGE(A3:A12,B14)
16			
17	Specific number	9.27	
18	Rank from top	4	<-- =RANK(B17,A3:A12)
19	Rank from bottom	7	<-- =RANK(B17,A3:A12,1)
20			
21	Percentile rank	0.8	
22	Percentile	11.01	<-- =PERCENTILE(A3:A12,B21)
23			
24	Specific number	9.27	
25	Percentile ranking	0.666	<-- =PERCENTRANK(A3:A12,B24)

Thus the third-largest number in the range A3:A12 is 10.98, and 9.27 is the fourth-largest number in the range A3:A12. If, as in cell B19, you specify an additional parameter in the function **Rank**, you will see that 9.27 is the seventh-ranking number from the bottom of the range A3:A12.

As illustrated, Excel has similar functions for percentiles: **Percentile** and **PercentRank**.

33.9 Count, CountA, CountIf

As their names suggest, all three of these functions count:

- **Count**: Counts the number of numeric entries in a range of cells.
- **CountA**: Counts all the nonblank cells in a range.
- **CountIf**: Counts cells that fulfill a specific condition.

Examples of **Count** and **CountIf** follow:

	A	B	C	D	E	F	G
1	**COUNT, COUNTA, COUNTIF**						
2	**Count**: Count only numerical values	5	<-- =COUNT(E2:G4)		1	two	3
3	**CountA**: count all nonblank cells	8	<-- =COUNTA(E2:G4)		4		six
4					seven	8	9

To use **CountIf** we have to specify a condition. The next spreadsheet gives a year of Merck's weekly stock returns (some rows have been hidden):

	A	B	C	D
1	**USING COUNTIF ON MERCK'S WEEKLY STOCK RETURNS**			
2	Number of returns	52	<-- =COUNT(C10:C61)	
3	Returns over 2%	13	<-- =COUNTIF(C10:C61,">2%")	
4				
5	Cutoff	5%		
6	Returns over cutoff	2	<-- =COUNTIF(C10:C61,">"&TEXT(B5,"0.00%"))	
7				
8	**Date**	**Merck price**	**Return**	
9	3-Jan-06	31.82		
10	9-Jan-06	32.15	1.03%	<-- =LN(B10/B9)
11	17-Jan-06	31.94	-0.66%	
12	23-Jan-06	33.33	4.26%	
13	30-Jan-06	33.04	-0.87%	
14	6-Feb-06	32.96	-0.24%	
15	13-Feb-06	34.63	4.94%	
16	21-Feb-06	33.72	-2.66%	
17	27-Feb-06	33.81	0.27%	
18	6-Mar-06	33.76	-0.15%	
19	13-Mar-06	34.61	2.49%	

In cell B3 we count all stock returns that are over 2 percent. In cells B5:B6 we illustrate a different technique. The cutoff in cell B5 is introduced into **CountIf** by means of the function **Text**.[6] Changing the entry in cell B5 allows us to count the number of returns above a certain level. Here is this information in a **Data Table**:

	A	B	C	D	E	F	G	H
1	**USING COUNTIF ON MERCK'S WEEKLY STOCK RETURNS**							
2	Number of returns	52	<-- =COUNT(C10:C61)					
3	Returns over 2%	13	<-- =COUNTIF(C10:C61,">2%")			**Data table: number of returns above cutoff**		
4								
5	Cutoff	5%				Cutoff	2	<-- =B6, data table header
6	Returns over cutoff	2	<-- =COUNTIF(C10:C61,">"&TEXT(B5,"0.00%"))			0%		
7						1%		
8	**Date**	**Merck price**	**Return**			2%		
9	3-Jan-06	31.82				3%		
10	9-Jan-06	32.15	1.03%			4%		
11	17-Jan-06	31.94	-0.66%			5%		
12	23-Jan-06	33.33	4.26%			6%		
13	30-Jan-06	33.04	-0.87%			7%		
14	6-Feb-06	32.96	-0.24%			8%		
15	13-Feb-06	34.63	4.94%			9%		
16	21-Feb-06	33.72	-2.66%			10%		
17	27-Feb-06	33.81	0.27%					

Table
Row input cell:
Column input cell: $B$5
OK
Cancel

Here is the resulting table:

	A	B	C	D	E	F	G	H
1	**USING COUNTIF ON MERCK'S WEEKLY STOCK RETURNS**							
2	Number of returns	52	<-- =COUNT(C10:C61)					
3	Returns over 2%	13	<-- =COUNTIF(C10:C61,">2%")			**Data table: number of returns above cutoff**		
4								
5	Cutoff	5%				Cutoff	2	<-- =B6, data table header
6	Returns over cutoff	2	<-- =COUNTIF(C10:C61,">"&TEXT(B5,"0.00%"))			0%	30	
7						1%	21	
8	**Date**	**Merck price**	**Return**			2%	13	
9	3-Jan-06	31.82				3%	8	
10	9-Jan-06	32.15	1.03%	<-- =LN(B10/B9)		4%	6	
11	17-Jan-06	31.94	-0.66%			5%	2	
12	23-Jan-06	33.33	4.26%			6%	1	
13	30-Jan-06	33.04	-0.87%			7%	1	
14	6-Feb-06	32.96	-0.24%			8%	1	
15	13-Feb-06	34.63	4.94%			9%	1	
16	21-Feb-06	33.72	-2.66%			10%	0	

6. This function and other text functions are discussed in Chapter 35.

Of the 52 weekly returns, 30 are over 0 percent, 21 over 1 percent, ...

33.10 Boolean Functions

When you include a question in parentheses, you are setting up a *Boolean function*:

	A	B	C
1	BASIC BOOLEAN FUNCTIONS		
2	x	22	
3	y	-15	
4			
5	Number	25	
6	Is number <= x?	FALSE	<-- =(B5<=B2)
7	Is number > y?	TRUE	<-- =(B5>B3)
8			
9	Multiplying	0	<-- =B6*B7

In cell B6 we have written **=(B5<=B2)**; this asks whether B5 is less than or equal to B2: If the answer is positive, Excel returns **False**, else it returns **True**. Multiplying **False** $*$ **True** or **False** $*$ **False** gives 0 (see cell B9), and multiplying **True** $*$ **True** gives 1:

	A	B	C
1	BASIC BOOLEAN FUNCTIONS		
2	x	22	
3	y	-15	
4			
5	Number	20	
6	Is number <= x?	TRUE	<-- =(B5<=B2)
7	Is number > y?	TRUE	<-- =(B5>B3)
8			
9	Multiplying	1	<-- =B6*B7

33.10.1 Using Boolean Functions

Boolean functions can be useful in the most unexpected places. In the next spreadsheet the first two columns contain the monthly returns for Marriott for a two-year period. The problem we encounter is counting the number of returns that are between two arbitrary bounds and taking the average of the returns that are between these bounds:

	A	B	C	D	E	F	G	H
1	USING BOOLEAN FUNCTIONS							
2	Date	Marriott stock price	Return					
3	7-Jan-05	31.20				How many data points?	24	<-- =COUNT(C4:C27)
4	1-Feb-05	31.65	1.43%	<-- =LN(B4/B3)		Maximal return	8.02%	<-- =MAX(C4:C27)
5	1-Mar-05	33.06	4.36%			Minimal return	-8.02%	<-- =MIN(C4:C27)
6	1-Apr-05	31.03	-6.34%					
7	2-May-05	33.40	7.36%					
8	1-Jun-05	33.78	1.13%			Upper bound	5%	
9	1-Jul-05	33.91	0.38%			Lower bound	-2%	
10	1-Aug-05	31.30	-8.01%					
11	1-Sep-05	31.25	-0.16%			How many < upper bound?	16	<-- =COUNTIF(C4:C27,"<"&G8)
12	3-Oct-05	29.58	-5.49%			How many > lower bound?	19	<-- =COUNTIF(C4:C27,">"&G9)
13	1-Nov-05	32.05	8.02%					
14	1-Dec-05	33.27	3.74%			How many between upper and lower bounds?	11	=SUMPRODUCT((C4:C27>G9)*(C4:C27<G8),(C4:C27>G9)*(C4:C27<G8))
15	3-Jan-06	33.11	-0.48%					
16	1-Feb-06	33.98	2.59%			Average of returns between the bounds	1.36%	=SUMPRODUCT((C4:C27>G9)*(C4:C27<G8),C4:C27)/SUMPRODUCT((C4:C27>G9)*(C4:C27<G8),(C4:C27>G9)*(C4:C27<G8))
17	1-Mar-06	34.14	0.47%					
18	3-Apr-06	36.36	6.30%					
19	1-May-06	35.99	-1.02%					
20	1-Jun-06	38.00	5.43%					
21	3-Jul-06	35.07	-8.02%					
22	1-Aug-06	37.61	6.99%					
23	1-Sep-06	38.59	2.57%					
24	2-Oct-06	41.71	7.77%					
25	1-Nov-06	45.09	7.79%					
26	1-Dec-06	47.72	5.67%					
27	3-Jan-07	45.10	-5.65%					

In cell G3 we use **Count** to determine the number of returns. Cells G11 and G12 use **Countif** to determine how many returns are below the upper bound in cell G8 and how many are above the lower bound in cell G9. But how many of the returns are between the two bounds? You can't do it with **Countif**, but we can do it (cell G14) with a trick involving Boolean functions:

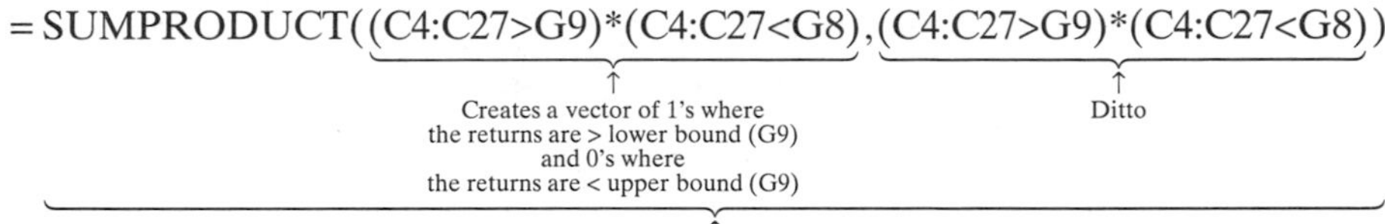
=SUMPRODUCT((C4:C27>G9)*(C4:C27<G8),(C4:C27>G9)*(C4:C27<G8))
Creates a vector of 1's where the returns are > lower bound (G9) and 0's where the returns are < upper bound (G9)
Ditto

Sumproduct multiplies the two vectors and sums the results.
This gives the number of data points between the two bounds.

A similar trick is employed in cell G16 to find the average of the returns that are between the two bounds:

$$= \frac{\text{SUMPRODUCT((C4:C27>G9)*(C4:C27<G8), C4:C27)}}{\text{SUMPRODUCT((C4:C27>G9)*(C4:C27<G8),(C4:C27>G9)*(C4:C27<G8))}}$$

$$= \frac{\text{Numerator: Multiplies vector of 1's and 0's times the returns, thus sums the returns that are between the bounds}}{\text{Counts the returns that are between the bounds}}$$

This is all very tricky, but it is also very useful!

33.11 Offset

The function **Offset** allows us to specify a cell or a block of cells in an array. It cannot be used by itself—rather, it must be part of another Excel function. The following example shows a large array of numbers. We want to sum a four-row, five-column array of the larger array (these numbers are specified in cells B6 and B7); as specified in cells B3 and B4, we want this summed array to start below the third row and to the right of the second column of the large block of numbers:

	A	B	C	D	E	F	G	H
1				**USING OFFSET**				
2	**Starting corner**							
3	Rows down	3						
4	Columns over	2						
5	**Range to be summed**							
6	Number of rows	4						
7	Number of columns	5						
8	Sum	811	<-- =SUM(OFFSET(A11:H31,B3,B4,B6,B7))					
9	**Check**	811	<-- =SUM(C14:G17)					
10								
11	89	34	72	42	41	89	75	41
12	33	6	49	7	62	50	38	17
13	71	69	42	68	39	75	32	77
14	1	69	8	79	40	8	67	46
15	70	12	44	48	88	27	38	51
16	85	0	23	35	83	30	17	52
17	30	50	16	28	73	4	55	68
18	35	56	31	24	15	47	89	88
19	99	31	55	60	45	24	28	3
20	93	72	7	75	90	81	52	71
21	62	56	55	19	73	81	33	76
22	87	27	80	38	65	61	38	68
23	10	59	27	81	6	83	51	1
24	70	88	44	35	70	35	0	82
25	98	45	17	45	89	19	58	42
26	83	75	21	13	80	9	18	64
27	32	23	4	86	88	52	52	69
28	76	61	72	28	83	1	32	38
29	64	87	32	67	50	73	19	83
30	54	55	57	64	80	29	17	92
31	12	95	66	59	48	78	87	23

The function OFFSET(A11:H31,B3,B4,B6,B7) in cell B8 specifies a block of cells within the range A11:H31. This range starts *3 rows below* (the value in cell B3) and *2 columns to the right* (the value in cell B4) of the top left-hand cell of the range A11:H31. The range itself is 4 rows deep (the value in cell B6) and 5 columns wide (the value in cell B7).

The values in cells B6 and B7 always have to be positive, but the values in B3 and B4 can be negative as well as positive. In the next example the initial reference range is B22:H31, and **Offset** indicates a range that starts above this block of cells (since the value in B3 is negative):

	A	B	C	D	E	F	G	H	I
1			**USING OFFSET with negative value**						
2	**Starting corner**								
3	Rows down	-5							
4	Columns over	1							
5	**Range to be summed**								
6	Number of rows	4							
7	Number of columns	5							
8	Sum	899	<-- =SUM(OFFSET(B22:H31,B3,B4,B6,B7))						
9	**Check**	899	<-- =SUM(C17:G20)						
10									
11	89	34	72	42	41	89	75	41	
12	33	6	49	7	62	50	38	17	
13	71	69	42	68	39	75	32	77	
14	1	69	8	79	40	8	67	46	
15	70	12	44	48	88	27	38	51	
16	85	0	23	35	83	30	17	52	
17	30	50	16	28	73	4	55	68	
18	35	56	31	24	15	47	89	88	
19	99	31	55	60	45	24	28	3	
20	93	72	7	75	90	81	52	71	
21	62	56	55	19	73	81	33	76	
22	87	27	80	38	65	61	38	68	
23	10	59	27	81	6	83	51	1	
24	70	88	44	35	70	35	0	82	
25	98	45	17	45	89	19	58	42	
26	83	75	21	13	80	9	18	64	
27	32	23	4	86	88	52	52	69	
28	76	61	72	28	83	1	32	38	
29	64	87	32	67	50	73	19	83	
30	54	55	57	64	80	29	17	92	
31	12	95	66	59	48	78	87	23	
32									

For an innovative use of **Offset**, see the chapter on event studies, section 14.5.

34 Using Array Functions and Formulas

34.1 Overview

An Excel array function or formula performs an operation on a rectangular block of cells. In the simplest cases, built-in Excel array functions such as **Transpose** or **MMult** take an array and transpose it or take two matrices and multiply them. Once you get the hang of array functions, you can design your own array formulas. In this chapter, for example, we show how to use array formulas to find the minimum or maximum of the off-diagonal elements of a matrix or to pick out the diagonal of a matrix—all useful tricks to know when doing portfolio calculations such as those discussed in Chapters 8–15.

The one critical thing to remember about array functions or formulas in that they are entered into a spreadsheet by pushing the [Ctrl] + [Shift] + [Enter] keys simultaneously; this procedure contrasts with the usual one whereby we enter a function or formula only by pushing [Enter].

34.2 Some Built-in Excel Array Functions

In this section we discuss some built-in Excel array functions: **Transpose**, **MMult**, **MInverse**, and **Frequency**. Other functions are discussed elsewhere in this book; for example, the function **Linest** is discussed in Chapter 33.

34.2.1 Transpose

Suppose we're trying to calculate the transpose of a 3 × 2 matrix (3 rows, 2 columns) that is in cells A2:B4 of the spreadsheet.

	A	B
2	1	5
3	2	6
4	3	7

Excel has a function called **Transpose( )**, but, like all array functions, its use requires care:

- First, block off the cells D3:F4 into which you intend to put the transposed matrix.

• Now type **=Transpose(A2:B4)**. This will appear in the top left-hand corner of the blocked-off cells. Of course you can use the usual tricks to show Excel which cells you want (for instance, pointing or using named ranges).

At this point your spreadsheet looks like this:

	A	B	C	D	E	F
1			USING TRANSPOSE			
2	1	5				
3	2	6		=transpose(A2:B4)		
4	3	7				
5						

• When you've finished typing the formula, *don't press Enter!* Instead use [Control] + [Shift] + [Enter]. This will put the array function into all of the blocked-off cells.

Here's what the final product will look like:

	A	B	C	D	E	F	G
1				USING TRANSPOSE			
2	1	5					
3	2	6		1	2	3	<-- {=TRANSPOSE(A2:B4)}
4	3	7		5	6	7	

Notice that the array function is surrounded by curly brackets { }. You don't type these in—Excel puts them in automatically.

There is, of course, another way to transpose an array: You can copy the original array, and then use **Edit|Paste Special** to transpose the range, clicking on **Transpose**:

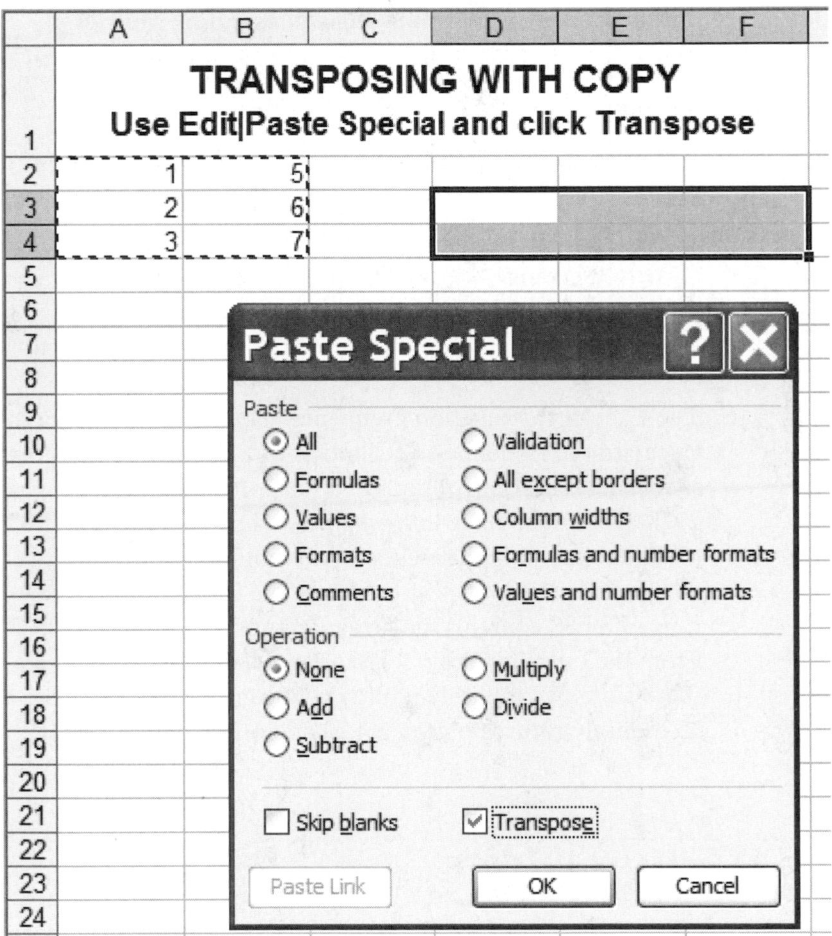

This will transpose the range, but it will not link the original with the target range—when you change something in the original range, the target range is unchanged. The neat thing about **Transpose** is that it's a *dynamic function*, as are all the array functions and formulas: When you change one of the initial set of cells, the transposed array also changes.

34.2.2 MMult and MInverse: Multiplying and Inverting Matrices

These two functions have been discussed in Chapter 31, so we only recapitulate briefly:

- **MMult(range1,range2)** multiplies the matrix in **range1** times that in **range2**. Of course, this is only possible if the number of columns in **range1** equals the number of rows in **range2**.
- **MInverse(range)** calculates the inverse of the matrix in **range**. Note that **range** must be rectangular.

34.2.3 Frequency

The Excel array function **Frequency(data_array,bins_array)** allows us to calculate the frequency distribution of a data set. The following spreadsheet shows monthly return data for Ford stock over the period January 1977–December 2006. In column E we have put the bins, taking care that the first bin will be *below* the minimum monthly return over the period and that the last bin will be *above* the maximum monthly return. The range F8:F38 contains the array function **Frequency (C4:C363,E8:E38)**. From the output we can, for example, deduce that in the 20-year period there were two monthly returns between –25.71 and –23.71 percent, and 33 monthly returns between 4.29 and 6.29 percent.

	A	B	C	D	E	F	G
1	**THE FREQUENCY ARRAY FUNCTION**						
2	**Date**	**Ford stock price**	**Monthly return**				
3	3-Jan-77	0.50					
4	1-Feb-77	0.48	-4.08%	<-- =LN(B4/B3)	Minimum	-24.71%	<-- =MIN(C4:C363)
5	1-Mar-77	0.45	-6.45%		Maximimum	32.48%	<-- =MAX(C4:C363)
6	1-Apr-77	0.47	4.35%				
7	2-May-77	0.46	-2.15%		**Bin**	**Frequency**	
8	1-Jun-77	0.50	8.34%		-25.71%	0	<-- {=FREQUENCY(C4:C363,E8:E38)}
9	1-Jul-77	0.48	-4.08%		-23.71%	2	
10	1-Aug-77	0.47	-2.11%		-21.71%	1	
11	1-Sep-77	0.50	6.19%		-19.71%	2	
12	3-Oct-77	0.47	-6.19%		-17.71%	6	
13	1-Nov-77	0.48	2.11%		-15.71%	3	
14	1-Dec-77	0.50	4.08%		-13.71%	5	
15	3-Jan-78	0.47	-6.19%		-11.71%	8	
16	1-Feb-78	0.47	0.00%		-9.71%	10	
17	1-Mar-78	0.51	8.17%		-7.71%	18	
18	3-Apr-78	0.58	12.86%		-5.71%	23	
19	1-May-78	0.56	-3.51%		-3.71%	26	
20	1-Jun-78	0.53	-5.51%		-1.71%	35	
21	3-Jul-78	0.53	0.00%		0.29%	35	
22	1-Aug-78	0.51	-3.85%		2.29%	37	
23	1-Sep-78	0.53	3.85%		4.29%	30	
24	2-Oct-78	0.48	-9.91%		6.29%	33	
25	1-Nov-78	0.49	2.06%		8.29%	22	
26	1-Dec-78	0.50	2.02%		10.29%	21	
27	2-Jan-79	0.50	0.00%		12.29%	9	
28	1-Feb-79	0.50	0.00%		14.29%	13	
29	1-Mar-79	0.53	5.83%		16.29%	5	
30	2-Apr-79	0.55	3.70%		18.29%	4	
31	1-May-79	0.53	-3.70%		20.29%	5	
32	1-Jun-79	0.53	0.00%		22.29%	2	
33	2-Jul-79	0.53	0.00%		24.29%	1	
34	1-Aug-79	0.55	3.70%		26.29%	1	
35	4-Sep-79	0.56	1.80%		28.29%	0	
36	1-Oct-79	0.48	-15.42%		30.29%	2	
37	1-Nov-79	0.40	-18.23%		32.29%	0	
38	3-Dec-79	0.42	4.88%		34.29%	1	
39	2-Jan-80	0.45	6.90%				
40	1-Fe						
41	3-M						
42	1-A						
43	1-Ma						
44	2-Ju						
45	1-J						
46	1-Au						
47	2-Se						
48	1-O						
49	3-No						
50	1-De						
51	2-Ja						
52	2-Fe						
53	2-M						
54	1-A						
55	1-Ma						
56	1-Ju						
57	1-J						
58	3-Au						
59	1-Se						
60	1-O						
61	2-No						
62	1-De						
63	4-Ja						
64	1-Fe						
65	1-M						
66	1-A						
67	3-Ma						
68	1-Ju						
69	1-J						
70	2-Au						
71	1-Sep-82	0.39	-7.41%				

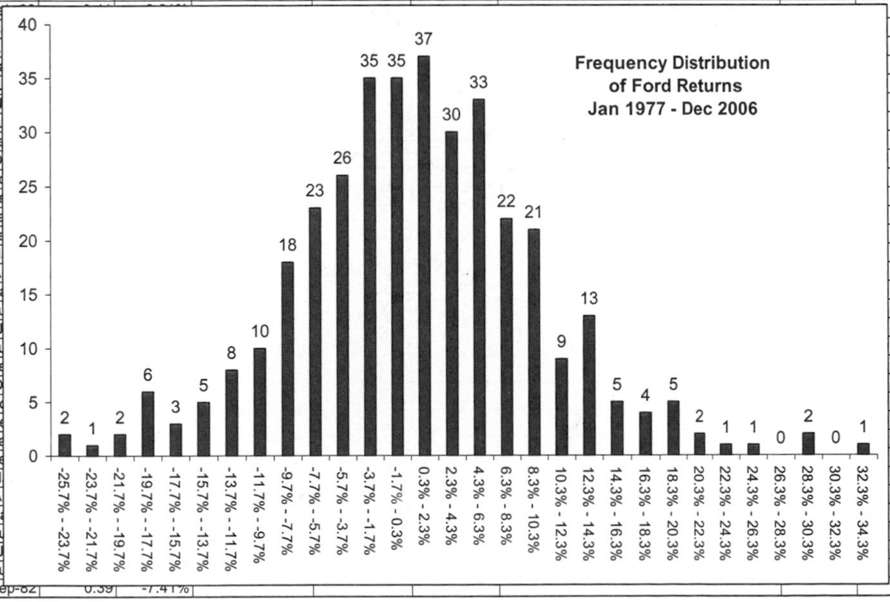

Frequency Distribution of Ford Returns Jan 1977 - Dec 2006

Bin range	Frequency
-25.7% - -23.7%	2
-23.7% - -21.7%	1
-21.7% - -19.7%	2
-19.7% - -17.7%	6
-17.7% - -15.7%	3
-15.7% - -13.7%	5
-13.7% - -11.7%	8
-11.7% - -9.7%	10
-9.7% - -7.7%	18
-7.7% - -5.7%	23
-5.7% - -3.7%	26
-3.7% - -1.7%	35
-1.7% - 0.3%	35
0.3% - 2.3%	37
2.3% - 4.3%	30
4.3% - 6.3%	33
6.3% - 8.3%	22
8.3% - 10.3%	21
10.3% - 12.3%	9
12.3% - 14.3%	13
14.3% - 16.3%	5
16.3% - 18.3%	4
18.3% - 20.3%	5
20.3% - 22.3%	2
22.3% - 24.3%	1
24.3% - 26.3%	1
26.3% - 28.3%	0
28.3% - 30.3%	2
30.3% - 32.3%	0
32.3% - 34.3%	1

34.3 Homemade Array Functions

In our experience array functions often arise out of situations where you are called upon to do long, repetitive calculations. You then discover that the same calculation can be done in a single array function. In many cases it is not clear why a particular array technique should work. For example, in this chapter we will use the fact that A3+B6:B8 adds the contents of cell A3 to each of cells B6:B8. Why? Heaven only knows! We also use the (undocumented, as far as we are aware) trick that B3:B7^A3:A7 raises cell B3 to the power A3, cell B4 to the power A4, ...

In this section we illustrate homemade array functions with two examples having to do with investment returns.

34.3.1 Computing the Compound Annual Return from 10 Years of Return Data

The following table gives the annual returns for the Podunk University endowment. You are asked to compute the compound annual return over the 10-year period. Assuming that the returns have been discretely computed (meaning that $r_t = \frac{\text{Endowment value}_t}{\text{Endowment value}_{t-1}}$, $t = 1, \ldots, 10$), you realize that the compounded annual return is $r = [(1 + r_1) * (1 + r_2) * \ldots * (1 + r_{10}))^{1/10} - 1$. In cell B14, we do this calculation with a single array function:

	A	B	C
1	PODUNK UNIVERSITY ENDOWMENT RETURNS		
2	Year	Return for the year	
3	1	25.80%	
4	2	20.50%	
5	3	12.20%	
6	4	32.20%	
7	5	-2.70%	
8	6	-0.50%	
9	7	12.50%	
10	8	21.10%	
11	9	19.20%	
12	10	16.70%	
13			
14	Using an array formula	15.23%	<-- {=PRODUCT(1+B3:B12)^(1/10)-1}

The Excel function **Product** multiplies the entries in a range of cells. The entry in cell B14 adds 1 to each cell in B3:B13, multiplies the cells, takes the tenth root, and subtracts 1 from the result—all in one cell (entered, of course, with [Ctrl] + [Shift] + [Enter]).

34.3.2 Computing the Compound Annual Continuous Return

Column B of the next spreadsheet gives the amounts that accumulated in a customer account of the Youngtalk Investment Fund. The annual continuously compounded return is computed by $r_t = \ln\left(\frac{\text{Account}_t}{\text{Account}_{t-1}}\right)$, and the average return over the period is $\frac{1}{10}\sum_{t=1}^{10} r_t$. In cell B15 we do this calculation by averaging the annual returns, and in cell B16 we show an array function that does the whole calculation in a single cell. Pretty neat!

	A	B	C	D
1	YOUNGTALK INVESTMENT FUND			
2	Year	Investment beginning of year	Continuous return for year	
3	1996	100.00		
4	1997	121.51	19.48%	<-- =LN(B4/B3)
5	1998	132.22	8.45%	
6	1999	98.63	-29.31%	
7	2000	75.65	-26.53%	
8	2001	140.48	61.90%	
9	2002	221.40	45.49%	
10	2003	243.46	9.50%	
11	2004	280.11	14.02%	
12	2005	398.72	35.31%	
13	2006	543.58	30.99%	
14				
15	Compound annual return		16.93%	<-- =AVERAGE(C4:C13)
16	Same calculation with array function		16.93%	<-- {=AVERAGE(LN(B4:B13/B3:B12))}
17			16.93%	<-- =LN(B13/B3)/10 , even simpler!

A final note: Look at cell C17—if you know some continuous-time mathematics, you will know that ln(B13/B3)/10 produces the same result. Simpler yet!

34.3.3 Computing

We are given a set of interest rates $r_1, r_2, \ldots$, and we want to compute the formula $\sum_{t=1}^{n} \frac{1}{(1+r_t)^t}$. This issue comes up in section 27.5. Excel's **NPV** function won't work for this purpose, so we'll have to build our own function. The following spreadsheet shows two methods:

	A	B	C	D
1	**COMPUTING PRESENT-VALUE FACTORS WITH AN ARRAY FUNCTION**			
2	Year	Interest rate		
3	1	6.23%		
4	2	4.00%		
5	3	4.20%		
6	4	4.65%		
7	5	4.80%		
8				
9	Present value	4.3746	<-- {=SUM(1/((1+B3:B7)^A3:A7))}	
10				
11	**Checking the formula with a recursive formula**			
12	Year	Interest rate	Sum of $1/(1+r_t)^t$	
13	1	6.23%	0.9414	<-- =1/(1+B13)^A13
14	2	4.00%	1.8659	<-- =C13+(1/(1+B14)^A14)
15	3	4.20%	2.7498	<-- =C14+(1/(1+B15)^A15)
16	4	4.65%	3.5836	
17	5	4.80%	4.3746	<-- =C16+(1/(1+B17)^A17)

In cell B9 we use an array function {= Sum(1/((1+B3:B7)^A3:A7))}. Writing (1 + B3:B7)^A3:A7) adds 1 to each of cells B3:B7 and raises the result to the power in cells A3:A7. Applying **Sum** gives the result (of course, this being an array function, you have to enter it with [Ctrl] + [Shift] + [Enter]).

An alternative, given in rows 13–17, is to build the result recursively. This gives the same result, but with more work.

34.4 Array Formulas with Matrices

In this section we create some array functions that have to do with matrices.

34.4.1 Subtracting a Constant from a Matrix

In the portfolio computations of Chapters 9–13, we often have to subtract a constant from a matrix. This task is easy with an array formula:

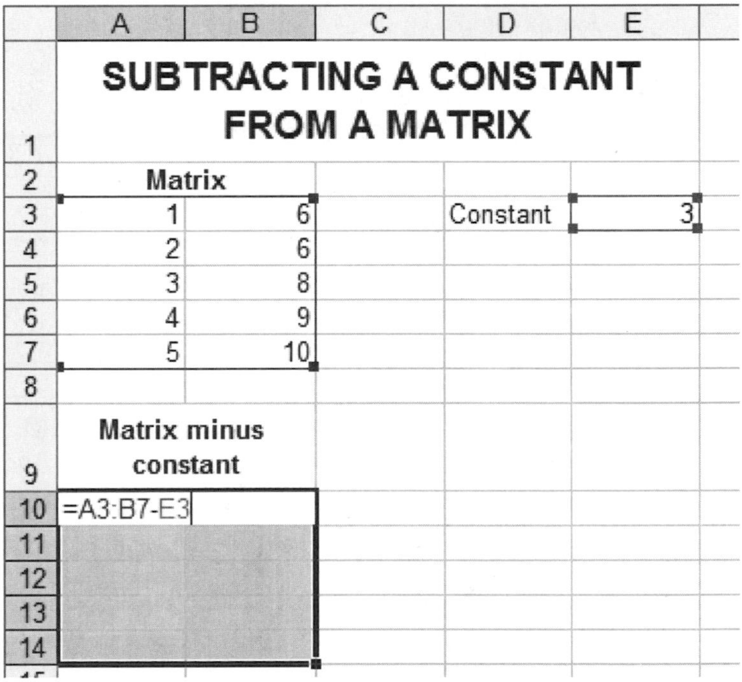

	A	B	C	D	E
1	SUBTRACTING A CONSTANT FROM A MATRIX				
2	Matrix				
3	1	6		Constant	3
4	2	6			
5	3	8			
6	4	9			
7	5	10			
8					
9	Matrix minus constant				
10	=A3:B7-E3				
11					
12					
13					
14					

Of course, since this is an array formula, you enter it with [Ctrl] + [Shift] + [Enter]. Here is the result:

	A	B	C	D	E
1	**SUBTRACTING A CONSTANT FROM A MATRIX**				
2	**Matrix**				
3	1	6		Constant	3
4	2	6			
5	3	8			
6	4	9			
7	5	10			
8					
9	**Matrix minus constant**				
10	-2	3			
11	-1	3	<-- {=A3:B7-E3}		
12	0	5			
13	1	6			
14	2	7			

As in all array formulas and functions, the result is dynamic: Changing entries in the source changes the target:

	A	B	C	D	E
1	**SUBTRACTING A CONSTANT FROM A MATRIX**				
2	**Matrix**				
3	1	6		Constant	16
4	2	6			
5	3	8			
6	4	9			
7	5	10			
8					
9	**Matrix minus constant**				
10	-15	-10			
11	-14	-10	<-- {=A3:B7-E3}		
12	-13	-8			
13	-12	-7			
14	-11	-6			

34.4.2 Creating a Matrix with Ones on the Diagonal and Zeros Elsewhere

This is a problem that comes up in Chapter 10: We want a matrix that has a diagonal of 1's but has zero off-diagonal elements. The following spreadsheet shows three ways of accomplishing this result:

	A	B	C	D	E	F
1	CREATING A MATRIX OF 1'S AND 0'S We want 1 on diagonal, and 0 elsewhere This problem comes up in Chapter 10					
2	Creating a diagonal matrix of 1's. The following cells contain the array formula =IF(B3:E3=A4:A7,1,0)}					
3		A	B	C	D	
4	A	1	0	0	0	
5	B	0	1	0	0	
6	C	0	0	1	0	
7	D	0	0	0	1	
8						
9	Creating a diagonal matrix of 1's. The following cells contain the array formula =IF(B$10=$A11,1,0)}					
10		A	B	C	D	
11	A	1	0	0	0	
12	B	0	1	0	0	
13	C	0	0	1	0	
14	D	0	0	0	1	
15						
16	Creating a diagonal matrix of 1's when there are no borders. The following cells contain the array formula =IF(ROW()-ROW($B$17)=COLUMN()-COLUMN($B$17),1,0)}					
17		1	0	0	0	
18		0	1	0	0	
19		0	0	1	0	
20		0	0	0	1	

The first and second methods rely on the labeling of the rows and the columns. In the first example, the formula =IF(B3:E3=A4:A7,1,0) tests whether the row label equals the column heading; if this is true, we put a 1 in the cell, and otherwise we put in a 0. In the second example, we use an **If** with mixed absolute and relative references to create the same effect. In the third example, there are no column or row labels, and we rely on the functions **Column** and **Row** to test the equality of the relative row and column places in the matrix.

34.4.3 Finding the Maximum and Minimum Off-Diagonal Elements of a Matrix

We want to find the maximal and minimal elements of the off-diagonal elements of a matrix. Two ways to do so are illustrated in the following spreadsheet:

	A	B	C	D	E	F
1	**FINDING THE MAX,MIN OF OFF-DIAGONAL ELEMENTS OF A MATRIX the long way**					
2		**The source matrix**				
3		**A**	**B**	**C**	**D**	
4	**A**	10	2	3	4	
5	**B**	-3	20	4	-3	
6	**C**	1	5	60	6	
7	**D**	4	2	-10	25	
8						
9	**RANGE below contains array formula =IF(B3:E3=A4:A7,"",B4:E7)**					
10		**A**	**B**	**C**	**D**	
11	**A**		2	3	4	<-- {=IF(B3:E3=A4:A7,"",B4:E7)}
12	**B**	-3		4	-3	
13	**C**	1	5		6	
14	**D**	4	2	-10		
15						
16	Max of off-diagonals	6	<-- =MAX(B11:E14)			
17	Min of off-diagonals	-10	<-- =MIN(B11:E14)			
18						
19						
20	**Using only nonarray formulas**					
21	**Range below contains the nonarray formula =IF(B$3=$A4,"",B4)**					
22		**A**	**B**	**C**	**D**	
23	**A**		2	3	4	<-- =IF(E$3=$A4,"",E4)
24	**B**	-3		4	-3	
25	**C**	1	5		6	
26	**D**	4	2	-10		
27						
28	Max of off-diagonals	6	<-- =MAX(B23:E26)			
29	Min of off-diagonals	-10	<-- =MIN(B23:E26)			

In this example, we first use an array function to replace all the diagonal elements with a blank cell. We can then use **Max** and **Min** to determine the extreme off-diagonal elements. As shown in rows 20–29, we could also have used the nonarray formula =IF(B$3=$A4,"",B4) in cell B11 and copied it to the rest of the matrix.

We can also find the maximum and minimum by incorporating the array formula directly into the **Max** and **Min**:

	A	B	C	D	E	F
1	FINDING THE MAX,MIN OF OFF-DIAGONAL ELEMENTS OF A MATRIX In one step					
2	The source matrix					
3		A	B	C	D	
4	A	10	2	3	4	
5	B	-3	20	4	-3	
6	C	1	5	60	6	
7	D	4	2	-10	25	
8						
9	Max of off-diagonals	6	<-- {=MAX(IF(B3:E3=A4:A7,"",B4:E7))}			
10	Min of off-diagonals	-10	<-- {=MIN(IF(B3:E3=A4:A7,"",B4:E7))}			

34.4.4 Replacing the Off-Diagonals Using VLookup

Now suppose that we want to replace the off-diagonal elements using a lookup table, as illustrated in this picture:

	A	B	C	D	E	F
1	REPLACING THE MAX,MIN OF OFF-DIAGONAL ELEMENTS OF A MATRIX Long way, nonarray formulas					
2	The source matrix					
3		A	B	C	D	
4	A	10	2	3	4	
5	B	-3	20	4	-3	
6	C	1	5	60	6	
7	D	4	2	-10	25	
8						
9	Lookup table for replacements					
10	-10	i				
11	-6	ii				
12	-2	iii				
13	2	iv				
14	6	v				
15	10	vi				
16						
17	The following range contains nonarray formula =IF(B$3=$A4,B4,VLOOKUP(B4,$A$10:$B$15,2)), which has been copied to all the cells					
18		A	B	C	D	
19	A	10	iv	iv	iv	<-- =IF(E$3=$A4,E4,VLOOKUP(E4,$A$10:$B$15,2))
20	B	ii	20	iv	ii	
21	C	iii	iv	60	v	
22	D	iv	iv	i	25	

Array formulas can simplify this procedure:

	A	B	C	D	E	F
1	**REPLACING THE MAX,MIN OF OFF-DIAGONAL ELEMENTS OF A MATRIX** **Using array formula**					
2		**The source matrix**				
3		**A**	**B**	**C**	**D**	
4	**A**	10	2	3	4	
5	**B**	-3	20	4	-3	
6	**C**	1	5	60	6	
7	**D**	4	2	-10	25	
8						
9	Lookup table for replacements					
10	-10	i				
11	-6	ii				
12	-2	iii				
13	2	iv				
14	6	v				
15	10	vi				
16						
17	**The following range contains array formula** **=IF(B3:E3=A4:A7,B4:E7,VLOOKUP(B4:E7,A10:B15,2))**					
18		**A**	**B**	**C**	**D**	
19	**A**	10	iv	iv	iv	<-- {=IF(B3:E3=A4:A7,B4:E7,VLOOKUP(B4:E7,A10:B15,2))}
20	**B**	ii	20	iv	ii	
21	**C**	iii	iv	60	v	
22	**D**	iv	iv	i	25	

Exercises

1. Use a homemade array function to multiply the vector {1,2,3,4,5} times the constant 3.

2. Use a the array functions **Transpose** and **MMult** to multiply the row vector {1,2,3,4,5} times the column vector $\begin{Bmatrix} -8 \\ -9 \\ 7 \\ 6 \\ 5 \end{Bmatrix}$.

3. The following spreadsheet shows the variance-covariance matrix of six stocks (you can find this matrix on the file **fm3_problems34.xls**). Use an array function to create a matrix with only variances on the diagonal and with zeros elsewhere.

	A	B	C	D	E	F	G
1		**GE**	**MSFT**	**JNJ**	**K**	**BA**	**IBM**
2	**GE**	**0.1035**	0.0758	0.0222	-0.0043	0.0857	0.1414
3	**MSFT**	0.0758	**0.1657**	0.0412	-0.0052	0.0379	0.1400
4	**JNJ**	0.0222	0.0412	**0.0360**	0.0181	0.0101	0.0455
5	**K**	-0.0043	-0.0052	0.0181	**0.0570**	-0.0076	0.0122
6	**BA**	0.0857	0.0379	0.0101	-0.0076	**0.0896**	0.0856
7	**IBM**	0.1414	0.1400	0.0455	0.0122	0.0856	**0.2993**

4. For exercise 3: Use an array function to create a matrix with zeros on the diagonal and the covariances off-diagonal.

5. The Fidelity Diversified International Fund's annual returns are given in the following spreadsheet. On the assumption that these returns are discretely computed, use an array function to compute the compound annual return over the period.[1]

	A	B	C	D
1	**FIDELITY DIVERSIFIED INTERNATIONAL FUND**			
2		Year	Return	
3		1998	14.39%	
4		1999	50.65%	
5		2000	-8.96%	
6		2001	-12.99%	
7		2002	-9.37%	
8		2003	42.38%	
9		2004	19.66%	
10		2005	17.23%	
11		2006	22.52%	
12		2007	11.10%	

1. Discretely compounded: The return in year t is $\frac{\text{Fund value}_t}{\text{Fund value}_{t-1}} - 1$. If the returns were continuously compounded, then the year-t return would be $\ln\left(\frac{\text{Fund value}_t}{\text{Fund value}_{t-1}}\right)$.

35 Some Excel Hints

35.1 Overview

This chapter covers a grab bag of Excel hints dealing with problems and needs that we sometimes run into. The chapter makes no pretence at uniformity or extensiveness of coverage. Topics covered include

- Fast fills and copy
- Graph titles that change when data change
- Creating multiline cells (useful for putting line breaks in cells and linked graph titles)
- Typing Greek symbols
- Typing sub- and superscripts (but not both)
- Naming cells
- Hiding cells
- Formula auditing
- Writing on multiple spreadsheets

35.2 Fast Copy: Filling in Data Next to Filled-In Column

Usually, we copy cells by dragging on the fill handle of the cell with the formula. There is sometimes an easier method. Consider the following situation:

	A	B	C
1	AUTO FILL/COPY		
2	1	2	
3	2	5	<-- =B2+3
4	3		
5	4		
6	5		
7	6		
8	7		
9	8		

Now double-click on "fill handle" (shown in the following figure with the cross). After double-clicking, the range B5:B10 will automatically fill with the formula in B4.

	A	B	C
1	AUTO FILL/COPY		
2	1	2	
3	2	5	<-- =B2+3
4	3		
5	4		
6	5		
7	6		
8	7		
9	8		

Here's the result:

	A	B	C
1	AUTO FILL/COPY		
2	1	2	
3	2	5	<-- =B2+3
4	3	8	
5	4	11	
6	5	14	
7	6	17	
8	7	20	
9	8	23	
10			
11	Double-clicking on the "fill handle" of a cell will fill in the rest of the column provided there's a filled cell next to it.		

35.3 Multiline Cells

It is sometimes useful to put a line break in a cell, thus creating a multiline cell. Perform this task with **[Alt] + [Enter]** where you want a line break.

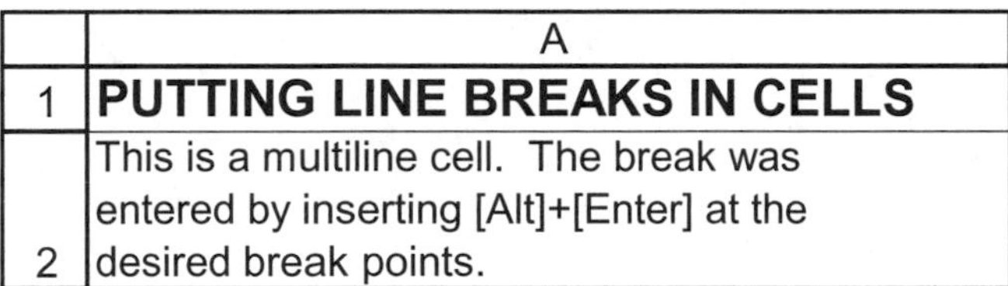

	A
1	**PUTTING LINE BREAKS IN CELLS**
2	This is a multiline cell. The break was entered by inserting [Alt]+[Enter] at the desired break points.

There are, of course, other ways to make a cell multilined. The most obvious of these is to use **Format|Cells|Alignment** and check **Wrap text**:

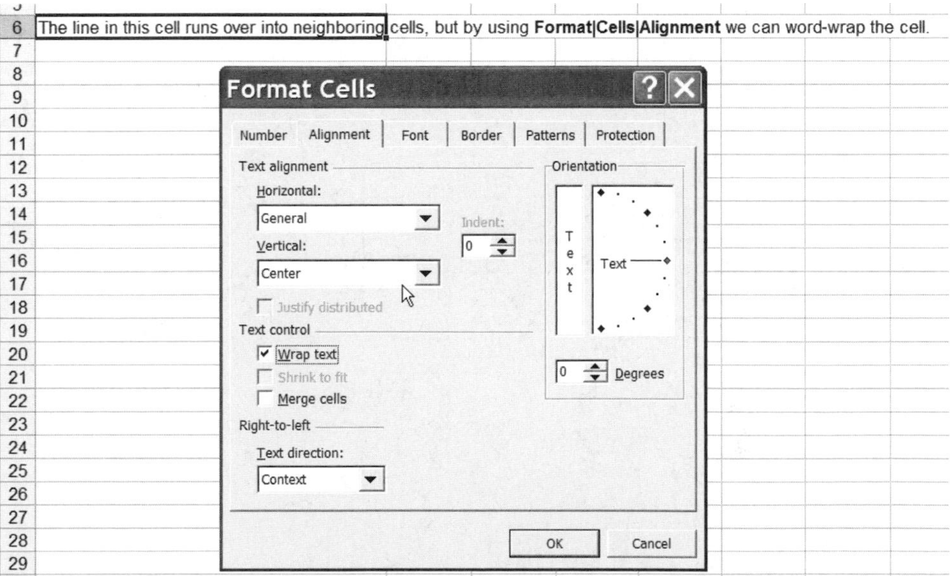

Here's the cell after we word-wrap it. (Note that in the dialogue box we've also set the vertical alignment of the cell to **Center**.)

	A
6	The line in this cell runs over into neighboring cells, but by using **Format|Cells|Alignment** we can word-wrap the cell.

35.3.1 Multiline Cells with Text Formulas

Sometimes you want to put a line break in a cell that has text formulas in it. In the next example, the text formula in cell A4 combines the text in cells A1 and A2.

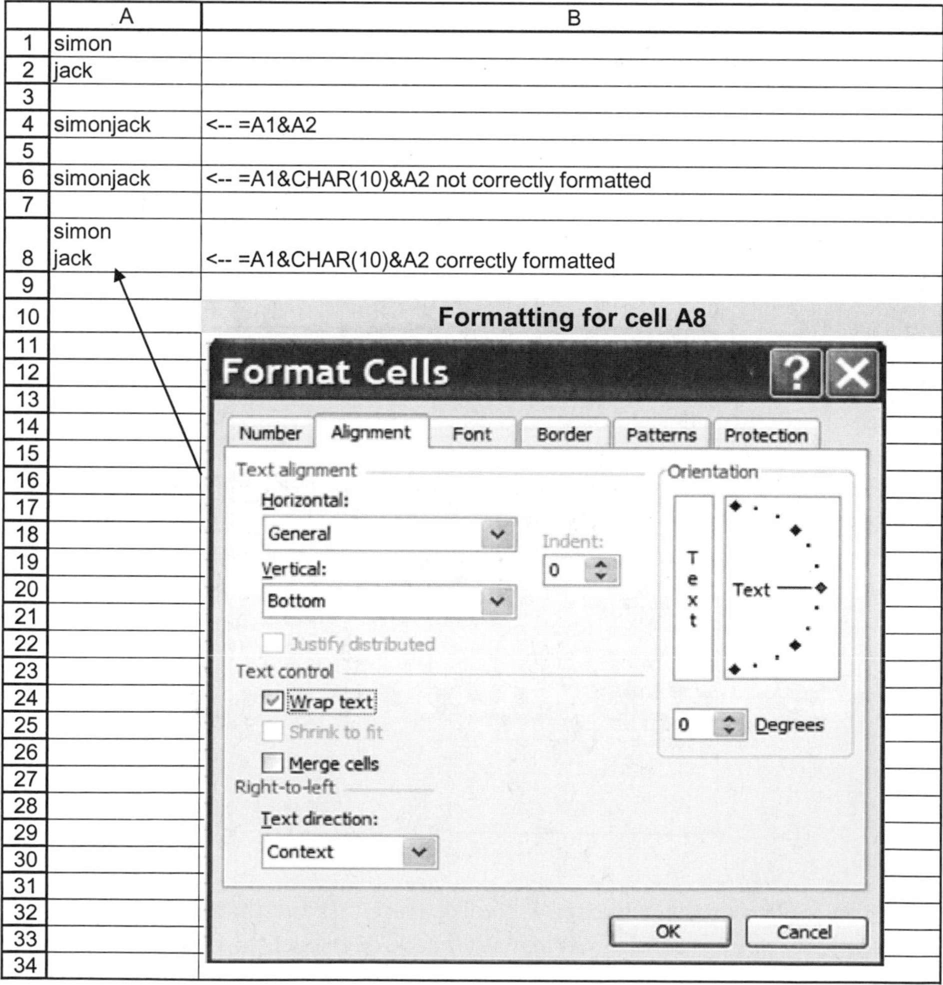

	A	B
1	simon	
2	jack	
3		
4	simonjack	<-- =A1&A2
5		
6	simonjack	<-- =A1&CHAR(10)&A2 not correctly formatted
7		
8	simon jack	<-- =A1&CHAR(10)&A2 correctly formatted
9		
10		**Formatting for cell A8**
11		
12		
13		
14		
15		
16		
17		
18		
19		
20		
21		
22		
23		
24		
25		
26		
27		
28		
29		
30		
31		
32		
33		
34		

We can put a line break into the text formula by doing two things:

1. Put Char(10) between A1 and A2—that is, write the formula =A1&Char(10)&A2 into the cell. Char(10) is the code for a hard line return.

2. Format the cell with **Format|Cells|Alignment** and click the box **Wrap text**. Now you will have a break between the contents of the two cells.

35.4 Writing on Multiple Spreadsheets

This Excel trick enables you to write in multiple spreadsheets at the same time.

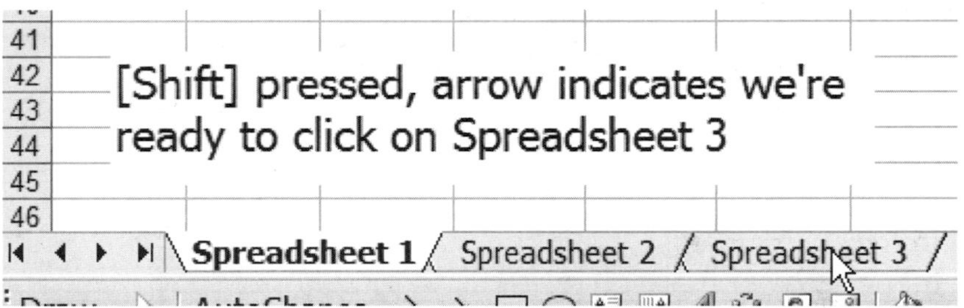

We hit **[Enter]** and choose all three spreadsheets:

Now anything we write in one of the sheets is also written in the same cells of all the others, so that we can produce three identical spreadsheets:

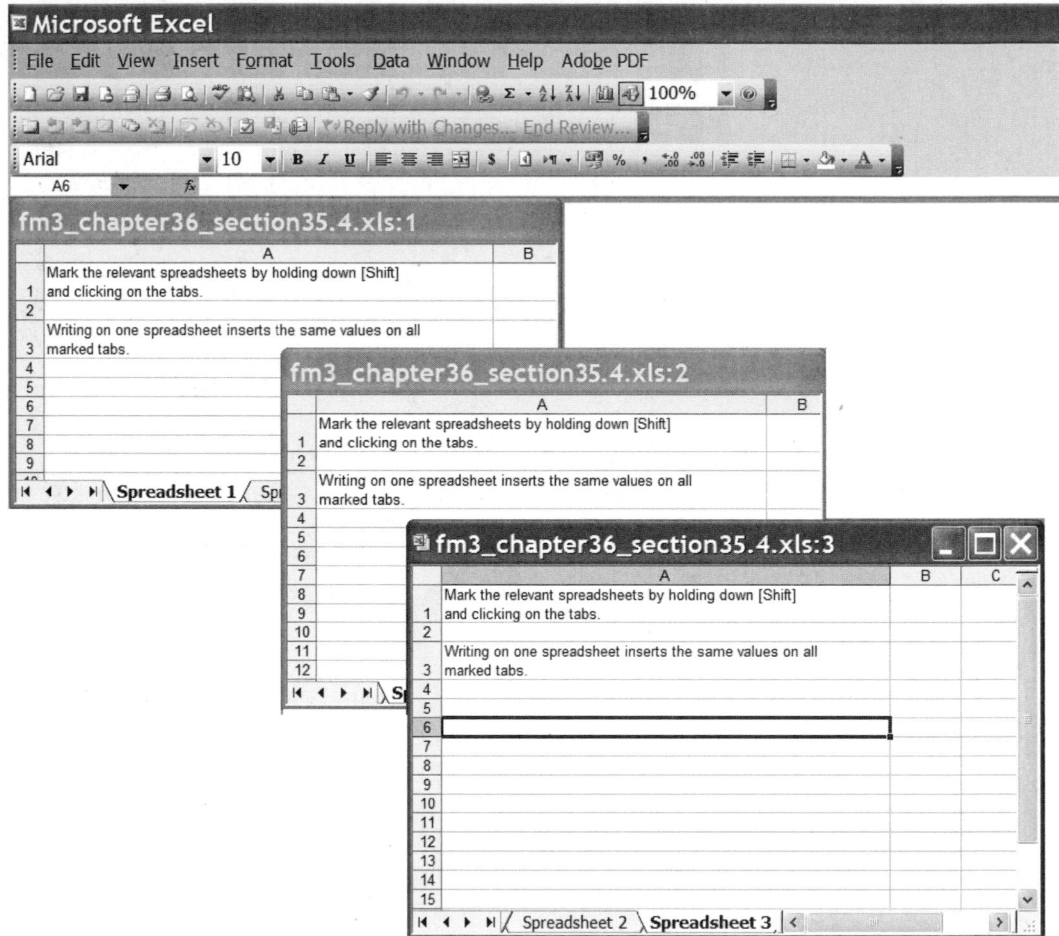

35.4.1 Moving Multiple Sheets of an Excel Notebook

We write on multiple sheets by holding down [Shift] and marking the tabs of the relevant spreadsheets. A similar trick works to move multiple sheets of the same Excel notebook:

- Mark the multiple sheets by holding down [Shift] and clicking on the appropriate sheets.
- Now use **Edit|Move** or **copy sheet** to move or copy the sheets to another location on the same spreadsheet or to a different spreadsheet.

35.5 Text Functions in Excel

Excel lets you change formulas to text. Here are some examples:

	A	B	C
1	**TEXT FUNCTIONS**		
2	Income	15,000	
3	Tax rate	35%	
4	Taxes owed	5,250	<-- =B3*B2
5			
6			
7	Tax rate as text	35.00%	<-- =TEXT(B3,"0.00%")
8		0.4	<-- =TEXT(B3,"0.0")
9			
10	Income as date	Jan. 24, 1941	<-- =TEXT(B2,"mmm. dd, yyyy")

Note that you can choose different ways of formatting cell B3 in text form. In cell B7 we have formatted the tax rate as a percentage with two decimal points, whereas in cell B8 we have formatted the tax rate as one decimal, causing it to be rounded off.

Note also the somewhat stupid example in cell B10: Since dates in Excel are just numbers that express the number of days from January 1, 1900, we can express the income of $15,000 in cell B2 as a date.

In the next section we use text functions to create chart titles that update themselves.

35.6 Chart Titles That Update

You want to have the chart title change when a parameter on the spreadsheet changes. For example, in the next spreadsheet, you want the chart title to indicate the growth rate.

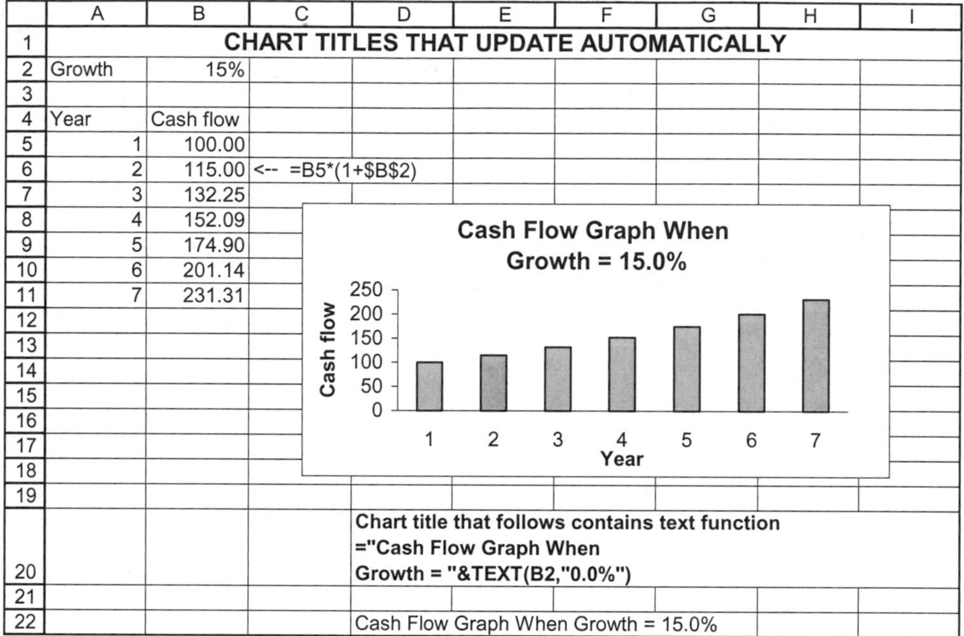

	A	B	C	D	E	F	G	H	I
1	CHART TITLES THAT UPDATE AUTOMATICALLY								
2	Growth	15%							
3									
4	Year	Cash flow							
5	1	100.00							
6	2	115.00	<-- =B5*(1+$B$2)						
7	3	132.25							
8	4	152.09							
9	5	174.90							
10	6	201.14							
11	7	231.31							
12									
13									
14									
15									
16									
17									
18									
19									
20				**Chart title that follows contains text function ="Cash Flow Graph When Growth = "&TEXT(B2,"0.0%")**					
21									
22				Cash Flow Graph When Growth = 15.0%					

Once we have completed the necessary steps, changing the growth rate will change both the graph *and* its title:

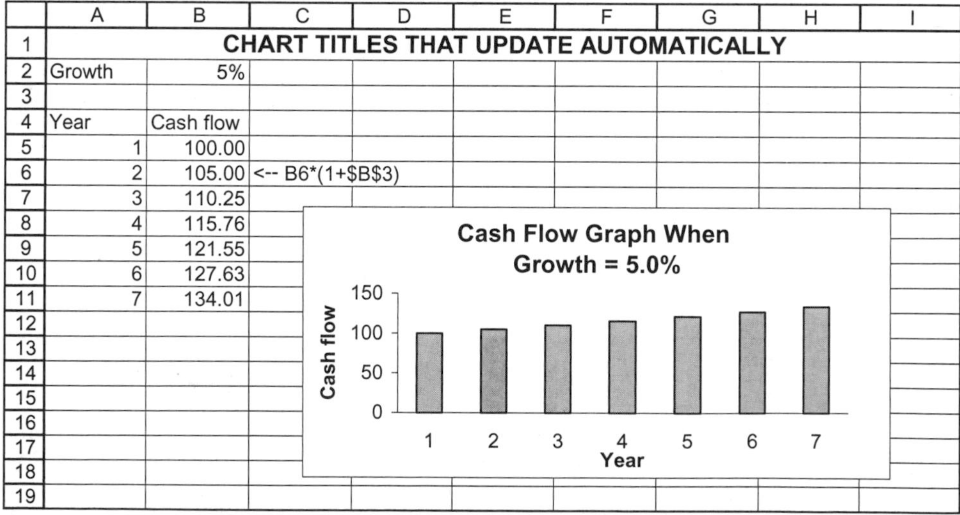

	A	B	C	D	E	F	G	H	I
1	CHART TITLES THAT UPDATE AUTOMATICALLY								
2	Growth	5%							
3									
4	Year	Cash flow							
5	1	100.00							
6	2	105.00	<-- B6*(1+$B$3)						
7	3	110.25							
8	4	115.76							
9	5	121.55							
10	6	127.63							
11	7	134.01							
12									
13									
14									
15									
16									
17									
18									
19									

To make graph titles update automatically, carry out the following steps:

• Create the graph you want in the format you want. Give the graph a "proxy title." (It makes no difference what, you're going to eliminate it soon.) At this stage your graph might look like this:

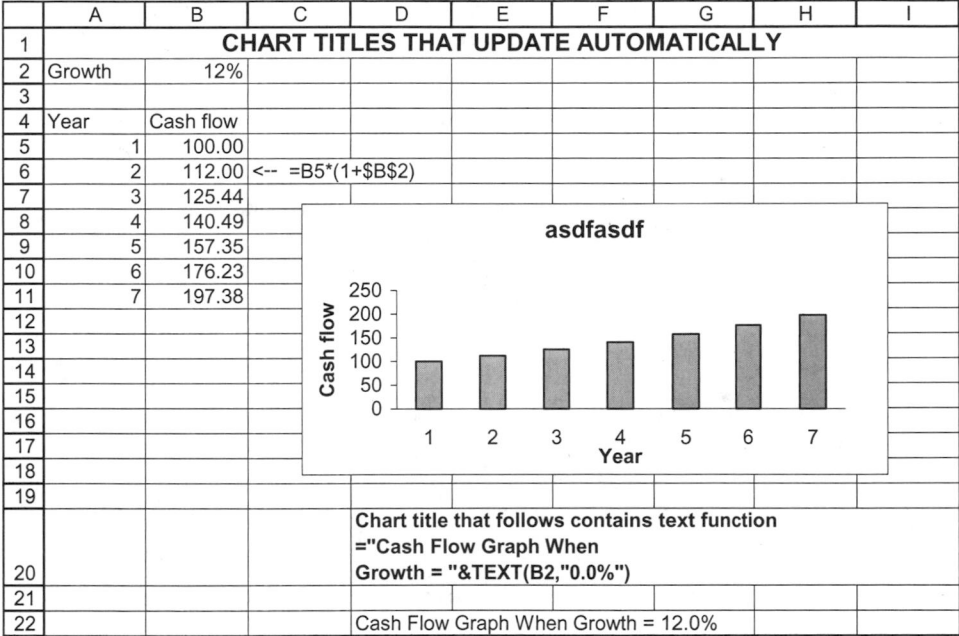

	A	B	C	D	E	F	G	H	I
1	CHART TITLES THAT UPDATE AUTOMATICALLY								
2	Growth	12%							
3									
4	Year	Cash flow							
5	1	100.00							
6	2	112.00	<-- =B5*(1+$B$2)						
7	3	125.44							
8	4	140.49							
9	5	157.35							
10	6	176.23							
11	7	197.38							
12									
13									
14									
15									
16									
17									
18									
19									
20				Chart title that follows contains text function ="Cash Flow Graph When Growth = "&TEXT(B2,"0.0%")					
21									
22				Cash Flow Graph When Growth = 12.0%					

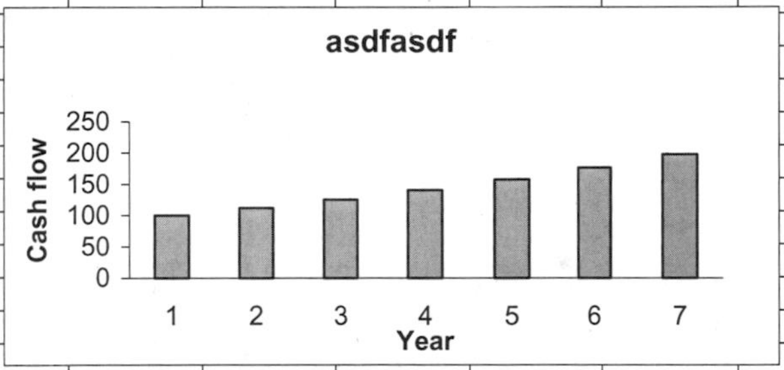

asdfasdf

Cash flow

250
200
150
100
50
0

1 2 3 4 5 6 7

Year

• Create the title you want in a cell. In this example, cell D21 contains the following formula: ="Cash Flow Graph When Growth = "&TEXT(B3,"0.0%")

• Click on the graph title to mark it, and then go to the formula bar and insert an equal sign to indicate a formula. Then **point** at cell D22 with the formula and click **[Enter]**. In the next picture, you see the chart title highlighted and in the formula bar "=Changing chart titles!$D$22" indicating the title of the graph.

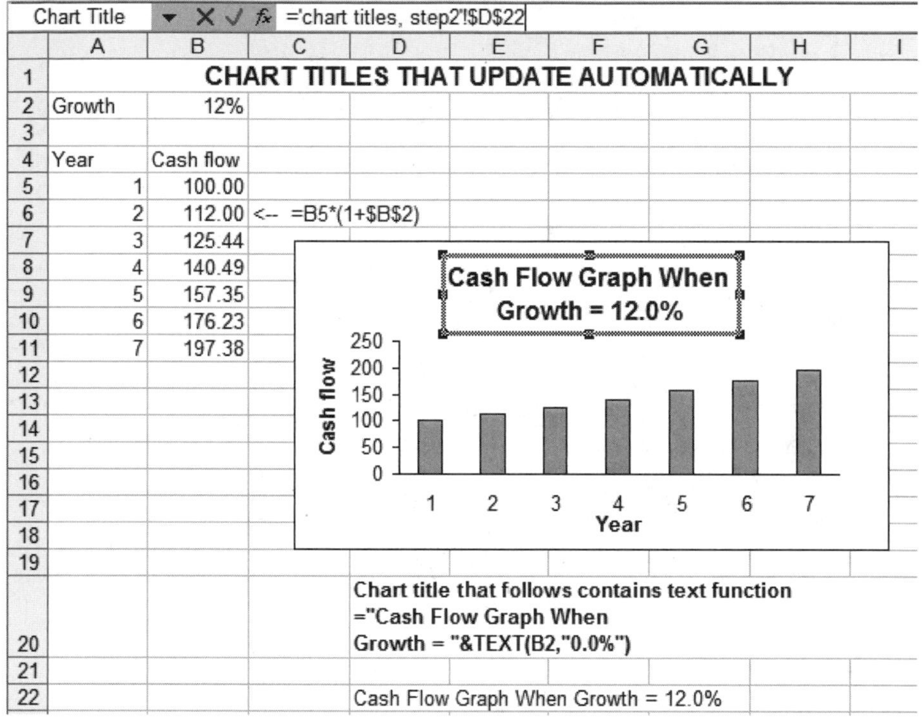

Chart Title =’chart titles, step2’!$D$22

	A	B	C	D	E	F	G	H
1	CHART TITLES THAT UPDATE AUTOMATICALLY							
2	Growth	12%						
3								
4	Year	Cash flow						
5	1	100.00						
6	2	112.00	<-- =B5*(1+$B$2)					
7	3	125.44						
8	4	140.49						
9	5	157.35						
10	6	176.23						
11	7	197.38						
20				Chart title that follows contains text function ="Cash Flow Graph When Growth = "&TEXT(B2,"0.0%")				
21								
22				Cash Flow Graph When Growth = 12.0%				

35.7 Getformula: A Useful Way of Annotating Spreadsheets

Throughout this book we have used a homemade Excel function to annotate our spreadsheets by showing the formulas inside cells. The formula, called **Getformula**,[1] is illustrated in the next spreadsheet:

	A	B	C	D	E	F
1	USING GETFORMULA IN A SPREADSHEET					
2	**Year**	**Cash flow**	**Discount rate**	**Present value**		
3	1	100	5%	95.24	<-- =B3/(1+C3)^A3	<-- =getformula(D3)
4	2	200	6%	178.00	<-- =B4/(1+C4)^A4	<-- =getformula(D4)
5	3	300	7%	244.89	<-- =B5/(1+C5)^A5	<-- =getformula(D5)
6	4	500	8%	367.51	<-- =B6/(1+C6)^A6	<-- =getformula(D6)
7						
8	Present value	885.64	<-- =SUM(D3:D6)			<-- =getformula(B8)
9		885.64	<-- {=SUM(B3:B6/(1+C3:C6)^A3:A6)}			<-- =getformula(B9)

1. I thank Maja Sliwinski and Benjamin Czaczkes for helping develop this formula.

The annotation in cell E3 is generated by the formula **Getformula(D3)**, and the annotations in other cells are similarly generated.

Getformula has two interesting properties:

• It is dynamic: If you change something in your spreadsheet, **Getformula** adjusts automatically. As a result, you will never have to worry about showing the correct cell contents! Here's an example: In the following spreadsheet, we've added a column and a row to the computations:

	A	B	C	D	E	F	G
1	**USING GETFORMULA IN A SPREADSHEET** **We've added a column and a row--Getformula automatically shows the adjusted cell formulas**						
2							
3		**Year**	**Cash flow**	**Discount rate**	**Present value**		
4		1	100	5%	95.24	<-- =C4/(1+D4)^B4	<-- =getformula(E4)
5		2	200	6%	178.00	<-- =C5/(1+D5)^B5	<-- =getformula(E5)
6		3	300	7%	244.89	<-- =C6/(1+D6)^B6	<-- =getformula(E6)
7		4	500	8%	367.51	<-- =C7/(1+D7)^B7	<-- =getformula(E7)
8							
9		Present value	885.64	<-- =SUM(E4:E7)			<-- =getformula(C9)
10			885.64	<-- {=SUM(C4:C7/(1+D4:D7)^B4:B7)}			<-- =getformula(C10)

• **Getformula** automatically adds curly brackets { } to array formulas. The contents of cell C10 (which was cell B9 in the original example) illustrate an array technique discussed in Chapter 34 for computing the present value where each cash flow has a separate discount rate: $\sum \frac{CF_t}{(1+r_t)^t}$. **Getformula** senses that this is an array formula and puts in the brackets.

35.7.1 Adding Getformula to Your Spreadsheet

Getformula is a VBA user-defined formula, a topic discussed in Chapter 36. To add such a formula to your spreadsheet, first open the spreadsheet in which you want the formula to work. Push [Alt] + F11. This action will open the VBA editor. The screen will look something like the following:

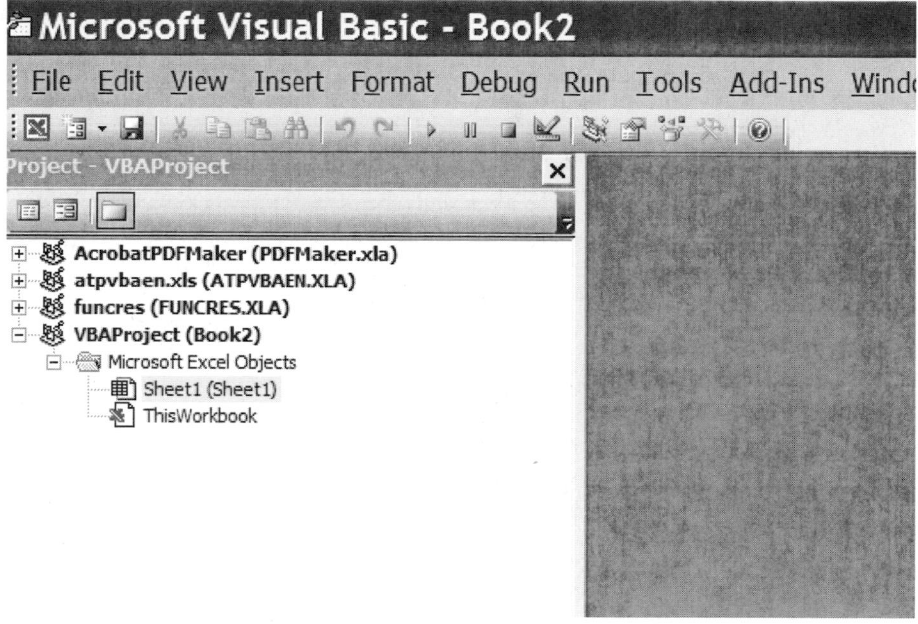

(Depending on all kinds of things, your screen may look different. Don't worry about the differences.)

Hit **Insert|Module**:

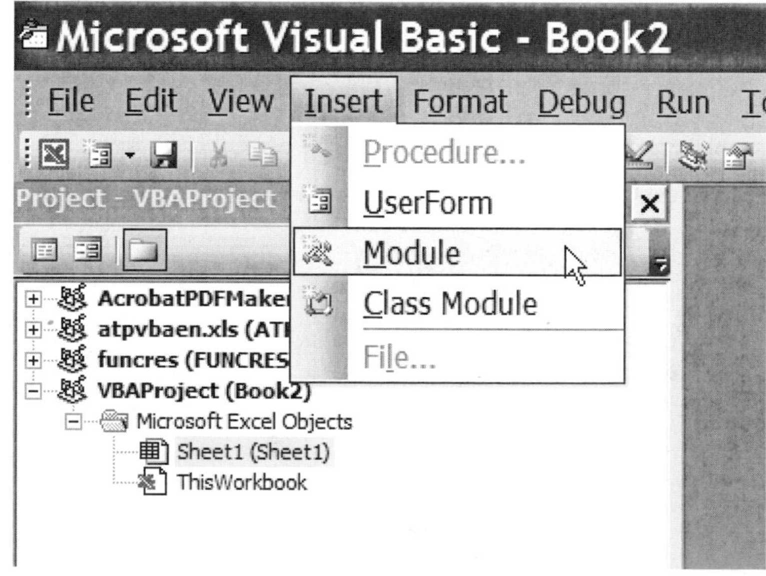

Now insert the following text into the module window. You can copy this text from any of the spreadsheets attached to this book.

```
Function getformula(r As Range) As String
  Application.Volatile
  If r.HasArray Then
  getformula = "<- " & " {" & _
  r.FormulaArray & "}"
  Else
  getformula = "<- " & " " & r.FormulaArray
  End If
End Function
Function ggetformula(r As Range) As String
  Application.Volatile
  If r.HasArray Then
  ggetformula = " {" & r.FormulaArray & "}"
  Else
  ggetformula = r.FormulaArray
  End If
End Function
```

Close VBA window (no need to save). The formula is now part of the spreadsheet and will be saved along with it.

35.8 Putting Greek Symbols in Cells

How do we type Greek letters in a spreadsheet?

	A	B
1	**GREEK AND SYMBOLS IN CELLS**	
2	Initial stock price	30
3	Mean, μ	15%
4	Standard deviation, σ	20%
5	Delta, Δt	0.004

This task is fairly simple, if you know the Latin = alphabet equivalents for the Greek letters. (For example, μ and σ are lowercase *m* and *s*, respectively; Σ and Δ are uppercase *S* and *D*.) For example, we first typed "Deltat, Dt" into cell A5 and then marked the *D* in the formula bar:

Arial 10

A5 fx Delta, Dt

	A	B
1	**GREEK AND SYMBOLS IN CELLS**	
2	Initial stock price	30
3	Mean, μ	15%
4	Standard deviation, σ	20%
5	Delta, Dt	0.004
6		

We then changed the font from "Arial" to "Symbol":

Symbol 10

A5 fx Delta, Dt

	A	B
1	**GREEK AND SYMBOLS IN CELLS**	
2	Initial stock price	30
3	Mean, μ	15%
4	Standard deviation, σ	20%
5	Delta, Δt	0.004

Pressing **[Enter]** produces the desired result.

35.9 Superscripts and Subscripts

It is not a problem to type subscripts or superscripts in Excel. Enter text into a cell, and then mark the letters you want to turn into a subscript or superscript:

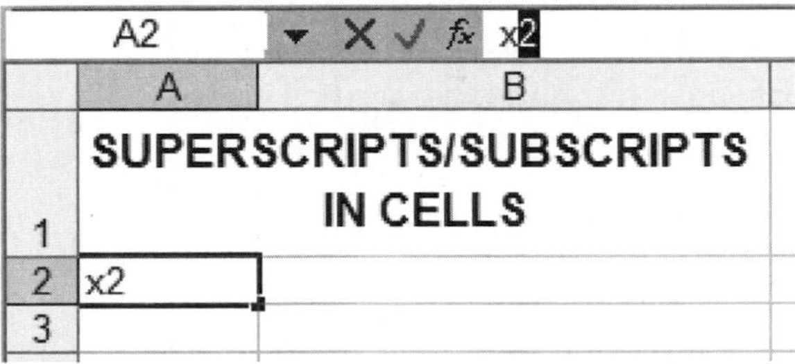

Now go to **Format|Cells** and mark the **Superscript** box:

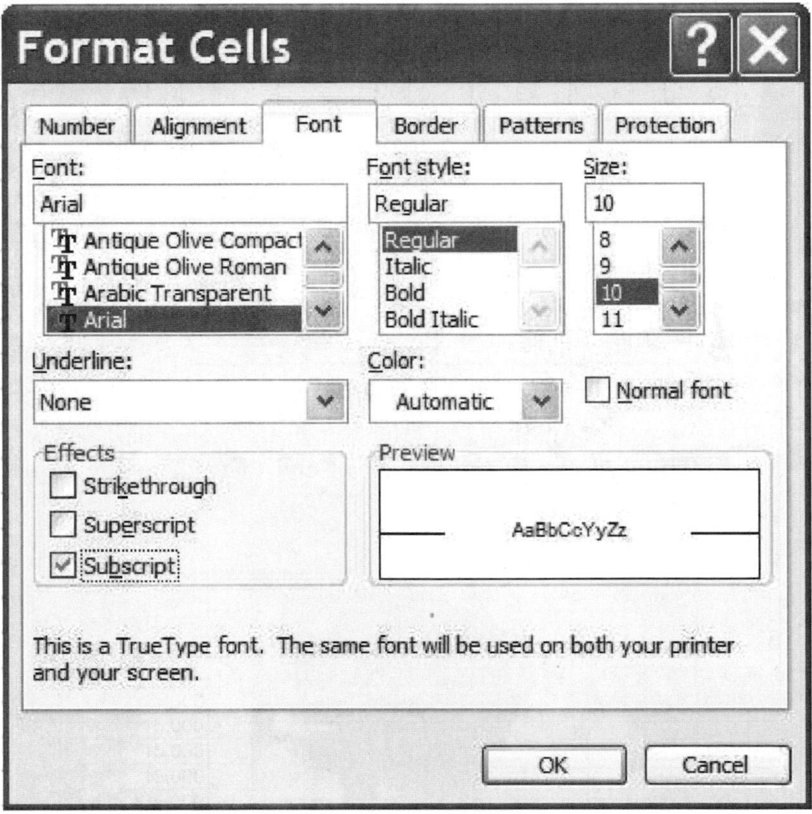

Here's the result:

	A	B
1	**SUPERSCRIPTS/SUBSCRIPTS IN CELLS**	
2	x^2	
3		
4	x^2 i	Cannot put superscript and subscript one above the other

As you can see in cell A4, you cannot put a subscript and a superscript on the same letter. That is, you cannot create x_i^2.

35.10 Named Cells

It is sometimes useful to give a name to a cell. Here's an example:

	A	B	C
1	**NAMED CELLS**		
2	Income	15,000	
3	Tax rate	33%	
4	Tax paid	4,950	<-- =B3*B2

We want to be able to refer to cell B3 by the name "tax." To achieve this purpose, we mark the cell and then go to the name tab on the toolbar:

B3 ▾ fx 33%

	A	B	C
1	**NAMED CELLS**		
2	Income	15,000	
3	Tax rate	33%	
4	Tax paid	4,950	<-- =B3*B2
5			

Typing in the word "tax" on the highlighted "B3" allows us to reference cell B3 by this name anywhere in the Excel notebook:

	A	B	C
1	**NAMED CELLS**		
2	Income	15,000	
3	Tax rate	33%	
4	Tax paid	4,950	<-- =tax*B2

Sometimes Excel lets us use cell names without ever actually going through the procedure just described. In the next example, Excel lets us use the column headers as cell names:

	A	B	C	D
7	**Sales**	**Margin**	**Profit**	
8	1000	20%	200	<-- =Sales*Margin
9	5000	30%	1500	<-- =Sales*Margin

35.11 Hiding Cells

In this text we have often hidden the cell contents of data table headers. (This topic is discussed in detail in Chapter 30.) Here's a simple data table:

	A	B	C	D
1	**HIDING CELLS**			
2	Payment	100		
3	Number of payments	15		
4	Discount rate	15%		
5	Present value	$584.74	<-- =PV(B4,B3,-B2)	
6				
7			**PV of payments**	
8	**Data table**		584.74	<-- =B5 , data table header
9		0%	1,500.00	
10		3%	1,193.79	
11		6%	971.22	
12		9%	806.07	
13		12%	681.09	
14		15%	584.74	
15		18%	509.16	
16		21%	448.90	

The data table header in cell C8 is necessary for the table to work, but it is ugly and may be confusing if the table is copied into other documents. To hide the contents of C8, mark the cell and go to the **Format|Cells** menu (or click on the right mouse button):

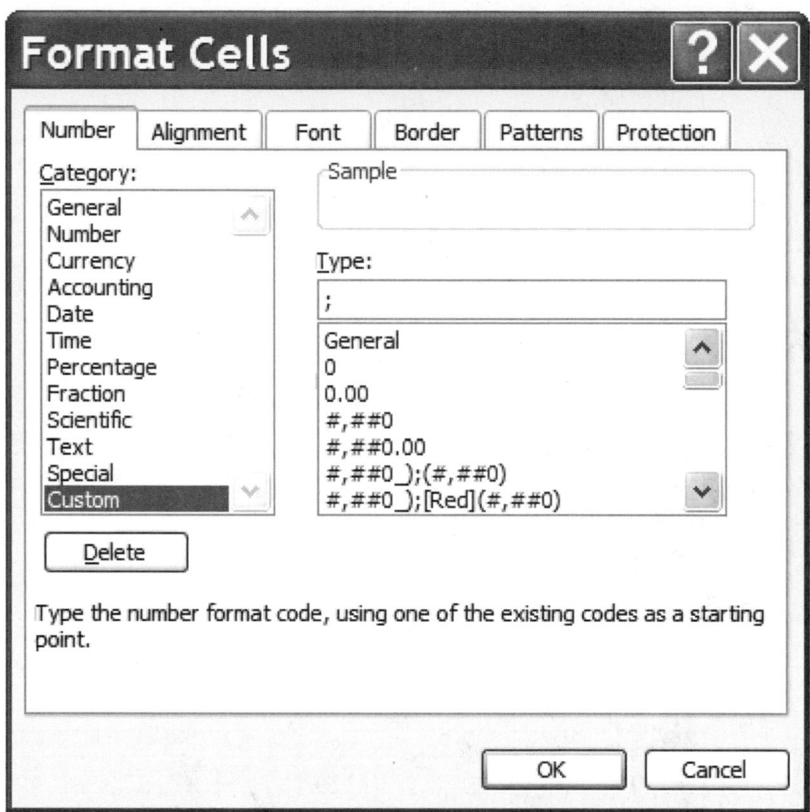

In the **Number|Custom|Type** box we have put in a semicolon. This preserves the cell contents but prevents them from being seen. Now when you copy the cells, this is the way they will appear:

	B	C	D
7		PV of payments	
8			<-- =B5 , data table header
9	0%	1,500.00	
10	3%	1,193.79	
11	6%	971.22	
12	9%	806.07	
13	12%	681.09	
14	15%	584.74	
15	18%	509.16	
16	21%	448.90	

Note the comment in cell D8: We advise you to always *annotate* your spreadsheet, so that when you come back to it after a few weeks or months, you will know that cell C8 really does have something in it!

One final note: To hide a cell that contains a reference to another cell containing a formula, three semicolons (;;;) may be necessary. In the next spreadsheet, cell B4 contains the function **IF**. Cell B6 refers to this cell. In order to hide B6, we use three semicolons instead of one in the **Format|Cells|Number|Custom|Type**. (If there's logic here, it escapes us!)

	A	B	C
1	**HIDING A CELL THAT REFERS TO A FORMULA**		
2	a	33	
3	b	8	
4	c	bbb	<-- =IF(B2+B3<15,"aaa","bbb")
5			
6	Cell to be hidden -->		<-- =B4

35.12 Formula Auditing

Excel can tell you where you've used a cell in your formulas, and which cells a particular formula depends on. Clicking on **Tools|Formula Auditing** brings up a menu that allows you to make use of this ability:

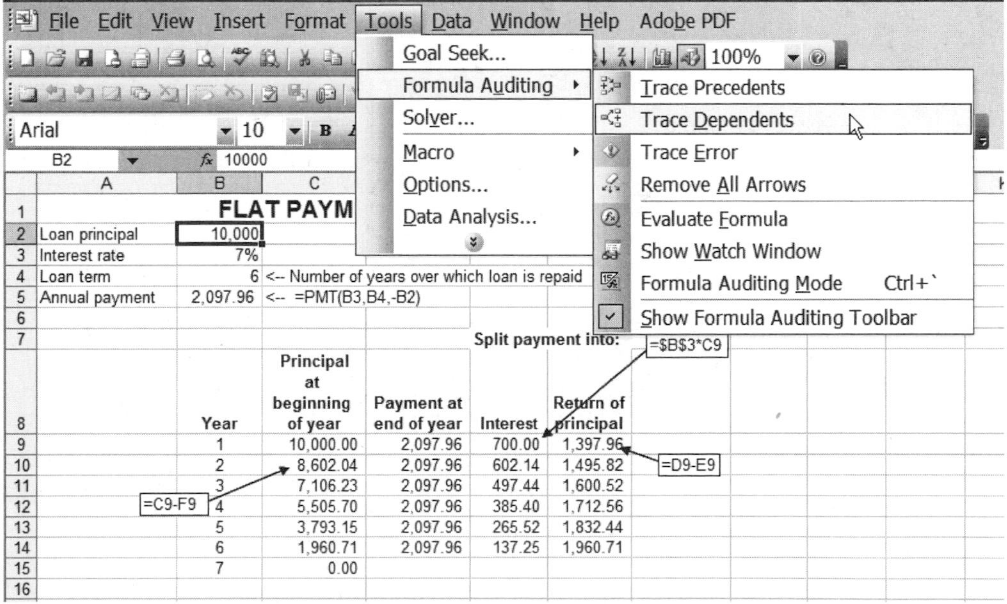

Here's the result:

	A	B	C	D	E	F	G
1	FLAT PAYMENT SCHEDULES						
2	Loan principal	10,000					
3	Interest rate	7%					
4	Loan term	6	<-- Number of years over which loan is repaid				
5	Annual payment	2,097.96	<-- =PMT(B3,B4,-B2)				
6							
7					**Split payment into:**		=$B$3*C9
8		**Year**	**Principal at beginning of year**	**Payment at end of year**	**Interest**	**Return of principal**	
9		1	10,000.00	2,097.96	700.00	1,397.96	
10		2	8,602.04	2,097.96	602.14	1,495.82	=D9-E9
11		3	7,106.23	2,097.96	497.44	1,600.52	
12	=C9-F9	4	5,505.70	2,097.96	385.40	1,712.56	
13		5	3,793.15	2,097.96	265.52	1,832.44	
14		6	1,960.71	2,097.96	137.25	1,960.71	
15		7	0.00				

In a similar way we can check to see which cells are precedents of a particular cell:

	A	B	C	D	E	F	G
1	FLAT PAYMENT SCHEDULES						
2	Loan principal	10,000					
3	Interest rate	7%					
4	Loan term	6	<-- Number of years over which loan is repaid				
5	Annual payment	2,097.96	<-- =PMT(B3,B4,-B2)				
6							
7					**Split payment into:**		=$B$3*C9
8		**Year**	**Principal at beginning of year**	**Payment at end of year**	**Interest**	**Return of principal**	
9		1	10,000.00	2,097.96	700.00	1,397.96	
10		2	8,602.04	2,097.96	602.14	1,495.82	=D9-E9
11		3	7,106.23	2,097.96	497.44	1,600.52	
12	=C9-F9	4	5,505.70	2,097.96	385.40	1,712.56	
13		5	3,793.15	2,097.96	265.52	1,832.44	
14		6	1,960.71	2,097.96	137.25	1,960.71	
15		7	0.00				

Formula auditing can help you implement a general rule of good spreadsheet writing: You should try to avoid cells that don't have either precedents or dependents.

35.13 Formatting Millions as Thousands

By using **Format|Cells|Custom** you can change millions into thousands. To see where this function is handy, consider the following income statement:

	A	B
1	**Income statement**	
2	Sales	31,235,689
3	Cost of goods sold	15,250,888
4	Sales, general and administrative	2,356,188
5	Interest	1,999,824
6	Profits before taxes	11,628,789
7	Taxes	4,418,940
8	Profits after taxes	7,209,849

We want to make the income statement appear in thousands. (In other words, instead of 31,235,689 we will see 31,235.) Here's how this can be done:

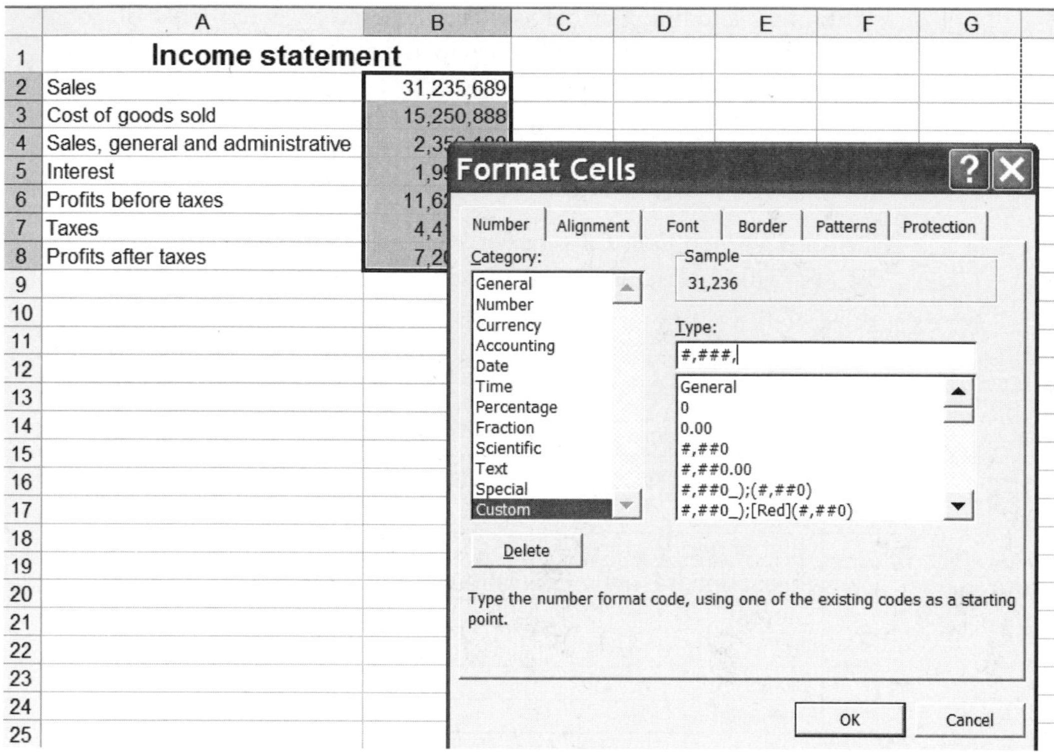

In the **Type** box we have indicated **#,###,**. The comma at the end indicates that we want Excel to drop the last three digits in the number, and the **#,###** indicates that we want the remaining numbers to appear with a comma. This procedure is merely a formatting change—the actual numbers are not changed: In cell B10 in the following output, we've multiplied the Sales by 2; the result is 62,471,378.

	A	B	C
1	**Income statement**		
2	Sales	31,236	
3	Cost of goods sold	15,251	
4	Sales, general and administrative	2,356	
5	Interest	2,000	
6	Profits before taxes	11,629	
7	Taxes	4,419	
8	Profits after taxes	7,210	
9			
10	The cells retain their values	62,471,378	<-- =2*B2

Adding another comma to the **Type** box (that is, **#,###,,**) will drop another three digits.

VI Introduction to Visual Basic for Applications

Chapters 36–41 (written by Benjamin Czaczkes) cover the Visual Basic for Applications (VBA) techniques needed in this book. While they are far from being a complete VBA programming guide, these chapters should enable you to do a competent job of programming financial functions.

Chapter 36 introduces VBA and shows you how to write user-defined functions. We have used these functions in several places throughout this book, including in Chapter 19 (to define the Black-Scholes option prices), Chapters 22 and 23 (Monte Carlo pricing), and Chapters 25 and 26 (to define the duration). Chapter 37 discusses types and loops. An example of the use of a loop is the function that calculates an option's implied volatility in Chapter 19. Chapter 38 discusses macros and user intervention, allowing you to write routines that ask the user for input—typically through a message box to be filled in on the spreadsheet. Chapter 39 shows you how to use VBA arrays (used in the lognormal simulations of Chapter 18). Chapter 40 discusses the use of VBA objects. The last chapter in this part, Chapter 41, shows how to use VBA to import information from the web into Excel.

36 User-Defined Functions with VBA

36.1 Overview

Chapters 36–41 discuss the uses of Excel's programming language, Visual Basic for Applications (VBA). VBA provides a complete programming language and environment fully integrated with Excel and all other Microsoft Office applications. In this chapter we introduce user-defined functions, which are used in various places in this book.

The examples and screen shots depict the Excel 2003 working environment but are fully compatible (unless otherwise noted) with all versions of Excel using Visual Basic for Applications (Version 5 and above).[1]

36.2 Using the VBA Editor to Build a User-Defined Function

A user function is a saved list of instructions for Excel that produces a value. Once defined, a user function can be used inside an Excel worksheet like any other function.[2]

In this section we will write our first user-defined function. Before you can perform this task, you need to activate the VBA editor. You can do so either from the Excel menu (**Tools|Macro|Visual Basic Editor**) or by using the keyboard shortcut [Alt] + F11. The result in both cases is a new window like the following screen shot (your window may look slightly different, but it will be functionally equivalent):

1. Up to and including Excel 2007.
2. User-defined functions are usually attached to a specific workbook and are only available if that workbook is currently open in Excel. One way of having access to a VBA function across worksheets is to put it in an add-in; see Chapter 40 for an introduction to add-ins in Excel.

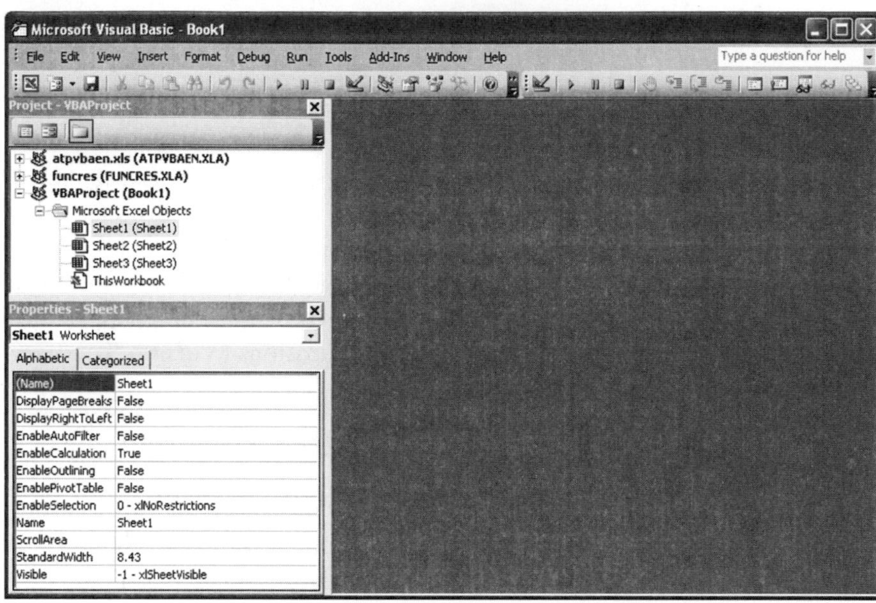

A user-defined function needs to be written in a module. To open a new module, select **Insert|Module** from the menu in the VBA editor environment. This step will open a new window, as follows:

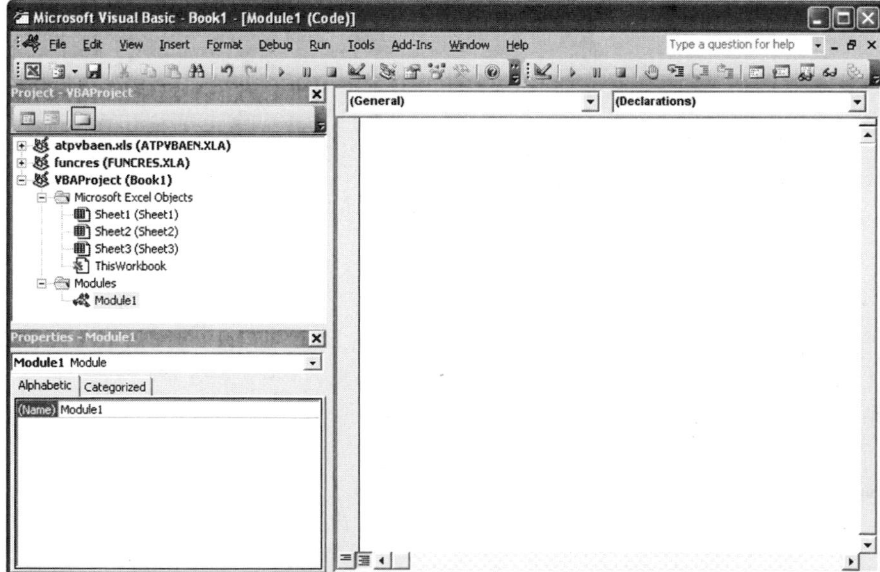

We are now ready to write our first function. A user-defined function in Excel has three obligatory elements:

1. A header line with the name of the function and a list of parameters.
2. A closing line (usually inserted by VBA).
3. Some program lines between the header and the closing line.

Start writing the first line of the function:

```
function Function1 (Parameter)
```

As soon as you end the line with a tap on the Enter key, VBA will do a cleanup job. The color of all the words that VBA recognizes as part of its programming language ("reserved words") will change. All reserved words will be capitalized. The closing line for the function will be inserted, and the cursor will be in position between the header and the closing line ready for you to go on typing.

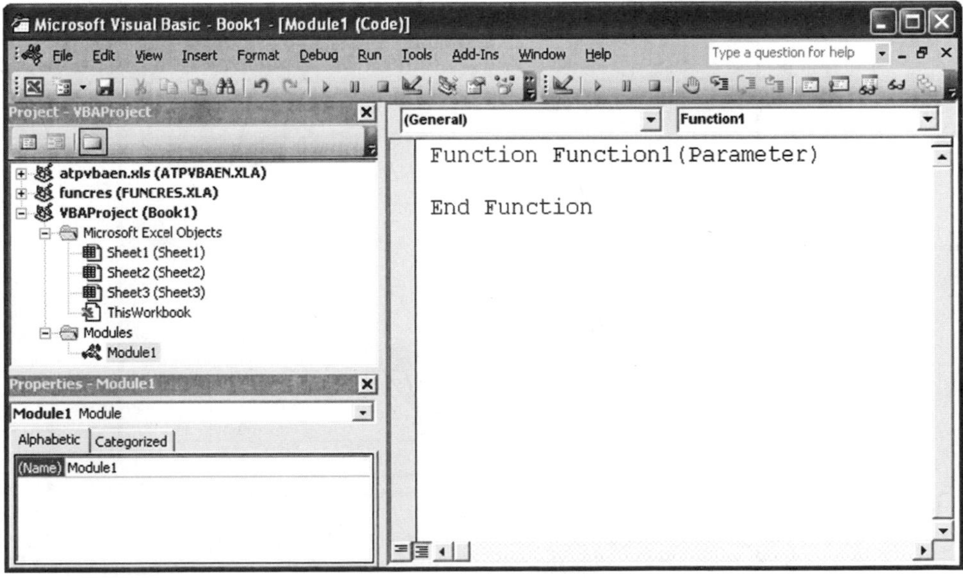

We are now ready to type our function line. This is the line that makes our function do something.[3] Our first function will take a variable, multiply it by 3, and add 1:

```
Function Function1(Parameter)
    Function1 = Parameter * 3 + 1
End Function
```

You can now use this function in your spreadsheet:

	A	B	C
1	**Functions in Action**		
2	Parameter	1.25	
3	Function1	4.75	<-- =Function1(B2)

You can also use the function in the Excel Function Wizard. Clicking on the *fx* icon on the toolbar will produce the following screen:

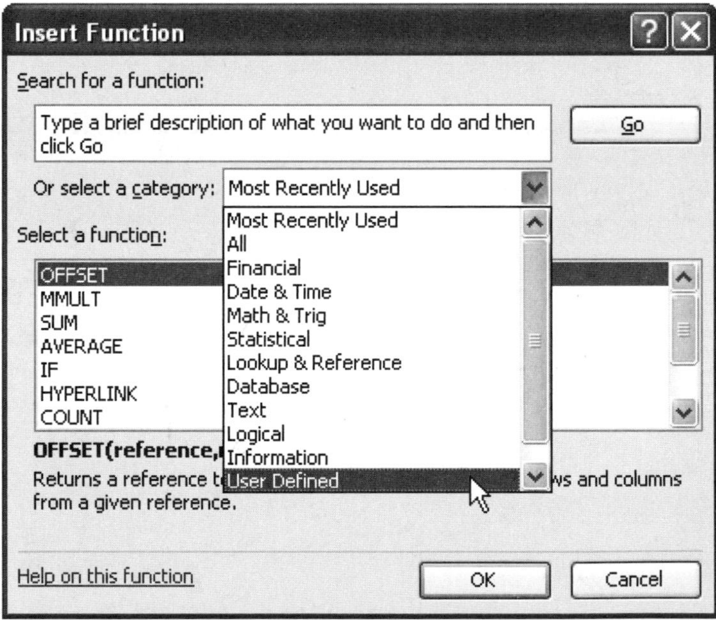

3. The indentation of lines in VBA code, which we added manually, is not required by VBA but makes reading the code much easier.

Selecting "User Defined" from the pull-down menu will present the following screen listing all user-defined functions; one of them should be the function **Function1**:

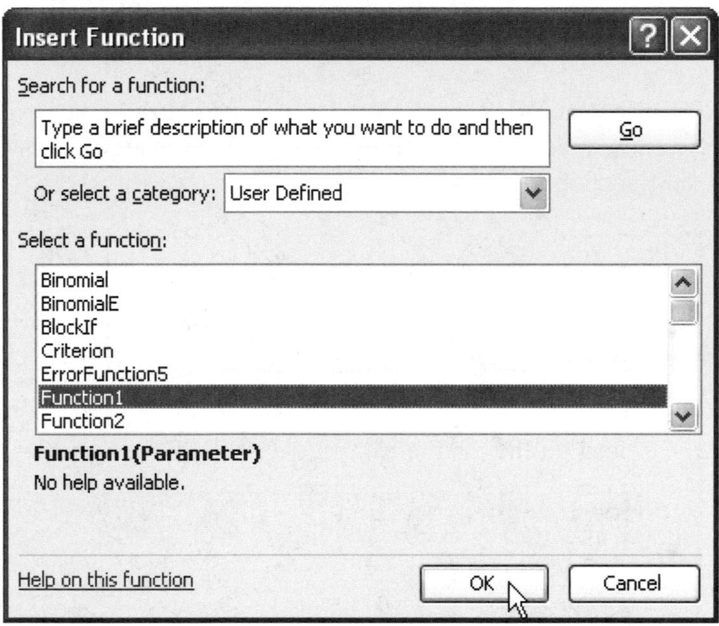

When you select **Function1** and click OK, you will see that Excel treats this like any other function, bringing up a dialogue box that asks for the location or value of **Parameter**:

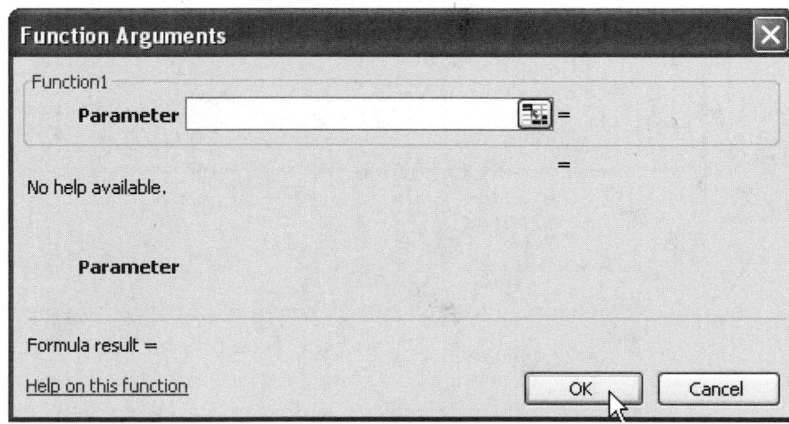

Notice that at this point there is no explanation or help for the function. The next section provides part of the remedy (the simple part); the full solution is beyond the scope of this book.

36.3 Providing Help for User-Defined Functions in the Function Wizard

Excel's Function Wizard provides a short help line (an explanation of what the function does). Here's how Excel explains its own functions in the Function Wizard:

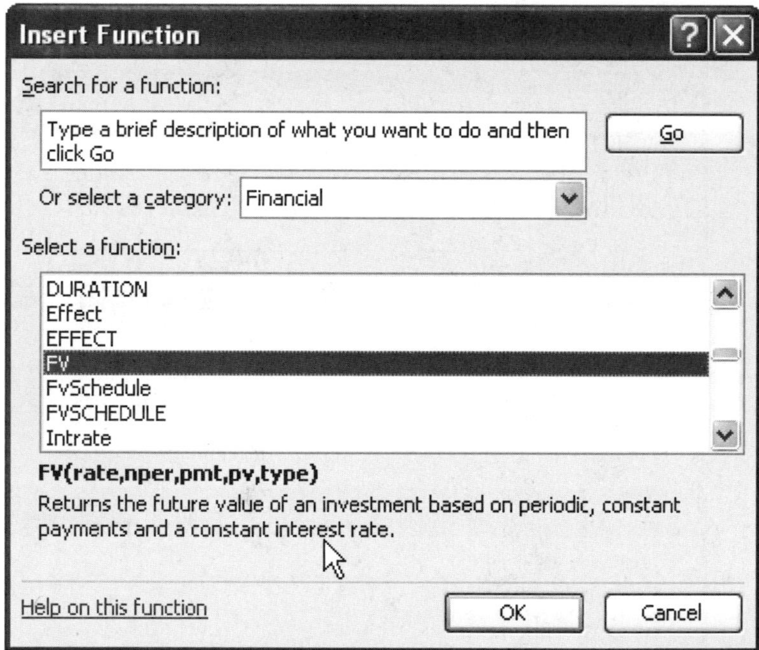

To attach a text description to **Function1**, activate the macro selection box. You can do so either from the Excel menu (**Tools|Macro|Macros**) or by using the keyboard shortcut [Alt] + F8.

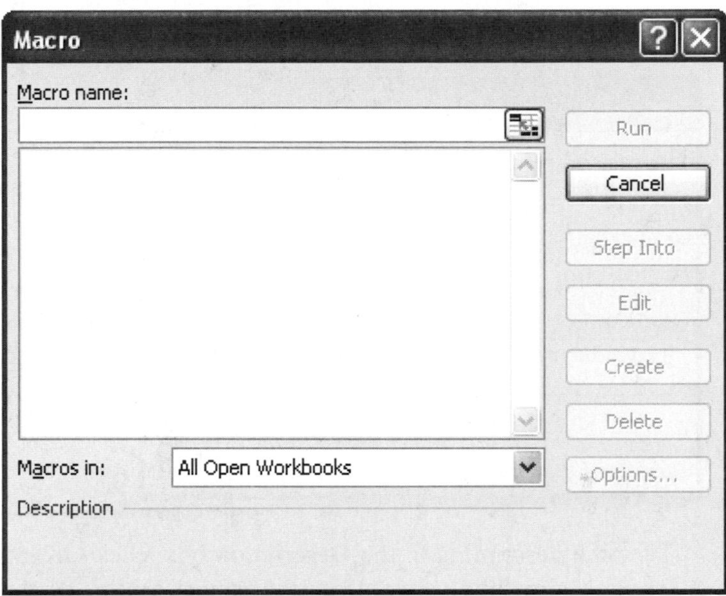

Click in the **Macro name** box, and type the name of the function. (Notice that you did not see the function name in the preceding macro dialogue box; you have to type it in.)

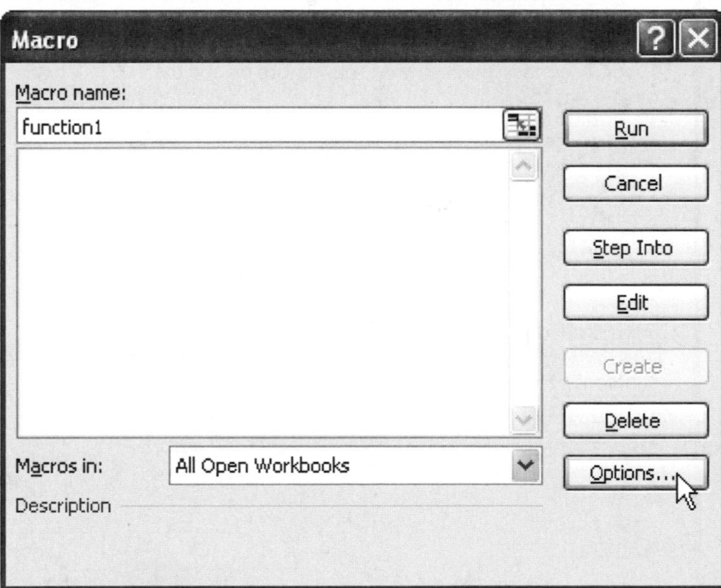

Click on the **Options** button.

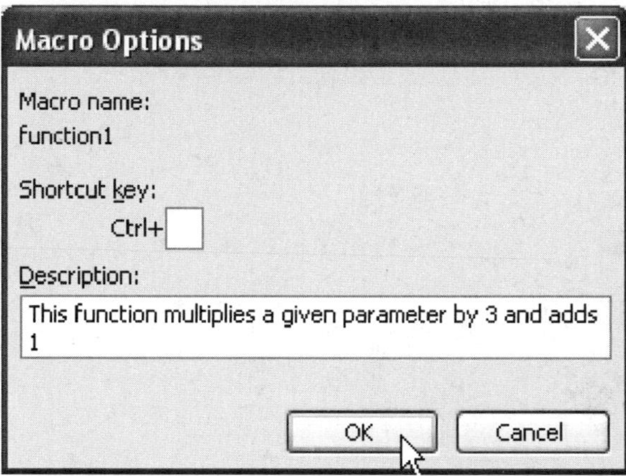

Type the description in the **Description** box, click OK, and close the macro selection box using either the cancel button or the corner X. **Function1** now has a help line.

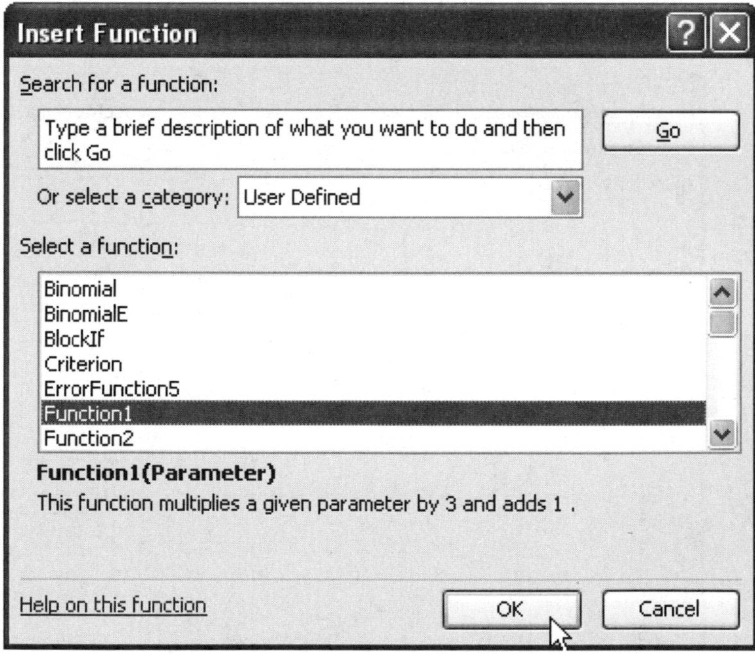

Excel functions have help lines attached to each of the parameters and a help file entry. We can supply the same for our function; sadly, the subject is beyond the scope of this introduction.

36.4 Fixing Mistakes in VBA

Once you start using VBA, you're sure to make mistakes. In this section we illustrate several typical mistakes and help you correct them. This list is not meant to be exhaustive—we have selected mistakes typically made by VBA beginners.

36.4.1 Mistake 1: Using the Wrong Syntax

Suppose that in writing **Function1** you forget the plus sign between **Parameter*3** and the **1** (recall that the function is supposed to return **Parameter*3+1**). Once you hit the Enter key, you get the following error message:

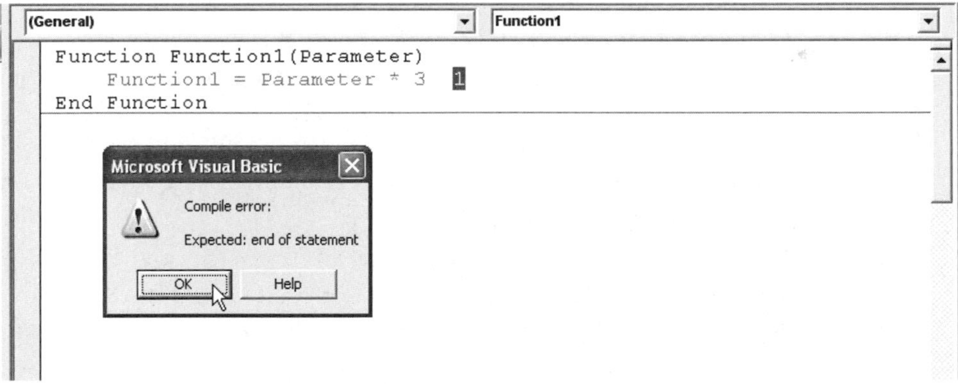

Clicking the OK button allows us to correct this problem.

36.4.2 Mistake 2: The Right Syntax with a Typing Error

It's easy to make typing errors that will only be detected once you try to use the function. In this example we define two functions—**Function1** and **Function2**. Unfortunately, the program line for **Function2** mistakenly calls the function "Function1":

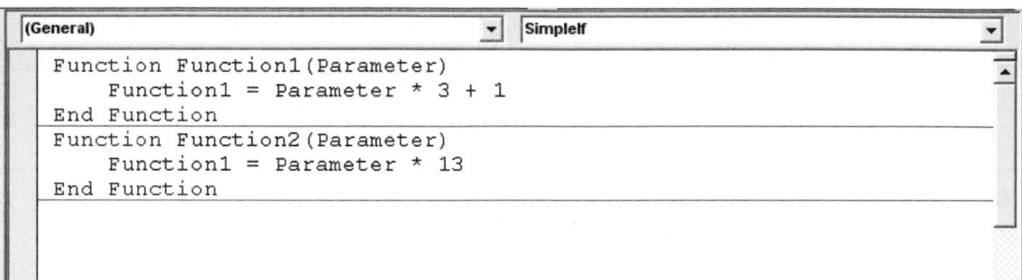

The VBA editor does not recognize this mistake. Only when you try to use the function in a worksheet will Excel notify you that you've made a mistake. This mistake will take you to the VBA editor:

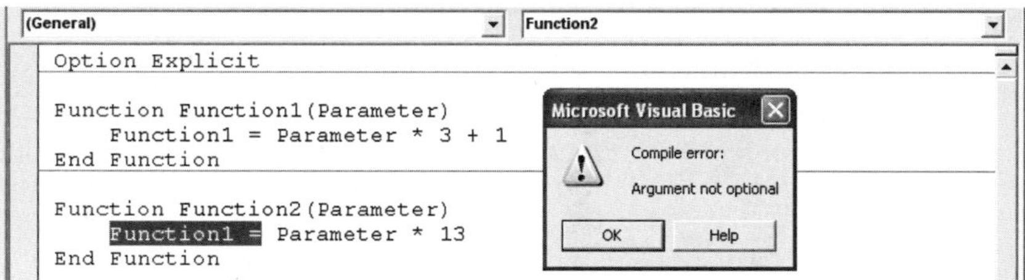

If you recognize your mistake, you can correct it. You can also try to go to the VBA help by clicking **Help** (in many cases this attempt will lead to an incomprehensibly complicated explanation).

Suppose you recognize your mistake. You click OK and get ready to correct the error by replacing the word "Function1" by "Function2." At this point your screen looks like this:

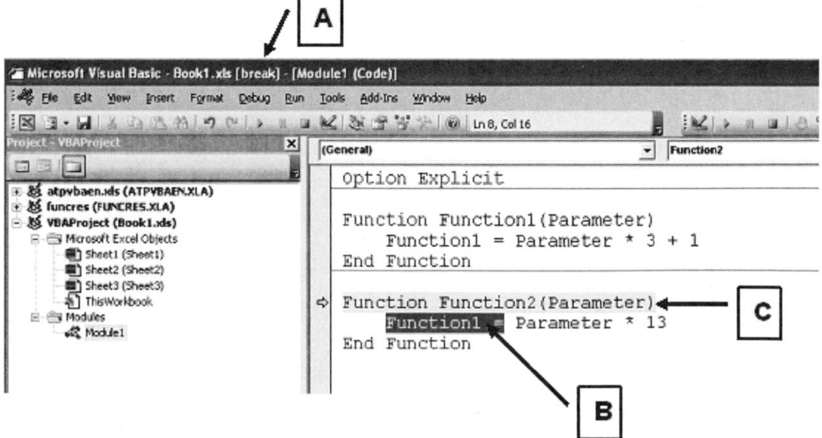

Notice the following:

A. The word "[break]" appears in the title bar.

B. The offending symbol is selected.

C. The function line is highlighted and pointed to by an arrow in the margin.

Because VBA found an error while trying to execute the function, it moved into a special execution mode called debug-break mode. For now all we need to do is get out of this special mode so we can get on with our work. We do so by clicking the appropriate icon on the VBA toolbar (a small dark square). Now you can fix the function and use it.

36.5 Conditional Execution: Using If Statements in VBA Functions

In this section we explore the **If** statements available to you in VBA. Not all things in life are linear, and sometimes decisions have to be made. **If** statements are one way of making decisions in VBA.

36.5.1 The One-Line If Statement

The one-line **If** statement is the simplest way to control the execution of a VBA function: One statement is executed if a condition is true, and another is executed if a condition is not true. The complete condition and its statement should be on one line. Here's an example:

```
Function SimpleIf(Parameter)
    If Parameter > 5 Then SimpleIf = 1 Else SimpleIf
    = 15
End Function
```

We can now use the function **SimpleIf** in Excel. When **Parameter** is greater than 5, **SimpleIf** returns 1, and when **Parameter** is less than or equal to 5, **SimpleIf** returns 15:

	A	B	C
1	SIMPLEIF IN ACTION		
2	Parameter		
3	12	1	<-- =SimpleIf(A3)
4	3	15	<-- =SimpleIf(A4)
5			
6	12	1	<-- =SimpleIf2(A6)
7	3	0	<-- =SimpleIf2(A7)
8			
9	12	1	<-- =SimpleIf3(A9)
10	3	-16	<-- =SimpleIf3(A10)

The one-line **If** statement doesn't even need the **Else** part. The next function, **SimpleIf2**, returns 0 if the condition "Parameter > 5" is not fulfilled:

```
Function SimpleIf2(Parameter)
    If Parameter > 5 Then SimpleIf2 = 1
End Function
```

	A	B	C
1	ONE-LINE SIMPLEIF2		
2	12	1	<-- =SimpleIf2(A2)
3	3	0	<-- =SimpleIf2(A3)

36.5.2 Good Programming Practice: Assign a Value to Your Function *First*

In the preceding functions, it would be good programming practice to first assign a value to the function before introducing the **If** statement. This way we know that **SimpleIf3** defaults to –16 if the condition on **Parameter** is not fulfilled.

```
Function SimpleIf3(Parameter)
    SimpleIf3 = -16
    If Parameter > 5 Then SimpleIf3 = 1
End Function
```

To see the difference this prior parameter assignment makes, look at the following spreadsheet:

	A	B	C
1	**ASSIGNING A PARAMETER VALUE FIRST**		
2	Parameter value	-7	
3	SimpleIf	15	<-- =SimpleIf(B2)
4	SimpleIf2	0	<-- =SimpleIf2(B2)
5	SimpleIf3	-16	<-- =SimpleIf3(B2)

36.5.3 If . . . ElseIf Statements

If more than one statement is to be conditionally executed, the block **If . . . ElseIf** statement can be used. It uses the following syntax:

```
If Condition0 Then
        Statements
ElseIf Condition1 Then
        Statements
[... More ElseIfs...]
Else
        Statements
End If
```

The **Else** and **ElseIf** clauses are both optional. You may have as many **ElseIf** clauses as you want following an **If**, but none can appear after an **Else** clause. **If** statements can be contained within one another.

Here's an example:

```
Function BlockIf(Parameter)
     If Parameter < 0 Then
          BlockIf = -1
     ElseIf Parameter = 0 Then
          BlockIf = 0
     Else
          BlockIf = 1
     End If
End Function
```

Here's how this function works in Excel:

	A	B	C
1	**BlockIf in Action**		
2	**Parameter**		
3	-3	-1	<-- =BlockIf(A3)
4	0	0	<-- =BlockIf(A4)
5	13	1	<-- =BlockIf(A5)

36.5.4 Nested If Structures

As stated in the previous subsection, **If** statements can be used as part of the statements used in another **If** statement. A program structure that has some **If** statements inside others is called a *nested If* structure. Each **If** statement in the structure must be a complete **If** statement. Either the one-line or the block version can be used.

The following function demonstrates the use of the nested **If** structure:

```
Function NestedIf(P1, P2)
    If P1 > 10 Then
       If P2 > 5 Then NestedIf = 1 Else
           NestedIf = 2
    ElseIf P1 < -10 Then
       If P2 > 5 Then
          NestedIf = 3
       Else
          NestedIf = 4
       End If
    Else
       If P2 > 5 Then
          If P1 = P2 Then NestedIf = 5 Else
          NestedIf = 6
       Else
          NestedIf = 7
       End If
    End If
End Function
```

This is how it looks in Excel:

	A	B	C	D
1	**NESTED IF FUNCTION**			
2	**P1**	**P2**	**NestedIf(P1, P2)**	
3	11	6	1	<-- =NestedIf(A3,B3)
4	22	3	2	
5	-22	6	3	
6	-57.3	4	4	
7	6	6	5	
8	-5	7	6	
9	4	3	7	

Here is a flow chart diagramming program flow for the function:

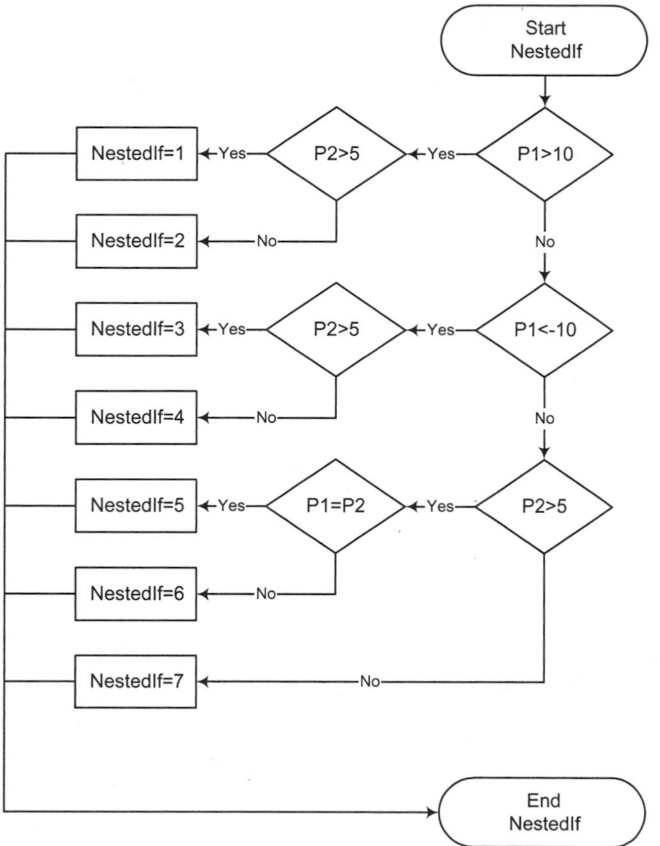

36.6 The Select Case Statement

The **Select Case** statement is used to execute one of several groups of statements, depending on the value of an expression. The following function demonstrates its use in a very simple case:

```
Function SimpleSelect(Parameter)
     Select Case Parameter
     Case 1
          SimpleSelect = 111
     Case 2
          SimpleSelect = 222
     Case 3, 5, 6
          SimpleSelect = 333
     Case 4, 2
          SimpleSelect = 444
     Case Else
          SimpleSelect = 555
     End Select
End Function
```

And this is how it looks in Excel:

	A	B	C
1	SIMPLESELECT IN ACTION		
2	Parameter	SimpleSelect	
3	0	555	<-- =simpleselect(A3)
4	1	111	
5	2	222	<-- Notice it's 222 and not 444
6	3	333	
7	3.5	555	
8	4	444	
9	5	333	
10	6	333	

Here is a flow chart of the function:

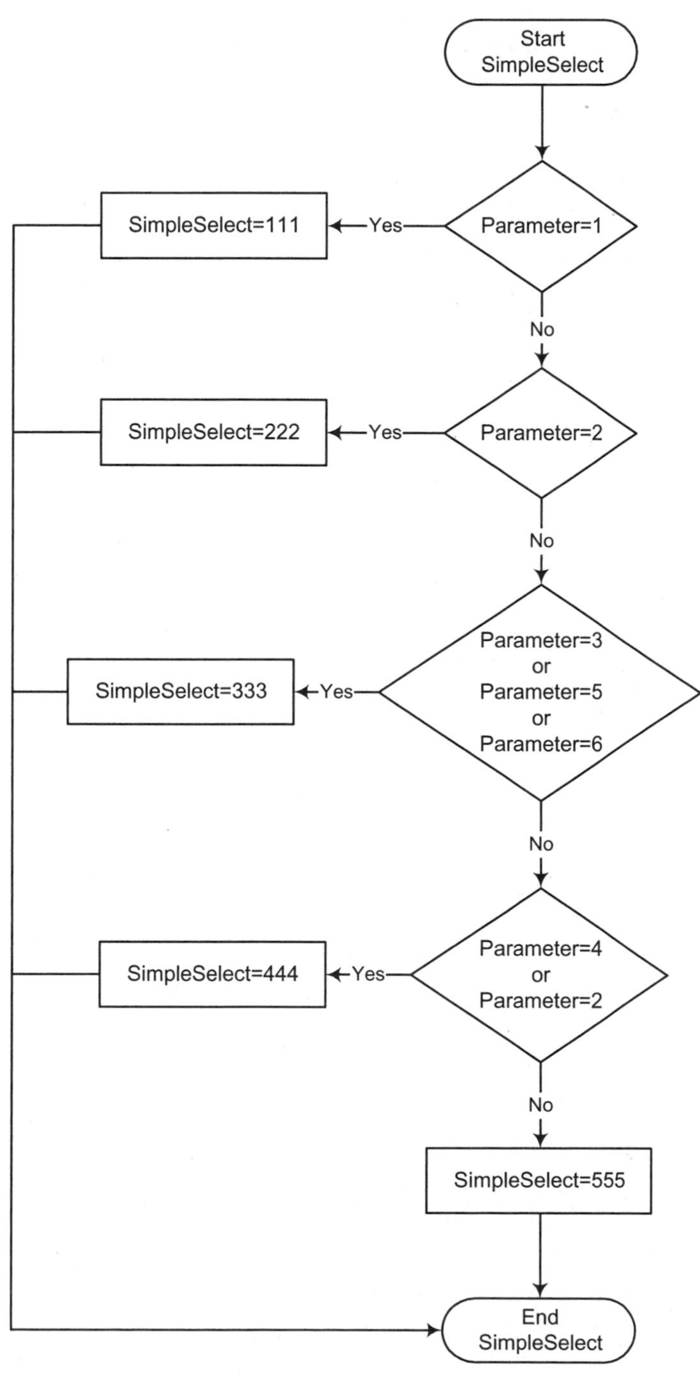
Start
SimpleSelect
Parameter=1
Yes
SimpleSelect=111
No
Parameter=2
Yes
SimpleSelect=222
No
Parameter=3
or
Parameter=5
or
Parameter=6
Yes
SimpleSelect=333
No
Parameter=4
or
Parameter=2
Yes
SimpleSelect=444
No
SimpleSelect=555
End
SimpleSelect

36.7 Using Excel Functions in VBA

VBA can make extensive use of Excel's worksheet functions. We illustrate by showing how to define the binomial distribution (even though this, itself, is an Excel function). The probability distribution of a binomial random variable is defined as

$$\text{binom}(p, n, x) = \binom{n}{x} p^x (1-p)^{n-x}$$

where p is the probability of success, x is the number of successes, and n the number of trials. The binomial coefficient is

$$\binom{n}{x} = \frac{n!}{(n-x)!x!}$$

which gives the number of ways of choosing x elements from among n elements. For example, suppose you want to form a two-person team from eight candidates and you want to know how many possible teams can be formed. The answer is given by

$$\binom{8}{2} = \frac{8!}{6!2!} = \frac{8 \cdot 7 \cdot 6 \cdot 5 \cdot 4 \cdot 3 \cdot 2 \cdot 1}{6 \cdot 5 \cdot 4 \cdot 3 \cdot 2 \cdot 1 * 2 \cdot 1} = 28$$

The Excel function **Combin**(8, 2) does this calculation.

We use this Excel function in the following VBA function:

```
Function Binomial(p, n, x)
    Binomial = Application.Combin(n, x) _
        * p ^ x * (1 - p) ^ (n - x)
End Function
```

As usual, this can be applied inside a spreadsheet:

	A	B	C
1	THE BINOMIAL FUNCTION		
2	p	0.5	
3	n	10	
4	x	6	
5	Binomial	0.205078125	<-- =Binomial(B2,B3,B4)

Note that we used **Application.Combin(n, x)** to compute $\binom{n}{x}$ in our function. As you might guess from its name (**Application.Something**), this function is the Excel worksheet function **Combin()**. Most, but not all,[4] Excel worksheet functions can be used in VBA in exactly the same way. Some examples will be given in subsequent parts of this section. For a complete list see the Help file.

One more thing to notice is the underscore (_) preceded by a space at the end of line 2. If a line gets too long to deal with,[5] it can be continued on the next line using this contraption (the second and third lines of Binomial are one line as far as VBA is concerned).

Suppose we try to use our **Binomial** function to calculate **Binomial(0.5,10,15)**. This attempt won't work:

	A	B	C
1	THE BINOMIAL FUNCTION		
2	p	0.5	
3	n	10	
4	x	15	
5	Binomial	#VALUE!	<-- =Binomial(B2,B3,B4)

The reason for the problem is that in the computation $\binom{n}{x}$ used in **Binomial**, we have to have $x < n$. In this case, VBA causes Excel to return the error message #**Value!** The subject of Excel error values is somewhat obscure, and therefore we cover it in the chapter appendix.

36.8 Using User-Defined Functions in User-Defined Functions

User-defined functions can be used in other user-defined functions, just like Excel functions. The next function is a replacement for the COMBIN worksheet function. COMBIN is defined as

4. When an equivalent function is available as a native VBA function, the corresponding Excel function is not available in VBA. For example, in VBA use **rnd()** and not **Application.Rand()**, and **sqr()** and not **Application.Sqrt()**.

5. What's too long? This is a matter of programming taste, but for our purposes 70–80 characters is considered too long.

$$c(n, x) = \frac{n!}{(n-x)!x!}$$

where ! stands for the factorial function. [Recall that the factorial function $n!$ is defined for any $n \geq 0$: $0! = 1$, and for $n > 0$, $n! = n * (n - 1) * (n - 2) \ldots 1$.]

We will now write our VBA version of the two functions: the factorial function and the COMBIN function.

```
1    Function HomeFactorial(n)
2          If Int(n) <> n Then
3                HomeFactorial = CVErr(xlErrValue)
4          ElseIf n < 0 Then
5                HomeFactorial = CVErr(xlErrNum)
6          ElseIf n = 0 Then
7                HomeFactorial = 1
8          Else
9                HomeFactorial = HomeFactorial _
                   (n - 1) * n
10         End If
11   End Function
```

Line 2 checks whether the input is an integer by comparing the integer part of "n" to "n." The function "Int" is a part of VBA. If we have erred, for example by asking for **HomeFactorial(3.3)**, then line 3 of the program will cause Excel to return **#VALUE!** Similarly, lines 4 and 5 check whether we have improperly asked for **HomeFactorial** of a negative number; if this is the case, then line 5 causes Excel to return **#NUM!**. For a fuller explanation of the use of error values, see the appendix.

Line 9 introduces a new concept, the function uses itself to calculate the value it should return. This new ability is called recursion. Here's an illustration of the function in action:

	A	B	C	D	E
1			**RECURSION IN ACTION**		
2	N	Factorial		HomeFactorial(n)	
3	0	1	<-- 1	1	<-- =HomeFactorial(A3)
4	1	1	<-- =B3*A4	1	<-- =HomeFactorial(A4)
5	2	2	<-- =B4*A5	2	
6	3	6	<-- =B5*A6	6	
7	4	24	<-- =B6*A7	24	
8	5	120	<-- =B7*A8	120	

We can now use **HomeFactorial** to create our VBA version of **Combin** (which we will call **HomeCombin**):

```
Function HomeCombin(n, x)
     HomeCombin = HomeFactorial(n) / _
          (HomeFactorial(n - x) * _
           HomeFactorial(x))
End Function
```

Finally, we can use **HomeCombin** to create a VBA version of the binomial function:

```
Function HomeBinom(p, n, x)
     If n < 0 Then
       HomeBinom = CVErr(xlErrValue) 'Make the function
                                     'return #VALUE!
     ElseIf x > n Or x < 0 Then
       HomeBinom = CVErr(xlErrNum)   'Make the 'function
                                     return #NUM!
     Else
       HomeBinom = HomeCombin(n, x) _
                   * p ^ x * p ^ (n - x)
     End If
End Function
```

Putting Comments in VBA Code

As illustrated in the preceding function, VBA will ignore anything that follows an apostrophe. (Note that each new line of comments has to begin with an apostrophe.)

Exercises

1. Write a VBA function for $f(x) = x^2 - 3$.

	A	B	C
1	Exercise 1		
2	x		
3	1	-2	<-- =Exercise1(A3)
4	2	1	<-- =Exercise1(A4)
5	3	6	<-- =Exercise1(A5)

2. Write a VBA function for $f(x) = \sqrt{2x^2} + 2x$. Note that there are two ways to carry out this assignment. The first is to use the VBA function **Sqr**. The second is to use the VBA operator ∧. We suggest you try both.

	A	B	C
1	Exercise 2		
2	x		
3	1	3.414213562	<-- =Exercise2(A3)
4	2	6.828427125	<-- =Exercise2(A4)
5	1	3.414213562	<-- =Exercise2a(A5)
6	2	6.828427125	<-- =Exercise2a(A6)

3. Suppose a share was priced at price P_0 at time 0, and suppose that at time 1 it will be priced P_1. Then the continuously compounded return is defined as $\ln\left(\frac{P_1}{P_0}\right)$. Implement this function in VBA. There are two ways to perform this calculation. You can use **Application.Ln** or the VBA function **Log**.

	A	B	C	D
1	Exercise 3			
2	P_0	P_1		
3	100	110	0.09531	<-- =Exercise3(A3,B3)
4	100	200	0.69315	<-- =Exercise3(A4,B4)
5	100	110	0.09531	<-- =Exercise3a(A5,B5)
6	100	200	0.69315	<-- =Exercise3a(A6,B6)

4. A bank offers different yearly interest rates to its customers based on the size of the deposit in the following way:

   For deposits up to 1,000 the interest rate is 5.5 percent.

   For deposits from 1,000 and up to 10,000 the interest rate is 6.3 percent.

   For deposits from 10,000 and up to 100,000 the interest rate is 7.3 percent.

   For all other deposits the interest rate is 7.8 percent.

   Implement the function **Interest(Deposit)** in VBA. Note that you can use the **Block If** structure or the **Select Case** structure.

	A	B	C
1	**Exercise 4**		
2	Deposit		
3	-1	#VALUE!	<-- =Interest(A3)
4	100	5.50%	<-- =Interest(A4)
5	1100	6.30%	
6	9999.99	6.30%	
7	10000	6.30%	
8	10000.001	7.30%	
9	100000.001	7.80%	
10	-1	#VALUE!	<-- =Interesta(A10)
11	100	5.50%	<-- =Interesta(A11)
12	1100	6.30%	
13	9999.99	6.30%	
14	10000	6.30%	
15	10000.001	7.30%	
16	100000.001	7.80%	

5. Using the function in exercise 4, implement a function **NewDFV(Deposit, Years)**. The function will return the future value of a deposit with the bank assuming the deposit and accrued interest are reinvested for a given number of years. For example, **NewDFV(10000,10)** will return 10000 ∗ (1.063) ^ 10.

	A	B	C	D
1	**Exercise 5**			
2	Deposit	Years		
3	10000	10	18421.82	<-- =NewDFV(A3,B3)
4	10000.001	10	20230.06	<-- =NewDFV(A4,B4)

6. An investment company offers a bond linked to the FT100 index. On redemption the bond pays the face value plus the largest of (a) the face value times the change in the index or (b) 5 percent yearly interest compounded monthly. For example, 100 invested when the index was 110 and redeemed a year later when the index was 125 will pay (a) 100 + 100 * (125 – 110)/110 = 113.636 and not (b) 100 * (1 + 0.05/12) ^ 12 = 105.116. Implement a VBA function **Bond(Deposit, Years, FT0, FT1)**.

	A	B	C	D	E	F
1				**Exercise 6**		
2	Deposit	Years	FT0	FT1		
3	100	1	110	125	113.636	<-- =Bond(A3,B3,C3,D3)
4	100	2	110	100	110.494	<-- =Bond(A4,B4,C4,D4)
5	100	12	2500	5000	200.000	<-- =Bond(A5,B5,C5,D5)
6	100	12	225	1387.5	616.680	-- =Bond(A6,B6,C6,D6)
7	150	5	3400	2500	192.504	<-- =Bond(A7,B7,C7,D7)

7. Implement a VBA function **ChooseBond(Deposit, Years, FT0, FT1)**. The function will return the value 1 if the superior investment is the bank in exercise 5 or the value 2 if it is the company in exercise 6.

	A	B	C	D	E	F
1				**Exercise 7**		
2	Deposit	Years	FT0	FT1		
3	100	1	110	125	2	<-- =ChooseBond(A3,B3,C3,D3)
4	100	1	110	110	1	
5	100	1	110	116.04	1	
6	100	1	110	116.05	2	
7	100,000	1	110	125	2	<-- =ChooseBond(A7,B7,C7,D7)
8	100,000	1	110	110	1	
9	100,000	1	110	118.02	1	
10	100,000	1	110	118.03	2	

8. A bank offers the following saving scheme: Invest a fixed amount on the first of each month for a set number of years. On the first of the month after your last installment get your money plus the accrued interest. The bank quotes a yearly interest rate, but interest is calculated and compounded on a monthly basis. Eight different interest rates are offered depending on the monthly deposit and the number of years the program is to run.

The following table lists the interest rates offered:

	For Sums ≤ 100 a Month	For Sums > 100 a Month
For a period of two years	3.5%	3.9%
For a period of three years	3.7%	4.5%
For a period of four years	4.2%	5.1%
For a period of five years	4.6%	5.6%

Write a two-argument function **DFV(Deposit, Years)**, returning the future value of such an investment.

	A	B	C	D
1	**Exercise 8**			
2	Deposit	Years	DFV	
3	1	1	#NUM!	<-- =DFV(A3,B3)
4	14.79846406	5	1000	<-- =DFV(A4,B4)
5	19.10180565	4	1000	<-- =DFV(A5,B5)
6	99.999999	2	2489.49	<-- =DFV(A6,B6)
7	100.000001	2	2499.97	<-- =DFV(A7,B7)

9. Using the information provided in exercise 8, write a two-argument function **DEP(DFV, Years)** that will return the monthly contribution necessary to get a certain sum in the future (two, three, four, or five years). Note: This problem is more interesting; remember that the interest rate is dependent on the monthly contribution.

	A	B	C	D
1	**Exercise 9**			
2	DFV	Years	DEP	
3	-1000	2	-40.169	<-- =DEP(A3,B3)
4	1000	5	14.7985	<-- =DEP(A4,B4)
5	1000	4	19.1018	<-- =DEP(A5,B5)
6	2489.488348	2	100	<-- =DEP(A6,B6)
7	2499.973424	2	100	<-- =DEP(A7,B7)

10. Fibonacci numbers (named after Leonardo Fibonacci, 1170–1230, an outstanding European mathematician of the medieval period) are defined as follows:

$$F(0) = 0$$
$$F(1) = 1$$
$$F(2) = F(0) + F(1) = 1$$
$$F(3) = F(1) + F(2) = 2$$
$$F(4) = F(2) + F(3) = 3$$
$$\ldots$$

In general, $F(n) = F(n - 2) + F(n - 1)$.

Write a VBA function that computes the nth number in the series. Note: Recursion is necessary.

Appendix: Cell Errors in Excel and VBA

Excel uses a special kind of value to report errors. The **CVErr()** function is part of VBA. It converts a value supplied by you to the special kind of value used for errors in Excel. Excel has a number of error values that a function can return to signal that something went wrong. Here's an example: The function **NewMistake(x,y)** returns the result x/y. However, if $y = 0$, the function outputs the (cryptic) error message #DIV/0!

```
Function NewMistake(x, y)
    If y <> 0 Then NewMistake = x / y Else _
        NewMistake = CVErr(xlErrDiv0)
End Function
```

> To anticipate future confusion, all the VBA error values are written "xlErr . . . ." Because the typed letter *l* also looks like the number 1, it would have been easier had Microsoft used capital letters "XLErr . . . ." But . . .

This is **NewMistake** in Excel:

	A	B	C	D
1	**NewMistake In Action**			
2	X	Y	NewMistake	
3	1	2	0.5	<-- =NewMistake(A3,B3)
4	2	1	2	<-- =NewMistake(A4,B4)
5	0	1	0	<-- =NewMistake(A5,B5)
6	1	0	#DIV/0!	<-- =NewMistake(A6,B6)

Error values and their explanation are listed in the following table. Each error is explained by a short example following the table.

Error Value	VBA Name	Possible Causes
#NULL!	XlErrNull	The #NULL! error value occurs when you specify an intersection of two areas that do not intersect.
#DIV/0!	XlErrDiv0	The #DIV/0! error value occurs when a formula divides by 0 (zero).
#VALUE!	XlErrValue	The #VALUE! error value occurs when the wrong type of argument is used.
#REF!	XlErrRef	The #REF! error value occurs when a cell reference is not valid.
#NAME?	XlErrName	The #NAME? error value occurs when Microsoft Excel doesn't recognize text in a formula.
#NUM!	XlErrNum	The #NUM! error value occurs when a problem occurs with a number in a formula or function.
#N/A	XlErrNA	The #N/A error value occurs when a value is not available to a function or formula.

The following worksheet demonstrates the most common causes for these errors:

	A	B	C	D
8				Notice comma omitted by mistake.
9	**#NULL! In Action**			
10				
11	1	4	#NULL!	<-- =SUM(A11:A13 B11:B13)
12	2	5	21	<-- =SUM(A11:A13,B11:B13)
13	3	6	21	<-- =SUM(A11:B13)

	A	B	C	D
16	#VALUE! In Action			
17	Ben		#VALUE!	<-- =A17+A18+A19
18	3		5	<-- =SUM(A17:A19)
19	2			

	A	B	C	D
20				
21	#REF! In Action			
22		#REF!	<-- =Sheet1!B1	

There is no Sheet 1 in this Excel notebook.

	A	B	C
26	#NAME! In Action		
27		#NAME?	<-- =Benny+3
28			
29			
30			

They don't know me!

	A	B	C
32	#NUM! In Action		
33		#NUM!	<-- =IRR(A33:A35,0.1)

	A	B	C	D
37	#N/A In Action			
38	3	#N/A	<-- =VLOOKUP(2,A38:A41,1)	
39	4	2	<-- =VLOOKUP(2,A38:A41,1,FALSE)	
40	1	#N/A	<-- =VLOOKUP(2,A38:A41,1,TRUE)	
41	2			
42				

37 Types and Loops

37.1 Overview

In this chapter we introduce variable and function types. Using typed variables and functions can make your program more readable and allow it to run faster and use less computer memory. (The jargon "typed variable" or "typed function" means a variable or function that has a type, not something that is typed on a keyboard.) Section 37.5 introduces the looping structures. Looping structures are a way to make your program perform a task repeatedly.

37.2 Using Types

When a function is used in a spreadsheet, the end result is a value. You can use VBA to categorize this value, so that your user-defined function returns only values of a particular type. Values in VBA are categorized into types, either by default or explicitly. The default type associated with a value returned from a function is **Variant**. **Variant** is a category of values that includes all other categories. If we know that a function should return a specific type of value, it is good practice to explicitly declare the function as returning that type. This technique makes the function work faster and uses less computer memory.

You can declare that a function must return a specific type of value by appending the reserved word **As**, followed by the type, to the function declaration line. We demonstrate by rewriting the Chapter 36 function **Function1** to return only an integer value. (This function from the previous chapter multiplies a variable by 3 and adds 1.) We start by writing the first line of the function:

```
function Function2(Parameter) as
```

As soon as you type the space after the word "as," VBA offers you a list of all the available types to choose from:

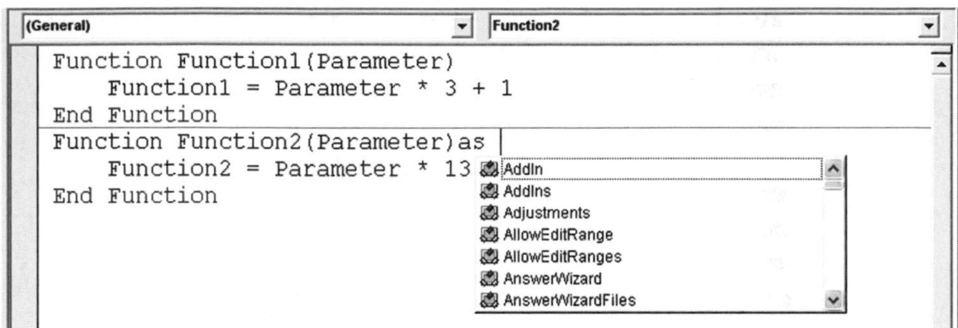

If you continue typing, the options will narrow automatically.

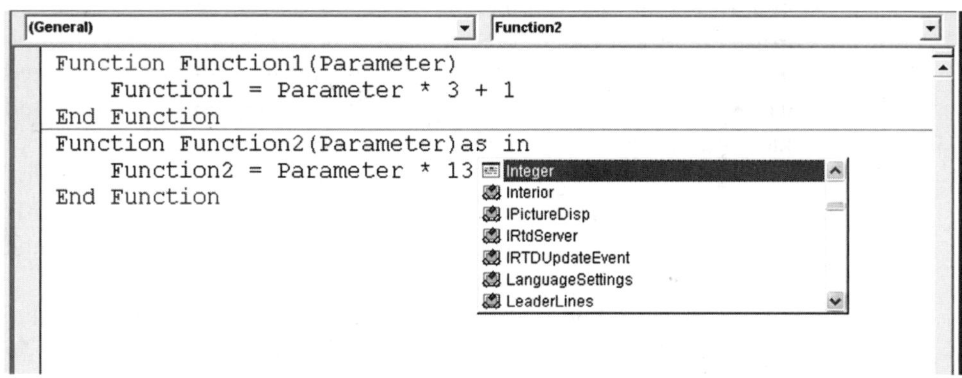

When the word you want is highlighted in the selection window, type the space to follow the word and the word will be inserted for you. Notice that we didn't type the reserved words **Function** and **As** with capitals (these will be added by the VBA editor). Now hit Enter or the "down arrow" key. VBA will do the capitalization for you. Continue typing; the full function should look like this:

```
Function Function2(Parameter) As Integer
    Function2 = Parameter * 3 + 1
End Function
```

You can now use the new function in Excel. Comparing the results returned with those of **Function1**, you can see that **Function2** returns an integer value by rounding off the results:

	A	B	C
1	**FUNCTIONS IN ACTION 1**		
2	Parameter	Function	
3	1.1667	4.5001	<-- =Function1(A3)
4	1.1667	5	<-- =Function2(A4)
5	1.16666	4.49998	<-- =Function1(A5)
6	1.1666	4	<-- =Function2(A6)

The list of Excel and VBA types is very extensive; some of the more important types will be covered in the next section.

37.3 Variables and Variable Types

This section looks at two kinds of variables: variables internal to the function and parameter variables. Here's an example:

```
Function Function3(Parameter)
     Temp = Parameter * 3 + 1
     Function3 = Temp
End Function
```

In **Function3** the variable **Parameter** is a "parameter variable," which gets its value from the applications that activate the function (either Excel or another function). Parameter variables, like most other variables, are recognized only in the function in which they were created. In contrast, the variable **Temp** stores the value to be returned before actually assigning it to the function's name. **Temp** is *internal* to **Function3** and is not recognized by Excel or by other VBA functions.

Whenever you assign a value to a name, VBA creates the corresponding variable. This is what happened in **Function3**—we simply typed `Temp`

`= Parameter * 3 + 1`, and VBA created the variable **Temp**. However, letting VBA create variables for you is not always a good idea, since a small typing mistake can completely alter the results of a function (for an example, see **Function4E** later in this section). A much better way of using variables is to explicitly declare our intention before actually using the variable. Variables are declared using the **Dim** statement. The following function uses the **Dim** statement to declare "Temp" before its use.

```
Function Function4(Parameter)
     Dim Temp
     Temp = Parameter * 3 + 1
     Function4 = Temp
End Function
```

	A	B	C
1	**FUNCTIONS IN ACTION 2**		
2	Parameter	Function	
3	1.1667	4.5001	<-- =Function3(A3)
4	1.1667	4.5001	<-- =Function4(A4)

We can make VBA alert us if we use an undeclared variable by inserting the **Option Explicit** statement as the first line in the module. With this statement any use of an undeclared variable will result in an error and not the creation of a new variable. The **Option Explicit** statement holds for all the routines in the module. Unfortunately there is no global **Option Explicit** statement. You can have VBA insert the **Option Explicit** statement to every *new* module. Select (**Tools|Options . . .**) from the VBA menu, tick the **Require Variable Declaration** line, and click the **OK** button.

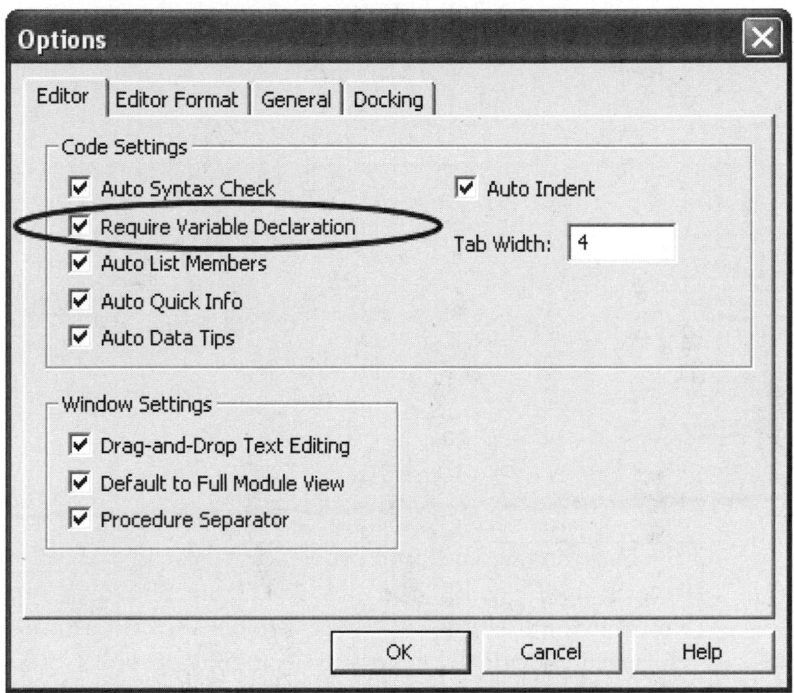

The following function contains a typing error:

```
Function Function4E(Parameter)
     Dim Temp
     remp = Parameter * 3 + 1
     Function4E = Temp
End Function
```

Without the **Option Explicit** statement, Excel merrily displays the following result:

	A	B	C
1	FUNCTIONS IN ACTION 3		
2	Parameter	Function	
3	1.1667	4.5001	<-- =Function4(A3)
4	1.1667	0	<-- =Function4E(A4)

However, inserting the **Option Explicit** statement before the VBA code and recalculating the worksheet results in the following "Run Time Error":

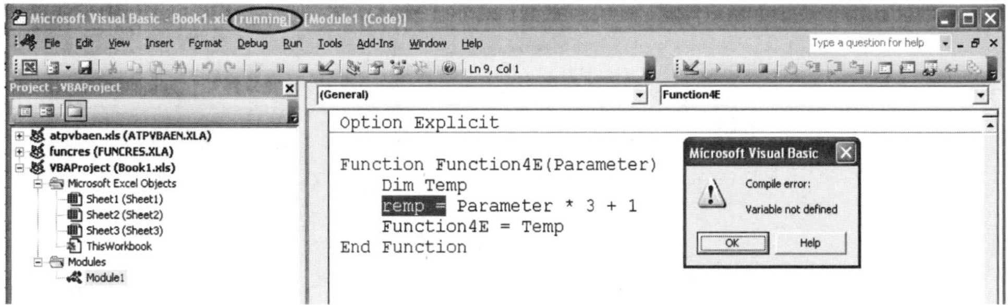

Once we are alerted to the problem, we can click the OK button, stop VBA from running, and fix the problem by replacing "remp" with "Temp." (Recall from Chapter 36 that after you fix the mistake in VBA, you have to press the button with a small square on the VBA editor toolbar.)

Like values, variables have types. Variables declared without a specific type (like Temp) are given the type **Variant**. Using variables and functions of the type **Variant** involves quite a lot of overhead. It is therefore recommended that functions and variables be given a specific type.[1]

You can declare a variable of a specific type by appending the reserved word **As** to the variable declaration. The following function is an integer version of **Function4**. We can now use this function in Excel and compare the results with **Function2** and **Function4**.

```
Function Function5(Parameter As Integer) As
  Integer
     Dim Temp As Integer
     Temp = Parameter * 3 + 1
     Function5 = Temp
End Function
```

1. Attentive readers will notice that we violate this rule quite often in this book! Oh well . . .

	A	B	C
1	FUNCTIONS IN ACTION 4		
2	Parameter	Function	
3	1.1667	5	<-- =Function2(A3)
4	1.1667	4.5001	<-- =Function4(A4)
5	1.1667	4	<-- =Function5(A5)
6	1.16666	4	<-- =Function2(A6)
7	1.16666	4.49998	<-- =Function4(A7)
8	1.16666	4	<-- =Function5(A8)

A Short List of VBA Types

Data Type	Range
Byte	0 to 255
Boolean	True or False
Integer	–32,768 to 32,767
Long (integer)	–2,147,483,648 to 2,147,483,647
Single (floating point)	–3.403E38 to –1.401E-45 for negative values; 1.401E-45 to 3.403E38 for positive values
Double (floating point)	–1.798E308 to –4.941E-324 for negative values; 4.941E-324 to 1.798E308 for positive values
Currency (scaled integer)	–922,337,203,685,477.5808 to 922,337,203,685,477.5807
Decimal	±79,228,162,514,264,337,593,543,950,335 with no decimal point; ±7.9228162514264337593543950 with 28 places to the right of the decimal
Date	January 1, 100, to December 31, 9999
String (variable length)	0 to approximately 2 billion
String (fixed length)	1 to approximately 65,400
Variant (with numbers)	Any numeric value up to the range of a Double
Variant (with characters)	Same range as for variable-length String

37.4 Boolean and Comparison Operators

Usually the expressions used as conditions in an **If** statement are constructed using the Comparison and/or Boolean operators. The following is a list of the most common comparison operators:

Operator	Meaning
<	Less than
≤	Less than or equal to
>	Greater than
≥	Greater than or equal to
=	Equal to
<>	Not equal to

The next function uses a Boolean operator to check both whether **Parameter1** < **10** *and* whether **Parameter2** > **15**:

```
Function AndDemo(Parameter1, Parameter2)
     If (Parameter1 < 10) And (Parameter2 > 15)
     Then
          AndDemo = 3
     Else
          AndDemo = 12
     End If
End Function
```

Here are two illustrations:

	A	B	C
1	**ANDDEMO IN ACTION 1**		
2	Parameter1	3	? < 10 ?
3	Parameter2	12	? > 15 ?
4	AndDemo	12	<-- =AndDemo(B2,B3)

	A	B	C
1	**ANDDEMO IN ACTION 2**		
2	Parameter1	3	? < 10 ?
3	Parameter2	33	? > 15 ?
4	AndDemo	3	<-- =AndDemo(B2,B3)

Notice what **AndDemo** does: It checks whether *both* Parameter1 < 10 *and* Parameter2 > 15. If both conditions hold, then the function returns a value of 3. Otherwise (i.e., if either one of the conditions is violated) it returns 12. (Note that both conditions are in parentheses.)

The following function and the activation screen shot demonstrate all four possible combinations of two conditions and the resulting combined condition:

```
Function AndDemoTable(Parameter1, Parameter2)
     AndDemoTable = Parameter1 And Parameter2
End Function
```

	A	B	C	D
1	**ANDDEMOTABLE IN ACTION**			
2	Parameter1	Parameter2		
3	TRUE	TRUE	TRUE	<-- =AndDemoTable(A3,B3)
4	TRUE	FALSE	FALSE	<-- =AndDemoTable(A4,B4)
5	FALSE	TRUE	FALSE	<-- =AndDemoTable(A5,B5)
6	FALSE	FALSE	FALSE	<-- =AndDemoTable(A6,B6)

The function **OrDemo**, as follows, checks whether at least one of the two conditions holds:

```
Function OrDemo(Parameter1, Parameter2)
     If (Parameter1 < 10) Or (Parameter2 > 15)
     Then
          OrDemo = 3
     Else
          OrDemo = 12
     End If
End Function
```

	A	B	C	D
1	ORDEMO IN ACTION			
2	Parameter1	Parameter2		
3	1	1	3	<-- =OrDemo(A3,B3)
4	1	30	3	<-- =OrDemo(A4,B4)
5	11	1	12	<-- =OrDemo(A5,B5)
6	11	30	3	<-- =OrDemo(A6,B6)

Notice what **OrDemo** does: It checks whether *either* Parameter1 < 10 *or* Parameter2 > 15 *or both* conditions hold. Only if both conditions are violated will the function return a value of 12. Otherwise (i.e., if either one or both of the conditions hold) it returns 3. (Note that both conditions are in parentheses.)

The following function and the activation screen shot demonstrate all four possible combinations of two conditions and the resulting combined condition:

```
Function OrDemoTable(Parameter1, Parameter2)
    OrDemoTable = Parameter1 Or Parameter2
End Function
```

	A	B	C	D
1	ORDEMOTABLE IN ACTION			
2	Parameter1	Parameter2		
3	TRUE	TRUE	TRUE	<-- =OrDemoTable(A3,B3)
4	TRUE	FALSE	TRUE	<-- =OrDemoTable(A4,B4)
5	FALSE	TRUE	TRUE	<-- =OrDemoTable(A5,B5)
6	FALSE	FALSE	FALSE	<-- =OrDemoTable(A6,B6)

37.5 Loops

Looping structures are used when you need to do something repeatedly. As always there is more than one way to achieve the desired effect. In general there are two major looping constructs:

- *A top-checking loop:* The loop condition is checked before anything else gets done. The something to be done can be left undone if the condition is not fulfilled on entry to the loop.
- *A bottom-checking loop:* The loop condition is checked after the something to be done is done. The something to be done will always be done at least once.

VBA has the two major looping structures covered from all possible angles by the **Do** statement and its variations. All the following subsections will use a version of the factorial function for demonstration purposes. The function used is defined as

$$f(0)=1 \qquad f(1)=1 \qquad f(2)=2*f(1)=2 \qquad \ldots f(n)=n*f(n-1)$$

37.5.1 The Do While Statement

The **Do While** statement is a member of the top-checking loops family. It makes VBA execute one or more statements zero or more times while a condition is true. The following function demonstrates this behavior:

```
Function DoWhileDemo(N As Integer) As Integer
     Dim i, j As Integer
     If N < 2 Then
          DoWhileDemo = 1
     Else
          i = 1
          j = 1
          Do While i <= N
               j = j * i
               i = i + 1
          Loop
          DoWhileDemo = j
     End If
End Function
```

	A	B	C
1	DOWHILEDEMO IN ACTION		
2	N		
3	1	1	<-- =DoWhileDemo(A3)
4	1.4	1	<-- =DoWhileDemo(A4)
5	2	2	<-- =DoWhileDemo(A5)
6	7	5040	<-- =DoWhileDemo(A6)
7	8	#VALUE!	<-- =DoWhileDemo(A7)

Notice that noninteger values get rounded to the nearest integer when transferred to an integer parameter in the function. Also notice that the function cannot handle values greater than 7, because—as explained in section 37.3—the type **Integer** is restricted to values between –32,678 and +32,767. The following function solves the problem by using the **Long** variable type, which allows larger integer values:

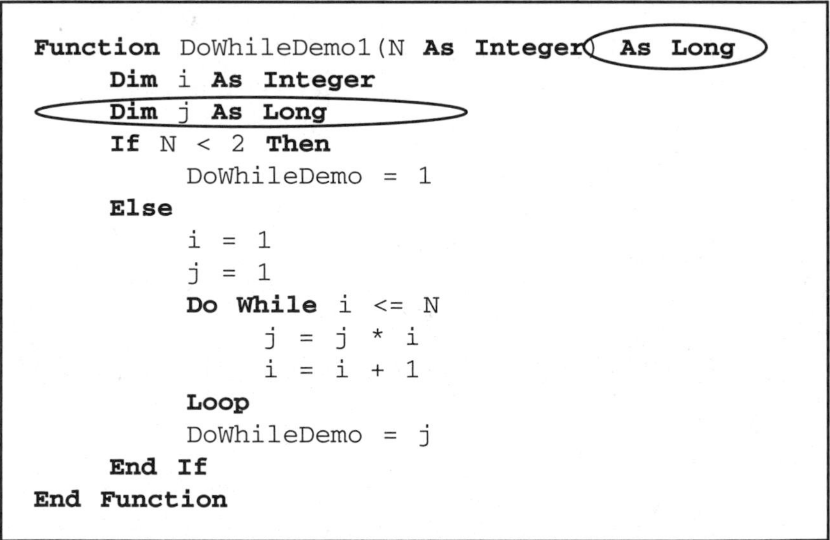

```
Function DoWhileDemo1(N As Integer) As Long
    Dim i As Integer
    Dim j As Long
    If N < 2 Then
        DoWhileDemo = 1
    Else
        i = 1
        j = 1
        Do While i <= N
            j = j * i
            i = i + 1
        Loop
        DoWhileDemo = j
    End If
End Function
```

	A	B	C
1	DOWHILEDEMO1 IN ACTION		
2	N		
3	1	1	<-- =DoWhileDemo1(A3)
4	1.4	1	<-- =DoWhileDemo1(A4)
5	2	2	<-- =DoWhileDemo1(A5)
6	7	5040	<-- =DoWhileDemo1(A6)
7	8	40320	<-- =DoWhileDemo1(A7)

37.5.2 The Do . . . Loop While Statement

The **Do** . . . **Loop While** statement is a member of the bottom-checking loops family. It makes VBA execute one or more statements one or more times while a condition is true. The following function demonstrates this behavior:

```
Function DoLoopWhileDemo(N As Integer) As Long
    Dim i As Integer
    Dim j As Long
    If N < 2 Then
        DoLoopWhileDemo = 1
    Else
        i = 1
        j = 1
        Do
            j = j * i
            i = i + 1
        Loop While i <= N
        DoLoopWhileDemo = j
    End If
End Function
```

	A	B	C
1	**DOLOOPWHILEDEMO IN ACTION**		
2	**N**		
3	1	1	<-- =DoLoopWhileDemo(A3)
4	1.4	1	<-- =DoLoopWhileDemo(A4)
5	2	2	<-- =DoLoopWhileDemo(A5)
6	7	5040	<-- =DoLoopWhileDemo(A6)
7	8	40320	<-- =DoLoopWhileDemo(A7)

37.5.3 The Do Until Statement

The **Do Until** is a member of the top-checking loops family. It makes VBA execute one or more statements zero or more times until a condition is met. The following function demonstrates this behavior:

```
Function DoUntilDemo(N As Integer) As Long
    Dim i As Integer
    Dim j As Long
    If N < 2 Then
        DoUntilDemo = 1
    Else
        i = 1
        j = 1
        Do Until i > N
            j = j * i
            i = i + 1
        Loop
        DoUntilDemo = j
    End If
End Function
```

	A	B	C
1	**DOUNTILDEMO IN ACTION**		
2	**N**		
3	1	1	<-- =DoUntilDemo(A3)
4	1.4	1	<-- =DoUntilDemo(A4)
5	2	2	<-- =DoUntilDemo(A5)
6	7	5040	<-- =DoUntilDemo(A6)
7	8	40320	<-- =DoUntilDemo(A7)

37.5.4 The Do . . . Loop Until Statement

The **Do . . . Loop Until** statement is a member of the bottom-checking loops family. It makes VBA execute one or more statements one or more times until a condition becomes true. The following function demonstrates this behavior:

```
Function DoLoopUntilDemo(N As Integer) As Long
    Dim i As Integer
    Dim j As Long
    If N < 2 Then
        DoLoopUntilDemo = 1
    Else
        i = 1
        j = 1
        Do
            j = j * i
            i = i + 1
        Loop Until i > N
        DoLoopUntilDemo = j
    End If
End Function
```

	A	B	C
1	**DOLOOPUNTILDEMO IN ACTION**		
2	**N**		
3	1	1	<-- =DoLoopUntilDemo(A3)
4	1.4	1	<-- =DoLoopUntilDemo(A4)
5	2	2	<-- =DoLoopUntilDemo(A5)
6	7	5040	<-- =DoLoopUntilDemo(A6)
7	8	40320	<-- =DoLoopUntilDemo(A7)

37.5.5 The While Statement

The **While** statement is a leftover from Quick Basic (a forerunner of VBA).[2] The **While** statement, a member of the top-checking loops family, executes a series of statements as long as a given condition is true. The following function demonstrates its workings:

2. A quotation from the Microsoft VBA Help file: "**Tip:** The **Do . . . Loop** statement provides a more structured and flexible way to perform looping."

```
Function WhileDemo(N As Integer) As Long
    Dim i As Integer
    Dim j As Long
    If N <= 1 Then
        WhileDemo = 1
    Else
        i = 1
        j = 1
        While i <= N
            j = j * i
            i = i + 1
        Wend
        WhileDemo = j
    End If
End Function
```

	A	B	C
1	**WHILEDEMO IN ACTION**		
2	**N**		
3	1	1	<-- =WhileDemo(A3)
4	1.4	1	<-- =WhileDemo(A4)
5	2	2	<-- =WhileDemo(A5)
6	7	5040	<-- =WhileDemo(A6)
7	8	40320	<-- =WhileDemo(A7)

37.5.6 The For Loop

One last (for now) variation on the loopy theme, the **For** loop, is used mainly for loops where the number of times the action is repeated is known in advance. The following functions demonstrate its use and variations:

```
Function ForDemo1(N As Integer) As Long
     Dim i As Integer
     Dim j As Long
     If N <= 1 Then
          ForDemo1 = 1
     Else
          j = 1
          For i = 1 To N Step 1
               j = j * i
          Next i
          ForDemo1 = j
     End If
End Function
```

	A	B	C
1	**FORDEMO1 IN ACTION**		
2	**N**		
3	1	1	<-- =ForDemo1(A3)
4	1.4	1	<-- =ForDemo1(A4)
5	2	2	<-- =ForDemo1(A5)
6	7	5040	<-- =ForDemo1(A6)
7	8	40320	<-- =ForDemo1(A7)

The **Step** part of the statement can be dropped if (as in this case) the increment is 1. For example,

```
For i = 1 To N
    j = j * i
Next i
```

If you want the loop to count down, the **Step** argument can be negative, as demonstrated in the next function:

```
Function ForDemo2(N As Integer) As Long
    Dim i As Integer
    Dim j As Long
    If N <= 1 Then
        ForDemo2 = 1
    Else
        j = 1
        For i = N To 1 Step -1
            j = j * i
        Next i
        ForDemo2 = j
    End If
End Function
```

	A	B	C
1	**FORDEMO2 IN ACTION**		
2	**N**		
3	1	1	<-- =ForDemo2(A3)
4	1.4	1	<-- =ForDemo2(A4)
5	2	2	<-- =ForDemo2(A5)
6	7	5040	<-- =ForDemo2(A6)
7	8	40320	<-- =ForDemo2(A7)

The **For** loop can be exited early by using the **Exit For** statement, as demonstrated in the next function:

```
Function ExitForDemo(Parameter1, Parameter2)
    Dim i As Integer
    Dim Sum As Long
    Sum = 0
    For i = 1 To Parameter1
        Sum = Sum + i
        If Sum > Parameter2 Then Exit For
    Next i
    ExitForDemo = Sum
End Function
```

	A	B	C	D
1	EXITFORDEMO IN ACTION			
2	Parameter1	Parameter2		
3	5	22	15	<-- =ExitForDemo(A3,B3)
4	6	22	21	<-- =ExitForDemo(A4,B4)
5	7	22	28	<-- =ExitForDemo(A5,B5)
6	8	22	28	<-- =ExitForDemo(A6,B6)

37.6 Summary

VBA Macros and functions use variables to store information. Variables can hold all sorts of information. Declaring and using variables that can hold only a specific type of information (**Typed Variables**) can make your program more readable and allow it to run faster and use less computer memory. Looping structures are a way to make your program perform a task repeatedly. In this chapter we reviewed the wide variety of looping structures offered by VBA and the Boolean and comparison operators used to control the looping and conditional execution structures. You will find this all very useful in writing homemade functions for your financial applications.

Exercises

1. Fibonacci numbers introduced in exercise 10 of Chapter 36 are defined as follows:

   $F(0)=0$
   $F(1)=1$
   $F(2)=F(0)+F(1)=1$
   $F(3)=F(1)+F(2)=2$
   $F(4)=F(2)+F(3)=3$
   ...

   In general, $F(n) = F(n-2) + F(n-1)$.

   Rewrite the function in exercise 10 of Chapter 36 without using recursion.

	A	B	C
1	FIBONACCI IN ACTION		
2	n	Fibonacci	
3	1	1	<-- =Fibonacci(A3)
4	2	1	<-- =Fibonacci(A4)
5	3	2	<-- =Fibonacci(A5)
6	6	8	<-- =Fibonacci(A6)
7	12	144	<-- =Fibonacci(A7)
8	24	46368	<-- =Fibonacci(A8)

2. Write a version of the function **HomeFactorial** (see section 36.8) that does not use recursion. Hint: We can describe the workings of the factorial function by saying, "To calculate 6! multiply the numbers from 1 to 6."

	A	B	C
1	HOMEFACTORIAL IN ACTION		
2	n	HomeFactorial	
3	-1	0	<-- =HomeFactorial(A3)
4	0	0	<-- =HomeFactorial(A4)
5	1	1	<-- =HomeFactorial(A5)
6	2	2	<-- =HomeFactorial(A6)
7	3	6	<-- =HomeFactorial(A7)
8	8	40320	<-- =HomeFactorial(A8)

3. Write a function **NewPV(CF, r)** that calculates the present value of a given cash flow *CF* at interest rate *r* for five periods:

$$NewPV(CF,r)=\frac{CF}{(1+r)^1}+\frac{CF}{(1+r)^2}+\frac{CF}{(1+r)^3}+\frac{CF}{(1+r)^4}+\frac{CF}{(1+r)^5}$$

	A	B	C	D
1	NEWPV IN ACTION			
2	CF	r	NewPV	
3	100.0000	10%	379.0787	<-- =NewPV(A3,B3)
4	50.0000	10%	189.5393	<-- =NewPV(A4,B4)
5	100.0000	1%	485.3431	<-- =NewPV(A5,B5)
6	50.0000	1%	242.6716	<-- =NewPV(A6,B6)

4. Rewrite the function in exercise 3 as **BetterNewPV(CF, r, n)**, so it could deal with *n* periods.

	A	B	C	D	E
1	BETTERNEWPV IN ACTION				
2	**CF**	**r**	**n**	**BetterNewPV**	
3	100.0000	5%	5	432.9477	<-- =BetterNewPV(A3,B3,C3)
4	50.0000	10%	5	189.5393	<-- =BetterNewPV(A4,B4,C4)
5	100.0000	1%	10	947.1305	<-- =BetterNewPV(A5,B5,C5)
6	50.0000	1%	10	473.5652	<-- =BetterNewPV(A6,B6,C6)

5. A bank offers different interest rates on loans. The rate is based on the size of the periodical repayment (**CF**) and the following table. Rewrite the function in exercise 4 as **BankPV(CF, r, n)** so that it reflects the present value of a loan in the bank.

For Periodical Repayments ≤	The Interest Rate Is
100.00	r
500.00	$r - 0.5\%$
1,000.00	$r - 1.1\%$
5,000.00	$r - 1.7\%$
1,000,000.00	$r - 2.1\%$

	A	B	C	D	E
1	BANKPV IN ACTION				
2	**CF**	**r**	**n**	**BankPV**	
3	£100.00	5%	5	£432.95	<-- =BankPV(A3,B3,C3)
4	£100.01	5%	5	£439.04	<-- =BankPV(A4,B4,C4)
5	£1,000.00	5%	5	£4,464.36	<-- =BankPV(A5,B5,C5)
6	£1,000.01	5%	5	£4,540.79	<-- =BankPV(A6,B6,C6)
7	£5,000.00	5%	5	£22,703.71	<-- =BankPV(A7,B7,C7)
8	£5,000.01	5%	5	£22,964.11	<-- =BankPV(A8,B8,C8)

6. A bank offers different interest rates on deposit accounts. The rate is based on the size of the periodical deposit (**CF**) and the following table. Write a future value function **BankFV(CF, r, n)**.

For Periodical Deposits	The Interest Rate Is
≤100.00	r
≤500.00	$r + 0.5\%$
≤1,000.00	$r + 1.1\%$
≤5,000.00	$r + 1.7\%$
>5,000.00	$r + 2.1\%$

	A	B	C	D	E
1	BANKFV IN ACTION				
2	CF	r	n	BankFV	
3	£100.00	5%	5	£580.19	<-- =BankFV(A3,B3,C3)
4	£100.01	5%	5	£588.86	<-- =BankFV(A4,B4,C4)
5	£1,000.00	5%	5	£5,992.91	<-- =BankFV(A5,B5,C5)
6	£1,000.01	5%	5	£6,099.47	<-- =BankFV(A6,B6,C6)
7	£5,000.00	5%	5	£30,497.07	<-- =BankFV(A7,B7,C7)
8	£5,000.01	5%	5	£30,856.78	<-- =BankFV(A8,B8,C8)

7. Another bank offers a 1 percent increase in interest rate to savings accounts with a balance of more than £10,000.00. Write a future value function **Bank1FV(CF, r, n)** that reflects this policy.

	A	B	C	D	E
1	BANK1FV IN ACTION				
2	CF	r	n	BankFV	
3	£100.00	5%	5	£580.19	<-- =Bank1FV(A3,B3,C3)
4	£1,000.00	5%	5	£5,801.91	<-- =Bank1FV(A4,B4,C4)
5	£5,000.00	5%	5	£29,691.39	<-- =Bank1FV(A5,B5,C5)

8. The bank in exercise 7 changed its bonus policy and now offers the interest rate increase based on the following table. Rewrite **Bank1FV(CF, r, n)** to reflect this change.

Balance	Interest Rate
≤1,000.00	$r + 0.2\%$
≤5,000.00	$r + 0.5\%$
≤10,000.00	$r + 1.0\%$
>10,000.00	$r + 1.3\%$

	A	B	C	D	E
1	**BANK2FV IN ACTION**				
2	**CF**	**r**	**n**	**BankFV**	
3	£1,000.00	5%	5	£5,884.33	<-- =Bank2FV(A3,B3,C3)
4	£1,000.01	5%	5	£5,884.39	<-- =Bank2FV(A4,B4,C4)
5	£5,000.00	5%	5	£30,033.93	<-- =Bank2FV(A5,B5,C5)
6	£5,000.01	5%	5	£30,033.99	<-- =Bank2FV(A6,B6,C6)

38 Macros and User Interaction

38.1 Overview

A macro is a VBA user routine used to automate routine or repetitive operations in Excel. Macros are also called subroutines; we use the names interchangeably. Some of the VBA user interaction routines are covered in sections 38.3 and 38.4. Modules (briefly mentioned in Chapter 36) are given fuller coverage in section 38.5.

38.2 Macro Subroutines

The first line of a macro subroutine gives the macro a name and lists the parameters if any. It is very similar to the first line of a function:

```
Sub MacroName()
```

The last line, put in automatically by VBA, indicates the end of the macro and so looks (very appropriately) like this:

```
End Sub
```

Separating the first and last line are the statements that the macro executes. The following is a very simple macro that puts a message on the screen.

```
Sub SayHi()
    MsgBox "Hi", , "I say Hi"
End Sub
```

The subroutine introduces a built-in VBA macro called **MsgBox**. It also introduces the way a macro is activated (called) from a VBA routine. **MsgBox** is named as a command on a line followed by its list of arguments separated by commas. Notice the syntax:

```
MsgBox "Hi", , "I say Hi"
```

There are three arguments:

- “Hi” is the message that will be displayed.
- The second argument is empty: notice the space between the commas. This argument can be used to define buttons for the message box. This topic is discussed in section 38.3.
- The third argument is “I say Hi”—this is the message box title.

A macro can be activated (run) from an Excel worksheet in various ways. The simplest way of running a macro is from the tools menu (**Tools|Macro|Macros**), or by using the keyboard shortcut [Alt + F8]. Either way, the macro selection box appears. The box lists all available macros alphabetically. Find our macro, click on its name, and click the run button.

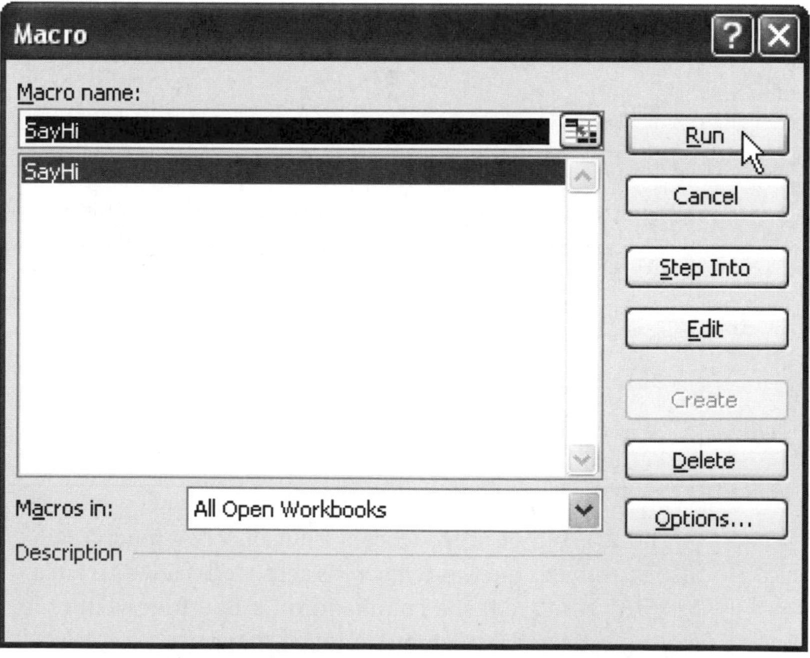

And this is what you will see:

At this point Excel is locked up. You have to click the **OK** button before you can proceed.

38.2.1 Keyboard Shortcut for Macros

Using a keyboard shortcut is a faster way to make a macro run. To attach a shortcut to our macro:

1. Select the **Options** button from the macro selection box.
2. Type a character in the provided space, and click **OK**.
3. Close the macro selection box using the corner **X**.

You can now activate the macro using the shortcut ([Ctrl + h] in our case).

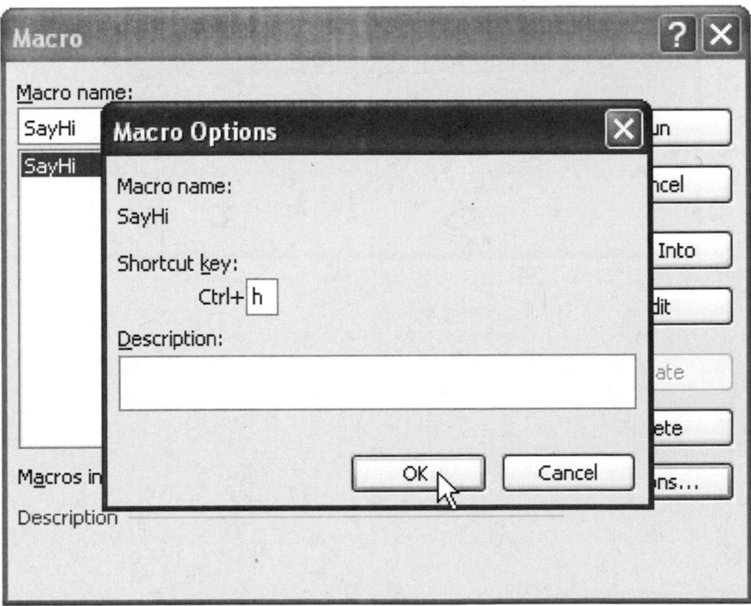

38.2.2 Attaching Macros to a Toolbar

You can attach macros to a button on a toolbar, and later activate the macro by clicking the button. To attach **SayHi** to a button, open the toolbars menu with **View|Toolbars|Customize** and select the **Commands** pane.

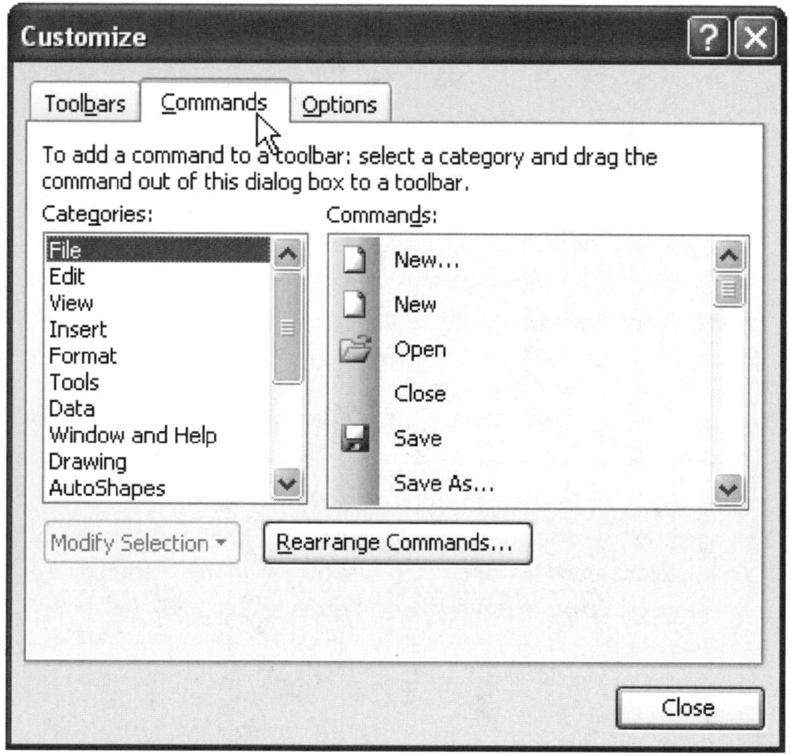

Scroll down the **Categories** subwindow to the Macros item.

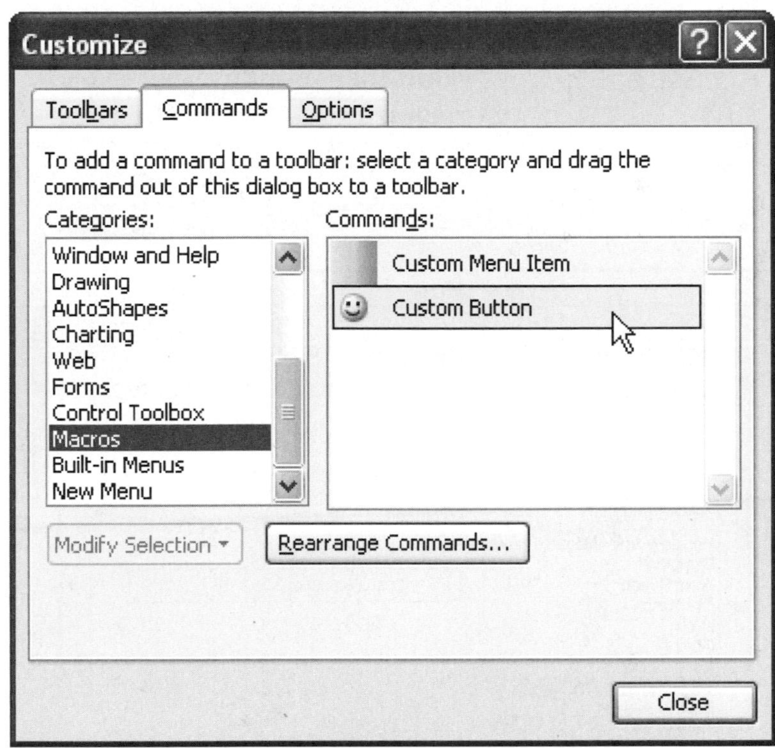

Select the Custom Button and drag it to a toolbar. (Keep the left mouse button pressed while dragging.)

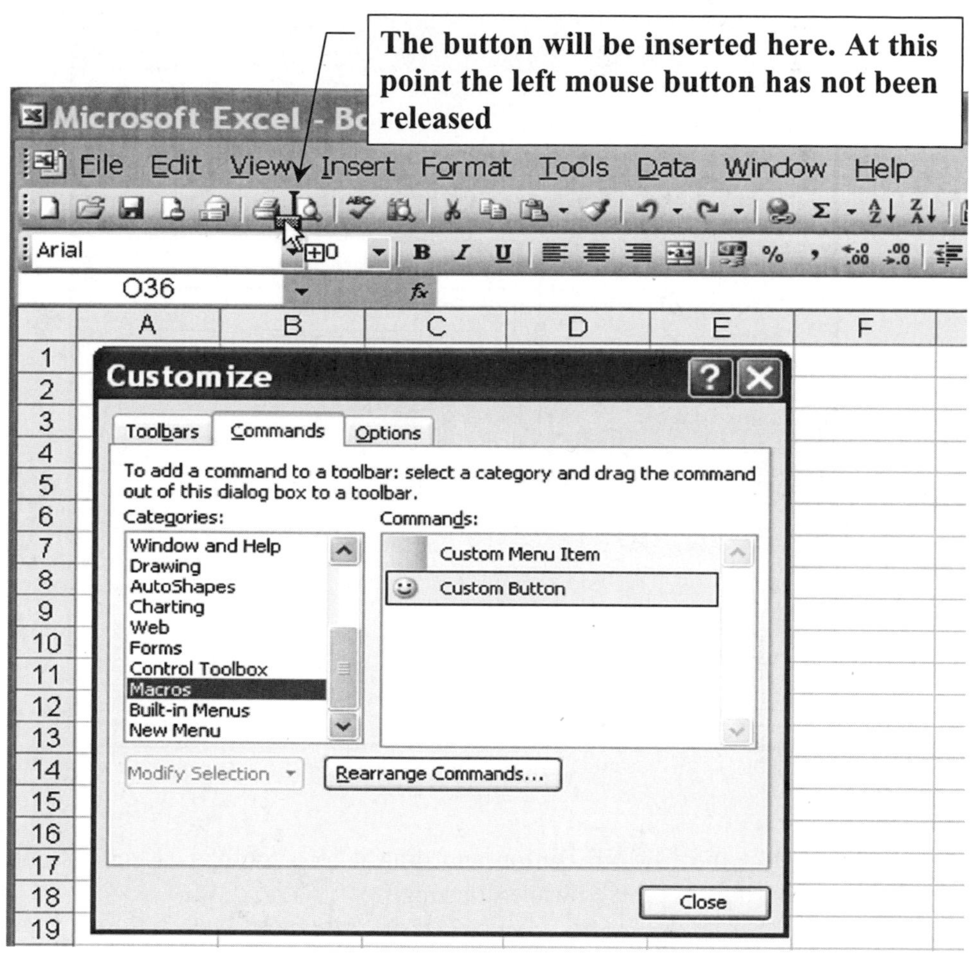

Right click on the newly inserted button and select **AssignMacro** from the menu.

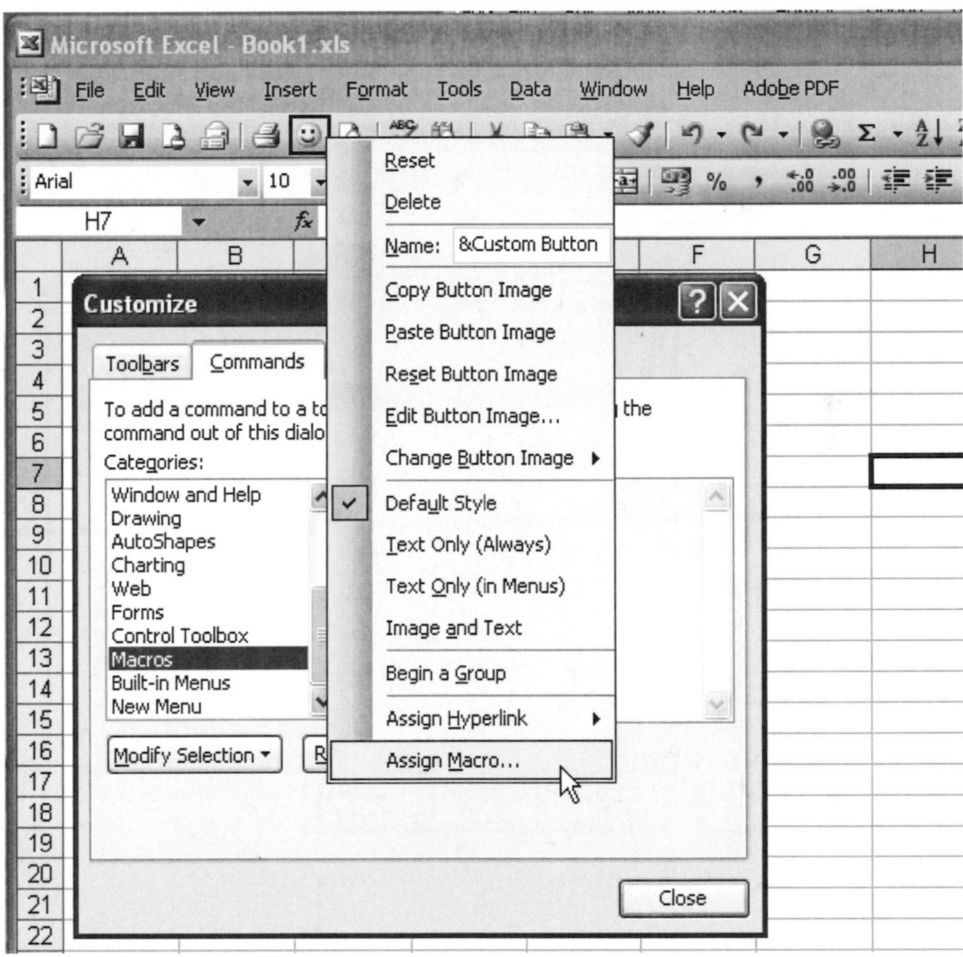

Select our macro from the list and click the **OK** button. Click the **Close** button. **SayHi** is now attached to the smiling button on the toolbar.

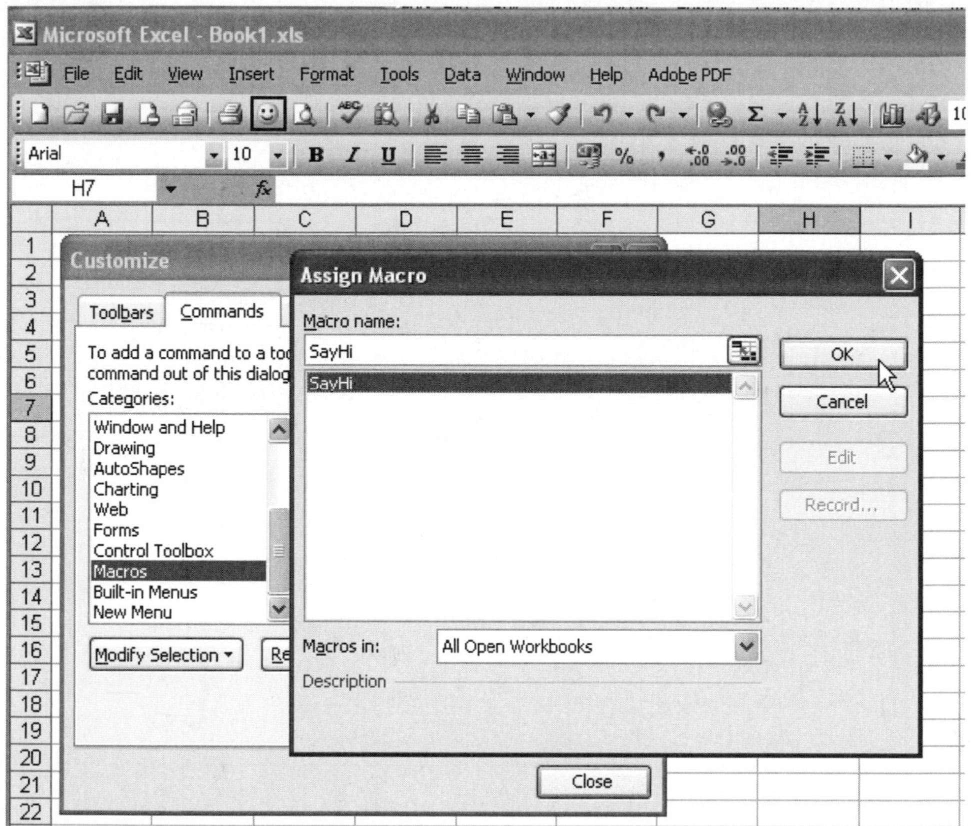

The image on the button and the tool tip attached to it can also be customized. For details refer to the Excel Help file.

38.3 User Output and the MsgBox Function

The **MsgBox** function displays a message on the screen and returns a value based on the button clicked. Some of the different options available with this function are demonstrated in the following macros:

```
Sub MsgBoxDefault()
     Dim Temp As Integer
     Temp = MsgBox("Default Message", ,
       "Default Title")
     MsgBox "The value returned by MsgBox is:" _
       & Temp
End Sub
```

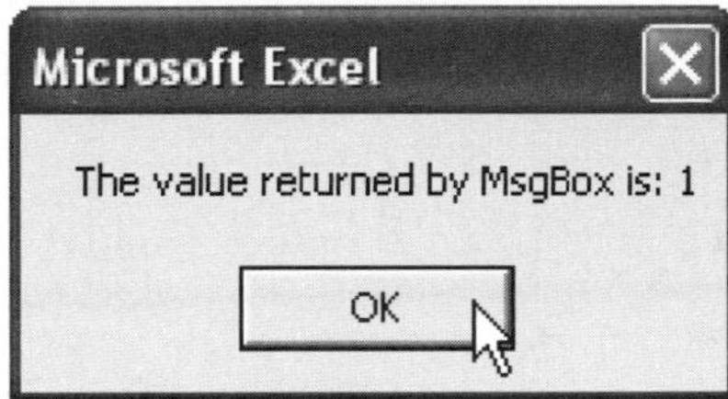

Note The default configuration of **MsgBox** produces one **OK** button. The Default title is "Microsoft Excel." Clicking the **OK** button makes **MsgBox** return the value 1.

```
Sub MsgBoxOKCancel()
     Dim Temp As Integer
     Temp = MsgBox("Default Message",
       vbOKCancel)
     MsgBox "The value returned by MsgBox is:" _
       & Temp
End Sub
```

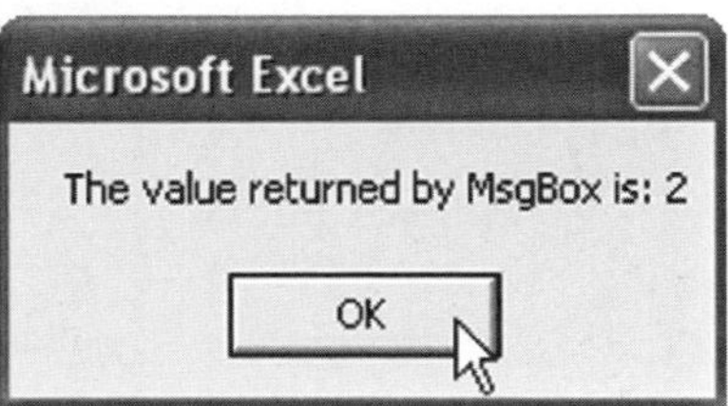

As previously noted, the second argument to **MsgBox** determines which buttons are displayed. This incarnation of the demo macro uses the constant **vbOKCancel** to produce the two buttons **OK** and **Cancel**. Note that if the **Cancel** button is clicked, **MsgBox** returns the value 2.

The following is a list of some of the constants that can be used as the second argument of **MsgBox**, together with the message box they produce:

VbOKOnly

VbOKCancel

VbAbortRetryIgnore

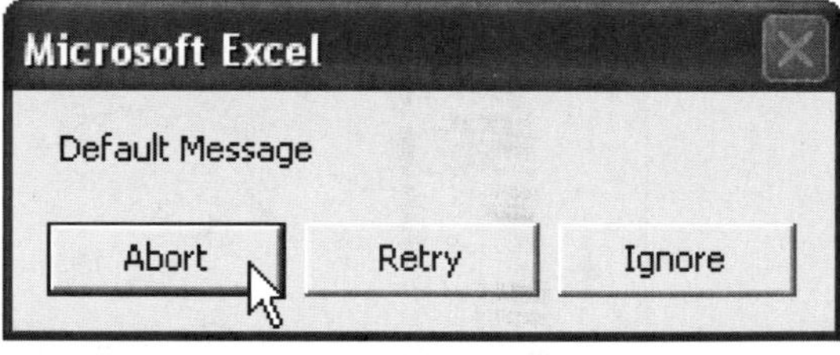

VbYesNoCancel

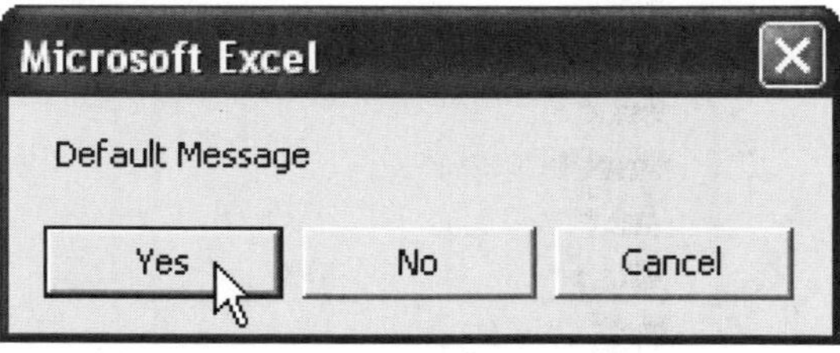

VbYesNo

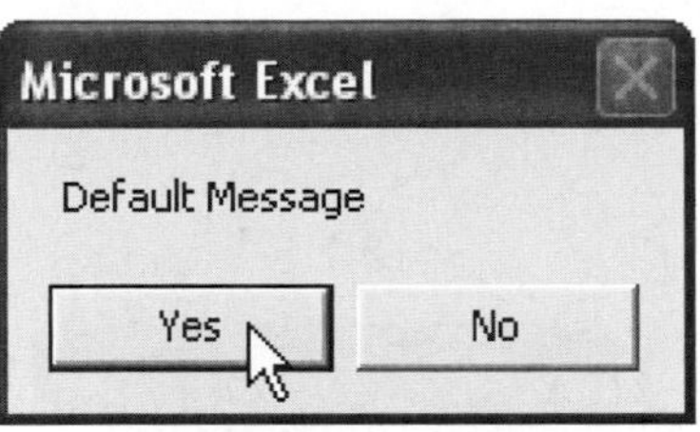

VbRetryCancel

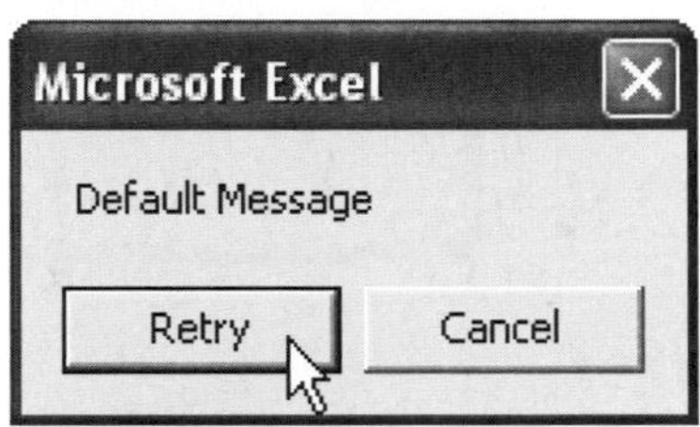

VbCritical

VbQuestion

VbExclamation

VbInformation 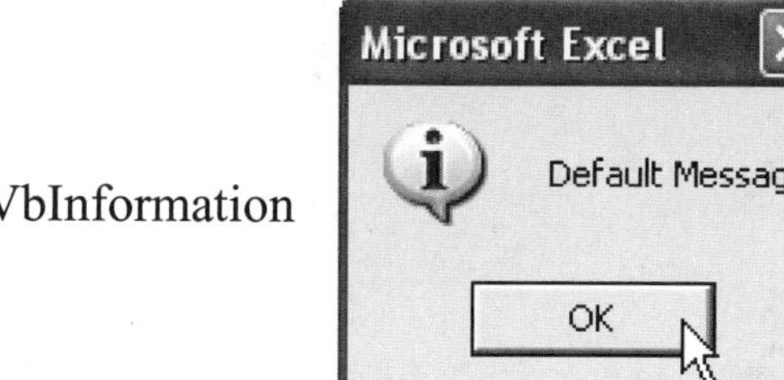

The values that can be returned by MsgBox are as follows:

Constant	Value	Description
vbOK	1	**OK** button clicked
vbCancel	2	**Cancel** button clicked
vbAbort	3	**Abort** button clicked
vbRetry	4	**Retry** button clicked
vbIgnore	5	**Ignore** button clicked
vbYes	6	**Yes** button clicked
vbNo	7	**No** button clicked

38.4 User Input and the InputBox Function

InputBox is an internal VBA function used to get textual information from the user into a variable in a subroutine (a macro by any other name . . .). The workings of the function are demonstrated in the following present-value calculator macro. The macro **PVCalculator** calculates $\sum_{t=1}^{10} \frac{CF}{(1.05)^t}$, where *CF* is a number entered by the user:

```
Sub PVCalculator ()
Dim CF
CF = InputBox ("Enter the cash flow value please", _
     "PV calculator", "100")
MsgBox "The present value of: " & CF & _
     " At 5% for 10 periods is: " & _
     Round (Application.PV (0.05, 10, -CF), 2), _
     vbInformation, "PV calculator"
End Sub
```

Note the syntax:

```
CF = InputBox ("Enter the cash flow value please", _
     "PV calculator", "100")
```

- "Enter . . . please," the first argument to **InputBox**, is the message to display.
- "PV calculator," the second argument, is the title for the box.
- "100," the third argument, is the default string to place in the box. If you do not replace this by some other value, running the macro should result in the following:

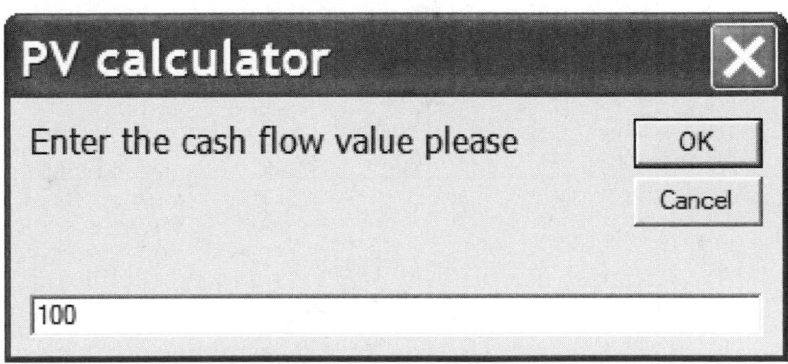

At this point you can replace "100" with some other number. (In this example, we've chosen to leave it.) Clicking on the OK box results in the following box:

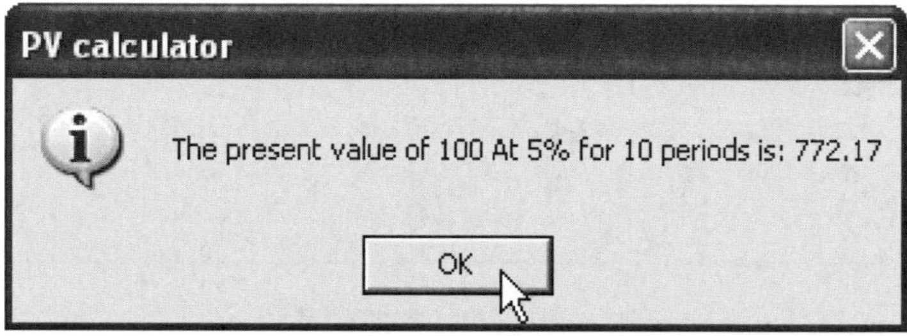

The macro also introduces a new VBA operator **&**. This operator is used to concatenate (combine) its two operands into one string of characters. It merits a small demo function on its own. Notice that nonstring operands are converted into strings.

```
Function ConcatDemo(Parameter1, Parameter2)
    ConcatDemo = Parameter1 & Parameter2
End Function
```

	A	B	C	D
1	**CONCATDEMO IN ACTION**			
2	**Parameter1**	**Parameter2**		
3	1	2	12	<-- =ConcatDemo(A3,B3)
4	Ben	Jerry	BenJerry	<-- =ConcatDemo(A4,B4)
5	Ben	1	Ben1	<-- =ConcatDemo(A5,B5)
6	Jerry	2	Jerry2	<-- =ConcatDemo(A6,B6)

38.5 Modules

VBA organizes user-defined functions and subroutines in units called modules. We can (and sometimes should) have more than one module in a VBA project (that is, the part of the workbook that has our functions and subroutines). Modules have names: By default VBA uses the name "Module" followed by a number to indicate the module's name, but you might find it useful (as we have done on the workbook accompanying this book) to give them somewhat more descriptive names.

To rename a module (in the VBA editor), select the module on the project explorer pane.

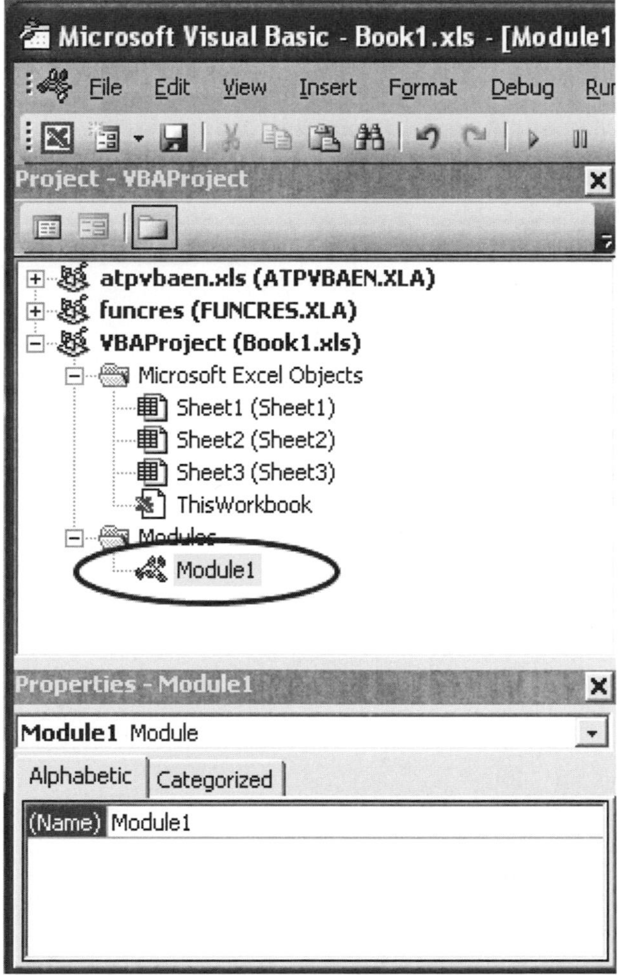

If the project explorer pane is not visible, select **Project Explorer** from the **View** menu.

Once a module is selected, the module's list of properties should appear in the properties pane. If the properties pane is not visible, select **Properties Window** from the **View** menu. Click on the module's name (it should be the only property available) and change it (use one word only, and only digits and alphabetic characters).

Once you tap the Enter key, the name is changed. Notice the change in the project explorer.

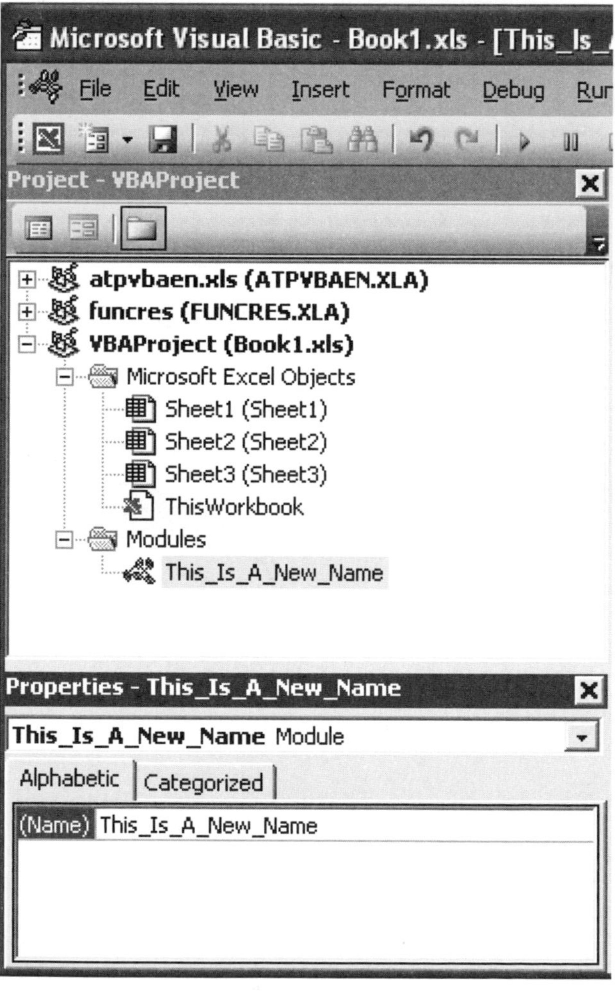

Hint Try to give your modules unique names. If a module called Tom has a function called Tom in it, the function Tom will not be available to the workbook. One common practice is to start module names (and only module names) with M_.

38.6 Summary

A macro is a VBA user routine used to automate routine or repetitive operations in Excel. VBA provides two important and very flexible functions for user interaction: **MsgBox** and **InputBox**. VBA groups macros and functions in units called modules. Keeping related functions and macros grouped is useful when dealing with large projects. All these topics, explored in this chapter, will help you in financial programming in Excel.

Exercises

1. Write a macro that displays the following message box. The message box should be on top of all other windows, and it should prevent the user from doing anything in any application until one of the buttons is clicked.

   Hint You need to use some options of **MsgBox** that were not covered in the text. Use the VBA Help system.

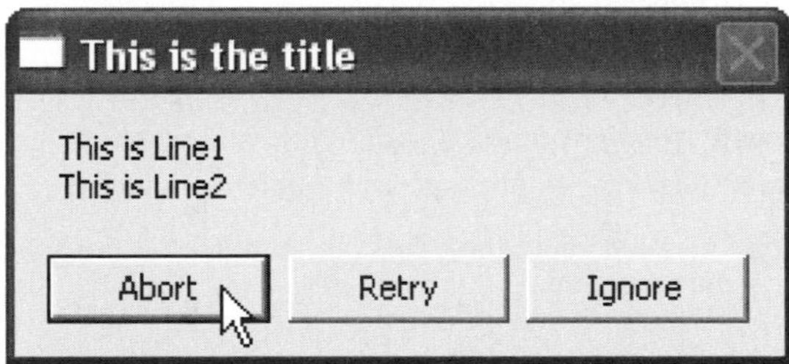

2. Write a present-value calculator macro similar to the one that appears in section 38.4. However—as illustrated here—your macro should ask the user for the cash flow value, the interest rate, and the number of periods. It should then display the result in a message box. Sensible default values should be supplied for all arguments. Do not use the Excel function **PV**; write your own present value function and use it. A reminder:

$$PV(CF, r, n) = \sum_{i=1}^{n} \frac{CF}{(1+r)^i}$$

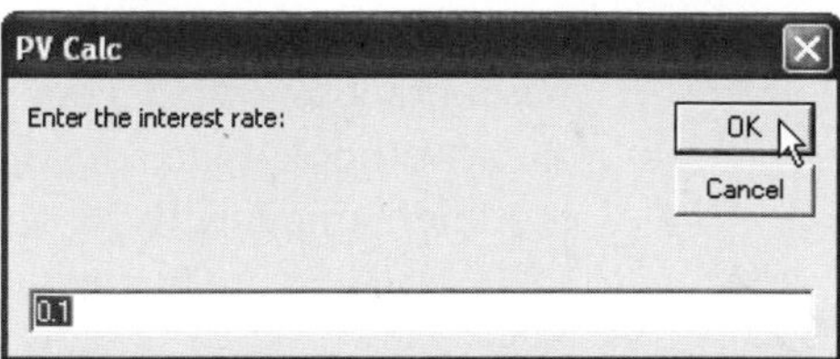

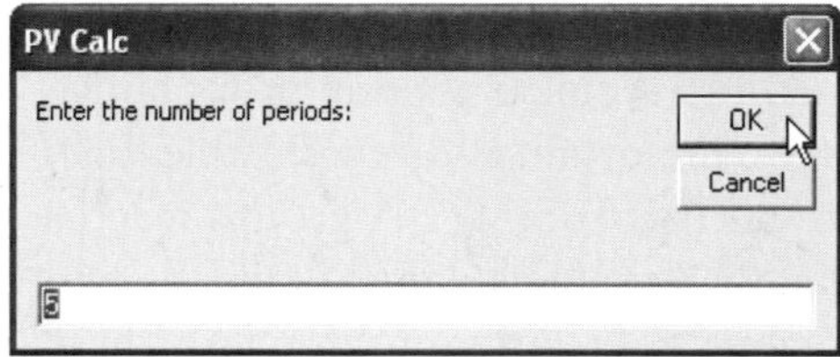

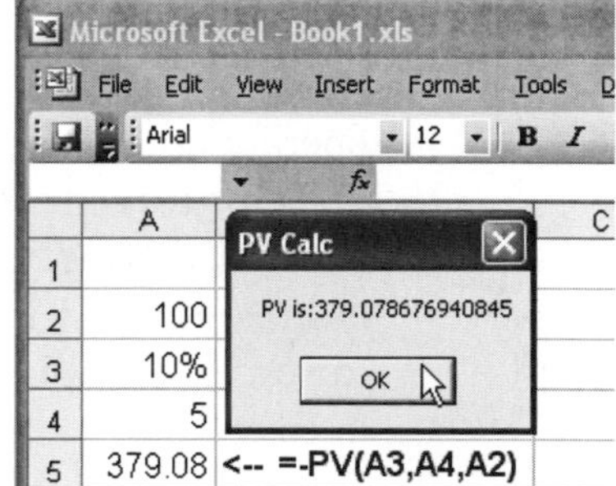

You can use the PV function provided by Excel, as we did, to verify the correctness of your macro.

3. Rewrite the macro in the previous exercise so that the user interface is as demonstrated in the following screen shots. Some of the functions needed to write the macro were not covered in the text. We used the following functions:

- **Val**—A function used to convert a string of digits to a number.
- **Left**—A function used to return the left part of a string.
- **Right**—A function used to return the right part of a string.
- **FormatPercent**—A function used to format a number.
- **FormatCurrency**—A function used to format a number.

More information about these functions is available from the VBA Help file. We recommend you use it.

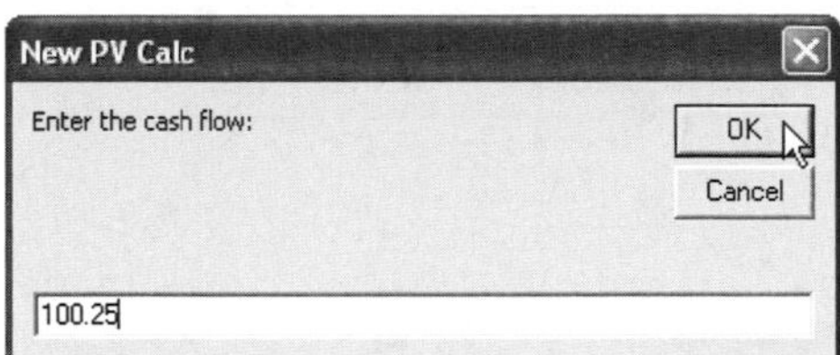

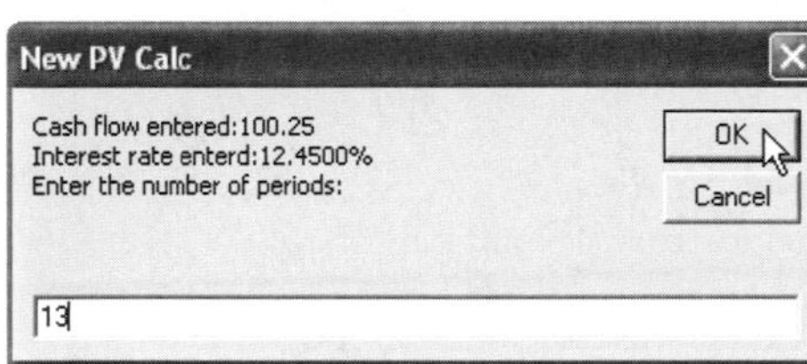

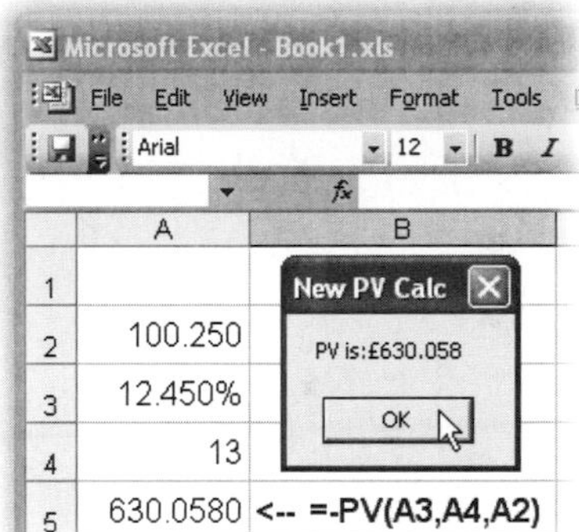

Note Your computer might display a different currency symbol.

4. Rewrite the macro in the previous exercise so it deals properly with the **Cancel** button.

   - A simple version of the new macro will abort the macro if **Cancel** is clicked in any stage.
   - A more sophisticated version of the new macro will allow the user to reenter the data from scratch.
   - The most sophisticated version of the new macro will allow reentering the data using the old data as a default.

   Note The last version is a slightly more complicated exercise using loops within loops.

5. Write a payment schedule calculator macro. The macro is to ask the user for the sum of the loan, the number of payments, and the interest rate. Assume payment at the end of the period. The output should look like the following example:

   Hints

   - You may want to use the worksheet function **PMT**.
   - The following macro and its output might be of interest.

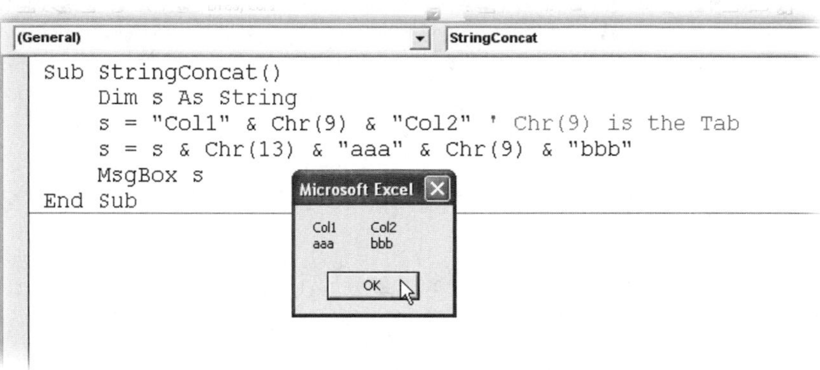

Here is an example of the requested macro in action:

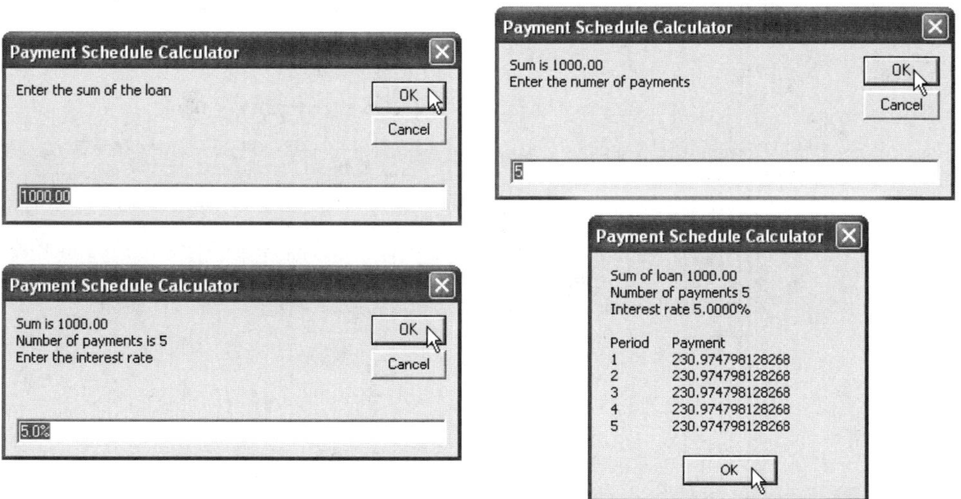

6. Rewrite the payment schedule calculator macro so that it displays the payments broken down to interest and capital payments. The input boxes in the example were removed for compactness.

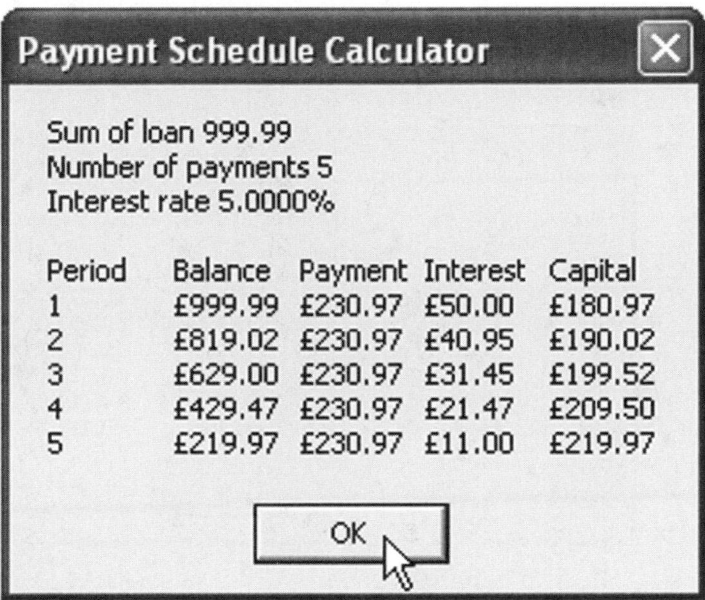

7. Write a payment schedule calculator macro. The macro is to ask the user for the sum of the loan, the payment, and the interest rate. Assume payment at the end of the period. The macro should display the payments broken down to interest and capital payments. Obviously, the last payment can be smaller (but not larger) than the payment supplied by the user. The output should look like the following example (input boxes removed for compactness):

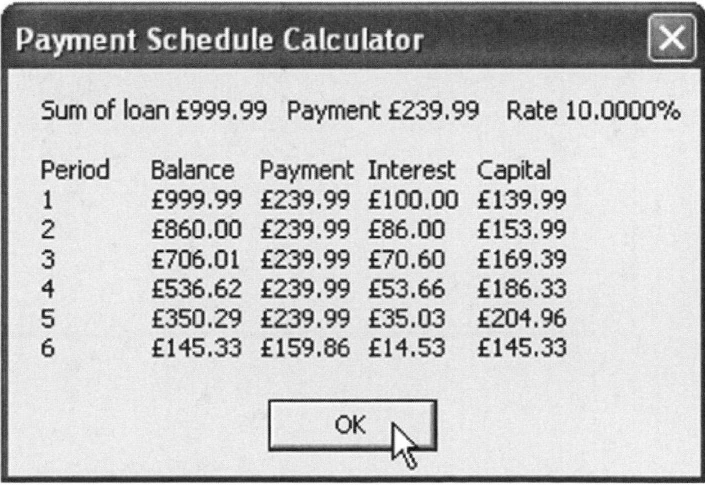

8. A somewhat more complicated version of the macro in exercise 7 would produce the following better-looking results. Write this version of the macro. *Note:* A quick look at the Help file for the **Format** function might be advantageous at this point.

Payment Schedule Calculator

Sum of loan £9,999.99 Payment £2,399.99 Rate 9.9900%

Period	Balance	Payment	Interest	Capital
1	£9,999.99	£2,399.99	£0,999.00	£1,400.99
2	£8,599.00	£2,399.99	£0,859.04	£1,540.95
3	£7,058.05	£2,399.99	£0,705.10	£1,694.89
4	£5,363.16	£2,399.99	£0,535.78	£1,864.21
5	£3,498.95	£2,399.99	£0,349.54	£2,050.45
6	£1,448.50	£1,593.21	£0,144.71	£1,448.50

OK

9. A sliding payment schedule involves payment that changes by a fixed percent over the life of the loan. Write a sliding-payment version of the payment schedule calculator in exercise 8. In addition to all the inputs described previously, the macro will get a payment rate of change (as percent) from the user. This is what it should look like in action:

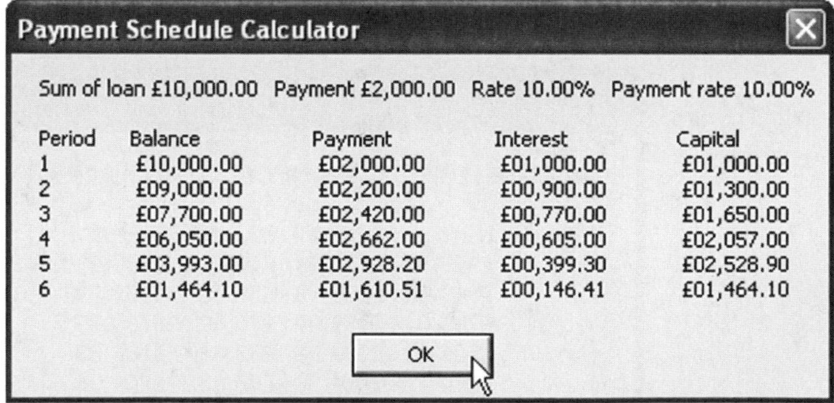

Payment Schedule Calculator

Sum of loan £10,000.00 Payment £2,000.00 Rate 10.00% Payment rate 10.00%

Period	Balance	Payment	Interest	Capital
1	£10,000.00	£02,000.00	£01,000.00	£01,000.00
2	£09,000.00	£02,200.00	£00,900.00	£01,300.00
3	£07,700.00	£02,420.00	£00,770.00	£01,650.00
4	£06,050.00	£02,662.00	£00,605.00	£02,057.00
5	£03,993.00	£02,928.20	£00,399.30	£02,528.90
6	£01,464.10	£01,610.51	£00,146.41	£01,464.10

OK

39 Arrays

39.1 Overview

This chapter deals with arrays. An array is a group of variables of the same type sharing the same name and referenced individually using an index. Vectors and matrices are good examples of one- and two-dimensional arrays. The first part of the chapter presents simple arrays. Dynamic arrays (whose size can be changed at run time) are discussed in the second part of the chapter. The chapter concludes with a section on the use of arrays as parameters, including a subsection on the relationship between arrays and worksheet ranges.

39.2 Simple Arrays

There are several ways to declare arrays, all using the **Dim** statement. The simplest way to declare an array is simply to tell VBA the largest value the array index can take. Unless you indicate otherwise, VBA arrays always start with index 0. In the following macro, **MyArray** has six elements numbered 0, 1, 2, . . . , 5.

```
Sub ArrayDemo1()
    Dim MyArray(5)
    Dim i As Integer
    Dim Temp As String
    For i = 0 To 5
        MyArray(i) = i * i
    Next i
    Temp = ""
    For i = 0 To 5
        Temp = Temp & " # " & MyArray(i)
    Next i
    MsgBox Temp
End Sub
```

If you use **ArrayDemo1** in a spreadsheet, here is the result:

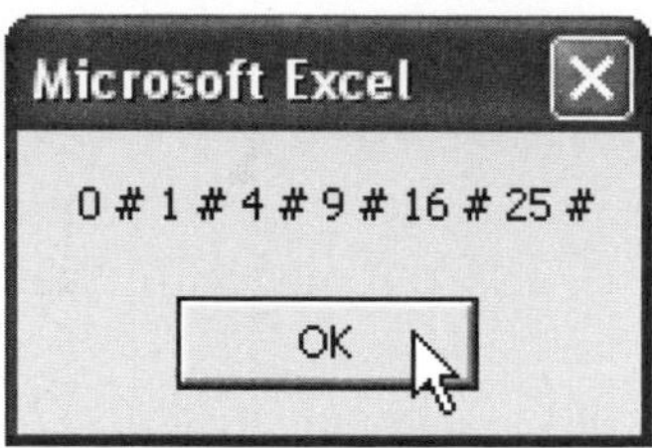

Notice the following:

- **MyArray** has six elements (variables), the first being **MyArray(0)** and the last **MyArray(5)**. All Excel arrays start from 0, unless you specify otherwise (see discussion of **Option Base** in section 39.2.3).
- An array element is treated just like a variable; that is, **MyArray(2)** is a variable and so is **MyArray(i-3)** (assuming that i-3 has an integer value >=0 and <=5).
- The use of the concatenation operator **&**. This operator concatenates (combines) its two operands to create a string. If an operand to the concatenation operator is not a string, it is converted to a string, and then the concatenation takes place.

If you try to access an array element that is not part of the array, VBA will complain, as demonstrated by the following macro:

```
Sub ArrayDemo2()
    Dim MyArray(5)
    Dim i As Integer
    i = 6
    MsgBox MyArray(i)
End Sub
```

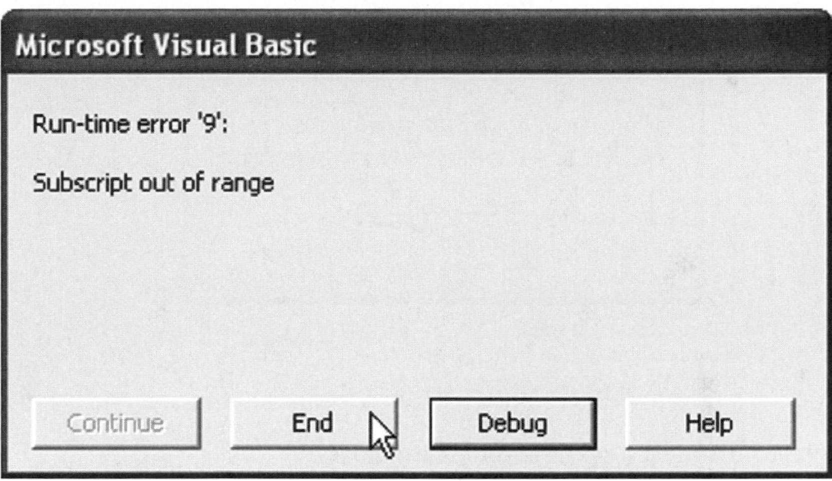

For now just click the **End** button and try to correct the problem. A full treatment of the debugger is beyond the scope of this book.

39.2.1 LBound and UBound

LBound and **UBound** are two internal VBA functions that are very useful when dealing with arrays. These functions return the minimum value (**LBound**) and maximum value (**UBound**) that an array index can have. The following macro demonstrates their use; the message box tells us that **MyArray** has lowest index 0 and highest index 5.

```
Sub ArrayDemo3()
    Dim MyArray(5)
    MsgBox "Minimum value for MyArray index is: " _
           & LBound (MyArray) & Chr (13) _
           & "Maximum value for MyArry index is: " _
           & UBound(MyArray), , "Lbound functions demo"
End Sub
```

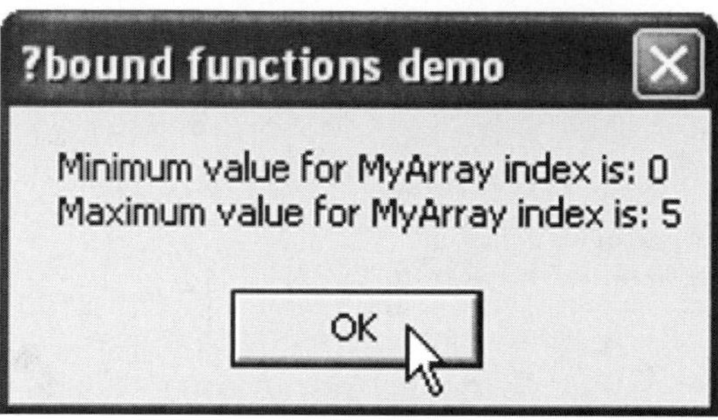

Note the use of **Chr(13)** to break the message line.

39.2.2 Explicitly Declared Index Boundaries

On occasion it is clearer to have an array with the index starting not at zero. You can create such an array by specifying a starting and ending value for the index. This approach is demonstrated in the following function:

```
Sub ArrayDemo4()
    Dim MyArray(6 To 10)
    Dim i As Integer
    MsgBox "Index of MyArray Starts at:" & _
    LBound(MyArray)
    MsgBox "Index of MyArray Stops at:" & _
    UBound(MyArray)
    For i = LBound(MyArray) To UBound(MyArray)
        MyArray(i) = i * i
    Next i
    MsgBox "The Value in MyArray(7) is: " & _
    MyArray(7)
End Sub
```

And here is the output in quick succession (click the **OK** button to close a message box and move to the next one):

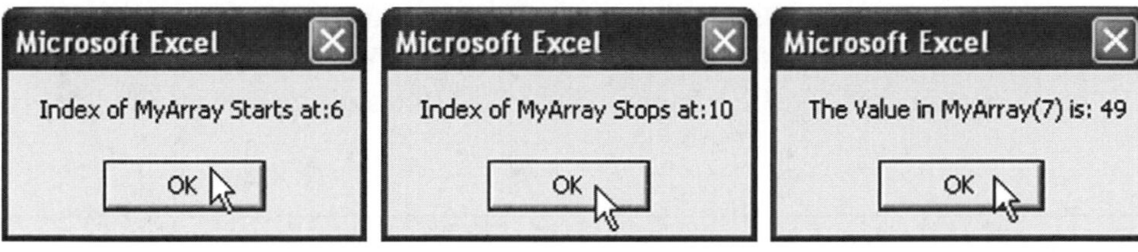

39.2.3 The Option Base Statement

Since most Excel (as opposed to VBA) array indices start at one, we can use a module option to make all not specifically declared array indices start at one. The following module demonstrates this procedure:

```
Option Explicit
Option Base 1
Sub ArrayDemoBase1()
    Dim MyArray(5)
    MsgBox "Minimum value for MyArray index is: " _
           & LBound (MyArray) & Chr (13) _
           & "Maximum value for MyArry index is: " _
           & UBound(MyArray), , "?bound functions demo"
End Sub
```

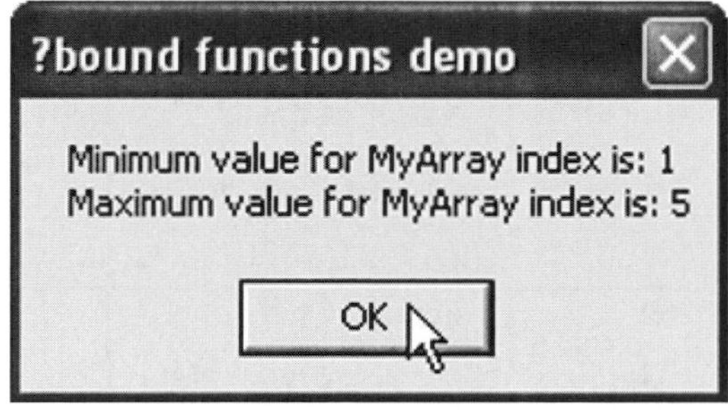

The **Option Base** 1 statement, like all options statements, should be inserted before all functions and subroutines in a module. Like all option statements, its effect is limited to all routines in the current module.

39.3 Multidimensional Arrays

Arrays can have more than one index. In a two-dimensional array the first index refers to the rows and the second to the columns. There is no formal limit to the number of indices you can declare in an array. The syntax for declaring a multidimensional array is demonstrated in the following macros; and so is the fact that array elements can (or indeed should) be typed.

```
Sub Matrix1()
    Dim MyMat(2, 2) As Integer
    Dim I, J As Integer
    Dim Temp As String
    For I = 0 To 2
        For J = 0 To 2
            MyMat(I, J) = I * J
        Next J
    Next I
    Temp = ""
    For I = 0 To 2
        For J = 0 To 2
            Temp = Temp & MyMat(I, J) & " # "
        Next J
        Temp = Temp & Chr(13)
    Next I
    MsgBox Temp
End Sub
```

Here's the output of this macro:

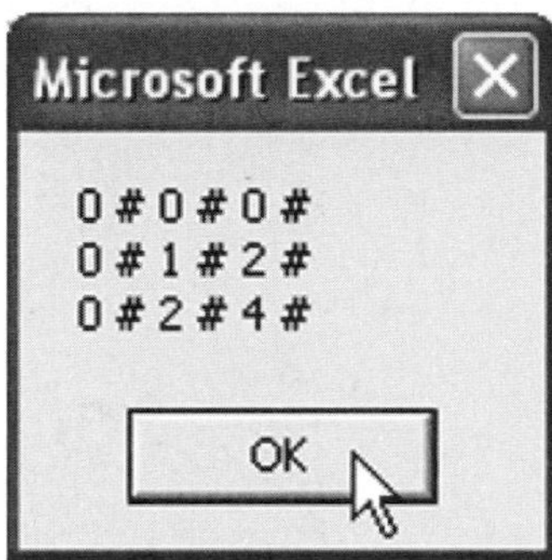

As the following macro demonstrates, we can use explicit index declaration for one or more of the dimensions in multidimensional arrays.

```
Sub Matrix2()
    Dim MyMat1(1 To 3, 1 To 2) As Integer
    Dim I, J As Integer
    Dim Temp As String
    For I = 1 To 3
        For J = 1 To 2
            MyMat1(I, J) = I * J
        Next J
    Next I
    Temp = ""
    For I = 1 To 3
        For J = LBound(MyMat1, 2) To
            UBound(MyMat1, 2)
           Temp = Temp & MyMat(I, J) & " # "
        Next J
        Temp = Temp & Chr(13)
    Next I
    MsgBox Temp
End Sub
```

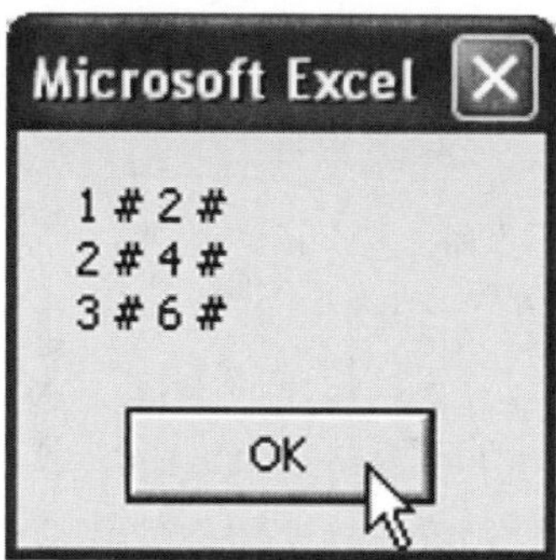

Note the use of the second argument to **LBound** and **UBound**. If used with only one argument, both functions return the largest index value the first dimension of the array can have. If the array has more than one dimension (as in this case) we can use a second argument to the function to specify the dimension we are interested in (the second dimension, in this case).

39.4 Dynamic Arrays and the ReDim Statement

Every so often it can be handy to have the size of an array set (and reset) when the program is running. Dynamic arrays are arrays that can have their size changed at run time. You declare dynamic arrays using the **Dim** statement but with nothing in the parentheses, as in

```
Dim SomeName() AsSomeType
```

For example, you might type the following to declare a dynamic array of doubles called Prices:

```
Dim Prices() As double
```

Before you can use the array you need to set its size using the **ReDim** Statement, as in

```
ReDim ArrayName(SomeIntegerExpression)
```

For example, you might type the following:

```
ReDim Prices(12)
```

To set the size of the dynamic array of doubles **Prices** to 12 elements, a more typical case would involve the use of a variable for the size as in the following:

```
Dim I as Integer
' I gets a value here some how
ReDim Prices(I)
```

This will set the size of **Prices** to the value of *I*.

The **ReDim** Statement can also be used to change the size of a dynamic array (or indeed any array). If you change the size of an array, all the data in the array are lost. Use **ReDim Preserve** to keep the old data, as in

```
ReDim Preserve ArrayName(SomeIntegerExpression)
```

The following macro calculates the present value of a series of future cash flows. To simplify the macro, the interest rate is fixed at 5 percent per period. The macro illustrates the use of a dynamic array (the variable *CF*) that derives its size from user input (the variable *n*).

```
Sub DynPV()
    Dim n As Integer              ' Number of periods
    Dim CF() As Double            ' Dynamic array for  cash
                                    flows
    Dim Temp As Double
    Dim i As Integer
    n = InputBox("Enter number of periods", _
        "Present value calculator", 3)
    ReDim CF(1 To n) ' redimension the array
    ' for demonstration purpose only
    MsgBox "Index starts at: " & LBound(CF) & _
        " and stops at: " & UBound(CF), _
        vbInformation, "Present value calculator"
    For i = 1 To n
        CF(i) = InputBox("Enter value for period " & _
        i, "Present value calculator", 0)
    Next i
    Temp = 0
    For i = 1 To n
        Temp = Temp + CF(i) / 1.05 ^ i
    Next i
    MsgBox "Present value is: " & Temp,
    vbInformation, _
        "Present value calculator"
End Sub
```

Running the macro produces the following in quick succession. Click **OK** to move from one message box to the next.

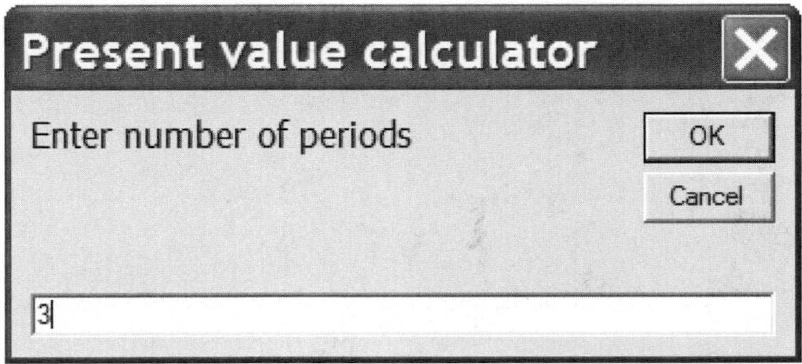

Notice that the 3 in the input box was provided by VBA as a default and that it is preselected, and so we can type a replacement value without selecting and clearing the default value.

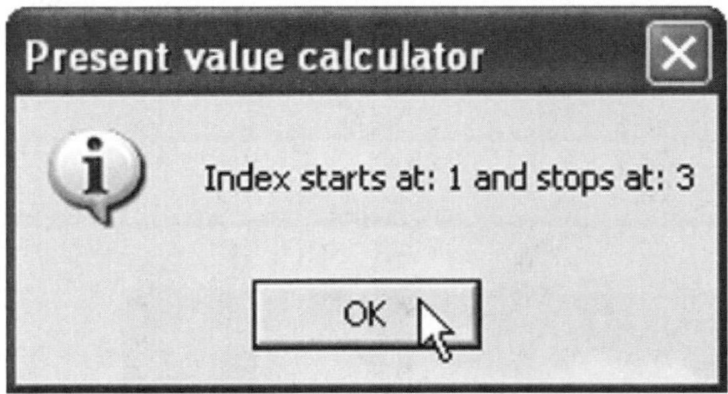

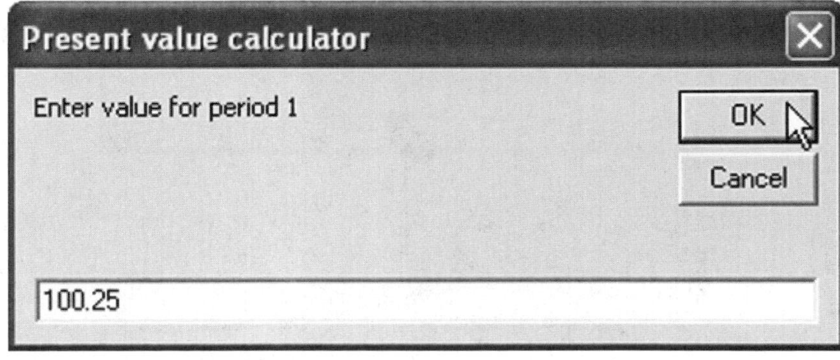

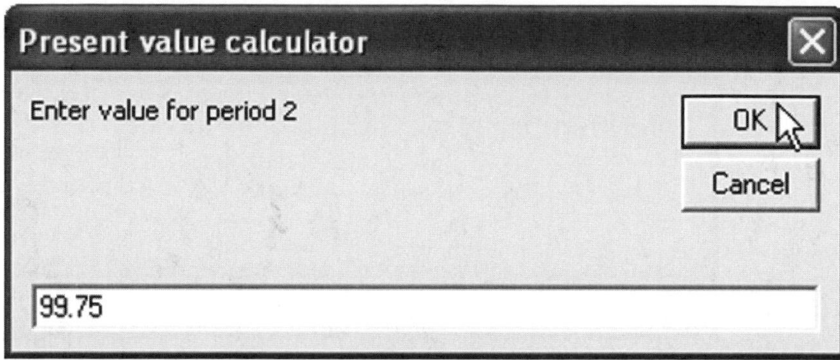

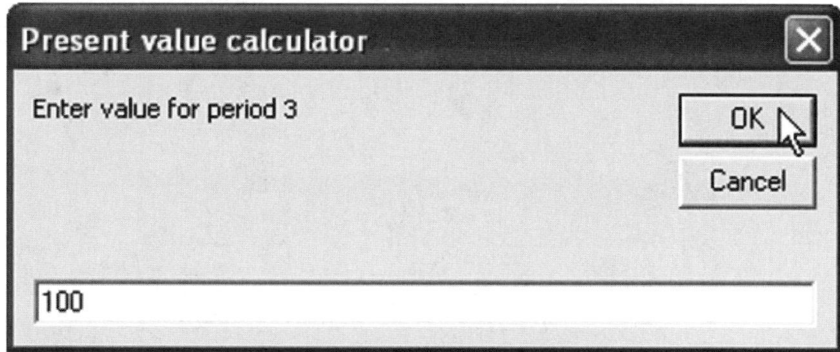

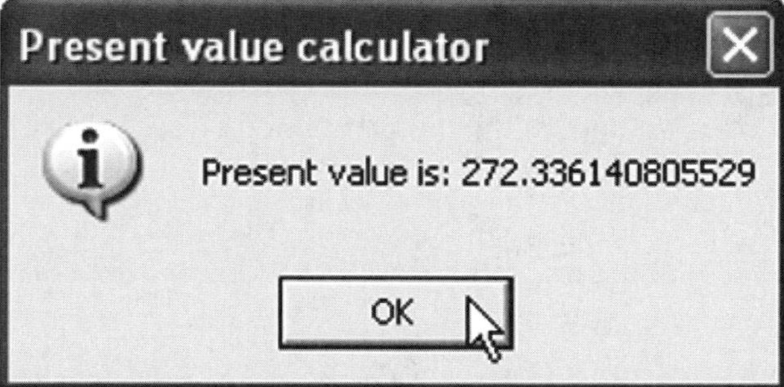

Trying to use a dynamic array that has not been initialized produces the following result:

```
Sub DynaArrayDemo1()
    Dim DynArray() As Integer
    MsgBox DynArray(0)
End Sub
```

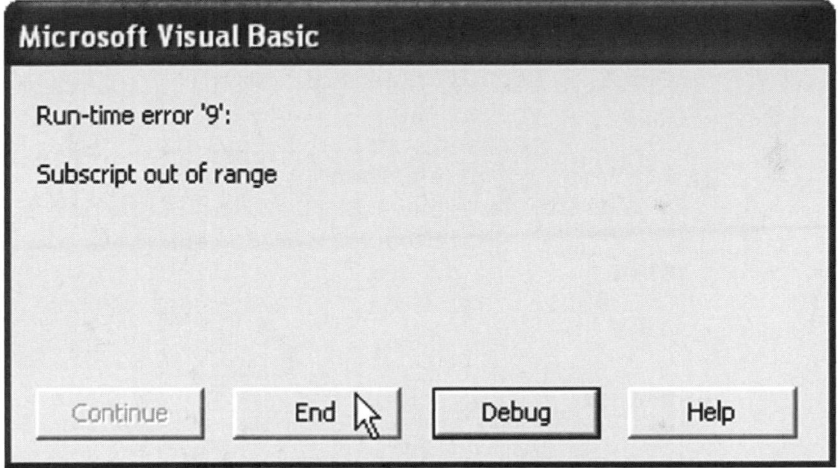

39.4.1 Using the ReDim Preserve Statement

As stated previously, the **Preserve** part of the **ReDim** statement prevents the loss of data from the redimensioned array. The use of **Preserve** imposes two major limitations on the use of **ReDim**.

- The inability to change the lower boundary of the index.
- The inability to change the number of dimensions.

The following macro is an interactive present-value calculator. It asks the user for the number of periods. Using the information supplied by the user, the macro redimensions an array to hold the cash flows for the periods. Once a present value has been calculated, the user is offered the choice of either stopping the macro or calculating the present value of another series of cash flows. As a by-product the macro demonstrates the use of **ReDim** and **Preserve**.

```
Sub MoreDynPV()
    Dim n, OldN As Integer ' Number of periods
    Dim CF() As Double ' Dynamic array for  cash flows
    Dim Temp As Double
    Dim i, Temp1 As Integer
    Do '******Begin main program loop
        OldN = n
        n = InputBox("Enter number of periods", _
            "Present value calculator", 3)
        Temp1 = MsgBox("Keep old Data?", _
                vbQuestion + vbYesNo, _
                "Present value calculator")
        If Temp1 = vbYes Then
            ReDim Preserve CF(1 To n) ' Redimension
                    ' the array and keep the old data
        Else
            ReDim CF(1 To n)  ' Redimension the array
                              ' do not keep the old
                              ' data
        End If
        For i = 1 To n
            CF(i) = InputBox("Enter value for period " _
                    & i, "Present value calculator", CF(i))
        Next i
        Temp = 0
        For i = 1 To n
            Temp = Temp + CF(i) / 1.05 ^ i
        Next i
        MsgBox "Present value is: " & Temp, _
                vbInformation, _
                "Present value calculator"
        Temp1 = MsgBox("Give it another go?", _
                vbQuestion + vbYesNo, _
                "Present value calculator")
    Loop While Temp1 = vbYes 'End main program loop
End Sub
```

One possible activation of the macro might look like the following screen shots, in which the button that has the arrow on it was clicked.

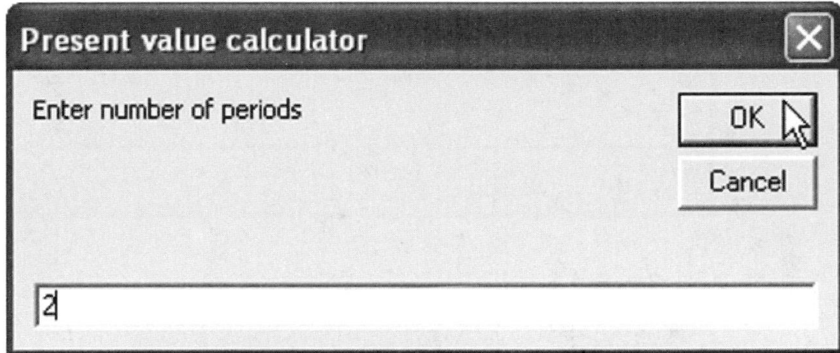

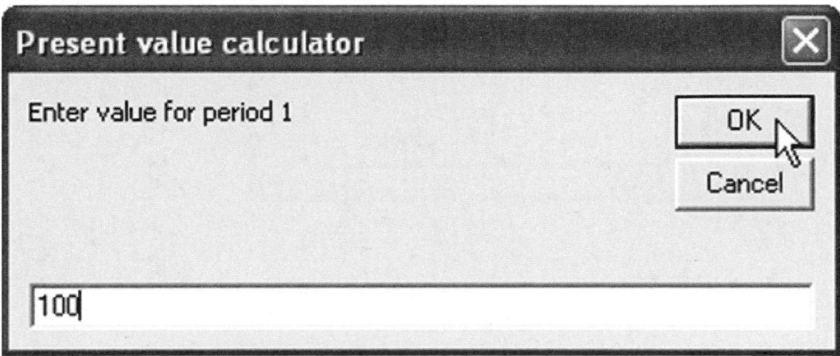

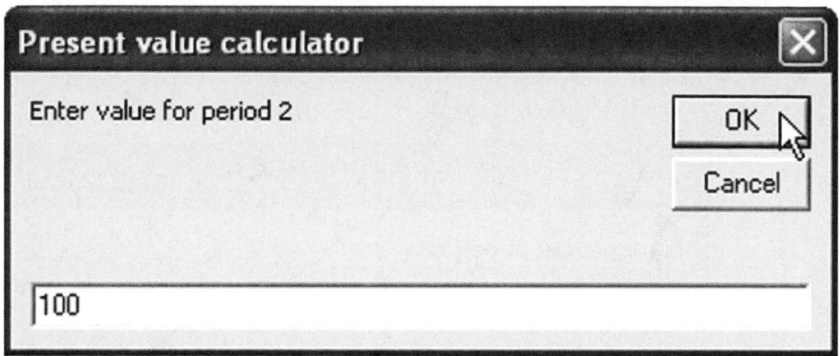
Present value calculator
Enter value for period 2
OK
Cancel
100

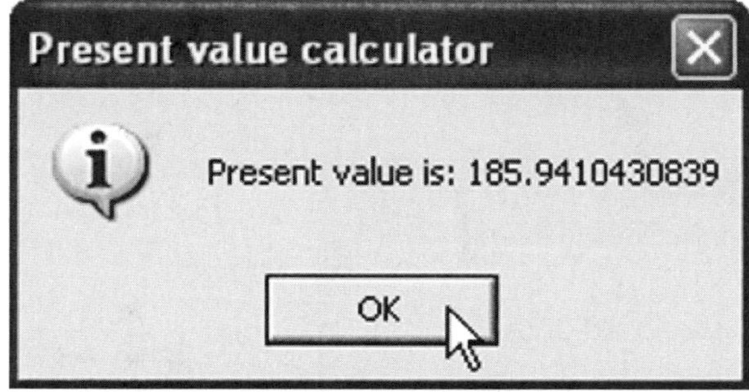
Present value calculator
Present value is: 185.9410430839
OK

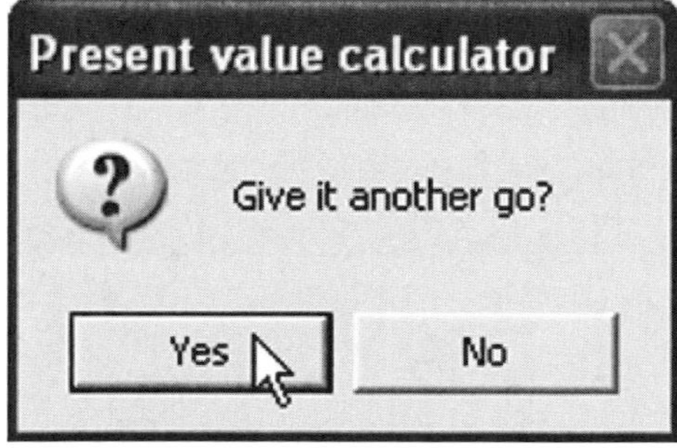
Present value calculator
Give it another go?
Yes
No

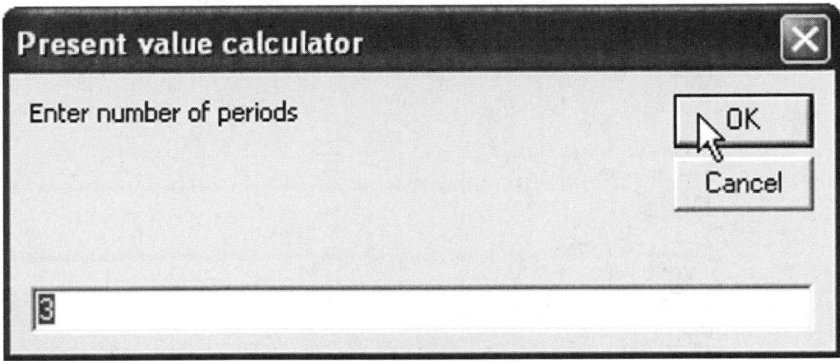
Present value calculator
Enter number of periods
OK
Cancel
3

Present value calculator
Keep old Data?
Yes
No

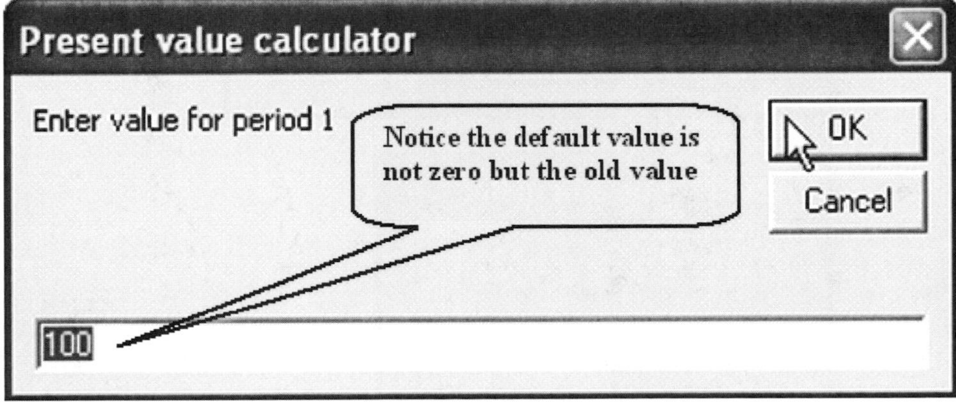
Present value calculator
Enter value for period 1
Notice the default value is not zero but the old value
OK
Cancel
100

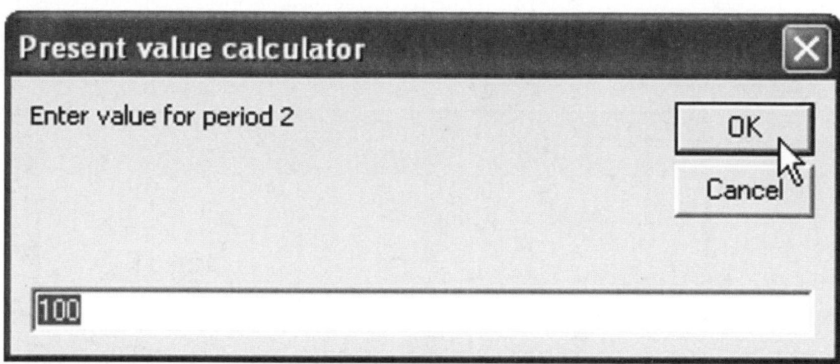
Present value calculator
Enter value for period 2
OK
Cancel
100

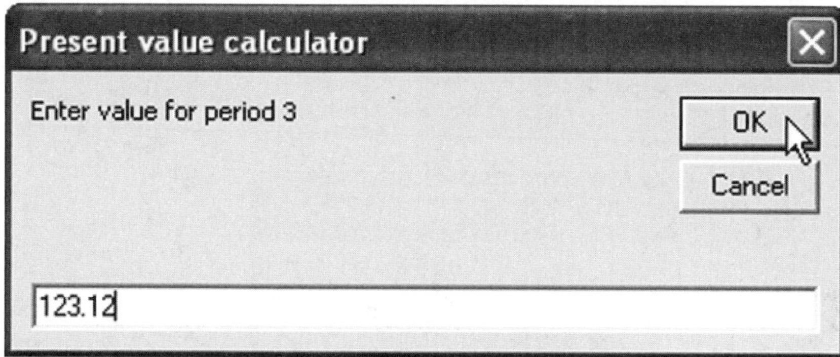
Present value calculator
Enter value for period 3
OK
Cancel
123.12

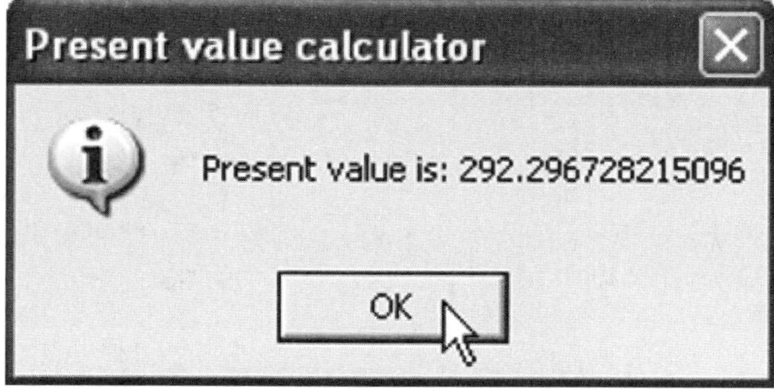
Present value calculator
Present value is: 292.296728215096
OK

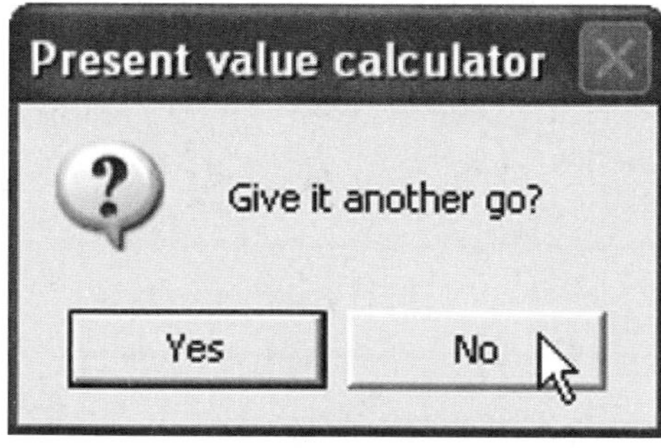
Present value calculator
Give it another go?
Yes
No

39.5 Array Assignment

Here's an error that's easy to make: In the following example we want to tell VBA that **Array2** is equal to **Array1**. VBA doesn't allow us to do so, as you can see:

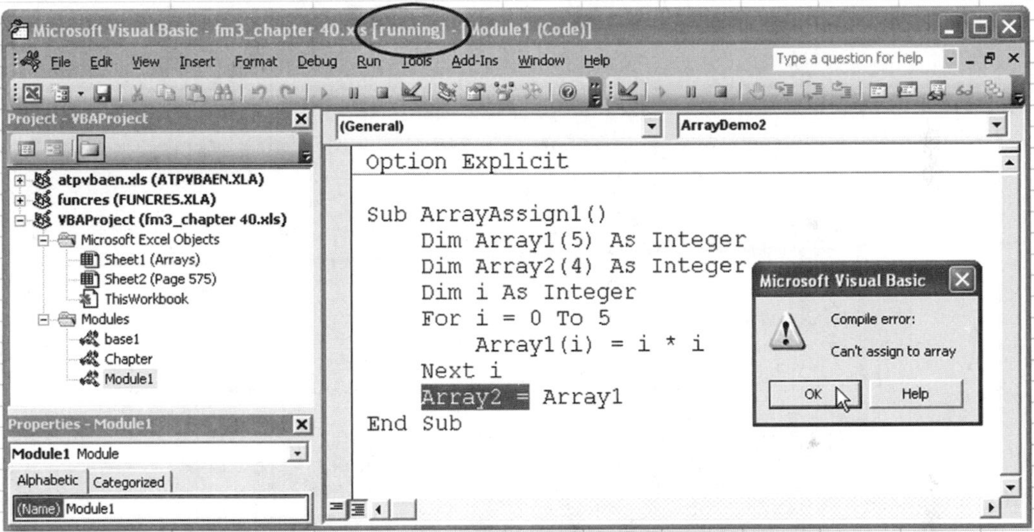

Obviously one way to assign arrays is to assign each element separately using a **For** loop.

```
Sub ArrayAssign()
    Dim Array1(5), Array2(4), I As Integer
    Dim Temp As String
    Temp = ""
    For I = 0 To 5: Array1(I) = I * I: Next I
    For I = 0 To 5
        Temp = Temp & Array1(I) & ":"
    Next I
    I = Len(Temp)
    Temp = Left(Temp, I - 1)
```

```
    MsgBox Temp, , "Array1"
    For I = 0 To 4: Array2(I) = Array1(I):
    Next I
    Temp = ""
    For I = 0 To 4
        Temp = Temp & Array2(I) & ":"
    Next I
    I = Len(Temp)
    Temp = Left(Temp, I - 1)
    MsgBox Temp, , "Array2"
End Sub
```

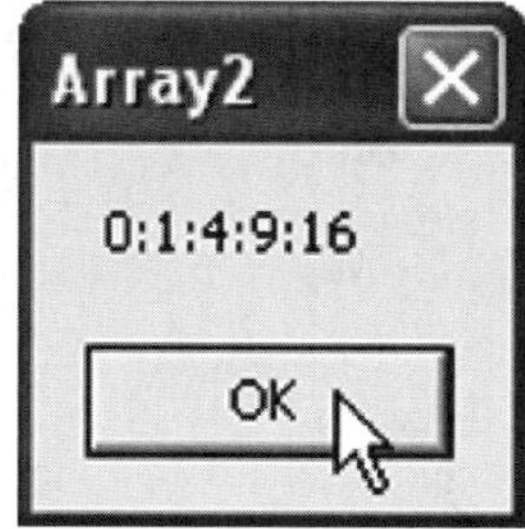

Note the following:

1. The use of the **:** operator to signal the end of a statement (line 5). This way we can put two or more short statements on the same line.
2. The use of the **Len** function to get the length of a string (line 9).
3. The use of the **Left** function to get the left part of a string (line 18). (Yes, a **Right** function is available.)

Another, much shorter, way of assigning arrays is discussed in the next section.

39.6 Variants Containing an Array

A **Variant** type variable can contain an array. The procedure is somewhat more complicated than the declaration of a normal array, but the reward in terms of assignment is sometimes worth the inconvenience (and the cost in program memory allocated to the array). The following macro demonstrates the use of a **Variant** containing an array:

```
Sub VarArrayAssign()
    Dim Array1   'This is a variant
    Dim I As Integer, Temp As String
    Array1 = Array()
    Temp = ""
    ReDim Array1(5) As Integer
    For I = LBound(Array1) To UBound(Array1)
        Array1(I) = I * I
    Next I
    For I = LBound(Array1) To UBound(Array1)
        Temp = Temp & Array1(I) & ":"
    Next I
    I = Len(Temp)
    Temp = Left(Temp, I - 1)
    MsgBox Temp, , "Array1"
End Sub
```

The **Array**() function (on the fourth line) returns an array. The assignment on the same line makes **Array1** into an array (not initialized at the moment). The **ReDim** statement two lines down makes **Array1** into a five-element **Integer** array.

And now for the reward, as demonstrated by the following macro (compare the macro with **ArrayAssign** in the preceding section):

```
Sub VarArrayAssign()
    Dim Array1   'This is a variant
    Dim Array2   'This is a variant
    Dim I As Integer
    Dim Temp As String
    Array1 = Array()
    Temp = ""
    ReDim Array1(5) As Integer
    For I = LBound(Array1) To UBound(Array1)
        Array1(I) = I * I
    Next I
    For I = LBound(Array1) To UBound(Array1)
        Temp = Temp & Array1(I) & ":"
    Next I
    I = Len(Temp)
    Temp = Left(Temp, I - 1)
    MsgBox Temp, , "VarArray1"
    Temp = ""
'********************Watch this spot
    Array2 = Array1 'Watch this spot
'********************Watch this spot
    For I = LBound(Array2) To UBound(Array2)
        Temp = Temp & Array2(I) & ":"
    Next I
    I = Len(Temp)
    Temp = Left(Temp, I - 1)
    MsgBox Temp, , "VarArray2"
End Sub
```

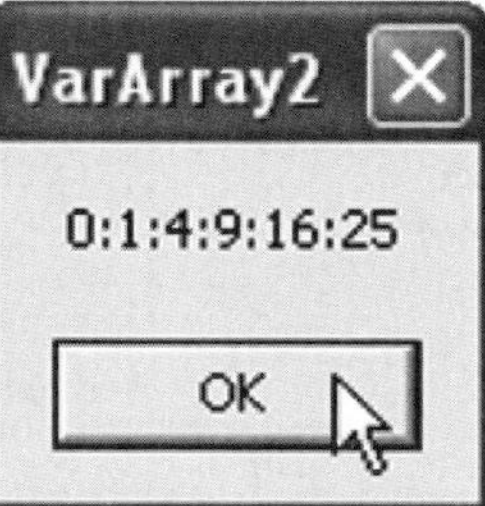

39.7 Arrays as Parameters to Functions

Arrays can be used as parameters to functions. The following set of functions and subroutines presents an improved version of **MoreDynPV.** Notice how mach easier it is to read the main macro **NewDynPV** when all the auxiliary tasks are relegated to separate functions and subroutines.

A function **ComputePV(CF(), n)** is used to compute the present value of a series of cash flows contained in an array of **Doubles.**

```
Function ComputePV(CF() As Double, n As
Integer) As Double
     Dim Temp As Double, i As Integer
     Temp = 0
     For i = 1 To n
          Temp = Temp + CF(i) / 1.05 ^ i
     Next i
     ComputePV = Temp
End Function
```

A subroutine **GetCF(CF(), n)** is used to query the user for the cash flow values and store them in the **CF** array.

```
Sub GetCf(CF() As Double, n As Integer)
    Dim i As Integer
    For i = 1 To n
        CF(i) = InputBox("Enter value for period " _
              & i, "Present value calculator", CF(i))
    Next i
End Sub
```

Note the fact that in both ComputePV**(CF(), n)** and **GetCF(CF(), n), CF()** has to be declared without index information. Consequently, index information has to be transferred to the function. We could use **Lbound** and **Ubound** as an alternative to providing index information.

This is the main macro:

```
Sub NewDynPV()
    Dim n As Integer ' Number of periods
    Dim OldN As Integer ' Old number of periods
    Dim CF() As Double ' Dynamic array for cash flows
    Dim Temp As Double
    Dim i As Integer, Temp1 As Integer
    Dim FirstTime As Boolean
    FirstTime = True
    Do    '**************************Begin main loop
        OldN = n
        n = GetN()
        If FirstTime Then
            ReDim CF(1 To n)     ' Redimension the array
                                 ' No old data to keep
            FirstTime = False    ' not the first time anymore
        Else
            If KeepOld() Then
                ReDim Preserve CF(1 To n)
                ' Redimension
                        ' the array and keep the old data
            Else
                ReDim CF(1 To n) ' Redimension
                the array
                                 ' do not keep the old data
            End If
        End If
       GetCf CF(), n
       Temp = ComputePV(CF, n)
        DisplayPV (Temp)
    Loop While AnotherGo()   '*****************End main loop
End Sub
```

Here are the auxiliary functions and subroutines, dealing with all sorts of maintenance tasks:

```
Function GetN() As Integer
     GetN = InputBox("Enter number of periods", _
               "Present value calculator", 3)
End Function

Function AnotherGo() As Boolean
     Dim Temp As Integer
     Temp = MsgBox("Give it another go?", vbQuestion _
                   + vbYesNo, "Present value calculator")
     AnotherGo = (Temp = vbYes)
End Function
Function KeepOld() As Boolean
     Dim Temp As Integer
     Temp = MsgBox("Keep old Data?", vbQuestion _
          + vbYesNo, "Present value calculator")
     KeepOld = (Temp = vbYes)
End Function
Sub DisplayPV(PV As Double)
     MsgBox "Present value is: " & PV, vbInformation, _
                   "Present value calculator"
End Sub
```

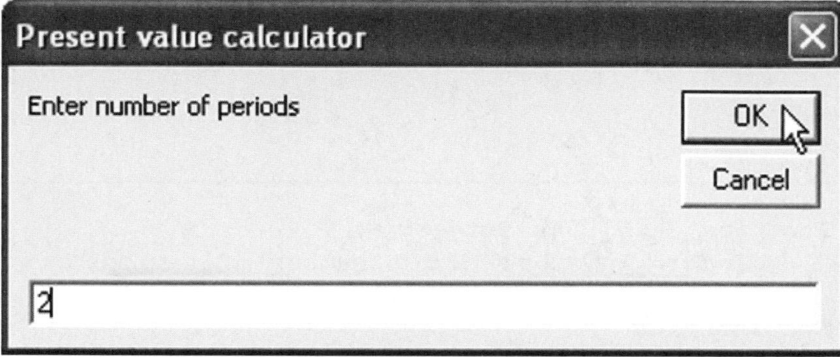
Present value calculator
Enter number of periods
OK
Cancel
2

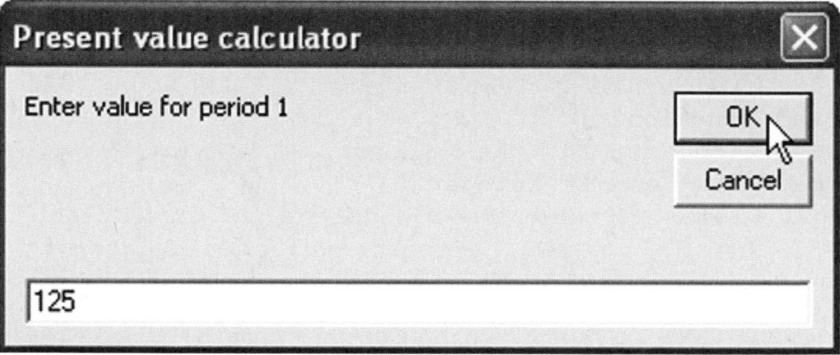
Present value calculator
Enter value for period 1
OK
Cancel
125

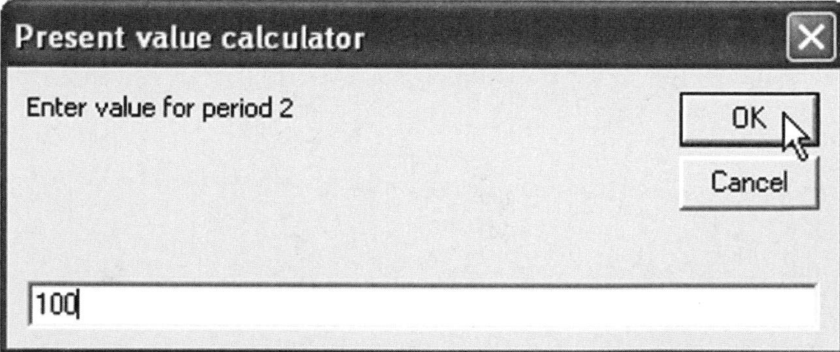
Present value calculator
Enter value for period 2
OK
Cancel
100

Present value calculator
Present value is: 209.750566893424
OK
Present value calculator
Give it another go?
Yes
No

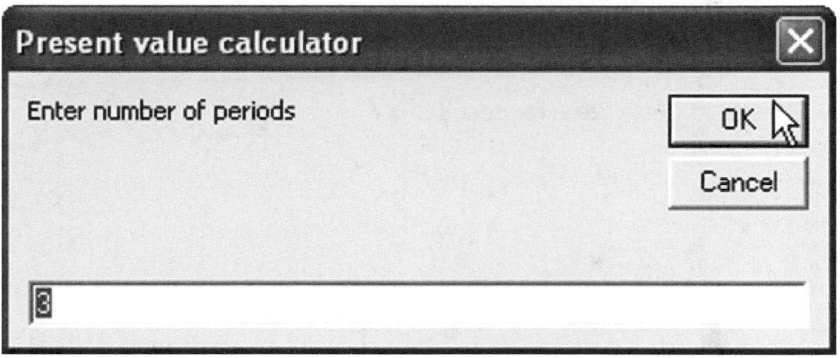

Present value calculator
Enter number of periods
OK
Cancel
3

Present value calculator
Keep old Data?
Yes
No

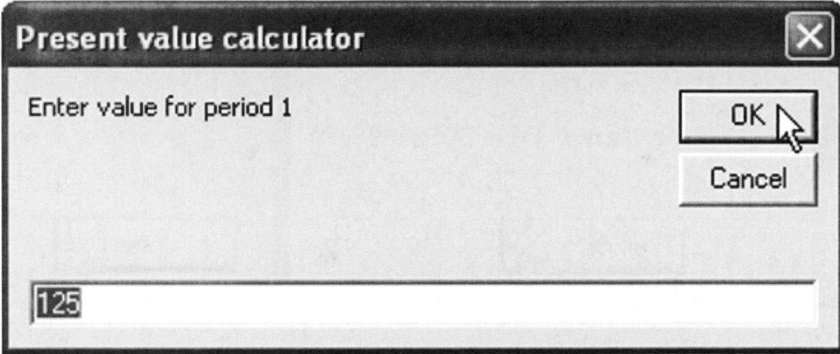
Present value calculator
Enter value for period 1
OK
Cancel
125

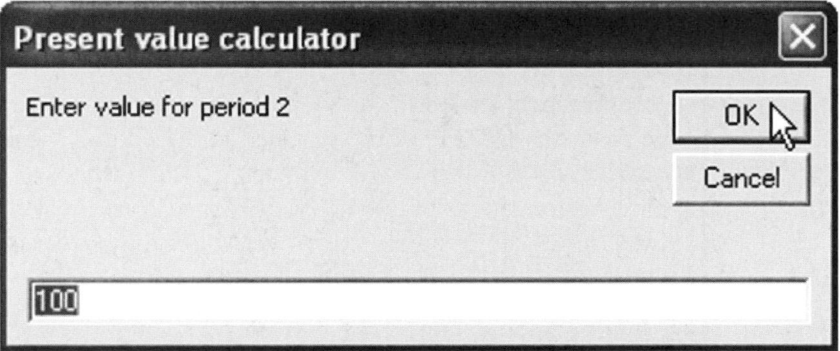
Present value calculator
Enter value for period 2
OK
Cancel
100

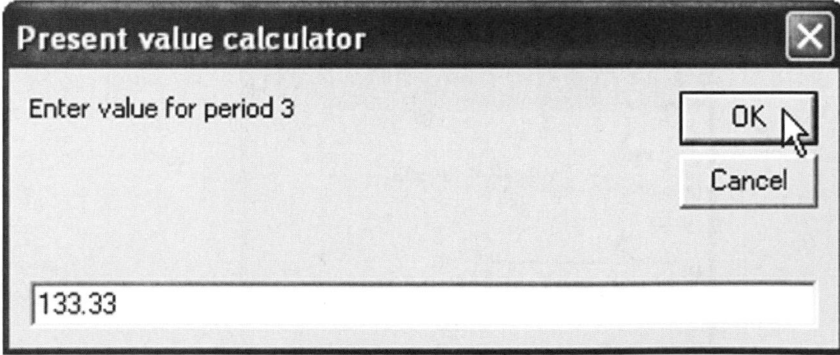
Present value calculator
Enter value for period 3
OK
Cancel
133.33

39.7.1 Arrays from a Worksheet

Arrays bear some resemblance to worksheet ranges. We might want to write a function that accepts a range as a parameter. Unfortunately the resemblance is only skin deep, and some manipulation is needed to achieve our goal. A full discussion of worksheet objects is beyond the scope of this book. The following function (based on **ComputePV** from the previous section) can actually accept a column range of cells as a parameter, because its parameter is defined as **Variant**. A range of cells is always a two-dimensional array (even if it is only a row or a column); the indices always run from one and not from zero.

```
Function VarPV(CF As Variant) As Double
    Dim X As Variant, Temp As Double, i As
    Integer
    X = CF
    Temp = 0
    For i = LBound(X) To UBound(X)
        Temp = Temp + X(i, 1) / 1.05 ^ i
    Next i
    VarPV = Temp
End Function
```

Note that the declaration of the internal variable “X as Variant” is necessary, and so is the assignment “X = CF” on the third line. Here is how **VarPV** looks in Excel:

	A	B	C	D	E
1	**VARPV IN ACTION**				
2	**CF**	**VarPV**		**NPV**	
3	100	432.9477	<-- =VarPV(A3:A$7)	432.9477	<-- =NPV(0.05,A3:A$7)
4	100	354.5951	<-- =VarPV(A4:A$7)	354.5951	<-- =NPV(0.05,A4:A$7)
5	100	272.3248	<-- =VarPV(A5:A$7)	272.3248	<-- =NPV(0.05,A5:A$7)
6	100	185.9410	<-- =VarPV(A6:A$7)	185.9410	<-- =NPV(0.05,A6:A$7)
7	100	#VALUE!	<-- =VarPV(A7:A$7)	95.2381	<-- =NPV(0.05,A7:A$7)

Notice the error value in cell B7. Our function expects an array, and a single cell (even if it represents itself as a range A7:A$7) is not an array.

If we want to emulate the way the worksheet function **NPV** works, then our function has to be modified.

```
Function NewVarPV(CF As Variant) As Double
     If IsArray(CF) Then
          NewVarPV = VarPV(CF) 'use the old
          function
     Else
          NewVarPV = CF / 1.05
     End If
End Function
```

	A	B	C	D	E
1	**NEWVARPV IN ACTION**				
2	**CF**	**VarPV**		**NPV**	
3	100	432.9477	<-- =NewVarPV(A3:A$7)	432.9477	<-- =NPV(0.05,A3:A$7)
4	100	354.5951	<-- =NewVarPV(A4:A$7)	354.5951	<-- =NPV(0.05,A4:A$7)
5	100	272.3248	<-- =NewVarPV(A5:A$7)	272.3248	<-- =NPV(0.05,A5:A$7)
6	100	185.9410	<-- =NewVarPV(A6:A$7)	185.9410	<-- =NPV(0.05,A6:A$7)
7	100	95.2381	<-- =NewVarPV(A7:A$7)	95.2381	<-- =NPV(0.05,A7:A$7)

Notice the use of the VBA function IsArray to determine whether a variable is an array. As a rule, always check function parameters to see whether they comply with the functions expectation before doing anything else in the function.

39.8 Summary

An array is a group of variables of the same type, sharing the same name, and referenced individually using one or more indices. In VBA an array index is an integer. By default the index of the first element in an array is 0; this can be changed to 1 for all arrays used in a module using the **Option Base 1** statement. The size and number of dimensions of an array are set at the time the array is declared and has to be known when the program is written. Dynamic arrays are arrays whose size (but not number of dimensions) can be set at run time.

Exercises

1. Write a version of the present value function **VarPV(CF())** that will work with column and row ranges. (Recall that the original version works only on column ranges.)

   Hint: Remember that

   - Ranges are always two-dimentional arrays.
   - The lower bound for ranges is always 1.
   - The upper bound is the boundary that sets the size of the array.

	A	B	C	D	E
1	**RCMYPV IN ACTION**				
2	100	100	100	272.325	<-- =RCMyPv(A2:C2)
3	100				
4	100				
5	272.325	<-- =RCMyPv(A2:A4)			

2. Write a version of the present value function with two interest rates, one for positive cash flows and another for negative cash flows. The function should be written for use in a worksheet and should accept both column and row ranges as parameters. The function declaration line should be

```
Function MyPV(CF As Variant, PositiveR As Double, _
                    NegativeR As Double) As Double
```

	A	B	C	D	E	F	G
1	**MYPV IN ACTION**						
2	PositiveR	5%	100	100	100	272.3248	<-- =MyPV(C2:E2,$B$2,$B$3)
3	NegativeR	10%	-100	-100	-100	-248.6852	<-- =MyPV(C3:E3,$B$2,$B$3)
4			-100	100	100	86.17762	<-- =MyPV(C4:E4,$B$2,$B$3)
5			-63	<-- =MyPV(C2:C4,$B$2,$B$3)			

3. Write a future-value version of the function in exercise 1.

4. Write a future-value version of the function in exercise 2.

5. A bank offers different interest rates on loans. The rate is based on the size of the periodical repayment (**CF**$_i$) and the following table. Write a present-value function BankPV(**CF, r**) so that it reflects the present value of a loan in the bank. The function should be usable as a worksheet function. **CF** could be either a row range or a column range.

For Periodical Repayments ≤	The Interest Rate Is
100.00	r
500.00	$r - 0.5\%$
1,000.00	$r - 1.1\%$
5,000.00	$r - 1.7\%$
1,000,000.00	$r - 2.1\%$

6. A bank offers different interest rates on deposit accounts. The rate is based on the size of the periodical deposit (**CF**$_i$) and the following table. Write a future-value function **BankFV(CF, r)**. The function should be usable as a worksheet function. **CF** could be either a row range or a column range.

For Periodical Deposits	The Interest Rate Is
≤100.00	r
≤500.00	$r + 0.5\%$
≤1,000.00	$r + 1.1\%$
≤5,000.00	$r + 1.7\%$
>5,000.00	$r + 2.1\%$

7. Another bank offers a 1 percent increase in interest rate for savings accounts with a balance of more than 10,000.00. Write a future-value function **Bank1FV(CF, r)** that reflects this policy. The function should be usable as a worksheet function. **CF** could be either a row range or a column range.

8. The bank in exercise 7 changed its bonus policy and now offers the interest rate increase based on the following table. Rewrite **Bank1FV(CF, r, n)** to reflect this change.

Balance	Interest Rate
≤1,000.00	$r + 0.2\%$
≤5,000.00	$r + 0.5\%$
≤10,000.00	$r + 1.0\%$
>10,000.00	$r + 1.3\%$

40 Objects and Add-Ins

40.1 Overview

This chapter deals with several of the more advanced subjects in VBA. Most of these subjects relate to the Excel Object Model. The bulk of the chapter describes some useful Excel objects and ways of dealing with them. Names, a way to make worksheets clearer and more readable, are presented in section 40.6. The use of VBA function across workbook boundaries is covered in sections 40.8 and 40.9. The chapter closes with a discussion of Excel add-ins, one easy way to make self-crafted functions automatically available across workbooks.

40.2 An Introduction to Worksheet Objects

Objects are the basic building blocks of VBA. Although you may not be aware that you are using objects, most things you do in VBA require the manipulation of objects. We can think of an object as a sort of a container with variables, functions, and subroutines inside. All of Excel's components (workbooks, worksheets, ranges, and so on) are represented by an object in the VBA Object Hierarchy (see appendix 1 for a chart). The object's data are held in special variables called properties that can be accessed using the dot **(.)** operator.

40.2.1 The Active Cell Range Object Variable

VBA has many variables predefined for our use; one of the more useful ones is **ActiveCell**. **ActiveCell** is a predefined **Range Object** variable that represents the cell in the worksheet with the cursor box around it. The following macro uses **ActiveCell** and three of its properties: **Address**, **Formula**, and **Value**.

```
Sub ActiveCellDemo( )
   Dim Msg As String
   Dim Title As String
   Title = "Active Cell Reporting"  ' Title for MsgBox
   Msg = "You are at:"     ' Start line one of message
   Msg = Msg & ActiveCell.Address     ' Add address of
                                      ' active cell
```

```
    Msg = Msg & Chr(13) ' Add a carriage Return
    ' The next line starts line two of message
    Msg = Msg & "The Formula in the cell is:"
    ' The next line Adds the text of the formula
    ' to the message
    Msg = Msg & ActiveCell.Formula
    Msg = Msg & Chr(13) ' Add a carriage return
    ' The next line starts line three of Message
    Msg = Msg & "The value of the cell is:"
    Msg = Msg & ActiveCell.Value     ' Add the value in
                                     ' the cell
    MsgBox Msg, vbInformation, Title  ' Report to user
    ' The next line adds "* 2" to the text in the
    ' cell
    ActiveCell.Formula = ActiveCell.Formula & "*2"
End Sub
```

The macro **ActiveCellDemo** first defines two string variables, one for the title of the message box and one for the message itself. We set the message variable in stages, adding bits to the string as we go along. In the process we use the values of three properties of **ActiveCell**. The first property we use is **Address**, which holds the absolute address of a range as a string. Obviously this property is read-only and cannot be changed.[1] The second property we use is **Formula**, which holds the text in the cell as a string and can be changed. The third property we use is **Value**, which holds the value in the cell as a variant and can be changed. We use the fact that the concatenation operator (**&**) converts its operands to strings to successively add values to the variable Msg. Once Msg is all set we use **MsgBox** to display it on screen.

The last line in the macro uses the **Formula** property again, but this time we change its value and add *2 to the end; this multiplies the last element in the formula by 2. Thus, if you have a formula =A2+3 in the active cell, the new formula will be =A2+3 ∗ 2. If you run the macro again on the same cell, the new formula will be = A2+3 ∗ 2 ∗ 2.

The Macro produces the following results.

1. If A1 is an address, then $A$1 is an absolute address.

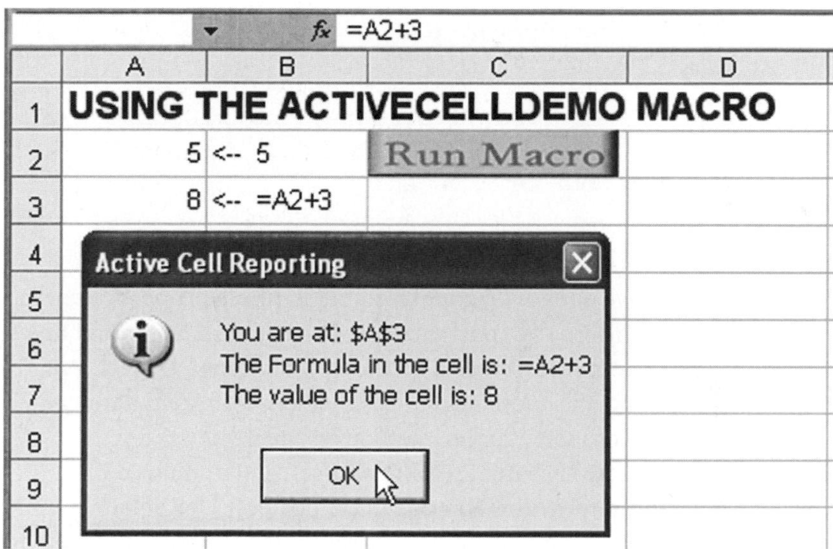

If you subsequently click **OK** on the dialogue box, you will see that the formula in the cell has been changed:

A3 =A2+3*2

	A	B	C	D
1	USING THE ACTIVECELLDEMO MACRO			
2	5	<-- 5	Run Macro	
3	11	<-- =A2+3*2		

40.2.2 Some Methods Using the Active Cell Range Object Variable

Methods are functions contained within an object. Methods are used to manipulate the object. Like properties, methods can be accessed using the dot **(.)** operator. The line between methods and properties is sometimes very fuzzy. In the following macro we use three of the methods available in a **Range Object** to move and change the border around the active cell:

```
Sub ActivecellDemo1( )
    MsgBox "You are at:" & ActiveCell.Address
    ActiveCell.BorderAround xlDouble, xlThick, 3
    ActiveCell.Cells(2, 2).Select
End Sub
```

We have already encountered the **Address** property used in the first line of the macro to report the current location. The second line of the macro uses the **BorderAround** method of the **Range Object**. As is evident from its name, this method changes the border around a range.[2] The third line uses a property and a method in quick succession; the **Cells** property accepts two parameters, a row offset, and a column offset (counting from 1) and returns the **Range** in that position; the **Select** method makes the **Range** that activates it the current selection, and if this **Range** is a single cell range, it also makes it the active cell. Once activated it looks like this:

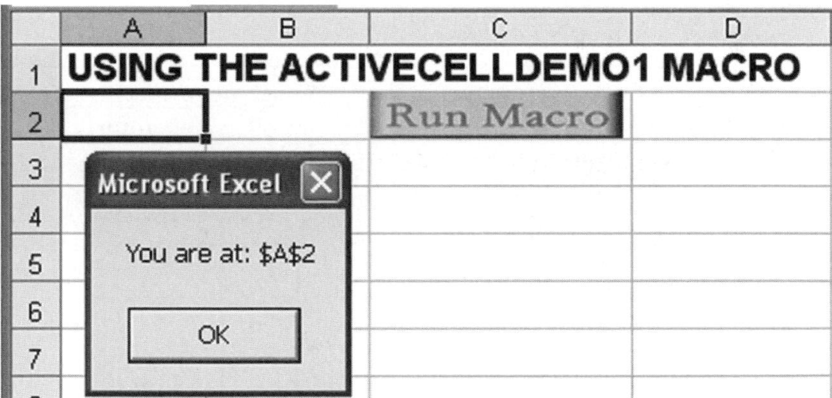

If you subsequently click **OK** on the dialogue box, you will see the former active cell has a line around it and that the active cell in the worksheet moved.

2. A full description of its parameters taken for the VBA Help files is presented in appendix 2.

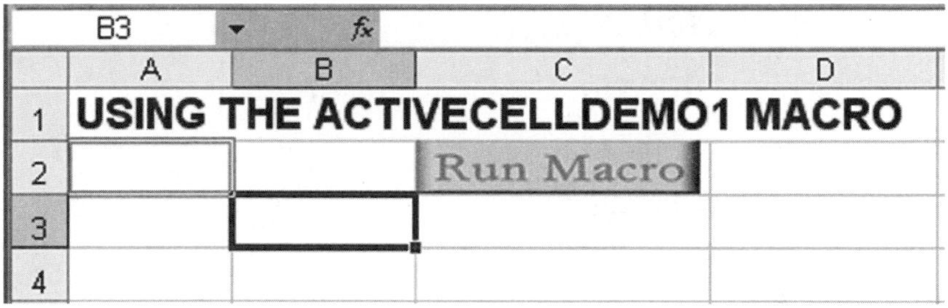

B3 | f_x

	A	B	C	D
1	USING THE ACTIVECELLDEMO1 MACRO			
2			Run Macro	
3				
4				

40.3 The Range Object

Objects have types. One of the most important object types in VBA is the **Range**. A worksheet cell and a range of cells are all objects of the type **Range**. For example, the VBA object variable **ActiveCell** that we encountered in the previous section is of the type **Range**. This section demonstrates the use of ranges in VBA and presents some more of the properties and methods of the **Range** object.

40.3.1 A Range as a Parameter to a Function

In this subsection we build a function that accepts a **Range** as a parameter. Our new function, named **MeanReturn**, accepts a column range of asset prices as a parameter and computes and returns the mean return of the assets in the column. Recall that the return of an asset for period t is $r_t = \frac{\text{Price}_t - \text{Price}_{t-1}}{\text{Price}_{t-1}}$ and the mean return of an asset is $\bar{r} = \frac{1}{N}\sum_{t=1}^{N} r_t$. An auxiliary function **AssetReturn** is used to compute r_t.

```
Function MeanReturn(Rng As Range) As Double
    Dim NumRows As Integer
    Dim Prices As Variant
    Dim T As Double
    Dim i As Integer
    NumRows = Rng.Rows.Count
    Prices = Rng.Value
    T = 0
```

```
    For i = 2 To NumRows
        T = T + AssetReturn(Prices(i - 1, 1), _
        Prices(i, 1))
    Next i
    MeanReturn = T / (NumRows - 1)
End Function
```

```
Function AssetReturn(P0 As Variant, P1 As _
  Variant) As Double
    AssetReturn = (P1 - P0) / P0
End Function
```

Lines of note:

```
NumRows = Rng.Rows.Count
```

In this line the **Dot** operator is used twice. **Rng** is our **Range** object. **Rows** is property of the **Range** object, so **Rng.Rows** is an object of the **Collection** type that represents all the rows in our range. **Count** is a property of **Collection** type objects that stores the number of members in the collection, so **Rng.Rows.Count** is a variable that stores the number of rows in our range.

```
Prices = Rng.Value
```

Value is a property of the **Range** object containing the values of all the cells in the range. **Value** is of the type **Variant**. If the range is more than one cell in size, **Value** is a two-dimensional array. The first index of **Value** is the row index starting from 1, and the second index is the column index starting from 1.

This is the function in action:

	A	B	C
1	MEANRETURN IN ACTION		
2	100.000	0.160	<-- =meanreturn(A2:A7)
3	110.000	0.100	<-- =meanreturn(A2:A4)
4	121.000	0.200	<-- =meanreturn(A4:A7)
5	145.200		
6	174.240		
7	209.088		

40.3.2 Type Considerations with Variants and Objects as Parameters

Unless we want to use a laborious and very time-consuming loop to move values from a Range in the worksheet to a function in VBA, we have to use a **Variant** variable to store the Range of values.[3] The sharp-eyed reader might have wondered why **AssetReturn** was defined with **Variant** parameters when we know perfectly well that the values supplied are doubles and a better declaration for the **AssetReturn** function would have been

```
Function AssetReturn(P0 As Double, P1 As
Double) As Double
```

Unfortunately, when we try to use the function, VBA checks the correctness of our program and finds that the **Prices(i-1,1)** is not a double. As a consequence the following error is issued:

3. This method is two orders of magnitude faster than the loop way.

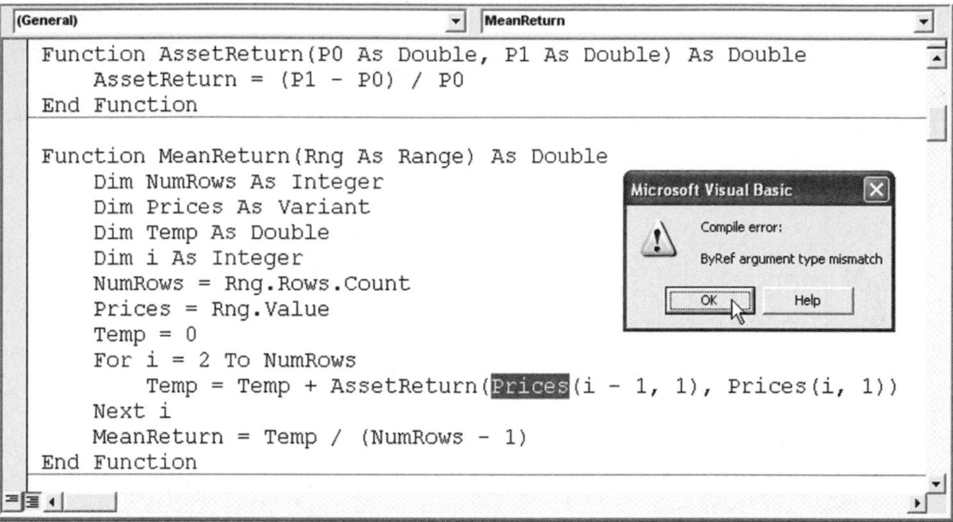

So, since we cannot have **Prices** as an array of doubles, we have to design **AssetReturn** to be flexible and accept **Variants** as input.

40.3.3 The Range Property

The **Range** property is one way to access a range on a worksheet. **Range** is a property of many Excel objects. When used on its own, as in the next macro, **Range** is a short way of writing **ActiveSheet.Range**.

```
Sub RangeDemo( )
    Range("A1").Formula = 23
End Sub
```

As expected, the macro will set the formula in cell A1 of the active worksheet to 23. The next macro sets the formula of each cell in the range A1:B2 of the active worksheet to 23.

```
Sub RangeDemo1( )
    Range("A1:B2").Formula = 23
End Sub
```

Another way of addressing a range of cells using the **Range** property is demonstrated by the next Macro. The Macro sets the formula of each cell in the range A1:B2 of the active worksheet to 23. The first argument to **Range** is the cell in the top left corner of the range, and the second is the cell in the bottom right corner of the range.

```
Sub RangeDemo2( )
    Range("A1", "B2").Formula = 23
End Sub
```

Range is also a property of the **Range** object. The range returned by **Range** when used this way is relative to the **Range** object. The next macro sets the formula of the cell C2 of the active worksheet to 23.

```
Sub RangeDemo3( )
    Range("B1").Range("B2").Formula = 23
End Sub
```

Note **Range("B1")** returns the range (or cell) B1 of the active worksheet. **Range("B1").Range("B2")** returns the cell B2 of the range that has B1 as the top left corner. In worksheet terms, **Range("B1"). Range("B2")** returns the cell C2.

The next macro sets the formula of each cell in the range C2:D3 of the active worksheet to 23. The macro uses the cell C2 as a starting point.

```
Sub RangeDemo4( )
    Range("C2").Range("A1", "B2").Formula = 23
End Sub
```

40.4 The With Statement

The **With** statement allows you to perform a series of statements on a specified object without restating the obvious (the object's name and its pedigree, which can be very long). If you have more than one property to change or more than one method to use for a single object, use the **With** statement. **With** statements make your procedures run faster and help you avoid repetitive typing. The following, somewhat contrived, macro sets some properties of the font of the cell in the top left-hand corner of the current region of the active cell. The font is set to be Arial, bold, red, and 15 points in size.

```
Sub WithoutDemo( )
    ActiveCell.CurrentRegion.Range("A1").Font _
        .Bold = True
    ActiveCell.CurrentRegion.Range("A1").Font _
        .ColorIndex = 3
    ActiveCell.CurrentRegion.Range("A1").Font _
        .Name = "Arial"
    ActiveCell.CurrentRegion.Range("A1").Font _
        .Size = 15
End Sub
```

And here is the same macro using the **With** statement:

```
Sub WithDemo( )
    With ActiveCell.CurrentRegion.Range("A1").
    Font
        .Bold = True
        .ColorIndex = 3
        .Name = "Arial"
        .Size = 15
    End With
End Sub
```

Notice the dot **(.)** operator before the properties in the **With** statement.

40.5 Collections

A **Collection** is an ordered set of items that can be referred to as a unit. The **Collection** object provides a convenient way to refer to a related group of items as a single object. The items, or members, in a **Collection** need only be related by the fact that they exist in the **Collection**. Members of a **Collection** don't have to share the same data type.

A **collection** can be created the same way other objects are created. Members can be added using the **Add** method and removed using the **Remove** method. Specific members can be referred to using an integer index. The number of members currently in a **Collection** is available via the **Count** method. Our use of **Collections** will be restricted to using the (quite numerous) arsenal of **Collections** that are part of the Excel Object Model, like the **Rows Collection** mentioned in section 40.3.1.

40.5.1 The For Each Statement in Use with Arrays and Collections

The **For Each** statement is a variation of the **For** loop unique to VBA. This statement comes in two distinct flavors. The first variation uses the statement to loop over an array as demonstrated in the following function:

```
Function ForEachSum(Rng As Range) As Double
    Dim Element As Variant
    Dim Sum As Double
    Sum = 0
    For Each Element In Rng.Value
        Sum = Sum + Element
    Next Element
    ForEachSum = Sum
End Function
```

	A	B	C	D	E
1	FOREACHSUM DEMO				
2	1	4	7	6	<-- =ForEachSum(A2:A4)
3	2	5	8	12	<-- =ForEachSum(A2:C2)
4	3	6	9	45	<-- =ForEachSum(A2:C4)

Points to note:

- The current member of the array is available to the statements within the loop body through the loop variable (**Element** in the preceding function).
- The loop variable (**Element** in the preceding example) has to be of the type **Variant** irrespective of the array type.
- Changes to **Element** will not be reflected in the actual array.
- You don't need to know the number of dimensions or the range of indices to loop over the array. The preceding function works on column ranges (as in cell E2), row ranges (as in cell E3), and rectangular ranges (as in cell E4) in the same fashion.

40.5.2 The For Each Statement in Use with Collections

The second version of the **For Each** statement loops over **Collections**:

```
Sub ZeroRange( )
    Dim Rng As Range
    Dim Cell As Variant
    Set Rng = ActiveCell.CurrentRegion
    MsgBox "The current region is: " & Rng.Address
    For Each Cell In Rng
        Cell.Formula = 0
    Next Cell
End Sub
```

Here is what happens when you run the macro:

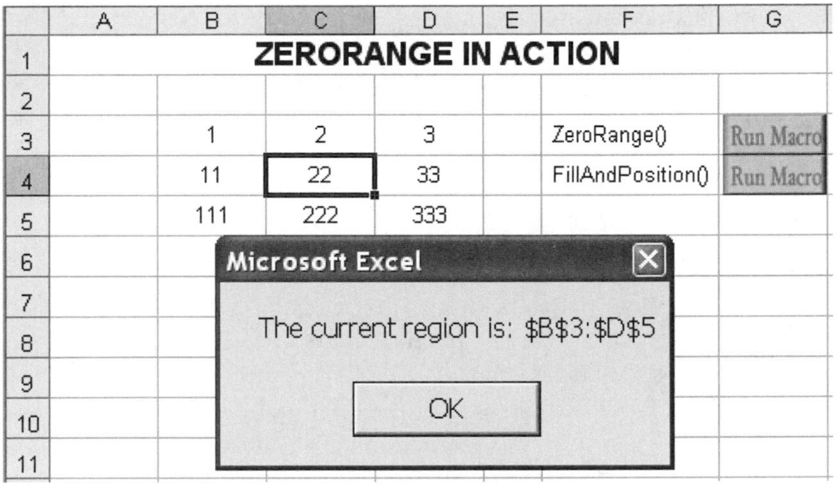

	A	B	C	D	E	F	G
1			ZERORANGE IN ACTION				
2							
3		1	2	3		ZeroRange()	Run Macro
4		11	22	33		FillAndPosition()	Run Macro
5		111	222	333			

Microsoft Excel

The current region is: $B$3:$D$5

OK

And when **OK** is clicked:

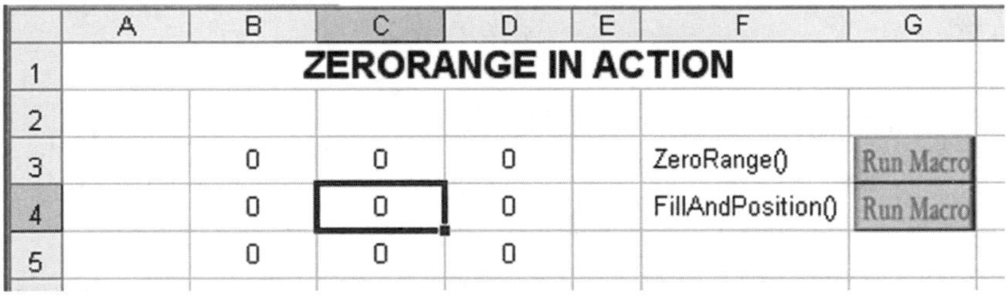

	A	B	C	D	E	F	G
1			ZERORANGE IN ACTION				
2							
3		0	0	0		ZeroRange()	Run Macro
4		0	0	0		FillAndPosition()	Run Macro
5		0	0	0			

Points to note:

- **Cell** is a variable used to iterate over *all* the members of the collection.
- **Cell** has to be one of the following types: **Variant**, **Object**, or the specific type of element the **Collection** is made of.
- **Cell** refers to the actual member of the **Collection**, and changes to **Cell** will be reflected in the **Collection**.
- **CurrentRegion** is a **Range** object that represents the current region. The current region is a range bounded by any combination of blank rows and blank columns.

• A complete explanation of the use of the **Set** statement is beyond the scope of this book. For our purposes just prefix the reserved word **Set** to all object assignments. If you don't, the following might ensue:

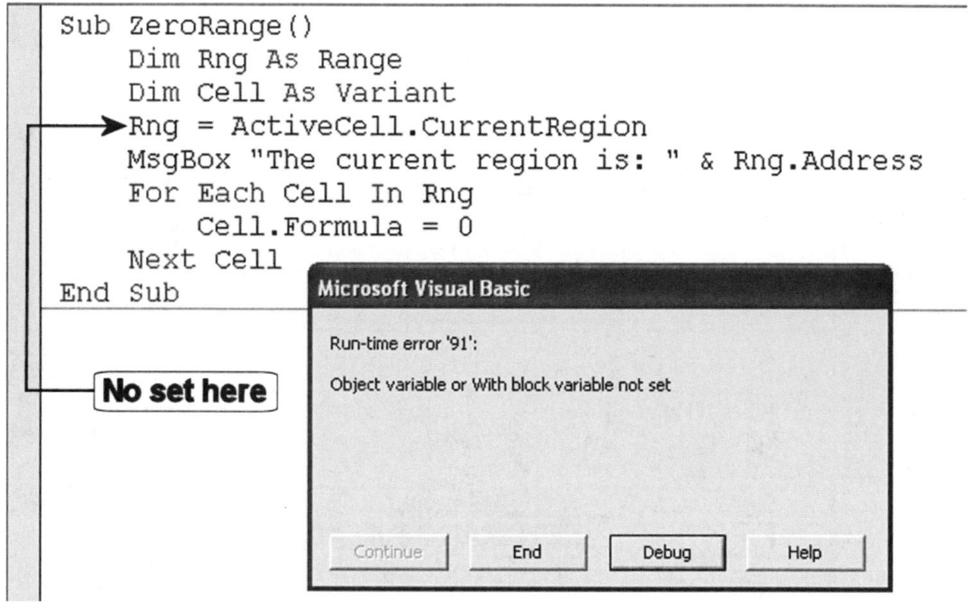
Sub ZeroRange()
Dim Rng As Range
Dim Cell As Variant
Rng = ActiveCell.CurrentRegion
MsgBox "The current region is: " & Rng.Address
For Each Cell In Rng
Cell.Formula = 0
Next Cell
End Sub
No set here
Microsoft Visual Basic
Run-time error '91':
Object variable or With block variable not set
Continue
End
Debug
Help

40.5.3 The Workbooks Collection and the Workbook Object

All the currently open workbooks are represented by a **Workbook** object in the **Workbooks Collection**. The following macro lists all open workbooks in a column of cells starting from the active cell:

```
Sub ListOpenWorkbooks( )
    Dim i As Integer
    Dim Element As Workbook
    ActiveCell.Item(2, 1).Formula = _
        "List of open Workbooks"
    ActiveCell.Item(4, 1).Formula = _
        "Created on:" & FormatDateTime(Date, _
        vbLongDate) _
```

```
            & " At: " & FormatDateTime(Time, _
            vbLongTime)
        With ActiveCell.Item(2, 1).Font
            .Bold = True
            .Name = "Arial"
            .Size = 12
        End With
        i = 5
        For Each Element In Workbooks
            ActiveCell.Item(i, 1).Formula = _
            Element.FullName
            i = i + 1
        Next Element
    End Sub
```

This is the worksheet after the macro was run:

	A	B	C	D
1	LISTOPENWORKBOOKS IN ACTION			
2	ListOpenWorkbooks()	Run Macro		
3				
4				
5	List of open Workbooks			
6				
7	Created on:Saturday, September 08, 2007 At: 4:23:02 PM			
8	C:\simon\WORK\FM3\Disk with book\Chapter files\fm3_chapter 40.xls			
9	C:\simon\WORK\FM3\Disk with book\Chapter files\fm3_chapter38.xls			
10	C:\simon\WORK\FM3\Disk with book\Chapter files\fm3_chapter07.xls			

Lines to note:

```
ActiveCell.Item(4, 1).Formula = _
    "Created on:" & FormatDateTime(Date, vbLongDate) _
    & " At:" & FormatDateTime(Time, vbLongTime)
```

- The **Date** function returns the current system date.
- The **Time** function returns the current system time.
- The **FormatDateTime** function formats **Date** and **Time** variables for display.

```
For Each Element In Workbooks
    ActiveCell.Item(i, 1).Formula = Element.
    FullName
    i = i + 1
Next Element
```

The **For** statement loops over the entire **Workbooks Collection.** On each iteration, **Element** is one of the **Workbook** objects in the **Collection**. **FullName** is a property of the **Workbook** object containing the full path name of the workbook.

The next macro adds a workbook to the **Workbooks Collection**:

```
Sub AddWorkbook( )
    Dim Wkbk As Workbook
    Dim OldWkbk As Workbook
    Set OldWkbk = ActiveWorkbook
    Set Wkbk = Workbooks.Add
    OldWkbk.Activate
    MsgBox Wkbk.FullName & " Added"
End Sub
```

Adding a workbook to the **Workbooks Collection** makes the newly added workbook the active workbook. If we want to stay where we are, we need to reactivate the old workbook.

40.5.4 The Worksheets Collection and the Worksheet Object

All the worksheets in a workbook are **Worksheet** objects in the **Worksheets Collection** that is a property of the **Workbook** object. We can use the **Worksheets Collection** without an object as a short form for **ActiveWorkbook.Worksheets**.

40.6 Names

In Excel you can use user-defined names to refer to a cell or a range of cells.[4] Use easy-to-understand names, such as Products, to refer to hard-to-understand ranges, such as Sales!C20:C30. Using names can make formulas easy to read: Compare the formula =sum('sheet12'!a10:a10) to =sum(lastYearSales). See appendix 2 for more examples. This section deals with the VBA side of names.

40.6.1 Naming a Range Using a Macro

The following macro names the current region:

```
Sub NameCurrentRegion( )
    Dim Rng As Range
    Dim MyName As String
    Set Rng = ActiveCell.CurrentRegion
    MyName = InputBox("The current region is: " & _
        Rng.Address & Chr(13) & "Enter Name please: ", _
        "Namer", "MyName")
    Names.Add Name:=MyName, RefersTo:="=" & _
    Rng.Address
End Sub
```

4. And a lot more, but that topic is beyond the scope of this book.

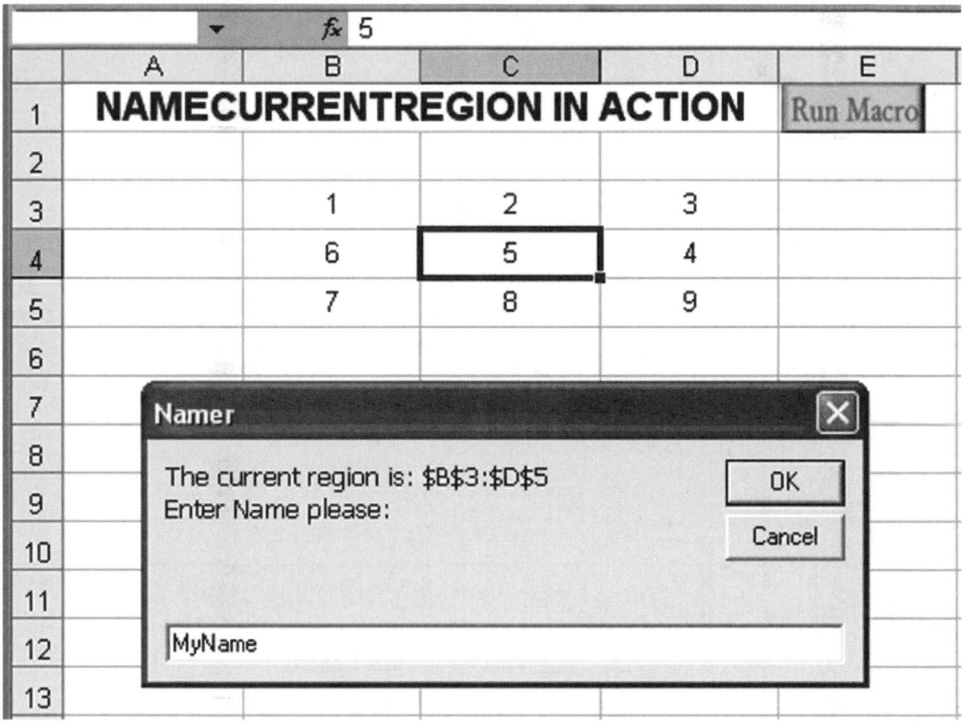

	A	B	C	D	E
1	NAMECURRENTREGION IN ACTION				Run Macro
2					
3		1	2	3	
4		6	5	4	
5		7	8	9	
6					

Namer

The current region is: $B$3:$D$5
Enter Name please:

OK
Cancel

MyName

Once we click OK, we can select "MyName" from the names box and see that it has been applied to the right range.

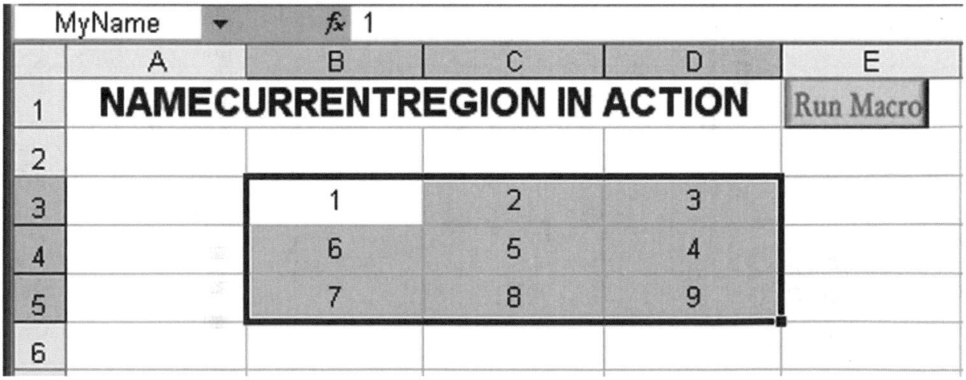

MyName

	A	B	C	D	E
1	NAMECURRENTREGION IN ACTION				Run Macro
2					
3		1	2	3	
4		6	5	4	
5		7	8	9	
6					

The interesting line in the macro is

```
Names.Add MyName, "=" & Rng.Address
```

Names is a **Collection** of all the names in the active workbook. **Add** is a method of the **Names Collection** used to add members to the collection. We use only the first two parameters of the method. The first parameter **MyName** is the name to add to the **Names Collection**. The second parameter is a string containing the address to which the added name is to refer, preceded by "=".

40.6.2 Looking for Defined Names

The name "Ben" has been defined in the "IsName" worksheet as demonstrated by the insert-name dialogue presented in the next screen capture:

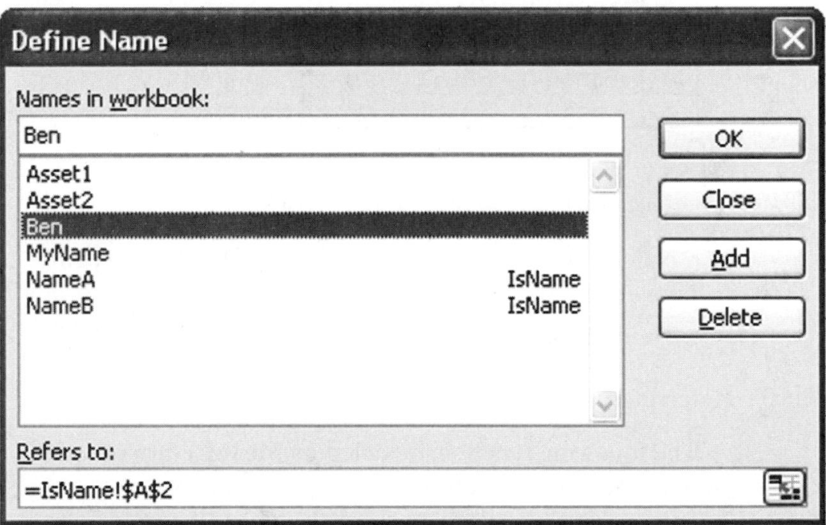

The following function looks for a defined name in the current workbook. The function returns the **Boolean** value "True" if the name is defined, and "False" if it is not part of the **Names Collection**.

```
Function IsName(Name As String) As Boolean
    Dim Element As Variant
    Dim Flag As Boolean
    Flag = False
    For Each Element In Names
        If Name = Element.Name Then
            Flag = True
            Exit For
        End If
    Next Element
    IsName = Flag
End Function
```

	A	B	C
1	**ISNAME IN ACTION**		
2	**Name**	**IsName**	
3	Ben	TRUE	<-- =IsName(A3)
4	Simon	FALSE	<-- =IsName(A4)
5	ben	FALSE	<-- =IsName(A5)

Note that

- Names are case sensitive. Thus the function recognizes "Ben" as a range name but not "ben."
- The **Exit For** statement can be used with **For Each**.

40.6.3 Referring to a Named Range

The following function, modeled on **MeanReturn** of section 40.3.1, computes the average return on a named range of asset prices.

```
Function NamedMeanReturn(RangeName As String)
As Double
    Dim Rng As Range
    Dim Prices As Variant
    Dim Temp As Double
    Dim i As Integer
    Set Rng = Range(RangeName)
    Prices = Rng.Value
    Temp = 0
    For i = 2 To UBound(Prices, 1)
        Temp = Temp + _
        (Prices(i, 1) - Prices(i - 1, 1)) / _
                Prices(i - 1, 1)
    Next i
    NamedMeanReturn = Temp / (UBound(Prices,
    1) - 1)
End Function
```

	A	B	C	D
1	**NAMEDMEANRETURN IN ACTION**			
2	**Asset1**	**Asset2**		
3	100	100	0.1	<-- =meanreturn(A3:A7)
4	110	120	0.2	<-- =meanreturn(B3:B7)
5	121	144	0.1	<-- =NamedMeanReturn("Asset1")
6	133.1	172.8	0.2	<-- =NamedMeanReturn("Asset2")
7	146.41	207.36	0.2	<-- =NamedMeanReturn("aSsEt2")

Note the new way to use the **Range** property introduced in the macro:

```
Set Rng = Range(RangeName)
```

40.7 Using the Object Browser

The **Object Browser** is a convenient way to learn about the different objects that are available for use in VBA. The object browser can be activated by pressing its button on the VBA toolbar or from the menu (**View|Object Browser)**. The toolbar button looks like this:

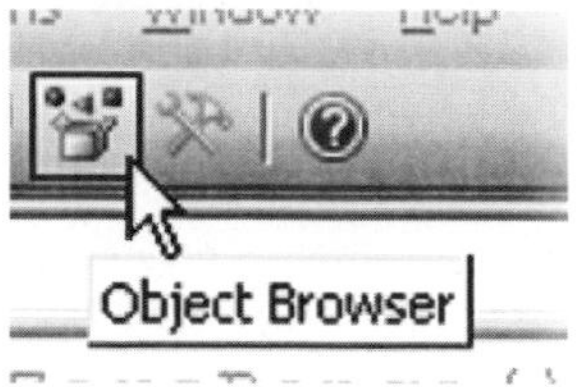

The object browser window is made of two panes, a selection box, and a few buttons. From the selection box you can choose a master set of objects to look at (two master sets, VBA and Excel, are always available). Select the VBA master set to look at objects that are internal to the working of VBA. The Excel master set deals with objects that are specific to Excel. (It's all part of a Microsoft master plan, no pun intended, where VBA is a center of many applications, not just Excel.)

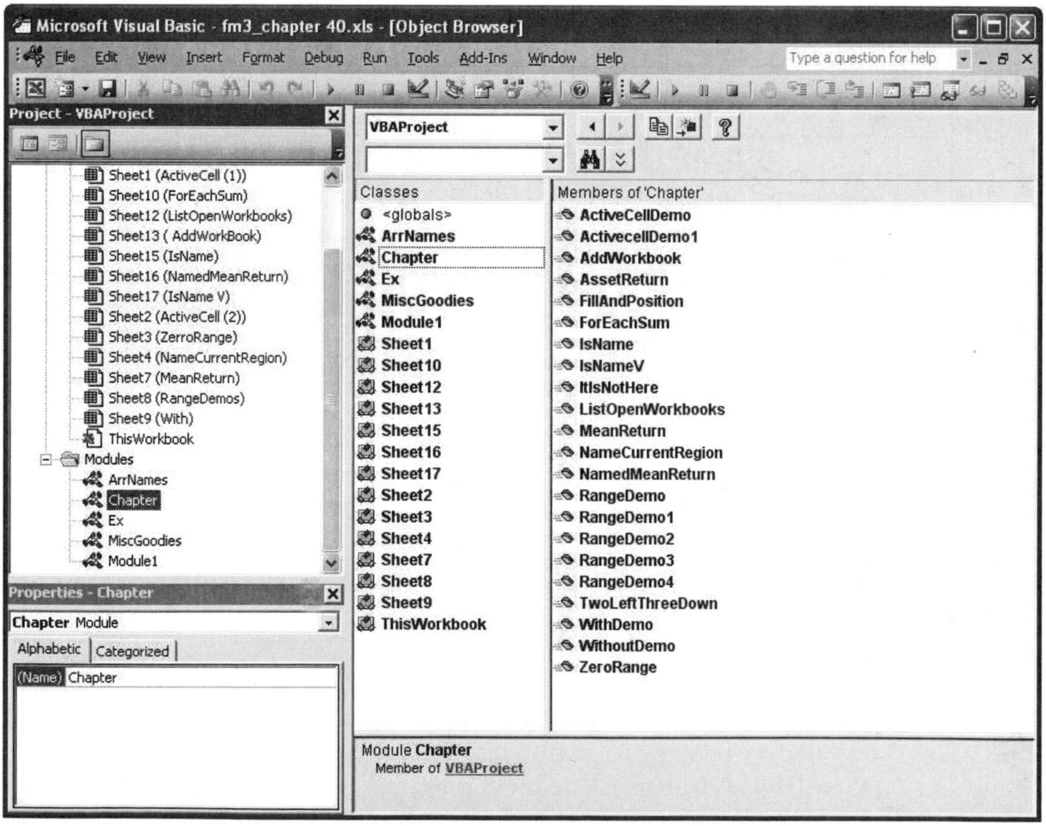

Once a master set of objects is selected, the two other panes change their contents to reflect the master set selected. The left pane is a list of categories (sorted in ascending alphabetical order). The right pane is a list of **Properties** or **Methods** attributable to the selected object in the left pane. Clicking the question-mark button causes the appropriate help screen to be displayed. The paste button causes the complete "calling sequence" for the selected **Method** or **Property** to be pasted at the current insertion point in the Module.

40.8 References to External Functions in Excel

All the macros and functions we have written so far were directly available only in the workbook in which they were written. Referring to a function in another workbook is almost like referring to a cell in another workbook, but unlike a cell reference the workbook needs to be open for the link to work. In later versions of Excel, using referents from external workbooks generates a few security warnings when you open a workbook containing the external reference. In light of this fact, we are going to use two separate workbooks for this section. The first workbook, **fm3_chapter40_server.xls**, will contain the externally referred to cells and functions, and from now on shall be referred to as the Server. The second workbook, **fm3_chapter40_client.xls**, will make use of the functions and cells, and from now on shall be referred to as the Client. The next screen shot demonstrates the two workbooks opened simultaneously in Excel:

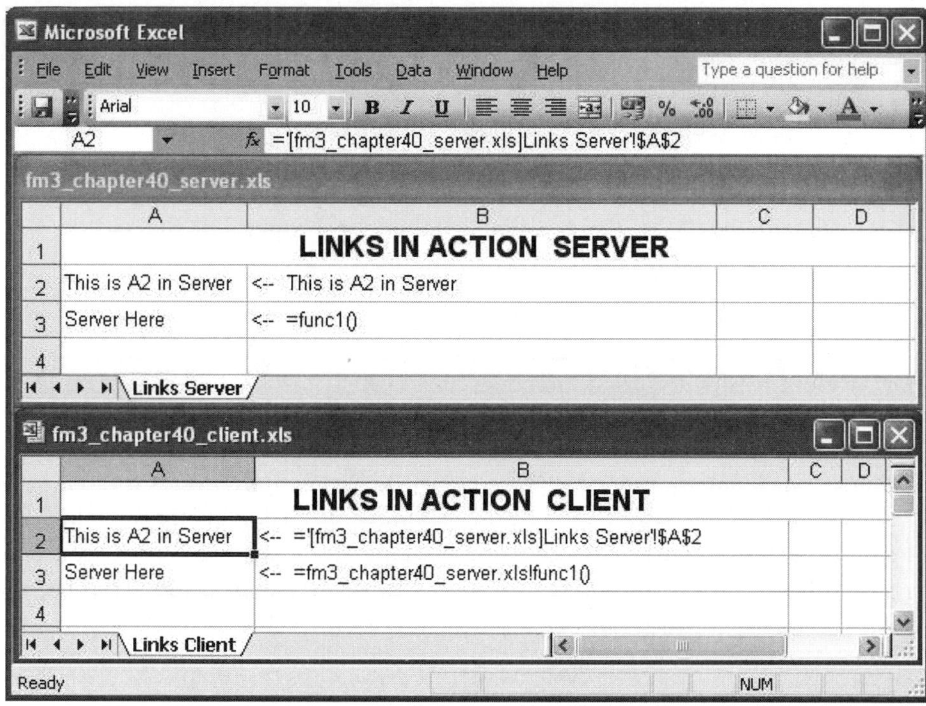

Note Cells A2 and A3 in the Client (**fm3_chapter40_client.xls**) contain a reference to a currently loaded workbook (no disk address).

The relevant function in the Server is

```
Function func1( )
    func1 = "Server Here"
End Function
```

All is well if both workbooks are currently loaded in Excel, but if you load just the Client, you get the following message:

This notice is produced any time a workbook containing a line (external reference) to another workbook is opened. If you click Update, the data will be updated as promised, but the function will not.

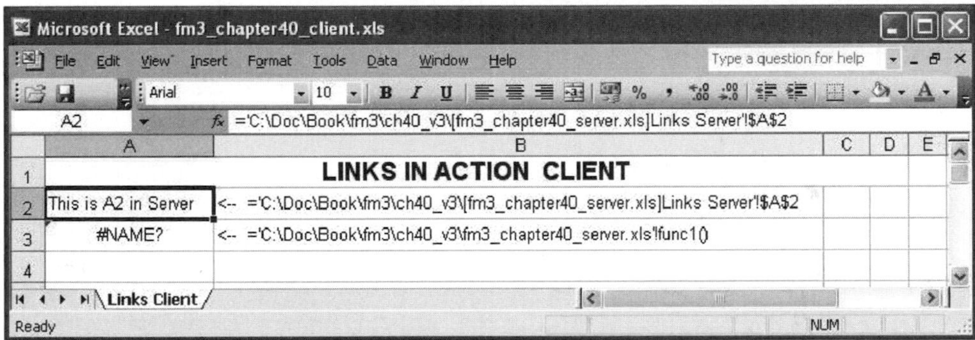

Note that the links in cells A2:A3 contain a full reference including a disk location. If we now open the Server, all will be fine because the references will now contain a disk location.

The moral of this section is, if we want to use functions in another workbook we have to make sure it is loaded into Excel. The next section shows one way of doing so automatically.

40.9 References to External Functions in VBA

Referring to functions in an external workbook in VBA is slightly more complicated than referencing external functions in the worksheet itself.

As in the previous section, this section uses two separate workbooks. The first workbook, **fm3_chapter40_vba_server.xls**, will contain the externally referred to cells and functions, and from now on shall be referred to as the Server. The second workbook, **fm3_chapter40_vba_client.xls**, will make use of the functions and cells, and from now on shall be referred to as the Client. Here are screen shots of the files in the original condition:

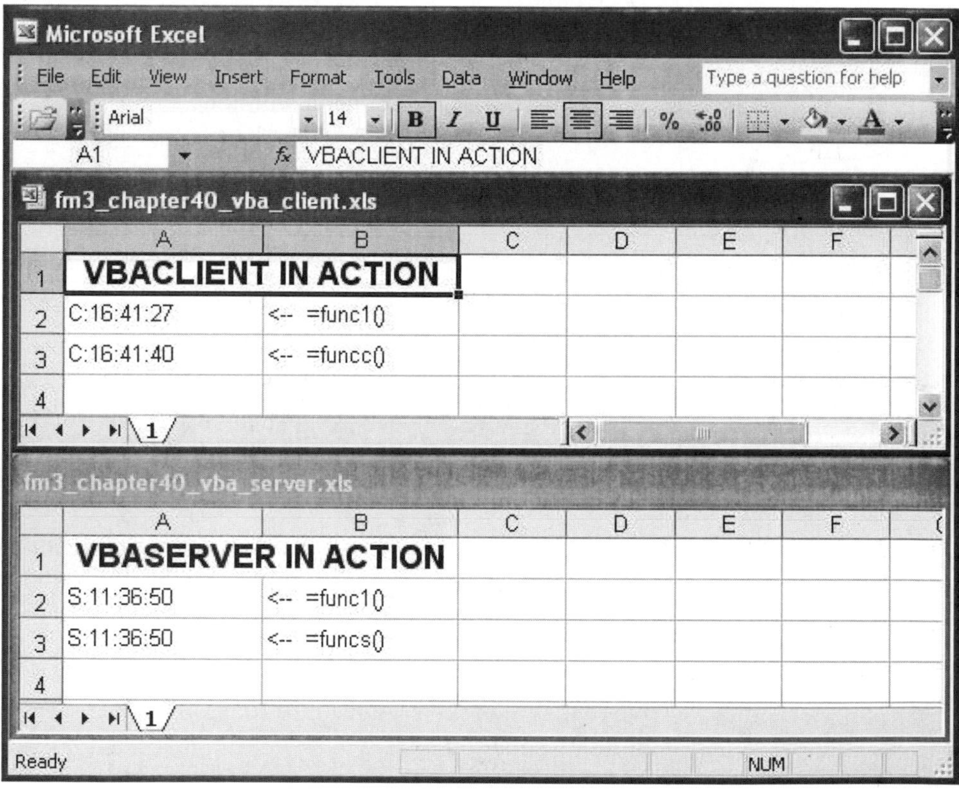

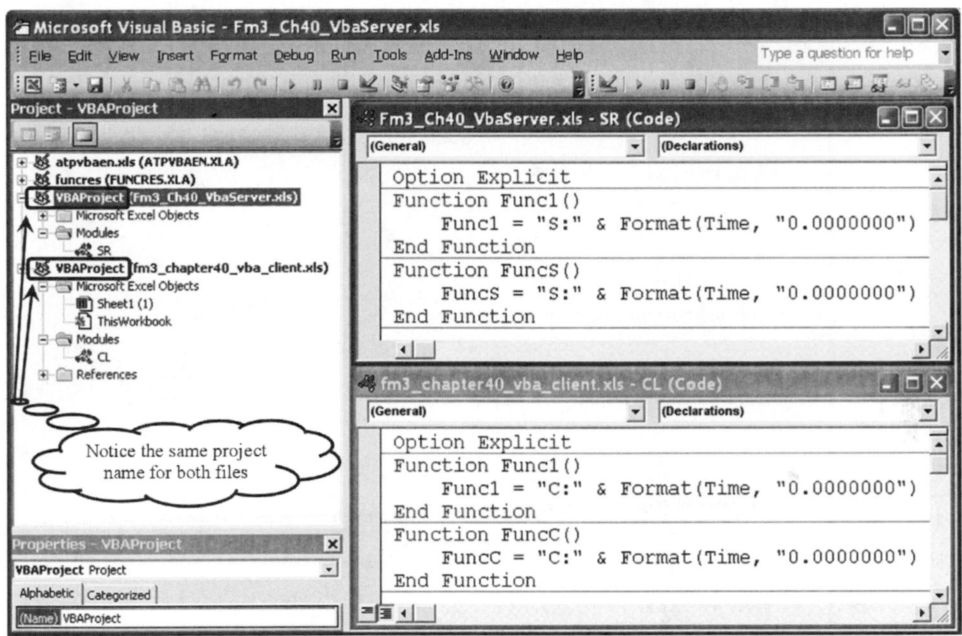

Now that the ground is set, we proceed with the actual work, which, as promised, will make us go through a few hoops. We are going to create a situation where a function defined in one workbook (the Server) can be used in VBA in another workbook (the Client). As a side benefit the Server will be loaded automatically whenever the Client is used, solving the problem presented at the end of the preceding section.

40.9.1 Give a Project a Name

The process begins on the Server side. We need to give the VBA project of the workbook a unique name. Normally all projects are called VBAProject and this is just fine, but since we are going to use the server project from another project (probably called VBAProject), our server project needs a proper name. To give it one, open the workbook and then open the VBA editor. On the toolbar of the VBA editor, select **Tools|VBAProject Properties** and change the name; you can add a description if you like.

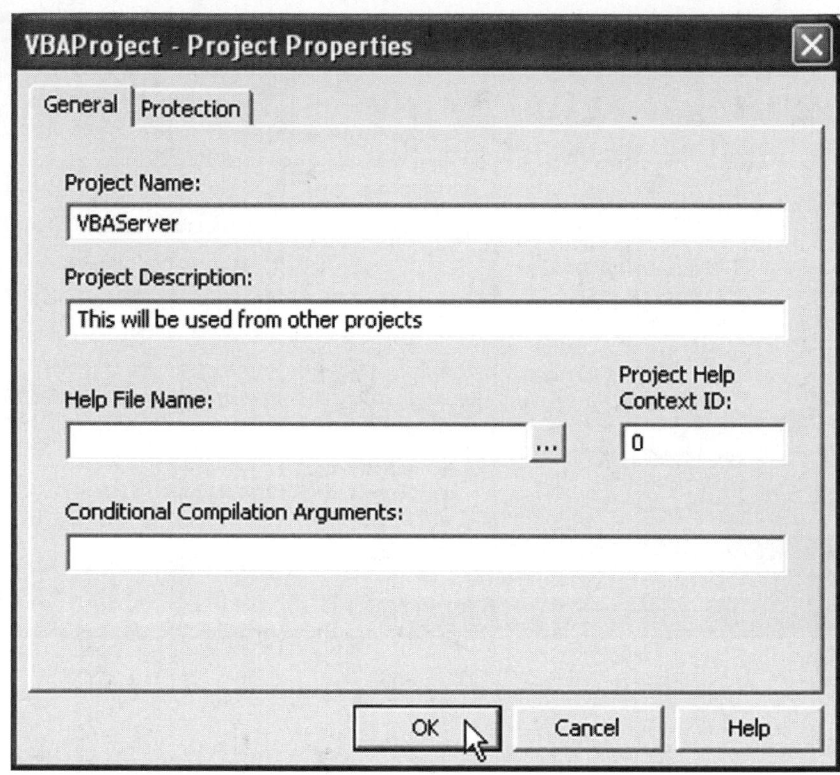

VBAServer (fm3_chapter40_vba_server.xls)
Microsoft Excel Objects
Modules

Notice that the project name has changed in the Project Explorer.

40.9.2 Attach a Reference to the Client Workbook

Open the Client workbook. Open the VBA editor. Select **Tools|References**.

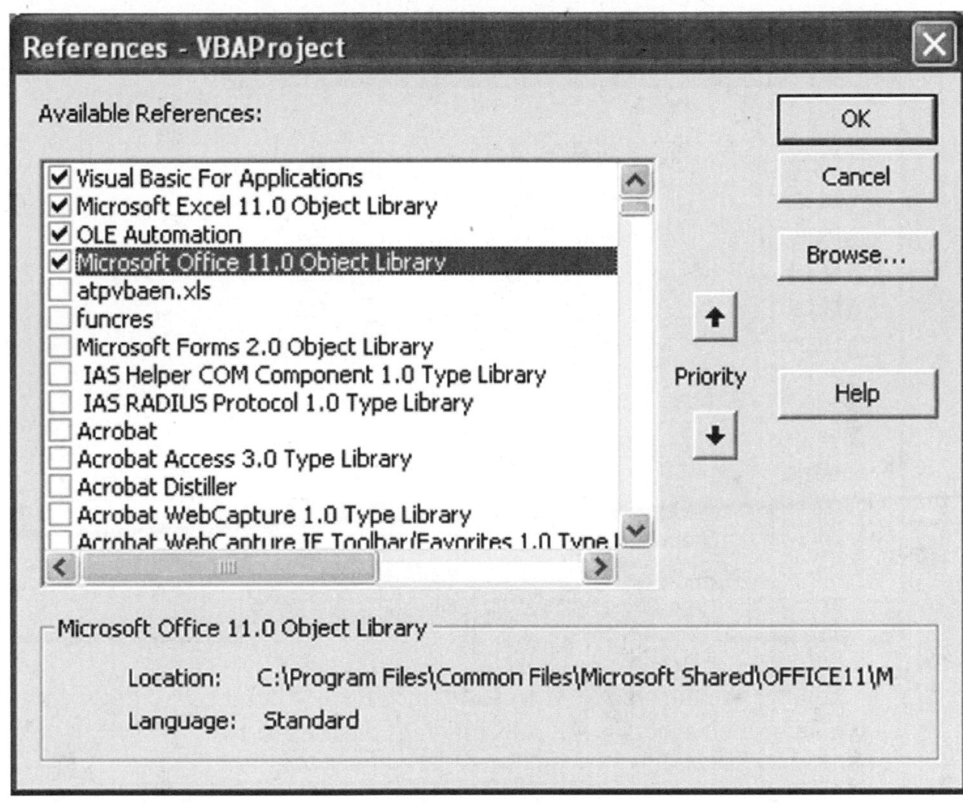

Select **Browse**.

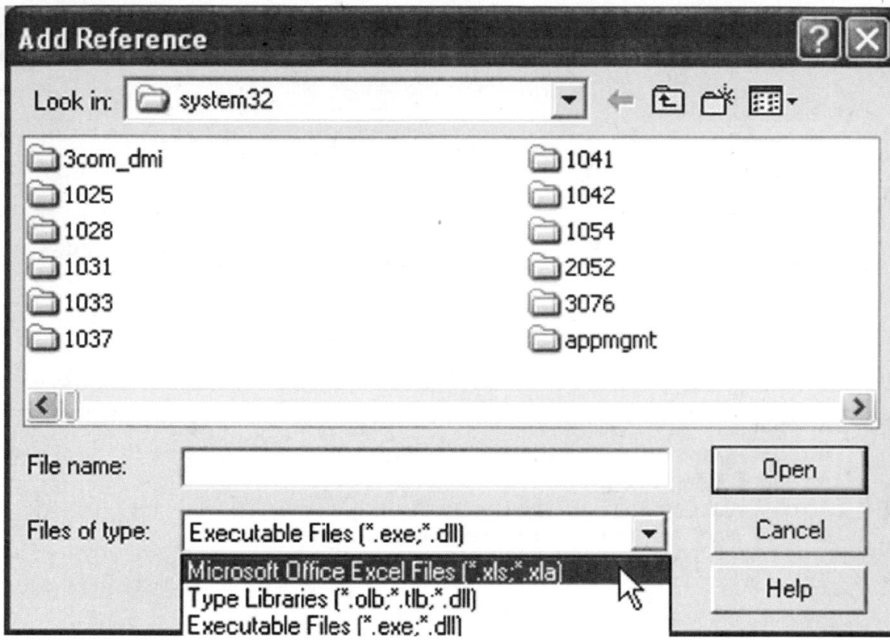

Change the file type to Microsoft Office Excel Files, browse to the location of the exporting file, select it, and select open.

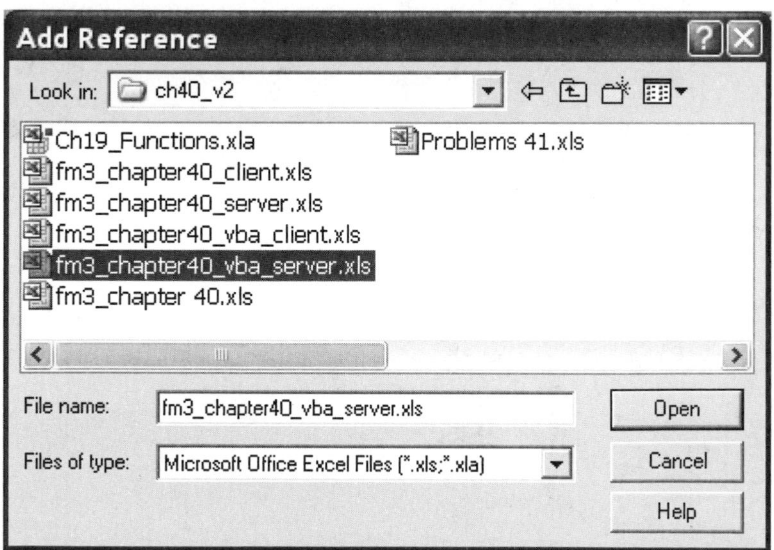

Once **Open** has been clicked, a reference to the file is now added to client workbook. Note that the reference is absolute (full path name) and not relative to the location of the client.

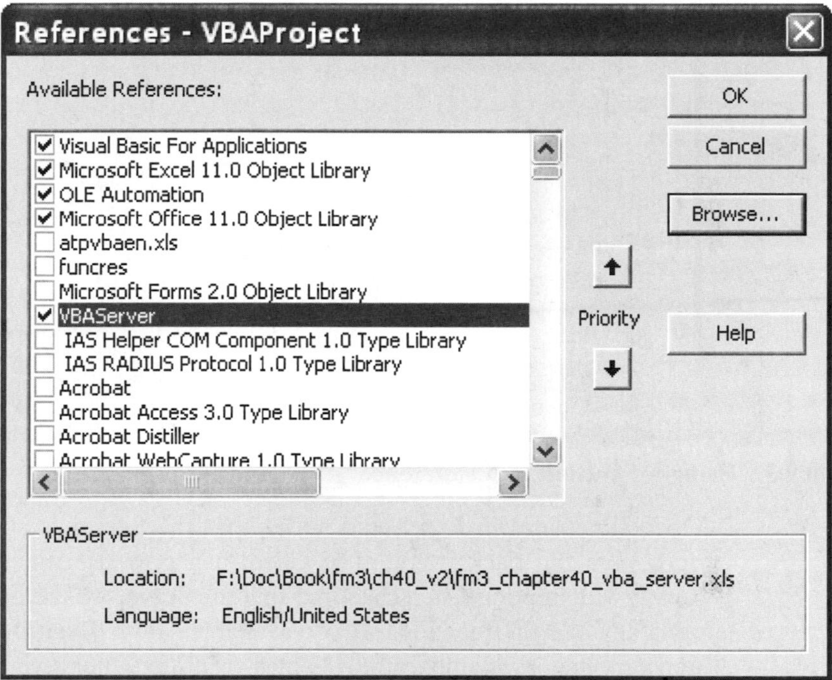

Click **OK** to apply the changes and close the references dialogue. Note: A new references category has been added to the project manager under the client project, and the Server is now open. Save the client.

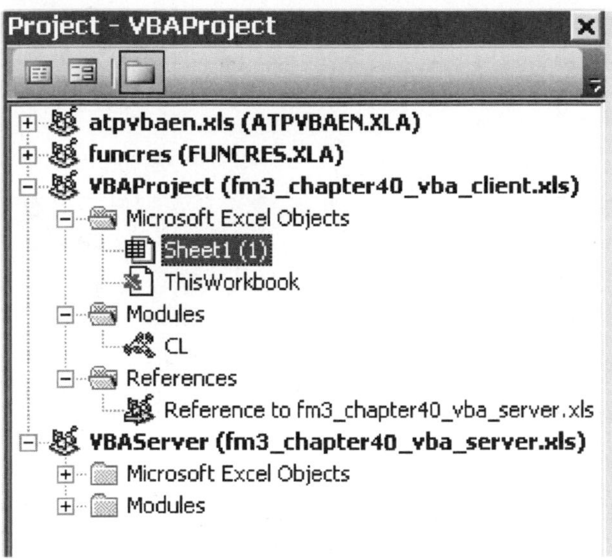

40.9.3 Using a Function in a Reference

Open the Client in Excel, and notice that the Server is automatically opened in the background. The Client can now use functions in the Server with impunity, being assured that the Server will be opened automatically and the functions will be available.[5] Four **User Defined** functions are now available in the Client[6]—from the Client we get Func1() and FuncC(), and from the server Func1() and FuncS(). The following, somewhat contrived, macro demonstrates their use.

5. This situation is unlike the one demonstrated near the end of section 40.8 where only references to cells in the server were updated automatically when the client was opened.

6. Actually the functions are available in both the Client and the Server, since both are currently loaded, but we are only assured that the Client will load the Server and not the other way around.

```
Sub ClientServer()
  Dim S As String                        ' The message string
  '--- Next line: Title for MsgBox
  Const T As String = "Client Server Demo Reporting"
  S = "Func1 is " & Func1 & vbCr      ' What is Func1
                                       ' Here?
  MsgBox S, vbInformation, T           ' Report progress
  '--- Next line adds to Message line What is FuncC
                                           ' Here?
  S = S & "FuncC is " & FuncC & vbCr '
  MsgBox S, vbInformation, T           ' Report progress
  '--- Next line adds to Message line    What is FuncS
                                            ' Here?
  S = S & "FuncS is " & FuncS & vbCr   '
  MsgBox S, vbInformation, T            ' Report progress
  '--- Next line adds to Message line   What is
                                          ' VBAServer.
                                          Func1 ' Here?
  S = S & "VBAServer.Func1 is " & VBAServer.Func1 &
  vbCr
  MsgBox S, vbInformation, T            ' Report progress
  '--- Next line adds to Message line; this is a
  'better way to refer
  '--- to external functions        What is VBAServer.
                                     ' FuncS Here?
  S = S & "VBAServer.FuncS is " & VBAServer.FuncS
  MsgBox S, vbInformation, T            ' Report progress
End Sub
```

Note the use of the dot (.) operator to refer to functions in the Server. Although we can use functions with unique names in the Server without explicitly referring to the Server, this practice is frowned upon, and we should always say that a function is not local when referring to it. Here is the output produced when this macro is run:

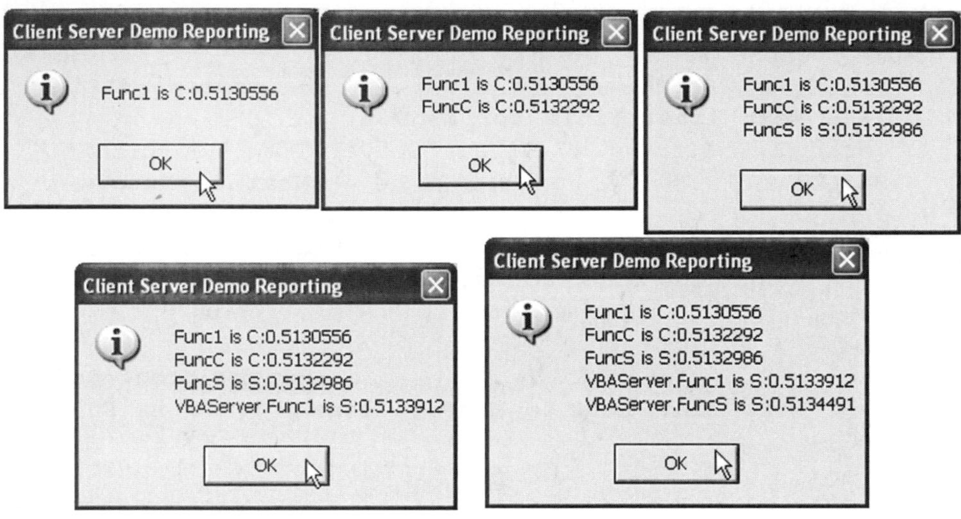

40.10 Add-Ins and Integration

An Excel Add-In is a file (usually with an **.xla** extension) that Excel can load when it starts up. The file contains VBA code that adds additional functionality to Excel, usually in the form of new functions. Add-Ins provide an excellent way of increasing the power of Excel and they are the ideal vehicle for distributing your custom functions. This section shows you how to convert an Excel workbook containing VBA functions to an Add-In, and how to load and use Add-Ins in Excel and VBA.

40.10.1 Converting a Workbook to an Add-In

To make an Add-In, save the workbook as an Add-In. To illustrate, suppose we want to use the option functions developed for Chapter 19 in other workbooks. We need to separate the functions from the actual workbook so as not to burden our Add-In with superfluous data. The easiest way to do so is by opening the file **fm3_chapter19.xls**, inserting a blank worksheet, eliminating all the other worksheets, and saving as a new file **fm3_chapter19_functions.xla**. Here is the file just before we saved it as an xla:

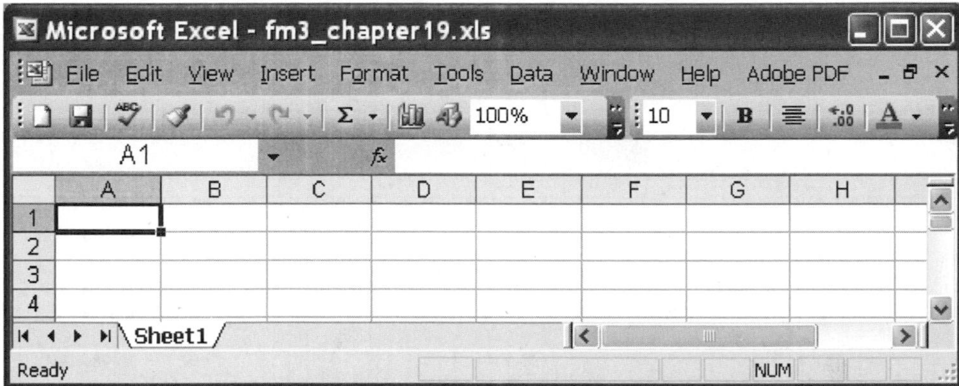

Select **Save as** from the Excel file menu, and change **Save as type** to "Microsoft Office Excel Add-In (*.xla)" (it's the last entry on the list). The **Save in** location will change to the Add-Ins directory on your computer.

You may want to navigate to a different location. (We tend to keep files together, so we navigated to the chapter 40 directory.) Now we can give the new name by clicking **Save**.

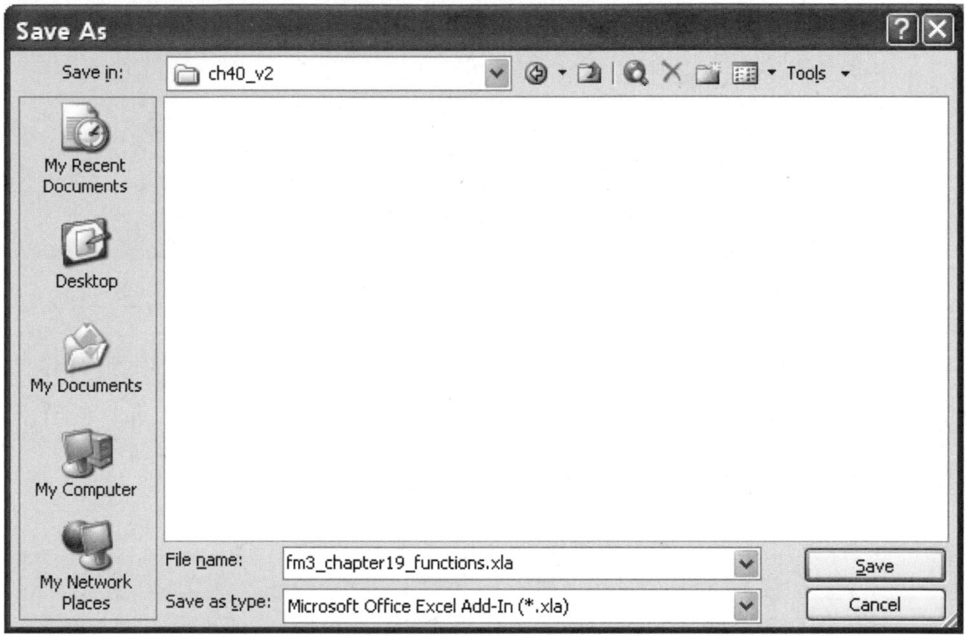

Notice that the original file is open but in a new mutilated state. *Be very careful not to save it.*

Close the original file without saving it by clicking *No*:

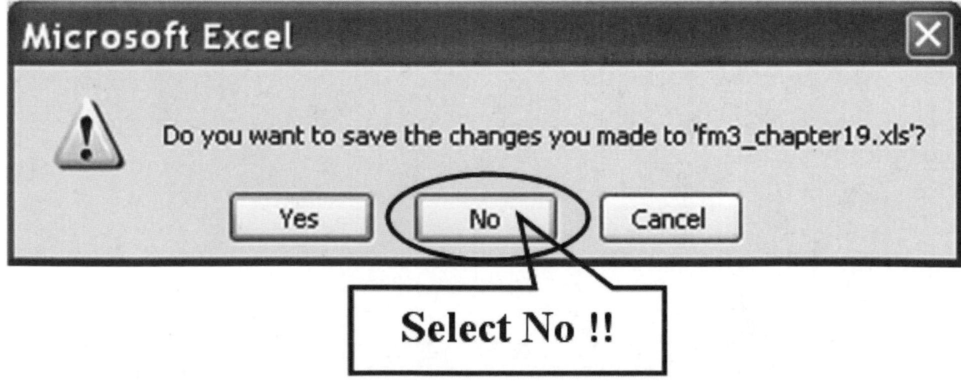

40.10.2 Install and Use an Add-In from an Excel Worksheet

Installing an Add-In is done on a per-computer basis (actually a per-computer-user basis). In Excel, select **Tools** and **Add-Ins**.[7] The following dialogue should be presented:

Click **Browse** and navigate to the location of your Add-In. Select it.

7. For reasons beyond our comprehension, this option will not be available unless a workbook (even a blank one) is loaded.

Then click **OK**.

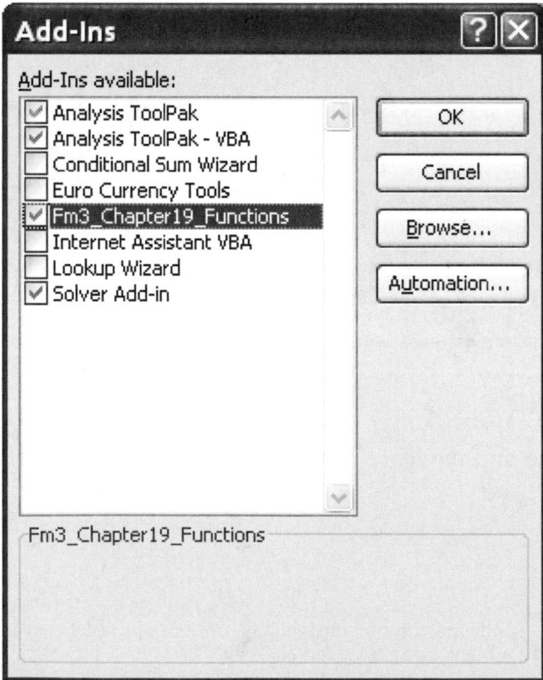

Notice that a new Add-In is available and activated. Click OK to close the Add-Ins dialogue. All the functions in our Add-In are now available to all workbooks in Excel. To verify, close and reopen Excel. Open the function wizard and navigate to **User Defined** functions. This (or something like it) is what you should get:

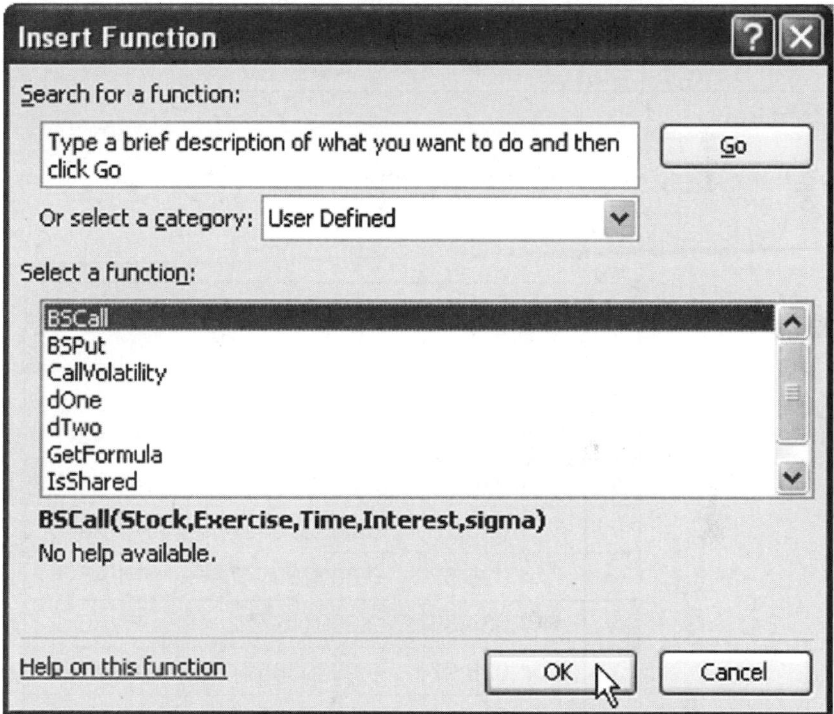

You may now use the functions to your heart's content.

40.10.3 Using an Add-In Function from VBA

To make functions in an Add-In available to a VBA project, we have to go through exactly the same process that we used to make a function in another workbook available in a VBA project. That is, we have to add a reference to the Add-In to the project. We covered this topic in section 40.8.

40.11 Summary

This chapter discusses two separate topics. We start with a more extensive discussion of objects, which underlie the VBA programming concept. Objects allow you to be much more parsimonious in expressing your programming references. We finish the chapter with a discussion of how to build add-ins in Excel, using the option functions from Chapter 19 as an example.

Exercises

1. Suppose you have a spreadsheet with a series of numbers and formulas:

	A	B	C
1	**Price**	**Return**	
2	1,000.00		
3	1,014.50	0.014497075	<-- =A3/A2-1
4	1,018.21	0.003664546	<-- =A4/A3-1
5	1,025.25	0.006910487	<-- =A5/A4-1
6	1,025.52	0.000260127	<-- =A6/A5-1
7	1,034.86	0.009107472	<-- =A7/A6-1
8	1,036.97	0.002038577	<-- =A8/A7-1
9	1,051.86	0.014357897	<-- =A9/A8-1
10	1,070.98	0.018181498	<-- =A10/A9-1

Suppose you want to turn this into the following:

	A	B	C
1	**Price**	**Return**	
2	1,000.00		
3	1,014.50	1.449707511	<-- =(A3/A2-1)*100
4	1,018.21	0.366454611	<-- =(A4/A3-1)*100
5	1,025.25	0.691048678	<-- =(A5/A4-1)*100
6	1,025.52	0.02601265	<-- =(A6/A5-1)*100
7	1,034.86	0.910747236	<-- =(A7/A6-1)*100
8	1,036.97	0.20385771	<-- =(A8/A7-1)*100
9	1,051.86	1.435789687	<-- =(A9/A8-1)*100
10	1,070.98	1.81814983	<-- =(A10/A9-1)*100

Write a macro that accomplishes this purpose. Your macro (roughly based on the macro **ActiveCellDemo** of section 40.2.1) should

- Put in a set of parentheses and multiply the cell contents by 100.
- Move down one cell (see **ActiveCellDemo1**, section 40.2.1).
- Ask if you want to repeat the process. (If "yes," the macro should do it; if "no," the macro should exit.)

Note The parentheses have to come after the "=." The **Right** function might be used for this operation.

You may want to refer to section 38.3 for more information on the MsgBox function and the values it returns.

2. Rewrite the macro in exercise 1 so that it deals correctly with the end of the series. One possible treatment is not to ask to repeat the process when the last cell in the series is dealt with.

   Hint For this macro it might be useful to think of the last cell in the series as the cell that fulfills the criterion `Cell.Item(2,1).Formula=""` (see section 38.3).

3. Write a macro that multiplies all cells in the current region by 2.

4. Rewrite the macro in exercise 3 so that its action is dependent on the cell's contents.

   - If the cell contents is a formula, it will be replaced by the same formula multiplied by 2.
   - If the cell contents is a number, it will be replaced by a number equal to the old number multiplied by 2.
   - On all other cells in the current region, nothing will be done.

Note For the purposes of this exercise a formula is anything beginning with =, and a number is anything beginning with the characters 0 to 9.

5. Rewrite the macro in exercise 4 so that it uses another method (the correct one) to detect the existence of a formula in a cell. Look at the different properties of the **Range** object in the Help file.

6. The annotations for worksheet formulas in this book were done with a macro. For example, running the macro on this worksheet, in which the active cell is A2,

	A	B
1	1	
2	2	
3	3	
4	4	

produces the following worksheet:

	A	B
1	1	
2	2	<-- =A1+1
3	3	
4	4	

Notice the changed column width. Write a macro to perform the annotation. If the cell immediately to the right of the active cell is not empty, the macro should overwrite it only after receiving confirmation from the user.

7. The **Selection** object represents the current selection in the worksheet. **Selection** is usually, and for our purposes always, a **Range** object. Rewrite the macro in exercise 6 so that it works on a selected range.

   Note the following:

   - If the selected range is a single cell, activate the macro in exercise 6.
   - If the selected range is a row range, the annotations should go below the selected range.
   - If the selected range is more than one column or one row, the macro should abort with an appropriate message.

8. Array functions are functions that return more than one value. For example, the **Transpose** worksheet function returns its argument turned by 90 degrees, as the following worksheet demonstrates:

	A	B	C	D	E	F
1	**TRANSPOSE IN ACTION**					
2	1	2	3	4	1	<-- {=TRANSPOSE(A2:D2)}
3					2	<-- {=TRANSPOSE(A2:D2)}
4					3	<-- {=TRANSPOSE(A2:D2)}
5					4	<-- {=TRANSPOSE(A2:D2)}

The curly brackets were not typed in but were added by Excel to indicate an array formula. The following macro created the preceding worksheet:

```
Sub TransposeMe()
    Range("E3:E6").FormulaArray = "=Transpose(A3:D3)"
End Sub
```

The next macro is a more complicated version that could deal with any size or place in the row range:

```
Sub TransposeMeToo()
   Dim R As Integer, C As Integer
   C = Selection.Columns.Count
   R = Selection.Rows.Count
   If C = 1 Then 'Its a Column
    MsgBox "I don't do Columns"
   ElseIf R = 1 Then 'Its a Row
    Selection.Cells(1, C + 1).Range("A1:A" & C). _
    FormulaArray = "=Transpose(" _
        & Selection.AddressLocal(False, False) & ")"
   Else 'What is it?
     MsgBox "What is it?"
   End If
End Sub
```

Rewrite **TransposeMeToo** so that it can deal with column ranges as well as row ranges.

9. Rewrite **TransposeMeToo** of exercise 8 so that it can deal with *all* ranges.

   Note It is not as easy as it looks at first sight.

Appendix 1: The Excel Object Model

This appendix presents the Excel object model—the way an Excel application looks from the VBA point of view. It shows an overview of the Excel application and can be used to find the exact name and pedigree of an object. This extract from the Excel Help files presents just the very top of the tree, and in the original Help file clicking on one of the branches expands it and provides more information about the branch.

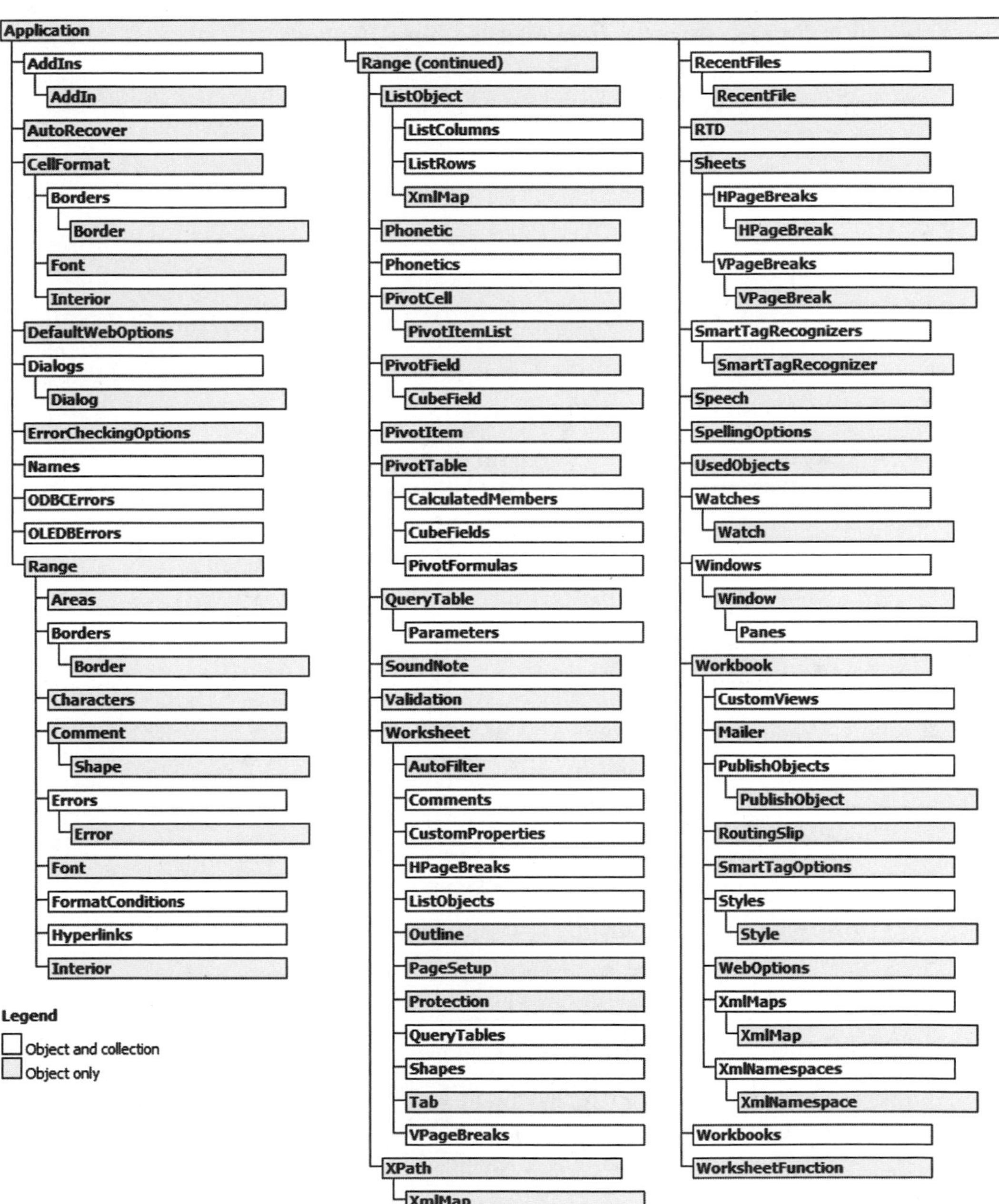
Application
AddIns
AddIn
AutoRecover
CellFormat
Borders
Border
Font
Interior
DefaultWebOptions
Dialogs
Dialog
ErrorCheckingOptions
Names
ODBCErrors
OLEDBErrors
Range
Areas
Borders
Border
Characters
Comment
Shape
Errors
Error
Font
FormatConditions
Hyperlinks
Interior
Range (continued)
ListObject
ListColumns
ListRows
XmlMap
Phonetic
Phonetics
PivotCell
PivotItemList
PivotField
CubeField
PivotItem
PivotTable
CalculatedMembers
CubeFields
PivotFormulas
QueryTable
Parameters
SoundNote
Validation
Worksheet
AutoFilter
Comments
CustomProperties
HPageBreaks
ListObjects
Outline
PageSetup
Protection
QueryTables
Shapes
Tab
VPageBreaks
XPath
XmlMap
RecentFiles
RecentFile
RTD
Sheets
HPageBreaks
HPageBreak
VPageBreaks
VPageBreak
SmartTagRecognizers
SmartTagRecognizer
Speech
SpellingOptions
UsedObjects
Watches
Watch
Windows
Window
Panes
Workbook
CustomViews
Mailer
PublishObjects
PublishObject
RoutingSlip
SmartTagOptions
Styles
Style
WebOptions
XmlMaps
XmlMap
XmlNamespaces
XmlNamespace
Workbooks
WorksheetFunction
Legend
Object and collection
Object only

Appendix 2: Extracts from the Help Files for Some Methods

The content of this appendix is a lightly edited version of the Excel VBA Help file.

BorderAround Method

Adds a border to a range and sets the **Color**, **LineStyle**, and **Weight** properties for the new border.

BorderAround (*LINESTYLE, WEIGHT, COLORINDEX, COLOR*)

LINESTYLE Optional. The line style for the border. Can be one of these constants:

xlContinuous xlDash xlDashDot xlDashDotDot xlDot xlDouble xlLineStyleNone xlSlantDashDot xlLineStyleNone

WEIGHT Optional. The border weight. Can be one of these constants:

xlHairline xlMedium xlThick xlThin

COLORINDEX Optional. The border color, as an index into the current color palette or as one of these constants:

xlColorIndexAutomatic xlColorIndexNone

COLOR Optional. The border color, as an RGB value.

Remarks

You must specify either ***ColorIndex*** or ***Color***, but not both.

You can specify either ***LineStyle*** or ***Weight***, but not both. If you don't specify either argument, Microsoft Excel uses the default line style and weight.

This method outlines the entire range without filling it in.

Range—Object and Collection

Represents a cell, a row, a column, a selection of cells containing one or more contiguous blocks of cells, or a 3-D range. The following properties and methods for returning a **Range** object are described in this section:

Range property

Cells property

Range and **Cells**

Offset property

Union method

Use Range(**arg**), where **arg** names the range, to return a **Range** object that represents a single cell or a range of cells. The following example places the value of cell A1 in cell A5.

```
Worksheets("Sheet1").Range("A5").Value = _
  Worksheets("Sheet1").Range("A1").Value
```

The following example fills the range A1:H8 with random numbers by setting the formula for each cell in the range. When it's used without an object qualifier (an object to the left of the period), the **Range** property returns a range on the active sheet. If the active sheet isn't a worksheet, the method fails. Use the **Activate** method to activate a worksheet before you use the Range property without an explicit object qualifier.

```
Worksheets("Sheet1").Activate
Range("A1:H8").Formula = "=Rand()"   'Range on
'the active sheet
```

The following example clears the contents of the range named Criteria.

```
Worksheets(1).Range("Criteria").ClearContents
```

If you use a text argument for the range address, you must specify the address in A1-style notation (you cannot use R1C1-style notation).

Cells Property

Use Cells(row, column) where row is the row index and column is the column index, to return a single cell. The following example sets the value of cell A1 to 24.

```
Worksheets(1).Cells(1, 1).Value = 24
```

The following example sets the formula for cell A2.

```
ActiveSheet.Cells(2, 1).Formula = "=Sum(B1:B5)"
```

Although you can also use Range("A1") to return cell A1, there may be times when the Cells property is more convenient because you can use a variable for the row or column. The following example creates column and row headings on Sheet1. Notice that after the worksheet has been activated, the Cells property can be used without an explicit sheet declaration (it returns a cell on the active sheet).

```
Sub SetUpTable()
Worksheets("Sheet1").Activate
For TheYear = 1 To 5
  Cells(1, TheYear + 1).Value = 1990 + _
  TheYear
Next TheYear
For TheQuarter = 1 To 4
  Cells(TheQuarter + 1, 1).Value = "Q" & _
  TheQuarter
Next TheQuarter
End Sub
```

Although you could use Visual Basic string functions to alter A1-style references, it's much easier (and much better programming practice) to use the Cells(1, 1) notation.

Use expression.Cells(row, column), where expression is an expression that returns a Range object, and row and column are relative to the upper-left corner of the range, to return part of a range. The following example sets the formula for cell C5.

```
Worksheets(1).Range("C5:C10").Cells(1, 1). _
Formula = "=Rand()"
```

Range and Cells
Use Range(cell1, cell2), where cell1 and cell2 are Range objects that specify the start and end cells, to return a Range object. The following example sets the border line style for cells A1:J10.

```
With Worksheets(1)
   .Range(.Cells(1, 1), _
     .Cells(10, 10)).Borders.LineStyle = _
     xlThick
End With
```

Notice the period in front of each occurrence of the Cells property. The period is required if the result of the preceding With statement is to be applied to the Cells property—in this case, to indicate that the cells are on worksheet one (without the period, the Cells property would return cells on the active sheet).

Offset Property
Use Offset(row, column), where row and column are the row and column offsets, to return a range at a specified offset to another range. The following example selects the cell three rows down from and one column to the right of the cell in the upper-left corner of the current selection. You cannot select a cell that isn't on the active sheet, so you must first activate the worksheet.

```
Worksheets("Sheet1").Activate
 'Can't select unless the sheet is active
Selection.Offset(3, 1).Range("A1").Select
```

Union Method

Use Union(range1, range2, . . .) to return multiple-area ranges—that is, ranges composed of two or more contiguous blocks of cells. The following example creates an object defined as the union of ranges A1:B2 and C3:D4, and then selects the defined range.

```
Dim r1 As Range, r2 As Range, myMultiAreaRange _
As Range
Worksheets("sheet1").Activate
Set r1 = Range("A1:B2")
Set r2 = Range("C3:D4")
Set myMultiAreaRange = Union(r1, r2)
myMultiAreaRange.Select
```

If you work with selections that contain more than one area, the **Areas** property is very useful. It divides a multiple-area selection into individual Range objects and then returns the objects as a collection. You can use the Count property on the returned collection to check for a selection that contains more than one area, as shown in the following example.

```
Sub NoMultiAreaSelection()
  NumberOfSelectedAreas = Selection.Areas.Count
  If NumberOfSelectedAreas > 1 Then
    MsgBox "You cannot carry out this command " & _
       "on multi-area selections"
  End If
End Sub
```

Names in Excel—From the Help Files

A defined name in a formula can make it easier to understand the purpose of the formula. For example, the formula `=SUM(FirstQuarterSales)` might be easier to identify than `=SUM(C20:C30)`.

Names are available to any sheet. For example, if the name ProjectedSales refers to the range A20:A30 on the first worksheet in a workbook, you can use the name ProjectedSales on any other sheet in the same workbook to refer to range A20:A30 on the first worksheet.

Names can also be used to represent formulas or values that do not change (constants). For example, you can use the name SalesTax to represent the sales tax amount (such as 6.2 percent) applied to sales transactions.

You can also link to a defined name in another workbook, or define a name that refers to cells in another workbook. For example, the formula `=SUM(Sales.xls!ProjectedSales)` refers to the named range ProjectedSales in the workbook named Sales.

Note By default, names use absolute cell references. (Absolute cell reference: In a formula, the exact address of a cell, regardless of the position of the cell that contains the formula. An absolute cell reference takes the form $A$1.)

Guidelines for Names

- What characters are allowed? The first character of a name must be a letter, an underscore character (_), or a backslash (\). Remaining characters in the name can be letters, numbers, periods, and underscore characters.
- Can names be cell references? Names cannot be the same as a cell reference, such as Z$100 or R1C1.
- Can more than one word be used? Yes, but spaces are not allowed. Underscore characters and periods may be used as word separators—for example, Sales_Tax or First.Quarter.
- How many characters can be used? A name can contain up to 255 characters.

Note If a name defined for a range contains more than 253 characters, you cannot select it from the Name box.

• Are names case sensitive? Names can contain uppercase and lowercase letters. Microsoft Excel does not distinguish between uppercase and lowercase characters in names. For example, if you have created the name Sales and then create another name called SALES in the same workbook, the second name will replace the first one.

Using Existing Row and Column Labels as Names

When you create a formula that refers to data in a worksheet, you can use the column and row labels in the worksheet to refer to the data. For example, to calculate the total value for the Product column, use the formula `=SUM(Product)`.

	Product	
	30	
	40	
	=SUM(Product)	

Using a Label

Or if you need to refer to the Product 3 amount for the East division (that is, the value 110.00), you can use the formula `=Product 3 East`. The space in the formula between "Product 3" and "East" is the intersection operator. (Operator: A sign or symbol that specifies the type of calculation to perform within an expression. There are mathematical, comparison, logical, and reference operators.) This operator designates that Microsoft Excel should find and return the value in the cell at the intersection of the row labeled East and the column labeled Product 3.

	A	B	C	D	E
1	Division A	Product 1	Product 2	Product 3	Total
2	East	30.00	70.00	110.00	
3	West	40.00	80 00	120.00	
4	Total	70.00			=SUM(B4:D4)

Note By default, Excel does not recognize labels in formulas. To use labels in formulas, click Options on the Tools menu, and then click the

Calculation tab. Under Workbook options, select the Accept labels in formulas check box.

Stacked Labels

When you use labels for the columns and rows on your worksheet, you can use those labels to create formulas that refer to data on the worksheet. If your worksheet contains stacked column labels—in which a label in one cell is followed by one or more labels below it—you can use the stacked labels in formulas to refer to data on the worksheet. For example, if the label West is in cell E5 and the label Projected is in cell E6, the formula `=SUM(West Projected)` returns the total value for the West Projected column.

THE ORDER FOR STACKED LABELS When you refer to information by using stacked labels, you refer to the information in the order in which the labels appear, from top to bottom. If the label West is in cell F5 and the label Actual is in cell F6, you can refer to the actual figures for West by using West Actual in a formula. For example, to calculate the average of the actual figures for West, use the formula `=AVERAGE(West Actual)`.

Using Dates as Labels

When you label a range by using the Label Ranges dialogue box and the range contains a year or date as a label, Excel defines the date as a label by placing single quotation marks around the label when you type the label in a formula. For example, suppose your worksheet contains the labels 2007 and 2008 and you have specified these labels by using the Label Ranges dialogue box. When you type the formula `=SUM(2008)`, Excel automatically updates the formula to `=SUM('2008')`.

41 Information from the Web

41.1 Overview

This chapter discusses the acquisition and updating of data from the Web to Excel. Our purpose is to illustrate a variety of techniques that can be used to capture data from a Web page and include them into an Excel spreadsheet.

Topics include the following:

- Copy-paste techniques for static data acquisition
- Dynamic data acquisition—that is, data acquisition that updates automatically
- VBA programming of dynamic data acquisition

41.2 Copy and Paste as a Simple Data-Acquisition Technique

By far the most common data Web acquisition task faced by most Excel users is to copy and paste data from a Web page into Excel. In many cases simple copy-paste will suffice to acquire data from the Web and put it into Excel. Suppose, for example, that we want to put the marked data of the following Yahoo price data into Excel (see appendix 2 of Chapter 2 for how to get to similar data):

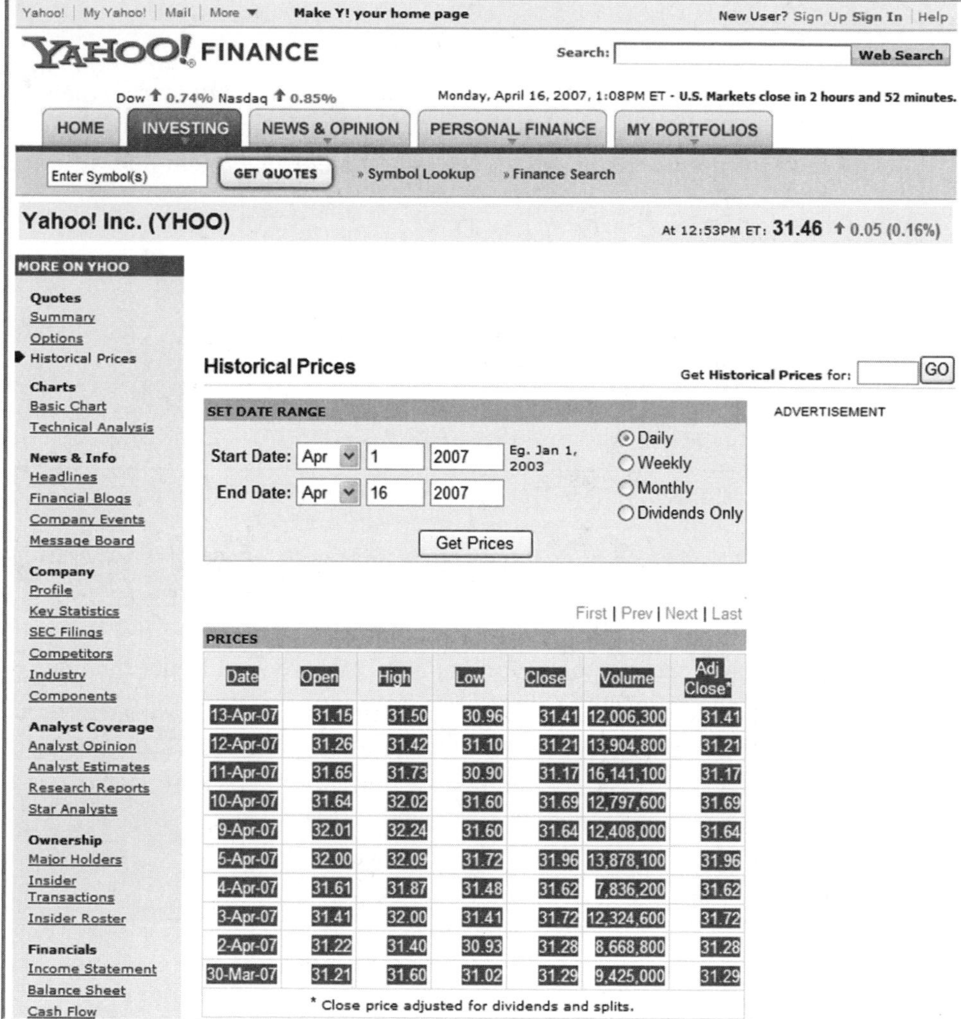

Yahoo! | My Yahoo! | Mail | More ▼ **Make Y! your home page** New User? Sign Up **Sign In** | Help

YAHOO! FINANCE Search: [ ] Web Search

Dow ↑ 0.74% Nasdaq ↑ 0.85% Monday, April 16, 2007, 1:08PM ET - **U.S. Markets close in 2 hours and 52 minutes.**

HOME | INVESTING | NEWS & OPINION | PERSONAL FINANCE | MY PORTFOLIOS

Enter Symbol(s) GET QUOTES » Symbol Lookup » Finance Search

Yahoo! Inc. (YHOO) At 12:53PM ET: **31.46** ↑ 0.05 (0.16%)

MORE ON YHOO

Quotes
Summary
Options
Historical Prices

Charts
Basic Chart
Technical Analysis

News & Info
Headlines
Financial Blogs
Company Events
Message Board

Company
Profile
Key Statistics
SEC Filings
Competitors
Industry
Components

Analyst Coverage
Analyst Opinion
Analyst Estimates
Research Reports
Star Analysts

Ownership
Major Holders
Insider Transactions
Insider Roster

Financials
Income Statement
Balance Sheet
Cash Flow

Historical Prices Get Historical Prices for: [ ] GO

ADVERTISEMENT

SET DATE RANGE

Start Date: Apr 1 2007 Eg. Jan 1, 2003
End Date: Apr 16 2007
Daily / Weekly / Monthly / Dividends Only
Get Prices

First | Prev | Next | Last

PRICES

Date	Open	High	Low	Close	Volume	Adj Close*
13-Apr-07	31.15	31.50	30.96	31.41	12,006,300	31.41
12-Apr-07	31.26	31.42	31.10	31.21	13,904,800	31.21
11-Apr-07	31.65	31.73	30.90	31.17	16,141,100	31.17
10-Apr-07	31.64	32.02	31.60	31.69	12,797,600	31.69
9-Apr-07	32.01	32.24	31.60	31.64	12,408,000	31.64
5-Apr-07	32.00	32.09	31.72	31.96	13,878,100	31.96
4-Apr-07	31.61	31.87	31.48	31.62	7,836,200	31.62
3-Apr-07	31.41	32.00	31.41	31.72	12,324,600	31.72
2-Apr-07	31.22	31.40	30.93	31.28	8,668,800	31.28
30-Mar-07	31.21	31.60	31.02	31.29	9,425,000	31.29

* Close price adjusted for dividends and splits.

The various possibilities that we will examine tend to depend on a combination of browser and your computer's setup. In this chapter Microsoft Internet Explorer 7 (MSIE) and Mozilla Firefox 2 (MF), which currently dominate the browser market, will be used to demonstrate the differences between Internet browsers.

41.2.1 Using Edit|Paste in Excel

In Excel, using **Edit|Paste** is the simplest possibility, and it may well work. Here's what happened to us, using Microsoft's Windows Internet Explorer:

	A	B	C	D	E	F	G
1	Date	Open	High	Low	Close	Volume	Adj Close*
2	13-Apr-07	31.15	31.5	30.96	31.41	12,006,300	31.41
3	12-Apr-07	31.26	31.42	31.1	31.21	13,904,800	31.21
4	11-Apr-07	31.65	31.73	30.9	31.17	16,141,100	31.17
5	10-Apr-07	31.64	32.02	31.6	31.69	12,797,600	31.69
6	09-Apr-07	32.01	32.24	31.6	31.64	12,408,000	31.64
7	05-Apr-07	32	32.09	31.72	31.96	13,878,100	31.96
8	04-Apr-07	31.61	31.87	31.48	31.62	7,836,200	31.62
9	03-Apr-07	31.41	32	31.41	31.72	12,324,600	31.72
10	02-Apr-07	31.22	31.4	30.93	31.28	8,668,800	31.28
11	30-Mar-07	31.21	31.6	31.02	31.29	9,425,000	31.29
12							

The table from the Web was imported into our Excel, though the formatting does not exactly match our default fonts (no big deal!). Note the *smart tag* to the side of the import. Clicking on this smart tag gives the following:

	A	B	C	D	E	F	G	H	I	J
1	Date	Open	High	Low	Close	Volume	Adj Close*			
2	13-Apr-07	31.15	31.5	30.96	31.41	12,006,300	31.41			
3	12-Apr-07	31.26	31.42	31.1	31.21	13,904,800	31.21			
4	11-Apr-07	31.65	31.73	30.9	31.17	16,141,100	31.17			
5	10-Apr-07	31.64	32.02	31.6	31.69	12,797,600	31.69			
6	09-Apr-07	32.01	32.24	31.6	31.64	12,408,000	31.64			
7	05-Apr-07	32	32.09	31.72	31.96	13,878,100	31.96			
8	04-Apr-07	31.61	31.87	31.48	31.62	7,836,200	31.62			
9	03-Apr-07	31.41	32	31.41	31.72	12,324,600	31.72			
10	02-Apr-07	31.22	31.4	30.93	31.28	8,668,800	31.28			
11	30-Mar-07	31.21	31.6	31.02	31.29	9,425,000	31.29			
12										
13								Keep Source Formatting		
14								Match Destination Formatting		
15								Create Refreshable Web Query...		
16										

Clicking on **Match Destination Formatting** reformats the import to the original formatting of the sheet. We will have more to say about this smart tag later on.

The preceding was in Internet Explorer. In contrast, when we used Firefox, **Copy|Paste** gave us all the data as one long line of text in one cell:

A1 | f_x DateOpenHighLowCloseVolumeAdj Close*13-Apr-0731.1531.5030.9631.411

	A	B	C	D	E	F	G	H	I
1	DateOpenHighLowCloseVolumeAdj Close*13-Apr-0731.1531.5030.9631.4112,006,30031.4112-Apr-07								
2									

One workaround for Yahoo data involves selecting the table including the header; notice that "PRICES" is selected.

First | Prev | Next | Last

PRICES ←

Date	Open	High	Low	Close	Volume	Adj Close*
13-Apr-07	31.15	31.50	30.96	31.41	12,006,300	31.41
12-Apr-07	31.26	31.42	31.10	31.21	13,904,800	31.21
11-Apr-07	31.65	31.73	30.90	31.17	16,141,100	31.17

Here is the result of a straightforward **Copy|Paste** into Excel when using Firefox:

G13 | f_x 31.29

	A	B	C	D	E	F	G
1	**PRICES**						
2							
3	Date	Open	High	Low	Close	Volume	Adj Close*
4	13-Apr-07	31.15	31.5	30.96	31.41	12,006,300	31.41
5	12-Apr-07	31.26	31.42	31.1	31.21	13,904,800	31.21
6	11-Apr-07	31.65	31.73	30.9	31.17	16,141,100	31.17
7	10-Apr-07	31.64	32.02	31.6	31.69	12,797,600	31.69
8	09-Apr-07	32.01	32.24	31.6	31.64	12,408,000	31.64
9	05-Apr-07	32	32.09	31.72	31.96	13,878,100	31.96
10	04-Apr-07	31.61	31.87	31.48	31.62	7,836,200	31.62
11	03-Apr-07	31.41	32	31.41	31.72	12,324,600	31.72
12	02-Apr-07	31.22	31.4	30.93	31.28	8,668,800	31.28
13	30-Mar-07	31.21	31.6	31.02	31.29	9,425,000	31.29

41.2.2 Using Edit|Paste Special

In most cases **Edit|Paste Special** gives you more control and options. We paste using **Edit|Paste Special** and then use **Text** as an import option. If the data are pasted into Firefox, the result looks like this:

	A	B	C	D	E	F	G
1	Date	Open	High	Low	Close	Volume	Adj Close*
2	13-Apr-07	31.15	31.5	30.96	31.41	12,006,300	31.41
3	12-Apr-07	31.26	31.42	31.1	31.21	13,904,800	31.21
4	11-Apr-07	31.65	31.73	30.9	31.17	16,141,100	31.17
5	10-Apr-07	31.64	32.02	31.6	31.69	12,797,600	31.69
6	09-Apr-07	32.01	32.24	31.6	31.64	12,408,000	31.64
7	05-Apr-07	32	32.09	31.72	31.96	13,878,100	31.96
8	04-Apr-07	31.61	31.87	31.48	31.62	7,836,200	31.62
9	03-Apr-07	31.41	32	31.41	31.72	12,324,600	31.72
10	02-Apr-07	31.22	31.4	30.93	31.28	8,668,800	31.28
11	30-Mar-07	31.21	31.6	31.02	31.29	9,425,000	31.29

Excel imported each value into a separate cell and differentiated between text, dates, and numbers. If, however, the data are pasted into Internet Explorer, the result looks like this:

A1 | *fx* Date Open High Low Close Volume Adj Close*

	A	B	C	D	E	F	G
1	Date Open High Low Close Volume Adj Close*						
2	13-Apr-07 31.15 31.50 30.96 31.41 12,006,300 31.41						
3	12-Apr-07 31.26 31.42 31.10 31.21 13,904,800 31.21						
4	11-Apr-07 31.65 31.73 30.90 31.17 16,141,100 31.17						
5	10-Apr-07 31.64 32.02 31.60 31.69 12,797,600 31.69						
6	9-Apr-07 32.01 32.24 31.60 31.64 12,408,000 31.64						
7	5-Apr-07 32.00 32.09 31.72 31.96 13,878,100 31.96						
8	4-Apr-07 31.61 31.87 31.48 31.62 7,836,200 31.62						
9	3-Apr-07 31.41 32.00 31.41 31.72 12,324,600 31.72						
10	2-Apr-07 31.22 31.40 30.93 31.28 8,668,800 31.28						
11	30-Mar-07 31.21 31.60 31.02 31.29 9,425,000 31.29						
12							
13							

Excel has imported the text as lines, and these need to be separated in order to be useful. All is not lost, however: Click on the smart tag (which was indicated with an arrow) and choose **Use Text Import Wizard**:

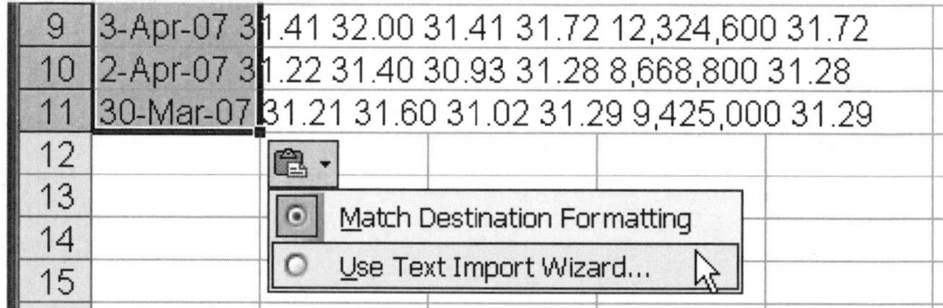

This option will take you to the Excel Text Import Wizard, which will walk you through a process that in the end will give you the columnar format of the numbers. The next illustration presents the first window from the text wizard—we trust you'll figure out how to proceed:

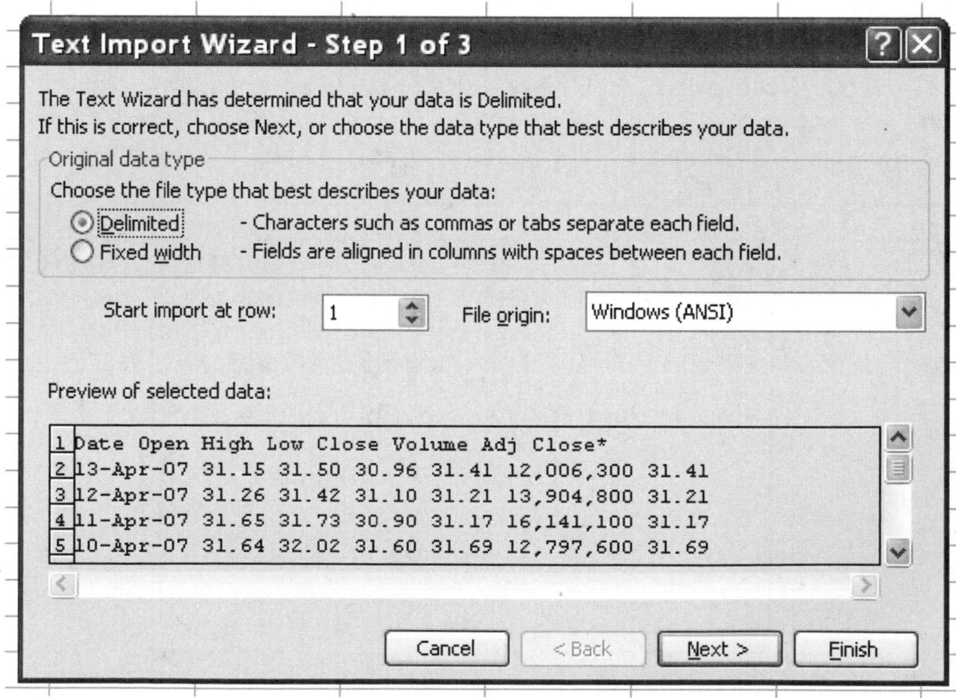

Here is the result (notice that the word "Close*" that was part of the header for column G got separated into its own column):

	A	B	C	D	E	F	G	H
1	Date	Open	High	Low	Close	Volume	Adj	Close*
2	13-Apr-07	31.15	31.5	30.96	31.41	12,006,300	31.41	↑
3	12-Apr-07	31.26	31.42	31.1	31.21	13,904,800	31.21	
4	11-Apr-07	31.65	31.73	30.9	31.17	16,141,100	31.17	
5	10-Apr-07	31.64	32.02	31.6	31.69	12,797,600	31.69	
6	09-Apr-07	32.01	32.24	31.6	31.64	12,408,000	31.64	
7	05-Apr-07	32	32.09	31.72	31.96	13,878,100	31.96	
8	04-Apr-07	31.61	31.87	31.48	31.62	7,836,200	31.62	
9	03-Apr-07	31.41	32	31.41	31.72	12,324,600	31.72	
10	02-Apr-07	31.22	31.4	30.93	31.28	8,668,800	31.28	
11	30-Mar-07	31.21	31.6	31.02	31.29	9,425,000	31.29	

41.3 Dynamic Web Queries

The copy-paste operations illustrated in the previous section are static: once copied the data do not change to reflect changes in the data stored on the Web page from which they came. In this section we illustrate the beginnings of dynamic Web queries—links between Excel and the data source that can be updated automatically.

If the data on the Web are updated frequently and we want the updates to be reflected in our worksheet, we can use a *Web query*. Web queries work on some but not all the data we can see on the Web.[1] Suppose we need information about the Dow Jones Industrial Average index; one place to get the information is the Web address (or URL) linking to Yahoo, http://finance.yahoo.com/q?s=DJI. Here is what the relevant part of the Yahoo Web site looks like:

1. In technical terms, the data generation should be done on the Web server and not on the client computer.

DOW JONES INDUSTRIAL AVERAGE IN (DJI:DJI) Delayed quote data	
Index Value:	12,720.46
Trade Time:	Apr 16
Change:	↑ 108.33 (0.86%)
Prev Close:	12,612.13
Open:	12,611.64
Day's Range:	12611.31 - 12731.18
52wk Range:	N/A

New! T

Chart

Market Updates

The way Microsoft envisaged the creation of Web queries involves the use of a wizard. From the **Data** menu select **Import External Data** and then **New Web Query**.

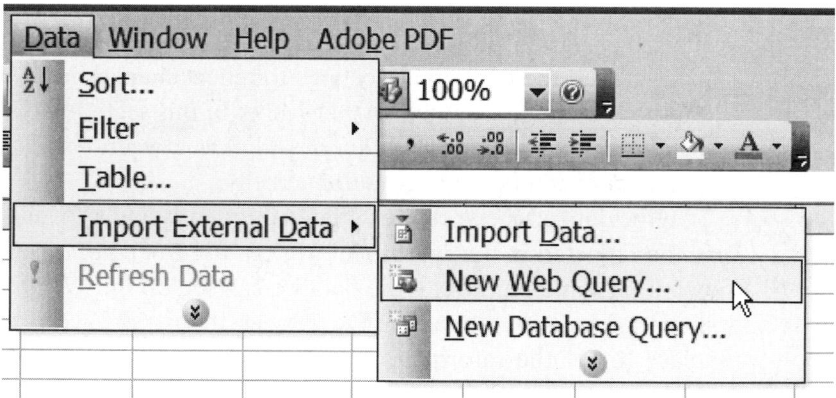

Once you have clicked on **New Web Query**, a window onto your Web home page opens.

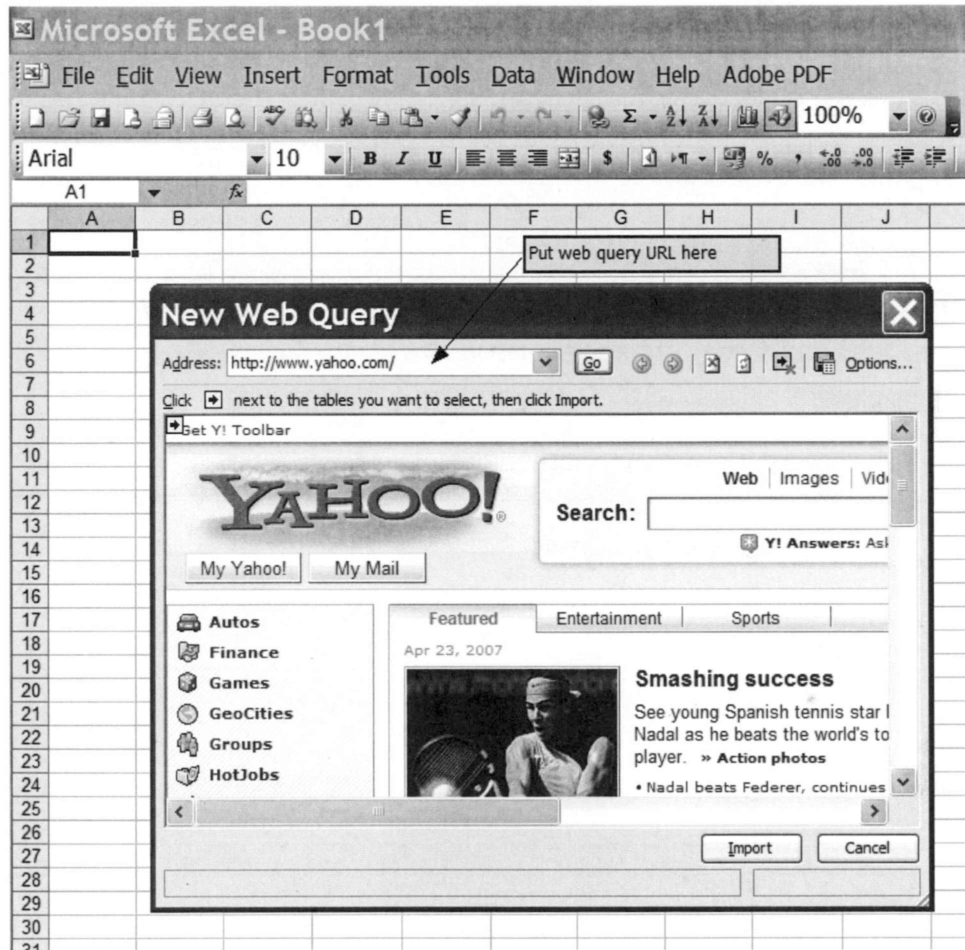

We now change the address in the address bar to the location of the document we want to load. In this instance the document is at http://finance.yahoo.com/q?s=^DJI. Once we click **Go** or press Enter, we should be presented with a view of the data and some yellow arrows pointing to parts of it. If the window is not sufficiently large, we can drag its corner to change its size.

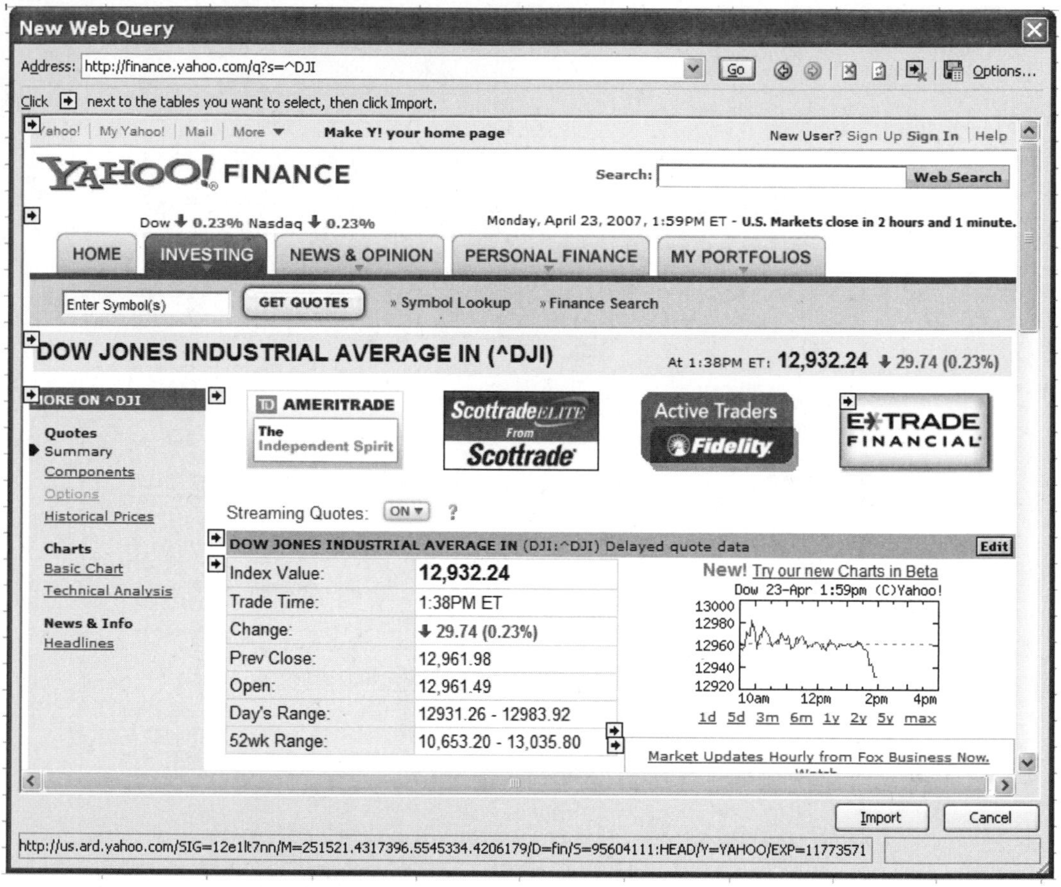

Clicking on an arrow changes it to a green tick mark to indicate that the item has been selected.

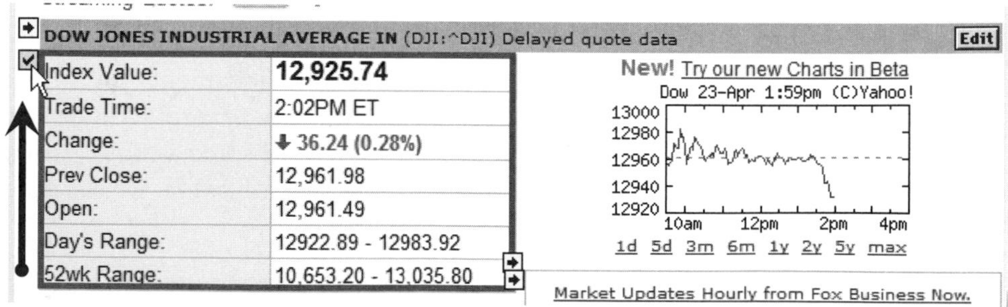

Once all the tables we are interested in have been selected, we can click the "Import" button.

The wizard now asks for a destination for the data; in the next example we put it in cell A1:

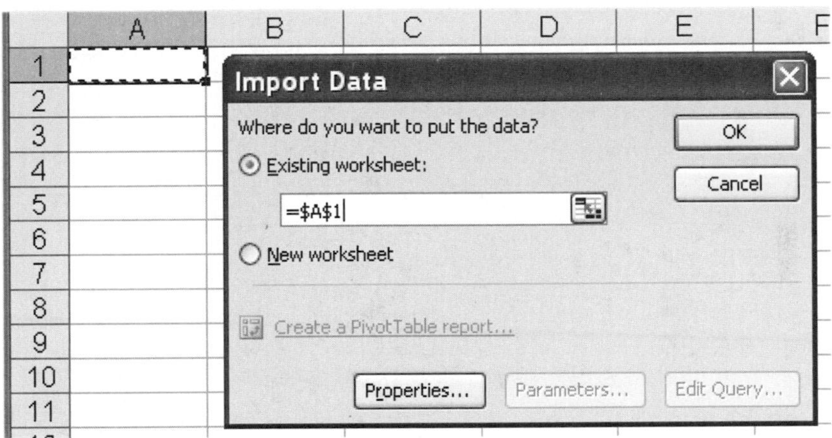

	A	B
1	q?s=DJI_1: Getting Data ...	
2		

Microsoft Excel - Book1

File Edit View Insert Format Tools Data

A1

	A	B
1	Index Value:	12,931.02
2	Trade Time:	2:13PM ET
3	Change:	Down 30.96 (0.24%)
4	Prev Close:	12,961.98
5	Open:	12,961.49
6	Day's Range:	12,922.89 - 12,983.92
7	52wk Range:	10,653.20 - 13,035.80

We can now update the data whenever we want by right-clicking on any cell in the query data range (cell B7 in the following screen capture) in Excel and selecting "Refresh Data" from the menu:

	A	B	C	D
1	Index Value:	12,720.46		
2	Trade Time:	Apr-16		
3	Change:	Up 108.33 (0.86%)		
4	Prev Close:	12,612.13		
5	Open:	12,611.64		
6	Day's Range:	12,611.31 - 12,731.18		
7	52wk Range:	N/A		

Cut
Copy
Paste
Paste Special...
Insert...
Delete...
Clear Contents
Insert Comment
Format Cells...
Edit Query...
Data Range Properties...
Parameters...
Refresh Data

If you use an up-to-date version of Excel, you might get the following message; click OK to make it go away:

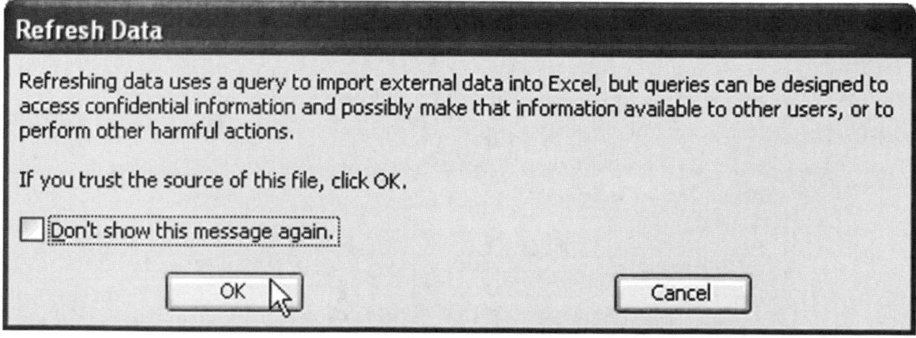
Refresh Data
Refreshing data uses a query to import external data into Excel, but queries can be designed to access confidential information and possibly make that information available to other users, or to perform other harmful actions.
If you trust the source of this file, click OK.
Don't show this message again.
OK
Cancel

The data will now be updated.

We can also set the data to refresh automatically by selecting the appropriate response from the "Data Range Properties . . ." on the right-click menu. While you are on that dialogue you may want to deselect the annoying "Adjust column width" option (circled and deselected on the screen cap):

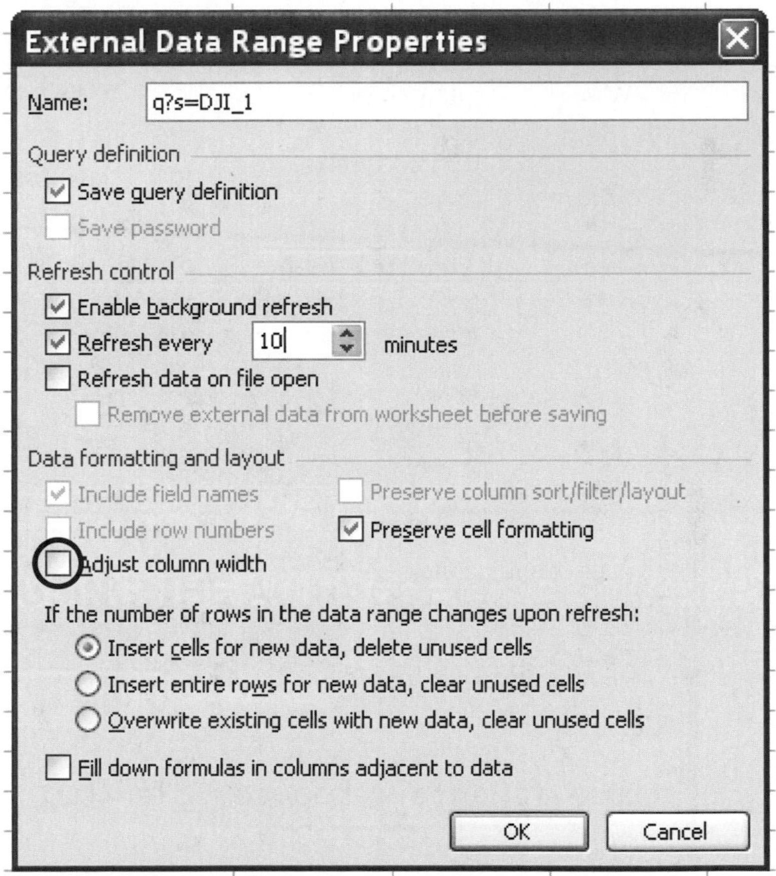

41.4 Web Queries: The iqy File

Information about a Web query can be kept in a simple text file with the extension iqy. You may create it using a text editor (like Notepad), or you may save a query created by the wizard as demonstrated in the next screen shot:

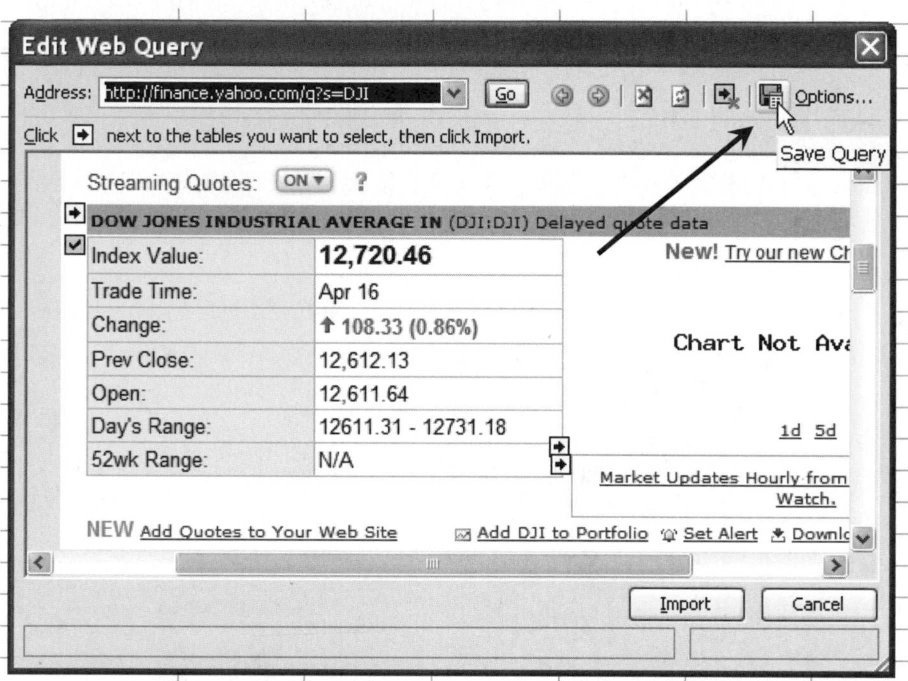

Here is the resulting file:

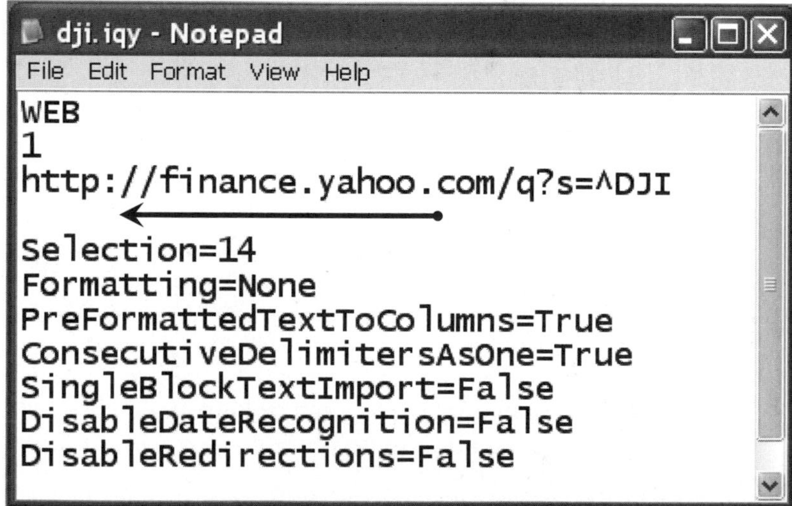


```
WEB
1
http://finance.yahoo.com/q?s=^DJI

Selection=14
Formatting=None
PreFormattedTextToColumns=True
ConsecutiveDelimitersAsOne=True
SingleBlockTextImport=False
DisableDateRecognition=False
DisableRedirections=False
```

The first four lines of the iqy file are mandatory; the third line is, of course, the full URL of the Web document from which the query is created. Note that the fourth line (mandatory, indicated with an arrow) is blank. In our case the only other necessary line is the fifth line—it selects the 14th element on the Web page as the target of our import.[2]

41.4.1 Running a Web Query

Web query files (having an iqy extension) can be run by Excel without going through the full procedure illustrated in the first part of this section. When you open a Web query file in Excel, the query is run.

To illustrate, we change the ticker symbol ^DJI in the previous Web query to GM, the symbol of General Motors. We save the resulting file as gm.iqy; when we open this file in Excel, this is what happens:

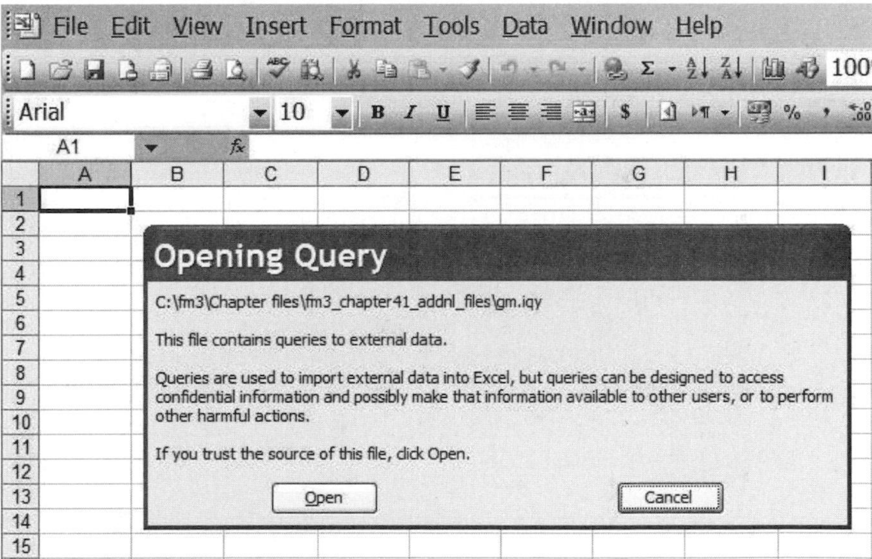

File Edit View Insert Format Tools Data Window Help
Arial
10
A1
Opening Query
C:\fm3\Chapter files\fm3_chapter41_addnl_files\gm.iqy
This file contains queries to external data.
Queries are used to import external data into Excel, but queries can be designed to access confidential information and possibly make that information available to other users, or to perform other harmful actions.
If you trust the source of this file, click Open.
Open
Cancel

Clicking on **Open** imports the data for GM:

2. This number is dependent on the structure of the Web page as recognized by the Web query.

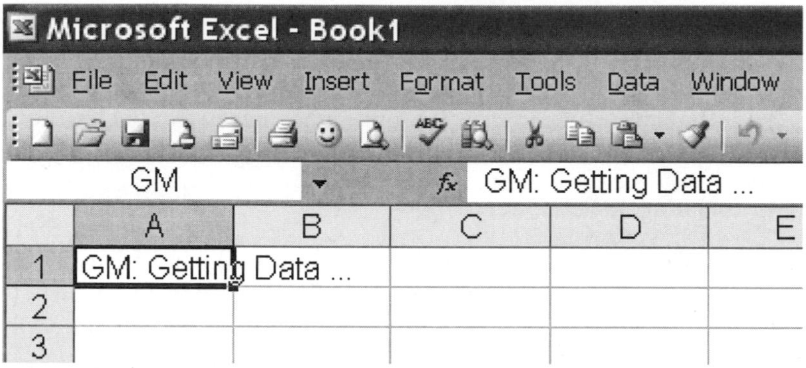

Microsoft Excel - Book1

File Edit View Insert Format Tools Data Window

GM | GM: Getting Data ...

	A	B	C	D	E
1	GM: Getting Data ...				
2					
3					

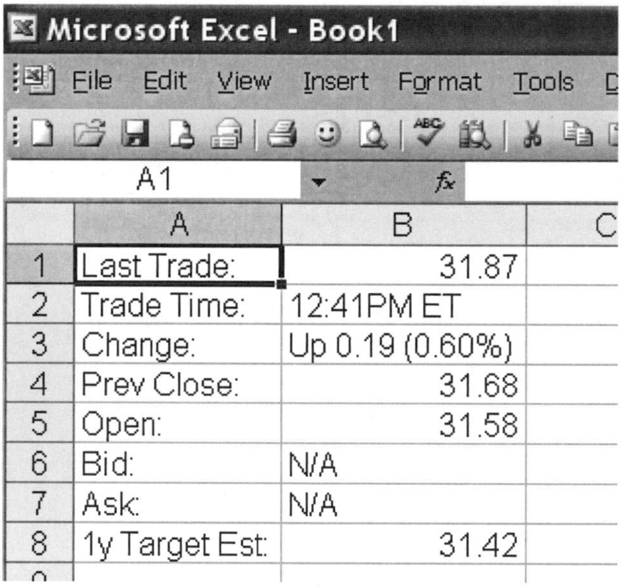

Microsoft Excel - Book1

File Edit View Insert Format Tools D

A1

	A	B	C
1	Last Trade:	31.87	
2	Trade Time:	12:41PM ET	
3	Change:	Up 0.19 (0.60%)	
4	Prev Close:	31.68	
5	Open:	31.58	
6	Bid:	N/A	
7	Ask:	N/A	
8	1y Target Est:	31.42	

If we compare the relevant Web pages, notice that the data retrieved are not the same as in the case of ^DJI, since Yahoo produces differently shaped pages for indexes and stocks.

To use an iqy file in the current worksheet, make the menu selection **Data|Import External Data|Import Data**; this should open the select data-source window. By default the window opens to "My Data Sources."

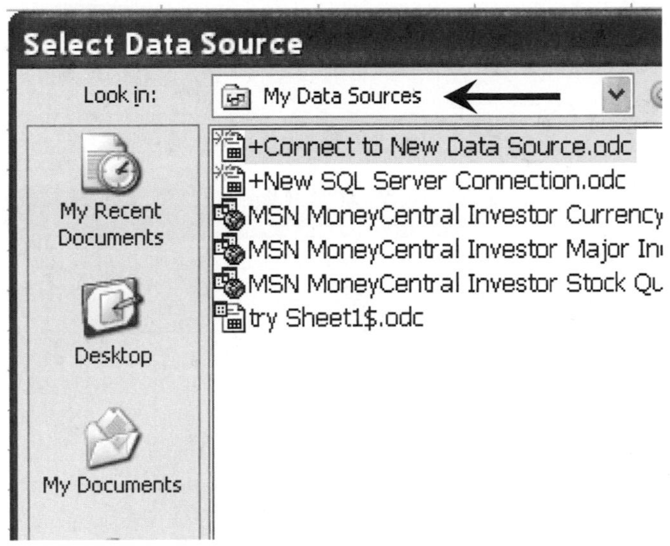

Navigate to the location of the iqy file and select it. Once the correct file is selected, Click **Open**:

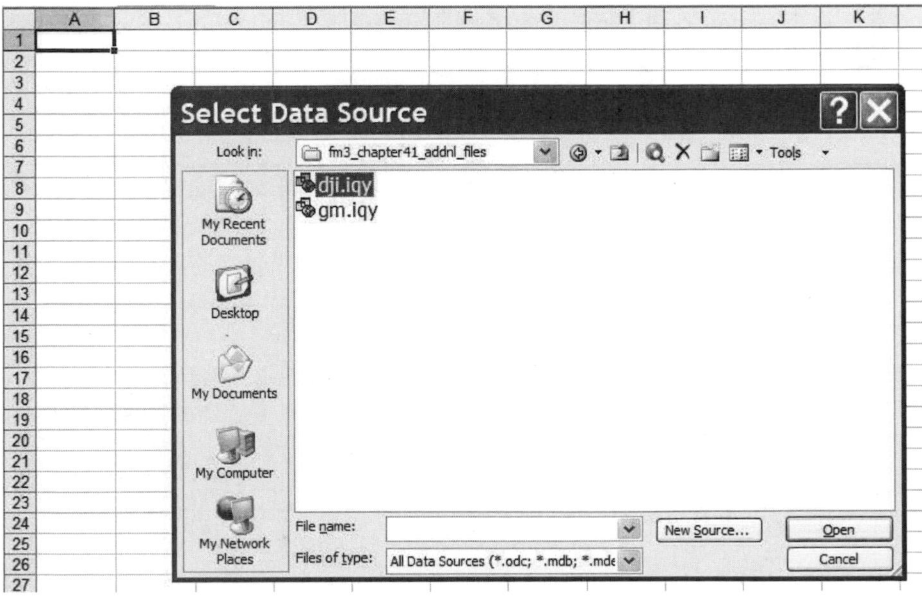

Now we select a location for the imported data:

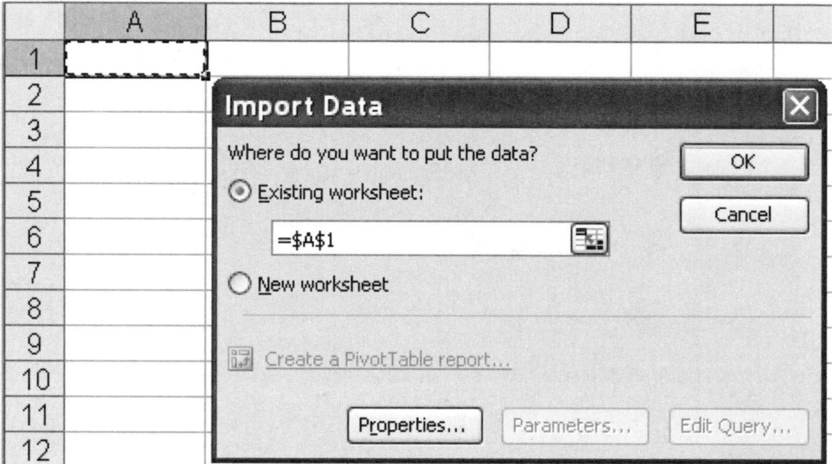

And a few seconds later the data are in the worksheet. If we repeat the process for the General Motors query (gm.iqy) and select the cell D1 as a target for the imported data, we can have two queries side by side on the same worksheet.

Microsoft Excel - Book1

File Edit View Insert Format Tools Data Window Help

M26

	A	B	C	D	E
1	Index Value:	12,936.38		Last Trade:	31.2
2	Trade Time:	2:42PM ET		Trade Time:	2:22PM ET
3	Change:	Down 25.60 (0.20%)		Change:	Down 0.48 (1.52%)
4	Prev Close:	12,961.98		Prev Close:	31.68
5	Open:	12,961.49		Open:	31.58
6	Day's Range:	12,919.88 - 12,983.92		Bid:	N/A
7	52wk Range:	10,653.20 - 13,035.80		Ask:	N/A
8				1y Target Est:	29.73
9					

41.5 Parametric Web Pages

The most common way of supplying a Web page with information is using parameters on the URL. We need to supply the information so the Web page can return the information we are interested in. Here is an example we used earlier:

The URL of this page has two parts separated by a question mark:

1. The actual address: http://finance.yahoo.com/q
2. Information for the page to act on: s=^DJI

The information in the second part of the URL consists of name=value pairs separated by "&." In this case we have only one such pair, "s=^DJI," and the separator is not necessary. As was demonstrated earlier, if we change the value in this pair from ^DJI to GM, the Web page returns the information for General Motors, and it is in a slightly different format.

This "?name1=value1&name2=value2. . ." arrangement is not unique to Yahoo.com. Here is another example taken from MSN MoneyCentral:

http://moneycentral.msn.com/investor/charts/chartdl.aspx?Symbol=$INDU&PT=2

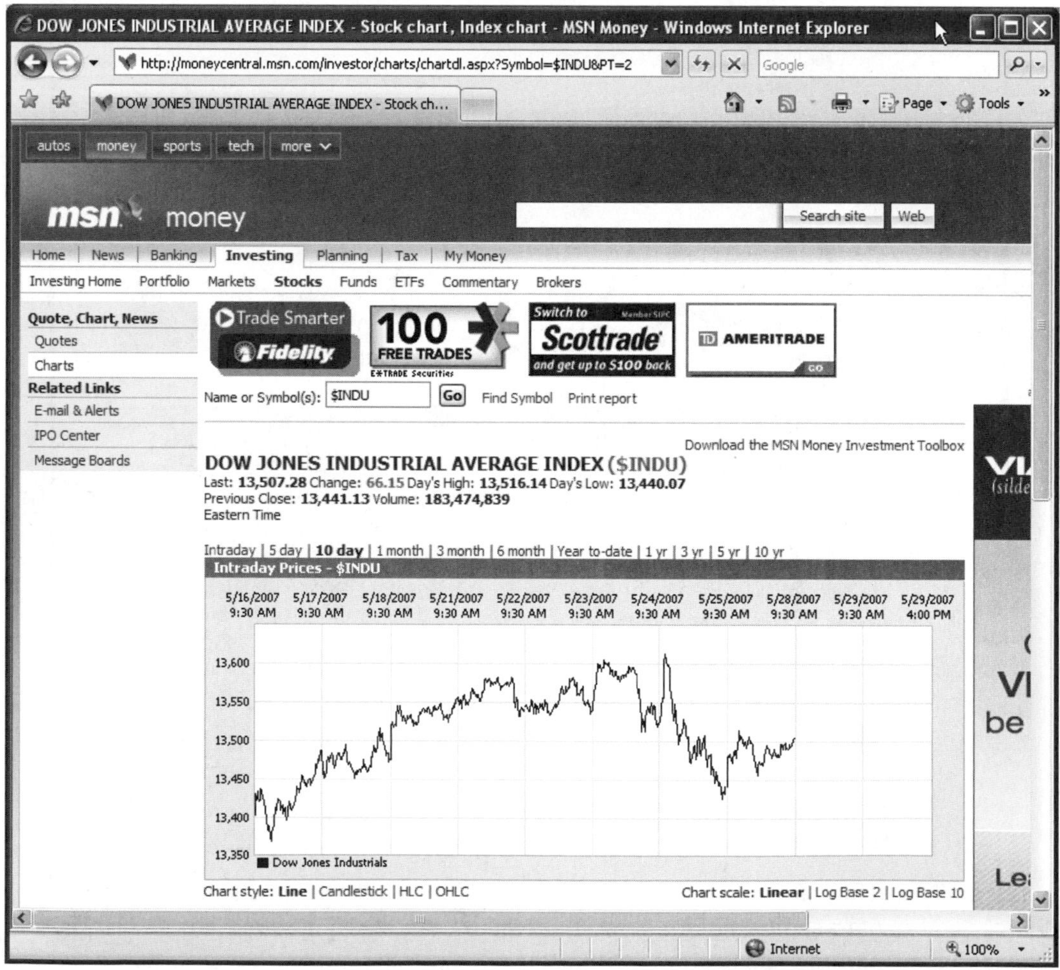

As before, the URL of this page has two parts separated by a question mark:

1. The actual address: http://moneycentral.msn.com/investor/charts/chartdl.aspx
2. Information for the page to act on: Symbol=$INDU&PT=2

The information in the second part of the URL is part of the HTML standard and is called a *get parameter structure*. It consists of name=value pairs separated by &. In this case,

• Symbol=$INDU: This pair selects the ticker-tape symbol, in this case the Dow Jones Industrial Average.

• PT=2: This pair selects the display period for the chart: PT=0 is intraday, PT=1 is five-day, PT=2 is 10-day (and is the current selection), and so on up to PT=10 for a 10-year chart.

41.6 Web Queries: Parameters

The interface presented by the Web query wizard has no provision for parameter information to be passed to the query. We can, however, use a roundabout way to force the issue.

Here is an iqy file querying a Web document that expects one numerical parameter called s.

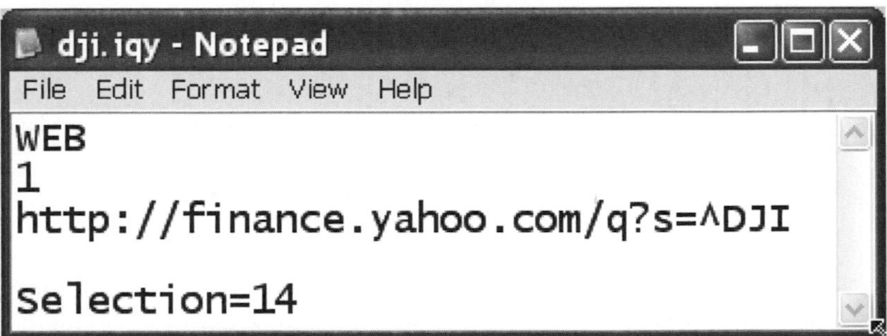

We make a small change to the iqy file, replacing s with ["Ticker-Tape Symbol?"]. This step results in a parametric query:

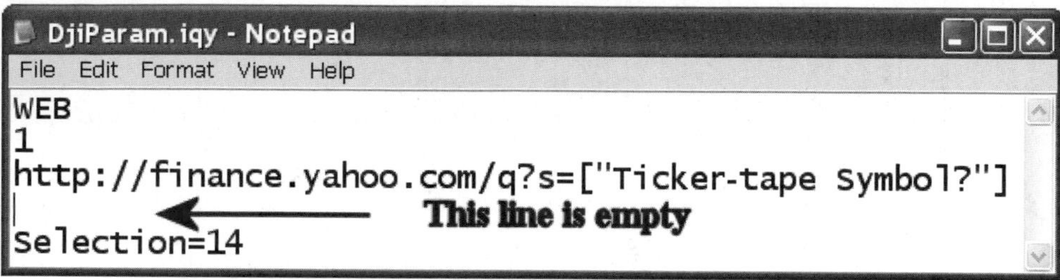

We can now activate the query by double-clicking the file DjiParam.iqy in Windows Explorer.

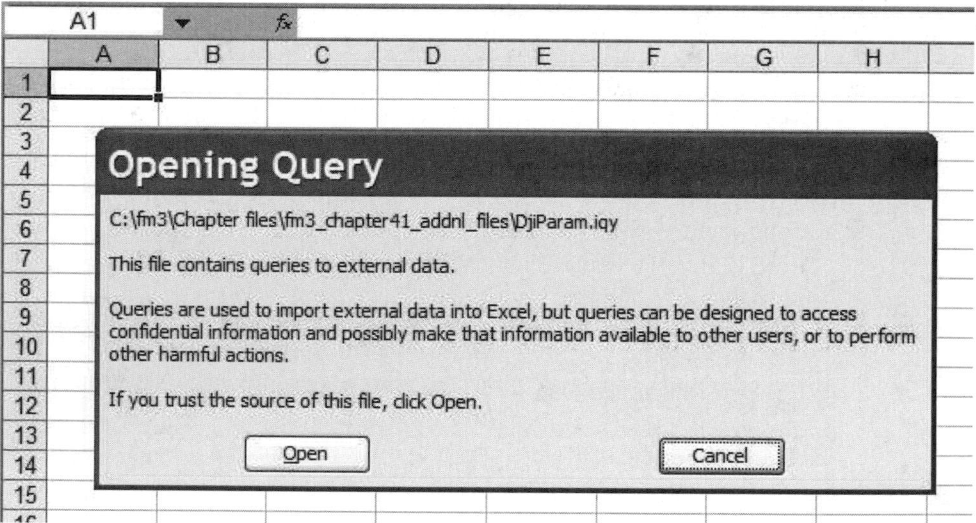

Once we click **Open** to activate the query, the parameterization of the query gets to work and we are presented with the following:

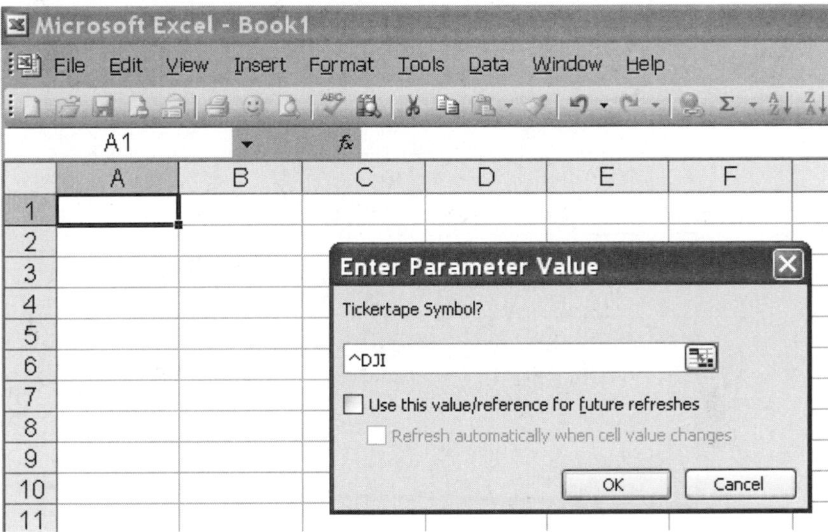

Notice that the question on the dialogue is taken from the quoted string in the iqy file (["Ticker-Tape Symbol?"]). Once we provide the value (^DJI) and click OK, the query is run with the value provided.

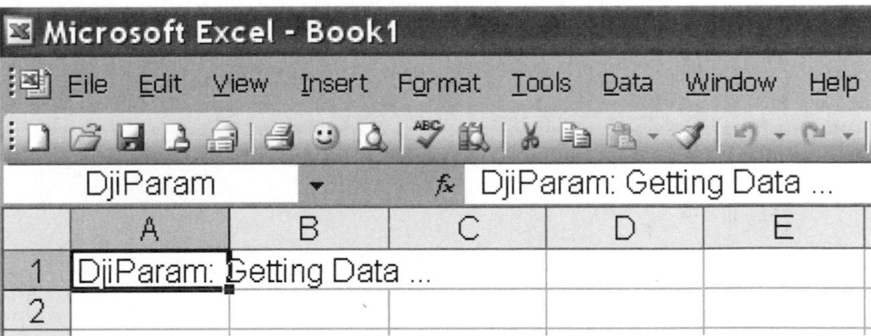

Microsoft Excel - Book1

File Edit View Insert Format Tools Data Window

A1

	A	B	C
1	Index Value:	**12,919.40**	
2	Trade Time:	Apr-23	
3	Change:	Down **42.58 (0.33%)**	
4	Prev Close:	12,961.98	
5	Open:	12,961.49	
6	Day's Range:	12,916.63 - 12,983.92	
7	52wk Range:	10,653.20 - 13,035.80	
8			

Every time we try to update the query, Excel will ask for a value for the first parameter. If we want to avoid the repeated queries (pun intended), we can direct Excel to take the value of a parameter from a cell in the worksheet. Some preparation is necessary, and the query itself needs to be activated using the data menu. The sequence of events is depicted in the following screen shots.

First we prepare a worksheet with a cell containing the value we want to give the query:

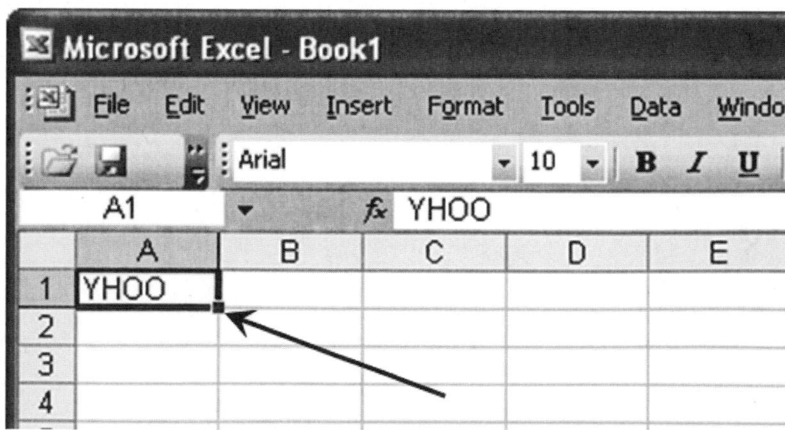

Then we open the file "DjiParam.iqy" using the menu selection **Data|Import External Data|Import Data**:

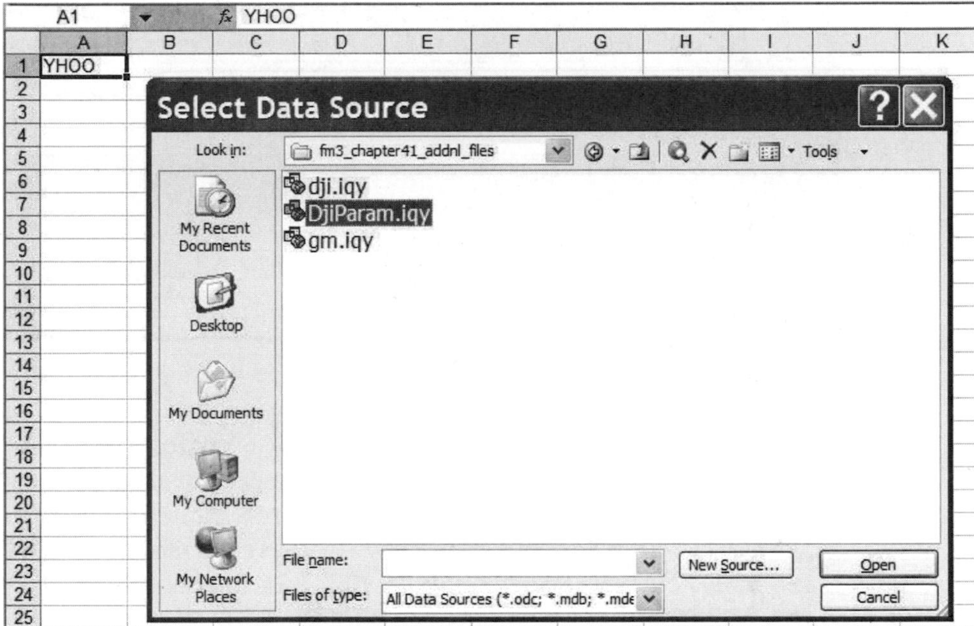

When presented with the import-data dialogue, we provide a destination ($A$1) for the data and select **Parameters** to provide information about the parameter:

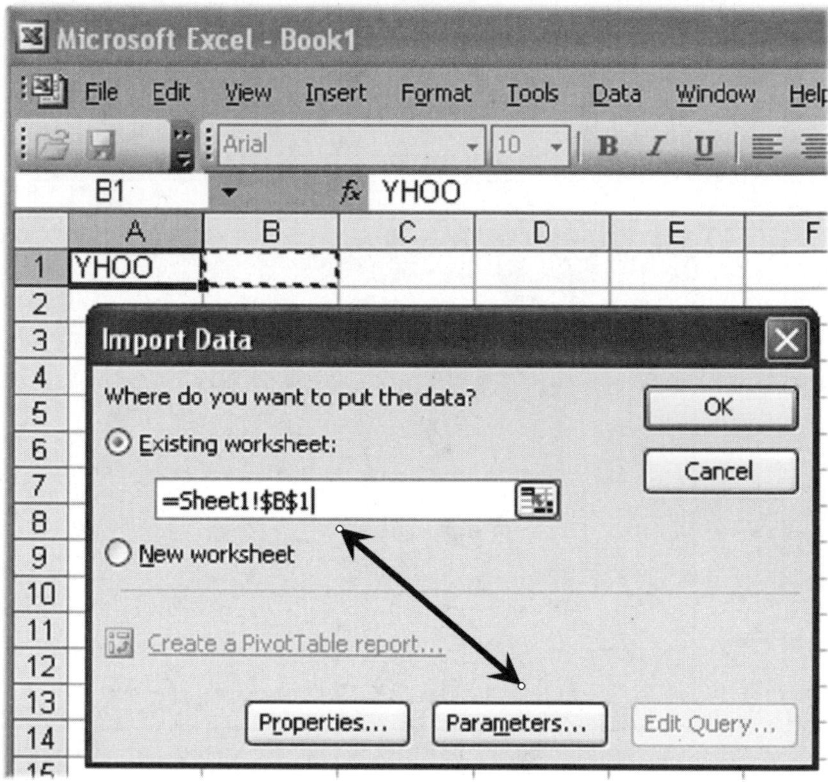
Microsoft Excel - Book1
File Edit View Insert Format Tools Data Window Help
Arial 10
B1 YHOO
YHOO
Import Data
Where do you want to put the data?
Existing worksheet:
=Sheet1!$B$1
New worksheet
Create a PivotTable report...
OK
Cancel
Properties...
Parameters...
Edit Query...

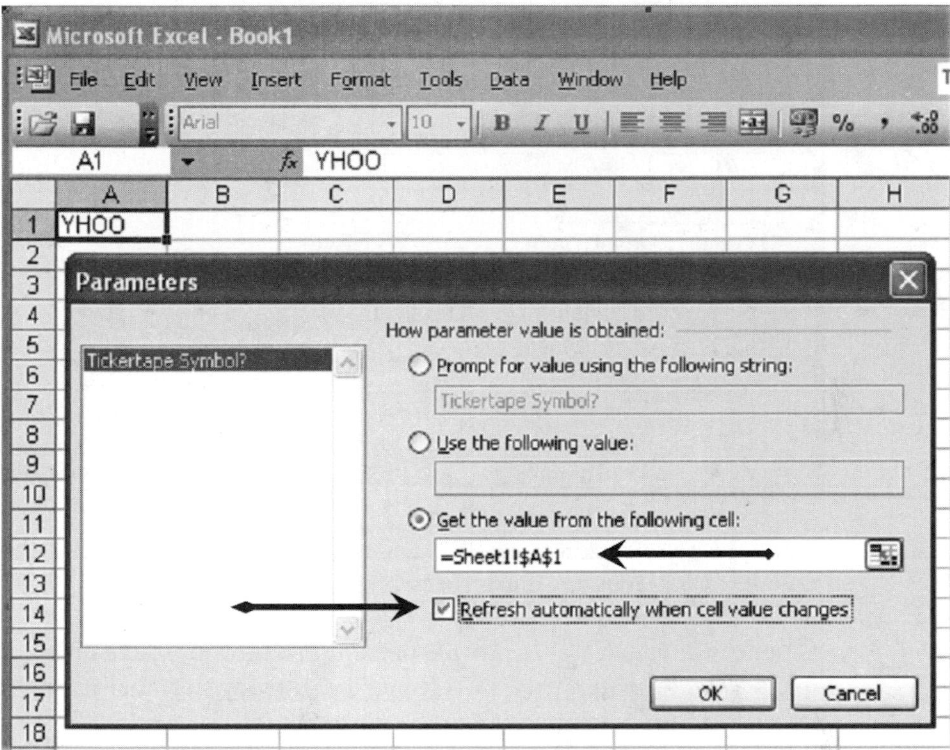

Having set up cell $A$1 to hold the value of the parameter, we choose the third option, supply the address, tick **Refresh automatically when cell value changes**, and click OK. This step gets us back to the import-data dialogue, and all we have to do now is click the OK button. Here is what we get:

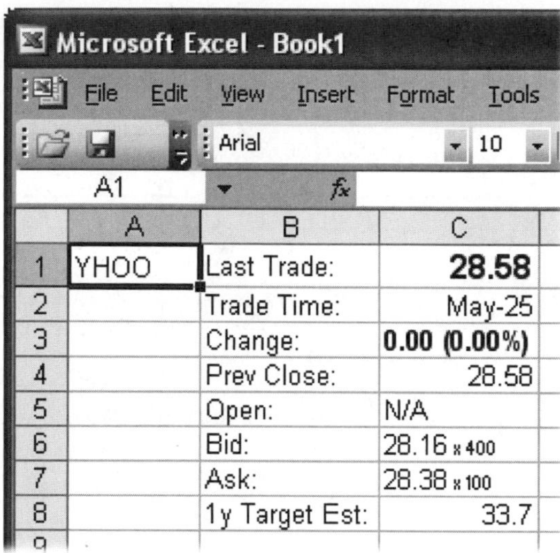

41.7 Web Queries: CSV Files and Postprocessing

A number of financial sites provide the option to download the information in a text format called CSV (comma separated values). For example, if we surf to the URL http://ichart.yahoo.com/table.csv?s=^FTSE using Firefox, we are presented with the option to save the file or open it.

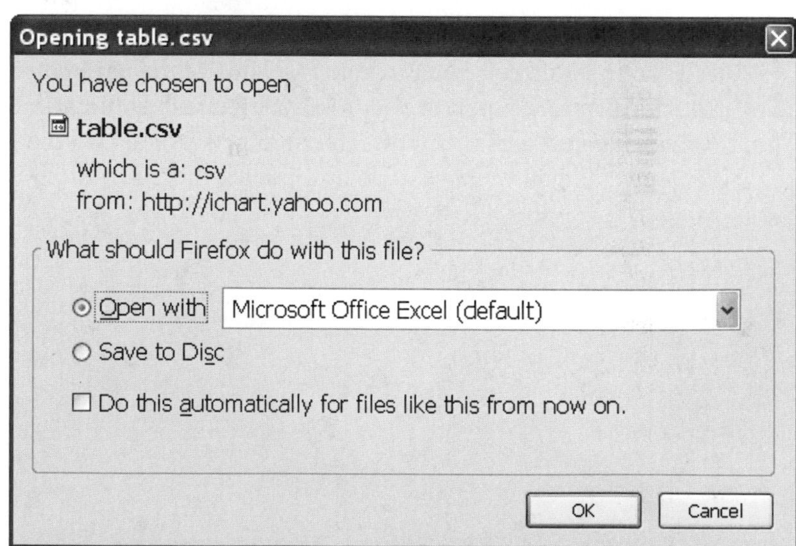

If we choose **Open**, then a new workbook with all the daily historical prices for the *Financial Times* FTSE100 index will open:

	A	B	C	D	E	F	G
1	Date	Open	High	Low	Close	Volume	Adj Close
2	23/04/2007	6486.8	6504.5	6466.1	6479.7	1.33E+09	6479.7
3	20/04/2007	6440.6	6508.9	6440.6	6486.8	2.14E+09	6486.8
4	19/04/2007	6449.4	6451.8	6386.2	6440.6	1.45E+09	6440.6
5	18/04/2007	6497.8	6497.8	6440.8	6449.4	1.49E+09	6449.4
6	17/04/2007	6516.2	6516.2	6456.4	6497.8	1.56E+09	6497.8
7	16/04/2007	6462.4	6516.2	6462.4	6516.2	1.5E+09	6516.2
8	13/04/2007	6416.4	6462.4	6416.4	6462.4	1.52E+09	6462.4
9	12/04/2007	6413.3	6419.6	6376.4	6416.4	1.49E+09	6416.4

As we can see, Excel can read this kind of file directly, but, sadly, there is no apparent way to link to such information and have it automatically updated. We can, however, use the Web query mechanism to achieve such integration with a bit of postprocessing.

Here is a URL that we can use to retrieve the daily prices for the FTSE 100 index for 2005 from Yahoo:

http://ichart.yahoo.com/table.csv?
s=^FTSE&a=00&b=1&c=2005&d=11&e=31&f=2005&g=d

If we copy the URL we used to get the information to a file and save it with the suffix iqy, we get a query file. Here is a screen shot of that file:

If we activate it (by double-clicking in the explorer) we get the following:

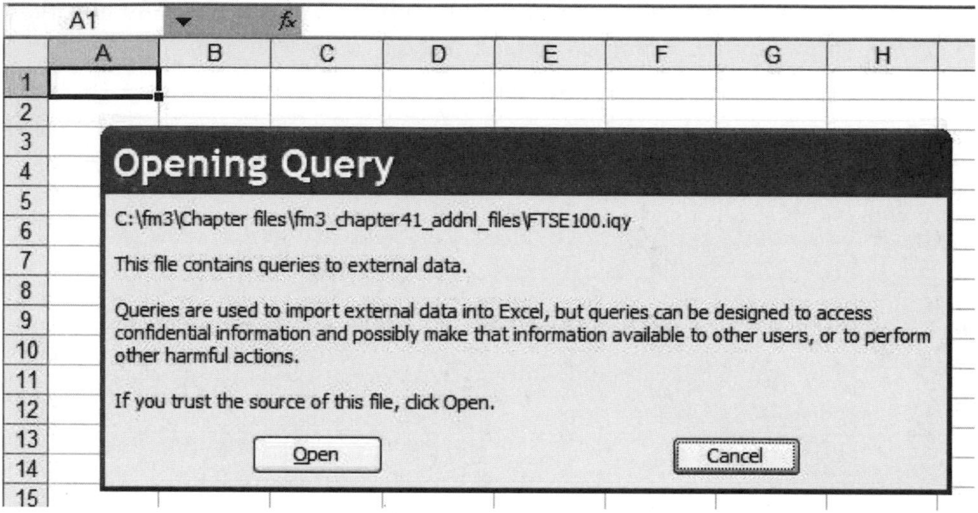

And if we select **Open**,

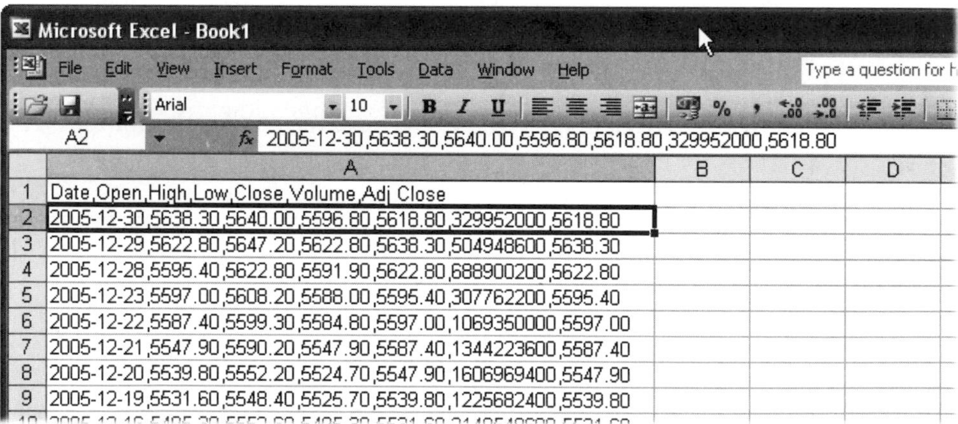

As seen, the output from the query is a single column of textual information. We now need to convert it to usable information; this operation is best done using the text-to-column conversion wizard already discussed in section 41.2.2.

41.8 A VBA Application: Importing Price Data from Yahoo

Up till now in this chapter we have discussed the direct import of Web data to Excel. In this section we show how to write routines in VBA that import the data and possibly manipulate them. As an example we show how to get price data for a selected stock, for a selected time period. Our stated purpose is to use the Yahoo price data for computing the historical volatility for a stock that was illustrated in Chapter 19. But of course our underlying motive is to illustrate an extensive use of the VBA connection between Excel and financial Web data. If you understand this application, you should be able to proceed on your own to more advanced implementations.

For clarity we proceed in three stages: First we show how to import data from Yahoo, and then we show how to use user interaction to supply Yahoo with the needed details. In the final stage we show how to deal with errors in user input and with Web connection problems.

41.8.1 Get Prices: A First Approximation

The first approximation retrieves some historical daily prices for the Nasdaq index QQQQ from Yahoo. Note that no error checking is performed and that all data are hardwired in the VBA code. The fact that the macro includes no error checking means that it might not run or that it might produce funny results if the Web connection misbehaves.

```
Sub GetPricesVer1()
    Dim Ws As Worksheet      'Our query is going to be
                             'stored here
    Dim Wq As QueryTable     'This will be our query
    Dim Url As String        'Full Web address on Yahoo
    Url = _
        "URL;" & _
        "http://ichart.finance.yahoo.com/table.csv?" & _
        "s=QQQQ&" & _
        "a=3&b=27&c=2007&" & _
        "d=4&e=6&f=2007&" & "g=d&" & _
        "ignore=.csv"
```

```
    'Use ActiveSheet for data; store reference in ws
    Set Ws = ActiveSheet
    'Add our query to the worksheet; results should
    'go to column A
    'down from A2; store reference in Wq
    Set Wq = Ws.QueryTables.Add(Connection:=Url, _
                                Destination:=Ws.Range("A2"))
    'Run our query in the foreground and wait for the
    'query to finish
    Wq.Refresh BackgroundQuery:=False
End Sub
```

Points of note:

• The URL string is composed of several strings on consecutive lines concatenated with the VBA concatenation operator **&**; also notice the VBA line-continuation operator _ at the end of some of lines.

• The first string—`"URL;"`—Sets the type of the query, in this case a Web query.

• The second string–`"http://ichart.finance.yahoo.com/table.csv?"`—provides the actual Web address for the data to be retrieved. Notice that it ends with the separator **?** used to separate the Web address of a parametric Web page from its parameters.

• The third string—`"s=QQQQ&"`—is the first parameter for the Web page and specifies the ticker-tape symbol of the stock; notice that it ends with the separator **&** used to separate one parameter of a parametric Web page from another.

The rest of the strings making the URL will be explained later in this section.

Here is the worksheet before the macro is run:

	A	B	C	D	E
1	**HISTORICAL VOLATILITY — REV1**				Run Macro
2					
3					

And here it is after the macro is run:

	A	B	C	D	E
1	HISTORICAL VOLATILITY — REV1				Run Macro
2	Date,Open,High,Low,Close,Volume,Adj Close				
3	2007-05-04,46.77,46.89,46.42,46.63,93591800,46.63				
4	2007-05-03,46.53,46.72,46.43,46.59,98003600,46.59				
5	2007-05-02,46.09,46.58,46.05,46.42,91971600,46.42				
6	2007-05-01,45.97,46.14,45.66,46.11,135044400,46.11				
7	2007-04-30,46.49,46.53,45.92,45.96,93290500,45.96				
8	2007-04-27,46.37,46.70,46.29,46.57,96536500,46.57				
9					
10					

The data are retrieved as a single column of text, and the column width is set to accommodate the data. If we rerun the macro, we get two columns of data next to each other. Because the destination range was not empty, Excel inserted a new column to the left of the destination range, loaded the data into the column, and reset its width to accommodate the data.

	A	B	C
1		HISTORICAL VOLATILITY — RI	
2	Date,Open,High,Low,Close,Volume,Adj Close	Date,Open,High,Low,Close,Volume,Adj Close	
3	2007-05-04,46.77,46.89,46.42,46.63,93591800,46.63	2007-05-04,46.77,46.89,46.42,46.63,93591800,46.63	
4	2007-05-03,46.53,46.72,46.43,46.59,98003600,46.59	2007-05-03,46.53,46.72,46.43,46.59,98003600,46.59	
5	2007-05-02,46.09,46.58,46.05,46.42,91971600,46.42	2007-05-02,46.09,46.58,46.05,46.42,91971600,46.42	
6	2007-05-01,45.97,46.14,45.66,46.11,135044400,46.11	2007-05-01,45.97,46.14,45.66,46.11,135044400,46.11	
7	2007-04-30,46.49,46.53,45.92,45.96,93290500,45.96	2007-04-30,46.49,46.53,45.92,45.96,93290500,45.96	
8	2007-04-27,46.37,46.70,46.29,46.57,96536500,46.57	2007-04-27,46.37,46.70,46.29,46.57,96536500,46.57	
9			

41.8.2 Get Prices: A Second Approximation

Our first approximation left us with two problems: First, the data are retrieved as one column of text, a configuration that is not very conducive to further analysis as numbers. Second, as we have shown, rerunning the macro causes duplication of the data in two parallel columns. We now take a small detour to demonstrate an unofficial way to solve the first problem and will return to the proper way shortly. The method illustrated is “unofficial” in that it uses a nondocumented behavior in Excel. Unlike regular queries, which can be set up using the query wizard, the query we use here can only be set up from a VBA macro. This "unofficial version" may be all you ever need to automate the import of data from the Web into Excel. It is simple and seems to work with most versions of Excel.

Here is our "unofficial" macro; differences from the official version are set in bold type on a shaded background for clarity:

```
Sub GetPricesVer1text()
     Dim Ws As Worksheet     'Our query is going to be
                             'stored here
     Dim Wq As QueryTable    'This will be our query
     Dim Url As String       'Full Web address on Yahoo
     Url = _
          "TEXT;" & _
          "http://ichart.finance.yahoo.com/table.csv?" & _
          "s=QQQQ&" & _
          "a=3&b=27&c=2007&" & _
          "d=4&e=6&f=2007&" & _
          "g=d&" & _
          "ignore=.csv"
     'Use ActiveSheet for data; store reference in ws
     Set Ws = ActiveSheet
     'Add our query to the worksheet; results should
     'go to column A
     'down from A2; store reference in wq.
     Set Wq = Ws.QueryTables.Add(Connection:=Url, _
                             Destination:=Ws.Range("A2"))
     'Set the text inport query type to dilimited
     Wq.TextFileParseType = xlDelimited
     'Set the text inport dilimiter type to comma
     Wq.TextFileCommaDelimiter = True
     'Run our query in the foreground, i.e., wait
     'for the query to finish
     Wq.Refresh BackgroundQuery:=False
End Sub
```

Points of note:

• The first part of the URL string, the part that sets the type of the query is not: "URL;" as for a Web query but "TEXT;" as for a text retrieval query.

• We added two lines to the macro:

```
Wq.TextFileParseType = xlDelimited
Wq.TextFileCommaDelimiter = True
```

These lines set the text-import query type to delimited, and the delimiter type to comma.

The end result of these changes is that we now have a Web query that behaves somewhat like a text-import query.

Here is the worksheet before the macro is run:

	A	B	C	D	E	F	G	H
1		HISTORICAL VOLATILITY — REV1TEXT						Run Macro
2								
3								

And here it is after the macro is run:

	A	B	C	D	E	F	G	H
1	HISTORICAL VOLATILITY — REV1TEXT							Run Macro
2	Date	Open	High	Low	Close	Volume	Adj Close	
3	04/05/2007	46.77	46.89	46.42	46.63	93591800	46.63	
4	03/05/2007	46.53	46.72	46.43	46.59	98003600	46.59	
5	02/05/2007	46.09	46.58	46.05	46.42	91971600	46.42	
6	01/05/2007	45.97	46.14	45.66	46.11	135044400	46.11	
7	30/04/2007	46.49	46.53	45.92	45.96	93290500	45.96	
8	27/04/2007	46.37	46.7	46.29	46.57	96536500	46.57	
9								
10								

Notice that the data are retrieved as multiple columns of the appropriate type and width. If we rerun the macro, we see that the "data-doubling" bug noticed in the first approximation still exists:

	A	B	C	D	E	F	G	H	I	J	K	L	M	N	O
1								HISTORICAL VOLATILITY — REV1TEXT							Run Macro
2	Date	Open	High	Low	Close	Volume	Adj Close	Date	Open	High	Low	Close	Volume	Adj Close	
3	04/05/2007	46.77	46.89	46.42	46.63	93591800	46.63	04/05/2007	46.77	46.89	46.42	46.63	93591800	46.63	
4	03/05/2007	46.53	46.72	46.43	46.59	98003600	46.59	03/05/2007	46.53	46.72	46.43	46.59	98003600	46.59	
5	02/05/2007	46.09	46.58	46.05	46.42	91971600	46.42	02/05/2007	46.09	46.58	46.05	46.42	91971600	46.42	
6	01/05/2007	45.97	46.14	45.66	46.11	135044400	46.11	01/05/2007	45.97	46.14	45.66	46.11	135044400	46.11	
7	30/04/2007	46.49	46.53	45.92	45.96	93290500	45.96	30/04/2007	46.49	46.53	45.92	45.96	93290500	45.96	
8	27/04/2007	46.37	46.7	46.29	46.57	96536500	46.57	27/04/2007	46.37	46.7	46.29	46.57	96536500	46.57	
9															
10															

The data-doubling bug is not disastrous and is easily "hand fixed." In succeeding subsections we show how to automate the process using the "official" Microsoft data-import method.

41.8.3 The Second Approximation in the "Official" Microsoft Way

Another approach to getting the data in columns is to postprocess the data retrieved by the query. This seems to be the prescribed Microsoft way and is shown in the following box. Again differences from version 1 are set in bold type on a shaded background for clarity.

```
Sub GetPricesVer2()
    Dim Ws As Worksheet        'Our query is going to be
                               'stored here
    Dim Wq As QueryTable       'This will be our query
    Dim Url As String          'Full Web address on Yahoo
    Url = _
        "URL;" & _
        "http://ichart.finance.yahoo.com/table.csv?" & _
        "s=QQQQ&" & _
        "a=3&b=27&c=2007&" & _
        "d=4&e=6&f=2007&" & _
        "g=d&" & _
        "ignore=.csv"
    'Use ActiveSheet for data; store reference in ws
    Set Ws = ActiveSheet
    'Add our query to the worksheet;
    'results should go to column A
    'down from A2; store reference in wq
```

```
    Set Wq = Ws.QueryTables.Add(Connection:=Url, _
                               Destination:=Ws.Range("A2"))
    'Run our query in the foreground, i.e., wait
    'for the query to finish
    Wq.Refresh BackgroundQuery:=False
    'Parse the text to columns; this is the approved
    'Microsoft way
    Wq.ResultRange.TextToColumns _
        Destination:=Wq.ResultRange.Range("A1"), _
        DataType:=xlDelimited, _
        TextQualifier:=xlDoubleQuote, _
        Comma:=True
    'Fit the column width to the data based on the
    'first 99 values
    Ws.Range("A2:G100").Columns.AutoFit
End Sub
```

Notice the use of **Wq.ResultRange**; **ResultRange** is a property of a **QueryTable** object that returns a range holding the returned data. Here is the worksheet before the macro is run:

	A	B	C	D	E	F	G	H
1	HISTORICAL VOLATILITY — REV2							Run Macro
2								
3								

And here it is after the macro is run:

	A	B	C	D	E	F	G	H
1	HISTORICAL VOLATILITY — REV2							Run Macro
2	Date	Open	High	Low	Close	Volume	Adj Close	
3	04/05/2007	46.77	46.89	46.42	46.63	93591800	46.63	
4	03/05/2007	46.53	46.72	46.43	46.59	98003600	46.59	
5	02/05/2007	46.09	46.58	46.05	46.42	91971600	46.42	
6	01/05/2007	45.97	46.14	45.66	46.11	135044400	46.11	
7	30/04/2007	46.49	46.53	45.92	45.96	93290500	45.96	
8	27/04/2007	46.37	46.7	46.29	46.57	96536500	46.57	
9								

Sadly, rerunning the macro is not without problems. The next screen capture shows the results returned by rerunning the query. The rerun deposits the data in column A, moving all the existing columns to the right. The macro then tries to convert the text in column A to numbers, but since the cells are already occupied by the results of the first run of the macro, we get the following question:

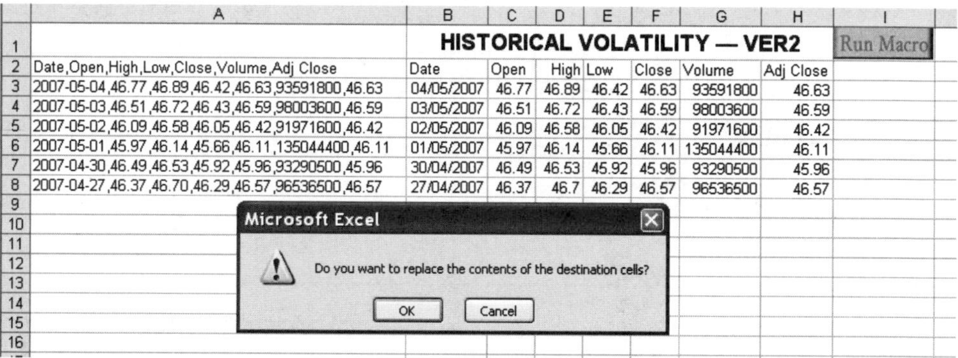

	A	B	C	D	E	F	G	H	I
1		HISTORICAL VOLATILITY — VER2							Run Macro
2	Date,Open,High,Low,Close,Volume,Adj Close	Date	Open	High	Low	Close	Volume	Adj Close	
3	2007-05-04,46.77,46.89,46.42,46.63,93591800,46.63	04/05/2007	46.77	46.89	46.42	46.63	93591800	46.63	
4	2007-05-03,46.51,46.72,46.43,46.59,98003600,46.59	03/05/2007	46.51	46.72	46.43	46.59	98003600	46.59	
5	2007-05-02,46.09,46.58,46.05,46.42,91971600,46.42	02/05/2007	46.09	46.58	46.05	46.42	91971600	46.42	
6	2007-05-01,45.97,46.14,45.66,46.11,135044400,46.11	01/05/2007	45.97	46.14	45.66	46.11	135044400	46.11	
7	2007-04-30,46.49,46.53,45.92,45.96,93290500,45.96	30/04/2007	46.49	46.53	45.92	45.96	93290500	45.96	
8	2007-04-27,46.37,46.70,46.29,46.57,96536500,46.57	27/04/2007	46.37	46.7	46.29	46.57	96536500	46.57	

When we click OK, the resulting worksheet has an extra column that needs deleting (H) and one column that needs reformatting as numbers and not dates (B):

	A	B	C	D	E	F	G	H	I
1		HISTORICAL VOLATILITY — VER2							Run Macro
2	Date	Open	High	Low	Close	Volume	Adj Close	Adj Close	
3	04/05/2007	15/02/1900	46.89	46.42	46.63	93591800	46.63	46.63	
4	03/05/2007	15/02/1900	46.72	46.43	46.59	98003600	46.59	46.59	
5	02/05/2007	15/02/1900	46.58	46.05	46.42	91971600	46.42	46.42	
6	01/05/2007	14/02/1900	46.14	45.66	46.11	135044400	46.11	46.11	
7	30/04/2007	15/02/1900	46.53	45.92	45.96	93290500	45.96	45.96	
8	27/04/2007	15/02/1900	46.7	46.29	46.57	96536500	46.57	46.57	
9									

We will deal with this annoying behavior later on in this section.

Both approaches (the "official" and the "unofficial") have their merits, but for the remainder of this section we will use the "official" approach.

41.8.4 Get Prices: A Third Approximation

One improvement our application could definitely do with is some control over the data retrieved. The third approximation gives us control of some of the relevant parameters for the Yahoo Web site from the user. It makes use of the user interaction described in Chapter 38. The macro gets the date of the last sample to be collected from the user. In order to keep the macro readable and of a manageable size, the actual interaction with the user will take place in a function. Notice that six of the parameters to the Yahoo Web site are affected by the end date and will be replaced by the results of the function.

The difference between **GetPricesVer3** and version 2 is the replacement of two of the parameter strings by the function **GetDates( )**; the function call is set in bold type on a shaded background for clarity:

```
Sub GetPricesVer3()
    Dim Ws As Worksheet         'Our query is going to be
                                'stored here
    Dim Wq As QueryTable        'This will be our query
    Dim Url As String           'Full Web address on Yahoo
    Url = _
        "URL;" & _
        "http://ichart.finance.yahoo.com/table.csv?" & _
        "s=QQQQ&" & _
        GetDates() & _
        "g=d&" & _
        "ignore=.csv"
    'Use ActiveSheet for data; store reference in ws
    Set Ws = ActiveSheet
    'Add our query to the worksheet;
    'results should go to column A
    'down from A2; store reference in wq
    Set Wq = Ws.QueryTables.Add(Connection:=Url, _
                         Destination:=Ws.Range("A2"))
    'Run our query in the foreground,
    'i.e., wait for the query to finish
    Wq.Refresh BackgroundQuery:=False
```

```
    'Parse the text to columns;
    'this is the approved Microsoft way
    Wq.ResultRange.TextToColumns _
        Destination:=Wq.ResultRange.Range("A1"), _
        DataType:=xlDelimited, _
        TextQualifier:=xlDoubleQuote, _
        Comma:=True
    'Fit the column width to the data based on the
    'first 99 values
    Ws.Range("A2:G100").Columns.AutoFit
End Sub
```

Note that the lines from **GetPricesVer2()**

```
"a=3&b=27&c=2007&" & _
"d=4&e=6&f=2007&" & _
```

were replaced by

```
GetDates() & _
```

The function **GetDates()** follows:

```
Function GetDates()
    Const p As String = _
    "Please enter last date to be retrieved"
    Dim Temp
    Dim ED ' end day here
    Dim EM ' end month here
    Dim EY ' end year
    Dim SD ' start day here
    Dim SM ' start month here
```

```
    Dim SY ' start year
    'Ask for a date; use current date as a default
    Temp = InputBox(p, Title, Date)
    'Did we get the correct answer?
    'If so, use its date value; if not, use current
    'date value
    If IsDate(Temp) Then
         Temp = DateValue(Temp)
    Else
         Temp = Date
    End If
    'Compute end and start day, month, and year;
    'Start date is 30 days before end date
    ED = Day(Temp)
    EM = Month(Temp) - 1 ' Yahoo month is 0-11
    EY = Year(Temp)
    SD = Day(Temp - 30)
    SM = Month(Temp - 30) - 1 ' Yahoo month is 0-11
    SY = Year(Temp - 30)
    'Compile the result string from the parameters
    GetDates = "a=" & SM & "&b=" & SD _
         & "&c" & SY & "&d=" & EM & "&e=" _
         & ED & "&f" & EY & "&"
End Function
```

Points of note:

• The VBA function **IsDate** returns TRUE if its argument is or can be converted to a Date Value; see appendix 1 for a full description.

• The VBA functions **Day**, **Month**, and **Year** return the appropriate part of their argument as a number; see appendix 1 for a full description.

• The variable **Title** used in the call to **InputBox** is defined as a global constant at the beginning of the module; it is going to be used as the title of all the input and message boxes in the application. Here is the definition line:

```
'This global constant
'is used by more than one function
Const Title As String = _
   "An Application - Get Historical Volatility"
```

Here is the worksheet before the macro is run:

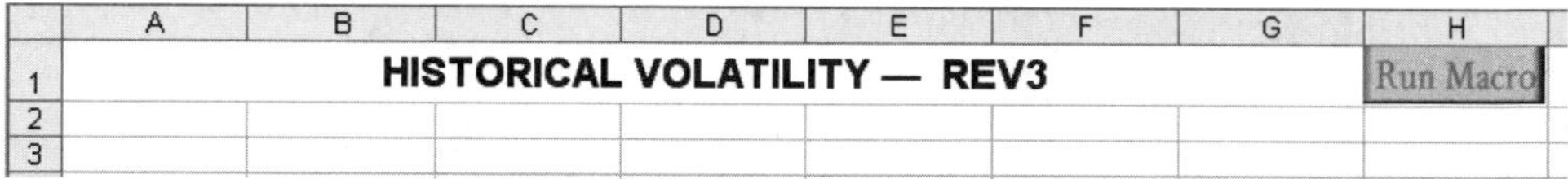

When we run the macro we are presented with an input box, into which we have inserted the date.[3]

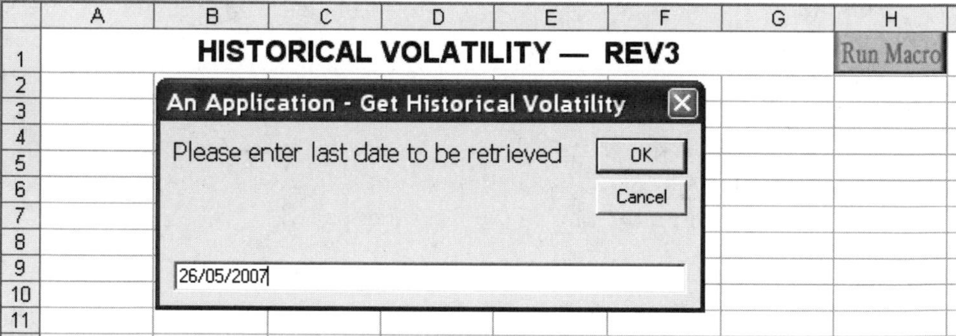

Following is the worksheet after we enter a date and select OK in the input box.

3. The input box accepts the following date versions: 22 May 2005, 22-May-2005, 22-5-2005, 22/5/2005, and more.

	A	B	C	D	E	F	G	H
1	HISTORICAL VOLATILITY — REV3							Run Macro
2	Date	Open	High	Low	Close	Volume	Adj Close	
3	25/05/2007	46.26	46.56	46.18	46.45	87143200	46.45	
4	24/05/2007	46.86	47.04	45.97	46.16	206268600	46.16	
5	23/05/2007	47.19	47.37	46.82	46.83	119220600	46.83	
6	22/05/2007	47.04	47.28	46.87	47.05	98029100	47.05	
7	21/05/2007	46.74	47.24	46.67	47.01	112831400	47.01	
8	18/05/2007	46.48	46.71	46.38	46.71	104961700	46.71	
9	17/05/2007	46.5	46.57	46.29	46.33	109869100	46.33	
10	16/05/2007	46.2	46.56	45.91	46.55	144420500	46.55	
11	15/05/2007	46.42	46.7	45.99	46.1	179438500	46.1	
12	14/05/2007	46.77	46.88	46.19	46.46	118899200	46.46	
13	11/05/2007	46.24	46.78	46.18	46.78	104767900	46.78	
14	10/05/2007	46.67	46.78	46.07	46.19	171196300	46.19	
15	09/05/2007	46.49	46.97	46.46	46.83	116021000	46.83	
16	08/05/2007	46.47	46.77	46.3	46.73	95138900	46.73	
17	07/05/2007	46.65	46.78	46.57	46.63	47487900	46.63	
18	04/05/2007	46.77	46.89	46.42	46.63	93591800	46.63	
19	03/05/2007	46.51	46.72	46.43	46.59	98003600	46.59	
20	02/05/2007	46.09	46.58	46.05	46.42	91971600	46.42	
21	01/05/2007	45.97	46.14	45.66	46.11	135044400	46.11	
22	30/04/2007	46.49	46.53	45.92	45.96	93290500	45.96	
23	27/04/2007	46.37	46.7	46.29	46.57	96536500	46.57	
24	26/04/2007	46.42	46.65	46.33	46.55	99308300	46.55	

If you rerun this macro, you will see that it does not completely solve the problems of data duplication and other deviant behavior. We will deal with these problems in the following pages.

41.8.5 Get Prices: The Penultimate Approximation

This version adds input routines for the number of samples and the ticker-tape symbol; once again the additions and alterations from version 3 are set in bold type on a shaded background.

```
Sub GetPricesVer4()
    Dim Ws As Worksheet      'Our query is going to be
                             'stored here
    Dim Wq As QueryTable     'This will be our query
    Dim Url As String        'Full Web address on Yahoo
    Url = _
           "URL; http://" & _
           ichart.finance.yahoo.com/table.csv?" & _
           GetTTS() & _
           GetDates() & _
           "g=d&" & _
           "ignore=.csv"
    'Use ActiveSheet for data; store reference in ws
    Set Ws = ActiveSheet
    'Add our query to the worksheet; results should
    'go to column A
    'down from A2; store reference in wq
    Set Wq = Ws.QueryTables.Add(Connection:=Url, _
                      Destination:=Ws.Range("A2"))
    'Run our query in the foreground, i.e., wait
    'for the query to finish
    Wq.Refresh BackgroundQuery:=False
    'Parse the text to columns; this is the approved
    'Microsoft way
    Wq.ResultRange.TextToColumns _
        Destination:=Wq.ResultRange.Range("A1"), _
        DataType:=xlDelimited, _
        TextQualifier:=xlDoubleQuote, _
        Comma:=True
    'Fit the column width to the data based on the
    'first 99 values
    Ws.Range("A2:G100").Columns.AutoFit
End Sub
```

```
Function GetDates()
     Const p As String = _
     "Please enter Date of last sample"
     Dim Temp
     Dim ED ' end day here
     Dim EM ' end month here
     Dim EY ' end year
     Dim SD ' start day here
     Dim SM ' start month here
     Dim SY ' start year
     Dim NDays 'the number of calendar days to sample
     'Ask for a date; use current date as a default
     Temp = InputBox(p, Title, Date)
     'Did we get the correct answer?
     'If so, use its date value; if not, use current
     'date value
     If IsDate(Temp) Then
          Temp = DateValue(Temp)
     Else
          Temp = Date
     End If
     'Get the number of calendar days to sample
     NDays = GetDays()
     ED = Day(Temp)
     EM = Month(Temp) - 1 ' Yahoo month is 0-11
     EY = Year(Temp)
     SD = Day(Temp - NDays)
     SM = Month(Temp - NDays) - 1 ' Yahoo month is
                                  ' 0-11
     SY = Year(Temp - NDays)
     GetDates = "a=" & SM & "&b=" & SD _
          & "&c" & SY & "&d=" & EM & "&e=" _
          & ED & "&f" & EY & "&"
End Function
```

And here are the two new functions **GetTTS ( )** and **GetDays ( )**:

```
Function GetTTS()
     Const p As String = _
     "Please enter" & "Ticker-Tape Symbol"
     Dim Temp
     'Ask for a TTS; use QQQQ as a default
     Temp = InputBox(p, Title, "QQQQ")
     'Did we get an answer? If so, use it; if
     'not, use "QQQQ"
     If Temp = "" Then
          Temp = "QQQQ"
     End If
     GetTTS = "s=" & Temp & "&"
End Function
```

```
Function GetDays()
     Const p As String = _
               "Please enter number of" & _
               "calendar days to sample"
     Dim Temp
     'Ask for the number of samples; use 15
     'as a default
     Temp = InputBox(p, Title, 15)
     'Did we get the correct answer? If so,
     'use it; if not, use 15
     If IsNumeric(Temp) Then
          GetDays = Temp
     Else
          GetDays = 15
     End If
End Function
```

Points of note:

• The VBA function **IsNumeric** returns TRUE if its argument is or can be converted to a numeric value; see appendix 1 for a full description.

• The variable **Title** used in the call to **InputBox** in all three user interaction functions is defined as a global constant at the beginning of the module.

Here is the macro when run:

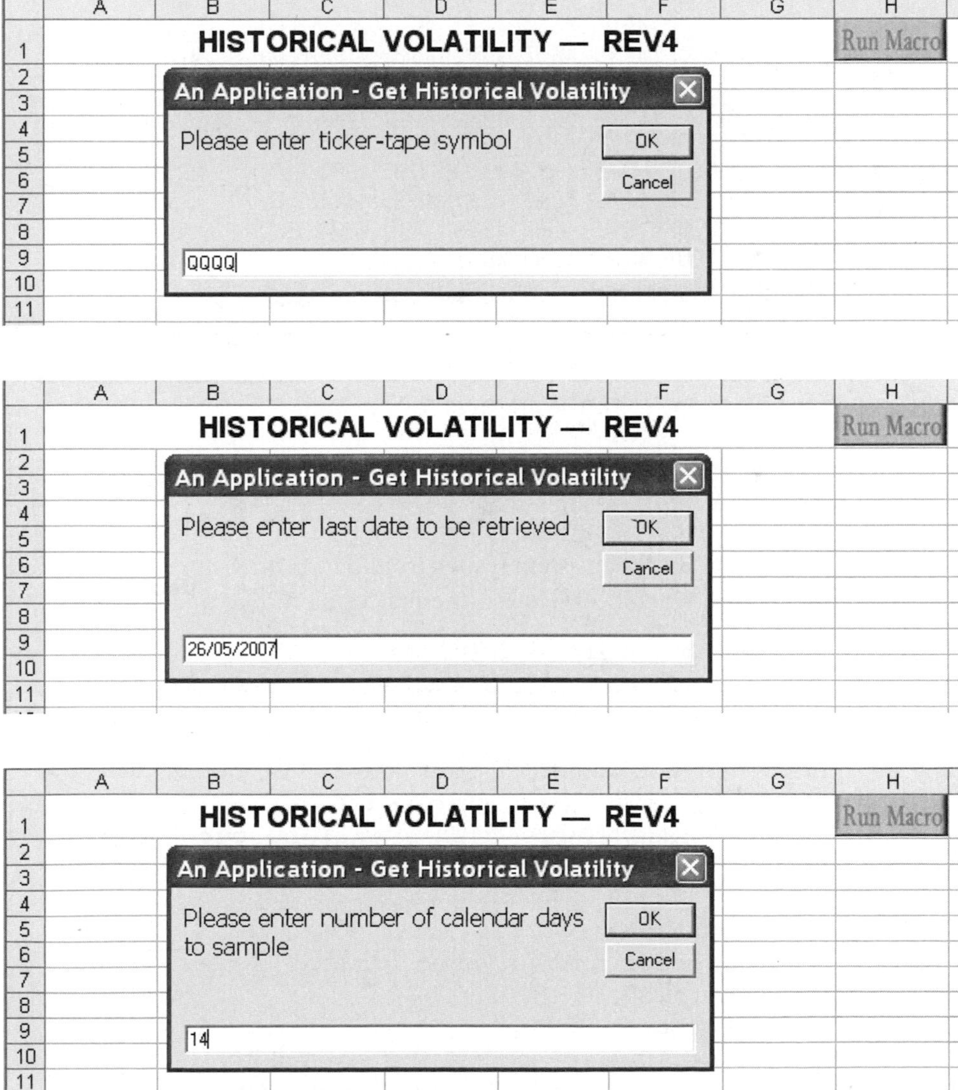

Here is the worksheet once the macro has run:

	A	B	C	D	E	F	G	H
1	HISTORICAL VOLATILITY — REV4							Run Macro
2	Date	Open	High	Low	Close	Volume	Adj Close	
3	25/05/2007	46.26	46.56	46.18	46.45	87143200	46.45	
4	24/05/2007	46.86	47.04	45.97	46.16	206268600	46.16	
5	23/05/2007	47.19	47.37	46.82	46.83	119220600	46.83	
6	22/05/2007	47.04	47.28	46.87	47.05	98029100	47.05	
7	21/05/2007	46.74	47.24	46.67	47.01	112831400	47.01	
8	18/05/2007	46.48	46.71	46.38	46.71	104961700	46.71	
9	17/05/2007	46.5	46.57	46.29	46.33	109869100	46.33	
10	16/05/2007	46.2	46.56	45.91	46.55	144420500	46.55	
11	15/05/2007	46.42	46.7	45.99	46.1	179438500	46.1	
12	14/05/2007	46.77	46.88	46.19	46.46	118899200	46.46	
13								

41.8.6 Get Prices: Using a New Worksheet for the Data

The time has come to deal with the "interesting behavior" of our macros when they are rerun. The reason behind this behavior is that Excel is trying not to overwrite information already in the worksheet. The easiest way to guarantee consistent results from our macro is for it to create and use its own worksheet. Here is the first version of a modified macro:

```
Sub GetPricesVer5()
    Dim Ws As Worksheet        'Our query is going to be
                               'stored here
    Dim Wq As QueryTable       'This will be our query
    Dim Url As String           'Full Web address on Yahoo
    Url = _
          "URL; http://" & _
          "ichart.finance.yahoo.com/table.csv?" & _
          GetTTS() & _
          GetDates() & _
          "g=d&" & _
          "ignore=.csv"
```

```
    'Create a new worksheet for the data; store
    'reference in Ws
    Set Ws = Worksheets.Add
    'Add our query to the worksheet; results should
    'go to column A
    'down from A1; store reference in wq
    Set Wq = Ws.QueryTables.Add(Connection:=Url, _
                        Destination:=Ws.Range("A1"))
    'Run our query in the foreground, i.e., wait
    'for the query to finish
    Wq.Refresh BackgroundQuery:=False
    'Parse the text to columns; this is the approved
    'Microsoft way
    Wq.ResultRange.TextToColumns _
         Destination:=Wq.ResultRange.Range("A1"), _
         DataType:=xlDelimited, _
         TextQualifier:=xlDoubleQuote, _
         Comma:=True
    'Fit the column width to the data based on the
    'first 100 values
    Ws.Range("A1:G100").Columns.AutoFit
End Sub
```

Once we run the macro, a new worksheet is added to the workbook, and the data are deposited and formatted in it. Here is the workbook before the macro is run (notice that the active worksheet is **Volatility Ver5**):

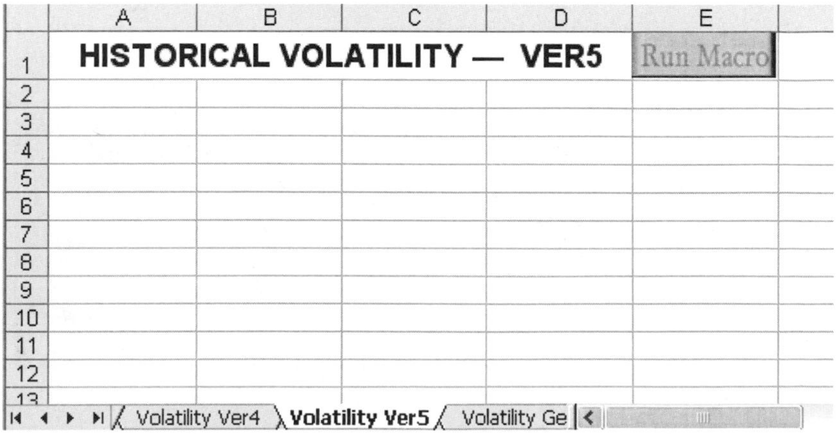

	A	B	C	D	E
1	HISTORICAL VOLATILITY — VER5				Run Macro
2					
3					
4					
5					
6					
7					
8					
9					
10					
11					
12					
13					

Volatility Ver4 | **Volatility Ver5** | Volatility Ge

Here is the macro being run:

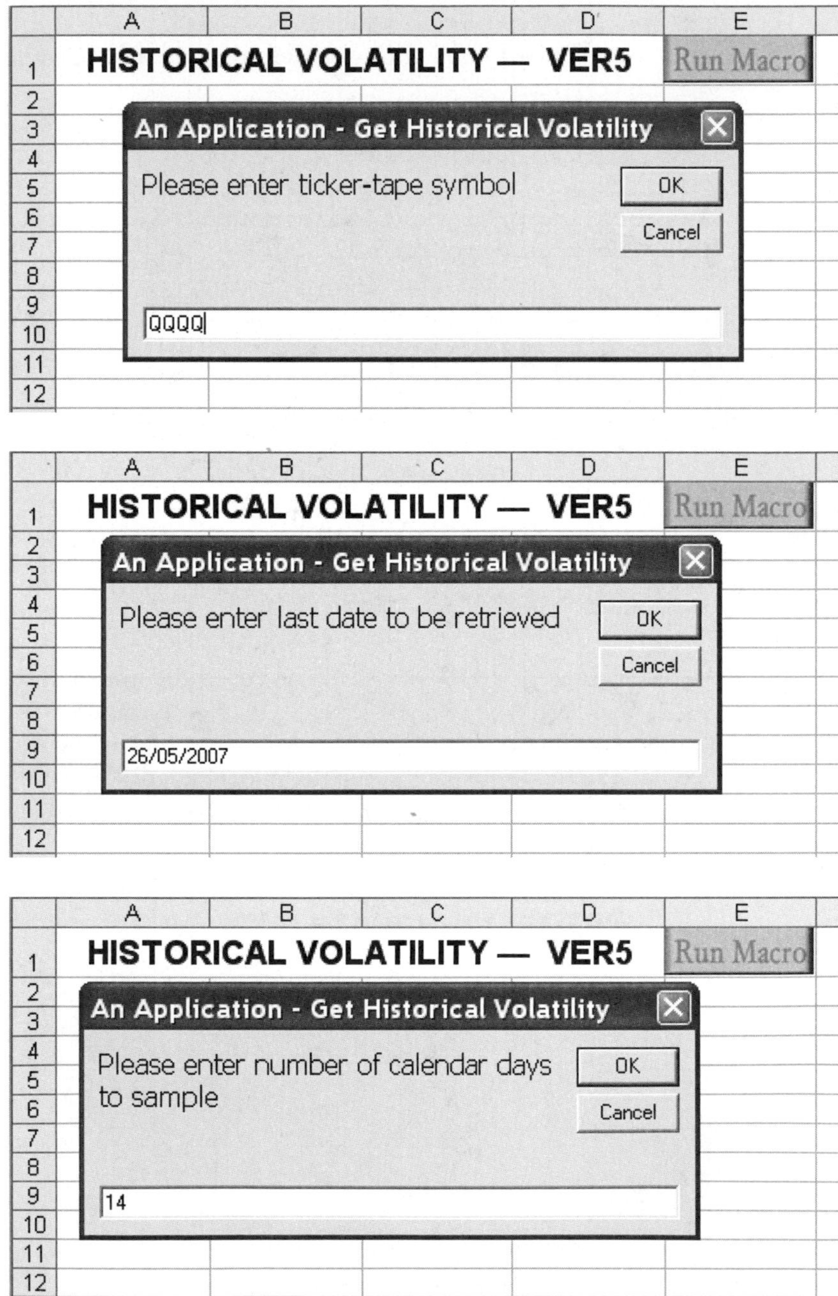

Once we click OK, a new worksheet is added. Notice that the active worksheet in the screen capture is **Sheet1**, the newly added worksheet, and not **Volatility Ver5** as before.

	A	B	C	D	E	F	G	H
1	Date	Open	High	Low	Close	Volume	Adj Close	
2	25/05/2007	46.26	46.56	46.18	46.45	87143200	46.45	
3	24/05/2007	46.86	47.04	45.97	46.16	206268600	46.16	
4	23/05/2007	47.19	47.37	46.82	46.83	119220600	46.83	
5	22/05/2007	47.04	47.28	46.87	47.05	98029100	47.05	
6	21/05/2007	46.74	47.24	46.67	47.01	112831400	47.01	
7	18/05/2007	46.48	46.71	46.38	46.71	104961700	46.71	
8	17/05/2007	46.5	46.57	46.29	46.33	109869100	46.33	
9	16/05/2007	46.2	46.56	45.91	46.55	144420500	46.55	
10	15/05/2007	46.42	46.7	45.99	46.1	179438500	46.1	
11	14/05/2007	46.77	46.88	46.19	46.46	118899200	46.46	
12								

Volatility Ver4 / **Sheet1** / Volatility Ver5 / V

If we go back to **Volatility Ver5** and rerun the macro, the same thing will happen again. For brevity, only the first and last screen captures are shown.

	A	B	C	D	E
1	**HISTORICAL VOLATILITY — VER5**				Run Macro
2					
3					
4					
5					
6					
7					
8					
9					
10					
11					

Volatility Ver4 / Sheet1 / **Volatility Ver5** / V

	A	B	C	D	E	F	G	H
1	Date	Open	High	Low	Close	Volume	Adj Close	
2	25/05/2007	46.26	46.56	46.18	46.45	87143200	46.45	
3	24/05/2007	46.86	47.04	45.97	46.16	206268600	46.16	
4	23/05/2007	47.19	47.37	46.82	46.83	119220600	46.83	
5	22/05/2007	47.04	47.28	46.87	47.05	98029100	47.05	
6	21/05/2007	46.74	47.24	46.67	47.01	112831400	47.01	
7	18/05/2007	46.48	46.71	46.38	46.71	104961700	46.71	
8	17/05/2007	46.5	46.57	46.29	46.33	109869100	46.33	
9	16/05/2007	46.2	46.56	45.91	46.55	144420500	46.55	
10	15/05/2007	46.42	46.7	45.99	46.1	179438500	46.1	
11	14/05/2007	46.77	46.88	46.19	46.46	118899200	46.46	
12								

Volatility Ver4 / Sheet1 / **Sheet2** / Volatility

Notice that a new worksheet, **Sheet2**, is added to the workbook and is the active worksheet.

Obviously, once we have made use of the data, the added worksheet should be disposed of, but this and more is the subject of the next subsection.

41.8.7 Get Returns

The next version of the macro uses a temporary worksheet for the query, calculates the returns, copies the returns to the current worksheet, and deletes the temporary worksheet.

```
Sub GetReturns()
    Dim Ws As Worksheet         'Our query is going to be
                                'stored here
    Dim Wq As QueryTable        'This will be our query
    Dim Url As String           'Full Web address on Yahoo
    Dim Cws As Worksheet        'To hold our current
                                'worksheet
    Dim Nrows As Integer        'the number of rows in the
                                'results
    Set Cws = ActiveCell.Worksheet
    Url = _
```

```
"URL;" & "http://ichart.finance.yahoo.com/table.csv?" & _
GetTTS() & _
GetDates() & _
"g=d&" & _
"ignore=.csv"
'Create a new worksheet for the data; store
'reference in ws
Set Ws = Worksheets.Add
'Add our query to the worksheet; results should
'go to column A
'down from A2; store reference in wq
Set Wq = Ws.QueryTables.Add(Connection:=Url, _
                        Destination:=Ws.Range("A1"))
'Run our query in the foreground, i.e., wait
'for the query to finish
Wq.Refresh BackgroundQuery:=False
'Parse the text to columns; this is the approved
'Microsoft way
Wq.ResultRange.TextToColumns _
     Destination:=Wq.ResultRange.Range("A1"), _
     DataType:=xlDelimited, _
     TextQualifier:=xlDoubleQuote, _
     Comma:=True
'Number of rows minus 1 = number of returns
Nrows = Wq.ResultRange.Rows.Count - 1
'insert returns formula in cloumn H down from H3
Ws.Range("H3", _
  Ws.Cells(Nrows, 8)).FormulaR1C1 =
  "=LN(R[-1]C[-1]/RC[-1])"
'Returns are in column H down from cell H3
'and for Nrows; so copy it
Ws.Range(Ws.Cells(3, 8), Ws.Cells(Nrows, 8)).Copy
Cws.Select 'this is the worksheet we started from
'Paste the values to the worksheet we started
'from
```

```
        Selection.PasteSpecial Paste:=xlPasteValues, _
                            Operation:=xlNone, _
                            SkipBlanks:=False, Transpose:=False
        'Uncomment the next line to stop Excel from
        'verifying
        'the deletion of the temporary worksheet
        'Application.DisplayAlerts = False
        'Clean up; delete the worksheet and the query
        'with it
        Ws.Delete
        Application.DisplayAlerts = True 'DO bother me
        'with questions now
End Sub
```

The formula that calculates the returns in this line

```
Ws.Range("H3", _
   Ws.Cells(Nrows, 8)).FormulaR1C1 = _
   "=LN(R[-1]C[-1]/RC[-1])"
```

uses the R1C1 style of reference. A complete explanation of this style of reference may be found in appendix 2.

And here are some screen captures of the macro in action:

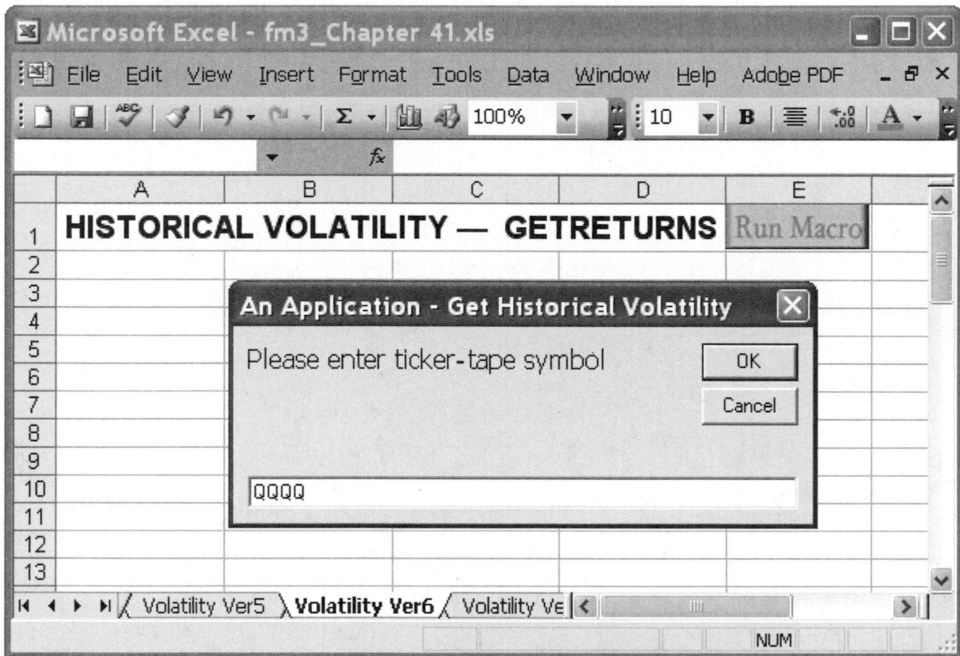
Microsoft Excel - fm3_Chapter 41.xls
File Edit View Insert Format Tools Data Window Help Adobe PDF
HISTORICAL VOLATILITY — GETRETURNS
Run Macro
An Application - Get Historical Volatility
Please enter ticker-tape symbol
OK
Cancel
QQQQ
Volatility Ver5
Volatility Ver6
NUM

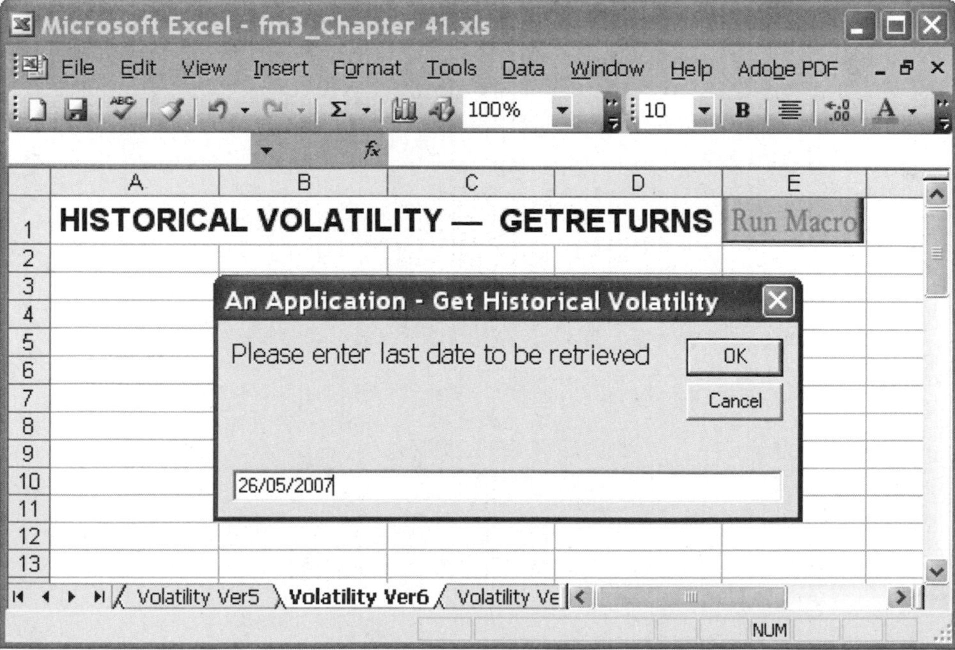
Microsoft Excel - fm3_Chapter 41.xls
File Edit View Insert Format Tools Data Window Help Adobe PDF
HISTORICAL VOLATILITY — GETRETURNS
Run Macro
An Application - Get Historical Volatility
Please enter last date to be retrieved
OK
Cancel
26/05/2007
Volatility Ver5
Volatility Ver6
NUM

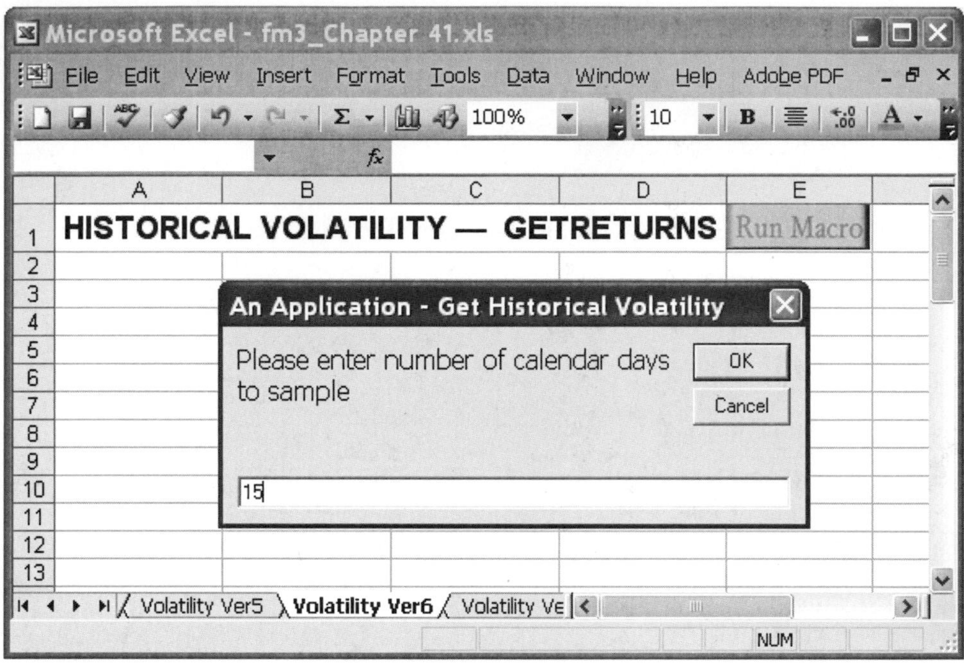
Microsoft Excel - fm3_Chapter 41.xls
File Edit View Insert Format Tools Data Window Help Adobe PDF
HISTORICAL VOLATILITY — GETRETURNS
Run Macro
An Application - Get Historical Volatility
Please enter number of calendar days to sample
OK
Cancel
15
Volatility Ver5
Volatility Ver6
NUM

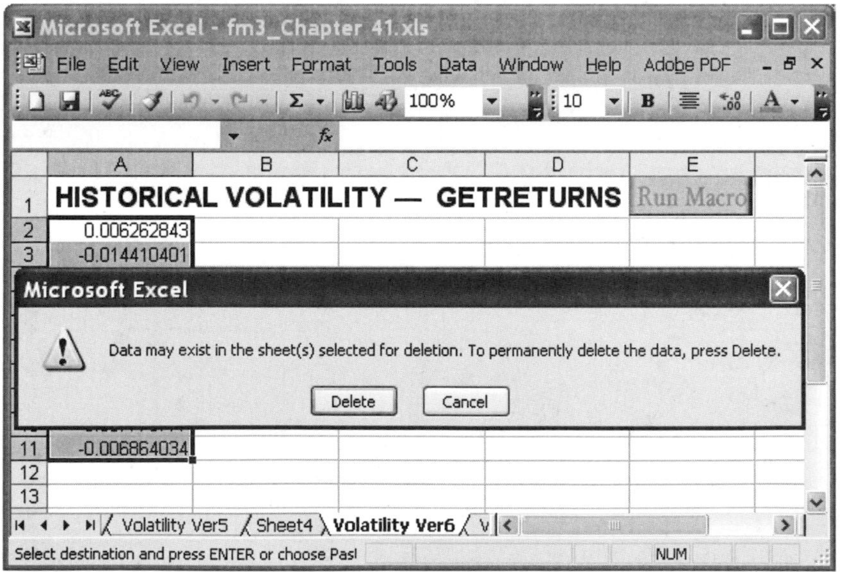
Microsoft Excel - fm3_Chapter 41.xls
File Edit View Insert Format Tools Data Window Help Adobe PDF
HISTORICAL VOLATILITY — GETRETURNS
Run Macro
0.006262843
-0.014410401
Microsoft Excel
Data may exist in the sheet(s) selected for deletion. To permanently delete the data, press Delete.
Delete
Cancel
-0.006864034
Volatility Ver5
Sheet4
Volatility Ver6
Select destination and press ENTER or choose Past
NUM

If we want to prevent Excel from querying the deletion of the temporary worksheet, we have to uncomment the following line near the end of the macro:

```
'Application.DisplayAlerts = False
```

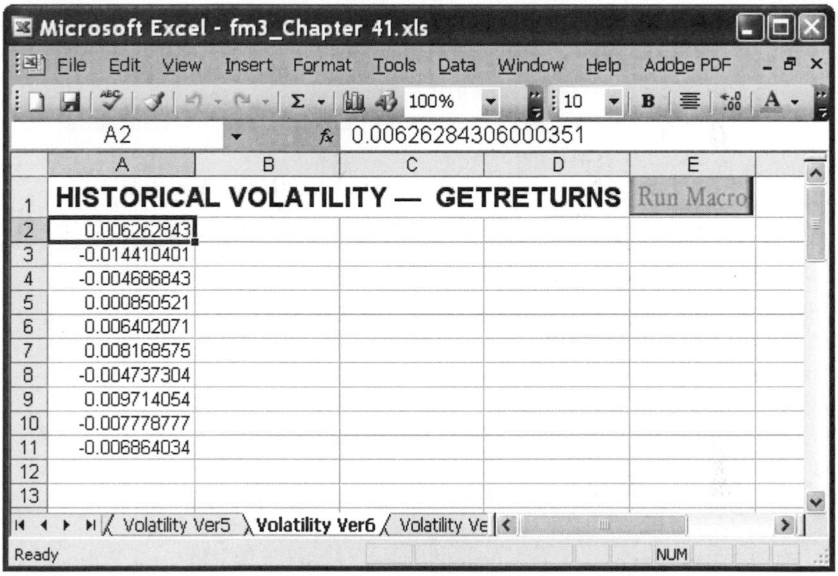

Microsoft Excel - fm3_Chapter 41.xls

A2 0.00626284306000351

	A	B	C	D	E
1	HISTORICAL VOLATILITY — GETRETURNS				Run Macro
2	0.006262843				
3	-0.014410401				
4	-0.004686843				
5	0.000850521				
6	0.006402071				
7	0.008168575				
8	-0.004737304				
9	0.009714054				
10	-0.007778777				
11	-0.006864034				
12					
13					

Volatility Ver5 | Volatility Ver6 | Volatility Ve

41.8.8 Get Volatility

The next version of the macro calculates the historical volatility using the array function from Chapter 19:

```
Sub GetVolatility()
    Dim Ws As Worksheet        'Our query is going to be
                               'stored here
    Dim Wq As QueryTable       'This will be our query
    Dim Url As String          'Full Web address on Yahoo
    Dim Cws As Worksheet       'To hold our current
                               'worksheet
```

```
Dim N As Integer        'A temporary number
Set Cws = ActiveCell.Worksheet
Url = _
       "URL; "http://" & _
       "ichart.finance.yahoo.com/table.csv?" & _
       GetTTS() & _
       GetDates() & _
       "g=d&" & _
       "ignore=.csv"
'Create a new worksheet for the data; store
'reference in ws
Set Ws = Worksheets.Add
'Add our query to the worksheet; results should
'go to column A
'down from A2; store reference in wq
Set Wq = Ws.QueryTables.Add(Connection:=Url, _
                       Destination:=Ws.Range("A1"))
'Run our query in the foreground, i.e.,
'wait for the query to finish
Wq.Refresh BackgroundQuery:=False
'Parse the text to columns; this is the approved
'Microsoft way
Wq.ResultRange.TextToColumns _
     Destination:=Wq.ResultRange.Range("A1"), _
     DataType:=xlDelimited, _
     TextQualifier:=xlDoubleQuote, _
     Comma:=True
N = Wq.ResultRange.Rows.Count - 4
'Insert volatility formula as an array formula in
'H3
Ws.Range("H3").FormulaArray = _
      "=SQRT(250)*STDEVP(LN(R[-1]C[-1]:R[" & _
      N - 1 & "]C[-1]/RC[-1]:R[" & N & "]C[-1]))"
Ws.Range("H3").Copy
Cws.Select 'This is the worksheet we started from
```

```
    'Paste the values to the worksheet we started
    'from
    Selection.PasteSpecial Paste:=xlPasteValues, _
                    Operation:=xlNone, _
                    SkipBlanks:=False, Transpose:=False
    Application.DisplayAlerts = False
    'Clean up; delete the worksheet and the query
    'with it
    Ws.Delete
    Application.DisplayAlerts = True 'DO bother me
    'with questions now
End Sub
```

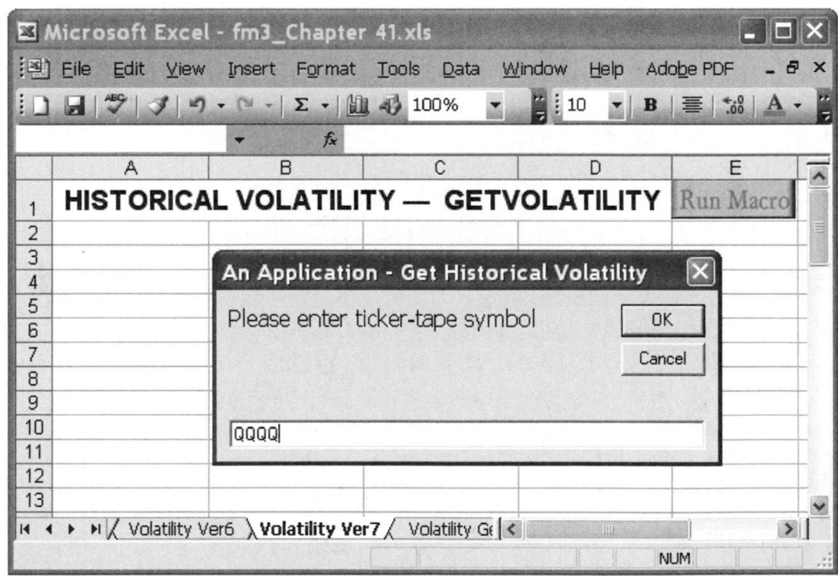

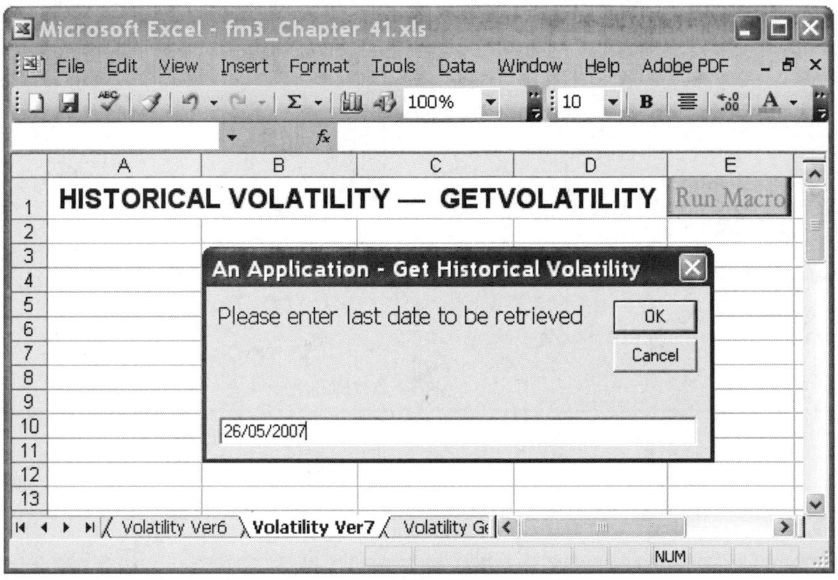
Microsoft Excel - fm3_Chapter 41.xls
File Edit View Insert Format Tools Data Window Help Adobe PDF
100%
10
HISTORICAL VOLATILITY — GETVOLATILITY
Run Macro
An Application - Get Historical Volatility
Please enter last date to be retrieved
OK
Cancel
26/05/2007
Volatility Ver6
Volatility Ver7
NUM

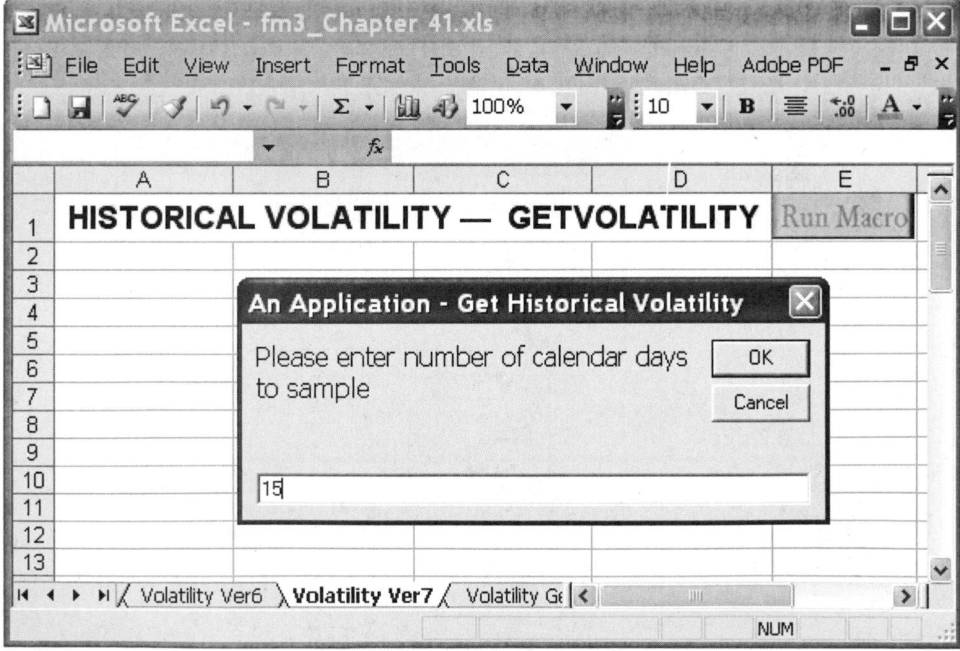
Microsoft Excel - fm3_Chapter 41.xls
File Edit View Insert Format Tools Data Window Help Adobe PDF
100%
10
HISTORICAL VOLATILITY — GETVOLATILITY
Run Macro
An Application - Get Historical Volatility
Please enter number of calendar days to sample
OK
Cancel
15
Volatility Ver6
Volatility Ver7
NUM

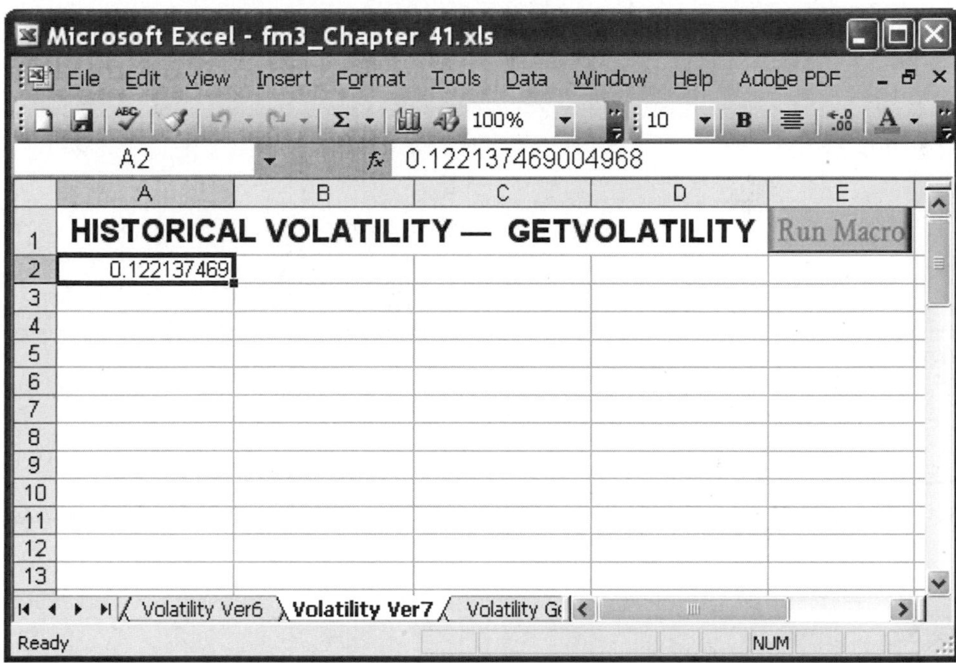

41.9 Summary

This chapter has covered the basics of the importation of data from the Web into Excel. The automation of the import process using VBA can include a myriad of applications. In the disk with this book we include a file (**fm3_chapter41_var_covar.xls**) that shows a more sophisticated application—the import of price data for the computation of the sample variance-covariance matrix discussed in Chapter 10. The sky is the limit.

Exercises

1. Create a query on the active worksheet to retrieve the current exchange rate from U.S. dollars to British pounds. Hint: See http://finance.yahoo.com/currency or http://uk.moneycentral.msn.com/investor/market/rates.asp for the rates.

2. Write macro to create the query in exercise 1. Hint: One way to do this might be to record the macro, subsequently changing it to make it work better.

3. Write a macro that takes the value of the currently selected cell, converts it from U.S. dollars to British pounds, and deposits the result as a value in the cell to the right of the currently selected cell. You may assume that a worksheet called "temp" in the current workbook can be used as a temporary storage space for the required query. Hint: As exercise 2, recording the macro and changing the recorded result might be the way to go.

4. Rewrite the macro from exercise 3. Use a new worksheet as a temporary storage space for the required query and delete it before the macro exists. Check that the input is a number. If the output cell is not empty, ask the user if it is OK to overwrite it.

Appendix 1: Excerpts from the Help File

The content of this appendix is a lightly edited version of the Excel VBA Help file, supplying technical information about objects and concepts covered in this chapter.

IsNumeric Function

Returns a Boolean value indicating whether an expression can be evaluated as a number.

Syntax
IsNumeric(expression)
The required expression argument is a Variant containing a numeric expression or string expression.

Remarks
IsNumeric returns True if the entire expression is recognized as a number; otherwise, it returns False. IsNumeric returns False if expression is a date expression.

IsDate Function

Returns a Boolean value indicating whether an expression can be converted to a date.

Syntax
IsDate(expression)
The required expression argument is a Variant containing a date expression or string expression recognizable as a date or time.

Remarks
IsDate returns True if the expression is a date or is recognizable as a valid date; otherwise, it returns False. In Microsoft Windows, the range of valid dates is January 1, 100, through December 31, 9999; the ranges vary among operating systems.

DateValue Function

Returns a Variant (Date).

Syntax
DateValue(date)

The required date argument is normally a string expression representing a date from January 1, 100, through December 31, 9999. However, date can also be any expression that can represent a date, a time, or both a date and time, in that range.

Remarks
If date is a string that includes only numbers separated by valid date separators, DateValue recognizes the order for month, day, and year according to the Short Date format you specified for your system. DateValue also recognizes unambiguous dates that contain month names, in either long or abbreviated form. For example, in addition to recognizing 12/30/1991 and 12/30/91, DateValue also recognizes December 30, 1991, and Dec 30, 1991.

If the year part of date is omitted, DateValue uses the current year from your computer's system date. If the date argument includes time information, DateValue doesn't return it. However, if date includes invalid time information (such as "89:98"), an error occurs.

DateSerial Function

Returns a Variant (Date) for a specified year, month, and day.

Syntax
DateSerial(year, month, day)

The DateSerial function syntax has these named arguments:

Part	Description
Year	Required; Integer. Number between 100 and 9999, inclusive, or a numeric expression.
Month	Required; Integer. Any numeric expression.
Day	Required; Integer. Any numeric expression.

Remarks

To specify a date, such as December 31, 1991, the range of numbers for each DateSerial argument should be in the accepted range for the unit; that is, 1–31 for days and 1–12 for months. However, you can also specify relative dates for each argument using any numeric expression that represents some number of days, months, or years before or after a certain date.The following example uses numeric expressions instead of absolute date numbers. Here the DateSerial function returns a date that is the day before the first day (1 – 1), two months before August (8 – 2), and 10 years before 1990 (1990 – 10); in other words, May 31, 1980:

DateSerial(1990 – 10, 8 – 2, 1 – 1).

When any argument exceeds the accepted range for that argument, it increments to the next larger unit as appropriate. For example, if you specify 35 days, it is evaluated as one month and some number of days, depending on where in the year it is applied. If any single argument is outside the range –32,768 to 32,767, an error occurs. If the date specified by the three arguments falls outside the acceptable range of dates, an error occurs.

Note For year, month, and day, if the Calendar property setting is Gregorian, the supplied value is assumed to be Gregorian.

Day Function

Returns a Variant (Integer) specifying a whole number between 1 and 31, inclusive, representing the day of the month.

Syntax

Day(date)

The required date argument is any Variant, numeric expression, string expression, or any combination, that can represent a date. If date contains Null, Null is returned.

Month Function

Returns a Variant (Integer) specifying a whole number between 1 and 12, inclusive, representing the month of the year.

Syntax
Month(date)

The required date argument is any Variant, numeric expression, string expression, or any combination, that can represent a date. If date contains Null, Null is returned.

Year Function

Returns a Variant (Integer) containing a whole number representing the year.

Syntax
Year(date)

The required date argument is any Variant, numeric expression, string expression, or any combination, that can represent a date. If date contains Null, Null is returned.

Appendix 2: The R1C1 Reference Style

You can also use a reference style where both the rows and the columns on the worksheet are numbered. The R1C1 reference style is useful for computing row and column positions in macros. In the R1C1 style, Excel indicates the location of a cell with an R followed by a row number and a C followed by a column number.

Reference	Meaning
R[−2]C	A relative reference to the cell two rows up and in the same column
R[2]C[2]	A relative reference to the cell two rows down and two columns to the right
R2C2	An absolute reference to the cell in the second row and in the second column
R[−1]	A relative reference to the entire row above the active cell
R	An absolute reference to the current row

When you record a macro, Excel records some commands by using the R1C1 reference style. For example, if you record a command such as clicking the **AutoSum** button to insert a formula that adds a range of cells, Excel records the formula by using R1C1-style, not A1-style, references.

To turn R1C1 reference style on or off,

Click **Options** on the **Tools** menu, and then click the **General** tab.

Under **Settings**, select or clear the **R1C1 reference style** check box.

Selected References

This bibliography is not intended to be extensive. We give the references cited in *Financial Modeling*, and we also include a limited number of books and articles that may help readers expand their horizons to more advanced topics. On occasion the same reference appears several times in different sections.

Chapters 1–5: Corporate Finance and Valuation

Benninga, S., and O. Sarig. 2003. Risk, Returns, and Values in the Presence of Differential Taxation. *Journal of Banking and Finance*, 27.

Benninga, S. Z., and O. H. Sarig. 1997. *Corporate Finance: A Valuation Approach*. McGraw-Hill.

Brealey, R. A., S. C. Myers, and F. Allen. 2005. *Principles of Corporate Finance*, 8th ed. McGraw-Hill.

Dittmar, A. K., and R. F. Dittmar. 2004. Stock Repurchase Waves: An Explanation of the Trends in Aggregate Corporate Payout Policy. Working paper, University of Michigan.

Gordon, M. J. 1959. Dividends, Earnings, and Stock Prices. *Review of Economics and Statistics*, 41.

McKinsey and Company, T. Koller, M. Goedhart, and D. Wessels, 2005. *Valuation: Measuring and Managing the Value of Companies*, 4th ed. Wiley.

Ross, S. A., R. W. Westerfield, and J. Jaffe. 2004. *Corporate Finance*, 7th ed. McGraw-Hill/Irwin.

Chapters 6–7: Leasing

Abdel-Khalik, R. 1981. *Economic Effects on Lessees of FASB*. Statement No. 13, Accounting for Leases. Stamford, CT: Financial Accounting Standards Board.

Copeland, T. E., and J. F. Weston. 1982. A Note on the Evaluation of Cancelable Operating Leases. *Financial Management*, 11.

El-Gazzar, S., S. Lilien, and V. Pastena. 1986. Accounting for Leases by Lessees. *Journal of Accounting and Economics*, 8.

Financial Accounting Standards Board, 1976. Statement No. 13, Accounting for Leases. Stamford, CT.

Franks, J. R., and S. D. Hodges. 1978. Valuation of Financial Lease Contracts: A Note. *Journal of Finance*, 33.

Levy, H., and M. Sarnat. 1979. On Leasing, Borrowing, and Financial Risk. *Financial Management*, winter.

Lewellen, W. G., M. S. Long, and J. J. McConnell. 1979. Asset Leasing in Competitive Capital Markets. *Journal of Finance*, 31.

McConnell, J. J., and J. S. Schallheim. 1983. Valuation of Asset Leasing Contracts. *Journal of Financial Economics*, 12.

Miller, M. H., and C. W. Upton. 1976. Leasing, Buying, and the Cost of Capital Services. *Journal of Finance*, 31.

Myers, S. C., D. A. Dill, and A. J. Bautista. 1976. Valuation of Financial Lease Contracts. *Journal of Finance*, 31.

Nakayama, M., S. Lilien, and M. Benis. 1981. Due Process and FAS No. 13. *Management Accounting*, 52.

Ofer, A. R. 1976. The Evaluation of the Lease versus Purchase Alternative. *Financial Management*, 5.

Schallheim, James S. 1994. *Lease or Buy? Principles for Sound Decision Making*, Harvard Business School.

Chapters 8–12: Portfolio Basics

Bengtsson, C., and J. Holst. 2002. On Portfolio Selection: Improved Covariance Matrix Estimation for Swedish Asset Returns. Working paper, Lund University and Lund Institute of Technology.

Black, F. 1972. Capital Market Equilibrium with Restricted Borrowing. *Journal of Business*, 45.

Bodie, Z., A. Kane, and A. J. Marcus. 2004, *Investments*, 6th ed. McGraw-Hill/Irwin.

Chan, L., J. Karceski, and J. Lakonishok. 1999. On Portfolio Estimation: Forecasting Covariances and Choosing the Risk Model. *Review of Financial Studies,* 12.

Disatnik, D. J., and S. Benninga. 2007. Shrinking the Covariance Matrix: Simpler Is Better. *Journal of Portfolio Management*, 33.

Efron, B., and C. Morris. 1977. Stein's Paradox in Statistics. *Scientific American,* 236.

Elton, E. J., M. J. Gruber, and T. Ulrich. 1978. Are Betas Best? *Journal of Finance*, 23.

Elton, E. J., M. J. Gruber, S. J. Brown, and W. N. Goetzmann. 2004. *Modern Portfolio Theory and Investment Analysis*, 6th ed. Wiley.

Fama, E., and K. French. 1997. Industry Costs of Equity. *Journal of Financial Economics,* 43.

Frost, P., and J. Savarino. 1986. An Empirical Bayes Approach to Efficient Portfolio Selection. *Journal of Financial and Quantitative Analysis,* 21.

D'Avolio, G. 2002. The Market for Borrowing Stock. *Journal of Financial Economics*, 66.

Green, R., and B. Hollifield. 1992. When Will Mean-Variance Efficient Portfolios Be Well Diversified? *Journal of Finance,* 47.

Green, R. C. 1986. Positively Weighted Portfolios on the Minimum-Variance Frontier. *Journal of Finance*, 41.

Haugen, R. A. 1997. *Modern Investment Theory*. Prentice Hall.

Jagannathan, R., and T. Ma. 2003. Risk Reduction in Large Portfolios: Why Imposing the Wrong Constraints Helps. *Journal of Finance,* 44.

Jensen, M. C., ed., 1972. *Studies in the Theory of Capital Markets*. New York: Praeger.

Jobson, J., and B. Korkie. 1981. Putting Markovitz Theory to Work. *Journal of Portfolio Management,* 7.

Jorion, P. 1986. Bayes-Stein Estimation of Portfolio Analysis. *Journal of Financial and Quantitative Analysis,* 213.

Ledoit, O., and M. Wolf. 2003. Improved Estimation of the Covariance Matrix of Stock Returns with an Application to Portfolio Selection. *Journal of Empirical Finance,* 10.

Ledoit, O., and M. Wolf. 2004. A Well-Conditioned Estimator for Large-Dimensional Covariance Matrices. *Journal of Multivariate Analysis,* 88.

Ledoit, O., and M. Wolf. 2004. Honey, I Shrunk the Sample Covariance Matrix. *Journal of Portfolio Management*, 31.

Lintner, J. 1965. The Valuation of Risky Assets and the Selection of Risky Investments in Stock Portfolios and Capital Budgets. *Review of Economics and Statistics*, 47.

Malkiel, B. G. 2005. Reflections on the Efficient Market Hypothesis: 30 Years Later. *Financial Review*, 40.

Markowitz, H. M. 1952. Portfolio selection. *Journal of Finance,* 7.

Merton, R. C. 1973. An Analytic Derivation of the Efficient Portfolio Frontier. *Journal of Financial and Quantitative Analysis*, 7.

Michaud, R. 1989. The Markowitz Optimization Enigma: Is Optimized Optimal? *Financial Analysts Journal,* 45.

Michaud, R. 1998. *Efficient Asset Management: A Practical Guide to Stock Portfolio Optimization and Asset Allocation*. Boston: Harvard Business School Press.

Mossin, J. 1966. Equilibrium in a Capital Market. *Econometrica*, 34.

Nielsen, L. T. 1987. Positively Weighted Frontier Portfolios: A Note. *Journal of Finance*, 42.

Press, W. H., B. P. Flannery, S. A. Teukolsky, and W. T. Vetterling. 1986. *Numerical Recipes: The Art of Scientific Computing*. Cambridge University Press.

Roll, R. 1977. A Critique of the Asset Pricing Theory's Tests, Part I: On Past and Potential Testability of the Theory. *Journal of Financial Economics*, 4.

Roll, R. 1978. Ambiguity When Performance Is Measured by the Securities Market Line. *Journal of Finance*, 33.

Sharpe, W. F. 1963. A Simplified Model for Portfolio Analysis. *Management Science*, 9.

Sharpe, W. F. 1964. Capital Asset Prices: A Theory of Market Equilibrium under Conditions of Risk. *Journal of Finance*, 19.

Stein, C. 1955. Inadmissibility of the Usual Estimator for the Mean of a Multivariate Normal Distribution. *Proceedings of the Third Berkeley Symposium on Probability and Statistics.* Berkeley: University of California Press.

Surowiecki, J. 2003. Get Shorty. *New Yorker* magazine. http://newyorker.com/talk/content/?031201ta_talk_surowiecki .

Wolf, M. 2004. Resampling vs. Shrinkage for Benchmarked Managers. Working paper, Department of Economics and Business, Universitat Pompeu Fabra.

Chapter 13: Black-Litterman

Best, M. J., and R. R. Grauer. 1985. Capital Asset Pricing Compatible with Observed Market Value Weights. *Journal of Finance*, 40.

Best, M. J., and R. R. Grauer. 1991. On the Sensitivity of Mean-Variance-Efficient Portfolios to Changes in Asset Means: Some Analytical and Computational Results. *Review of Financial Studies*, 2.

Bevan, A., and K. Winkelmann. 1998. Using the Black-Litterman Global Asset Allocation Model: Three Years of Practical Experience. Goldman Sachs.

Black, F., and R. Litterman. 1991. Global Asset Allocation with Equities, Bonds, and Currencies. Goldman Sachs.

Carhart, M. M. 2000. Forecasting the Size and Value Risk Premia. Powerpoint presentation available on Web. http://leeds.colorado.edu/uploadedFiles/FacultyandResearch/ResearchCenters/BurridgeCenterforSecuritiesAnalysisandValuation/Conferences/2000/carhart.ppt

Chopra, V., and William Ziemba. 1993. The Effect of Errors in Means, Variances, and Covariances on Optimal Portfolio Choice. *Journal of Portfolio Management*, 19.

DeMiguel, V., L. Garlappi, and R. Uppal. 2007. Optimal versus Naive Diversification: How Inefficient Is the 1/*N* Portfolio Strategy? *Review of Financial Studies*, 21.

Frost, P. A., and J. E. Savarino. 1986. An Empirical Bayes Approach to Portfolio Selection. *Journal of Financial and Quantitative Analysis*, 21.

Goldman Sachs. 1999. The Intuition Behind Black-Litterman Model Portfolios.

Jagannathan, R., and T. Ma. 2003. Risk Reduction in Large Portfolios: Why Imposing the Wrong Constraint Helps. *Journal of Finance*, 54.

Jorion, P. 1986. Bayes-Stein Estimation for Portfolio Analysis. *Journal of Financial and Quantitative Analysis*, 21.

Kandel, S., and R. F. Stambaugh. 1995. Portfolio Inefficiency and the Cross-Section of Expected Returns. *Journal of Finance*, 50.

Litterman, R. 2003. *Modern Investment Management: An Equilibrium Approach*. Wiley.

Satchell, S., and A. Scowcroft. 2000. A Demystification of the Black–Litterman Model: Managing Quantitative and Traditional Portfolio Construction. *Journal of Asset Management*, 1.

Stambaugh, R. 2000. Optimization and Views about Expected Returns: The Black-Litterman Model. Wharton class note.

Chapter 14: Event Studies

Ball, C., and W. Torous. 1988. Investigating Security Price Performance in the Presence of Event Date Uncertainty. *Journal of Financial Economics*, 22.

Binder, J. 1985. On the Use of the Multivariate Regression Model in Event Studies. *Journal of Accounting Research*, 23.

Boehmer, E., J. Musumeci, and A. Poulsen. 1991. Event- Study Methodology under Conditions of Event-Induced Variance. *Journal of Financial Economics*, 30.

Brown, S., and J. Warner. 1985. Using Daily Stock Returns: The Case of Event Studies. *Journal of Financial Economics*, 14.

Campbell, J. Y., A. W. Lo, and A. C. McKinley. 1996. *The Econometrics of Financial Markets*. Princeton University Press.

Fama, E., L. Fisher, M. Jensen, and R. Roll. 1969. The Adjustment of Stock Prices to New Information. *International Economic Review*, 10.

MacKinlay, A. C. 1997. Event Studies in Economics and Finance. *Journal of Economic Literature*, 35.

Malatesta, P. 1986. Measuring Abnormal Performance: The Event Parameter Approach Using Joint Generalized Least Squares. *Journal of Financial and Quantitative Analysis*, 21.

Salinger, Michael. 1992. Value Event Studies. *Review of Economics and Statistics*, 74.

Scholes, M., and J. Williams. 1977. Estimating Betas from Nonsynchronous Data. *Journal of Financial Economics*, 5.

Sefcik, S., and R. Thompson. 1986. An Approach to Statistical Inference in Cross-Sectional Models with Security Abnormal Returns as Dependent Variable. *Journal of Accounting Research*, 24.

Thompson, R. 1985. Conditioning the Return-Generating Process on Firm Specific Events: A Discussion of Event Study Methods, *Journal of Financial and Quantitative Analysis*, 20.

Thompson, R. 1995. Empirical Methods of Event Studies in Corporate Finance. Chapter 29 in *Handbooks in Operations Research and Management Science*, vol. 9, ed. R. Jarrow et al. Elsevier Science.

Chapter 15: Value at Risk

Beder T. 1996. VAR: Seductive but Dangerous. *Financial Analyst Journal*, 52.

Hull, J. C. 2006. *Options, Futures, and Other Derivatives*, 6th ed. Prentice Hall.

Jorion, P. 1997. *Value at Risk, the New Benchmark for Controlling Market Risk*. McGraw-Hill.

Linsmeier, T., and N. Pearson. 1997. Risk Measurement: An Introduction to Value at Risk. Mimeo, University of Illinois.

RiskMetrics, Introduction to RiskMetrics™. 1995. This and other documents can be found at http://www.riskmetrics.com/techdoc.html.

Chapters 16–21: Options and Portfolio Insurance

Benninga, S., and M. Blume. 1985. On the Optimality of Portfolio Insurance. *Journal of Finance*, 40.

Benninga, S., R. Steinmetz, and J. Stroughair. 1993. Implementing Numerical Option Pricing Models. *Mathematica Journal*, 3.

Bhaghat, S., J. Brickley, and U. Loewenstein. 1987. The Pricing Effects of Interfirm Cash Tender Offers. *Journal of Finance*, 42.

Billingsley, P. 1968. *Convergence of Probability Measures*. Wiley.

Black, F., and M. Scholes. 1973. The Pricing of Options and Corporate Liabilities. *Journal of Political Economy*, 81.

Bodie, Z., A. Kane, and A. J. Marcus. 2004. *Investments*, 6th ed. Irwin.

Brennan, M. J., and E. S. Schwartz. 1979. Alternative Investment Strategies for the Issuers of Equity-Linked Life Insurance Policies with an Asset Value Guarantee. *Journal of Business*, 52.

Brennan, M. J., and E. S. Schwartz. 1976. The Pricing of Equity-Linked Life Insurance Policies with an Asset Value Guarantee. *Journal of Financial Economics*, 3.

Brennan, M. J., and R. Solanki. 1981. Optimal Portfolio Insurance. *Journal of Financial and Quantitative Analysis*, 16.

Copeland, T. E., J. F. Weston, and J. Shastri. 2003. *Financial Theory and Corporate Policy*. Pearson.

Cox, J., and M. Rubinstein. 1985. *Options Markets*. Prentice Hall.

Cox, J., and S. A. Ross. 1976. The Valuation of Options for Alternative Stochastic Processes. *Journal of Financial Economics*, 3.

Cox, J., S. A. Ross, and M. Rubinstein. 1979. Option Pricing: A Simplified Approach. *Journal of Financial Economics*, 7.

Cvitanić, J., Z. Wiener, and F. Zapatero. 2007. Analytic Pricing of Employee Stock Options. *Review of Financial Studies*, 21.

Gatto, M. A., R. Geske, R. Litzenberger, and H. Sosin. 1980. Mutual Fund Insurance. *Journal of Financial Economics*, 8.

Haug, E. G. 2006. The Complete Guide to Option Pricing Formulas, 2nd ed. McGraw-Hill.

Hull, J. 2006. *Options Futures, and Other Derivative Securities*, 6th ed. Prentice Hall.

Hull, J., and A. White. 2004. How to Value Employee Stock Options. *Financial Analysts Journal*, 60.

Jacobs, B. 1983. The Portfolio Insurance Puzzle. *Pensions and Investment Age*, 26.

Jacques, W. E. 1987. Portfolio Insurance or Job Insurance? *Financial Analysts Journal*, 7.

Jarrow, R. A., and A. Rudd. 1983. *Option Pricing*. Irwin.

Knuth, D. E. 1981. *The Art of Computer Programming,* vol. 2: *Seminumerical Algorithms*, 2nd ed. Addison-Wesley.

Leland, H. E. 1980. Who Should Buy Portfolio Insurance? *Journal of Finance*, 35.

Leland, H. E. 1985. Option Pricing and Replication with Transaction Costs. *Journal of Finance*, 40.

Merton, R. 1973. Theory of Rational Option Pricing. *Bell Journal of Economics and Management Science*, 4.

Merton, R. 1976. Option Pricing When Underlying Stock Returns Are Discontinuous. *Journal of Financial Economics*, 3.

Omberg, E. 1987. A Note on the Convergence of Binomial-Pricing and Compound-Option Models. *Journal of Finance*, 42.

Pozen, R. C. 1978. When to Purchase a Protective Put. *Financial Analysts Journal*, 34.

Rubinstein, M. 1985. Alternative Paths to Portfolio Insurance. *Financial Analysts Journal*, 41.

Rubinstein, M., and H. E. Leland. 1981. Replicating Options with Positions in Stock and Cash. *Financial Analysts Journal*, 37.

Schwartz, E. S. 1986–87. Options and Portfolio Insurance. *Finanzmarkt und Portfolio Management*, 1.

Somes, S. P., and M. A. Zurack. 1987. Pension Plans, Portfolio Insurance, and FASB Statement No. 87: An Old Risk in a New Light. *Financial Analysts Journal*, 33.

Taleb, N. N. 1997. *Dynamic Hedging: Managing Vanilla and Exotic Options*. Wiley.

Chapters 22–23: Monte Carlo

Acworth, P., M. Broadie, and P. Glasserman. 1996. A Comparison of Some Monte Carlo and Quasi–Monte Carlo Techniques for Option Pricing. In H. Niederreiter et al., eds., *Monte Carlo and Quasi–Monte Carlo Methods*. Springer-Verlag, Lectures Notes in Statistics.

Bailey, D. H., J. M. Borwein, and P. B. Borwein. 1987. Ramanujan, Modular Equations, and Approximations to π Or How to Compute One Billion Digits of Pi. *American Mathematical Monthly*, 96.

Barone-Adesi, G., and R. E. Whaley. 1987. Efficient Analytic Approximation of American Option Values. *Journal of Finance*, 42.

Boyle, P., M. Broadie, and P. Glasserman. 1997. Monte Carlo Methods for Security Pricing *Journal of Economic Dynamics and Control*, 21.

Boyle, P. 1977. Options: A Monte Carlo Approach. *Journal of Financial Economics*, 4.

Boyle, P. P., A. W. Kolkiewicz, and K. S. Tan. 2002. Pricing American Derivatives Using Simulation: A Biased Low Approach. In K.-T. Fang, F. J. Hickernell, and H. Niederreiter, eds., *Monte Carlo and Quasi–Monte Carlo Methods 2000.* Springer-Verlag.

Boyle, P., and S. H. Lau. 1994. Bumping Up Against the Barrier with the Binomial Method. *Journal of Derivatives,* 2.

Boyle, P. P., and Y. K. Tse. 1990. An Algorithm for Computing Values of Options on the Maximum or Minimum of Several Assets. *Journal of Financial and Quantitative Analysis*, 25.

Broadie, M., and P. Glasserman. 1997. Pricing American-Style Securities Using Simulation. *Journal of Economic Dynamics and Control*, 21.

Broadie, M., P. Glasserman, and G. Jain. 1997. Enhanced Monte Carlo Estimates for American Option Prices. *Journal of Derivatives*, 5.

Broadie, M., P. Glasserman, and S. Kou. 1997. A Continuity Correction for Discrete Barrier Options. *Mathematical Finance*, 7.

Douady, R. 2001. Bermudan Option Pricing with Monte-Carlo Methods. In Marco Avellaneda, ed., *Quantitative Analysis in Financial Markets,* vol. 3. World Scientific Publishing.

Duffie, D., and P. Glynn. 1995. Efficient Monte Carlo Simulation of Security Prices. *Annals of Applied Probability*, 5.

Dupire, B., and A. Savine. 1998: Dimension Reduction and Other Ways of Speeding Monte Carlo Simulation. In Dupire, B. ed., *Monte Carlo—Methodologies and Applications for Pricing and Risk Management*. Risk Books.

Fu, M. C., S. B. Laprise, D. B. Madan, Y. Su, and R. Wu. 2001. Pricing American Options: A Comparison of Monte Carlo Simulation Approaches. *Journal of Computational Finance*, 4.

Gentle, J. E. 1998. *Random Number Generation and Monte Carlo Methods.* Springer-Verlag.

Glasserman, P. 2004. *Monte Carlo Methods in Financial Engineering*. Springer-Verlag.

Ibáñez, A. 2004. Valuation by Simulation of Contingent Claims with Multiple Early Exercises Opportunities. *Mathematical Finance*, 14.

Jäckel, P. 2002. *Monte Carlo Methods in Finance*. Wiley.

Joy, C., P. P. Boyle, and K. S. Tan. 1996. Quasi–Monte Carlo Methods in Numerical Finance. *Management Science*, 42.

Kanigel, Robert. 1991. *The Man Who Knew Infinity: A Life of the Genius Ramanujan*. Charles Scribner.

Knuth, D. E. 1998. *The Art of Computer Programming*, vol. 2: *Seminumerical Algorithms*, 3rd ed. Addison-Wesley.

Longstaff, F. A., and E. S. Schwartz. 2001. Valuing American Options by Simulation: A Simple Least-Square Approach. *Review of Financial Studies*, 14.

Metropolis, N., and S. Ulam. 1949. The Monte Carlo Method. *Journal of the American Statistical Association*, 44.

Morokoff, W. J. 1998. Generating Quasi-Random Paths for Stochastic Processes. *SIAM Review*, 40.

Paskov, S. H. 1997. New Methodologies for Valuing Derivatives. In Dempster M. A. H., and S. R. Pliska, eds., *Mathematics of Derivatives Securities*. Cambridge University Press.

Raymar, S. B., and M. J. Zwecher. 1997. Monte Carlo Estimation of American Call Option on the Maximum of Several Assets. *Journal of Derivatives*, 5.

Rubinstein, M., and E. Reiner. 1991. Breaking Down the Barriers. *Risk*, 4.

Tavella, D. 2002. *Quantitative Methods in Derivatives Pricing—An Introduction to Computational Finance*. Wiley.

Chapter 24: Real Options

Amram, M., and N. Kulatilaka. 1998. *Real Options: Managing Strategic Investment in an Uncertain World*. Harvard Business School Press.

Benninga, S., and E. Tolkowsky. 2004. Real Options—An Introduction and an Application to R&D Valuation. *Engineering Economist*, 47.

Dixit, A. K., and R. S. Pindyck. 1995. The Options Approach to Capital Investment. *Harvard Business Review*, 73.

Kellogg, D., and J. M. Charnes. 2000. Real-Options Valuation for a Biotechnology Company. *Financial Analysts Journal*, 56.

Luehrman, T. A. 1998. Investment Opportunities as Real Options: Getting Started on the Numbers. *Harvard Business Review*, 76.

Trigeorgis, L. 1993. Real Options and Interactions with Financial Flexibility. *Financial Management*, 22.

Trigeorgis, L. 1995. *Real Options in Capital Investment: Models, Strategies, and Applications*. Praeger.

Trigeorgis, L. 1996. *Real Options: Managerial Flexibility and Strategy in Resource Allocation*. MIT Press.

Chapters 25–26: Duration and Immunization

Altman, E. 1989. Measuring Corporate Bond Mortality and Performance. *Journal of Finance*, 44.

Altman, E., and V. M. Kishore. 1996. Almost Everything You Wanted to Know about Recoveries on Defaulted Bonds. *Financial Analysts Journal*, 52.

Babcock, G. 1985. Duration as a Weighted Average of Two Factors. *Financial Analysts Journal*, 41.

Benninga, S., and A. Protopapadakis. 1986. General Equilibrium Properties of the Term Structure of Interest Rates. *Journal of Financial Economics*, 16.

Bierwag, G. O. 1977. Immunization, Duration, and the Term Structure of Interest Rates. *Journal of Financial and Quantitative Analysis*.

Bierwag, G. O. 1978. Measures of Duration. *Economic Inquiry*, 16.

Bierwag, G. O., G. G. Kaufman, and A. Toevs. 1983a. Duration: Its Development and Use in Bond Portfolio Management. *Financial Analysts Journal*, 38.

Bierwag, G. O., G. G. Kaufman, and A. Toevs. 1983b. *Innovations in Bond Portfolio Management: Duration Analysis and Immunization*. JAI Press.

Bierwag, G. O., G. G. Kaufman, R. Schweitzer, and A. Toevs. 1981. The Art of Risk Management in Bond Portfolios. *Journal of Portfolio Management,* 7.

Billingham, C. J. 1983. Strategies for Enhancing Bond Portfolio Returns. *Financial Analysts Journal*, 39.

Chance, D. M. 1983. Floating Rate Notes and Immunization. *Journal of Financial and Quantitative Analysis,* 18.

Chance, D. M., and J. V. Jordan. 1996. Duration Convexity, and Time as Components of Bond Returns. *Journal of Fixed Income*, 6.

Chua, J. H. 1984. A Closed-Form Formula for Calculating Bond Duration. *Financial Analysts Journal.*

Cooper, I. A. 1977. Asset Values, Interest Rate Changes, and Duration. *Journal of Financial and Quantitative Analysis*, 12.

Cox, J., J. Ingersoll, and S. Ross. 1979. Duration and Measurement of Basis Risk. *Journal of Business*, 52.

Cox, J. C., J. E. Ingersoll, and S. A. Ross. 1985. A Theory of the Term Structure of Interest Rates. *Econometrica* 53.

Fisher, L., and R. L. Weill. 1971. Coping with the Risk of Market-Rate Fluctuations: Returns to Bondholders from Naive and Optimal Strategies. *Journal of Business*, 44.

Gultekin, B., and R. J. Rogalski. 1984. Alternative Duration Specifications and the Measurement of Basis Risk: Empirical Tests. *Journal of Business*, 57.

Gushee, C. H. 1981. How to Immunize a Bond Investment. *Financial Analysts Journal.*

Hicks, J. 1939. *Value and Capital.* Clarendon Press.

Ingersoll, J. E., Jr., J. Skelton, and R. L. Weil. 1978. Duration Forty Years Later. *Journal of Financial and Quantitative Analysis*, 13.

Joehnk, M. D., H. R. Fogler, and C. E. Bradley. 1978. The Price Elasticity of Discounted Bonds: Some Empirical "Evidence." *Journal of Financial and Quantitative Analysis*, 13.

Lanstein, R., and W. F. Sharpe. 1978. Duration and Security Risk. *Journal of Financial and Quantitative Analysis*, 13.

Macaulay, F. R. 1938. *Some Theoretical Problems Suggested by Movements of Interest Rates, Bond Yields, and Stock Prices in the United States Since 1856.* National Bureau of Economic Research.

Macauley, F. R. 1983. *The Movement of Interest Rates, Bonds, Yields, and Stock Prices in the United States Since 1865.* Columbia University Press.

McCullogh, J. H. 1990. U.S. Term Structure Data. 1946–1987. *Handbook of Monetary Economics*, vol 1. North-Holland.

Morgan, G. E. 1986. Floating Rate Securities and Immunization: Some Further Results. *Journal of Financial and Quantitative Analysis*, 21.

Ott, R. A., Jr. 1986. The Duration of an Adjustable-Rate Mortgage and the Impact of the Index. *Journal of Finance*, 41.

Redington, F. M. 1952. Review of the Principle of Life-Office Valuations. *Journal of the Institute of Actuaries*, 78. Reprinted in *Bond Duration and Immunization: Early Developments and Recent Contributions*, ed. G. A. Hawawini. Garland. 1972.

Samuelson, P. A. 1945. The Effects of Interest Rate Increases on the Banking System. *American Economic Review*, 35.

Smith, Donald J. 1998. A Note on the Derivation of Closed-Form Formulas for Duration and Convexity Statistics on and between Coupon Dates. *Journal of Financial Engineering*, 7.

Standard and Poor's. 1996. *Standard and Poor's Corporate Ratings Criteria.*

Vasicek, O. 1977. An Equilibrium Characterization of the Term Structure. *Journal of Financial Economics*, 5.

Weil, R. L. 1973. Macaulay's Duration: An Appreciation. *Journal of Business*, 46.

Chapter 27: Fitting the Term Structure

Adams, K. J., and D. R. Van Deventer. 1994. Fitting Yield Curves and Forward Rate Curves with Maximum Smoothness. *Journal of Fixed Income*, 4.

Chambers, D., W Carleton, and D. Waldman. 1984. A New Approach to Estimation of Term Structure of Interest Rates. *Journal of Financial and Quantitative Studies*, 19.

Coleman, T. S., L. Fisher, and R. Ibbotson. 1992. Estimating the Term Structure of Interest From Data That Include the Prices of Coupon Bonds. *Journal of Fixed Income*, 2.

Coleman, T. S., R. Ibbotson, and L. Fisher. 1993. *Historical U.S. Treasury Yield Curves.* Ibbotson Associates.

Diament, Paul. 1993. Semi-empirical Smooth Fit to the Treasury Yield Curve. *Journal of Fixed Income*, 3.

Fabozzi, F. J. 2003. *Bond Markets, Analysis and Strategies,* 5th ed. Prentice Hall.

Fisher, M., and D. Zervos. 1996. Yield Curve. In *Computational Economics and Finance: Modeling and Analysis with Mathematica*, ed. H. R. Varian. Springer.

Gürkaynak, R. S., B. Sack, and J. H. Wright. 2006. The U.S. Treasury Yield Curve: 1961 to the Present. http://www.federalreserve.gov/Pubs/feds/2006/

Jarrow, Robert A. 1996. *Modeling Fixed Income Securities and Interest Rate Options.* McGraw-Hill.

Jordan, J. V. 1984. Tax Effects in Term Structure Estimation. *Journal of Finance*, 39.

Litterman, R., and J. Scheinkman. 1991. Common Factors Affecting Bond Returns. *Journal of Fixed Income*, 1.

Mann, S. V., and P. Ramanlal. 1997. Relative Performance of Yield Curve Strategies. *Journal of Portfolio Management,* 23.

McCulloch, J. F. 1971. Measuring the Term Structure of Interest Rates. *Journal of Business*, 44.

McCulloch, J. F. 1975. The Tax-Adjusted Yield Curve. *Journal of Finance*, 30.

Nelson, C., and A. Siegel. 1987. Parsimonious Modeling of Yield Curves. *Journal of Business*, 60.

Shea, G. 1984. Pitfalls in Smoothing Interest Rate Term Structure Data: Equilibrium Models and Spline Approximations. *Journal of Financial and Quantitative Analysis*, 19.

Shea, G. 1985. Interest Rate Term Structure Estimation with Exponential Splines: A Note. *Journal of Finance*, 40.

Stigum, Marcia, and Franklin L. Robinson. 1996. *Money Market and Bond Calculations.* Irwin Professional.

Suits, D. B., A. Mason, and L. Chan. 1978. Spline Functions Fitted by Standard Regression Methods. *Review of Economics and Statistics*, 60.

Sundaresan, S. 1997. *Fixed Income Markets and Their Derivatives.* South-Western College Publishing.

Taggart, Robert A., Jr. 1996. *Quantitative Analysis for Investment Management*. Prentice Hall.

Tuckman, B. 1996. *Fixed-Income Securities.* Wiley.

Vasicek, O., and G. Fong. 1982. Term Structure Estimation Using Exponential Splines. *Journal of Finance*, 38.

Chapter 28: Expected Bond Returns

Altman, E., and V. M. Kishore. 1996. Almost Everything You Wanted to Know about Recoveries on Defaulted Bonds. *Financial Analysts Journal*, 52.

Altman, E. I., and A. C. Eberhart. 1994. Do Seniority Provisions Protect Bondholders' Investments? *Journal of Portfolio Management*, 20.

Altman, E. I., and S. Nammacher. 1984. The Default Rate Experience of High Yield Corporate Debt. *Financial Analysts Journal*, 40.

Amihud, Y., and H. Mendelson. 1991. Liquidity, Asset Prices, and Financial Policy. *Financial Analysts Journal*, 47.

Amihud, Y., and H. Mendelson. 1991. Liquidity, Maturity, and the Yields on U.S. Treasury Securities. *Journal of Finance*, 46.

Antonov, A., and Y. Yanakieva. 2004. Transition Matrix Generation. International Conference on Computer Systems and Technologies, CompSysTech'2004.

Bakshi G., D. B. Madan, and F. X. Zhang. 2004. Understanding the Role of Recovery in Default Risk Models: Empirical Comparisons and Implied Recovery Rates. EFA 2004 Maastricht Meetings Paper No. 3584; AFA 2004 San Diego Meetings; FEDS Working Paper No. 2001–37.

Cochrane, J. H. 2001. *Asset Pricing*. Princeton University Press.

Duffie, D., and K. J. Singleton. 1997. An Econometric Model of the Term Structure of Interest-Rate Swap Yields. *Journal of Finance*, 52.

Duffie, D., and K. J. Singleton. 1999. Modeling Term Structures of Defaultable Bonds. *Review of Financial Studies*, 12.

Dynkin L., A. Gould, J. Hyman, V. Konstantinovsky, and B. Phelps. 2006. *Quantitative Management of Bond Portfolios*. Princeton University Press.

Jafry, Y., and T. Schuermann. 2003. Metrics for Comparing Credit Migration Matrices. Wharton Financial Institutions Working Paper 03–08.

Jarrow, R. A., D. Lando, and S. M. Turnbull. 1997. A Markov model for the term structure of credit spreads. *Review of Financial Studies*, 10.

Jarrow, R. A., and S. M. Turnbull. 1995. Pricing Derivatives on Financial Securities Subject to Credit Risk. *Journal of Finance*, 50.

Lando, D. 1998. On Cox Processes and Credit Risky Securities. *Review of Derivatives Research*, 2.

Lando, D. 2004. *Credit Risk Modeling Theory and Applications*. Princeton University Press.

Löffler, G. 2004. An Anatomy of Rating through the Cycle. *Journal of Banking and Finance*, 28.

Löffler, G. 2005. Avoiding the Rating Bounce: Why Rating Agencies Are Slow to React to New Information. *Journal of Economic Behavior and Organization*, 56.

Merton, R. 1974. On the Pricing of Corporate Debt: The Risk Structure of Interest Rates. *Journal of Finance*, 22.

Moody's Special Report. 1992. *Corporate Bond Defaults and Default Rates*. Moody's Investors Service.

Nelson, C., and A. Siegel. 1987. Parsimonious Modeling of Yield Curves. *Journal of Business*, 60.

Standard & Poor's. Rating Transitions 2004: U.S. CMBS Upgrades Overwhelm Downgrades Amid Improved Real Estate Fundamentals. http://www2.standardandpoors.com/spf/pdf/fixedincome/RatingTransitionsCMBS04.pdf?vregion=apandvlang=en.

Walder, R. 2002. A Historical Primer on the Business of Credit Ratings: Modeling the Joint Dynamics of Default-Free and Defaultable Bond Term Structures. Research Paper No. 26, November.

Yu, F. 2002. Modeling Expected Return on Defaultable Bonds. *Journal of Fixed Income*, 122.

Chapter 29: Random Numbers

Abramowitz, M., and I. A. Stegun. 1965. *Handbook of Mathematical Functions.* Dover.

Box, G. E. P, and M. E. Muller. 1958. A Note on the Generation of Random Normal Deviates. *Annals of Mathematical Statistics*, 29.

Knuth, D. E. 1981. *The Art of Computer Programming*, vol. 2: *SemiNumerical Algorithms*. Addison-Wesley.

D. H. Lehmer. 1951. Mathematical Methods in Large-Scale Computing Units. Proceedings of the Second Symposium on Large-Scale Digital Calculating Machinery, 26. Annals of the Computational Laboratory of Harvard University, Harvard University Press.

Index

Note: Page numbers followed by f indicate figures; those followed by t indicate tables.

T